Contemporary Theatre, Film, and Television

A Note About
Contemporary Theatre, Film, and Television
and
Who's Who in the Theatre

Contemporary Theatre, Film, and Television is a continuation of *Who's Who in the Theatre*, expanded to include film and television personalities. The editors believe this change in coverage of the series makes for a more representative and useful reference tool.

To provide continuity with *Who's Who in the Theatre (WWT)*, the cumulative index at the back of this volume interfiles references to *Contemporary Theatre, Film, and Television*, Volumes 1-4, with references to *Who's Who in the Theatre*, 1st-17th Editions, and *Who Was Who in the Theatre* (Gale Research Co., 1978).

ISSN 0749-064X

Contemporary Theatre, Film, and Television

A Biographical Guide Featuring Performers,
Directors, Writers, Producers, Designers, Managers,
Choreographers, Technicians, Composers, Executives,
Dancers, and Critics in the United States and Great Britain

A Continuation of
Who's Who in the Theatre

Monica M. O'Donnell, Editor

Paul Gallagher, Associate Editor

Volume 4

Includes Cumulative Index Containing References to
Who's Who in the Theatre and *Who Was Who in the Theatre*

GALE RESEARCH COMPANY • BOOK TOWER • DETROIT, MICHIGAN 48226

STAFF

Monica M. O'Donnell, *Editor*

Paul Gallagher, *Associate Editor*

J. Peter Bergman, Mel Cobb, James R. Kirkland, *Sketchwriters*
Sharon Gamboa, Vincent Henry, *Editorial Assistants*

Marilyn K. Basel, Peter Dolgenos, Cheryl Gottler,
Anne Janette Johnson, Joanne M. Peters, Thomas Wiloch, *Contributing Editors*

Mary Beth Trimper, *Production Manager*
Michael Vargas, *Production Associate*
Roger D. Hubbard, *Graphic Arts Coordinator*
Arthur Chartow, *Art Director*

Frederick G. Ruffner, *Chairman*
J. Kevin Reger, *President*
Dedria Bryfonski, *Publisher*
Ellen Crowley, *Associate Editorial Director*
Christine Nasso, *Director, Biography Division*
Linda Hubbard, *Senior Editor*

Computerized photocomposition by
Roberts/Churcher

Printed in the United States of America

Contents

Preface

The worlds of theatre, film, and television hold an undeniable appeal, and the individuals whose careers are devoted to these fields are subjects of great interest. The people both behind the scenes and in front of the lights and cameras—writers, directors, producers, performers, and others—all have a significant impact on our lives, for they enlighten us as they entertain.

Contemporary Theatre, Film, and Television
Provides Broad Coverage in the
Entertainment Field

Contemporary Theatre, Film, and Television (CTFT) is a comprehensive biographical series designed to meet the need for information on theatre, film, and television personalities. Prior to the publication of *CTFT*, biographical sources covering entertainment figures were generally limited in scope; for more than seventy years *Who's Who in the Theatre (WWT)*, for example, provided reliable information on theatre people. But today few performers, directors, writers, producers, or technicians limit themselves to the stage. And there are also growing numbers of people who, though not active in the theatre, make significant contributions to other entertainment media. With its broad scope, encompassing not only stage notables but also film and/or television figures, *CTFT* is a more comprehensive and, the editors believe, more useful reference tool. Its clear entry format, allowing for the quick location of specific facts, combines with hundreds of photographs to further distinguish *CTFT* from other biographical sources on entertainment personalities.

Moreover, since *CTFT* is a series, new volumes can cover the steady influx of fresh talent into the entertainment media. The majority of the entries in each *CTFT* volume present information on people new to the series, but *CTFT* also includes updated versions of previously published *CTFT* sketches on especially active figures as well as complete revisions of *WWT* entries. The *CTFT* cumulative index makes all listings easily accessible.

Scope

CTFT is a biographical series covering not only performers, directors, writers, and producers but also designers, managers, choreographers, technicians, composers, executives, dancers, and critics from the United States and Great Britain. With nearly 700 entries in *CTFT* Volume 4, the series now provides biographies for more than 3,200 people involved in all aspects of the theatre, film, and television industries.

Primary emphasis is given to people who are currently active. *CTFT* includes major, established figures whose positions in entertainment history are assured, such as choreographer Peter Gennaro; television personality Monty Hall; actress and singer Melba Moore; screenwriter and director Paul Schrader; and television and film producer, director, and executive George Stevens, Jr. New and highly promising individuals who are beginning to make their mark are represented in *CTFT* as well—people such as D. J. Giagni, who has choreographed several recent Broadway shows; actress and singer Audrey Landers and her sister Judy, who have appeared in numerous film and television productions; Ari Meyers, the young actress currently appearing on *Kate and Allie;* Emma Samms, of *Dynasty* and *The Colbys* fame; and John Stamos, who got his start on *General Hospital* and has since moved on to such prime time series as *Dreams* and *You Again.*

CTFT also includes sketches on people no longer professionally active who have made significant contributions to their fields and whose work remains of interest today. This volume, for example, contains entries on actress Joan Bennett; producer and director Stanley Kramer; producer, director, and screenwriter Billy Wilder; and actress Shelley Winters. Selected sketches also record the achievements of theatre, film, and television personalities deceased since 1960. Among such notables with listings in this volume are Cary Grant, Siobhan McKenna, Forrest Tucker, and Hal Wallis.

With its broad coverage and detailed entries, *CTFT* is designed to assist a variety of users—a student preparing for a class, a teacher drawing up an assignment, a researcher seeking a specific fact, a librarian searching for the answer to a question, or a general reader looking for information about a favorite personality.

Compilation Methods

Every effort is made to secure information directly from biographees. The editors consult industry directories, biographical dictionaries, published interviews, feature stories, and film, television, and theatre reviews to identify people not previously covered in *WWT* or *CTFT*. Questionnaires are mailed to prospective listees or, when addresses are unavailable, to their agents, and sketches are compiled from the information they supply. The editors also select major figures included in *WWT* whose entries require updating and send them copies of their previously published entries for revision. *CTFT* sketches are then prepared from the new information submitted by these well-known personalities or their agents. Among the notable figures whose *WWT,* seventeenth edition, entries have been completely revised for this volume of *CTFT* are Denholm Elliott, A. R. Gurney, Jr., Doris Roberts, and Tony Walton. If people of special interest to *CTFT* users are deceased or fail to reply to requests for information, materials are gathered from reliable secondary sources. Sketches prepared solely through research are clearly marked with an asterisk (*) at the end of the entries.

The emphasis is on people currently active in theatre, film, and television who are not already covered in *WWT* or *CTFT*. However, to ensure *CTFT*'s timeliness and comprehensiveness, each volume includes updated *WWT* entries as well as revisions of *CTFT* sketches that have become outdated. The entry for a given biographee may be revised as often as there is substantial new information to provide. This volume, for example, contains updates of earlier *CTFT* listings on such personalities as Pam Dawber, Catherine Deneuve, Judd Hirsch, Shirley MacLaine, and Roger Rees.

Format

CTFT entries, modeled after those in the Gale Research Company's highly regarded *Contemporary Authors* series, are written in a clear, readable style with few abbreviations and no limits set on length. So that a reader needing specific information can quickly focus on the pertinent portion of an entry, typical *CTFT* listings are clearly divided into the following sections:

Entry heading—Cites the form of the name by which the listee is best known followed by birth and death dates, when available.

Personal—Provides the biographee's full or original name if different from the entry heading, date and place of birth, family data, and information about the listee's education (including professional training), politics, religion, and military service.

Vocation—Highlights the individual's primary fields of activity in the entertainment industry.

Career—Presents a comprehensive listing of principal credits or engagements. The career section lists theatrical debuts (including Broadway and London debuts), principal stage appearances, and major tours; film debuts and principal films; television debuts and television appearances; and plays, films, and television shows directed and produced. Related career items, such as professorships and lecturing, are also included as well as non-entertainment career items.

Writings—Lists published and unpublished plays, screenplays, and scripts along with production information. Published books and articles, often with bibliographical data, are also listed.

Recordings—Cites album and single song releases with recording labels, when available.

Awards—Notes theatre, film, and television awards and nominations as well as writing awards, military and civic awards, and fellowships and honorary degrees received.

Member—Highlights professional, union, civic, and other association memberships, including official posts held.

Sidelights—Cites favorite roles, recreational activities, and hobbies. Frequently this section includes portions of agent-prepared biographies or personal statements from the listee. In-depth sidelights providing an overview of an individual's career achievements are compiled on selected personalities of special interest.

Addresses—Notes home, office, and agent addresses, when available. (In those instances where an individual prefers to withhold his or her home address from publication, the editors make every attempt to include at least one other address in the entry.)

Enlivening the text in many instances are large, clear photographs. Often the work of theatrical photographers, these pictures are supplied by the biographees to complement their sketches. This volume, for example, contains over 290 such portraits received from various individuals profiled in the following pages.

Brief Entries

CTFT users have indicated that having some information, however brief, on individuals not yet in the series would be preferable to waiting until full-length sketches can be prepared as outlined above under "Compilation Methods." Therefore, *CTFT* includes abbreviated listings on notables who presently do not have sketches in *CTFT*. These short profiles, identified by the heading "Brief Entry," highlight the person's career in capsule form.

Brief entries are not intended to replace sketches. Instead, they are designed to increase *CTFT*'s comprehensiveness and thus better serve *CTFT* users by providing pertinent and timely information about well-known people in the entertainment industry, many of whom will be the subjects of full sketches in forthcoming volumes.

This volume, for example, includes brief entries on such up-and-coming people as Lisa Bonet, Judd Nelson, Charlie Sheen, and Tracey Ullman.

Cumulative Index

To facilitate locating sketches on the thousands of notables profiled in *CTFT*, each volume contains a cumulative index to the entire series. As an added feature, this index also includes references to all seventeen editions of *WWT* and to the four-volume compilation *Who Was Who in the Theatre* (Gale, 1978). Thus by consulting only one source—the *CTFT* cumulative index—users have easy access to the tens of thousands of biographical sketches in *CTFT, WWT,* and *Who Was Who in the Theatre.*

Suggestions are Welcome

If readers would like to suggest people to be covered in future *CTFT* volumes, they are encouraged to send these names (along with addresses, if possible) to the editor. Other suggestions and comments are also most welcome and should be addressed to: The Editor, *Contemporary Theatre, Film, and Television,* 150 E. 50th Street, New York, NY 10022.

Forthcoming *CTFT* Entries

A Partial List of Theatre, Film, and Television Personalities
Who Will Appear in Forthcoming Volumes of *CTFT*

Aiello, Danny
Anderson, Harry
Anderson, Michael, Jr.
Antony, Scott
Arnott, Mark
Askin, Peter
Aston, John
Avalos, Luis
Averback, Hy
Babcock, Debra Lee
Baer, Max, Jr.
Baldwin, Alec
Barnes, Joanna
Barris, Chuck
Baxter, Cash
Beatty, Ned
Belafonte-Harper, Shari
Berman, Shelly
Bernhard, Sandra
Bernstein, Jay
Blades, Ruben
Blakely, Susan
Bledsoe, Tempestt
Boorman, John
Boris, Robert
Botsford, Sara
Brimley, Wilford
Brokaw, Tom
Brosnan, Pierce
Byrne, David
Carter, Dixie
Cates, Phoebe
Clayton, Jack
Cole, Toby
Collins, Pat
Copperfield, David
Cosell, Howard
Craven, Wes
Crisp, Quentin
Cronkite, Walter
Cross, Ben
Cunningham, Merce
Curry, Tim
Curtis, Jamie Lee
Cwikowski, Bill
Dahl, Roald
Daltry, Roger
Daly, Tyne
D'Apollonia, James
Davis, Brad
Davis, Clifton
De Angelis, Rosemary

DeSilva, Albert
DeSilva, David
De Vito, Danny
Dixon, Donna
Donahue, Phil
Douglas, Mike
Down, Lesley-Ann
Downs, Hugh
Duff, Howard
Durning, Charles
Dzundza, George
Eikenberry, Jill
Elcar, Dana
Ellis, Leslie
Estabrook, Christine
Fabares, Shelley
Falabella, John
Feldon, Barbara
Ferrer, Mel
Field, Jules
Fingerhut, Arden
Flanagan, Kit
Flanders, Ed
Foreman, John
Foreman, Richard
Frankenheimer, John
Franz, Elizabeth
Fraser, Alison
Friedkin, William
Fuller, Penny
Gardner, Herb
Geffen, David
Gerard, Gil
Gero, Frank
Gerrianne, Raphael
Gibson, Mel
Gilliam, Terry
Glass, Philip
Gleason, Jackie
Gless, Sharon
Godfrey, Lynnie
Goldthwait, Bob
Gossett, Lou
Griffith, Melanie
Grimes, Scott
Hagerty, Julie
Hailey, Arthur
Hannah, Daryl
Harper, Jessica
Harper, Valerie
Heard, John
Hill, Benny

Hill, Debra
Holliday, Jennifer
Holloway, Sterling
Hopkins, Telma
Hughes, John
Hunt, Pamela
Hunter, Marion
Hyams, Peter
Idle, Eric
Jaffe, Herb
Jarre, Maurice
Jennings, Peter
Joffe, Roland
Kasdan, Lawrence
Kasem, Casey
Keitel, Harvey
Kellerman, Sally
Kelsey, Linda
Kennedy, Kathleen
Kinney, Terry
Kinski, Klaus
Kotto, Yaphet
Kristofferson, Kris
Kuralt, Charles
Kurosawa, Akira
Lamas, Lorenzo
Lang, Stephen
Lange, Hope
Larson, Penny
Laughlin, Tom
Lauter, Ed
Lazar, Irving Paul
LeBeauf, Sabrina
Lee, Spike
Leno, Jay
Lenz, Kay
Leone, Sergio
LeVine, David
Levine, Joseph E.
Lewis, Emmanuel
Lewis, Jerry
Locke, Sondra
Lollabrigida, Gina
Long, Shelly
Lunden, Joan
Lynch, David
MacCormick, Cara Duff
MacGraw, Ali
Madigan, Amy
Malkovich, John
Mann, Michael
Margolin, Janet

Margolin, Stuart
Martin, Steve
Mason, Jackie
Mastroianni, Marcello
McAnuff, Des
McArdle, Andrea
McCambridge, Mercedes
McDowell, Malcolm
McGavin, Darren
McGovern, Maureen
McHattie, Stephen
Mercouri, Melina
Mifune, Toshiro
Miles, Vera
Mimieux, Yvette
Mr. T
Miyori, Kim
Moore, Roger
Morgenstern, Susan
Mudd, Roger
Murdoch, Rupert
Nesmith, Michael
Neuberger, Jay
Newman, Edwin
Newton-John, Olivia
Nykvist, Sven
O'Connor, Glynnis
Overmeyer, Eric
Palance, Jack
Paley, William
Palin, Michael
Pare, Michael
Parker, Eleanor
Parks, Bert
Parton, Dolly
Pauley, Jane
Pinchot, Bronson
Plunkett, Maryann
Post, Markie
Pressman, Lawrence
Prince
Purl, Linda
Quinlan, Kathleen
Raffin, Deborah
Rapf, Matthew
Rashad, Phylicia
Rather, Dan
Reddy, Helen
Reed, Alaina
Reedy, Pat
Reiner, Carl
Reiner, Rob

Reinhold, Judge	Scheider, Roy	Stigwood, Robert	Vonnegut, Kurt, Jr.
Reiss, Stuart	Schell, Maximilian	Stockwell, Dean	Von Sydow, Max
Reisz, Karel	Schepisi, Fred	Strauss, Peter	Walcott, Derek
Rich, Frank	Schifrin, Lalo	Stykes, Eric	Walters, Barbara
Richard, Cliff	Schoenfeld, Gerald	Takei, George	Ward, Rachel
Riddle, Nelson	Scott, Tony	Tesich, Steve	Warfield, Marsha
Rinehart, Elaine	Sears, Austin	Tewson, Josephine	Warner, Malcolm-Jamal
Robinson, Charlie	Selby, David	Thomas, Gerald	Wasserman, Dale
Roman, Ruth	Semple, Lorenzo	Thorne, Raymond	Weege, Reinhold
Rooney, Andy	Shapiro, Ken	Tillinger, John	Wenders, Wim
Ross, Diana	Shukat, Scott	Tinker, Grant	Wiest, Dianne
Rourke, Mickey	Sikking, James	Tisch, Laurence	Williams, Hal
Roussel, Pamela	Simmons, Jonathan	Tryon, Tom	Winters, Jonathan
Rowlands, Gena	Simpson, Don	Turner, Kathleen	Winters, Time
Rush, Barbara	Sinatra, Frank	Turner, Ted	Woods, James
Rusler, Robert	Snodgress, Carrie	Vadim, Roger	Wurtzel, Stuart
Russell, Ken	Soyinka, Wole	Venora, Diane	Yniguez, Richard
Salmi, Albert	Spano, Joe	Villard, Tom	York, Susannah
Sarrazin, Michael	Stander, Lionel	Vincent, Jan Michael	Young, Burt
Savage, John	Stanton, Harry Dean		

To ensure that *CTFT* meets users' needs for biographical information on entertainment figures of special interest, the editor welcomes your suggestions for additional personalities to be included in the series.

Contemporary Theatre, Film, and Television

Contemporary Theatre, Film, and Television

* Indicates that a listing has been compiled from secondary sources believed to be reliable.

ABADY, Josephine R.   1949-

PERSONAL: Born August 21, 1949, in Richmond, VA; married H. Michael Krawitz. EDUCATION: Syracuse University, B.S.; Florida State University, M.F.A.

VOCATION: Director, administrator, consultant, and teacher.

CAREER: PRINCIPAL STAGE WORK—Director: *Private Lives,* Ensemble Theatre Company, Tampa, FL, 1973; *Thurber Carnival, Private Ear, Public Eye, The Owl and the Pussycat,* and *Just So So Stories,* all at the Roundhouse Theatre, Manchester, VT, 1974; *Hay Fever,* Ensemble Theatre Company, Tampa, 1975; *West Side Story,* Fanfare Series, Richmond, VA, 1976; *Thurber Carnival,* Paul Arts Center, Durham, NH, 1978; *Kings,* New York Theatre Ensemble, New York City, 1979; *A Coupla White Chicks Sitting Around Talking,* Cincinnati Playhouse in the Park, then Charles Playhouse, Boston, MA, 1981; *The Dresser,* Cincinnati Playhouse in the Park, 1982; *Tally's Folly,* Merrimack Regional Theatre, Lowell, MA, 1982; *Territorial Rites,* American Place Theatre, New York City, 1982.

Since 1982, has directed: *The Dresser* and *Painting Churches,* Alley Theatre, Houston, TX; *A Grand Romance,* Long Wharf Theatre, New Haven, CT; *The Little Foxes,* Walnut Street Theatre, Philadelphia, PA; *A Lesson from Aloes,* Syracuse Stage, Syracuse, NY.

As artistic director, Berkshire Theatre Festival, Stockbridge, MA: *The Petrified Forest* and *Sexual Perversity in Chicago,* both 1979; *The Little Foxes, The Palace of Amateurs,* and *The Glass Menagerie,* all 1980; *A View from the Bridge* and *A Safe Place,* both 1981; *Sunrise at Campobello* and *A Thousand Clowns,* both 1982. Since 1982: *Caught; The Member of the Wedding; The Big Knife; Fanny; A Loss of Roses; Sabrina Fair.*

PRINCIPAL TELEVISION WORK—Consultant, *Kate and Allie,* CBS.

RELATED CAREER—Director of theatre and visiting professor of theatre, Hampshire College, Amherst, MA; guest director, North Adams State College and Smith College; professor of theatre, Virginia Union University, Indian Hill Arts Workshop, and Ben-

JOSEPHINE R. ABADY

nington College; director and teacher, New York University, New York City.

AWARDS: Artist in Residence, National Education Association, University of Washington, Seattle; President's Council on Scholarship in the Arts; Sawyer Falk Memorial Award.

MEMBER: Society of Stage Directors and Choreographers.

ADDRESSES: OFFICE—Berkshire Theatre Festival, P.O. Box 797, Stockbridge, MA 01262. AGENT—c/o Ron Muchnik, 432 S. Ogden Drive, Los Angeles, CA 90036.

ABRAHAM, F. Murray 1939-

PERSONAL: Born October 24, 1939. EDUCATION: Attended University of Texas at El Paso, 1959-61; trained for the stage with Uta Hagen at the Herbert Berghof Studio in New York City.

VOCATION: Actor.

CAREER: STAGE DEBUT—Mr. Shumway, *The Wonderful Ice Cream Suit,* Coronet Theatre, Los Angeles, 1965. BROADWAY DEBUT—Rudin, *The Man in the Glass Booth,* Royale Theatre, New York City, 1968. PRINCIPAL STAGE APPEARANCES—Old Actor, *The Fantasticks,* Sullivan Street Playhouse, 1966; Player A, *Adaptation Next,* 13th Street Theatre, New York City, 1967; Jonathan, *To-Nite in Living Color,* Actors Playhouse, New York City, 1967; Reverend, *Little Murders,* Circle in the Square, New York City, 1969; Bummer, *Last Chance Saloon,* La Mama Experimental Theatre Club (E.T.C.), New York City, 1970; Monsignor, *The Survival of St. Joan,* Anderson Theatre, New York City, 1971; Harold, *Scuba Duba,* Studio Arena Theatre, Buffalo, NY, 1972; the Men, *Where Has Tommy Flowers Gone?,* Playhouse 74, New York City, 1973; Roy Pitt, *Bad Habits,* Booth Theatre, New York City, 1974; Chris, *The Ritz,* Longacre Theatre, New York City, 1975-76.

Doc, *Legend,* Barrymore Theatre, New York City, 1977; Detective Hoolihan, *Landscape of the Body,* New York Shakespeare Festival (NYSF), Public Theatre, New York City, 1977; Bernie, *Sexual Perversity in Chicago,* Cherry Lane Theatre, New York City, 1977; Master, *Master and Margarita,* NYSF, Public Theatre, New York City, 1978; Demon, *Teibele and Her Demon,* Brooks Atkinson Theatre, New York City, 1979-80; title role, *Cyrano de Bergerac,* Baltimore Center Stage, 1980; Dorn, *The Seagull,* NYSF, Public Theatre, New York City, 1980; Player Man, *Window,* Time and Space Ltd. Theatre, New York City, 1980; Davies, *The Caretaker,* Roundabout Theatre, New York City, 1982; Creon, *Antigone,* NYSF, Public Theatre, New York City, 1982; Astrov, *Uncle Vanya,* La Mama E.T.C., New York City, 1983; the Rabbi, *The Golem,* NYSF, Delacorte Theatre, New York City, 1984; Ragpicker, *Madwoman of Chaillot,* Mirror Repertory Theatre, New York City, 1985; with the NYSF, Delacorte Theatre: Rabbi of Prague, *The Golem,* 1985, Malvolio, *Twelfth Night,* 1986, and title role, *Macbeth,* 1987.

In addition to the productions listed above, Abraham has done much children's theatre with Jay Harnick's musical company, Theatreworks, Inc.

MAJOR TOURS—Father Drobney, *Don't Drink the Water,* Florida cities, 1966-67; also, *And Miss Reardon Drinks a Little,* 1972.

FILM DEBUT—Detective Levy, *Serpico,* Paramount, 1974. PRINCIPAL FILM APPEARANCES—Mechanic, *The Sunshine Boys,* United Artists, 1975; Detective Rafferty, *All the President's Men,* Warner Brothers, 1976; Chris, *The Ritz,* Warner Brothers, 1976; Cohen, *Madman,* Israeli film, 1978; Epis, *The Big Fix,* Universal, 1979; Omar, *Scarface,* Universal, 1983; Salieri, *Amadeus,* Orion, 1985; *The Name of the Rose,* 1986.

TELEVISION DEBUT—*Love of Life,* NBC. PRINCIPAL TELEVISION APPEARANCES—Series: Big Tony, *Kojak,* CBS. Episodic: *All in the Family,* CBS. Movies: Jakopo, *Marco Polo;* also *How to Survive a Marriage, Dream West.*

RELATED CAREER—Performed as Santa Claus, Macy's Department Store, New York City, 1965.

MEMBER: Actors' Equity Association, Screen Actors Guild, American Federation of Television and Radio Artists.

AWARDS: Best Actor, Academy Award, Golden Globe, and Los Angeles Film Critics, Albert Schweitzer Award for Classic Film Acting, all 1985, for *Amadeus;* also, Obie Award.

ADDRESSES: AGENT—William Morris Agency, 1350 Sixth Avenue, New York, NY 10019.

* * *

ABRAHAMS, Jim 1944-

PERSONAL: Born May 10, 1944, in Milwaukee, WI. EDUCATION: Attended the University of Wisconsin.

VOCATION: Producer, writer, and director.

CAREER: PRINCIPAL STAGE WORK—(With David and Jerry Zukor) Co-founder, Kentucky Fried Theatre, specializng in improvisation mixed with videotaped skits, Madison, WI; opened a Kentucky Fried Theatre in Los Angeles, 1972.

PRINCIPAL FILM WORK—(All with David and Jerry Zukor) Screenwriter, *The Kentucky Fried Movie,* United Film, 1977; co-screenwriter, co-director, and co-executive producer, *Airplane!,* Paramount, 1980; co-screenwriter (also with Martyn Burke), co-director, and co-producer *Top Secret!,* Paramount, 1984; co-screenwriter, co-director, and co-producer, *Ruthless People,* Buena Vista, 1986.

ADDRESSES: AGENT—c/o Len Hirshan, William Morris Agency, 151 El Camino Drive, Beverly Hills, CA 90212.*

* * *

ACKLES, Kenneth V. 1916-1986

PERSONAL: Born 1916; died of a stroke in Pasadena, TX, November 5, 1986. EDUCATION: Trained with Lee Strasberg and Sanford Meisner.

VOCATION: Actor.

CAREER: PRINCIPAL STAGE APPEARANCES—Broadway: *Li'l Abner;* Off-Broadway: *The Lower Depths; Scarecrow.*

PRINCIPAL FILM APPEARANCES—*Rachel, Rachel,* Warner Brothers/Seven Arts, 1968; *Death Wish,* Paramount, 1974; *Night of the Juggler,* Columbia, 1980.

PRINCIPAL TELEVISION APPEARANCES—Episodic: *Steve Allen's Tonight Show,* NBC; *The Shirley Temple Storybook,* NBC; *Your Show of Shows,* NBC; also appeared on *The Guiding Light* and *The Edge of Night.* Movies: *Izzy and Moe,* 1985.

NON-RELATED CAREER—National Wrestling Alliance's light

heavyweight champion in the 1940s and wrestled in the U.S. and Europe as "Cowboy" Ken Ackles.*

* * *

ADAMS, Mason

PERSONAL: Married Margot Adams (a writer); children: Betsy, Bil. EDUCATION: University of Wisconsin, B.A., 1940, M.A., 1941; trained for the stage at the Neighborhood Playhouse.

VOCATION: Actor.

CAREER: STAGE DEBUT—Hilltop Theatre, Baltimore, summer, 1940. BROADWAY DEBUT—Joe Rigga, *Get Away Old Man,* Cort Theatre, 1943. LONDON DEBUT—Playwright, bed salesman, and Herbert, *You I Can't Hear You When the Water's Running,* New Theatre, 1968. PRINCIPAL STAGE APPEARANCES—Broadway productions: *Career Angel, Public Relations, Violet, Shadow of My Enemy, Inquest, The Sign in Sidney Brustein's Window, Tall Story, The Trial of the Catonsville Nine, Checking Out.* Off-Broadway, appeared in *The Shortchanged Review,* New York Shakespeare Festival, New York City; *Paradise Lost,* 1984, and *Time of Your Life,* 1985, both with the Mirror Repertory Company at the Theatre at St. Peter's Church, New York City; *Danger: Memory,* Lincoln Center, New York City, 1987.

PRINCIPAL FILM APPEARANCES—President of the United States, *The Final Conflict,* Twentieth Century-Fox, 1981; Colonel Mason, *F/X,* Orion, 1986.

MASON ADAMS

PRINCIPAL TELEVISION APPEARANCES—Series: Charlie Hume, *Lou Grant,* CBS, 1977-82; *Morning Star, Evening Star,* NBC, 1985. Episodic: *Flamingo Road,* NBC; *Family Ties,* NBC. Movies: *The Deadliest Season,* 1977; *And Baby Makes Six,* 1979; *A Shining Season,* 1979; *The Revenge of the Stepford Wives,* 1980; *The Kid with the Broken Halo,* 1982; *Rage of Angels,* 1982; *Passions,* CBS, 1984; also, *Freedom to Speak, Under Siege,* and *Solomon Northup's Odyssey.*

RELATED CAREER—Performed on most major radio shows originating in New York; title role for sixteen years, *Pepper Young's Family.*

AWARDS: Three Emmy award nominations, Charlie Hume, *Lou Grant,* CBS.

MEMBER: Actors' Equity Association, Screen Actors Guild, American Federation of Television and Radio Artists; The Players Club; Delta Sigma Rho; Phi Kappa Phi.

ADDRESSES: HOME—Westport, CT; Los Angeles, CA. AGENT—Don Buchwald Associates, Ten E. 44th Street, New York, NY 10017.

* * *

ADLER, Larry 1914-

PERSONAL: Full name, Lawrence Cecil Adler; born February 10, 1914, in Baltimore, MD; son of Louis (a plumber) and Sadie (Hack) Adler; married Eileen Walser, April 11, 1938 (divorced, 1959); married Sally Cline, 1967 (divorced, 1976); children: (first marriage) Carole, Peter, Wendy; (second marriage) Katelyn. EDUCATION: Attended Baltimore City College, 1926-28; trained in music at the Peabody Conservatory.

VOCATION: Composer and musician.

CAREER: BROADWAY DEBUT—Harmonica player, Paramount Theatre, 1928. LONDON DEBUT—Harmonica player, *Streamline Revue,* Palace Theatre, 1934. PRINCIPAL STAGE WORK—Harmonica soloist: Sydney Symphony Orchestra, Australia, 1939; New York Philharmonic Orchestra and other orchestras in England, Japan, and Europe; additional appearances at the Edinburgh Festival, Scotland in 1963, and a one man show titled, *From Hand to Mouth,* at the Edinburgh Festival, 1965.

MAJOR TOURS—Harmonica soloist and accompanist for Paul Draper, U.S. cities, 1941-49; war tours for allied troops in 1943-45, European cities and in Germany, 1947 and 1949, Korea, 1951, and Israel in 1967 and 1973.

FILM DEBUT—*Many Happy Returns,* Paramount, 1933. PRINCIPAL FILM APPEARANCES—*Music for the Millions,* 1944; *Three Daring Daughters,* 1948.

PRINCIPAL FILM WORK—Composer: *Genevieve,* Rank Sirus, 1953; *The Great Chase,* 1963; *King and Country,* Allied Artists, 1965; *High Wind in Jamaica,* Twentieth Century-Fox, 1965.

PRINCIPAL TELEVISION WORK—Composer: *Midnight Men,* BBC; also composed music for television plays, documentaries, and commercials.

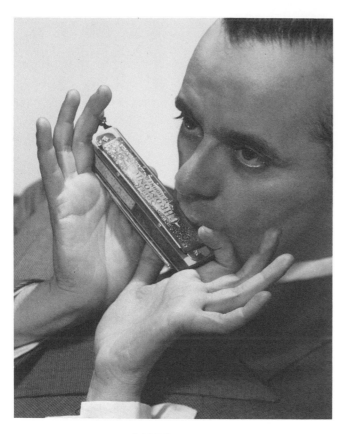

LARRY ADLER

WRITINGS: BOOKS—*How I Play,* 1937; *Larry Adler's Own Arrangements,* 1960; *Jokes and How to Tell Them,* Doubleday, 1963; *It Ain't Necessarily So,* Cohons, 1984. CONCERT MUSIC—*Theme and Variations; Camera III.*

AWARDS: Best Film Score, Academy Award nomination, 1954, for *Genevieve.*

MEMBER: Actors' Equity Association, Musicians Union.

ADDRESSES: OFFICE—c/o Michael Bakewell, 118 Tottenham Court Road, London W1, England. AGENT—c/o Bob Gardner, 610 West End Avenue, New York, NY 10024.

                    *   *   *

ADLER, Richard   1921-

PERSONAL: Born August 3, 1921, in New York, NY; son of Clarence and Elsa Adrienne (Richard) Adler; married Marion Hart (divorced); married Sally Ann Howes (divorced); children: (first marriage) Andrew H., Christopher E. (died, 1984). EDUCATION: Attended University of North Carolina. MILITARY: U.S. Navy, 1941-46.

VOCATION: Composer, lyricist, producer, and director.

CAREER: PRINCIPAL STAGE WORK—(With Jerry Ross) Composer and lyricist, *John Murray Anderson's Almanac,* New York City, 1953; (with Jerry Ross) composer and lyricist, *The Pajama Game,*

New York City, 1954, and London, 1955; (with Jerry Ross) composer and lyricist, *Damn Yankees,* New York City, 1955, and London, 1957; co-producer, *The Sin of Pat Muldoon,* New York City, 1957; composer and lyricist, *Kwamina,* New York City, 1961. Producer and director: *New York's Birthday Salute for President Kennedy,* 1962, *Inaugural Anniversary Salute for President Kennedy,* 1963, *Washington Salutes President Johnson,* 1964, *New York Salutes President Johnson,* 1964, all at the National Guard Armory, Washington, DC, then Madison Square Garden, New York City. Director, *Inaugural Gala for President Lyndon B. Johnson,* Washington, DC, 1965; composer and lyricist, *A Mother's Kisses,* New York City, 1968; co-producer, *The Pajama Game,* New York City, 1973; producer, *Rex,* New York City, 1976; co-producer and composer, *Music Is,* St. James Theatre, New York City, 1976.

PRINCIPAL FILM WORK—(Both with Jerry Ross) Composer and lyricist: *Pajama Game,* Warner Brothers, 1957; *Damn Yankees,* Warner Brothers, 1958.

PRINCIPAL TELEVISION WORK—Teleplays: Composer, lyricist, and co-producer, *Little Women* and *Gift of the Magi,* both 1957; producer, composer, and lyricist, "Olympus 7-0000," *Stage 67,* ABC, 1966.

RELATED CAREER—Consultant, North Carolina School of the Arts, 1963—; White House consultant on talent and the arts, 1965-69; advisory board, Institute of Outdoor Drama, NC, 1968—; founder, performance unit, Duke University, NC, 1977.

NON-RELATED CAREER—Member of the advertising department of Celanese Corporation of America, 1946-50.

RICHARD ADLER

WRITINGS: MUSIC—Composer: (In addition to the above) *Memory of a Childhood,* Detroit Symphony Orchestra, 1978; *Retrospectrum,* Soviet Emigre Chamber Orchestra, Carnegie Hall, New York City, 1979; *Yellowstone Overture,* American Philharmonic Orchestra, Carnegie Hall, New York City, 1980; *Yellowstone,* premiered in New York City, 1981; *Wilderness Suite,* commissioned by the Department of the Interior, performed first at Symphony Hall, Salt Lake City, 1983; *The Lady Remembers, the Statue of Liberty Suite,* first performed at the Kennedy Center, Washington, DC, 1985.

RECORDINGS: ALBUMS—*Wilderness Suite,* with the Utah Symphony, RCA Red Seal, 1983; *The Lady Remembers,* RCA Red Seal, 1986.

AWARDS: Antoinette Perry Award, Donaldson Award, and *Variety* Critics Poll Award, all 1954, for *Pajama Game,* and all 1955, for *Damn Yankees;* Antoinette Perry Award nomination, 1962, for *Kwamina;* Pulitzer Prize nominations, 1980, for *Retrospectrum,* 1981, for *Yellowstone Overture,* 1983, for *Wilderness Suite,* and 1986, for *The Lady Remembers, the Statue of Liberty Suite;* Songwriters Hall of Fame, 1984; Honorary Ranger Award, National Park Service, 1984.

MEMBER: John F. Kennedy Center for the Performing Arts, (trustee, 1964-77, executive committee, 1975-77), New Dramatists (board of directors, 1974—), Dramatists Guild (executive council, 1958-68), American Guild of Authors and Composers (executive council, 1962-68), American Society of Composers, Authors and Publishers (ASCAP; director, chairman, executive committee, 1964-69), American National Theatre Association (board of directors, executive committee), Songwriters Guild of America (first vice president, 1984); National Hypertension Association.

ADDRESSES: OFFICE—Eight E. 83rd Street, New York, NY 10028.

*   *   *

AITKEN, Maria   1945-

PERSONAL: Born September 12, 1945, in Dublin, Ireland; daughter of Sir William (a member of Parliament) and Penelope (Maffey) Aitken; married Richard Durden (divorced); married Nigel Davenport. EDUCATION: St. Anne's College; Oxford University, M.A.

VOCATION: Actress.

CAREER: STAGE DEBUT—With the Oxford University Dramatic Society, U.K., 1963. LONDON DEBUT—Clara, *Ellen,* Hampstead Theatre, 1971. PRINCIPAL STAGE APPEARANCES—Prostitute, *A Streetcar Named Desire,* Belgrade Theatre, Coventry, U.K., 1967; in repertory at Northampton Theatre and Theatre Royal, U.K., 1970-71; Mrs. Honeydew, *The High Bid,* Arts Theatre, Cambridge, U.K., 1971; Gwendolyn, *Travesties,* Aldwych Theatre, London, 1974; Countess Malcolm, *A Little Night Music,* Adelphi Theatre, London, 1975; Elvira, *Blithe Spirit,* with the National Theatre Company, Lyttelton Theatre, London, 1976; Susannah, *Bedroom Farce,* Lyttelton Theatre, London, 1977; Lady, *The Man of Destiny,* Open Air Theatre, Regent's Park, London, 1978; Rosalind, *As You Like It,* Bristol Old Vic Theatre, 1978; Millamant, *The Way of the World,* Northcott Theatre, Exeter, U.K., 1979.

MAJOR TOURS—Viola, *Twelfth Night* and Hermione, *The Winter's Tale,* both Far Eastern cities, 1972.

FILM DEBUT—*Some Girls Do,* 1969. PRINCIPAL FILM APPEARANCES—*Mary Queen of Scots,* Universal, 1971.

PRINCIPAL TELEVISION APPEARANCES—Appearances since 1969: *The Regiment, Quiet as a Nun,* and *Company & Co.*

SIDELIGHTS: RECREATIONS—Cooking, poultry-keeping, arguing.

ADDRESSES: AGENT—Leading Artists, 60 St. James's Street, London SW1, England.*

*   *   *

AKERS, Karen   1945-

PERSONAL: Born November 13, 1945, in New York, NY; daughter of Heinnick Christian and Mary Louise (a chaplain; maiden name, Adams) Orth-Pallavilini; married James Earl Akers (a lawyer), May 11, 1968; children: Jeremy Todd, Christopher Jordan. EDUCATION: Graduated from Hunter College; studied in acting workshops at the Arena Stage, Washington, DC; studied voice with Joseph K. Scott in New York City.

VOCATION: Actress and singer.

CAREER: BROADWAY DEBUT—Luisa Contini, *Nine,* 46th Street Theatre, for nine months, 1982. PRINCIPAL STAGE APPEARANCES—In concert at Carnegie Hall, New York City, 1983.

FILM DEBUT—Kitty Haynes, *The Purple Rose of Cairo,* Orion, 1985. PRINCIPAL FILM APPEARANCES—Thelma Rice, *Heartburn,* Paramount, 1986.

TELEVISION DEBUT—*Presenting Karen Ackers,* PBS Special, 1982. PRINCIPAL TELEVISION APPEARANCES—Episodic: *Hart to Hart,* ABC, 1983; *The Equalizer,* NBC, 1985.

AWARDS: Best Featured Actress, Antoinette Perry Award nomination and *Theatre World* Award, both 1982, for *Nine.*

MEMBER: Actors' Equity Association, Screen Actors Guild, American Federation of Radio and Television Artists.

ADDRESSES: AGENT—c/o Bob Duva, The Lantz Office, 888 Seventh Avenue, New York, NY 10106.

*   *   *

ALBEE, Edward   1928-

PERSONAL: Full name, Edward Franklin Albee III; born March 12, 1928, in Washington, DC; adopted son of Reed A. (a co-owner of the Keith-Albee theatre circuit) and Frances (Cotter) Albee. EDUCATION: Attended Lawrenceville School, Valley Forge Military Academy, and Choate School; attended Trinity College, 1946-47. RELIGION: Christian.

VOCATION: Writer, producer, and director.

CAREER: PRINCIPAL STAGE WORK—Director: *The Sandbox,* Cherry Lane Theatre, New York City, 1962; *The American Dream* and *The Palace at 4 a.m.,* John Drew Theatre, East Hampton, NY, 1972; *Seascape,* Shubert Theatre, New York City, 1975; *Three Albee One-Acts,* Wollman Auditorium, Columbia University, 1979; *The Man Who Had Three Arms,* New World Festival, Miami, then Goodman Theatre, Chicago, 1982, and Lyceum Theatre, New York City, 1983.

With Richard Barr and Clinton Wilder, co-produced: *Corruption in the Palace of Justice,* 1963; *Play, The Lover, Funnyhouse of a Negro, Two Executioners, The Dutchman,* and *Tiny Alice,* all 1964; *Lovey, Hunting the Jingo Bird, Do Not Pass Go, Happy Days, That Thing at the Cherry Lane, Up to Thursday, Balls, Home Free, Pigeons,* and *Conserico Was Here to Stay,* all 1965; *The Butter and Egg Man* and *Night of the Dunce,* both 1966; *The Long Christmas Dinner, Queens of France, The Happy Journey from Trenton to Camden, The Rimers of Eldritch,* and *The Party on Greenwich Avenue,* all 1967; *The Death of Bessie Smith, The American Dream, Krapp's Last Tape, The Zoo Story,* and *Happy Days,* all 1968; *The Front Page,* 1969; *Water Color* and *Criss-Crossing,* both 1970; *All Over,* 1971.

MAJOR TOURS—Director, *Albee Directs Albee,* U.S. cities, 1978-79.

RELATED CAREER—Continuity writer for WNYC radio; founder, William Flanagan Center for Creative Persons, Montauk, NY, 1971; co-director, Vivian Beaumont Theatre at Lincoln Center for the Performing Arts, New York City, 1979—; president, Edward F. Albee Foundation.

NON-RELATED CAREER—Office boy, Warwick and Legler Advertising Agency; record salesman, G. Schirmer, Inc.; counterman, Manhattan Towers Hotel Luncheonette; messenger, Western Union, 1955-58.

WRITINGS: PLAYS, PRODUCED AND PUBLISHED—*The Zoo Story* (in German), Schiller Theatre Werkstatt, Berlin, 1959, then Provincetown Playhouse, New York City, 1960; *The Death of Bessie Smith* (in German), Schlosspark, Berlin, 1960, then York Playhouse, New York City, 1961; *The Sandbox,* Jazz Gallery, New York City, 1960, then Cherry Lane Theatre, New York City, 1962, published together in one volume entitled *The Zoo Story, The Death of Bessie Smith, The Sandbox: Three Plays,* Coward, 1960, with "The American Dream," published as *The Zoo Story and Other Plays,* J. Cape, 1962; (libretto, with James Hinton, Jr.) *Bartleby,* York Playhouse, New York City, 1961; *The American Dream,* York Playhouse, New York City, 1961, published by Coward, 1961; *Fam and Yam,* White Barn Theatre, Westport, CT, 1960, published by Dramatists Play Service, 1961; *Who's Afraid of Virginia Woolf?,* Billy Rose Theatre, New York City, 1962, published by Atheneum, 1962; (adaptation) *The Ballad of the Sad Cafe,* Martin Beck Theatre, New York City, 1963, published by Houghton, 1963; *Tiny Alice,* Billy Rose Theatre, New York City, 1964, published by Atheneum, 1965.

(Adaptation) *Malcolm,* Shubert Theatre, New York City, 1966, published by Atheneum, 1966; *A Delicate Balance,* Martin Beck Theatre, New York City, 1966, published by Atheneum, 1966; (musical adaptation, with music by Bob Merrill) *Breakfast at Tiffany's,* produced in Philadelphia, then Majestic Theatre, New York City, 1966; (from the play by Giles Cooper) *Everything in the Garden,* Plymouth Theatre, New York City, 1967, published by Atheneum, 1968; *Box* and *Quotations from Chairman Mao Tse-*

Tung, Studio Arena Theatre, Buffalo, NY, 1968, then Billy Rose Theatre, New York City, 1968, published by Atheneum, 1969.

All Over, Martin Beck Theatre, New York City, 1971, then by the Royal Shakespeare Company at the Aldwych Theatre, London, 1972, published by Atheneum, 1971; *Seascape,* Shubert Theatre, New York City, 1975, published by Atheneum, 1975; *Counting the Ways,* produced by the National Theatre Company of Great Britain, London, 1976, then Hartford Stage Company, CT, 1977; *Listening: A Chamber Play,* Hartford Stage Company, 1977, published together in one volume entitled, *Counting the Ways* and *Listening: Two Plays,* Atheneum, 1977; *The Lady from Dubuque,* Hartford State Company, then Morosco Theatre, New York City, 1980, published by Atheneum, 1979.

(Adaptation) *Lolita,* Wilbur Theatre, Boston, 1981, then Brooks Atkinson Theatre, New York City, 1981; *The Man Who Had Three Arms,* New World Festival, Miami, 1982, then Goodman Theatre, Chicago, 1982.

SCREENPLAYS—*A Delicate Balance,* AFT Distributing, 1973; (adaptation) *Le Locataire (The Tenant,),* 1976; *The Death of Bessie Smith;* also screenplays concerning Nijinsky, Stanford White, and Evelyn Nesbitt.

TELEVISION—*The Death of Bessie Smith,* ITV, London, 1965; *The American Dream,* ITV, London, 1965; also, *All Over,* 1976. RADIO PLAYS—*Listening: A Chamber Play,* BBC, 1976.

BOOKS—Author of introductions: *Three Plays by Noel Coward: Blithe Spirit, Hay Fever, Private Lives,* Delta, 1965; *National Playwrights Directory,* edited by Phyllis Johnson Kaye, second edition, Eugene O'Neill Theatre Center, 1981; (with Sabina Lietzmann) *New York,* Vendome Press, 1981; *Louise Nevelson: Atmospheres and Environments,* Clarkson N. Potter, Inc., 1981.

AWARDS: Best New Foreign Play, Berlin Festival Award, 1959, for *The Zoo Story* and 1960, for *The Death of Bessie Smith;* Outstanding Contribution to the Off-Broadway Theatre, Vernon Rice Memorial Award and Obie Award, 1960, and Argentine Critics Circle Award, 1961, all for *The Zoo Story;* Best Plays of 1960-61, Foreign Press Association Award, 1961, for *The Death of Bessie Smith* and *The American Dream;* Lola D'Annunzio Award, 1961, for *The American Dream;* Most Promising Playwright, New York Drama Critics Award, 1963; Best Play, Antoinette Perry Award, New York Drama Critics Circle Award, Outstanding American Playwright, Outer Circle Award, Best American Play, Foreign Press Association, American National Theatre Association Award, *Saturday Review* Drama Critics Award, and *Variety* Drama Critics Poll Award, all 1963, and the *Evening Standard* Award, 1964, all for *Who's Afraid of Virginia Woolf?;* co-recipient (with Richard Barr and Clinton Wilder), Margo Jones Award, 1965; Pulitzer Prize Awards, 1967, for *A Delicate Balance* and 1975, for *Seascape;* American Academy and Institute of Arts and Letters Gold Medal Award, 1980; Creative Arts Award, 1983, 1984.

Honorary Degrees: Doctor of Letters, Emerson College, 1967, Trinity College, 1974.

MEMBER: Dramatists Guild, P.E.N., National Institute of Arts and Letters; National Endowment (grant-giving council); New York State Council for the Arts (governing commission); National Society of Arts and Letters, Brandeis University (committee chairman).

SIDELIGHTS: With his early one-acts, notably *The Zoo Story* (1959) and *The American Dream* (1961), Edward Albee established himself as a leader of the younger generation of American playwrights whose home was New York's Off-Broadway theater. His first Broadway play, *Who's Afraid of Virginia Woolf?* (1962), widely regarded as the greatest American play of the last twenty-five years, made him a culture hero and the apparent successor to Eugene O'Neill and Tennessee Williams as the United States' leading playwright. While Albee is still considered his country's most important practitioner of the so-called "theater of the absurd," his post-1962 plays have failed, for some critics and much of the public, to meet the expectations created by his early works. For C. W. Bigsby, the editor of the 1975 anthology *Edward Albee: A Collection of Critical Essays,* part of the problem is that "Albee has remained at heart a product of Off-Broadway, claiming the same freedom to experiment and, indeed, fail, which is the special strength of that theatre. . . . [yet] he continues to offer his plays to a Broadway audience who, even given their tolerance for anything which can be officially ratified as 'art,' find his refusal to repeat the formula of *Who's Afraid of Virginia Woolf?* increasingly perverse."

The adopted son of millionaire Reed Albee, whose father had founded the Keith-Albee chain of vaudeville theatres, Edward Albee was expelled from several prep schools and, in 1947, Trinity College. For the next eleven years, he worked at assorted odd jobs. "Then at thirty, a kind of explosion took place in my life," he explained to a reporter for the Hartford Stage Company's publication *On the Scene* in 1980. "I'd been drifting and I got fed up with myself. I decided to write a play." Accordingly, he quit his job as a Western Union messenger and wrote *The Zoo Story* in three weeks. The play was rejected by several Broadway producers, and received its first production through a highly circuitous route described by Albee in his introduction to its published edition: ". . . a young composer friend of mine. . . looked at the play, liked it, and sent it to several friends of his, among them David Diamond, another American composer, resident in Italy; Diamond liked the play and sent it on to a friend of *his,* a Swiss actor, Pinkas Braun; Braun liked the play, made a tape recording of it, playing both its roles, which he sent on to [an editor at] the S. Fischer Verlag, a large publishing house in Frankfurt; she, in turn. . . well, through her it got to Berlin, and to production."

The Zoo Story was successful enough in Berlin so that producers Richard Barr and Clinton Wilder brought it to New York's Off-Broadway Provincetown Playhouse on a double bill with Samuel Beckett's *Krapp's Last Tape.* After that opening, which took place on January 14, 1960, the critics hailed the play, in the words of *The Nation's* (February 13, 1960) Harold Clurman, as "the introduction to what could prove to be a major talent on the American stage." Clurman also claimed that "*The Zoo Story* interested me more than any other new American play thus far this season." Richard Watts, Jr. of the *New York Post* (January 15, 1960) echoed Clurman's judgement: "*The Zoo Story* demonstrates that the hitherto unproduced American is a playwright who writes with power, skill and freshness, and he is clearly a man with a claim to attention." What made the play striking, in Watts's opinion, was "that Mr. Albee can make his narrative seem ominous and his climax chilling while writing with unhackneyed vigor, observing with humor, insight and sympathy, and drawing character with vividness and force."

A simple, two-character play, *The Zoo Story* describes the encounter, on a Central Park bench, of Peter, an executive, and Jerry, who looks like a typical "beatnik" of the period but steadfastly resists stereotyping. The play revolves around Jerry's attempt to intrude on Peter's space, both physically (the bench) and psychologically. At its end, Jerry forces Peter to kill him. This ending has been viewed by commentators in two ways. Some have seen it as positive, feeling that Jerry, by his death, has at last awakened the human feelings in Peter; others have viewed it more pessimistically.

In the year following the New York premiere of *The Zoo Story,* Albee produced four more one-acts Off-Broadway, *The Death of Bessie Smith, The Sandbox, Fam and Yam,* and *The American Dream.* Of these works, *The American Dream,* a savage satire on the so-called "typical" American family, received the most favorable reception from the critics. Richard P. Cooke of the *Wall Street Journal* (January 26, 1961) wrote: "Mr. Albee provides [the characters] with just about every cliche of family life, and then, by his gift for the unfriendly comic twist, endows them with an almost frightening vitality. We are aghast that such gusto can be generated in such hollow bosoms."

Albee's first full-length play and, in the opinion of many, his masterpiece, *Who's Afraid of Virginia Woolf?* depicts a night of bickering between a couple in a New England college town: George, a history professor and Martha, the daughter of the college president. At first, the shrewish Martha appears to dominate her quieter husband. At the play's climax, however, George spoils an elaborate game the couple has been playing in which they pretend to have a son. He reveals, in front of a visiting couple, that the son has died.

The Broadway opening night of *Who's Afraid of Virginia Woolf?* was described by John McClain of the *New York Journal-American* (October 15, 1962) as "the most enthusiastic outing of the past several seasons." McClain added: "From almost the first entrance, there was that indefinable yet infallible aura of success seeping from the stage through the audience. This is a Big One." These words were echoed by most of McClain's fellow critics, who used phrases like "No one will depart unshaken" (Norman Nadel of the *New York World-Telegram and Sun*) and "It need not be liked, but it must be seen" (Walter Kerr of the *New York Herald Tribune*).

Howard Taubman of the *New York Times* (October 15, 1962) was somewhat less enthusiastic than Kerr, McClain, and the others, but still called the play "a wry and electric evening in the theater." He went on to say: "Although Mr. Albee's vision is grim and sardonic, he is never solemn. With the instincts of a born dramatist and the shrewdness of one whose gifts have been tempered in the theater, he knows how to fill the stage with vitality and excitement." Although Taubman understood that not all playgoers would sympathize with Albee's characters, he felt that everyone would find them "vibrant with dramatic urgency. In their anger and terror they are pitiful as well as corrosive, but they are also wildly and humanly hilarious." Taubman was also an admirer of Albee's dialogue which, in the critic's words, "is dipped in acid, yet ripples with a relish of the ludicrous."

Who's Afraid of Virginia Woolf? also had its detractors, who focused largely on the play's language and frank treatment of sexual themes. The Boston city censor threatened to revoke the license of the theater where *Virginia Woolf* was playing until Albee and the producers agreed to delete one word, the name of Jesus Christ used as an expletive. The Pulitzer Prize drama jury, consisting of critic John Mason Brown and Yale professor John Gassner, nominated the play for the prize but the advisory board rejected it. Brown and Gassner then resigned from the jury in protest.

Since its original Broadway run ended, *Virginia Woof* has continued to be a source of controversy among literary critics who offer differing interpretations of the play. It has been suggested, among other things, that George and Martha are actually homosexuals; that their names stand for George and Martha Washington; and that the play is actually, metaphorically, about the hydrogen bomb.

Albee's next major play, *Tiny Alice*, also provoked a large controversy when it opened on Broadway in 1964, in that it was possibly too obscure. The bulk of the plot is simple enough: a lay brother in the Catholic Church is seduced by, and subsequently marries, a wealthy woman who is donating a large sum to the church, but he is then shot by her lawyer. Only the last scene, in which the dying lay brother either is confronted by an unseen god or abstraction or hallucinates that this happens, is actually difficult to understand. Most people felt, however, that the entire play was allegorical in some way that they could not comprehend. Even Albee's publisher asked him to write an introduction to the published version of the play explaining it. He at first agreed to do so but then changed his mind, as he explained in the brief "Author's Note" that he did write, "because I find. . . that I share the view of even more people: that the play is quite clear."

The frequently perplexed reviewers gave *Tiny Alice* mixed reviews, with their attitude often depending on how well they were able to accept their own bafflement. In his *New York World-Telegram and Sun* review (December 30, 1964), Norman Nadel referred to the play as "massive theater. . . an allegory in conventional dramatic form, which transcends conventional dramas in almost every dimension." He also found *Tiny Alice* to be "superlative in the lofty literacy of its speech, the awesome depth of its several mysteries, and the shocking audacity of its premise." Critics Martin Gottfried, Walter Kerr, and Michael Smith were all more negative than Nadel, although all saw some merit in the work. Gottfried described it in *Women's Wear Daily* (December 30, 1964) as "at once extraordinary and ridiculous." While, in his opinion, the play "wriggled and slipped through an assortment of philosophical pretensions as disorganized as a student notebook," it was also "a play of exhilarating theatricality." For Kerr, on the other hand, it was precisely theatricality that was missing in the play, due to the goals Albee had set for himself—which Kerr nonetheless respected. "If the play is to say that no true human union can be achieved, then Mr. Albee must. . . refuse himself people. . . That he has done. . . The universe is indifferent, impenetrable, from the beginning." Writing in the *New York Herald Tribune* of December 30, 1964, Kerr saw the play as uninteresting, but felt that this had to be the case if the playwright were to avoid cheating. In his view, the play "is moving toward an absolute negation. It cannot, in honesty, occupy us with sham positives—real goals, actual tensions, promises of satisfaction—along the way."

In Smith's analysis, as expressed in the *Village Voice* of January 14, 1965, "the play exists on two levels, the naturalistic and the mythic. Each is fascinating as far as it goes, but the intended interaction barely occurs." Although Smith believed that Albee "conceived the play on an ambitious scale," as he viewed it "the play remains fragmented, its pieces uneven in quality, structurally out of mind to the raw creation." Nonetheless, Smith concluded that the errors of the play were "relatively superficial—in choice of metaphor, in formal application," but that the sensibility behind it was "contemporary, original and authentic."

With *A Delicate Balance* in 1966, Albee returned to a more realistic mode. Albee's previous plays had featured essentially unsympathetic characters, and the first thought that struck critic Richard Watts about this play was that "it reveals a new note that might almost be described as compassion." In the *New York Post* of September 23, 1966, Watts went on to say that the play "has all the quality of brilliantly corroding and lacerating wit that has marked his previous work. But, amid the mutual exchange of biting insults in his dialogue, there is a sympathetic feeling for the embattled characters that represents an advance in the understanding of human inner-torment." Watts perhaps alluded to the *Tiny Alice* controversy when he wrote that the new play "suggests thoughtful depths of meaning but is not cast in the form of a puzzling enigma." As he saw it, *A Delicate Balance* was "written with not only the author's characteristic sharpness of humor but also with the grace of style that gives his work for the theater its quality of literary distinction." *A Delicate Balance* was awarded the Pulitzer Prize for Drama—an honor that many felt was Albee's compensation for losing the prize he should have received for *Virginia Woolf*.

Albee's most audaciously avant-garde work came two years later in the bill of the one-act plays *Box* and *Quotations from Chairman Mao Tse-Tung*. The first of these consists of a series of random musings suggested by the word "box," which are recited by an offstage woman's voice while a large cube stands alone on stage. In *Quotations*, three disparate characters recite lines which have no evident connection with each other, while a fourth character, dressed as a minister, stands on the stage without speaking. Albee, in his introduction to the published version of the play, explained that "I have attempted, in these two related plays, several experiments having to do—in the main—with the application of musical form to dramatic structure." He also stated that audiences could appreciate the plays very simply: "All that one need do is—quite simply—relax and let the plays happen. That, and be willing to approach the dramatic experience without a preconception of what the nature of the dramatic experience should be."

Clive Barnes was evidently willing to follow Albee's advice. In his *New York Times* review of the play (October 1, 1968), Barnes commented: "I enjoyed it. I don't say I understood it—actually, I presumed, perhaps wrongly, that there wasn't very much to understand—but I let the works lap over me like creative foam over a more than usually receptive stone, heard some of them, let them run around in my mind, and this way or that way gathered an experience. Which, in the theater, is what we are fundamentally talking about."

Other critics, however, felt that the plays were pretentious and lacked any real meaning; Martin Gottfried in *Women's Wear Daily* of October 1, 1968, characterized them as "sloppy, boring and frankly, stupid." Perhaps the most interesting critical comment on the double bill was the left-handed compliment tendered by Walter Kerr in the Sunday *New York Times* (October 13, 1968): "I have noticed people asleep at the playlets. . . but I have yet to discover anyone who has been infuriated by them."

Since then, Albee has produced a wide variety of plays in various styles, all of which have received a sharply divided response from reviewers. He won his second Pulitzer Prize in 1975 for *Seascape*, a comedy in which a human couple meets a pair of lizards about to evolve. Clive Barnes, who had emerged as the playwright's most consistent advocate, called that play "a major dramatic event" (*New York Times*, January 27, 1975), adding, "As Mr. Albee has matured as a playwright, his work has become leaner, sparer and simpler. He depends on strong theatrical strokes to attract the attention of the audience, but the tone of the writing is always thoughtful, even careful, even philosophic." On the other hand, John Simon of *New York* magazine (February 10, 1975), a "self-proclaimed Albeephobe," wrote, "This simple-minded allegory can be interpreted in a dozen convenient, wishy-washy ways. . .

Albee endows it only with doughy verbiage, feebly quivering inaction, and grandly gesticulating pretentiousness.''

For his own part, Albee, in his public statements, has insisted that he cares little about the critical and public response to his plays. In the program for the Hartford Stage Company's 1980 production of his *The Lady from Dubuque*, he is quoted as saying, ''The popularity of a piece of writing will always tell you more about the state of critical letters and public taste than it will about the excellence of the work.'' He went on to address specifically the charge that his plays were ''obscure'': ''If I limited my plays to only those questions to which I have the answers they'd be pretty dull plays, and I think a play should be an open-ended experience rather than a solved experience.''

In his most recent play, *The Man Who Had Three Arms* (1983), Albee struck back directly at some of the more negative critical judgments of his work, and in particular at the widespread notion that he has accomplished little of value since *Virginia Woolf*. Its obviously autobiographical protagonist, referred to only as ''Himself,'' had once become a celebrity because he possessed a third arm, but faded into obscurity when the extra limb withered away.

Perhaps predictably, reviewers responded to *The Man Who Had Three Arms* with more invective. ''The sad thing,'' Jack Kroll commented in *Newsweek* (April 18, 1983), ''is not his attack on us, but his apparent retroactive definition of himself as a circus sideshow.'' Frank Rich of *The New York Times* (April 6, 1983) was also largely negative but did admire the play's ending, in which Himself is torn between asking the audience to leave or stay. ''It's a painful, if embarrassing, spectacle,'' Rich wrote, ''because it shows us the real and sad confusion that exists somewhere beneath the narcissistic arrogance and bile that the author uses as a dodge to avoid introspection the rest of the time.''

When he is not writing his own plays, Albee is a frequent guest lecturer at colleges and universities throughout the United States. In 1981, as a member of the Artistic Directorate of the Vivian Beaumont Theatre at New York's Lincoln Center, he sponsored a program of one-acts by young North and South American playwrights. An admirer of contemporary art, Albee has also been a patron for young artists through his Albee Foundation, based at his home in Montauk, New York. He is an avid champion of the avant-garde and experimental in all arts—the ''dangerous'' as opposed to the ''safe,'' as he put it in a 1981 interview for *Contemporary Authors* (Gale Research, 1981). In 1962, he commented in the *New York Times Magazine*: ''The health of a nation, of a society, can be determined by the art it demands.''

ADDRESSES: HOME—14 Harrison Street, New York, NY 10013. AGENT—William Morris Agency, 1350 Sixth Avenue, New York, NY 10019.*

*   *   *

ALDA, Rutanya

PERSONAL: Born Rutanya Skrastins, October 13, in Riga, Latvia; daughter of Janis (a poet) and Vera (a businesswoman; maiden name, Ozolins) Skrastins; married Richard Bright (an actor), June 11, 1977. EDUCATION: University of Northern Arizona, B.S.; studied acting with Barbara Loden and Paul Mann in New York City.

RUTANYA ALDA

VOCATION: Actress.

CAREER: STAGE DEBUT—Ellen, *Sunday in New York,* Yarmouth Playhouse, Cape Cod, MA, 1965. PRINCIPAL STAGE APPEARANCES—Teresa, *Every Place Is Newark,* Theatre at St. Clements, New York City, 1980; also: Julia, *A Thing Called Child* and Sister Johanna, *The Cradle Song,* both at the Berkshire Playhouse, MA; Ellen, *Luv,* Cellar Theatre, Los Angeles; the Actress, *The Exercise,* Actors Studio, Los Angeles; Falidia, *And They Put Handcuffs on the Flowers,* Inner City Cultural Center, Los Angeles; Jennifer, *Middle Class White,* Los Angeles Actors Theatre; Esther, *A Cat in the Ghetto,* Whole Theatre Company, Montclair, NJ; Miss Gilpin, *The Straw,* Barbara Loden Workshop, New York City; Ern, *Sacraments,* Harold Clurman Theatre, New York City.

PRINCIPAL STAGE WORK—Director, *And They Put Handcuffs on the Flowers,* Inner City Cultural Center, Los Angeles.

FILM DEBUT—Linda, *Greetings,* Sigma III, 1969. PRINCIPAL FILM APPEARANCES—*Hi Mom,* Sigma III, 1970; Nurse Anne, *Panic in Needle Park,* Twentieth Century-Fox, 1971; hippie, *Scarecrow,* Warner Brothers, 1973; Rutanya Sweet, *The Long Goodbye,* 1973; Assassination Team B, *Executive Action,* National General, 1973; Ruthie Lee, *Pat Garrett and Billy the Kid,* Metro-Goldwyn-Mayer (MGM), 1973; Apple Mary, *Deadly Hero,* AVCO-Embassy, 1976; Kristen, *The Fury,* Twentieth Century-Fox, 1978; Angela, *The Deer Hunter,* Universal, 1978; Mrs. Mandrakis, *When a Stranger Calls,* Columbia, 1979; Carol Ann, *Mommie Dearest,* Paramount, 1981; Dolores, *Amityville II: The Possession,* Orion, 1982; Vicki, *Vigilante,* Films Around the World, 1982; Mrs. Nash, *Racing with the Moon,* Paramount, 1983; *Girls' Nite Out,* Aries

International, 1984; *Rappin,* Cannon Films, 1985; *Hot Shot,* Twentieth Century-Fox, 1986; *Black Widow,* Twentieth Century-Fox, 1986; Alma, *The Long Lost Friend,* 1986; also appeared in *The Nap* (short).

TELEVISION DEBUT—Rachel, *Can Ellen Be Saved,* ABC, 1975. PRINCIPAL TELEVISION APPEARANCES—Episodic: *Doc Elliot,* ABC; Mrs. Degnan, *Cannon,* CBS; *As the World Turns,* CBS; *General Hospital,* ABC. Movies: Jess, *Battered,* NBC, 1978; also, *Nobody Ever Died of Old Age,* PBS.

MEMBER: Actors' Equity Association, Screen Actors Guild, American Federation of Radio and Television Artists.

SIDELIGHTS: Rutanya Alda told *CTFT:* "Growing up in displaced persons camps after World War II, I saw my first play, a fairy tale, done in the camps. It showed a better life than I was living in, it was magical and I said to myself then and there, that's what I want to do. . . . My favorite role is really the one I'm currently working on, whatever it may be. But there are some that stand out—Angela in *The Deer Hunter,* Linda in *Greetings,* the 'be black baby sequence' in *Hi Mom,* Carol Ann in *Mommie Dearest,* and Alma in *The Long Lost Friend.*"

ADDRESSES: HOME—New York, NY. MANAGER—Jerry Silverhardt, Moorehardt Management, 231 W. 58th Street, New York, NY 10019.

*   *   *

ALDREDGE, Theoni V.   1932-

PERSONAL: Born Theoni Athanasios Vachlioti, August 22, 1932, in Salonika, Greece; daughter of Athanasios (an army general) and Meropi (Gregoriades) Vachlioti; married Tom Aldredge (an actor), December 10, 1953. EDUCATION: Attended the American School, Athens; studied at the Goodman Theatre School, Chicago, 1949-52.

VOCATION: Costume designer.

CAREER: FIRST STAGE WORK—Costume designer, *The Distaff Side,* Goodman Theatre, Chicago, 1950. PRINCIPAL STAGE WORK—Costume designer: *The Importance of Being Earnest,* stock production, 1953; *The Immoralist,* Studebaker Theatre, Chicago, 1956; *Much Ado About Nothing, A View from the Bridge, Lysistrata,* and *The Guardsman,* all at the Studebaker Theatre, Chicago, 1957.

The following costume design all for New York City productions unless indicated: *Heloise* and *The Golden Six,* both 1958; *The Nervous Set, The Saintliness of Margery Kempe, Chic, The Geranium Hat, Flowering Cherry, Silent Night Lonely Night,* and Geraldine Page's costumes in *Sweet Bird of Youth,* all 1959.

A Distant Bell, The Best Man, Measure for Measure, Hedda Gabler, Rosemary, The Alligators, all 1960; *Mary, Mary, Under Milkwood, Smiling the Boy Fell Dead, First Love, Ghosts, A Short Happy Life, Much Ado About Nothing, A Midsummer Night's Dream, The Devil's Advocate,* all 1961; *The Umbrella, Rosmersholm, I Can Get It for You Wholesale, Macbeth, King Lear, The Tempest, The Merchant of Venice, Mr. President, Tchin-Tchin, Who's Afraid of Virginia Woolf?,* all 1962; *The Blue Boy in Black, Memo, The Time of the Barracudas, Anthony and Cleopatra, As You Like*

It, The Winter's Tale, The Trojan Women, and Geraldine Page's costumes in *Strange Interlude,* all 1963; *But for Whom Charlie, Anyone Can Whistle, The Three Sisters, Hamlet, The Knack, Othello, Electra, Any Wednesday, Luv, Poor Richard, Ready When You Are CB!,* and Geraldine Page's costumes in *P.S. I Love You,* all 1964; *Coriolanus, Troilus and Cressida, Minor Miracle, The Porcelain Year, Skyscraper, The Playroom, Cactus Flower,* all 1965.

UTBU, First One Asleep, Whistle, Happily Never After, A Time for Singing, Sergeant Musgrave's Dance, All's Well That Ends Well, Measure for Measure, Richard III, A Delicate Balance, all 1966; *You Know I Can't Hear You When the Water's Running, That Summer . . . That Fall, Ilya Darling, Little Murders, The Comedy of Errors, Hamlet, Hair, King John, Titus Andronicus, Daphne in Cottage D, The Trial of Lee Harvey Oswald,* all 1967; *Before You Go, I Never Sang for My Father, Portrait of a Queen, Weekend, The Only Game in Town, Ergo, The Memorandum, King Lear, Ballad for a Firing Squad, Huui Huui, Henry IV,* Parts I and II, *Hamlet, Romeo and Juliet, Don Rodrigo,* all 1968; *Zelda, Billy, The Gingham Dog, Cities in Bezique, Invitation to a Beheading, Peer Gynt, Electra, Twelfth Night,* all 1969.

The Wars of the Roses, Parts I and II, *Richard III, The Happiness Cage, Trelawny of the Wells, Colette,* Jack Macgowran's costumes in the *Works of Samuel Beckett,* all 1970; *Subject to Fits* (also designed the costumes in the London production), *Blood, Underground, The Basic Training of Pavlo Hummel, Timon of Athens, Two Gentlemen of Verona, The Tale of Cymbeline, The Incomparable Max, Sticks and Bones, The Wedding of Iphigenia, Iphigenia in Concert,* all 1971; *The Sign in Sidney Brustein's Window, Voices, That Championship Season, Older People, The Hunter, The Corner, Hamlet, Ti-Jean and His Brothers, Much Ado About Nothing, The Wedding Band, Children,* all 1972; *A Village Romeo and Juliet, The Three Sisters, No Hard Feelings, The Orphan, Nash at Nine, As You Like It, King Lear, The Boom Boom Room, The Au Pair Man,* and the London production of *Two Gentlemen of Verona,* all 1973; *Find Your Way Home, The Killdeer, The Dance of Death, Music! Music!, An American Millionaire, In Praise of Love, Mert & Phil, Kid Champion,* and the London production of *That Championship Season,* 1974; *A Doll's House, Little Black Sheep, A Chorus Line, Trelawny of the Wells,* and the Los Angeles production of *Souvenir,* all 1975.

Rich and Famous, Mrs. Warren's Profession, The Belle of Amherst, The Baker's Wife, Threepenny Opera, The Eccentricities of a Nightingale, all 1976; *Marco Polo Sings a Solo, Annie,* and the Philadelphia production of *The Dream,* all 1977; *Ballroom,* 1978; *The Grand Tour, Break a Leg, The Madwoman of Central Park West,* all 1979; *Barnum, 42nd Street,* both 1980; *Woman of the Year, Dreamgirls,* both 1981; New York Shakespeare Festival (NYSF) production of *Hamlet, Ghosts, A Little Family Business,* all 1982; *Merlin,* 1983, NYSF production of *Buried Inside Extra,* 1983; *Private Lives, La Cage aux Folles,* both 1983; *The Rink,* 1984.

PRINCIPAL FILM WORK—Costume Designer: *Girl of the Night,* Warner Brothers, 1960; *You're a Big Boy Now,* Seven Arts, 1967; *No Way to Treat a Lady,* Paramount, 1968; *Uptight,* 1968; *Last Summer,* Paramount, 1969; *I Never Sang for My Father,* Columbia, 1970; *Promise at Dawn,* AVCO-Embassy, 1971; *The Great Gatsby,* Paramount, 1974; *Network,* United Artists, 1977; *Semi-Tough,* United Artists, 1977; *The Cheap Detective,* Columbia, 1978; *Fury!,* Twentieth Century-Fox, 1978; *Eyes of Laura Mars,* Columbia, 1978; *The Champ,* United Artists, 1979; *The Rose,*

Twentieth Century-Fox, 1979; *Middle Age Crazy,* Twentieth Century-Fox, 1980; *Racing with the Moon,* Paramount, 1984.

PRINCIPAL TELEVISION WORK—Mini-Series: Costume designer, *Nutcracker,* NBC, 1987.

AWARDS: Academy Award, 1974, for *The Great Gatsby;* Distinguished Service to the Off-Broadway Theatre, Obie Award, 1976; British Academy of Motion Picture Arts Award, 1976, for *The Great Gatsby;* Antoinette Perry Awards: 1977, for *Annie,* 1980, for *Barnum,* and 1984, for *La Cage aux Folles;* Marharam Award, for *Peer Gynt;* also received numerous Drama Desk and New York Drama Critics Awards; received the honorary degree of Doctor of Humane Letters from DePaul University.

MEMBER: United Scenic Artists, Costume Designers Guild, Academy of Motion Picture Arts and Sciences.

SIDELIGHTS: "The terror of designing costumes is that you never *really* know what anything will look like until the curtain goes up," costume designer Theoni V. Aldredge told John Gruen of the *New York Times* (April 8, 1984). "It's always something of a shock to me when the images you've carried in your head or produced in a sketch assume reality on the stage. But that's the magic of it." Between 1958 and 1984, the award-winning designer Aldredge created costumes for approximately one hundred sixty-five Broadway productions, including such hit musicals as *A Chorus Line, 42nd Street,* and *La Cage aux Folles,* as well as numerous Off-Broadway shows, films, operas, and ballets. In the Gruen article, one of her mentors, producer Joseph Papp explained: "Theoni never actually creates a costume; it's real clothing that comes out of character. She has an incomparable sense of what is psychologically and dramatically appropriate, and with an almost maternal instinct will bring a loving and human touch to it."

A member of a distinguished Greek family, Aldredge decided to become a costume designer when she saw the 1945 British movie version of *Caesar and Cleopatra.* She left her war-ravaged native land and came to America at age seventeen to enroll at the Goodman Theatre School, then a division of the Art Institute of Chicago. She originally planned to remain in the United States for only one or two years, but that plan changed after she married actor Tom Aldredge, a fellow Goodman student.

The couple moved to New York in 1957, and two years later Aldredge received her first big break when actress Geraldine Page, who had appeared with the Goodman company, asked Aldredge to design her costumes for the Broadway production of Tennessee William's *Sweet Bird of Youth.* Several more Broadway jobs followed. Another pivotal assignment came in 1960, when a then-obscure producer named Joseph Papp hired Aldredge for his Central Park production of *Measure for Measure.* Aldredge would go on to design costumes for over fifty of Papp's productions, and for several years she held the title of "principal costume designer" for his New York Shakespeare Festival.

One show that Aldredge designed for Papp was the blockbuster 1975 musical *A Chorus Line.* She found this a difficult assignment because each character wore only one outfit—until the show's finale. "It is more difficult to do a rehersal garment than it is to do a beaded gown," she told Sheryl Flatow of *Dramatics* (May, 1983). Feeling that each costume had to reflect the character of the individual who wore it, she based her designs largely on the outfits the actors wore to rehearsal. "To find a character in each dancer took us six months. I was in rehearsal every day with my Polaroid,

and I watched the kids because they brought their own personalities. And I just borrowed from what they brought." The designer told Flatow: "I took it as a compliment if people said, 'Well, they're wearing their own clothes.' That is what it should look like." So it did not bother her to receive little recognition for her work on this production.

In fact, Aldredge firmly believes that if the audience comes out of a show praising the costumes, the designer has not done the job properly. "You don't take over a show. What you do is enhance it, because the costumes are there to serve a producer's vision, a director's viewpoint and, most importantly, an actor's comfort." She concluded: "To me, good design is design you're not aware of. It must exist as part of the whole—as an aspect of characterization."

In sharp contrast to her work for *A Chorus Line* were Aldredge's lavish outfits for *Dreamgirls,* director Michael Bennett's 1981 musical about a rock group's rise and fall. The costumes for the show cost more than one million dollars, and thanks to Bennett, she was given a year to complete her work on the show, including eight weeks—more time than she usually spends on an entire show—just for the accessories. Sheryl Flatow pointed out in *Playbill* (July, 1982) that one second-act scene, in which the singing group poses for a spread in *Vogue* magazine, created an especially strong effect: "The costumes are stunning, their effect is magical and the audience inevitably breaks into applause."

Her next major musical, *La Cage aux Folles,* gave Aldredge a new sort of challenge, since mmost of its cast consisted of men dressed as women. In fact, she originally did not want to do the show, but relented when director Arthur Laurents explained that it was to be a love story rather than just a "drag" show. "As it turned out," she told Gruen, "none of our boys, including our lead, George Hearn, had ever worn a dress in their lives." Aldredge had the men wear high heels and dresses at all rehearsals so that they could adjust to the women's clothing. "Had I designed the same costumes for women, the effect would not be the same. The real impact is seeing the costumes on the men, because they project a heightened sense of female glamour—a more outrageous delight in flaunting the image of show-girl razzmatazz."

Aldredge first branched out into films in 1960 with *Girl of the Night.* Of the many films she has worked on, probably the best-known (as far as her work goes) is *The Great Gatsby,* the 1974 movie adaptation of F. Scott Fitzgerald's novel. The film not only brought Aldredge an Oscar, but it spawned a fad for 1920's clothing, particularly white suits.

ADDRESSES: OFFICE—890 Broadway, New York, NY 10003.

*   *   *

ALEXANDER, Jane   1939-

PERSONAL: Born Jane Quigley, October 28, 1939, in Boston, MA; daughter of Thomas B. (an M.D.) and Ruth Elizabeth (Pearson) Quigley; married Robert Alexander (an actor and director), July 23, 1962 (divorced, 1969); married Edwin Sherin (a director), March 29, 1975; children: (first marriage) Jason. EDUCATION: Attended Sarah Lawrence College, 1957-58, University of Edinburgh, 1959-60.

VOCATION: Actress, producer, and writer.

CAREER: BROADWAY DEBUT—Eleanor Bachman, *The Great White Hope,* Alvin Theatre, October 3, 1968. PRINCIPAL STAGE APPEARANCES—Member, Arena Stage acting company, Washington, DC, 1965-68; Katrina, *Mother Courage and Her Children,* Arena Stage, Washington, DC, 1970; Mistress Page, *The Merry Wives of Windsor* and Lavinia, *Mourning Becomes Electra,* both 1970, and title role, *Major Barbara,* 1971, all with the American Shakespeare Festival, Stratford, CT; Kitty Duval, *The Time of Your Life,* Eisenhower Theatre, Kennedy Center, Washington, DC, Philadelphia, Chicago, and at the Huntington Hartford Theatre, Los Angeles, 1972; Anne Miller, *Six Rms Riv Vu,* Helen Hayes Theatre, New York City, 1972; Jacqueline Harrison, *Find Your Way Home,* Brooks Atkinson Theatre, New York City, 1974; Liz Essendine, *Present Laughter,* Eisenhower Theatre, Kennedy Center, Washington, DC, 1974; Gertrude, *Hamlet,* Vivian Beaumont Theatre, Lincoln Center, New York City, 1975; Catherine Sloper, *The Heiress,* Broadhurst Theatre, New York City, 1976; Hilda, *The Master Builder,* Eisenhower Theatre, Kennedy Center, Washington, DC, 1977; Judge Ruth Loomis, *First Monday in October,* Majestic Theatre, New York City, 1978; Joanne, *Losing Time,* Manhattan Theatre Club, New York City, 1979.

Natalia, *Goodbye Fidel,* Ambassador Theatre, New York City, 1980; Cleopatra, *Antony and Cleopatra,* Alliance Theatre, Atlanta, 1981; title role, *Hedda Gabler,* Hartman Theatre, Stamford, CT, then Boston, 1981; Annie, *Monday After the Miracle,* Spoleto Festival, Charleston, SC, then Eisenhower Theatre, Kennedy Center, Washington, DC, both 1982, then Eugene O'Neill Theatre, New York City, 1983; Anna, *Old Times,* Roundabout Theatre, Stage One, New York City, 1983-84.

FILM DEBUT—Eleanor Bachman, *The Great White Hope,* Twentieth Century-Fox, 1970. PRINCIPAL FILM APPEARANCES—*A Gunfight,* Paramount, 1971; Dorothy, *The New Centurions,* Columbia, 1972; *All the President's Men,* Warner Brothers, 1976; *The Betsy,* Allied Artists, 1978; *Kramer vs. Kramer,* Columbia, 1979; *Brubaker,* Twentieth Century-Fox, 1980; *Night Crossing,* Buena Vista, 1982; *Testament,* Paramount, 1983; *City Heat,* Warner Brothers, 1984; Juanelle, *Square Dance,* Island Pictures, 1987; Anna, *Sweet Country,* Cinema Group, 1987.

PRINCIPAL FILM WORK—Co-producer, *Square Dance,* Island Pictures, 1987.

PRINCIPAL TELEVISION APPEARANCES—Movies: *Welcome Home Johnny Bristol,* 1971; *Miracle on 34th Street,* 1973; *Death Be Not Proud,* 1974; *Eleanor and Franklin,* 1976; *Eleanor and Franklin: The White House Years,* 1977; *A Circle of Children,* 1977; *Lovey: A Circle of Children, Part II,* 1978; *Dear Liar,* PBS, 1978; *A Question of Love,* 1978; *Playing for Time,* CBS, 1980; *Calamity Jane: The Diary of a Frontier Woman,* CBS Cable, 1983; *In the Custody of Strangers,* 1983; *Calamity Jane,* CBS, 1984; *When She Says No,* 1984; *Malice in Wonderland,* CBS, 1985; *Blood & Orchids,* CBS, 1986; Mrs. Stockdale, *In Love and War,* NBC, 1987; *Open Admissions,* CBS, 1987. Teleplays: *The Time of Your Life, Find Your Way Home.*

PRINCIPAL TELEVISION WORK—Co-producer, *Calamity Jane,* CBS, 1984.

WRITINGS: PLAYS, TRANSLATED—(With Sam Engelstad) *The Master Builder.* BOOKS—(With Greta Jacobs) *The Bluefish Cookbook.*

RECORDINGS: AUDIO CASSETTES—*Wuthering Heights,* Random House; *Rebecca,* Warner.

AWARDS: Best Supporting Actress, Antoinette Perry Award, Drama Desk Award and *Theatre World* Award, all 1969, for *The Great White Hope;* Antoinette Perry Award nominations: 1973, for *Six Rms Riv Vu,* 1975, for *Find Your Way Home,* and 1979, for *First Monday in October;* Academy Award nominations: 1969, for *The Great White Hope,* 1976, for *All the President's Men,* 1979, for *Kramer vs. Kramer,* 1983, for *Testament;* Television Critics Circle Award, Emmy Award nomination, both 1976, for *Eleanor and Franklin: The White House Years;* Outstanding Supporting Actress in a Limited Series or a Special, Emmy Award, 1981, for *Playing for Time;* St. Botolph Club Achievement in Dramatic Arts, 1979; Israel Cultural Award, 1982; Emmy Award nominations, 1984, for *Calamity Jane* and 1985, for *Malice in Wonderland;* Helen Caldicott Leadership Award, 1984.

MEMBER: Actors' Equity Association, Screen Actors Guild, American Federation of Television and Radio Artists.

ADDRESSES: AGENT—William Morris Agency, 1350 Avenue of the Americas, New York, NY 10019.

*   *   *

ALLEN, Bob   1906-

PERSONAL: Born Irvine E. Theodore Baehr, March 28, 1906, in Mount Vernon, NY; son of Eugene Blasius (an importer and manufacturer) and Katherine (Braun) Baehr; married Evelyn Peirce (an actress and real estate broker), January 2, 1932; children: Katherine, Robert E. Theodore. EDUCATION: Dartmouth College, A.B. RELIGION: Evangelical Christian. MILITARY: United Service Organization, 1943-44.

VOCATION: Actor.

CAREER: PRINCIPAL FILM APPEARANCES—*The Quarterback,* Paramount, 1926; *Animal Crackers,* Paramount, 1926; *Revenge Rider,* Columbia, 1934; *Law Beyond the Range,* Columbia, 1934; *Fighting Shadows,* Columbia, 1934; "Range Rider" Series, Columbia, 1936-37: *The Unknown Ranger, Ranger Courage, Rio Grande Ranger, Law of the Range, The Ghost Ranger, The Rangers Step In.*

Also appeared in *Big Business Girl, Party Husband, Reckless Hour,* and *Night Nurse,* all 1931; *Menace* and *Winner Take All,* both 1932; *The Captain Hates the Sea,* 1934; *White Lies, Death Flies East, Crime and Punishment, Love Me Forever, Party Wire, Guard That Girl,* and *The Black Room,* all 1935; *Lady of Secrets* and *Craig's Wife,* both 1936; *The Awful Truth,* 1937; *Holiday* and *Kentucky* both 1938; *Winter Carnival,* 1939; *Jealousy* and *Pride of the Marines,* both 1945; *Perils of Pauline,* 1947; *Bodyguard,* 1948; *Brimstone, the Amish Horse,* Buena Vista, 1949.

Appeared in: *Guard That Girl; Race Track; Air Fury; Fighting Squadron; Air Hawks; I'll Love You Always; Meet the Girls; Life of Lafayette; Keep Smiling; Up the River; City of Chance; Everybody's Baby; Fighting Thoroughbreds; Fire Away;* the Judge, *Lenny Bruce, Dirty Mouth;* as Vermont father, *Pie in the Sky;* as Arizona lawyer, *Arizona Slim;* title role, *Fire Away, the Story of*

BOB ALLEN

Trotter, for Paramount, and recently *Raiders of the Living Dead*, 1986.

STAGE DEBUT—Dartmouth Players, Dartmouth College Theatre, 1924. PRINCIPAL STAGE APPEARANCES—Broadway: Standby for Melvyn Douglas, *Time Out for Ginger;* bellhop, standby for Roger Pryor, *Blessed Event;* lead, *A Few Wild Oats;* lead, *Popsy;* B.K. Froy, *I Killed the Count,* Cort Theatre; Turbill, *Kiss Them for Me,* Belasco Theatre; Steve, *Show Boat,* Ziegfeld Theatre; Mr. Babcock, *Auntie Mame;* Judson Morgan, *Whoopee,* American National Theatre Academy, 1980.

Regional and stock: J.B. Biggley, *How to Succeed in Business without Really Trying,* Equity Library Theatre, 1972; John Graham Whitfield, *Night of January 16th,* McAlpin Theatre; *Penthouse Legend,* MacAlpin Rooftop Theatre, 1973; *Laughing Feather,* 73rd Street Stage, 1975; *Mornings at Seven,* Syracuse Repertory Theatre, NY, 1975; Judson Morgan, *Whoopee,* Goodspeed Opera House, East Hadam, CT, 1979.

Also appeared on stage in: *Papa Is All; Jeannie; Pygmalion; Elmer the Great; The Show Off; The Hottentot; Cupcake; It's a Wise Child; That Ferguson Family; Finale; Goodbye Again; Coquette; Her Cardboard Lover; The Party's Over; Monna Vanna; Adam, the Creator; The Second Mrs. Tanqueray; The Late Christopher Bean; Baby Cyclone; Counsellor at Law; As Husbands Go; Unexpected Husband; Children of the Moon; Penny Arcade; Left Bank; There's Always Juliet; Holiday; Criminal at Large; Vinegar Tree; Church Mouse; Who'll Take Papa; The Bride the Sun Shines On; The Cat and the Canary; Junior Miss; Janie; Kiss and Tell; Society Girl;*

The Petrified Forest; Brief Holiday; Watch on the Rhine; The Shining Threshold and as Dr. *Benderley* in *Portrait of a Teacher.*

MAJOR TOURS—U.S. cities: Bert Jefferson, *The Man Who Came to Dinner,* Biltmore Theatre, Los Angeles and Curran Theatre, San Francisco, 1939-40; *The Greeks Had a Word for It;* Harry Graves, *Junior Miss;* Colonel H.C. Foley, *Over 21;* Dr. Shelby, *Blind Alley;* the Boss, *Time for Elizabeth.*

PRINCIPAL TELEVISION APPEARANCES—Series: Harold, *Ethel and Albert,* NBC; also General Blair, *First Love,* Judge Parker, *The Greatest Gift,* Dr. Wayland, *Fairmeadows, U.S.A.,* and Pritchard, *Atom Squad.* Episodic: *Kraft Theatre,* NBC; *Lux Playhouse,* CBS; *Armstrong Circle Theatre,* NBC; *Philco Television Playhouse,* NBC; *Theatre of the Mind,* NBC, 1949; *Pulitzer Prize Playhouse,* ABC; *The Web,* CBS; *Plainclothesman,* DuMont; *Danger,* CBS; *Suspense,* CBS; Judge Bishop, *Somerset,* NBC; also *Hollywood Doctor, Lamp Unto My Feet,* and *The First Hundred Years.*

NON-RELATED CAREER—Real estate broker, 1964—.

MEMBER: Seawanhaka, Corinthian Yacht Club.

ADDRESSES: OFFICE—Two Summit Court, Oyster Bay, NY 11771.

                    *   *   *

ALLEN, Karen   1951-

PERSONAL: Full name, Karen Jane Allen; born October 5, 1951, in Carrollton, IL; daughter of Carroll Thompson (an FBI Agent) and Patricia (a teacher; maiden name, Howell) Allen. EDUCATION: George Washington University, 1974-76; studied at the Washington Theatre Laboratory with Anthony Abeson and at the Theatre Institute with Lee Strasberg.

VOCATION: Actress.

CAREER: STAGE DEBUT—Jane, *The Innocent Party,* Washington Theatre Laboratory, Washington, DC, 1975. BROADWAY DEBUT—Helen Keller, *Monday After the Miracle,* Eugene O'Neill Theatre, 1982. PRINCIPAL STAGE APPEARANCES—Gittel, *Two for the Seesaw,* Berkshire Theatre Festival, Stockbridge, MA, 1981; Helen Keller, *Monday After the Miracle,* Eisenhower Theatre, Kennedy Center, Washington, DC, then Dock Street Theatre, Spoleto Festival, Charleston, SC, 1982; Laura, Esmerelda, and Miriam, *Tennessee Williams: A Celebration,* Williamstown Theatre Festival, MA, 1982; Marjorie, *Extremities,* West Side Arts Theatre, New York City, 1983; Laura, *The Glass Menagerie,* Williamstown Theatre Festival, 1985, the Longwharf Theatre, New Haven, CT, 1986; Annie Sullivan, *The Miracle Worker,* Roundabout Theatre, New York City, 1987.

FILM DEBUT—Katy, *National Lampoon's Animal House,* Universal, 1977. PRINCIPAL FILM APPEARANCES—*The Whidjit-Maker,* 1977; *Manhattan,* United Artists, 1979; *The Wanderers,* Orion, 1979; *A Small Circle of Friends,* United Artists, 1980; *Cruising,* United Artists, 1980; *Raiders of the Lost Ark,* Paramount, 1981; *Split Image,* Orion, 1982; *Shoot the Moon,* Metro-Goldwyn-Mayer/United Artists (MGM/UA), 1982; *Strange Invaders,* Orion, 1983; *Until September,* MGM/UA, 1983; *Starman,* Columbia, 1984; *The End of the Line,* 1986; *Backfire,* 1986; Laura, *The Glass Menagerie,* upcoming.

KAREN ALLEN

PRINCIPAL TELEVISION APPEARANCES—Movies: *Lovey: A Circle of Children, Part II*, 1978; Abra, *East of Eden*, 1979.

AWARDS: Best Actress, Academy of Science Fiction, Fantasy and Horror, 1982, for *Raiders of the Lost Ark; Theatre World* Award, 1983, for *Monday After the Miracle.*

MEMBER: Actors' Equity Association, Screen Actors Guild.

ADDRESSES: AGENT—c/o Joan Hyler, William Morris Agency, 151 El Camino Blvd., Beverly Hills, CA 90212.

*   *   *

ALLEN, Penelope

PERSONAL: EDUCATION: Trained for the theatre at the Actors Studio in New York City.

VOCATION: Actress.

CAREER: STAGE DEBUT—*Under Milk Wood*, Circle in the Square Theatre, New York City. PRINCIPAL STAGE APPEARANCES—*The Good Woman of Setzuan, Caucasian Chalk Circle, Ashes*, all at the Circle in the Square Theatre, New York City; *The Water Engine*, New York Shakespeare Festival, Public Theatre, New York City; Lady Ann, *Richard III*, Lyceum Theatre, New York City; *Chekhov Sketchbook*, Broadway production; performed for

many years with the Theatre Company of Boston, the Tyrone Guthrie Theatre, Minneapolis, MN, and Arena Stage in Washington, DC.

FILM DEBUT—Annie, *Scarecrow*, Warner Brothers, 1973. PRINCIPAL FILM APPEARANCES—Head bank teller, *Dog Day Afternoon*, Warner Brothers, 1975; Sara, *Resurrection*, Universal, 1980; Rose, *On the Nickle.*

TELEVISION DEBUT—Mother, *Gardners Son*, PBS. PRINCIPAL TELEVISION APPEARANCES—Movies: School teacher, *Sybil*, 1976; Mistress Hibbins, *Scarlet Letter*, PBS; Mary, *Mother Seton*, PBS; Miss Becker, *Until She Talks*, PBS.

ADDRESSES: HOME—42 Grand Street, New York, NY 10013.

*   *   *

ALLEN, Roland
See Ayckbourn, Alan

*   *   *

ALLEN, Steve   1921-

PERSONAL: Born December 26, 1921, in New York, NY; son of Billy (a vaudeville performer) and Belle (a vaudeville comedienne; maiden name, Montrose) Allen; married Dorothy Goodman (an actress; divorced, 1952); married Jayne Meadows (an actress and comedienne), July 31, 1954; children: (first marriage) Steve Jr., Brian, David; (second marriage) William Christopher. EDUCATION: Attended Drake University, 1940-41; attended Arizona State Teachers College, 1941-42. MILITARY: U.S. Army, infantry, 1942.

VOCATION: Comedian, actor, writer, producer, composer, lyricist, and musician.

CAREER: PRINCIPAL STAGE APPEARANCES—*The Pink Elephant*, Broadway production, 1953.

MAJOR TOURS—*Tonight at 8:30*, 1975; *The Wake*, Eastern theatre circuit, 1978.

PRINCIPAL CABARET AND CONCERT APPEARANCES—As a musician: The Blue Note and Michaels' Pub, both New York City; engagements with symphonies and pop orchestras around the U.S.

PRINCIPAL FILM APPEARANCES—*Down Memory Lane*, 1949; *I'll Get By*, 1950; *The Benny Goodman Story*, Universal, 1956; *College Confidential*, Universal, 1960; *Warning Shot*, Paramount, 1967.

PRINCIPAL RADIO WORK—Announcer, writer, pianist, and producer, KOY, Phoenix, 1943; (with announcer Wendell Noble) *Smile Time*, Mutual Broadcasting Company, Los Angeles, 1945; half-hour talk show on KNX, CBS, Los Angeles, 1947-1950.

PRINCIPAL TELEVISION APPEARANCES—Series: Emcee, *Songs for Sale*, CBS, 1950-51; *The Steve Allen Show*, CBS, 1950-52; emcee, *Talent Patrol*, ABC, 1953; panelist, *What's My Line*, CBS, 1953-54; host, *The Tonight Show*, NBC, 1953-57; *The Steve Allen*

Show, NBC, 1956-59 (re-titled *The Steve Allen Plymouth Show*), NBC, 1959-60, then ABC, 1960-61; moderator, *I've Got a Secret,* CBS, 1964-67; syndicated daily series, *Steve Allen,* Filmways/ Golden West Broadcasters, 1968-72; *Steve Allen's Laughback,* in syndication, 1976-77; host, *Meeting of the Minds,* PBS, 1977-81; host, *The Big Show,* NBC, 1980; co-host, *The Book of Lists,* CBS, 1982; host, *Life's Most Embarrassing Moments,* ABC, 1984; *Inside Your Schools,* Cable TV Learning Channel, 1985.

Guest: *This Is Show Business,* CBS, 1950; *What's My Line,* CBS, 1951; *Mike Wallace Interviews,* ABC, 1957; *Showtime,* CBS, 1968. Episodic: *Max Liebman Presents,* NBC, 1955; *The Love Boat,* ABC; *Darkroom,* ABC, 1981. Mini-series: Nichols, *Rich Man, Poor Man—Book I,* ABC, 1976-77. Specials: Host and producer, *The Unofficial Miss Las Vegas Showgirl Beauty Pageant,* premiered on ABC, 1974; emcee, *The Emmy Awards,* NBC, 1980; *Steve Allen's Music Room* and *Steve Allen's Comedy Room,* both Disney Channel, 1984; also *American Academy of Humor,* NBC.

NON-RELATED CAREER—Guest lecturer of philosophy and history, Radford University, 1986.

WRITINGS: PLAYS, PRODUCED—*The Wake,* first produced at Masquers Theatre, Los Angeles, 1971, published by Doubleday, 1972; *The Al Chemist Show,* Los Angeles Actors' Theatre, 1980; book, score, and lyrics, *Seymour Glick Is Alive But Sick,* St. Regis Hotel, New York City, and The Horn, Los Angeles, CA, 1983-84; also, *Belle Star;* book, score and lyrics, *Sophie,* New York City.

SONGS—Words and music, "This Could Be the Start of Something Big," lyrics: "South Rampart Street Parade," "Pretend You Don't See Her," "Gravy Waltz," "Impossible," title lyrics for the films *Picnic, Houseboat, On the Beach, Sleeping Beauty,* and *Bell, Book and Candle.* Allen has written over four thousand songs.

SCORES—Films: *A Man Called Dagger,* Metro-Goldwyn-Mayer, 1968. Television: *Meeting of the Minds,* PBS, 1977-81; episode of *Fantasy Island,* ABC, 1983; documentary, *I Remember Illinois,* NBC; special, *The Bachelor,* NBC; also wrote lyrics for Irwin Allen's all-star production of *Alice In Wonderland,* CBS, 1985.

SPECIAL COMPOSITIONS—Commemorative march, "The Mort Glosser March," 1985; "Ten Feet Tall," for the Professional Football Hall of Fame, 1985.

ARTICLES—Published for *Look Magazine, The Saturday Review, Television Quarterly, New York Times, Cavalier, Frontier, Redbook, The Progressive, The Los Angeles Times, Chicago American, Indianapolis News, United Press International, Chicago Tribune, Associated Press, Coronet, Playboy, America, Cosmopolitan, National Review, Esquire, Inter-Continental Press,* and others.

BOOKS—*Bop Fables,* Simon & Schuster, 1955; (short stories) *Fourteen for Tonight,* Henry Holt & Company (Holt), 1955; *The Funny Men,* Simon & Schuster, 1956; (poetry) *Wry on the Rocks,* Holt, 1956; (short stories) *The Girls on the Tenth Floor and Other Stories,* Holt, 1958; *The Question Man,* Bellmeadow Press, with Bernard Geis Associates, 1959.

(Autobiography) *Mark It and Strike It,* Holt, Reinhart & Winston, 1960; (pamphlet) *Morality and Nuclear War,* World Peace Broadcasting Foundation, 1961; *Not All Your Laughter, Not All Your Tears,* Bernard Geis Associates, 1962; (with others, as told to Henry Kane) *How to Write a Song,* Avon, 1962; (with William F. Buckley, Jr., Robert M. Hutchins, L. Brent Bozell, James MacGregor Burns, and Willmoore Kendall) *Dialogues in Americanism* (series

of three debates held in Pasadena, CA), Regnery, 1964; *Letter to a Conservative,* Doubleday & Company, 1965; *The Ground Is Our Table* (on migrant labor), Doubleday & Company, 1966; *Bigger Than a Breadbox,* Doubleday & Company, 1967; (poems) *A Flash of Swallows,* Droke House, 1969, second edition, 1972.

Curses; Or, How Never to Be Foiled Again, Hawthorn, 1973; *Princess Snip-Snip and the Puppy-Kittens,* Platt & Munk, 1973; *What to Say When It Rains,* Price, Stern & Sloan, 1975; *Schmock! Schmock!,* Doubleday & Company, 1975; *Ripoff: The Corruption That Plagues America,* Lyle Stuart, 1979; *Funny People,* Stein & Day, 1982; *The Talk Show Murders,* Delacorte, 1983; *More Funny People,* Stein & Day, 1982; *How to Make a Speech,* McGraw-Hill, 1985; (with Jane Wollman) *How to Be Funny,* McGraw-Hill, 1987. Also wrote: *Meeting of Minds,* volumes one and two and *Explaining China,* all Crown Publishers Inc.; *Chopped-Up Chinese,* Price, Stern & Sloan; *Beloved Son: A Story of the Jesus Cults,* Bobbs-Merrill.

RECORDINGS: Allen has recorded over thirty albums.

AWARDS: Sylvania Award for words and music, 1954, for *The Bachelor;* Best Comedy Television Show, Peabody Award, 1960, for *The Steve Allen Show;* Grammy Award, 1964, for "The Gravy Waltz"; Peabody Award, Emmy Award, three additional Emmy nominations, Television Critics Circle Award, *Encyclopedia Brittanica* Award, and Film Advisory Board Award, all 1977-78, for *Meeting of Minds;* Best Play Los Angeles Television Critics' Circle Award nomination, 1978, for *The Wake;* included in the *Guiness Book of World Records* as the most prolific composer of modern times, 1984; inducted into the Television Academy's Hall of Fame, 1986.

SIDELIGHTS: From the publicity biography submitted for this volume of *CTFT,* Steve Allen comments on the various aspects of his career: "When I ad-lib something, I laugh . . . I laugh for the same reason the audience does; I've never heard that joke before— and I'm just as surprised as they are." Asked where he gets his ideas, Allen responds, "Creativity, of just about any sort, is a mysterious process . . . nobody knows how the world's poets and writers get ideas. You're brushing your teeth and suddenly you think, hey, there's an idea for a book. Obviously it wasn't brushing your teeth that gave you the idea." On the medium of television: "Much of TV is what I call junk food for the mind, like junk food for the stomach, it's not terribly harmful in itself. It's just that it's something to pass the time. This was brought to my mind during a visit to a veteran's hospital during the Vietnam War. Here were these kids in those damn beds—some of them are probably still there—and what a godsend television is to people in that kind of predicament."

ADDRESSES: OFFICE—15201 Burbank Blvd., Suite B, Van Nuys, CA 91411. AGENT—c/o Irvin Arthur, 9200 Sunset Blvd., Los Angeles, CA 90069.

*   *   *

ALLISON, Nancy   1954-

PERSONAL: Born Nancy Alison Cohen, February 28, 1954, in Baltimore, MD; daughter of Philip Kader (a civil servant) and Florence Joan (a secretary; maiden name, Dowinsky) Cohen; married Robert E. Mahaffay, August 12, 1982 (divorced, 1986). EDUCATION: Ohio University, B.F.A., 1976.

NANCY ALLISON

VOCATION: Dancer, choreographer, and teacher.

CAREER: STAGE DEBUT—Dancer, *Ballet School,* in a Bolshoi Ballet production, Baltimore Civic Center, 1963, for four performances. PRINCIPAL STAGE WORK—Dancer, *The Tamed Hunter,* Theatre of the Open Eye, New York City, 1976; dancer and choreographer, *The Cobra and the Crows,* Theatre of the Open Eye, New York City, 1976.

Choreographer: *Raven's Dance,* 1976 and *Isle of the Seal,* 1977, both at the Theatre of the Open Eye, New York City; *Demeter's Daughters,* St. Michel Theatre, Orge, France, 1979; *Images of Vinalhaven,* Vinalhaven, ME, 1980; *Duet for Flute and Dancer,* Fairfield County Flute Festival, Stamford, CT, 1980; *In the Eye of the Whale Swims the Sea,* American Museum of Natural History, New York City, 1982; *Rafting, an Oregon Journey,* Artquake, Portland, OR, 1983; *Marsyus, an Attic Resurrection,* Theatre for the New City, New York City, 1985; *Fiddlemania,* Ballet Oregon, 1985; *Faces of the Great Goddess,* Herodes Atticus Theatre, Athens, Greece, 1985; *Samsara* and *What Can I Tell My Bones?,* both Nickolais-Louis Dance Space, New York City, 1986.

MAJOR TOURS—Principal dancer, *Op Odyssey,* Theatre of the Open Eye, Rotterdam, Holland, and Paris and Bordeaux, France, 1977; principal dancer with Theatre of the Open Eye, National Endowment for the Arts tour of U.S. colleges and universities, 1976-78; co-producer, artistic director, choreographer, and dancer, *Contemporary Mythmakers,* U.S. and European cities, 1979-85; assistant choreographer and dancer, Theatre of the Open Eye, Athens Festival, Greece, 1986.

FIRST TELEVISION WORK—Choreographer and dancer, *Inner Visions,* cable television, 1980. PRINCIPAL TELEVISION WORK—

Choreographer and dancer, *Nancy Allison & Company,* WNYC-TV, New York City, 1986.

RELATED CAREER—Solo dancer and associate choreographer, Theatre of the Open Eye, New York City, 1976—; producing co-artistic director, choreographer, and solo dancer, Contemporary Mythmakers, New York City, 1980-85; choreographer and solo dancer, Solo Performance Company, National Academy of Dance and Music, Denpasar, Bali, 1984; producing artistic director, choreographer, and solo dancer, Nancy Allison in Concert Company, Nikolais-Louis Dance Space, New York City, 1986.

Teacher: Children's dance program, Theatre of the Open Eye, New York City, 1976-77; Understanding the Kinesthetic Experience, Lincoln Center Library, New York City, 1979; modern dance technique, New York Loft Studios, New York City, 1981-85; the Pilates method, Pilates Studio, New York City, 1982-85; State University of New York at Purchase, 1986—.

AWARDS: Outstanding Graduate Award, Ohio University School of Dance, 1976; International Festival De La Danse Award, Paris, France, 1977; grants and fellowships: American University of Dance at Jacob's Pillow, 1973, Ohio University School of Dance, 1974-76, Royal Society of the Arts, London, 1979, Experimental Intermedia Foundation, 1981, and Ohio University Performing Arts Alumni Fund, 1981, 1983.

MEMBER: Dance Theatre Workshop, American Dance Guild, Laban-Bartenieff Institute of Movement Studies.

SIDELIGHTS: Nancy Allison told *CTFT,* "I got started dancing because my sister had weak ankles and the doctor told my mother to send her to dancing school. My mother took us both and I've been dancing ever since."

ADDRESSES: OFFICE—325 E. 21st Street, Apt. 22, New York, NY 10010.

*   *   *

ALMQUIST, Gregg   1948-

PERSONAL: Born December 1, 1948, in Minneapolis, MN; son of A.E. "Buzz" (a salesman) and Margaret (a teacher; maiden name, Yost) Almquist. EDUCATION: University of Minnesota, B.A.

VOCATION: Actor and writer.

CAREER: STAGE DEBUT—Servant to Angelo, *Measure for Measure,* American Shakespeare Theatre, Kennedy Center, Washington, DC, 1973. OFF-BROADWAY DEBUT—Conrad Carver, *Kerouac,* Lion Theatre. PRINCIPAL STAGE APPEARANCES—With the American Shakespeare Theatre, Stratford, CT, 1973-75; with the Denver Center Theatre, 1979-83; Danforth, *I'm Not Rappaport,* Booth Theatre, New York City, 1985-86.

MAJOR TOURS—Gloucester, *King Lear* and Don Quixote, *Camino Real,* both with the Acting Company, U.S. cities, 1977-78.

FILM DEBUT—Man at Georgetown party, *Heartburn,* 1986.

NON-RELATED CAREER—Lab worker, J.W. French, Ltd. Flour Mills, London, 1971.

GREGG ALMQUIST

WRITINGS: BOOKS—*Beast Rising,* Pocket Books, 1987.

MEMBER: Actors' Equity Association; Players Club.

ADDRESSES: AGENT—Ambrosio/Mortimer and Associates, 165 W. 46th Street, New York, NY 10036.

*   *   *

AMOS, John   1941-

PERSONAL: Born December 27, 1941, in Newark, NJ; son of John A. and Annabelle P. Amos; children: Shannon Patrice, K.C. (a son). EDUCATION: Attended Colorado State University and Long Beach City College.

VOCATION: Actor, producer, and director.

CAREER: PRINCIPAL TELEVISION APPEARANCES—Series: Gordy Howard, *Mary Tyler Moore Show,* CBS, 1970-73; regular, *The Funny Side,* NBC, 1971; Henry Evans, *Maude,* CBS, 1973-74; James Evans, *Good Times,* CBS, 1974-79; Captain Dolan, *Hunter,* NBC, 1984; *South by Southwest,* PBS.

Mini-Series: Kunte Kinte, *Roots,* ABC, 1977. Movies: *The President's Plane Is Missing,* 1971; *Willa,* 1979. Episodic: *Tim Conway Comedy Hour,* CBS, 1970; also *Love, American Style,* ABC; *Police Story,* NBC. Guest: *The Tonight Show; The Merv Griffin Show; The Mike Douglas Show.*

STAGE DEBUT—Ben Chambers, *Norman, Is That You?,* Ebony Showcase Theatre, Los Angeles, 1971, for one hundred and fifty performances. BROADWAY DEBUT—Luther, *Tough to Get Help,* Royale Theatre, for six performances. PRINCIPAL STAGE APPEARANCES—*The Emperor Jones,* 1979; Sam, *Master Harold. . .and the Boys,* Birmingham Theatre, Detroit, MI, 1983; Rusty, *Split Second,* Mayfair Theatre, 1985.

PRINCIPAL STAGE WORK—Director, *And Miss Reardon Drinks a Little* and *Twelve Angry Men,* both at the Bahamian Repertory Company.

FILM DEBUT—*Vanishing Point,* Twentieth Century-Fox, 1971. PRINCIPAL FILM APPEARANCES—Coach Archer, *The World's Greatest Athlete,* Buena Vista, 1973; *Let's Do It Again,* Warner Brothers, 1975; *The Beastmaster* and *Dance of the Dwarfs,* both 1983; *American Flyers,* Warner Brothers, 1984.

PRINCIPAL FILM WORK—Producer, director, and writer, *Grambling Takes It All Back Home.*

NON-RELATED CAREER—Professional football player; social worker for the Vera Institute of Justice in New York City.

AWARDS: Most Outstanding Performance, Los Angeles Drama Critics Award nomination, 1971, for *Norman, Is That You?;* Most Outstanding Actor, Emmy Award nomination, 1977, for *Roots;* Best Actor, Black Image Award nomination, National Association for the Advancement of Colored People (NAACP), 1985, for *Split Second.*

MEMBER: Screen Actors Guild, American Federation of Television and Radio Artists; Young Men's Christian Association.

SIDELIGHTS: RECREATIONS—Scuba-diving, horseback riding, flying.

John Amos told *CTFT* that he was a professional football player for three years in the American, Continental, and Canadian football leagues, including the Vancouver, British Columbia Lions.

ADDRESSES: HOME—Summit, NJ. AGENT—Barry Douglas Talent Agency, 1650 Broadway, New York, NY 10036.

*   *   *

ANDERSON, Haskell V. III   1942-

PERSONAL: Born November 26, 1942, in Queens, NY; son of Haskell Clay (a postman) and Sara Smith (an accountant; maiden name, Ray) Anderson. EDUCATION: St. Procopius College, B.S., 1966; Temple University, M.A., 1972; trained for the stage with Jose Quintero and the Harvey Lembeck Comedy Workshop. MILITARY: U.S. Navy Medical Corps, 1966-69.

VOCATION: Actor.

CAREER: STAGE DEBUT—Gabe Gabriel, *No Place to Be Somebody,* Karamu House of Performing Arts, Cleveland, OH, 1974. OFF-BROADWAY DEBUT—Kookie, *Benny Leonard and the Brooklyn Bridge,* Open Space Theatre, 1977, for sixteen performances. PRINCIPAL STAGE APPEARANCES—Habu and Baby San, *Tracers,* Los Angeles Public Theatre, then as Habu at the Annenberg Center, Philadelphia, 1986; Wiggins and Major, *Hard Laughs,* Santa Monica Playhouse, CA, 1986; Lenny Munk, *Rounds,* CAST Theatre, Los Angeles, 1987; also appeared as: Duke of Norfolk,

Richard III, Cleveland Playhouse; Homer and Baily, *The Skin of Our Teeth*, Beverly Hills Playhouse; Lodovico, *Othello;* Camillo and Cleomenes, *The Winter's Tale;* Billy Boy, *All Kinds of Blue*, American National Theatre Academy (ANTA) West; Donald, *You Can't Take It with You*. Performed at the Barter Theatre, the Globe Playhouse.

MAJOR TOURS—Habu, *Tracers*, Australian cities, 1986, U.S. cities, 1987.

FILM DEBUT—*Brotherhood of Death*, Cinema Shares International. PRINCIPAL FILM APPEARANCES—*Getting Straight*, Columbia, 1970; *Victim*, U.S. Navy Productions; also appeared in *Street Love; Brother's Keeper; Grey Area; Keep in Touch; Pas De Trois;* as well as voiceovers for *A Soldier's Story*, Columbia, 1984.

TELEVISION DEBUT—Diplomat, *The Master*, NBC, 1984. PRINCIPAL TELEVISION APPEARANCES—Episodic: *Gimme a Break*, NBC.

NON-RELATED CAREER—American Youth Association.

AWARDS: Best Supporting Actor, National Association for the Advancement of Colored People (NAACP) Image Award nomination, 1985, for *Hard Laughs*.

MEMBER: Actors' Equity Association; Ensemble Studo Theatre, American Film Institute's Alumni Writer's Workshop Actors Repertory.

ADDRESSES: AGENT—c/o Beverly Hecht Agency, 8949 Sunset Blvd., Los Angeles, CA 90069.

HASKELL V. ANDERSON III

ANDERSON, Judith 1898-

PERSONAL; Born Frances Margaret Anderson-Anderson, February 10, 1898, in Adelaide, South Australia; daughter of James and Jessie Margaret (Saltmarsh) Anderson-Anderson; married Benjamin Harrison Lehman (divorced); married Luther Greene (divorced). EDUCATION: Attended schools in Adelaide.

VOCATION: Actress.

CAREER: STAGE DEBUT—Stephanie, *A Royal Divorce*, Theatre Royal, Sydney, New South Wales, 1915. OFF-BROADWAY DEBUT—At the 14th Street Theatre, 1918. LONDON DEBUT—Lady Macbeth, *Macbeth*, Old Vic Theatre, 1937. PRINCIPAL STAGE APPEARANCES—As Frances Anderson, played Mrs. Bellmore in *On the Stairs* and in *A Crooked Square*, Playhouse Theatre, New York City, 1922; as Judith Anderson: Jessie Weston, *Peter Weston*, Sam H. Harris Theatre, New York City, 1923; Elise Van Zile, *Cobra*, Hudson Theatre, New York City, 1924; Dolores Romero, *The Dove*, Empire Theatre, New York City, 1925; Elise, *Cobra*, the Wife, *Tea for Three*, and Iris Fenwick, *The Green Hat*, all in Australia, 1927; Antoinette Lyle, *Behold the Bridegroom*, Cort Theatre, New York City, 1927; Anna Plumer, *Anna*, Lyceum Theatre, New York City, 1928; Nina Leeds, *Strange Interlude*, John Golden Theatre, New York City, 1928.

Unknown One, *As You Desire Me*, Maxine Elliott Theatre, New York City, 1931; Lavinia Mannon, *Mourning Becomes Electra*, Alvin Theatre, New York City, 1932; Karola Lovasdy, *Firebird*, Empire Theatre, New York City, 1932; Helen Nolte, *Conquest*, Plymouth Theatre, New York City, 1933; Savina Grazia, *The Mask and the Face*, Guild Theatre, New York City, 1933; Valerie Latour, *The Drums Begin*, Shubert Theatre, New York City, 1933; the Woman, *Come of Age*, Maxine Elliott Theatre, New York City, 1934; Mimea Sheller, *The Female of the Species*, Pittsburgh, PA, 1934; Delia Lovell, *The Old Maid*, 1935 and Gertrude, *Hamlet*, 1936, both at the Empire Theatre, New York City; Lady Macbeth, *Macbeth*, New Theatre, New York City, 1937; Mary, *Family Portrait*, Morosco Theatre, New York City, 1939.

Lady Macbeth, *Macbeth*, National Theatre, New York City, 1941; Olga, *The Three Sisters*, Ethel Barrymore Theatre, New York City, 1942; title role, *Medea*, National Theatre, New York City, 1947, repeated role at the City Center, New York City, 1949; Clytemnestra, *Tower Beyond Tragedy*, American National Theatre Academy (ANTA) Playhouse, New York City, 1950; the Woman, *Come of Age*, City Center, New York City, 1952; *John Brown's Body*, New Century Theatre, New York City, 1953; Gertrude Eastman-Cuevas, *In the Summer House*, Playhouse Theatre, New York City, 1953; Isabel Lawton, *Comes a Day*, Ambassador Theatre, New York City, 1958; Irina Arkadina, *The Seagull*, with the Old Vic Company, Edinburgh Festival, Scotland, 1960; Alice Christie, *Black Chiffon*, Sombrero Playhouse, Phoenix, AZ, 1964.

Performed excerpts from *Medea, Tower Beyond Tragedy*, and *Macbeth*, Elder Hall, Adelaide, Australia, 1966; Clytemnestra, *The Oresteia*, Greek Theatre, Ypsilanti, MI, 1966; title role, *Elizabeth the Queen*, City Center, New York City, 1966; title role, *Hamlet*, Carnegie Hall, New York City, 1971; Nurse, *Medea*, Cort Theatre, New York City, 1982.

MAJOR TOURS—*Monsieur Beaucaire, The Scarlet Pimpernel*, and *David Garrick*, Australian cities, 1916; *Dear Brutus*, U.S. cities, 1920; Nina Leeds, *Strange Interlude*, U.S. cities, 1929; Unknown One, *As You Desire Me*, U.S. cities, 1930-31; Lavinia Mannon,

Mourning Becomes Electra, U.S. cities, 1932; Delia Lovell, *The Old Maid,* U.S. cities, 1935; Clytemnestra, *Tower Beyond Tragedy,* U.S. West Coast cities, 1939; Miss Madrigal, *The Chalk Garden,* U.S. cities, 1956; scenes from *Medea, Tower Beyond Tragedy,* and *Macbeth,* U.S. and Canadian cities, 1961; excerpts from *Medea* and *Macbeth,* Australian cities, 1966; title role, *Hamlet,* U.S. cities, 1970.

FILM DEBUT—*Blood Money,* 1933. PRINCIPAL FILM APPEARANCES—Mrs. Danvers, *Rebecca,* 1940; *Forty Little Mothers,* 1940; *Free and Easy,* 1941; *King's Row,* 1941; *All Through the Night,* 1942; *The Edge of Darkness,* 1943; *Jane Eyre,* 1944; *Laura,* Twentieth Century-Fox, 1944; *And Then There Were None,* Twentieth Century-Fox, 1945; *Strange Love of Martha Ivers,* Paramount, 1946; *Diary of a Chambermaid,* 1946; *Spectre of the Rose,* 1946; *Red House,* 1947; *Tycoon,* RKO, 1947; *Pursued,* 1947; *The Furies,* 1950; *Salome,* 1953; *Don't Bother to Knock,* 1953; Memnet, *The Ten Commandments,* Paramount, 1956; Big Mama Pollitt, *Cat on a Hot Tin Roof,* Metro-Goldwyn-Mayer (MGM), 1958; *Cinderfella,* Paramount, 1960; Lady Macbeth, *Macbeth,* 1960; *A Man Called Horse,* National General, 1970; *Inn of the Damned,* 1974; *Star Trek III: The Search for Spock,* Paramount, 1984; *Hitchcock, Il Brivido Del Genio,* 1985; also appeared in *Come of Age.*

PRINCIPAL TELEVISION APPEARANCES—Series: Minx Lockridge, *Santa Barbara,* NBC, 1984—. Episodic: *Telephone Time,* CBS, 1956. Dramatic Specials: Lady Macbeth, "Macbeth," *Hallmark Hall of Fame,* NBC, 1954 and 1960; Prioress, *The Cradle Song,* 1956; Flatateena, *Caesar and Cleopatra,* 1956; Tiare, *The Moon and Sixpence,* 1959; title role, *Elizabeth the Queen,* 1968; Aunt Sophy, *The Borrowers,* 1973. Movies: Elisabeth Devlin, *The File on Devlin,* 1969; *The Chinese Prime Minister,* 1974. Specials: *Light's Diamond Jubilee,* 1954; *A Salute to Television's Twenty-Fifth Anniversary,* 1972.

AWARDS: Dame Commander of the British Empire, Birthday Honours, 1960; Best Actress in a Play, Antoinette Perry Award, 1947, for *Medea;* Donaldson Award, 1948; New York Critics Award, 1948; Best Speech Award, American Academy of Arts and Sciences, 1948; Best Actress in a Single Performance, Emmy Award, 1954, for *Macbeth;* Outstanding Performance by an Actress in a Leading Role, Emmy Award, 1960, for *Macbeth.*

SIDELIGHTS: During World War II, Dame Judith was an overseas entertainer for the U.S. Army. FAVORITE ROLES —The Woman, *Come of Age.* RECREATIONS—Riding and reading.

ADDRESSES: HOME—808 San Ysidro Lane, Santa Barbara, CA 93103.*

*   *   *

ANDERSON, Melody

PERSONAL: Born in Edmonton, AB, Canada. EDUCATION: Carlton University, B.A.; trained for the stage with Stella Adler.

VOCATION: Actress.

CAREER: PRINCIPAL TELEVISION APPEARANCES—Movies: *Elvis,* 1979; Barbara Shantz, *Police Woman Centerfold,* 1983; *High*

MELODY ANDERSON

School USA, 1983; Edie Adams, *Ernie Kovacs: Between the Laughter,* 1984; Claudia, *Beverly Hills Madam,* NBC, 1986.

Series: Brooke McKenzie, *Manimal,* NBC, 1983. Episodic: *Dallas,* CBS; *St. Elsewhere,* NBC.

PRINCIPAL FILM APPEARANCES—Dale Arden, *Flash Gordon,* Universal, 1980; *Dead and Buried,* 1981; *The Boy in Blue,* Twentieth Century-Fox, 1986; *The Firewalker,* Cannon (upcoming).

RELATED CAREER—Reporter, CBC Radio, Ottawa, Canada.

ADDRESSES: AGENT—c/o Monique Moss, Michael Levine Public Relations, 9123 Sunset Blvd., Los Angeles, CA 90069.

*   *   *

ANDREWS, Dana   1912-

PERSONAL: Born January 1, 1912, in Collins, MS; son of Charles Forrest and Annis (Speed) Andrews; married Janet Murray (died); married Mary Todd. EDUCATION: Attended Sam Houston State College; trained for the stage at the Pasadena Playhouse and in voice with Isadore Braggiotti and Florence Russell.

VOCATION: Actor.

CAREER: STAGE DEBUT—The Frenchman, *Cymbeline,* Pasadena Playhouse, CA, 1935. BROADWAY DEBUT—Jerry Ryan, *Two for the Seesaw,* Booth Theatre, 1958. PRINCIPAL STAGE APPEAR-

ANCES—Appeared in repertory with the Pasadena Playhouse, CA, 1935-38; Richard Kohner, *The Captains and the Kings,* Playhouse Theatre, New York City, 1962; Sir Thomas More, *A Man for All Seasons,* Royal Poinciana Playhouse, Palm Beach, FL, then Papermill Playhouse, Milburn, NJ 1965; Julian Armstone, *Calculated Risk,* Sombrero Playhouse, Phoenix, AZ, 1966; *Child's Play,* Bucks County Playhouse, New Hope, PA, 1971; Sam Nash, Jesse Kiplinger, and Roy Hubley, *Plaza Suite,* Little Theatre, Albuquerque, NM, 1971; *Marriage-Go-Round,* Golden Palace, Arlington, TX, 1972; Stage Manager, *Our Town,* Bucks County Playhouse, New Hope, 1972-73, then Thorndike Theatre, Surrey, U.K.; Gil, *Janus,* Royal Poinciana Playhouse, Palm Beach, 1975. Dinner theatre appearances include *The Best of Friends, Angel Street, The Gang's All Here,* and *Any Wednesday.*

MAJOR TOURS—Tom, *The Glass Menagerie,* New England cities, 1952; Kenneth Higman, *A Remedy for Winter,* U.S. cities, 1965; Oscar Madison, *The Odd Couple,* U.S. cities, 1967-68; *Conflict of Interest,* U.S. cities, 1972; *Together Tonight,* U.S. cities, 1976.

FILM DEBUT—*Lucky Cisco Kid,* Twentieth Century-Fox, 1939. PRINCIPAL FILM APPEARANCES—*The Westerner,* Metro-Goldwyn-Mayer (MGM), 1939; *Swamp Water* and *Tobacco Road,* 1941; *The Ox-Box Incident,* Twentieth Century-Fox, and *Crash Dive,* both 1943; *Laura,* Twentieth Century-Fox, 1944; *State Fair,* Twentieth Century-Fox, and *Fallen Angel,* 1945; *The Best Years of Our Lives,* RKO, *A Walk in the Sun,* Twentieth Century-Fox, and *Canyon Passage,* all 1946; *Daisy Kenyon, Night Song,* and *Boomerang,* all 1947; *Iron Curtain, No Minor Vices,* and *Deep Waters,* all 1948; *My Foolish Heart* and *Britannia Mews,* 1949; *Where the Sidewalk Ends,* Twentieth Century-Fox, and *The Edge of Doom,* 1950; *I Want You, Sealed Cargo,* and *The Frogmen,* all 1951; *Assignment, Paris,* Columbia, 1952; *Elephant Walk,* 1953; *Duel in the Jungle,* 1954; *Smoke Signal,* Universal, and *Strange Lady in Town,* Warner Brothers, both 1955; *Comanche,* United Artists, and *Beyond a Reasonable Doubt,* RKO, both 1956.

Zero Hour, Paramount, *Night of the Demon,* Columbia, *Spring Reunion,* United Artists, all 1957; Abner Bedford, *Enchanted Island,* RKO, *While the City Sleeps,* Twentieth Century-Fox, and *The Fear Makers,* United Artists, all 1958; *The Crowded Sky,* Warner Brothers, 1960; *Madison Avenue,* Twentieth Century-Fox, and *Two for the See-Saw,* United Artists, both 1962; *The Battle of the Bulge,* Warner Brothers, *The Satan Bug,* United Artists, *A Crack in the World,* and *In Harm's Way,* both Paramount, and *The Loved One,* MGM, all 1965; *The Frozen Dead,* 1967; *The Devil's Brigade,* United Artists, 1968; Blake, *Innocent Bystanders,* Paramount, 1973; small plane pilot, *Airport, 1975,* Universal, 1974; Morgan, *Take a Hard Ride,* 1975; *Born Again,* AVCO-Embassy, 1978; Edgar Harolds, *Good Guys Wear Black,* Mar Vista, and *The Last Tycoon,* Paramount, both 1978; Cardinal, *Prince Jack,* 1983. Also appeared in *Forbidden Street* and *Three Hours to Kill.*

TELEVISION DEBUT—"Crazy Sunday," *Four Star Playhouse,* CBS. PRINCIPAL TELEVISION APPEARANCES—Series: *Checkmate,* CBS, 1960; also appeared in *One Small Step Forward.* Episodic: "The Right Hand Man," *Playhouse 90,* 1958; "The Playoff," *General Electric Theatre,* CBS; *The Barbara Stanwyck Show,* NBC, 1960; "Mutiny," *The Dupont Show of the Week,* NBC, 1961; "The Town That Died" and "The Boy Who Wasn't Wanted," *Alcoa Theatre,* NBC, 1957; "No Time Like the Past," *Twilight Zone,* CBS, 1959; "The Last of the Big Spenders," *The Dick Powell Show,* NBC, 1961; "A Wind of Hurricane Force," *Bob Hope Presents the Chrysler Theatre,* NBC, 1963; also appeared on *The Horror of It All,* 1983.

Movies: Thomas Boswell, *Bright Promise,* 1969; Allan McDonald, *The Failing of Raymond,* 1971; Len Raeburn, *Shadow in the Streets* and Dr. Hutchins, *The First 36 Hours of Dr. Durant,* both 1975; Roger Shanley, *The Last Hurrah,* 1977; Gen. George C. Marshall, *Ike: The War Years,* ABC, 1978; also *Alas, Babylon* and *Shadow in the Streets.*

NON-RELATED CAREER—Accountant with the Gulf Refining Company, 1930; chief accountant with Tobins, Inc., CA, 1931.

MEMBER: Screen Actors Guild (vice-president, 1957-63, president, 1964-65).

SIDELIGHTS: RECREATIONS—Photography and sailing.

ADDRESSES: OFFICE—4238 Beeman Avenue, Studio City, CA 91604.*

*   *   *

ANGEL, Heather   1909-1986

PERSONAL: Born Heather Grace Angel, February 9, 1909, in Oxford, England; died of cancer, in Santa Barbara, CA, December 13, 1986; married Ralph Forbes (an actor; divorced); married Henry Wilcoxon (an actor; divorced); married Robert B. Sinclair (a direc.or; died, 1970); children: one son. EDUCATION: Attended Wycombe Abbey School and the London Polytechnic of Dramatic Arts.

CAREER: PRINCIPAL STAGE APPEARANCES—Appeared in *Leave It to Psmith, Money Money,* and others, with the Old Vic Company, London, 1926-30; *The Wookie,* New York City production, 1944.

MAJOR TOURS—Appeared in *Leave It to Psmith, Money Money,* and others, with the Old Vic Company, India, Egypt, and other countries.

FILM DEBUT—*City of Song,* England, 1930. PRINCIPAL FILM APPEARANCES—*Sookey,* 1931; *Frail Women,* 1931; *Self Made Lady,* 1931; *Bill the Conqueror,* 1932; *After Office Hours,* 1932; *A Night in Montmartre,* 1932; *Men of Steel,* 1932; *Berkeley Square,* 1933; *Pilgrimage,* 1933; *The Informer,* 1935; *The Mystery of Edwin Drood,* 1935; *The Three Musketeers,* 1935; *Charlie Chan's Greatest Case,* 1935; *The Orient Express,* 1936; *Murder in Trinidad,* 1936; *Springtime for Henry,* 1936; *It Happened in New York,* 1936; *The Last of the Mohicans,* 1936; *Daniel Boone,* 1937; *Bulldog Drummond Escapes,* 1937; *Army Girl,* 1937; *Bulldog Drummond in Africa,* 1938; *Arrest Bulldog Drummond,* 1939; *Bulldog Drummond's Secret Police,* 1939; *Undercover Doctor,* 1939; *The Hound of the Baskervilles,* 1939.

Pride And Prejudice, 1940; *That Hamilton Woman,* 1941; *Suspicion,* 1941; *Singapore Woman,* 1941; *Half a Sinner,* 1941; *The Undying Monster,* 1942; *Time to Kill,* 1942; *Devotion,* 1943; *Cry Havoc,* 1943; *In the Meantime Darling,* 1944; *Lifeboat,* 1944; *The Saxon Charm,* 1948; *Premature Burial,* 1962; also in *Peter Pan* and *Alice in Wonderland.*

PRINCIPAL TELEVISION APPEARANCES—Episodic: *Studio 57,* DuMont, 1954-55; *Perry Mason,* CBS; *Mr. Novak,* NBC. Series: *Peyton Place,* ABC; *Family Affair,* CBS; *Backstairs at the White House,* NBC, 1979.

RELATED CAREER—Voice-over actress for animated features for Walt Disney Studios.*

* * *

ANGLIM, Philip 1953-

PERSONAL: Born February 11, 1953, in San Francisco, CA. EDUCATION: Yale University, B.A.

VOCATION: Actor.

CAREER: STAGE DEBUT—Rosencrantz, *Rosencrantz and Guildenstern Are Dead,* Yale Theatre, New Haven, CT, 1970. BROADWAY DEBUT—John Merrick, *The Elephant Man,* Booth Theatre, 1979. PRINCIPAL STAGE APPEARANCES—In repertory at the Southbury Playhouse, CT, 1972; *What the Butler Saw* and *The Contrast,* both at the Cincinnati Playhouse in the Park, OH, 1975-76; Kevin, *Snow White,* American Place Theatre, New York City, 1976; Geoffrey, *The Lion in Winter,* Berkshire Theatre, Stockbridge, MA; John Merrick, *The Elephant Man,* Theatre of St. Peter's Church, New York City, 1979; Captain Andrei Vukhov, *Judgment,* Theatre of St. Peter's Church, New York City, 1980-81; title role, *Macbeth,* Vivian Beaumont Theatre, New York City, 1981; Michael Cape, *Welded,* Horace Mann Theatre, New York City, 1981.

PRINCIPAL FILM APPEARANCES—*The All-American Boy,* Warner Brothers, 1973.

PRINCIPAL TELEVISION APPEARANCES—Mini-Series: *The Adams Chronicles; Tomorrow's Families.*

Dramatic specials: *The Elephant Man.*

ADDRESSES: OFFICE—1160 Fifth Avenue, New York, NY 10029.*

* * *

ANSTEY, Edgar 1907-

PERSONAL: Full name, Edgar Harold MacFarlane Anstey; born February 16, 1907, in Watford, England; son of Percy Edgar (a chef) and Kate (a concert singer; maiden name, Clowes) Anstey; married Daphne Lilly (a film editor), April 2, 1949; children: John Edgar, Caroline. EDUCATION: Attended Birkbeck College, University of London.

VOCATION: Director, critic, and producer.

CAREER: FIRST FILM WORK—Director and cameraman, *Uncharted Waters* and *Eskimo Village* (silent), 1933. PRINCIPAL FILM WORK—Director: *Housing Problems, Enough to Eat?,* and *On the Way to Work,* all between 1935-36. Producer: *Journey into Spring,* 1957; *Between the Tides,* 1958; *Terminus,* 1961; *Wild Wings,* 1965.

RELATED CAREER—Empire Marketing Board and GPO Film Units, British Documentary, 1931-33; founder, Shell Film Unit, 1933-34; director, social documentaries, 1934-35; director of productions, "March of Time," London, 1936; foreign editor, "March of Time," New York, 1937-38; producer of films for Ministry of Information and Armed Services, 1939-46; producer, Venezualan Oil Industry Documentary Film Unit, 1947-49; producer and supervisor, British Transportation Commission Film Unit, 1949-74; lecturer, "History of Documentary Film: London," Temple University, Philadelphia, PA, 1978-85; chairman, production committee, Children's Film Foundation, 1981-83; also film critic, *The Spectator,* 1940s; panel member, *The Critics,* BBC Radio.

AWARDS: Order of the British Empire, 1969; British Film Academy Award and Venice Film Award, both 1957, for *Journey into Spring;* Venice Film Award, 1958, for *Between the Tides;* British Film Academy Award and Venice Film Award, both 1961, for *Terminus;* Academy Award, 1965, for *Wild Wings.*

MEMBER: Cinematograph Films Council (1947-49), British Film Academy (chairman, 1956), International Scientific Film Association (president, 1961-63), British Association of Film and Television Arts (chairman, 1967), British Industrial and Scientific Film Association (president, 1974-81), British Film Institute (governor, 1965-75), Royal College of Art (senior fellow), British Kinematograph Society (honorary fellow), Academy of Motion Picture Arts and Sciences, British Academy of Film and Television Arts; Saville Club, London.

SIDELIGHTS: Edgar Anstey wrote *CTFT,* "In 1931, I was lucky enough to join John Grierson in the pioneering of the documentary film movement and most of what I know about films—and, indeed, about life—I learned from him."

ADDRESSES: HOME—Six Hurst Close, London NW11 7BE, England.

* * *

ARLEDGE, Roone 1931-

PERSONAL: Full name, Roone Pinckney Arledge, Jr.; born July 8, 1931, in Forest Hills, NY; son of Roone and Gertrude (Stritmater) Arledge; married Joan Heise, December 27, 1953 (divorced, 1971); married a second time; separated; children: (first marriage) Elizabeth Ann, Susan Lee, Patricia Lu, Roone Pinckney. EDUCATION: Columbia University, B.B.A., 1952. MILITARY: U.S. Army, 1953-54.

VOCATION: Television producer and executive.

CAREER: FIRST TELEVISION WORK—An entry level position with the DuMont Television Network, 1952-53. PRINCIPAL TELEVISION WORK—Producer and director, *The Shari Lewis Show* and public affairs programs, NBC, 1955-60.

With ABC Television, 1960—: producer, network sports, 1960-61; producer and creator, *Wide World of Sports,* 1961; vice president in charge of sports, originating *Monday Night Football,* 1963-68; executive producer of all sports programs, including the Olympic Games, 1964, 1968, and 1972; president ABC News, 1968-85; creator, *Nightline,* 1980; president, ABC Sports Inc., 1977-85; group president, ABC News and Sports, 1985—; producer of entertainment specials, including for Frank Sinatra, and *The Main Event at Madison Square Garden.*

RELATED CAREER—Producer and director of radio programs

while serving in the army, Aberdeen Proving Ground, MD, 1953-54.

AWARDS: Nineteen Emmy Awards since 1958; four George Foster Peabody Awards for International Understanding; National Headlines special citation; *Saturday Review* Award; Distinguished Service Award, New York chapter of Broadcast Pioneers, 1968; Kennedy Family Award, 1972; New York Chapter, National Football Foundation and Hall of Fame Award, 1972; named Man of the Year, National Association of Television Program Executives; Man of the Year, Philadelphia Advertising and Sales Club; Man of the Year, *Football News;* Man of the Year, Ohio State University; Man of the Year, Gallagher Report.

MEMBER: President's Council on Physical Fitness (chairman, sports committee).

ADDRESSES: OFFICE—American Broadcasting Company, 1330 Avenue of the Americas, New York, NY 10019.*

*　　　*　　　*

ARMITAGE, Richard   ?-1986

PERSONAL: Died of a heart attack in Stebbing, Essex, England, November 16, 1986; son of Noel Gay (a composer); children: Charles, Alex. EDUCATION: Attended Eton and King's College, Cambridge University.

VOCATION: Producer and talent agent.

CAREER: PRINCIPAL STAGE WORK—Producer, *Me and My Girl,* Haymarket Theatre, London, 1985, then Marquis Theatre, New York City, 1986; also *High Society* and *The Entertainer,* both upcoming London productions.

RELATED CAREER—Chairman of the Noel Gay Organization, a London music publisher and management company.

SIDELIGHTS: CTFT learned that Richard Armitage produced the New York and London revivals of *Me and My Girl* as a tribute to his father, the composer of the musical. The original London production ran for 1,646 performances in 1937-38.*

*　　　*　　　*

ARNAZ, Desi   1917-1986

PERSONAL: Full name, Desiderio Alberto Arnaz III; born March 2, 1917, in Santiago, Cuba; died of cancer in Del Mar, CA, December 2, 1986; married Lucille Ball (an actress and producer) November 30, 1940 (divorced, 1960); married Edith Mack Hirsch, 1963 (died, 1985); children: (first marriage) Lucie Desiree, Desiderio Alberto (Desi Jr.) IV. EDUCATION: Attended Colegio Dolores, Jesuit Preparatory School, Santiago, Cuba. MILITARY: U.S. Army Medical Corps, sergeant, 1943-45.

VOCATION: Actor, singer, producer, and writer.

CAREER: PRINCIPAL STAGE APPEARANCES—*Too Many Girls,* New York City, 1939. MAJOR TOURS—Singer with Xavier Cugat

Band, national tour, 1935-36; as singer and musician with his own band, national tour, 1945-46.

PRINCIPAL FILM APPEARANCES—*Too Many Girls,* RKO, 1940; *Father Takes a Wife,* RKO, 1941; *Four Jacks and a Jill,* RKO, 1942; *The Navy Comes Through,* RKO, 1942; *Bataan,* Metro-Goldwyn-Mayer (MGM), 1943; *Holiday in Havana,* Columbia, 1949; *Cuban Pete,* Universal, 1950; *The Long Long Trailer,* MGM, 1953; *Forever Darling,* MGM, 1956; *The Escape Artist,* Warner Brothers, 1982.

PRINCIPAL FILM WORK—Producer, *Forever Darling,* 1956.

PRINCIPAL TELEVISION APPEARANCES—Series: Ricky Ricardo, *I Love Lucy,* CBS, 1951-57; host and performer, *Westinghouse Desilu Playhouse,* CBS, 1958-60; Ricky Ricardo, *The Lucy-Desi Comedy Hour,* CBS, summers, 1962-65, and 1967; *Ironside* (pilot for spinoff series), NBC. Guest: *The Kraft Music Hall,* CBS; *Saturday Night Live,* NBC.

PRINCIPAL TELEVISION WORK—Producer: *I Love Lucy,* CBS; *Westinghouse Desilu Playhouse,* CBS; *The Mothers-in- Law,* NBC, 1967-79.

RELATED CAREER—Music director, Bob Hope's radio show, 1946-47; president and co-founder, Desilu Productions Inc., 1951-62; president, Desi Arnaz Productions, Inc., 1965.

NON-RELATED CAREER—Owner of Corona Breeding Farm.

WRITINGS: NON-FICTION—*A Book* (autobiography), 1976.

AWARDS: Best Performance of the Month, *Photoplay* Magazine, 1943, for *Bataan.*

SIDELIGHTS: CTFT notes that industry analysts credit Desi Arnaz as being the progenitor of the ''re-run'' and syndicated shows with his decision to film the *I Love Lucy* television series in the early 1950s. Until that time, only the rather crude ''kinescope recording'' of television programs had been used.*

*　　　*　　　*

ARNOLD, Tom   1947-

PERSONAL: Born January 25, 1947, in London, England; son of Thomas Charles (a theatrical producer) and Helen (Breen) Arnold; married Elizabeth Jane Smithers, 1984. EDUCATION: Pembroke College, Oxford University, M.A.

VOCATION: Producing manager and Member of Parliament.

CAREER: PRINCIPAL STAGE WORK—Producer: *Christmas Ice Pantomime,* Wembley Arena and Conference Center, U.K., 1969-78; *Danny La Rue at the Palace,* London, 1970; *Peter Pan,* London, 1971-79; *The Sunshine Boys,* London, 1975; *The King and I,* London, 1979; *Dancin',* London, 1983.

MAJOR TOURS—*Peter Pan,* U.K. cities, 1971-79.

NON-RELATED CAREER—Member of the British Parliament for Hazel Grove, U.K., since 1974.

MEMBER: Society of West End Theatres.

ADDRESSES: OFFICE—House of Commons, London SW1A 0AA, England.

*   *   *

ARNOTT, James Fullarton   1914-1982

PERSONAL: Born April 29, 1914, in Glasgow, Scotland; died November 22, 1982, in London; son of Hezekiah Merricks and Susie Willock (Fullarton) Arnott; married Martha Lawrence Grant. EDUCATION: Attended Ardrossan Academy, University of Glasgow, M.A., Merton College, Oxford University, M.Litt., and Peterhouse University, Cambridge, U.K.; studied at the Royal Scottish Academy of Music and Dramatic Art.

VOCATION: Director, theatre administrator, educator, editor, and author.

CAREER: PRINCIPAL STAGE WORK— Director: *Murder in the Cathedral*, 1952; *Love's Labour's Lost*, 1964; *The Play of Daniel* and *Curlew River*, both 1968; *A Satyre of the Thrie Estaitis*, 1969; *The Forrigan Reel*, 1970; *Valentine*, 1976, all in Glasgow. Also directed the Scottish Ballet and the Citizens' Theatre, Scotland.

RELATED CAREER—Educator: Hull University; University of Glasgow, 1939 (head of drama department, 1966, reader, 1971, professor of drama, 1973, retired, 1979); United Kingdom National Commission for the United Nations Education, Scientific, and Cultural Organization (UNESCO; 1980-82).

WRITINGS: BOOKS—(With J. W. Robinson) *English Theatrical Literature, 1559-1900*, 1970. JOURNALS—Editor, ''Theatre Research,'' re-titled, ''Theatre Research International,'' 1964-82.

MEMBER: International Federation for Theatre Research (president, 1975-79), Scottish Arts Council (chairman of drama committee, 1976-79), Arts Council of Great Britain, 1977-79, Theatres Trust (trustee, 1980), Scottish Theatre Trust (governor).*

*   *   *

ARONSTEIN, Martin   1936-

PERSONAL: Born November 2, 1936, in Pittsfield, MA; son of Milton David and Selma Frances (Herman) Aronstein. EDUCATION: Attended Queen's College.

VOCATION: Lighting designer.

CAREER: PRINCIPAL STAGE WORK—Lighting designer, all New York City productions: *Carousel*, Equity Library Theatre, 1959; *The Taming of the Shrew*, 1960; *King Richard II*, *Black Nativity*, *Romeo and Juliet*, *Julius Caesar*, *Electra*, and *Mister Roberts*, all 1961; *The Tempest*, 1962; *The Winter's Tale* and *Morning Sun*, both 1963; *The White Rose and the Red*, *Cindy*, *The Milk Train Doesn't Stop Here Anymore*, *A Severed Head*, *I Was Dancing*, *Tiny Alice*, *Othello*, *Electra*, and *A Midsummer Night's Dream*, all 1964; *The Impossible Years*, *The Royal Hunt of the Sun*, *Cactus*

Flower, *Love's Labour's Lost*, *Coriolanus*, *Troilus and Cressida*, and *King Henry V*, all 1965.

Slapstick Tragedy, *The Condemned of Altona*, *All's Well That Ends Well*, *Measure for Measure*, *Richard III*, *The Investigation*, and *Those That Play the Clowns*, all 1966; *Marat/Sade*, *The Astrakhan Coat*, *The East Wind*, *Galileo*, *The Comedy of Errors*, *King John*, *Titus Andronicus*, *Song of the Grashopper*, *Hair*, *How Now Dow Jones*, and *Hamlet*, all 1967; *The Education of H*Y*M*A*N K*A*P*L*A*N*, *George M!*, *I'm Solomon*, *The Memorandum*, *Henry IV*, Parts I and II, *Romeo and Juliet*, *Her First Roman*, *Huui Huui*, *Morning, Noon and Night*, *Promises, Promises*, *Dames at Sea*, and *Forty Carats*, all 1968; *Cities in Bezique*, *The Owl Answers*, *Play It Again Sam*, *The Dozens*, *Invitation to a Beheading*, *Billy*, *Peer Gynt*, *Twelfth Night*, *The Reckoning*, *The Penny Wars*, *Buck White*, *La Strada*, and *Sambo*, all 1969.

Paris Is Out!, *The Chinese and Dr. Fish*, *Grin and Bare It*, *Postcards*, *The Effect of Gamma Rays on Man-in-the-Moon Marigolds*, *Park*, *Mod Donna*, *The Wars of the Roses*, Parts I and II, *Richard III*, *The Happiness Cage*, *Trelawny of the 'Wells'*, *Jack MacGowran in the Works of Samuel Beckett*, and *The Gingerbread Lady*, all 1970; *Four on a Garden*, *And Miss Reardon Drinks a Little*, *The Basic Training of Pavlo Hummel*, *Charlie Was Here and Now He's Gone*, *Timon of Athens*, *The Tale of Cymbeline*, *The Incomparable Max*, and *Ain't Supposed to Die a Natural Death*, all 1971; *Moonchildren*, *Sugar*, *Promenade, All!*, *The Little Black Book*, *Different Times*, *Don't Play Us Cheap*, *Hamlet*, *Ti-Jean and His Brothers*, *Much Ado About Nothing*, *Hurry Harry*, *Wedding Band*, and *Ambassador*, all 1972.

Tricks, *Echoes*, *Nash at Nine*, *Smith*, *As You Like It*, *King Lear*, *Boom Boom Room*, *The Three Sisters*, *The Beggar's Opera*, *Measure for Measure*, *The Au Pair Man*, and *Scapin*, all 1973; *Next Time I'll Sing to You*, *More than You Deserve*, *What the Wine-Sellers Buy*, *Dear Nobody*, *Once I Saw a Boy Laughing*, *My Fat Friend*, *Music! Music!*, *An American Millionaire*, *Pericles*, *The Merry Wives of Windsor*, *Mert & Phil*, *Fame*, and *In the Boom Boom Room*, all 1974; *The Ritz*, *A Doll's House*, *A Matter of Time*, *Little Black Sheep*, *Hamlet*, *Kennedy's Children*, and *Souvenir* (in Los Angeles), all 1975; *The Poison Tree*, *Hamlet*, *The Comedy of Errors*, *Mrs. Warren's Profession*, *I Have a Dream*, *The Mikado*, *The Pirates of Penzance*, and *HMS Pinafore*, all 1976; *Absent Friends* (Toronto), 1977; *Hello, Dolly!* and *Players*, both 1978; *The Grand Tour*, 1979.

Cause Celebre and *On Golden Pond*, both Ahmanson Theatre, Los Angeles, 1979-80; *Home*, Cort Theatre, New York City, 1980; *Blackstone!*, Majestic Theatre, New York City, 1980; *Says I, Says He*, Mark Taper Forum, Los Angeles, 1980; *Division Street*, Ambassador Theatre, New York City, 1980; *Mixed Couples*, Brooks Atkinson Theatre, New York City, 1980-81; *Chekhov in Yalta* and *Twelfth Night*, both Mark Taper Forum, 1981; *Medea*, Cort Theatre, New York City, 1982; *The Chalk Garrden*, Roundabout Theatre, Stage One, New York City, 1982; *Another Part of the Forest*, Ahmanson Theatre, 1982; *Ghosts*, Brooks Atkinson Theatre, 1982; *Whodunnit*, Biltmore Theatre, New York City, 1982-83; *A Soldier's Play*, *A Month in the Country*, and *Richard III*, all at the Mark Taper Forum, 1982-83; *Hay Fever*, Ahmanson Theatre, 1983; *The American Clock*, *Wild Oats*, and *Moby Dick—Rehearsed*, all at the Mark Taper Forum, 1983-84; *Beethoven's Tenth* and *Detective Story*, both Ahmanson Theatre, 1983-84; *Noises Off*, Brooks Atkinson Theatre, 1983-85; *Beethoven's Tenth*, Nederlander Theatre, New York City, 1984; *A Woman of Independent Means*, Biltmore Theatre, New York City, 1984; *Passion Play*, *Undiscovered*

Country, and *Measure for Measure,* all at the Mark Taper Forum, 1984-85; *Noises Off,* Ahmanson Theatre, 1985; *Benefactors,* Brooks Atkinson Theatre, New York City, 1985; *Romance Language,* '*Night, Mother, The Immigrant, Hedda Gabler,* and *The Real Thing,* all at the Mark Taper Forum, 1986; *The Petrified Forest* and *The Faire Penitent,* both Los Angeles Theatre Center, 1986; *Sweet Bird of Youth,* Ahmanson Theatre, 1986; *Pump Boys and Dinettes,* Las Palmas Theatre, Los Angeles, 1986; *Wild Honey,* Virginia Theatre, New York City, 1986; *The Film Society* and *The Importance of Being Earnest,* both Los Angeles Theatre Center, 1987.

MAJOR TOURS—All U.S. cities tours: *Rich Little Rich Girl,* 1964; *Hello, Dolly!,* 1977-83; *Daisy Mayme,* 1979-80; *The Winslow Boy,* 1981; *Torch Song Trilogy,* 1983-84.

ADDRESSES: OFFICE—4851 Sylmar Ave., Sherman Oaks, CA 91423.

* * *

ARTHUR, Beatrice　1926-

PERSONAL: Born Bernice Frankel, May 13, 1926, in New York, NY; daughter of Philip and Rebecca Frankel; married Gene Saks (an actor and director), May 28, 1950 (divorced); children: two sons. EDUCATION: Attended Blackstone College and Franklin Institute of Science and Arts; trained for the stage at the New School for Social Research with Erwin Piscator.

VOCATION: Actress.

CAREER: STAGE DEBUT—Title role, *Lysistrata,* Dramatic Workshop of the New School, New York City, 1947. BROADWAY DEBUT—Madame Suze, *Seventh Heaven,* American National Theatre Academy (ANTA) Theatre, 1955. PRINCIPAL STAGE APPEARANCES—Appeared in *Gas,* member of the chorus, *Dog Beneath the Skin,* and title role, *Yerma* all at the Cherry Lane Theatre, New York City, 1947; Inez, *No Exit,* Kate, *The Taming of the Shrew,* Mother, *Six Characters in Search of an Author,* and Mother, *The Owl and the Pussycat,* all 1948; Marchioness, *Le Bourgeois Gentilhomme,* Constance, *Yes Is for a Very Young Man,* Tekla, *The Creditors,* and Hesione Hushabye, *Heartbreak House,* all 1949.

Regional theatre performances include: *Personal Appearance, Candlelight, Love or Money, The Voice of the Turtle,* and *Gentlemen Prefer Blondes,* 1950-53; also appeared in *Fiddler on the Roof,* Circle Theatre, Atlantic City, 1951, Music Circus Theatre, Lambertville, NJ and State Fair Music Hall, Dallas, TX, 1953; Clotilde Lombaste, *The New Moon,* State Fair Music Hall, Dallas, 1953; Lucy Brown, *The Threepenny Opera,* Theatre de Lys, New York City, 1954; *The Shoestring Revue,* President Theatre, New York City, 1954; *The Threepenny Opera,* Theatre de Lys, New York City, 1955; *The Ziegfeld Follies,* Shubert Theatre, Boston, 1956; appeared in *What's the Rush?,* 1956; Queen Gertrude, *Hamlet,* Theatre de Lys, New York City, 1957; Nadine Fesser, *Nature's Way,* Coronet Theatre, New York City, 1957; Bella-Bello, *Ulysses in Nighttown,* Rooftop Theatre, New York City, 1958; *Chic,* Orpheum Theatre, New York City, 1959.

Hortense, *Gay Divorcee,* Cherry Lane Theatre, New York City, 1960; Mrs. Miller, *A Matter of Position,* Walnut Street Theatre,

Philadelphia, PA, 1962; Yente, *Fiddler on the Roof,* Imperial Theatre, New York City, 1964; Vera Charles, *Mame,* Winter Garden Theatre, New York City, 1966; Meg, *A Mother's Kisses,* Shubert Theatre, New Haven, CT, 1968; Enid Pollack, *The Floating Light Bulb,* Vivian Beaumont Theatre, New York City, 1981; *Hey, Look Me Over!,* Avery Fisher Hall, New York City, 1981; *Night of 100 Stars,* Radio City Music Hall, New York City, 1982.

MAJOR TOURS—*The Ziegfeld Follies,* U.S. cities, 1956.

FILM DEBUT—*That Kind of Woman,* Paramount, 1959. PRINCIPAL FILM APPEARANCES—*Lovers and Other Strangers,* Cinerama, 1970; Vera, *Mame,* Warner Brothers, 1974; unemployment clerk, *History of the World: Part I,* Brooksfilms, 1981.

TELEVISION DEBUT—*Once Upon a Time,* DuMont, 1951. PRINCIPAL TELEVISION APPEARANCES—Series: Maude Findlay, *All in the Family,* CBS, 1971; Maude Findlay, *Maude,* CBS, 1972-78; co-host, *On the Air,* CBS, 1978; Amanda Cartwright, *Amanda's,* ABC, 1983; Dorothy, *The Golden Girls,* NBC, 1985—. Episodic: *The Steve Allen Show,* CBS, 1952; *The George Gobel Show,* NBC, 1958; *The Sid Caesar Show,* ABC, 1963.

Pilots: Rosalyn Gordon, *P.O.P.,* 1984. Specials: Host, *The Beatrice Arthur Special,* 1980. Guest: *The Bob Hope Special: Bob Hope—Hope, Women and Song,* 1980; *The Bob Hope Special: Bob Hope's Women I Love—Beautiful but Funny,* 1982; *The Dean Martin Celebrity Roast,* 1984; *The 37th Annual Prime Time Emmy Awards,* 1985; *The 38th Annual Prime Time Emmy Awards,* 1986; *The All-Star Party for Clint Eastwood,* 1986.

RELATED CAREER—Has performed in nightclubs since 1948; was the resident commedienne with the Tamiment Theatre, PA, 1953.

AWARDS: Best Supporting Actress in a Musical, Antoinette Perry Award, 1966, for *Mame;* Outstanding Leading Actress in a Comedy Series, Emmy Award, 1977, for *Maude.*

MEMBER: Actors' Equity Association, Screen Actors Guild, American Federation of Television and Radio Artists.

ADDRESSES: AGENT—William Morris Agency, Inc., 151 El Camino Dr., Beverly Hills, CA 90212.*

* * *

ARTHUR, Robert　1909-1986

PERSONAL: Born Robert Arthur Feder, November 1, 1909, in New York, NY; died after a long illness in Beverly Hills, CA, October 28, 1986; married. EDUCATION: Attended Southwestern University and University of Southern California. MILITARY: U.S. Army, 1942-45.

VOCATION: Producer and screenwriter.

CAREER: PRINCIPAL FILM WORK—Producer: *Buck Privates Come Home,* Universal, 1947; *Wistful Widow of Wagon Gap,* Universal, 1947; *Abbott and Costello Meet Frankenstein,* Universal, 1948; *For the Love of Mary,* Universal, 1948; *Mexican Hayride,* Universal, 1948; *Abbott and Costello in the Foreign Legion,* Universal, 1950; *Louisa,* Universal, 1950; *Francis,* Universal, 1950; *Golden Horde,* Universal, 1951; *Starlift,* Warner Brothers,

1951; *The Story of Will Rogers*, Warner Brothers, 1952; *Big Heat*, Columbia, 1953; *The Black Shield of Falworth*, Universal, 1954; *Richochet Romance*, Universal, 1954; *The Long Gray Line*, Columbia, 1955; *Francis in the Haunted House*, Universal, 1956; *Day of Fury*, Universal, 1956; *Pillars of the Sky*, Universal, 1956; *Kelly and Me*, Universal, 1957; *Mister Cory*, Universal, 1957; *Midnight Story*, Universal, 1957; *Man of a Thousand Faces*, Universal, 1957; *A Time to Love*, Universal, 1958; *A Perfect Furlough*, Universal, 1959; *Operation Petticoat*, Universal, 1959.

The Great Imposter, Universal, 1961; *Come September*, Universal, 1961; *Lover Come Back*, Universal, 1962; *The Spiral Road*, Universal, 1962; *That Touch of Mink*, Universal, 1962; *For Love or Money*, Universal, 1963; *Brass Bottle*, Universal, 1964; *Captain Newman M.D.*, Universal, 1964; *Bedtime Story*, Universal, 1964; *Father Goose*, Universal, 1965; *Shenandoah*, Universal, 1965; *Blindfold*, Universal, 1966; *A Man Could Get Killed*, Universal, 1966; *Hellfighters*, Universal, 1969; *Sweet Charity*, Universal, 1969; *One More Train to Rob*, Universal, 1971.

RELATED CAREER—Producer of approximately six hundred Air Force training films between 1942-45.

NON-RELATED CAREEER—Oil company executive, 1929-36.

WRITINGS: SCREENPLAYS—Contributed to: *New Moon*, Metro-Goldwyn-Mayer (MGM), 1940; *Chip Off the Old Block*, MGM, 1944.*

*   *   *

ASHBY, Harvey

PERSONAL: EDUCATION: Graduate, Royal Academy of Dramatic Art.

VOCATION: Actor and director.

CAREER: PRINCIPAL STAGE APPEARANCES—*Treasure Island*, Mermaid Theatre, London; *The Killing Game*, Apollo Theatre, London; *Dick Turpin*, Mermaid Theatre, London; *The Importance of Being Earnest*, English Theatre, Vienna, Austria; *Dead Ringer*, London production; *The Cherry Orchard*, London production.

MAJOR TOURS—*Night and Day* and *The Taming of the Shrew*, both Number One tours, England.

PRINCIPAL STAGE WORK—Director: *Night and Day*, Windsor Festival, 1982; *Flarepath*, Windsor Festival, 1983; *Dick Whittington*, Malcolm Knight Productions, 1984; also: *Relatively Speaking*, Henley, England; *The Life and Death of Almost Everybody*, Webber Douglas Academy of Dramatic Art, London; *Arms and the Man*, Paris, France; *Schweyk in the Second World War*, Welsh National Youth Theatre; *Rose*, South Africa; *Macbeth*, Norway; *The Importance of Being Earnest*, English Theatre, Vienna, Austria; *No Time for Love* and *The Willing Ram*, both Cheltenham, England; *The Boston Story*, Watford, England; *Spring and Port Wine*, Liverpool Playhouse, England; *Night and Day*, Windsor Festival.

Directed tours of *The Gentle Trap*, 1981; *Fallen Angels*, Number One tour, 1982; *Who Killed William Hickey*, Number One tour, 1982; *Privates on Parade*, 1985; *On Approval*, Number One tour,

HARVEY ASHBY

1986; assistant director, *Son Et Lumiere*, Warwick Castle, Blenheim Palace, Hampton Court, Canterbury Cathedral.

PRINCIPAL FILM APPEARANCES—*Eye of the Devil*, Metro-Goldwyn-Mayer (MGM), 1967; *Scrooge*, National General, 1970; *High Road to China*, Warner Brothers, 1983; *The Importance of Being Earnest*, Wien Films, 1985; also, *The Periguin Hunters*, C.F.F.

PRINCIPAL TELEVISION APPEARANCES *The Secret Servant*, BBC; *The Naked Civil Servant*, ITV; *Lytton's Diary*, ITV; *War and Peace*, BBC; *The Onedin Line*, BBC; *The Importance of Being Earnest* and *My Wife Next Door*, both for German television; *Danger Man*, ITV; *The Avengers*, ITV; *The Prisoner*, ITV; *Die Kleine Warheid*, N.C.R. TV; *Zakarov*.

MEMBER: British Actors' Equity Association (councillor, 1984).

ADDRESSES: AGENT—Eric Glass Ltd., 28 Berkeley Square, London W1X 6HD, England.

*   *   *

ASHCROFT, Peggy   1907-

PERSONAL: Full name, Edith Margaret Emily Ashcroft; born December 22, 1907, in Croydon, England; daughter of William Worsley and Violetta Maud (Bernheim) Ashcroft; married Rupert Charles Hart-Davis, 1929 (divorced); married Theodore Komisarjevsky, 1934 (divorced); married Jeremy Nicholas Hutchinson, 1940 (divorced, 1966); children: one son and one daughter. EDUCATION: Attended Woodford School, Croydon; trained for the stage at the Central School of Dramatic Art with Miss Elsie Fogerty.

VOCATION: Actress.

CAREER: STAGE DEBUT—Margaret, *Dear Brutus,* Birmingham Repertory Theatre, U.K., 1926. LONDON DEBUT—Bessie, *One Day More,* Playroom Six Theatre, 1927. BROADWAY DEBUT—Lise, *High Tor,* Martin Beck Theatre, 1937. PRINCIPAL STAGE APPEARANCES—Mary Dunn, *The Return,* Everyman Theatre, London, 1927; Eve, *When Adam Delved,* Q Theatre, London, 1927; Betty, *The Way of the World,* Wyndham's Theatre, London, 1927; Anastasia Vulliamy, *The Fascinating Foundling* and Mary Bruin, *The Land of Heart's Desire,* both at the Arts Theatre, London, 1928; Edith Strange, *Earthbound,* Q Theatre, London, 1928; Kristina, *Easter,* Arts Theatre, London, 1928; Eulalia, *A Hundred Years Old,* Lyric Theatre, Hammersmith, London, 1928; Lucy Deren, *Requital,* Everyman Theatre, London, 1929; Sally Humphries, *Bees and Honey,* with the Repertory Players, Strand Theatre, London, 1929; Naomi, *Jew Suss,* Duke of York's Theatre, London, 1929; Desdemona, *Othello,* Savoy Theatre, London, 1930; Judy Battle, *The Breadwinner,* Vaudeville Theatre, London, 1930.

Pervaneh, *Hassan,* 1931, and Juliet, *Romeo and Juliet,* 1932, both for the Oxford University Dramatic Society (OUDS), Oxford, U.K.; Angela, *Charles the 3rd,* Wyndham's Theatre, London, 1931; Anne, *A Knight Passed By,* Ambassadors Theatre, London, 1931; Fanny, *Sea Fever,* New Theatre, London, 1931; Marcela, *Take Two from One,* Haymarket Theatre, London, 1931; Stella, *Le Cocu Magnifique,* Globe Theatre, London, 1932; Salome Westaway, *The Secret Woman,* Duchess Theatre, then leading role at Old Vic Theatre and Sadler's Wells Theatre, all London, 1932; Cleopatra, *Caesar and Cleopatra,* Imogen, *Cymbeline,* and Rosalind, *As You Like It,* all Old Vic Theatre and Sadler's Wells Theatre, London, 1932; title role, *Fraulein Elsa,* with the Independent Theatre Club, Kingsway Theatre, London, 1932; Portia, *Merchant of Venice,* Kate Hardcastle, *She Stoops to Conquer,* Perdita, *The Winter's Tale,* title role, *Mary Stuart,* Juliet, *Romeo and Juliet,* Lady Teazle, *School for Scandal,* and Miranda, *The Tempest,* all at the Old Vic Theatre, London, 1932-33; Inken Peters, *Before Sunset,* Shaftesbury Theatre, London, 1933; Vasantesena, *The Golden Toy,* Coliseum Theatre, London, 1934; Lucia Maubel, *The Life that I Gave Him,* Little Theatre, London, 1934; Therese Paradis, *Mesmer,* King's Theatre, Glasgow, Scotland, 1935; Juliet, *Romeo and Juliet,* New Theatre, London 1935.

Queen, *Richard II,* Lady Teazle, *School for Scandal,* Irina, *Three Sisters,* and Portia, *The Merchant of Venice,* all at the Queen's Theatre, London, 1937-38; Yeleina Talberg, *The White Guard,* Phoenix Theatre, London, 1938; Viola, *Twelfth Night,* Phoenix Theatre, London, 1939; Cecily Cardew, *The Importance of Being Earnest,* Globe Theatre, London, 1939; Dinah Sylvester, *Cousin Muriel,* Globe Theatre, London, 1940; Miranda, *The Tempest,* Old Vic Theatre, London, 1940; Cecily Cardew, *The Importance of Being Earnest,* Phoenix Theatre, London, 1942; Catharine Lisle, *The Dark River,* Whitehall Theatre, London, 1943; Ophelia, *Hamlet,* Titania, *A Midsummer Night's Dream,* and the title role, *The Duchess of Malfi,* all at the Haymarket Theatre, London, 1944-45; Evelyn Holt, *Edward, My Son,* His Majesty's Theatre, London, 1947, then Martin Beck Theatre, New York City, 1948; Catherine Sloper, *The Heiress,* Haymarket Theatre, London, 1949.

Beatrice, *Much Ado About Nothing* and Cordelia, *King Lear,* both

with the Royal Shakespeare Company, Stratford-on-Avon, U.K., 1950; Viola, *Twelfth Night,* 1950, title role, *Electra,* 1951, and Mistress Page, *The Merry Wives of Windsor,* 1951, all at the Old Vic Theatre, London; Hester Collyer, *The Deep Blue Sea,* Duchess Theatre, London, 1952; Portia, *The Merchant of Venice* and Cleopatra, *Antony and Cleopatra,* both with the Royal Shakespeare Company, Stratford-on-Avon, 1953; title role, *Hedda Gabler,* Lyric Theatre, Hammersmith, then Westminster Theatre, both London, 1954, repeated at the New Theatre, Oslo, Norway, 1955; Beatrice, *Much Ado About Nothing,* with the Royal Shakespeare Company, Palace Theatre, London, 1955; Miss Madrigal, *The Chalk Garden,* Haymarket Theatre, London, 1956; Shen Te, *The Good Woman of Setzuan,* Royal Court Theatre, London, 1956; Rosalind, *As You Like It* and Imogen, *Cymbeline,* both with the Royal Shakespeare Company, Stratford-on-Avon, 1957; *Portraits of Women,* Edinburgh Festival, Scotland, then Lyceum Theatre, London, 1958; Julia Raik, *Shadow of Heroes,* Piccadilly Theatre, London, 1958; Rebecca West, *Rosmersholm,* Royal Court Theatre, London, 1959, then Comedy Theatre, London, 1960.

With the Royal Shakespeare Company, appeared as Katharina, *The Taming of the Shrew,* Paulina, *The Winter's Tale,* both at the Shakespeare Memorial Theatre, Stratford-on-Avon, title role, *The Duchess of Malfi,* Aldwych Theatre, London, all 1960; *The Hollow Crown* and Ranevsky, *The Cherry Orchard,* both at the Aldwych Theatre, London, and Emilia, *Othello,* Stratford-on-Avon, all 1961; *The Vagaries of Love,* Belgrade Theatre, Coventry, U.K., 1962; Margaret of Anjou, *The Wars of the Roses,* a trilogy consisting of *Henry VI, Edward IV,* and *Richard III,* Stratford-on-Avon, then Aldwych Theatre, London, 1964.

Madame Arkadina, *The Seagull,* with the English Stage Company, Queen's Theatre, London, 1964; Margaret of Anjou, *The Wars of the Roses,* with the Royal Shakespeare Company, Stratford-on-Avon, 1964; Mother, *Days in the Trees,* 1966, and Mrs. Alving, *Ghosts,* 1967, both at the Aldwych Theatre, London; appeared in *The Hollow Crown,* 1968; Agnes, *A Delicate Balance,* 1969; Beth, *Landscape,* 1969; Queen Katherine, *Henry VIII,* Stratford-on-Avon, 1969; Volumnia, *The Plebeians Rehearse the Uprising,* Aldwych Theatre, London, 1970; Queen Katherine, *Henry VIII,* Aldwych Theatre, London, 1970; Claire Lannes, *The Lovers of Viorne,* Royal Court Theatre, London, 1971; the Wife, *All Over,* Aldwych Theatre, London, 1972; Lady Boothroyd, *Lloyd George Knew My Father,* Savoy Theatre, London, 1972; appeared in *Old Times,* 1972; Beth, *Landscape* and Flora, *A Slight Ache,* both at the Aldwych Theatre, London, 1973; Ella Rentheim, *John Gabriel Borkman* and Winnie, *Happy Days,* both with the National Theatre Company, Old Vic Theatre, London, 1975; Lilian Baylis, *Tribute to the Lady,* with the National Theatre Company, Old Vic Theatre, London, 1976; Lidya, *Old World,* with the Royal Shakespeare Company, Aldwych Theatre, London, 1976; Winnie, *Happy Days,* Lyttleton Theatre, London, 1977. Also appeared in *Watch on the Rhine,* 1980; *Family Voices* and *All's Well that Ends Well,* 1981.

MAJOR TOURS—Hester, *The Silver Cord,* U.K. cities, 1928; Constance Neville, *She Stoops to Conquer,* U.K. cities, 1929; Isolde, *Weep for the Spring,* U.K. cities, 1939; Mrs. de Winter, *Rebecca,* U.K. cities, 1941; Ophelia, *Hamlet,* U.K. cities, 1944; Cleopatra, *Antony and Cleopatra,* The Hague, Amsterdam, Antwerp, Brussels, Paris, 1953; Eva Delaware, *The Coast of Coromandel,* U.K. cities, 1959; *The Hollow Crown,* European cities, 1962.

FILM DEBUT—1933. PRINCIPAL FILM APPEARANCES—*The Thirty-Nine Steps,* Gaumont, 1935; *The Nun's Story,* Warner Brothers, 1959; *Three into Two Won't Go,* Universal, 1969; *Sunday*

Bloody Sunday, United Artists, 1971; Mrs. Moore, *A Passage to India,* Columbia, 1984. Also appeared in *The Wandering Jew.*

TELEVISION DEBUT—*The Shadow of Heroes,* 1959. PRINCIPAL TELEVISION APPEARANCES—Dramatic specials: Madame Ranevsky, *The Cherry Orchard,* 1962; Margaret, *The Wars of the Roses,* 1965; the Mother, *Days in the Trees,* 1967; also *Cream in my Coffee, Caught on a Train,* 1980, and *The Jewel in the Crown,* 1984.

AWARDS: Dame of the British Empire, birthday honors, 1956; King's Gold Medal Award, Norway, 1955, for *Hedda Gabler; Evening Standard* Drama Award, 1956, for *The Chalk Garden;* Best Actress, Paris Theatre Festival Award, 1962, for *The Hollow Crown;* Best Actress, New York Film Critics Award, 1984, for *A Passage to India;* Best Supporting Actress, Academy Award and Los Angeles Film Critics Award, both 1984, for *A Passage to India;* honorary degrees: Doctor of Letters, Oxford University, 1961, Leicester University, 1964; Doctor of Literature, London University, 1965, Cambridge University, 1972.

MEMBER: English Stage Company (council), 1957, Shakespeare Memorial Theatre Council, 1962-65, Apollo Society (president), 1964, Royal Shakespeare Company (director) 1968—.

SIDELIGHTS: FAVORITE ROLES—Winnie, *Happy Days.*

CTFT learned that Dame Peggy Ashcroft spoke the prologue at the opening production at the Ashcroft Theatre, Croydon, which had been named in her honour.

ADDRESSES: OFFICE—Manor Lodge, 40 Frognal Lane, Hampstead, London NW3, England.*

*   *   *

ASHTON, Ellis   1919-

PERSONAL: Born December 1, 1919, in Liverpool, England; son of Joseph and Beatrice Ashton; married Margaret Mitchell (a dancer). EDUCATION: Attended Holy Trinity, Liverpool and Army Formation College, U.K.

VOCATION: Comedian and theatre historian.

CAREER: STAGE DEBUT—Comedian, *The Silloth Follies,* Pavilion Theatre, Silloth, U.K., 1947. PRINCIPAL STAGE WORK—Comedian, manager, and director of variety and seasonal shows and tours, U.K.

RELATED CAREER—Co-founder and member, Theatres Trust and the British Theatre Institute.

WRITINGS: PERIODICALS—Regular contributor, *The Stage.*

MEMBER: Royal Society of Arts (fellow), British Music Hall Society (chairman), National Association of Theatrical, Television and Kine Employees (past president); governor, Ruskin College, Oxford, U.K. and vice-president, Ruskin Fellowship, London; Zoologican Society (fellow), Royal Geographical Society (fellow), Linnaean Society (fellow).

SIDELIGHTS: CTFT has learned that Ellis Ashton is a member of

many theatrical committees and associations for the preservation of rare buildings in the U.K., especially theatres and cinemas.

ADDRESSES: OFFICE—One King Henry Street, London N16, England.*

*   *   *

ASSANTE, Armand   1949-

PERSONAL: Born October 4, 1949, in New York, NY. EDUCATION: Attended the American Academy of Dramatic Art in New York City.

VOCATION: Actor.

CAREER: OFF-BROADWAY DEBUT—*The Lake of the Woods,* 1971. PRINCIPAL STAGE APPEARANCES—Teddy, *Comedians,* Music Box Theatre, New York City, 1976; Tybalt, *Romeo and Juliet,* Circle in the Square, New York City, 1977; Emperor Napoleon I, *Kingdoms,* Cort Theatre, New York City, 1981; also appeared in *Yankees 3, Detroit 0, Rubbers,* and *Boccaccio,* all New York City.

PRINCIPAL FILM APPEARANCES—*The Lords of Flatbush,* Columbia, 1974; *Paradise Alley,* Universal, 1978; *Prophecy,* Paramount, 1979; *Little Darlings,* Paramount, 1980; *Private Benjamin,* Warner Brothers, 1980; *I, the Jury,* Twentieth Century-Fox, 1982; *Love and Money,* Paramount, 1982; *Unfaithfully Yours,* Twentieth Century-Fox, 1984; also *Belizaire the Cajun* and *Animal Behavior.*

PRINCIPAL TELEVISION APPEARANCES—Movies: *Human Feelings,* 1978; *The Lady of the House,* 1978; *The Pirate* (also known as *Harold Robbins' The Pirate*), 1978; *Sophia Loren: Her Own Story,* 1980; *Rage of Angels,* 1983; *Why Me?,* ABC, 1984; *A Deadly Business,* CBS, 1986. Mini-Series: *Evergreen,* NBC, 1985.

ADDRESSES: AGENT—c/o Lou Pitt, International Creative Management, Inc., 8899 Beverly Blvd., Los Angeles, CA 90048.*

*   *   *

ATHERTON, William   1947-

PERSONAL: Born William Atherton Knight, II, June 30, 1947, in New Haven, CT; son of Robert Atherton and Myrtle (Robison) Knight. EDUCATION: Attended Carnegie-Mellon University of Drama; trained for the stage with the Aesthetic Realism Foundation, New York City, with Consultation with Three, Ted van Griethuysen, Roy Harris, Sheldon Kranz, and Eli Siegel.

VOCATION: Actor.

CAREER: STAGE DEBUT—*The Boyfriend,* Clinton Playhouse, Clinton, CT, 1964. BROADWAY DEBUT—David Ragin, *The Sign in Sidney Brustein's Window,* Longacre Theatre, 1972. PRINCIPAL STAGE APPEARANCES—Kenny, *Little Murders,* Civic Theatre, Chicago, IL, 1970; Victor, *Goodbye and Keep Cold,* Loft Theatre, New York City, 1970; Ronnie Shaughnessy, *House of Blue Leaves,* Truck and Warehouse Theatre, New York City, 1971; title role, *The Basic Training of Pavlo Hummel,* New York Shakespeare Festival,

Newman Theatre, New York City, 1971; title role, *Suggs,* Forum Theatre, Lincoln Center, New York City, 1972; Leonidik, *The Promise,* Bucks County Playhouse, PA, 1974; Lord Ravensbane, *The Scarecrow,* Kennedy Center, Washington, DC, 1975; Aubrey, *The Show-Off,* Long Wharf Theatre, New Haven, CT, 1975; Bing Ringling, *Rich and Famous,* New York Shakespeare Festival, Public Theatre, New York City, 1976; Percival, *Misalliance,* Lake Forest, IL, 1976; Richard, *Passing Game,* American Place Theatre, New York City, 1977; Roy Lane, *Broadway,* Wilbur Theatre, Boston, MA, 1978; *William Atherton: Acting, Ethics, Person,* Terrain Gallery, New York City, 1978; Johnny Case, *Happy New Year,* Morosco Theatre, New York City, 1980; Lee Baum, *The American Clock,* Biltmore Theatre, New York City, 1980; Richard, *Three Acts of Recognition,* New York Shakespeare Festival, Public/Anspacher Theatre, New York City, 1982; Lt. Cmdr. John Challee, *The Caine Mutiny Court-Martial,* Circle in the Square Theatre, New York City, 1983.

FILM DEBUT—*The New Centurions,* Columbia, 1972. PRINCIPAL FILM APPEARANCES—*Class of '44,* Warner Brothers, 1972; *Sugarland Express,* Universal, 1974; *The Day of the Locust,* Paramount, 1975; *The Hindenburg,* Universal, 1975; *Looking for Mr. Goodbar,* Paramount, 1977; *Real Genius,* Tri-Star, 1985.

PRINCIPAL TELEVISION APPEARANCES—Mini-Series: Jim Lloyd, *Centennial,* NBC, 1978. Dramatic specials: *The House of Mirth,* WNET, NY.

ADDRESSES: AGENT—Writers and Artists Agency, 11726 San Vincente Blvd., Suite 300, Los Angeles, CA 90049.*

*   *   *

ATKINS, Eileen   1934-

PERSONAL: Born June 16, 1934, in London, England; daughter of Arthur Thomas and Annie Ellen (Elkins) Atkins; married Julian Glover (divorced). EDUCATION: Trained for the stage at the Guildhall School of Music and Drama.

VOCATION: Actress.

CAREER: STAGE DEBUT—Nurse, *Harvey,* Repertory Theatre, Bangor, Ireland, 1952. LONDON DEBUT—Jacquenetta, *Love's Labour's Lost,* Open Air Theatre, Regent's Park, 1953. BROADWAY DEBUT—Childie, *The Killing of Sister George,* Belasco Theatre, 1966. PRINCIPAL STAGE APPEARANCES—Diana, *Pericles,* among other roles with the Memorial Theatre Company, Stratford-Upon-Avon, 1957-59; Beattie, *Roots,* Bristol Old Vic Theatre, 1960; the Girl, *The Square,* Bromley Theatre, London, 1961; Viola, *Twelfth Night,* Lady Anne, *Richard III,* and Miranda, *The Tempest,* all with the Old Vic Company, London, 1962; Eileen Midway, *Semi-Detached,* Saville Theatre, London, 1962; Lady Brute, *The Provok'd Wife,* Vaudeville Theatre, London, 1963; Juliette, *Exit the King,* Edinburgh Festival, Scotland, then Royal Court Theatre, London, 1963; Viola, *Twelfth Night* and Ophelia, *Hamlet,* both at the Ravinia Festival, IL, 1964; Childie, *The Killing of Sister George,* Bristol Old Vic Theatre, then Duke of York's Theatre, London, 1965.

Joan Middleton, *The Restoration of Arnold Middleton,* Royal Court Theatre, London, 1966; Lika, *The Promise,* Henry Miller's Theatre, New York City, 1967; Celia Coplestone, *The Cocktail Party,*

Chichester Festival, U.K., then Wyndhams Theatre, then Haymarket Theatre, both London, 1968; Joan Shannon, *The Sleeper's Den,* Royal Court Theatre, London, 1969; Elizabeth I, *Vivat! Vivat Regina!,* Chichester Festival, then Piccadilly Theatre, London, 1970, then Broadhurst Theatre, New York City, 1972; title role, *Suzanna Andler,* Aldwych Theatre, London, 1973; Rosalind, *As You Like It,* with the Royal Shakespeare Company, Stratford-Upon-Avon, 1973; Hesione Hushabye, *Heartbreak House,* with the National Theatre Company at the Old Vic Theatre, London, 1975; title role, *Saint Joan,* Old Vic Theatre, London, 1977; Viola, *Twelfth Night* and Jennet Jourdemayne, *The Lady's Not for Burning,* both at the Old Vic Theatre, London, 1978; title role, *Mary Barnes,* Long Wharf Theatre, New Haven, CT, 1980.

TELEVISION DEBUT—Maggie, *Hilda Lessways,* BBC, 1959. PRINCIPAL TELEVISION APPEARANCES—Dramatic specials (British): *The Age of Kings; The Lady's Not for Burning; Electra.*

SIDELIGHTS: FAVORITE ROLES—Celia Coplestone, *The Cocktail Party.*

ADDRESSES: AGENT—Larry Dalzell Associates, 126 Kennington Park Road, London SE11, England.*

*   *   *

AUMONT, Jean-Pierre   1913-

PERSONAL: Born January 5, 1913, in Paris, France; son of Alexandre and Suzanne (Berr) Aumont; married Maria Montez (an actress), July 13, 1943 (died, September 7, 1951); married Marisa Pavan (an actress), 1951; children: (first marriage) Maria-Christina; (second marriage) Jean-Claude, Patrick. MILITARY: Free French Forces, 1939-45.

VOCATION: Actor and writer.

CAREER: STAGE DEBUT—Oedipe, *La Machine Infernale,* Comedie Champs-Elysees, Paris, April 10, 1934. BROADWAY DEBUT—Pierre Renault, *My Name Is Aquilon,* Lyceum Theatre, February 9, 1949. PRINCIPAL STAGE APPEARANCES—*Le Coeur,* Gymnase Theatre, Paris, 1937; Pelleas, *Pelleas et Melisande,* Theatre des Champs-Elysees, Paris, 1938; Orlando, *As You Like It,* Theatre des Champs-Elysees, Paris, 1939; Pierre, *Rose Burke,* Curran Theatre, San Francisco, CA, 1942; Pierre Renault, *L'Empereur de Chine,* Theatre des Maturins, Paris, 1948; Otto, *Design for Living,* Westport Country Playhouse, CT, 1948; Mark Antony, *Julius Caesar,* Arena Theatre, Arles, France, 1953; Henri and Pierre Belcourt, *The Heavenly Twins,* Booth Theatre, New York City, 1955.

Jupiter, *Amphitryon 38,* Comedie des Champs-Elysee, Paris, 1957; *Mon Pere Avait Raison,* Theatre de la Madeleine, Paris, 1960; Farou, *Second String,* Eugene O'Neill Theatre, New York City, 1960; title role, *The Affairs of Anatol,* Boston Arts Festival, MA, 1961; appeared in *Incident at Vichy,* Los Angeles, CA, 1962; appeared in *Flora,* Varietes, Paris, 1962; Prince Mikail, *Tovarich,* Broadway Theatre, New York City, 1963; Emile de Becque, *South Pacific,* Los Angeles, then San Francisco, CA, 1964; appeared in *Hostile Witness,* 1967; appeared in *There's a Girl in My Soup,* 1969; Jacques Casanova, *Camino Real,* Vivian Beaumont Theatre, New York City, 1970; Mark Antony, *Julius Caesar,* Jules Cesar Theatre, Paris, 1970; Dag Hammersjold, *Murderous Angels,* Theatre National Populaire, Paris, then Playhouse Theatre, New York

City, 1971; appeared in *Jacques Brel Is Alive and Well and Living in Paris,* Tappan Zee Playhouse, Nyack, NY, 1972; Nicholas Astrov, *Perfect Pitch,* Eisenhower Theatre, Kennedy Center, Washington, DC, 1974; appeared in *Janus,* Royal Poinciana Playhouse, Palm Beach, FL, 1975; appeared in *Jacques Des Journees Entieres dans les Arbres,* Ambassador Theatre, New York City, 1976; Ulysse, *La Guerre de Troie N'Aura Pas Lieu,* City Center, New York City, 1977; appeared in *Heartbreak House,* 1978; appeared regionally in *Gigi,* 1977 and *The Sound of Music,* 1978; Dr. Paul Marchand, *A Talent for Murder,* Biltmore Theatre, New York City, 1981.

PRINCIPAL CABARET APPEARANCES—Created a cabaret act and appeared in it at The Persian Room, New York City, and in Chicago, Miami, Montreal, and Mexico City, all 1966.

MAJOR TOURS—*Rose Burke,* U.S. cities, 1942; *The Sound of Music,* U.S. cities, 1978.

FILM DEBUT—*Jean de la Lune,* 1932. PRINCIPAL FILM APPEAR-ANCES—*L'Equipage,* 1936; *Lac aux Dames,* 1936; *Drole de Dame,* 1938; *Hotel du Nord,* 1938; *Le Deserteur,* 1939; *Assignment in Brittany,* Metro-Goldwyn-Mayer (MGM), 1943; *The Cross of Lorraine,* 1943; *Heartbeat,* RKO, 1945; *Sheherazade,* 1945; *Siren of Atlantis,* 1947; *Lili,* MGM, 1952; *Charge of the Lancers,* 1954; *Hilda Crane,* Twentieth Century-Fox, 1956; *Royal Affairs in Versailles,* Times, 1957; *The Seventh Sin,* MGM, 1957; *Gigi,* MGM, 1958; *John Paul Jones,* Warner Brothers, 1959; *The Enemy General,* Columbia, 1960; *The Blonde from Buenos Aires,* 1960; *The Devil at Four O'Clock,* Columbia, 1961; *The Horse without a Head,* 1962; *Blind Man's Bluff,* 1967; *Cauldron of Blood,* 1968; *Castle Keep,* Columbia, 1969; *Cat and Mouse,* Grove, 1970; *Day for Night,* Warner Brothers, 1973; *The Happy Hooker,* 1975; *Catherine & Co.,* Warner Brothers, 1976; *Mahogany,* Paramount, 1976; *Blackout,* 1978; *Two Solitudes,* 1979; *Something Short of Paradise,* Orion, 1979; also, *Life Begins Tomorrow.*

PRINCIPAL TELEVISION APPEARANCES—Episodic: *Westinghouse Playhouse,* NBC, 1961; *The Patty Duke Show,* ABC, 1963; *The Name of the Game,* NBC, 1968; *The Love Boat,* ABC, 1977. Movies: *Beggerman Thief,* 1979; *The Memory of Eva Ryker,* 1980; also *Hold Back the Dawn, The Imposter, Crime and Punishment, Intermezzo,* and *The French Atlantic Affair.* Guest: *The Perry Como Show,* NBC; *The Sid Caesar Show,* ABC, 1963. Teleplays: *No Time for Comedy,* 1951; *Arms and the Man,* 1952; *Crime and Punishment,* 1953; also, *A Month in the Country* and *The Tempest.*

WRITINGS: PLAYS, PRODUCED—*L'Empereur de Chine,* Theatre des Mathurins, Paris, France, 1948, then adapted and produced under the title of *My Name Is Aquilon,* Lyceum Theatre, New York City, 1949; *L'Ile Heureuse,* Theatre Edouard VII, Paris, 1951; *Un Beau Dimanche,* Theatre de la Michodiere, 1952; *Ange le Bienheureux,* Theatre Municipal, Nice, France, 1956; *Farfada,* Comedie Wagram, Paris, 1957; *Lucy Crown,* Theatre de Paris, Paris, 1958.

PLAYS, PUBLISHED—*L'Empereur de Chine,* Nagel, 1948; *Un Beau Dimanche,* published in supplement to "France Illustration," Number 119, 1952; *Lucy Crown,* 1958.

FICTION—*La Pomme de son Oeil,* Julliard, 1969. NON-FICTION—*Souvenirs Provisoires,* Julliard, 1957; (autobiography) *Sun and Shadow,* 1978.

AWARDS: *Variety* New York Critics Poll nomination, 1963, for *Tovarich;* Chevalier Legion of Honour; Croix de Guerre.

MEMBER: Actors' Equity Association, Screen Actors Guild, American Federation of Television and Radio Artists.

SIDELIGHTS: FAVORITE ROLES—Prince Mikail, *Tovarich* and Jacques Casanova, *Camino Real.*

ADDRESSES: AGENT—International Creative Management, 40 W. 57th St., New York, NY 10019.*

*   *   *

AUSTRIAN, Marjorie 1934-

PERSONAL: Born February 3, 1934, in New York, NY; daughter of Samuel (a doctor) and Gladys (Englander) Austrian; married Arthur L. Terr, December 18, 1955 (divorced, 1982); children: Michael, Allison. EDUCATION: Syracuse University, B.S., speech and drama, 1955; University of Kansas, M.S., audiology, 1957; studied acting at the Herbert Berghof Studios in New York City with Stephen Strimpell, Aaron Frankel, and Bill Hickey; also studied at the Warren Robertson Theatre Workshop in New York City.

VOCATION: Actress.

CAREER: PRINCIPAL STAGE APPEARANCES—Bara, *Ritual,* Persona Cafe Theatre, New York City, 1978; Angustias, *The House of Bernarda Alba,* I.N.T.A.R., New York City, 1979; Mrs. Van Daan, *The Diary of Anne Frank,* No Smoking Playhouse, New York City, 1984; Hippolyta, *A Midsummer Night's Dream,* Norma

MARJORIE AUSTRIAN

Henshaw, *The Diviners,* and Betty Meeks, *The Foreigner,* all at the Lyceum Theatre, Arrow Rock, MO, 1986.

Also: Magnolia Lustgarden, *Dune Road* and Dora, *Lucky Rita,* both American Theatre Academy, New York City; Emilie Ducotel, *My Three Angels,* Annabelle Fuller, *George Washington Slept Here,* and Elizabeth, *Angel Street,* all at Theatre-at-the-Inn; Edith, *Never Too Late,* Hunterdon Hills Playhouse; Marian Jellicoe, *Absence of a Cello,* Host Inn Dinner Theatre; Donna Lucia, *Charley's Aunt,* Seton Hall Summer Theatre, NJ; Audrey, *As You Like It* and the Actress, *La Ronde,* both New Jersey Shakespeare Festival; Marian, *Father's Day* and Clarisse, *When You Coming Back, Red Ryder?,* both Cabaret Playhouse; Rosie Montefalco, *Opal's Million Dollar Duck,* Fortuna Mill Theatre; Zinaida, *Ivanov* and Lady Asela, *Loyalties,* both Jewish Repertory Theatre, New York City; Sylvia 2, *Sylvia Plath: A Dramatic Portrait,* Nameless Theatre, New York City; Concetta, *The Wooing of Lady Sunday,* Joseph Jefferson Company, Chicago.

FILM DEBUT—Hooker, *The Man Who Loved Women,* Columbia, 1983. PRINCIPAL FILM APPEARANCES—*Annie,* Columbia, 1983.

TELEVISION DEBUT—Intern, *Ryan's Hope,* ABC, 1979.

MEMBER: Actors' Equity Association, Screen Actors Guild, American Federation of Radio and Television Artists.

ADDRESSES: HOME—484 W. 43rd Street, Apt. 4L, New York, NY 10036.

*   *   *

AXELROD, George   1922-

PERSONAL: Born June 9, 1922, in New York, NY; son of Herman (in real estate) and Beatrice (formerly a silent picture actress; maiden name, Carpenter) Axelrod; married Gloria Washburn (an actress) February 28, 1942 (divorced, 1954); married Joan Stanton, October, 1954; children: (first marriage) Peter, Steven; (second marriage) Nina. MILITARY: U.S. Army Signal Corps, World War II.

VOCATION: Writer, director, and producer.

CAREER: FIRST STAGE WORK—Assistant stage manager, *Kind Lady,* Playhouse Theatre, New York City, 1940. PRINCIPAL STAGE WORK—Director, *Will Success Spoil Rock Hunter?,* Belasco Theatre, New York City, 1955; (with Clinton Wilder) co-producer, *Visit to a Small Planet,* Booth Theatre, New York City, 1957; director, *Once More, with Feeling,* National Theatre, New York City, 1958; director, *Goodbye Charlie,* Lyceum Theatre, New York City, 1959; director, *The Star Spangled Girl,* Plymouth Theatre, New York City, 1966.

PRINCIPAL FILM WORK—(With John Frankenheimer) Co-producer, *The Manchurian Candidate,* United Artists, 1962; co-producer, *Paris When It Sizzles,* Paramount, 1964; co-producer, *How to Murder Your Wife,* United Artists, 1965; producer and director, *Lord Love a Duck,* United Artists, 1966; producer and director, *The Secret Life of an American Wife,* Twentieth Century-Fox, 1968.

WRITINGS: PLAYS, PRODUCED AND PUBLISHED—Contributor, *Small Wonder,* Coronet Theatre, New York City, 1948; *The Seven*

Year Itch, Fulton Theatre, New York City, 1952, published by Random House, 1953, and Dramatists Play Service; *Will Success Spoil Rock Hunter?,* Belasco Theatre, New York City, 1955, published by Random House, 1956, and Samuel French, Inc.; *Goodbye Charlie,* Longacre Theatre, New York City, 1959, published by Samuel French, Inc., 1959.

SCREENPLAYS—*Phffft,* Columbia, 1954; (co-adaptor, with Billy Wilder) *The Seven Year Itch,* Twentieth Century-Fox, 1955; *Bus Stop,* Twentieth Century-Fox, 1956; *The Catbird Seat,* Paramount, 1961; *Breakfast at Tiffany's,* Paramount, 1961; *The Manchurian Candidate,* United Artists, 1962; *Paris When It Sizzles,* Paramount, 1964; *How to Murder Your Wife,* United Artists, 1965; (with Larry H. Johnson) *Lord Love a Duck,* United Artists, 1966; *The Secret Life of an American Wife,* Twentieth Century-Fox, 1968.

TELEVISION—*Celebrity Time,* CBS, 1950. RADIO—*Midnight in Manhattan,* 1940; *The Grand Ole Opry,* NBC, 1950-52; also wrote for *The Shadow.*

CABARET—*All About Love,* Versailles, New York City, 1951.

FICTION—*Beggar's Choice,* Howell, Soskin, 1947 (published in England as *Hobson's Choice,* Elek, 1951); *Blackmailer,* Fawcett, 1952; *Where Am I Now When I Need Me?,* Viking, 1971 (also published as *Where Am I Now That I Need Me?),* Pocket Books, 1972.

MEMBER: Dramatists Guild, Authors League of America.

ADDRESSES: AGENT—c/o Irving Paul Lazar Agency, 211 S. Beverly Drive, Suite 209, Beverly Hills, CA 90212.*

*   *   *

AYCKBOURN, Alan   1939-
(Roland Allen)

PERSONAL: Surname is pronounced Ache-born; born April 12, 1939, in London, England; son of Horace (a musician) and Irene Maud (Worley) Ayckbourn; married Christine Roland, May 9, 1959; children: Steven Paul, Philip Nicholas. EDUCATION: Attended Haileybury and Imperial Service College, Hertfordshire, England, 1952-57.

VOCATION: Playwright, director, producer, and actor.

CAREER: PRINCIPAL STAGE APPEARANCES—With the Victoria Theatre, Stoke-on-Trent, U.K.: Fred, *The Birds and the Wellwishers,* Robert, *An Awkward Number,* Aston, *The Caretaker,* James, *The Collection,* Ben, *The Dumb Waiter,* title role, *O'Flaherty, V.C.,* Roderick Usher, *Usher,* Bill Starbuck, *The Rainmaker,* Crimson Gollywog, *Xmas v. Mastermind,* the Count, *The Rehearsal,* Vladimir, *Waiting for Godot,* Thomas More, *A Man for All Seasons,* Jordan, *The Rainbow Machine,* Anderson, *Ted's Cathedral,* Jerry Ryan, *Two for the Seesaw,* Mr. Manningham, *Gaslight,* the Interrogator, *The Prisoner,* a Jew and Martin del Bosco, *The Jew of Malta,* all 1962-64.

PRINCIPAL STAGE WORK—Director, at the Victoria Theatre, Stoke-on-Trent: *The Caretaker,* (co-director) *Xmas v. Mastermind, The Referees, The Mating Season, The Rainbow Machine,*

Standing Room Only, Mr. Whatnot, Miss Julie, The Glass Menagerie, all 1962-64.

Director, at the Library Theatre, Scarborough, U.K.: *How the Other Half Loves,* 1969, *The Story So Far, Wife Swapping—Italian Style,* and *The Shy Gasman,* all 1970, *Time and Time Again,* 1971, *Absurd Person Singular, Carmilla, Uncle Vanya,* and *Tom, Dick and Harry,* all 1972, *The Norman Conquests: Table Manners, Living Together, Round and Round the Garden,* all 1973, *Absent Friends, Away from It All, The Breadwinner, But Fred Freud Is Dead,* and *Frost at Midnight,* all 1974, *Confusions: Mother Figure, Drinking Companion, Between Mouthfuls, Gosforth's Fete, A Talk in the Park, Bedroom Farce* (also co-director of National Theatre production at the Prince of Wales's Theatre, and the subsequent New York City production), *Angels in Love,* and *An Englishman's Home,* all 1975, *Just Between Ourselves,* 1976, *Ten Times Table,* 1977, *Family Circles,* 1978, *Joking Apart,* 1979.

PRINCIPAL RADIO WORK—Producer of more than one hundred performances, BBC-Radio, Leeds, U.K., 1964-70.

RELATED CAREER—Stage manager, Donald Wolfit's Company at Edinburgh, Worthing, Leatherhead, and Oxford, U.K.; founding member, Victoria Theatre, Stoke-on-Trent, 1962-64; artistic director, Scarborough Theatre Trust Ltd.

WRITINGS: PLAYS, PRODUCED—(As Roland Allen) *The Square Cat,* Library Theatre, Scarborough, U.K., 1959; (as Roland Allen) *Love After All,* Library Theatre, Scarborough, 1960; (as Roland Allen) *Dad's Tale,* Library Theatre, Scarborough, 1960; (as Roland Allen) *Standing Room Only,* Library Theatre, Scarborough, 1961; *Xmas v. Mastermind,* Victoria Theatre, Stoke-on-Trent, U.K., 1962; *Mr. Whatnot,* Victoria Theatre, Stoke-on-Trent, 1963, and the Arts Theatre, London, 1964; *Meet My Father,* Library Theatre, Scarborough, 1965, re-titled *Relatively Speaking,* Duke of York's Theatre, London, 1967; *The Sparrow,* Library Theatre, Scarborough, 1967; "Countdown" (one-act), included in *We Who Are About To. . .,* Hampstead Theatre Club, London, 1969, re-titled *Mixed Doubles: An Entertainment on Marriage,* Comedy Theatre, London, 1970; *How the Other Half Loves,* Library Theatre, Scarborough, 1969, Lyric Theatre, London, 1970; *The Story So Far,* Library Theatre, Scarborough, 1970, revised and retitled *Me Times Me Times Me,* toured, 1972, later produced as *Family Circles,* Orange Tree Theatre, Richmond, U.K., 1978; *Ernie's Incredible Illucinations,* London, 1971; *Time and Time Again,* Library Theatre, Scarborough, 1971, Comedy Theatre, London, 1972.

Absurd Person Singular, Library Theatre, Scarborough, 1972, then Criterion Theatre, London, 1973; *Mother Figure* (one-act), first produced in *Mixed Blessings,* Capitol Theatre, Horsham, Sussex, U.K., 1973, produced again in *Confusions* (see below); *The Norman Conquests* (a trilogy, including "Table Manners," "Living Together," and "Round and Round the Garden") Library Theatre, Scarborough, 1974, then Globe Theatre, London, transferred to Apollo Theatre, London, 1975; *Absent Friends,* Library Theatre, Scarborough, 1974, then Garrick Theatre, London, 1975; *Confusions: Mother Figure, Drinking Companion, Between Mouthfuls, Gosforth's Fete, A Talk in the Park,* Library Theatre, Scarborough, 1974, then Apollo Theatre, London, 1976; (book and lyrics) *Jeeves,* Her Majesty's Theatre, London, 1976; *Bedroom Farce,* Library Theatre, Scarborough, 1975, then produced by the National Theatre at the Lyttelton Theatre, 1977, transfered to the Prince of Wale's Theatre, London, 1978; *Just Between Ourselves,* Library Theatre, Scarborough, 1976, then Queen's Theatre, London, 1977; *Ten Times Table,* Stephen Joseph Theatre-in-the-Round, Scarbo-

rough, 1977, then Globe Theatre, London, 1979; *Joking Apart,* Stephen Joseph Theatre-in-the-Round, Scarborough, 1978, then Globe Theatre, London, 1979; *Men on Women on Men* (music by Paul Todd), Stephen Joseph Theatre-in-the-Round, Scarborough, 1978; *Sisterly Feelings,* Stephen Joseph Theatre-in-the-Round, Scarborough, 1979, then Olivier Theatre, London, 1980; *Taking Steps,* Stephen Joseph Theatre-in-the-Round, 1979, then Lyric Theatre, London, 1980.

Suburban Strains (music by Paul Todd), Stephen Joseph Theatre-in-the-Round, Scarborough, 1980, then Round House Theatre, London, 1981; *Season's Greetings,* Stephen Joseph Theatre-in-the-Round, 1980, then Round House Theatre, London, 1982, Greenwich Theatre, Greenwich, U.K., 1982, and Apollo Theatre, London, 1982; *Way Upstream,* Stephen Joseph Theatre-in-the-Round, 1981, then Lyttelton Theatre, London, 1982; *Making Tracks* (music by Paul Todd), Stephen Joseph Theatre-in-the-Round, 1981; *Intimate Exchanges,* Stephen Joseph Theatre-in-the-Round, 1982; *Incidental Music* (music by Paul Todd), 1983; *It Could Be Any One of Us,* 1983; *The Seven Deadly Virtues* (music by Paul Todd), 1984; *A Chorus of Disapproval,* 1984; *The Westwoods,* 1984.

PLAYS, PUBLISHED—*Relatively Speaking,* Evans Plays, London, 1968, Samuel French, Inc., New York, 1968; *Ernie's Incredible Illucinations,* Samuel French Inc., 1969; *Mixed Doubles: An Entertainment on Marriage,* Methuen, London, 1970; *How the Other Half Loves,* Samuel French Inc., 1971, Evans Plays, London, 1972; *Time and Time Again,* Samuel French Inc., 1973; *Absurd Person Singular,* Samuel French Inc., 1974; *The Norman Conquests* (a trilogy, including "Table Manners," "Living Together," and "Round and Round the Garden"), Samuel French Inc., 1975, Chatto & Windus, London, 1975, Grove Press, New York, 1979; *Absent Friends,* Samuel French Inc., 1975, Grove Press, 1979.

Confusions: Mother Figure, Drinking Companion, Between Mouthfuls, Gosforth's Fete, A Talk in the Park, Samuel French Inc., 1977, Methuen, 1983; *Bedroom Farce,* Samuel French Inc., 1977; *Three Plays* (includes "Absurd Person Singular," "Absent Friends," and "Bedroom Farce"), Chatto & Windus, London, 1977, Samuel French Inc., 1979; *Just Between Ourselves,* Samuel French Inc., 1978; *Ten Times Table,* Samuel French Inc., 1978; *Joking Apart,* Samuel French Inc., 1979; *Joking Apart and Other Plays* (includes "Joking Apart," "Just Between Ourselves," and "Ten Times Table"), Chatto & Windus, London, 1979; *Sisterly Feelings and Taking Steps,* Chatto & Windus, London, 1981; *Woman in Mind,* Methuen, 1983; *A Chorus of Disapproval,* Faber & Faber, 1986.

TELEPLAYS—*Service Not Included,* BBC, 1974; *Theatre,* BBC, 1976.

AWARDS: Evening Standard Awards: Best New Comedy, 1973, for *Absurd Person Singular,* Best New Play, 1974, for *The Norman Conquests,* and 1977, for *Just Between Ourselves;* Best New Play, *Plays and Players* Award, 1974, for *The Norman Conquests; Variety* Club of Great Britain Playwright of the Year Award, 1974; Best New Comedy, *Plays and Players* Award, 1979, for *Joking Apart.* Hon. D.Litt., Hull University, 1981.

SIDELIGHTS: RECREATIONS—Music, cricket, and astronomy.

ADDRESSES: OFFICE—Theatre in the Round Company, 32 Manor Road, Scarborough, North Yorkshire, England. AGENT—Margaret Ramsay Ltd., 14a Goodwin's Court, St. Martin's Lane, London WC2N 4LL, England.*

B

BACKUS, Richard   1945-

PERSONAL: Born March 28, 1945, in Goffstown, NH. EDUCA-TION: Graduated Harvard University.

VOCATION: Actor.

CAREER: BROADWAY DEBUT—Standby Don Baker, occasional-ly playing the role, *Butterflies Are Free,* Booth Theatre, 1971. PRINCIPAL STAGE APPEARANCES—Willie, Wesley, Walter, and Wendell, *Promenade, All!,* Alvin Theatre, New York City, 1972; appeared in repertory with the American Shakespeare Festival, Stratford, CT, 1973; title role, *Studs Edsel,* Ensemble Studio Theatre, New York City, 1974; Robert Mayo, *Beyond the Horizon,* McCarter Theatre, Princeton, NJ, 1974; Richard Miller, *Ah, Wil-derness!,* Long Wharf Theatre, New Haven, CT, 1974; King of France, *King Lear,* George Gibbs, *Our Town* and Florizel, *The Winter's Tale,* with the American Shakespeare Festival, Stratford, CT, 1975; Richard Miller, *Ah, Wilderness!,* Circle in the Square Theatre, New York City, 1975; *The Winter's Tale,* McCarter Theatre, Princeton, NJ, 1976; performed with the O'Neill Play-wright's Conference, O'Neill Center, Waterford, CT, 1976-77; Albert Prosser, *Hobson's Choice,* Long Wharf Theatre, New Haven, CT, 1977; Kev, *Gimme Shelter,* Brooklyn Academy of Music (BAM), NY, 1978; William, *Sorrows of Stephen,* New York Shakespeare Festival (NYSF), Public Theatre, New York City, 1979.

Hat, *Missing Persons,* The Production Company, New York City, 1981; Mordred, *Camelot,* Winter Garden Theatre, New York City, 1981; *Beloved Friend,* Hartman Theatre, Stamford, CT, 1984; Constable of France, *Henry V,* NYSF, Delacorte Theatre, New York City, 1984; Algernon, *The Importance of Being Earnest* and *Dramatic License,* both American Stage Festival, Milford, NH, 1983; Nick Alameda, *Beyond Your Command,* White Barn Thea-tre, CT, 1985; Richard Allen, *Tomorrow's Monday* and Harvey Campbell, *Talley and Son,* both Circle Repertory Company, New York City, 1985; Danny Luches, *Fugue,* Long Wharf Theatre, New Haven, 1986; Lathan Kane, *Rhymes with Evil,* American Stage Festival, 1986; Mr. Bohun, *You Never Can Tell,* Circle in the Square, New York City, 1986-87.

PRINCIPAL TELEVISION APPEARANCES—Series: Jason Saxton, *Lovers and Friends,* NBC, 1976-77; Jason Saxton, *For Richer, For Poorer,* NBC, 1978; Ted Bancroft, *Another World,* NBC, 1979; Barry Ryan, *Ryan's Hope,* ABC, 1980-81; Russ Elliot, *As the World Turns,* CBS, 1984-85. Episodic: *Remington Steele,* NBC, 1983. Movies: *Mothers Against Drunk Driving,* 1982; *Bare Essence,* 1983; *Why Me?,* 1983; *Flight 90: Disaster on the Poto-mac,* 1984; *Crime Story,* 1986; *Kayo,* 1986.

PRINCIPAL FILM APPEARANCES—*Dead of Night,* 1974.

AWARDS: Theatre World Award, Straw Hat Award, Clarence Derwent Award, and *Variety* Critics Poll, all 1972, for *Promenade, All!;* New Jersey Drama Critics Award, 1975.

MEMBER: Actors' Equity Association, American Federation of Television and Radio Artists.

ADDRESSES: AGENT—STE Representation, 888 Seventh Ave-nue, New York, NY 10106.

*   *   *

BADDELEY, Hermione   1906-1986

PERSONAL: Full name, Hermione Clinton-Baddeley; born No-vember 13, 1906, in Broseley, Shropshire, England; died of com-plications from a stroke, at Cedars Sinai Medical Center, Los Angeles, CA, August 19, 1986; daughter of W.H. and Louise (Bourdin) Clinton-Baddeley; married David Tennant (divorced); married J.H. Willis. EDUCATION: Trained for the dance at Marga-ret Morris's School of Dancing.

VOCATION: Actress.

CAREER: LONDON DEBUT—Le Negre, *La Boite a Joujoux,* Court Theatre, 1918. BROADWAY DEBUT—Helen, *A Taste of Honey,* Booth Theatre, 1961. PRINCIPAL STAGE APPEARANCES—Paste, *Make Believe,* Lyric Theatre, Hammersmith, U.K., 1918; Michael, *The Knight of the Burning Pestle,* Kingsway Theatre, London, 1920; Balk, *Balk and the Bighead,* 1922; Lea, *The Mental Athletes,* performed for the Stage Society at Lyric Theatre, Hammersmith, 1923; Florrie Small, *The Likes of Her,* St. Martin's Theatre, London, 1923; Jeanne, *The Fledglings,* London, 1923; Amina, *The Forest,* London, 1924; *The Punch Bowl,* Duke of York's Theatre, London, 1924; *The Co-Optimists,* Palace Theatre, London, 1924; *On with the Dance,* London Pavillion, 1925; Daisy Odiham, *The Show,* St. Martin's Theatre, London, 1925; *Nine to Eleven,* Little Theatre, London, 1925; *Still Dancing* and *Cochran's Revue (1926),* both London Pavilion, 1926; title role, *Minetta,* with the Repertory Players at Strand Theatre, London, 1926; Coddles, *Queen High,* Queen's Theatre, London, 1926; Ninetta Crummles, *When Crummles Played,* Lyric Theatre, Hammersmith, 1927; Clara, *Lord Babs,* Vaudeville Theatre, London, 1928; Vera, *Holding Out the Apple,* Globe Theatre, London, 1928; Amelie, *Excelsior,* Playhouse Thea-tre, London, 1928; Susie Snow, *The Five O'Clock Girl,* Hippodrome, London, 1929; Poppy, *The Shanghai Gesture,* Scala Theatre, London, 1929.

Faith Bly, *Windows,* Duchess Theatre, London, 1932; Sara, *Tobias and the Angel,* Westminster Theatre, London, 1932; *After Dinner,* Gaiety Theatre, London, 1932; *Ballyhoo,* Comedy Theatre, London, 1932; *Paris Fantaisie,* Prince of Wales Theatre, London, 1933; Polaire, *The Greeks Had a Word for It,* Fulham Theatre, London, 1933; *Why Not To-Night,* Vaudeville Theatre, London, 1934; Polaire, *The Greeks Had a Word for It,* Duke of York's Theatre, London, 1934; *To and Fro,* Comedy Theatre, London, 1936; *Floodlight,* Saville Theatre, London, 1937; *Nine Sharp,* Little Theatre, London, 1938; *The Little Revue,* Little Theatre, London, 1939; Margery Pinchwife, *The Country Wife,* Little Theatre, London, 1940; *Rise Above It,* Comedy Theatre, London, 1941; *Sky High,* Phoenix Theatre, London, 1942; Ida Arnold, *Brighton Rock,* Garrick Theatre, London, 1943; Minnie, *Cinderella,* Winter Garden Theatre, London, 1944; *The Gaieties,* Winter Garden Theatre, London, 1945; Babs Coates and Pinkie Collins, *Grand National Night,* Apollo Theatre, London, 1946; *A la Carte,* Savoy Theatre, London, 1948; Doris, *Fumed Oak* and Julia Sterroll, *Fallen Angels,* both Ambassadors Theatre, London, 1949.

Arabella, *For Love or Money,* Ambassadors Theatre, London, 1950; Ada, *The Martin's Nest,* Westminster Theatre, London, 1951; Christine Foskett, *The Pink Room,* Lyric Theatre, Hammersmith, 1952; Noo-Ga, *Pagan in the Parlour,* Royal Theatre, Bath, U.K., then Wimbledon Theatre, London, both 1952; *At the Lyric,* Lyric Theatre, Hammersmith, 1953, re-titled *Going to Town,* St. Martin's Theatre, London, 1954; Mrs. Pooter, *The Diary of a Nobody,* Duchess Theatre, London, 1955; Laura Saintsbury, *Postman's Knock!,* Royal Theatre, Newcastle, 1955, re-titled, *Breakfast in Salisbury,* Streatham Hill, 1955; Six-Gun Kate, *Adventures of Davy Crockett,* Olympia Theatre, Dublin, Ireland, 1956; Mother, *Jezebel,* Oxford Playhouse, U.K., 1958.

Sonia Mann, *The Dream of Peter Mann,* Edinburgh Festival, Scotland, 1960; Flora Goforth, *The Milk Train Doesn't Stop Here Anymore,* Spoleto Festival of Two Worlds, Italy, 1962, then Morosco Theatre, New York City, 1963; Bessie Linstrom, *Cool Off,* Forrest Theatre, Philadelphia, PA, 1964; Marty Owen, *Anna Christie,* Los Angeles, CA, 1966; title role, *The Killing of Sister George,* St. Martin's Theatre, London, 1966; *I Only Want an Answer,* Stage 73, New York City, 1968; the Wife of Bath, *Canterbury Tales,* Eugene O'Neill Theatre, New York City, 1969; Mrs. Gwynne, *Nell,* Richmond Theatre, London, 1970; Mrs. Peachum, *The Threepenny Opera,* Prince of Wales Theatre, London, then Picadilly Theatre, London, 1972; Mother, *Mother Adam,* Hampstead Theatre, London, 1973; Dame Edith Runcible, *Whodunnit,* Biltmore Theatre, New York City, 1982.

MAJOR TOURS—Mrs. Curtis Honey, *Your Young Wife,* U.K. citics, 1956; Helen, *A Taste of Honey,* U.S. cities, 1961-62; cabaret performances, Indian cities, 1965.

PRINCIPAL FILM APPEARANCES—*Room at the Top,* Continental, 1959; *The Black Windmill,* Universal, 1974; also *Brighton Rock.*

PRINCIPAL TELEVISION APPEARANCES—Series: Mrs. Nell Naugatuck, *Maude,* CBS, 1974-77. Episodic: *Julia,* NBC, 1971.

ADDRESSES: AGENT—Peter Campbell, 31 King's Road, London SW3.*

BAILEY, Pearl   1918-

PERSONAL: Born March 29, 1918, in Newport News, VA; daughter of Joseph James (a minister) and Pearl Bailey; married John Randolph Pinkett, Jr., August 31, 1948 (divorced, March, 1952); married Louis Bellson, Jr. (a drummer), November 19, 1952; children: one son, one daughter.

VOCATION: Actress and singer.

CAREER: STAGE DEBUT—Singer in vaudeville, Pearl Theatre, Philadelphia, 1933. BROADWAY DEBUT—Butterfly, *St. Louis Woman,* Martin Beck Theatre, 1946. LONDON DEBUT—A cabaret appearance at Talk of the Town, 1972. PRINCIPAL STAGE APPEARANCES—Connecticut, *Arms and the Girl,* 46th Street Theatre, New York City, 1950; *Bless You All,* Mark Hellinger Theatre, New York City, 1950; Madame Fleur, *House of Flowers,* Alvin Theatre, New York City, 1954; Sally Adams, *Call Me Madam,* Melodyland Theatre, Berkeley, CA, 1966; Dolly Gallagher Levi, *Hello, Dolly!,* St. James Theatre, New York City, 1967; *Festival at Ford's,* Circle in the Square at Ford's, Ford's Theatre, Washington, DC, 1970; *The Pearl Bailey Show,* Starlight Theatre, Kansas City, MO, 1973; repeated title role, *Hello, Dolly!,* Minskoff Theatre, New York City, 1975; *Night of 100 Stars,* Radio City Music Hall, New York City, 1982.

MAJOR TOURS—Dolly Gallagher Levi, *Hello Dolly!,* U.S. cities, 1969-71 and U.S. and Canadian cities, 1975-76.

PRINCIPAL CONCERT APPEARANCES—*An Evening with Pearl Bailey,* for the Youth Welfare and Community Service Fund in Albany, NY, 1966; performed in concert with Al Hirt, O'Keefe Center, Toronto, Canada, 1966; appeared at the Philharmonic Hall, Lincoln Center, New York City, 1967.

PRINCIPAL CABARET APPEARANCES—Village Vanguard, 1941; Blue Angel, 1942; La Vie en Rose, 1945; Cafe Zanzibar, 1950; Royal Box in the Americana Hotel, New York City, 1963; Cafe Pompeii in the Eden Roc Hotel, Miami Beach, FL, and at the Flamingo, Las Vegas, NV, 1966; Coconut Grove, Los Angeles, 1971; Royal Box, New York City, 1972; Empire Room, Waldorf-Astoria Hotel, New York City, 1973; Talk of the Town, London, 1973; appeared in a variety program for Weight Watchers, Madison Square Garden, New York City, 1973.

FILM DEBUT—*Variety Girl,* Paramount, 1947. PRINCIPAL FILM APPEARANCES—*Isn't It Romantic,* Paramount, 1948; *Carmen Jones,* Twentieth Century-Fox, 1954; Gussie, *That Certain Feeling,* Paramount, 1956; Aunt Hagar, *Saint Louis Blues,* Paramount, 1957; Maria, *Porgy and Bess,* Columbia, 1959; *All the Fine Young Cannibals,* Metro-Goldwyn-Mayer (MGM), 1960; *The Landlord,* United Artists, 1970; Beatrice Chambers, *Norman, Is That You?,* United Artists, 1976; voice of Big Mama, *The Fox and the Hound,* Buena Vista; also appeared in *Lost Generation.*

PRINCIPAL TELEVISION APPEARANCES—Series: *The Pearl Bailey Show,* ABC, 1971; Lulu Baker, *Silver Spoons,* NBC, 1982—. Episodic: *As the World Turns,* 1956; *One More Time,* 1974; Mrs. Washington, *The Love Boat,* 1977. Teleplays: Bernice, *Member of the Wedding,* 1982.

Specials: *Carol Channing and Pearl Bailey on Broadway,* ABC, 1966; also Bob Hope specials, 1956, 1968, 1978, 1981, 1982; *The Big Party for Revlon,* 1959; *Something Special,* 1966; *Mike and Pearl,* 1968; *The Bob Hope Show,* 1968; *Bing Crosby and His*

Friends, 1972; *Bing!. . .A Fiftieth Anniversary Special,* 1977; Martha Dermody, *Cindy Eller: A Modern Fairy Tale,* 1985.

Guest: Appearances include *The Ed Wynn Show,* NBC, *The Nat "King" Cole Show,* NBC, *The Milton Berle Show,* NBC, *What's My Line?,* CBS, *The Perry Como Show,* NBC, *The Danny Kaye Show,* CBS, *The Johnny Carson Show,* NBC, *The Jack Paar Show,* NBC, *The Mike Douglas Show,* CBS, and *Johnny Mann's Stand Up and Cheer,* syndicated.

WRITINGS: TELEVISION—*The Pearl Bailey Show,* ABC, 1971. BOOKS—(Autobiographies) *Raw Pearl,* Harcourt, Brace, Jovanovich, Inc., 1969, *Talking to Myself,* Harcourt, Brace, Jovanovich, Inc., 1971. Also, *Pearl's Kitchen: An Extraordinary Cookbook,* Harcourt, Brace, Jovanovich, Inc., 1973; *Duey's Tale* (juvenile), Harcourt, Brace, Jovanovich, Inc., 1975; *Hurry Up, America, and Spit,* Harcourt, Brace, Jovanovich, Inc., 1976.

AWARDS: Donaldson Award, 1946, for *St. Louis Woman;* Entertainer of the Year, *Cue* Magazine Award, 1967; Antoinette Perry Award, 1968, for *Hello, Dolly!;* March of Dimes Award, 1968; Woman of the Year Award, U.S.O., 1969; John V. Lindsay New York City Award; appointed by President Gerald R. Ford special advisor to the U.S. Mission of the United Nations General Assembly, 30th session, 1975.

SIDELIGHTS: RECREATIONS—Cooking.

ADDRESSES: HOME—P.O. Box L, Lake Havasu City, AZ 86403. AGENT—William Morris Agency, 1350 Avenue of the Americas, New York, NY 10019.*

*   *   *

BAIN, Conrad 1923-

PERSONAL: Born February 4, 1923, in Lethbridge, Alberta, Canada; son of Stafford Harrison and Jean Agnes Bain; married Monica Sloan. EDUCATION: Attended Banff School of Fine Arts; trained for the stage at the American Academy of Dramatic Arts, 1948.

VOCATION: Actor.

CAREER: STAGE DEBUT—Stage Manager, *Our Town,* in a high school production. BROADWAY DEBUT—Larry Slade, *The Iceman Cometh,* Circle in the Square Theatre, 1956. PRINCIPAL STAGE APPEARANCES—Albert Kummer, *Dear Ruth,* Ivoryton Playhouse, CT, 1947; played with stock companies in the U.S. and the Bahamas, 1949-56; Dr. Peter Hoenig, *Sixth Finger in a Five Finger Glove,* Longacre Theatre, New York City, 1956; King of Hesse, the Captain, and Old Inquisitor, *Candide,* Martin Beck Theatre, New York City, 1956; Vitek, *The Makropoulos Secret,* Phoenix Repertory Theatre, New York City, 1957; Smelicue, *Dark of the Moon,* Carnegie Hall Playhouse, New York City, 1958; Mark Eland, *Lost in the Stars,* City Center, New York City, 1958; Earl of Northumberland, *Henry IV, Part I,* Antonio, *Much Ado About Nothing,* and Antigonus, *The Winter's Tale,* all at the Stratford Shakespeare Festival, Ontario, Canada, 1958; Dr. Warburton, *Family Reunion,* Phoenix Repertory Theatre, 1958; Mr. Juno, *Overruled,* the Solicitor, *Buoyant Billions,* General Bridgenorth,

Getting Married, all at the Provincetown Playhouse, New York City, 1959.

Nicholas, *A Country Scandal,* Greenwich Mews Theatre, New York City, 1960; Senator Winthrop, *Advise and Consent,* Cort Theatre, New York City, 1960; Mr. Norah, "It's All Yours," Daddy Jack, "A Summer Ghost," in repertory with the overall title, *A Pair of Pairs,* Van Dam Theatre, New York City, 1962, Older Man, *Lunatic View,* Theatre de Lys, New York City, 1962; George Higgins, *Hot Spot,* Majestic Theatre, New York City, 1963; Duke of Cornwall, *King Lear,* 1963, Biedermann, *The Firebugs,* Howard, *The Death of a Salesman,* Rakosi, *The Shadow of Heroes,* all 1964, with the Seattle Repertory Theatre, WA; Raim, *The Queen and the Rebels,* Theatre Four, New York City, 1965; Doc, *Square in the Eye,* Theatre de Lys, New York City, 1965; James Palsy Murphy, *Hogan's Goat,* The American Place Theatre, New York City, 1965; Max, *The Kitchen,* Eighty-First Street Theatre, New York City, 1966; Mr. Hopp, *Willie Doesn't Live Here Anymore,* Theatre de Lys, New York City, 1966; Tourist, *Scuba Duba,* The New Theatre, New York City, 1967; Appleby, *The Cuban Thing,* Henry Miller's Theatre, New York City, 1968.

George Griffith, *Nobody Hears a Broken Drum,* Fortune Theatre, New York City, 1970; Oldtimer, *Steambath,* Truck and Warehouse Theatre, New York City, 1970; Aslaksen, *An Enemy of the People,* Vivian Beaumont Theatre, New York City, 1971; Kurt, *Play Strindberg,* Forum Theatre, New York City, 1971; Swede, *Twigs,* Broadhurst Theatre, New York City, 1971; Ilya Telegin, *Uncle Vanya,* Circle in the Square Theatre, New York City, 1973; F. Sherman, *The Owl and the Pussycat,* Palm Springs Center, CA, 1976; *Country Cops,* Elitch Theatre, Denver, 1986.

MAJOR TOURS—Alfred Moulton-Barrett, *The Barretts of Wimpole Street,* U.S. cities, 1949; Mr. Nicklebush, *Rhinoceros,* U.S. cities, 1962.

PRINCIPAL FILM APPEARANCES—*A Lovely Way to Die,* Universal, 1968; Madison Avenue Man, *Coogan's Bluff,* Universal, 1968; Dan's Father, *Last Summer,* Allied Artists, 1969; Lester, *Jump,* Cannon, 1971; Dr. Rubicoff, *The Anderson Tapes,* Columbia, 1971; Semple, *Bananas,* United Artists, 1971; *New Leaf,* Paramount, 1971; Val, *Who Killed Mary What's Ername?,* Cannon, 1971; Poppy, *A Fan's Notes,* 1972; Ralph Norton, *C.H.O.M.P.S.,* American International, 1979.

PRINCIPAL TELEVISION APPEARANCES—Series: Dr. Facciola, *Search for Tomorrow,* NBC, 1951; Dr. Arthur Harmon, *Maude,* CBS, 1974-78; Philip Drummond, *Diff'rent Strokes,* NBC, 1978-86. Movies: Lawyer, *The Borgia Stick,* 1967; *Strangers,* 1979; Frank King, *Child Bride of Short Creek,* 1981; *The Choice,* 1981. Host: *TV Funnies,* 1982. Dramatic Specials: Title role, *Candide,* 1956; Swede, *Twigs,* 1975; also appeared in *Little Women, The Last Dictator,* and *Quartet.*

NON-RELATED CAREER—Founder and president of the Actors Federal Credit Union.

MEMBER: Actors' Equity Association, Screen Actors Guild, American Federation of Television and Radio Artists; Players Club.

SIDELIGHTS: RECREATIONS—Swimming, sculpture, sailing, and guitar playing.

ADDRESSES: AGENT—Henderson/Hogan Agency, Inc., 405 W. 44th Street, New York, NY 10036.*

ROD BAKER

BAKER, Rod   1945-

PERSONAL: Born October 11, 1945, in Sewannee, TN; son of Gordon Darrell and Edythe Mary (Sanders) Baker; married Pattie Corinne Williams, October 27, 1984; children: Corinne Anne, Casseday Darrell. EDUCATION: Long Beach State University, B.A., radio, television, and cinema, 1973. MILITARY: U.S. Navy, 1966-68.

VOCATION: Writer.

WRITINGS: TELEVISION—Episodes of *Hawaii Five-O,* CBS: "Hookman," 1973, "Right Grave—Wrong Body," 1974, "The Flip Side Is Death," 1974, "A Woman's Work Is with a Gun," 1974, and "A Sentence to Steal," 1975; "A Covenant with Evil," *Petrocelli,* NBC, 1974; "The Night of the Strangler," *Charlie's Angels,* ABC, 1976; "The Cannibals," *The Streets of San Francisco,* ABC, 1976; "Plastique," *Jigsaw John,* NBC, 1976; *Baa Baa Blacksheep,* NBC: "Last One for Hutch," 1977, and "Operation Standown," 1978; story editor, *CHiPs,* NBC, 1977, writer, "Rainey Day," 1978; "The Starships Are Coming," *The New Adventures of Wonder Woman,* CBS, 1979; "Oil and Water," *240 Robert,* ABC, 1979; "Death Fare," *Strike Force,* ABC, 1982.

Novel adaptations for television: *ABC Weekend Specials:* "The Ghost of Thomas Kempe," 1979, "The Joke's on Mr. Little," 1981, "The Haunted Mystery Mansion," 1982, "All the Money in the World," 1983, and "The Dog Days of Arthur Kane," 1983. Short story adaptations: *The Notorious Jumping Frog of Calaveras County,* ABC, 1981. Animation: *M.A.S.K.,* Dic Enterprises, twelve episodes in syndication, 1984-84.

BOOKS—*The Adventures of Gabby Bear,* ten young persons books with accompanying cassette recordings, Select Merchandising, Inc., 1986-87.

RELATED CAREER—Lecturer on writing for television at New Mexico State University and the University of Wisconsin.

AWARDS: Best Adaptation, Youth in Film Award, Cine Golden Eagle Award 1981-82, for *The Notorious Jumping Frog of Calaveras County;* National Association for the Advancement of Colored People Image Award and Emmy Award nomination, 1983-84, for "All the Money in the World," *ABC Weekend Special.*

MEMBER: Writers Guild of America West.

ADDRESSES: AGENT—c/o Gary Salt, Paul Kohner Agency, 9169 Sunset Blvd., Los Angeles, CA 90069.

*   *   *

BALFOUR, Katharine

PERSONAL: Born in New York, NY; daughter of Raphael and Gertrude Balfour; married Leonard Sillman (a psychoanalyst); children: Mary. RELIGION: Jewish.

VOCATION: Actress and writer.

KATHARINE BALFOUR

CAREER: BROADWAY DEBUT—R.U.R., Barrymore Theatre. PRINCIPAL STAGE APPEARANCES—Alma Winemiller, Summer and Smoke, Dallas, TX; title role, Helen of Troy and A Scrap of Paper, both Off-Broadway productions.

MAJOR TOURS—Alma, Summer and Smoke, U.S. cities.

FILM DEBUT—Music for Millions, Metro-Goldwyn-Mayer (MGM), 1944. PRINCIPAL FILM APPEARANCES—Sophia, America, America, Warner Brothers, 1964; Love Story, Paramount, 1970; The Adventurers, Paramount, 1970; school psychologist, Teachers, MGM/United Artists, 1984.

PRINCIPAL TELEVISION APPEARANCES—Movies: A Day with Conrad Green; The Shady Hill Kidnapping.

PRINCIPAL RADIO WORK—Host of a talk show, New York City, 1968-85.

WRITINGS: ARTICLES—Freelance writer for Family Circle and other magazines.

AWARDS: Best Supporting Actress, Hollywood Reporter Award, 1964, for America, America; Best Actress, Joseph Jefferson Award, for Summer and Smoke; Emmy Award nomination, for A Day with Conrad Green.

ADDRESSES: HOME—New York, NY. AGENT—Jerry Kahn Agency, 853 Seventh Avenue, New York NY 10019.

*   *   *

BANBURY, Frith 1912-

PERSONAL: Born Frederick Harold Banbury, May 4, 1912, in Plymouth, Devon, England; son of Frederick Arthur Frith (a career naval officer) and Winifred (Fink) Banbury. EDUCATION: Attended Hertford College, Oxford University; trained for the stage at the Royal Academy of Dramatic Art.

VOCATION: Actor, director, and manager.

CAREER: LONDON DEBUT—If I Were You, Shaftesbury Theatre, June 15, 1933. PRINCIPAL STAGE APPEARANCES—Barry Green, The Dark Tower, Shaftesbury Theatre, London, 1934; Courier, Hamlet, New Theatre, London, 1934; Monsieur Moi, Ambassadors Theatre, London, 1935; Love of Women, Arts Theatre, London, 1935; The Hangman, Duke of York's Theatre, London, 1935; Unicorn, Alice Through the Looking Glass, Little Theatre, London, 1935; appeared at the Perranporth Summer Theatre, 1936-38; Eustace, Oscar Wilde, Gate Theatre, London, 1936; Gerald Perkins, Adventure, Victoria Palace Theatre, London, 1936; Michael, First Night, Arts Theatre, London, 1937; Ridgeway's Late Joys, Players Theatre, London, 1938; Peter Thropp, Goodness, How Sad!, Vaudeville Theatre, London, 1938; Let's Face It, Chanticleer Theatre, London, 1939; Quetsch, Follow My Leader, Apollo Theatre, London, 1940; New Faces, Comedy Theatre, London, 1940; Algernon, The Importance of Being Earnest and Horace Bream, Sweet Lavender, both Stratford-Upon-Avon, U.K., 1940;

Rise Above It, Q Theatre, London, 1941; The New Ambassadors Revue, Ambassadors Theatre, London, 1941; Peter Blakiston, Jam To-day, St. Martin's Theatre, London, 1942; Light and Shake, Ambassadors Theatre, London, 1942; Gregers Werle, The Wild Duck, title role, The Gay Lord Quex, Muishkin, The Idiot, the Actor, The Guardsman, Joseph, The School for Scandal, Sneer, The Critic, and Cusins, Major Barbara, all in repertory at the Arts Theatre, Cambridge, U.K., 1943; Astrov, Uncle Vanya, Westminster Theatre, London, 1943; Lord Foppington, A Trip to Scarborough and Cyril Beverley, Bird in the Hand, both at the Arts Theatre, London, 1944; White Rabbit and White Knight, Alice in Wonderland, Palace Theatre, London, 1944; Hlestakov, The Government Inspector, Citizen's Theatre, Glasgow, Scotland, 1945; Gestapo Man, Jacobowsky and the Colonel, Piccadilly Theatre, London, 1945; Colbert, While the Sun Shines, Globe Theatre, London, 1945; Captain Hawtree, Caste, Lyric Theatre, Hammersmith, London, 1946, then Duke of York's Theatre, London, 1947.

MAJOR TOURS—Richard of Bordeaux, U.K. cities, 1934; Colbert, While the Sun Shines, European cities, 1945. Directed The Day After the Fair, U.S. cities, 1973.

PRINCIPAL STAGE WORK—Directed in London unless otherwise indicated: Dark Summer, 1947; Shooting Star, 1949; The Holly and the Ivy, Always Afternoon, and The Old Ladies, 1950; The Silver Box, Waters of the Moon, and All the Year Round, 1951; The Pink Room and The Deep Blue Sea (both London and New York City), 1952; A Question of Fact, 1953; Marching Song and Loves' Labour's Lost (with the Old Vic Company), 1954; The Bad Seed, 1955; The Good Sailor, The Diary of Anne Frank, 1956; A Dead Secret, Flowering Cherry, 1957; A Touch of the Sun, The Velvet Shotgun, and Moon on a Rainbow Shawl, 1958; The Ring of Truth and Flowering Cherry (produced in New York City), 1959; The Tiger and the Horse, Mister Johnson, 1960.

Director, unless otherwise stated: A Chance in the Daylight, 1960; director and co-producer, Life of the Party, 1960; Big Fish Little Fish, 1962; The Unshaven Cheek (produced at the Edinburgh Festival, Scotland), The Wings of the Dove, 1963; director and co-producer, I Love You, Mrs. Patterson, 1964; Do Not Pass Go (produced in New York City), 1965; The Right Honourable Gentleman (produced in New York City), 1965; Do Not Pass Go, 1966; Howard's End, Dear Octopus, 1967; Enter a Free Man, A Day in the Death of Joe Egg (produced in Tel Aviv, Israel), Le Valet (produced in Paris, France), 1968; On the Rocks (produced in Dublin, Ireland), 1969; director and co-producer, My Darling Daisy, 1970; The Winslow Boy, 1970; Captain Brassbound's Conversion, 1971; Reunion in Vienna, 1972 (also produced at Chichester Festival, U.K., 1971); director and co-producer, The Day After the Fair, 1973; Glasstown, 1973; Ardele, 1975; Family Matter, 1976; On Approval, 1977 (also produced in South Africa, 1976); Equus (produced in Kenya), 1977; The Aspern Papers (produced in U.S.), 1979; The Day After the Fair (produced in Australia), 1979; Mother-dear, 1980; Dear Liar, 1982; Fallen Angels, Coconut Grove Playhouse, Miami, FL, 1982; The Aspern Papers, 1984; The Corn Is Green, 1985. Also has directed other productions in Hong Kong, Toronto, New York, Paris, Tel Aviv, Johannesburg, Nairobie, Sydney, and Melbourne.

SIDELIGHTS: RECREATIONS—Playing piano.

ADDRESSES: HOME—Four St. James Terrace, Prince Albert Road, London NW8, England.*

BANNERMAN, Kay   1919-

PERSONAL: Born October 11, 1919, in Hove, Sussex, England; daughter of Robert George and Chicot (Mowat) Bannerman; married Harold Brooke. EDUCATION: Trained for the stage at the Royal Academy of Dramatic Art, London.

VOCATION: Actress and playwright.

CAREER: STAGE DEBUT—Emmanuele, *Asmodee,* Gate Theatre, London, 1939. PRINCIPAL STAGE APPEARANCES—Suzanne, *Prison without Bars,* Q Theatre, London, 1939; Doreen Pierce, *Rhondda Roundabout,* Globe Theatre, London, 1939; Deborah, *Music at Night* and Sarah, *Major Barbara,* both at the Westminster Theatre, London, 1939; Virginia Farquharson, *Temporary Residence,* Q Theatre, London, 1940; Ann Sheldon, *Other People's Houses,* Phoenix Theatre, London, 1942; Mary Jefferson, *One Flight Up,* Q Theatre, London, 1942; Portia, *The Merchant of Venice,* with the Old Vic Company at the New Theatre, London, 1943; Suzanne, *Guilty,* also titled *Therese Raquin,* Lyric Theatre, Hammersmith, London, 1944; Joan Manby, *We Are Seven,* Q Theatre, London, 1945; Hazel Crawford, *Myself a Stranger* and Polina, *The Gambler,* both at the Embassy Theatre, London, 1945; Frau Fruhling, *The Dove and the Carpenter,* Arts Theatre, London, 1946; Diana Temple, *High Horse,* New Lindsey Theatre, London, 1946.

MAJOR TOURS—Portia, *The Merchant of Venice,* Miss Neville, *She Stoops to Conquer,* and Raina, *Arms and the Man,* with the Old Vic Company, U.K. cities, 1943.

WRITINGS: PLAYS, PRODUCED—(With Harold Brooke) *Fit for Heroes,* 1945; *The Nest Egg,* 1952; *All for Mary,* 1954; *The Call of the Dodo,* 1955; *Love and Marriage,* 1956; *Once a Rake,* 1957; *How Say You?,* 1958; *Handful of Tansy,* 1959; *Death and All That Jazz,* 1961; *Don't Tell Father,* 1962; *The Call of the Dodo,* later retitled *There's a Yank Close Behind Me,* then *Let's Be Frank,* 1963; *The Snowman,* 1965; *Let Sleeping Wives Lie,* 1967; *It Shouldn't Happen to a Dog,* 1970; *She Was Only an Admiral's Daughter,* 1972; *Take Zero,* 1974.

SIDELIGHTS: RECREATIONS—Work.

ADDRESSES: HOME—Babergh Hall, Great Waldingfield, Sudbury, Suffolk, England.*

*   *   *

BARANSKI, Christine   1952-

PERSONAL: Born May 2, 1952, in Buffalo, NY; daughter of Lucien and Virginia (Mazcrowski) Baranski; married Matthew Cowles (an actor), October 15, 1983. EDUCATION: Juilliard School of Music and Dramatic Arts, B.A., 1974.

VOCATION: Actress.

CAREER: STAGE DEBUT—Annabella, *'Tis Pity She's a Whore,* McCarter Theatre, Princeton, NJ. BROADWAY DEBUT—Elly Bart, *Hide and Seek,* Belasco Theatre, May 4, 1980. PRINCIPAL STAGE APPEARANCES—With the Marymount Manhattan Theatre, New York City: Wanda, *One Crack Out,* 1978, Maeve Macpherson, *Says I, Says He,* 1979, and Amanda Gracie, Madame Igrec, and

CHRISTINE BARANSKI

second underworld figure, *The Trouble with Europe,* 1980; Angela, *Operation Midnight Climax,* Off Center Theatre, New York City, 1981; *Coming Attractions,* Playwrights Horizons, New York City, 1980-81; *Tally's Folly,* Studio Arena Theatre, Buffalo, NY, 1981; Helena, *A Midsummer Night's Dream,* New York Shakespeare Festival, Delacorte Theatre, New York City, 1982; Elvira, *Blithe Spirit,* McCarter Theatre, Princeton, 1982; Clarissa, *Sunday in the Park with George,* Playwrights Horizons, New York City, 1983; Charlotte, *The Real Thing,* Plymouth Theatre, New York City, 1984; Bonnie, *Hurlyburly,* Ethel Barrymore Theatre, New York City, 1985.

Also appeared as Lady Capulet, *Romeo and Juliet* and Maggie, *Cat on a Hot Tin Roof,* both American Shakespeare Festival, Stratford, CT; Constance, *She Stoops to Conquer,* Dunyasha, *The Cherry Orchard,* Lina, *Misalliance,* Dorine, *Tartuffe,* and Billie Dawn, *Born Yesterday,* all with the Center Stage Company, Baltimore, MD; Miss Scoons, *Angel City,* McCarter Theatre, Princeton; Miss Harris, *The Undefeated Rumba Champ,* Ensemble Studio Theatre, New York City; Marsha, *Sally and Marsha,* Manhattan Theatre Club, New York City.

MAJOR TOURS—Davina Saunders, *Otherwise Engaged,* U.S. cities.

FILM DEBUT—*Soup for One,* Warner Brothers, 1982. PRINCIPAL FILM APPEARANCES—*Lovesick,* Warner Brothers, 1983; *Crackers,* Universal, 1984.

TELEVISION DEBUT—*The Adams Chronicles.* PRINCIPAL TELEVISION APPEARANCES—Series: *All My Children,* ABC; *Texas,*

NBC; *Another World*, NBC. Movies: *Playing for Time*, CBS, 1980; also *Murder Ink*.

AWARDS: Obie Award, 1983, for *A Midsummer Night's Dream*.

MEMBER: Actors' Equity Association, American Federation of Television and Radio Artists, Screen Actors Guild.

ADDRESSES: AGENT—Paul Doherty, Schumer-Oubre, 1697 Broadway, New York, NY 10019.*

*   *   *

BARBEAU, Adrienne

PERSONAL: Born in Sacramento, CA; married John Carpenter (a director), January 1, 1979; children: a son. EDUCATION: Attended Foothill College, Los Altos, CA; trained privately in voice and ballet.

VOCATION: Actress.

CAREER: STAGE DEBUT—*The King and I*, San Jose Light Opera Company. BROADWAY DEBUT—Hodel, *Fiddler on the Roof*. PRINCIPAL STAGE APPEARANCES—Various roles with the San Jose Light Opera Company for two years; Rizzo, *Grease*, Broadway production, 1971-72.

MAJOR TOURS—In a musical revue, San Jose Light Opera and U.S. State Department, South East Asian cities.

ADRIENNE BARBEAU

PRINCIPAL TELEVISION APPEARANCES—Series: Carol, *Maude*, CBS, 1974-78. Movies: *Having Babies*, 1976; *Red Alert*, 1977; *Crash, the True Story of Flight 401*, 1978; *Someone's Watching Me!*, 1978; *Tourist*, 1980; *Seduced*, 1985; *Bridge Across Time*, NBC, 1985. Episodic: *Sweepstakes*, NBC, 1979; *Twilight Zone, the Series*, CBS, 1985; *Murder, She Wrote*, CBS, 1985.

FILM DEBUT—*The Fog*, AVCO-Embassy, 1980. PRINCIPAL FILM APPEARANCES—*Escape from New York*, AVCO-Embassy, 1981; *Cannonball Run*, Twentieth Century-Fox, 1981; *Swamp Thing*, Embassy, 1982; *The Next One*, 1984.

AWARDS: Antoinette Perry Award nomination, Most Promising Actress in a Musical and *Theatre World* Award, both 1971-72, for *Grease;* honorary chairperson, Entertainment Industry Committee for Safety Belts; Concern II (for children's cancer research).

ADDRESSES: PUBLICIST—c/o Monique Moss, Michael Levine Agency, 9123 Sunset Blvd., Los Angeles, CA 90069.

*   *   *

BARCELO, Randy   1946-

PERSONAL: Born September 19, 1946, in Havana, Cuba; son of Ramon (an architect) and Ondina (an architect; maiden name, Lopez) Barcelo.

VOCATION: Set and costume designer.

CAREER: PRINCIPAL STAGE WORK—Costume designer, Broadway productions: *Ain't Misbehavin'; The Magic Show; Jesus Christ Superstar; Lenny; The Leaf People; Sergeant Pepper's Lonely Hearts Club Band; A Broadway Musical; The Night That Made America Famous*.

Off-Broadway productions: Costume designer, *Lady Day*, Chelsea Theatre Center; set and costume designer, *Blood Wedding* and *Rice and Beans*, INTAR Theatre; costume designer, *The Tempest, Caligula*, and *The Moondreamers*, all at La Mama ETC (Experimental Theatre Club); costume designer, *A Midsummer Night's Dream*, New York Shakespeare Festival, Delacorte Theatre; set designer, "Philip Morris Superband Series," Beacon Theatre and European tour; set and costume designer, *Mayor*, Village Gate Theatre.

Opera: Costume designer, *Mass*, Kennedy Center, Washington, DC; set and costume designer, *L'Histoire du Soldat*, Carnegie Hall, New York City; costume designer, *Les Troyen*, Vienna State Opera; costume designer, *Salome* and *Lily*, both New York City Opera.

Dance: Costume designer, *Fuenteovejuna* and *The Street Dancer*, Ballet Hispanico; designed sets and costumes for *Mondrian, Predicaments for Five*, and *Lovers*, for Jennifer Muller and the Works, and for *The Mooche, Crosswords, Spells*, and *For Bird with Love*, for the Alvin Ailey Dance Theatre.

PRINCIPAL TELEVISION WORK—Costume designer: *Ailey Celebrates Ellington*, CBS, 1975; *Ain't Misbehavin'*, NBC, 1982; *Duke Ellington, the Music Lives On*, PBS, 1983.

PRINCIPAL FILM WORK—Set and costume design of theatre

RANDY BARCELO

sequence, *Fat Chance;* costume design of dance sequence, *Secret Life of Plants;* costume design, *The Cop and the Anthem;* art director and costume designer for *The Two Worlds of Angelita, Welcome to Miami, Cubanos,* and *Tainted.*

AWARDS: Antoinette Perry Award nomination; Maharam Award; *Variety* Critics Poll Award.

MEMBER: United Scenic Artists, Local 829.

ADDRESSES: OFFICE—200 W. 90th Street, Studio 14B, New York, NY 10024.

*   *   *

BARNES, Wade   1917-

PERSONAL: Born May 15, 1917, in Alliance, OH; son of J. Ralph (a grocer and meat dealer) and Flora Ellen (Borem) Barnes; married Georgene O'Donnell (a writer and public relations director), July 13, 1957. EDUCATION: Hunter College, B.A.; studied music at the American Society of Composers, Authors and Publishers Seminars and with Jan Gorbaty. POLITICS: Democrat.

VOCATION: Actor and writer.

CAREER: STAGE DEBUT—Leading player, *The Devil Passes,* Canton Players Guild Theatre, Canton, OH, 1938, for seven performances. OFF-BROADWAY DEBUT—Kiepert, *Three Acts of Recognition,* New York Shakespeare Festival, Anspacher Theatre,

1982, for eighty performances. PRINCIPAL STAGE APPEARANCES— Little John, *Robin Hood,* Dallas Little Theatre, TX, 1946.

PRINCIPAL FILM APPEARANCES—*Serpico,* Paramount, 1974; *The Turning Point,* Twentieth Century-Fox, 1977; *Annie Hall,* United Artists, 1977; *Exorcist II: The Heretic,* Warner Brothers, 1977; *Manhattan,* United Artists, 1979; *Stardust Memories,* United Artists, 1980; *Diner,* Metro-Goldwyn-Mayer/United Artists, 1982; *Easy Money,* Orion, 1983; *The Purple Rose of Cairo,* Orion, 1984; *The Money Pit,* Universal, 1986; *Outrageous Fortune,* Touchstone, 1987; also appeared in *Cold River,* 1982.

PRINCIPAL TELEVISION APPEARANCES—Movies: *Johnny, We Hardly Knew Ye,* 1977. Episodic: *Andros Targets,* CBS, 1977; also *Kojak,* CBS. Mini-Series: *Seventh Avenue,* NBC, 1977.

PRINCIPAL RADIO WORK—Announcer, director, actor, and writer for WHBC, Canton, OH, and NBC, Cleveland, OH; announcer and writer for WCAU, Philadelphia. Appeared as a guest and later served as news director for WNYC, New York City. Host, WTFM and WPIX, New York City; news announcer, WINS, New York City; sales manager, recording division, NBC, New York City.

NON-RELATED CAREER—Sales representative, Hughes Tool and Gulf Brewing; public relations and advertising executive, Barnes Associates, New York City.

WRITINGS: TELEPLAYS and RADIO PLAYS—(with Ralph Blane) *Quillow and the Giant,* BBC, 1960 and NBC, 1962; *Circus* and *Lefgook,* both WNYC, 1980. PLAYS—*The Stoop, The Mighty Pen, Poolside,* and *Noah Webster's Words with Music.*

WADE BARNES

AWARDS: Ohio State University Best Show of the Year Award, 1962, for *Quillow and the Giant.*

MEMBER: National Academy of Television Arts and Sciences, International Radio and Television Society, Screen Actors Guild, Affiliated Federation of Musicians; Variety Club.

ADDRESSES: HOME—20 Beekman Place, New York, NY 10022. OFFICE—Barnes Associates, 19 W. 44th Street, New York, NY 10036.

* * *

BARRE, Gabriel 1957-

PERSONAL: Full name, James Gabriel Barre; born August 26, 1957, in Brattleboro, VT; son of James Lyman (a state medicaid administrator) and Susan (a bank systems analyst; maiden name, Hebb) Barre. EDUCATION: Trained for the stage at the American Academy of Dramatic Arts, attaining an associate degree and with Richard Morse and Julie Bovasso.

VOCATION: Actor and composer.

CAREER: STAGE DEBUT—One of the kids, *Mr. Flanagan's Ocean,* tour of Northern Vermont cities, 1967. OFF-BROADWAY DEBUT—Narrator, *Cheers,* 13th Street Theatre, 1977, for twenty performances. PRINCIPAL STAGE APPEARANCES—Klezmer lead-

GABRIEL BARRE

er and as part of the ensemble, *Rags,* Mark Hellinger Theatre, New York City, 1986. Appeared Off-Broadway in: *Jabberwock,* Truck and Warehouse Theatre; *Gimpel the Fool,* 92nd Street YMHA; *T.N.T.,* Players Theatre; *The Plagues,* La Mama E.T.C. (Experimental Theatre Club); Priest, *The Baker's Wife,* York Theatre. With the Mirror Repertory Theatre appeared as George, *The Circle,* Troshin, *Children of the Sun,* and Harry, *The Time of Your Life.* Regional: *Bodo,* Goodspeed Opera House, East Haddam, CT; Wazir, *Kismet,* An Evening Dinner Theatre.

MAJOR TOURS—*Richard Morse Mime Theatre,* Middle Eastern and European cities, 1978; Ringmaster, *Barnum,* U.S. cities, 1981.

PRINCIPAL STAGE WORK—Composer and lyricist of original music for *Home Free,* Haven Theatre, New York City, 1986.

PRINCIPAL TELEVISION APPEARANCES—Episodic: *Kate and Allie,* CBS; *Fame,* NBC; *Bloodhound Gang,* PBS; *All My Children,* ABC; *Another World,* NBC.

FILM DEBUT—Mime, *Can't Stop the Music,* ITC, 1980. PRINCIPAL FILM APPEARANCES—*Stardust Memories,* United Artists, 1980; *Luggage of the Gods,* General Pictures, 1983; also in *Mangia.*

RELATED CAREER—Writer, producer, and director of 16mm films.

MEMBER: Actors' Equity Association, Screen Actors Guild, American Federation of Television and Radio Artists, American Society of Composers, Authors, and Publishers (ASCAP).

ADDRESSES: AGENT—c/o Louis Ambrosio, Ambrosio/Mortimer, 165 W. 46th Street, Suite 1109, New York, NY 10036.

* * *

BARRETT, Leslie 1919-

PERSONAL: Born Leslie Klein, October 30, 1919, on Staten Island, NY; son of Cecil and Theresa (Leonhardt) Klein; married Diana Newman Barth (divorced); married Ruth W. Livingston. EDUCATION: Trained for the stage at the American Theatre Wing and with Lee Strasberg. MILITARY: U.S. Army, 1942-46.

VOCATION: Actor.

CAREER: STAGE DEBUT—Under the name Leslie Klein as Bosco, *But for the Grace of God,* Guild Theatre, New York City, 1937. PRINCIPAL STAGE APPEARANCES—A boy, *An Enemy of the People,* Hudson Theatre, New York City, 1937; as Leslie Barrett: Tommy, *Dead End,* Belasco Theatre, New York City, 1937; Pogriski, *Sunup to Sundown,* Hudson Theatre, New York City, 1938; Tommy Hammond, *There's Always a Breeze,* Windsor Theatre, New York City, 1938; Davy Wallace, *The Primrose Path,* Biltmore Theatre, New York City, 1939; Newsboy, *At the Stroke of Eight,* Biltmore Theatre, New York City, 1940; Jockey Lane, *Horse Fever,* Mansfield Theatre, New York City, 1940.

Western Union boy, *Good Neighbor,* Windsor Theatre, New York City, 1941; Marco, *All in Favor,* Henry Miller's Theatre, New York City, 1942; Henry Susskind, *Counsellor-at-Law,* Royale Theatre, New York City, 1942; Lee Brady, *The Love Wagon,* Paper Mill Playhouse, Milburn, NJ, 1947; *Much Ado About Nothing* and

LESLIE BARRETT

As You Like It, both at the Shakespeare Theatre Workshop, New York City, 1955; Clerk of the Court, *Deadfall,* Holiday Theatre, New York City, 1955; Postmaster, *Purple Dust,* Cherry Lane Theatre, New York City, 1957; Grigory, *The Trial of Dmitri Karamazov,* Jan Hus Theatre, New York City, 1958; *From Classics to Contemporaries: Lives of the Poets,* Donnell Library, New York City and Equity Library Theatre, Los Angeles.

Old Gentleman, *Rhinoceros,* Longacre Theatre, New York City, 1961; Cat, *The Dragon,* Phoenix Repertory Theatre, New York City, 1963; Henry, *Slapstick Tragedy,* Longacre Theatre, New York City, 1966; Waiter, *Incident at Vichy,* Playhouse in the Park, Philadelphia, PA, 1966; First Witness and Second Witness, *The Investigation,* Ambassador Theatre, New York City, 1966; Padre, *Hamp,* Renata Theatre, New York City, 1967; *The Day the Lid Blew Off,* Jan Hus Theatre, New York City, 1967; Uncle Eugene, *Tango,* Pocket Theatre, New York City, 1969.

Appeared at the Loretto-Hilton Theatre, St. Louis, MO, 1970; Jim Heeler, *Hobson's Choice,* Canada, 1971; Judge Gaffney, *Harvey,* Barter Theatre, Abingdon, VA, 1972; de Pinna, *You Can't Take It with You,* Actors Theatre of Louisville, KY, 1972; Old Mr. Ewbank, *The Contractor,* Chelsea Westside Theatre, New York City, 1973; Pedant, *The Taming of the Shrew,* Walnut Theatre, Philadelphia, 1974; Mr. Wilbur, *Once More with Feeling,* Westgate Theatre, Toledo, OH, 1974; Major Brigg, *Savages,* Hudson Guild Theatre, New York City, 1977; Bertram, *The Last Analysis,* Berkshire Playhouse, Stockbridge, MA, 1977; Rosas, *Semmelweiss,* Studio Arena Theatre, Buffalo, NY, 1977, then repeated the role at the Hartman Theatre, Stamford, CT, 1981; John of Gaunt, *Richard II,* American Musical and Dramatic Academy (AMDA) Studio

Theatre, New York City, 1978; Fineberg, *My Old Friends,* Orpheum Theatre, then 22 Steps Theatre, New York City, 1979.

Friar Laurence, *Romeo and Juliet,* Equity Library Theatre, New York City, 1980; De Lacey, *Frankenstein,* Palace Theatre, New York City, 1981; understudy Jasper, *Close of Play,* Manhattan Theatre Club, New York City, 1981; Geoffrey and understudy Gloucester, *The Dresser,* Brooks Atkinson Theatre, New York City, 1981; Starkeeper, *Carousel,* Music Hall, Dallas, TX, 1983; understudy Selsden Mowbray, *Noises Off,* Kennedy Center, Washington, DC, then Brooks Atkinson Theatre, New York City, 1983; Harvey, *Season's Greetings,* Whole Theatre, Montclair, NJ, 1985.

PRINCIPAL STAGE WORK—Director, *The Crucible,* Equity Library Theatre, New York City, 1959.

MAJOR TOURS—Old Gentleman, *Rhinoceros,* U.S. cities, 1961; Doc, *West Side Story,* U.S. cities, 1965; Herr Schlick, *Bitter Sweet,* toured Ohio with the Kenley Players, 1975; Josef, *The Student Prince,* U.S. cities, 1976.

SIDELIGHTS: RECREATIONS—Gallery-going, tennis.

ADDRESSES: HOME—New York City. AGENT—Beverly Anderson Agency, 1472 Broadway, New York, NY 10036.

*   *   *

BARRETT, Rona   1936-

PERSONAL: Born Rona Burstein, October 8, 1936, in New York, NY; daughter of Harry J. (a food market entrepreneur) and Ida (Lefkowitz) Burstein; married William Allan Trowbridge (a businessman), September 22, 1973. EDUCATION: Attended New York University, 1953-55.

VOCATION: Writer, columnist, television interviewer, and host.

CAREER: PRINCIPAL TELEVISION APPEARANCES—With ABC, Los Angeles: Host, *Dateline, Hollywood,* 1967, and host, *Rona Barrett's Hollywood,* 1969; syndicated journalist with Metromedia Network, 1969-74; arts and entertainment editor, featured journalist, and interviewer, *Good Morning, America,* ABC, 1975-80. interviewer and news correspondent, *Today Show* and *Tomorrow,* NBC, 1980—; senior correspondent, *Entertainment Tonight,* syndicated, 1981.

Specials: *Rona Looks at the Oscars,* 1972; *Rona Looks at Raquel, Liza, Cher, and Ann-Margret,* 1975; *Rona Looks at James Caan, Michael Caine, Elliot Gould, and Burt Reynolds,* 1976. Episodic: As herself, *Moonlighting,* ABC, 1987. Guest Host: *Larry King Show,* CNN, 1987.

RELATED CAREER—President, Rona Barrett Communications, Inc.

WRITINGS: BOOKS—*The Love-Maniacs* (novel), Nash, 1972; *Miss Rona* (autobiography), Nash, 1974. PERIODICALS—Columnist: *Rona Barrett's Young Hollywood,* syndicated 1957; *Motion Picture* magazine, 1960; syndicated columnist with the North American Newspaper Alliance, 1961-64. Also, publisher of *Rona Barrett's Hollywood,* 1969, and *Rona Barrett's Gossip;* publisher and executive editor, *The Rona Barrett Report* (a newsletter), 1985—.

ADDRESSES: HOME—P.O. Box, 1410, Beverly Hills, CA 90213. OFFICE—National Broadcasting Company, 3000 W. Alameda Ave., Burbank, CA 91523.*

*   *   *

BARRY, John   1933-

PERSONAL: Born 1933, in York, England.

VOCATION: Composer, arranger, and conductor.

CAREER: PRINCIPAL FILM WORK—Composer, arranger, and conductor: *Beat Girl* (also known as *Wild for Kicks*), 1962; *The Amorous Mr. Prawn,* 1962; *Never Let Go,* Continental, 1963; *From Russia with Love,* United Artists, 1964; *Seance on a Wet Afternoon,* Artixo, 1964; *Zulu,* Embassy, 1964; *Goldfinger,* United Artists, 1964; *The Ipcress File,* Universal, 1965; *The Knack,* United Artists, 1965; *King Rat,* Columbia, 1965; *Thunderball,* United Artists, 1965; *Born Free,* Columbia, 1966; *The Chase,* Columbia, 1966; *The Wrong Box,* Columbia, 1966; *The Quiller Memorandum,* Twentieth Century-Fox, 1967; *The Whisperers,* Lopert, 1967; *You Only Live Twice,* United Artists, 1967; *Deadfall,* Twentieth Century-Fox, 1968; *Petulia,* Warner Brothers/Seven Arts, 1968; *The Lion in Winter,* AVCO-Embassy, 1968; *Midnight Cowboy,* United Artists, 1969; *The Appointment,* 1969.

The Tamarind Seed, AVCO-Embassy, 1974; *The Dove,* Paramount, 1974; *The Day of the Locust,* Paramount, 1975; *Robin and Marian,* Columbia, 1976; *King Kong,* Paramount, 1976; *The Deep,* Columbia, 1977; *The Betsy,* Allied Artists, 1978; *Moonraker,* United Artists, 1979; *The Black Hole,* Buena Vista, 1979; *Somewhere in Time,* Universal, 1980; *Frances,* Universal, 1982; *Hammett,* Zoetrope, 1983; *Mike's Murder,* Warner Brothers, 1984; *Until September,* Metro-Goldwyn-Mayer/United Artists (MGM/UA), 1984; *The Cotton Club,* Orion, 1984; *A View to a Kill,* MGM/UA, 1985; *Out of Africa,* Universal, 1985; *Peggy Sue Got Married,* Tri-Star, 1986.

PRINCIPAL TELEVISION WORK—Specials: Composer, arranger, and conductor for *Elizabeth Taylor in London* and *Sophia Loren in Rome.*

RELATED CAREER—Artist and producer, Columbia Broadcasting System Records.

AWARDS: Best Original Score, Academy Award, 1985, for *Out of Africa.*

ADDRESSES: AGENT—c/o Marion Rosenberg, The Lantz Office, 9255 Sunset Blvd., Suite 505, Los Angeles, CA 90069.*

*   *   *

BAXTER, Keith   1935-

PERSONAL: Born Keith Stanley Baxter-Wright, April 29, 1935, in Newport, Monmouthshire, Wales; son of Stanley (a dockmaster) and Emily Marian (Howell) Baxter-Wright. EDUCATION: Trained

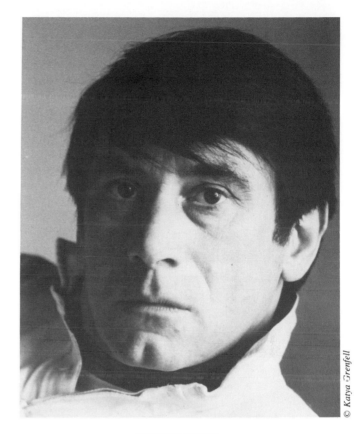

KEITH BAXTER

for the stage at the Royal Academy of Dramatic Art, 1952-53, 1955-56. MILITARY: British Army, 1953-55.

VOCATION: Actor and writer.

CAREER: STAGE DEBUT—Oxford and Worthing Repertories, 1956-57. LONDON DEBUT—Ralph, *Tea and Sympathy,* Comedy Theatre, April 25, 1957. BROADWAY DEBUT—Henry VIII, *A Man for All Seasons,* American National Theatre Academy (ANTA) Theatre, November 22, 1961. PRINCIPAL STAGE APPEARANCES—Hippolytus, *Phedre,* Theatre in the Round, London, 1958; Vasse, *Change of Tune,* Strand Theatre, London, 1959; Prince Hal, *King Henry IV,* Parts I and II, Belfast, then Dublin, Ireland, 1960; Roger Balion, *Time and Yellow Roses,* St. Martin's Theatre, London, 1961; David Glyn, *Unfinished Journey,* Pembroke Theatre, Croydon, U.K. 1961; Donald Howard, *The Affair,* Henry Miller's Theatre, New York City, 1962; Gino Carella, *Where Angels Fear to Tread,* Arts Theatre, then St. Martin's Theatre, both London, 1963; Valentine, *You Never Can Tell* and Bob Acres, *The Rivals,* both at the Haymarket Theatre, London, 1966; Baldassare Pantaleone, *Avanti!,* Booth Theatre, New York City, 1968; Horner, *The Country Wife* and Octavius Caesar, *Antony and Cleopatra,* both at the Chichester Festival, U.K., 1969; Milo Tindle, *Sleuth,* St. Martin's Theatre, London, then Music Box Theatre, New York City, 1970.

Title role, *Macbeth,* Birmingham Repertory Theatre, 1972; Vershinin, *Three Sisters,* Greenwich Theatre, London, 1973; Benedick, *Much Ado About Nothing,* Royal Lyceum Theatre, Edinburgh, Scotland, 1973; Ricco Verri, *Tonight We Improvise,* Chichester Festival,

1974; the Dead Poet, the Preacher, and the Politician, *Sap,* Sherman Theatre, Cardiff, Wales, 1974; title role, *Antony and Cleopatra,* Witwoud, *The Way of the World* and Vershinin, *Three Sisters,* both Stratford, Ontario, Canada, 1976; King, *The Red Devil Battery Sign,* Round House Theatre, then Phoenix Theatre, both London, 1977; Lord Illingworth, *A Woman of No Importance* and Dorante, *The Inconstant Couple,* both at the Chichester Festival, 1978; Patrick, *A Meeting by the River,* Palace Theatre, New York City, 1979; Bill Cardew, *Home and Beauty,* Kennedy Center, Washington, DC, 1979; title role, *Hamlet,* Edmonton, Alberta, Canada, 1979; Ken Harrison, *Whose Life Is It Anyway?,* Parker Playhouse, Ft. Lauderdale and Gussman Theatre, Miami, 1979.

Sherlock Holmes, *The Penultimate Case of Sherlock Holmes,* Hudson Guild Theatre, New York City, 1980; Jason Carmichael, *Romantic Comedy,* Ethel Barrymore Theatre, New York City, then Royal Alexandra Theatre, Toronto, and Auditorium, Denver, all 1980; Friedrich, *Undiscovered Country,* Antony, *Antony and Cleopatra,* and Edmund Kean, *Kean,* all the the Hartford Stage Company, CT, 1981; Gwilym, *56 Duncan Terrrace,* Edmonton, Alberta, 1982; narrator of the opera *Oedipus Rex,* Philadelphia Opera Company, 1982; Antony, *Antony and Cleopatra,* Young Vic Theatre, London, 1982; Sherlock Holmes, *Murder, Dear Watson,* Bromley Theatre, Kent, U.K., 1983; Evelyn/Rupert, *Corpse!,* Apollo Theatre, London, 1984, then Helen Hayes Theatre, New York City, 1986.

MAJOR TOURS—Sanyamo, *South Sea Bubble,* U.K. cities, 1957; Evelyn/Rupert, *Corpse!,* U.S. cities and Australia, 1985-86.

PRINCIPAL STAGE WORK—Co-director, *The Red Devil Battery Sign,* Round House Theatre, then Phoenix Theatre, London, 1977.

FILM DEBUT—1956. PRINCIPAL FILM APPEARANCES—Charles Moulton-Barrett, *The Barretts of Wimpole Street,* Metro-Goldwyn-Mayer (MGM), 1957; Alexander, *Family Doctor,* Twentieth Century-Fox, 1957; Young Detective, *Peeping Tom,* Rank, 1959; Prince Hal, *Chimes at Midnight,* Welles, 1967; Tony, *With Love in Mind,* Associated British, 1969; David, *Ash Wednesday,* Paramount, 1973; *Golden Rendezvous,* 1977.

PRINCIPAL TELEVISION APPEARANCES—Dramatic Specials: Thomas, *She Stoops to Conquer,* BBC, 1956; *Man and Superman,* 1958; *The Reward of Silence,* BBC, 1963; *For Tea on Sunday,* BBC, 1963; Dunois, *Saint Joan,* BBC, 1968; *Love Story,* 1968; *Orson Welles Great Mysteries,* 1973; *The Vineyard,* BBC, 1974; also appeared in *The Miracle Man* and *The Bonus.*

WRITINGS: PLAYS, PRODUCED—*56 Duncan Terrace,* Edmonton, Alberta, Canada, 1982; *Cavell,* Chichester Festival, U.K., 1982; *Barnaby and the Old Boys,* Theatre Clwyd, Wales, 1987.

AWARDS: Bronze Medal Award, Royal Academy of Dramatic Art, 1956; *Theatre World* Award, 1962, for *A Man for All Seasons;* Fanny Kemble Award, 1962; Drama Desk Award and Outer Circle Award, both 1971, for *Sleuth.*

MEMBER: Actors' Equity Association, Screen Actors Guild.

SIDELIGHTS: FAVORITE ROLES—Bob Acres from *The Rivals* and Antony from *Antony and Cleopatra.* RECREATIONS—The sea.

ADDRESSES: HOME—London, England. AGENT—International Creative Management Ltd., 388 Oxford Street, London W1, England.

BAY, Howard   1912-1986

PERSONAL: Born May 3, 1912, in Centralia, WA; died of a heart attack in New York, NY, November 21, 1986; son of William D. (a teacher) and Bertha A. (a teacher; maiden name, Jenkins) Bay; married Ruth Jonas, November 23, 1932; children: Ellen, Timothy. EDUCATION: Attended University of Washington, 1928; Chappell School of Art, Denver, CO, 1928-29; University of Colorado, 1929; Marshall College, 1929-30; Carnegie Institute of Technology, 1930-31; Westminster College, 1931-32; studied in Europe, 1939.

VOCATION: Designer, director, teacher, and writer.

CAREER: FIRST STAGE WORK—Designer, *There's a Moon Tonight,* New York City, 1933. PRINCIPAL STAGE WORK—For the Federal Theatre Project in New York City, designed sets for: *Chalk Dust* and *Battle Hymn,* both Experimental Theatre, 1936, *Power (The Living Newspaper),* Ritz Theatre, 1937, *Native Ground,* Venice Theatre, 1937, *One Third of a Nation,* Adelphi Theatre, 1938, *Trojan Incident,* St. James Theatre, 1938, and *The Life and Death of an American,* Maxine Elliott's Theatre, 1939. While still with the Federal Theatre project, he designed the sets for *Marching Song,* Bayes Theatre, New York City, 1937, *Sunup to Sundown,* Hudson Theatre, 1938, *The Merry Wives of Windsor,* 1938, *The Little Foxes,* National Theatre, New York City, 1939, and *The Dog Beneath the Skin,* 1939.

Designed sets and lighting for four operas for the National Orchestral Association: *Pagliacci, Gianni Schicchi, Suor Angelica,* and *The Abduction from the Seraglio,* all at Carnegie Hall, New York City, 1939-40.

Set and lighting designer for all, unless otherwise noted: *The Fifth Column,* Alvin Theatre, New York City, 1940; *Morning Star,* Longacre Theatre, New York City, 1940; *The Corn Is Green,* National Theatre, New York City, 1940; *The Man with Blond Hair,* Belasco Theatre, New York City, 1941; *Brooklyn, USA,* Forrest Theatre, New York City, 1941; *Johnny 2x4,* Longacre Theatre, New York City, 1942; *The Moon Is Down,* Martin Beck Theatre, New York City, 1942; *The Strings, My Lord, Are False,* Royale Theatre, New York City, 1942; *Uncle Harry,* Broadhurst Theatre, New York City, 1942; *The Eve of St. Mark,* Cort Theatre, New York City, 1942; *Count Me In,* Ethel Barrymore Theatre, New York City, 1942; *The Great Big Doorstep,* Morosco Theatre, New York City, 1942; *Something for the Boys,* Alvin Theatre, New York City, 1943; *The Patriots,* National Theatre, New York City, 1943; *The Merry Widow,* Majestic Theatre, New York City, 1943; *A New Life,* Royale Theatre, New York Theatre, 1943; *One Touch of Venus,* Imperial Theatre, New York City, 1943; *Carmen Jones,* Broadway Theatre, New York City, 1943; *Listen, Professor!,* Forrest Theatre, New York City, 1943.

(Sets only) *Storm Operation,* Belasco Theatre, New York City, 1944; (sets only) *The Peep Show,* Fulton Theatre, New York City, 1944; *Chicken Every Sunday,* Henry Miller's Theatre, New York City, 1944; *Follow the Girls,* Century Theatre, New York City, 1944; *The Searching Wind,* Fulton Theatre, New York City, 1944; *Ten Little Indians,* Broadhurst Theatre, New York City, 1944; *Catherine Was Great,* Shubert Theatre, New York City, 1944; pre-Broadway tryout of *Franklyn Street,* 1944; pre-Broadway tryout of *Spring in Brazil,* 1944; *Men to the Sea,* National Theatre, New York City, 1944; *The Visitor,* Henry Miller's Theatre, New York

City, 1944; *Violet*, Belasco Theatre, New York City, 1944; pre-Broadway tryout of *Glad to See You*, 1944.

Up in Central Park, Century Theatre, New York City, 1945; *Marinka*, Winter Garden Theatre, New York City, 1945; *Devils Galore*, Royale Theatre, New York City, 1945; *Deep Are the Roots*, Fulton Theatre, New York City, 1945; *Polonaise*, Alvin Theatre, New York City, 1945; *Show Boat*, Ziegfeld Theatre, New York City, 1946; *The Would-Be Gentleman*, Booth Theatre, New York City, 1946; *Woman Bites Dog*, Belasco Theatre, New York City, 1946; *The Big Knife*, National Theatre, New York City, 1949; *Montserrat*, Fulton Theatre, New York City, 1949; *Magdelena*, Philharmonic Auditorium, Los Angeles, CA, 1949.

Come Back Little Sheba, Booth Theatre, New York City, 1950; *Michael Todd's Peepshow*, Winter Garden Theatre, New York City, 1950; *Parisienne*, Fulton Theatre, New York City, 1950; *Hilda Crane*, Coronet Theatre, New York City, 1950; *Flahooley*, Broadhurst Theatre, New York City, 1951; *The Autumn Garden*, Coronet Theatre, New York City, 1951; *Two on the Aisle*, Mark Hellinger Theatre, New York City, 1951; *The Grand Tour*, Martin Beck Theatre, New York City, 1951; *The Shrike*, Cort Theatre, 1952; (sets, lighting, and costumes) *Les Noces*, Brandeis University, Boston, 1952; *The Children's Hour*, Coronet Theatre, New York City, 1952; *Mid-Summer*, Vanderbilt Theatre, New York City, 1953.

(Sets only) *Show Boat*, New York City Center, 1954; (sets only) *Sandhog*, Phoenix Theatre, 1954; pre-Broadway tryout, *Top Man*, 1955; *The Desparate Hours*, Ethel Barrymore Theatre, New York City, 1955; *Red Roses for Me*, Booth Theatre, New York City, 1955; *Carmen Jones*, New York City Center, 1956; *A Very Special Baby*, Playhouse, New York City, 1956; pre-Broadway tryouts, *Build with One Hand* and *A Certain Joy*, both 1956; *Night of the Auk*, Playhouse Theatre, New York City, 1956; *Tevya and His Daughters*, 1957; *Look Back in Anger*, 1957; *The Music Man*, 1957; *Interlock*, American National Theatre Academy (ANTA), New York City, 1958; *Regina*, revival, 1958; *Jolly Anna*, Philharmonic Auditorium, Los Angeles, 1959; *A Desert Incident*, John Golden Theatre, New York City, 1959; (lighting design only) *The Fighting Cock*, 1959; *Carmen*, San Francisco Opera Company, 1959.

The Cut of the Axe, Ambassador Theatre, New York City, 1960; *The Cool World*, Eugene O'Neill Theatre, New York City, 1960; *Toys in the Attic*, Hudson Theatre, New York Theatre, 1960; *Show Boat*, Los Angeles Civic Light Opera Company, 1960; *The Wall*, Billy Rose Theatre, New York City, 1960; *The Music Man*, London, 1961; *Pal Joey*, New York City Center, 1961; *Milk and Honey*, Martin Beck Theatre, New York City, 1961; *Carmen*, San Francisco Opera Company, 1961; *Isle of Children*, Cort Theatre, New York City, 1962; *My Mother, My Father, and Me*, Plymouth Theatre, New York City, 1963; *Bicycle Ride to Nevada*, Cort Theatre, New York City, 1963; *Never Live Over a Pretzel Factory*, Eugene O'Neill Theatre, New York City, 1964; *The Music Man*, New York City Center, 1965; (sets, lighting, and costumes) *Man of La Mancha*, ANTA Theatre, New York City, 1965, also produced in London, 1968; *Capriccio* and *Natalya Petrovna*, New York City Opera, 1965; *Chu Chem*, Locust Theatre, Philadelphia, 1966; *The Little Foxes*, Vivian Beaumont Theatre, 1967; *Man of La Mancha*, London, 1968; *Fire!*, Longacre Theatre, New York City, 1969.

Cry for Us All, Broadhurst Theatre, New York City, 1970; *Knickerbocker Holiday*, Curran Theatre, San Francisco, 1971; *Halloween*, Bucks County Playhouse, New Hope, PA, 1972; (supervisor of

American scenery and lighting) *Equus*, Plymouth Theatre, New York City, 1974; *Home Sweet Homer*, 1976; *Poor Murderer*, Ethel Barrymore Theatre, New York City, 1976; revival of *Man of La Mancha*, Palace Theatre, New York City, 1977; *The Utter Glory of Morrissey Hall*, Mark Hellinger Theatre, New York City, 1979. Bay was working on a Peking Opera production of *The Music Man* at the time of his death.

Director and designer: *As the Girls Go*, Winter Garden Theatre, New York City, 1948; *Crimes and Crimes*, Brattle Theatre, Cambridge, MA, 1955, then Carnegie Institute of Technology, 1963; *The Cage*, University of Ohio, 1964; *Ping Pong*, Brandeis University, 1966; *The Workhouse Donkey*, Brandeis University, 1967; *Colombe*, Brandeis University, 1968; *The Cradle Will Rock*, Brandeis University, 1976; *Pal Joey*, 1976.

MAJOR TOURS—Set and lighting designer unless otherwise noted: *It's Up to You*, 1944; *Up in Central Park*, 1945; *Hallowe'en*, national, 1972; (costumes with Ray Diffen, in addition to decor and lights) *Odyssey* (re-titled *Home Sweet Homer*) national, 1976.

PRINCIPAL FILM WORK—Designer of puppets and sets, *Pete Roleum and His Cousins*, 1939; art director: *The Exile*, Universal, 1947; *Up in Central Park*, Universal, 1948; *A Midsummer Night's Dream*, Columbia, 1962.

PRINCIPAL TELEVISION WORK—Series: Art director, *Fred Waring Show*, CBS, 1953-55; *Somerset Maugham Theatre*, CBS and NBC, 1954-56; *Mr. Broadway*, CBS, 1964. Episodic: Art director, "Peer Gynt," *Hallmark Hall of Fame*, NBC, 1956. Movies: Art director, *The Pueblo Incident*, 1973.

RELATED CAREER—Instructor with Drama Department, University of Michigan, 1941; resident designer, Bucks County Playhouse, 1941; designer, Universal-International Pictures, 1946-48; guest lecturer and instructor of drama, Perdue University, 1962; instructor with Circle in the Square School of the Theatre, New York City, 1962-63; guest director, Drama Department, Carnegie Institute of Technology, 1963; professor of Theatre Arts, Brandeis University from 1965, chairman of department, 1966-67; visiting critic in stage lighting, Yale University School of Drama, 1966; lecturer, University of Michigan, Ohio University, and Purdue.

WRITINGS: BOOKS, PUBLISHED—(Contributor) "Navy on Stage," *U.S. Navy Handbook*, 1945; wrote "Scene Design for Stage and Screen" for the "Staging and Stage Design" section of the *Encyclopaedia Britannica*, 1961; *Stage Design*, 1974; wrote Broadway section of *Contemporary Stage Design, U.S.A.*, 1974.

AWARDS: *Variety* New York Drama Critics Award for set design, 1942, for *Brooklyn, U.S.A.*; Best Set Design for a Musical, Donaldson awards, 1944, for *Carmen Jones* and 1945, for *Up in Central Park*; Best Set Design, Antoinette Perry awards, 1960 for *Toys in the Attic* and 1966 for *Man of La Mancha*; Best Setting, Maharam Award, 1966, for *Man of La Mancha*; Guggenheim fellow, 1940-41.

MEMBER: United Scenic Artists of America (president, 1941-46, 1952-63), National Society of Interior Designers (national board, 1960-62), International Theatre Institute (advisory board), Society of Motion Picture Art Directors; Players Club.

SIDELIGHTS: Howard Bay was blacklisted from the film and television industries during the late 1940s and early 1950s.*

BEACHAM, Stephanie 1947-

PERSONAL: Born February 28, 1947; married John McEnery. EDUCATION: Trained for the stage with Etienne de Creux, Paris, 1964, and at the Royal Academy of Dramatic Art, 1965-67.

VOCATION: Actress.

CAREER: STAGE DEBUT—Clarice, *The Servant of Two Masters*, Liverpool Everyman Theatre, U.K., 1964. LONDON DEBUT—Jane, *The Basement*, Duchess Theatre, 1970. PRINCIPAL STAGE APPEARANCES—First Witch, *Macbeth*, Liverpool Everyman Theatre, 1964; appeared in *Monsieur Barnett*, Bristol Old Vic Theatre, 1967; Irma, *The Madwoman of Chaillot* and Louka, *Arms and the Man*, both at Oxford Playhouse, U.K., 1967-68; Ruth, *The Homecoming*, Juno, *The Tempest*, and Nora, *A Doll's House*, all at Nottingham Playhouse, U.K., 1972; Helen, *On Approval*, Theatre Royal, Haymarket, London, 1976; Eva, *Absurd Person Singular*, Crucible Theatre, Sheffield, U.K., 1977; Hubert Page, *The Singular Life of Albert Nobbs*, New End Theatre, London, 1978; Berthe, *An Audience Called Edouard*, Greenwich Theatre, London, 1978; Eugenia, *The London Cuckolds*, Royal Court Theatre, London, 1979; Margery Harnoll, *Can You Hear Me at the Back?*, Piccadilly Theatre, London, 1979.

FILM DEBUT—*The Games*, Universal, 1967. PRINCIPAL FILM APPEARANCES—*The Nightcomers*, AVCO-Embassy, 1972; *Schizo*, 1977.

PRINCIPAL TELEVISION APPEARANCES—Series: *Dynasty II: The Colbys*, ABC, 1985—; also, *Marked Personal; Call My Bluff*. Dramatic Specials: *Jane Eyre; A Sentimental Education*.

SIDELIGHTS: RECREATIONS—Making dollhouse furniture.

ADDRESSES: AGENT—Fraser and Dunlop, 91 Regent Street, London W1, England.*

*   *   *

BECK, Julian 1925-1985

PERSONAL: Born May 31, 1925, in New York City; died September 14, 1985; son of Irving (a businessman) and Mabel Lucille (a teacher; maiden name Blum) Beck; married Judith Malina (a writer, actress, producer, and director) October 30, 1948. EDUCATION: Attended Yale University and City College of New York. RELIGION: Jewish. POLITICS: "Pacifist anarchist."

VOCATION: Producer, director, designer, and actor.

CAREER: PRINCIPAL STAGE WORK—Co-founder (with Judith Malina), producer, director, and actor, Living Theatre Productions, Inc., New York City, 1947; portrayed in Living Theatre productions: The Regisseur, *Childish Jokes*, Teacher, *He Who Says Yes and He Who Says No*, and Young Man, *Dialogue of the Young Man and the Manikin;* director, *Gertrude Stein's Ladies' Voices;* designer, *The 13th God*, Cherry Lane Theatre, New York City, 1951.

With the Living Theatre, in New York City and Europe: producer, *Dr. Faustus Lights the Lights, Beyond the Mountains*, 1951; *Desire Trapped by the Tail, Ladies' Voices, Sweeney Agonistes, Faustina, Ubu Roi*, produced and appeared as Theseus, *The Heroes*, 1952;

Quant, *The Age of Anxiety*, Colonel, *The Spook Sonata*, Azrael, *Orpheus*, title role, *The Idiot King*, 1954; produced, directed, and appeared as The Director, *Tonight We Improvise*, produced and appeared as Theramenes, *Phaedra*, produced and directed, *The Young Disciple*, 1955; produced, *The Connection, Madrigal of War, All That Fall, Embers, Act without Words, I and II, Bertha, Theory of Comedy, Love's Labors*, produced, directed, and appeared as The Director, *Tonight We Improvise*, produced and directed, *Many Loves, The Cave at Machpelah*, 1959; produced, *The Devil's Mother, Faust Foutu, The Herne's Egg, Purgatory, A Full Moon in March*, produced and directed, *The Marrying Woman, The Women of Trachis*, produced and appeared as The Director, *The Election*, Shink, *In the Jungle of Cities*, 1960.

Produced, *The Mountain Giants*, produced and appeared as Peter, *Many Loves*, Ajax, *The Apple*, 1961; produced and directed, *Man Is Man*, 1962; *The Brig*, 1963; co-produced, designed, *The Brig*, Mermaid Theatre, London, 1964; produced and appeared with the Living Theatre at the Academy of Liberal Arts, West Berlin, Germany, 1964; wrote, produced, and directed, *Mysteries*, Theatre 140, Brussels, 1965; co-authored, co-directed (with Judith Malina), *Frankenstein*, Brussels, 1966; produced, *Antigone, The Maids, Mysteries*, Teatro Parioli, Rome, 1967; produced, *Mysteries and Smaller Pieces*, co-authored (with Malina) and produced, *Paradise Now*, produced, designed, and appeared in *Frankenstein*, produced and appeared as Kreon, *The Antigone of Sophokles*, Brooklyn Acadmey of Music, New York City, 1968; co-authored (with Malina) and produced, *The Legacy of Cain: Three Pilot Projects*, produced, *Rituals, Rights and Transformations*, Rio Clara, Embu, Brazil, 1971; co-authored (with Malina) and produced, *Seven Meditations on Political Sado-Masochism*, Washington Square Methodist Church, New York City, 1974; *Prometheus*, Round House, London, 1979; produced and appeared in *The Archeology of Sleep, The Antigone of Sophokles, The Yellow Methuselah* and *The One and the Many*, Joyce Theatre, New York City, 1984.

MAJOR TOURS—With the Living Theatre Repertory Company: *The Connection, Many Loves, In the Jungle of Cities*, Rome, Turin, Milan, Paris, Berlin, Frankfurt, 1961; *The Connection, In the Jungle of Cities, The Apple*, Switzerland, France, The Netherlands, Germany, Belgium, 1962; *Antigone, The Maids, Mysteries*, European cities, 1967; *Paradise Now, Mysteries and Smaller Pieces*, appeared in *Frankenstein*, Kreon, *The Antigone of Sophokles*, U.S. cities, 1971.

PRINCIPAL FILM APPEARANCES—*Narcissus*, 1957; *Living and Glorious*, 1965; *Amore, Amore*, 1966; *Agonia*, 1967; *Oedipus Rex*, 1967; *Le Compromis*, 1968; *Etre Libre*, 1968; *Paradise Now*, 1969; *Poltergeist II: The Other Side*, Metro-Goldwyn-Mayer/United Artists, 1986. Also, work appears in a filmed version of *The Brig*.

PRINCIPAL TELEVISION WORK—*The Brig*.

RELATED CAREER—Formed theatre group in Bordeaux, France, 1975.

WRITINGS: PLAYS—All with Judith Malina: *Frankenstein: A Collective Creation of the Living Theatre*, La Fiacola, 1972; *Paradise Now: A Collective Creation of the Living Theatre*, Random House, 1971; *The Legacy of Cain: Three Pilot Projects; A Collective Creation of the Living Theatre*, Belibaste, 1972; *Seven Meditations on Political Sado-Masochism: A Collective Creation of the Living Theatre*, Fag Rag, 1973; also *Six Public Acts*, and *The Money Tower*.

POEMS—*Songs of the Revolution: One to Thirty-Five,* Interim, 1963; *Twenty-One Songs of the Revolution,* April Verlag, 1969; *Songs of the Revolution: Thirty-Six to Eighty-Nine,* Union Generale d'Editions, 1974.

NON-FICTION—*Revolution and Counterrevolution,* Nuovi Argumenti, 1968; *Conversations with Julian Beck and Judith Malina,* edited by Jean-Jacques Lebel, Belfond, 1969; (with Judith Malina and Aldo Rostagno) *We, the Living,* Ballantine, 1970; *The Life of the Theatre,* City Lights, 1972; (contributor) John Lahr and Jonathan Price, editors, *The Great American Life Show,* Bantam, 1974.

AWARDS: Lola D'Annunzio Award, 1959, for outstanding contribution to Off-Broadway; Obie Awards, 1960, for *The Connection,* 1969, for direction and production, *The Brig,* and for acting, *Antigone of Sophokles,* 1975, for Best New Play, *Frankenstein;* Page One Award, Newspaper Guild, 1960; Grand Prix de Theatre des Nations Award, 1961; Prix de l'Universite Award, 1961; Creative Arts Theatre Citation, Brandeis University, 1961; Paris Critics Circle medallion, 1961; New England Theatre Conference award, 1962; Olympio Prize, 1967, for *Antigone of Sophokles;* Maharam Award, 1969, for stage design, *Frankenstein.**

*   *   *

BECKETT, Samuel   1906-

PERSONAL: Full name, Samuel Barclay Beckett; born April 13, 1906, in Dublin, Ireland; son of William Frank (a quantity surveyor) and Mary (an interpreter; maiden name, Roe) Beckett; married Suzanne Dechevaus-Dumensnil (a pianist). EDUCATION: Attended Portora Royal School, Enniskillen; Trinity College, B.A., French and Italian, 1927, M.A., 1931. MILITARY: Served in French Resistance, 1941-42, and with Irish Red Cross, 1945.

VOCATION: Writer, director, translator, and educator.

CAREER: PRINCIPAL STAGE WORK—Writer and director: *Va et Vient* (*Come and Go*), Odeon Theatre, Paris, 1966; *Waiting for Godot,* Royal Court Theatre, London, 1976; *Happy Days,* Royal Court Theatre, London, 1979.

PRINCIPAL TELEVISION WORK—Writer and director, *He, Joe,* Suddeutscher Rundfunk, West Germany, 1955.

RELATED CAREER—Teacher: Campbell College, 1927-28; English lecturer, Ecole Normale Superieure, 1928; assistant lecturer in French, Trinity College, Dublin, 1930-32.

WRITINGS: PLAYS, PRODUCED AND PUBLISHED—(All works originally written in French unless otherwise noted): *En Attendant Godot,* Theatre de Babylone, Paris, 1953, English translation by Beckett entitled *Waiting for Godot,* Coconut Grove Playhouse, Miami Beach, then John Golden Theatre, New York City, 1956, revived with an all black cast at the Ethel Barrymore Theatre, New York City, 1957, revived again at the Royal Court Theatre, London, 1976, published by Editions de Minuit, 1952, and Grove Press, 1954; *Fin de partie,* Royal Court Theatre, London, 1957, English translation by Beckett entitled *Endgame,* Cherry Lane Theatre, New York City, 1958, published by Editions de Minuit, 1957, and Grove Press, 1958; *Acte sans Paroles,* Royal Court Theatre, London, 1957, English translation by Beckett entitled *Act without Words,* Living Theatre, New York City, 1959, published

by Editions de Minuit, 1957, and Grove Press, 1958; *Krapp's Last Tape,* Royal Court Theatre, London, 1958, then Provincetown Playhouse, New York City, 1960, published in the "Evergreen Review," Volume 2, Number 5, 1958, then published with *Embers,* by Faber & Faber, 1959, then published as *Krapp's Last Tape and Other Dramatic Pieces* (including "All That Fall," "Act without Words (I)," and "Act without Words II"), Grove Press, 1960, French translation by Beckett, with Pierre Leyris and Robert Pinget, entitled *La Derniere bande* (and) *Cendres,* published by Editions de Minuit, 1959.

Happy Days, Cherry Lane Theatre, New York City, 1961, then Royal Court Theatre, London, 1979, published by Grove Press, 1961, French translation by Beckett entitled *Oh les beaux jours,* published by Editions de Minuit, 1963; *Play,* produced in Ulm, Germany, 1963, then Cherry Lane Theatre, New York City, 1964, published as *Play, and Two Short Pieces for Radio* (including "Words and Music" and "Cascando"), Faber & Faber, 1964; "Words and Music" published in "Evergreen Review," 1962, French translation by Beckett published as *Paroles et musiques,* in *Comedie et actes divers,* (including "Comedie," "Va et vient," "Dis Joe," and "Acte sans paroles II"), Editions de Minuit, 1966; *Cascando,* published in *Dublin* Magazine, 1936, "Evergreen Review," 1963, and by Faber and Faber, 1964, and Grove Press, 1968.

Kommen und Gehen, Werkstatt des Schiller Theatres, Berlin, 1965, then produced under the direction of Beckett as *Va et vient,* Odeon Theatre, Paris, France, 1966, translated by Beckett into English and entitled *Come and Go,* Peacock Theatre, Dublin, 1968, published in *Comedie et actes divers* (above) and by Calder & Boyars, 1967; "Breath," a sketch for the production *Oh, Calcutta!,* Edison Theatre, New York City, 1969, produced by itself in Glasgow, Scotland, 1969; *Not I,* Forum Theatre, Lincoln Center, New York City, 1972, then Royal Court Theatre, London, 1973.

PLAYS, UNPUBLISHED—"Eleutheria," 1947.

SCREENPLAYS—*Film,* M.K. Productions, 1966. TELEVISION PLAYS—*He, Joe,* Suddeutscher Rundfunk, West Germany, 1955, produced in English under the title, *Eh Joe,* BBC, then New York Television Theatre, 1966; also *Ghost Trio and. . .But the Clouds,* 1977. RADIO PLAYS—*All That Fall,* BBC, 1957; *Embers,* BBC, 1959; *Words and Music,* BBC, 1962; *Cascando,* France, 1963.

BOOKS—Fiction: *More Pricks than Kicks* (short stories), Chatto & Windus, 1934, Calder & Boyars, 1966; *Murphy,* Routledge and Kegan Paul, 1938, Grove Press, 1957, French translation by Beckett published by Bordas, 1947; *Molloy,* Editions de Minuit, 1951, English translation by Beckett, with Patrick Bowles, published by Grove Press, 1955, also published with an earlier fragment of *Malone Dies,* under the collective title "Two Fragments," in *transition,* Number 6, 1950; *Malone Meurt,* Editions de Minuit, 1951, English translation by Beckett entitled, *Malone Dies,* Grove Press, 1956, also published with an earlier fragment of *Malloy* under the collective title "Two Fragments" (see above); *Watt,* Olympia Press, 1953, Grove Press, 1959, rewritten and translated into French by Beckett and published by Editions de Minuit, 1968; *L'Innommable,* Editions de Minuit, 1953, English translation by Beckett entitled *The Unnamable,* Grove Press, 1958.

Nouvelles et textes pour rien (contains "L'Expulse," "Le Calmant," "la Fin," revised edition of novella originally published as "Suite" in *Les Temps Modernes,* 1946, English translation by Beckett and Richard Seaver entitled "The End" in *Merlin,* 1954, and thirteen monologues including "Text for Nothing I," "From an Abandoned Work," "Enough," "Imagination Dead Imagine," and "bing") Editions de Minuit, 1955, Calder & Boyars, 1967, published as *Short Stories and Texts for Nothing,* Grove Press, 1967; *Comment c'est,* Editions de Minuit, 1961, English translation by Beckett entitled *How It Is,* Grove Press, 1964, excerpts published in *X,* 1951, and under the title "From an Unabandoned Work," in "Evergreen Review," 1960; *Imagination morte imaginez,* Editions de Minuit, 1965, English translation by Beckett entitled *Imagination Dead Imagine,* Calder and Boyars and Grove Press (see above); *bing,* Editions de Minuit, 1966 (see above); *Assez,* Editions de Minuit, 1966; *Tete-mortes,* Editions de Minuit, 1967; *Mercier et camiers,* Grove Press, 1975; also *Premier amour,* published in French and English.

Also contributor to *transition, New Review, Evergreen Review, Contempo, Les Temps Modernes, Merlin, Spectrum,* and other periodicals.

POEMS—*Whoroscope: Poem on Time* (written in English), Hours Press, Paris, 1930; *Echo's Bones, and Other Precipitates* (written in English), Europa Press, Paris, 1935; *Collected Giedichte* (French and German languages; German translations by Eva Hesse), Limes Verlag, Wiesbaden, 1959; *Poems in English,* Calder & Boyers, 1961, Grove Press, 1962.

CRITICISM—"Dante. . .Bruno, Vico. . .Joyce" (essay on James Joyce, written in English), published in *Our Examination Round His Factification for Incamination of Work in Progress,* by Beckett, Eugene Jolas, William Carlos Williams, and others, published by Shakespeare & Co., Paris, 1929, New Directions, 1939, second edition, 1962; *Proust* (written in English), Chatto & Windus, 1931, Grove Press, 1957; (with Georges Duthuit) *Proust, and Three Dialogues* (new criticism; not the same as *Proust* above; "Three Dialogues" first published in *transition,* number 5, 1949), Calder & Boyers, 1965.

TRANSLATIONS—(With Alfred Peron) James Joyce, "Anna Livia Plurabelle" (section of *Finnegans Wake*), published in *Nouvelle Revue Francaise,* May, 1931, then in *Souvenirs de James Joyce,* by Philippe Soupault, Charlot (Algiers), 1943; Paul Eluard, "Seven Poems," published in *Thorns of Thunder,* edited by G. Reavey, published jointly by Europa Press and Stanley Nott (London), 1936; (with Jean Wahl) Marc Chagall and Jean Wahl, *Illustrations for the Bible,* Harcourt, 1956; Octavio Paz, compiler, *Anthology of Mexican Poetry,* preface by C.M. Bowra, Indiana University Press, 1958; Robert Pinget, *The Old Tune* (translation of the play *La Manivelle;* bilingual text), Editions de Minuit, 1960, published in *Three Plays,* by Robert Pinget, Hill & Wang, 1966; (with others) Alain Bosquet, *Selected Poems,* New Directions, 1963.

AWARDS: Best Poem Concerning Time, Hours Press Award, Paris, 1930, for *Whoroscope;* Italia Prize, 1957, for *All That Fall,* and 1959, for *Embers;* Obie Awards: Best New Play, 1958, for *Endgame,* 1964, for *Play,* Distinguished Play, 1960, for *Krapp's Last Tape,* Best Foreign Play, 1962, for *Happy Days,* also 1973, for *Not I;* Prix Formentor, 1959; co-recipient (with Jorge Luis Borges), International Publishers Prize, 1961, for literary accomplishment; Nobel Prize for Literature, 1969. Honorary degrees: Doctor of Literature, Trinity College, Dublin, 1959.

MEMBER: American Academy of Arts and Sciences.

ADDRESSES: AGENT—Faber and Faber, Ltd., Three Queen Square, London WC1, England.*

ED BEGLEY, JR.

BEGLEY, Ed, Jr.   1949-

PERSONAL: Born September 16, 1949, in Hollywood, CA; son of Edward J. (an actor) and Allene (an actress; maiden name, Sanders) Begley; married Ingrid Taylor, October 31, 1976; children: Amanda. EDUCATION: Attended Valley College; trained for the stage with Peggy Fuery. POLITICS: Democrat. RELIGION: Roman Catholic.

VOCATION: Actor and comedian.

CAREER: TELEVISION DEBUT—Marv, *My Three Sons,* CBS, 1967. PRINCIPAL TELEVISION APPEARANCES—Series: Lieutenant Robert W. Chapman, *Roll Out,* CBS, 1973-74; Doctor Victor Erlich, *St. Elsewhere,* NBC, 1982—.

Episodic: *Mary Hartman, Mary Hartman,* 1975; host, *Saturday Night Live,* NBC, 1984.

FILM DEBUT—Lester, *Stay Hungry,* United Artists, 1975. PRINCIPAL FILM APPEARANCES—*Transylvania 6-5000,* New World, 1985.

RELATED CAREER—As a stand-up comic, has appeared at the Troubadour, the Ice House, the Bottom Line, and Max's Kansas City.

AWARDS: Emmy Award nominations, 1982, 1984, 1985, all for *St. Elsewhere;* Golden Globe Award nomination, 1986, for *St. Elsewhere.*

MEMBER: Academy of Television Arts and Sciences, Academy of

Motion Picture Arts and Sciences, Society of Motion Picture and Television Engineers.

ADDRESSES: OFFICE—760 N. La Cienega Blvd., Los Angeles, CA 90069. AGENT—Belson and Klass, 211 S. Beverly Drive, Beverly Hills, CA 90212.

*   *   *

BENNETT, Joan   1910-

PERSONAL: Born February 27, 1910, in Palisades, NJ; daughter of Richard and Adrienne (Morrison) Bennett; married John Marion Fox, 1926 (divorced, 1928); married Gene Markey (a writer), March 16, 1932 (divorced, 1937); married Walter Wanger (a producer), 1940 (divorced, 1965); married David Wilde, February 14, 1978; children: (first marriage) Diana; (second marriage) Melinda; (third marriage) Stephanie, Shelley. EDUCATION: Attended St. Margaret's School, CT and L'Hermitage, Versailles, France.

VOCATION: Actress and writer.

CAREER: BROADWAY DEBUT—Daisy, *Jarnegan*, Longacre Theatre, September, 1928. LONDON DEBUT—Edith Lambert, *Never Too Late*, Prince of Wales Theatre, September, 1963. PRINCIPAL STAGE APPEARANCES—Soledad, *The Pirate*, Biltmore Theatre, New York City, 1928; Mother, *Love Me Little*, Helen Hayes Theatre, New York City, 1958; Edith Lambert, *Never Too Late*, Coconut Grove Theatre, Miami, FL, 1963; appeared with the

JOAN BENNETT

Bucks County Playhouse, New Hope, PA, 1972-73; Jessica, *Janus*, Royal Poinciana Playhouse, Palm Beach, FL, 1975.

Also appeared in *Fallen Angels, Jane, The Man Who Came to Dinner, The Boy Friend*, and *Butterflies Are Free*.

MAJOR TOURS—All U.S. cities: *Stage Door*, 1937; Susan, *Susan and God*, 1948 and 1951; Gillian Holroyd, *Bell, Book and Candle*, 1952-53; Film Star, *Best Foot Forward*, 1953; Alice Walters, *Anniversary Waltz*, 1956; Jessica, *Janus*, 1956-57; Dolly Fabian, *Once More with Feeling*, 1959; Katherine Dougherty, *The Pleasure of His Company*, 1960-61.

FILM DEBUT—*Bulldog Drummond*, 1929. PRINCIPAL FILM APPEARANCES—*Disraeli*, 1929; *Crazy That Way*, 1930; *Doctors' Wives*, 1931; *The Careless Lady*, 1932; *Arizona to Broadway*, 1933; *Little Women*, RKO, 1933; *The Man Who Reclaimed His Head*, 1934; *Mississippi*, 1935; *Big Brown Eyes*, 1936; *Artists and Models Abroad*, 1938; Jerry Stokes, *Man Hunt*, 1941; *Confirm or Deny*, 1941; *Reckless Moment*, 1942; Alice Reed, *The Woman in the Window*, 1944; Kitty March, *Scarlet Street*, Universal, 1945; *The Macomber Affair*, 1947; Celia, *Secret Beyond the Door*, Universal, 1948; *Hollow Triumph* (also known as *The Scar*), 1948; *For Heaven's Sake*, 1950; *Father of the Bride*, Metro-Goldwyn-Mayer (MGM), 1950; *Father's Little Dividend*, MGM, 1951; *The Guy who Came Back*, 1951; *Highway Dragnet*, 1954; Amelie Ducotel, *We're No Angels*, Paramount, 1955; Peg Blain, *Navy Wife*, Allied Artists, 1956; Marion Groves, *There's Always Tomorrow*, Universal, 1956; *Moby Dick*, Warner Brothers, 1956; *Desire in the Dust*, Twentieth Century-Fox, 1960; *The Pursuit of Happiness*, Columbia, 1971; Miss Blank, *Suspiria*, Twentieth Century-Fox, 1977. Also appeared in *Three Live Ghosts*.

TELEVISION DEBUT—1949. PRINCIPAL TELEVISION APPEARANCES—Series: Mary Blake, *Too Young to Go Steady*, NBC, 1959; Elizabeth, Flora, and Naomi Collins, *Dark Shadows*, ABC, 1966. Episodic: *Danger*, CBS, 1950; *Somerset Maugham's TV Theatre*, CBS, 1950; *Nash Airflyte Theatre*, CBS, 1950; *Ford Television Theatre*, NBC, 1952; Lorraine Sheldon, "The Man Who Came to Dinner," *The Best of Broadway*, CBS, 1955; *Playhouse 90*, CBS, 1956; *Pursuit*, CBS, 1958.

Pilots: Grace Graves, *Junior Miss*, 1957; Claire Ramsey, *Gidget Gets Married*, 1972. Movies: Aunt Alexandra, *The Eyes of Charles Sand*, 1972; Mrs. Graham, *Suddenly Love*, 1978; Rag Lady, *This House Possessed*, 1980; *Divorce Wars*, 1981. Specials: *The Spencer Tracy Legacy*, 1986.

RELATED CAREER—Vice-president and treasurer of Diana Productions, 1945-48.

WRITINGS: BOOKS—*How to Be Attractive*, 1951; (with Lois Kibbee) *The Bennett Playbill*, 1970.

ADDRESSES: HOME—67 Chase Road, Scarsdale, NY 10583.

*   *   *

BERG, Greg

PERSONAL: Reared in Akron and Cleveland, OH. EDUCATION: Trained for the stage at the Harvey Lembeck Comedy Workshop.

VOCATION: Actor and comedian.

GREG BERG

CAREER: PRINCIPAL TELEVISION APPEARANCES—Episodic: Billy, *Knots Landing*, CBS; *Days of Our Lives*, NBC; also *On the Air with Roger and Roger.*

PRINCIPAL TELEVISION WORK—Series: Voice over work on *Dallas*, CBS, *The A Team*, NBC, *Fame*, syndicated, *Magnum P.I.*, CBS, *Solid Gold*, syndicated; supplies voices for Fozzie and Scooter on *Jim Henson's Muppet Babies*, CBS.

PRINCIPAL FILM WORK—Voice over, *Revenge of the Nerds*, Twentieth Century-Fox, 1984.

PRINCIPAL STAGE APPEARANCES—Mr. Shears, *Finian's Rainbow*, Akron, OH; *Butterscotch*, Hollywood, CA; also comedy sketches at N.O.T.E. Theatre, Los Angeles, CA.

PRINCIPAL RADIO WORK—Series regular, *Rick Dees Weekly Top 40*, Los Angeles, CA.

RELATED CAREER—As a comedian, has appeared at the Comedy Store, the Improvisation, the Laff Stop, the Masquers Club, and Disneyland, all in Los Angeles.

MEMBER: Screen Actors Guild, American Federation of Television and Radio Artists.

SIDELIGHTS: From material supplied by Greg Berg, *CTFT* learned that he is a master of over one hundred voices and impressions and at least thirteen dialects.

ADDRESSES: AGENT—c/o Bob Colvin, International Creative

Management, 8899 Beverly Blvd., Los Angeles, CA 90048. PUBLICIST—Nan Herst Public Relations, 8733 Sunset Blvd., Suite 103, Los Angeles, CA 90069.

*   *   *

BERGESE, Micha   1945-

PERSONAL: Born Michael Bergese, February 19, 1945, in Munich, West Germany; son of Hans (a professor of music) and Brigitte (a movement teacher; maiden name, Fuchs) Bergese; married Rebecca Neil (a costume designer); children: Jocasta. EDUCATION: Attended Andrew Hardie Ballet School, 1967-68; London School of Contemporary Dance, 1968-69.

VOCATION: Dancer, choreographer, and teacher.

CAREER: PRINCIPAL STAGE APPEARANCES—With the London Contemporary Dance Theatre, danced in the following productions between 1970-73: *Stages, People Alone, Tiger Balm, Cold, Hunter of Angels, Changing Your Mind,* and *Diversion of Angels.* Also danced with the London Contemporary Dance Theatre, 1975-76.

PRINCIPAL STAGE WORK—Choreographer: Workshops with the X Group of the London Contemporary Dance Theatre for the ICES Contemporary Music Festival, 1970-73; *Hinterland*, London Contemporary Dance Theatre, 1974; *Da Capo Al Fine*, London Contemporary Dance Theatre, 1976; *El Amor Brujo*, Cycles Dance Company, 1976; *Nema* and *When Summer's Breath*, both with the

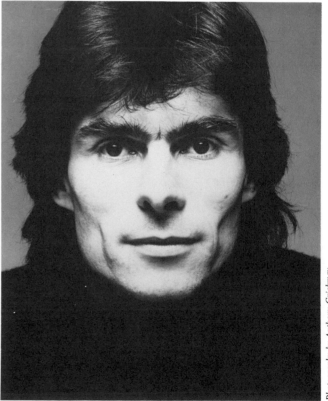

Photography by Anthony Crickmay

MICHA BERGESE

London Contemporary Dance Theatre, 1977; *Act of Waiting,* Junction Dance Company, 1977; *Box* and *Solo Ride,* both with the London Contemporary Dance Theatre, 1978; *Changes,* Ballet Rambert, 1979; *Scene Shift,* London Contemporary Dance Theatre, 1979; *18 Fifty-Nine Second Pieces* and *Underground,* both with the Extemporary Dance Company, 1979.

Some Dance and Some Duet, London Contemporary Dance Theatre, 1980; *Chasing Rainbows,* Manchester, U.K., 1980; *Telos* for deaf dancers in Stuttgart, Germany, 1980; *Of Clocks and Clouds,* video dance project, London School of Contemporary Dance, 1980; *Ghost Dances,* Mantis Dance Company, 1980; *Undercurrents,* Jazzart, Cape Town, South Africa, 1981; *Social Life,* East Anglian Dance Theatre, 1981; *Encore,* Jumpers Dance Company, 1981; *Dots and Dashes,* Mantis Dance Theatre, 1981; *Transit Breakdown,* solo work for Lise Ferner, 1982; *Suite Italienne,* City Contemporary Dance Company, Hong Kong, 1982; untitled piece for Hovik Ballet, Oslo, Norway, 1982; *Pick Up,* Mantis Dance Theatre, 1982; *Crickets,* Edinburgh Fringe Festival and ICA Theatre, London, 1983; *Performing Clothes,* ICA Theatre and Mantis Dance Theatre, 1983; *Stage 7,* Mantis Dance Theatre, 1983; *Mouth of the Night,* Mantis Dance Theatre, 1984; *Faust,* Mantis Dance Theatre, 1985; also producer, *Scenes from the Life of Beethoven,* 1986.

MAJOR TOURS—With the London Contemporary Dance Theatre, international tours 1975-76; Mantis Dance Theatre, international tours, 1980-85.

PRINCIPAL FILM WORK—The huntsman, *The Company of Wolves,* Cannon, 1985; Malinov, *Zina,* 1985.

PRINCIPAL TELEVISION WORK—Dancer, *People Alone,* BBC, 1973; *Let's Dance,* BBC, 1973; *Kontakion,* ITV, 1974; *Playaway,* BBC, 1974; *Ballet Workshop,* BBC, 1974; choreographer, *Love of Three Oranges,* BBC Opera production, 1979; performer and choreographer, "Signs," *Riverside Show,* BBC2, 1983; performer and choreographer of a four part series, *Map of Dreams,* Channel 4-TV, London, 1986; "A Walk in the European Countryside," from *Scenes from the Life of Beethoven,* Channel 4-TV, London, 1986.

RELATED CAREER Teacher with the London Contemporary Dance Theatre, 1975-79, associate choreographer, London Contemporary Dance Theatre, 1976-79; executive director and founder, Mantis Dance Theatre, 1980—.

MEMBER: British Actors' Equity Association.

ADDRESSES: OFFICE—1/2 Alfred Place, London WC1, England. AGENT—Kate Feast Management, 43A Princess Road, Regents Park, London NW1, England.

*   *   *

BERGHOF, Herbert   1909-

PERSONAL: Born September 13, 1909, in Vienna, Austria; son of Paul (a railroad station-master) and Regina Berghof; married Alice Hermes (an acting teacher; divorced); married Uta Hagen (an actress and acting teacher). EDUCATION: Attended University of Vienna; trained for the stage at the Vienna State Academy of Dramatic Art, and studied with Alexander Moissi and Max Reinhardt.

VOCATION: Actor, director, and teacher.

CAREER: STAGE DEBUT—*Don Carlos,* Duetsches Volkstheatre, Vienna, Austria, September, 1927. BROADWAY DEBUT—Director, *From Vienna,* for the Refugee Artists Group at the Music Box Theatre, June 20, 1939. PRINCIPAL STAGE APPEARANCES—Resident member, St. Gallen Repertory Company, Zurich, Switzerland, 1927-29; member of Volkstheatre, Vienna, 1929-30; appeared at the Salzburg Festivals, Austria, 1933-38; performed in more than one hundred twenty plays in Vienna, Zurich, Paris, Berlin and at the Salzburg Festivals, including: Romeo, *Romeo and Juliet,* Louis Dubedat, *The Doctor's Dilemma,* title role, *Hamlet,* Death, *Everyman,* Oswald, *Ghosts,* Orlando, *As You Like It,* Marchbanks, *Candida,* title role, *Marius,* title role, *The Unknown Soldier;* also appeared in *Journey's End, All God's Chillun Got Wings, Crime for Crime, Six Characters in Search of an Author,* and *An American Tragedy.*

Reunion in New York, Little Theatre, New York City, 1940; Captain Miller, *Somewhere in France,* National Theatre, Washington, DC, 1941; Fool, *King Lear* and Kummerer, *The Criminals,* both at the New School for Social Research, New York City, 1941; title role, *Nathan the Wise,* Shubert Theatre, New York City, 1942; Tieck, *Winter Soldiers,* Studio Theatre, New York City, 1942; Panin, *The Russian People,* Guild Theatre, New York City, 1942; Otto, *The Innocent Voyage,* Belasco Theatre, New York City, 1943; Hakim, *Oklahoma!,* St. James Theatre, New York City, 1944; Jacobowski, *Jacobowski and the Colonel,* Martin Beck Theatre, New York City, 1944; Gustav Eberson, *The Man Who Had All the Luck,* Forrest Theatre, New York City, 1944; Maurice, *Beggars Are Coming to Town,* Coronet Theatre, New York City, 1945.

Captain Karel Palivec, *Temper the Wind,* Playhouse Theatre, New York City, 1946; Dmitri Savalev, *The Whole World Over,* Biltmore Theatre, New York City, 1947; Pastor Manders, *Ghosts* and Judge Brack, *Hedda Gabler,* both at the Cort Theatre, New York City, 1948; Bartholdi, *Miss Liberty,* Imperial Theatre, New York City, 1949; title role, *Torquato Tasso,* Barbizon Plaza, New York City, 1949; Dr. Wangel, *The Lady from the Sea,* Fulton Theatre, New York City, 1950; the Critic, *The Guardsman,* Erlanger Theatre, Buffalo, NY, 1951; Prince Mikail Alexandrovitch Ouratieff, *Tovarich,* City Center, New York City, 1952; Mr. Miller, *The Deep Blue Sea,* Morosco Theatre, New York City, 1952; appeared in *Michael and Lavinia,* Theatre-by-the-Sea, Matunuck, RI, 1954; M. Prunelles, *Cyprienne,* Norwich Summer Theatre, CT, 1955; directed and appeared in *The Affairs of Anatol,* for the Ann Arbor Dramatic Festival, MI, at the Lydia Mendelssohn Theatre, 1957; Henry Wirz, *The Andersonville Trial,* Henry Miller's Theatre, New York City, 1959; title role, *Krapp's Last Tape,* Provincetown Playhouse, New York City, 1960; title role, *Enrico IV,* Arena Stage, Washington, DC, 1964; Edward Teller, *In the Matter of J. Robert Oppenheimer,* Vivian Beaumont Theatre, New York City, 1969.

MAJOR TOURS—Jean, *Dr. Lazare's Pharmacy,* U.S. and Canadian cities, 1945-46.

PRINCIPAL STAGE WORK—Director: *The Melody That Got Lost,* Volles Theatre, Vienna, Austria, 1929; (with Ezra Stone) *Reunion in New York,* Little Theatre, New York City, 1940; *The Key,* Old Knickerbocker Music Hall, New York City, 1947; *Rip Van Winkle,* City Center, New York City, 1947; *Protective Custody,* Ambassador Theatre, New York City, 1956; *Waiting for Godot,* John Golden Theatre, New York City, 1956, then with an all black cast at the Ethel Barrymore Theatre, New York City, 1957; *The Affairs of Anatol,* Ann Arbor Festival, MI, 1957; *The Infernal Machine,* Phoenix Theatre, New York City, 1958; *Twelfth Night,* Cambridge Drama Festival, Boston, 1959; *The Queen and the Rebels,* Bucks County Playhouse, New Hope, PA, 1959; *Men, Women and Angels,* Vancouver, Canada, 1961; *Do You Know the Milky Way?,* Vancouver, Canada, then Billy Rose Theatre, New York City, 1961; *This Side of Paradise,* Sheridan Square Playhouse, New York City, 1962; *The Sponsor,* Peachtree Playhouse, Atlanta, GA, 1975; *Poor Murder* (his own translation), Ethel Barrymore Theatre, New York City, 1976.

Also directed for the Herbert Berghof Playwright's Foundation: *Tomorrow, Seize the Day, Democracy and Esther, Kaspar.*

PRINCIPAL FILM APPEARANCES—*Assignment Paris,* Columbia, 1952; *Diplomatic Courier,* Twentieth Century-Fox, 1952; *Five Fingers,* Twentieth Century-Fox, 1952; *Red Planet Mars,* United Artists, 1952; *Cleopatra,* Twentieth Century-Fox, 1963; *Fraulein,* Twentieth Century-Fox, 1963; *Harry & Tonto,* Twentieth Century-Fox, 1974.

PRINCIPAL TELEVISION APPEARANCES—Episodic: "For Whom the Bell Tolls," *Playhouse 90,* CBS, 1959; "Chez Rouge," *Desilu Playhouse,* NBC, 1965; also appeared on *Producer's Showcase* and *Kraft Television Theatre,* NBC. Dramatic Specials: *And the Bones Come Together,* ABC, 1973. Movies: *Kojak: The Belarus File,* CBS, 1985.

PRINCIPAL RADIO WORK—Has performed on *Report to the Nation, The Goldbergs,* and *Norman Corwin Presents.*

RELATED CAREER—Acting teacher, New York City: New School for Social Research, American Theatre Wing, Neighborhood Playhouse, Columbia University; founder and teacher, Herbert Berghof Studio, 1946—, founder, HB Playwright's Foundation, 1964—.

WRITINGS: TRANSLATIONS—*Poor Murder,* Ethel Barrymore Theatre, New York City, 1976.

MEMBER: Actors' Equity Association, American Federation of Television and Radio Artists, Screen Actors Guild.

SIDELIGHTS: FAVORITE ROLES—Hamlet, Oedipus, Dubedat, from *The Doctor's Dilemma,* Nathan, from *Nathan the Wise.*

ADDRESSES: OFFICE—27 Washington Square, New York, NY 10014; 120 Bank Street, New York, NY 10014.*

*			*			*

BERNHARD, Harvey 1924-

PERSONAL: Born March 5, 1924, in Seattle, WA. EDUCATION: Attended Stanford University.

VOCATION: Producer.

CAREER: PRINCIPAL FILM WORK—Producer: *The Mack,* Cinerama, 1973; *The Omen,* Twentieth Century-Fox, 1976; *Damien: Omen II,* 1978; *The Final Conflict,* Twentieth Century-Fox, 1981; *The Beast Within,* Metro-Goldwyn-Mayer, 1981; *Ladyhawke,* Warner Brothers, 1985; *The Goonies,* Warner Brothers, 1985.

RELATED CAREER—Entertainer, Last Frontier Hotel, Las Vegas, NV, 1950; production partner with Sandy Howard, 1958-60; vice-president of production, David L. Wolper Productions, 1961-68; vice-president of production, MPC, 1968-70; president, Harvey Bernhard Entertainment, Inc.

NON-RELATED CAREER—Formerly a real estate executive in Seattle, 1947-50.*

*			*			*

BERNSTEIN, Elmer 1922-

PERSONAL: Born April 4, 1922, in New York, NY; son of Edward and Selma (Feinstein) Bernstein; married Pearl Glusman, December 21, 1946 (divorced); married Eve Adamson, October 25, 1965; children: (first marriage) Peter Matthew, Gregory Eames; (second marriage) Emily Adamson, Elizabeth Campbell. EDUCATION: Attended Walden School, Juilliard School, and New York Universtiy. MILITARY: U.S. Army Air Force, radio unit.

VOCATION: Composer and conductor.

CAREER: PRINCIPAL FILM WORK—Composer and conductor: *Sudden Fear,* 1952; *The Man with the Golden Arm,* United Artists, 1956; *The Ten Commandments,* Paramount, 1957; *The Sweet Smell of Success,* United Artists, 1957; *Desire Under the Elms,* Paramount, 1958; *Some Came Running,* Metro-Goldwyn-Mayer (MGM), 1959; *From the Terrace,* Twentieth Century-Fox, 1960; *The Magnificent Seven,* United Artists, 1960; *The Birdman of Alcatraz,* United Artists, 1962; *Walk on the Wild Side,* Columbia, 1962; *To Kill a Mockingbird,* Universal, 1963; *The Caretakers,* United Artists, 1963; *The Carpetbaggers,* Paramount, 1964; *Love with a Proper Stranger,* Paramount, 1964; *Baby the Rain Must Fall,* Columbia, 1965; *The Sons of Katie Elder,* Paramount, 1965; *Hallelujah Trail,* United Artists, 1965; *The Reward,* Twentieth Century-Fox, 1965; *Seven Women,* MGM, 1966; *Cast a Giant Shadow,* United Artists, 1966; *Hawaii,* United Artists, 1966; *Thoroughly Modern Millie,* Universal, 1967; *True Grit,* Paramount, 1969.

Cahill: U.S. Marshall, Warner Brothers, 1973; *McQ,* Warner Brothers, 1974; *Gold,* Allied Artists, 1974; *The Trial of Billy Jack,* Taylor-Laughlin, 1974; *Report to the Commissioner,* United Artists, 1975; *From Noon Till Three,* United Artists, 1976; *The Shootist,* Paramount, 1976; *National Lampoon's Animal House,* Universal, 1978; *Blood Brothers,* Warner Brothers, 1979; *Meatballs,* Paramount, 1979; *Airplane!,* Paramount, 1980; *Stripes,* Columbia, 1981; *An American Werewolf in London,* Universal, 1981; *Honky Tonk Freeway,* Universal, 1981; *Going Ape,* Paramount, 1981; *The Chosen,* Twentieth Century-Fox, 1982; *Five Days One Summer,* Warner Brothers, 1982; *Airplane II: The Sequel,* Paramount, 1982; *Spacehunter,* Columbia, 1983; *Class,* Orion, 1983; *Trading Places,* Paramount, 1983; *Ghostbusters,* Columbia, 1984; *The Black Cauldron,* Buena Vista, 1984; *Spies Like Us,* 1985; *Legal Eagles,* Universal, 1986; *The Three Amigos,* Orion, 1986. Also, *Sarah* and *Genocide.*

PRINCIPAL TELEVISION WORK—Specials: Composer and conductor—*The Race for Space,* parts I and II; *D-Day; The Making of the President: 1960; Hollywood and the Stars; Voyage of the Brigantine Yankee; The Crucifixion of Jesus.* Movies: Composer and conductor—*Little Women,* 1978; *The Guyana Tragedy: The*

Story of Jim Jones, 1980. Series: Composer and conductor—*Owen Marshall,* ABC, 1971-74; *The Rookies,* ABC, 1972-76; *Serpico,* NBC, 1976-77; *Ellery Queen,* CBS, 1983-84; also *Gulag.*

RELATED CAREER—Employed with the United Nations radio department after military service; currently, music director, Valley Symphony Orchestra, CA.

AWARDS: Motion Picture Exhibitors Laurel Awards, 1956, 1957, 1962; Golden Globe Award, Hollywood Foreign Press, 1962, for *To Kill a Mockingbird;* Best Music Written for Television, Emmy Award, 1964, for *Making of the President;* Best Original Score, Academy Award, 1968, for *Thoroughly Modern Millie.*

MEMBER: Academy of Motion Picture Arts and Sciences (first vice-president, 1963—; co-chairman, music branch), Screen Composers Association (director), Composers and Lyricists Guild of America (president, 1982—), National Academy of Recording Arts and Sciences (director), Young Musicians Foundation (president); Thalians Club (vice president, 1959-62).

ADDRESSES: OFFICE—c/o Academy of Motion Picture Arts and Sciences, 8949 Wilshire Blvd., Beverly Hills, CA 90211.*

*   *   *

BERTOLUCCI, Bernardo   1940-

PERSONAL: Born March 16, 1940, in Parma, Italy; son of Attilio (a poet, film critic, and teacher) and Ninetta Bertolucci; married Clare Peptoe. EDUCATION: Attended University of Rome, 1960-62. POLITICS: Communist.

VOCATION: Screenwriter, director, and poet.

CAREER: FIRST FILM WORK—Assistant director, *Accatone,* 1962. PRINCIPAL FILM WORK—Director and (with Pier Paolo Pasolini and Sergio Citti) co-screenwriter, *La commare secca (The Grim Reaper),* Cinematografica Cervi, 1962; director and (with Gianni Amico) co-screenwriter, *Prima della rivoluzione (Before the Revolution),* Iride Cinematografica, 1964; director and screenwriter, "Il fico infruttuoso" (included in the motion picture *Vangela 70*), Castoro Films, 1967; director and (with Amico) co-screenwriter, *Partner,* Red Films, 1968.

Director and (with Marilu Paolini and Edoardo De Gregorio) co-screenwriter, *La strategia del ragno (The Spider's Strategy),* Red Films, 1970; director *Il conformista (The Conformist),* Mars Film/Marianne Productions/Maran Films, 1970; director and (with Arcalli) co-screenwriter, *Ultimo tango a Parigi (Last Tango in Paris),* United Artists, 1973; director and (with Arcalli and Giuseppe Bertolucci) co-screenwriter, *Novecento (1900),* Paramount, 1977; director and (with A. and G. Bertolucci) co-screenwriter, *La luna* (released in the U.S. as *Luna*), Twentieth Century-Fox, 1979; director, *Tragedio dell uomo ridiculo (Tragedy of a Ridiculous Man),* Fiction Cinematografica, 1981, and Ladd, 1982; also director, *The Last Emperor,* filmed in Red China.

PRINCIPAL TELEVISION WORK—Writer and director: *La via del petrolio,* (an omnibus containing "Le origini," "Il viaggio," and "Attraverso L'Europe,") RAI-TV, 1965-66; *I poveri muoino prima,* 1971; also *La salute e malata* (film about health reforms), for the Italian Communist Party, 1972.

RELATED CAREER—Lecturer, Museum of Modern Art, 1969; advisory committee, Orson Welles Motion Picture Directorial Achievement Award, 1987.

WRITINGS: PLAYS, PRODUCED—"Agonia" (from the production *Amore e Rabbia,* title means "Love and Anger"), with the Living Theatre, 1967. SCREENPLAYS—(In addition to those listed above; with Sergio Leone) *Once Upon a Time in the West,* Paramount, 1968; also *Ballata de un milliardo.*

POEMS—*In cerca del mistero (In Search of Mystery),* Longanesi, Milan, 1962. Also contributor of poems to Italian periodicals.

AWARDS: Premio Viareggio, 1962, for *In cerca del mistero;* Young Critics Award, Cannes Film Festival Award, and Max Ophuls Award, all 1964, for *Prima della revoluzione;* Best Director, National Society of Film Critics Award and Best Screenplay, Academy Award nomination, both 1971, for *Il conformista (The Conformist);* Raoul Levy Prize and Silver Ribbon Award, both 1973, for *Last Tango in Paris.*

ADDRESSES: OFFICE—Via del Babuino 51, Rome, Italy.*

*   *   *

BICKFORD, David   1953-

PERSONAL: Born September 25, 1953, in New Britain, CT; son of John Herbert (an engineer) and Anne Rosie (an architect; maiden name, Chalmers) Bickford; married Kazumi Tanaka (a musical manager), July 14, 1984. EDUCATION: Wesleyan University, B.A., 1975; trained for the stage at Herbert Berghof Studio with Bill Hickey; also studied with Warren Robertson, Clyde Vinson, and Paul Sills.

VOCATION: Actor, writer, composer, and magician.

CAREER: STAGE DEBUT—Mute, *The Fantasticks,* Sharon Playhouse, Sharon, CT, 1976, for ten performances. OFF-BROADWAY DEBUT—Policeman, *Poison or Petrification,* Festival Theatre Foundation, 1977. PRINCIPAL STAGE APPEARANCES—Alyoshka, *The Lower Depths,* Spectrum Theatre, New York City, 1981; Snodgrass, *Gethsemene Springs,* Spectrum Theatre, New York City, 1981; Lorenzo, *Money Back Guarantee,* Quaigh Theatre, New York City, 1982.

MAJOR TOURS—Magician, comic, and pianist, with Le Clique Theatrical Company, New York City, Atlantic City, NJ, Las Vegas, Los Angeles, and other U.S. cities, as well as Canada, Bermuda, Barbados, 1980—.

PRINCIPAL CABARET APPEARANCES—*Seasoned Woman in the Salad of Life,* at Don't Tell Mama and the Duplex, both New York City, 1983-85.

FILM DEBUT—Extra, *Willie and Phil,* Twentieth Century-Fox, 1980. PRINCIPAL FILM APPEARANCES—*Ragtime,* Paramount, 1981; Rojax's son-in-law, *Seize the Day,* Cannon, 1987; *Radio Days,* Orion, 1987.

TELEVISION DEBUT—Magician, *Bob and Ray Special,* PBS, 1975. PRINCIPAL TELEVISION APPEARANCES—Series: Dick Entwhistle, *The Edge of Night,* ABC, 1979; George, *The Guiding Light,* CBS, 1980-84.

DAVID BICKFORD

WRITINGS: PLAYS, PRODUCED—*Terrorist in a Teapot,* Theatre Matrix, New York City, 1982; (with Susan McCarthy) *Revenge in C-Minor,* 1987. COMPOSITIONS—Scores: *Snake in the Garden,* T.O.M.I. Theatre, New York City, 1977; (with Shelby Bufford) *Victory Girls,* Red Parrot Theatre, New York City, 1983.

MEMBER: American Federation of Television and Radio Artists, Actors' Equity Association, Screen Actors Guild, Society of America's Magicians, American Federation of Musicians.

SIDELIGHTS: David Bickford told *CTFT* that he began his performing career as a magician at age three.

ADDRESSES: OFFICE—P.O. Box 252, Madison Square Station, New York, NY 10159.

*   *   *

BILLINGTON, Ken 1946-

PERSONAL: Born December 29, 1946, in White Plains, NY; son of Kenneth Arthur (an automobile dealer) and Ruth (Roane) Billington. EDUCATION: Studied at the Lester Polakov Studio and Form of Stage Design. RELIGION: Presbyterian.

VOCATION: Lighting designer.

CAREER: FIRST STAGE WORK—Lighting designer, *Carnival,* Berkshire Playhouse, Stockbridge, MA, 1965. FIRST OFF-BROAD-

WAY STAGE WORK—Lighting designer, *Fortune and Men's Eyes,* Stage 73, 1969. FIRST LONDON STAGE WORK—Lighting designer, *Sweeney Todd,* Drury Lane Theatre, 1980. PRINCIPAL STAGE WORK—Lighting designer, Broadway productions, all New York City: *The Visit, Chemin de Fer,* and *Holiday,* all Barrymore Theatre, 1973; *Bad Habits,* Booth Theatre, 1974; *Hosanna,* Bijou Theatre, 1974; *Love for Love* and *The Rules of the Game,* both Helen Hayes Theatre, 1974; *The Hashish Club,* Bijou Theatre, 1974; *Member of the Wedding* and *Rodgers and Hart,* both Helen Hayes Theatre, 1975; *The Skin of Our Teeth,* Mark Hellinger Theatre, 1975; *Sweet Bird of Youth,* Harkness Theatre, 1975.

Continuing on Broadway: *Wheelbarrow Closers,* Bijou Theatre, 1976; *Checking Out,* Longacre Theatre, 1976; *Fiddler on the Roof,* Winter Garden Theatre, 1976; *She Loves Me,* Town Hall, 1977; *Side by Side by Sondheim,* Music Box Theatre, 1977; *Knickerbocker Holiday,* Town Hall, 1977; *Ethel Merman and Mary Martin Together on Broadway,* Winter Garden Theatre, 1977; *Some of My Best Friends,* Longacre Theatre, 1977; *Do You Turn Somersaults?,* 46th Street Theatre, 1978; *On the Twentieth Century,* St. James Theatre, 1978; *Working,* 46th Street Theatre, 1978; *Sweeney Todd,* Uris Theatre, 1979; *Lerner and Loewe: A Very Special Evening,* Winter Garden Theatre, 1979; *The Madwoman of Central Park West,* Princess Theatre, 1979; *But Never Jam Today,* Longacre Theatre, 1979.

On Broadway: *Happy New Year,* Morosco Theatre, 1980; *Perfectly Frank,* Helen Hayes Theatre, 1980; *Copperfield,* American National Theatre Academy (ANTA) Theatre, 1981; *Wally's Cafe,* Brooks Atkinson Theatre, 1981; *My Fair Lady,* Uris Theatre, 1981; *Fiddler on the Roof,* New York State Theatre, 1981; *A Talent for Murder,* Biltmore Theatre, 1981; *Blues in the Night,* Rialto Theatre, New York City, 1982; *A Doll's Life,* Mark Hellinger Theatre, 1982; *Foxfire,* Barrymore Theatre, 1982; *Shirley MacLaine on Broadway,* Gershwin Theatre, 1984; *Play Memory,* Longacre Theatre, 1984; *End of the World,* Music Box Theatre, 1984; *The Three Musketeers,* Broadway Theatre, 1984; *Home Front,* Royale Theatre, 1985; *Grind,* Mark Hellinger Theatre, 1985; *Jerome Kern Goes to Hollywood,* Ritz Theatre, 1986; *A Little Like Magic,* Lyceum Theatre, 1986; *Sweet Sue,* Music Box Theatre, 1987; *Stardust,* Biltmore Theatre, 1987.

Pre-Broadway productions: *Step Lively Boy,* Locust Theatre, Philadelphia, 1973; *$600 and a Mule,* Huntington Hartford Theatre, Los Angeles, 1973; *Snoopy!!!,* Forest Theatre, Philadelphia, 1975; *The Philantropist,* National Theatre, Washington, DC, 1975; *Long Days Journey into Night,* Eisenhower Theatre, Kennedy Center, Washington, DC, 1976; *Seven Brides for Seven Brothers,* Bob Carr Auditorium, Orlando, FL, 1979; *Noel,* Goodspeed Opera House, East Haddam, CT, 1981; *Chaplin,* Dorothy Chandler Pavilion, Los Angeles, 1984; *Queenie Pie,* Eisenhower Theatre, Kennedy Center, Washington, DC, 1986.

Off-Broadway productions, all New York City: *The Dream on Monkey Mountain,* St. Mark's Playhouse, 1971; *Heloise,* Equity Library Theatre, 1971; *Nightride,* Van Dam Theatre, 1971; *Don't Bother Me, I Can't Cope,* Playhouse Theatre, 1972; *A Meeting by the River,* Edison Theatre, 1972; *Strike Heaven on the Face, Games After Liverpool,* and *The Government Inspector,* all Playhouse Theatre, 1973; *Thoughts,* Theatre de Lys, 1973; *A Breeze from the Gulf,* Eastside Playhouse, 1973; *The Great MacDaddy,* St. Mark's Playhouse, 1974; *Pretzels,* Theatre Four, 1974; *When Hell Freezes Over I'll Skate,* Mitzi Newhouse Theatre, Lincoln Center, 1979; *People in Show Business Make Long Goodbye's,* Orpheum Theatre, 1979; *Styne after Styne,* Manhattan Theatre, Club, 1980;

KEN BILLINGTON

Snoopy, Lambs Theatre, 1982; *Talullah,* West Side Arts Theatre, 1984; *Diamonds,* Circle in the Square, Downtown, 1984; *Ann Reinking: A Lady and Her Music,* Joyce Theatre, 1984, also Westwood Playhouse, Los Angeles, 1985; *Three Guys Naked from the Waist Down,* Minetta Lane Theatre, 1985; *Stardust,* Theatre-Off-Park, 1986.

Regional: With the Milwaukee Repertory Theatre, WI: *Journey of the Fifth Horse,* 1972, *The Play's the Thing* and *Two Gentlemen of Verona,* 1973, and *Doctor Faustus,* 1974; *The Philanthropist,* Goodman Theatre, Chicago, 1975; *King Lear, Our Town,* and *The Winter's Tale,* all with the American Shakespeare Festival, Stratford, CT, 1975; *Kiss Me, Kate,* Wolf Trap Farm, VA, 1979; *Play Memory,* McCarter Theatre, Princeton, NJ, 1983; *Get Happy,* Westwood Playhouse, Los Angeles, 1984; *Three Guys Naked from the Waist Down,* Playmakers Repertory Theatre, 1984; *The Music Is Kern,* Emelin Theatre, 1985; *Gentlemen Prefer Blondes,* Theatre of the Stars, Atlanta, 1986; *Queenie Pie,* American Music Theatre Festival, 1986; *Roza,* Center Stage, Baltimore, 1986.

Opera: *Simon Boccanegra,* Phildelphia Lyric Opera, 1973; *Le Coq D'Or,* Dallas Civic Opera, 1973; *Il Tabarro/Gianni Schicchi,* Phildelphia Lyric Opera, 1974; *Anna Bolena,* Dallas Civic Opera, 1975; *Ashmedai,* New York City Opera, 1976; *L'Histoire Soldat* and *The Voice of Ariadne,* New York City Opera, 1977; *The Merry Widow* and *Naughty Marietta,* New York City Opera, 1978; *La Fanciulla del West,* Lyric Opera of Chicago, 1978; *Un Ballo in Maschera,* Dallas Civic Opera, 1978; *La Fanciulla del West,* San Francisco Opera, 1979; *The Pearl Fishers,* Dallas Civic Opera, 1979; *Silverlake,* New York City Opera, 1980; *The Merry Widow,* Greater Miami Opera, 1981; *Willie Stark,* Houston Grand Opera,

1981; *Ernani,* Dallas Civic Opera, 1981; *Candide,* New York City Opera, 1982; *Lucia di Lammermoor,* Dallas Civic Opera, 1982; *Faust,* Greater Miami Opera, 1983; *Turandot,* Vienna State Opera, 1983; *Cosi Fan Tutte,* Greater Miami Opera, 1984; *Sweeney Todd,* Houston Grand Opera, then New York City Opera, 1984; *Madama Butterfly,* Houston Grand Opera, 1985; *Faust,* Houston Grand Opera, 1985; *Cavalleria Rusticana* and *Pagliacci,* both at the Greater Miami Opera, 1986; *La Fanciulla Del West,* Dallas Civic Opera, 1986; *Orpheus in the Underworld,* Houston Grand Opera, also Michigan Opera, 1986; *Faust,* Seattle Opera, 1987.

MAJOR TOURS—*Mame,* Los Angeles, 1970; *International Ice Review,* Brooklyn, 1971; *Fiddler on the Roof,* Los Angeles, 1976; *Equus,* Burlington, VT, 1976; *My Fair Lady,* St. Louis, 1977; *On the Twentieth Century,* Detroit, 1979; *Da,* Amherst, MA, 1979; *Snow White and the Seven Dwarfs,* Baltimore, 1980; *Da,* Portland, OR, 1980; *My Fair Lady,* New Orleans, 1980; *Sweeny Todd,* Washington, DC, 1980; *Foxfire,* Los Angeles, 1985; *Pippin,* Dallas, 1986.

AWARDS: Lumen Award, Illuminating Engineering Society of North America Edwin F. Guth Memorial Lighting Design Award of Merit; Antoinette Perry Award nominations, Best Lighting Design, 1973, for *The Visit* and 1978, for *Working,* 1978; Antoinette Perry Award nomination, Drama Desk Award nomination, Los Angeles Drama Critics Award, Best Lighting Design, all 1979, for *Sweeney Todd;* Ace Award, Monitor Award nomination, Best Lighting Design, 1982, Antoinette Perry Award nomination, Drama Desk Award nomination, Boston Drama Critics Award, Maharam Award nomination, Best Lighting Design, all 1982, for *Foxfire;* Antoinette Perry Award nomination, Best Lighting Design, 1984, for *End of the World;* also received Boston Drama Critics Award, Antoinette Perry Award nomination, Drama Desk nomination, Maharam Award nomination, and Los Angeles Drama Critics Award, all for work in 1986.

MEMBER: United Scenic Artists.

ADDRESSES: OFFICE—200 W. 70th Street, New York, NY 10023.

*   *   *

BLACK, Karen   1942-

PERSONAL: Born Karen Blanche Ziegler, July 1, 1942, in Park Ridge, IL; daughter of Norman A. and Elsie (Reif) Zeigler; married Charles Black (divorced); married Robert Burton (divorced, 1974); married L. Minor Carson (a writer), July 4, 1975; children: Hunter (a son). EDUCATION: Attended Northwestern University; trained for the stage with Lee Strasberg.

VOCATION: Actress.

CAREER: FILM DEBUT—*You're a Big Boy Now,* Warner Brothers, 1966. PRINCIPAL FILM APPEARANCES—*Hard Contract,* 1969; *Easy Rider,* Columbia, 1969; *Five Easy Pieces,* Columbia, 1970; *Drive, He Said,* Columbia, 1971; *A Gunfight,* Paramount, 1971; *Born to Win,* United Artists, 1971; *Portnoy's Complaint,* Warner Brothers, 1972; *The Pyx,* Cinerama, 1973; *Rhinocerous,* American Film Theatre, 1974; *The Outfit,* United Artists, 1974; *The Great Gatsby,* Paramount, 1974; *Airport, 1975,* Universal, 1974; *Law and Disorder*, Columbia, 1974; *The Day of the Locust*, Paramount, 1975; *Nashville*, Paramount, 1975.

Family Plot, Universal, 1976; *Crime and Passion*, 1976; *Burnt Offerings*, United Artists, 1976; *Capricorn One*, Warner Brothers, 1978; *Because He's My Friend*, Australian, 1978; *The Rip Off*, 1978; *In Praise of Older Women*, AVCO-Embassy, 1979; *Killer Fish*, 1979; *The Last Word*, 1979; *Valentine*, 1979; *Greed* and *Miss Right*, both 1980; *Danny Travis* and *Chanel Solitaire*, both 1981; *Come Back to the Five and Dime Jimmy Dean, Jimmy Dean*, Cinecom, 1982; *Growing Pains*, Hammer, 1982; *Breathless*, Orion, 1983; *Killing Heat*, 1984; Karen, *Martin's Day*, Metro-Goldwyn-Mayer/United Artists, 1985; *The Blue Man*, New Century, upcoming; *Invaders from Mars*, Cannon, upcoming; also, *Cut and Run*, *Animal Behavior*, *A Stroke of Genius*.

PRINCIPAL TELEVISION APPEARANCES—Series: Marcia Garroway, *The Second Hundred Years*, ABC, 1968. Movies: *The Strange Possession of Mrs. Oliver*, 1977. Guest: *Celebrity Challenge of the Sexes*, CBS, 1978. Episodic: "Hired Help," *The Hitchhiker*, HBO, 1985.

PRINCIPAL STAGE APPEARANCES—Broadway: *The Playroom*, 1965; *Keep It in the Family*, 1968; also appeared in *Happily Never After*, and with the Heckscher House Company in several Shakespearean plays.

AWARDS: Best Actress, New York Drama Critics Award nomination, 1965, for *The Playroom;* Academy Award nomination and New York Film Critics Award, both 1970, for *Five Easy Pieces.**

*   *   *

BLACKMAN, Honor

PERSONAL: Married Maurice Kaufmann. EDUCATION: Trained for the stage at the Guildhall School of Music and Drama.

VOCATION: Actress.

CAREER: LONDON DEBUT—Monica Cartwright, *The Gleam*, Globe Theatre, 1946. PRINCIPAL STAGE APPEARANCES—Mary Dering, *The Blind Goddess*, Apollo Theatre, London, 1947; Lorraine McKay, *The Fifth Season*, Cambridge Theatre, London, 1954; Susy Henderson, *Wait Until Dark*, Strand Theatre, London, 1966; Doris and Laura Jesson, *Mr. and Mrs.*, Palace Theatre, London, 1968; Barbara Love, *Who Killed Santa Claus?*, Theatre Royal, Windsor, U.K., 1969, then Piccadilly Theatre, London, 1970; Margaret, *The Exorcism*, Comedy Theatre, London, 1975; Mrs. Millamant, *The Way of the World*, 1975, and Paula Cramer, *Motive*, 1976, both at the Arnaud Theatre, Guildford, U.K.; Mrs. Millamant, *The Way of the World* and Desiree, *A Little Music*, both at the Northcott Theatre, Exeter, U.K., 1979.

MAJOR TOURS—Title role, *Move Over Mrs. Markham*, Australian and North American cities, 1972-73; Hester, *The Deep Blue Sea*, U.K. cities, 1977; Desiree, *A Little Night Music*, U.K. cities, 1979.

FILM DEBUT—*Fame Is the Spur*, Two Cities, 1947. PRINCIPAL FILM APPEARANCES—*Conspirator*, 1949; *So Long at the Fair*, 1950; *Green Grow the Rushes*, 1951; *Come Die My Love*, 1952; *The Rainbow Jacket*, 1953; *The Glass Cage*, 1954; *Dead Man's Evidence*, 1955; *A Night to Remember*, Rank, 1959; *A Matter of*

Who, 1961; *Serena*, 1962; *Jason and the Argonauts*, Columbia, 1963; Pussy Galore, *Goldfinger*, United Artists, 1964; *Life at the Top*, Royal International and *The Secret of My Success*, Metro-Goldwyn-Mayer (MGM), both 1965; *Quartet*, Ajay Pictures and *Moment to Moment*, Universal, both 1966; *A Twist of Sand*, United Artists and *Shalako*, Cinerama, both 1968; *The Virgin and the Gypsy*, Chevron and *The Last Grenade*, Cinerama, both 1970; *Something Big*, National General and *Fright*, both 1971; *To the Devil a Daughter*, EMI, 1975; *Summer Rain*, 1976; *The Cat and the Canary*, Grenadier Films Ltd., 1978; *Ragtime*, Paramount, 1981. Also appeared in *Daughter of Darkness*, *A Boy, a Girl and a Bike*, *Diamond City*, *Set a Murderer*, *The Outsiders*, *The Delavine Affair*, *The Three Musketeers*, *Breakaway*, *The Homecoming*, *Suspended Alibi*, *Dangerous Drugs*, *The Square Peg*, *Present Laughter*, *The Recount*, *The Struggle for Rome*, and *Twinky*.

TELEVISION DEBUT—1950. PRINCIPAL TELEVISION APPEARANCES—Series: *The Vise*, ABC, 1955; *The Invisible Man*, CBS, 1958; *The Avengers*, BBC, 1962-64; *The Saint*, NBC, 1967; also *Probation Officer*.

Movies: *Four Just Men*, 1959; *Man of Honour*, 1960; *Ghost Squad*, 1961; *Top Secret*, 1962; *The Explorer*, 1968; *Visit from a Stranger*, 1970; *Out Damned Spot*, 1972; *The Winds of Change*, 1977; *Robin's Nest*, 1982; *Never the Twain*, 1982; *Secret Adversary*, 1983.

WRITINGS: BOOKS—*Honor Blackman's Book of Self-Defence.*

SIDELIGHTS: RECREATIONS—Watching soccer, reading.

ADDRESSES: AGENT—London Management, 235 Regent Street, London W1A 2JT, England.*

*   *   *

BLAKELY, Colin   1930-1987

PERSONAL: Born September 23, 1930, in Bangor, County Down, Northern Ireland; died of leukemia in London, May 7, 1987; son of Victor Charles and Dorothy Margaret Ashmore (Rodgers) Blakely; married Margaret Whiting (an actress and singer). EDUCATION: Attended Sedbergh School, Yorkshire.

VOCATION: Actor and director.

CAREER: STAGE DEBUT—Dick McCardle, *Master of the House*, with the Ulster Group, Belfast, Ireland, 1958. LONDON DEBUT—Second rough fellow, *Cock-a-Doodle-Dandy*, with the English Stage Company at the Royal Court Theatre, 1959. PRINCIPAL STAGE APPEARANCES—Kevin McAlinden, *The Bonfire*, Lyceum Theatre, Edinburgh, U.K., 1958. With the English Stage Company at the Royal Court Theatre, London: A Pugnacious Collier, *Serjeant Musgrave's Dance*, Thomas Noon (alias Kelly), *The Naming of Murderer's Rock*, 1959, and repeating role in 1960; Phil Hogan, *A Moon for the Misbegotten*, Arts Theatre, London, 1960; Warren Baxter, *Over the Bridge*, Princes Theatre, London, 1960; Josh, *Dreaming Bandsmen*, Belgrade Theatre, Coventry, U.K., 1960.

Lord Hastings, *Richard III*, Touchstone, *As You Like It*, and the Duke of Venice, *Othello*, all with the Royal Shakespeare Comany, Stratford-on-Avon, U.K., 1961; Cox, *Box and Cox* and Schmitz, *The Fire-Raisers*, both at the Royal Court Theatre, London, 1961; Bottom, *A Midsummer Night's Dream*, Royal Court Theatre,

London, 1962. With the National Theatre Company at the Old Vic Theatre, London: Fortinbras, *Hamlet*, Kite, *The Recruiting Officer*, Peider, *Andorra*, title role, *Philoctetes*, Pizarro, *The Royal Hunt of the Sun* (also produced at the Chichester Festival, U.K.), John Proctor, *The Crucible*, title role, *Hobson's Choice*, Sergeant, *Mother Courage and Her Children*, and Ben, *Love for Love*, all 1963-65, Captain Jack Boyle, *Juno and the Paycock* and Creon, *Oedipus Rex*, 1965-68.

Astrov, *Uncle Vanya*, Royal Court Theatre, 1970; Deeley, *Old Times*, with the Royal Shakespeare Company, 1971; *Titus Andronicus*, with the Royal Shakespeare Company, Stratford-on-Avon, 1972, then and at the Aldwych Theatre, London, 1973; Torvald Helmer, *A Doll's House*, Criterion Theatre, London, 1973; Blakey, *The Illumination Of Mr. Shannon*, Soho Poly Theatre, London, 1973; Casement, *Cries from Casement* and General Muster, *Section Nine*, both with the Royal Shakespeare Company at The Place, London, 1973; Captain Shotover, *Heartbreak House*, with the National Theatre Company at the Old Vic Theatre, London, 1975; Vukhov, *Judgement*, Institute of Contemporary Arts (ICA) and at the Old Vic Theatre, London, 1975; Martin Dysart, *Equus*, Albery Theatre, London, 1976; Dennis, *Just Between Ourselves*, Queen's Theatre, London, 1977; Domenico Soriano, *Filumena*, Lyric Theatre, London, 1977; title role, *Semmelweiss*, Eisenhower Theatre, Kennedy Center, Washington, DC, 1978.

MAJOR TOURS—With the National Theatre Company of Great Britain, toured Moscow and Berlin, 1965.

PRINCIPAL STAGE WORK—Director, *The Illumination of Mr. Shannon*, Soho Poly Theatre, London, 1973.

PRINCIPAL FILM APPEARANCES—*Murder on the Orient Express*, Paramount, 1974; *Equus*, Warner Brothers, 1977; *Nijinsky*, Paramount, 1980. Also, *Saturday Night and Sunday Morning*, 1960; *Man Friday*, 1976.

PRINCIPAL TELEVISION APPEARANCES—Movies: *When Silver Drinks*, *Son of Man*, *Donkey's Years*.

NON-RELATED CAREER—Formerly employed as a merchant in his family's sports retail business.

MEMBER: British Actors' Equity Association, Screen Actors Guild.

SIDELIGHTS: RECREATIONS—Golf, sailing, sketching, and the piano.

ADDRESSES: AGENT—Julian Belfrage Associates, 60 St. James Street, London SW1, England.*

*   *   *

BLATTY, William Peter   1928-

PERSONAL: Born January 7, 1928, in New York, NY; son of Peter (a carpenter) and Mary (Mouakad) Blatty; married Mary Margaret Rigard, February 18, 1950 (annulled); married Elizabeth Gilman, 1950 (marriage ended); married Linda Tuero (a professional tennis player), July 20, 1975; children: (second marriage) Christine Ann, Michael Peter, Mary Joanne; (third marriage) two children. EDUCATION: Georgetown University, A.B., 1950, M.A., 1954. RELIGION: Roman Catholic. MILITARY: U.S. Air Force, 1951-54.

VOCATION: Writer and producer.

CAREER: PRINCIPAL FILM WORK—Writer (see below); also producer, *The Exorcist*, Warner Brothers, 1973; producer and director, *Twinkle, Twinkle, "Killer" Kane* (also known as *The Ninth Configuration*), United Film, 1980.

RELATED CAREER—Editor, *News Review*, United States Information Agency, Beirut, Lebanon, 1955-57.

NON-RELATED CAREER—Door-to-door Electrolux vacuum cleaner salesman, 1950; beer truck driver for Gunther Brewing Company, 1950; publicity director, University of Southern California, Los Angeles, 1957-58; public relations director, Loyola University of Los Angeles, 1959-60.

WRITINGS: SCREENPLAYS—*The Man from the Diner's Club*, Columbia, 1963; *John Goldfarb, Please Come Home!*, Twentieth Century-Fox, 1965; *A Shot in the Dark*, United Artists, 1966; *Promise Her Anything*, British, 1966; *What Did You Do in the War, Daddy?*, United Artists, 1966; *Gunn*, Paramount, 1967; *The Great Bank Robbery*, Warner Brothers, 1969; *Darling Lili*, Paramount, 1970; *The Exorcist*, Warner Brothers, 1973; *Twinkle, Twinkle, "Killer" Kane* (also known as *The Ninth Configuration*), United Film, 1980.

TELEVISION—Movies: *The Baby Sitter*, 1980. Episodic: *Insight*.

BOOKS—*Which Way to Mecca, Jack?*, Bernard Geis Associates, 1960; *John Goldfarb, Please Come Home!*, Doubleday, 1963; *I, Billy Shakespeare!*, Doubleday, 1965; *Twinkle, Twinkle, "Killer" Kane*, Doubleday, 1967; *The Exorcist*, Harper, 1971; *I'll Tell Them I Remember You*, Norton, 1973; *William Peter Blatty on "The Exorcist": From Novel to Film*, Bantam, 1974; *The Ninth Configuration*, Harper, 1978; *Legion*, Simon & Schuster, 1983.

AWARDS: Gabriel Award, National Catholic Broadcasters Association and Blue Ribbon, American Film Festival, both 1969, for *Insight;* Silver Medal, California Literature Medal Award, 1972, for *The Exorcist;* Best Screenplay Based on a Work in Another Medium, Academy Award, and Best Film, August Derleth Award, both 1973, for *The Exorcist;* Best Movie Screen Play, Golden Globe Award, 1980, for *Twinkle, Twinkle, "Killer" Kane*. Honorary degrees: Seattle University, L.H.D., 1974.

MEMBER: Writers Guild of America.

ADDRESSES: AGENT—Brandt and Brandt Literary Agents, Inc., 1501 Broadway, New York, NY 10036.*

*   *   *

BLECKNER, Jeff

PERSONAL: Born in Brooklyn, NY; son of Jack S. and Etta (Paluba) Bleckner; married Jeanne Hepple. EDUCATION: Amherst College, B.A.; Yale University, M.F.A.

VOCATION: Director.

CAREER: FIRST STAGE WORK—Director, *Little Malcolm and His Struggle Against the Eunuchs*, Yale University Experimental Theatre, New Haven, CT, 1967. PRINCIPAL STAGE WORK: Director:

Worked at the Long Wharf Theatre, New Haven, CT, 1967-68; *Coriolanus*, 1968; *The Unseen Hand* and *Forensic and the Navigators*, Astor Place Theatre, New York City, 1970; *Twelfth Night*, Arena Stage, Washington, DC, 1971; *The Basic Training of Pavlo Hummel* and *Sticks and Bones*, both New York Shakespeare Festival, Public Theatre, New York City, 1971; *The Secret Affairs of Mildred Wild* and *Old Times*, Mark Taper Forum, Los Angeles, CA, 1972; *The Orphan*, 1973; *The Death and Life of Jesse James*, Mark Taper Forum, Los Angeles, 1974; *The Father*, Yale Repertory Theatre, 1975; *FDR*, Washington, DC, 1977; *The Goodbye People*, Belasco Theatre, New York City, 1979.

PRINCIPAL TELEVISION WORK—Episodic: Director—*Doc*, CBS, 1975; "Life in the Minors," *Hill Street Blues*, NBC, 1983; *Another World*, NBC; *The Guiding Light*, CBS. Teleplays: *Sticks and Bones*, 1972; "Concealed Enemies," *American Playhouse*, PBS, 1984.

AWARDS: Best Director, Antoinette Perry Award, 1971, for *Sticks and Bones;* Outstanding Directing in a Drama Series, Emmy Award, 1983, for "Life in the Minors," *Hill Street Blues;* Outstanding Directing in a Limited Series or a Special, Emmy Award, 1984, for "Concealed Enemies," *American Playhouse.*

ADDRESSES: AGENT—Howard Rosenstone, Rosenstone-Wender, Three E. 48th St., New York, NY 10017.*

*   *   *

BLEY, Maurice G.   1910-

PERSONAL: Surname pronounced "Bly"; full name Maurice George Bley; born December 7, 1910, in Hamburg, NY; son of Lawrence Henry (an architect) and Matilda Anna (Schummer) Bley; married Anna Kowalska (a concert pianist), December 14, 1942. EDUCATION: Carnegie Institute of Technology, B.A., 1933; trained for the stage at the Studio Theatre School, Buffalo, NY, with Jane Keeler. POLITICS: "Liberal" Democrat. RELIGION: Roman Catholic. MILITARY: U.S. Army, 1942-45.

VOCATION: Producer, director, actor, and designer.

CAREER: STAGE DEBUT—Uncle, *The Youngest*, Hamburg High School Theatre, NY, 1928. PRINCIPAL STAGE APPEARANCES—Mulatto, *The Night of January 16th*, Erlanger Theatre, Buffalo, during the 1930s.

At the Studio Theatre, Buffalo: Jay, *Post Road*, 1935; Epihodov, *The Cherry Orchard*, John Shaw, *The Great Adventure*, Kimo, *Petticoat Fever*, waiter, *The Good Fairy*, Roger Crosby, *The Cat and the Canary*, and Bennie Fox, *June Moon*, all 1936; Counsel, *Libel*, Walter Havan, *Another Language*, Burleigh, *Milky Way*, the man, *Noah*, and Reverend Alex Mill, *Candida*, all 1937; waiter, *Candlelight*, Aiken, *Excursion*, Jeeter Fry, *Green Grow the Lilacs*, Erwin, *Three Men on a Horse*, and Leo Davis, *Room Service*, all 1938; Prefect, *Right You Are*, 1939; *The Play's the Thing*, 1940; Austin Love, *The Second Man*, Walter Manners, *When Ladies Meet*, and Roosevelt, *Knickerbocker Holiday*, all 1941.

Grant Bottome, *Brother Rat*, George Kent, *Up Pops the Devil*, and Bennie Fox, *June Moon*, all at the Roadside Theatre, 1939.

PRINCIPAL STAGE WORK—Musical researcher and accompanist,

Studio Theatre, Buffalo, NY: *Ten Nights in a Barroom*, 1936; *Maria Marten*, 1937; *Sweeney Todd*, 1938; *Hawkshaw*, 1940.

Director and producer at the Hamburg Little Theatre, Hamburg, NY: *Years Ago* and *Adam and Eva*, both 1949; *Mr. Pim, Milky Way, Laura*, and *One Night in Bethlehem*, all 1950; *Big Hearted Herbert, Christopher Bean, Post Road*, and *The Christmas Story*, all 1951; *Parlor Story, The Happiest Years*, and *First Lady*, all 1952; *Good Housekeeping, But Not Goodbye*, and *Ladies in Retirement*, all 1953; *January Thaw, Papa Is All*, and *The Curious Savage*, all 1954; *Great Big Doorstop* and *Cat and the Canary*, both 1955; *Goodbye My Fancy, Late Love*, and *Silver Whistle*, all 1956; *The Little Foxes, Blithe Spirit*, and *King of Hearts*, all 1957; *Accent on Youth, Sand Sprite*, and *Jenny Kissed Me*, all 1958; *Anastasia* and *Time Out for Ginger*, both 1959; *Mr. Barry's Etchings*, 1960; *All for Mary*, 1961; *White Sheep of the Family*, 1962; also designed for sets for *Mr. Barry's Etchings, All for Mary*, and *White Sheep of the Family*.

NON-RELATED CAREER—Design engineer for a restaurant equipment house.

MEMBER: New York State Community Theatre Association (area representative and board member, 1959-60; vice president and state conference chairman, 1960-61; president, 1961-63; board member ex-officio, 1963-65; vice-president and state conference chairman, 1965-66).

SIDELIGHTS: RECREATIONS—Music, cooking, and travel.

Maurice Bley told *CTFT* that he was honored at a testimonial dinner in celebration of the twentieth anniversary of his founding of the Hamburg Little Theatre in Buffalo. He also informed us that he was the only director for the first twelve years of the theatre.

ADDRESSES: HOME—140 S. Lake Street, Hamburg, NY 14075.

*   *   *

BLOOM, Claire   1931-

PERSONAL: Full name, Patricia Claire Bloom; born February 15, 1931; daughter of Edward Max (an executive) and Elizabeth (Grew) Bloom; married Rod Steiger (an actor) September 19, 1959 (divorced, 1969); married Hillard Elkins (a director), August 14, 1969 (divorced, 1972); children: (first marriage) Anna-Justine. EDUCATION: Attended Badminton School, Bristol, England, Fern Hill Manor, New Milton, England, and New York City public schools; trained for the stage with Eileen Thorndike at the Guildhall School of Music and Drama, 1946-48; also attended the Central School of Speech and Drama, 1947-48.

VOCATION: Actress.

CAREER: STAGE DEBUT—Private Jessie Killigrew, *It Depends What You Mean*, with the Oxford Repertory Theatre, U.K., 1946. LONDON DEBUT—*The White Devil*, Duchess Theatre, 1947. BROADWAY DEBUT—Juliet, *Romeo and Juliet*, Winter Garden Theatre, 1956. PRINCIPAL STAGE APPEARANCES—Helen, *An Italian Straw Hat*, Jessie, *Pink String and Sealing Wax*, both with the Oxford Repertory Theatre, 1946; *He Who Gets Slapped*, with the Under Thirty Group, Duchess Theatre, London, 1947; Erinna, *The Wanderer*, His Majesty's Theatre, London, 1947; Lady Blanche,

King John, Ophelia, *Hamlet*, and Perdita, *The Winter's Tale*, all at the Stratford-on-Avon Memorial Theatre, U.K., 1948; Daphne Randall, *The Damask Cheek*, Lyric Theatre, Hammersmith, U.K., 1949; Alizon Eliot, *The Lady's Not for Burning*, Globe Theatre, London, 1949.

Isabelle, *Ring Round the Moon*, Globe Theatre, London, 1950; Juliet, *Romeo and Juliet* and Jessica, *Merchant of Venice*, with the Old Vic Company, Old Vic Theatre, London, 1952-53; Ophelia, *Hamlet*, Edinburgh Festival, Scotland, 1953; Ophelia, *Hamlet*, Helena, *All's Well That Ends Well*, Viola, *Twelfth Night*, Virgilia, *Coriolanus*, and Miranda, *The Tempest*, all with the Old Vic Company, Old Vic Theatre, London, 1953-54; Cordelia, *King Lear*, Palace Theatre, London, 1955; Juliet, *Romeo and Juliet*, with the Old Vic Company, Old Vic Theatre, London, 1956; Lucile, *Duel of Angels*, Apollo Theatre, London, 1958; Wife, *Rashomon*, Music Box Theatre, New York City, 1959; Johanna, *Altona*, Royal Court Theatre, London, then Saville Theatre, London, 1961; Andromache, *The Trojan Women*, Spoleto Festival of Two Worlds, Italy, 1963; Sasha, *Ivanov*, Phoenix Theatre, London, 1965.

Nora, *A Doll's House*, Playhouse Theatre, New York City, then repeated role at Eisenhower Theatre, Kennedy Center, Washington, DC, 1971; title role, *Hedda Gabler*, Playhouse Theatre, New York City, 1971; Mary Queen of Scots, *Vivat! Vivat Regina!*, Broadhurst Theatre, New York City, 1972; repeated role of Nora, *A Doll's House*, Criterion Theatre, London, 1973; Blanche du Bois, *A Streetcar Named Desire*, Piccadilly Theatre, London, 1974; Miss Giddens, *The Innocents*, Morosco Theatre, New York City, 1976; Rebecca West, *Rosmersholm*, Haymarket Theatre, London, 1977; also appeared in *The Cherry Orchard*, Chichester Festival, U.K., 1981.

MAJOR TOURS—Juliet, *Romeo and Juliet*, Canadian and U.S. cities, 1956-57; one woman show, *These Are Women, a Portrait of Shakespeare's Heroines*, U.K. and U.S. cities, 1982-83.

FILM DEBUT—*The Blind Goddess*, 1948. PRINCIPAL FILM APPEARANCES—Teresa, *Limelight*, United Artists, 1952; *The Man Between*, United Artists, 1953; *Innocents in Paris*, Tudor, 1955; *Richard III*, Lopert, 1956; *Alexander the Great*, United Artists, 1956; *The Brothers Karamazov*, Metro-Goldwyn-Mayer (MGM), 1958; *Look Back in Anger*, Warner Brothers, 1959; *Three Steps to Freedom*, 1960; *Royal Game*, Ufa, 1960; *Brainwashed*, Associated Artists, 1961; *The Wonderful World of the Brothers Grimm*, MGM, 1962; *The Chapman Report*, Warner Brothers, 1962; *The Haunting*, MGM, 1963; *80,000 Suspects*, 1963; *Alta Infedelita*, De Laurentiis, 1963; *Il Maestro di Vigevano*, De Laurentiis, 1963; *The Outrage*, MGM, 1964; *The Spy Who Came in from the Cold*, Paramount, 1966; *Charly*, Cinerama, 1966; *Three into Two Won't Go*, Universal, 1969; *The Illustrated Man*, Warner Brothers-Seven Arts, 1969; *Red Sky at Morning*, Universal, 1970; *A Severed Head*, Columbia, 1971; *A Doll's House*, Paramount, 1973; *Islands in the Stream*, Paramount, 1977; *Clash of the Titans*, United Artists, 1981; *Shadowlands*, 1985; *Always*, 1985.

PRINCIPAL TELEVISION APPEARANCES—Episodic: *Shirley Temple's Storybook*, NBC, 1959; "Claire Bloom Reads Poetry," *Camera Three*, CBS, 1964. Movies: *A Legacy*, 1975; *Promises to Keep*, 1985; *Anna Karenina*, 1985. Mini-series: Lady Marchmain, *Brideshead Revisited*, 1979; Edith Galt Wilson, *Backstairs at the White House*, NBC, 1979; *Ellis Island*, 1984; *Florence Nightingale*, 1984; *Liberty*, 1985.

Teleplays: Roxanne, "Cyrano de Bergerac," *Producers Show-*case, NBC, 1956; Cleopatra, "Caesar and Cleopatra," *Producers Showcase*, NBC, 1956; Juliet, "Romeo and Juliet," *Producers Showcase*, NBC, 1957; "Misalliance," *Playhouse 90*, CBS, 1959; title role, "Anna Karenina," *Twenty-Fifth Anniversary of BBC-TV*, 1961; Kathy, *Wuthering Heights*, BBC, 1962; Margaret Chapman, "A Time to Love," *Bob Hope Theatre*, NBC, 1967; Queen Anne, "Soldier in Love," *Hallmark Hall of Fame*, NBC, 1967; Sasha, *Ivanov*, CBS, 1967; *The Orestea*, 1978; Katherine of Aragon, *Henry VIII*, 1979; *Hamlet*, 1980; *Cymbeline*, 1982; Miss Cooper, *Separate Tables*, 1982; Hope Louff, *The Ghost Writer*, 1982; *King John*, 1983; *Time and the Conways*, 1984; *Oedipus the King*, 1985; *Lightning Always Strikes Twice*, 1985. Also appeared in *Wessex Tales*, *An Imaginative Woman*, *In Praise of Love*, and *Ann and Debbie*.

WRITINGS: *Limelight and After: The Education of an Actress* (autobiography), Harper & Row, 1982.

AWARDS: British Film Award and Elle Award, both 1952, for *Limelight*; Drama Desk Award and Outer Circle Award, both for *Hedda Gabler*; Best Actress awards, *London Evening Standard* Variety Club, and *Plays and Players*, both 1974, for Blanche du Bois, *A Streetcar Named Desire*.

MEMBER: Actors' Equity Association, Screen Actors Guild, American Federation of Television and Radio Artists; Guildhall School of Music (fellow).

SIDELIGHTS: FAVORITE ROLES—Blanche du Bois, *A Streetcar Named Desire*. RECREATIONS—Ballet, reading, walking, and music.

ADDRESSES: AGENT—Michael Linnit, Globe Theatre, Shaftesbury Avenue, London W1, England.*

*   *   *

BLOOM, Michael   1950-

PERSONAL: Born January 1, 1950, in Hartford, CT; son of David H. and Anne (Sigel) Bloom. EDUCATION: George Washington University, B.A., 1972; Stanford University, Ph.D., directing and dramatic criticism, 1976.

VOCATION: Director.

CAREER: PRINCIPAL STAGE WORK—Director: *Medal of Honor Rag*, Los Angeles Actors' Theatre, 1978; *The Birthmark*, New York City, 1981; *Americans Abroad*, Manhattan Theatre Club, New York City, 1984; *Holiday Sampler*, Hartman Theatre, Stamford, CT, 1985; *Split Decision*, Philadelphia Festival Theatre, Philadelphia, PA, 1985; *The Day Room*, American Repertory Theatre, Cambridge, MA, 1986. Also directed: *The House of Blue Leaves*, *Mandragola*, and *Electra*, all at Scripps College, Claremont, CA; *Lysistrata*, Gateway Playhouse; *The Strong Box* and *Domino Courts*, both Circle in the Square Acting Program, New York City; *Cowboy Mouth* and *The Golden Fleece*, Williamstown Theatre Festival, MA; *Home Fires* and *Fanshen*, both Soho Repertory Theatre, New York City. Adaptor: *The Birthmark*, New York City, 1981.

RELATED CAREER—Associate professor, Great Lakes Colleges Association, New York City, 1980—; associate artistic director, Hartman Theatre, Stamford, CT, 1985—.

MICHAEL BLOOM

AWARDS: Best Adaptation, Villager Award, 1981, for *The Birthmark.*

MEMBER: Society of Stage Directors and Choreographers.

ADDRESSES: HOME—16 Jane Street, Apt. 1C, New York, NY 10014. OFFICE—Hartman Theatre, 61 Atlantic Street, Stamford, CT 06904. AGENT—Helen Merrill, 361 W. 17th Street, New York, NY 10011.

*   *   *

BLOUNT, Helon   1929-

PERSONAL: Born January 15, 1929, in Big Spring, TX; daughter of Ralph Eugene, Sr. and Alma Helon (Shipp) Blount; married Keith Kaldenberg. EDUCATION: University of Texas at Austin, M.A., music.

VOCATION: Actress and singer.

CAREER: STAGE DEBUT—State Fair Music Hall, Dallas, TX, 1951. BROADWAY DEBUT—Neighbor, standby for Cleo, *The Most Happy Fella,* Imperial Theatre, 1956. PRINCIPAL STAGE APPEARANCES—All New York City, except when indicated otherwise: Police Matron Jonsen, *Fly Blackbird,* Mayfair Theatre, 1962; Mrs. Farrell, *Riverwind,* Actor's Playhouse, 1962; Miss

Jones, *How to Succeed in Business without Really Trying,* 46th Street Theatre, 1963-65; Mrs. Victoria Haslam, *Do I Hear a Waltz?,* 46th Street Theatre, 1965; Katie, *My Wife and I,* Theatre Four, 1966; Sarah, *Curley McDimple,* Bert Wheeler Theatre, 1967; Mother-in-Law, *The Fig Leaves Are Falling,* Broadhurst Theatre, 1969; Deedee West, *Follies,* Winter Garden Theatre, 1971, then Shubert Theatre, Century City, CA, 1972; Attendant, *A Quarter for the Ladies Room,* Village Gate Theatre, 1972; Mrs. Farrell, *Riverwind,* Masters Theatre, 1973; standby for Madame Matroppo, *Very Good Eddie,* Booth Theatre, 1975; Sophie Tucker, *Last of the Red Hot Mamas,* Manhattan Theatre Club, 1977; Roberta, *Musical Chairs,* Rialto Theatre, 1980; chairperson, *Woman of the Year,* Palace Theatre, 1981-82; Aunt Sally Phelps, *Downriver,* Musical Theatre Workshop, 1985.

Stock appearances include: Fraulein Schneider, *Cabaret,* mother, *Babes in Toyland,* Meg, *Damn Yankees,* and Rose, *Destry.*

MAJOR TOURS—Cleo, *The Most Happy Fella,* U.S. cities, 1957-58; chairperson, *Woman of the Year,* U.S. cities, 1983; stock tours, U.S. cities: Nettie, *Carousel;* Rosalie, *Carnival;* Mother Abbess, *The Sound of Music;* Housekeeper, *Man of La Mancha,* 1979.

ADDRESSES: HOME—346 Littleworth Lane, Sea Cliff, NY 11579.*

*   *   *

BOGDANOVICH, Peter   1939-

PERSONAL: Born July 30, 1939, in Kingston, NY; son of Borislav (an artist) and Herma (Robinson) Bogdanovich; married Polly Platt (a costume designer), 1962 (divorced, 1970); married Cybil Shepherd (a model and actress), 1971 (divorced, 1978); children: (first marriage) Antonia, Alexandra. EDUCATION: Attended Collegiate School, NY; studied acting at the Stella Adler Theatre Studio, NY.

VOCATION: Director, writer, actor, and producer.

CAREER: STAGE DEBUT—With the American Shakespeare Festival, Stratford, CT, 1956. PRINCIPAL STAGE APPEARANCES—Actor, New York Shakespeare Festival, New York City, 1958. PRINCIPAL STAGE WORK—Director and producer of the following Off-Broadway productions: *The Big Knife,* 1959, *Camino Real,* 1961, *Ten Little Indians,* 1961, *Rocket to the Moon,* 1961, and *Once in a Lifetime,* 1964.

FIRST FILM WORK—Second-unit director, co-writer, and actor, *The Wild Angels,* American International Pictures, 1966. PRINCIPAL FILM WORK—Co-producer, director, writer, and actor, *Targets,* Paramount, 1968; director and co-writer, *The Last Picture Show,* Columbia, 1971; producer, director, and writer, *What's Up, Doc?,* Warner Brothers, 1972; producer, director, and writer, *Paper Moon,* Paramount, 1973; producer, director, and writer, *Directed by John Ford,* American Film Institute, California Arts Commission, 1974; producer and director, *Daisy Miller,* Paramount, 1974; producer, director, and writer, *At Long Last Love,* Twentieth Century-Fox, 1975; director and co-writer, *Nickelodeon,* Columbia, 1976; director, co-writer, and actor, *Saint Jack,* Copa de Oro Pictures, Orion, and New World Pictures, 1979; director and writer, *They All Laughed,* Moon Pictures, PSO, and Time/Life, 1981; director, *Mask,* Marstar-Universal, 1985; director, *Whereabouts,* 1985.

PETER BOGDANOVICH

PRINCIPAL RADIO WORK—Associated with *The Film Scene,* New York City, 1960-61.

RELATED CAREER—Editor, ''Showbill,'' 1960-61; organizer of film series and showings for the New Yorker Theatre, 1960-61; owner, Saticoy Productions Inc., Los Angeles, CA, 1968—; cofounder, Directors Company, 1972; owner, Copa de Oro Productions, 1973; general partner, Bogdanovich Film Partners, 1982—; owner, Crescent Moon Productions, Inc., Los Angeles, 1986—.

WRITINGS: BOOKS—*The Cinema of Orson Welles,* Museum of Modern Art, 1961; *The Cinema of Howard Hawks,* Museum of Modern Art and Doubleday, 1962; *The Cinema of Alfred Hitchcock,* Museum of Modern Art and Doubleday, 1963; *John Ford,* Studio Vista, 1967, expanded and revised, University of California Press, 1978; *Fritz Lang in America,* 1969; *Allan Dwan: The Last Pioneer,* 1971; *Pieces of Time: Peter Bogdanovich on the Movies,* Arbor House, 1961, 1973, enlarged 1985; *The Killing of the Unicorn: Dorothy Ruth Stratten (1960-1980): A Memoir,* Morrow, 1984, Bantam, 1985.

ARTICLES—Appearing in *Esquire, Frontier, Saturday Evening Post, TV Guide, Vogue, Movie, Cahiers du Cinema, New York Times, Variety, Los Angeles Times.*

AWARDS: Best Screenplay, New York Film Critic's Award and British Academy Award, both 1971, for *The Last Picture Show;* Best Screenplay, Writers Guild of America Award, 1972, for *What's Up Doc?;* Silver Shell, Mar del Plata, Spain, 1973, for *Paper Moon;* Best Director, Brussells Film Festival, 1974, for

Daisy Miller; Pasinetti Award, Critics Prize, Venice Film Festival, 1979, for *Saint Jack.*

MEMBER: Directors Guild of America, Writers Guild of America, Academy of Motion Picture Arts and Sciences.

SIDELIGHTS: Mr. Bogdanovich is competent in Serbian.

ADDRESSES: AGENT—Camp & Peiffer, 2040 Avenue of the Stars, Century City, CA, 90067.

*   *   *

BOLT, Robert   1924-

PERSONAL: Full name Robert Oxton Bolt, born August 15, 1924, in Sale, Manchester, England; son of Ralph (a shopkeeper) and Leah (a teacher; maiden name, Binnion) Bolt; married Celia Anne Roberts (a painter), November 6, 1949 (divorced, 1967); married Sarah Miles (an actress), 1967 (divorced); married Ann Zane, 1980 (divorced); children: (first marriage) Sally Simmons, Benedict, Joanna; (second marriage) Thomas. EDUCATION: Manchester University, B.A., 1950; University of Exeter, teaching diploma, 1950. POLITICS: Left-wing. MILITARY: Royal Air Force, 1943-44; Royal West African Frontier Force, 1944-46.

VOCATION: Writer and director.

CAREER: PRINCIPAL STAGE WORK—Playwright.

PRINCIPAL FILM WORK—Screenwriter; director, *Lady Caroline Lamb,* United Artists, 1972.

NON-RELATED CAREER—Office boy, Sun Life Assurance, Manchester, England, 1942, Devon, 1950-52; teacher, head of English department, Millfield School, Street, Somerset, England, 1952-58.

WRITINGS: PLAYS, PRODUCED AND PUBLISHED—*Flowering Cherry,* Haymarket Theatre, London, 1957, and Lyceum Theatre, New York City, 1959, published by Heinemann, 1958; *A Man for All Seasons,* London, 1960, then American National Theatre Academy (ANTA) Theatre, New York City, 1961, published by Samuel French, 1960, and Random House, 1962; *The Tiger and the Horse,* London, 1960, published by Heinemann, 1961; *Gentle Jack,* London, 1960, published by Samuel French, 1964, and Random House, 1965; *The Thwarting of Baron Bolligrew,* produced in London, 1966, published by Samuel French, 1966; *Vivat! Vivat Regina!,* Picadilly Theatre, London, and Chichester Festival, U.K., 1970, published by Random House, 1971.

PLAYS, PRODUCED AND UNPUBLISHED—''The Last of the Wine,'' London, 1956; ''The Critic and the Heart,'' Oxford, U.K., 1957; ''Brother and Sister,'' Brighton, U.K., 1967; ''State of Revolution,'' National Theatre, London, 1978.

SCREENPLAYS—*Lawrence of Arabia,* Columbia, 1962; *Doctor Zhivago,* United Artists, 1966; *A Man for All Seasons,* Columbia, 1966; *Ryan's Daughter,* Metro-Goldwyn-Mayer (MGM), 1970; *Lady Caroline Lamb,* United Artists, 1972; *The Bounty,* Orion, 1984.

TELEPLAYS—*A Man for All Seasons,* BBC, 1957.

RADIO PLAYS—*The Master,* 1953; *Fifty Pigs,* 1953; *Ladies and Gentlemen,* 1954; *The Last of the Wine,* 1955; *Mr. Sampson's Sundays,* 1955; *The Window,* 1958; *The Drunken Sailor,* 1958; *The Banana Tree,* 1961.

BOOKS—*Dr. Zhivago: The Screenplay,* Random House, 1966; also work included in anthology, *The New Theatre of Europe,* Volume I, edited by Robert W. Corrigan, Dell, 1962. His work has appeared in *Esquire, Theatre Arts, Saturday Review,* and other periodicals.

AWARDS: Evening Standard Drama Award, 1957, for *Flowering Cherry;* New York Drama Critics Circle Award, 1962, for *A Man for All Seasons;* British Film Academy Award and Academy Award nomination, both 1962, for *Lawrence of Arabia;* Best Screenplay Adaptation, Academy Award, 1966, for *Doctor Zhivago;* Best Picture of the Year, New York Film Critics Award, 1966, Golden Globe Press Award, 1967, and Best Screenplay Adaptation, Academy Award, 1967, all for *A Man for All Seasons;* Antoinette Perry Award nomination, 1972, for *Vivat! Vivat Regina!;* Commander of the British Empire, 1972.

MEMBER: Writers Guild of Great Britain, Association of Cinematography and Television Technicians (former president); Campaign for Nuclear Disarmament, Spares Club (honorary life member).

SIDELIGHTS: RECREATIONS—Walking, sailing.

ADDRESSES: AGENT—Margaret Ramsay, 14A Goodwin's Court, St. Martin's Lane, London WC2N 4LL, England.*

*   *   *

BOND, Edward   1934-

PERSONAL: Born July 18, 1934, in London; married Elisabeth Pable, 1971. POLITICS: Socialist. RELIGION: Atheist. MILITARY: Served two years with British Army Infantry.

VOCATION: Writer and director.

CAREER: PRINCIPAL STAGE WORK—Director: *The Woman: Scenes of War and Freedom,* with the National Theatre, Olivier Theatre, London, 1978; *The Worlds,* New Half Moon Theatre, London, 1979; *Restoration,* Royal Court Theatre, London, 1981; *Summer,* National Theatre, Cottesloe Stage, London, 1982; *The War Plays:* part one, "Red, Black and Ignorant," part two, "The Tin Can People," part three, "Great Peace," Royal Shakespeare Company, London, 1986.

NON-RELATED CAREER—Former factory and office worker.

WRITINGS: PLAYS, PRODUCED AND PUBLISHED—(All performed first at the Royal Court Theatre, London, unless noted otherwise) *The Pope's Wedding,* 1962, published in *The Pope's Wedding and Other Plays,* Methuen, 1971, revised, 1977; *Saved,* 1965, also performed at the Chelsea Theatre Center of Brooklyn, Brooklyn Academy of Music, NY, 1970, published by Methuen, 1966, Hill & Wang, 1966; *Narrow Road to the Deep North,* Belgrade Theatre, Coventry, U.K., 1968, then Charles Playhouse, Boston, 1969, published by Methuen, 1968, Hill & Wang, 1969; *Early Morning,* 1968, also La Mama Experimental Theatre Club

(E.T.C.), New York City, 1970, published by Calder & Boyers, 1968, Hill & Wang, 1969; *Black Mass,* 1970, published in *Plays: Two: Lear, The Sea, Narrow Road to the Deep North, Black Mass, Passion,* Methuen, 1978; *Passion,* 1971, also performed at Yale Repertory Theatre, New Haven, CT, 1972, published in *Plays: Two:. . .,* Methuen, 1978; *Lear,* 1971, also performed at Yale Repertory Theatre, 1973, published by Methuen, 1972, revised, 1978, Hill & Wang, 1972; *The Sea,* 1973, also performed at Goodman Theatre, Chicago, 1974, published in *Plays: Two:. . .,* Methuen, 1978.

Bingo: Scenes of Money and Death, Northcott Theatre, Exeter, U.K., 1973, then at Cleveland Playhouse, OH, 1975, published by Methuen, 1974; *The Fool: Scenes of Bread and Love,* 1975, published in *The Fool and We Come to the River,* Methuen, 1976; *Stone,* Institute of Contemporary Arts Theatre, London, 1976, published in *A-A-America! and Stone,* Methuen, 1976, revised, 1981; *A-A-America!* (two plays entitled "Grandma Faust: A Burlesque" and "The Swing: A Documentary"), Almost Free Free Theatre, London, 1976, published in *A-A-America! and Stone,* Methuen, 1976; *The Bundle, or, New Narrow Road to the Deep North,* Warehouse Theatre, London, 1978, published in *Plays One: Saved, Early Morning, The Pope's Wedding, The Bundle, or, New Narrow Road to the Deep North,* Methuen, 1978; *The Woman: Scenes of War and Freedom,* with the National Theatre, Olivier Theatre, London, 1978, published by Methuen, 1978, Hill & Wang, 1979; *The Worlds,* Newcastle Playhouse, Newcastle-upon-Tyne, U.K, 1979, then New Half Moon Theatre, London, 1981, published by Methuen, 1980; *Restoration,* 1981, published by Methuen, 1981, revised version, in *Restoration and The Cat,* Methuen, 1982; *Summer: A Play for Europe,* Cottesloe Theatre, London, 1982, published by Methuen, 1982. Also produced, *Human Cannon,* 1985; *The War Plays:* part one, "Red, Black and Ignorant," part two, "The Tin Can People," part three, "Great Peace," Royal Shakespeare Company, London, 1986.

Also, resident theatre writer, University of Essex, 1982-83.

OPERA—Libretto, *We Come to the River,* Royal Opera House, London, 1976, published in *The Fool and We Come to the River,* Methuen, 1976; libretto, *The English Cat,* 1982, published in *Restoration and the Cat,* Methuen, 1982. BALLET—*Orpheus,* 1978.

TRANSLATIONS—*The Three Sisters,* Royal Court Theatre, London, 1967; *Spring Awakening,* with the National Theatre, London, 1974. ADAPTATIONS—*The White Devil,* Old Vic Theatre, London, 1976.

SCREENPLAYS—*Blow-Up,* Metro-Goldwyn-Mayer, 1967; *Laughter in the Dark,* Lopert, 1969; (co-writer) *Michael Kohlhaas,* Columbia, 1969; *Walkabout,* Twentieth Century-Fox, 1971.

BOOKS—*Choruses from After the Assassinations,* Methuen, 1985; *Theatre Poems and Songs,* Methuen, 1978; *Poems 1978-1985,* Methuen, 1987.

AWARDS: George Devine Award, English Stage Society, 1968, for *Early Morning;* co-recipient, John Whiting Playwrights Award, Arts Council, 1969, for *Narrow Road to the Deep North.* Honorary degrees: Doctor of Letters, Yale University.

ADDRESSES: AGENT—Margaret Ramsay, 14A Goodwin's Court, St. Martin's Lane, London, WC2N 4LL, England.

BONET, Lisa

BRIEF ENTRY: Born in Los Angeles. Actress. At the age of fifteen, Lisa Bonet first appeared to American audiences as Denise Huxtable on the popular television show, *The Cosby Show*. Although she had originally intended to be a veterinarian, her success in acting has led her to expand her horizons beyond her work on the series. She recently made her film debut as Epiphany Proudfoot in the much-talked about 1987 movie *Angel Heart*, from Tri-Star Pictures. As Epiphany, Bonet turns in a performance that proves just how versatile her talents can be. Saying that she originally chose to star in the film because she didn't want to restrict herself to teen roles, she explained, ''Anyone who is a fan of mine will be pleased with the movie. Anyone who is a fan of Denise (from *The Cosby Show*) will be surprised.'' Bonet is a vegetarian, who enjoys running four to six miles four times a week in New York City's Central Park. She also practices yoga for relaxation.*

*   *   *

BOOKE, Sorrell   1930-

PERSONAL: Born January 4, 1930, in Buffalo, NY. EDUCATION: Columbia University, A.B.; Yale School of Drama, M.F.A. MILITARY: Served in the U.S. Armed Forces.

VOCATION: Actor.

CAREER: STAGE DEBUT—*Right You Are, If You Think You Are,* July, 1950. OFF-BROADWAY DEBUT—Doctor Julio, *The White Devil,* Phoenix Theatre, March 17, 1955. BROADWAY DEBUT—Baron Schwarz, *The Sleeping Prince,* Coronet Theatre, November 1, 1956. PRINCIPAL STAGE APPEARANCES—*Moby Dick* and a soldier, *The Carefree Tree,* both at the Phoenix Theatre, New York City, 1955; Duke of Albany, *King Lear,* City Center, New York City, 1956; a footman and Dr. Shpichelsky, *A Month in the Country,* Phoenix Theatre, 1956; Rip Voorhees, *Nature's Way,* Coronet Theatre, New York City, 1957; Abramovitch, Erbstein, Jimmy Jones, Corky, and Morrie, *Winkelberg,* Renata Theatre, New York City, 1958; Mayor Honorat, *The Gay Felons,* Ford's Theatre, Baltimore, MD, 1959; the burglar, *Heartbreak House,* Billy Rose Theatre, New York City, 1959.

Darling, *Caligula,* 54th Street Theatre, New York City, 1960; the father, *Jennette,* Maidman Playhouse, New York City, 1960; Senator Billboard Rawkins, *Finian's Rainbow,* City Center, New York City, 1960; understudy title role, *Fiorello!,* Broadhurst Theatre, New York City, 1960; *Evenings with Chekhov,* Key Theatre, New York City, 1961; Ol' Cap'n Cotchipee, *Purlie Victorious,* Cort Theatre, New York City, 1961; title role, *Fiorello!,* City Center Theatre, New York City, 1962; Daniel Webster, Reverend Fuller, Stephen Douglas, Ulysses S. Grant, Dr. W.W. Keen, and John Hay, *The White House,* Henry Miller's Theatre, 1964; title role, *Jonah,* American Place Theatre, New York City, 1966; Milton Rademacher, *Come Live with Me,* Billy Rose Theatre, 1967; Updike, ''Morning,'' Cecil, ''Noon,'' and Fibber Kidding, ''Night,'' in *Morning, Noon, and Night,* Henry Miller's Theatre, New York City, 1968; *Richard II,* Ahmanson Theatre, Los Angeles, 1972.

PRINCIPAL FILM APPEARANCES—*Gone Are the Days,* Hammer Brothers, 1963; *Black Like Me,* Reade, 1964; *Fail Safe,* Columbia, 1964; *Joy House,* Metro-Goldwyn-Mayer, 1965; *A Fine Madness,* Warner Brothers, 1966; *What's Up Doc?,* Warner Brothers, 1972;

Freaky Friday, Buena Vista, 1977; *The Take,* Columbia, 1974; *The Bank Shot,* United Artists, 1974.

PRINCIPAL TELEVISION APPEARANCES—Series: Jefferson Davis ''Boss'' Hogg, *The Dukes of Hazzard,* CBS, 1979-86. Episodic: ''The Life of Samuel Johnson,'' *Omnibus,* NBC, 1957; ''Little Moon of Alban,'' *Hallmark Hall of Fame,* NBC, 1958; ''The Iceman Cometh,'' *Play of the Week,* 1960; ''Pere Goriot,'' *Masterpiece Theatre,* PBS, 1971. Also appeared on *Dr. Kildare,* NBC; *The Bob Hope Chrysler Theatre,* NBC; *Twelve O'Clock High,* ABC; *Slattery's People,* CBS; *The Great Adventure,* CBS; *The Naked City,* ABC; *The DuPont Show of the Week,* NBC; *Route 66,* CBS; *What's Happening,* ABC; *Soap,* ABC.

MEMBER: Actors' Equity Association, Screen Actors Guild, American Federation of Television and Radio Artists.

ADDRESSES: AGENT—David Shapira & Associates, Inc., 15301 Ventura Blvd., Suite 345, Sherman Oaks, CA 91403.*

*   *   *

BOOTH, Shirley   1907-

PERSONAL: Born Thelma Booth Ford, August 30, 1907, in New York, NY; daughter of Albert James (a sales manager for I.B.M.) and Virginia (Wright) Ford; married Edward F. Gardner (an actor and producer), 1931 (divorced, 1944); married William H. Baker (an investment counselor), 1946 (died, 1950). EDUCATION: Attended public schools in New York City.

VOCATION: Actress.

CAREER: STAGE DEBUT—*The Cat and the Canary,* Poli Stock Company, Hartford, CT, 1919. BROADWAY DEBUT—Nan Winchester, *Hell's Bells,* Wallack's Theatre, January 26, 1925. PRINCIPAL STAGE APPEARANCES—Peggy Bryant, *Laff That Off,* Wallack's Theatre, 1925; Betty Hamilton, *Buy, Buy, Baby,* Princess Theatre, New York City, 1926; Mary Marshall, *High Gear,* Wallack's Theatre, 1927; Emily Rosen, *The War Song,* National Theatre, New York City, 1928; Marg, *The School for Virtue,* Longacre Theatre, New York City, 1928; Bobby Marchante, *The Camels Are Coming,* President Theatre, New York City, 1931; Annie Duval, *Coastwise,* Provincetown Playhouse, 1931; Elisa Zanotti, *The Mask and the Face,* Guild Theatre, New York City, 1933; *After Such Pleasure,* Bijou Theatre, New York City, 1934; *Sunday Nights at Nine,* Barbizon-Plaza Theatre, New York City, 1934; Mabel, *Three Men on a Horse,* The Playhouse, New York City, 1935; Mrs. Loschavio, *Excursion,* Vanderbilt Theatre, New York City, 1937; Carrie Nolan, *Too Many Heroes,* Hudson Theatre, New York City, 1937; Elizabeth Imbrie, *The Philadelphia Story,* for the Theatre Guild at the Shubert Theatre, New York City, 1939-40; Ruth Sherwood, *My Sister Eileen,* Biltmore Theatre, 1940-42; Leona Richards, *Tomorrow the World,* Barrymore Theatre, New York City, 1943-44; Louhedda Hopsons, *Hollywood Pinafore,* Alvin Theatre, New York City, 1945; Susan Pengilly, *Land's End,* The Playhouse, 1946; Maggie Welch, *The Men We Marry,* Mansfield Theatre, New York City, 1948; Grace Woods, *Goodbye, My Fancy,* Morosco Theatre, New York City, 1948; Abby Quinn, *Love Me Long,* 48th Street Theatre, 1949.

Lola, *Come Back, Little Sheba,* Booth Theatre, New York City, 1950; Cissy, *A Tree Grows in Brooklyn,* Alvin Theatre, New York

City, 1951; Leona Samish, *The Time of the Cuckoo*, Empire Theatre, New York City, 1952; Lottie Gibson, *By the Beautiful Sea*, Majestic Theatre, New York City, 1954; Bunny Watson, *Desk Set*, Broadhurst Theatre, New York City, 1955; Lola, *Come Back, Little Sheba*, Valley Music Theatre, Woodland, CA, 1956; Mrs. Ackroyd, *Miss Isobel*, Royale Theatre, New York City, 1957; Juno Boyle, *Juno*, Winter Garden Theatre, New York City, 1959; title role, *Nina*, Ivoryton Playhouse, CT, 1959; Fanny, *A Second String*, O'Neill Theatre, New York City, 1960; *The Torchbearers*, Ogunquit Playhouse, ME, 1967; Mother Maria, *Look to the Lilies*, Lunt-Fontanne Theatre, New York City, 1970; Judith Bliss, *Hay Fever*, Helen Hayes Theatre, New York City, 1970; Veta Louise, *Harvey*, Colorado Opera House, Central City, CO, 1971.

MAJOR TOURS—U.S. cities: Bunny Watson, *Desk Set*, 1955; Veta Louise, Simmons, *Harvey*, 1971; Mrs. Gibson, *Mourning in a Funny Hat*, 1972.

PRINCIPAL FILM APPEARANCES—Lola, *Come Back, Little Sheba*, Paramount, 1952; *About Mrs. Leslie*, Paramount, 1954; *Hot Spell* and *The Matchmaker*, both Paramount, 1958.

PRINCIPAL TELEVISION APPEARANCES—Series: Hazel Burke, *Hazel*, NBC, 1961-65, CBS, 1965-66; Grace Simpson, *A Touch of Grace*, ABC, 1973. Movies: *The Pearl Mesta Story*. Teleplays: Amanda, *The Glass Menagerie*, CBS, 1966.

PRINCIPAL RADIO APPEARANCES—Miss Duffy, *Duffy's Tavern*, NBC, 1940-42.

AWARDS: Best Actress, Antoinette Perry Awards, 1949, for *Goodbye, My Fancy*, 1950, for *Come Back, Little Sheba;* Best Actress, National Board of Review, New York Film Critics, Academy Award, all 1952, Cannes International Film Festival, 1953, all for *Come Back, Little Sheba;* Best Actress, Antoinette Perry Award and Delia Austrian Medal, Drama League of New York, both 1953, for *Time Time of the Cuckoo;* Best Actress, Sarah Siddons Award, 1957, for *The Desk Set;* Outstanding Performance in a Series, Emmy Awards, 1962 and 1963, for *Hazel.* Also received many other awards for *Hazel.*

MEMBER: Actors' Equity Association, Screen Actors Guild, American Federation of Television and Radio Artists.

SIDELIGHTS: FAVORITE ROLES—Lola, *Come Back, Little Sheba.* RECREATIONS—Painting, knitting, needlework, gardening, and interior decorating.

ADDRESSES: HOME—P.O. Box 103, Chatham, MA 02633.*

*   *   *

BOOTHE, Powers   1949-

PERSONAL: Born 1949, in Snyder, TX.

VOCATION: Actor.

CAREER: PRINCIPAL FILM APPEARANCES—*Cruising*, United Artists, 1980; *Southern Comfort*, Twentieth Century-Fox, 1981; *A Breed Apart*, 1984; *The Emerald Forest*, Embassy, 1985; also *Extreme Prejudice*.

PRINCIPAL TELEVISION APPEARANCES—Movies: *The Guyana*

Tragedy: The Story of Jim Jones, CBS, 1980. Series: Whalen, *Skag*, NBC, 1980; *Philip Marlowe*, HBO.

PRINCIPAL STAGE APPEARANCES—Roderigo, *Othello*, Roundabout Theatre, New York City, 1978; Roy, *Lone Star*, Century Theatre, New York City, 1979.

AWARDS: Outstanding Lead Actor in a Limited Series or Special, Emmy Award, 1980, for *The Guyana Tragedy: The Story of Jim Jones.*

MEMBER: Actors' Equity Association, Screen Actors Guild, American Federation of Television and Radio Artists.*

*   *   *

BOSCO, Philip   1930-

PERSONAL: Born September 26, 1930, in Jersey City, NJ; son of Philip Lupo and Margaret Raymond (Thik) Bosco; married Nancy Ann Dunkle (formerly a carnival worker and truck driver); children: Diane, Philip, Chris, Jenny, Lisa, Celia, John. EDUCATION: Attended Catholic University, Washington, DC; studied for the stage with James Marr, Josephine Callan, and Leo Brady.

VOCATION: Actor.

CAREER: STAGE DEBUT—Machiavelli the Cat, *The Fairy Cobbler*, St. John's School, Jersey City, NJ, 1944. BROADWAY DEBUT—Brian O'Bannion, *Auntie Mame*, City Center Theatre, 1958. PRINCIPAL STAGE APPEARANCES—Title roles, *Hamlet* and *Richard III*, and Malvolio, *Twelfth Night*, all at Catholic University; resident actor with Arena Stage, Washington, DC, appearing in twenty plays, 1957-60; Angelo, *Measure for Measure*, Belvedere Lake Amphitheatre, Central Park, New York City, 1960; Heracles, *The Rape of the Belt*, Martin Beck Theatre, New York City, 1960; Will Danaher, *Donnybrook*, 46th Street Theatre, New York City, 1961; Hawkshaw, *The Ticket-of-Leave Man*, Mayfair Theatre, New York City, 1961. At the American Shakespeare Festival, Stratford, CT: Henry Bolingbroke, *Richard II* and the title role, *Henry IV*, Part I, both 1962; Kent, *King Lear*, Rufio, *Antony and Cleopatra*, Pistol, *Henry V*, and Aegeon, *Comedy of Errors*, all 1963; Benedick, *Much Ado About Nothing* and Claudius, *Hamlet*, both 1964; title role, *Coriolanus*, 1965.

Duke of Buckingham, *Richard III*, New York Shakespeare Festival (NYSF), Delacorte Theatre, New York City, 1966. As resident actor with the Lincoln Center Repertory Company at the Vivian Beaumont Theatre, New York City: Lovewit, *The Alchemist*, 1966; Jack, *The East Wind* and Sagredo, *Galileo*, both 1967; the Bastard of Orleans, *Saint Joan*, Hector, *Tiger at the Gates*, Comte de Guiche, *Cyrano de Bergerac*, and Kent, *King Lear*, all 1968; still with the Lincoln Center Repertory Company, at the Forum Theatre, New York City: Zelda and Mr. Gray, *An Evening for Merlin Finch*, 1968; Anselme, *The Miser*, Nick, *The Time of Your Life*, Baron de Charlus, *Camino Real*, Captain Bovine, *Operation Sidewinder*, and Jupiter, *Amphitryon*, all 1970.

At the Vivian Beaumont Theatre, New York City: Cutis Moffat Jr., *In the Matter of J. Robert Oppenheimer*, 1968-69; First God, *The Good Woman of Setzuan*, Jimmy Farrell, *The Playboy of the Western World*, Peter Stockman, *An Enemy of the People*, and Creon, *Antigone*, all 1971; Earl of Leicester, *Mary Stuart*, Prime Minister, *Narrow Road to the Deep North*, Antonio, *Twelfth Night*, and Reverend Hale, *The Crucible,* all 1972; Mikhail Sktobotov, *Enemies,* Gratiano, *The Merchant of Venice,* and Harold Mitchell, *A Streetcar Named Desire,* all 1973; Crofts, *Mrs. Warren's Profession,* 1976.

Pistol, *Henry V,* NYSF, Delacorte Theatre, New York City, 1976; Mack the Knife, *The Threepenny Opera,* 1976; Sgt. Cokes, *Streamers,* Mitzi E. Newhouse Theatre, Lincoln Center, New York City, 1977; *Stages,* Belasco Theatre, New York City, 1978; Col. Pieter Goosen, *The Biko Inquest,* Theatre Four, New York City, 1978; Dr. Emerson, *Whose Life Is It, Anyway?,* Trafalgar Theatre, New York City, 1979.

At the Roundabout Theatre, New York City: Dr. Spigelsky, *A Month in the Country,* 1979; the Devil, *Don Juan in Hell,* 1980; Hudson, *Inadmissible Evidence* and Judge Brack, *Hedda Gabler,* both 1981; Chrysale, *Learned Ladies* and Gaetano Altobelli, *Some Men Need Help,* both 1982; John Tarlton, *Misalliance* and Nat Miller, *Ah! Wilderness,* both 1983; Doc, *Come Back, Little Sheba,* 1984.

At Circle in the Square, New York City: Warwick, *St. Joan,* 1977; Mendoza, *Man and Superman,* 1978; Cadmus, *The Bacchae* and Andrew Undershaft, *Major Barbara,* both 1980; Holmes Bradford, *Eminent Domain,* 1982; Lt. Commander John Challee, *The Caine Mutiny Court Martial,* 1983; Boss Mangan, *Heartbreak House,* 1984; Max, *The Loves of Anatol,* 1985; Waiter, *You Never Can Tell,* 1986; Sir Thomas More, *A Man for All Seasons,* Christian C. Yegen Theatre, NY, 1987.

FILM DEBUT—*Requiem for a Heavyweight,* 1961. PRINCIPAL FILM APPEARANCES—Fuller, *A Lovely Way to Die,* Universal, 1968; *The Money Pit,* Universal, 1986; *Children of a Lesser God,* Paramount, 1986; also *Walls of Glass.*

TELEVISION DEBUT—"The Prisoner of Zenda," *DuPont Show of the Month,* CBS, 1960. PRINCIPAL TELEVISION APPEARANCES—Episodic: *Armstrong Circle Theatre,* CBS; "An Enemy of the People" and "A Nice Place to Visit," both *Play of the Month,* PBS; *Esso Repertory Theatre,* syndicated; *The Nurses,* CBS; *Trials of O'Brien,* NBC; *Hawk,* NBC.

AWARDS: Shakespeare Society Award, New York Drama Critics Award, and Antoinette Perry Award nomination, all 1960, for *The Rape of the Belt;* general excellence, Clarence Derwent Award, 1966-67; Best Featured Actor, Antoinette Perry Award nomination, 1984, *Heartbreak House.*

MEMBER: Actors' Equity Association, American Federation of Television and Radio Artists, Screen Actors Guild.

SIDELIGHTS: RECREATIONS—Horses. FAVORITE ROLES—*Richard III,* Pistol in *Henry V,* Hamlet, Malvolio in *Twelfth Night,* Benedick in *Much Ado About Nothing,* and Cyrano in *Cyrano de Bergerac.**

*   *   *

BOSLEY, Tom   1927-

PERSONAL: Born October 1, 1927, in Chicago, IL; son of Benjamin and Dora (Heyman) Bosley; married Jean Eliot, March 8, 1962 (died, 1978); married Patricia Carr, December 21, 1980; children: (first marriage) one daughter. EDUCATION: Attended De Paul

University; trained for the stage with Lee Strasberg. MILITARY: U.S. Navy, World War II.

VOCATION: Actor.

CAREER: TELEVISION DEBUT—1952. PRINCIPAL TELEVISION APPEARANCES—Episodic: *Naked City,* ABC; *The Nurses,* CBS; *The Law and Mr. Jones,* ABC; *Route 66,* CBS; *Profiles in Courage,* NBC; *Ben Casey,* ABC; *The F.B.I.,* ABC; *Bonanza,* NBC; *Joanie Loves Chachie,* ABC; Henry Elliott, *The Castaways on Gilligan's Island,* NBC, 1979.

Series: Bob Landers, *The Debbie Reynolds Show,* NBC, 1968-70; *The Dean Martin Show,* NBC, 1971-72; Harry Boyle, *Wait Till Your Father Gets Home,* 1972-74; Bert Quinn, *Sandy Duncan Show,* CBS, 1972; Howard Cunningham, *Happy Days,* ABC, 1974-83; narrator, *That's Hollywood,* syndicated, 1977; Amos, *Murder, She Wrote,* CBS, 1984—.

Dramatic specials: Knave of Hearts, *Alice in Wonderland,* 1953; Throttlebottom, *The Right Man,* 1960; Teddy Brewster, *Arsenic and Old Lace,* 1962; Judge Harper, *Miracle on 34th Street,* 1973; Lawyer Cribbs, *The Drunkard,* 1982; also appeared in *Deathtrap.*

Movies: Jack Berger, *Step Out of Line,* 1971; Johnny Cavanaugh, *Vanished,* 1971; Herb, *Congratulations, It's a Boy!,* 1971; Mr. Jones, *Mr. & Mrs. Bo Jo Jones,* 1971; Dr. Sam Golinski, *No Place to Run,* 1972; Harold, *The Girl Who Came Gift Wrapped,* 1974; David Mason, *Death Cruise,* 1974; Bevo Means, *Who is the Black Dahlia?,* 1975; Norman Smith, *The Night that Panicked America,* 1975; Marcus Damian, *The Last Survivors,* 1975; narrator and appeared as Dr. Louis Hedler, *Testimony of Two Men,* 1977; Dr. Andrew Brantford, *Black Market Baby,* 1977; Edward, *With This Ring,* 1978; Morris Feldman, *The Triangle Factory Fire Scandal,* 1979; Frank Webber, *The Return of the Mod Squad,* 1979; Norman, *For the Love of It,* 1980; Jimmy Hoffa, *The Jesse Owens Story,* 1984; Harry O'Reilly, *Private Sessions,* NBC, 1985.

Pilots: Tiny Baker, *Marcus Welby, M.D.,* ABC, 1969; Sidney Resnick (story two), *Night Gallery,* NBC, 1969; Saretti, *The Streets of San Francisco,* 1972; George Havlicek, *Love Boat,* ABC, 1976; Henry Elliott, *Castaways on Gilligan's Island,* 1979; Mini-Series: Benjamin Franklin, *The Bastard,* 1978; Benjamin Franklin, *The Rebels,* 1979. Guest: *What's Up, America?,* 1971; *Mitzi and a Hundred Guys,* 1975; *A Special Olivia Newton-John,* 1976; *Rich Little's Washington Follies,* 1978; guest host, *Evening at the Improv,* 1980.

FILM DEBUT—*Love with a Proper Stranger,* Paramount, 1964. PRINCIPAL FILM APPEARANCES—*The World of Henry Orient,* United Artists, 1964; *Divorce American Style,* Columbia, 1967; *Yours, Mine and Ours,* United Artists, 1968; *The Secret War of Harry Frigg,* Universal, 1968; Mr. Katchaturian, *To Find a Man,* Columbia, 1972; Al, *Mixed Company,* United Artists, 1974; *Gus,* Buena Vista, 1976; Fred O'Hara, *O'Hara's Wife,* 1982.

STAGE DEBUT—Simon Stimson, *Our Town,* with the Canterbury Players, Fine Arts Theatre, Chicago, IL. OFF-BROADWAY DEBUT—Dupont-Dufour, *Thieves' Carnival,* Cherry Lane Theatre, 1955. PRINCIPAL STAGE APPEARANCES—Papa Bonaparte, *Golden Boy,* Eleventh Street Theatre, Chicago, IL, 1947; with the Woodstock Summer Playhouse, Woodstock, IL, 1947-48; Homer Bolton, *Mornings at Seven,* Cherry Lane Theatre, New York City, 1955; Yakov, *The Seagull,* Fourth Street Theatre, New York City, 1956; *The Power and the Glory,* Phoenix Theatre, New York City, 1956;

Scrub, *The Beaux Stratagem,* Phoenix Theatre, New York City, 1959; Fiorello LaGuardia, *Fiorello!,* Broadhurst Theatre, New York City, 1959-61; Izzy Einstein, *Nowhere to Go but Up,* Winter Garden Theatre, New York City, 1962; Vince Brinkman, *Natural Affection,* Booth Theatre, New York City, 1963; Cabouche, *A Murderer Is Among Us,* Morosco Theatre, New York City, 1964; Inspector Levine, *Catch Me If You Can,* Morosco Theatre, New York City, 1965; title role, *The Education of H*Y*M*A*N K*A*P*L*A*N,* Alvin Theatre, New York City, 1968; *A Shot in the Dark,* Ivanhoe Theatre, Chicago, IL, 1970.

MAJOR TOURS—Milt Manville, *LUV,* U.S. cities, 1965-66.

AWARDS: Best Actor in a Musical, Antoinette Perry Award, American National Theatre Academy (ANTA) Award, *Variety* New York Drama Critics Poll Award, and Page One Award, all 1960, for *Fiorello!;* Festival of Leadership Award, Chicago.

MEMBER: Actors' Equity Association (governing council, 1961-69), Screen Actors Guild, American Federation of Television and Radio Artists.

ADDRESSES: AGENT—Burton Moss Agency, 113 N. San Vincente Blvd., Beverly Hills, CA 90211.*

*   *   *

BOTTOMS, Joseph   1954-

PERSONAL: Born April 22, 1954, in Santa Barabara, CA. EDUCATION: Attended Sanata Barbara Public Schools.

VOCATION: Actor.

CAREER: FILM DEBUT—*The Dove,* Paramount, 1974. PRINCIPAL FILM APPEARANCES—*Crime and Passion,* 1976; *King of the Mountain,* Universal, 1981; *Blind Date,* New Line Cinema, 1984.

PRINCIPAL TELEVISION APPEARANCES—Episodic: *Owen Marshall,* ABC. Movies: *Celebrity,* NBC; *Winesburg, Ohio.*

BROADWAY DEBUT—*The Fifth of July,* New Apollo Theatre, 1981. PRINCIPAL STAGE APPEARANCES—Performed with community theatre, Santa Barbara.*

*   *   *

BOTTOMS, Sam   1955-

PERSONAL: Born October 17, 1955, in Santa Barbara, CA.

VOCATION: Actor.

CAREER: PRINCIPAL FILM APPEARANCES—*The Last Picture Show,* Columbia, 1971; *Class of '44,* Warner Brothers, 1973; *Zandy's Bride,* Warner Brothers, 1974; *The Outlaw Josey Wales,* Warner Brothers, 1976; *Apocalypse Now,* United Artists, 1979; *Up From the Depths,* New World, 1979; *Bronco Billy,* Warner Brothers, 1980.

PRINCIPAL TELEVISION APPEARANCES—Movies: *Savages,* 1974;

Greatest Heroes of the Bible, 1979; *Desperate Lives.* Mini-Series: *East of Eden,* 1980.*

*   *   *

BOVA, Joseph   1924-

PERSONAL: Born May 25, 1924, in Cleveland, OH; son of Anthony and Mary (Catalano) Bova; married Lee Lawson. EDUCATION: Attended Northwestern University; trained for the stage at the Actors Studio with Lee Strasberg and Alvina Krause.

VOCATION: Actor.

CAREER: STAGE DEBUT—David, *It Can't Happen Here,* Federal Theatre Project, Cleveland, OH, 1936. OFF-BROADWAY DEBUT—Chip, *On the Town,* Carnegie Hall Playhouse, 1959. PRINCIPAL STAGE APPEARANCES—*Stalag 17,* Cleveland Playhouse, OH, 1953; Francis X Dignan, *King of Hearts,* Cleveland Playhouse, 1954; Sakini, *Teahouse of the August Moon,* Cleveland Playhouse, 1957; Prince Dauntless, *Once Upon a Mattress,* Phoenix Theatre, New York City, then Alvin Theatre, New York City, 1959.

Tranio, *The Taming of the Shrew,* New York Shakespeare Festival, Delacorte Theatre, New York City, 1960; Theseus, *The Rape of the Belt,* Martin Beck Theatre, New York City, 1960; Bob, *Irma la Douce,* Plymouth Theatre, New York City, 1961; Charlie, *Never Too Late,* 46th Street Theatre, New York City, 1963; Shim, *Hot Spot,* Majestic Theatre, New York City, 1964; Junior Mister, *The Cradle Will Rock,* Theatre Four, New York City, 1964. With the New York Shakespeare Festival, Delacorte Theatre: Costard, *Love's Labour's Lost* and Thersites, *Troilus and Cressida,* both 1965, title role, *King Richard III,* 1966, Antipholus of Ephesus, *The Comedy of Errors,* 1967, Mercutio, *Romeo and Juliet,* 1968; also appeared as M'sieur Pierre, *Invitation to a Beheading,* Public Theatre, New York City, 1969.

Mr. Lee, *The Chinese and Dr. Fish,* Ethel Barrymore Theatre, New York City, 1970; Coviello, *Comedy,* Colonial Theatre, Boston, 1972; Jake Jackson, *An American Millionaire,* Circle in the Square Theatre, New York City, 1974; Ford, *The Merry Wives of Windsor,* New York Shakespeare Festival, Delacorte Theatre, New York City, 1974; various roles, *The Beauty Part,* American Place Theatre, New York City, 1974; Milt, *LUV,* Papermill Playhouse, Milburn, NJ, 1976; Fluellen, *Henry V* and Sgt. Rooney, *Streamers,* both New York Shakespeare Festival, 1976; Dunois, *Saint Joan,* Goodman Theatre, Chicago, IL, then Circle in the Square Theatre, New York City, 1977; Sir Toby Belch, *Twelfth Night,* American Shakespeare Festival, Stratford, CT, 1978; Bert Barry, *Forty-Second Street,* Winter Garden Theatre, New York City, 1980-81, then Majestic Theatre, 1981—.

MAJOR TOURS—Bob, *Irma la Douce,* U.S. cities, 1962.

FILM DEBUT—*The Young Doctors,* United Artists, 1961. PRINCIPAL FILM APPEARANCES—*Pretty Poison,* Twentieth Century-Fox, 1968; *Serpico,* Paramount, 1974.

PRINCIPAL TELEVISION WORK—Producer and actor for children's programming, Cleveland, OH, 1951-54.

PRINCIPAL TELEVISION APPEARANCES—Dramatic specials—

Oscar, *The Tin Drum*, PBS; *Once Upon a Mattress*. Episodic—*Kojak*, CBS; *Barney Miller*, ABC. Movies—*Johnny, We Hardly Knew Ye*, 1977.

AWARDS: Antoinette Perry Award nomination, 1970, for *The Chinese and Dr. Fish;* Emmy Award nomination, for *The Tin Drum.*

MEMBER: Actors' Equity Association.

SIDELIGHTS: RECREATIONS—Golf, tennis, bridge.

ADDRESSES: AGENT—Richard Astor Agency, 119 W. 57th Street, New York, NY 10019.*

* * *

BRAINE, John   1922-1986

PERSONAL: Full name, John Gerard Braine; born April 13, 1922, in Bradford, Yorkshire, England; died of a burst stomach ulcer in London, October 28, 1986; son of Fred and Katherine (Henry) Braine; married Helen Patricia Wood, 1955; children: Anthony, Frances, Felicity. EDUCATION: Leeds School of Librarianship, A.I.A., 1949. POLITICS: Conservative. RELIGION: Roman Catholic. MILITARY: Royal Navy, 1942-43.

VOCATION: Writer.

CAREER: PRINCIPAL FILM WORK—Screenwriter: *Room at the Top*, Continental, 1959; *Life at the Top*, Royal International, 1966; *Man at the Top*, British, 1975.

PRINCIPAL STAGE WORK—Playwright, *The Desert in the Mirror*, Bingley, England, 1951; also *The Stirrer*, 1975.

PRINCIPAL TELEVISION WORK—Series: Writer, *Man at the Top*, Thames, 1970, 1972.

RELATED CAREER—Contributing writer to newspapers and periodicals in Great Britain and the United States.

NON-RELATED CAREER—Assistant librarian, Bingley Public Library, Bingley, U.K., 1940-48, chief assistant librarian, 1948-51; librarian, Northumberland County Library, U.K., 1954-56; librarian, West Riding County Library, U.K., 1956-57; member of North Regional Advisory Council, British Broadcasting Corporation, 1960-64.

WRITINGS: BOOKS—*Room at the Top*, Houghton, 1957, reprinted, Methuen, 1980; *The Vodi*, Eyre & Spottiswoode, 1959, published in America as *From the Hand of the Hunter*, Houghton, 1960; *Life at the Top*, Houghton, 1962, Methuen, 1980; *The Jealous God*, Eyre & Spottiswoode, 1964, Houghton, 1965; *The Crying Game*, Houghton, 1968; *Stay with Me Till Morning*, Eyre & Spottiswoode, 1970, published as *The View from Tower Hill*, Coward, 1971; *The Queen of a Distant Country*, Methuen, 1972, Coward, 1973; *Writing a Novel*, Coward, 1974; *The Pious Agent*, Eyre Methuen, 1975, Atheneum, 1975; *Waiting for Sheila*, Eyre Methuen, 1976; *Finger of Fire*, Eyre Methuen, 1977; *J.B. Priestley*, Barnes & Noble, 1979. Also *The Stirrer*, 1975; *These Golden Days*. PERIODICALS—Contributor to many periodicals and newspapers in Great Britain and the United States.

MEMBER: Arts Theatre Club, Authors' Club, Bingley Little Theatre, Bradford Civic Theatre; Library Association.

SIDELIGHTS: John Braine was a leading figure in the British group of writers known as the "Angry Young Men." The common theme for this group was disenchantment with the traditional British class system

In an interview given in the 1970s, Braine said, "Let this be my epitaph: As a writer, I never tried to please anybody but myself."

ADDRESSES: AGENT—David Higham Associates, Ltd., 5-8 Lower John Street, Golden Square, London W1R 4HA, England.*

* * *

BRIDGES, James   1936-

PERSONAL: Born February 3, 1936, in Little Rock, AR; son of Doy and Celestine (McKeen) Bridges. EDUCATION: Attended Arkansas Teachers College and the University of Southern California.

VOCATION: Actor, writer, director, and producer.

CAREER: FILM DEBUT—*Johnny Trouble*, Warner Brothers, 1957. PRINCIPAL FILM APPEARANCES—*Faces*, Continental, 1968.

PRINCIPAL FILM WORK—Writer (see below); also director: *The Baby Maker*, National General, 1970; *The Paper Chase*, Twentieth Century-Fox, 1973; *September 30, 1955*, Universal, 1978; *The China Syndrome*, Columbia, 1979; *Urban Cowboy*, Paramount, 1980; *Mike's Murder*, Warner Brothers, 1982; producer and director, *Perfect*, Columbia, 1985.

PRINCIPAL STAGE WORK—Director: At the Edinburgh Festival, Scotland, Mark Taper Forum and Ahmanson Theatre, Los Angeles, and in New York City.

PRINCIPAL TELEVISION APPEARANCES—Appeared in more than fifty television programs.

WRITINGS: SCREENPLAYS—*The Appaloosa*, Universal, 1966; *Colossus: The Forbin Project*, Universal, 1970; *The Baby Maker*, National General, 1970; *Limbo*, Universal, 1972; *The Paper Chase*, Twentieth Century-Fox, 1973; *September 30, 1955*, Universal, 1978; (with Mike Gray and T.S. Cook) *The China Syndrome*, Columbia, 1979; *Urban Cowboy*, Paramount, 1980; *Mike's Murder*, Warner Brothers, 1984; *Perfect*, Columbia, 1985.

TELEVISION—Episodic: "Unlocked Window" and seventeen other episodes, for *Alfred Hitchcock Presents*, NBC; "Go Down Moses," *Great Adventure*, CBS. Pilots: *The Paper Chase*, CBS, 1978.

PLAYS—Has written more than sixteen plays, some published in New Theatre for Now.

AWARDS: Mystery Writer's Award, for "Unlocked Window," *Alfred Hitchcock Presents;* Best Screenplay, Academy Award nomination, and Best Screenplay, Best Picture, and Best Director, Atlanta Film Festival Awards, all 1973, for *The Paper Chase;* Best Drama, Writers Guild Award, Best Writer, American Movie Award, Best Writer and Best Director, Christopher Awards, Best Screenplay, Japanese Academy Award, Best Writer, Best Director, and Best Picture, Golden Globe nominations, Best Screenplay, Academy Award nomination, all 1979, for *The China Syndrome.*

MEMBER: Writers Guild of America, Directors Guild of America, Screen Actors Guild, American Federation of Television and Radio Artists.

ADDRESSES: AGENT—c/o Steven Roth, Creative Artists Agency, 1888 Century Park E., Los Angeles, CA 90067.*

*   *   *

BRIGHT, Richard

PERSONAL: Born June 11, in Brooklyn, NY; son of Ernest (a shipbuilder) and Matilda (Scott) Bright; married Rutanya Alda (an actress), June 11, 1977; children: Diane. EDUCATION: Attended New York City public schools; trained for the stage with Frank Crosano, John Lehne, and Paul Mann.

VOCATION: Actor.

CAREER: PRINCIPAL FILM APPEARANCES—Coco, *Odds Against Tomorrow,* 1959; Billy the Kid, *Lion's Love,* Max L. Rabb, 1969; Hank, *Panic in Needle Park,* Twentieth Century-Fox, 1971; locker thief, *The Getaway,* National General, 1972; Holly, *Pat Garrett and Billy the Kid,* Metro-Goldwyn-Mayer (MGM), 1972; Al Neri, *The Godfather,* Paramount, 1972; Al Neri, *The Godfather II,*

RICHARD BRIGHT

Paramount, 1974; Burt, *Rancho Deluxe,* United Artists, 1975; Karl, *Marathon Man,* Paramount, 1977; Smilin' Jack, *Citizens Band,* Paramount, 1977; Prince George, *Looking for Mr. Goodbar,* Paramount, 1977; Nunn, *On the Yard,* Midwest, 1977; Sergeant Fenton, *Hair,* United Artists, 1979; Uncle Tony, *The Idolmaker,* Twentieth Century-Fox, 1981; Burke, *Vigilante,* Artists Releasing Corporation, 1982; Chicken Joe, *Once Upon a Time in America,* Warner Brothers, 1984; Stuart, *Two of a Kind,* Twentieth Century-Fox, 1985; Bob, *Cut and Run,* 1986; Sergeant, *Brighton Beach Memoirs,* Universal, 1986; *Fifty-Two Pickup,* Cannon, 1986.

TELEVISION DEBUT—*Lamp Unto My Feet.* PRINCIPAL TELEVISION APPEARANCES—Episodic: *Armstrong Circle Theatre,* NBC; *The Verdict Is Yours,* CBS; *Kraft Television Theatre,* ABC; *Studio One,* CBS; *Cagney and Lacey,* CBS; *Beacon Hill,* CBS, 1975; *Hill Street Blues,* NBC, 1986; also appeared on *Kayo, Look Up and Live, CBS Television Workshop, Somerset, Texas,* and *From These Roots.*

Pilots: Houston Knights, Columbia Television, 1986. Movies: *A Death of Innocence,* CBS, 1971; *The Connection,* 1973; *The Gun,* ABC, 1974; *Cops and Robin,* NBC, 1978; *Sizzle,* ABC, 1981; the detective, *There Must Be a Pony,* ABC, 1986; judge, *Penalty Phase,* 1986; also appeared in *Police Brass,* CBS. Specials: appeared on "Baby Face," *ABC Afterschool Special.* Mini-Series: *From Here to Eternity,* 1979; *Skag,* NBC; *Sizzle,* ABC.

BROADWAY DEBUT—The slave, *The Balcony,* Circle in the Square Theatre, 1959. LONDON DEBUT—Billy the Kid, *The Beard,* Royal Court Theatre, 1968-69. PRINCIPAL STAGE APPEARANCES—Billy the Kid, *The Beard,* Evergreen Theatre, New York City, 1968; Mute Shepherd, *The Salvation of St. Joan,* Anderson Theatre, New York City, 1971; the resurrection man, *Gogol,* New York Shakespeare Festival, Public Theatre, New York City, 1976; Sergeant Brisbey, *The Basic Training of Pavlo Hummel,* Longacre Theatre, New York City, 1977; first murderer, *Richard III,* Cort Theatre, New York City, 1979-80; Abe Reles, *Kid Twist,* Soho Repertory Theatre, New York City, 1983; Mr. Nett, *Short Eyes,* Second Stage Theatre, New York City, 1984.

Other New York City productions: Roy Zinc, *Black Hole in Space,* Gate Theatre; Mumon and the master, *Koolaid,* Forum Theatre; Victor, *Vinyl Visits an FM Station,* Playwrights Unit; Bickham, *Does a Tiger Wear a Necktie?,* New Dramtists Workshop; and at Theatre Genesis: title role, *Forgotten American;* Rocky, *Waterworks at Lincoln;* Mr. Williams, *Flite Cage;* Pedro, *Mission Beach;* the Vesuvian, *Are You Lookin'?*

Productions in San Francisco: Billy the Kid, *The Beard* and Jeriah Jip, *A Man's Man,* both at the Encore Theatre; the Orator, *The Chairs,* Committee Theatre; Bertram, *The Last Analysis,* Peter Quince, *A Midsummer Night's Dream,* and Lightborn, *Edward II,* all at the Marine's Memorial Theatre. Also appeared as Pablo and Stanley, *A Streetcar Named Desire,* Pittsburgh Playhouse.

MAJOR TOURS—Billy the Kid, *The Beard,* Warner Playhouse, Los Angeles, Theatres des Nations, Paris, and other U.S., U.K., and European cities, 1964-70.

MEMBER: Actors' Equity Association, Screen Actors Guild, American Federation of Television and Radio Artists.

SIDELIGHTS: FAVORITE ROLES—Al Niri, *Godfather I* and *Godfather II;* Hank, *Panic in Needle Park;* Billy the Kid, *The Beard;* Abe Reles, *Kid Twist.*

RECREATIONS—Bonsai gardening, coin collecting, and motorcycling.

ADDRESSES: AGENT—c/o Jeff Hunter, Triad Agency, 888 Seventh Avenue, Suite 1602, New York, NY 10106; c/o Jerry Silverhardt, Moorehardt Management Company, 231 W. 58th Street, New York, NY 10019.

*   *   *

BRISBANE, Katharine   1932-

PERSONAL: Born January 7, 1932, in Singapore; daughter of David William (a civil engineer) and Myra Gladys Brisbane; married Philip Edward Parsons (an academic). EDUCATION: University of Western Australia, B.A., 1953. RELIGION: Anglican.

VOCATION: Critic and publisher.

CAREER: PRINCIPAL STAGE WORK—Critic for *West Australian*, Perth, Australia, 1959-61, 1962-65; *Australian*, Sydney, Australia, national critic, 1967-74; *National Times*, national theatre writer, 1981-82.

WRITINGS: CONTRIBUTOR—*The Literature of Australia*, Penguin, 1976; *World Drama*, Harrap, 1977; (also co-editor) *New Currents in Australian Writing*, Angus & Robertson, 1978; *Contemporary Australian Drama: Perspectives Since 1955*, Currency Press, 1981, revised edition, 1987; *Contemporary Dramatists*, St. James Press, 1977, revised editions, 1982, 1987.

Author of introductions, all for plays published by Currency Press: *Three Plays*, by Alexander Buzo, 1973; *A Hard God*, by Peter Kenna, 1974; *Brumby Innes*, by K.S. Prichard, 1974; *Bid Me to Love*, by K.S. Prichard, 1974; *How Does Your Garden Grow*, by Jim McNeil, 1975; *The Floating World*, by John Romeril, 1975; *Summer of the Seventeenth Doll*, by Ray Lawler, 1978; *Big Toys*, by Patrick White, 1979; *Furtive Love*, by Peter Kenna, 1980; *Collected Plays*, Volume I, by Patrick White, 1985; *Collected Plays*, Volume I, by David Williamson, 1986.

RELATED CAREER—Co-founder, with Philip Edward Parsons, Currency Press, Sydney, Australia, 1971—.

AWARDS: For Outstanding Service to the Theatre, Dorothy Crawford Award, Australian Writers Guild, 1985.

MEMBER: Australian Journalists Association, Australian National Playwrights Conference (chairman, 1977-84); Griffin Theatre Company (board of management, 1985—).

ADDRESSES: OFFICE—Currency Press Ltd., 330 Oxford Street, Paddington, 2021, Australia.

*   *   *

BRODERICK, Matthew   1962-

PERSONAL: Born March 21, 1962, in New York, NY; son of James (an actor) and Patricia (a painter; maiden name, Biow) Broderick. EDUCATION: Attended Walden High School, New York City.

VOCATION: Actor.

CAREER: STAGE DEBUT—Brother Vaughn, *Valentine's Day*, Herbert Berghof Studio, New York City, 1980, for twelve performances. PRINCIPAL STAGE APPEARANCES—David, *Torch Song Trilogy*, Actors' Playhouse, New York City, 1982; Eugene M. Jerome, *Brighton Beach Memoirs*, Neil Simon Theatre, New York City, 1983; Eugene M. Jerome, *Biloxi Blues*, Neil Simon Theatre, New York City, 1985; *The Widow Claire*, Circle in the Square Downtown, New York City, 1986-87.

FILM DEBUT—Michael McPhee, *Max Dugan Returns*, Twentieth Century-Fox, 1983. PRINCIPAL FILM APPEARANCES—David Lightman, *WarGames*, Metro-Goldwyn-Mayer, 1983; Phillipe, *Ladyhawke*, Warner Brothers, 1984; title role, *Ferris Bueller's Day Off*, Paramount, 1986; Jimmy, *Project X*, Twentieth Century-Fox, 1987.

TELEVISION DEBUT—Mike, *Lou Grant*, CBS, 1982. PRINCIPAL TELEVISION APPEARANCES—Teleplays: Hallie, "Master Harold. . .and the Boys," shown on *Great Performances*, PBS, 1984.

AWARDS: Villager Award and Outer Critics Circle Award, both 1982, for *Torch Song Trilogy*; Los Angeles Critics Award, Drama League Award, *Theatre World* Award and Antoinette Perry Award, all 1983, for *Brighton Beach Memoirs*.

MEMBER: Actors' Equity Association, Screen Actors Guild.

SIDELIGHTS: With his performances on Broadway in the play *Brighton Beach Memoirs* and in the movies *Max Dugan Returns* and *WarGames*, then twenty-one-year-old Matthew Broderick became a leader of the group of younger actors and actresses active in the American cinema and stage. Broderick's youthful appearance and mannerisms kept him playing teenaged roles into his mid-twenties.

Broderick told *CTFT* that he had "wanted to be an actor since I was little." Having devoted more attention to school plays than to his classwork in high school, he decided to study acting with renowned teacher Uta Hagen instead of going to college. Broderick made his professional stage debut alongside his father, stage and television actor James Broderick, in the 1980 Off Off-Broadway production of Horton Foote's *Valentine's Day*.

Broderick's first major break came in 1982, when he was cast as a "street kid" whom the transvestite protagonist wishes to adopt in the New York stage hit *Torch Song Trilogy*. Although the part was relatively small, Broderick received excellent reviews. Jack Kroll wrote in *Newsweek*, "Teenager Matthew Broderick gives one of the most original, touching and witty performances I've ever seen from a young actor." *Variety*'s reviewer commented, "Broderick has a distinctive presence that augurs a bright future."

While still in *Torch Song Trilogy*, Broderick won the lead role of Eugene Jerome in *Brighton Beach Memoirs*, Neil Simon's semi-autobiographical 1983 comedy about a Brooklyn family during the Depression. Brendan Gill of the *New Yorker* credited Broderick with "a virtuoso acting performance" and added, "Without him, much of the pleasing humaneness of the play would degenerate into slapstick."

Broderick's performance prompted Simon to give the young actor a leading role in the movie *Max Dugan Returns*, for which the playwright had written the script. During the filming of *Max Dugan Returns*, producer Leonard Goldberg was similarly impressed with Broderick and gave him the starring role in *WarGames*. That film, in which Broderick played a young computer whiz who inadvertently comes close to starting a nuclear war, was one of the biggest hits of the summer of 1983, and its release, soon after the Broadway opening of *Brighton Beach Memoirs*, established Broderick as a star.

Broderick's character in his next movie, *Ladyhawke,* was likened by Pauline Kael of the *New Yorker* to "a contemporary American adolescent placed in the Middle Ages." However, Kael went on to note that though Broderick was cast in the role for comic relief, he "has more of a fairy-tale quality than anyone else, and he gives this limp movie . . . its only traces of inspiration."

Returning to the stage early in 1985, Broderick again portrayed Eugene Jerome, this time in *Biloxi Blues.* "Mr. Broderick is even more appealing here than in his last appearance as Eugene," *New York Times* critic Frank Rich said of the actor's performance in Simon's sequel to *Brighton Beach Memoirs.* Noting that the character is now six years older and undergoing basic training for service in World War II, the critic felt that "the performer no longer seems a practical stand-up comic masquerading in little boy's clothing but an assured actor at one with a full-bodied role." He concluded, Broderick's "comic timing, now as much physical as verbal, has attained a textbook perfection."

As David Ansen of *Newsweek* saw it, Broderick's 1986 film, *Ferris Bueller's Day Off,* is a kind of daydream of adolescent omnipotence: an account of a high-school hero's perfect day of playing hooky." Ansen also wrote that "Broderick, who has been trained on the stage, doesn't hide his efforts to entertain and seduce us. He's like a new-age magician who lets the audience see his bag of tricks, but still pulls off wonders."

Despite his success, Broderick prefers hobbies such as watching reruns of the 1950's television series *The Honeymooners.* In 1983, he told David Richards of the *Washington Post:* "I used to wonder what it would be like to see my name on a billboard. I couldn't imagine something like that. Then you see it and, well, it just makes billboards not as special as they used to be."

ADDRESSES: AGENT—Arnold Stiefel, 9200 Sunset Blvd., Los Angeles, CA 90069.

*   *   *

BROOK, Faith   1922-

PERSONAL: Born February 16, 1922, in York, England; daughter of Clive and Mildred (Evelyn) Brook; married Charles Moffett (a physician; divorced); married Michael Horowitz (divorced). EDUCATION: Trained for the stage with Kate Rorke, Dame May Whitty, and at the Royal Academy of Dramatic Art.

VOCATION: Actress.

CAREER: STAGE DEBUT—Rose, *Lottie Dundass,* Lobero Theatre, Santa Barbara, CA, August, 1941. BROADWAY DEBUT—Marion Curwood, *Letters to Lucerne,* Cort Theatre, December 23, 1941. LONDON DEBUT—Marie, *Aren't Men Beasts?,* Garrick Theatre, November 11, 1942. PRINCIPAL STAGE APPEARANCES—Dorinda, *The Beaux Stratagem,* Pauline, *Jenny Villiers,* Lady Macduff, *Macbeth,* Olivia, *Twelfth Night,* and Olga, *Keep in a Cool Place,* all with the Bristol Old Vic Company, U.K., 1946; Louisa Packard, *Truant in Park Lane,* St. James's Theatre, London, 1947; Alice Langdon, *Deep Are the Roots,* Wyndham's Theatre, London, 1947; Gloria Clandon, *You Never Can Tell,* Martin Beck Theatre, New York City, 1948; Olivia, *Twelfth Night,* Helen of Troy, *Dr. Faustus,* Mrs. Millamant, *The Way of the World,* and Charlotte Ivanovna, *The Cherry Orchard,* all with the Old Vic Company, London, 1948-49; Celia Coplestone, *The Cocktail Party,* Henry Miller's Theatre, New York City, 1950.

Appeared in *The Devil's Disciple, The Tempest, Too True to Be Good,* and *Don Juan in Hell,* summer stock, 1951; Sheila Vendice, *Dial M for Murder,* with the National Company, Chicago and New York City, 1952-53; Mary Terriford, *The Burning Glass,* Apollo Theatre, London, 1954; Inez, *Vicious Circle,* New Watergate Theatre, London, 1955; Anne Irving, *The Leopard,* Connaught Theatre, Worthing, U.K., 1955; the visitor, *The Whole Truth,* Aldwych Theatre, London, 1955; Helene Donaldo, *No Laughing Matter,* Arts Theatre, London, 1957; Agnes Potter, *The Kidders,* St. Martin's Theatre, London, 1958; Lady Dungavel, *Roar Like a Dove,* Phoenix Theatre, London, 1959; Frances Darling, *Little Darlings,* Adelphi Theatre, London, 1960.

Paula Tanqueray, *The Second Mrs. Tanqueray,* Pembroke Theatre, Croydon, U.K., 1961; Laura Foster, *Licence to Murder,* Vaudeville Theatre, London, 1963; Kathy and Angela Wallace, *Games,* New Arts Theatre, London, 1964; Antonia, *A Severed Head,* Criterion Theatre, London, 1964; Dalila, *Samson Agonistes,* Yvonne Arnaud Theatre, Guildford, U.K., 1965; Patricia, *Minor Murder,* Savoy Theatre, London, 1967; woman, *Fill the Stage with Happy Hours,* Vaudeville Theatre, London, 1967; Mrs. Forbes, *Backbone,* Royal Court Theatre, London, 1968; Olivia, *His, Hers and Theirs,* Apollo Theatre, London, 1969; Gertrude, *Hamlet,* Cambridge Theatre, London, 1971; appeared in *The Ride Across Lake Constance,* Hampstead Theatre, London, 1973; the daughter, *All Over,* Gardner Arts Centre Theatre, Brighton, U.K., 1976; Veronica, *The Old Country,* Queen's Theatre, London, 1977.

MAJOR TOURS—Patricia, *Flare Path,* Mable Crum, *While the Sun Shines* and other roles, with a military ATS Unit called, "Stars in Battledress," 1943-45; Gertrude, *Hamlet* and Lady Macsycophant, *The Man of the World,* U.K. cities, 1969; the daughter, *All Over,* U.K. cities, 1976.

PRINCIPAL TELEVISION APPEARANCES—Series: Julia Naughton, *Claudia, the Story of a Marriage,* NBC, 1952. Teleplays: Appearances in more than thirty teleplays, including *War and Peace, Angels,* and *After Julius.*

SIDELIGHTS: RECREATIONS—Painting and cooking.

ADDRESSES: AGENT—Boyack and Conway, Ltd., 8 Cavendish Place, London W1, England.*

*   *   *

BROOKS, Joel

PERSONAL: Born in New York City. EDUCATION: Attended Hunter College and the University of Minnesota.

VOCATION: Actor.

CAREER: TELEVISION DEBUT—*Three's Company,* CBS. PRINCIPAL TELEVISION APPEARANCES—Series: *Hail to the Chief;* Lieutenant Billy Dean, *Private Benjamin,* CBS, 1982; Barney Betelman, *Teachers Only,* NBC, 1985; J.D. Lucas, *My Sister Sam,* CBS, 1986—. Episodic: *M*A*S*H,* CBS; *The Twilight Zone,* CBS; *Night Court,* NBC; *It Takes Two,* ABC; *The Facts of Life,* NBC. Movies: *The Mating Season,* 1980; Phil Garrett, *Stranded,* NBC, 1986; also, *Help Wanted: Kids.*

PRINCIPAL FILM APPEARANCES—*Stir Crazy,* Columbia, 1980;

JOEL BROOKS

NORMAN G. BROOKS

Honky Tonk Man, Warner Brothers, 1982; *Best Defense,* Paramount, 1984; *Protocol,* Warner Brothers, 1984.

PRINCIPAL STAGE APPEARANCES—With the New York Shakespeare Festival, New York City: *The Taming of the Shrew, New Jerusalem, All's Well That Ends Well, Museum,* and *Flux.* Off-Broadway and Regional: *Sweet Apple Cider, Aaron Weiss, Oedipus Rex, The Prague Spring, Fog and Mismanagement, Auto-Destruct, The Rivals,* and *Cracks.*

ADDRESSES: PUBLICIST—c/o Monique Moss, Michael Levine Public Relations, 9123 Sunset Blvd., Los Angeles, CA 90069.

*   *   *

BROOKS, Norman G.   1926-

PERSONAL: Born Norman Geller, March 24, 1926 in Chicago, IL; son of Abraham (self employed) and Esther (Halperin) Geller; married Fern Field (a director and producer) May 13, 1979; children: Melinda Robin, Bobbi Lee, Mark Steven. EDUCATION: Northwestern University. RELIGION: Jewish.

VOCATION: Executive producer.

PRINCIPAL TELEVISION WORK—Producer and executive producer, 1977—; executive producer, *Henry Hamilton, Graduate Ghost,* 1984.

MEMBER: Masonic Order, Scottish Rite, Al Malaikah Shrine

Temple; Sholom Aleichem Temple of Creative Art (president, 1981-84); media access committee, Employment for the Disabled.

AWARDS: National Association for the Advancement of Colored People (NAACP) Image Award; Humanitas and Silver Cloud awards, both 1986.

ADDRESSES: HOME—Marina Del Rey, CA. OFFICE—11600 Washington Place, Suite 203, Los Angeles, CA, 90060.

*   *   *

BROWN, Kenneth H.   1936-

PERSONAL: Born March 9, 1936, in Brooklyn, NY; son of Kenneth F. (a New York City policeman) and Helen (department head, Swiss Bank Corporation; maiden name, Bella) Brown. MILITARY: U.S. Marine Corp, 1954-57.

VOCATION: Writer, teacher, and actor.

CAREER: Playwright in residence and playwriting tutor, Yale University School of Drama, 1966-69; created performing theatre group, Hollins College, VA, 1969; drama teacher, Hunter College, New York City, 1969-70; producer and director, University of Iowa, 1971; lecturer and reader.

NON-RELATED CAREER—Construction worker, bartender, and restaurant manager.

WRITINGS: PLAYS, PRODUCED—*The Brig,* Living Theatre, New York City, 1963, for a two year run, toured Europe in repertory of the Living Theatre for four years, performed in over thirty professional productions, and was made into a film by Jonas Mekis; *The Happy Bar,* Actors Studio, New York City, 1966; *Devices,* Yale School of Drama, New Haven, CT, Judson Poets Theatre, New York City, Actors Studio, New York City, and Manhattan Theatre Club, New York City; *Blake's Design,* Yale School of Drama, 1968, and Theatre for the New City, New York City, 1974; *The Green Room,* University of Iowa, 1971; *The Cretan Bull,* O'Neill Theatre Center, Waterford, CT, 1972, Drake University, 1972, and Manhattan Theatre Club, New York City, 1973; *Nightlight,* Hartford Stage Company, CT, 1973.

PLAYS, PUBLISHED—*The Brig,* Hill and Wang, 1963; *The Narrows,* Dial Press, 1970; *Nightlight,* Samuel French Inc., 1973; has completed ten other plays, two are under option, one is in progress.

ARTICLES—"The Living Theatre," *Tulane Drama Review,* Fall, 1963; "Dada Drama Daddy," *Arts Magazine,* April, 1969; "Theatre of God," *Plays & Players,* London, September, 1964, and *City Lights Journal,* San Francisco, 1966; "The Illusion," *Encore,* London, 1965; "Lincoln Center," *Plays & Players,* London, November, 1965; "The Night Club," *City Lights Journal,* 1966; "Theatre, a Reflection of the National Personality," *Arts Magazine,* November, 1967; "Whose Cup of Tea Shall We Fill," *New York Times,* Sunday Drama section, April 2, 1967; "Homerun," *The Evergreen Review,* March, 1969; "The Death of the Artist in His Own Time," *New York Times,* Sunday Drama section, September, 1973; "The O'Neill Theatre," *New York Times,* Sunday Drama section, September, 1973; "Eulogy to Warren Finnerty," *The Village Voice,* December, 1974; "The Bright Side of Fifty," *New York Times Magazine,* January, 1986.

POEMS—"My Seed Grows Wilder," published in *Kulchur Magazine,* No. 14, Spring, 1964; "For Julian and Judith," *Intermission Magazine,* Hull House, Chicago, 1966, *Yale/Theatre Magazine,* Vol. 1, Spring, 1966; "Through a Cage Brightly," *Intermission Magazine,* Hull House, Chicago, 1965.

BOOKS, UNPUBLISHED—Three novels completed and one in progress.

AWARDS: Three Obie Awards, 1963-65, for *The Brig;* Guggenheim Fellowship, Writing for the Theatre, 1965; Rockefeller Fellowship, Writing for the Theatre, and study with Paul Sills in Chicago on the Story Theatre, 1966; ABC/Yale University Fellowship, Writing for the Theatre, 1967 and 1968; National Endowment for the Arts grant, Writing for the Theatre, 1972; CAPS grant, Writing for the Theatre, New York State Council on the Arts, 1974; Gold Medal, Venice Film Festival, for *The Brig.*

MEMBER: The Living Theatre, 1963—.

ADDRESSES: AGENT—c/o Richard O'Shea, 72 Second Street, Garden City, NY 11530.

*   *   *

BROWNE, Coral   1913-

PERSONAL: Born July 23, 1913, in Melbourne, Australia; daughter of Leslie Clarence and Victoria Elizabeth (Bennett) Browne; married Phillip Westrope Pearman (died); married Vincent Price (an actor), 1974. EDUCATION: Attended Melbourne schools.

VOCATION: Actress.

CAREER: STAGE DEBUT—Margaret Orme, *Loyalties,* Comedy Theatre, Melbourne, Australia, 1931. LONDON DEBUT—Helen Storer, *Lover's Leap,* Vaudeville Theatre, 1934. PRINCIPAL STAGE APPEARANCES—Wanda, *The Calendar,* Mimi, *A Warm Corner,* Myra, *Hay Fever,* Madge, *Let Us Be Gay,* Mrs. Murdo Fraser, *The First Mrs. Fraser,* Suzy, *Topaze,* Manuela, *The Command to Love,* Diane, *The Quaker Girl,* Orinthia, *The Apple Cart,* Fraulein von Bernberg, *Children in Uniform,* title role, *Hedda Gabler,* Mrs. Dearth, *Dear Brutus,* all performed in Australia, 1931-34.

Concordia, *Mated* and Lady Ameridine, *Basalik,* both at the Arts Theatre, London, 1935; Mary Penshott, *This Desirable Residence,* 1935 and Victoria, *The Golden Gander,* 1936, both at the Embassy Theatre, London; Connie Crawford, *Heroes Don't Care,* St. Martins Theatre, London, 1936; Lydia Latimer, *Death Asks a Verdict,* Royalty Theatre, London, 1936; the Widow, *The Taming of the Shrew,* New Theatre, London, 1937; Adah Isaacs Menken, *The Great Romancer,* Strand Theatre, London, 1937; Ida Ferrier, *The Great Romancer,* New Theatre, London, 1937; Jacqueline, *The Gusher,* Prince's Theatre, London, 1937; Empress Poppaea, *Emperor of the World,* Strand Theatre, London, 1939; Madeleine, *Believe It or Not,* New Theatre, London, 1940.

Maggie Cutler, *The Man Who Came to Dinner,* Savoy Theatre, London, 1941; Ruth Sherwood, *My Sister Eileen,* London, 1943; title role, *The Last of Mrs. Cheyney,* London, 1944; Lady Frederick Berolles, *Lady Frederick,* Savoy Theatre, London, 1946; Elma Melton, *Canaries Sometimes Sing,* Garrick Theatre, London, 1947; Bathsheba, *Jonathan,* Aldwych Theatre, London, 1948; Boss Trent, *Castle in the Air,* Adelphi Theatre, London, 1949; Emilia, *Othello* and Regan, *King Lear,* both at the Old Vic Theatre, London, 1951; Constance Russell, *Affairs of State,* Cambridge Theatre, London, 1952; Laura Foster, *Simon and Laura,* Strand Theatre, London, 1954; Nina Tessier, *Nina,* Haymarket Theatre, London, 1955.

Lady Macbeth, *Macbeth,* Old Vic Theatre, 1956; Zabina, *Tamburlaine the Great* and Helen, *Troilus and Cressida,* both at the Winter Garden Theatre, New York City, 1956; Gertrude, *Hamlet,* Helena, *A Midsummer Night's Dream,* Goneril, *King Lear,* all at the Old Vic Theatre, London, 1957-58; Katherine Dougherty, *The Pleasure of His Company,* Haymarket Theatre, London, 1959; Albertine Prine, *Toys in the Attic,* Piccadilly Theatre, London, 1960; Marie Paule, *Bonne Soupe,* Comedy Theatre, London, 1961, then Wyndham's Theatre, London, 1962; Countess, *The Rehearsal,* Theatre Royal, Brighton, U.K., 1963, then Royale Theatre, New York City, 1963; Mrs. Rossiter, *The Right Honourable Gentleman,* Her Majesty's Theatre, London, 1964, then Billy Rose Theatre, New York City, 1965.

Mrs. Erlynne, *Lady Windermere's Fan,* Phoenix Theatre, New York City, 1966; Mrs. Prentice, *What the Butler Saw,* Queen's Theatre, London, 1969; Lady Warwick, *My Darling Daisy,* Lyric Theatre, London, 1970; title role, *Mrs. Warren's Profession,* National Theatre, London, 1970; Louise Rafi, *The Sea,* Royal Court Theatre, London, 1973; Emily, *The Waltz of the Toreadors,* Haymarket Theatre, London, 1974; the Countess, *Ardele,* Queen's Theatre, London, 1975; Mrs. Lenin, *Travesties* and Lady Bracknell, *The Importance of Being Earnest,* both at the Mark Taper Forum, Los Angeles, 1976.

MAJOR TOURS—Lady Macbeth, *Macbeth,* with the Old Vic Company, U.S. cities, 1956; Gertrude, *Hamlet,* with the Shakespeare Memorial Theatre Company, Moscow, Soviet Union, 1958.

PRINCIPAL FILM APPEARANCES—*The Amateur Gentleman*, British, 1936; Vera Charles, *Auntie Mame*, Warner Brothers, 1958; Mercy Croft, *The Killing of Sister George*, Cinerama, 1969; Lady Claire, *The Ruling Class*, AVCO-Embassy, 1972; Miss Chloe Moon, *Theatre of Blood*, United Artists, 1973; Olivia Devereaux, *The Drowning Pool*, Warner Brothers, 1975; voice of heavenly female, *Xanadu*, Universal, 1980; Margaret McMann, *American Dreamer*, Warner Brothers, 1984; Alice Hargreaves, *Dreamchild*, Universal, 1985.

PRINCIPAL TELEVISION APPEARANCES—Margaret Winters, *Time Express*, CBS, 1979. Movies: Lady Stella Reading, *Eleanor, First Lady of the World*, 1982.

NON-RELATED CAREER—Painter.

SIDELIGHTS: RECREATIONS—Collecting art and needlepoint.

ADDRESSES: HOME—16 Eaton Place, London SW1, England.*

*　　*　　*

BROWNE, Roscoe Lee   1925-

PERSONAL: Born in 1925, in Woodbury, NJ; son of a minister. EDUCATION: Attended Lincoln University, Middlebury College, and Columbia University.

VOCATION: Actor, director, and writer.

CAREER: STAGE DEBUT—Soothsayer and Pindarus, *Julius Caesar*, East River Park Amphitheatre, New York Shakespeare Festival (NYSF), New York City, 1956. PRINCIPAL STAGE APPEARANCES—*Taming of the Shrew*, NYSF, 1956; Aaron, *Titus Andronicus* and Balthazar, *Romeo and Juliet*, NYSF, 1957; understudy title role, *Othello*, NYSF, 1958; Cothurnus, *Aria da Capo*, Theatre Marquee, New York City, 1958.

Archibald, *The Blacks*, St. Mark's Playhouse, New York City, 1961; *Brecht on Brecht*, Theatre de Lys, New York City, 1962; Corporal, *General Seeger*, Lyceum Theatre, New York City, 1962, Deacon Sitter Morris, *Tiger, Tiger, Burning Bright*, Booth Theatre, New York City, 1962; Fool, *King Lear*, Delacorte Theatre, NYSF, 1962; *Brecht on Brecht* and Street Singer, *Threepenny Opera*, Arena Stage, Washington, DC, 1963; *Brecht on Brecht*, Sheridan Square Playhouse, New York City, 1963; Autolycus, *The Winter's Tale*, Delacorte Theatre, NYSF, 1963; Narrator, *The Ballad of the Sad Cafe*, Martin Beck Theatre, New York City, 1963; Babu, *Benito Cereno*, American Place Theatre, New York City, 1964; Ulysses, *Troilus and Cressida*, Delacorte Theatre, NYSF, 1965; St. Just, *Danton's Death*, Vivian Beaumont Theatre, New York City, 1965; *A Hand Is on the Gate*, Longacre Theatre, New York City, 1966; Babu, *Benito Cereno*, Playhouse in the Park, Cincinnati, OH, 1966; Sheridan Whiteside, *The Man Who Came to Dinner*, Long Wharf Theatre, New Haven, CT, 1966; Mosca, *Volpone*, Mobile Theatre for the NYSF, 1967.

Makak, *The Dream on Monkey Mountain*, Mark Taper Forum, Los Angeles, 1970, then St. Mark's Playhouse, New York City, 1971; *A Rap on Race*, New Theatre for Now, Los Angeles, 1971-72; Ephraim Cabot, *Desire Under the Elms*, Academy Festival Theatre, Chicago, 1974; Babu, *Benito Cereno*, American Place Theatre, New York City, 1976; *A Hand Is on the Gate*, Afro-American

Studio, New York City, 1976-77; Albert Perez Jordan, *Remembrance*, the Other Stage at the Public Theatre, NYSF, 1979; *My One and Only*, St. James Theatre, New York City, 1983.

PRINCIPAL STAGE WORK—Writer and director, *A Hand Is on the Gate*, Longacre Theatre, New York City, 1966.

FILM DEBUT—*The Connection*, 1962. PRINCIPAL FILM APPEARANCES—*The Cool World*, Cinema V, 1964; *The Comedians*, Metro-Goldwyn-Mayer, 1967; *Uptight*, Paramount, 1968; *Topaz*, Universal, 1969; *The Liberation of L.B. Jones*, Columbia, 1970; *The Cowboys*, Warner Brothers, 1972; *The World's Greatest Athlete*, Buena Vista, 1973; *Superfly TNT*, Paramount, 1973; *Black Like Me*, Reade-Sterling, 1974; *Uptown Saturday Night*, Warner Brothers, 1974; *Logan's Run*, United Artists, 1976; *Twilight's Last Gleaming*, Allied Artists, 1977; also appeared in *The Fifth Door*.

TELEVISION DEBUT—*Green Pastures*, 1952. PRINCIPAL TELEVISION APPEARANCES—Series: Gideon Gibbs, *The Big Rip-Off*, NBC, 1975-76; Harold Devore Neistadter, *Miss Winslow and Son*, CBS, 1979; Sounders, *Soap*, ABC, 1980-81. Episodic: *Espionage*, NBC; *The Defenders*, CBS. Teleplays: *Benito Cereno*. Movies: Gideon Gibbs, *The Big Rip-Off*, NBC, 1975. Mini-Series: *Space*, CBS, 1985.

NON-RELATED CAREER—National sales representative, Shenley Import Corporation, 1946-56; literature and French teacher, Lincoln University, 1952.

WRITINGS: Poems and short stories.

AWARDS: Best Actor, Obie Award, 1965, for *Benito Cereno;* Best Actor, Los Angeles Drama Critics Award, 1970, for *The Dream on Monkey Mountain*.

SIDELIGHTS: Before beginning his acting career, the distinguished black actor Roscoe Lee Browne was an internationally acclaimed track and field runner. A member of ten Amateur Athletic Union teams, he was twice the American indoor champion in the 1000-yard run and in 1951, in Paris, he was the world champion in the 800-yard dash. A heel injury kept him from making the 1952 U.S. Olympic team.

When his running career ended, Browne became a national sales representative for the Schenley Import Corporation, where his chief job was speaking on the after-dinner circuit. Tiring of that life, he quit his job in June, 1956, and decided to try to become an actor. That afternoon he went to an audition for an upcoming production of *Julius Caesar* being staged by a then-unknown producer named Joseph Papp at the East River Park Amphitheatre. Browne won the parts of the Soothsayer and Pindarus—for which he received no pay.

Over the next nine years, Browne performed in seven more Shakespearean plays for Papp, primarily in New York's Central Park. His two most highly acclaimed portrayals were the Fool in the 1962 *King Lear* and Autolycus in the 1963 production of *A Winter's Tale*. Reviewing *Lear*, Joseph Morgenstern of the New York *Herald Tribune* (August 14, 1962) wrote that Browne "makes the most of his license with a delicious melange of foppishness, sweetness, infantilism and wisdom," while *Variety*'s critic (August 19, 1962) felt that he "conveys both the compassion and the pungency of the Fool." Browne's Autolycus was described by Michael Smith of the *Village Voice* (August 22, 1963) as "a baroque, eccentric, expansive, wholly effective portrayal," while Milton Esterow commented in the *New York Times* (August 16, 1963): "Mr. Browne is a graceful and joyous scoundrel. As a pickpocket, he has no peer. He deserves the key to the city, if he hasn't already walked off with it."

From 1958 on, between Central Park appearances, Browne took roles in several other Off-Broadway and Broadway productions. He made his Broadway debut in 1960 as a comic narcotics peddler in *The Cool World*, but two notable Off-Broadway plays of the early 1960's—Jean Genet's *The Blacks* and *Benito Cereno*, Robert Lowell's adaptation of the Herman Melville story—proved to be even more important in his career. In particular, his portrayal in *Benito Cereno* of Babu, a seemingly docile servant aboard a nineteenth-century Portuguese slave ship who actually has taken over the vessel, brought him to the attention of several critics and much of the public. Sydney Schubert Walter of the *Village Voice* (November 12, 1964) remarked that Browne's "transformation from a fawning servant to an African king is a frightening demonstration of a brilliant mind and an iron will forced by circumstance into the service of destruction."

Following *Benito Cereno*, Browne took part in two more classical revivals in 1965: Papp's park production of Shakespeare's *Troilus and Cressida* and the Repertory Theatre of Lincoln Center's revival of George Buchner's drama of the French Revolution, *Danton's Death*. In his *Newark Evening News* review of the latter production (October 22, 1965), Edward Sothern Hipp noted that none of the other actors "succeeds in matching the power of . . . Browne as the implacable St. Just, with every measured word heavy with venom and the lust of a compulsive killer."

The next year Browne organized, directed, and was one of the eight participants in *A Hand Is on the Gate*, an evening of poetry and folk music written by blacks. After opening as part of Papp's summer Shakespeare Festival in Central Park, the production was successful enough to transfer to the Longacre Theatre on Broadway, where it received mixed reviews. Richard Watts, Jr. deemed it "a moving and beautiful evening of stirring lyric grandeur," in the *New York Post* (September 22, 1966). He added, "The spirit can in turn be bitter, scornful, defiant, tragic, humorous, sardonic, wistful, proud and brooding, but it is always brave, poignant and filled with unvanquishable beauty." The *Village Voice*'s Joseph LeSueur, on the other hand, was more critical (September 29, 1966), calling the show "something middlebrow audiences will take to their hearts."

Since the mid-1960s, Browne has continued to appear in a wide variety of plays in New York and around the country. In 1979, he was widely acclaimed for his Off-Broadway portrayal of an aging Trinidadian who longs for British colonial days in Derek Walcott's play *Remembrance*. Douglas Watt of the *New York Daily News* (May 10, 1979) wrote that "Browne has a marvelous time with [the character], conveying the man's humor, vigor, bemusement and foolishness skillfully and winningly." In a 1983 Broadway appearance, Browne played a Harlem minister who moonlights as a bootlegger in the hit musical *My One and Only*.

Browne's film career began in the early 1960s with the movie version of the Off-Broadway play *The Connection*. His performance as the cook on a cattle drive headed by John Wayne in the 1972 film *The Cowboys* prompted *New Yorker*'s Pauline Kael (January 22, 1972) to say, "With his reserves of charm to call upon, and with that deep voice rising from his great chest, Browne acts Wayne right off the screen, and without raising a bead of sweat." She continued: "Not only does Browne come off as the only real actor in the movie but the cook is by far the verbal and intellectual superior of everyone

else. He's wickedly, incongruously suave, like a Shakespearean ham lost in the sticks but dressing for dinner every night."

An accusation that has sometimes been made against Browne is that his manner of speech is too polished and refined for a black actor. The actor, who acquired his accent (which some have found vaguely British) from his father (a New Jersey minister), has generally been able to laugh these complaints off. Once, when a producer asked him why he spoke "like a white person," he replied that it was because "we had a white maid."

In addition to his acting, Browne is an accomplished poet and short-story writer. Some of his own poetry was included in *A Hand Is on the Gate*, and after that show's Broadway opening, *Women's Wear Daily*'s reviewer said in the September 22, 1966 issue that Browne's verse was "as arch, deft, and to-the-point as his acting." In the *New York Post* (March 21, 1965), Jerry Tallmer reported that writing and reading poetry is "the deepest part of his [Browne's] private life." Browne frequently gives public readings of his own poetry and the works of other poets at colleges, high schools, and libraries throughout the United States and over the radio.

ADDRESSES: AGENT—George Gilly, 8721 Sunset Blvd., Los Angeles, CA 90069.*

*   *   *

BROWNING, Susan 1941-

PERSONAL: Born February 25, 1941, in Baldwin, Long Island, NY. EDUCATION: Attended Pennsylvania State University.

VOCATION: Actress and singer.

CAREER: BROADWAY DEBUT—Elizabeth Pringle, *Love and Kisses*, Music Box Theatre, 1963. PRINCIPAL STAGE APPEARANCES—Meg, *Jo*, Orpheum Theatre, New York City, 1964; appeared with The Theatre Group, Los Angeles, CA, 1965-66; *Collision Course*, Cafe au Go Go, New York City, 1968; April, *Company*, Alvin Theatre, New York City, 1970; Wednesday November, *Shelter*, John Golden Theatre, New York City, 1973; *Sondheim: A Musical Tribute*, Shubert Theatre, New York City, 1973; Southern Comfort, *Whiskey*, St. Clement's Theatre, New York City, 1973; Phebe, *As You Like It*, New York Shakespeare Festival, Delacorte Theatre, New York City, 1973; Kate, *The Removalists*, Playhouse II, New York City, 1974; Agnes Sorel, *Goodtime Charley*, Palace Theatre, New York City, 1975; Tree, *The Butterfingers Angel*, Stockbridge, MA, 1975; *Chapter Two*, New York City, 1977; *Overruled* and *Village Wooing*, Nassau Repertory Theatre, Hempstead/New Hyde Park, NY, 1982; Maisie, *Miss Liberty*, Goodspeed Opera House, East Haddam, CT, 1983; *Cyrano de Bergerac*, Huntington Theatre Company, Boston, 1984; *Hang on to Me*, Guthrie Theatre, Minneapolis, MN, 1984; Widow Douglas and Sally Phelps, *Big River*, Eugene O'Neill Theatre, New York City, 1985-86.

Appeared Off-Off Broadway in *Dime a Dozen, The Night Little Girl Blue Made Her Social Debut, Seventeen, The Boys from Syracuse*.

MAJOR TOURS—Felice, *After the Fall*, 1964-65.

PRINCIPAL TELEVISION APPEARANCES—Series: Pat Gimble, *Mary Hartman, Mary Hartman,* syndicated, 1976-77. Specials: *First Ladies' Diaries; Broadway Showstoppers.*

AWARDS: *Theatre World Award* and Antoinette Perry Award nomination, 1970, for *Company;* Antoinette Perry Award nomination, 1975, for *Goodtime Charley;* Emmy Award nomination, for *First Ladies' Diaries.*

MEMBER: Actors' Equity Association, Screen Actors Guild, American Federation of Television and Radio Artists.

ADDRESSES: AGENT—Gage Group, 1650 Broadway, New York, NY 10019.*

*   *   *

BUCKLEY, Betty Lynn   1947-

PERSONAL: Born July 3, 1947, in Fort Worth, TX; daughter of Ernest (dean of engineering; lieutenant colonel, U.S. Air Force) and Betty Bob (a dancer and journalist; maiden name, Diltz) Buckley; married Peter Flood, 1972 (divorced, 1974). EDUCATION: Texas Christian College, B.A., journalism; studied voice with Paul Gavert and acting with Stella Adler.

VOCATION: Actress.

CAREER: BROADWAY DEBUT—Martha Jefferson, *1776,* 1969. LONDON DEBUT—Fran Kubelik, *Promises, Promises.* PRINCIPAL STAGE APPEARANCES—*Johnny Pott,* New York City production; *What's a Nice Country Like You Doing in a State Like This?,* Upstairs at Jimmy's, New York City, 1972; *Pippin,* Imperial Theatre, New York City, 1973-75; Heather, *I'm Getting My Act Together and Taking It on the Road,* Circle in the Square Downtown, New York City, 1981; Grizabella, *Cats,* Winter Garden Theatre, New York City, 1982-85; Cecilia Miller, *Juno's Swans,* Second Stage Theatre, New York City, 1985; Edmund Drood/Miss Alice Nutting, *The Mystery of Edmund Drood,* New York Shakespeare Festival, Delacorte Theatre, New York City, 1985, then Imperial Theatre, New York City, 1985-86; *Song and Dance,* Royale Theatre, New York City, 1986. Also appeared in *Circle of Sound,* Off-Broadway production, New York City.

PRINCIPAL FILM WORK—Miss Collins, *Carrie,* United Artists, 1976; Dixie Scott, *Tender Mercies,* Universal, 1983.

PRINCIPAL TELEVISION WORK—Series: Abby Bradford, *Eight Is Enough,* ABC, 1977-81. Movies: *The Ordeal of Bill Carney,* 1981; *The Three Wishes of Billy Grier,* 1984; also, *The Devil's Work,* PBS. Mini-Series: *Evergreen,* NBC, 1985.

AWARDS: Best Featured Actress in a Musical, Antoinette Perry Award, 1983, for *Cats.*

MEMBER: Actors' Equity Association, Screen Actors Guild, American Federation of Television and Radio Artists.

ADDRESSES: AGENT—c/o John Kimble, Triad Artists, 888 Seventh Avenue, Suite 1602, New York, NY 10106.*

BUFMAN, Zev   1930-

PERSONAL: Born October 11, 1930, in Tel-Aviv, Israel; son of Mordekhai and Hayah (Torban) Bufman; married Leah Debora Habas (divorced); married Vilma Greul Auld. EDUCATION: Los Angeles State College, M.A., 1957.

VOCATION: Producer and actor.

CAREER: STAGE DEBUT—As a cabaret entertainer in *The Israeli Danny Kaye,* Tel-Aviv, 1950. PRINCIPAL STAGE APPEARANCES—Stock: Quack Doctor, *The Imaginary Invalid,* Tustin Playbox, CA, 1951; Russian Spy, *See How They Run,* 1951; Eddie, *Lady in the Dark,* Mr. Lundie, *Brigadoon,* Theodatus, *Caesar and Cleopatra,* all 1952; Harry, *Merton of the Movies,* Huntington Hartford Theatre, Hollywood, CA, 1956.

PRINCIPAL STAGE WORK—Producer: *A Hole in the Head,* Civic Playhouse, Los Angeles, 1958; *Laffcapades of '59, Fair Game, Murder in the Red Barn, The Barber of Seville, Mendel the Beatnik, Our Town, Pajama Tops,* all in Hollywood, CA, 1959.

Vintage '60, Hollywood and New York City, *A Timid Evening with Don Rickles,* Los Angeles, *Carnival Island,* Hollywood, *Only in America,* Hollywood, all 1960; *Second City,* Hollywood, *The Fantasticks,* Los Angeles and San Francisco, *The Egg,* Chicago, *Elsa Lanchester Herself,* Hollywood, all 1961; *The Egg,* New York City, *Little Mary Sunshine, A Curious Evening with Gypsy Rose Lee, Under the Yum-Yum Tree,* all Hollywood, *Write Me a Murder,* Los Angeles, *The Premise,* Miami, FL, all 1962; *The Tenth Man,* Los Angeles and Miami, *Sunday in New York,* Los Angeles, *Pajama Tops,* New York City, *Lord Pengo, A Calculated Risk, The Tender Trap, Come Blow Your Horn, Tchin-Tchin, King of Hearts, Madly in Love, A Shot in the Dark,* all Miami, *A Thousand Clowns, Mary Mary,* all 1963; *Fair Game for Lovers,* Miami and New York City, 1964; *Minor Miracle,* New York City, 1965; *Marat/Sade* and *Spofford,* both New York City, 1967; *Mike Downstairs, Soldiers, Your Own Thing, Jimmy Shine, Big Time Buck White,* all New York City, 1968; *Spitting Image, Big Time Buck White,* both New York City, 1969.

Story Theatre, New York City, 1970; *Ovid's Metamorphoses,* New York City, 1971; *The American Revolution, Part I,* Ford's Theatre, Washington, DC, 1973; *The Trouble with People,* Miami, 1974; *The Magnificent Yankee,* Washington, DC, 1976; *Peter Pan,* Lunt-Fontanne Theatre, New York City, 1979-80; *Oklahoma!,* Palace Theatre, New York City, 1979-80.

West Side Story, Minskoff Theatre, New York City, 1980; *Brigadoon,* Majestic Theatre, New York City, 1980-81; *The Little Foxes,* Martin Beck Theatre, New York City, then at the Ahmanson Theatre, Los Angeles, both 1981; *Oh, Brother!,* American National Theatre Academy (ANTA) Theatre, New York City, 1981; *The First,* Martin Beck Theatre, New York City, 1981; *Joseph and the Amazing Technicolor Dreamcoat,* Royale Theatre, New York City, 1982-83; *A View from the Bridge,* Ambassador Theatre, New York City, 1983; *Private Lives,* Lunt-Fontanne Theatre, New York City, 1983; *The Corn Is Green,* Lunt-Fontanne Theatre, New York City, 1983; *Peg,* Lunt-Fontanne Theatre, New York City, 1983; *Requiem for a Heavyweight,* Martin Beck Theatre, New York City, 1985.

MAJOR TOURS—Producer: *Pajama Tops,* West Coast cities, 1962; *God Bless Our Bank,* U.S. cities, 1963; *In One Bed. . .And Out the*

Other, U.S. cities, 1964; *Any Wednesday,* U.S. cities, 1966; *On a Clear Day You Can See Forever,* U.S. and Canadian cities, 1967; *The Star-Spangled Girl,* U.S. cities, 1968; *Your Own Thing,* U.S. cities and London, 1969; *Oklahoma!,* U.S. cities, 1980-81; *Peter Pan,* U.S. cities, 1982-83; *Jerry's Girls,* U.S. cities, 1984; *On Your Toes,* U.S. cities, 1984.

FILM DEBUT—Farrid, *Bengal Rifles,* 1952. PRINCIPAL FILM APPEARANCES—*Flight to Tangiers,* 1953; *The Prodigal,* Metro-Goldwyn-Mayer (MGM), 1955; *The Ten Commandments,* Paramount, 1957; *Buccaneer,* Paramount, 1959.

AWARDS: Mayor's Citation Award, City of Los Angeles, 1964.

ADDRESSES: OFFICE—2980 McFarlane Road, Coconut Grove, FL 33133.*

*   *   *

BULLOCK, Eldon   1952-

PERSONAL: Born February 8, 1952, in Richmond, VA; son of Dorothy Perlele Brown (a domestic worker); married Judi Byrd (an actress), July 27, 1985. EDUCATION: Norfolk State College, B.S., 1975; Virginia Commonwealth University, M.F.A., 1978. RELIGION: Baptist.

VOCATION: Actor.

ELDON BULLOCK

CAREER: STAGE DEBUT—Gitlow, *Purlie,* Virginia Museum Theatre, Richmond, 1976, for thirty performances. OFF-BROADWAY DEBUT—Preacher Haglar, *Dark of the Moon,* Ensemble Studio Theatre, 1979, for sixteen performances. PRINCIPAL STAGE APPEARANCES—Cassius, *Julius Caesar,* Gaslight Theatre, Richmond; Jeff, *The River Niger,* Barksdale Dinner Theatre, Richmond; Chuck Stone, *The Trial of Adam Clayton Powell, Jr.,* Henry Street Settlement Theatre, New York City; Friar Peter, *Measure for Measure,* New York Shakespeare Festival, New York City; B.T. Washington, *Cast Me Down,* Hunter College Theatre, New York City; multiple roles, *In a Dry and Thirsty Land,* 1986.

MAJOR TOURS—Shylock, *The Merchant of Venice,* Shakespeare and Company, U.S. cities.

PRINCIPAL TELEVISION APPEARANCES—Episodic: *The Equalizer.*

PRINCIPAL FILM APPEARANCES—*Falling in Love,* Paramount, 1984; *Muppets Take Manhattan,* Tri-Star, 1984; *Turk 182!,* Twentieth Century-Fox, 1985; *Brewster's Millions,* Universal, 1985; also appeared in *Once Upon a Midnight Clear,* Columbia.

MEMBER: Actors' Equity Association, Screen Actors Guild; Site Five Tenants Association (president).

ADDRESSES: HOME—500 W. 55th Street, New York, NY 10019.

*   *   *

BURBRIDGE, Edward

VOCATION: Scenic designer.

CAREER: FIRST OFF-BROADWAY STAGE WORK—Designer, *Misalliance,* Sheridan Square Playhouse, September 25, 1961. PRINCIPAL STAGE WORK—Designer, *Marat/Sade,* New York City production, 1967; with the Negro Ensemble Company, New York City: *The Song of the Lustanian Bogey, Summer of the Seventeenth Doll, Kongi's Harvest, Mike Downstairs, Daddy Goodness, Jimmy Shine, Big Time Buck White, God Is a (Guess What?),* all 1968; *Does a Tiger Wear a Necktie, Spitting Image, Malcochon, Contribution, String, Man Better Man, The Reckoning, Our Town, Buck White,* all 1969; *Five on the Black Hand Side, Steal the Old Man's Bundle, The Shepherd of Avenue B, Ododo,* all 1970; *Perry's Mission, Rosalie Pritchett, The Dream on Monkey Mountain, Ride a Black Horse, The Sty of the Blind Pig,* all 1971; *Ti-Jean and His Brothers, A Ballet Behind the Bridge, Frederick Douglas. . .Through His Own Words,* all 1972; *Status Quo Vadis, The Visit, Chemin de Fer, Holiday,* all 1973; *Absurd Person Singular,* 1974; *The First Breeze of Summer,* 1975; *The Last Minstrel Show,* 1978; *In an Upstate Motel,* 1981.

Costume designer, *What the Wine-Sellers Buy,* with the Negro Ensemble Company, 1974.

MAJOR TOURS—Designer, *Absent Friends,* U.S. cities, 1977.

PRINCIPAL TELEVISION WORK—Production designer, *The First Breeze of Summer,* 1976.*

MURIEL BURGESS

BURGESS, Muriel   1926-

PERSONAL: Born July 8, 1926, in Birmingham, England; daughter of Percy James (an engineer) and Edith Burgess; married Laurence Murray Kelly (a physician), April, 1957. RELIGION: Church of England.

VOCATION: Writer.

WRITINGS: BOOKS—*Doctor Sahib; Over My Shoulder; All of Me; Gracie Fields; The Unsinkable Hermione Baddeley; The Doctor's Cabin* (also known as *Love Boat*). TELEPLAYS—*Father Doyle.* ARTICLES—Contributor to women's magazines and newspapers.

MEMBER: Writers Guild.

ADDRESSES: HOME—Lowood, The Street, Betchworth, Surrey R.H.3. 7DJ, England. AGENT—Eric Glass Ltd., 28 Berkeley Square, London W1X 6HD, England.

*   *   *

BURRELL, Pamela   1945-

PERSONAL: Born August 4, 1945, in Tacoma, WA; daughter of Donald A. (an employee of American Telephone and Telegraph) and Mickey Rose (a store owner and manager; maiden name, Curtiss) Burrell; married Monty Silver, July 19, 1965 (divorced, 1978); married Peter J. Gatto (an actor), April 21, 1979; children:

(first marriage) Deirdre Paige, Emily Beth. EDUCATION: Trained for the stage with Sandy Miesner and as a dancer at the San Francisco Ballet and the New York City Ballet. POLITICS: Democrat. RELIGION: Religious Science.

VOCATION: Actress and dancer.

CAREER: BROADWAY DEBUT—Singer and showgirl, *Funny Girl,* Imperial Theatre, 1966. PRINCIPAL STAGE APPEARANCES—Raina, *Arms and the Man,* Sheridan Square Playhouse, New York City, 1967; Gwen, *Where's Charley?,* Broadway production, 1974; Duchess, *Berkeley Square,* Manhattan Theatre Club, New York City, 1976; Mrs. Cuyler, *The Boss,* Chelsea Theatre, New York City, 1976; *Tatyana Repina,* Judson Poet's Theatre, New York City, 1978; Antoinette, *Biography,* Chelsea Theatre, New York City, 1979; Viazapurikha, *Strider,* Westside Theatre, then Helen Hayes Theatre, New York City, 1979; Yvonne and Naomi, *Sunday in the Park with George,* Booth Theatre, New York City, 1985.

Regional: *Quality Street* and *Lyrics of Oscar Hammerstein II,* both at the Bucks County Playhouse, New Hope, PA, 1967; Jennifer, *Do I Hear a Waltz?,* Cohasset Theatre, Hyannis, MA, 1967; Yelena, *Uncle Vanya,* Center Stage, Baltimore, MD, 1973; Thelma, *After Magritte,* Felicity, *The Real Inspector Hound,* and Antoinette, *Biography,* all at the Seattle Repertory Theatre, WA, 1975; Joanne, *Come Back to the Five and Dime, Jimmy Dean, Jimmy Dean,* Alliance Theatre, Atlanta, GA, 1977; Alma, *Eccentricities of a Nightingale,* Nassau Repertory, NY, 1981; Chelsea, *On Golden Pond,* North Shore Playhouse, Beverly, MA, 1981; Belle, *Rocket to the Moon,* Nassau Repertory, NY, 1982; Hippolyta, *A Midsummer Night's Dream,* Pittsburgh Public Theatre, 1982; Grace, *Bus*

PAMELA BURRELL

Stop, Nassau Repertory, NY, 1983; Regina, *The Little Foxes,* Nassau Repertory, NY, 1984; Clara, *The Show-Off,* Syracuse Playhouse, NY, then Paper Mill Playhouse, Milburn, NJ, 1983-84; Gladys, *A Lesson from Aloes,* Long Island Stage Company, NY, 1986.

MAJOR TOURS—Clara, *The Show-Off,* U.S. cities, 1983-84.

FILM DEBUT—Inga, *Da Duva,* Independent, 1967. PRINCIPAL FILM APPEARANCES—Mrs. Stonefeller, *Popeye,* Paramount, 1980.

TELEVISION DEBUT—Toby's mother, "Toby," *CBS Afternoon Special.* PRINCIPAL TELEVISION APPEARANCES—Series: Annabelle Catlin, *The Catlins,* 1984-85. Episodic: Mrs. Conti, *Search for Tomorrow,* NBC; Dr. Evelyn Blai, *Ryan's Hope,* ABC; Jessie Finnly, *Spenser for Hire,* ABC, 1986.

AWARDS: Theatre World Award, 1968, for *Arms and the Man;* Antoinette Perry Award nomination, 1980, for *Strider.*

MEMBER: Actors' Equity Association, Screen Actors Guild, American Federation of Television and Radio Artists.

SIDELIGHTS: FAVORITE ROLES—Antoinette in *Biography,* Viazapurikha in *Strider,* Alma in *Eccentricities of a Nighingale,* and Regina in *The Little Foxes.*

ADDRESSES: HOME—New York, NY. AGENT—Monty Silver Agency, 200 W. 57th Street, New York, NY 10019.

* * *

BUSH, Norman 1933-

PERSONAL: Born April 11, 1933, in Louisville, KY; married wife Myrna, February 25, 1961; children: Hector Martin. EDUCATION: Trained for the stage with American Academy of Dramatic Arts, at the American Mime Theatre with Paul Curtis, and with Paul Mann and Michael Schulz. MILITARY: U.S. Air Force.

VOCATION: Actor.

CAREER: OFF-BROADWAY DEBUT—*The Goose,* Sullivan Street Playhouse, 1959. LONDON DEBUT—*Song of the Lusitanian Bogey,* with the Negro Ensemble Company, Old Vic Theatre, 1969. PRINCIPAL STAGE APPEARANCES—*The Connection,* Living Theatre, New York City; *The New York Nativity Plays,* Judson Poets Theatre, New York City; *Funnyhouse of a Negro,* East End Theatre, New York City; *Sarah and the Sax,* Theatre de Lys, New York City; *The Toilet,* St. Mark's Playhouse, New York City; *Servant of Two Masters,* Theatre in the Street, New York City; *Weary Blues,* Lincoln Center Theatre, New York City; *In a New England Winter,* Henry Street Playhouse, New York City; *Sleep,* American Place Theatre, New York City; with the Negro Ensemble Company, New York City: *Akokawe, Day of Absence, Man Better Man, Malcochon, God Is a (Guess What?), Summer of the Seventeenth Doll, Kongi's Harvest, Daddy Goodness,* and *Blackbody Blues.*

PRINCIPAL STAGE WORK—Director: *The One,* Negro Ensemble Company Works in Progress.

MAJOR TOURS—With the Negro Ensemble Company, U.S. and European cities.

PRINCIPAL TELEVISION APPEARANCES—Episodic: *N.Y.P.D.,* ABC; "Alamo," *You Are There,* CBS; *Catholic Hour; Search for Tomorrow; As the World Turns; All My Children; Ryan's Hope; Love of Life; Best of Families.* Movies: *Hardhat and Legs,* 1980. Mini-Series: *The Adam's Chronicles.* Pilots: *The Connection.* Dramatic Specials: *Day of Absence.*

PRINCIPAL FILM APPEARANCES—*Across 110th Street,* United Artists, 1972; *The Super Cops,* United Artists, 1974; *Serpico,* Paramount, 1974; *Harry and Tonto,* Twentieth Century-Fox, 1974; *Death Wish,* Paramount, 1974; *Three Days of the Condor,* Paramount, 1975; *Muppets Take Manhattan,* Tri-Star, 1984; *Banquet of Horror.*

PRINCIPAL RADIO WORK—*Funnyhouse of a Negro,* BBC.

RECORDINGS: Profiles in Courage; History Records.

MEMBER: Actors' Equity Association, American Federation of Television and Radio Artists, Screen Actors Guild; Negro Ensemble Company (founding member, 1967).

ADDRESSES: HOME—New York City.

C

CABOT, Susan 1937-1986

PERSONAL: Full name, Susan Cabot-Roman; born 1937; died as the result of a beating in her home in Encino, CA, December 10, 1986.

VOCATION: Actress.

CAREER: FILM DEBUT—*On the Isle of Samoa*, 1950. PRINCIPAL FILM APPEARANCES—*Tomahawk*, Universal, 1951; *Flame of Araby*, Universal, 1951; *Battle at Apache Pass*, Universal, 1952; *Duel at Silver Creek*, Universal, 1952; *Son of Ali Baba*, Universal, 1952; *Gunsmoke*, Universal, 1953; *Ride Clear of Diablo*, Universal, 1954; *Carnival Rock*, Howco Films, 1957, *Sorority Girl*, 1957; *Saga of the Viking Women and Their Voyage to the Waters of the Great Sea Serpent*, 1957; *War of the Satellites*, 1957; *Machine Gun Kelly*, 1958; *The Wasp Woman*, 1958; *Surrender—Hell!*, 1959.*

*   *   *

CAMPION, Clifford 1949-

PERSONAL: Born December 26, 1949, in Santa Monica, CA; son of Royal A. (a cattle breeder) and Jean (Hendricks) Campion. EDUCATION: University of Southern California, B.A., 1972.

VOCATION: Producer and writer.

CAREER: PRINCIPAL TELEVISION WORK—Co-producer, "The Marva Collins Story," *Hallmark Hall of Fame*, CBS, 1981; co-producer, *Samaritan*, CBS, 1985; producer, *Growing Up*, CBS, 1985.

WRITINGS: TELEVISION—Series: *Westbrook Hospital; This Is the Life;* (co-creator) *Rituals*, syndicated. Episodic: "Ghost of Cell Block Two," *Next Step Beyond*, syndicated. Movies: *Image in a Glass;* "The Marva Collins Story," *Hallmark Hall of Fame*, CBS, 1981; *Love, Mary*, CBS, 1985; *Samaritan*, CBS, 1985; *Growing Up*, CBS, 1985; *Race Against Time*, CBS, 1986; *Celebration Family*, ABC; *Kingsley*, CBS. Documentaries: *Having a Baby; Portrait of a First Lady* (about Nancy Reagan), ABC. Animated movies: *The Little Troll Prince*, Lutheran TV; *Musco, Blue Whale*, ABC; *Captain Caveman*, ABC; *Dinky Dog*, ABC; also, *The Witch Who Stole Marineland* and *Clyde's Ride*. Specials: *Upbeat Aesop*, KABC and syndicated.

SCREENPLAYS—*The Bottom Line*, Odyssey; seven films for the U.S. Army Chaplain's Board.

REVUES—*Gotta Get Away*, Radio City Music Hall summer show.

ARTICLES—"Sister," *The Christian Science Monitor*.

AWARDS: Christopher Award; FAB Award; Humanitas Prize Award Finalist; National Association for the Advancement of Colored People (NAACP) Image Award nomination; Best Original Dramatic Anthology, Writers' Guild of America Award; Luminas Award.

MEMBER: Writers' Guild of America, Academy of Television Arts and Sciences, Delta Kappa Alpha (Cinema Honorary).

ADDRESSES: AGENT—Creative Artist Agency, 1888 Century Park E., Los Angeles, CA 90067.

*   *   *

CANBY, Vincent 1924-

PERSONAL: Born July 27, 1924, in Chicago, IL; son of Lloyd and Katharine Anne (Vincent) Canby. EDUCATON: Dartmouth College, B.A., 1947. MILITARY: U.S. Navy, 1944-46.

VOCATION: Journalist, critic, playwright, and novelist.

CAREER: Assistant to drama editor, *Chicago Journal of Commerce*, 1949-51; critic and reporter, *Motion Picture Herald-Motion Picture Daily*, 1951-58; movie, theatre, and television reporter and critic, *Variety*, New York City, 1959-67; member of theatre and film criticism staff, *New York Times*, New York City, 1967-69, film critic, 1969—; lecturer on history of film criticism, Yale University, 1970-71; associate fellow, Pierson College.

WRITINGS: FICTION—*Living Quarters*, Knopf, 1975; *Unnatural Scenery*, Knopf, 1979. PLAYS, PRODUCED—*End of the War*, Ensemble Studio Theatre, New York City, 1978; *After All*, Manhattan Theatre Club, New York City, 1981; *The Old Flag*, George Street Playhouse, New Brunswick, NJ, 1984.

ADDRESSES: OFFICE—c/o *The New York Times*, 229 W. 43rd Street, New York, NY 10036.*

*   *   *

CAPRI, Mark 1951-

PERSONAL: Born July 19, 1951, in Washington, DC; son of Charles and Billie (Kenney) Capri. EDUCATION: Attended Stanford University, 1969-73; trained for the stage at the Royal Academy of Dramatic Art, 1973-75.

VOCATION: Actor.

CAREER: STAGE DEBUT—Solanio and Arragon, *The Merchant of Venice,* Watford Palace Theatre, Watford, U.K., 1976, for thirty-two performances. LONDON DEBUT—Hector Malone, *Man and Superman,* Royal Shakespeare Company, 1977, for two-hundred-fifty performances. OFF-BROADWAY DEBUT—George, *On Approval,* Roundabout Theatre, 1984, for two-hundred-eight performances. PRINCIPAL STAGE APPEARANCES—Title role, *Macbeth,* American Shakespeare Festival Theatre, Stratford, CT, 1980; Iachimo, *Cymbeline,* Hartford Stage Company, CT, 1981.

Berowne, *Love's Labor's Lost,* Thorndyke Theatre, U.K.; El Gallo, *The Fantasticks* and Freddy, *My Fair Lady,* both Crucible Theatre, Sheffield, U.K.; Mortimer, *Edward II,* Royal Lyceum Theatre Company, Edinburgh Festival, Scotland; Polixenes, *Winter's Tale,* Yale Repertory Theatre; Geoffry, *Absurd Person Singular,* Philadelphia Drama Guild; Chee Chee, *Pirandello Festival,* Philadelphia Drama Guild; Stanislawski, *Chekhov in Yalta,* Walnut Street Theatre, Philadelphia; Christian, *Cyrano de Bergerac,* Santa Fe Festival Theatre, NM; Antonio, *The Tempest,* Sergius, *Arms and the Man,* and Slim, *Of Mice and Men,* Denver Center Theatre, CO; Paul Kreindle, *Undiscovered Country,* Hartford Stage Company; Hovstad, *An Enemy of the People,* Roundabout Theatre, New York City.

MAJOR TOURS—Solanio and Arragon, *The Merchant of Venice,* British Council tour of India and Southeast Asian cities, 1976; Hector Malone, *Man and Superman,* Royal Shakespeare Company, U.K. cities, 1977.

TELEVISION DEBUT—Hal Bristow, *Horse in the House,* BBC, 1977. PRINCIPAL TELEVISION APPEARANCES—Series: *Citizen Smith,* BBC; *A Family Affair,* BBC; *Horse in the House,* Thames. Teleplays: "A Greenish Man," *Play for Today,* BBC. Episodic: "Season of Belief," *Tales of the Unexpected,* NBC, 1986.

FILM DEBUT—Vadar officer, *Star Wars,* Twentieth Century-Fox, 1977. PRINCIPAL FILM APPEARANCES—Bridge controller, *The Empire Strikes Back,* Twentieth Century-Fox, 1980.

AWARDS: Theatre World Award, 1984, for *On Approval.*

MEMBER: Actors' Equity Association, British Actors' Equity Association, Screen Actors Guild, American Federation of Television and Radio Artists.

ADDRESSES: AGENT—c/o David Williams, International Creative Management, 40 W. 57th Street, New York, NY 10019.

*   *   *

CAPTAIN KANGAROO
See Keeshan, Robert J.

*   *   *

CARDEN, William   1947-

PERSONAL: Born February 3, 1947, in New York, NY; son of George Alexander (a physician) and Constance Seager (Sullivan) Carden; married Pamela Berlin (a director), June 15, 1986. EDUCATION: Attended St. Lawrence Univeristy, 1966-68; Brandeis

WILLIAM CARDEN

University, 1968-70; trained for the stage with Wynn Handman and Uta Hagen.

VOCATION: Actor.

CAREER: BROADWAY DEBUT—Clark Davis, *Short Eyes,* Vivien Beaumont Theatre, 1974, for two hundred performances. PRINCIPAL STAGE APPEARANCES—Johnny, *The Marriage,* 1972, Saunders, *Life Class,* 1975, Lionel, *In the Summerhouse,* 1977, all at the Manhattan Theatre Club, New York City; Ben, *Leaving Home,* 1974, lawyer, *Innocent Pleasures,* 1978, Callie, *The Bloodletters,* 1984, title role, *Dennis,* 1985, all at the Ensemble Studio Theatre, New York City; Jonathan Edwards, *Back in the Race,* Circle Repertory Company, New York City, 1980; Bertram, *The Captivity of Pixie Shedman,* Phoenix Theatre, New York City, 1981; Skreeb, *Thin Ice,* WPA Theatre, New York City, 1984.

FILM DEBUT—Johnny, *In Another Place,* independent, 1981. PRINCIPAL FILM APPEARANCES—Michael, *The Passage,* independent, 1983.

TELEVISION DEBUT—Nick, "Valley Forge," *Hallmark Hall of Fame,* NBC, 1976. PRINCIPAL TELEVISION APPEARANCES—Series: Peter Rafferty, *Best of Families,* NET, 1978. Episodic: *Barnaby Jones,* NBC; *Nurse,* CBS; *As the World Turns,* CBS; *One Life to Live,* ABC.

RELATED CAREER—Program co-ordinator, director and acting teacher, Boston University Theatre Institute, 1984-86; acting teacher, Ensemble Studio Theatre Institute, New York City, 1984—.

MEMBER: Actors' Equity Association, American Federation of

Television and Radio Artists; Ensemble Studio Theatre (chairman of member's council and board of directors).

ADDRESSES: AGENT—Ambrosio-Mortimer and Associates, 165 W. 46th Street, New York, NY 10036.

✝   *   *

CARDINALE, Claudia   1938-

PERSONAL: Born April 15, 1938, In Tunis, Tunisia; daughter of Franco and Yolanda Cardinale; married Franco Cristaldi (a film producer and director), 1966; children: one son. EDUCATION: Lycee Carnot and College Paul Cambon, Tunis.

VOCATION: Actress.

CAREER: FILM DEBUT—*Goha,* Italian, 1957. PRINCIPAL FILM APPEARANCES—*I Soliti Ignoti* (*Big Deal on Madonna Street*), Italian, 1958; *Upstairs and Downstairs,* British, 1958; *La Prima Notte,* Italian, 1959; *Un Maledetto Imbroglio,* Italian, 1959; *I Bell Antonio,* Italian, 1959; *Austerlitz,* French, 1959; *Il Delfini,* Italian, 1960; *La Ragazza con la Valigia* (*The Girl with the Suitcase*), Titanus, 1960; *Rocco e i Suoi Fratelli* (*Rocco and His Brothers*), Titanus, 1960; *La Viaccia,* Arco, 1961; *Cartouche,* Italian, 1961; *Senilita,* Zebra, 1962; *8 1/2,* Cineriz, 1963; *Il Gattopardo* (*The Leopard*), Twentieth Century-Fox, 1963; *La Ragazza di Bube,* Italian, 1963; *The Pink Panther,* United Artists, 1964; *The Magnificent Showman,* British, 1964; *Gli Indifferenti,* Italian, 1964; *Blindfold,* Universal, 1965; *Of a Thousand Delights,* Italian, 1965; *Lost Command,* Columbia, 1966; *The Professionals,* Columbia, 1966; *Le Fate,* Italian, 1966; *Don't Make Waves,* Metro-Goldwyn-Mayer, 1967; *Il Giorno della Civetta,* Italian, 1967; *Once Upon a Time in the West,* Paramount, 1969; *A Fine Pair,* National General, 1969; *The Adventures of Gerard,* 1970.

La Scoumoune, Italian, 1972; *Il Giorno del Furore,* Italian, 1973; *Libera, Amore Mio,* Italian, 1973; *Escape to Athens,* Associated Film Distributors, 1979; *Fitzcarraldo,* New World Pictures, 1982; also appeared in *The Legend of Frenchie King,* 1971; *The Red Tent,* 1971; *La Part du Feu,* 1977; *Corleone,* 1977; *L'Arma,* 1978; *La Petite Fille en Velours Bleu,* 1978; *Le Ruffian,* 1982; *Conversation Piece, The Immortal Bachelor, Circus World,* and *The Queens.*

PRINCIPAL TELEVISION APPEARANCES—*Princess Daisy,* NBC, 1983.

RELATED CAREER—Professional model.

AWARDS: Nastro d'Argento Award; David di Donatello Award; Grolla d'Oro; voted most beautiful girl in Tunis.

ADDRESSES: OFFICE—Via Flamina Km. 17,200, 1-0018 Rome, Italy.*

*   *   *

CAREY, Denis   1909-1986

PERSONAL: Born August 3, 1909 in London, England; died in London, England, September 28, 1986; son of William Denis and May (Wilkinson) Carey; married Yvonne Coulette (an actress). EDUCATION: St. Paul's School, London, England; Trinty College, Dublin, Ireland.

VOCATION: Actor and director.

CAREER: STAGE DEBUT—Mickey, *The Great Big World,* Royal Court Theatre, London, 1921. BROADWAY DEBUT—Second priest, *Murder in the Cathedral,* Ritz Theatre, 1938. PRINCIPAL STAGE APPEARANCES—Appeared at the Gate Theatre and Abbey Theatre, Dublin, Ireland, 1929-34, including, at the Abbey: *Deirdre, Is Life Worth Living,* as the Greek in *The Resurrection,* as the title role in *Parnell of Avondale,* and in *Summer's Day;* appeared in London and New York City, 1935-39, Second Priest, *Murder in the Cathedral,* Duchess Theatre, London, 1936, Michael Byrne in *Spring Meeting,* Ambassadors Theater, London, then Morosco Theatre, New York City, both 1938; Dermot Francis O'Flingsley, *Shadow and Substance,* Duke of York's Theatre, London, 1943; with the Glasgow Citizen's Theatre Company, 1943-45; appeared at the Midland Theatre, Coventry, U.K., 1945-46.

Jack Manders, *Galway Handicap* and Clochet, *Men without Shadows,* both at the Lyric Theatre, Hammersmith, London, 1947; Telyegin, *Uncle Vanya,* Royal Court Theatre, London, 1970; Ocean, *Prometheus Bound,* Mermaid Theatre, 1971; Gunga Din, *Chez Nous,* Globe Theatre, London, 1974; Dr. Lombardi, *The Artful Widow,* Greenwich, 1976; Feste, *Twelfth Night,* Greenwich, 1976; Jawan, *Kismet,* Shaftesbury, 1978.

MAJOR TOURS—Toured England with the Pilgrim Players, 1940-43; Egeus and Quince, *A Midsummer Night's Dream,* Royal Shakespeare Company, world tour, 1972-73.

FIRST STAGE WORK—Director, *A Pound on Demand* and *Happy as Larry,* Mercury Theatre, then Criterion Theatre, London, 1947. PRINCIPAL STAGE WORK—Director: *Georgia Story,* New Lindsay Theatre, London, 1948; *Playboy of the Western World,* Mercury Theatre, London, 1948.

As director of the Bristol Old Vic Theatre Company, 1949-54, he directed over thirty plays for the company including: *The Cocktail Party, Traveller without Luggage,* and *Two Gentlemen of Verona* (also performed at the Old Vic Theatre, London, 1952). Also for the Bristol Old Vic directed: *Romanoff and Juliet* and *Much Ado About Nothing,* both 1956; *Free as Air* and *Man of Distinction,* both 1957; *Henry V* (also at the Old Vic Theatre, London, 1957); *Waiting for Godot,* 1957; *The Heart's a Wonder* (musical adaptation of *Playboy of the Western World;* presented in London at the Westminster Theatre, 1958); *Mr. Fox of Venice* (Picadilly Theatre, 1959); *The Flanders Mare,* 1961; *A Scent of Flowers,* 1965; *The Happiest Days of Your Life,* 1965; *The Playboy of the Western World,* 1966; *Hedda Gabler* and *I'll Get My Man* both produced at the Royal Theatre, Bristol, 1966; *The Way of the World,* 1967; *D.P.,* produced at the Little Theatre, Bristol, 1967.

As first director of the American Shakespeare Festival, Stratford, CT, directed *Julius Caesar* and *The Tempest,* both 1955.

Also directed: *Salad Days,* London production, 1954; *A Kind of Folly,* London production, 1955; *The Cherry Orchard* and *The Taming of the Shrew,* both Ottawa, 1959; *Follow That Girl,* Vaudeville Theatre, London, 1960; *Othello,* Theatre Nationale de Belgique, Brussels, 1960; *The Truth About Billy Newton,* Playhouse Theatre, Salisbury, U.K., 1960; *Hooray For Daisy,* Lyric Theatre, Hammersmith, London, 1960; *Mam'zelle Nitouche,* Nottingham Playhouse, U.K., 1961; *The Golden Years,* Royal Court Theatre, Liverpool, U.K., 1961; *Twelfth Night,* Ludlow Castle and Open Air, Regent's Park, 1962; *The Golden Rivet,*

Royale Theatre, Bristol, 1963; *The Life in My Hands,* Nottingham Playhouse, 1964; *Armstrong's Last Goodnight,* Glasgow Citizens' Theatre Company, 1964; *The Cherry Orchard* and *Volpone,* both Nottingham Playhouse, 1965; *When the Saints Go Cycling In,* Gate Theatre, Dublin Festival, 1965; *Juno and the Paycock,* Gaiety Theatre, Dublin, 1966; *Hobson's Choice,* Alhambra Theatre, Bradford, England, 1968.

Directed tours of *The Golden Years,* 1961, *Hamlet* and *A Man for All Seasons,* with the Bristol Old Vic Company for a fourteen week tour of Pakistan, India and Ceylon, 1963, and *The Pilgrim's Progress,* 1973.

PRINCIPAL FILM APPEARANCES—*The Day of the Jackal,* Universal, 1973.

PRINCIPAL TELEVISION APPEARANCES—Series: *General Hospital,* ABC; also, *Sutherland's Law.*

RELATED CAREER—Associate director, Arts Theatre, Salisbury, England, 1948; director, Bristol Old Vic Theatre Company, 1949-54, and 1963-66; first director of the American Shakespeare Festival, Stratford, CT, 1955.

NON-RELATED CAREER—Worked in an income tax consultant's office.

SIDELIGHTS: Denis Carey's biggest box office success was the revue *Salad Days,* which ran for 2,283 performances in the 1954-55 London season.*

* * *

CARMEL, Roger C.   1932-1986

PERSONAL: Born 1932; died of an apparent drug overdose in Hollywood, CA, November 11, 1986.

VOCATION: Actor.

CAREER: PRINCIPAL TELEVISION APPEARANCES—Series: Roger Buell, *Mothers-in-Law,* NBC, 1967-68; Lawrence Brody, *Fitz and Bones,* NBC, 1981. Episodic: *Naked City,* ABC; *Alfred Hitchcock Presents,* CBS and ABC; *Route 66,* CBS; *The Dick Van Dyke Show,* CBS; *I Spy,* NBC; *Batman,* ABC; Harcourt Fenton Mudd, *Star Trek,* NBC; *The Defenders,* CBS; *Hart to Hart,* ABC; *All in the Family,* CBS.

PRINCIPAL FILM APPEARANCES—*The Greatest Show Earth,* 1952; *North by Northwest,* Metro-Goldwyn-Mayer (MGM), 1959; *Goodbye Charlie,* Twentieth Century-Fox, 1964; *A House Is Not a Home,* Embassy, 1964; *The Silencers,* Columbia, 1966; *Gambit,* Universal, 1966; *Alvarez,* Columbia, 1966; *The Venetian Affair,* MGM, 1967; *Skullduggery,* Universal, 1970; *Breezy,* Universal, 1973; *Hardly Working,* 1981.

PRINCIPAL STAGE APPEARANCES—Broadway: *A Man for All Seasons; Half a Sixpence; Rhinoceros; Caligula; Purlie Victorious; Once There Was a Russian.*

SIDELIGHTS: CTFT learned that Roger Carmel was the voice of "Smokey the Bear," in television advertisements for fire prevention.*

CARNEY, Art   1918-

PERSONAL: Full name, Arthur William Matthew Carney; born November 4, 1918, in Mount Vernon, NY; son of Edward M. and Helen (Farrell) Carney; married Jean Myers, August 15, 1940 (divorced, 1965), remarried Jean Myers, March, 1977 (divorced); married Barbara Isaac; children: (first marriage) Eileen, Brian, Paul. EDUCATION: Attended A.B. Davis High School, Mount Vernon. MILITARY: U.S. Army, 1944-45.

VOCATION: Actor.

CAREER: TELEVISION DEBUT—*Morey Amsterdam Show,* CBS, 1948. PRINCIPAL TELEVISION APPEARANCES—Series: Regular, *Henry Morgan's Great Talent Hunt,* NBC, 1951; Ed Norton, "The Honeymooners," *Cavalcade of Stars,* DuMont, 1951-52; appeared as series regular in "The Honeymooners" sketches on *The Jackie Gleason Show,* CBS, 1952-55; Ed Norton, *The Honeymooners,* CBS, 1955-56; appeared as series regular in "The Honeymooners" sketches on *The Jackie Gleason Show,* CBS, 1956-57, then 1966-70; Chief Paul Lanigan, *Lanigan's Rabbi,* NBC, 1977.

Teleplays: *Uncle Harry,* 1954; *Burlesque,* 1954; *Panama Hattie,* 1954; *Charlie's Aunt,* 1957; *Incredible Irishman,* 1957; "Harvey," *Dupont Show of the Month,* 1958; *Art Carney Meets Peter and the Wolf,* 1958; *Our Town,* 1959; *Call Me Back,* 1960. Movies: *Death Scream,* 1975; *Katherine,* 1975; *Scott Joplin, King of Ragtime,* 1978; *Terrible Joe Moran,* CBS, 1984; *The Night They Saved Christmas,* ABC, 1984; *Izzy and Moe,* CBS, 1985; also appeared in *A Doctor's Story; Velvet Alley; Art Carney Meets the Sorcerer's Apprentice; Very Important People; Man in the Dog Suit.*

Episodic: *Studio One,* CBS; *Kraft Television Theatre,* NBC; *Omnibus,* ABC; *Chevy Show,* NBC; *Playhouse 90,* CBS; *Batman,* ABC. Specials: *Sid Caesar-Art Carney Show,* ABC.

Guest: *The Jackie Gleason Show,* CBS, 1961; *Carol Burnett Show,* CBS; *Jonathan Winters Show,* NBC; *Tonight Show,* NBC.

FILM DEBUT—*Pot of Gold,* 1941. PRINCIPAL FILM APPEARANCES—*The Yellow Rolls Royce,* Metro-Goldwyn-Mayer, 1965; Harry, *Harry and Tonto,* Twentieth Century-Fox, 1974; *W.W. and the Dixie Dance Kings,* Twentieth Century-Fox, 1975; *Won Ton Ton,* Paramount, 1976; *The Late Show,* Warner Brothers, 1977; Dr. Blaine, *Movie Movie,* Warner Brothers, 1978; Dr. Willoughby, *House Calls,* Universal, 1978; *Better Late Than Never,* 1979; *Sunburn,* Paramount, 1979; *Going in Style,* Warner Brothers, 1979; *Defiance,* American International, 1980; *Roadie,* United Artists, 1980; *Steel,* 1980; *Take This Job and Shove It,* AVCO-Embassy, 1981; *Firestarter,* Universal, 1984; *The Naked Face,* 1984.

BROADWAY DEBUT—James Hyland, *The Rope Dancers,* Cort Theatre, 1957. PRINCIPAL STAGE APPEARANCES—Elmer P. Dowd, *Harvey,* Ivoryton Playhouse, CT, 1956; James Hyland, *The Rope Dancers,* Henry Miller's Theatre, New York City, 1957; Frank Michaelson, *Take Her, She's Mine,* Biltmore Theatre, New York City, 1961; Felix Ungar, *The Odd Couple,* Plymouth Theatre, New York City, 1965; Andy Tracey, *Lovers,* Vivian Beaumont Theatre, then Music Box Theatre, New York City, 1968; Mel Edison, *The Prisoner of Second Avenue,* Eugene O'Neill Theatre, New York City, then Ahmanson Theatre, Los Angeles, 1972; Oscar Madison, *The Odd Couple,* Arlington Park Theatre, Chicago, 1974; Mel Edison, *The Prisoner of Second Avenue,* Westbury Music Fair, Long Island, NY, 1974.

MAJOR TOURS—Richard Sherman, *The Seven Year Itch*, New England cities, 1956.

PRINCIPAL RADIO WORK—Philly, *Joe and Ethel Turp*; numerous voice characterizations.

RELATED CAREER—Appeared extensively in vaudeville and cabaret.

AWARDS: Best Series Supporting Actor, Emmy Award, 1954, for *The Jackie Gleason Show;* Sylvania Award, 1954, and two in 1959; Outstanding Individual Achievement, Emmy Awards, 1967, 1968; Best Actor, Academy Award, 1974, for *Harry and Tonto;* Outstanding Supporting Actor in a Special, Emmy Award, 1984, for *Terrible Joe Moran.*

MEMBER: Actors' Equity Association, Screen Actors Guild, American Federation of Television and Radio Artists; Players Club, Lambs Club.

SIDELIGHTS: "How would you like to go through life with your name synonymous with sewage?," actor Art Carney asked columnist Earl Wilson during an August 3, 1974, interview in the *New York Post.* Carney was then still best known for playing Ed Norton, the self-styled "underground sanitation expert," on the popular 1950s television situation comedy series *The Honeymooners.* Within a year, however, Carney won an Academy Award for his performance as Harry, a retired professor who embarks on a cross-country tour when he is thrown out of his New York City apartment, in the 1974 comedy-drama *Harry and Tonto.* That movie and the ones that immediately followed, notably *The Late Show* in 1977 and *House Calls* in 1978, gave Carney a new reputation—as one of Hollywood's most effective actors portraying elderly men. In a *New York Times* article (February 20, 1977) just after after the release of *The Late Show,* Joseph Morgenstern wrote: "He's shown men playing through their lives to feel the wholeness of their lives. . . . Young audiences, as well as old, are looking up to [Carney] as a hero."

Through his brother Jack, a musical booking agent, Carney landed his first show-business job in 1936, as a mimic and novelty singer for Horace Heidt's band. He worked with the band in vaudeville, on radio, and in one movie. Able to imitate Franklin D. Roosevelt, Winston Churchill, and other world figures, Carney held several more radio jobs in the years just before and after his World War II Army service. His role as "Philly" on the *Joe and Ethel Turp* show foreshadowed his characterization of Ed Norton.

Carney first appeared as Norton, the foil for star Jackie Gleason's Ralph Kramden, when "The Honeymooners" was a regular skit between 1951-52 on the DuMont Network's *Cavalcade of Stars* television program. The feature was used again on CBS's *Jackie Gleason Show* (1952-55 and 1956-57). Most of the episodes so often broadcast in syndication in the decades since then, however, were originally shown during the one year (1955-56) that *The Honeymooners* was a separate series. Carney's dumb but good-hearted Norton remained one of the best remembered characters of sitcom history. The actor's contribution was acknowledged when, in 1966, Gleason and Carney were temporarily reunited for a new set of "Honeymooners" segments on the *Jackie Gleason Show;* a reporter for *Look* (November 15, 1966) asserted that Carney "brings to comedy all the deftness, imagination and pathos of yesterday's most eloquent loser, Charlie Chaplin."

Indeed, even during his *Honeymooners* years, Carney thought of himself as an actor rather than just a comic. Wanting to prove he

could handle more serious work, in 1957, he left Gleason and accepted one of the lead roles in Morton Wishengrad's Broadway drama *The Rope Dancers.* The play was only a moderate success, but Carney received virtually unanimous raves from the rather surprised critics. Robert Coleman of the *New York Mirror* (November 21, 1957) felt Carney was "the dramatic find of the year," while Hobe Morrison of *Variety* (November 27, 1957) called him "a revelation." Morrison elaborated, "His portrayal starts on a low key, as does the part, but grows in depth and color as the indolent would-be writer is engulfed in tragedy." Carney's success in *The Rope Dancers* led to more Broadway parts, the most famous one being that of Felix Ungar, the obsessively neat roommate in Neil Simon's *Odd Couple.* In his *Variety* review of the play (March 17, 1965), Morrison stated, "Carney gives a mercurial, flexible, articulate and effectively contrasting portrayal of the maniacally neurotical, hypochondriac border."

While appearing in *The Odd Couple,* Carney suffered a nervous breakdown brought on by the failure of his twenty-five-year first marriage, and he left the play to enter a sanitarium for nearly six months. Over the next nine years, he fought addictions to alcohol, amphetamines, and barbituates, finally bringing his alcoholism under control at about the time he made *Harry and Tonto.*

Originally Carney was not interested in portraying Harry in *Harry and Tonto* at all, feeling the film sentimentalized old age and that at fifty-five he was too young to play a seventy-two-year-old. Soon convinced, however, by director Paul Mazursky, that "this part was not that of an 'old' 72-year-old-man," and as the actor explained to a reporter for the *National Enquirer* (October 7, 1974), little change was necessary to become Harry: "I used my own voice, very slight makeup, bushier eyebrows, grew my own mustache and whitened my hair." In addition, Carney wore his own hearing aid and did not try to mask the limp that was the result of a World War II injury.

In his *Christian Science Monitor* (August 12, 1974) review of *Harry and Tonto,* David Sterritt asserted, "We fans . . . have always known that Carney has the makeup of a first-rate movie star." Describing Carney's work in the film as a "tour de force of performing skill," he went on to say, "Carney presides over [the movie] like a wizened wizard, aged 20 years by makeup magic and acting nuance, onscreen nearly every moment, filling the screen with his unique warmth." Sterritt's opinion was shared by nearly all of his fellow critics; Virginia Gray of *The Lively Arts* (September, 1974) wrote, "Art Carney's performance is remarkable in its range and honesty, as he conveys Harry's confusion, his determination to remain independent, and his abiding sense of the absurdity of it all without a trace of self-pity or self-consciousness."

Carney's next important part was in *The Late Show,* writer-director Robert Benton's 1977 homage to the classic detective thrillers of such actors as Humphrey Bogart. In this film, Carney's character, aging detective Ira Wells, has trouble pursuing his profession because of physical disabilities, but manages to outwit the villains anyway. Critics generally felt that the movie did not work as a thriller, but they admired the chemistry between Carney and co-star Lily Tomlin. Clancy Sigal of the British publication *The Spectator* (July 16, 1977) remarked, "It's startlingly easy to identify with [these] likeable losers but stubborn survivors."

Carney's comic portrayals of physicians in two later films were also noted by critics. Frank Rich, in the April 10, 1978, issue of *Time,* described Dr. Willoughby, the senile, incompetent hospital chief of staff portrayed by Carney in *House Calls* as "the film's one outright hilarious character, played with vaudevillian relish.'' The actor's crusty Dr. Blaine in *Movie Movie*, a satiric re-creation of 1930's double features, prompted *New Yorker*'s Pauline Kael (December 4, 1978) to comment, ''It's easy to forget him [Carney], because he's the kind of good actor who does things so instinctively that you don't see any actor's tension or control—he just plays his part, as if there were nothing to it.''

Although Carney's film roles since 1978 have been in less successful movies, he has won a new generation of admirers due to the growing popularity of *The Honeymooners* in reruns. Back in 1964, Carney had told Vernon Scott of UPI that he did not mind people calling him 'Norton' on the street: ''That's okay. I look back on *The Honeymooners* as having the same quality as Laurel and Hardy. The audiences believed in them.'' In a press release for his 1979 movie *Going in Style*, however, the actor denied that he was actually like Norton: ''I love Ed Norton and what he did for my career. But the truth is that we couldn't have been more different. Norton was the total extrovert, there was no way you could put down his infectious good humor. Me? I'm a loner and a worrier.''

ADDRESSES: AGENT—International Creative Management, 8899 Beverly Blvd., Los Angeles, CA 90048.*

*   *   *

CARRADINE, David   1936-

PERSONAL: Full name, John Arthur Carradine; born December 8, 1936; son of John (an actor) and Ardanelle Abigail (McCool) Carradine; married Barbara Hershey (divorced); children: Calista, Tom, Kansas. EDUCATION: Attended San Francisco State College and University of California at Berkeley; trained for the stage with Justin Smith. POLITICS: Jeffersonian Democrat. RELIGION: Christian Science. MILITARY: U.S. Army, 1960-62.

VOCATION: Actor, composer, writer, and editor.

CAREER: FILM DEBUT—*Bus Riley's Back in Town*, Universal, 1965. PRINCIPAL FILM APPEARANCES—*Taggart*, 1965; *Too Many Thieves*, 1967; *The Violent Ones*, 1967; *Heaven with a Gun*, Metro-Goldwyn-Mayer (MGM), 1969; *Young Billy Young*, United Artists, 1969; *The Good Guys and the Bad Guys*, Warner Brothers, 1969; *Gallery of Horrors*, 1970; *The McMasters*, Chevron, 1970; *Macho Callahan*, AVCO-Embassy, 1970; *McCabe and Mrs. Miller*, Warner Brothers, 1971; *Boxcar Bertha*, 1972; *Mean Streets*, Warner Brothers, 1973; *The Long Goodbye*, 1973; *Death Race 2000*, New World, 1975.

Cannonball, New World Pictures, 1976; *Bound for Glory*, United Artists, 1976; *Thunder and Lightning*, Twentieth Century-Fox, 1977; *Serpent's Egg*, Embassy, 1977; *Mr. Horn*, 1978; *Gray Lady Down*, Universal, 1978; *Deathsport*, New World Pictures, 1978; *Circle of Iron*, New World Pictures, 1980; *Cloud Dancer*, Blossom Pictures, 1980; *The Long Riders*, United Artists, 1980; *Safari 3000*, 1981; *Lone Wolf McQuade*, Orion, 1983; *Americana*, Crown International, 1983; *Kain of the Dark Planet*, 1984.

TELEVISION DEBUT—*East Side/West Side*, CBS, 1963. PRINCIPAL TELEVISION APPEARANCES—Series: Title role, *Shane*, ABC, 1966; Kwai Chang Caine, *Kung Fu*, ABC, 1972-75. Episodic: *Darkroom*, ABC; *Amazing Stories*, NBC, 1986. Movies: *Gaugin the Savage*, CBS, 1978; *Johnny Belinda*, 1982; *Jealousy*, 1984; *The Bad Seed*, 1985. Mini-Series: *North and South*, ABC, 1985.

DAVID CARRADINE

STAGE DEBUT—Tybalt, *Romeo and Juliet*, Playbox Theatre, Berkeley, CA, for twenty-four performances. BROADWAY DEBUT—*The Deputy*, Brooks Atkinson Theatre, 1963, for two-hundred and fifty performances. PRINCIPAL STAGE APPEARANCES—Atahualpa, *The Royal Hunt of the Sun*, American National Theatre Academy (ANTA), New York City, 1965; *Black Elk Speaks*, American Indian Theatre, Tulsa, OK.

WRITINGS: BOOKS, UNPUBLISHED—(With Christopher Sergel) Troublemaker; The Spirit of Shaolin. MUSICAL COMPOSITIONS—Score for *Mata Hari* and seventy five songs for Catahoula and Carlin publishing companies.

AWARDS: Most Promising Personality, *Theatre World* Award, 1965; Man of the Year Award, Fraternal Order of Police, 1985.

MEMBER: Screen Actors Guild, American Federation of Television and Radio Artists, Directors Guild of America; Muscular Distrophy Association, National Rifle Association, 1199 Club, Fraternal Order of Police (honorary).

SIDELIGHTS: RECREATIONS—Music, horses, sculpture, painting, filmmaking, philosophy, art, science, children, French, and the American Revolution.

David Carradine told *CTFT* that one of his favorite activites is acting as a coach for the Special Olympics.

ADDRESSES: AGENT—Contemporary Artists, Ltd., 132B Laskey Drive, Beverly Hills, CA 90212.

CARRADINE, John 1906-

PERSONAL: Born Richmond Reed Carradine, February 5, 1906, in New York, NY; son of William Reed and Genevieve Winifred (Richmond) Carradine; married Ardanelle McCool (divorced); married Sonia Henius (divorced); married Doris I. Rich (divorced); married Emily Cisneros; children: Bruce John, John Arthur, Christopher John, Keith Ian, Robert Reed. EDUCATION: Attended the Graphic Art School, Philadelphia.

VOCATION: Actor.

CAREER: PRINCIPAL FILM APPEARANCES—As John Peter Richmond: *Tol'able David,* First National, 1920; *The Invisible Man,* 1933; *Cleopatra,* 1934; *Black Cat,* Universal, 1934. As John Carradine: *Bride of Frankenstein,* Universal, 1935; *Les Miserables,* 1935; *The Crusades,* 1935; *Winterset,* 1936; *Jesse James,* 1939; *Adventures of Mark Twain,* 1944; *House of Frankenstein,* 1944; *Fallen Angel,* 1945; *House of Dracula,* 1945; *Captain Kidd,* 1945; *Face of Marble,* 1946; *Private Affairs of Bel Ami,* 1947; *C-Man,* 1949; *Casanova's Big Night,* 1954; *Thunder Pass,* 1954; *Johnny Guitar,* 1954; *The Egyptian,* 1954; *Stranger on Horseback,* United Artists, 1955; *Desert Sands,* United Artists, 1955; *The Kentuckian,* United Artists, 1955; *Hidden Guns,* Republic, 1956; *Dark Venture, Black Sheep,* and *Good Guys and Bad Guys,* Warner Brothers, 1969; *Boxcar Bertha* American International, 1972; *Everything You Always Wanted to Know About Sex,* United Artists, 1972; *The Shootist,* Paramount, 1976; *The Sentinal,* Universal, 1977; *Zorro, the Gay Blade,* Twentieth Century-Fox, 1981; *House of Long Shadows,* 1983.

STAGE DEBUT—*Camille,* St. Charles Theatre, New Orleans, LA, 1925. PRINCIPAL STAGE APPEARANCES—*Window Panes,* Egan Theatre, Los Angeles, 1927; Louis XI, *The Vagabound King,* Los Angeles and San Francisco, 1941; Allan Manville, *My Dear Children,* Brighton Theatre, Brooklyn, NY, 1945; Matthew, *Murder without Crime,* Bridgeport, CT, 1945; Jonathan Brewster, *Arsenic and Old Lace,* Town Hall Theatre, New York City, 1946; Cardinal, *The Duchess of Malfi,* Ethel Barrymore Theatre, New York City, 1946; Rupert Cadell, *Rope,* Toledo Theatre, New York City, 1946; Inquisitor, *Galileo,* Maxine Elliott Theatre, New York City, 1947; Voltore, *Volpone* and Nyunin, *The Wedding,* both City Center, New York City, 1948; Walter Fowler, *The Cup of Trembling,* Music Box Theatre, New York City, 1948; Benjy, *The Leading Lady,* National Theatre, New York City, 1948; the ragpicker, *The Madwoman of Chaillot,* Belasco Theatre, New York City, 1948. Summer stock performances: Dr. Austin Sloper, *The Heiress,* 1949, Brutus, *Julius Caesar,* Sir Robert, *The Winslow Boy,* and in *Shadow and Substance,* 1950, leading role, *Silver Whistle,* Mephistopheles, *Dr. Faustus,* and Jeeter Lester, *Tobacco Road,* 1951.

Kit Carson, *The Time of Your Life,* City Center, New York City, 1955; Lycus, *A Funny Thing Happened on the Way to the Forum,* Alvin Theatre, New York City, 1962-64; Jeeter Lester, *Tobacco Road,* Alhambra Dinner Theatre, Jacksonville, FL, 1970; *The Fantasticks* and *You Never Can Tell,* Arlington Park, IL, 1973; Sir Thomas More, *A Man for All Seasons,* Episcopal Academy Theatre, Philadelphia, PA, 1974; also appeared in *Boo,* 1984.

MAJOR TOURS—Shylock, *The Merchant of Venice,* title role and Iago, *Othello,* title role, *Hamlet,* in his own repertory company, U.S. cities, 1943-44; the ragpicker, *The Madwoman of Chaillot,* U.S. cities, 1949-50; Nickles, *JB,* U.S. cities, 1960-61; Fagin, *Oliver!,* U.S. cities, 1966; *Arsenic and Old Lace,* U.S. cities, 1974.

PRINCIPAL STAGE WORK—Director: *A Man for All Seasons,* Episcopal Academy Theatre, Philadelphia, PA, 1974.

PRINCIPAL TELEVISION APPEARANCES—Series: Mr. Corday, *My Friend Irma,* CBS, 1953-54. Episodic: *NBC Repertory Theatre,* NBC, 1949; *Sure as Fate,* CBS, 1950; *Suspense,* CBS; *The Web,* CBS.

MEMBER: Screen Actors Guild, Actors' Equity Association, American Federation of Television and Radio Artists; Players Club, Channel Island Yacht Club.

SIDELIGHTS: FAVORITE ROLES—Jeeter Lester in *Tobacco Road,* Othello, Sir Thomas More in *A Man for All Seasons,* Sir Robert in *The Winslow Boy,* Shylock in *The Merchant of Venice,* and Dr. Sloper in *The Heiress.* RECREATIONS—Sculpture, tennis, sailing.

ADDRESSES: OFFICE—c/o The Players Club, 16 Gramercy Park South, New York, NY 10003.*

*   *   *

CARTER, T.K.

VOCATION: Actor and songwriter.

CAREER: PRINCIPAL FILM APPEARANCES—*Seems Like Old Times,* Columbia, 1980; *The Hollywood Knights,* Columbia, 1980; *Dr. Detroit,* Universal, 1983; *Runaway Train,* Cannon Films, 1985; Reggie and Regina, *Pulling It Off,* 1986.

T.K. CARTER

PRINCIPAL TELEVISION APPEARANCES—Series: Shabu, *Just Our Luck,* ABC, 1983; Mike Fulton, *Punky Brewster,* NBC, 1984-85.

PRINCIPAL STAGE APPEARANCES—Toured in his own act from Caesar's Palace in Atlantic City and Universal Amphitheatre in Los Angeles.

WRITINGS: SONGS—Contributed one of the songs used in the film *Dr. Detriot,* 1983.

SIDELIGHTS: RECREATIONS—Softball and cooking.

T.K. Carter told *CTFT* that he enjoys taking long rides in his jeep. "I've come up with many of my best ideas there and it helps me to get away from it all and put my life in perspective—I never want to lose that."

ADDRESSES: PUBLICIST—Jo-Ann Geffen & Associates, 3151 Cahuenga Blvd. W., Suite 235, Los Angeles, CA 90068.

*   *   *

CASH, Rosalind   1938-

PERSONAL: Born December 31, 1938, in Atlantic City, NJ; daughter of John and Martha (Curtis) Cash. EDUCATION: Attended the City College of New York; studied with Vinnette Carol and at the Negro Ensemble Company in New York City.

VOCATION: Actress.

CAREER: STAGE DEBUT—*Soul Gone Home,* Harlem YMCA, New York City, 1958. BROADWAY DEBUT—Mrs. Hoyt, *The Wayward Stork,* 46th Street Theatre, January 19, 1966. LONDON DEBUT—Third extraordinary spook, *God Is a (Guess What?),* with the Negro Ensemble Company at the Aldwych Theatre as part of the World Theatre Season, May 5, 1969. PRINCIPAL STAGE APPEARANCES—*Fiorello!,* City Center Theatre, New York City, 1962; Sonja, *Junebug Graduates Tonight!,* Chelsea Theatre Center, New York City, 1967; Lita, *To Bury a Cousin,* Bouwerie Lane Theatre, New York City, 1967; as a member of the Negro Ensemble Company at the St. Marks Playhouse, New York City: *Song of the Lusitanian Bogey,* Segi and Ogbo Aberi, *Kongi's Harvest,* Fanny, *Daddy Goodness,* and third extraordinary spook, *God Is a (Guess What?),* all 1968; Inez Briscoe, *Man Better Man,* 1969; Ayo, *The Harangues* and Mary, *Day of Absence,* both 1970; Carla, *Charlie Was Here and Now He's Gone,* Eastside Playhouse, 1971; Adele Eloise Parker, *Ceremonies in Dark Old Men,* Philadelphia Drama Guild, PA, 1973; Goneril, *King Lear,* New York Shakespeare Festival, Delacorte Theatre, 1973; *Boesman and Lena,* 1976; *Evolution of the Blues,* 1978; Marsha, *The Sixteenth Round,* Negro Ensemble Company, Theatre Four, 1980; *Orchards in the Moonlight,* American Repertory Theatre, Cambridge, MA, 1981-82.

FILM DEBUT—*All-American Boy,* Warner Brothers, 1969. PRINCIPAL FILM APPEARANCES—*The Omega Man,* Warner Brothers, 1971; *Melinda,* Metro-Goldwyn-Mayer, 1972; *Hickey and Boggs,* United Artists, 1972; *The New Centurions,* Columbia, 1972; *Amazing Grace,* United Artists, 1974; *Uptown Saturday Night,* Warner Brothers, 1974; *Cornbread, Earl and Me,* 1975; *The Class of Miss MacMichael,* British, 1978; *Wrong Is Right,* Columbia, 1982.

PRINCIPAL TELEVISION APPEARANCES—Episodic: *Barney Miller,* ABC; *Starsky & Hutch,* ABC; *Police Story,* NBC; *Kojak,* CBS; *What's Happening,* ABC; *Good Times,* CBS; *The Mary Tyler Moore Show* CBS. Movies: *A Killing Affair,* 1977; *The Guyana Tragedy: The Story of Jim Jones,* 1980; *The Sophisticated Gents,* 1981; *Sister, Sister,* 1982; also, *Many Mansions; South by Northwest; Denmark Vesey; Up & Coming.* Teleplays: *Ceremonies in Dark Old Men, King Lear,* and *Go Tell It on the Mountain.*

NON-RELATED CAREER—Employed as a hospital aide, waitress, and salesgirl.

MEMBER: Actors' Equity Association, Screen Actors Guild, American Federation of Television and Radio Artists.

SIDELIGHTS: FAVORITE ROLES—Those she played while a member of the Negro Ensemble Company. RECREATIONS—Painting, sewing, guitar, and poetry.

ADDRESSES: AGENT—John Sekura, 1133 N. Vista, Hollywood, CA 90046.*

*   *   *

CASTILLO, Helen   1955-

PERSONAL: Born February 5, 1955, in Santurce, PR; daughter of Amerigo and Victoria (Encarnacion) Castillo. EDUCATION: Juilliard School of Music, B.F.A., dance, 1978; studied music with Richard Harper at Jazzmobile.

HELEN CASTILLO

VOCATION: Actress, choreographer, dancer, and singer.

CAREER: STAGE DEBUT—Singer and dancer, *Don't Bother Me, I Can't Cope*, bus and truck tour, U.S. cities, 1975. BROADWAY DEBUT—Alter-ego, *They're Playing Our Song*, Imperial Theatre, 1978-81.

MAJOR TOURS—Actress, singer, and dancer, *Dreamgirls*, Los Angeles, San Francisco, and Chicago, 1983-86.

FILM DEBUT—Dancer, *The Wiz*, United Artists, 1977.

TELEVISION DEBUT—*Loving*, ABC, 1986.

RELATED CAREER—Dance teacher, New York City Board of Education, 1986.

MEMBER: Actors' Equity Association, Screen Actors Guild, American Federation of Television and Radio Aritsts.

SIDELIGHTS: Ms. Castillo is fluent in both Spanish and English.

ADDRESSES: OFFICE—P.O. Box 1745, Cathedral Station, New York, NY 10025.

*   *   *

CAZENOVE, Christopher   1945-

PERSONAL: Born December 17, 1945, in Winchester, U.K.; son of Arnold de Lerisson and Elizabeth Laura (Gurney) Cazenove; married Angharad Rees (an actress), 1974; children: two sons.

CHRISTOPHER CAZENOVE

EDUCATION: Attended Eton and Oxford University; trained for the stage at the Bristol Old Vic Theatre School.

VOCATION: Actor.

CAREER: STAGE DEBUT—*Man and Superman*, Phoenix Theatre, Leicester, U.K., 1967. LONDON DEBUT Courtenay, *The Lionel Touch*, Lyric Theatre, November 5, 1969. BROADWAY DEBUT—James Sinclair, *Goodbye Fidel*, Ambassador Theatre, April 10, 1980. PRINCIPAL STAGE APPEARANCES—Played two seasons at Pitlochry Theatre in many roles including the title role in *Hamlet*, 1967-69; Guy Vivian, *My Darling Daisy*, Lyric Theatre, London, 1970; John Watherstone, *The Winslow Boy*, New Theatre, London, 1970; Christian De Neuvillette, *Cyrano de Bergerac* and Cassio, *Othello*, both at the Chichester Festival Theatre, U.K., 1975, then later at the Hong Kong Festival; Richard, *Joking Apart*, Globe Theatre, London, 1979.

PRINCIPAL FILM APPEARANCES—*Royal Flash*, Twentieth Century-Fox, 1975; *East of Elephant Rock*, 1977; *Zulu Dawn* and *The Girl in Blue Velvet*, 1979; *Eye of the Needle*, United Artists, 1981; *Heat and Dust*, Universal, 1983; *Until September*, Metro-Goldwyn-Mayer/United Artists, 1984; *Mata Hari*, 1985.

PRINCIPAL TELEVISION APPEARANCES—Series: In the U.K.— *The Regiment; The Duchess of Duke Street*, and *Jennie*. In the U.S.—Ben Carrington, *Dynasty*, ABC, 1986—. Mini-Series: *Kane and Abel*, CBS, 1985.

ADDRESSES: OFFICE—Aaron Spelling Productions, 1041 N. Formosa, Los Angeles, CA 90046; Ten Trinity Close, London SW4, England. AGENT—Chatto and Linnet, Globe Theatre, Shaftesbury Avenue, London W1, England.*

*   *   *

CHAMBERLIN, Lee

PERSONAL: Born Elise La Pallo, February 14, in New York, NY; daughter of Bernando (a chef) and Ida Roberta (Small) La Pallo; children: Erika, Matthew. EDUCATION: Washington Square College of New York University, B.A.; also attended University of Paris; trained for the stage at the Herbert Berghof Studios with Uta Hagen and Walt Witcover; studied voice with Carlo Minotti.

VOCATION: Actress, composer, and writer.

CAREER: OFF-BROADWAY DEBUT—Various roles, *The Believers*, Martinique Theatre, 1968. PRINCIPAL STAGE APPEARANCES— Alice, *Hospice*, Henry Street, New Federal Theatre, New York City, 1983; Laveer, *Long Time Since Yesterday*, Henry Street, New Federal Theatre, New York City, 1985; also appeared as Cordelia, *King Lear*, New York Shakespeare Festival, New York City; *Slaveship*, Chelsea Theatre Center, New York City; Olivia, *Your Own Thing*, Orpheum Theatre, New York City; title role, *Medea*, Pennsylvania Festival of the Arts; Billie, *Nevis Mountain Dew*, Los Angeles Actors Theatre.

TELEVISION DEBUT—Various roles, *The Electric Company*, PBS, 1970-72. PRINCIPAL TELEVISION APPEARANCES—Series: Pat

LEE CHAMBERLIN

CHANNING, Marvin   1944-

PERSONAL: Born August 11, 1944, in New York, NY; son of Harry (a laborer) and Emma (Charn) Channing; married Arline Rita Kallem (a teacher), August 21, 1965. EDUCATION: Brooklyn College, B.A., 1964; studied acting with Peter Thompson and Terry Schrieber in New York. MILITARY: U.S. Army, military police.

VOCATION: Actor and writer.

CAREER: PRINCIPAL STAGE APPEARANCES—Barney, *Caine Mutiny Court Martial,* Show Boat Theatre; Steve Purcell, *Eagle in a Cage,* No Smoking Playhouse, New York City; Milt, *Luv* and Oscar, *The Odd Couple,* both St. Petersburg Dinner Theatre; Arthur, *The 75th,* Will, *Hopscotch,* and Peter, *The Zoo Story,* all Center Stage Theatre; Doctor Bessner, *Murder on the Nile,* National Theatre; Grigory Smirnov, *The Brute,* Royal Court Repertory; Joel Kane, *Barbara & Ruth,* West End (London) production.

MAJOR TOURS—Carl Goldstein, *The Shohet,* five state tour.

PRINCIPAL FILM APPEARANCES—Homicide detective, *Still of the Night,* Metro-Goldwyn-Mayer, 1982; Broadway backer, *Author! Author!,* Twentieth Century-Fox, 1982; waiter, *Tootsie,* Columbia, 1982.

PRINCIPAL TELEVISION APPEARANCES—Patient, *Nurse,* CBS.

PRINCIPAL RADIO WORK—*Marv Channing Show,* WPAC; *Music*

Baxter, *All My Children,* ABC; Lucy Daniels, *All's Fair,* CBS, 1976-77; Barbara Paris, *Paris,* CBS, 1979-80; *Tuned In,* PBS.

Mini-Series: *Roots: The Next Generations,* ABC, 1979. Episodic: *The White Shadow,* CBS; *Diff'rent Strokes,* NBC; *What's Happening,* ABC; *Lou Grant,* CBS; *James at 15,* NBC; *Secrets of Midland Heights,* CBS. Movies: *Once Upon a Family,* 1980; *Brave New World,* 1980. Pilots: *Full House,* ABC; *Ryan's Four,* ABC; *Up and Comin',* KQED, Los Angeles; *The Apples,* KQED, Los Angeles.

PRINCIPAL FILM APPEARANCES—*Up the Sandbox,* National General, 1972; Madame Zenobia, *Uptown Saturday Night,* First Artists, 1973; *Let's Do It Again,* Warner Brothers, 1975; *Beat Street,* Orion, 1984.

WRITINGS: PLAYS, PRODUCED—*Struttin',* AMAS Repertory, New York City, 1987.

RECORDINGS: Two albums for Disques Festival, France; *Electric Company,* Cast Album.

AWARDS: Co-winner, Grammy Award, 1972, for *Electric Company;* Best Actress, Audelco Award, 1983, for *Hospice;* Best Actress, Audelco Award nomination, 1985, for *Long Time Since Yesterday.*

ADDRESSES: HOME—New York, NY. AGENT—c/o Michael Thomas Agency, Inc., 305 Madison Avenue, New York, NY 10165.

MARVIN CHANNING

in the Night, WILI; *1360 Club*, WWBZ; *Here's Channing*, WKAL; *Insight*; *Celebrity*.

WRITINGS: TELEVISION—*Eagle in a Cage*. MAGAZINES—Chief writer, Red Circle Publications.

MEMBER: Actors' Equity Association, American Federation of Television and Radio Artists, Screen Actors' Guild.

SIDELIGHTS: Marvin Channing told *CTFT* that the motivation in his career is "love of performing—hopefully to make the world a slightly better place."

ADDRESSES: HOME—105-15 66th Road, Forest Hills, NY 11375.

*   *   *

CHAPMAN, Lonny   1920-

PERSONAL: Born October 1, 1920, in Tulsa, OK; son of Elmer William (a truck mechanic) and Eunice (Presley) Chapman; married Erma Gibbons, February 13, 1944; children: Wyley Dean. EDUCATION: University of Oklahoma, B.A., drama. MILITARY: U.S. Marine Corps, served in the South Pacific, 1941-45.

VOCATION: Actor, director, and writer.

CAREER: STAGE DEBUT—Wiley, *Mr. Roberts*, Erlanger Theatre, Chicago, IL, 1948. BROADWAY DEBUT—Turk, *Come Back, Little Sheba*, Booth Theatre, 1950. PRINCIPAL STAGE APPEARANCES—*The Closing Door*, Empire Theatre, New York City, 1950; *In Any Language* and Harry, *Ladies of the Corridor*, both at the Cort Theatre, New York City, 1952; *Whistler's Grandmother*, Presidents Theatre, New York City, 1953; Nub, *The Chase*, Playhouse Theatre, New York City, 1954; Tom, *The Time of Your Life*, City Center, New York City, 1956; *The Traveling Lady*, Playhouse Theatre, New York City, 1956; Jim, *The Glass Menagerie*, City Center, New York City, 1957; *Marathon 33*, New York City, 1963.

MAJOR TOURS—Tom, *The Time of Your Life*, Brussels, Belgium, 1958.

PRINCIPAL STAGE WORK—Director: Directed over one-hundred plays for the Cecilwood Theatre, Fishkill, NY, between 1959-66; *The Glass Menagerie, The Rothschilds, West Side Story*, all for the Inner City Cultural Committee, Los Angeles, 1969-71; *Chicago*, Gate Theatre, Los Angeles, 1982.

FILM DEBUT—Roy, *East of Eden*, Warner Brothers, 1953. PRINCIPAL FILM APPEARANCES—*Young at Heart*, Warner Brothers, 1954; *Baby Doll*, Warner Brothers, 1956; Johnson, *Hour of the Gun*, Warner Brothers, 1966; *I Walk the Line*, Columbia, 1970; *Norma Rae*, Twentieth Century-Fox, 1979; also appeared in *The Sterling Moon*.

PRINCIPAL TELEVISION APPEARANCES—Series: Jeff Prior, *The Investigator*, NBC, 1958; Frank Malloy, *For the People*, CBS, 1965. Episodic: Has appeared in over four-hundred television programs, 1949-86.

RELATED CAREER—Acting teacher, Studio of New York, 1956-61.

WRITINGS: PLAYS, PRODUCED—*The Buffalo Skinner*, New York City, 1958; *Cry of the Raindrop*, St. Marks Playhouse, New York City, 1960; *Hoot Sudie*, Merle Oberon Theatre, Los Angeles, 1970; *Go Hang the Moon*, Los Angeles, 1974; *Night at the Red Dog*, Los Angeles, 1979; *Happy Days Are Here Again Blues*, Los Angeles, 1979.

ADDRESSES: AGENT—Contemporary Artists, 132 Lasky Drive, Beverly Hills, CA 90212.

*   *   *

CHARLESON, Ian   1949-

PERSONAL: Born August 11, 1949, in Edinburgh, Scotland; son of John and Jane Charleson. EDUCATION: Attended Edinburgh University, M.A., 1970; trained for the stage at the Royal Academy of Dramatic Art, London.

VOCATION: Actor.

CAREER: STAGE DEBUT—(At age eight) *Kith and Kin*, Edinburgh. LONDON DEBUT—Jimmy Porter, *Look Back in Anger*, Young Vic, 1972. PRINCIPAL STAGE APPEARANCES—Guildenstern, *Rosencrantz and Guildenstern Are Dead*, with the Young Vic Theatre Company, London, 1974; Lucentio, *The Taming of the Shrew*, Ottavio, *Scapino*, and Brian Curtis, *French without Tears*, all with the Young Vic Theatre Company, at the Brooklyn Academy of Music, NY, 1974; title role, *Hamlet*, Cambridge Theatre Company, U.K., 1975; Dave, *Otherwise Engaged*, Queen's Theatre, London, 1975; Octavius, *Julius Caesar* and Peregrine, *Volpone*, with the National Theatre Company, London, 1977; Ariel, *The Tempest*, Tranio, *The Taming of the Shrew*, and Longaville, *Love's Labour's Lost*, all with the Royal Shakespeare Company, Stratford, U.K., 1978, and at the Aldwych Theatre, London, 1979; *Piaf*, Other Place Theatre, London, 1978; Joe Maguire, *The Innocent*, Warehouse Theatre, London, 1979; *Piaf*, Warehouse Theatre, Aldwych Theatre, and Wyndham's Theatre, London, 1979; Sky Masterson, *Guys and Dolls*, National Theatre, London, 1982-83.

MAJOR TOURS—Gad, *Joseph and the Amazing Technicolor Dreamcoat*, with the Young Vic Theatre Company, Edinbrugh Festival, 1972.

PRINCIPAL FILM APPEARANCES—*Jubilee*, Megalovision, 1978; Eric Liddell, *Chariots of Fire*, Warner Brothers, 1981; *Gandhi*, Columbia, 1982; *Ascendancy*, 1983; *Greystoke: The Legend of Tarzan, Lord of the Apes* Warner Brothers, 1984; *Car Trouble*.

PRINCIPAL TELEVISION APPEARANCES—*Something's Got to Give*, Scot TV, 1982; *Louisiana*, Cinemax Cable, 1985; also *Rock Follies, Churchill's People, The Paradise Run, Antony and Cleopatra, All's Well That Ends Well, Master of the Game, Oxbridge Blues, A Month in the Country*, and *The Devil's Lieutenant*.

SIDELIGHTS: RECREATIONS—Collecting jigsaws, reading, and painting.

ADDRESSES: AGENT—Jeremy Conway, Eight Cavendish Place, London W1M 9DJ, England.*

CLARK, Brian 1932-

PERSONAL: Born June 3, 1932, in Bournemouth, England; son of Leonard (a blacksmith) and Selina (Smith) Clark. EDUCATION: Redland College of Education, teaching certificate, 1954; University of Nottingham, B.A., 1964; trained for the stage at the Central School of Speech and Drama, London, 1954-55. RELIGION: Agnostic. MILITARY: British Army, Signal Corps, 1950-52.

VOCATION: Writer and publisher.

WRITINGS: PLAYS, PRODUCED—*Truth or Dare,* Hull Arts Center, U.K., 1972; *Whose Life Is It Anyway?,* Mermaid and Savoy Theatres, London, both 1978, then Folger Shakespeare Theatre, Washington, DC, 1978, and Trafalgar Theatre, New York City, 1979, revised and re-staged at the Royale Theatre, New York City, 1980; *Kipling,* Oxford Playhouse, London, then Royale Theatre, New York City, both 1984; *The Petition,* John Golden Theatre, New York City, 1986.

Contributed to *Lay-By,* 1971 and *England's Ireland,* 1972. Also wrote *Can You Hear Me at the Back?,* 1979; *Post Mortem; Campion's Interview.*

TELEVISION—Series: *Telford's Change,* BBC, 1979.

Teleplays: *Ten Torrey Canyons,* BBC, 1972; *Operation Magic Carpet,* ITV, 1973; *Achilles Heel,* ITV, 1973; *The Greeting,* ITV, 1973; *Parole,* Granada, 1975; *Post Mortem,* BBC, 1976; *The Saturday Party,* BBC, 1976; *Campion's Review,* BBC, 1977; *Happy Returns,* Granada, 1977; *There's No Place,* BBC, 1977; *The Country Party,* BBC, 1977; *Whose Life Is It Anyway?,* BBC, 1980. Also the author of about twenty additional television plays and two radio plays.

BOOKS—*Group Theatre,* Pitman, 1971, and Theatre Arts, 1972.

RELATED CAREER—Publisher, Amber Lane Press.

MEMBER: Writers Guild.

ADDRESSES: HOME—Amber Lane Farm, The Slack, Ashover S45 0EB, Derbyshire, England. AGENT—Judy Daish Associates, 83 Eastbourne Mews, London W2 6LQ, England.*

*   *   *

CLAYTON, Tony 1935-

PERSONAL: Born March 2, 1935; son of Richard Joseph and Catherine (McLoughlin) Clayton; married Ann Hamilton (an actress); children: Michael Anthony.

VOCATION: Manager, director, and writer.

CAREER: FIRST STAGE WORK—Assistant stage manager, Southport Repertory Company, U.K. PRINCIPAL STAGE WORK—Company manager, Royal Shakespeare Company, Aldwych Theatre, also in Los Angeles, CA; general manager, Belgrade Theatre, Coventry, U.K.; director, Wyvern Theatre, Swindon, U.K.; director, Palace Theatre, West Cliff-on-Sea, Essex, U.K.; director, Key Theatre, Peterborough, U.K.

Director of National British and international touring productions;

TONY CLAYTON

producer and director, British national tour, *Jesus Christ Superstar;* director, *Who's Been Sleeping in My Bed?*

WRITINGS: PLAYS, PRODUCED—*Policy for Murder,* British national tour; *Who's Been Sleeping in My Bed?,* British national tour; *Murder Assured,* British national tour, published by Samuel French, Ltd.; (with Alison Sargent) *It Sticks Out a Mile and a Bit!*

Has also written pantomimes and drama documentaries.

MEMBER: British Actors' Equity Association, Writers Guild of Great Britain.

SIDELIGHTS: Tony Clayton told *CTFT* that his son is a sound engineer and has worked on productions of *Cats, Song & Dance, Evita,* and *Starlight Express.*

ADDRESSES: HOME—Bennetts Mill Road, Buxhall near Stowmarket, Suffolk, England. OFFICE—Key Theatre, Peterborough, Cambridgeshire, England. AGENT—Eric Glass, Ltd., 28 Berkeley Square, London, WIX 6HD, England.

*   *   *

CLEESE, John 1939-

PERSONAL: Full name, John Marwood Cleese; born October 27, 1939, in Weston-super-Mare, Somerset, England; son of Reginald (in insurance sales) and Muriel (an acrobat; maiden name, Cross) Cleese; married Connie Booth (an actress and writer), February 20,

1968 (divorced, 1978); married Barbara Trentham (a director, actress, and artist), February 15, 1981; children: (first marriage) Cynthia; (second marriage) Camilla. EDUCATION: Attended Downing College, Cambridge, M.A., 1963. POLITICS: Social-Democrat Liberal.

VOCATION: Comedian, actor, and writer.

CAREER: PRINCIPAL STAGE APPEARANCES—*Footlights Revue*, London production, 1963, re-titled *Cambridge Circus*, for the New York City production, 1963; also *Half a Sixpence*, 1965.

PRINCIPAL FILM APPEARANCES—*Interlude*, Columbia, 1968; *The Rise and Rise of Michael Rimmer*, 1970; *The Magic Christian*, Commonwealth United, 1970; *The Statue*, Cinerama, 1971; *And Now for Something Completely Different*, Columbia, 1971; *Monty Python and the Holy Grail*, Cinema 5, 1975; *Monty Python's Life of Brian*, Warner Brothers, 1977; *The Secret Policeman's Ball*, 1979; *Time Bandits*, AVCO-Embassy, 1981; *The Great Muppet Caper*, Universal, 1981; *The Secret Policeman's Other Ball*, Amnesty International, 1982; *Monty Python Live at the Hollywood Bowl*, Columbia, 1982; *Monty Python's The Meaning of Life*, Universal, 1983; *Yellowbeard*, Orion, 1983; *Privates on Parade*, Orion Classics, 1984; *Silverado*, Columbia, 1985; *Clockwise*, 1986.

PRINCIPAL TELEVISION APPEARANCES—Series: *The Frost Report*, BBC, 1966-67, *At Last the 1948 Show*, BBC, 1966-67; *Monty Python's Flying Circus*, BBC, 1969-73, broadcast in the United States on PBS, 1974-82; *Fawlty Towers*, BBC, 1975-79, broadcast in the United States on PBS. Dramatic Specials: *The Taming of the Shrew*, BBC, 1980. Episodic: *Cheers*, NBC, 1987.

RELATED CAREER—Creator of commerical advertisements for radio and television. As president and owner of Video Arts Ltd., creator of business training films, including "Meetings, Bloody Meetings," "The Secretary and Her Boss," "The Balance Sheet Barrier," and "Time Management Delegation," 1972—.

WRITINGS: SCREENPLAYS—Contributor: *And Now for Something Completely Different*, Columbia, 1972; *Monty Python and the Holy Grail*, Cinema 5, 1975; *Monty Python's Life of Brian*, Warner Brothers, 1979; *Monty Python Live at the Hollywood Bowl*, Columbia, 1982; *Monty Python's The Meaning of Life*, Universal, 1983

TELEVISION—Contributor, *The Frost Report*, BBC, 1966-67; contributor, *At Last the 1948 Show*, BBC, 1966-67; (with Graham Chapman, Terry Gilliam, Eric Idle, Terry Jones, and Michael Palin) contributor, *Monty Python's Flying Circus*, BBC, 1969-73, PBS, 1974-82; (with Connie Booth) co-author, *Fawlty Towers*, BBC, 1975-79, also PBS. Movies: Contributor, *Pythons in Deutschland*, Batavia Atelier, 1972.

BOOKS—(With Jack Hobbs and Joe McGrath) *The Strange Case of the End of Civilisation as We Know It*, Star Books, 1970; (with Connie Booth) *Fawlty Towers*, Futura, Volume I, 1977, Volume II, 1979; (with Robin Skynner) *Families and How to Survive Them*, 1983.

Contributor: *Monty Python's Big Red Book*, Methuen, 1972, Warner Books, 1975; *The Brand New Monty Python Bok*, Metheun, 1973, also published as *The Brand New Monty Python Paperbok*, 1974; *Monty Python and the Holy Grail*, Methuen, 1977, also published as *Monty Python's Second Film: A First Draft*, 1977; *Monty Python's Life of Brian (of Nazareth)* (and) *Montypythonscrapbook*, Grosset, 1979; *The Complete Works of Shakespeare and Monty*

Python (contains "Monty Python's Big Red Book" and "The Brand New Monty Python Paperbok"), Methuen, 1981.

RECORDINGS: COMEDY ALBUMS—(With Tim Brooke-Taylor, David Frost, and others) Contributor, *The Frost Report on Britain*, Starline, 1966; (with Connie Booth) contributor, *Fawlty Towers*, BBC Records, 1979; (with Booth) contributor, *Fawlty Towers/ Second Sitting*, BBC Records, 1981; (with Booth) contributor, *Fawlty Towers/At Your Service*, BBC Records, 1982.

Contributor to Monty Python recordings: *Monty Python's Flying Circus*, BBC Records, 1969; *Another Monty Python Record*, Charisma, 1970; *Monty Python's Previous Record*, Charisma, 1972; *Monty Pyton's Matching Tie and Handkerchief*, Charisma, 1974, Arista, 1975; *Monty Python Live at Drury Lane*, Charisma, 1974; *The Album of the Soundtrack of the Trailer of the Film Monty Python and the Holy Grail*, Arista, 1975; *Monty Python Live at City Center*, Arista, 1976; *Monty Python's Instant Record Collection*, Charisma, 1977; *Monty Python's Life of Brian*, Warner Brothers, 1979; *Monty Python's Contractual Obligation Album*, 1980; *Monty Python's The Meaning of Life*, CBS Records, 1983.

AWARDS: Co-winner, Golden Palm Award, Cannes Film Festival, 1983, for *Monty Python's The Meaning of Life;* Queen's Award for Exports, for an American radio commercial series created by Video Arts Ltd., 1982. Honorary degrees: LL.D., St. Andrews University, 1971.

SIDELIGHTS: John Cleese achieved fame as a member of the Monty Python comedy group, creating and performing in outlandish and wacky satire. In one of his most remembered skits, he presided over the Ministry of Silly Walks interviewing prospective grantee's and demonstrating various disjointed ways of walking. Their collective sense of humor spared no topic or institution in the sometimes bawdy depiction of man vs. bureaucracy. Cleese has now turned his attention to his Video Arts Ltd. company. "I've enjoyed my twenty-two years in the world of jokes but now that Video Arts has given me financial independence, I intend to spend more time exploring other fields."

ADDRESSES: OFFICE—Eight Clarendon Road, London W11 3AA, England.*

*   *   *

CLIMENHAGA, Joel   1922-

PERSONAL: Born April 9, 1922, in Bulawayo, South Rhodesia; son of John Arthur (a preacher) and Emma Light (a missionary; maiden name, Smith) Climenhaga; married Zoe Lenore Motter (a writer and weaver), December 21, 1955; children: Neal, Anna, Greta, Miriam. EDUCATION: Chaffey College, A.A., 1949; University of California at Los Angeles, B.A., 1953, M.A., 1958.

VOCATION: Writer, director, teacher, and producer.

CAREER: PRINCIPAL STAGE WORK—Has appeared in fifty-seven stage productions, directed one hundred twenty-nine productions, and produced twenty-two plays in summer repertory and stock theatre.

PRINCIPAL RADIO WORK—Producer, *One Man's Journey*, KKSU, Manhattan, KS.

RELATED CAREER—Teacher of English and drama, Central Dauphin High School, Harrisburg, PA, 1956-57; assistant professor of English, director of creative writing, Wilmington College, OH, 1958-61; visiting associate professor of dramatic art, University of North Carolina, Chapel Hill, 1962-63; associate professor of speech, drama, and English, then chairman, department of speech and drama, Culver-Stockton College, Canton, MO, 1963-68; associate professor of theatre, Kansas State University, Manhattan, 1968—, and director of theatre, 1968-72. Also has served as publisher and editor of several literary magazines.

WRITINGS: BOOKS—*Heathen Pioneer,* 1956; *Marriage Wheel,* 1963; *Hawk and Chameleon,* 1972; *Report on the Progress of the Bearded One's Homework,* 1985; also plays written for stage, film, and radio.

MEMBER: American Film Institute, American Theatre Association, International Society of Dramatists; Poets and Writers, Inc., Theta Alpha Phi National Honorary Fraternity of Theatre Arts, University-College Theatre Association, Modern Language Association, Phi Delta Kappa National Honorary Society of Education.

SIDELIGHTS: Through material provided by Joel Climenhaga, *CTFT* learned he has written and published 1,116 poems, as well as numerous short stories, essays, and reviews of productions of plays. He has also contributed writings to eighty-six different magazines and journals.

ADDRESSES: OFFICE—Department of Speech, Kansas State University, Manhattan, KS 66506.

BIJOU CLINGER

CLINGER, Bijou   1955-

PERSONAL: Born Eleanore Clinger, September 16, 1955, in Sharon, PA; daughter of William Floyd (a U.S. senator) and Julia Forker (Whitla) Clinger; married Gregory J. Miller (a composer), June 18, 1983. EDUCATION: State University of New York at Purchase, B.F.A., 1979; trained for the stage at Herbert Berghof Studio and the Actors Space with Bill Hickey and Alan Langdon; also studied voice with Marge Rivingston.

VOCATION: Actress and singer.

CAREER: OFF-BROADWAY DEBUT—Title role, *Susan B.,* Town Hall Theatre. PRINCIPAL STAGE APPEARANCES—Eleanor Roosevelt, *First Lady,* Promenade Theatre, New York City, 1982, 1984; Emily Roebling, *The Brooklyn Bridge,* Quaigh Theatre, New York City, 1983; Stephanie, *Rubbings,* Quaigh Theatre, New York City, 1984; *Laughter in the Dark,* Hartley House Theatre, New York City, 1984; *When the Cookie Crumbles You Can Still Pick Up the Pieces,* Promenade Theatre, New York City, 1984; Callie, *Attack of the Three Sisters,* True Ensemble Theatre, New York City, 1985; Marie, *Louis Braille,* T.O.M.I. Theatre, New York City, 1986.

MAJOR TOURS—Title role, *Susan B.,* Florida cities, 1981-82; Eleanor Roosevelt, *First Lady,* New Orleans Worlds Fair, and Florida cities, 1983-84.

TELEVISION DEBUT—Sarah Good, *Three Sovereigns for Sarah,* PBS, 1985.

JOEL CLIMENHAGA

RELATED CAREER—Acting teacher, Theatreworks U.S.A., New York City, 1981-86.

MEMBER: Actors' Equity Association, Screen Actors Guild, American Federation of Television and Radio Artists; Actors Space, True Ensemble Theatre.

SIDELIGHTS: Bijou Clinger told *CTFT* that after a special command performance of *First Lady* at the White House in which she played the singing, dancing Eleanor Roosevelt, Franklin Delano Roosevelt, Jr. approached her and said, "You were great, Mom!"

ADDRESSES: HOME—New York, NY. AGENT—c/o Molly McCarthy, Barry Agency, 165 W. 46th Street, New York, NY 10036.

*   *   *

COLE, Dennis

PERSONAL: Born July 19, in Detroit, MI; son of Harold Wilson (a musician) and Dorothy Cleo (West) Cole; married Sally Ann Bergeron, November, 1960 (divorced, 1965); married Jaclyn Smith (an actress), 1977 (divorced); children: Joseph Dennis. EDUCATION: Attended University of Detroit; trained for the stage with Robert Graham Park

VOCATION: Actor.

CAREER: TELEVISION DEBUT—Series: Duke Spaulding, *Paradise Bay,* NBC, 1965. PRINCIPAL TELEVISION APPEARANCES—Series: Jim Briggs, *Felony Squad,* ABC, 1966-69; Davey Evans, *Brackens' World,* NBC, 1969-70; Johnny Read, *Bearcats,* CBS, 1971; also appeared in *Big Shamus, Little Shamus,* CBS, 1979 and *The Young and the Restless,* CBS, for two years.

Episodic: *Lancer,* CBS; *Medical Center,* CBS; *Barnaby Jones,* CBS; *Police Story,* CBS; *Police Woman,* NBC; *The Streets of San Francisco,* ABC; *Charlies' Angels,* ABC; *Love Boat,* ABC; *Fantasy Island,* ABC; *Trapper John,* CBS; *Love, American Style,* ABC; *Man Called Sloan,* NBC; *The A Team,* NBC; *Fall Guy,* ABC; *Vegas,* ABC; *Murder She Wrote,* CBS, also appeared in *Honeymoon Suite; Capra; Star Games; Celebrity Dare-Devil.*

Movies: *Cave-In,* NBC, 1983. Pilots: *Men Against Evil,* ABC; *Bracken's World,* NBC; *Powder Keg,* CBS; *Barbary Coast,* ABC.

FILM DEBUT—Mr. Crawley, *Pretty Funny,* New World, 1986.

STAGE DEBUT—Ronnie Ames, *All the Girls Came Out to Play,* Pheasant Run Dinner Theatre. BROADWAY DEBUT—Ronnie Ames, *All the Girls Came Out to Play,* Cort Theatre, 1972, for twenty performances. PRINCIPAL STAGE APPEARANCES—*Tender Trap; Accomodations; Lovers and Other Strangers; Boys in the Band; Run for Your Wife.*

MEMBER: American Federation of Television and Radio Artists, Screen Actors Guild, Actors' Equity Association; American Cancer Society (honorary chairman); March of Dimes (honorary chairman for three years); Arthritus Foundation (honorary chairman for two years).

ADDRESSES: AGENT—Harry Gold and Associates, 12725 Ventura Blvd., Suite E., Studio City, CA 91604.

KAY COLE

COLE, Kay   1948-

PERSONAL: Born Kathleen Adele Colominas, January 13, 1948, in Miami, FL; daughter of Guillermo Dario (a mechanic) and Beatrice (a registered nurse; maiden name, Stewart) Colominas. EDUCATION: Studied dance with Eugene Loring, Edna McCrae, and Paul Petroff and acting with Milton Katsales, Jeff Corey, Uta Hagen, and Herbert Berghof.

VOCATION: Actress, dancer, and choreographer.

CAREER: STAGE DEBUT—*Me Candido,* Players Ring Gallery, Los Angeles. BROADWAY DEBUT—Second sad girl, *Bye Bye Birdie,* Shubert Theatre, 1960-61. PRINCIPAL STAGE APPEARANCES—Broadway: Maggie, *A Chorus Line;* Strawberry Fields, *Sergeant Pepper;* soloist, *Words and Music;* Veronica, *Jesus Christ Superstar;* Amaryllis Zaneeta, *Music Man;* Jeanie and Sheila, *Hair;* Jane, *Stop the World I Want to Get Off;* lead urchin, *The Roar of the Greasepaint, the Smell of the Crowd.*

Off-Broadway: Babs Gamz, *Road to Hollywood;* Minerva, *Best Foot Forward;* Sister Mister, *Cradle Will Rock;* girl, *Rainbow;* Rosannah, *White Nights;* soloist, *Peter Link Concert;* Mick Jagger and Golden Oldie, *Lemmings;* Vera, *On the Swing Shift;* Woman, *One Man Band.*

In Los Angeles: Title role, *Alison,* Paul Aaron Company; Crissy, Sheila, and Jeanie, *Hair,* Aquarius Theatre; Boo, *Salvation,* Las Palmas Theatre; Annie, *Nevada,* Mark Taper Lab; Maggie, *A Chorus Line,* Shubert Theatre; Number 13, *Zen Boogie,* Solari Theatre; Cheryl, *I'm Getting My Act Together and Taking It on the*

Road; Miriam, *In the Valentine Lounge;* also appeared in various roles with the Los Angeles Repertory Company.

Regional: *Karen Akers Concert,* Kentucky Opera House; *Mass,* Kennedy Center, Washington, DC; has appeared at the Shubert Theatre in New Haven, CT.

FIRST LONDON STAGE WORK—Choreographer, *Snoopy,* Duchess Theatre, 1983-84. PRINCIPAL STAGE WORK—Choreographer: *Blockheads,* Mermaid Theatre, London, 1984; *One Man Band,* South Street Theatre, New York City; *Hang on to the Good Times,* Manhattan Theatre Club, New York City; *Gin Game,* Goodspeed Opera House, East Haddam, CT.

TELEVISION DEBUT—*Playhouse 90,* CBS, 1956. PRINCIPAL TELEVISION APPEARANCES—Episodic: *It Takes a Thief,* ABC; *Police Story,* CBS; *Carol Burnett Show,* CBS; *Szysnyk,* CBS; *The Judge.*

Guest: *Mike Douglas Show; Celebrity Review.*

FILM DEBUT—Tina, *Dino,* Allied Artists, 1957. PRINCIPAL FILM APPEARANCES—*Black Orchid,* Paramount, 1956; *Hello Down There,* Universal, 1965; *Coma,* Metro-Goldwyn-Mayer (MGM), 1977.

WRITINGS: PLAYS, PRODUCED—(Co-writer) *Blockheads,* Mermaid Theatre, London, 1984.

MEMBER: Actors' Equity Association, Screen Actors Guild, American Federation of Television and Radio Artists.

ADDRESSES: AGENT—Rickey Barr Agency, 9100 Sunset Blvd., Los Angeles, CA 90069; Fifi Oscard, 19 W. 44th Street, New York, NY 10036.

*　　　*　　　*

COLONNA, Jerry　1904-1986

PERSONAL: Full name, Gerald Colonna; born October 17, 1904, in Boston, MA; died of kidney failure in Woodland Hills, CA, November 21, 1986; married; children: one son.

VOCATION: Actor, comedian, singer, and musician.

CAREER: PRINCIPAL STAGE APPEARANCES—Entertained U.S. troops abroad with the *Bob Hope Show,* 1941-1966; cabaret musician (trombonist), Leo Reisman Band, Benny Goodman Band, Artie Shaw Band, Red Nichols Band, Dorsey Brothers Band, and the Ozzie Nelson Orchestra.

FILM DEBUT—*52nd Street,* 1937. PRINCIPAL FILM APPEARANCES—*Rosalie,* 1937; *Little Miss Broadway,* 1938; *Garden of the Moon,* 1938; *College Swing,* 1938; *The Road to Singapore,* 1940; *Sis Hopkins,* 1941; *Star Spangled Rhythm,* 1942; *True to the Army,* 1942; *Atlantic City,* 1944; *The Road to Rio,* 1947; *Coming Round the Mountain,* 1951; *Meet Me in Las Vegas,* 1956; *Andy Hardy Comes Home,* 1958; *The Road to Hong Kong,* 1962; also appeared in *Ice Capades.*

PRINCIPAL TELEVISION APPEARANCES—Bob Hope specials, in the 1960s and 1970s.

PRINCIPAL RADIO WORK—Staff trombonist with CBS Orchestra, New York City, 1931; guest on *The Fred Allen Show, Bing Crosby's Kraft Music Hall Show,* 1937, and the *Bob Hope Show,* 1938.

WRITINGS: BOOKS—*Who Threw That Coconut?; The Loves of Tullio,* 1970.

RECORDINGS: SINGLE—*Ebb Tide.*

AWARDS: Air Force Scroll of Appreciation for his service with Bob Hope.

SIDELIGHTS: Jerry Colonna's comedy trademarks were his bulging eyes, walrus mustache and his ability to hold a note for over seventy-two seconds. He travelled over four million miles with Bob Hope entertaining U.S. servicemen and performed in more than fifteen hundred shows. he became identified with his reading of the line "Whattsa matter, you crazy or something?"*

*　　　*　　　*

COLUMBU, Franco

PERSONAL: Born in Sardinia, Italy. EDUCATION: Ph.D., nutrition.

CAREER: PRINCIPAL FILM APPEARANCES—*Stay Hungry,* United Artists, 1976; *Pumping Iron,* Cinema 5, 1977; *Conan the Barbarian,* Universal, 1982; *The Terminator,* Orion, 1984; *Raw Deal,* Twentieth Century-Fox, 1986.

FRANCO COLUMBU

PRINCIPAL TELEVISION APPEARANCES—Episodic: *Streets of San Francisco*, ABC; *Sixty Minutes*, CBS. Movies: *Hustler of Muscle Beach*, ABC, 1980; *Getting Physical*, CBS, 1984; also *Shepherd to Superstar*.

Guest: *Real People*, NBC; *To Tell the Truth*, CBS; *Wide World of Sports*, ABC; *That's Incredible!*, ABC; also *The Merv Griffin Show*; *The Phil Donahue Show*; *Afternoon Exchange*; *AM Los Angeles*; *AM Washington*; *Daybreak*; *The Mike Douglas Show*; *The Guinness Show*; *Tommy Hawkins*; *Morning Exchange*; *Noonbreak*; *Noon Day*; *Sunday Open House*; *Sun Up*; *Viewpoint on Nutrition*; *Dorothy Fuldheim*; *Kelley and Company*; *Kids Are People Too*; *Mid Morning L.A.*; *World's Strongest Men*; *P.M. Magazine*.

RELATED CAREER—Doctor of Chiropractic; physical trainer and body builder for Sylvester Stallone, Gregory Harrison, Gary Busey, Kevin Dobson, Fred Dryer, Sandahl Bergman, others; nutritional supplements developer, "Body by Dr. Franco Columbu," Rich Life, Inc.

WRITINGS: NON-FICTION—*Winning Bodybuilding*, CBI, 1977; *Coming on Strong*, CBI, 1978; *Starbodies: The Women's Weight Training Book*, E. P. Dutton, 1978; *Weight Traning for the Young Athlete*, CBI, 1979; *Winning Powerlifting and Weightlifting*, CBI, 1979; *Bodybuilding for the Young Athlete*, Simon & Schuster, 1979; *Franco Columbu's Complete Book of Bodybuilding*, CBI, 1982; *The Businessman's Minutes-a-Day Guide to Shaping-Up*, CBI, 1983; *Redesign Your Body*, E. P. Dutton, 1985; *The Body-builder's Nutrition Book*, CBI, 1985. MAGAZINES—Staff writer for "Muscle and Fitness" and "Flex Magazine."

AWARDS: Bodybuilding Titles: Mr. Olympia, Mr. Universe, Mr. World, Mr. International, Mr. Europe, Mr. Italy. Also, power and weightlifting world records: bench press, squat, deadlift, snatch, jerk. Amateur boxing champion of Italy.

MEMBER: Screen Actors Guild, American Federation of Television and Radio Artists; American Chiropractic Association (ACA), ACA Council on Sports Injuries, California Chiropractic Association, National Health Federation, International Federation of Bodybuilders.

SIDELIGHTS: CTFT has learned through material provided by Dr. Columbu that he has, on occasion, been referred to as the "Sardinian Superman," and that his recreational activities include raising many varieties of roses. He also owns an aviary containing some eighty finches, doves, and canaries.

ADDRESSES: HOME—West Los Angeles, CA. PUBLICIST—Selfman and Others Public Relations, 2491 Purdue Avenue, Los Angeles, CA 90064.

*   *   *

CONTI, Bill   1943-

PERSONAL: Born 1943, in Providence, RI. EDUCATION: Studied piano at age seven; attended the Juilliard School of Music.

VOCATION: Composer and musician.

CAREER: PRINCIPAL FILM WORK—Music supervisior, *Blume in Love*, Warner Brothers, 1973. Composer: *Candidate for a Killing*,

1972; *Harry and Tonto*, Twentieth Century-Fox, 1974; *Rocky*, United Artists, 1977; *Handle with Care*, Metro-Goldwyn-Mayer, 1978; *F.I.S.T.*, United Artists 1978; *Slow Dancing in the Big City*, United Artists, 1978; *An Unmarried Woman*, Twentieth Century-Fox, 1978; *Paradise Alley*, Universal, 1978; *The Big Fix*, Universal, 1979; *Uncle Joe Shannon*, United Artists, 1979; *Hurricane*, Paramount, 1979; *Rocky II*, United Artists, 1979; *Golden Girl*, AVCO-Embassy, 1979; *A Man, a Woman, and a Bank*, AVCO-Embassy, 1979; *Big Trouble*, Universal, 1979; *Gloria*, Columbia, 1980; *Private Benjamin*, Warner Brothers, 1980; *For Your Eyes Only*, United Artists, 1981; *Carbon Copy*, 1981; *Split Image*, Orion, 1982; *Bad Boys*, Universal, 1983; *The Right Stuff*, Warner Brothers, 1983; *Unfaithfully Yours*, Twentieth Century-Fox, 1984; *The Bear*, Embassy, 1984; *Mass Appeal*, Universal, 1984; *Gotcha!*, Universal, 1985; *Beer*, Orion, 1985; *Nomads*, Atlantic Releasing, 1986; *Big Trouble*, Columbia, 1986; *F/X*, Orion, 1986.

PRINCIPAL TELEVISION WORK—Movies: Composer, *Kill Me If You Can*, 1977; *Stark*, CBS, 1985.

PRINCIPAL CONCERT APPEARANCES—Toured Italy with a jazz trio.

AWARDS: Best Original Score, Academy Award nomination, 1984, for *Mass Appeal*.*

*   *   *

COOK, Peter   1937-

PERSONAL: Full name, Peter Edward Cook; born November 17, 1937, in Torquay, Devonshire, England; son of Alexander E. and Margaret Cook; married Wendy Snowden (an artist), October 28, 1964 (divorced); married Judy Huxtable, February 14, 1974; children: (first marriage) two daughters. EDUCATION: Attended Radley and Pembroke Colleges, Cambridge University.

VOCATION: Actor, writer, comedian, and producer.

CAREER: LONDON DEBUT—*Beyond the Fringe*, Fortune Theatre, May 10, 1961. BROADWAY DEBUT—*Beyond the Fringe*, John Golden Theatre, October, 1962. PRINCIPAL STAGE APPEARANCES—*Beyond the Fringe*, Edinburgh Festival, Scotland, Lyceum Theatre, London, 1959, then Fortune Theatre, London, 1961, and John Golden Theatre, New York City, 1962; *Beyond the Fringe 1964*, John Golden Theatre, New York City, 1964; *Artists Against Apartheid*, Prince of Wales Theatre, London, 1965; *Behind the Fridge*, Cambridge Theatre, London, 1972, retitled *Good Evening*, Plymouth Theatre, New York City, 1973.

MAJOR TOURS—*Behind the Fridge*, Australian cities, 1972; *Good Evening*, U.S. cities, 1973-75.

PRINCIPAL STAGE WORK—Producer: (With John Krimsky) *The Establishment*, Strollers Theatre Club, New York City, 1963; (with Krimsky) *The Muffled Report*, Strollers Theatre Club, 1964; *Square in the Eye*, Theatre de Lys, New York City, 1965; *The Mad Show*, New Theatre, New York City, 1966; *Monopoly*, Stage 73, New York City, 1966; *Serjeant Musgrave's Dance*, Theatre de Lys, New York City, 1966; (with Rita Fredericks and Paul Stoudt) *The Kitchen*, 81st Street Theatre, New York City, 1966; (with Fredericks) *A Hand Is on the Gate*, Longacre Theatre, New York City, 1966.

PRINCIPAL FILM APPEARANCES—*The Wrong Box,* Columbia, 1966; *Bedazzled,* Twentieth Century-Fox, 1966; *A Dandy in Aspic,* Columbia, 1968; *Monte Carlo or Bust,* 1969; *The Bed Sitting Room,* United Artists, 1969; *The Rise and Rise of Michael Rimmer,* 1971; *The Adventures of Barry McKenzie,* 1972; *Pleasure at Her Majesty's,* Amnesty International, 1976; *The Hound of the Baskervilles,* 1977; *Derek and Clive Get the Horn,* 1978; *Beauborg,* 1980; voice of secret policeman, *The Secret Policeman's Other Ball,* Amnesty International, 1981; *Yellowbeard,* Orion, 1983; Sir Mortimer Chris, *Whoops Apocalypse,* 1983; *Supergirl,* Tri-Star, 1984.

PRINCIPAL FILM WORK—Executive producer, *Haunted,* 1983.

PRINCIPAL TELEVISION APPEARANCES—Episodic: *The New London Palladium Show,* ATV, 1965; *Laughter Makers,* 1966. Specials: *Beyond the Fringe,* BBC, 1964; *Alice in Wonderland,* BBC, 1967; *Where Do I Sit?*

Series: *Not Only . . .But Also,* BBC, 1964-66; *Revolver,* 1978.

RELATED CAREER—Owner, The Establishment Theatre Co. (a satirical nightclub), 1962; director, *Private Eye* magazine.

WRITINGS: PLAYS, PRODUCED—*Pieces of Eight,* Apollo Theatre, London, 1959; *One Over the Eight,* Duke of York's Theatre, London, 1961; (with Alan Bennett, Jonathan Miller, and Dudley Moore) *Beyond the Fringe,* Edinburgh Festival, Scotland, Lyceum Theatre, London, 1959, then Fortune Theatre, London, 1961, and John Golden Theatre, New York City, 1962; *The Establishment,* Strollers Theatre Club, New York City, 1963; (with Bennett, Moore, and Paxton Whitehead) *Beyond the Fringe 1964,* John Golden Theatre, New York City, 1964; (with John Bird) *The Establishment: 1964,* Lindy Opera House, Los Angeles, 1964; (with Dudley Moore) *Behind the Fridge,* Cambridge Theatre, London, 1972, and Australian cities, re-titled *Good Evening,* Plymouth Theatre, New York City, 1973, and U.S. cities.

SCREENPLAYS—*The Secret Policeman's Other Ball,* Amnesty International, 1981.

TELEPLAYS—*Not Only. . .But Also,* BBC, 1964-66.

BOOKS—(Both with Dudley Moore) *Dud and Pete* and *The Dagenham Dialogues,* 1971. Also contributes to various humorous and satirical periodicals.

AWARDS: Best Musical or Revue, London *Evening Standard* Award, 1962, Antoinette Perry Award, 1963, and a Special Citation by the New York Drama Critics Circle, 1963, all for *Beyond the Fringe;* (with Dudley Moore) Comedian of the Year, Guild of Television Producers and Directors, 1973; (with Moore) special Antoinette Perry Award for contributions to the theatre of comedy, 1974.

MEMBER: Actors' Equity Association, American Federation of Television and Radio Artists, American Guild of Variety Artists, Screen Actors Guild; Footlights Club at Cambridge University (former president).

SIDELIGHTS: RECREATIONS—Gambling, gossip, and golf.

ADDRESSES: AGENT—Wright and Webb, Ten Soho Square, London W1, England.*

DENNIS COONEY

COONEY, Dennis   1938-

PERSONAL: Born September 19, 1938, in Yonkers, NY; son of Dennis James (a New York City detective) and Katherine (Horgan) Cooney; married Barbara Deitchman (an agent), August 27, 1967 (divorced, 1970). EDUCATION: Fordham University, B.S.S., 1960; studied acting with Wynn Handman, Sanford Meisner, and Phillip Burton in New York City. POLITICS: Democrat.

VOCATION: Actor, producer, and writer.

CAREER: STAGE DEBUT—Tom Lee, *Tea & Sympathy,* Legion Star Playhouse, Ephrata, PA, 1957. BROADWAY DEBUT—Evans, *Ross,* Eugene O'Neill Theatre, 1961. PRINCIPAL STAGE APPEARANCES—Broadway productions: Dr. Watson, *Sherlock Holmes,* Young Senator, *The Last of Mrs. Lincoln,* Geoffrey, *The Lion in Winter,* Buzzy Pringle, *Love and Kisses,* and standby, *A Loss of Roses;* Paris, *Tiger at Gates* and Christian, *Cyrano de Bergerac,* both at Lincoln Center, New York City; Lysander, *A Midsummer Night's Dream,* New York Shakespeare Festival; the boy, *In the Summer House,* Tom Jefferson, *Young Jefferson,* and Jamesie, *Every Other Evil,* all Off-Broadway productions.

Ben *Star Spangled Girl,* Sullivan Little Theatre, Sullivan, IL; D.H. Lawrence, *I Rise in Flame Cried the Phoenix,* Hartman Theatre Company, Stamford, CT; at the Shaw Festival, Westport, CT: Johnny Tarleton, *Misalliance,* Freddy, *Pygmalion,* Steven Undershaft, *Major Barbara,* Tom, *Tea & Sympathy,* Bentley, *Misalliance,* Alan, *Picnic,* and Gustav, *Thieves' Carnival.*

MAJOR TOURS—Michael, *The Boys in the Band,* Los Angeles, San Francisco, Baltimore, Eastern summer circuit, 1969-70.

PRINCIPAL CABARET APPEARANCES—Little Theatre, Sullivan, IL; Knott's Berry Farm; Catskill circuit.

PRINCIPAL STAGE WORK—Producer, Kennebunkport Playhouse, ME.

FILM DEBUT—Elliot Adams, *Fitzwilly,* United Artists, 1967 PRINCIPAL FILM APPEARANCES—*Sole Survivor,* CBS Cinema Center.

TELEVISION DEBUT—Alan, *Love of Life,* CBS, 1959. PRINCIPAL TELEVISION APPEARANCES—Series: Alan Sterling, *Love of Life,* CBS, 1965-67; Kevin Kincaid, *The Secret Storm,* NBC, 1970-71; Jay Stallings, *As the World Turns,* CBS, 1974-80. Episodic: "Magnificent Yankee," *Hallmark Hall of Fame,* NBC; Northrop, *The Lunts; U.S. Steel Hour; CBS Workshop; Ironside,* NBC; *Hawaii Five-O,* CBS; *The Virginian,* NBC; *The Flying Nun,* ABC.

RELATED CAREER—Chairman of the board, Bandwagon Inc., a not for profit producing organization dedicated to producing "vintage" musicals of the American theatre, 1979-83.

WRITINGS: SCREENPLAYS, UNPRODUCED—"Little Boy Blue."

AWARDS: Theatre World Award, 1961, for *Every Other Evil.*

MEMBER: Actors' Equity Association, Screen Actors Guild, American Federation of Television and Radio Artists.

SIDELIGHTS: Dennis Cooney tells us, "I wanted to act since I first went on stage playing Santa Claus in grade school. My favorite roles are Geoffrey in *The Lion in Winter* and Michael, *The Boys in the Band.* I love to travel and I speak some French and have studied Italian."

ADDRESSES: HOME—484 W. 43rd Street, New York, NY 10036. AGENT—Bret Adams, 448 W. 44th Street, New York, NY 10036.

*   *   *

JIM CORDES

writer, *New Jersey Herald,* 1986—; magazine contributor, *Quadrifoglio* and *Singles Unlimited.*

WRITINGS: SCREENPLAYS—*Immigrants in Chains,* Encyclopaedia Brittanica Films, 1972; *Sexual Identities,* Harper and Row, 1975; *Toward Justice Supreme,* National Park Service Bi-Centennial Films, 1976. UNPUBLISHED NOVELS—"Phroots" and "The Lion's Jaw."

MEMBER: Actors' Equity Association, Screen Actors Guild, American Federation of Television and Radio Artists, American Guild of Variety Artists; Players Club.

SIDELIGHTS: RECREATIONS—Skiing and sailing.

ADDRESSES: AGENT—c/o Doris Mantz, International Creative Management, 40 W. 57th Street, New York, NY 10019.

*   *   *

CORDES, Jim   1932-

PERSONAL: Full name, James J. Cordes; born December 25, 1932, in Brooklyn, NY; son of Charles J. (a municipal supervisor) and Anna (Ford) Cordes; married Carole Munderloh, February 20, 1960 (divorced, 1976); children: Jessica, Justin. EDUCATION: Attended High School of the Performing Arts, New York City.

VOCATION: Actor and writer.

CAREER: STAGE DEBUT—Charlie, *Detective Story,* Erie Playhouse, Erie, PA, 1952. OFF-BROADWAY DEBUT—Boswell, *Dr. Johnson,* Jan Hus Theatre, 1954. PRINCIPAL STAGE APPEARANCES—Standby, *Come Blow Your Horn,* Brooks Atkinson Theatre, New York City, 1961.

MAJOR TOURS—Jerry, *Two for the Seesaw,* national, 1959-60.

FILM DEBUT—Captain Watts, *F/X,* Orion, 1986.

RELATED CAREER—Columnist: "Impressions," *Bergen Record,* 1972-73; "Easier Said," Riverdale newspapers, 1977-79; feature

CORZATTE, Clayton

PERSONAL: Last name rhymes with "for what"; born in Fairhope, AL; son of William C. and Grace (Smith) Corzatte; married Susan Heinrich; children: Christopher, Felicity Katharine. EDUCATION: Attended University of Alabama. MILITARY: U.S. Navy.

VOCATION: Actor and director.

CAREER: STAGE DEBUT—Lachlan MacLachlan, *The Hasty Heart*, Barter Theatre, Abingdon, VA. PRINCIPAL STAGE APPEARANCES— Ensign Pulver, *Mr. Roberts*, Eben, *Desire Under the Elms*, Richard, *The Lady's Not for Burning*, Covey, *The Plough and the Stars*, Sakini, *Teahouse of the August Moon*, and Harry the Hoofer, *The Time of Your Life*, all at the Cleveland Playhouse, OH; Romeo, *Romeo and Juliet* and Bing, *Brother Rat*, both at Arena Stage, Washington, DC; Oberon, *A Midsummer Night's Dream* and Feste, *Twelfth Night*, both at Antioch Shakespeare Festival, Yellow Springs, OH; Ariel, *The Tempest*, Sebastian, *Twelfth Night*, and Puck, *A Midsummer Night's Dream*, all at the American Shakespeare Festival, Stratford, CT; Feste, *Twelfth Night*, Mercutio, *Romeo and Juliet*, and Clarence, *Richard III*, all at the San Diego Shakespeare Festival, CA.

With the Association of Producing Artists (APA)-Phoenix Repertory Theatre, New York City: Charles Surface, *A School for Scandal*, Folksbiene Theatre, then Lyceum Theatre; Aubrey Piper, *The Show Off*, Tony Kirby, *You Can't Take It with You*, Gregers Werle, *The Wild Duck*, Oswald, *Ghosts*, Constantine, *The Seagull*, Narrator, *War and Peace*. Also performed as the Duke, *Measure for Measure*, Goodman Theatre, Chicago, IL; Vagabond, *The Tavern*, Milwaukee Repertory Theatre, WI; Cleante, *The Miser* and Kulygin, *The Three Sisters*, both at the Tyrone Guthrie Theatre, Minneapolis, MN; Brian, *A Day in the Death of Joe Egg*, Mosca, *Volpone*, Walter, *The Price*, Tom Olley, *Make and Break*, and Polonius, *Hamlet*, all at the Seattle Repertory Theatre, WA; Sidney Bruhl, *Deathtrap*, and title role, *Billy Bishop Goes to War*, both with the Alaska Repertory Theatre; Hogan, *A Moon for the Misbegotten*, Pastor Manders, *Ghosts*, Professor, *Bus Stop*, and Yens, *Vikings*, all at the Intiman Theatre, Seattle, WA; Henry Carr,

Travesties, title role, *Quartermaine's Terms*, professor, *Angels Fall*, and Her Father, *The Fantasticks*, all at A Contemporary Theatre, Seattle.

MAJOR TOURS—Puck, *A Midsummer Night's Dream*, national tour with the American Shakespeare Festival; Aubrey Piper, *The Show Off*, national tour with the APA-Phoenix Repertory Company.

PRINCIPAL STAGE WORK—Director: *Getting Married, Entertaining Mr. Sloan, Summertree, Misalliance*, and *The Tavern*, all at the Seattle Repertory Theatre; *Brighton Beach Memoirs, On Golden Pond*, and *The Fourposter*, all with the Alaska Repertory Theatre; *Whose Life Is It Anyway?, Butterflies Are Free, The Prime of Miss Jean Brodie, Fridays*, and *Holy Ghosts*, all at A Contemporary Theatre, Seattle; *The Importance of Being Earnest*, Intiman Theatre, Seattle; *The Importance of Being Earnest, Six Characters in Search of an Author, The Three Sisters*, and *Bus Stop*, all at the University of Washington Professional Actor Training Program.

PRINCIPAL FILM APPEARANCES—*The Prodigal*, Metro-Goldwyn-Mayer (MGM), 1955; *Cinderella Liberty*, Twentieth Century-Fox, 1970.

PRINCIPAL TELEVISION APPEARANCES—Movies: *Jacqueline Bouvier Kennedy*, 1981.

RELATED CAREER: Head of acting division, drama department, Cornish Institute, Seattle.

AWARDS: Omar Ranney Award, Cleveland, 1953; Obie Award, 1962, for Constantine, *The Seagull;* Antoinette Perry Award nomination, 1966, for Charles Surface, *A School for Scandal.*

MEMBER: Actors' Equity Association, Screen Actors Guild, American Federation of Television and Radio Artists, Society of Stage Directors and Choreographers.

ADDRESSES: HOME—2520 11th Avenue West, Seattle, WA, 98119.

*   *   *

COTTEN, Joseph   1905-

PERSONAL: Born May 15, 1905, in Petersburg, VA; son of Joseph Cheshire and Sally (Wilson) Cotten; married Lenore Kipp (died); married Patricia Medina, 1960. EDUCATION: Trained for the stage at the Hickman School of Expression, Washington, DC.

VOCATION: Actor.

CAREER: BROADWAY DEBUT—Appeared in and was assistant stage manager for *Dancing Partner*, Belasco Theatre, 1930. PRINCIPAL STAGE APPEARANCES—Appeared in and was assistant stage manager for *Tonight or Never*, Belasco Theatre, New York City, 1930; appeared in summer stock productions in Boston, MA, 1931-32, and in Bar Harbor, ME, 1932; Larry, *Absent Father*, Vanderbilt Theatre, New York City, 1932; Dick Ashley, *Jezebel*, Ethel Barrymore Theatre, New York City, 1933; *Accent on Youth*, Plymouth Theatre, New York City, 1935; Ralph Mendes, *Loose Moments*, Vanderbilt Theatre, New York City, 1935; Policeman, *The Postman Always Rings Twice*, Lyceum Theatre, New York City, 1936. With the Federal Theatre Project: *Horse Eats Hat*,

CLAYTON CORZATTE

Maxine Elliott Theatre, New York City, 1936; Scholar, *Dr. Faustus*, Maxine Elliott Theatre, New York City, 1937; Publius, *Julius Caesar*, Mercury Theatre, New York City, 1937; Rowland Lacy, *The Shoemaker's Holiday*, Mercury Theatre, New York City, 1938; Barrere, *Danton's Death*, Maxine Elliott Theatre, New York City, 1938; C.K. Dexter Haven, *The Philadelphia Story*, Shubert Theatre, New York City, 1939

Appeared in summer stock with David O. Selznick Productions, La Jolla, CA, 1947; Linus Larrabee, Jr., *Sabrina Fair*, National Theatre, New York City, 1953; Victor Fabian, *Once More, with Feeling*, National Theatre, New York City, 1958; Julian Armstone, *Calculated Risk*, Ambassador Theatre, New York City, 1962; *The Reluctant Debutante*, Country Dinner Playhouse, Dallas, TX, 1974.

MAJOR TOURS—C.K. Dexter Haven, *The Philadelphia Story*, U.S. cities, 1940; Dr. Flemming, *Prescription: Murder*, U.S. cities, 1962; *Seven Ways of Love*, U.S. cities, 1964.

FILM DEBUT—*Citizen Kane*, RKO, 1940. PRINCIPAL FILM APPEARANCES—*Lydia*, 1941; *The Magnificent Ambersons*, RKO, 1942; *Journey into Fear*, RKO, 1942; *Shadow of a Doubt*, 1943; *Since You Went Away*, 1944; *The Stranger*, RKO, 1946; *Duel in the Sun*, 1946; Dr. Lewis Moline, *Beyond the Forest*, 1949; Jonathan Adams, *Special Delivery*, Columbia, 1955; *Bottom of the Bottle*, Twentieth Century-Fox, 1956; Sam Wagner, *A Killer Is Loose*, United Artists, 1956; Daniel, *Halliday Brand*, United Artists, 1957; *From the Earth to the Moon*, Warner Brothers, 1958; *The Angel Wore Red*, Metro-Goldwyn-Mayer (MGM), 1960; *A Touch of Evil*, Universal, 1960; *The Last Sunset*, Universal, 1961; *The Great Souix Massacre*, Columbia, 1965; *The Oscar*, Embassy, 1966; *The Tramplers*, Embassy, 1966; *The Money Trap*, MGM, 1966; *Petulia*, Warner Brothers-Seven Arts, 1968.

Henry Stimson, *Tora! Tora! Tora!*, Twentieth Century-Fox, 1970; *The Grasshopper*, National General, 1970; Dr. Vesalius, *The Abominable Dr. Phibes*, American International, 1971; Becker, *Baron Blood*, American International, 1972; Simonson, *Soylent Green*, MGM, 1973; Harry, *A Delicate Balance*, American Film Theatre, 1973; Arthur Renfrew, *Twilight's Last Gleaming*, Allied Artists, 1977; Nicholas St. Downs, III, *Airport '77*, Universal, 1977; Elwood Crandall, *Caravans*, 1978; Richard Gable, *Guyana: Cult of the Damned*, 1979; Reverend Doctor, *Heaven's Gate*, United Artists, 1980; Walter Prichard, *The Hearse*, 1980; Ivar Langrock, *The House Where Death Lives*, 1980; Priest, *The Survivor*, 1981. Also appeared in *Half Angel*, *Peking Express*, *Man with a Cloak*, *The Untamed Frontier*, *The Steel Trap*, *Niagara*, *Blueprint for Murder*, *Two Flags West*, *September Affair*, *Walk Softly*, *Hers to Hold*, *They Also Killed*, *The White Comanche*, and *The Hellbenders*.

TELEVISION DEBUT—*The High Green Wall*, 1954. PRINCIPAL TELEVISION APPEARANCES—Series: Host, *The Twentieth Century-Fox Hour*, CBS, 1955; Dan McCorn, *Broadway*, 1955; host, *The Joseph Cotten Show*, NBC, 1956; host, *Hollywood and the Stars*, NBC, 1963.

Episodic: *Light's Diamond Jubilee*, 1954; William Meredith, "On Trial," *Star Stage*, NBC, 1955; *Fireside Theatre*, NBC, 1955; *Alfred Hitchcock Presents*, CBS, 1955; *Texaco Command Performance*, 1957; *The Westinghouse Desilu Playhouse*, CBS, 1958; *The DuPont Show with June Allyson*, CBS, 1959; *Notorious*, 1961; "The Massacre at Wounded Knee," *The Great Adventure*, CBS,

1963. Pilots: General Antigonus, *Alexander the Great*, 1968; Dr. Zeigler, *City Beneath the Sea*, 1971; Ed Booker, *Casino*, 1980.

Movies: Dr. Ben Stern, *Split Second to an Epitaph*, 1968; Martin Bannister, *The Lonely Profession*, 1969; Gerlad Spalding, *Cutter's Trail*, 1970; Dr. Robert Carson, *Do You Take This Stranger?*, 1971; Admiral, *Assault on the Wayne*, 1971; George Tresvant, *The Screaming Woman*, 1972; Judge Wetherby, *The Devil's Daughter*, 1973; Dr. John Francis Condon, *The Lindbergh Kidnapping Case*, 1976; Horton Paine, *Aspen*, 1977; Mr. Grant, *Return to Fantasy Island*, 1978.

PRINCIPAL TELEVISION WORK—Director, *Peter Hunter, Private Eye*, 1948.

WRITINGS: BOOKS—*Vanity Will Get You Somewhere* (autobiography), Mercury House, 1987.

MEMBER: Players Club, New York Racquet Club, Bucks Club, London.

SIDELIGHTS: CTFT learned Joseph Cotten began his career in the theatre as an understudy and assistant stage manager for David Belasco in his last two productions.

ADDRESSES: OFFICE—6363 Wilshire Blvd., Los Angeles, CA 90048.*

* * *

COUSIN BUBBA
   See Emmons, Wayne

* * *

COVINGTON, Julie

PERSONAL: EDUCATION: Attended Cambridge University.

VOCATION: Actress and singer.

CAREER: STAGE DEBUT—*Godspell*, Round House, U.K., 1971. PRINCIPAL STAGE APPEARANCES—*Godspell*, Wyndham's Theatre, London, 1971; Marea Garga, *In the Jungle of Cities*, The Place, London, 1973; Charmian, *Antony and Cleopatra*, Bankside Globe Theatre, London, 1973; Gale, *The Pleasure Principle*, Theatre Upstairs, London, 1973; Iris, *The Tempest*, Old Vic Theatre, London, 1974; Janice, *Weapons of Happiness*, Lyttelton Theatre, London, 1976; Varya, *The Cherry Orchard*, Riverside Studios, London, 1978; Alice Park, *Plenty*, Lyttleton Theatre, London, 1978; Anna I, *The Seven Deadly Sins of Ordinary People*, Coliseum Theatre, London, 1978; Edward/Betty, *Cloud 9*, Royal Court Theatre, London, 1979; Shelly, *Buried Child*, Hampstead Theatre, London, 1980; Viv, *Tom & Viv*, New York Shakespeare Festival, Public Newman Theatre, 1985.

MAJOR TOURS—*A Midsummer Night's Dream*, U.K. and U.S. cities, 1968.

FILM DEBUT—*The Adventures of Barry McKenzie,* 1972.

PRINCIPAL TELEVISION APPEARANCES—*Rock Follies; Censored Scenes from King Kong; The Voysey Inheritance.*

RECORDINGS: ALBUMS—*Evita,* Original Cast Album.

ADDRESSES: AGENT—Kate Feast Management, 43A Princess Road, London NW1, England.*

*   *   *

COX, Ronny   1938-

PERSONAL: Born July 23, 1938, in Cloudcroft, NM; son of Bob P. (a carpenter) and Lounette (Rucker) Cox; married Mary Griffith (a writer), September 10, 1960; children: Brian, John. EDUCATION: Eastern New Mexico University, B.A., 1963.

VOCATION: Actor, producer, and writer.

CAREER: STAGE DEBUT—Bruz, *King KoKo,* Portales, NM, 1951. BROADWAY DEBUT—Jesse James, *Indians,* Brooks Atkinson Theatre, 1969, for one-hundred-thirty performances. PRINCIPAL STAGE APPEARANCES—Miles, *The Happiness Cage,* New York Shakespeare Festival, Public Theatre, then Delacorte Theatre, New York City, 1970.

MAJOR TOURS—Johnny Buccannon, *Summer and Smoke,* summer tour ending in the Huntington Hartford Theatre, Los Angeles.

FILM DEBUT—Drew Ballinger, *Deliverance,* Warner Brothers, 1972. PRINCIPAL FILM APPEARANCES—*The Happiness Cage,* Cinerama, 1972; *Hugo the Hippo,* Twentieth Century-Fox, 1976; Ozark, *Bound for Glory,* United Artists, 1977; *Gray Lady Down,* Universal, 1978; *Harper Valley PTA,* 1978; Pierce Brooks, *The Onion Field,* AVCO-Embassy, 1979; Colonel Kerby, *Taps,* Twentieth Century-Fox, 1981; Colonel Powers, *Some Kind of Hero,* Paramount, 1982; Pete Caufield, *Courage,* 1983; *Beverly Hills Cop,* Paramount, 1984; *Vision Quest,* Warner Brothers, 1985.

TELEVISION DEBUT—Jerry Rubin, *Chicago 7 Trial,* BBC, 1970. PRINCIPAL TELEVISION APPEARANCES—Series: George Apple, *Apple's Way,* CBS, 1974-75. Movies: *A Case of Rape,* 1974; *Transplant,* 1979; *When Hell Was in Session,* 1979; *Fugitive Family,* 1980; *Alcatraz: The Whole Shocking Story,* 1980; *Fallen Angel,* 1981; *The Jesse Owens Story,* 1984; also, Editor Webb, *Our Town, Hatter Fox.*

WRITINGS: SCREENPLAYS—(With Mary Cox) *Courage,* 1983.

MEMBER: Actors' Equity Association, American Federation of Television and Radio Artists, Screen Actors Guild, Academy of Motion Picture Arts and Sciences, Academy of Television Arts and Sciences, Writers Guild, American Society of Composers Authors and Publishers (ASCAP).

ADDRESSES: AGENT—c/o Merritt Blake, Blake-Glenn Agency, 409 N. Camden Drive, Beverly Hills, CA 90210.*

CRAWFORD, Cheryl   1902-1986

PERSONAL: Born September 24, 1902, in Akron, OH; died after a long hospitalization as a result of a fall in New York City, October 7, 1986; daughter of Robert K. (a realtor) and Luella Elizabeth (Parker) Crawford. EDUCATION: Attended Buchtel College; Smith College, A.B., 1925.

VOCATION: Director, producer, and actress.

CAREER: STAGE DEBUT—Lady Macbeth, *Macbeth,* Central High School, 1917. PRINCIPAL STAGE APPEARANCES—Madame Barrio (also assistant stage manager), *Juarez and Maximilian,* Guild Theatre, New York City, 1926; *Brothers Karamazov,* Guild Theatre, 1927.

PRINCIPAL STAGE WORK—Casting director for the Theatre Guild, 1928-30; founding member and directed for the Group Theatre, New York City: *The House of Connelly,* Martin Beck Theatre, 1931; *Big Night,* Maxine Elliott's Theatre, 1933; *Till the Day I Die,* Longacre Theatre, 1935; *Weep for the Virgins,* 46th Street Theatre, 1935. Producer, with the Group Theatre, New York City, 1931-37: *Men in White, Waiting for Lefty, Awake and Sing, Golden Boy,* and *Bury the Dead.*

Producer: (With John Stillman) *All the Living,* Fulton Theatre, New York City, 1938; (with Day Tuttle and Richard Skinner) *Family Portrait,* Morosco Theatre, New York City, 1939; *Another Sun,* National Theatre, New York City, 1940; with John Wildberg, founded the Maplewood (NJ) Theatre, where they presented revival, *Porgy and Bess,* then transferred to the Majestic Theatre, New York City, 1942; *The Flowers of Virtue,* Royale Theatre, New York City, 1942; (with Richard Krakeur) *A Kiss for Cinderella,* Music Box Theatre, New York City, 1942; (with Wildberg) *Porgy and Bess,* 44th Street Theatre, New York City, 1943; (with Wildberg) *One Touch of Venus,* Imperial Theatre, New York City, 1943; (with Wildberg) *Porgy and Bess,* City Center, New York City, 1944; *The Perfect Marriage,* Ethel Barrymore Theatre, New York City, 1944; *The Tempest,* Alvin Theatre, then New York City Center, 1945.

With Eva Le Gallienne and Margaret Webster, founded the American Repertory Theatre and was managing director of its following productions, all at the International Theatre, New York City: *Henry VIII,* 1946, *What Every Woman Knows,* 1946, *John Gabriel Borkman,* 1946, *Androcles and the Lion,* 1946, *A Pound on Demand,* 1946, *Alice in Wonderland,* 1947, *Through the Looking Glass,* 1947.

Producer: *Brigadoon,* Ziegfeld Theatre, New York City, 1948; *Skipper Next to God* and (with T. Edward Hambleton) *A Temporary Island,* both Maxine Elliott's Theatre, New York City, 1948; *Love Life,* 46th Street Theatre, New York City, 1948; (with Clinton Wilder) *Regina,* 46th Street Theatre, 1949; *The Closing Door,* Empire Theatre, New York City, 1949; *Brigadoon,* City Center, New York City, 1950.

As joint general director (with Robert Breen), presented the American National Theatre Academy (ANTA) play series at the ANTA Playhouse New York City which included *The Tower Beyond Tragedy,* 1950 and *Peer Gynt,* 1951.

Producer: *The Rose Tattoo,* Martin Beck Theatre, New York City, 1951; (with E.Y. Harburg and Fred Saidy) *Flahooley,* Broadhurst Theatre, New York City, 1951; *Paint Your Wagon,* Shubert Theatre, New York City, 1951; (with Ethel Reiner) *Camino Real,*

National Theatre, New York City, 1953; (with Anderson Lawler) *Oh, Men! Oh, Women!*, Henry Miller's Theatre, New York City, 1953; *The Honeys,* Longacre Theatre, New York City, 1955; pre-Broadway tryout, *Reuben Reuben,* 1955; (with Robert Lewis) *Mister Johnson,* Martin Beck Theatre, New York City, 1956; *Girls of Summer,* Longacre Theatre, New York City, 1956; (with William Myers) *Good as Gold,* Belasco Theatre, New York City, 1957; (with Alan Pakula) *Comes a Day,* Ambassador Theatre, New York City, 1958; (with Joel Schenker) *The Shadow of a Gunman,* Bijou Theatre, New York City, 1958; (with Schenker) *The Rivalry,* Bijou Theatre, 1959; *Sweet Bird of Youth,* Martin Beck Theatre, New York City, 1959.

Producer: (With Schenker) *The Long Dream,* Ambassador Theatre, New York City, 1960; (with Schenker) *Kula, Burr, and Ollie,* Hotel Astor, New York City, 1960; *Period of Adjustment,* Helen Hayes Theatre, New York City, 1960; *Brecht on Brecht,* Theatre de Lys, New York City, 1961; (with Roger L. Stevens) *Andorra,* Biltmore Theatre, New York City, 1963; (with Jerome Robbins) *Mother Courage and Her Children,* Martin Beck Theatre, New York City, 1963; (with Richard Halliday) *Jennie,* Majestic Theatre, New York City, 1963; (with Roger L. Stevens) *Double Talk,* Theatre de Lys, New York City, 1964; (with Mitch Leigh) *Chu Chem,* Locust Theatre, Philadelphia, 1966; (with Carl Schaeffer) *The Freaking Out of Stephanie Blake,* Eugene O'Neill Theatre, New York City, 1967; (with Richard Chandler) *Celebration,* Ambassador Theatre, New York City, 1969; (with Mary W. John) *Colette* (original production and return engagement), Ellen Stewart Theatre, New York City, 1970; (with Konrad Matthaei, Hale Matthews, and Robert Weinstein) *The Love Suicide at Schofield Barracks,* ANTA Theatre, New York City, 1972; (with Jean Dalrymple) *The Web and the Rock,* Theatre de Lys, New York City, 1972; also: *Yentl,* 1975; *Do You Turn Somersaults,* 1978; co-producer, *So Long on Lonely Street,* 1985; *Legends,* 1986.

In addition to the above, founded the Actors Studio with Elia Kazan, Lee Strasberg, and Robert Lewis where she was member of the board of directors and executive producer of the producing unit; produced for the Actors Studio Theatre, New York City, 1962-65: *Blues for Mister Charlie, Baby Want a Kiss,* and *The Three Sisters* (also produced in London).

WRITINGS: BOOKS—Autobiography, *One Naked Individual: My Fifty Years in the Theater,* Bobbs-Merrill Company, 1977.

AWARDS: Lawrence Langner Award for Lifetime Achievement in the Theatre, 1977; induction into the Theatrical Hall of Fame, Gershwin Theatre Lobby; honorary doctor of fine arts, Smith College, 1962; Brandeis University Medal of Achievement for Distinguished Contribution to American Theatre Arts, 1964.*

*   *   *

CRAWFORD, Joanna   1942-

PERSONAL: Born January 14, 1942, in Shippensburg, PA; daughter of William Warden (a horse trainer) and Miriam Elizabeth (Whorle) Crawford; children: Anonna. EDUCATION: Attended Shippensburg University for three years; Bennington College, B.A. RELIGION: Presbyterian.

VOCATION: Screenwriter and novelist.

WRITINGS: SCREENPLAYS—*Birch Interval* (adaption of her own novel), United Artists, 1965, later refilmed by B. Radnitz Productions, 1973; *My Side of the Mountain,* Paramount, 1967; *The Little Ark,* Cinema Center Films, 1968; *The Margaret Sanger Story,* Stephen Friedman Productions, 1969; *Mother,* Warner Brothers, 1970; *Love Sounds,* Paramount, 1971; *Dollmaker,* Paramount, 1974; *Piombino,* Grimaldi/Playboy Productions, 1975; *King Kong II,* De Laurentiis, 1976; *Trans-Siberian Express,* Marble Arch, 1979; *You and Me Together,* United Artists, 1980; *The Jean Seberg Story,* Warner Brothers, 1983.

TELEVISION—Movies: *Born Innocent II,* NBC, 1972; *Apartment to Share,* ABC, 1972; *Mother Jones,* CBS, 1975; *The Elsie Giorgi Story,* Universal, 1976; *Secrets,* ABC, 1977; *Forever,* CBS, 1977; *Betrayal,* NBC, 1978; *Friends, Secrets and Lies,* NBC, 1978; *The Sophia Loren Story,* NBC, 1982; *Her Life as a Man,* NBC, 1983; *Of the Children,* CBS, 1984; *The Trail of the Lonesome Pine,* CBS, 1984; *The Pat Moore Story* (also known as *Double Identity*) CBS, 1985.

BOOKS—*Birch Interval,* Houghton-Mifflin, 1973; *Primrose,* Harcourt, Brace, Jovanovich, 1974. SHORT STORIES—"Great Responsibilities from Small Jellyfish Grow."

MEMBER: Writers Guild of America, Authors Guild, Academy of Motion Picture Arts and Sciences, Screen Actors Guild.

SIDELIGHTS: RECREATIONS—Folklore, antiques, seventeenth-century music, people, and sailing.

ADDRESSES: HOME—1291 Oreta Terrace, Los Angeles, CA 90069. AGENT—Robinson, Weintraub Gross & Associates, 8428 Melrose Place, Suite C, Los Angeles, CA, 90038.

*   *   *

CROUSE, Lindsay   1948-

PERSONAL: Born May 12, 1948, in New York City; daughter of Russell (a playwright) Crouse; married David Mamet (a playwright). EDUCATION: Attended Radcliffe College.

VOCATION: Actress.

CAREER: BROADWAY DEBUT—*Much Ado About Nothing,* 1972. PRINCIPAL STAGE APPEARANCES—*Holiday,* Tyrone Guthrie Theatre, Minneapolis, MN, 1978. With the Circle Repertory Company at the Circle Repertory Theatre, New York City: *Reunion* and Ophelia, *Hamlet,* both 1979; Viola, *Twelfth Night,* 1980; Ada, *Childe Byron,* 1981; and Queen to Richard, *Richard II,* with the Circle Repertory Company at the Entermedia Theatre, New York City, 1982.

Mary, *Serenading Louie,* New York Shakespeare Festival, Public Theatre, New York City, 1984; *The Cherry Orchard,* with the New Theatre Company at the Goodman Theatre, Chicago, 1984; *The Shawl,* Mitzi Newhouse Theatre at Lincoln Center, New York City, 1986. Also appeared in *The Foursome, Fishing, Long Day's Journey into Night, Total Recall,* and *Father's Day,* all Off-Broadway productions, New York City.

PRINCIPAL FILM APPEARANCES—*All the President's Men,* Warner Brothers, 1976; *Slap Shot,* Universal, 1977; *Between the Lines,*

CROWE   **CONTEMPORARY THEATRE, FILM, AND TELEVISION ● Volume 4**

Midwest Film Productions, 1977; *The Verdict,* Twentieth Century-Fox, 1982; *Daniel,* Paramount, 1983; *Iceman,* Universal, 1984; *Places in the Heart,* Tri-Star, 1984.

PRINCIPAL TELEVISION APPEARANCES—Movies: *Eleanor and Franklin,* 1976; *The Tenth Level.* Episodic: *Hill Street Blues,* NBC, 1987.

AWARDS: Obie Award, 1980, for *Reunion.*

SIDELIGHTS: Lindsay Crouse began her performing career as a modern and jazz dancer. She plays the flute and piano.

ADDRESSES: OFFICE—Circle Repertory Theatre, 99 Seventh Avenue South, New York, NY 10014. AGENT—c/o Mary Goldberg, William Morris Agency, 1350 Avenue of the Americas, New York, NY 10019.*

*   *   *

CROWE, Christopher 1948-

PERSONAL: Born August 1, 1948, in Racine, WI; son of Jack Francis (a graphic artist) and Lorraine Edith Crowe. EDUCATION: Dominican College, B.A., communications.

VOCATION: Director, producer, and writer.

CHRISTOPHER CROWE

CAREER: PRINCIPAL FILM WORK—Writer and producer, *Nightmares,* Universal, 1983.

TELEVISION DEBUT—Story editor, *Baretta,* ABC, 1978. PRINCIPAL TELEVISION WORK—Executive producer and director, *Streets of Justice,* 1985; executive producer, *Alfred Hitchcock Presents,* 1985-86.

WRITINGS: The Last Chase, Argosy, 1977; *Nightmares,* Universal, 1983; *The Mean Season,* Orion, 1984; (with Brian DePalma) *Rapture,* Tri-Star (upcoming), and *Nops Trials,* Columbia (upcoming).

MEMBER: Writers Guild of America, Directors Guild of America, Producers Guild of America.

ADDRESSES: OFFICE—100 Universal Plaza, Universal City, CA 91608. AGENT—Bauer-Benedict Agency, 9522 Sunset Blvd., Hollywood, CA 90069.

*   *   *

CRYER, Gretchen 1935-

PERSONAL: Born Gretchen Kiger, October 17, 1935, in Dunreith, IN; married David Cryer (an actor, producer, and singer; divorced); children: Jon. EDUCATION: Attended DePauw University, IN.

VOCATION: Playwright, actress, singer, and lyricist.

CAREER: BROADWAY DEBUT—Miss Kepplewhite, *Little Me,* Lunt-Fontanne Theatre, 1962. PRINCIPAL STAGE APPEARANCES—Chorus, *110 in the Shade,* Broadhurst Theatre, New York City, 1963; lead role, *Now Is the Time for All Good Men,* Theatre de Lys, New York City, 1967; lead role, *I'm Getting My Act Together and Taking It on the Road,* New York Shakespeare Festival (NYSF), Anspacher Theatre, then transferring to the Circle in the Square Downtown, 1978; *A Circle of Sounds,* Manhattan Theatre Club, New York City, 1978; Della Juracko, *Blue Plate Special,* Manhattan Theatre Club, New York City, 1983.

PRINCIPAL CONCERT APPEARANCES—Appeared with Nancy Ford in a program of their songs at Town Hall Theatre and the Cookery, New York City.

WRITINGS: PLAYS, PRODUCED—(All with Nancy Ford as composer, unless otherwise noted) Book and lyrics, *Now Is the Time for All Good Men,* Theatre de Lys, New York City, 1967; *The Last Sweet Days of Issac,* 1970; (with Doug Dyer and Peter Link) *The Wedding of Iphigenia,* and *Iphigenia in Concert,* both 1971; *Shelter,* Broadway production, 1973; *I'm Getting My Act Together and Taking It on the Road,* NYSF, Anspacher Theatre, then transferring to the Circle in the Square Downtown, New York City, 1978; *Hang on to the Good Times,* Manhattan Theatre Club at City Center, New York City, 1985.

PLAYS, PUBLISHED—All plays with Nancy Ford, published by Samuel French, Inc.: *Now Is the Time for All Good Men, The Last Sweet Days of Issac, Shelter,* and *I'm Getting My Act Together and Taking It on the Road.*

AWARDS: Obie Award, 1970, for *The Last Sweet Days of Issac.*

MEMBER: Actors' Equity Association, Dramatists Guild.

ADDRESSES: HOME—885 West End Avenue, New York, NY 10025.*

*   *   *

CRYER, Jon 1965-

PERSONAL: Born April 16, 1965; son of David (an actor) and Gretchen (a writer and actress) Cryer. EDUCATION: Bronx School of Science; attended the Royal Academy of Dramatic Art, London.

VOCATION: Actor.

CAREER: STAGE DEBUT—David, Torch Song Trilogy, Helen Hayes Theatre, New York City and in Los Angeles, 1983. PRINCI-PAL STAGE APPEARANCES—Eugene, Brighton Beach Memoirs, Alvin Theatre (now Neil Simon Theatre), New York City, 1984.

FILM DEBUT—No Small Affair, Columbia Pictures, 1984. PRINCI-PAL FILM APPEARANCES—Pretty in Pink, 1986; Superman IV, Warner Brothers, 1987; title role, Morgan Stewart's Coming Home, New Century/Vista, 1987; Dudes, 1987.

TELEVISION DEBUT—"Noon Wine," American Playhouse Series, PBS, 1985. PRINCIPAL TELEVISION APPEARANCES—Episodic: Amazing Stories, NBC, 1986.

MEMBER: Screen Actors Guild, Actors' Equity Association, American Federation of Television and Radio Artists.

ADDRESSES: OFFICE—Martin Tudor Productions, 125 W. Third Street, New York, NY 10012. AGENT—c/o David Lewis, International Creative Management, 40 W. 57th Street, New York, NY 10019.

*   *   *

CULLUM, John 1930-

PERSONAL: Born March 2, 1930, in Knoxville, TN; married Emily Frankel (a dancer and choreographer); children: John David. EDUCATION: University of Tennessee, B.A. MILITARY: U.S. Army.

VOCATION: Actor and singer.

CAREER: STAGE DEBUT—Citizen, Cobbler, Servant, Julius Caesar, Shakespearewrights, New York City, 1957. PRINCIPAL STAGE APPEARANCES—Grimaldi, 'Tis Pity She's a Whore, Players Theatre, New York City, 1959; Mastax, The Jackass, Barbizon-Plaza Theatre, New York City, 1960; Duke of Orleans, King Henry V, Gentleman, Measure for Measure, Lord, The Taming of the Shrew, all with the New York Shakespeare Festival at Belvedere Lake, New York City, 1960; Sir Dinadan, Camelot, Majestic Theatre, New York City, 1960; Johnny Sykes, We Take the Town, Shubert Theatre, New Haven, CT, 1962; Cassius, Infidel Caesar, Music Box Theatre, New York City, 1962; King of France, King

Lear, New York Shakespeare Festival, New York City, 1963; Cyril Bellamy, The Saving Grace, Writer's Stage, New York City, 1963; Timothy, Thistle in My Bed, Gramercy Arts Theatre, New York City, 1963; Laertes, Hamlet, Lunt-Fontanne Theatre, New York City, 1964; title role, Hamlet, Pabst Theatre, Milwaukee, WI, 1964; Dr. Mark Bruckner, On a Clear Day You Can See Forever, Mark Hellinger Theatre, New York City, 1965.

Don Quixote, Man of La Mancha, American National Theatre Academy (ANTA) Theatre, New York City, 1966; Father Jerome Fogarty, "The Frying Pan," Tom Dorgan, "Eternal Triangle," Denis Sullivan, "The Bridal Night," in the triple-bill Three Hand Reel, Renata Theatre, New York City, 1966; Edward Rutledge, 1776, 46th Street Theatre, New York City, 1969; Lord Bothwell, Vivat! Vivat Regina!, Broadhurst Theatre, New York City, 1972; King, The King and I, Jones Beach Theatre, Long Island, NY, 1972; Thomas Mendip, The Lady's Not for Burning, Goodman Theatre, Chicago, IL, 1973; Billy Bigelow, Carousel, Jones Beach Theatre, 1973; Don Medigua, El Capitan, Ford's Theatre, Washington, DC, 1973; Charlie Anderson, Shenandoah, Alvin Theatre, New York City, 1975; Bobby Horvath, The Trip Back Down, Longacre Theatre, New York City, 1977; Sigmund, The Archbishop's Ceiling, Eisenhower Theatre, Kennedy Center, Washington, DC, 1977; Oscar Jaffe, On the Twentieth Century, St. James Theatre, New York City, 1978; Sidney Bruhl, Deathtrap, Music Box Theatre, New York City, 1979.

Ebenezer Scrooge, A Christmas Carol, Ford's Theatre, Washington, DC, 1980; Hey, Look Me Over, Avery Fisher Hall, New York City, 1981; The Magistrate, Hartman Theatre, Stamford, CT, 1982; The Portage to San Cristobal of A.H., Hartford Stage Company, Hartford, CT, 1983; Victor Prynne, Private Lives, Lunt-Fontanne Theatre, New York City, 1983; title role, Cyrano de Bergerac, Syracuse Stage, Syracuse, NY, then with the Alliance Theatre Company, Atlanta, both 1984; Guy, Doubles, Ritz Theatre, New York City, 1985; in The Yearling, Alliance Theatre, Atlanta, 1985; Tom Sawyer, The Boys in Winter, Circle in the Square Theatre, New York City, 1986.

Has also appeared in The Rehearsal, Kings, The Elizabethans, In the Voodoo Parlor of Marie Leveau, and Whistler.

PRINCIPAL STAGE WORK—Director: The Red Blue Grass Western Flyer Show, Goodspeed Opera House, East Haddam, CT, 1977; Zinnia, Colonnades Theatre, New York City, 1977; People in Show Business Make Long Goodbyes, Orpheum Theatre, New York City, 1979.

PRINCIPAL FILM APPEARANCES—All the Way Home, Paramount, 1963; Hawaii, United Artists, 1966; Edward Rutledge, 1776, Columbia, 1972.

PRINCIPAL TELEVISION APPEARANCES—Movies: The Man without a Country, 1973; Summer, 1980; Carl Sandburg, 1981; The Day After, 1984; also appeared in Androcles and the Lion.

NON-RELATED CAREER—Tennis professional; real estate salesman.

AWARDS: Theatre World Award, 1965-66, for On a Clear Day You Can See Forever; Best Actor in a Musical, Antoinette Perry Awards, 1975, for Shenandoah and 1979, for On the Twentieth Century.

ADDRESSES: AGENT—International Creative Management, 40 W. 57th Street, New York, NY 10019.*

CONSTANCE CUMMINGS

CUMMINGS, Constance 1910-

PERSONAL: Born Constance Halverstadt, May 15, 1910, in Seattle, WA; daughter of Dallas Vernon (a lawyer) and Kate Logan (Cummings) Halverstadt; married Benn Wolf Levy (a playwright), 1933 (died, 1973); children: Jonathan, Jemina. EDUCATION: Attended St. Nicholas School, Seattle, WA.

VOCATION: Actress.

CAREER: BROADWAY DEBUT—Chorus, *Treasure Girl,* Alvin Theatre, November 8, 1928. LONDON DEBUT—Alice Overton, *Sour Grapes,* with the Repertory Players at the Comedy Theatre, July 22, 1934. PRINCIPAL STAGE APPEARANCES—*The Little Show,* Music Box Theatre, New York City, 1929; Carrie, *This Man's Town,* Ritz Theatre, New York City, 1930; continued role of Alice Overton, *Sour Grapes,* Apollo Theatre, London, 1934; Linda Brown, *Accent on Youth,* Plymouth Theatre, New York City, 1934; Regina Conti, *Young Madame Conti,* Savoy Theatre, London, 1936, then Music Box Theatre, New York City, 1937; Emma Bovary, *Madame Bovary,* Broadhurst Theatre, New York City, 1937; Nellie Blunt, *If I Were You,* Mansfield Theatre, New York City, 1938; Katherine, *Goodbye, Mr. Chips,* Shaftesbury Theatre, London, 1938; Kate Settle, *The Jealous God,* Lyric Theatre, London, 1939; Juliet, *Romeo and Juliet,* Miss Richland, *The Good Natured Man,* and title role, *Saint Joan,* all with the Old Vic Theatre company at the Buxton Festival, then Streatham Hill, U.K., 1939.

Lydia Kenyon, *Skylark,* Duchess Theatre, London, 1942; Gabby Maple, *The Petrified Forest,* Globe Theatre, London, 1942; Racine Gardner, *One-Man Show,* Ethel Barrymore Theatre, New York

City, 1945; Jane Pugh, *Clutterbuck,* Wyndham's Theatre, London, 1946; Anna Luise Klopps, *Happy with Either* and Madeleine, *Don't Listen, Ladies!,* both St. James's Theatre, London, 1948; Laura Whittingham, *Before the Party,* St. Martin's Theatre, London, 1949; Martha Cotton, *Return to Tyassi,* Duke of York's Theatre, London, 1950; Georgie Elvin, *Winter Journey,* St. James's Theatre, London, 1952; Ann Downs, *The Shrike,* Prince's Theatre, London, 1953; Andrea, *Trial and Error,* Vaudeville Theatre, London, 1953; title role, *Lysistrata,* Oxford Playhouse, U.K., 1957; Antiope, *The Rape of the Belt,* Piccadilly Theatre, London, 1957, then Martin Beck Theatre, New York City, 1960.

Sarah, *JB,* Phoenix Theatre, London, 1961; Inez, *In Camera (Huis Clos)* and Countess of Amersham, *A Social Success,* Oxford Playhouse, U.K., 1962; Katy Maartens, *The Genius and the Goddess,* Oxford Playhouse, U.K., then Comedy Theatre, London, 1962; Catherine Gurnee, *The Strangers,* Westport Country Playhouse, CT, 1963; Martha, *Who's Afraid of Virginia Woolf?,* Piccadilly Theatre, London, 1964; Liza Foote, *Public and Confidential,* Malvern Festival, U.K., then Duke of York's Theatre, London, 1966; Julia Stanford, QC, *Justice Is a Woman,* Vaudeville Theatre, London, 1966; Jane Banbury, *Fallen Angels,* Vaudeville Theatre, London, 1967; Gertrude, *Hamlet,* Round House Theatre, London, then Lunt-Fontanne Theatre, New York City, 1969; Mrs. Goforth, *The Milk Train Doesn't Stop Here Any More,* Citizen's Theatre, Glasgow, Scotland, 1969.

Claire, *The Visit,* Belgrade Theatre, Coventry, U.K., 1970; Volumnia, *Coriolanus,* with the National Theatre, London, 1971; Leda, *Amphitryon 38,* and Mary Tyrone, *Long Day's Journey into Night,* both with the National Theatre at the New Theatre, London, 1971; Madame Ranevsky, *The Cherry Orchard* and Agave, *The Bacchae,* both at the Old Vic Theatre, London, 1973; Mother, *Children,* Mermaid Theatre, London, 1974; Lady Champion-Cheney, *The Circle,* Arnaud Theatre, Guildford, U.K., 1974; Dodie, *Stripwell,* Royal Court Theatre, London, 1975; title role, *Mrs. Warren's Profession,* Bristol Old Vic Theatre, U.K., 1976; Emily Stilson, *Wings,* New York Shakespeare Festival, Newman Theatre, then Lyceum Theatre, New York City, then the Cottesloe Theatre, London, 1979; *Hay Fever,* London, 1980; *The Golden Age,* 1981; Mrs. St. Maugham, *The Chalk Garden,* Roundabout Theatre, Stage One, New York City, 1982; Amanda, *The Glass Menagerie,* Coconut Grove Playhouse, Miami, 1984, the in a London production, 1985; *Crown Matrimonial,* U.K. production, 1987.

MAJOR TOURS—The Wife, *All Over,* U.K. cities, 1976; in a one-woman show, *Fanny Kemble,* U.K. production, 1986.

FILM DEBUT—*Movie Crazy,* Paramount, 1932. PRINCIPAL FILM APPEARANCES—*Behind the Mask, Doomed Cargo,* and *Washington Merry-Go-Round,* all Columbia, 1932; *Broadway Through a Keyhole,* United Artists, 1933; *Glamour,* Universal, 1934; *Looking for Trouble,* United Artists, 1934; *Heads We Go,* B.I.P., 1934; *Channel Crossing,* Gaumont-British, 1934; *Remember Last Night,* Universal, 1935; *The Northing Tramp,* Ealing, 1936; *Seven Sinners* and *Strangers on a Honeymoon,* both Gaumont-British, 1937; *Haunted Honeymoon* (also known as *Busman's Honeymoon*), Metro-Goldwyn-Mayer (MGM), 1940; *Blithe Spirit,* United Artists, 1940; *This England,* World, 1941; *The Foreman Went to France,* Ealing, 1942; *Into the Blue,* Wilcox, 1950; *Three's Company,* 1953; *The Finger of Guilt,* RKO, 1956; *With all My Heart,* 1956; *The Intimate Stranger,* Anglo-Amalgamated, 1956; *John and Julie,* DCA, 1957; *The Battle of the Sexes,* Continental, 1960; *The Outsider,* 1961; *Sammy Going South,* Seven Arts, 1962; *In the Cool of the Day,* MGM, 1963; *A Boy Ten Feet Tall,* Paramount, 1965; also, *The Scream.*

PRINCIPAL TELEVISION APPEARANCES—Teleplays: Roxanne, *Cyrano de Bergerac*, 1938; Martha, *Return to Tyassi*, 1956; title role, *The Trial of Mary Dugan*, 1957; Harriet Craig, *Craig's Wife*, 1957; Kathleen, *The Last Tycoon*, 1959; Jane, *Clutterbuck*, 1959; title role, *Ruth*, 1962; Helga, *Late Summer*, 1963; *The Old Ladies*, BBC, 1983; also *Wings*, PBS; *Touch of the Sun*.

PRINCIPAL RADIO WORK—Performed on *Showmen of England*, 1938; *The White Cliffs*, 1941; title role, *Saint Joan*, 1941; *The Rebirth of Venus*, 1941; *Man's Company*, 1942; Amy, *They Knew What They Wanted*, 1942; Cleopatra, *Antony and Cleopatra*, 1942; panelist, *Women on Stage*, 1949; title role, *Hedda Gabler*, 1952; Georgie Elgin, *Winter Journey*, 1954; Emma Bovary, *Madam Bovary*, 1955; performed on *Variety Playhouse*, 1955; performed on *Call the Tune*, 1957.

RELATED CAREER—During World War II, appeared in six plays for the benefit of the British forces.

AWARDS: Order of the British Empire, 1974; Antoinette Perry Award, Obie Award, Drama Desk Award, all 1979, for *Wings*.

MEMBER: Actors' Equity Association, British Actors' Equity Association (member of council), American Federation of Television and Radio Artists, Screen Actors Guild; Labour Party, Chelsea Arts Club, Young People's Theatre Panel (chairman), Arts Council (1963-69), Royal Society for the Encouragement of Arts and Commerce.

SIDELIGHTS: RECREATIONS—Anthropology, needlework, gardening, swimming, and reading.

ADDRESSES: OFFICE—68 Old Church Street, London SW3, England.

*   *   *

CUSHING, Peter   1913-

PERSONAL: Born May 26, 1913, in Kenley, Surrey, England; son of George Edward and Nellie Marie (King) Cushing; married Helen Beck, 1943 (died). EDUCATION: Attended Purley School, Surrey; trained for the stage at the Guildhall School of Music and Drama with Cairns James.

VOCATION: Actor.

CAREER: STAGE DEBUT—Captain Randall, *The Middle Watch*, Connaught Theatre, Worthing, U.K., 1935. BROADWAY DEBUT—Percival, *The Seventh Trumpet*, Mansfield Theatre, 1941. LONDON DEBUT—Alexander I and Captain Ramballe, *War and Peace*, Phoenix Theatre, 1943. PRINCIPAL STAGE APPEARANCES—Valentine Christie, *The Dark Potential* and Kevin Ormond, *The Crime of Margaret Foley*, both at the Q Theatre, London, 1944; Private Charles, *Happy Few*, Cambridge Theatre, London, 1944; Lieutenant Colbert, *While the Sun Shines*, Globe Theatre, London, 1944-45; Faulkland, *The Rivals*, Criterion Theatre, London, 1945; title role, *The Curious Dr. Robson*, Q Theatre, London, 1946; Joseph Surface, *The School for Scandal*, Duke of Clarence, *Richard III*, and Ivan Lomov, *The Proposal*, all at the New Theatre, London, 1949.

Valentine, *The Gay Invalid*, Garrick Theatre, London, 1951; Bel Affris and Brittanus, *Caesar and Cleopatra* and Alexas Diomedes, *Antony and Cleopatra*, both at the St. James's Theatre, London,

PETER CUSHING

1951; *The Wedding Ring*, London, 1952; Oliver Erwenter, *The Silver Whistle*, Duchess Theatre, London, 1956; Charles Norbury, *The Sound of Murder*, Aldwych Theatre, London, 1959; Sir Hector Benbow, *Thark*, Yvonne Arnaud Theatre, Guildford, U.K., 1956, then repeated the role at Garrick Theatre, London, 1965; Dr. Austin Sloper, *The Heiress*, Haymarket Theatre, Basingstoke, U.K., 1975.

MAJOR TOURS   Joseph Surface, *The School for Scandal*, Duke of Clarence, *Richard III*, and Ivan Lomov, *The Proposal*, all with the Old Vic Company, Australian and New Zealand cities, 1948; Soldier, *The Soldier and the Lady*, U.K. cities, 1954.

FILM DEBUT—*Vigil in the Night*, 1939. PRINCIPAL FILM APPEARANCES—Osric, *Hamlet*, Universal, 1948; Henry Milies, *The End of the Affair*, Columbia, 1955; Memnon, *Alexander the Great*, United Artists, 1956; Otto Wesendonk, *Magic Fire*, Republic, 1956; *Abominable Snowman*, Twentieth Century-Fox, 1957; Captain Pearson, *John Paul Jones*, Warner Brothers, 1959; Sherlock Holmes, *The Hound of the Baskervilles*, United Artists, 1959; Dr. Victor Stein, *The Revenge of Frankenstein*, Columbia, 1958; Professor Van Helsing, *The Horror of Dracula*, Universal International, 1958; *The Brides of Dracula*, Universal, 1960; *The Sword of Sherwood Forest*, Columbia, 1961; *The Naked Edge*, United Artists, 1961; *Cash on Demand*, Columbia, 1962; *Night Creatures*, Universal, 1962; *Fury at Smuggler's Bay*, Embassy, 1963; *The Evil of Frankenstein*, Universal, 1964; *The Gorgon*, Columbia, 1965; *Dr. Terror's House of Horrors*, Paramount, 1965; Major Holly, *She*, Metro-Goldwyn-Mayer (MGM), 1965; *The Skull*, Paramount, 1965; *Dr. Who and Daleks*, Continental, 1966; *Frankenstein Created Woman*, Twentieth Century-Fox, 1967; *Island of Terror*,

Universal, 1967; *The Torture Garden,* Columbia, 1968; *Corruption,* Columbia, 1968.

Baron Frankenstein, *Frankenstein Must Be Destroyed,* Warner Brothers, 1970; Major Heinrich, *Scream and Scream Again,* American International Pictures, 1970; Philip, "Waxworks," *The House That Dripped Blood,* Cinerama, 1971; Grimsdyke, "Poetic Justice," *Tales from the Crypt,* Cinerama, 1972; Professor Van Helsing, *Dracula A.D. 1972,* Warner Brothers, 1972; *Fear in the Night,* Hammer Films, 1972; Captain, *Asylum,* Cinerama, 1972; Emanuel Hildern, *The Creeping Flesh,* Columbia, 1972; *Horror Express,* Scotia International, 1973; *Dynasty of Fear,* Hammer Films, 1973; Baron Frankenstein, *Frankenstein and the Monster from Hell,* Paramount, 1974; Dr. Christopher Lundgren, *The Beast Must Die,* Cinerama, 1975; *The Legend of the Werewolf,* Tyburn Films, 1975; Dr. Abner Perry, *At the Earth's Core,* American International, 1976; Grand Moff Tarkin, *Star Wars,* Twentieth Century-Fox, 1977; *Shock Waves,* 1977; Wilbur Gray, *The Uncanny,* Astral Films, 1978; Wazir Al Wuzara, *Arabian Adventure,* Associated Film Distributors, 1979; Dr. Lawrence, *The Ghoul,* Tyburn Films, 1981; Seneschal, *Sword of the Valiant,* Cannon Films, 1983; bookstore owner, *Top Secret!,* Paramount, 1984; *Bloodsuckers,* VCL Communications, 1985; Colonel Raymond, *Biggles,* Yellowbill Productions, 1985.

Also appeared in *A Chump at Oxford,* 1941; *Moulin Rouge,* 1951; *Black Knight,* 1954; *Time without Pity,* 1956; *The Curse of Frankenstein,* 1957; John Banning, *The Mummy,* 1959; *The Man Who Finally Died,* 1962; *Daleks—Invasion Earth 2150 A.D.,* 1966; *Some May Live,* 1967; *The Night of the Big Heat,* 1967; General Spielsdorf, *The Vampire Lovers,* 1971; *I, Monster,* 1972; *Nothing but the Night,* 1972; Dr. Wells, *Panico en el Transiberiano,* 1972; Dr. Pope, *And Now the Screaming Starts,* 1973; *The Satanic Rites of Dracula,* 1973; *From Beyond the Grave,* 1973; Professor Van Helsing, *Count Dracula and His Vampire Bride,* 1974; MacGregor, *La Grande Trouille,* 1974; Professor Van Helsing, *Dracula and the Seven Golden Vampires,* 1975; SS Commander, *Almost Human,* 1975; Rattwood, *Call Him Mr. Shatter,* 1976; *Trial by Combat,* 1976; *Die Standarte,* 1977; Kolderup, *Monster Island,* 1981; Sebastian, *The House of the Long Shadows,* 1983; *Code of Silence,* 1985; Colonel Raymond, *Biggles,* 1986. Also appeared in *Battleflag, Hitler's Son, Touch of the Sun, Black Jack, Violent Playground, Suspect, The Flesh and the Friends, The Devil's Agent, The Hell-Fire Club, The Frighten Bed Island, Death's Head Moth, Doctors Wear Scarlet, The Bride of Fengriffen, The Revenge of Dr. Death, Tender Dracula, The Devil's People,* and *Death Corps.*

PRINCIPAL TELEVISION APPEARANCES—Series: Title role, *Dr. Who,* 1973. Movies: Dr. Manetee, *A Tale of Two Cities,* 1980; Professor Charles Copeland, *Helen Keller: The Miracle Continues,* 1984; Sherlock Holmes, *The Masks of Death,* 1984. Also has appeared in numerous teleplays since 1951, including *Nineteen Eighty Four,* 1955.

NON-RELATED CAREER—Prior to acting career, was employed as a clerk in a surveyor's office.

WRITINGS: AUTOBIOGRAPHY—*Peter Cushing: An Autobiography,* Weidenfeld and Nicolson, 1986.

AWARDS: Outstanding Actor of the Year, National Television Award, *Daily Mail,* 1954; Best Performance, Guild of Television Producers and Directors, 1955, for *Nineteen Eighty Four;* Best Actor, Television Top Ten, *News Chronicle,* 1956; Best Actor, Licorne d'or Award (France), 1973, for *Tales from the Crypt.*

SIDELIGHTS: RECREATIONS—Country walks and collecting books, cigarette cards, and model soldiers.

ADDRESSES: AGENT—John Redway, 16 Berners Street, London W1P 3DD, England.

*   *   *   **

CUTTER, Lise

PERSONAL: EDUCATION: California State University at Fullerton, B.A.; studied film and television acting with Roy London.

VOCATION: Actress.

CAREER: PRINCIPAL TELEVISION APPEARANCES—Series: *Perfect Strangers,* ABC, 1986—. Episodic: *Dallas,* CBS; *Remington Steele,* NBC; *Hollywood Beat.* Movies: *Fatal Vision,* 1984.

PRINCIPAL STAGE APPEARANCES—In productions at California State University at Fullerton: *Anne of the Thousand Days; The Moon Is Down; A Month in the Country.*

SIDELIGHTS: RECREATIONS—Designing and sewing her own clothing, photography, painting.

ADDRESSES: HOME—Los Angeles, CA. PUBLICIST—Guttman and Pam Ltd., 120 El Camino Drive, Beverly Hills, CA 90212.

LISE CUTTER

D

DAMES, Rob 1944-

PERSONAL: Full name, Robert L. Dames; born June 13, 1944, in St. Louis, MO; son of George F. (a salesman) and Mercedes C. (Lyons) Dames; married Diane Yates (an art director), April 5, 1986; children: Damien Susan. EDUCATION: St. Louis University, B.S., 1966. MILITARY: U.S. Air Force, 1966-70.

VOCATION: Director, producer, and writer.

CAREER: FIRST TELEVISION WORK—Writer, *The Love Boat,* ABC, 1978. PRINCIPAL TELEVISION WORK—Story editor, *Phyll and Mikhy,* CBS, 1979; producer, *Mr. & Mrs. & Mr,* CBS, 1979; producer and director, *Benson,* ABC, 1979-86; (with Bob Fraser) co-producer, *Marblehead Manor,* NBC, 1987.

RELATED CAREER—Formerly an actor in university, stock, and dinner theatre; producer and director, Barn and Plantation Dinner Theatres, 1973-75; (with Bob Fraser) co-producer, Dames/Fraser Productions, Paramount Studios, 1986—.

WRITINGS: PLAYS, PRODUCED—*Frozen Stiff,* Hollywood Actors Theatre, Los Angeles, 1978. SCREENPLAYS—(With Fraser) *Firecrackers,* Twentieth Century-Fox, 1980.

ADDRESSES: AGENT—c/o Richard Weston, Major Clients Agency, 1900 Avenue of the Stars, Los Angeles, CA 90067.

*   *   *

DANCE, Charles 1946-

PERSONAL: Born October 10, 1946, in Rednal England; son of Walter (an engineer) and Eleanor (Perks) Dance; married Joanna Haythorn (an artist) July 18, 1970; children: Oliver, Rebecca. EDUCATION: Plymouth College of Art; Leicester College of Art, diploma in graphic design; studied privately with Leonard Bennett and Martin St. John Burchardt.

VOCATION: Actor.

CAREER: STAGE DEBUT—Sven, *It's a Two Foot Six Inches Above the Ground World,* post West End tour of England, 1970. LONDON DEBUT—Reynaldo and Fortinbras, *Hamlet,* Royal Shakespeare Company, 1975. PRINCIPAL STAGE APPEARANCES—Title role, *Henry V,* Royal Shakespeare Company at Brooklyn Academy of Music, Brooklyn, NY; Badger, *Toad of Toad Hall,* Swindon, U.K.; Beaudricourt, *St. Joan,* Oxford, U.K.; Henry Carr, *Travesties,* Leeds, U.K.; Soliony, *The Three Sisters* and the hotel manag-

er, *Born Yesterday,* both Greenwich, U.K.; understudy Macheath, *The Beggars' Opera,* Chichester Festival, U.K.; Morris Townsend, *The Heiress,* Nottingham Playhouse, U.K.

Lancaster, *Henry IV,* Parts I and II, Catesby, *Richard III,* Spanish Envoy, *Perkin Warbeck,* Williams and Scroop, *Henry V,* Oliver, *As You Like It,* Tomazo, *The Changeling,* Freeman, *The Jail Diary of Albie Sachs,* and Tullus Aufidius, *Coriolanus,* all with Royal Shakespeare Company, 1975-79; title role, *Coriolanus,* Odeon Nationale, Paris; Nestor, *Irma La Douce,* West End production, London, 1980; Frank, *Turning Over,* Bush, U.K., 1983.

FILM DEBUT—Klaus, *For Your Eyes Only,* United Artists, 1981. PRINCIPAL FILM APPEARANCES—Raymond Brock, *Plenty,* Pressman Films, 1985; Sardo, *The Golden Child,* Paramount, 1986; also: Hatcher, *The Macguffin,* BBC Films; D.W. Griffith, *Good Morning Babylon,* Italy; Richards, *Hidden City,* Lee International.

CHARLES DANCE

PRINCIPAL TELEVISION APPEARANCES—Duke of Clarence, *Edward VII*, ATV; Edward Hartford Jones, *Nancy Astor*, BBC; Siegfried Sassoon, *The Fatal Spring*, BBC; Alan, *Saigon: The Last Day*, BBC; Reynaed Callaghan, *Frost in May*, BBC; O'Brien, *Father Brown;* Teddy, *Raffles;* Parker, *The Professionals;* Borghejm, *Little Eyolf*, BBC; Captain Truman, *Rainy Day Women*, BBC; James Latimer, *This Lightning Always Strikes Twice*, Granada; Charleston, *Thunder Rock*, BBC; Guy Perron, *The Jewel in the Crown*, Granada. Movies: *The Secret Servant*, BBC, 1984; Gerry Hampton, *Out on a Limb*, ABC, 1987.

AWARDS: Scottish Academy of Television Arts, Best Actor, 1984, for *The Secret Servant;* British Academy of Film and Television Arts, Best Actor nomination, 1984.

MEMBER: British Actors' Equity Association, Screen Actors Guild.

SIDELIGHTS: Mr. Dance was an active member of the Royal Shakespeare Company from 1975 until 1979.

ADDRESSES: AGENT—c/o Marion Rosenberg, The Lantz Office, 9255 Sunset Blvd., Suite 505, Los Angeles, CA 90069.

*   *   *

DANIELS, Danny
See Giagni, D.J.

*   *   *

DANIELS, Jeff

PERSONAL: Born in Georgia. EDUCATION: Attended Central Michigan University; trained for the stage as an apprentice with the Circle Repertory Company, New York City.

VOCATION: Actor.

CAREER: PRINCIPAL STAGE APPEARANCES—Arthur, *The Farm*, 1976, Young Eddie, *My Life*, Nephew, *Brontosaurus*, and Wesley, *Feedlot*, all 1977, Schwartz, *Lulu*, 1978, all Circle Repertory Theatre, New York City; Slugger, PAF Playhouse, Huntington Station, NY, 1978; Jed Jenkins, *The Fifth of July*, Circle Repertory Theatre, New York City, 1978, Ahmanson Theatre, Los Angeles, 1979, and New Apollo Theatre, New York City, 1980-81; Joe Bonham, *Johnny Got His Gun*, Circle Repertory Theatre, New York City, 1982; Andrei, *Three Sisters*, Manhattan Theatre Club, New York City, 1982-83; *The Golden Age*, Jack Lawrence Theatre, New York City, 1984; also appeared in an Off-Broadway production of *Short Changed Review*.

FILM DEBUT—*Ragtime*, Paramount, 1981. PRINCIPAL FILM APPEARANCES—*Terms of Endearment*, Paramount, 1983; *The Purple Rose of Cairo*, Orion, 1985; *Marie*, Metro-Goldwyn-Mayer/United Artists, 1985; *Something Wild*, Orion, 1986; Biff Baxter, *Radio Days*, Orion, 1987.

PRINCIPAL TELEVISION APPEARANCES—Pilots: *Breaking Away*, ABC; *Hawaii Five-O*, CBS. Movies: *A Rumor of War*, CBS, 1980; *An Invasion of Privacy*, ABC, 1983; *The Fifth of July*, American Playhouse, PBS.

ADDRESSES: AGENT—Hildy Gottlieb, International Creative Management, Inc. 40 West 57th Street, New York NY, 10019. PUBLICIST—Catherine Olim, PMK Public Relations, One Lincoln Plaza, New York, NY 10023.*

DANSON, Ted   1947-

PERSONAL: Born December 29, 1947; son of Edward B. (an archeologist) and Jessica (MacMaster) Danson; married Randall Lee Gosch, August, 1970 (divorced, 1977); married Cassandra Coates (a designer), July 30, 1977; children: Kate. EDUCATION: Attended Stanford University, 1966-68; attended Carnegie-Mellon University, 1968-72; studied at the Actors Institute with Dan Fauci.

VOCATION: Actor and producer.

CAREER: OFF-BROADWAY DEBUT—Reginald, *The Real Inspector Hound*, Theatre Four, 1972. PRINCIPAL STAGE APPEARANCES—*Comedy of Errors*, New York Shakespeare Festival, New York City; *Comedians* and *Status Quo Vadis*, both New York City productions.

FILM DEBUT—Policeman, *The Onion Field*, AVCO-Embassy, 1979. PRINCIPAL FILM APPEARANCES—Lawyer, *Body Heat*, Warner Brothers, 1981; *Creepshow*, Warner Brothers, 1983; *Little Treasure*, Tri-Star, 1985; *A Fine Mess*, Columbia, 1986; *Just Between Friends*, Orion, 1986; *The Music Box*, Columbia, 1987.

TELEVISION DEBUT—*The Doctors*. PRINCIPAL TELEVISION AP-

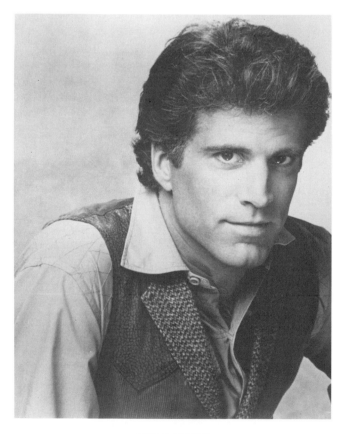

TED DANSON

PEARANCES—Series: Sam Malone, *Cheers,* NBC, 1982—. Episodic: *Somerset;* "Dear Teacher," *Comedy Theatre,* NBC, 1981. Movies: *The Women's Room,* 1980; *Cowboy,* 1983; *Something About Amelia,* ABC, 1984; Duffy Lynch, *We Are the Children,* ABC, 1987; also, *The Good Witch of Laurel Canyon.*

PRINCIPAL TELEVISION WORK—Movies: Co-producer, *We Are the Children,* ABC, 1987.

RELATED CAREER—Acting teacher, Actors Institute, Los Angeles, 1978-80.

AWARDS: Outstanding Lead Actor in a Comedy Series, Emmy Award nomination, 1983, for *Cheers;* Discovery of the Year, Women's Press Association, 1983; Best Actor in a Mini-Series or Motion Picture Made for Television, Golden Globe Award, 1984, for *Something About Amelia.*

MEMBER: Actors' Equity Association, American Federation of Television and Radio Aritsts, Screen Actors Guild.

ADDRESSES: OFFICE—c/o Paramount Studios, Bldg D, Room 201, 5555 Melrose, Los Angeles, CA 90028. AGENT—Bauman & Hiller, 9220 Sunset Blvd., Los Angeles, CA 90069.*

*   *   *

DAVIES, Robertson   1913-

PERSONAL: Born August 28, 1913, in Thamesville, Ontario, Canada; son of William Rupert (a publisher) and Florence Sheppard (McKay) Davies; married Brenda Mathews (a theatrical stage manager at time of marriage), February 2, 1940; children: Miranda, Jennifer, Rosamond. EDUCATION: Attended Upper Canada College, Toronto, Queen's University, Kingston, Ontario and Balliol College, Oxford, B. Litt, 1938.

VOCATION: Writer, publisher, teacher, and actor.

CAREER: STAGE DEBUT—Appeared with the Oxford University Dramatic Society and in provincial U.K. theatres. LONDON DEBUT—Thomas Howard, *Traitor's Gate,* Duke of York's Theatre, 1938. PRINCIPAL STAGE APPEARANCES—With the Old Vic Company, London: Snout, *A Midsummer Night's Dream,* the Widow and others, *The Taming of the Shrew,* and the Archbishop, *St. Joan,* 1938-39.

RELATED CAREER—Teacher and literary evaluator, Old Vic Drama School, 1938-39; literary editor, *Saturday Night* magazine, 1940-42; editor, *Peterborough Examiner,* 1942, publisher, 1958-68; visiting professor, Trinity College, University of Toronto, 1960-62; first master, Massey College, University of Toronto, 1962-81; senator, Stratford Shakespeare Festival, Stratford, Ontario, Canada.

WRITINGS: PLAYS, PRODUCED AND PUBLISHED—*Fortune, My Foe,* International Players Theatre, Kingston, Ontario, 1948, published by Clarke, Irwin, 1949; *Overlaid,* Peterborough Little Theatre, Ontario, Canada, 1947, *Eros at Breakfast,* Montreal Repertory Theatre, Quebec, Canada, 1948, *The Voice of the People,* Montreal Repertory Theatre, Quebec, 1948, *At the Gates of the Righteous,* Peterborough Little Theatre, Ontario, 1948, *Hope Deferred,* Montreal Repertory Theatre, Quebec, 1948, all published under the

title, *Eros at Breakfast and Other Plays,* Clarke, Irwin, 1949 and later revised in an edition titled *Four Favorite Plays,* Clarke, Irwin, 1968, *The Voice of the People* published separately, Book Society of Canada, 1968; *At My Heart's Core,* Peterborough Little Theatre, Ontario, 1950, published by Clarke, Irwin, 1952; *A Masque of Aesop,* Upper Canada College Theatre, Toronto, Ontario, 1952, published by Clarke, Irwin, 1952; *A Jig for the Gypsy,* Crest Theatre, Toronto, 1954, published by Clarke, Irwin, 1955.

Love and Libel Royal Alexandra Theatre, Toronto, 1960, then Martin Beck Theatre, New York City, 1960, published by Studio Duplicating Service, 1960; *A Masque of Mr. Punch,* Upper Canada College Theatre, Toronto, 1962, published by Oxford University Press, 1963; *King Phoenix,* Peterborough Little Theatre, Ontario, 1950, *Hunting Stuart,* Crest Theatre, Toronto, 1955, *General Confession,* all published under the title *Hunting Stuart and Other Plays,* New Press, 1972; *Question Time,* St. Lawrence Center Theatre, Toronto, 1975, published by Macmillan, 1975. Also, *Pontiac and the Green Man,* Macmillan Theatre, Toronto, 1977 (not published).

TELEPLAYS—*Brothers in the Black Art,* CBC, 1974; also *Fortune, My Foe.* RADIO PLAYS—*A Jig for the Gypsy.*

NON-FICTION—*Shakespeare's Boy Actors,* Dent, 1939, Russell, 1964; *Shakespeare for Young Players: A Junior Course,* Clarke, Irwin, 1942; *The Diary of Samuel Marchbanks,* Clarke, Irwin, 1947; *The Table Talk of Samuel Marchbanks,* Clarke, Irwin, 1949; (with Tyrone Guthrie and Grant Macdonald) *Renown at Stratford: A Record of the Shakespearean Festival in Canada,* Clarke, Irwin, 1953, 1971; (with Guthrie and Macdonald) *Twice Have the Trumpets Sounded: A Record of the Stratford Shakespearean Festival in Canada,* Clarke, Irwin, 1954; (with Guthrie, Boyd Neal, and Tanya Moiseiwitsch) *Thrice the Brinded Cat Hath Mew'd: A Record of the Stratford Shakespearean Festival in Canada,* Clarke, Irwin, 1955; *A Voice from the Attic,* Knopf, 1960, published in England as *The Personal Art: Reading to Good Purpose,* Secker and Warburg, 1961, reprinted by Darby Books, 1983; *Le Jeu de centenaire,* Commission du Centenaire, 1967; *Samuel Marchbanks' Almanack,* McClelland and Stewart, 1967; *The Heart of a Merry Christmas,* Macmillan, Toronto, 1970; *Stephen Leacock,* McClelland and Stewart, 1970.

Editor and author of introduction, *Feast of Stephen: An Anthology of Some of the Less Familiar Writings of Stephen Leacock,* McClelland & Stewart, 1970; (with Michael R. Booth, Richard Southern, Frederick Marker, and Lise-Lone Marker) *The Revels History of Drama in English, Volume VI: 1750-1880,* Methuen, 1975; *One Half of Robertson Davies: Provocative Pronouncements on a Wide Range of Topics,* Macmillan, Toronto, 1977, also published as *One Half of Robertson Davies,* Viking, 1978; *The Enthusiasms of Robertson Davies,* McClelland and Stewart, 1979; contributor, *Studies in Robertson Davies' Deptford Trilogy,* Robert G. Lawrence and Samuel L. Macey, editors, English Literary Studies, University of Victoria, 1980; *Robertson Davies, the Well-Tempered Critic: One Man's View of Theatre and Letters in Canada,* McClelland and Stewart, 1981; *The Mirror of Nature,* University of Toronto Press, 1983; *The Papers of Samuel Marchbanks* (includes portions of *The Diary of Samuel Marchbanks, The Table Talk of Samuel Marchbanks,* and *Samuel Marchbanks' Almanack),* Irwin Publishing, 1985.

FICTION—*Tempest-Tost,* Clarke, Irwin, 1951, Rinehart, 1952, Penguin, 1980, *Leaven of Malice,* Clarke, Irwin, 1954, Scribner, 1955, Penguin, 1980, *A Mixture of Frailties,* Macmillan, 1958,

Scribner, 1958, Penguin, 1980, also known collectively under the title, *The Salterton Trilogy; Fifth Business,* Macmillan, 1970, Viking, 1970, *The Manticore,* Macmillan, 1972, Viking, 1972, *World of Wonders,* Macmillan, Toronto, 1975, Viking, 1976, also known collectively under the ttitle, *The Deptford Trilogy; The Rebel Angels,* Macmillan, 1982, Viking, 1982; *High Spirits,* Penguin, 1982, Viking, 1983; *What's Bred in the Bone,* Macmillan, 1985, Viking, 1985, Penguin, 1986.

AWARDS: Companion of the Order of Canada, 1972; also: Louis Jouvet Prize for directing, Dominion Drama Festival, 1949; Stephen Leacock Medal for Humour, 1954, for *Leaven of Malice;* Lorne Pierce Medal, Royal Society of Canada, 1961; Governor General's Award for Fiction, 1973, for *The Manticore;* World Fantasy Award, 1984, for *High Spirits;* City of Toronto Book Award, 1986; Canadian Authors Association Literary Award for Fiction, 1986; Banff Centre School of Fine Arts National Award, 1986; Toronto Arts Awards: Lifetime Achievement Award, 1986; Canadian National Arts Club Medal, 1987.

Honorary degrees: LL.D. (Doctor of Laws), University of Alberta, 1957, Queen's University, 1962, University of Manitoba, 1972, University of Calgary, 1975, University of Toronto, 1981; D. Litt. (Doctor of Literature), McMaster University, 1959, University of Windsor, 1971, York University, 1973, Mount Allison University, 1973, Memorial University of Newfoundland, 1974, University of Western Ontario, 1974, McGill University, 1974, Trent University, 1974, University of Lethbridge, 1981, University of Waterloo, 1981, University of British Columbia, 1983, University of Santa Clara, 1985; D.C.L. (Doctor of Classical Literature), Bishop's University, 1967; D.Hum.Litt. (Doctor of Humane Letters), University of Rochester, 1983.

MEMBER: Authors Guild, Authors League of America, Dramatists Guild, Writers Union of Canada, P.E.N. International; Royal Society of Canada (fellow), 1967—, Royal Society of Literature (fellow), American Academy and Institute of Arts and Letters (honorary), 1980—; Balliol College, Oxford University (honorary fellow), 1986.

ADDRESSES: OFFICE—Massey College, University of Toronto, Four Devonshire Place, Toronto, Ontario, Canada M5S 2E1. AGENT—Curtis Brown Ltd., Ten Astor Place, New York, NY 10003.

*   *   *

DAVIS, Allen III   1929-

PERSONAL: Born March 9, 1929, in Cincinnati, OH; son of Allen, Jr. (a manufacturer) and Rose (Gershon) Davis. EDUCATION: Syracuse University, B.A., 1950; Yale School of Drama, M.F.A., 1956; studied acting with Paul Mann and Lloyd Richards, 1957-60. MILITARY: U.S. Marine Corps, 1951-53.

VOCATION: Writer, administrator, and teacher.

CAREER: PRINCIPAL STAGE WORK—Stage manager: Karamu House, Cleveland, OH, 1950-51, Cherry County Playhouse, Traverse City, MI, 1955, Northland Theatre, Southfield, MI, 1956; special arts coordinator, East New York Young Men's and Women's Hebrew Associations, Brooklyn, NY, 1961-63; executive director, North Shore Community Arts Center, Roslyn, NY, 1963-

64; administrator and general manager, Playhouse in the Park, Cincinnati, OH, 1966; general manager, Santa Fe Theatre Company, NM, 1967-68; writer-in-residence, University of Alaska, 1975; administrator, Puerto Rican Traveling Theatre, New York City, 1970-78, then director of playwrights workshop, 1980-86; member of board of directors for Theatre at St. Clements, 1980; treasurer, Literary Managers and Dramaturgs of America, Inc., 1985-86.

WRITINGS: PLAYS, PRODUCED—*Leroy and the Ark,* Brooklyn, NY, 1962; *Rocco, the Rolling Stone,* Playhouse in the Park, Cincinnati, OH, 1966; *The Head of Hair,* Milwaukee Repertory Theatre, WI, 1968, and New Theatre Workshop, New York City, 1970; *Where the Green Bananas Grow,* Herbert Berghof Studio Foundation, New York City, 1972; *The Rag Doll,* University of Texas at Austin, 1972, and New Dramatists, New York City, 1974; *Bull Fight Cow,* New Dramatists, 1976; *Montezuma's Revenge,* Theatre at St. Clements, New York City, 1978.

PLAYS, UNPRODUCED—"High Stakes" and "Song of a Consumptive Canary."

AWARDS: Yaddo Fellowship, 1965 and 1970; Helen Wurlitzer Foundation Fellowship, 1967 and 1968; MacDowell Colony Fellowship, 1969 and 1971; Ossabow Island Project Fellowship, 1973, National Endowment for the Arts, 1978; Creative Artists Public Service (CAPS) Grant, New York State, 1980; Ragdale Fellowship, 1982; Virginia Center for the Creative Arts Fellowship.

ALLEN DAVIS III

MEMBER: Dramatists Guild, Actors' Equity Association, New Dramatists (1968-78).

ADDRESSES: HOME—484 W. 43rd Street, Apt. 20F, New York, NY 10036.

* * *

DAVIS, Kevin   1945-

PERSONAL: Born January 9, 1945, in Milwaukee, WI; son of Emmett Matthew (a factory worker) and Mary Ruth (an office worker; maiden name, McCarten) Davis; married Karen Susanne Veley, November 9, 1963 (divorced, 1979); children: Christopher, Cameron. EDUCATION: University of Wisconsin, B.S., 1967; studied writing with Jerry McNeely and Robert McKee.

VOCATION: Actor and writer.

CAREER: STAGE DEBUT—Captain Bluntschli, *Arms and the Man,* Belfry Theatre, Williams Bay, WI, 1963. PRINCIPAL STAGE APPEARANCES—At the University of Wisconsin: Willie, *Wildcat Willie in the Doghouse,* soldier, *A Peacetime Episode,* president, *The Mouse That Roared,* in the chorus and dancer, *The King and I,* Jigger, *Carousel,* and Professor Hill, *The Music Man;* Pleusicles, *The Swaggering Soldier* and Biff, *Death of a Salesman,* both Belfry Theatre, Williams Bay, WI; in the chorus and dancer, *On a Clear Day You Can See Forever,* Long Beach Civic Light Opera; Phil, *Run-Through,* Pan-Andreas Theatre.

KEVIN DAVIS

PRINCIPAL FILM APPEARANCES—Gypsy blacksmith, *The Inner Man* IOTA Productions; draftsman, *Love Minus One,* Tempo Productions; John, *The Hoax.*

PRINCIPAL TELEVISION APPEARANCES—Episodic: *General Hospital,* ABC.

NON-RELATED CAREER—Computer salesman, International Buisness Machines, Madison, WI, 1967-69; computer analyst and programmer, Hughes Aircraft Company, Los Angeles, CA, 1969-75; president and owner, Davis Management Corporation, Los Angeles, CA, 1977—.

WRITINGS: SCREENPLAYS—*The Hoax,* 1972. TELEVISION—Episodic: *Owen Marshall, Counselor at Law,* ABC, 1974. PLAYS, PRODUCED—*Run Through,* Los Angeles, 1980. SCREENPLAYS, UNPRODUCED—The Jail, 1970; The Heirhunters, 1971; Great Adventure, 1973; Campus Town Rapist, 1975; Strangers in Blood, 1986.

MEMBER: Writers Guild of America, Screen Actors Guild, Actors Equity Association, American Federation of Television and Radio Artists; Mensa, Amnesty International, Century Park East Homeowners Association (president, board of directors).

ADDRESSES: HOME—Beverly Hills, CA. OFFICE—Davis Management Corporation, 2029 Century Park E., Suite 1110, Los Angeles, CA 90067. AGENT—c/o Ida Fischer, Emerald Artists, 6565 Sunset Blvd., Suite 525A, Los Angeles, CA 90028.

* * *

DAVIS, Sammy, Jr.   1925-

PERSONAL: Born December 8, 1925, in New York, NY; son of Sammy (an entertainer) and Elvira (an entertainer; maiden name, Sanchez) Davis; married Loray White, 1958 (divorced, 1959); married May Britt (an actress), November 13, 1960 (divorced, 1967); married Altovise Gore, May 11, 1970; children: (second marriage) Tracey, Mark, Jeff. MILITARY: U.S. Army, 1943-45.

VOCATION: Singer, dancer, actor, comedian, writer, and producer.

CAREER: STAGE DEBUT—In vaudeville with uncle and father as the Will Mastin Trio, 1930-48. BROADWAY DEBUT—Charley Welch, *Mr. Wonderful,* Broadway Theatre, 1956. LONDON DEBUT—*An Evening with Sammy Davis, Jr.,* Prince of Wales Theatre, 1961. PRINCIPAL STAGE APPEARANCES—In variety show, Olympia Theatre, Paris, 1964; Joe Wellington, *Golden Boy,* Majestic Theatre, New York City, 1964, Chicago Auditorium, and Palladium Theatre, London, 1968; one man show, *Sammy Davis. . .That's All,* Forrest Theatre, Philadelphia, 1966; *Sammy on Broadway!,* Uris Theatre, 1974; Littlechap, *Stop the World, I Want to Get Off,* New York State Theatre, Lincoln Center, New York City, 1978.

MAJOR TOURS—Toured in cabaret, 1966-67; European cities, 1967; South Vietnam, 1972.

PRINCIPAL CABARET APPEARANCES—Miller's Riviera, Fort Lee, NJ, 1949; performed with the Will Mastin Trio, El Rancho, Las Vegas, 1953; Ciro's, Hollywood, 1956; appearances in 1972 include: Variety show, Westbury Music Fair, Long Island, NY,

Alice Tully Hall, New York City, Elmwood Casino, Windsor, Ontario, Canada, Harrah's Lake Tahoe, NV; appearance at the White House, Washington, DC, 1973; Sands Hotel, Las Vegas, 1973; Kennedy Center Concert Hall, 1973; in concert at The Front Row, Cleveland, OH, 1974; Grosvenor House, London, 1974; Latin Casino, Phildelphia, 1975; Caesar's Palace, Las Vegas, 1975; the Palladium, London, 1976; also appeared at the Copacabana Club, New York City, Eden Rock Hotel and the Deauville Hotel, Miami Beach, also two Royal Variety Shows.

FILM DEBUT—*Rufus Jones for President*, 1928. PRINCIPAL FILM APPEARANCES—*The Benny Goodman Story*, 1956; *Anna Lucasta*, United Artists, 1958; *Porgy and Bess*, Columbia, 1959; *Oceans Eleven*, Warner Brothers, 1960; *Pepe*, Columbia, 1960; *Johnny Cool*, United Artists, 1963; *Convicts Four*, Allied Artists, 1963; *Robin and the Seven Hoods*, RKO, 1964; *Threepenny Opera*, Embassy, 1964; *A Man Called Adam*, Embassy, 1966; *Salt and Pepper*, United Artists, 1968; *Sweet Charity*, Universal, 1968; *One More Time*, United Artists, 1970; *The Pigeons*, Metro-Goldwyn-Mayer, 1970; *Save the Children*, Paramount, 1973; *The Cannonball Run*, Twentieth Century-Fox, 1981; *Cannonball Run II*, Warner Brothers, 1984.

PRINCIPAL TELEVISION APPEARANCES—Debut in 1950. Variety: Host, *Hollywood Palace*, ABC; *The Sammy Davis, Jr. Show*, NBC, 1966; host, *NBC Follies*, NBC, 1973; *G.E. Presents Sammy Davis, Jr.*, NBC, 1973; *Sammy and Company*, in syndication, 1975-77. Series: *Poor Devil*, 1973. Episodic: *The Mod Squad*, ABC; *The Name of the Game*, NBC; *The Rifleman*, ABC; *Laugh-In*, NBC; *The Lucy Show*, CBS; *I Dream of Jeannie*, NBC; *All in the Family*, CBS; *Wednesday Night Mystery Movie*, NBC; *Ben Casey*, ABC. Guest: *The Big Party*, CBS, 1959; *Ed Sullivan Show*, CBS; *The Jerry Lewis Show*, ABC, 1963; *The Nat King Cole Show*, in syndication; *The Tonight Show*, NBC.

PRINCIPAL TELEVISION WORK—Producer, *The Trackers*, ABC, 1971.

RELATED CAREER—Wrote, produced, and directed camp shows with the U.S. Army, Special Services.

WRITINGS: BOOKS—(Autobiographies) *Yes I Can*, 1965, and *Hollywood in a Suitcase*, 1980.

RECORDINGS: ALBUMS—*Hey There, What Kind of Fool Am I?*, *As Long as She Needs Me, At Town Hall, Porgy and Bess, Mr. Entertainment*, all with Decca Records; *Belts Best of Broadway, Shelter of Your Arms, The Sounds of '66, Sammy Davis, Jr., at the Cocoanut Grove*, all with Reprise Records. Also recording artist for Twentieth Century Records and Warner Records.

AWARDS: Special citation, 1974, for contribution to television entertainment, National Academy of Television Arts and Sciences.

MEMBER: Actors' Equity Association, Screen Actors Guild, American Guild of Variety Artists, American Federation of Television and Radio Artists, Negro Actors Guild; National Association for the Advancement of Colored People (co-chairman, Membership Drive, Los Angeles Chapter); appointed to National Advisory Council on Economic Opportunity, 1971, American Society of Magazine Photographers; Friars Club.

ADDRESSES: OFFICE—c/o Mecca Artists, 1650 Broadway, Suite 1410, New York, NY 10019.*

BRUCE DAVISON

DAVISON, Bruce   1946-

PERSONAL: Born June 28, 1946, in Philadelphia, PA; son of Clair W. (an architect and musician) and Marian E. (a secretary; maiden name, Holman) Davison. EDUCATION: Attended Pennsylvania State University; New York University, B.F.A.; trained for the stage at New York University School of the Arts with Ted Hoffman.

VOCATION: Actor and writer.

CAREER: STAGE DEBUT—Jonathan, *Oh Dad, Poor Dad, Mamma's Locked You in the Closet and I'm Feelin So Bad*, Pennsylvania Festival Theatre, 1966, for fifteen performances. BROADWAY DEBUT—Troilus, *Tiger at the Gate*, Vivian Beaumont Theatre, 1967, for fifty performances. PRINCIPAL STAGE APPEARANCES—*King Lear*, Lincoln Center, New York City, 1968; *A Home Away from Home*, Off-Broadway, 1969; *Streamers*, Westwood Playhouse, Los Angeles, 1978; *A Life in the Theatre*, Matrix Theatre, Los Angeles, 1980; John Merrick (title role), *The Elephant Man*, Booth Theatre, New York City, 1980; title role, *Sorrows of Stephen*, Old Globe Theatre, San Diego, CA, 1981; *The Front Page*, Long Wharf Theatre, New Haven, CT, 1982; Clarence, *Richard III*, New York Shakespeare Festival, Delacorte Theatre, New York City, 1984; the Son, *The Glass Menagerie*, Eugene O'Neill Theatre, New York City, 1984; *Caine Mutiny Court Martial*, Ahmanson Theatre, Los Angeles, 1984; *The Normal Heart*, Las Palmas Theatre, Los Angeles, 1986. Also appeared in *A Cry of Players*, Lincoln Center, New York City; *As You Like It*, Long Beach Shakespeare Festival, Long Beach, CA; *Little Foxes*, Westwood Playhouse, Los Angeles.

FILM DEBUT—*Last Summer,* Allied Artists, 1969. PRINCIPAL FILM APPEARANCES—*Strawberry Statement,* Metro-Goldwyn-Mayer (MGM), 1970; *Willard,* Cinerama, 1971; *Jerusalem File,* MGM, 1972; *Peege,* 1972; *Ulzana's Raid,* Universal, 1973; *Mame,* Warner Brothers, 1974; *Mother, Jugs & Speed,* Twentieth Century-Fox, 1975; *Short Eyes,* 1978; *Brass Target,* MGM, 1978; *High Risk,* Hemdale, 1981; *A Texas Legend,* Qui Productions, 1982; *Lies,* New World, 1983; *Crimes of Passion,* China Blue Productions, 1984; *Spies Like Us,* Warner Brothers, 1985; *Lady's Club,* 1986.

PRINCIPAL TELEVISION APPEARANCES—Series: Captain Ben Wyler, *Hunter,* NBC, 1984-86.

Movies: *Deadman's Curve,* CBS, 1978; *Summer of My German Soldier,* NBC, 1979; *The Lathe of Heaven,* PBS, 1980; *Mind Over Murder,* 1980; *Tomorrow's Child,* 1982; *The Gathering, Parts I and II,* 1982; *Incident at Crestridge,* 1982; *Ghost Dancing,* ABC, 1983. Also appeared in *The Wave,* ABC.

Episodic: *Amazing Stories,* NBC, 1985; *Alfred Hitchcock Presents,* NBC, 1985. Pilots: *The Astronauts,* CBS. Teleplays: *Mourning Becomes Electra,* PBS; *Taming of the Shrew,* 1983.

WRITINGS: SCREENPLAYS—*Retreat.*

AWARDS: Los Angeles Drama Critics Award, 1978, for *Streamers;* New York Dramalogue Award, 1980, for *The Elephant Man;* Los Angeles Drama Critics Award and Los Angeles Dramalogue Award, both 1986, for *The Normal Heart;* Golden Scroll Award, for *The Lathe of Heaven.*

MEMBER: Actors' Equity Association, Screen Actors Guild, American Federation of Television and Radio Artists, Actors Institute.

ADDRESSES: AGENT—Oppenheim, Appel, Dixon, Inc., 2029 Century Park East, Los Angeles, CA 90067. PUBLICIST—Nanci Ryder Public Relations, 8380 Melrose Avenue, Suite 310A, Los Angeles, CA 90069.

*   *   *

DAWBER, Pam   1954-

PERSONAL: Born October 18, 1954, in Detroit, MI; daughter of Eugene E. (a commercial artist) and Thelma M. (Fisher) Dawber. EDUCATION: Attended Oakland Community College, Farmington Hills, MI, for one year; studied voice with Jack Woltzer and Nate Lam in Los Angeles, and with Pappy Earnhart in New York City.

VOCATION: Actress.

CAREER: STAGE DEBUT—Jennie, *Sweet Adeline,* Goodspeed Opera House, East Haddam, CT, 1977. BROADWAY DEBUT—Mabel, *Pirates of Penzance,* Minskoff Theatre, 1982. PRINCIPAL STAGE APPEARANCES—Eliza, *My Fair Lady,* Kenley Theatre, OH, 1980; Mabel, *Pirates of Penzance,* Ahmanson Theatre, Los Angeles, 1981.

MAJOR TOURS—Eliza Doolittle, *My Fair Lady,* Kenley Theatres, Columbus, Dayton, and Akron, OH, 1980; Marion, *The Music Man,* St. Louis, MO, Indianapolis, IN, and Dallas, 1984.

PAM DAWBER

FILM DEBUT—Tracy, *A Wedding,* 1977.

TELEVISION DEBUT—Mindy Beth McConnell, *Mork & Mindy,* ABC, 1978-82. PRINCIPAL TELEVISION APPEARANCES—Series: Samantha Russell, *My Sister Sam,* CBS, 1986. Movies: *The Girl, the Gold Watch and Everything,* 1980; *Remembrance of Love,* 1982; *Through Naked Eyes,* ABC, 1983; *Voyeurs,* 1983; *Last of the Great Survivors,* CBS, 1984; *This Wife for Hire,* ABC, 1985; *Wild Horses,* CBS, 1985; *American Geisha,* CBS, 1986. Specials: *Texaco Star Theatre: Salute to the American Musical,* NBC, 1982; *Tony Award Show,* 1982; *Parade of Stars,* 1983; *Candid Camera: The First 40 Years,* CBS, 1987. Episodic: "The Little Mermaid," *Faerie Tale Theatre,* Showtime Cable Television, 1985.

RELATED CAREER—Former model; teacher of television commercial class, Wilhemina Modeling Agency, 1977-78; founder and president, Pony Productions.

AWARDS: People's Choice Award, Favorite Newcomer, and *Photoplay* Award, Favorite Actress in a New Series, both 1978, for *Mork and Mindy.*

MEMBER: Actors' Equity Association, Screen Actors Guild, American Federation of Television and Radio Artists; Solar Lobby, Washington, DC (board of directors).

SIDELIGHTS: RECREATIONS—Canoeing, cooking, horseback riding, reading, listening to classical music and swimming.

ADDRESSES: HOME—Los Angeles and New York. OFFICE—Pony Productions, 4000 Warner Blvd., Producers Building 4,

Room 1, Burbank, CA 91522. MANAGER—Mimi Weber, 9738 Arby Drive, Beverly Hills, CA 90210. PUBLICIST—Rogers and Cowen, 10000 Santa Monica Blvd., Los Angeles, CA 90067.

* * *

DEACON, Brian 1949-

PERSONAL: Born February 13, 1949, in Oxford, England; son of Robert Thomas and Eileen Mary (a nurse; maiden name, Maher) Deacon; married Rula Lenska (an actress) April 6, 1977 (divorced, 1982); children: Cara Elizabeth. EDUCATION: Studied acting and stage fighting at the Webber Douglas Academy of Dramatic Art, London.

VOCATION: Actor.

CAREER: STAGE DEBUT—John, *The Lion in Winter*, Belgrade Theatre, Coventry, U.K. PRINCIPAL STAGE APPEARANCES— Glendenning, *The Contractor*, Troilus, *Troilus and Cressida*, Dauphin, *Saint Joan*, and Roland Maule, *Present Laughter*, all at the Belgrade Theatre, Coventry. With the Bristol Old Vic: Mellefont, *The Double Dealer*, Lucentio, *The Taming of the Shrew*, Crow, *The Tooth of Crime*, Len, *Early Morning*, and the son, *London Assurance*.

Various roles, *A Bunch of Fives, Coal,* and *Fanny*, all at the Soho Poly Theatre, London; Young Marlow, *She Stoops to Conquer*, Mercury Theatre, U.K.; Hotspur, *Henry IV, Part I*, Redgrave Theatre, U.K.; Guildenstern, *Hamlet*, Guildenstern, *Rosencrantz and Guildenstern Are Dead*, and Jerry, *The Zoo Story*, all with the

BRIAN DEACON

New Shakespeare Company, U.K.; the son, *Shay*, Lyceum Theatre, Edinburgh; Bassanio, *The Merchant of Venice*, Leeds Playhouse, U.K.; Edmund, *King Lear* and *As You Like It*, both at the Northcott Theatre, Exeter, Ludlow Festival, U.K.; the son, *Curse of the Starving Class*, Royal Court Theatre, London; Otavius, *Anthony and Cleopatra*, Young Vic Theatre, London; Bluntschli, *Arms and the Man*, Regents Park Open Air Theatre, London.

MAJOR TOURS—Bernard and Bob, *Great and Small*, Triumph Tour with the W.E. Vaudeville Theatre.

FILM DEBUT—Gunner Barton, *The Triple Echo*, Altura Films, 1973. PRINCIPAL FILM APPEARANCES—Title role, *Jesus, His Life and Times*, Warner Brothers, 1979; *Vampires; Il Bacio;* Oswald, *A Zed and Two Noughts.*

TELEVISION DEBUT—*The Guardians*, LWT. PRINCIPAL TELEVISION APPEARANCES—Title role, *Love and Mr. Lewisham*, BBC; *Thirty Minute Theatre*, BBC; *Churchill's People*, BBC; *The Feathered Serpent*, Thames TV; *Country Dance*, HTV; *Good Girl*, YTV; Oswald, *Ghosts*, YTV; *The Emmigrants*, BBC; *Centre Play-Risking It*, BBC; *Leap in the Dark*, BBC; Frank Miles, *Lillie*, LWT; *Shock of the New*, BBC; Somerset and Oxford, *Henry VI*, Parts I,II, and III, BBC; Henry Richmond, *Richard III*, BBC; Charles, *Separate Tables*, HBO Cable Films; David, *The Rewards of Virtue*, Channel 4; Alan Woodcourt, *Bleak House*, BBC; Clive Grey, *Mr. Palfrey of Westminster*, Thames TV; Alex, *Inappropriate Behaviour*, BBC; Alan and Martin Yardly, *Hammer Horror: And the Wall Came Tumbling Down.*

AWARDS: Best Performance by a Drama Student, Rodney Millington Gold Award; Best Newcomer, Bronze Award, Teramo Film Festival, for *The Triple Echo.*

ADDRESSES: AGENT—Kate Feast Management, 43A Princess Road, Regents Park, London N.W.1, England.

* * *

DEBUSKEY, Merle 1923-

PERSONAL: Full name, Basil Merle Debuskey; born March 24, 1923, in Baltimore, MD; son of Robert M. (an insurance broker) and Freda B. (Blaustein) Debuskey. EDUCATION: Attended University of Virginia, 1940-43; Johns Hopkins University, B.A., English literature, 1947; attended the New School for Social Research, public relations, 1948. MILITARY: Lieutenant, U.S. Navy, 1941-46.

VOCATION: Press representative.

CAREER: FIRST STAGE WORK—Joined a cooperative theatre company, the Interplayers, in New York City, which presented four plays at the Provincetown Playhouse, 1948. PRINCIPAL STAGE WORK—Member of Off-Broadway, Inc., which presented *Yes Is for a Very Young Man* and *The Bourgeois Gentleman*, Cherry Lane Theatre, New York City, 1949; apprentice press representative, *Regina*, 46th Street Theatre, New York City, 1949; served as apprentice press representative for three years in New York City; press representative for Theatre-by-the-Sea, Matunuck, RI, 1950-52.

Press representative for the following Broadway and Off-Broadway productions: *The Rose Tattoo, Falhooley, Buy Me a Blue*

Ribbon, Paint Your Wagon, all 1951; *One Bright Day, Shuffle Along,* both 1952; *The World of Sholom Aleichem, The Crucible,* both 1953; *Abie's Irish Rose, Mrs. Patterson, Anastasia, Trouble-makers, The Saint of Bleecker Street,* all 1954; *Plain and Fancy, A View from the Bridge, The Diary of Anne Frank, Inherit the Wind,* all 1955; *Tevya and His Daughters, Look Homeward Angel,* both 1957; *The Trial of Dmitri Karamazov, Cloud 7, Chapparral, Curtains Up,* all 1958; *A Raisin in the Sun, Mistress and Maidens, Summer of the Seventeenth Doll, Marching Song,* all 1959.

Continuing Broadway and Off-Broadway: *Semi-Detached, The Wall, The Good Soup,* all 1960; *How to Succeed in Business without Really Trying, Come Blow Your Horn, There Is a Play Tonight,* all 1961; *Little Me, The Portrait of the Artist as a Young Man, The Barroom Monks, The Pinter Plays,* all 1962; *To the Water Tower, Nobody Loves an Albatross, Cafe Crown, Antony and Cleopatra, On an Open Roof, The Heroine, The Riot Act, Semi-Detached,* all 1963; *Traveller without Luggage, Absence of a Cello, The Sign in Sidney Brustein's Window, The Owl and the Pussycat, Bajour, Peterpat, And Things That Go Bump in the Night, A View from the Bridge, New Cambridge Circus, The Decline and Fall of the Entire World as Seen Through the Eyes of Cole Porter Revisited, From The Second City, How to Succeed in Business without Really Trying, A Sign of Affection,* all 1964; *The Royal Hunt of the Sun, The Zulu and the Zayda, Skyscraper, The White Devil, New Cole Porter Revue, Phedre, Six from La Mama, The Return of the Second City in '20,000 Frozen Grenadiers,' The Butterfly Dream,* all 1965.

Broadway and Off-Broadway: *The Investigation, Walking Happy, Hallelujah Baby, Eh?, Drums in the Night, Man of La Mancha, What Do You Really Know About Your Husband,* all 1966; *The Ninety-Day Mistress, Before You Go, Portrait of a Queen, A Midsummer Night's Dream, Hair, Iphigenia in Aulis,* all 1967; *Lovers and Other Strangers, Morning Noon and Night, The Good-bye People, But Seriously, Does a Tiger Wear a Necktie?, Come Summer, Trumpets of the Lord, A Moon for the Misbegotten, Little Murders, Philosophy in the Boudoir, No Place to Be Somebody,* all 1968; *Love Is a Time of Day, No Place to Be Somebody, Purlie, Man of La Mancha, From the Second City, Seven Days of Mourn-ing, The White House Murder Case, Billy Noname, Chicago 70,* all 1969; *No No Nanette, Boesman and Lena, House of Blue Leaves,* all 1970.

Broadway and Off-Broadway: *Jesus Christ Superstar, Ain't Sup-posed to Die a Natural Death, Unlikely Heroes, Two Gentlemen of Verona, Sticks and Bones, The Last Analysis, F. Jasmine Addams,* all 1971; *Much Ado About Nothing, Mourning Becomes Electra, Medea, Here Are the Ladies,* all 1972; *Uncle Vanya, The Waltz of the Toreadors, The Good Doctor, The Iceman Cometh, Thieves, An American Millionaire, Scapino,* all 1973; *The National Health, Where's Charley?, Shenandoah, Hughie, Duet, All God's Chillun Got Wings,* all 1974; *Death of a Salesman, Ah!, Wilderness, A Chorus Line, The Leaf People, The Glass Menagerie, The Poison Tree, Songs of the Street, The Lady from the Sea,* all 1975.

Broadway and Off-Broadway: *Pal Joey, Days in the Trees, King, Sly Fox, The Night of the Iguana, The Trip Back Down, Romeo and Juliet, The Club,* all 1976; *The Importance of Being Earnest, Tartuffe, Miss Margarida's Way, The Act, The Merchant, Saint Joan, The Water Engine, Mr. Happiness, 13 Rue de L'Amour, Dancin', Angel, Runaways,* 1977; *The Inspector General, Once in a Lifetime, Ballroom, Man and Superman, Spokesong or The Common Wheel, Zoot Suit, Bosoms and Neglect, Oh Kay!,* all 1978; *Loose Ends, Comin' Uptown, Charlotte, Major Barbara, Past Tense,* all 1979.

Also Broadway and Off-Broadway: *The Man Who Came To Dinner, The Bacchae, Tricks of the Trade, Amadeus, John Gabriel Borkman, Frankenstein, Woman of the Year, The Father,* all 1980; *Scenes and Revelations, Candida, Dreamgirls, Macbeth, The World of Sholom Aleichem, Eminent Domain, The Little Prince and the Aviator,* all 1981; *Present Laughter, The Queen and the Rebels, 84 Charing Cross Road, Plenty, The Misanthrope, The Caine Mutiny Court-Martial,* all 1982; *Ben Kingsley as Edmund Kean, La Tragedie de Carmen, Heartbreak House, The Rink, Awake and Sing!, The Human Comedy, Play Memory,* all 1983; *Design for Living, Accidental Death of an Anarchist, The Loves of Anatol, Arms and the Man, Danny and the Deep Blue Sea,* all 1984; *The Marriage of Figaro, Arms and the Man,* both 1985; *The Boys in Autumn, The Flying Karamazov Brothers, Terrors of Pleasure, Swimming to Cambodia, Sex and Death to the Age 14, The Front Page, You Never Can Tell, Transposed Heads, House of Blue Leaves, The Caretaker, Prairie du Chien, The Shawl,* all 1986.

As press representative for the New York Shakespeare Festival: *As You Like It,* 1957; *Richard III, Othello,* 1958; *Julius Caesar,* 1959; *Henry V, Measure for Measure, The Taming of the Shrew,* 1960; *King Lear, The Tempest, The Merchant of Venice,* 1962; *Hamlet, Othello, Electra, A Midsummer Night's Dream,* 1964; *Love's Labour's Lost, Coriolanus, Troilus and Cressida, Henry V, The Taming of the Shrew,* 1965; *All's Well That Ends Well, Measure for Measure, Potluck!, Richard III, Macbeth,* 1966; *Hamlet, Ergo, The Memorandum, The Comedy of Errors, King John, Titus Andronicus, Volpone,* 1967; *Huui Huui, Cities in Bezique, Invita-tion to a Beheading, Henry IV, Parts I and II, Hamlet, Romeo and Juliet,* 1968; *Stomp, Mod Donna, Sambo, Peer Gynt, Twelfth Night, Electra,* 1969.

Continuing for the New York Shakespeare Festival: *The Happiness Cage, MacGowran in the Works of Beckett, Trelawny of the Wells, Subject to Fits, Slag, Here Are Ladies, Blood, Candide, The Basic Training of Pavlo Hummel, Richard III, Sambo,* 1970; *Dance Wi' Me, Nigger Nightmare, The Black Terror, The Wedding of Iphigenia and Iphigenia in Concert, Black Visions, That Championship Season, Older People, The Hunter, Timon of Athens, Cymbeline,* 1971; *The Children, The Cherry Orchard, Siamese Connections, The Orphan, Hamlet, Ti-Jean and his Brothers, Much Ado About Nothing,* 1972; *In the Boom Boom Room, Troilus and Cressida, The Au Pair Man, The Tempest, What the Wine-Sellers Buy, The Dance of Death, Macbeth, Short Eyes, Lotta, or the Best Thing Evolution's Ever Come Up With, More Than You Deserve, Les Femmes Noires, Barbary Shore, The Emperor of Late Night Radio, The Killdeer, As You Like It, King Lear,* 1973; *Richard III, Mert and Phil, Black Picture Show, A Midsummer Night's Dream, A Doll's House, The Taking of Miss Janie, Little Black Sheep, Naked Lunch, The Measure Taken, Where Do We Go from Here?, Sweet Talk, The Last Days of British Honduras, The Sea Gull, Our Late Night, Kid Champion, Fishing, Time Trial, Ghosts, A Chorus Line, Pericles, The Merry Wives of Windsor, Miss Moffat,* 1974; *Trelawny of the Wells, Hamlet, The Shortchanged Review, Mrs. Warren's Profession, Streamers, The Threepenny Opera, So Nice They Named It Twice, Rich and Famous, The Comedy of Errors,* 1975.

Also for the Festival: *The Cherry Orchard, Agamemnon, For Colored Girls Who Have Considered Suicide When the Rainbow Is Enuf, Rebel Women, Marco Polo Sings a Solo, Ashes, Museum, Hagar's Children, On the Lock-In, The Stronger, Creditors, Streamers, Henry V, Measure for Measure,* 1976; *The Cherry Orchard, The Misanthrope, Landscape of the Body, Tales of Hasidim, The Mandrake, Where the Mississippi Meets the Amazon, The Dybbuk, A Photograph: A Study of Cruelty, A Prayer for My*

Daughter, Curse of the Starving Class, Unfinished Women, 1977; *Sganarelle, Wings, I'm Getting My Act Together and Taking It on the Road, Springs Awakening, Drinks Before Dinner, Fathers and Sons, Wonderland in Concert, Julius Caesar, New Jerusalem, The Umbrellas of Cherbourg, Taken in Marriage, Coriolanus, Sancocho, Leave It to Beaver Is Dead, Nasty Rumors and Final Remarks, Dispatches, Remembrance, Wake Up It's Time to Go to Bed, The Woods, All's Well That Ends Well, The Taming of the Shrew,* 1978; *Happy Days, Spell Number Seven, Poets from the Inside, Mercier & Camier, Sorrows of Stephen, Tongues with Savage/Love, The Art of Dining, Hard Sell, Salt Lake City Skyline, Marie and Bruce, The Haggadah: A Passover Cantata, The Music Lessons, Sunday Runners in the Rain, Mother Courage and Her Children, Coriolanus, The Mighty Gents,* 1979.

Also: *The Pirates of Penzance, Long Day's Journey into Night, F.O.B. (Fresh Off the Boat), Girls Girls Girls, The Sea Gull, Dead End Kids, Alice in Concert, True West, Penquin Touquet, Mary Stuart, Texts, Il Campiello: A Venetian Comedy, Waiting for Godot, A Midsummer Night's Dream,* 1980; *How It All Began, The Dance and the Railroad, The Laundry Hour, Dexter Creed, Family Devotions, Specimen Days, Twelve Dreams, Zastrozzi, Lullabye and Goodnight, The Haggadah, Three Acts of Recognition, Goose and Tomtom, The Tempest, Henry IV, Part I,* 1981; *The Comedy of Errors, The Death of von Richthofen as Witnessed from Earth, Uncle Vanya, Hamlet, Necessary Ends, Top Girls, Company, Cold Harbor, Hajj, Egyptology, Buried Inside Extra, Fen, A Midsummer Night's Dream,* 1982; *Goodnight Ladies!, Funhouse, Emmett: A One Mormon Show, My Uncle Sam, Sound & Beauty, A Private View, Samuel Beckett's Company, Lenny and the Heartbreakers, Serenading Louie, Cinders, Pieces of 8, Found a Peanut, Ice Bridge, The Nest of the Wood Grouse, Richard III, Non Pasquale,* 1983; *Through the Leaves, The Ballad of Soapy Smith, La Boheme, Coming of Age in Soho, Tom and Viv, Virginia, Salonika, The Normal Heart, The Marriage of Bette and Boo, Rat in the Skull, Henry V, The Golem,* 1984.

For the Meadow Brook Theatre, Rochester, MI: *The Caucasian Chalk Circle, Love's Labour's Lost, You Never Can Tell, The Imperial Nightingale, The Waltz of the Toreadors,* and *The Three Sisters,* all 1966, and *The Importance of Being Earnest, John Gabriel Borkman, Charley's Aunt, And People All Around, King Lear, No Exit, The Firebugs, The Sea Gull,* all 1967.

Was press representative for *Romance* and *Meeting the Bike Rider* for the Young Playwrights Festival, New York City, 1983.

MAJOR TOURS—Press representative: *A Certain Joy,* 1953; *Maiden Voyage,* 1957; *One for the Dame,* 1960; *How to Succeed in Business without Really Trying,* 1963; *Man of La Mancha,* 1968; two companies, *A Chorus Line,* 1975-82; *For Colored Girls Who Have Considered Suicide When the Rainbow Is Enuf,* 1977; *Shenandoah,* 1977; *Sly Fox,* 1977; *The Club,* 1977; *Dancin',* 1978-79; *Dreamgirls,* 1982-83.

PRINCIPAL FILM WORK—Press representative: *Rome 11 O'Clock,* 1953; *Justice Is Done,* 1953; *We Are All Murderers,* 1957; *The Crucible,* 1958; *Orders to Kill,* 1958; *Spartacus,* 1960; *A Midsummer Night's Dream,* 1962.

PRINCIPAL TELEVISION WORK—Press representative for many Antoinette Perry Award broadcasts and for *Night of 100 Stars, II.*

NON-RELATED CAREER—Worked as a sports reporter, on a

bottling line at a whiskey distillery, as an office cleaner, and as a catcher on a paper box cutting press.

AWARDS: Five combat stars and a citation for valor from the U.S. Navy, 1946.

MEMBER: Association of Theatrical Press Agents and Managers (president, 1967—); Actors Fund of America (board of directors), the Eliot Feld Ballet (board of directors).

ADDRESSES: HOME—411 West End Avenue, New York, NY 10024.

*　　*　　*

De FORE, Don   1919-

PERSONAL: Born August 25, 1919, in Cedar Rapids, IA; son of Joseph E. (a locomotive engineer) and Albia (Nezerka) De Fore; married Marion Holmes (a singer), February 14, 1942; children: Penny, David, Dawn, Ronald, Amy. EDUCATION: Attended University of Iowa; trained for the stage at the Pasadena Playhouse, 1934-37. MILITARY: U.S. Army.

VOCATION: Actor.

CAREER: STAGE DEBUT—In church plays, Cedar Rapids, IA. BROADWAY DEBUT—Rennie, *Where Do We Go from Here?,* Vanderbilt Theatre, 1938. PRINCIPAL STAGE APPEARANCES—

DON De FORE

Rennie, *Where Do We Go from Here?*, New Hampshire Playhouse, Hollywood, during the 1930s; *Railroads on Parade*, New York World's Fair Theatre, 1939; Hunky, *Steel*, Provincetown Playhouse, New York City, 1939; Wally Myers, *The Male Animal*, Cort Theatre, New York City, 1940; Mike O'Connor, *Judy O'Connor*, Shubert Theatre, New Haven, CT, 1946; *Claudia*, La Jolla Summer Theatre, CA, 1950; title role, *Mike McCauley*, Lobero Theatre, Santa Barbara, CA, and later Harris Theatre, Chicago, 1951; Clark Redfield and a Mexican, *Dream Girl*, City Center, New York City, 1951; *Susan Slept Here*, New England, 1964; *Never Too Late*, Pheasant Run Playhouse Theatre, St. Charles, IL, 1965; *Generation*, San Diego, and Pheasant Run Theatre, St. Charles, 1967; *Any Wednesday*, Dallas, 1969; *Never Too Late*, Jacksonville, FL, 1970; *Light Up the Sky*, 1971.

MAJOR TOURS—Wally Myers, *The Male Animal*, U.S. cities, 1940; solo performances, Viet Nam theatre of operations, United Service Organization, 1966; *Any Wednesday*, U.S. cites, 1972; *The Subject Was Roses*, Florida and Texas cities, 1973-74.

FILM DEBUT—*Kid Galahad*, Warner Brothers, 1937. PRINCIPAL FILM APPEARANCES—*Submarine D-1*, Warner Brothers, 1937; *We Go Fast*, Twentieth Century-Fox, 1941; *The Male Animal*, Warner Brothers, 1942; *A Girl in Every Port*, RKO, 1942; *City without Men*, Columbia, 1943; *The Human Comedy*, Metro-Goldwyn-Mayer (MGM), 1943; *A Guy Named Joe*, MGM, 1943; *Thirty Seconds Over Tokyo*, MGM, 1944; *The Affairs of Susan*, Paramount, 1945; *You Came Along*, Paramount, 1945; *The Stork Club*, Paramount, 1945; *Without Reservations*, RKO, 1946; *Ramrod*, United Artists, 1947; *It Happened on Fifth Avenue*, Allied Artists, 1947; *Romance on the High Seas*, Warner Brothers, 1948; *One Sunday Afternoon*, Warner Brothers, 1948; *My Friend Irma*, Paramount, 1949.

Too Late for Tears, United Artists, 1949; *Southside 1-1000*, Allied Artists, 1950; *Dark City*, Paramount, 1950; *The Guy Who Came Back*, Twentieth Century-Fox, 1951; *No Room for the Groom*, Universal, 1952; *She's Working Her Way Through College*, Warner Brothers, 1952; *Jumping Jacks*, Paramount, 1952; *Susan Slept Here*, RKO, 1954; *Battle Hymn*, Universal, 1956; *A Time to Love and a Time to Die*, Universal, 1958; *Facts of Life*, United Artists, 1960.

PRINCIPAL TELEVISION APPEARANCES—Series: Thorny Thornberry, *The Adventures of Ozzie and Harriet*, ABC, 1952-58; George Baxter, *Hazel*, NBC, 1961-65. Episodic: *Lux Video Theatre*, NBC; *Philco Television Playhouse*, NBC; *Goodyear Playhouse*, NBC; *My Three Sons*, ABC, 1968; *Mod Squad*, ABC, 1969; *Mannix*, CBS, 1970; *Men of Shiloh*, 1970; *Murder, She Wrote*, CBS; Harry Kline, *St. Elsewhere*, NBC. Dramatic specials: "A Punt, a Pass, and a Prayer," *Hallmark Theatre*, NBC, 1968. Guest: *What's My Line*, CBS, 1969; *All-American College Show*, 1969. Pilot: *Home Team*, 1960.

NON-RELATED CAREER—Owner, Don Defore's Silver Banjo Restaurant, Disneyland, CA, 1957.

WRITINGS: BOOKS—*With All My Love, Penny*, 1965; (autobiography) *Hollywood De Fore 'N After*.

AWARDS: Honorary Mayor of Brentwood, CA, 1967; honorary degrees: Saint Mary of the Plains College, Dodge City, KS, doctor of human letters, 1982.

MEMBER: Actors' Equity Association, Screen Actors Guild, American Federation of Television and Radio Artists, National Academy of Television Arts and Sciences (president, 1954-56); Advisory Committee on California Rehabilitation, 1970; Peace Corps (National Advisory Board, 1981-83).

SIDELIGHTS: De Fore told *CTFT* that he was a special delegate to the Moscow Film Festival in 1969, and in 1980, he and his wife were asked by President Reagan to serve on a goodwill Ambassadorial delegation to the Kingdom of Swaziland during that country's diamond jubilee celebration.

ADDRESSES: HOME—Los Angeles, CA.

*   *   *

de la ROCHE, Elisa   1949-

PERSONAL: Born Elizabeth Paula Morgan, May 28, 1949, in New York, NY; daughter of Sava Tarkanovskia (an artist and professor); married Con Roche (an actor), 1972 (divorced, 1982); children: Theseus, Alexander. EDUCATION: University of Wisconsin, B.A.; Columbia University, M.A.; currently working toward Ph.D., New York University; trained for the stage at the Herbert Berghof Studio.

VOCATION: Actress.

CAREER: OFF-BROADWAY DEBUT—Hembra, *Yerma*, Green-

ELISA de la ROCHE

wich Mews Theatre, 1971, for over one hundred performances. PRINCIPAL STAGE APPEARANCES—Adela, *House of Bernarda Alba,* INTAR Theatre, New York City, 1977; Anita, *Deli's Fable,* Playhouse 46, New York City, 1978; Mina, *D.K.,* Puerto Rican Travelling Theatre, New York City, 1983.

MAJOR TOURS—*Last One in Is a Rotten Egg,* New York City Public Schools, 1979-80; title role, *Dona Francisquita,* Miami, Washington, DC, and Grammercy Arts Theatre, New York City, 1983-84.

PRINCIPAL TELEVSION APPEARANCES—Episodic: *One Life to Live,* ABC, 1980; Nurse, *Bill Cosby Show,* NBC, 1985.

RELATED CAREER—Artist in residence: New York Foundation for the Arts, 1979-86; Committee for Young Audiences, New York City, 1977-86; adjunct lecturer, Brooklyn College, 1984-86.

MEMBER: Actors' Equity Association, Screen Actors Guild, American Federation of Television and Radio Artists.

ADDRESSES: HOME—New York, NY.

*   *   *

DELOY, George   1953-

PERSONAL: Born Jorge Del Hoyo, November 23, 1953, in Canelones, Uruguay; son of Juan Angel (a machinist) and Maria Lerida (Fernandez) Del Hoyo; married Deborah Sue May (an actress), August 27, 1983; children: Alexandra May. EDUCATION: Attended the University of Utah; trained for the stage with Michael Shurtleff and Laura Rose, and studied voice with Gwen Omeron and David Craig.

VOCATION: Actor.

CAREER: OFF-BROADWAY DEBUT—Pepe Hernandez, *El Grande de Coca-Cola,* Plaza 9 Theatre, 1975, for one-hundred- fifty performances. PRINCIPAL STAGE APPEARANCES—Jamie Lockhart, *The Robber Bridegroom,* Biltmore Theatre, New York City, 1976; Cleante, *The Imaginary Invalid,* Cincinnati Playhouse, OH, 1977; Orlando, *As You Like It,* Old Globe Theatre, San Diego, CA, 1982; Dennis, *Loot,* American Conservatory Theatre (ACT), San Francisco, 1983; Deeley, *Old Times,* ACT, San Francisco, 1984; Demetrius, *A Midsummer Night's Dream* and Fred Ritter, *The Torch-Bearers,* both Old Globe Theatre, San Diego, 1985; Henry, *The Real Thing,* Seattle Repertory Theatre, WA, 1986; Eilert Lovberg, *Hedda Gabler,* Mark Taper Forum, Los Angeles, 1986.

MAJOR TOURS—Jamie Lockhart, *The Robber Bridegroom,* U.S. and Canadian cities, 1978.

TELEVISION DEBUT—*Quincy, M.E.,* NBC, 1978. PRINCIPAL TELEVISION APPEARANCES—Series: Rosetti, *Star of the Family,* ABC, 1982; Michael, *9 to 5,* ABC, 1983; Ken Valere, *St. Elsewhere,* NBC, 1985-86; Carlos Mariono, *Hunter,* NBC, 1986; Orpheus, *Days of Our Lives,* NBC, 1986—. Movies: *The Secret War of Jackie's Girls,* NBC, 1979; Gilbert Kent, *The Seekers,* 1979. Episodic: *Battlestar Gallactica,* ABC, 1980; Peter, "Downhill to Death," *Hart to Hart,* ABC, 1980; *Quincy, M.E.,* NBC, 1981. Pilots: Tony, *One Night Band,* CBS, 1981; Sal, *Family Business,* ABC, 1983.

GEORGE DELOY

MEMBER: Actors' Equity Association, American Federation of Television and Radio Artists, Screen Actors Guild; Big Brothers of Greater Los Angeles (1978-83); Hospice Volunteer Program of Los Angeles (1983-87).

ADDRESSES: AGENT—Bauman, Hiller, and Strain, 9220 Sunset Blvd., Los Angeles, CA 90069 and 250 W. 57th Street, New York, NY 10019. MANAGER—Financial Management International, 9200 Sunset Blvd., Suite 831, Los Angeles, CA 90069.

*   *   *

DENCH, Judi   1934-

PERSONAL: Full name, Judith Olivia Dench; born December 9, 1934, in York, England; daughter of Reginald Arthur and Eleanora Olave (Jones) Dench; married Michael Williams, 1971. EDUCATION: Attended the Mount School, York; trained for the stage at the Central School of Speech Training and Dramatic Art.

VOCATION: Actress.

CAREER: STAGE DEBUT—Ophelia, *Hamlet,* for the Old Vic Company, Royal Court Theatre, Liverpool, England, 1957. LONDON DEBUT—Ophelia, *Hamlet,* Old Vic Theatre, 1957. BROADWAY DEBUT—Katherine, *Henry V,* with the Old Vic Company, 1958. PRINCIPAL STAGE APPEARANCES—Juliet, *Measure for Measure,* First Fairy, *A Midsummer Night's Dream,* 1957, Maria, *Twelfth Night,* Katherine, *Henry V,* 1958, Phebe, *As You Like It,*

Cynthia, *The Double Dealer*, Cecily Cardew, *The Importance of Being Earnest*, Anne Page, *The Merry Wives of Windsor*, 1959, Katherine, *Henry V*, Juliet, *Romeo and Juliet*, Kate Hardcastle, *She Stoops to Conquer*, Hermia, *A Midsummer Night's Dream*, 1960, all with Old Vic Company, London; Anya, *The Cherry Orchard*, with the Royal Shakespeare Company, Aldwych Theatre, London, 1961; Isabella, *Measure for Measure*, and Titania, *A Midsummer Night's Dream*, with Royal Shakespeare Company, Stratford-Upon-Avon, U.K., 1962; Dorcas Bellboys, *A Penny for a Song*, Aldwych Theatre, London, 1962; Lady Macbeth, *Macbeth*, Nottingham Playhouse, U.K., 1963; Josefa Lautenay, *A Shot in the Dark*, Lyric Theatre, London, 1963; Irina, *The Three Sisters*, and Anna, *The Twelfth Hour*, both 1964, Dol Common, *The Alchemist*, Jeannette, *Romeo and Jeanette*, and Jacqueline, *The Firescreen*, all 1965, all with Oxford Playhouse Company, U.K.

Isabella, *Measure for Measure*, 1965, Amanda, *Private Lives*, Barbara, *The Astrakhan Coat*, title role, *St. Joan*, all 1966, with Nottingham Playhouse, U.K.; Lika, *The Promise*, and Sila, *The Rules of the Game*, both Oxford Playhouse, U.K., 1966; Lika, *The Promise*, Fortune Theatre, London, 1967; Sally Bowles, *Cabaret*, Palace Theatre, London, 1968; Bianca, *Women Beware Women*, Hermione and Perdita, *Winter's Tale*, and Viola, *Twelfth Night*, with the Royal Shakespeare Company, Stratford-Upon-Avon, U.K., 1969; Viola, *Twelfth Night*, Hermione and Perdita, *The Winter's Tale*, Grace Harkaway, *London Assurance*, Barbara Undershaft, *Major Barbara*, all at Aldwych Theatre, London, 1970-71; Portia, *Merchant of Venice*, Viola, *Twelfth Night*, title role, *The Duchess of Malfi*, First Fieldmouse, a Brave Stoat, and Mother Rabbit, *Toad of Toad Hall*, all with the Royal Shakespeare Company, Stratford-Upon-Avon, 1971; Grace Harkaway, *London*

JUDI DENCH

Assurance, New Theatre, London, 1972; *Content to Whisper*, Theatre Royal, York, U.K., 1973; Vilma, *The Wolf*, Apollo Theatre, then Queen's Theatre, then New London Theatre, London, all 1973; Miss Trant, *The Good Companions*, Her Majesty's Theatre, London, 1974.

Sophie Fullgarney, *The Gay Lord Quex*, Albery Theatre, London, 1975; Nurse, *Too True to Be Good*, with the Royal Shakespeare Company, Aldwych Theatre, then Globe Theatre, London, 1975; Beatrice, *Much Ado About Nothing*, Lady Macbeth, *Macbeth*, Adriana, *The Comedy of Errors*, Regan, *King Lear*, all with the Royal Shakespeare Company, Stratford-Upon-Avon, 1976; Adriana, *The Comedy of Errors*, Beatrice, *Much Ado About Nothing*, Lona Hessell, *Pillars of the Community*, Millament, *The Way of the World*, Lady Macbeth, *Macbeth*, all at Aldwych Theatre, London, 1977-78; Imogen, *Cymbeline*, with the Royal Shakespeare Company, Stratford-Upon-Avon, 1979.

Also appeared in *Juno and the Paycock*, 1980-81; Lady Bracknell, *The Importance of Being Earnest*, 1982; Deborah, *A Kind of Alaska*, 1982; *Pack of Lies*, 1983; *Mother Courage*, 1984; *Mr. and Mrs. Nobody*, Garrick Theatre, London, 1987; *Anthony and Cleopatra*, National Theatre, London, 1987.

MAJOR TOURS—With the Royal Shakespeare Company, U.S., Canadian, and Yugoslavian cities and Edinburgh, Scotland, 1957-61; Lady Macbeth, *Macbeth*, and Viola, *Twelfth Night*, with the Nottingham Playhouse, West African cities, 1963; Viola, *Twelfth Night*, Australian cities, 1970, Japanese cities, 1972.

PRINCIPAL FILM APPEARANCES—*A Study in Terror*, Columbia, 1966; *He Who Rides a Tiger*, 1966; *Four in the Morning*, 1966; *A Midsummer Night's Dream*, Royal Shakespeare Company, 1968; *The Third Secret*, 1978; *Dead Cert*, 1985; *Weatherby*, Metro-Goldwyn-Mayer/United Artists, 1985; Nora Doel, *84 Charing Cross Road*, Brooks Films, 1987.

PRINCIPAL TELEVISION APPEARANCES—All in the U.K.: *Hilda Lessways; Talking to a Stranger; An Age of Kings; Village Wooing; Love in a Cold Climate; Major Barbara; Pink String and Sealing Wax; The Funambulists; Jackanory; Luther; Neighbours; Parade's End; Marching Song; On Approval; Days to Come; Emilie; Comedy of Errors; Macbeth; Langrishe Go Down; On Giants Shoulders; A Fine Romance; The Cherry Orchard; Going Gently; Saigon—Year of the Cat* 1982; *Mr. and Mrs. Edgehill; The Browning Version*, BBC, 1985.

WRITINGS: BOOKS—Autobiography, *Judi Dench: A Great Deal of Laughter*.

AWARDS: Received Order of the British Empire, 1970; Paladino d'Argentino Award, Venice Festival, 1961, *Romeo and Juliet*; Most Promising Newcomer, British Film Academy, 1965, for *Four in the Morning*; Best Actress, *Variety* London Critics, 1967, for *The Promise*; Best Actress, Guild of Directors, 1967, for *Talking to a Stranger*; Best Actress, Society of West End Theatres (SWET) Award, 1977, for *Macbeth*; Best Actress, New Standard Drama Award, 1980, for *Juno and the Paycock*; and 1983 for *The Importance of Being Earnest*, and *A Kind of Alaska*; Best Television Actress, British Academy of Film and Television Arts (BAFTA) Award, 1981; honorary degrees: Doctor of Letters, Warwick University, 1978 and York University, 1983.

SIDELIGHTS: RECREATIONS—Painting, drawing, sewing, swimming, catching up with letters.

ADDRESSES: AGENT—Julian Belfrage Associates, 60 St. James's Street, London SW1, England.

*   *   *

DENEUVE, Catherine   1943-

PERSONAL: Born Catherine Dorleac, October 22, 1943, in Paris, France; daughter of Maurice (an actor) and Renee (an actress) Dorleac; married David Bailey, 1965 (divorced, 1970); children: Christian Vadim, Chiara Mastroianni. EDUCATION: Attended Lycee La Fontaine, Paris.

VOCATION: Actress.

CAREER: PRINCIPAL FILM APPEARANCES—*Les Petits Chats*, 1956; *Les Collegiennes*, 1956; *Les Portes Claquent* (*The Doors Slam*), 1960; *Les Parisiennes*, 1961; *Le Vice et la Vertu*, 1961; *Vacances Portugaises*, 1961; *Et Satan Conduit le Bal*, 1962; *Les Plus Belles Escroqueries du Monde*, 1963; *Les Parapluies de Cherbourg* (*The Umbrellas of Cherbourg*), 1963; *La Chasse a l'Homme*, 1964; *Un Monsieur de Compagnie*, 1964; *Repulsion*, 1965; *Coeur a la Gorge*, 1965; *Le Chant du Monde*, 1965; *La Vie de Chateau*, 1965; *Das Liebenskarussel*, 1965; *Les Creatures*, 1966; *Le Dimanche de la Vie*, 1966; *Les Demoiselles de Rochefort* (*The Young Girls of Rochefort*), 1967; *Manon 70*, 1967; *Benjamin*, Paramount, 1967; *Belle de Jour*, 1967; *La Chamade*, 1968; *La Sirene du Mississippi* (*Mississippi Mermaid*), 1968; *The April Fools*, National General, 1969; *Mayerling*, Metro-Goldwyn-Mayer (MGM), 1969; *Tristana*, 1969.

Peau d'Ane, 1970; *It Only Happens to Others*, Cinerama, 1971; *Dirty Money*, 1972; *The Slightly Pregnant Man*, 1973; *Les Sauvages*, 1975; *Hustle*, Paramount, 1975; *Lovers Like Us*, 1975; *Act of Aggression*, 1976; *March or Die*, Columbia, 1977; *La Grande Bourgeoise*, 1977; *Coup de Foudre*, 1977; *L'Argent des Autres*, 1978; *Ecoute Voir*, 1978; *Ils Sont Grands Ces Petits*, 1979; Marion Steiner, *The Last Metro*, 1980; *A Second Chance*, 1981; *Reporters*, 1982; *The Hunger*, MGM/United Artists, 1983; *Le Bon Plaisir*, 1983; *Fort Saganne*, 1983; *Love Songs*, Spectrafilms, 1985; Lili, *Scene of the Crime*, Kino International, 1986; *Paroles et Musique*, 1986.

AWARDS: Golden Palm Award, Cannes Film Festival, 1963, for *Parapluies de Cherbourg;* Golden Lion Award, Venice Film Festival, 1967, for *Belle de Jour*.

SIDELIGHTS: Once called "the most beautiful woman in the world" by *Look* magazine, French-born Catherine Deneuve is well known in Europe not only as one of that continent's leading sex symbols, but also as a serious actress. She has won several awards for her performances and has worked with such important directors as Roman Polanski, Luis Bunuel, and Francois Truffaut. In the United States, however, she may be best known for her television advertisements on behalf of Chanel No. 5 perfume, Mercury automobiles, and—since 1985—her own "Deneuve" brand of perfume. "For countless American males, who sit riveted in front of their television sets as certain commercials flash across the screen," Diane de Dubovay of the *New York Daily News* wrote in 1978, "Catherine Deneuve is a fantasy—an image of glossy blonde elegance and glamour with which their wives and girlfriends could never hope to compete."

Although both her parents were actors, Deneuve went to the theatre only rarely as a child and did not plan on an acting career, wanting instead to become an interior designer. Her sister, Francoise Dorleac, did become an actress, however, and when a woman was needed to play Dorleac's sister in *Les Portes Claquent* (*The Doors Slam*, 1960), Deneuve was hired. Director Roger Vadim, already famous as the discoverer of France's then-reigning sex symbol, Brigitte Bardot, saw the film and cast Deneuve as Virtue in *Le Vice et la Virtu* (*Vice and Virtue*, 1961). He also fathered Deneuve's son, Christian, in 1963.

In 1963, Deneuve's performance as the heroine of Jacques Demy's sentimental musical *The Umbrellas of Cherbourg* brought her to the attention of international audiences. Richard Oulahan of *Life* felt that Deneuve was "enchanting as Genevieve—a lovely, dewy child who grows, in the course of the picture, into a cool young matron."

Her next important film was a very different type of picture—*Repulsion*, Roman Polanski's 1965 case study of a woman driven insane by a pathological fear of sex who eventually commits two murders. In the *New York Post*, Archer Winsten wrote, "Among the performers, . . . Deneuve stands out both for the difficulty of her role and the perfection with which she succeeds in making [the character's descent into madness] seem so progressive."

Early in 1967, Deneuve teamed up with her sister for Jacques Demy's *The Young Girls of Rochefort*. It was the last film they made together before Dorleac's death in a plane crash. Later in that year, Deneuve had what is probably her best known film role, the lead in Luis Bunuel's *Belle de Jour*. In the opinion of several critics, Deneuve's "icy" image served her well in portraying a sexually frustrated housewife who secretly becomes a prostitute during the day while her husband is at work. To Richard Schickel, Deneuve seemed "a breathtaking beautiful sleepwalker who, when she emerges from her trances, flutters with bourgeoise, even virginal embarrassment at what she is doing." The details of her performance earned this comment from him in *Life:* "Every gesture says, 'I am not responsible,' every glance is a muted cry for release from the dark, unfathomable forces that enslave her."

Deneuve worked for Bunuel again in *Tristana*. In the course of that 1969 film, her character ages several years, which led Vincent Canby of the *New York Times* to write, "Deneuve is beautiful, of course, but never before has her beauty seemed more precise and enigmatic, so that while, at the beginning, there is just the slightest hint of the erotic woman inside the school girl, there is, at the end, an awareness of the saint that once lived within the majestically deformed woman."

Another distinguished European director, the Frenchman Francois Truffaut, who had previously used Deneuve in his lighthearted *Mississippi Mermaid*, cast her in 1980's *The Last Metro* as Marion Steiner, an actress who becomes romantically involved with her leading man, played by Gerard Depardieu, while she is hiding her Jewish husband from the Nazis and trying to keep their theatre going. Truffaut explained his choice of Deneuve, saying he wanted "to give her the role of a responsible woman." Reviewer Molly Haskell commented in *Ms* magazine, "It is difficult, even in European cinema, for a beautiful star to mature, to cease being a paragon of beauty and become a woman of parts." She observed, however, that with Truffaut's help, "Deneuve manages the transition as gracefully as one could wish."

Haskell found the actress "still beautiful, but with a wise womanly intelligence'' and deemed her ''more convincing as an efficient administrator than as an actress, or a woman with a wild crush on her leading man.'' The reason, she suggested, ''may be that Deneuve herself radiates a sort of sane self-sufficiency, a quality that militates against the twin madnesses of theatre and love.'' In *Time* (February 23, 1981), Richard Schickel called Deneuve ''more beautiful than ever,'' and agreed that she ''displays a knowing humanity.'' For this critic, however, what was new was Deneuve's sensuality. Feeling that in the past ''she had been used more as icon than actress,'' the critic alleged that, ''When she and Depardieu finally acknowledge their passion for each other, there is a sheer eroticism—without so much as a button being unbuttoned—that one finds in few movie love scenes.''

Further proof of Deneuve's stature as an actress came in 1985, when she was selected by the French Ministry of Culture to replace Brigitte Bardot as the new model for Marianne, a symbol of the French Republic. Copies of a statue of Deneuve as Marianne are now displayed in town halls throughout France. Pierre Boute, the French radio and television personality who originally suggested the change, explained, ''Bardot represented the ideal French woman in the 1960's, but we wanted to find a woman for the '80's.''

ADDRESSES: AGENT—c/o Place St. Sulpice 76, Rue Bonapart, Paris 6, France 75008.

*   *   *

De NIRO, Robert   1943-

PERSONAL: Born August 17, 1943, in New York, NY; son of Robert (an artist) and Virginia (Admiral) De Niro; married Diahnne Abbott (an actress); children: Drena, Raphael. EDUCATION: Studied with Stella Adler and Lee Strasberg at the Actors Studio.

VOCATION: Actor.

CAREER: PRINCIPAL STAGE APPEARANCES—*Night of 100 Stars*, Radio City Music Hall, New York City, 1982; *Cuba and His Teddy Bear*, with the New York Shakespeare Festival, Public Theatre, then Longacre Theatre, New York City, 1986; also *One Night Stand of Noisy Passenger*, New York City production.

PRINCIPAL FILM APPEARANCES—*Greetings*, Sigma III, 1968; *The Wedding Party*, Ondine Productions, 1969; *Bloody Mama*, American International, 1970; *Hi, Mom*, Sigma III, 1970; *Jennifer on My Mind*, United Artists, 1971; *Born to Win*, United Artists, 1971; *The Gang That Couldn't Shoot Straight*, Metro-Goldwyn-Mayer, 1971; *Bang the Drum Slowly*, Paramount, 1973; *Mean Streets*, Warner Brothers, 1973; Vito Corelone, *The Godfather, Part II*, Paramount, 1974; *1900*, Paramount, 1977; Travis Bickle, *Taxi Driver*, Columbia, 1976; *The Last Tycoon*, Paramount, 1977; Jimmy Doyle, *New York, New York*, United Artists, 1977; *The Deer Hunter*, Universal, 1979; Jake la Motta, *Raging Bull*, United Artists, 1981; *True Confessions*, United Artists, 1981; *The King of Comedy*, Twentieth Century-Fox, 1983; *Once Upon a Time in America*, Warner Brothers, 1984; *Falling in Love*, Paramount, 1984; *Brazil*, Universal, 1985; *The Mission*, Warner Brothers, 1986; Louis Cypher, *Angel Heart*, Tri-Star, 1987.

AWARDS: Best Supporting Actor, Academy Award, 1974, for *The Godfather, Part II;* Hasty Pudding Award, Harvard University, 1979; Best Actor, Academy Award, 1981, for *Raging Bull*.

MEMBER: Screen Actors Guild, Actors' Equity Association.

ADDRESSES: AGENT—Jay Julien, 1501 Broadway, New York, NY 10036.*

*   *   *

DENISON, Michael   1915-

PERSONAL: Full name, John Michael Terence Wellesley Denison; born November 1, 1915, in Doncaster, Yorkshire, England; son of Gilbert Dixon (a paint manufacturer) and Marie Louise (Bain) Denison; married Dulcie Gray (an actress and writer), April 29, 1939. EDUCATION: Magdalen College, Oxford University, B.A., 1937; trained for the stage at the Webber-Douglas School in London. MILITARY: British Army, Intelligence Corps, 1940-46.

VOCATION: Actor, director, and writer.

CAREER: STAGE DEBUT—Lord Fancourt Babberley, *Charley's Aunt*, Frinton-on-Sea, U.K., August, 1938. LONDON DEBUT—Paris, *Troilus and Cressida*, Westminster Theatre, 1938. PRINCIPAL STAGE APPEARANCES—Gordon Whitehouse, *Dangerous Corner*, Ghazan Khan, *Marco Millions*, Robert Devizes, *The Will*, Redpenny, *The Doctor's Dilemma*, Rev. Alexander Mill, *Candida*, Peter Horlett, *Music at Night*, and Stephen Undershaft, *Major Barbara*, all at the Westminster Theatre, London, 1939; also appeared with the A.R. Whatmore Players, Aberdeen, Scotland, 1939; appeared with the H.M. Tennent Players, Edinburgh and Glasgow, Scotland, 1939; Nicholas Corbel, *Rain on the Just*, Aldwych Theatre, London, 1948; Michael Fuller, *Queen Elizabeth Slept Here*, Strand Theatre, London, 1949.

Michael, *Fourposter*, Ambassadors Theatre, 1950; Stuart, *Dragon's Mouth*, Winter Garden Theatre, New York City, 1952; Clive Jevons, *Sweet Peril*, St. James Theatre, New York City, 1952; Brian, *The Bad Samaritan*, Criterion Theatre, London, 1953; the White Knight, Tweedledee, and Humpty Dumpty, *Alice Through the Looking Glass*, Prince's Theatre, London, 1954, then the Chelsea Palace Theatre, London, 1955; Francis Oberon, *We Must Kill Toni*, Westminster Theatre, London, 1954; as a member of the Shakespeare Memorial Theatre Company, Stratford-on-Avon: Andrew Aguecheek, *Twelfth Night*, Bertram, *All's Well That Ends Well*, Dr. Caius, *The Merry Wives of Windsor*, and Lucius, *Titus Andronicus*, 1955.

Philip Grant, *Love Affair*, Lyric Theatre, Hammersmith, London, 1956; A, *A Village Wooing*, and Lieutenant Duvallet, *Fanny's First Play*, Lyceum Theatre, London, then Edinburgh Festival, Scotland, and Berlin Festival, Germany, 1956; Charles Cuttinghame, *Meet Me by Moonlight*, Aldwych Theatre, London, 1957; Duke of Hampshire, *Let Them Eat Cake*, Cambridge Theatre, London, 1959; Reverend James Morell, *Candida*, Piccadilly Theatre, then Wyndham's Theatre, London, 1960; Hector Hushabye, *Heartbreak House*, Wyndham's Theatre, London, 1961; Henry Higgins, *My Fair Lady*, Melbourne and Brisbane, Australia, 1962; A, *A Village Wooing* and Harrison Crockstead, *A Marriage Has Been Arranged*, both at the City Center Theatre, Hong Kong, 1962; Henry VIII, *The Royal Gambit*, Ashcroft Theatre, London, 1962; Philip Herriton, *Where Angels Fear to Tread*, New Arts Theatre, then St. Martin's Theatre, London, 1963; Simon Crawford, *Hostile Witness*, Haymarket Theatre, London, 1964; Sir Robert Chiltern, *An Ideal Husband*, Strand Theatre, London, 1965.

Duke of Bristol, *On Approval*, St. Martin's Theatre, London, 1966; Mark, *Happy Family*, St. Martin's Theatre, London, 1967; Sebastian Fleming, *Number Ten*, Strand Theatre, London, 1967; Charlie, *Vacant Possession* and Major Hissling, *Confession at Night*, both Nottingham Playhouse, U.K. 1968; Andrew Pilgrim, *Out of the Question*, St. Martin's Theatre, London, 1968.

A, *A Village Wooing* and Balsquith, *Press Cuttings*, both Fortune Theatre, London, 1970; Hjalmar Ekdal, *The Wild Duck*, Criterion Theatre, London, 1970; Prospero, *The Tempest* and Malvolio, *Twelfth Night*, both at the Open Air Theatre, Regents Park, London, 1972; Tweedledee and White Knight, *Alice Through the Looking Glass*, Ashcroft Theatre, London, 1972; Lew Trent, *At the End of the Day*, Savoy Theatre, London, 1973; Norman Banks, *The Sack Race*, Ambassadors Theatre, London, 1974; Captain Hook and Mr. Darling, *Peter Pan*, Coliseum, London, 1974; Pooh-Bah, *The Black Mikado*, Cambridge Theatre, London, 1975; Malvolio, *Twelfth Night*, Hebble Tyson, *The Lady's Not for Burning*, and Ledbedev, *Ivanov*, all at the Old Vic Theatre, London, 1978; Ernest, *Bedroom Farce*, with the National Theatre Company at the Prince of Wales Theatre, London, 1979. Also at the Old Vic: *The Kingfisher, Relatively Speaking, Coat of Varnish, Captain Brassbound's Conversion, School for Scandal, Song at Twilight,* and *See How They Run.*

MAJOR TOURS—*The Fourposter* and *Private Lives*, tour of South Africa, 1954-55; Jeffery Banning, *Double Cross*, 1958; toured England and Europe with his wife in a Shakespeare program, 1964; toured U.K. cities: Lord Ogleby, *The Clandestine Marriage*, 1971, Prospero, *The Tempest* and Malvolio, *Twelfth Night*, 1972, six roles in *The Dragon Variation*, 1972, appeared in *The Earl and the Pussycat* and as James Fraser, *The First Mrs. Fraser*, 1976, Edward Moulton Barrett, *Robert and Elizabeth*, 1976, Sir Julian Twombley, *The Cabinet Minister*, 1977, Malvolio, *Twelfth Night*, Hebble Tyson, *The Lady's Not for Burning* and Lebedev, *Ivanov*, 1978.

PRINCIPAL STAGE WORK—Director: *Love Affair*, Alexandra Theatre, Birmingham, U.K., 1955, then at the Lyric Theatre, Hammersmith, London, 1956; *How He Lied to Her Husband*, Fortune Theatre, London, 1970; director of the New Shakespeare Company, 1971—.

FILM DEBUT—*Tilly of Bloomsbury*, British, 1940. PRINCIPAL FILM APPEARANCES—*Hungry Hill*, British, 1947; *The Glass Mountain*, 1950; *My Brother Jonathan; The Blind Goddess; Landfall; The Franchise Affair; Angels One Five; Tall Headlines; The Importance of Being Earnest; There Was a Young Lady; Contraband Spain; The Truth About Women; Faces in the Dark.*

PRINCIPAL TELEVISION APPEARANCES—Series: *Boyd, QC*, BBC, 1957-63. Episodic: *Funeral Games; Unexpectedly Vacant.* Movies: *Tale of Piccadilly*, 1973; *The Twelve Pound Look; The Provincial Lady; Bedroom Farce; Private Schultz; Blood Money; The Critic; Scorpion; Cold Warrior; Good Behavior.*

WRITINGS: BOOKS—(With Dulcie Gray) *The Actor and His World* (juvenile), Gollancz, 1964; *Overture and Beginners* (memoirs), Gollancz, 1973. PLAYS, PRODUCED—(Adaptator) *The Cabinet Minister*, touring production, 1978.

AWARDS: Queen's Jubilee Medal from Queen Elizabeth II, 1977.

MEMBER: British Actors' Equity Association (council, 1949-55, 1959-77; vice-president, 1952, 1961-63, and 1974).

SIDELIGHTS: RECREATIONS—Golf, gardening, painting, and motoring.

ADDRESSES: HOME—Shardeloes, Amersham, Buckinghamshire, England. OFFICE—c/o Midland Bank, Ltd, Buckingham Palace Road, London SW1, England.*

*   *   *

DENNEHY, Brian

PERSONAL: Born in Bridgeport, CT. EDUCATION: Attended Columbia University. MILITARY: U.S. Marine Corps, until 1965.

VOCATION: Actor.

CAREER: FILM DEBUT—T.J. Lambert, *Semi-Tough*, United Artists, 1977. PRINCIPAL FILM APPEARANCES—Fergie, *Foul Play*, Paramount, 1978; Frank Vasko, *F.I.S.T.*, United Artists, 1978; Bartender, *10*, Warner Brothers, 1979; O.C. Hanks, *Butch and Sundance: The Early Days*, Twentieth Century-Fox, 1979; Herbie, *Little Miss Marker*, Universal, 1980; Kevin, *Split Image*, Orion, 1982; Sheriff Will Teasle, *First Blood*, Orion, 1982; William Kirwill, *Gorky Park*, Orion, 1983; Rosie Little, *Never Cry Wolf*, Buena Vista, 1983; Mayor Frizzoli, *Finders Keepers*, Warner Brothers, 1984; Doc, *River Rat*, 1984; Cobb, *Silverado*, Columbia, 1985; Walter, *Cocoon*, Twentieth Century-Fox, 1985; Nick, *Twice in a Lifetime*, 1985; Leo McCarthy, *F/X*, Orion, 1986; C.J. Cavanaugh, *Legal Eagles*, Universal, 1986. Also appeared in *The Check is in the Mail*, 1985.

PRINCIPAL TELEVISION APPEARANCES—Series: Arnie Sutter, *Big Shamus, Little Shamus*, CBS, 1979; Lester "Buddy" Krebs, *Star of the Family*, ABC, 1982. Movies: Fire Chief, *It Happened at Lake Wood Manor*, 1977; Longshoreman, *Johnny We Hardly Knew Ye*, 1977; Sergeant Otto Chain, *Pearl*, 1978; Buford Pusser, *Real American Hero*, 1978; Barney Parsons, *A Death in Canaan*, 1978; George Paulsen, *Ruby and Oswald*, 1978; Ragoti, *Dummy*, 1979; Dr. D, *The Jericho Mile*, 1979; Mr. O'Neil, *Silent Victory: The Kitty O'Neil Story*, 1979; Sergeant Ned Coleman, *A Rumor of War*, 1980; Bliss Dawson, *The Seduction of Miss Leona*, 1980; Chief Arthur Buchanan, *Skokie*, 1981; Tim Arnold, *Fly Away Home*, 1981; Edward G. Partin, *Blood Feud*, 1983; Phil Zakarian, *I Take These Men*, 1983; Sergeant Cheever, *Off Sides*, 1984; Cook, *The Last Place on Earth*, 1985; Matthew Malone, *Evergreen*, 1985; Buffalo Bill, *Annie Oakley*, 1985; *The Lion of Africa*, Home Box Office, 1987. Pilots: Colonel Marvin Richardson, *Handle with Care*, 1977; Ernie Stapp, *Bumpers*, 1977; Tim Arnold, *Fly Away Home*, 1981.

PRINCIPAL STAGE APPEARANCES—Pete Hannafin, *Says I, Says He*, Marymount Manhattan Theatre, New York City, then Center Group at the Ahmanson Theatre, Los Angeles, both 1979; *The Front Page*, Long Wharf Theatre, New Haven, CT, 1981; with the New Theatre for Now Productions, Center Theatre Group, Mark Taper Forum, Los Angeles, 1983-84.

MEMBER: Actors' Equity Association, Screen Actors Guild, American Federation of Television and Radio Artists.

ADDRESSES: AGENT—c/o Susan Smith, Smith-Freedman, 123 N. San Vincente Blvd., Beverly Hills, CA 90211.*

DENOFF, Sam 1928-

PERSONAL: Born July 1, 1928, in Brooklyn, NY; son of Harry (a salesman) and Esther (Rothbard) Denoff; married Bernice Levey, November 27, 1955 (divorced); married Sharon L. Shore (a former dancer), May 30, 1965; children: Douglas, Leslie, Melissa, Matthew. EDUCATION: Attended Adelphi College, Garden City, NY.

VOCATION: Writer and producer.

CAREER: PRINCIPAL TELEVISION WORK—Creator and producer, *That Girl,* ABC, 1967-71; also writer for several series.

WRITINGS: TELEVISION—Series: *The Dick Van Dyke Show,* CBS, 1963-65; (also creator and producer) *That Girl,* ABC, 1967-71; *Good Morning World,* CBS, 1967-68; *The Funnyside,* NBC, 1971; *The Don Rickles Show,* CBS, 1972; *Lotsa Luck,* NBC, 1973; *The Montefuscos,* NBC, 1975; *Big Eddie,* CBS, 1975; *Turnabout,* NBC, 1979; *The Lucie Arnaz Show,* NBC, 1984. Specials: *Sid Caesar Special; First Bill Cosby Special.*

AWARDS: Outstanding Writing Achievement in Comedy or Variety, Emmy Awards, 1964 and 1965, for *The Dick Van Dyke Show;* Outstanding Writing for a Special, Emmy Awards, 1967 for *Sid Caesar Special* and 1968, for *Bill Cosby Special;* Writers Guild Award, for *The Dick Van Dyke Show.*

MEMBER: Writers Guild of America (board of directors, two-terms), Screen Actors Guild, American Federation of Radio and Television Artists, Producers Guild, American Society of Composers, Authors, and Publishers (ASCAP), American Guild of Authors and Composers, Academy of Television Arts and Sciences, National Academy of Recording Arts and Sciences, Caucus for Producers, Writers, and Directors (steering committee, four years).

ADDRESSES: HOME—Los Angeles, CA. AGENT—George Shapiro, 151 El Camino Drive, Beverly Hills, CA 90212.

*   *   *

DEUTSCH, Helen 1906-

PERSONAL: Born March 21, 1906, in New York, NY; daughter of Heyman (a furniture manufacturer) and Ann (Freeman) Deutsch. EDUCATION: Barnard College, B.A., 1927. RELIGION: Jewish.

VOCATION: Writer.

CAREER: Play reader, general executive, Provincetown Playhouse, New York City, 1927-29; free-lance writer, New York City, 1929-42; founder, secretary, New York Drama Critics Circle, 1934-39; assistant to executive director, New York Theatre Guild, 1937-38; also taught screen-writing as an adult education course in Los Angeles and at New York University.

WRITINGS: SCREENPLAYS—(With Theodore Reeves) *National Velvet,* Metro-Goldwyn-Mayer (MGM), 1944; *The Seventh Cross,* MGM, 1944; *Golden Earrings,* MGM, 1947; *The Loves of Carmen,* MGM, 1948; *Kim,* MGM, 1950; *King Solomon's Mines,* MGM, 1950; (with William Ludwig, Ray Chordes, and others) *It's a Big Country,* MGM, 1952; *Plymouth Adventure,* MGM, 1952; *Lili,* MGM, 1953; (also author of ballet libretto and lyrics) *The Glass Slipper,* MGM, 1955; *I'll Cry Tomorrow,* MGM, 1956; *Forever Darling,* MGM, 1956; *The Unsinkable Molly Brown,* MGM, 1964; (with Dorothy Kingsley) *The Valley of the Dolls,* Twentieth Century-Fox, 1967.

PLAYS, PRODUCED—*Love on an Island,* Westport Country Playhouse, CT, 1934; book for the musical, *Carnival,* 1961.

TELEVISION—*Jack and the Beanstalk,* NBC, 1956; *The General Motors Fiftieth Anniversary Show,* NBC, 1957; *The Hallmark Christmas Tree,* NBC, 1958.

BOOKS—(With Stella B. Hanau) *The Provincetown: A Story of the Theatre,* Farrar and Rinehart, 1931, reprinted by Atheneum, 1972. POEMS—*The White Magnolia Tree.* SHORT STORIES—Contributor to such magazines as: *Saturday Evening Post; McCall's; Ladies' Home Journal; Cosmopolitan; Redbook.*

SONGS—"Hi-Lilli-Hi-Lo," "Take My Love," "The Ballad of Jack and the Beanstalk," "Twelve Feet Tall," "Sweet World," "I'll Go Along with You," "Looka Me," "He Never Looks My Way," "March of the Ill-Assorted Guards."

AWARDS: One of the Year's Ten Best Films, *New York Times* Award, 1944, for *National Velvet;* Best Screenplay, Academy Award nomination, Best Musical, Writers Guild of America Award, One of the Year's Ten Best Films, *New York Times* Award, *Film Daily* Award, National Board of Review of Motion Pictures Award, Best Screenplay, Golden Globe Award, Hollywood Press Association Award, and many others, all 1953, for *Lili;* Exhibitor Laurel Award, Film Buyers Association, 1953-54, for *Lili;* Books and Authors Association Award, 1956, for *I'll Cry Tomorrow;* All-American Award of the Year, *Radio Daily,* 1956, for *Jack and the Beanstalk;* seven separate awards, 1957, for *The General Motors Anniversay Show;* Gold Medal Award, *Photoplay,* 1964, for *The Unsinkable Molly Brown;* Certificate of Recognition Award, American Film Institute, 1982.

MEMBER: American Society of Composers, Authors and Publishers (ASCAP), Writers Guild of America, Academy of Motion Picture Arts and Sciences, Dramatists Guild.

SIDELIGHTS: From material provided by Helen Deutsch, *CTFT* learned that she reads Twelfth Century middle Latin, middle French, middle English, French, and German and she has written and published verse in middle English. She has also studied and recites passages from Sanskrit classics. She is currently working on a Twelfth Century novel which she says she "will never complete."

ADDRESSES: HOME—1185 Park Avenue, New York, NY 10128.

*   *   *

DEVLIN, Dean

PERSONAL: Born in New York, NY. EDUCATION: Graduated from North Hollywood High School, CA.

VOCATION: Actor, writer, and musician.

CAREER: PRINCIPAL TELEVISION APPEARANCES—Series: Jeffrey Sullivan, *L.A. Law,* NBC, 1986; David Delvalle, *Hard Copy,* CBS, 1987—.

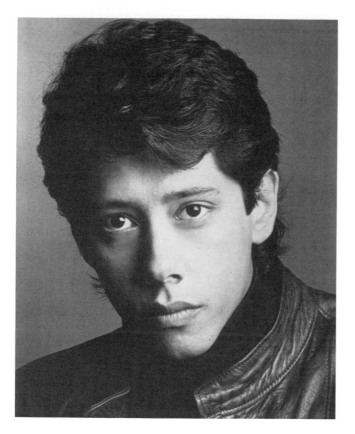

DEAN DEVLIN

Episodic: *Two Close for Comfort,* ABC; *Hill Street Blues,* NBC; *Misfits of Science,* NBC; *Insiders.*

PRINCIPAL FILM APPEARANCES—*Wild Life; City Limits.*

PRINCIPAL STAGE APPEARANCES—*Comedies by Shakespeare,* Los Angeles, CA; *There Must Be a Pony,* New York City.

RELATED CAREER—Comedian, *Something Clever Revue,* New York City.

AWARDS: Best Film Maker Award, California Super Eight-Millimeter Film Festival.

SIDELIGHTS: Through material provided by him, *CTFT* learned that Dean Devlin has written a television pilot for Taliafilms II. He has also made a demonstration record with his band "Nervous Service," for which he sings and plays rhythm guitar and keyboards.

ADDRESSES: PUBLICIST—Guttman and Pam, Ltd., 8500 Wilshire Blvd., Suite 801, Beverly Hills, CA 90211.

*   *   *

DEWHURST, Colleen   1926-

PERSONAL: Born June 3, 1926, in Montreal, PQ, Canada; married James Vickery (divorced); married George C. Scott (divorced); remarried George C. Scott (divorced); children: (second marriage)

two sons. EDUCATION: Attended Downer College for Young Ladies, Milwaukee, WI; trained for the stage at the American Academy of Dramatic Arts and with Harold Clurman and Joseph Anthony.

VOCATION: Actress.

CAREER: STAGE DEBUT—Julia Cavendish, *The Royal Family,* Carnegie Lyceum Theatre, Pittsburgh, PA, 1946. BROADWAY DEBUT—Neighbor, *Desire Under the Elms,* American National Theatre Academy (ANTA) Theatre, 1952. PRINCIPAL STAGE APPEARANCES—Memphis Virgin and Turkish Concubine, *Tamburlaine the Great,* Winter Garden Theatre, New York City, 1956; Tamora, *Titus Andronicus,* New York Shakespeare Festival, New York City, 1956; title role, *Camille,* Cherry Lane Theatre, New York City, 1956; Kate, *The Taming of the Shrew,* Emanuel Presbyterian Church, New York City, 1956; Queen, *The Eagle Has Two Heads,* Actors Playhouse, New York City, 1956; Penelope, *Maiden Voyage,* Forrest Theatre, Philadelphia, 1957; Lady Macbeth, *Macbeth,* New York Shakespeare Festival, New York City, 1957; Mrs. Squeamish, *The Country Wife,* Adelphi Theatre, New York City, 1957; Laetitia, *Children of Darkness,* Circle in the Square Theatre, New York City, 1958; Josie Hogan, *A Moon for the Misbegotten,* Festival of Two Worlds, Spoleto, Italy, 1958; Cleopatra, *Antony and Cleopatra,* Heckscher Theatre, New York City, 1959.

Caesonia, *Caligula,* 54th Street Theatre, New York City, 1960; Mary Follet, *All the Way Home,* Belasco Theatre, New York City, 1960-61; Phoebe Flaherty, *Great Day in the Morning,* Henry Miller's Theatre, New York City, 1962; Abbie Putnam, *Desire Under the Elms,* Circle in the Square Theatre, New York City, 1963; Cleopatra, *Antony and Cleopatra,* New York Shakespeare Festival, Delacorte Theatre, New York City, 1963; Amelia Evans, *The Ballad of the Sad Cafe,* Martin Beck Theatre, New York City, 1963; Josie Hogan, *A Moon for the Misbegotten,* Studio Arena Theatre, Buffalo, NY, 1965; Sara, *More Stately Mansions,* Broadhurst Theatre, New York City, 1967; Hester, *Hello and Goodbye,* Sheridan Square Playhouse, New York City, 1969.

Shen Teh, *The Good Woman of Setzuan,* Vivian Beaumont Theatre, New York City, 1970; the Mistress, *All Over,* Martin Beck Theatre, New York City, 1971; Nel Denton, *The Big Coca-Cola Swamp in the Sky,* Westport Country Playhouse, CT, 1971; Gertrude, *Hamlet,* New York Shakespeare Festival, Delacorte Theatre, 1972; Christine Mannon, *Mourning Becomes Electra,* Circle in the Square Theatre, New York City, 1972; Josie Hogan, *A Moon for the Misbegotten,* Morosco Theatre, New York City, 1973, and repeated role at the Ahmanson Theatre, Los Angeles, CA, 1974; Margaret, *Artichoke,* Long Wharf Theatre, New Haven, CT, 1975; Martha, *Who's Afraid of Virginia Woolf?,* Music Box Theatre, New York City, 1976; Irene Porter, *An Almost Perfect Person,* Belasco Theatre, New York City, 1977; Lillian Hellman, *Are You Now or Have Ever Been . . .?,* Promenade Theatre, New York City, 1978; Ruth Chandler, *Taken in Marriage,* Newman Room at the New York Shakespeare Festival, Public Theatre, New York City, 1979; *O'Neill and Carlotta,* New York Shakespeare Festival, Public Theatre, New York City, 1979.

Night of 100 Stars, Radio City Music Hall, 1982; Argia, *The Queen and the Rebels,* Plymouth Theatre, New York City, 1982; Olga, *You Can't Take It with You,* Paper Mill Playhouse, Milburn, NJ, then moved to the Plymouth Theatre, New York City, 1983; "The Only Woman General," part of the *Festival of One-Act Plays,* American Place Theatre, New York City, 1984; *Rainsnakes,* Long Wharf Theatre, New Haven, CT, 1984; *Night of 100 Stars II,* Radio

City Music Hall, 1985; Carlotta O'Neill, *My Gene*, New York Shakespeare Festival, Public Theatre, 1987.

Also appeared on Broadway in *The Dance of Death.*

PRINCIPAL STAGE WORK—Director, *Ned and Jack*, Hudson Guild Theatre, then moved to the Little Theatre, both in New York City, 1981.

MAJOR TOURS—Martha, *Who's Afraid of Virginia Woolf?*, U.S. cities, 1965.

FILM DEBUT—*The Nun's Story*, Warner Brothers, 1959. PRINCIPAL FILM APPEARANCES—*A Fine Madness*, Warner Brothers, 1966; *The Last Run*, Metro-Goldwyn-Mayer (MGM), 1971; *The Cowboys*, Warner Brothers, 1971; *McQ*, Warner Brothers, 1974; *Annie Hall*, United Artists, 1977; *When a Stranger Calls*, Columbia, 1979; *Ice Castles*, Columbia, 1979; *Final Assignment*, 1980; *Tribute*, Twentieth Century-Fox, 1980; *The Dead Zone*, Paramount, 1983; *The Boy Who Could Fly*, Twentieth Century-Fox, 1986.

PRINCIPAL TELEVISION APPEARANCES—Dramatic Specials: Inez, *No Exit;* Cleopatra, *Antony and Cleopatra; Medea; Focus; The Price; The Crucible; The Hands of Cormac Joyce; Jacob and Joseph; Studs Lonigan; The Kitty O'Neal Story.* Movies: *And Baby Makes Six*, 1979. *The Glitter Dome*, 1984. Mini-Series: *The Blue and the Gray*, NBC, 1984; *A.D.*, CBS, 1985; Marilla, *Anne of Green Gables*, PBS, 1985.

AWARDS: Obie Award and *Theatre World* Award, both 1958, for *Children of Darkness;* Sylvania Award, 1960; Lola D'Annunzion Award, 1961; Antoinette Perry Award, 1962, for *All the Way Home;* Obie Award, 1963, for *Antony and Cleopatra;* Antoinette Perry and Sarah Siddons awards, 1974, for *Moon for the Misbegotten;* Best Supporting Actress, Gemini Award, 1986, for *Anne of Green Gables.*

MEMBER: Actors' Equity Association, Screen Actors Guild.

ADDRESSES: AGENT—STE Representation, Ltd., 888 Seventh Avenue, New York, NY 10106.*

*　　　*　　　*

De YOUNG, Cliff 1946-

PERSONAL: Born February 12, 1946, in Los Angeles, CA; married. EDUCATION: Attended California State College at Los Angeles and Illinois State University.

VOCATION: Actor and singer.

CAREER: PRINCIPAL TELEVISION APPEARANCES—Mini-Series: John Skimmerhorn, *Centennial*, NBC, 1978; John F. Kennedy, *Robert Kennedy and His Times*, CBS; Robert F. Kennedy, *King;* also in *Captains and Kings; Master of the Game.* Episodic: "Annie Oakley," *Tall Tales*, Showtime, 1986.

Movies: Sam Hayden, *Sunshine*, NBC, 1973; Charles Lindbergh, *The Lindbergh Kidnapping Case*, 1876; Sam Hayden, *Sunshine Christmas*, NBC, 1977; *Scared Straight: Another Story*, 1980;

CLIFF De YOUNG

Deadly Intentions, ABC, 1985. Series: Sam Hayden, *Sunshine*, NBC, 1975.

PRINCIPAL FILM APPEARANCES—*Harry and Tonto*, Twentieth Century-Fox, 1974; *Blue Collar*, Universal, 1978; *Shock Treatment*, 1981; *Independence Day*, Warner Brothers, 1982; *The Hunger*, Metro-Goldwyn-Mayer (MGM)/United Artists, 1983; *Reckless*, MGM/United Artists, 1984; John Hilley, *Protocol*, Warner Brothers, 1984; *Secret Admirer*, Orion, 1985; *F/X*, Orion, 1986.

PRINCIPAL STAGE APPEARANCES—*Sticks and Bones* and *Hair*, both Broadway productions; Vershinin, *Three Sisters*, Los Angeles Theatre Center, 1985; *Ice*, Mark Taper Forum; *Two by South*, Los Angeles Actors' Theatre.

RECORDINGS: ALBUMS—*Sunshine*. SINGLES—"Sunshine," "Call Me Mr. Blue."

ADDRESSES: HOME—Santa Monica, CA. PUBLICIST—c/o Monique Moss, Michael Levine Public Relations, 9123 Sunset Blvd., Los Angeles, CA 90069.

*　　　*　　　*

DIENER, Joan 1934-

PERSONAL: Born February 24, 1934, in Cleveland, OH; married Albert Marre; children: one son, one daughter. EDUCATION: Attended Sarah Lawrence College.

VOCATION: Actress and singer.

CAREER: STAGE DEBUT—*H.M.S. Pinafore*, Cleveland Playhouse, OH, 1947. BROADWAY DEBUT—*Small Wonder*, Coronet Theatre, September 15, 1948. LONDON DEBUT—Lalume, *Kismet*, Stoll Theatre, 1955. PRINCIPAL STAGE APPEARANCES—Deedy Barton, *Season in the Sun*, Cort Theatre, New York City, 1950; title role, *Kiss Me, Kate*, Sacramento Music Circus Theatre, CA, 1952; Lalume, *Kismet*, Ziegfeld Theatre, New York City, 1953; *The Ziegfeld Follies*, Shubert Theatre, Boston, then Shubert Theatre, Philadelphia, 1956; Isola Parelli, *At the Grand*, Philharmonic Auditorium, Los Angeles, then Curran Theatre, San Francisco, 1958; appeared in a musical revue, Palladium Theatre, London, 1959; soprano roles, various operas in Italy and Germany, 1959-60; title role, *La Belle Helene*, Cambridge Drama Festival, MA, 1960; Frenchy, *Destry Rides Again*, North Shore Theatre, Beverly, MA, 1961; repeated title role, *La Belle* (revised version of *La Belle Helene*), Shubert Theatre, Philadelphia, 1962.

Aldonza, *Man of La Mancha*, Goodspeed Opera House, East Haddam, CT, 1965, American National Theatre Academy (ANTA)-Washington Square Theatre, New York City, 1965, Ahmanson Theatre, Los Angeles, 1967, Piccadilly Theatre, London, 1968, (in French version) Opera House, Brussels, Belgium and Champs Elysees Theatre, Paris, 1968-69, and (in revival) Vivian Beaumont Theatre, New York City, 1972.

Kathleen Stanton, *Cry for Us All*, Broadhurst Theatre, New York City, 1970; Penelope, *Home Sweet Homer*, Palace Theatre, New York City, 1976; Lalume, *Kismet*, with the Los Angeles Civic Light Opera at the Shaftesbury Theatre, London, 1978.

MAJOR TOURS—Title role, *La Belle* (revised version of *La Belle Helene*,) U.S. cities, 1962; Penelope, *Odyssey*, U.S. cities, 1974-76.

NIGHT CLUBS—Appeared at the Blue Angel, New York City, 1950.

PRINCIPAL TELEVISION APPEARANCES—Series: Regular, *The Fifty-Fourth Street Revue*, CBS, 1949-50. Episodic: "Androcles and the Lion," *Omnibus*, CBS, 1956. Guest: *The Today Show*, NBC; *The Ed Sullivan Show*, CBS; *The Johnny Carson Show*, NBC.

AWARDS: Theatre World Award, 1954, for *Kismet*.

MEMBER: Actors' Equity Association, American Federation of Television and Radio Artists, Screen Actors Guild, American Guild of Variety Artists.

ADDRESSES: AGENT—c/o Floria Lasky, Fitelson, Lasky, Aslan and Couture, 551 Fifth Avenue, 34th Fl., New York, NY 10176.*

*   *   *

DILLON, Mia   1955-

PERSONAL: First name pronounced with a long "i"; born July 9, 1955, in Colorado Springs, CO.

VOCATION: Actress.

CAREER: STAGE DEBUT—Virginia, *The Canterville Ghost*, Des Moines Community Theatre, IA. BROADWAY DEBUT—Mary Tate, *Da*, Morosco Theatre, 1978-79, for five-hundred-sixty-performances. PRINCIPAL STAGE APPEARANCES—Mary Tate, *Da*, Hudson Guild Theatre, New York City, 1978; Mary Mooney, *Once a Catholic*, Helen Hayes Theatre, New York City, 1979; Babe Botrell, *Crimes of the Heart*, Golden Theatre, New York City, then Ahmanson Theatre, Los Angeles, 1981-82; Irina, *Three Sisters*, Manhattan Theatre Club, New York City, 1982; title role, *Agnes of God*, Music Box Theatre, New York City, 1983; *Much Ado About Nothing*, Yale Repertory Theatre, New Haven, CT, 1983; Bessie Watty, *The Corn Is Green*, Lunt-Fontanne Theatre, New York City, 1983; Lillian, *Wednesday*, Hudson Guild Theatre, New York City, 1983; Marie, *Come Back, Little Sheba*, Roundabout Theatre, New York City, 1984; Georgia, *The Vienna Notes*, The Second Stage Theatre, New York City, 1985; *Paris Bound*, Berkshire Theatre Festival, MA, 1985; Sorel Bliss, *Hay Fever*, Music Box Theatre, New York City, 1985-86, then Eisenhower Theatre, Kennedy Center, Washington, DC, 1986; also, with the New Amsterdam Theatre Company, appeared as Sophie, *Roberta* and Hulde, *Music in the Air*, both at Town Hall, New York City.

TELEVISION DEBUT—Hapsy, "The Jilting of Granny Weatherall," *American Short Story*, PBS. PRINCIPAL TELEVISION APPEARANCES—Movies: *Lots of Luck*, Disney Cable.

AWARDS: Drama Desk nomination, 1979, for *Once a Catholic;* Clarence Derwent Award, 1981, Antoinette Perry Award nomination and Drama-Logue Award, both 1982, all for *Crimes of the Heart.*

MEMBER: Actors' Equity Association.

ADDRESSES: AGENT—Milton Goldman, International Creative Management, 40 W. 57th Street, New York, NY 10019.*

*   *   *

DINNER, William
(Surrey Smith)

PERSONAL: Born April 27, in Bournemouth, England.

VOCATION: Playwright.

WRITINGS: PLAYS—(With William Morum) *The Late Edwina Black*, Ambassador Theatre, London, 1949, and Booth Theatre, New York City, produced as *L'Hommed au Paraplue*, Paris; *Two Soon for Daisies; The Magnificent Mr. Booth;* also over one-hundred one-act plays.

MEMBER: Authors and Composers Society.

ADDRESSES: AGENT—Eric Glass, Ltd., 28 Berkeley Square, London W1X 6HD, England.

Photography by Douglas Kirkland/SYGMA

WILLIAM DINNER

* * *

DOUGLAS, Michael   1944-

PERSONAL: Born September 25, 1944, in New Brunswick, NJ; son of Kirk (an actor) and Diana (an actress; maiden name, Dill) Douglas; married Diandra Luker, March 20, 1977; children: Cameron Morrell. EDUCATION: Attended the University of California at Santa Barbara; trained for the stage by attending three summers in residence at the O'Neill Center's National Playwrights Conference; studied acting with Wynn Handman at the American Place Theatre in New York City.

VOCATION: Actor and producer.

CAREER: PRINCIPAL STAGE APPEARANCES—Appeared in half-dozen off-Broadway plays, including *City Scene* and *Pinkville*, all New York City; *Night of 100 Stars, II,* Radio City Music Hall, New York City, 1985.

PRINCIPAL FILM APPEARANCES—*Hail Hero,* National General, 1969; *Adam at 6:00 A.M.,* National General, 1970; *Summertree,* Columbia, 1971; *Napoleon and Samantha,* Buena Vista, 1972; *Coma,* United Artists, 1978; *The China Syndrome,* Columbia, 1979; *Running,* Universal, 1979; *It's My Turn,* Columbia, 1980; *Star Chamber,* Twentieth Century-Fox, 1983; *Romancing the Stone,* Twentieth Century-Fox, 1984; *The Jewel of the Nile,* Twentieth Century-Fox, 1985; *A Chorus Line,* Columbia, 1985.

PRINCIPAL FILM WORK—Assistant director: *Lonely Are the Brave,* Universal, 1962; *Heroes of Telemark,* British, 1965; *Cast a Giant*

Shadow, 1966. Co-producer, *One Flew Over the Cuckoo's Nest,* United Artists, 1975; producer, *The China Syndrome,* Columbia, 1979; producer, *Romancing the Stone,* Twentieth Century-Fox, 1984; executive producer, *Starman,* Columbia, 1984; producer, *The Jewel of the Nile,* Twentieth Century-Fox, 1985.

TELEVISION DEBUT—"The Experiment," *CBS Playhouse,* PRINCIPAL TELEVISION APPEARANCES—Series: Inspector Steve Keller, *Streets of San Francisco,* ABC, 1972-76; Episodic: *The FBI,* ABC; *Medical Center,* CBS. Movies: *When Michael Calls,* 1971.

PRINCIPAL TELEVISION WORK—Producer, *Conquistador, the Conquest of Mexico.*

AWARDS: Theatre World Award, 1970-71; Best Picture, Academy Award, 1975, for *One Flew Over the Cuckoo's Nest.*

ADDRESSES: OFFICE—Twentieth Century-Fox, 10201 W. Pico Blvd., Los Angeles, CA, 90035. AGENT—Ron Meyer, Creative Artists Agency, 1888 Century Park East, Suite 1400, Los Angeles, CA 90067.*

* * *

DOUGLAS, Sarah

PERSONAL: Daughter of Edward (a career member of the Royal Air Force) and Beryl (a physiotherapist; maiden name, Smith); married Richard Le Parmentier, April 25, 1981 (divorced, 1986). EDUCATION: Trained for the stage at the Rose Bruford Drama School. POLITICS: Conservative. RELIGION: Church of England.

© *Evening Argus, Brighton*

SARAH DOUGLAS

VOCATION: Actress.

CAREER: PRINCIPAL TELEVISION APPEARANCES—Series: Pamela Lynch, *Falcon Crest,* CBS, 1983—. Episodic: *V,* NBC; *Murder She Wrote,* CBS; *Space 1999; Return of the Saint,* NBC.

Movies (All for the BBC): *Harlequinade; She; Black and Blue; Warship; Esther Waters; The Ghost Girl; The Inheritors; Justice; Room Service; Howerd Confessions; Thundercloud; The Professionals; Bergerac.*

PRINCIPAL FILM APPEARANCES—*Last Days of Man on Earth* (also known as *The Final Programme*) 1973; *People That Time Forgot,* American International, 1977; *Superman,* Warner Brothers, 1978; *Superman II,* Warner Brothers, 1981; *Conan the Destroyer,* Universal, 1984; *Solarbabies,* Metro-Goldwyn-Mayer, 1986; also, *The Brute.*

PRINCIPAL STAGE APPEARANCES—Appeared in U.K. productions of *Gnomes, Zigger Zagger, Fuzz, Spring Heeled Jack.*

MAJOR TOURS—*Don't Just Lie There, Say Something,* U.K. cities.

SIDELIGHTS: RECREATIONS—Gardening.

ADDRESSES: HOME—Los Angeles, CA. AGENT—J. Michael Bloom, 9200 Sunset Blvd., Suite 710, Los Angeles, CA 90069.

* * *

DOYLE, Jill 1965-

PERSONAL: Born January 12, 1965, in Dublin, Ireland; daughter of Daniel Eric (a lab technician) and Eileen (a film hairdresser; maiden name, Clarke) Doyle. EDUCATION: Holy Child Community School, 1978-83; Audrey Meredith Speech & Drama School, 1970-82; diploma, Leinster School of Music and Drama; studied dance with the Irish Professional Teachers of Old-Time Dancing Society, associate qualification, 1982; one month intensive course, Alexander Technique of Acting, Glynn and Robert MacDonald, London.

VOCATION: Actress.

CAREER: STAGE DEBUT—Carmel, *All the Way Back,* Abbey Theatre, Dublin, Ireland, 1985-86. PRINCIPAL STAGE APPEARANCES—Linda, *Blood Brothers,* Olympia Theatre, Dublin, 1986.

FILM DEBUT—Baba, *The Country Girls,* London Films, 1983. PRINCIPAL FILM APPEARANCES—*Eat the Peach,* Strongbow Productions, Ireland, 1986.

TELEVISION DEBUT—Rene, *Night in Tunsia,* R.T.E., 1982. PRINCIPAL TELEVISION APPEARANCES—Movies: Ita, *Dying for a Drink,* Radharc Production, 1982; Movies: Mary Canty, *The Irish R.M.,* Littlebird Films, Channel Four Production, 1983; Bridget, *The Ballinish Bowl,* German television, 1984; *The Woman Who Married Clark Gable,* Irish Film Board and Channel Four Production, 1985; Denise, *An Invitation to a Party,* BBC, 1985. Documentaries: *Secret Languages,* Ann McCabe Production, R.T.E., 1982; *Country and Irish,* Octagon Films, Channel Four Production, 1983.

JILL DOYLE

RELATED CAREER—Drama and dance teacher, Dance Centre, 1984-86; management, Children's Agency, 1986—.

ADDRESSES: HOME—173 Glenageary Park, Glenageary, Dublin, Ireland. AGENT—Kate Feast Management, 43A Princess Road, London N.W.1, England.

* * *

DUBERSTEIN, Helen 1926-

PERSONAL: Born June 3, 1926, in New York, NY; daughter of Jacob M. (a businessman) and Beatrice Duberstein; married Victor Lipton (a writer), April 10, 1949; children: Jackie Frances, Irene Judith.

VOCATION: Writer.

CAREER: PRINCIPAL STAGE WORK—Playwright, Circle Theatre Repertory Company, New York City, 1968-72 and Woodstock, NY, 1972; adjunct community advisor, University of Boston, 1972; adjunct community advisor, University of Michigan, 1972; artistic director, Theatre for the New City, New York City, 1974-79; playwright in residence, University of Hartford, CT, 1977-78; playwright in residence, Interlochen Academy of the Arts, 1979; creative writing teacher, P.S. 97, Queens, NY, 1981; president, Playwrights Group, Inc.

WRITINGS: PLAYS—Manuscripts performed as readings: *Street*

Scene, Chelsea Theatre Center and Heritage Theatre; *The Kingdom by the Sea,* Provincetown Playhouse, Circle in the Square, and Cubiculo, New York City; *The Affair,* Circle Repertory Company at Westbeth Theatre, New York City and Old Reliable Theatre; *Five Thousand Feet,* Westbeth Theatre Cabaret, New York City; *A Visit from Grandma,* Dove Theatre Company; *Love/Hate,* Omni Theatre Club, New York City; *Your Unhappiness with Me Is of No Concern to Readers,* Omni Theatre Club and ASTA Theatre; *The Visit,* Assembly Theatre and Westbeth Theatre, New York City; *Time Shadows,* Circle Repertory Theatre and Roudabout Theatre, New York City; *The Monkey of the Inkpot,* Actors Experimental Unit with Playwrights Cooperative; *Copout!,* New York Theatre Ensemble, New York City and University of Hartford, CT; *The Play Within,* New York Theatre Ensemble, New York City; *When I Died My Hair in Venice,* Circle Theatre Company, New York City; *Foggia,* Theatre-in-Zimmer, Hamburg, Germany; *The Brain,* Open Space Theatre and Playwrights Group Theatre, New York City; *The Puppeteers,* Uptaught Theatre; *Under the Bridge There Is a Lonely Spot with Gregory Peck,* Plaza Theatre at Lincoln Center and Theatre for the New City, New York City; *Four Corners,* Quaigh Theatre and Circle Theatre Repertory Company, New York City; *We Never Thought a Wedding,* Theatre for the New City, New York City; *The Broken Lease.* PLAYS, PUBLISHED—Plays have been published in *Dramatica, Janus,* and *Quixote* magazines.

POETRY—*Arrive Safely, Changes, The Voyage Out, Succubus/Incubus, The Human Dimension.* Her poetry has also appeared in *The Living Underground, City College Annual Poetry Awards, Provincetown Poets, Confrontation, The Village Voice, The Outsider, Liberation.* FICTION—Has written for *Semiotext, Catalyst 87, New Letters, for Now, Jewish Dialogue, Confrontation, Shantih, Ingenue.*

AWARDS: Grants: National Foundation for the Arts, 1972; Best Play, Interlochen Award, 1979; New York State Council for the Arts.

MEMBER: Dramatists Guild, Poetry Society of America.

ADDRESSES: AGENT—Helmut Meyer, 330 E. 79th Street, New York, NY 10021.

*   *   *

DUCLOW, Geraldine   1946-

PERSONAL: Born Geraldine Anne Hodzima, September 20, 1946, in Chicago, IL; daughter of Steve (a sales representative) and Irene (Halat) Hodzima; married Donald F. Duclow (a college professor), July 11, 1969. EDUCATION: DePaul University, B.A., 1967; Rosary College, River Forest, IL, M.L.S., 1968.

VOCATION: Performing arts librarian.

CAREER: Reference librarian, Chicago Public Library, 1968-69; reference librarian, literature department, Free Library of Philadelphia, PA, 1969-71; curator, Theatre Collection, Free Library of Philadelphia, 1972—.

WRITINGS: BOOKS—Contributor, *Preserving America's Performing Arts,* Theatre Library Association, 1985.

MEMBER: Philadelphia Drama Guild, Pennsylvania Library Asso-

ciation, American Society for Theatre Research, Theatre Library Association (executive board, 1980—).

SIDELIGHTS: RECREATIONS—Art, needlework, and horticulture.

ADDRESSES: HOME—1914 Nectarine Street, Philadelphia, PA 19130. OFFICE—Free Library of Philadelphia, Logan Circle, Philadelphia, PA 19103.

*   *   *

DUFFY, Julia   1951-

PERSONAL: Born Julia Hinds, June 27, 1951, in St. Paul, MN; daughter of Joseph and Mary Katherine (a real estate agent; maiden name, Duffy) Hinds; married Jerry Lacy (an actor), June 21, 1984; children: Kerry Kathleen. EDUCATION: American Academy of Dramatic Arts, graduate 1972.

VOCATION: Actress.

CAREER: STAGE DEBUT—Leslie, *The Girl in the Freudian Slip,* Old Log Theatre, Excelsior, MN, 1969. BROADWAY DEBUT—Susan, *Once in a Lifetime,* Circle in the Square Theatre, 1978.

PRINCIPAL STAGE APPEARANCES—Daisy, *The Enchanted,* Kennedy Center, Washington, DC, 1973; Kate, *Never Too Late,* Kenley Players, Warren, OH, 1977; Emma, *Curse of the Starving Class,* Loretto-Hilton Repertory Company, St. Louis, MO, 1978; Irina, *The Three Sisters,* Loretto-Hilton Repertory Company,

JULIA DUFFY

1979; Corie, *Barefoot in the Park,* Aspen Theatre Festival, CO, 1980; Bianca, *The Taming of the Shrew,* Globe Theatre, Hollywood, CA, 1981.

FILM DEBUT—Julie, *Night Warning,* Carruthers/Hennessey, 1981. PRINCIPAL FILM APPEARANCES—Mary, *Wacko,* 1981; Mol, *Battle Beyond the Stars,* Roger Corman Productions, 1981.

TELEVISION DEBUT—Gerry, *Love of Life,* CBS, 1972. PRINCIPAL TELEVISION APPEARANCES—Series: Penny Davis, *The Doctors,* NBC, 1973-77; Princess Ariel, *Wizards and Warriors,* CBS, 1983; Stephanie Vanderkellen, *Newhart,* CBS, 1983—. Specials: Juliet, *Romeo and Juliet,* PBS, 1975. Mini-Series: Mary, *The Blue and the Gray,* CBS, 1981. Movies: Dee, *Children in the Crossfire,* NBC, 1984. Pilot: Lois, *Irene,* NBC, 1981.

AWARDS: Best Supporting Actress, Emmy Award nominations, 1984, 1985, 1986, for *Newhart;* Best Supporting Actress in a Comedy, Viewers for Quality Television, 1986, for *Newhart.*

MEMBER: Screen Actors Guild, American Federation of Television and Radio Artists, Actors' Equity Association.

ADDRESSES: OFFICE—c/o MTM 4024 Radford Avenue, Studio City, CA, 91604. AGENT—ATM, 870 N. Vine Street, Suite G, Los Angeles, CA 90038.

*   *   *

DULLEA, Keir   1936-

PERSONAL: Born May 30, 1936, in Cleveland, OH; son of Robert and Margaret (Ruttan) Dullea; married Margo Bennett (divorced); married Susan Coe, 1971. EDUCATION: Attended San Francisco State College; trained for the stage at the Neighborhood Playhouse.

VOCATION: Actor.

CAREER: STAGE DEBUT—Resident juvenile, Totem Pole Playhouse, PA. OFF-BROADWAY DEBUT—Timmie Redwine, *Season of Choice,* Barbizon-Plaza Theatre, 1959. PRINCIPAL STAGE APPEARANCES—Appeared at the Berkshire Playhouse, the Hedgerow Theatre in Philadelphia, and at the John Drew Theatre in stock productions; Nick, *A Short Happy Life,* Moore Theatre, Seattle, WA, then Huntington Hartford Theatre, Los Angeles, CA, 1961; Dr. Jim Tennyson, *Dr. Cook's Garden,* Belasco Theatre, New York City, 1967; Don Baker, *Butterflies Are Free,* Booth Theatre, New York City, 1969; Brick, *Cat on a Hot Tin Roof,* American Shakespeare Festival, Stratford, CT, then at the American National Theatre Academy (ANTA) Theatre, New York City, 1974; Jimmy, *P.S. Your Cat Is Dead!,* John Golden Theatre, New York City, 1975; Guy, *Doubles,* Ritz Theatre, New York City, 1985. Also appeared in the Off-Broadway production of *Sweet Prince.*

FILM DEBUT—*Hoodlum Priest,* United Artists, 1961. PRINCIPAL FILM APPEARANCES—*David and Lisa,* Continental, 1962; *The Thin Red Line,* Allied Artists, 1964; *Mail Order Bride,* Metro-Goldwyn-Mayer (MGM), 1964; *The Naked Hours,* 1964; *Bunny Lake Is Missing,* Columbia, 1965; *Madame X,* Universal, 1966; David Bowman, *2001: A Space Odyssey,* MGM/United Artists, 1968; *The Fox,* Claridge, 1968; *De Sade,* American International, 1969; Dr. Stevens, *Pope Joan,* 1972; *Devil in the Brain,* 1972; Rick, *Paperback Hero,* 1973; Garry, *Paul and Michelle,* Paramount, 1974; Peter, *Black Christmas,* 1975; *Silent Night, Evil*

Night, Warner Brothers, 1975; Lewis, *Welcome to Blood City,* EMI, 1977; Magnus Lofting, *Full Circle,* 1977; *Leopard in the Snow,* Harlequin, 1977; Julian Bedford, *Brainwaves,* 1982; Dr. Steiger, *Blind Date,* 1983; David Bowman, *2010,* MGM/United Artists, 1984.

PRINCIPAL TELEVISION APPEARANCES—Series: Larry Franklin, *Channing,* ABC, 1963. Movies: Elisha, *Give Us Barabbas!,* 1961; Dr. Chris Perdeger, *Black Water Gold,* 1970; Devon, *The Starlost,* 1973; Johnny Morrison, *Law and Order,* 1976; General George Custer, *The Legend of the Golden Gun,* 1978; *Hostage Tower,* 1979; Thomas Grambell, *Brave New World,* 1979; Mr. Smith, *The Hostage Tower,* 1981; Cliff Letterman, *No Place to Hide,* 1981; Glenn, *The Next One,* Showtime, 1985; also, *All Summer Long.*

AWARDS: Best Actor, San Francisco International Film Festival Award, 1962, for *David and Lisa.*

MEMBER: Actors' Equity Association, Screen Actors Guild.

ADDRESSES: OFFICE—c/o M.J. Mitosky, 150 Central Park South, New York, NY 10019.*

*   *   *

DUNCAN, Fiona

PERSONAL: Full name, Fiona Mary Duncan; born in Yorkshire, England; children: Stella Duncan-Petely. EDUCATION: Royal Academy of Dramatic Art, London.

FIONA DUNCAN

VOCATION: Actress.

CAREER: STAGE DEBUT—Harold, *Warp and Weft,* Bradford Girl's Grammar School. LONDON DEBUT—Flower Girl, *Duel of Angels,* Apollo Theatre, 1958. PRINCIPAL STAGE APPEARANCES— Leading roles in *Major Barbara, Crime on Goat Island, The King of Nowhere, Dear Brutus,* and *Love's Labour's Lost,* all in repertory at Croydon, Edinburgh, Glasgow, and Windsor.

MAJOR TOURS—*Duel of Angels; So Wise So Young; Foursome Reel; The Two Noble Kinsmen.*

TELEVISION DEBUT—*The Skin of Our Teeth,* BBC. PRINCIPAL TELEVISION APPEARANCES—*Ruth,* BBC; Mary Warren, *The Crucible,* Granada TV; also *The Old Road; The Leather Jungle; Dismissal Leading to Lustfulness; Search Party; Point Counter Point; Kippers and Curtains; The Old Curiosity Shop; A Tale of Two Cities; The Second Mrs Tanqueray,* BBC and Granada TV.

SIDELIGHTS: FAVORITE ROLES—From the plays of George Bernard Shaw, especially *Major Barbara.* RECREATIONS—Drawing, walking, and listening to chamber music.

ADDRESSES: AGENT—Eric Glass Ltd., 28 Berkeley Square, London W1X 6HD, England.

*   *   *

DUNCAN-PETLEY, Stella   1975-

PERSONAL: Born June 25, 1975; daughter of Roderick Hugh and Fiona Mary (an actress) Duncan. EDUCATION: Attended South Hampstead High School.

VOCATION: Actress.

CAREER: FILM DEBUT—Elizabeth Colt, *Hearts of Fire,* Torrenado Ltd., 1986. PRINCIPAL FILM APPEARANCES—Julie, *A Dance by the Light of the Moon,* 1986.

SIDELIGHTS: RECREATIONS—Music, reading, piano, violin, swimming, and riding.

ADDRESSES: AGENT—Eric Glass Ltd., 28 Berkeley Square, London W1X 6HD, England.

*   *   *

DUNLOP, Vic, Jr.

PERSONAL: Born in New York City; son of Vic (an actor; stage name, Victor Marko) Dunlop, Sr. MILITARY: U.S. Army.

VOCATION: Comedian, actor, and inventor.

CAREER: PRINCIPAL STAGE APPEARANCES—As member of improvisational group, "Natural Gas," at the Comedy Store, Hollywood, CA.

PRINCIPAL CABARET APPEARANCES—One-man stand-up show, tours throughout clubs in the U.S.

PRINCIPAL FILM APPEARANCES—*The Devil and Max Devlin,* Buena Vista, 1981; *Meatballs II,* Tri-Star, 1984; *Skateboard USA.*

PRINCIPAL TELEVISION APPEARANCES—Series: Regular with "Natural Gas" on *Don Kirshner's Rock Concert,* syndication; *Make Me Laugh,* ABC, 1979-81; Dolie Peterson, *Safe at Home,* WTBS, 1986. Movies: *Spot Marks the X,* Disney Movie of the Week, 1986.

NON-RELATED CAREER—Invents and markets novelty items, such as "Crazy Comic Eyes," and other "eyeball" products, including jackets and T-shirts.

AWARDS: Third place in the Los Angeles Stand-up Comedy Competition.

SIDELIGHTS: Concerning Vic Dunlop's creativity and inventions, Jo-Ann Geffen & Associates supplied *CTFT* with a biography stating, "Vic still finds time to be a brilliant inventor and entrepreneur. Dunlop has slipped from the sublime to the ridiculous with his new line of products. . . eyeballs that you can wear and eat. 'It was a happy accident, I was wearing a pair of plastic bloodshot eye balls in my act and it became such a hit that I built a regular routine around them. Next thing I knew members of the audience asked me where they could buy them. They even started wearing them to my shows!'"

ADDRESSES: PUBLICIST—Jo-Ann Geffen & Associates, 3151 Cahuengha Blvd. W., Suite 235, Los Angeles, CA 90068.

VIC DUNLOP, JR.

DUNNE, Griffin   1955-

PERSONAL: Born June 8, 1955; son of Dominick (a writer) and Ellen (Griffin) Dunne. EDUCATION: Trained for the stage at the Neighborhood Playhouse.

VOCATION: Actor and producer.

CAREER: PRINCIPAL STAGE APPEARANCES—*Marie and Bruce*, New York Shakespeare Festival, New York City, 1980; *Coming Attractions*, Playwright's Horizons, New York City, 1982; *Hooters*, Hudson Guild Theatre, New York City, 1984.

PRINCIPAL FILM APPEARANCES—*Chilly Scenes of Winter*, United Artists, 1979; *American Werewolf in London*, Universal, 1981; *Johnny Dangerously*, Twentieth Century-Fox, 1984; *Almost You*, 1984; *After Hours*, Warner Brothers, 1985.

PRINCIPAL FILM WORK—Producer, *Chilly Scenes of Winter*, United Artists, 1979; producer, *Baby It's You*, Paramount, 1982; producer, *After Hours*, Warner Brothers, 1985.

PRINCIPAL TELEVISION WORK—Movies: *The Wall*, CBS, 1980. Episodic: *Alfred Hitchcock*, 1985; *Amazing Stories*, 1985.

MEMBER: Actors' Equity Association, Screen Actors Guild, American Federation of Television and Radio Artists.

ADDRESSES: AGENT—International Creative Management, 8899 Beverly Blvd., Los Angeles, CA 90048. PUBLICIST—c/o Neil Koeningsberg, P/M/K Public Relations, Inc., 8436 W. Third St., Suite 650, Los Angeles, CA 90048.

*   *   *

DURAS, Marguerite   1914-

PERSONAL: Born Marguerite Donnadieu, April 4, 1914, in Giadinh, Indochina (now Vietnam); daughter of Henri (a mathematics teacher) and Marie (Legrand) Donnadieu; divorced; children: one son. EDUCATION: Attended the Lycee de Saigon, Indochina, University of Paris, and the Sorbonne, France; degrees in law and political science; also studied mathematics.

VOCATION: Playwright, screenwriter, film director, film producer, novelist, journalist, and composer.

CAREER: PRINCIPAL FILM WORK—Director and screenwriter: (Co-director) *La Musica* (film version of her play), United Artists, 1966; *Detruire, dit-elle* (also known as *Destroy, She Said*, film version of her novel), Ancinex/Madeline Films, 1969; (also producer and co-editor) *Jaune le Soleil* (also known as *Yellow, the Sun*, from her novel *Abahn, Sabana, David*), 1971; (also composer) *Nathalie Granger*, Monelet & Co., 1972; *La Femme du Ganges*, 1974; (also voice-over) *India Song*, 1975; *Des journees entieres dans les arbres* (also known as *Days in the Trees*), 1976; *Son Nom de Venise dans Calcutta desert*, 1976; *Baxter, Vera Baxter*, 1977; (also appeared in) *Le Camion*, 1977; the four-part film series *Aurelia Steiner:* "Cesaree," 1978, "Les Mains negatives," 1978, "Aurelia Steiner—Melbourne," 1979, and "Aurelia Steiner—Vancouver," 1979; *Agatha et les Lectures Illimitees* (also known as *Agatha*), 1981.

RELATED CAREER—Contributor to *Vogue;* was employed in publishing houses in Paris.

NON-RELATED CAREER—Secretary with the Colonies Ministry, 1935-41.

WRITINGS: PLAYS, PRODUCED—*The Viaducts of Seine-et-Oise*, produced as *The Viaduct*, Yvonne Arnaud Theatre, Guildford, U.K., 1967; (with James Lord) *The Beast in the Jungle*, 1962; *La Musica*, produced as *The Music*, West Side Actors Workshop and Repertory Theatre, New York City, 1967; *Days in the Trees*, Theatre de France, Paris, 1967; *Suzanna Andler*, Theatre Mathurins, Paris, 1969, English translation by Barbara Bray produced at Aldwych Theatre, London, 1973; *L'Amante anglaise*, Theatre National Populaire, Paris, 1969, then Royal Court Theatre, London, 1969, then Barbizon-Plaza Theatre, New York City, 1971, English translation by Bray produced under the title of *A Place without Doors*, Long Wharf Theatre, New Haven, CT, 1970, then Staircase Theatre, New York City, 1970, then produced under the title of *Lovers of Viorne*, Royal Court Theatre, London, 1971.

PLAYS, PUBLISHED—*Theatre I* (contains "Les Eaux et forets," "Le Square," and "La Musica"), Gallimard, 1965; *Three Plays*, English translation by Barbara Bray and Sonia Orwell (contains "The Square," "Days in the Trees," and "The Viaducts of Seine-et-Oise"), Calder & Boyars, 1967; *Theatre II* (contains "Suzanna Andler," "Des Journees entieres dan les arbres," "Yes, peut-etre," "Le Shaga," and "Un Homme est venue me voir"), Gallimard, 1968; *Ah! Ernesto*, F. Ruy-Vidal, 1971; *India Song*, Gallimard, 1973, translation by Bray published under the same title, Grove Press, 1976.

SCREENPLAYS—*Hiroshima, Mon Amour*, 1959; *Moderato Cantabile*, Royal Films International, 1960; *Une Aussi Longue Absence* (also known as *The Long Absence*, film version of her novel), 1961; *Nuit noire, Calcutta*, 1964; *Ten-thirty p.m. Summer* (film version of her novel *Ten-thirty on a Summer Night*) Lopert, 1966; *L'Homme assis dans le couloir*, 1980.

Screenwriter and director: (Co-director) *La Musica* (film version of her play), United Artists, 1966; *Detruire, dit-elle* (also known as *Destroy, She Said*, film version of her novel), Ancinex/Madeline Films, 1969; (also producer and co-editor) *Jaune le Soleil* (also known as *Yellow, the Sun*, from her novel *Abahn, Sabana, David*), 1971; (also composer) *Nathalie Granger*, Monelet & Co., 1972; *La Femme du Ganges*, 1974; (also voice-over) *India Song*, 1975; *Des journees entieres dans les arbres* (also known as *Days in the Trees*), 1976; *Son Nom de Venise dans Calcutta desert*, 1976; *Baxter, Vera Baxter*, 1977; (also appeared in) *Le Camion*, 1977; the four-part film series *Aurelia Steiner:* "Cesaree," 1978, "Les Mains negatives," 1978, "Aurelia Steiner—Melbourne," 1979, and "Aurelia Steiner—Vancouver," 1979; *Agatha et les Lectures Illimitees* (also known as *Agatha*), 1981.

FICTION—*Les Impudents*, Plon, 1943; *Le Vie tranquille*, Gallimard, 1944; *Un Barrage contre le Pacifique*, Gallimard, 1950, translation by Herma Briffault published as *The Sea Wall*, Pellegrini & Cudahy, 1952, same translation published with preface by Germaine Bree, Farrar, Strauss, 1967, translation by Antonia White published as *A Sea of Troubles*, Methuen, 1953; *Le Marin de Gibralter*, Gallimard, 1952, translation by Barbara Bray published as *The Sailor from Gibraltar*, Grove Press, 1966; *Les Petits Chevaux de Tarquinia*, Gallimard, 1953, translation by Peter DuBerg published as *The Little Horses of Tarquinia*, J. Calder, 1960; *Des Journees entieres dans les arbres* (short stories), Gallimard, 1954; *Le Square*, Gallimard, 1955, translation by Sonia Pitt-Rivers and Irina Morduch published as *The Square*, Grove Press, 1959, French language edition published under original French title, edited by Claude

Morhange Begue, Macmillan, 1965; *Moderato Cantabile*, Editions de Minuit, 1958, translation by Richard Seaver published as *Moderato Cantabile*, Grove Press, 1960, French language edition edited by Thomas Bishop, Prentice-Hall, 1968, another French language edition, edited by W.S. Strachan, Methuen, 1968, also published with supplemental material as *Moderato cantabile* (suivi de) *L'Univers romanesque de Marguerite Duras*, Plon, 1962.

Dix heures et demie du soir en ete, Gallimard, 1960, translation by Anne Borchardt published as *Ten-thirty on a Summer Night*, J. Calder, 1962, Grove Press, 1963; *L'Apres Midi de Monsieur Andesmas*, Gallimard, 1962, translation by Borchardt, published together with Bray's translation of the play *Les Eaux et forets* as *The Afternoon of Monsieur Andesmas* and *The Rivers and Forests*, J. Calder, 1965; *Le Ravissement de Lol V. Stein*, Gallimard, 1964, translation by Seaver published as *The Ravishing of Lol Stein*, Grove Press, 1966, translation by Eileen Ellenbogen published as *The Rapture of Lol V. Stein*, Hamlish Hamilton, 1967; *Four Novels* (contains "The Square," "Moderato Cantabile," "Ten-thirty on a Summer Night," and "The Afternoon of Monsieur Andesmas"), translations by Pitt-Rivers and others, introduction by Bree, Grove Press, 1965; *Le Vice-consul*, Gallimard, 1966, translation by Ellenbogen published as *The Vice-consul*, Hamlish Hamilton, 1968; *L'Amante anglaise*, Gallimard, 1967, translation by Bray published as *L'Amante anglaise*, Grove Press, 1968; *Detruire, dit-elle*, Editions de Minuit, 1969, translation by Bray published as *Destroy, She Said*, Grove Press, 1970; *Abahn, Sabana, David*, Gallimard, 1970; *L'Amour*, Gallimard, 1972; (with Xaviere Gauthier) *Les Parleuses*, Editions de Minuit, 1974; also *Savannah Bay* and *La Maladice de la Mort*, both 1983, and *Les Enfants*, 1984.

NON-FICTION—(With Jacques Lacan and Maurice Blanchot) *Etude sur l'oeuvre litteraire, theatrale, et cinematographique de Marguerite Duras*, Albatros, 1976.

AWARDS: Prix Jean Cocteau, for *India Song;* Grand Prix and Academe du cinema awards, for *L'Amant anglaise;* Prix Goncourt, 1984; Ritz Paris Hemingway Award, 1986. Also won an award for *Des journees entieres dans les arbres*.

ADDRESSES: HOME—5 rue St. Benoit, 75006, Paris, France. AGENT—MLR Ltd., 194 Old Brompton Road, London SW5, England.*

*   *   *

DUSSAULT, Nancy   1936-

PERSONAL: Born June 30, 1936, in Pensacola, FL; daughter of George Adrian (a naval officer) and Sarah Isabel (Seitz) Dussault; married James D. Travis, October 4, 1958. EDUCATION: Northwestern University, B. Music, 1957; studied acting with Alvina Kraus and singing with Lotte Lehmann in New York City.

VOCATION: Singer and actress.

CAREER: STAGE DEBUT—A nurse, *South Pacific*, Highland Park Music Theatre, IL, 1955. OFF-BROADWAY DEBUT—*Diversions*, Downtown Theatre, November 7, 1958. PRINCIPAL STAGE APPEARANCES—Appeared in *Guys and Dolls, Lady in the Dark, Kismet, The Golden Apple,* and *Pal Joey*, all at the Highland Park Music Theatre, 1955-56; Jeanne, *Street Scene*, City Center, New York City, 1959; Judy, *Dr. Willy Nilly*, Barbizon Plaza Theatre, New York City, 1959; Pitti-Sing, *The Mikado*, 1959, and Sister

Mister, *The Cradle Will Rock,* both at the City Center, New York City, 1960; Bobbie, *No for an Answer,* Circle in the Square Theatre, New York City, 1960; Hilaret, *Lock Up Your Daughters!,* Shubert Theatre, New Haven, CT, 1960; Tilda Mullen, *Do Re Mi,* St. James Theatre, New York City, 1960; Maria, *The Sound of Music,* Lunt-Fontanne Theatre, New York City, 1962; Miss Agnes, *Apollo and Miss Agnes,* State Music Fair, Dallas, TX, 1963; Beatrice, *Beatrice and Benedict,* with the Washington, DC Opera Company, 1964; repeated role of Maria, *The Sound of Music,* with the Pittsburgh Civic Light Opera and the St. Louis Municipal Opera companies, 1964; appeared in *What Makes Sammy Run,* Valley Music Theatre, 1964; Emily Kirsten, *Bajour,* Shubert Theatre, New York City, 1964; appeared in *Phoebe,* Bucks County Playhouse, New Hope, PA, 1965; Carrie Pipperidge, *Carousel,* City Center, New York City, 1966.

Sharon McLonergan, *Finian's Rainbow,* City Center, New York City, 1967; Marie, *Fiorello!,* command performance at the White House, Washington, DC, 1968; Nellie Forbush, *South Pacific,* summer stock, Dallas, 1967; title role, *Peter Pan,* the Girl, *On Time,* and appeared in *After You, Mr. Hyde,* all at the Goodspeed Opera House, East Haddam, CT, 1968; Daisy, *On a Clear Day You Can See Forever,* with the St. Paul Civic Light Opera Company, MN, 1968; repeated role of Nellie Forbush, *South Pacific,* Jones Beach Theatre, Long Island, NY, 1969; the First Lady, *Whispers on the Wind,* Theatre de Lys, New York City, 1970; Rose Trelawny, *Trelawny of the Wells,* New York Shakespeare Festival, The Other Stage, then Anspacher Theatre, all New York City, 1970; Elaine, *The Last of the Red Hot Lovers,* North Shore Music Theatre, Beverly, MA, 1972; Mary McLeod, *Detective Story,* Shubert Theatre, Philadelphia, 1973; appeared in *6 Rms Riv Vu,* Playhouse-on-the-Mall, Paramus, NJ, 1973; repeated role of Nellie Forbush, *South Pacific,* in Sacramento, CA, 1974; title role, *Irene,* Paper Mill Playhouse, Millburn, NJ, 1975; appeared in *Winter Interludes,* Town Hall Theatre, New York City, 1976; appeared in *Side by Side by Sondheim,* Music Box Theatre, New York City, 1977; *Night of 100 Stars,* Radio City Music Hall, New York City, 1982; *Night of 100 Stars II,* Radio City Music Hall, 1985.

Special musical performances include: Soloist with the Chicago Symphony Orchestra, 1957; *Broadway Answers Selma,* Majestic Theatre, New York City, 1965; *ASCAP Salute,* 1967; *The Magic of Cole Porter,* Lincoln Center Music Theatre, New York City, 1967; *The Music of Vincent Youmens, Harold Arlen, Noel Coward,* 1968, and *The Music of Kurt Weil* and *The Heyday of Rodgers and Hart,* both 1969, all Philharmonic Hall, New York City; *A Salute of Rudolph Friml,* Shubert Theatre, New York City, 1969; *A Hammerstein Salute,* Philharmonic Hall, New York City, 1972; *The Revue of Revues,* Avery Fisher Hall, Lincoln Center, New York City, 1973; *A Salute to Jule Styne,* Palace Theatre, New York City, 1974.

MAJOR TOURS—Ann, *Half a Sixpence,* U.S. cities, 1967; Daisy Gamble, *On a Clear Day You Can See Forever,* U.S. cities, 1968; *The Gershwin Years,* U.S. cities, 1973.

PRINCIPAL FILM APPEARANCES—*The In-Laws,* Warner Brothers, 1979.

TELEVISION DEBUT—*The Ed Sullivan Show,* CBS, 1961. PRINCIPAL TELEVISION APPEARANCES—Series: Carol Davis, *The New Dick Van Dyke Show,* CBS, 1971; host, *Good Morning, America,* ABC, 1975; Muriel Rush, *Too Close for Comfort,* ABC, 1980-83; host, Program 3, *The Shape of Things,* 1982. Episodic: *Calendar,* CBS, 1962; *The Gary Moore Show,* CBS, 1963; *Bell Telephone Hour,* NBC, 1965; *Love, American Style,* ABC.

Pilots: Nancy Clancy, *The Nancy Dussault Show*, CBS, 1973; Muriel Rush, *Family Business*, 1983. Teleplays: Polly, *The Beggar's Opera*, PBS, 1967; also, *Love Is*. Specials: Has appeared on *Alan King Looks Back in Anger: A Review of 1972*, 1973; *Burt and the Girls*, 1973; *The Many Faces of Comedy*, 1973; *The Lily Tomlin Show*, 1973; *Night of 100 Stars, II*, 1985.

Guest: *The Tonight Show*, NBC; *The Mike Douglas Show*, CBS; *The Merv Griffin Show*, syndicated. Panelist: *The $10,000 Pyramid*, ABC; *The Match Game*, CBS; *Beat the Clock*, CBS; *What's My Line*, CBS; *To Tell the Truth*, CBS.

AWARDS: Young Artists Award, Society of American Musicians, for performance with Chicago Symphony, 1957; *Theatre World* Award, Antoinette Perry Award nomination, both 1960, for *Do Re Mi;* Best Actress, Kit Kat Club Award, for *The Sound of Music;* Applause Award, Northwestern University, 1963, for contribution to the arts; Antoinette Perry Award nomination, 1965, for *Bajour.*

MEMBER: Actors' Equity Association, American Federation of Television and Radio Artists, Screen Actors Guild, American Guild of Musical Artists, American Guild of Variety Artists; Delta Delta Delta (former vice president).

SIDELIGHTS: RECREATIONS—Needlework, cooking, reading, and music.

ADDRESSES: HOME—New York, NY. AGENT—Shapiro, Taxon, and Kopell, 111 W. 40th Street, New York, NY 10018.*

*   *   *

DYSART, Richard A.

PERSONAL: Born in Augusta, ME. EDUCATION: Attended Emerson College, Boston.

VOCATION: Actor.

CAREER: NEW YORK DEBUT—Orderly, *The Quare Fellow*, Circle in the Square Theatre, 1958. PRINCIPAL STAGE APPEARANCES—Howie Newsome, *Our Town*, Circle in the Square Theatre, New York City, 1959; Barney Evans, *Epitaph for George Dillon*, Actors Playhouse, New York City, 1960; prison guard, *The Seven at Dawn*, Actors Playhouse, New York City, 1961; the Father, *Six Characters in Search of an Author*, Martinique Theatre, New York City, 1963; Uncle Fred, *All in Good Time*, Royale Theatre, New York City, 1965; Horace Giddens, *The Little Foxes*, Vivian Beaumont Theatre, then Ethel Barrymore Theatre, both New York City, 1967; Mike, "The Ruffian on the Stair" and title role, "The Erpingham Camp," both part of *Crimes of Passion*, Astor Place Theatre, New York City, 1969; Pierre Lannes, *A Place without Doors*, Long Wharf Theatre, New Haven, CT, then Staircase Theatre, New York City, 1970; Coach, *That Championship Season*, New York Shakespeare Festival, Newman Theatre, then Booth Theatre, both New York City, 1972; Louis Puget, *Black Angel*, Mark Taper Forum, Los Angeles, CA, 1978; Marcus, *Another Part of the Forest*, with the Center Theatre Group, Ahmanson Theatre, Los Angeles, 1982.

MAJOR TOURS—The Common Man, *A Man for All Seasons*, U.S. cities, 1963-64; *Uncle Vanya*, with the American Conservatory Theatre, Connecticut, Illinois, and California cities, 1966.

PRINCIPAL FILM APPEARANCES—*The Crazy World of Julius Vrooder*, Twentieth Century-Fox, 1974; *The Terminal Man*, Warner Brothers, 1974; *Warning Signs*, Twentieth Century-Fox, 1985.

PRINCIPAL TELEVISION APPEARANCES—Series: Leland McKensie, *L.A. Law*, NBC, 1986—.

ADDRESSES: AGENT—Writers and Artists Agency, 162 W. 56th Street, New York, NY 10019.*

E

ECKART, William J. 1920-

PERSONAL: Born October 21, 1920, in New Iberia, LA; son of William J. (a salesman) and Annette Cecile (Brown) Eckart; married Jean Levy (a designer and producer), August 28, 1943; children: one son and one daughter. EDUCATION: Attended Tulane University, B.S., architecture, Yale University, M.F.A., stage design. MILITARY: U.S. Army translator, 1942-46.

VOCATION: Designer and producer.

CAREER: PRINCIPAL STAGE WORK—Scenic designer (unless otherwise noted; all with his wife Jean Eckart): *Glad Tidings,* Lyceum Theatre, New York City, 1951, *To Dorothy, a Son,* John Golden Theatre, New York City, 1951; *Gertie,* Plymouth Theatre, New York City, 1952; scenic design, costumes, and lights, *Maya,* scenic design and lighting, *The Scarecrow, The School for Scandal,* and *The Little Clay Cart,* all at Theatre de Lys, New York City, 1953; *Oh Men! Oh Women!,* Henry Miller's Theatre, New York City, 1953; scenic design and lighting, *Dead Pigeon,* Vanderbilt Theatre, New York City, 1953; *The Golden Apple,* Phoenix Repertory Theatre, 1954; scenic design and lighting design, *Wedding Breakfast,* 46th Street Theatre, New York City, 1954; *Portrait of a Lady,* American National Theatre and Academy (ANTA) Theatre, New York City, 1954; scenic design, costumes, and lighting, *Damn Yankees,* 46th Street Theatre, New York City, 1955; *Reuben Reuben,* Shubert Theatre, Boston, 1955; scenic design and lighting, *L'il Abner,* St. James Theatre, New York City, 1956; scenic design, costumes, and lighting, *Mister Johnson,* Martin Beck Theatre, New York City, 1956; *Damn Yankees,* London, 1957; *Livin' the Life,* Phoenix Repertory Theatre, New York City, 1957; scenic design and lighting, *Copper and Brass,* Martin Beck Theatre, New York City, 1957; *The Body Beautiful,* Broadway Theatre, New York City, 1958; co-producer, scenic designer, and costumes, *Once Upon a Mattress,* Phoenix Repertory Theatre, New York City, 1959; scenic design, costumes, and lighting, *Fiorello!,* Broadhurst Theatre, New York City, 1959.

Scenic design and lighting, *Viva Madison Avenue!,* Longacre Theatre, New York City, 1960; *Once Upon a Mattress,* London, 1960; scenic design and lighting, *The Happiest Girl in the World,* Martin Beck Theatre, New York City, 1961; *Let It Ride,* Eugene O'Neill Theatre, New York City, 1961; *Take Her She's Mine,* Biltmore Theatre, New York City, 1961; *Oh Dad, Poor Dad, Mama's Hung You in the Closet and I'm Feelin' So Sad,* Phoenix Repertory Theatre, New York City, 1962; scenic design and lighting, *Never Too Late,* Playhouse Theatre, New York City, 1962; *Here's Love,* Shubert Theatre, New York City, 1963; *She Loves Me* Eugene O'Neill Theatre, New York City, 1963; *Never Too Late,* London, 1963; *Too Much Johnson,* New York City, 1964; *Anyone Can Whistle,* Majestic Theatre, New York City,

1964; scenic design and lighting, *Fade Out—Fade In,* Mark Hellinger Theatre, New York City, 1964; *All About Elsie,* New York World's Fair Theatre, New York City, 1964; *She Loves Me,* London, 1964.

A Sign of Affection, Shubert Theatre, New Haven, CT, then Walnut Street Playhouse, Philadelphia, 1965; *Flora the Red Menace,* Alvin Theatre, New York City, 1965; scenic design and lighting, *The Zulu and the Zayda,* Cort Theatre, New York City, 1965; *Oh Dad Poor Dad Mama's Hung You in the Closet and I'm Feelin' So Sad,* London, 1965; *Mame,* Winter Garden Theatre, New York City, 1966; *Agatha Sue I Love You,* Henry Miller's Theatre, New York City, 1966; *A Midsummer Night's Dream,* for the American Shakespeare Festival, Stratford, CT, 1967; *Hallelujah, Baby,* Martin Beck Theatre, New York City, 1967; *The Education of H*Y*M*A*N K*A*P*L*A*N,* Alvin Theatre, New York City, 1968; *Maggie Flynn,* ANTA Theatre, New York City, 1968; *A Mother's Kisses,* Shubert Theatre, New Haven, CT, then the Morris A. Mechanic Theatre, Baltimore, 1968, and New York City, 1968; *The Fig Leaves Are Falling,* Broadhurst Theatre, New York City, 1969; *A Way of Life,* ANTA Theatre, New York City, 1969; *Mame,* London production, 1969.

Norman, Is That You?, Lyceum Theatre, New York City, 1970; *Sensations,* Theatre Four, New York City, 1970; also *Of Mice and Men,* New York City, 1971; with the Milwaukee Repertory Theatre, 1980-81; *The Dining Room,* Plaza Theatre, Dallas, 1984.

PRINCIPAL FILM WORK—Costume designer, *The Pajama Game,* Warner Brothers, 1957; set and costume designer, *Damn Yankees,* Warner Brothers, 1958; set and costume designer, *The Night They Raided Minsky's,* United Artists, 1968.

PRINCIPAL TELEVISION WORK—With NBC, 1943; with CBS, 1950-51; work includes design for *Excursions,* NBC, 1953-54; *Adventure in Music,* NBC, 1959. Teleplays: Scenic design, *Cinderella,* CBS, 1957.

RELATED CAREER—Has designed for industrial productions, including *Glamour* magazine fashion shows, 1950-57, the Oldsmobile show, 1955, the Martex show, 1957, and the DuPont-Borden show for the 1964 World's Fair, New York City; head of Theatre Design Studies, Southern Methodist University, Dallas, TX, 1971.

AWARDS: Recipient (with Jean Eckart) of the Donaldson Award, 1954, for *The Golden Apple.*

MEMBER: United Scenic Artists.

ADDRESSES: OFFICE—14 St. Luke's Place, New York, NY 10014.*

NICOLE EGGERT

EGGERT, Nicole

PERSONAL: Born in Southern California.

VOCATION: Actress.

CAREER: TELEVISION DEBUT—*When She Was Bad,* 1979. PRINCIPAL TELEVISION APPEARANCES—Series: Marci Ferguson, *Who's the Boss?,* ABC, 1985-86; *Charles in Charge,* syndicated, 1986—; Chrissie Hooker, *T.J. Hooker,* ABC.

Movies: *When Hell Was in Session,* 1979; *I Dream of Jeannie, 15 Years Later,* 1985; *Annihilator,* 1986; also, "Dead Wrong: The John Evans Story," *ABC Afterschool Special,* ABC. Mini-Series: Young Golda, *Golda;* Lucia, *Marco Polo.* Episodic: "Dear Pen Pal," *Still the Beaver;* Marci, "Kiddie Porn," *Today's F.B.I; Fantasy Island.*

Specials: *Circus of the Stars,* 1986; voice of Margaret, "May Day for Mothers," *Dennis the Menace;* voice of the little girl, *She's the One, Charlie Brown.*

PRINCIPAL FILM APPEARANCES—*Rich and Famous,* Metro-Goldwyn-Mayer, 1981; *Hambone and Hillie,* New World, 1984; young Ayla, *Clan of the Cave Bear,* Warner Brothers, 1985; *Omega 7,* New World, 1986.

PRINCIPAL STAGE APPEARANCES—Eydie, *Grown Ups,* Mark Taper Forum, Los Angeles, CA.

SIDELIGHTS: RECREATIONS—Biking, skiing.

Through material provided by Nicole Eggert's public relations agent, *CTFT* learned that she began her public career at the age of five and one-half years, when she won the Miss Universe Petite Division Pageant.

ADDRESSES: HOME—Orange County, CA. PUBLICIST—c/o Monique Moss, Michael Levine Public Relations, 9123 Sunset Blvd., Los Angeles, CA 90069.

*   *   *

EISELE, Robert   1948-

PERSONAL: Surname pronounced "Eyes-lee"; born June 9, 1948, in Altadena, CA; son of Lawrence C. (a shoe business executive) and Helen (Klimek) Eisele; married Diana G. Ryterband (a dancer and teacher), June 21, 1975; children: Nicholas A. EDUCATION: University of California at Los Angeles, B.A., 1971, M.F.A., 1974.

VOCATION: Writer.

WRITINGS: PLAYS, PRODUCED—*Goats,* University of California at Los Angeles, 1973, American College Theatre Festival, Kennedy Center, Washington, DC, 1974; *Animals Are Passing from Our Lives,* University of California at Los Angeles, 1973, American Conservatory Theatre, San Francisco, CA, 1975-76, Waterloo Playhouse, IA, 1977, Grassroots Experience, San Francisco, CA, 1978, Bonfils Theatre, Denver Center for the Performing Arts, CO, 1978; Hedgerow Theatre, Philadelphia, PA, 1978, St. Clements Theatre, New York City, 1979, Kentucky Cooperative, Louisville, 1983; *A Garden in Los Angeles,* The Breughel Project, San Francisco, CA, 1976; *The Greenroom,* University of Colorado, 1979; *A Dark Night of the Soul,* St. Nicholas Theatre, Chicago, IL, 1979; *The Murder of Einstein,* Alliance Theatre, Atlanta, GA, 1980.

PLAYS, PUBLISHED—*Animals Are Passing from Our Lives,* "West Coast Plays," *Volume 3,* Berkeley, 1979. POEMS—Published in *Poem* magazine and *Westwinds* magazine.

TELEVISION—Episodic: "Ordinary Hero," *Cagney and Lacey,* CBS, 1985; "Schedule One," *Cagney and Lacey,* CBS, 1986. Dramatic specials: *The Murder of Einstein,* PBS, 1980.

SCREENPLAYS—*Breach of Contract,* Atlantic, 1985.

BOOKS—*The Rat, the Gypsy and the Young Man,* 1973.

RELATED CAREER—Associate professor of theatre arts, Rio Hondo College, Whittier, CA, 1976—.

NON-RELATED CAREER—Worked at Camarillo State Mental Hospital, 1974.

AWARDS: Samuel Goldwyn Writing Award, 1973, for *The Rat, the Gypsy and the Young Man;* Donald Davis Dramatic Writing Award, 1974, for *Animals Are Passing from Our Lives;* Best Original Play, American College Theatre Festival, 1974, for *Goats;* First Prize, Theatre Arts Corporation National Playwriting Competition Award, 1979, for *The Greenroom;* Humanitas Prize Award and Imagen Award, both 1986, for "Ordinary Hero," *Cagney and Lacey.* Fellowships: Oscar Hammerstein Playwriting, 1974; American Conservatory Theatre Playwriting, 1975-76.

MEMBER: Writers Guild of America West, Dramatists Guild, Screen Actors Guild, Actors' Equity Association.

ADDRESSES: HOME—404 N. Sweetzer Avenue, Los Angeles, CA 90048. AGENT—c/o Ken Sherman, Paul Kohner Agency, 9169 Sunset Blvd., Los Angeles, CA 90069.

*　　*　　*

ELIAS, Michael   1940-

PERSONAL: Born September 20, 1940 in Monticello, NY; son of Frederick (a physician) and Sylvia (a librarian and teacher; maiden name, Lifschite) Elias. EDUCATION: St. Johns College, Annapolis, B.S., 1962; studied with Peggy Feury at the Corner Loft and Bill Hickey and Alice Spivak at the Herbert Berghof Studios in New York.

VOCATION: Actor and producer.

CAREER: STAGE DEBUT—Prisoner Number Five, *The Brig,* Living Theatre, New York City, then transferred to Mermaid Theatre, London, 1963. PRINCIPAL STAGE APPEARANCES—Performed at the Judson Poets Theatre, New York City, 1964-68; *The Pitch,* Padua Playwrights Festival, Los Angeles, CA.

FILM DEBUT—*The Night They Raided Minsky's,* United Artists, 1968. PRINCIPAL FILM APPEARANCES—*The Brig; The Frisco Kid,* Warner Brothers, 1979; *Young Doctors in Love,* Twentieth Century-Fox, 1982.

TELEVISION DEBUT—As part of the comedy team Elias & Shaw, *The Tonight Show,* six appearances, NBC, 1964-67. PRINCIPAL TELEVISION APPEARANCES—Series: *The Cosby Show,* NBC; *All in the Family,* CBS; *The Mary Tyler Moore Show,* CBS; *The Odd Couple,* ABC.

PRINCIPAL TELEVISION WORK—Co-creator and co-executive producer, *Head of the Class,* ABC, 1986—; also, co-executive producer, *Eye to Eye,* ABC.

ADDRESSES: OFFICE—100 N. Pass Avenue, Burbank, CA 91522. AGENT—Contemporary Artists Agency, 1888 Century Park East, Los Angeles, CA 90067.

*　　*　　*

ELLIOTT, Alice   1946-

PERSONAL: Born August 22, 1946, in Durham, NC; daughter of Charles Ray (a professor) and Mary (a therapist; maiden name, Farquhar) Elliott; married Russell L. Treyz (a director), May 15, 1971; children: Amanda Mary, Ross Denney. EDUCATION: Attended Carnegie Mellon University; Goodman School of Drama, B.F.A., 1968; studied voice with Clyde Vinson.

VOCATION: Actress and teacher.

CAREER: STAGE DEBUT—Emily, *Our Town,* Totem Pole Playhouse. PRINCIPAL STAGE APPEARANCES—Mary Alden, *To-*

MICHAEL ELIAS

ALICE ELLIOTT

wards Zero, Woodstock Playhouse, NY; Ursula, *Much Ado About Nothing*, Goodman Theatre, Chicago; Cecily, *The Importance of Being Earnest*, McCarter Theatre, Princeton, NJ; Sybil, *Private Lives*, State West; Celia, *As You Like It*, North Shore Music Theatre, Long Island, NY; Amy, *The Show Off*, Carnegie Mellon Theatre Company, Pittsburgh; Jo Ann, *Vanities*, Virginia Museum Theatre, Richmond, VA; Laura, *The Glass Menagerie*, Theatre by the Sea, Portsmouth, NH; Margery Pinchwife, *The Country Wife*, Alabama Shakespeare Festival, Montgomery, AL.

Off-Broadway appearances: Sis II, *Don't Fail Your Lovin' Daddy*, Public Theatre; Elsa, *Spring's Awakening*, Public Theatre Workshop; various roles, *American Gothics*, Roundabout Theatre; Shirley Preston, *Professor George* and Susie Friend, *Uncommon Women*, both Playright's Horizons Theatre; Celia, *As You Like It*, La Mama Experimental Theatre Club (E.T.C.).

TELEVISION DEBUT—Amy Wolfe, *As the World Turns*, CBS, 1974. PRINCIPAL TELEVISION APPEARANCES—*All My Children*, ABC; Louise, *Loving*, ABC.

FILM DEBUT—Bridget, *Four Friends*, Filmways, 1981.

ADDRESSES: AGENT—Dulce Eisen Agency, 154 E. 61st Street, New York, NY 10023.

*   *   *

ELLIOTT, Denholm   1922-

PERSONAL: Full name, Denholm Mitchell Elliott; born May 31, 1922, in London, England; son of Myles Layman Farr and Nina (Mitchell) Elliott; married Virginia McKenna, March 1, 1954 (divorced); married Susan Robinson, June 15, 1962; children: Jennifer, Mark. EDUCATION: Attended Malvern College, 1936-39; trained for the stage at the Royal Academy of Dramatic Art, 1939. MILITARY: Royal Air Force, 1939-45.

VOCATION: Actor.

CAREER: FILM DEBUT—*Dear Mr. Prohack*, 1948. PRINCIPAL FILM APPEARANCES—*Breaking the Sound Barrier*, United Artists, 1951; *The Ringer*, 1952; Mick Gregory, *The Holly and the Ivy*, 1953; *The Cruel Sea*, 1953; Wilson, *Heart of the Matter*, Associated Artists, 1954; *They Who Dare*, Associated Artists, 1955; Denis, *The Man Who Loved Red Heads*, United Artists, 1955; Flight Lt. McKenzie, *The Night My Number Came Up*, 1955; Martin Blake, *Lease of Life*, I.F.E., 1956; *Pacific Destiny*, 1956; *Scent of Mystery*, 1960; *Marco Polo*, American International, 1962; *Nothing but the Best*, Royal, 1964; *Station Six Sahara*, Allied Artists, 1964; *King Rat*, Columbia, 1965; *You Must Be Joking*, Columbia, 1965.

Alfie, Paramount, 1966; *Here We Go Round the Mulberry Bush*, Lopart, 1968; *The Night They Raided Minsky's*, United Artists, 1968; Dorn, *The Sea Gull*, Warner Brothers-Seven Arts, 1968; Captain Hornsby, *Too Late the Hero*, Cinerama, 1970; *The Rise and Rise of Michael Rimmer*, Warner Brothers, 1970; Charles, *The House that Dripped Blood*, Cinerama, 1971; Emmanuel Whitebread, *Percy's Progress*, Metro-Goldwyn-Mayer (MGM), 1971; *The Hero*, AVCO-Embassy, 1972; Diltant, *Vault of Horror*, Cinerama, 1973; Krogstad, *A Doll's House*, Paramount, 1973; Friar, *The Apprenticeship of Duddy Kravitz*, Paramount, 1974; *Percy's Prog-*

ress, MGM, 1974; Commander Petapiece, *Russian Roulette*, AVCO-Embassy, 1975; Henry Beddows, *To the Devil a Daughter*, 1976; Admiral Canaris, *Voyage of the Damned*, AVCO-Embassy, 1976; John Grey, *Partners* (Canada), 1976; Will Scarlett, *Robin and Marion*, Columbia, 1976; voice, *Watership Down*, AVCO-Embassy, 1978; Jupp, *Sweeney 2*, 1978; Sidney Beynon, *The Boys from Brazil*, Twentieth Century-Fox, 1978; Lt. Colonel Pulleine, *Zulu Dawn*, 1979; Raglan Thistle, *A Game for Vultures*, 1979; Skinner, *Cuba*, United Artists, 1979; William Leigh, *Saint Jack*, 1979.

Stefan Vognic, *Bad Timing/A Sensual Obsession*, World Northal, 1980; Seymor, *Rising Damp*, 1980; Marcus Brody, *Raiders of the Lost Ark*, Paramount, 1981; Parker, *Sunday Lovers*, United Artists, 1981; Thomas Bates, *Brimstone and Treacle*, Namara Films, 1982; The Bishop of London, *The Missionary*, Columbia, 1982; Sir Ralph Skelton, *The Wicked Lady*, MGM/United Artists, 1983; Dr. Mortimer, *The Hound of the Baskervilles*, 1983; Coleman, *Trading Places*, Paramount, 1983; *Illusions*, 1983; Dr. Swaby, *A Private Function*, 1984; Elliott Templeton, *The Razor's Edge*, Columbia, 1984; Victor, *Past Caring*, 1985; Dr. Savary, *Underworld*, 1985; Vernon Bayliss, *Defence of the Realm*, 1985; *A Room with a View*, Cinecom, 1986; Sir Henry Broughton, *The Happy Valley*, 1986; Colonel Hugh Phelps, *Whoopee Boys*, 1986.

Also appeared in *The High Bright Sun*.

STAGE DEBUT—Arden Rencelaw, *The Drunkard*, Playhouse, Amersham, U.K., 1945. LONDON DEBUT—Grimmett, *The Guinea Pig*, Criterion Theatre, 1946. BROADWAY DEBUT—Hugo and Frederic, *Ring Round the Moon*, Martin Beck Theatre, 1950. PRINCIPAL STAGE APPEARANCES—Jan-Erik, *Frenzy*, St. Martin's Theatre, London, 1948; Albin, *The Green Cockatoo*, Lyric Theatre, Hammersmith, London, 1948; Pierre Blandinet, *Don't Listen, Ladies!*, St. James Theatre, London, 1948; Frank Shire, *Horn of the Moon*, Bolton's Theatre, London, 1949; title role, *John Keats Lived Here*, Wyndham's Theatre, London, 1949; Junius, *Buoyant Billions*, Malvern Festival, U.K., then Prince's Theatre, London, 1949.

Edgar, *Venus Observed*, St. James's Theatre, London, 1950; Julian, *The Green Bay Tree*, John Golden Theatre, New York City, 1951; Private Peter Able, *A Sleep of Prisoners*, St. Thomas's Church, Regent Street, London, 1951; Kip Ames, *Third Person*, Arts Theatre, then Criterion Theatre, London, 1951-52; Giles Seabrook, *A Fiddle at the Wedding*, Royal Theatre, Brighton, U.K., 1952; Colby Simpkins, *The Confidential Clerk*, Edinburgh Festival, Scotland, then Lyric Theatre, London, 1953; Jan Wicziewsky, *South*, Arts Theatre, London, 1955; Alan Bretherton, *The Delegate*, Opera House, Manchester, U.K., 1955; Alex Shanklin, *The Long Echo*, St. James's Theatre, London, 1956; Stefan, *Who Cares?*, Fortune Theatre, London, 1956; Kilroy, *Camino Real*, Phoenix Theatre, New York City, 1957; Fernand, *Monique*, John Golden Theatre, New York City, 1957; Francis X. Digman, *King of Hearts*, New Shakespeare Theatre, Liverpool, U.K., 1958; Gaston, *Traveller without Luggage*, Arts Theatre, London, 1959; Shem, *The Ark*, Westminster Theatre, London, 1959.

Bassanio, *The Merchant of Venice*, Troilus, *Troilus and Cressida*, Valentine, *The Two Gentlemen of Verona*, all at the Shakespeare Memorial Theatre, Stratford-upon-Avon, U.K., 1960; Jan Wicziewsky, *South*, Lyric Theatre, Hammersmith, London, 1961; Honorable Clive Rodingham, *Write Me a Murder*, Belasco Theatre, New York City, 1961; title role, *Domino*, Royal Theatre, Brighton, 1963; Trigorin, *The Seagull* and Reverend John Hale, *The Crucible*, both at the Belasco Theatre, New York City, 1964; Chrystal,

The Game as Played, New Arts Theatre, London, 1964; Dr. Diaforus, *The Imaginary Invalid,* Alec Harvey, *Still Life,* and Cornelius Melody, *A Touch of the Poet,* all at the American National Theatre Academy (ANTA) Theatre, New York City, 1967.

Come as You Are, New Theatre then Strand Theatre, London, 1970; Leo, *Design for Living,* Los Angeles Music Centre, 1971; Judge Brack, *Hedda Gabler,* Royal Court Theatre, London, 1972; Hughes Humphrey, *Turn On,* Royal Theatre, Windsor, U.K., 1973; James Ludlow, *Mad Dog,* Hampstead Theatre, London, 1973; Dick, *Chez Nous,* Globe Theatre, London, 1975; title role, *The Return of A.J. Raffles,* with the Royal Shakspeare Company at the Aldwych Theatre, London, 1975; *Heaven and Hell,* Greenwich Theatre, London, 1976; Sir Wilfred Cates-Darby, *The New York Idea* and Mar and Vershinin, *Three Sisters,* with the Royal Shakespeare Company at the Brooklyn Academy of Music, New York City, 1977; title role, *The Father,* Open Space Theatre, London, 1979.

MAJOR TOURS—Patrice, *Ring Round the Moon,* Trigorin, *The Seagull* and Reverend John Hale, *The Crucible,* U.S. cities with the National Repertory Company, 1963-64.

PRINCIPAL TELEVISION APPEARANCES—*Sextet; Clayhanger; Donkey's Years.*

AWARDS: Best Supporting Actor, Clarence Derwent Award, 1950, for *Venus Observed;* Donaldson Award, 1950, for *Ring Round the Moon;* Best Actor (television), British Academy of Film and Television Arts (BAFTRA) Award nomination, 1986, for *Hotel du Lac;* Best Supporting Actor, Academy Award and BAFTRA Award, both 1986, for *A Room with a View.*

MEMBER: Actors' Equity Association, Screen Actors Guild, American Federation of Television and Radio Artists, British Academy of Film and Television Arts; Garrick Club.

SIDELIGHTS: RECREATIONS—Piano playing, swimming.

ADDRESSES: AGENT—McCartt, Oreck, Barrett, 9200 Sunset Blvd., Suite 1009, Los Angeles, CA 90026.

                          *   *   *

EMMONS, Wayne
(Cousin Bubba)

BRIEF ENTRY: Emmons spent sixteen years as a Church of Christ minister and fifteen years after that as a prosecutor and defense lawyer before turning to stand-up comedy. He bills himself as being from Ash Flat, Arkansas where he grew up. He served in the prosecutor's office in Dyersburg, Tennessee before moving to Memphis to practice criminal law. He created the character of "Cousin Bubba" as a joke when he was speaking at legal seminars in New York. His character wears overalls and his act plays on the traditions of the southern "good ole' boys," using lawyers and the law as a target for his humor. "Do you know why they're using lawyers in laboratory experiments? Because there's more of them than white mice, and you don't get so attached to them." Emmons refuses to use bad language in his routine and is determined to stay out of the law business. "You're dealing in laughter," he says about comedy, "not in human misery."

DAVID ENGELBACH

ENGELBACH, David

PERSONAL: EDUCATION: Fairleigh Dickinson University, B.A., drama and psychology, 1968; trained in film at the University of Southern California.

VOCATION: Writer, producer, and director.

CAREER: PRINCIPAL FILM WORK—Producer, director, and editor, *Alice's Army,* 1969; producer, director, and writer, *Street Scene,* Universal, 1970; director and editor for Furman Films, 1970-72; director of photography, *Hello Fool, Goodbye,* Isis, 1971; producer, *Coming On,* American Film Institute, 1973; assistant to the director, *Jaws,* Universal, 1974; writer and director, *America 3000,* Cannon, 1986.

PRINCIPAL TELEVISION WORK—Dialogue director, *The Night Stalker,* ABC, 1974-75; writer and co-producer, *Lottery!,* ABC, 1982.

PRINCIPAL STAGE WORK—Co-director and managing producer, National Student Touring Company, 1966-68; director, *The Inspector General,* 1967.

RELATED CAREER—Contributing editor, *Millimeter* magazine, 1974-76; creative consultant, Darren McGavin Company, 1974-76.

WRITINGS: SCREENPLAYS—*Street Scene,* Universal, 1970; *Fiste,* New World, 1972; *Harry in the Middle,* 1973; *Hong Kong Export,* Premier, 1973; *Trapspace,* Metromedia, 1973; *Overthere,* 1975;

Crossroads, Warner Brothers, 1976; *Keystone,* Columbia, 1977; *Starforce,* Twentieth Century-Fox, 1978; *Olympiad: A Love Story,* Columbia, 1979; *Death Wish II,* Cannon, 1981; *Deja Vu,* Cannon, 1982; *Time Zero: The Day the Earth Stood Still,* Twentieth Century-Fox, 1983; *America 3000,* Cannon, 1986; *Over the Top,* Cannon, 1986.

TELEVISION—Movies: *Lottery!,* ABC, 1982; *Goldie and the Bears,* ABC, 1984.

SIDELIGHTS: RECREATIONS—Racquetball, tennis, cooking, reading, and snorkeling.

David Engelback told *CTFT* that two of his goals are to "win an Oscar for best director and hop a ride on the space shuttle."

ADDRESSES: HOME—Venice, CA. PUBLICIST—Nan Herst Public Relations, 8733 Sunset Blvd., Suite 103, Los Angeles, CA 90069.

*   *   *

EPSTEIN, Pierre   1930-

PERSONAL: Born July 27, 1930, in Toulouse, France; son of Abraham and Henriette (Castex) Epstein; married Doree Lanouette (divorced). EDUCATION: Attended University of Paris, Goddard College, and Columbia University; trained for the stage at Ecole de l'Atelier in Paris and with Harold Clurman.

VOCATION: Actor and director.

CAREER: STAGE DEBUT—*The Mountebanks,* St. John's Church, New York City, 1955. BROADWAY DEBUT—The Guard, *A Shot in the Dark,* Booth Theatre, 1961. PRINCIPAL STAGE APPEARANCES—Morestan, *A Shot in the Dark,* Booth Theatre, New York City, 1961; Don Baxter, *Enter Laughing,* Henry Miller's Theatre, New York City, 1963; Schuppanzigh, *Black Comedy,* Ethel Barrymore Theatre, New York City, 1967; Prosecutor, *The People Versus Ranchman,* Fortune Theatre, New York City, 1968; Jailer, *Promenade,* Promenade Theatre, New York City, 1969; Jose Rodriques, *Fun City,* Morosco Theatre, New York City, 1972; Harry, *Thieves,* Broadhurst Theatre, New York City, 1974; Henry Morlino, *Little Black Sheep,* Vivian Beaumont Theatre, New York City, 1975.

Raymond, *A Memory of Two Mondays,* Phoenix Theatre, New York City, 1975-76; Barnaby, *The Baker's Wife,* Washington DC, 1976; Beethoven, *Beethoven/Karl,* Manhattan Theatre Club, New York City, 1979; Sam, *Manny,* Century Theatre, New York City, 1979; Kilgore Trout, *God Bless You Mr. Rosewater,* Entermedia Theatre, New York City, 1979; Nocella, *Filumena,* St. James Theatre, New York City, 1980; *The Front Page,* Long Wharf Theatre, New Haven, CT, 1982; Frenchman Number Two, *Plenty,* Plymouth Theatre, New York City, 1983; *The Diary of Anne Frank,* Philadelphia Drama Guild, 1983; Colonel Jesus Schneider, *Breakfast Conversations in Miami,* American Place Theatre, New York City, 1984; Rev. Dickey, *The Ballad of Soapy Smith,* New York Shakespeare Festival, Public Theatre, 1984; French Soldier, *Henry V,* New York Shakespeare Festival, Delacorte Theatre, 1984.

Has also appeared on Broadway in *Bajour,* and Off-Broadway in *Incident at Vichy, Threepenny Opera, Too Much Johnson, Second*

City, Cakes with Wine, Comedy of Errors, They Knew What They Wanted, Museum, The Bright and Golden Land,* and *The Itch.*

Also appeared regionally with the Arena Stage, Washington DC, and the PAF Playhouse, Huntington, Long Island, NY.

PRINCIPAL STAGE WORK—Director: *The Lesson,* NY, 1963; *Savage Amusement,* American Renaissance Theatre, New York City, 1984.

PRINCIPAL FILM APPEARANCES—*Popi,* United Artists, 1969; *Diary of a Mad Housewife,* Universal, 1970; *Love and Death,* United Artists, 1974; *Simon,* Warner Brothers, 1980.

RELATED CAREER—Translator of plays from the French.

AWARDS: Best Director, Obie Award, 1963, for *The Lesson.*

ADDRESSES: AGENT—Dulcina Eisen, 154 E. 61st Street, New York, NY 10021.*

*   *   *

ERDMAN, Jean   1916-

PERSONAL: Born February 20, 1916, in Honolulu, HI; daughter of John Pinney (a director of the Hawaiian Board of Missions) and Marion Elinor (a singer; maiden name, Dillingham) Erdman; mar-

JEAN ERDMAN

ried Joseph Campbell (a professor of comparative mythology and writer), May 5, 1938. EDUCATION: Sarah Lawrence College, 1938; trained for dance at the Martha Graham Dance School, the Hisamatsu School of Japanese Dance, and the Muriel Stuart School of American Ballet.

VOCATION: Dancer, director, and choreographer.

CAREER: STAGE DEBUT—Russian Princess, *Ways and Means,* Dillingham Hall, Honolulu, HI, 1937. BROADWAY DEBUT—The Ideal Spectator, *Every Soul Is a Circus,* with the Martha Graham Dance Company, St. James Theatre, 1939, for three performances. PRINCIPAL STAGE WORK—Dancer with the Martha Graham Dance Company, 1939-43 and had leading roles in *Punch and the Judy* and *Letter to the World;* choreograher, *The Transformation of Medusa,* Bennington Summer Festival, VT, 1942; founder, dancer, and choreographer, the Jean Erdman Dance Company, 1944-1959 and created during this time: *Daughters of the Lonesome Isle,* 1945, *Ophelia,* 1946; *The Perilous Chapel,* 1949; *Changingwoman,* 1951; *Otherman—Or the Beginning of a New Nation,* 1954; *Duet for Flute and Dancer,* 1956, *Fearful Symmetry,* 1957, *Harlequinade,* 1957, *Four Portraits from Duke Ellington's Shakespeare Album,* 1958, and *Now and Zen—Remembering,* 1959; founder and choreographer, the Jean Erdman Theatre of Dance, 1960 and created for it *Twenty Poems of e.e. Cummings,* 1960, *Ensembles, Voracious,* and *Safari,* all 1969, and *The Castle,* 1970.

Also, choreographer, *The Flies,* Vassar College, New York City, 1947; choreographer, *The Enchanted,* Lyceum Theatre, New York City, 1950; writer, director, choreographer, and danced the part of Anna Livia Plurabelle, *The Coach with the Six Insides,* Village South Theatre, New York City, 1962; choreographer, *Yerma,* Vivian Beaumont Theatre, New York City, 1966; director, *The Municipal Water System Is Not Trustworthy,* Sullivan Street Theatre, New York City, 1967; choreographer, *The Two Gentlemen of Verona,* New York Shakespeare Festival, Delacorte Theatre, 1971, then at the Mobile Theatre, New York City, 1973; choreographer, director, and appeared as the Queen, *Moon Mysteries,* Theatre at St. Clement's, New York City, 1972; artistic director, Theatre of the Open Eye, 1972.

MAJOR TOURS—Solo dancer and choreographer with the Jean Erdman Dance Company, world cities, 1955; writer, tour director, choreographer, and danced the part of Anna Livia Plurabelle, *The Coach with the Six Insides,* world cities, 1964.

PRINCIPAL TELEVISION APPEARANCES—Writer, director, choreographer, and danced the part of Anna Livia Plurabelle, *Coach with the Six Insides,* PBS, 1965.

AWARDS: Best New Work of the Season, *Dance Magazine* Award, 1949, for *The Perilous Chapel;* Obie Award and Vernon Rice Award, 1962, for *The Coach with the Six Insides;* Best Choreography, Drama Desk Award and Antoinette Perry Award nomination, 1972, for *The Two Gentlemen of Verona;* American Dance Guild Award, 1986.

MEMBER: Actors' Equity Association, Society of Stage Directors and Choreographers (executive committee, 1972-1973).

ADDRESSES: HOME—136 Waverly Place, New York, NY 10014. OFFICE—Theatre of the Open Eye, 220 W. 89th Street, New York, NY 10024.

EWELL, Tom   1909-

PERSONAL: Born Yewell Tompkins, April 29, 1909, in Queensboro, KY; son of Samuel William and Martine (Yewell) Tompkins; married Judith Ann Abbott (a director, producer, and actress), March 18, 1946 (divorced, 1946); married Marjorie Gynne Sanborn (an advertising copywriter), April 29, 1948; children: one son. EDUCATION: Attended University of Wisconsin. MILITARY: U.S. Naval Reserve, 1941-45.

VOCATION: Actor.

CAREER: STAGE DEBUT—Mike, *The Spider,* Park Theatre, Madison, WI, February 18, 1928. BROADWAY DEBUT—Red, *They Shall Not Die,* Royale Theatre, February 21, 1934. LONDON DEBUT—*Thurber Carnival,* Savoy Theatre, February, 1964. PRINCIPAL STAGE APPEARANCES—Novice and member of the choir, *The First Legion,* 46th Street Theatre, New York City, 1934; Denver, *Geraniums in My Window,* Longacre Theatre, New York City, 1934; stage manager and waiter, *DeLuxe,* Booth Theatre, New York City, 1934; young Frank Martin and small Hardy, *Let Freedom Ring,* Broadhurst Theatre, New York City, 1935; Dennis Eady, *Ethan Frome,* National Theatre, New York City, 1936; Captain Tim, *Tobacco Road,* Forrest Theatre, New York City, 1936; Larry Westcott, *Stage Door,* Music Box Theatre, New York City, 1936; Cornelius Hackl, *The Merchant of Yonkers,* Guild Theatre, New York City, 1938; Simon, *Family Portrait,* Morosco Theatre, New York City, 1939; Brother Galusha, *Susanna and the Elders,* Morosco Theatre, New York City, 1940.

Dick Brown, *Liberty Jones,* for the Theatre Guild at the Shubert Theatre, New York City, 1941; Daniel Marshall, *Sunny River,* St. James Theatre, New York City, 1941; Elkins, *Of All People,* Town Hall, Toledo, OH, then Ford's Theatre, Baltimore, 1945; Huckleberry Haines, *Roberta,* Philharmonic Auditorium, Los Angeles, then Curran Theatre, San Francisco, 1946; Glen Stover, *Apple of His Eye,* Biltmore Theatre, New York City, 1946; Fred Taylor, *John Loves Mary,* Booth Theatre, New York City, 1947; appeared in revue, *Small Wonder,* Coronet Theatre, New York City, 1948; Tommy Turner, *The Male Animal,* summer stock theatres, 1949.

Title role, *Kin Hunter,* Westport Country Playhouse, CT, 1951; Fred Taylor, *John Loves Mary* and Elwood P. Dowd, *Harvey,* both at Bahama Playhouse, Nassau, Bahamas, 1951; Kenneth Bixby, *Goodbye Again,* Bahama Playhouse, 1952; Richard Sherman, *The Seven Year Itch,* Fulton Theatre, New York City, 1952; Vladimir, *Waiting for Godot,* Coconut Grove Playhouse, Miami, FL, 1956; Augie Poole, *The Tunnel of Love,* Royale Theatre, New York City, 1957; Leon Rollo, *Patate,* Henry Miller's Theatre, New York City, 1958; Elliott Nash, *The Gazebo,* Central City, CO, 1959; appeared in *A Thurber Carnival,* American National Theatre and Academy (ANTA) Theatre, New York City, 1960.

Edward T. Wellspot, *Christmas in Las Vegas,* Ethel Barrymore Theatre, New York City, 1965; John O'Rourke, *The Armored Dove,* Palm Beach Playhouse, FL, 1967; Richard Pawling, George, Chuck, and Herbert, *You Know I Can't Hear You When the Water's Running,* New Theatre, London, 1968; Vladimir, *Waiting for Godot,* Actors Playhouse, 1971; Captain Jack Boyle, *Juno and the Paycock,* Walnut Street Theatre, Philadelphia, 1973.

MAJOR TOURS—U.S. cities: Dan, *Brother Rat,* 1936-37; Frank Michaelson, *Take Her, She's Mine,* 1962-63; *Thursday Is a Good Night,* 1964; Harry Lambert, *Never Too Late,* 1965; *We've Had Some Fun,* 1965-66; Mr. Day, *Life with Father,* 1966; John

O'Rourke, *The Armored Dove,* 1967; Dr. Jack Kingsley, *The Impossible Years,* 1967-68; *The Apple Tree,* 1969; *What Did We Do Wrong?,* 1974.

FILM DEBUT—*Kansas Kid,* Republic, 1939. PRINCIPAL FILM APPEARANCES—*They Knew What They Wanted,* RKO, 1940; *Adamb's Rib,* Metro-Goldwyn-Mayer (MGM), 1949; *Mr. Music,* Paramount, 1950; *A Life of Her Own,* MGM, 1950; *American Guerilla in the Phillipines,* Twentieth Century-Fox, 1950; *Finders Keepers* and *Up Front,* both Universal, 1951; *Lost in Alaska,* Universal, 1952; *Willie and Joe Back at the Front,* Twentieth Century-Fox, 1955; *Seven Year Itch,* Twentieth Century-Fox, 1955; *The Lieutenant Wore Skirts,* Twentieth Century-Fox, 1956; *The Girl Can't Help It,* Twentieth Century-Fox, 1956; *Tender Is the Night,* Twentieth Century-Fox, 1962; *State Fair,* Twentieth Century-Fox, 1962; *Suppose They Gave a War and Nobody Came,* Cinerama, 1970; *To Find a Man,* Columbia, 1972; *They Only Kill Their Masters,* 1972; *The Great Gasby,* Paramount, 1974.

PRINCIPAL TELEVISION APPEARANCES—Series: Tom Potter, *The Tom Ewell Show,* CBS, 1960-61; Billy Truman, *Baretta,* ABC, 1975-78; Doctor Jerome Kullens, *Best of the West,* ABC, 1981-82. Episodic: "Daisy, Daisy," *Playwrights '56,* NBC, 1955; *The Alfred Hitchcock Show,* CBS, 1955; *The Perry Como Show,* NBC, 1956; "The Square Egghead," *U.S. Steel Hour,* CBS, 1959; narrator, "The Fourposter," *Golden Showcase,* CBS, 1962.

PRINCIPAL RADIO WORK—Episodic: *The March of Time,* NBC, 1935; *Ellery Queen,* NBC, 1936. Series: *The Ewells,* 1966-68.

RELATED CAREER—Appeared in a number of travel-related films produced by Paramount between 1948-49.

AWARDS: Best Actor, *Variety* New York Drama Critics' Poll, the Clarence Derwent Award, and the Donaldson Award, all 1947, for *John Loves Mary;* Best Actor, Antoinette Perry Award, 1952, for *The Seven Year Itch.*

SIDELIGHTS: RECREATIONS—Golf, farming.

ADDRESSES: OFFICE—267 Palos Verde Drive W., Palos Verdes Estates, CA 90274.*

F

FABRAY, Nanette 1920-

PERSONAL: Born Ruby Nanette Fabares, October 27, 1920, in San Diego, CA; daughter of Raoul Bernard and Lillian (McGovern) Fabares; married David Tebet, October 26, 1947 (divorced, 1951); married Ranald MacDougall, 1957 (died, 1973); children: Jamie. EDUCATION: Attended Los Angeles City College; trained for the stage at the Max Reinhardt School of the Theatre; studied music and voice at the Juilliard Conservatory of Music with Arthur Rodzinski and studied dancing with Bill Robinson, Ernest Belcher, George Danbury, and Danny Daniels.

VOCATION: Actress, singer, and dancer.

CAREER: STAGE DEBUT—As Baby Nanette, vaudeville circuit. BROADWAY DEBUT—Meet the People, Mansfield Theatre, 1940. PRINCIPAL STAGE APPEARANCES—Sister Beatrice, The Miracle, the Daughter, Six Characters in Search of an Author, and Smeraldina, Servant of Two Masters, all with Max Reinhardt School for the Theatre, New York City, 1939; Jean Blanchard, Let's Face It, Imperial Theatre, New York City, 1941; Antiope, By Jupiter, Shubert Theatre, New York City, 1943; Jean, My Dear Public, 46th Street Theatre, New York City, 1943; Sally Madison, Jackpot, Alvin Theatre, New York City, 1944; Evelina, Bloomer Girl, Shubert Theatre, New York City, 1945; Sara Longstreet, High Button Shoes, Shubert Theatre, New York City, 1947; Susan Cooper, Love Life, 46th Street Theatre, New York City, 1948; Jo Kirkland, Arms and the Girl, 46th Street Theatre, New York City, 1950; Janette, Make a Wish, Winter Garden Theatre, New York City, 1951; Nell Henderson, Mr. President, St. James Theatre, New York City, 1962; Roberta Bartlett, No Hard Feelings, Martin Beck Theatre, New York City, 1973; Applause, Palace Theatre, New York City, 1973-74; Karen Nash, Muriel Tate, and Norma Hubley, Plaza Suite, Cirque Theatre, Seattle, WA, 1975; Ruth, Wonderful Town, Dorothy Chandler Pavilion, Los Angeles, CA, 1975; appeared in The Secret Affairs of Mildred Wild, 1977 and in Night of 100 Stars II, Radio City Music Hall, New York City, 1985; appears regularly in dinner theatres.

FILM DEBUT—1927. PRINCIPAL FILM APPEARANCES—The Private Lives of Elizabeth and Essex, Warner Brothers, 1938; A Child Is Born, 1939; Lily Marton, The Band Wagon, Metro-Goldwyn-Mayer (MGM), 1952; Agnes, The Happy Ending, 1970; The Cockeyed Cowboys of Calico County, Universal, 1970; That's Entertainment, Part 2, United Artists, 1976; Alice Finely, Harper Valley PTA, April Fool Productions, 1978; Malvina, Amy, Walt Disney Productions, 1981.

PRINCIPAL TELEVISION APPEARANCES—Series: Ann Victor, Caesar's Hour, NBC, 1954-56; Nan McGovern, Westinghouse Playhouse, NBC, 1961 (syndicated title, Yes, Yes Nanette); Dotty Richards, The Mary Tyler Moore Show, CBS, 1970; panelist, I've Got a Secret, CBS, 1972; Grandma Katherine Romano, One Day at a Time, CBS, 1979. Episodic: Chevrolet Tele-Theatre, NBC, 1948; The Alcoa Hour, NBC, 1955; The Kaiser Aluminum Hour, NBC, 1956; Love, American Style, ABC, 1969.

Pilots: Patricia, Fame is the Name of the Game, NBC, 1966. Movies: Mrs. Vale, But I Don't Want to Get Married!, 1970; Marion Randolph, The Couple Takes a Wife, 1972; Virginia Woolfe, Magic Carpet, 1972; Dora Dayton, The Man in the Santa Claus Suit, 1979; Specials: March of Dimes Fashion Show, 1948; Sara Longstreet, High Button Shoes, 1956; Sally, So Help Me, Aphrodite, 1960; Chevrolet Golden Anniversary Show, 1961; Hollywood Melody, 1962; the white queen, Alice Through the Looking Glass, 1966; The Wonderful World of Burlesque, III, 1967; Nellie Cohan, George M!, 1970; The Bob Hope Show, 1970, 1971, 1982; Burt and the Girls, 1973; substitute dice roller, High Rollers, 1974; Fay Lucas, Happy Anniversary and Goodbye, 1974; Night of 100 Stars II, 1985; NBC 60th Anniversary Celebration, 1986; Irving Berlin's America, 1986. Guest: The Dean Martin Show, NBC, 1960.

AWARDS: Best Performance in a Musical and Best Supporting Performance, both Donaldson Awards, 1947, for High Button Shoes; Best Musical Actress of the Year, Antoinette Perry Award, 1949, for Love Life; Best Actress in Supporting Role, 1955, Best Continuing Performance by a Comedienne in a Series, 1955, 1956, all Emmy Awards, for Caesar's Hour; Woman of the Year, Radio and TV Editors of America, 1955; Hollywood Women's Press Club Award, 1960; President's Distinguished Service Award, 1970. Also: One of Ten Best Dressed Women in America, Fashion Academy Award, 1950; Achievement Award, Women's Division of Albert Einstein College, 1963; Eleanor Roosevelt Humanitarian Award, 1964; Honorary Mayor of Pacific Palisades, 1967-68; Human Relations Award, Anti-Defamation League of B'nai B'rith, 1969; Woman of the Year, Jewish War Veterans of America, 1969; Cogswell Award, Gallaudet College, 1970. Honorary degrees: Doctor of Humane Letters, Gallaudet College, 1972; Doctor of Fine Arts, Western Maryland College, 1972.

MEMBER: Eugene O'Neill Memorial Foundation (trustee); National Theatre of the Deaf; Muses of California Music Foundation; National Association of Hearing and Speech Agencies (vice president, board of directors); President's National Advisory Committee on Education for the Deaf (board of directors); President's Committee on Employment for the Handicapped; National Council on the Handicapped, 1982—.

SIDELIGHTS: RECREATIONS—Rock collecting, fishing, boating.

ADDRESSES: AGENT—Writers and Artists Agency, 11726 San Vincente Blvd., Suite 300, Los Angeles, CA 90049.*

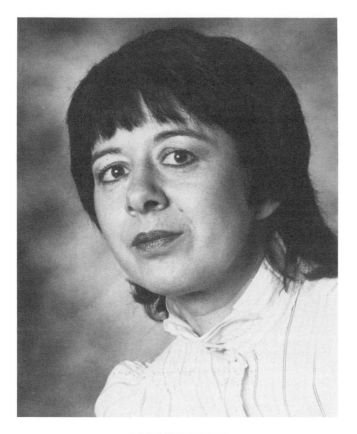

ROSEMARY FAITH

FAITH, Rosemary

PERSONAL: Born March 20, in Belfast, Northern Ireland; daughter of Percy (a jeweller) and Winnie (a bookkeeper; maiden name, Thomson) Faith; married Trevor Ronald Gray (a theatre manager) April 15, 1978. EDUCATION: Studied acting at the Weber-Douglas Academy of Dramatic Art, London.

VOCATION: Actress.

CAREER: STAGE DEBUT—Actress and assistant stage manager, *Lock Up Your Daughters,* Belgrade, Coventry, U.K. LONDON DEBUT—Lucy Rabbit, *Toad of Toad Hall,* Duke of York Theatre, 1970. PRINCIPAL STAGE APPEARANCES—*Gypsy,* Piccadilly Theatre, London; *Once Upon a Time,* Duke of York Theatre, London; *The Rupert Show,* Victoria Palace Theatre, London; *Seven Brides for Seven Brothers,* Old Vic Theatre Company, London; also: Hermia, *A Midsummer Night's Dream;* Mary McGregor, *The Prime of Miss Jean Brodie;* Biondello, *The Taming of the Shrew;* Doris, *Same Time, Next Year.*

Has also appeared at the Little Theatre in Bangor, Northern Ireland, the Grand Theatre in Swansea, Leas Pavilion in Folkstone, Gulbenkian Theatre in Canterbury, Connaught Theatre in Worthing, and the Gardner Arts Centre in Brighton.

MAJOR TOURS—*The Reluctant Debutante, Lock Up Your Daughters, Lady Frederick, Under Milk Wood, One for the Pot, Joseph and His Amazing Technicolor Dreamcoat, The Chiltern Hundreds, Seven Brides for Seven Brothers,* all British national tours and a season in Toronto, Canada.

FILM DEBUT—Title role, *Call Me Cleo,* ARC Films.

TELEVISION DEBUT—Deirdre Garvey, *Beggar My Neighbour,* BBC. PRINCIPAL TELEVISION APPEARANCES—*Dad's Army,* BBC; *The Goodies,* BBC; *Oppenheimer,* BBC; *Please Sir,* LWT; *No Honestly,* LWT; *People Like Us,* LWT.

AWARDS: Principal's Prize for Comedy, Weber-Douglas Academy of Dramatic Art.

SIDELIGHTS: FAVORITE ROLES—Hermia, Mary McGregor, Biondello, and Doris in *Same Time, Next Year.*

Rosemary Faith told *CTFT* that she in interested in "mysticism, comparative religion, and psychology. My main hobby is reading." She has had poetry published as a child in the Poetry Society's *Voice of Youth.*

ADDRESSES: HOME—Eleven Cranworth Road, Worthing BN11 2JE, Sussex, England. AGENT—Eric Glass Ltd., 28 Berkeley Square, London W1X 6HD, England.

*   *   *

FARRELL, Mike   1939-

PERSONAL: Born February 6, 1939, in St. Paul, MN; son of Joe Farrell (a motion picture studio carpenter); married Judy Hayden (an actress), 1963 (divorced); married Shelley Fabares (an actress); children: (first marriage) Michael Joshua, Erin. EDUCATION: Trained

MIKE FARRELL

for the stage with Jeff Corey and David Alexander. MILITARY: U.S. Marine Corps.

VOCATION: Actor, producer, director, and writer.

CAREER: PRINCIPAL TELEVISION APPEARANCES—Series: Dr. Sam Marsh, *The Interns*, CBS, 1970-71; Andy Hayes, *The Man and the City*, ABC, 1971-72; B.J. Hunnicutt, *M*A*S*H*, CBS, 1975-83; also, Scott Banning, *Days of Our Lives*, ABC. Episodic: *The Bold Ones*, NBC; *Marcus Welby, M.D.*, ABC; *Owen Marshall, Counselor at Law*, ABC; *Mannix*, CBS. Movies: *The Longest Night*, 1972; *The Questor Tapes*, 1974; *Battered*, 1978; *Sex and the Single Parent*, 1979; *Damien: The Leper Priest*, 1980; *Prime Suspect*, 1982; *Memorial Day*, 1983; *Choices of the Heart*, 1983: *Private Sessions*, NBC, 1985; *Vanishing Act*, 1987.

PRINCIPAL TELEVISION WORK—Wrote and directed episodes of *M*A*S*H*, CBS, 1975-83; co-producer, *Memorial Day*, 1983.

FILM DEBUT—*Captain Newman, M.D.*, 1964. PRINCIPAL FILM APPEARANCES—*The Americanization of Emily*, Metro-Goldwyn-Mayer, 1964; *The Graduate*, Embassy, 1967; *Targets*, Paramount, 1968.

PRINCIPAL STAGE APPEARANCES—*Rain*, Los Angeles Civic Stage; *A Thousand Clowns, Mary, Mary, Under the Yum-Yum Tree*, and *The Skin of Our Teeth*, all at the Laguna Beach Playhouse, CA.

MEMBER: American Federation of Television and Radio Artists, Screen Actors Guild.

SIDELIGHTS: RECREATION—Chess, reading (politics and psychology), motorcycling.

ADDRESSES: AGENT—Triad Artists, 10100 Santa Monica Blvd., Los Angeles, CA 90067.

*　　*　　*

FAWCETT, Farrah 1947-

PERSONAL: Born February 2, 1947, in Corpus Christi, TX; daughter of James William (an oil field contractor) and Pauline Alice (Evans) Fawcett; married Lee Majors (an actor), July 28, 1973 (divorced, 1982); children: Redmond O'Neal. EDUCATION: Attended the University of Texas at Austin.

VOCATION: Actress and model.

CAREER: STAGE DEBUT—Jill, *Butterflies Are Free*, Burt Reynolds Dinner Theatre, Jupiter, FL. OFF-BROADWAY DEBUT—Marjorie, *Extremities*, West Side Arts Theatre, 1983.

PRINCIPAL TELEVISION APPEARANCES—Series: *Harry-O*, ABC, 1974-76; Jill Munroe, *Charlie's Angels*, ABC, 1976-77. Episodic: *McCloud*, NBC; *Apple's Way*, CBS; *The Six-Million Dollar Man*, ABC; *Marcus Welby, M.D.*, ABC; *Owen Marshall, Counselor at Law*. Movies: *The Feminist and the Fuzz*, 1970; *Murder in Texas*, 1981; *The Red-Light Sting*, 1984; *The Burning Bed*, NBC, 1984; *Between Two Women*, ABC, 1986.

PRINCIPAL FILM APPEARANCES—*Love Is a Funny Thing*, United

FARRAH FAWCETT

Artists, 1970; *Myra Breckinridge*, Twentieth Century-Fox, 1970; *Logan's Run*, United Artists, 1976; *Somebody Killed Her Husband*, Columbia, 1978; *Sunburn*, Paramount, 1979; *Strictly Business*, 1979; *The Helper*, 1979; *Saturn III*, Associated Film Distribution, 1979; *Cannonball Run*, Twentieth Century-Fox, 1981; Marjorie, *Extremities*, Atlantic Releasing, 1986.

RELATED CAREER—Model; has appeared in more that one hundred television commercials.

AWARDS: People's Choice Award; *Bravo* Magazine Award.

SIDELIGHTS: RECREATION—Sculpture, painting, drawing, tennis, racquetball, and golf.

ADDRESSES: AGENT—c/o Sue Mengers, International Creative Management, 8899 Beverly Blvd., Los Angeles, CA 90048.*

*　　*　　*

FIANDER, Lewis 1938-

PERSONAL: Born January 12, 1938, in Melbourne, Victoria, Australia; son of Walter Lewis and Mona Jane (King) Fiander; married Claire Loise Curzon-Price. EDUCATION: Attended schools in Melbourne, Australia.

VOCATION: Actor.

CAREER: STAGE DEBUT—Tom, *Accolade,* National Theatre, Melbourne, Australia, 1954. LONDON DEBUT—Hughie, *The One Day of the Year,* Theatre Royal, Stratford East, 1962. PRINCIPAL STAGE APPEARANCES—Launcelot Gobbo, *The Merchant of Venice,* and Feste, *Twelfth Night,* both with the National Company, Melbourne, 1954-56; Ishmael, *Moby Dick-Rehearsed,* and ten other productions for the Union Repertory Company, Melbourne, 1959-60; Leslie, *The Hostage,* Geoff, *A Taste of Honey,* Launcelot Gobbo and two performances as Shylock, *The Merchant of Venice,* all with the Elizabethan Theatre Trust, Sydney, Australia, 1960-62; first gentleman, *The School for Scandal,* Haymarket Theatre, London, 1963; Lory, *Virtue in Danger,* Mermaid Theatre, then Strand Theatre, London, 1963; understudy title role, *Hamlet,* de Courcelles, *St. Joan,* and Domingo, *The Royal Hunt of the Sun,* all with the National Theatre, Old Vic Theatre, 1963-64.

Title role, *Stephen D.,* Citizen's Glasgow Theatre, Scotland, 1966; Deacon Pobyedov, *The Duel,* Duke of York's Theatre, London, 1968; Christian Talbot, *The Pursuit of Love,* Bristol Old Vic, U.K., 1967; John Adams, *1776,* New Theatre (Albery), London, 1970, and at Her Majesty's Theatre, Melbourne then Theatre Royal, Sydney, both 1971; Mosca, *Volpone,* Bristol Old Vic, U.K., 1971; Lord Melbourne and Benjamin Disraeli, *I and Albert,* Piccadilly Theatre, London, 1972; King Herod, *Follow the Star,* Chichester Festival Theatre, 1974 and Westminster, U.K., 1975; George, *Same Time Next Year,* Her Majesty's Theatre, Melbourne, then Theatre Royal, Sydney, both 1976; Jack Rover, *Wild Oats,* Royal Shakespeare Company, Piccadilly Theatre, London, 1977; Bluntschli, *Arms and the Man,* Greenwich Theatre, London, 1978; Owen Shorter, *Clouds,* Criterion Theatre, London, 1979; Littleton Coke, *Old Heads and Young Hearts,* Chichester Festival, U.K., 1980.

MAJOR TOURS—Antipholus of Syracuse, *The Comedy of Errors,* with the Royal Shakespeare Company, New Zealand cities, 1966; Truwit, *The Silent Woman,* Warwick, *Saint Joan,* and title role, *Peer Gynt,* with the Oxford Playhouse Company, U.K. cities, 1967-70.

FILM DEBUT—*The Password Is Courage,* Metro-Goldwyn-Mayer (MGM), 1963. PRINCIPAL FILM APPEARANCES—*Sweeney 2.*

PRINCIPAL TELEVISION APPEARANCES—*Pride and Prejudice; Notorious Woman; Smith.*

SIDELIGHTS: FAVORITE ROLES—Leslie, *The Hostage;* John Adams, *1776;* and Jack Rover, *Wild Oats.*

ADDRESSES: OFFICE—Chatto and Linnit, Prince of Wales Theatre, Coventry Street, London SW1, England.*

*　　　*　　　*

FIBICH, Felix   1917-

PERSONAL: Born Felix Goldblat, August 5, 1917, in Warsaw, Poland; son of Symehia (a merchant) and Seve (a merchant; maiden name, Fibich) Goldblat; married Judith Berg, August, 1942. EDUCATION: Attended schools in Warsaw, Poland, the Soviet Union, and Juilliard School in New York City.

VOCATION: Actor, choreographer, dancer, and lecturer.

CAREER: NEW YORK DEBUT—Dancer, Carnegie Recital Hall, 1950. PRINCIPAL STAGE WORK—Choreographer: Concerts at

FELIX FIBICH

Brooklyn Academy of Music, Carnegie Hall, Cooper Union, Museum of New York, and the Brooklyn Museum; *Let's Sing Yiddish,* Brooks Atkinson Theatre, New York City, 1966; *Sing, Israel, Sing,* Brooks Atkinson Theatre, New York City, 1967; *Light, Lively, and Yiddish,* Belasco Theatre, New York City, 1969; actor with the Jewish Repertory Theatre, New York City, 1983.

MAJOR TOURS—Choreographer and dancer: Appeared in U.S., South American, Canadian, Israeli, Soviet, and European cities; special bond drives for Israel in U.S. cities of Philadelphia, Chicago, Montreal, Milwaukee, Cleveland, Boston, and New York.

PRINCIPAL TELEVISION WORK—Choreographer and dancer: *Look Up and Live,* CBS; *Lamp unto My Feet,* CBS; also dance performance specials on WOR, New York and WNET, Newark, NJ.

PRINCIPAL FILM WORK—Choreographer, *The Chosen,* Twentieth Century-Fox, 1982.

RELATED CAREER—Dancer, Byelostock Jewish Theatre, 1939-41; dancer, Ashkhabad Opera and Ballet, Turkmenian, Soviet Union, 1941-43; dancer, Tashkent Philharmonic, 1943-46; dancer, Polish Review Theatre, 1946-47; organizer (with Judith Fibich), School of Jewish Dance, Poland, 1947-49; dancer, UNESCO International Archives of Dance, 1949-50; choreographer, Jewish Theatre for Children, 92nd Street YMHA and Board of Jewish Education, New York City, 1954-69; choreographer, dancer, Yiddish Village Theatre, New York City, 1964-66; director of dance department, B. Horwich Jewish Community Center, Chicago, 1970-75; teacher, Stevens College, Columbia, MO, 1977; director, choreographer, Felix Febich School of Dance, Chicago,

1971-78; lecturer, teacher, B'nai Brith and Tarbuth Foundation for the Perpetuation of Jewish Culture, New York City, 1978—; Shalow Theatre, Town Hall, New York City, 1979-81; Folksbine Theatre, New York City, 1981-84.

MEMBER: Society of Stage Directors and Choreographers, Screen Actors Guild, Hebrew Actors Union.

ADDRESSES: HOME—50 W. 97th Street, #15L, New York, NY 10025.

*   *   *

FIELD, Fern   1934-

PERSONAL: Born June 28, 1934, in Milan, Italy; daughter of William (a businessman) and Betty (a business person; maiden name, Dosnansky) Field; married Norman G. Brooks (a producer), May 13, 1979. EDUCATION: Attended Columbia University, Hunter College, and University of California at Westwood.

VOCATION: Producer, director, and writer.

CAREER: PRINCIPAL TELEVISION WORK—Assistant to executive producer, (pilot) *King of the Road,* CBS, 1970's; assistant to executive producer, *Maude,* CBS, 1972-78, *All's Fair,* CBS, 1976-77, and *The Nancy Walker Show,* ABC, 1976; producer, *The Baxters,* syndicated, 1979-81; producer, director, and writer, *Second Annual Media Awards,* 1980; production executive, *The Facts of Life,* NBC, 1980; producer, *Joe's World,* NBC, 1980;

FERN FIELD

producer, director, and writer, *Third Annual Media Awards,* 1981; producer, *Please Don't Hit Me Mom,* ABC, 1981; producer, *The Wave,* ABC, 1981; producer, director, and co-writer, *Movin' On,* 1982; producer, *But It's Not My Fault,* ABC, 1982; co-writer, "Jenny and the Giraffe," *Afterschool Special,* ABC, 1982; producer, *Eleanor, First Lady of the World,* CBS, 1982; director, Disney/Epcot Foundation Films, 1982; producer and co-director, "Mr. Wizard's World," *Nickelodeon,* 1983; director, co-producer, and co-writer, "The Celebrity and the Arcade Kid," *Afterschool Special,* ABC, 1983; (with Norman G. Brooks) executive co-producer, *One More Hurdle,* NBC, 1984; (with Norman G. Brooks) executive co-director, *Henry Hamilton: Graduate Ghost,* ABC, 1984; (with Fay Kanin) co-producer, *Heartsounds,* ABC, 1984; producer, "No Greater Gift," *Afterschool Special,* ABC, 1985; (with Stan Kallis) producer, *Kane and Abel,* CBS, 1985; executive producer, *The American Ticket,* KCET, 1986; producer, *Justice Delayed: The Lenell Geter Story,* CBS, 1986.

PRINCIPAL FILM WORK—Producer and director, *A Different Approach,* filmed during the 1970s and producer, *It's a New Day,* both for the South Bay Mayor's Committee for Employment of the Handicapped, 1980; director and producer, *Just the Way You Are,* California Department of Mental Health, 1983.

WRITINGS: BOOKS—*They Call Me Destiny,* 1962.

SCREENPLAYS—*It's a New Day,* 1980.

AWARDS: Academy Award nomination, 1970s, for *A Different Approach;* Cold Camera Award, Silver Cindy Award, Chris Statuette, and Cine Golden Eagle Award, all 1980, for *It's a New Day;* Golden Halo Award, Emmy Award nomination, 1981, for *Please Don't Hit Me Mom;* Ohio State Award, Gabriel Award, George Foster Peabody Award, Emmy Award, all 1981, for *The Wave;* Golden Globe Award nomination, Emmy Award nomination, both 1982, for *Eleanor, First Lady of the World;* FAB Award of Excellence, Cine Golden Eagle Award, Chris Bronze Plaque Award, all 1983, for *Just the Way You Are;* Emmy Award nomination, 1983, for *The Celebrity and the Arcade Kid;* National Association for the Advancement of Colored People (NAACP) Award and Golden Halo Award, both 1984, for *One More Hurdle;* Emmy Award nomination, 1984, for *Henry Hamilton: Graduate Ghost;* Emmy Award nomination, George Foster Peabody Award, both 1984, for *Heartsounds;* Sponsor's Recognition Award, FAB Award of Excellence, both 1985, for *Kane and Abel;* also Emmy Award and Glen Media Award, for *The Baxters.*

MEMBER: Women in Film, Academy of Television Arts and Sciences, Directors' Guild, Writers Guild; Governor's Committee for Employment of the Handicapped, Coalition for Clean Air.

ADDRESSES: HOME—13078 Mindanau Way, Apt. 309, Marina Del Rey, CA 90292. OFFICE—11600 Washington Place, Suite 203, Los Angeles, CA 90066.

*   *   *

FIELD, Leonard S.   1908-

PERSONAL: Born July 10, 1908, in St. Paul, MN; son of M. Louis (a movie house chain owner) and Rachel (a pianist; maiden name, Blumenthal) Field; married Ruth Dietrich Malcomson, August 4, 1942 (divorced, 1955); married Virginia Clayburgh, June 9, 1959;

children: (first marriage) Ruth, Katharine. EDUCATION: University of Minnesota, B.A., 1930; trained for the stage with the National Collegiate Players and Ed Stadt. POLITICS: Democrat. MILITARY: U.S. Army Signal Corps, 1942-45.

VOCATION: Producer and general manager.

CAREER: FIRST STAGE WORK—Producer, *Three Men on a Horse,* Plymouth Theatre, Boston, 1935. FIRST BROADWAY WORK—Producer, *Good Hunting,* Lyceum Theatre, 1936, for two performances. FIRST LONDON WORK—Producer, *LUV,* Arts Theatre, 1963, for twenty-eight performances. PRINCIPAL STAGE WORK—General manager, *Porgy and Bess,* Ziegfeld Theatre, New York City 1953-55; co-adaptor and producer, *The Hostage,* New York City, 1960; co-producer, *The Birthday Party,* Booth Theatre, New York City, 1967; producer, *Three Bags Full,* New York City, 1967.

MAJOR TOURS—General manager, *Bell, Book, and Candle,* Philadelphia, Pittsburgh, St. Louis, Chicago, 1952; manager, *Clearing in the Woods,* national, 1956.

FIRST FILM WORK—General manager, *Never Wave at a WAC,* RKO, 1957.

MEMBER: Actors' Equity Association, 1935; Association of Theatrical Managers, 1947; National Collegiate Players, University of Minnesota, 1930.

ADDRESSES: HOME—535 Park Avenue, New York, NY 10021.

DAVID FIRTH

FIRTH, David   1945-

PERSONAL: Full name, David Firth Coleman; born March 15, 1945, in Bedford, England; son of Ivor Firth and Beatrice (Jenkins) Coleman; married Julia Elizabeth Gould. EDUCATION: Bedford Modern School; Sussex University; studied for the theatre at the Guildhall School of Music and Dramatic Art.

VOCATION: Actor, singer, director, and writer.

CAREER: STAGE DEBUT—Fyodor, *Notes from the Underground,* N.U.S. Drama Festival, Garrick Theatre, London, 1967. PRINCIPAL STAGE APPEARANCES—The courier, *1776,* New Theatre, London, 1970; Orlando, *As You Like It* and Mercutio, *Romeo and Juliet,* Phoenix Theatre, Leicester, London, 1971; Roger, *After Haggerty* and Jo Jo, *Irma La Douce,* Belgrade Theatre, Coventry, U.K., 1972; Gawain, *The Green Knight* and *Happy as a Sandbag,* Phoenix Theatre, Leicester, 1973; Donalbain, *Macbeth* and Yasha, *The Cherry Orchard,* National Theatre, London, 1973; Lucio, *Measure for Measure,* Old Vic Theatre, London, 1973; Attilio, *Saturday, Sunday, Monday,* National Theatre Company, Queen's Theatre, London, 1974; Massingham, *All Good Men,* Young Vic Theatre, London, 1975; Parolles, *All's Well That Ends Well* and Lucio, *Measure for Measure,* Greenwich Theatre, London, 1975; Nickleby, *Nickleby and Me,* Royal Theatre, Stratford, U.K., 1975; Richard Pershore, *The Chairman,* Globe Theatre, London, 1976; *Side by Side by Sondheim,* Wyndham's Theatre, London, 1977; Courtall, *She Would and If She Could,* Greenwich Theatre, London, 1979; Captain Loveit, *Miss in Her Teens* and Leander, *The Padlock,* Old Vic Theatre, London, 1979.

LEONARD S. FIELD

Tesman, *Hedda Gabler*, Roundhouse Theatre, London, 1980; *Beatlemania*, St. Bart's Playhouse, New York, 1980; Gaston, *Gigi*, Haymarket Theatre, Leicester, London, 1980; Tony, *Wonderland*, Kings Head Theatre, London, 1981; Nicholas Nickleby, *Nickleby and Me*, Chichester, 1981; Guildenstern, *Hamlet*, Warehouse Theatre, then Piccadilly Theatre, London, 1982; Arthur Miller, *Marilyn* and Jack Idle, *Poppy*, both Adelphi Theatre, London, 1983; Algernon, *The Importance of Being Earnest*, Ambassadors Theatre, London, 1984; Saatchi One, *The Ratepayers Iolanthe*, Queen Elizabeth Hall and Phoenix Theatre, London, 1984; David, *Canary Blunt*, Latchmere Theatre, London, 1985; Sir Alistair Pish, *Metropolitan Mikado*, Queen Elizabeth Hall and Royal Festival Hall, London, 1985; Dr. Col. Frank Inglehurst, *Young England*, Adelphi Theatre, London, 1986; Firmin, *The Phantom of the Opera*, Her Majesty's Theatre, London, 1986.

MAJOR TOURS—With the Royal Shakespeare Company: Amiens, *As You Like It*, Helenus, *Troilus and Cressida*, and Sordido, *The Revenger's Tragedy*, Stratford, London, U.S., and Europe, 1967-70; James, *Me Times Me*, British Isles, 1972.

PRINCIPAL STAGE WORK—Director, *Purity*, Phoenix Theatre, Leicester, London, 1973.

PRINCIPAL TELEVISION APPEARANCES—*Search for the Nile*, 1971; *Love for Lydia; Nanny's Boy; Whodunit; Yes Minister; Lucky Jim; Drummonds; Troilus and Cressida; Card Trick*, and *Sorry, I'm a Stranger Here Myself.* Movies: *Out on a Limb*, CBS, 1987.

WRITINGS: PLAYS—Book and lyrics, *Canary Blunt*, Latchmere Theatre, London, 1985. TELEVISION—*Card Trick* and *I'm a Stranger Here Myself.*

AWARDS: Most Promising Actor, *Plays and Players*, Awards, 1970, for *1776.*

MEMBER: British Actors' Equity Association.

ADDRESSES: HOME—One Newry Road, St. Margaret's Twickenham, Middlesex, TW1 1PJ, England.

*   *   *

FISHER, Jules   1937-

PERSONAL: Born November 12, 1937, in Norristown, PA; son of Abraham (a retailer) and Anne (Davidson) Fisher. EDUCATION: Attended Pennsylvania State University; Carnegie Institute of Technology, B.F.A., 1960.

VOCATION: Lighting designer, director, and producer.

CAREER: FIRST STAGE WORK—Lighting designer, *January Thaw*, high school, March, 1954. FIRST OFF-BROADWAY WORK—Lighting designer, *All the King's Men*, 74th Street Theatre, 1959. PRINCIPAL STAGE WORK—Lighting designer, *Death of a Salesman*, *The Girl on the Via Flaminia*, and *End as a Man*, all with Circle in the City Theatre, Philadelphia, 1956.

Lighting designer, New York City (except where indicated otherwise): *Parade*, Players Theatre, *Tobacco Road*, Cricket Theatre, *Here Come the Clowns*, Actors Playhouse, *Greenwich Village USA*, One Sheridan Square Theatre, and *Marcus in the High Grass*,

Greenwich Mews Theatre, all 1960; *Ballet Ballads* (a trilogy consisting of "The Eccentricities of Davy Crockett," "Riding Hood Revisited," and "Willie the Weeper"), 74th Street Theatre, *Donogoo* and *Red Roses for Me*, both Greenwich Mews Theatre, *Cicero*, St. Mark's Playhouse, *The Tiger Rag*, Cherry Lane Theatre, *Go Show Me a Dragon*, Maidman Theatre, and *All in Love*, Martinique Theatre, all 1961; *Moon on a Rainbow Shawl*, East Eleventh Street Theatre, *The Bunker's Daughter*, Jan Hus House Theatre, *The Creditors*, Mermaid Theatre, *Fly Blackbird*, Mayfair Theatre, *The Book of Job*, Christ Church Methodist Theatre, *The Golden Apple*, York Theatre, *This Side of Paradise*, Sheridan Square Playhosue, *Nathan the Wise*, 78th Street Playhouse, *Half-Past Wednesday*, Orpheum Theatre, *Porgy and Bess*, City Center Theatre, *O Say Can You See!*, Provincetown Playhouse, and *Riverwind*, Actors Playhouse, all 1962; also designed lights for the Casa Manana Theatre, Fort Worth, TX and the Old Globe Shakespeare Festival, San Diego, CA, 1962.

Continuing as lighting designer in New York City: *The Love Nest* and *Telemachus Clay*, both at the Writers Stage Theatre, *An Evening with Maurice Chevalier*, Ziegfeld Theatre, *Six Characters in Search of an Author*, Martinique Theatre, *Best Foot Forward*, Stage Seventy-Three, *The Dragon*, Phoenix Repertory Theatre, *Spoon River Anthology*, Booth Theatre, *The Ginger Man*, Orpheum Theatre, *The Trojan Women*, Circle in the Square Theatre, *The Establishment*, Strollers Theatre, *Enter Laughing*, Henry Miller's Theatre, *A Rainy Day in Newark*, Belasco Theatre, *Ole! Ole!*, Little Fox Theatre, *A Midsummer Night's Dream* and *Don Giovanni*, both at the City Center, all 1963; *Anyone Can Whistle*, Majestic Theatre, *High Spirits*, Alvin Theatre, *Wonderful World*, for the New York World's Fair, *The White House* and *P.S. I Love You*, both at Henry Miller's Theatre, *The Subject Was Roses*, Royale Theatre, *A Girl Could Get Lucky*, Cort Theatre, *The Tragical Historie of Doctor Faustus*, Phoenix Repertory Theatre, *I Had a Ball*, Martin Beck Theatre, *Gogo Loves You*, Theatre de Lys, *Natalia Petrovna*, City Center, and *The Sign in Sidney Brustein's Window*, Longacre Theatre, all 1964; also lighting for *Royal Flush*, Shubert Theatre, New Haven, CT, and *South Pacific*, Toronto, Canada, both 1964.

Continuing as lighting designer, New York City: *Do I Hear a Waltz?* and *Pickwick*, both at the 46th Street Theatre, *The Decline and Fall of the Entire World as Seen Through the Eyes of Cole Porter Revisited*, Square East Theatre, *Half a Sixpence*, Broadhurst Theatre, *And Things That Go Bump in the Night*, Royale Theatre, *Square in the Eye* and *Leonard Bernstein's Theatre Songs*, both at Theatre de Lys, *The Devils*, Broadway Theatre, *The White Devil*, Circle in the Square, *The Yearling*, Alvin Theatre, and *Ben Bagley's New Cole Porter Revue*, Square East Theatre, all 1965; *Serjeant Musgrave's Dance*, Theater de Lys; *Hooray! It's a Glorious Day. . . and All That*, Theatre Four, *The Kitchen*, 81st Street Theatre, *A Hand Is on the Gate*, Longacre Theatre, *Eh?*, Circle in the Square, *Jeux*, for the New York City Ballet at the State Theatre, *The Threepenny Opera*, Billy Rose Theatre, *Hail Scrawdyke!*, Booth Theatre, *Young Marrieds Play Monopoly*, Stage 73, and *The Office*, Henry Miller's Theatre, all 1966; also, *Macbeth*, Arena Stage, Washington, DC, and *Suburban Tragedy*, Princess Rebecca Birnbaum, and *Make Like a Dog*, 1966.

Lighting designer in New York City: *Black Comedy* and *White Lies*, both at the Ethel Barrymore Theatre, *You're a Good Man Charlie Brown*, St. Mark's Theatre, *The Natural Look*, Longacre Theatre, *You Know I Can't Hear You When the Water's Running*, Ambassador Theatre, *Little Murders*, Broadhurst Theatre, *South Pacific*, New York State Theatre, *The Unknown Soldier and His Wife*, Vivian Beaumont Theatre, *A Minor Adjustment*, Brooks Atkinson

Theatre, *Scuba Duba*, New Theatre, *The Trial of Lee Harvey Oswald*, American National Theatre Academy (ANTA) Theatre, and *Iphigenia in Aulis*, Circle in the Square, all 1967; *Before You Go*, Henry Miller's Theatre, *The Grand Music Hall of Israel*, Palace Theatre, *Here's Where I Belong*, Billy Rose Theatre, *Kongi's Harvest*, St. Mark's Playhouse, *Hair*, Biltmore Theatre, *The Only Game in Town*, Broadhurst Theatre, *A Moon for the Misbegotten*, Circle in the Square, *The Happy Hypocrite*, Bouwerie Lane Theatre, *The Cuban Thing*, Henry Miller's Theatre, *The Canterbury Tales*, Eugene O'Neill Theatre, and *The Man in the Glass Booth*, Royale Theatre, all 1968.

Continuing as lighting designer, New York City: *But Seriously. . .*, Henry Miller's Theatre, *The Watering Place*, Music Box Theatre, *Peter and the Wolf*, City Center, *Someone's Comin' Hungry*, Pocket Theatre, *Trumpets of the Lord*, Brooks Atkinson Theatre, *Promenade*, Promenade Theatre, and *Butterflies Are Free*, Booth Theatre, all 1969; *Sheep on the Runway*, Helen Hayes Theatre, *Gantry*, George Abbott Theatre, *Minnie's Boys*, Imperial Theatre, *Dear Janet Rosenberg, Dear Mr. Kooning*, Gramercy Arts Theatre, *Inquest*, Music Box Theatre, *The Engagement Baby*, Helen Hayes Theatre, *Steambath*, Truck and Warehouse Theatre, *Home*, Morosco Theatre, and *Jakey Fat Boy*, all 1970; also designer for the premier season of the American Ballet at the Brooklyn Academy of Music, 1969-70.

Lighting designer, New York City: *Soon*, Ritz Theatre, *Hamlet*, Carnegie Hall, *No, No, Nanette*, 46th Street Theatre, *Jesus Christ Superstar*, Mark Hellinger Theatre, and *Lenny*, Brooks Atkinson Theatre, all 1971; *Fun City*, Morosco Theatre, *Pippin*, Imperial Theatre, *Lysistrata*, Brooks Atkinson Theatre, *Mourning Becomes Electra*, Circle in the Square, *The Trials of Oz*, Anderson Theatre, all 1972; *Seesaw*, Uris Theatre, *Molly*, Alvin Theatre, *Full Circle*, ANTA Theatre, *The Iceman Cometh* and *Uncle Vanya*, both at the Circle in the Square, and *Rachel Lily Rosenbloom and Don't You Ever Forget It*, Broadhurst Theatre, all 1973; also *Joseph and the Amazing Technicolor Dreamcoat*, Albery Theatre, London, and *Pippin*, London production, both 1973; *Ulysses in Nighttown* and *Liza*, both at the Winter Garden Theatre, *Thieves*, Broadhurst Theatre, and *Sergeant Pepper's Lonely Hearts Club Band on the Road*, Beacon Theatre, all 1974; also *Billy*, Theatre Royal, London, 1974.

Continuing as lighting designer, New York City: *Man on the Moon*, Little Theatre and *Chicago*, 46th Street Theatre, both 1975; *Rockabye Hamlet*, 1976; *American Buffalo*, Ethel Barrymore Theatre, *Beatlemania*, Winter Garden Theatre, revival of *Hair*, Biltmore Theatre, *Golda*, Morosco Theatre, all 1977; *Dancin'*, Broadhurst Theatre, 1978; *Beatlemania*, produced in London, 1979; *Rock 'N' Roll! The First 5,000 Years*, St. James Theatre, 1982; *La Cage aux Folles*, Palace Theatre, 1983; *Song and Dance*, Royale Theatre, 1985; *Big Deal*, Broadway Theatre, 1986; *Rags*, Mark Hellinger Theatre, New York City, 1986.

Co-Producer, *Jesus Christ Superstar*, Mark Hellinger Theatre, New York City, 1971. Producer: *Lenny*, Brooks Atkinson Theatre, New York City, 1971; *Dancin'*, Broadhurst Theatre, New York City, 1978; *Frankenstein*, Palace Theatre, New York City, 1981; *Rock 'N' Roll! The First 5,000 Years*, St. James Theatre, New York City, 1982; *The Rink*, Martin Beck Theatre, New York City, 1984. Executive producer, *Big Deal*, Broadway Theatre, New York City, 1986.

Co-originator and production supervisor, *Beatlemania*, Winter Garden Theatre, New York City, 1977.

MAJOR TOUR WORK—Lighting designer, *West Side Story*, U.S. cities, 1960; lighting designer, *The Mikado* and *H.M.S. Pinafore*, U.S. cities, 1963; production supervisor, *Tommy*, U.S. cities, 1973.

PRINCIPAL CONCERT WORK—Supervisor and lighting designer, Laura Nyro, 1969-70, David Bowie, U.S. cities, 1974, and Rolling Stones, world tour, 1975; also Kiss; lighting designer, Simon and Garfunkel, Central Park, New York City, 1981; Revues: *Hallelujah Hollywood*, MGM Grand Hotel, Las Vegas, NV, 1974; *Revue*, Le Scala, Barcelona, Spain, 1974.

PRINCIPAL TELEVISION WORK—Lighting designer, Academy Awards presentation, 1977.

PRINCIPAL FILM WORK—Lighting designer: *A Star Is Born*, Warner Brothers, 1976; *Can't Stop the Music*, Associated Films, 1980. Appeared as himself in *All That Jazz*, Twentieth Century-Fox, 1979. Also has made several short experimental films.

RELATED CAREER—Assistant stage manager and carpenter, Valley Forge Music Fair, Devon, PA, 1955; assistant electrician, Shubert Theatre, Philadelphia, PA, 1956 for *The Most Happy Fella*, *The Ziegfeld Follies*, and *Mr. Wonderful*.

Lighting consultant: Circle in the Square, New York City; Westbury Music Fair, Long Island, NY; Deauville Star Theatre, Miami, FL; Rebekah Harkness Theatre, New York City; Studio Theatre New York City, Broooklyn Academy of Music, New York City.

President, Jules Fisher Associates, Inc., 1963-73; partner, Jules Fisher and Paul Marantz, Inc. Architecural Lighting Design, 1971—; president, Jules Fisher Enterprises, Inc., Lighting Design and Theatrical Production, 1973—.

AWARDS: Best Lighting, Antoinette Perry Awards, 1973, for *Pippin*, 1974, for *Ulysses in Nighttown*, 1978, for *Dancin'*; Best Lighting, Antoinette Perry Award nomination, 1972, for *Jesus Christ Superstar;* received honors from the Joseph Maharam Foundation for his lighting of *Pippin;* Best Lighting, Drama Desk Award, 1976, for *Chicago;* Best Lighting, Los Angeles Drama Critics Circle Award, 1979, for *Dancin';* Best Lighting, Drama Desk Award, 1980, for *Frankenstein*.

MEMBER: United Scenic Artists, League of American Theatres and Producers; United States Institute for Theatre Technology, American National Theatre Association.

SIDELIGHTS: RECREATIONS—Magic, music, and film making.

CTFT learned that another of Jules Fisher's recreations is inventing and he is the inventor who created the remote control spotlight.

ADDRESSES: OFFICE—Jules Fisher Enterprises, Inc., 126 Fifth Avenue, New York, NY 10011.

*			*			*

FISHER, Robert

PERSONAL: Son of Irving and Mollie (Cytron) Fisher; children: Mark. EDUCATION: University of California at Los Angeles, A.A., 1941.

ROBERT FISHER

VOCATION: Writer, director, teacher, designer, and composer.

CAREER: PRINCIPAL TELEVISION WORK—Executive story editor, *Alice*, CBS.

PRINCIPAL STAGE WORK—Director: *My Daughter's Rated X*, U.S. tours.

RELATED CAREER—Acting and directing teacher; comedy writer for Jack Benny, George Burns, Milton Berle, Fanny Brice, Bob Hope, Red Skelton, Alan King, and Amos and Andy.

WRITINGS: TELEVISION—*Make Room for Daddy*, ABC, CBS, 1953-71; *Bachelor Father*, CBS, NBC, ABC; *All in the Family*, CBS; *The Jeffersons*, CBS; *Maude*, CBS; *Good Times*, CBS; *Alice*, CBS.

PLAYS, PRODUCED—Broadway productions: (With Arthur Marx) *The Impossible Years*, 1965; (with Marx) *Minnie's Boys*, 1970; (with Marx) *My Daughter's Rated X*, 1970; (with Marx) *Groucho, a Life in Revue*, 1983; (with Robert Sacchi) *Bogart*, Hanna Theatre, New York City. PLAYS, PUBLISHED—*The Impossible Years*, *Minnie's Boys*, and *My Daughter's Rated X*, all published by Samuel French.

SCREENPLAYS—Seven films, four of which starred Bob Hope and his latest titled *The Cowboy and the Angel*, scheduled for upcoming release.

RADIO—Over four hundred radio comedies.

AWARDS: Best Play of the Summer Season, Straw Hat Award, for *My Daughter's Rated X;* received the Sylvania Award and the St. Christopher Award for Best Television Comedies; two Humanitas Award nominations.

ADDRESSES: HOME—Beverly Hills, CA.

✝   ✝   ✝

FLETCHER, Duane   1953-

PERSONAL: Born September 23, 1953, in Philadelphia, PA. EDUCATION: La Salle University, B.A., 1975; trained for the stage at the Royal Academy of Dramatic Art, London, and the Classical Theatre, Philadelphia.

VOCATION: Actor, choreographer, director, producer, and teacher.

CAREER: STAGE DEBUT—Richard Henry Lee, *1776,* Riverfront Dinner Theatre, Philadelphia, PA, 1976, for one-hundred-twenty performances. PRINCIPAL STAGE WORK—Director, *You're a Good Man, Charlie Brown*, La Salle Music Theatre, Philadelphia, PA, 1972; director and choreographer, *I've Come a Long Way*, Duplex Theatre, New York City, 1978; director, *The Genvieve Duvall Affair*, Main Street Theatre, New York City, 1983; director, *Blood Dues*, Main Street Theatre, New York City, 1984; director, *Ophelia*, Theatre Lab at the Princess Theatre, 1984; director, *The Queen's Pawn*, Theatre Lab at Lincoln Center, New York City,

DUANE FLETCHER

1985; director and choreographer, *The Comeback of Colby Clyman*, Theatre Lab at the Princess Theatre, New York City, 1985.

TELEVISION DEBUT—William Penn, *The Treaty Never Broken*, with the Germantown Theatre Guild, WHYY-TV, Philadelphia, 1976.

RELATED CAREER—Founder and artistic director, the School House Players, Philadelphia, 1970-73; assistant to the managing director, La Salle Music Theatre, Philadelphia, 1972-74; production manager, the Greek Theatre of New York, New York City, 1980-82; associate artistic director, Main Street Theatre, New York City, 1982-85; resident director, the Barbara Barondess Theatre Lab, New York City, 1983-85; teaches acting, directing, and tap-dancing, New York City.

AWARDS: Philadelphia Catholic Youth Organization Service Award, 1976; Outstanding Young Men of America Award, National Jaycees, 1984.

MEMBER: Philadelphia Catholic Youth Organization, Senior Citizens' Association, Manhattan Plaza Volunteers.

ADDRESSES: HOME—400 W. 43rd Street, Apt. 14P, New York, NY 10036. AGENT—Jack W. Batman Theatrical Consultants Ltd., 252 W. 46th Street, New York, NY 10036.

*   *   *

FOCH, Nina   1924-

PERSONAL: Born Nina Consuelo Maud Fock, April 20, 1924, in Leyden, Holland; daughter of Dirk (a conductor) and Consuelo (an actress; maiden name, Flowerton) Fock; married James Lipton, June 6, 1954 (divorced, 1958); married Dennis Brite, November 27, 1959 (divorced, 1963); married Michael Dewell, October 31, 1967; children: one son. EDUCATION: Attended Columbia University and Parsons Art School; trained for the stage at the American Academy of Dramatic Arts, studied acting with Stella Adler, Lee Strasberg, Harold Clurman, and David Alexander.

VOCATION: Actress, teacher, director, and producer.

CAREER: STAGE DEBUT—On tour, *Western Union, Please*, U.S. cities, 1941. BROADWAY DEBUT—Mary McKinley, *John Loves Mary*, Booth Theatre, February 4, 1947. PRINCIPAL STAGE APPEARANCES—Countess Olivia, *Twelfth Night*, Empire Theatre, New York City, 1949; *Congressional Baby*, Albany, NY, 1950; Dynamene, *A Phoenix Too Frequent*, Fulton Theatre, New York City, 1950; appeared in *The Philadelphia Story* and *Light Up the Sky*, summer stock, 1950; Cordelia, *King Lear*, National Theatre, New York City, 1950; Isabella, *Measure for Measure* and Katharine, *The Taming of the Shrew*, both at the American Shakespeare Festival, Stratford, CT, 1956, then at the Phoenix Theatre, New York City, 1957; Jane, *A Second String*, Eugene O'Neill Theatre, New York City, 1960; Masha, *The Three Sisters*, University of California at Los Angeles, 1960.

At the University of California at Los Angeles: appeared in *USA Revue*, 1962, *Brecht on Brecht*, 1965, appeared as Freda Lawrence, *I Rise in Flames Cried the Phoenix* and Frances, *Windows* in a program with the overall title, *An Evening of Williams, Pinter and Schisgal*, 1965; appeared as the Wife, *All Over*, 1972, and Madame

NINA FOCH

Arkadina, *The Seagull*, 1974, both with the Seattle Repertory Theatre, WA.

PRINCIPAL STAGE WORK—Director, "Ways and Means," from a triple bill with the overall title, *Tonight at 8:30*, for the National Repertory Theatre at the American National Theatre Academy (ANTA) Theatre, New York City, 1967; associate producer of inaugural night reopening, Ford's Theatre, Washington, DC, 1968.

FILM DEBUT—*Nine Girls*, Columbia, 1944. PRINCIPAL FILM APPEARANCES—*Return of the Vampire*, 1944; *Cry of the Werewolf*, 1944; *Shadows in the Night*, 1944; *Song to Remember*, Columbia, 1945; *My Name Is Julia Ross*, Columbia, 1945; *Escape in the Fog*, Columbia, 1945; *I Love a Mystery*, 1945; *Johnny O'Clock*, 1947; *The Guilt of Janet Ames*, 1947; *The Dark Past*, 1948; *Johnny Allegro*, 1949; *Undercover Man*, 1949; *An American in Paris*, Metro-Goldwyn-Mayer (MGM), 1951; *Scaramouche*, MGM, 1952; *Young Man with Ideas*, 1952; *Sombrero*, MGM, 1953; *Fast Company*, MGM, 1953; *Executive Suite*, MGM, 1954; *Four Guns to the Border*, Universal, 1954; *Illegal*, Warner Brothers, 1955; *You're Never Too Young*, Paramount, 1955; *Three Brave Men*, Twentieth Century-Fox, 1957; *The Ten Commandments*, Paramount, 1957; *Spartacus*, Universal, 1960; *Cash McCall*, Warner Brothers, 1960; *Such Good Friends*, Paramount, 1971; *Salty*, 1973; *Mahogany*, Paramount, 1975; *Jennifer*, 1978; *Rich and Famous*, MGM, 1981; *Indian Summer*, 1986; also appeared in and *Prison Ship*.

PRINCIPAL FILM WORK—Associate director, *The Diary of Anne Frank*, Twentieth Century-Fox, 1959.

TELEVISION DEBUT—1947. PRINCIPAL TELEVISION APPEAR-

ANCES—Episodic: *Danger*, CBS; *Lux Video Theatre*, CBS; *Philip Morris Playhouse*, CBS; *Studio One*, CBS; *Kraft Suspense*, CBS; *U.S. Steel Hour*, CBS; *Playhouse 90*, CBS; *Producer's Showcase*, NBC; *Route 66*, CBS; *Naked City*, ABC; *Burke's Law*, ABC; *The Outer Limits*, syndicated; *Bus Stop*, syndicated; *The Trailmaster*, ABC; *Arrest and Trial*, ABC; *Mr. Broadway*, CBS, 1964; *Lou Grant*, CBS, 1980.

Series: Panelist, *Q.E.D.*, ABC, 1951; panelist, *It's News to Me*, CBS, 1954; moderator, *Let's Take Sides*, 1957-59; *Shadowchaser*, ABC, 1985-86. Guest: *The Steve Allen Show*, CBS, 1956. Mini-Series: *War and Remembrance*, ABC, 1987.

RELATED CAREER—Founder, Los Angeles Theatre Group, 1960-65; adjunct professor, University of Southern California, Los Angeles, 1965-66, 1978-80, professor, 1966-67; artist in residence, University of North Carolina, 1965-66; artist in residence, University of Ohio, 1966; artist in residence, California Institute of Technology, 1969; faculty member, Center of Advanced Film Studies of the American Film Institute, 1971-74, senior faculty, 1974-77; founder and teacher, Nina Foch Studio, Hollywood, 1973—; adjunct professor of film and television, University of Southern California graduate school.

AWARDS: Best Supporting Actress, Academy Award nomination, 1954, for *Executive Suite;* recipient of *Film Daily* Awards, 1949, 1953; Best Supporting Actress, Emmy Award nomination, 1980, for *Lou Grant.*

MEMBER: Actors' Equity Association, American Federation of Television and Radio Artists, Screen Actors Guild, National Repertory Theatre (board of directors, 1967-75), American Film Institute (board of governors), Hollywood Academy of Television Arts and Sciences, (board of governors, 1976-77), Foreign Film Academy (executive committee), Academy of Motion Picture Arts and Sciences, 1970—; Actors Fund of America.

SIDELIGHTS: RECREATIONS—Painting, cooking, and needlepoint.

ADDRESSES: OFFICE—Nina Foch Studio, P.O. Box 1884, Beverly Hills, CA 90213.

*   *   *

FOOTE, Horton   1916-

PERSONAL: Born March 14, 1916, in Wharton, TX; son of Albert Horton (a shopkeeper) and Hallie (Brooks) Foote; married Lillian Vallish, June 4, 1945; children: Barbarie Hallie, Albert Horton, Walter Vallish, and Daisy Brooks. EDUCATION: Trained for the stage at the Pasadena Playhouse School of Theatre, CA, 1933-35, and Tamara Daykarhanova School of Theatre, New York City, 1937-39.

VOCATION: Playwright, screenwriter, novelist, actor, teacher, and production manager.

WRITINGS: PLAYS, PRODUCED—*Texas Town*, Weidman Studio, 1941, then Provincetown Playhouse, 1942, both New York City; *Out of My House*, New York City, 1942; *Only the Heart*, Bijou Theatre, New York City, 1944; *Celebration*, Maxine Elliott Theatre, New York City, 1948; *The Chase*, Playhouse, New York City,

1952; *The Trip to Bountiful*, Henry Miller's Theatre, New York City, 1953; *The Traveling Lady*, Playhouse, New York City, 1954; *John Turner Davis* and *The Midnight Caller*, both one-acts produced in New York City, 1958; book, *Gone with the Wind*, Drury Lane Theatre, London, 1972, then Dorothy Chandler Pavilion, Los Angeles, 1973; *Valentine's Day*, Herbert Berghof Studio, New York City, 1980; *The Roads to Home*, Manhattan Punch Line Theatre, New York City, 1982; *The Road to the Graveyard* (one-act), as part of "Marathon '85," Ensemble Studio Theatre, New York City, 1985; *Courtship/Valentine's Day*, Stage One, Dallas, TX, 1985; *Tomorrow*, Off-Broadway production, 1985; *Blind Date* (one-act), as part of "Marathon '86," Ensemble Studio Theatre, New York City, 1986; *Lily Dale*, Samuel Beckett Theatre, New York City, 1986-87; *The Widow Claire*, Circle in the Square Downtown, New York City, 1986-87.

PLAYS, PUBLISHED—*Only the Heart*, Dramatists Play Service, 1944; *The Chase*, Dramatists Play Service, 1952; *A Young Lady of Property* (volume of six plays: "The Dancers," "A Young Lady of Property," "The Old Beginning," "John Turner Davis," "Death of the Old Man," and "The Oil Well"), Dramatists Play Service, 1954; *Harrison, Texas: Eight Television Plays*, Harcourt, Brace, Jovanovich, 1959; *Roots in a Parched Ground*, Dramatists Play Service, 1962; *Three Plays* ("Roots in a Parched Ground," "Old Man," and "Tomorrow"), Harcourt, Brace, Jovanovich, 1962; *Tomorrow*, Dramatists Play Service, 1963; also published by Dramatists Play Service: *The Traveling Lady, The Midnight Caller, The Trip to Bountiful, The Roads to Home, Courtship,* and *Blind Date.*

SCREENPLAYS—*Storm Fear*, United Artists, 1956; *To Kill a Mockingbird*, Universal, 1963; *The Chase*, Columbia, 1965; *Baby, the Rain Must Fall*, Columbia, 1965; *Hurry Sundown*, Paramount, 1967; *The Stalking Moon*, Warner Brothers, 1968; *Tomorrow*, Filmgroup, 1971; *Tender Mercies*, Universal, 1983; *1918*, Cinecom International, 1984; *On Valentine's Day*, Angelika Films, 1985; (also co-producer) *The Trip to Bountiful*, Island Pictures, 1985.

TELEVISION PLAYS—*Only the Heart*, NBC, 1947; *Ludie Brooks*, CBS, 1951; *The Travelers*, NBC, 1952; *The Old Beginning*, NBC, 1953; "A Young Lady of the Property," *Philco Television Playhouse*, NBC, 1953; *The Trip to Bountiful*, NBC, 1953; "The Oil Well," *Goodyear Television Playhouse*, NBC, 1953; *Rocking Chair*, NBC, 1953; *Expectant Relations*, NBC, 1953; *Tears of My Sister*, NBC, 1953; "Midnight Caller," *Philco Television Playhouse*, NBC, 1953; "John Turner Davis," *Philco Television Playhouse*, NBC, 1953; *The Death of the Old Man*, NBC, 1953; *Shadow of Willie Greer*, NBC, 1954; "The Dancers," *Philco Television Playhouse*, NBC, 1954; *Roads to Home*, ABC, 1955; *Flight*, NBC, 1956; *Drugstore: Sunday Noon*, ABC, 1956; *Member of the Family*, CBS, 1957; *Old Man*, CBS, 1959; *The Shape of the River*, CBS, 1960; "The Night of the Storm," *DuPont Show of the Month*, CBS, 1960; "Tomorrow," *Playhouse 90*, CBS, 1960; *The Gambling Heart*, NBC, 1964; *The Displaced Person*, PBS, 1977; *Barn Burning*, PBS, 1980; "Keeping On," *American Playhouse*, PBS. Also a contributor to *The DuPont Show of the Week*, NBC, 1961.

NOVELS—*The Chase*, Holt Rhinehart & Winston, Inc., 1956.

RELATED CAREER—Actor from 1939-42; appeared in *Texas Town*, Provincetown Playhouse, New York City, 1942; also appeared in *The Eternal Road, The Fifth Column, The Coggerers,* and *Mr. Banks of Birmingham*, all New York City. Manager, Productions, Inc., a semi-professional theatre, Washington, DC, 1942-45. Teacher of playwriting.

AWARDS: Best Screenplay, Academy Award, Writers Guild of America Screen Award, 1962, for *To Kill a Mockingbird;* Best Original Screenplay, Academy Award, 1983, for *Tender Mercies.*

MEMBER: Texas Institute of Letters.

ADDRESSES: HOME—Ferris Lane, Grand View, NY 10960. AGENT—Lucy Kroll, 390 West End Avenue, New York, NY 10024; c/o Dramatists Play Service, 440 Park Avenue South, New York, NY 10016.*

*   *   *

FORMAN, Milos   1932-

PERSONAL: Born February 18, 1932, in Kaslov, Czechoslovakia; immigrated to the United States, 1968; naturalized citizen, 1977. EDUCATION: Attended the Academy of Music and Dramatic Art, Prague and Laterna Magika, Prague, 1958-62.

VOCATION: Director.

CAREER: FILM DEBUT—Screenwriter, *Dedecek Automobil,* 1956. PRINCIPAL FILM WORK—Director: *Talent Competition,* 1963; *Black Peter,* 1963; *Peter and Pavla,* 1963; *If There Was No Music,* 1964; *Loves of a Blonde,* Prominent, 1966; *The Firemen's Ball,* Cinema V, 1967; *Taking Off,* Universal, 1971; "The Decathlon," episode from *Visions of Eight,* Cinema V, 1973; *One Flew Over the*

MILOS FORMAN

Cuckoo's Nest, United Artists, 1975; *Hair,* United Artists, 1979; *Ragtime,* Paramount, 1981; *Amadeus,* Orion, 1984.

RELATED CAREER—Teacher of film, Columbia University.

AWARDS: Czechoslovak Film Critics Award, 1963, for *Peter and Pavla;* Grand Prix Award, 17th International Film Festival, Locarno, 1964; Best Director, Academy Awards, 1975, for *One Flew Over the Cuckoo's Nest* and 1984, for *Amadeus.*

SIDELIGHTS: With three comedies in the mid-1960s, *Black Peter, Loves of a Blonde,* and *The Firemen's Ball,* Milos Forman achieved renown as one of the outstanding young directors of Czechoslovakia's so-called cinematic "new wave." Although he had studied film at Prague's Academy of Music and Dramatic Art only after the drama division rejected his application, these films quickly gave him a reputation beyond his own country. Thus, after the 1968 Russian invasion of his country, Forman was soon able to establish himself in the American film industry with successful motion picture adaptations of popular novels and plays. *One Flew Over the Cuckoo's Nest* and *Amadeus,* in particular, won praise for his ability to retain the essence of the original works while transforming them for the film medium.

Forman's earliest films, however, were closer to his own experiences. Having lost both parents to concentrations camps during World War II, he spent the war years with relatives and family friends in different parts of Czechoslovakia. Forman's first feature film, *Black Peter,* was a comedy about an adolescent boy's coming of age. Forman followed it with *Loves of a Blond,* the simple story of a girl in a provincial town who is seduced by a travelling musician and follows him to Prague. *Loves of a Blonde* enjoyed the biggest commercial success of any Czech film up to that time, both because it was a comedy and, as the director put it, "people like to laugh" and because it contained the first nude scene in a Czech movie.

Both *Black Peter* and *Loves of a Blonde* were well received when they when shown at the New York Film Festival, in 1965 and 1966 respectively. Reviewing *Loves of a Blonde* for the *New York Times,* Bosley Crowther called it "delightful and unusual—comic and sad and comprehending in a curiously inarticulate way . . . human, true but understated—inconclusive, indeed as is life."

Forman's last Czech film, *The Firemen's Ball* (1967), a comedy about a ball being given for a retiring fire chief, aroused the ire of two separate groups. Czech firemen, angry over being satirized in the movie, staged a brief strike, while the communist government later banned the film entirely, understanding that the government was the actual target of the allegorical humor. In the West, however, *The Firemen's Ball,* like its predecessors, was received with acclaim. Renata Adler of the *New York Times* described it as "a hilarious shaggy dog story, with the pessimism of the exquisite logic that leads nowhere." Calling Forman's comedy "muted Rabelaisian in its view of human character," Adler further stated: "The timing and involutions of the humor are such that there is escalating laughter, while an awareness of the sadness of things— real fire, monumental pettiness—deepens as well. That a director who sees things so bitterly and clearly can be this funny now may mean that we are in for a comic renaissance after all."

At the time the Russians occupied Prague, Forman had already left the country and arranged to direct his first American film, *Taking Off* (1971). Immersing himself immediately in his new country's culture, he selected a peculiarly American subject—youthful runaways and their parents—and, while preparing to make the film, acquired an apartment in Greenwich Village and took in several actual runaways. As in his Czech movies, he filled many parts with non-professional actors, some of whom he found in New York streets and Central Park.

On the whole, critics welcomed *Taking Off*. In *New York* magazine, Judith Crist wrote, "Forman reveals not only his eye for all the varieties of youngness in its endless combinations of beauty and blemish but his infatuation with life itself, his appreciation of the moment's reach for self-fulfillment, his joyous zest in meeting humans on their own terms . . . Forman has caught the silences, the frustrations and the foolishness of our relationships and held up a poignant mirror." Despite similar comments from most critics, however, the movie was a commercial failure.

After the financial failure of *Taking Off*, Forman did not receive another offer to direct an American film for four years, and while he was willing to go back to Czechoslovakia to make movies, the Czech film industry no longer wanted him. Finally, producers Michael Douglas and Saul Zaentz hired him to make *One Flew Over the Cuckoo's Nest*, their version of Ken Kesey's novel. In the film of this counterculture favorite of the 1960s, Jack Nicholson took the role of an inmate in a mental institution who sparks a revolt against a tyrannical nurse, played by Louise Fletcher. In her *New Yorker* review of the movie, Pauline Kael explained that Forman "has understood how crude the poetic-paranoid system of the book would look on the screen now that the sixties' paranoia has lost its nightmarish buoyancy, and he and the scenarists . . . have done a very intelligent job of loosening Kesey's schematism. It had to be done . . . The movie (set in 1963) retains most of Kesey's ideas but doesn't diagram them; we're not cued at every step." The finished product, according to Kael, was "a powerful, smashingly effective movie—not a great movie but one that will probably stir audiences' emotions and join the ranks of . . . pop-mythology films." *One Flew Over the Cuckoo's Nest* did become one of the biggest critically and popular hits of the 1970s, and only the second film ever to sweep all five of the most important Academy Awards— Best Picture, Best Actor (Nicholson), Best Actress (Fletcher), Best Screenplay and, the Best Director award for Forman.

Sticking to counterculture themes, Forman, for his next film, chose to adapt the 1967 "American Tribal Love-Rock Musical" *Hair*, which he had seen during one of his first trips to America. The show's very slight plot revolves around a young man, about to be drafted to fight in Vietnam, who falls in with a group of hippies. It seemed to be an artifact of the 1960s and Frank Rich of *Time* was not alone in believing, before the movie opened, that "if ever a project looked doomed, it was this one," since "even at the time [the original show opened], it was dated." After seeing the finished 1979 film, however, Rich rhapsodized, "*Hair* succeeds at all levels—as lowdown fun, as affecting drama, as exhilarating spectacle and as provocative social observation." He went on to praise the director's technique saying, "Though every cut and camera angle . . . appears to have been carefully conceived, the total effect is spontaneous." Jack Kroll of *Newsweek* concurred in the praise: "Forman's new film . . . treats the [musical] exactly as it should be treated—as a myth of our popular consciousness, no more dated than your last dream of happiness after a bad day in the real world . . . [the] movie glows, dances and clangs with the euphoria of the flower-child insurrection."

After two hits in a row, Forman failed critically with *Ragtime* (1981), his version of E. L. Doctorow's sprawling novel which mixed real and fictional characters from turn-of-the-century America. The book had many interrelated plots, and Forman chose to focus on one involving the black pianist-turned-revolutionary Coalhouse Walker (played by Howard E. Rollins, Jr.). A friend of the eighty-two-year-old actor James Cagney, Forman scored a major coup when he persuaded Cagney to portray Police Commissioner Rhinelander Waldo, who foils Walker's attempt to blow up the Morgan library in New York City.

Richard Corliss of *Time* admired Cagney and most of the other actors in *Ragtime*, but added, "To dwell on the performances is to admit to the ultimate failure of Forman's enterprise. His commitment to the actors allows them the time to bring their characters to quirky behavioral life, but every reaction show, every unfinished phrase or repeated sentence means that many moments stolen from the Doctorow overview." Corliss felt the director had "reduced a pageant to an anecdote, and sacrificed sweep for nuance."

Forman came back strongly in 1984 with *Amadeus*, based on Peter Shaffer's play about the rivalry of two eighteenth-century composers, Wolfgang Amadeus Mozart and the now lesser-known Antonio Salieri. In Shaffer's fictionalized view, Salieri becomes angry because he sees himself as a pious man and Mozart as an "obscene child," and yet feels that God his using Mozart as "His instrument." Salieri's frustration increases because, in the play and movie, he is the only person who truly appreciates Mozart's genius. At the director's urging, Shaffer dramatically altered his work in writing the film's screenplay. Forman felt, as the playwright explained in the introduction to the "film edition" of the play, that "the film of a play is really a new work, another fulfillment of the same impulse that had created the original. The adapter's task was to explore many new paths to emerge in the end at the same emotional place."

In his *Time* review of the cinematic *Amadeus*, Richard Corliss asserted that Forman "saw a way to retain the play's intellectual breadth and formal audacity without betraying the movie medium's demand for matter of fact naturalism . . . The result is a grand, sprawling entertainment that incites enthrallment." Specifically, in Corliss's words, Mozart's "music, which in the play served only as an allusive *ostinato*, sizes center stage with significant excerpts from four Mozart operas, several concerti and the *Requiem*. . . . Shaffer's screenplay retains many of the play's epigrammatic fulminations, deftly synopsizes whole sections, transforms Mozart's father from a hectoring apparition to an on-screen tyrant, and provides a thrilling new climax in which the dying Mozart dictates his *Requiem* to a Salieri racked with guilt, jealousy and awe." Several other critics echoed the judgment of *Rolling Stone*'s Chris Hodenfiled, who felt that *Amadeus* "might be one of the best movies about music ever made." As with *Cuckoo's Nest*, Forman won every virtually every major American directorial award, including the Academy Award, for *Amadeus*.

ADDRESSES: AGENT—Robert Lantz, 888 Seventh Avenue, New York, NY 10016.

* * *

FORSYTHE, Colin   1961-

PERSONAL: Born Ron Johnstone, January 5, 1961, in London, England; son of George Edward (a psychotherapist) and Maude (a teacher; maiden name, Keaveney) Johnstone. EDUCATION: Attended Cambridge University, 1980-84.

VOCATION: Actor and director.

CAREER: PRINCIPAL STAGE APPEARANCES—Title role, *Agamemnon,* A.D.C. Theatre, U.K., 1980; *Flying Blind,* Cambridge Union, U.K., 1980; Connor, *Comedians,* Cambridge Mummers, U.K., 1981; Christy Mahon, *Playboy of the Western World,* Cambridge and in Harlech, Wales, 1981; Frank, *If You'll be Glad, I'll be Frank,* Cambridge, U.K., 1981; Fred, *Saved,* Cambridge, U.K., 1981; Moriarty, *Sherlock Holmes* and Quasi, *Terror in Toytown,* both Edinburgh Festival, U.K., 1981; Ballad Singer, *Threepenny Opera,* Peterhouse Mayweek Garden production, 1983.

PRINCIPAL STAGE WORK—Director: *City Sugar,* A.D.C. Theatre, Cambridge, 1981; *Twelfth Night,* Dryden Society, Trinity May Week production, 1982; *La Machine Infernale,* Emmanuel Old Library, Cambridge, 1983; *The Suicide,* Belgrade Youth Theatre, 1984; (assistant director) *Annie* and *Aladdin,* Belgrade Theatre, Coventry, U.K., 1984; *America Hurrah,* Belgrade Studio Theatre, 1985; (trainee director) *The Hunchback of Notre of Dame,* Belgrade Theatre, 1985; *The Sea,* Belgrade Studio Theatre, 1985.

PRINCIPAL FILM APPEARANCES—*It Wisnae Me, Mister,* Scottish production.

PRINCIPAL TELEVISION APPEARANCES—*Sutherland's Law,* BBC, 1974; interviewed on *Nationwide,* BBC, 1974; *Cavern Deep,* STV, 1976; *Playfair,* STV, 1977; *Teenage Talk,* 1977; Tom, *Middle English,* Thames TV, 1983; title role, *Houseman's Tale,* BBC, 1985.

RELATED CAREER—Writer and adaptor for radio productions in

COLIN FORSYTHE

England and has recorded songs for various programs. Served as as a stage manager for the Shakespeare Festival in Oakland, CA.

MEMBER: British Actors' Equity Association.

ADDRESSES: AGENT—Kate Feast Management, 43A Princess Road, Regents Park, London NW1, England.

*   *   *

FORSYTHE, Henderson   1917-

PERSONAL: Born September 11, 1917, in Macon, MO; son of Cecil Proctor and Mary Katherine (Henderson) Forsythe; married Dorothea M. Carlson, May 26, 1942; children: Eric, Jason. EDUCATION: Iowa State University, B.A., 1939, M.F.A., 1940. RELIGION: Presbyterian. MILITARY: U.S. Army, 1941-46.

VOCATION: Actor and director.

CAREER: STAGE DEBUT—Dickie Reynolds, *Accent on Youth,* Erie Summer Theatre, Point Chautauqua, NY, August, 1940. BROADWAY DEBUT—Mr. Hubble, *The Cellar and the Well,* American National Theatre Academy (ANTA) Theatre, 1950. PRINCIPAL STAGE APPEARANCES—Geoffrey Cole, *The Vinegar Tree* and Prince Rudolph, *Candlelight,* both Erie Summer Theatre, Point Chautauqua, NY, 1940; Reporter, *Margin for Error,* Spencer Grant, *Here Today,* and Cupid Holliday, *We Were Here First,* all 1940, Tim Shields, *Tony Draws a Horse,* Paul Rambusch, *Middletown Mural,* and James, *Family Portrait,* all 1941, all at Cleveland Playhouse, OH.

At the Erie Playhouse, PA: Rough, *Angel Street,* Harry Archer, *Kiss and Tell,* Benjamin Griggs, *But Not Goodbye,* all 1946; Ernest Friedman, *Design for Living,* Tommy Turner, *The Male Animal,* Norman, *Out of the Frying Pan,* Dr. Shelby, *Blind Alley,* Horace Giddens, *The Little Foxes,* various roles, *My Sister Eileen,* Albert Kummer, *Dear Ruth,* Kingsley, *Stage Door,* title role, *Uncle Harry,* Dennis Curtin, *Anything Can Happen,* all 1947; Dr. Ferguson, *Men in White,* David Bellow, *I Like It Here,* Ned Farrar, *Her Master's Voice,* title role, *The Late George Apley,* John, *John Loves Mary;* Grant Matthews, *State of the Union,* Dr. Johnson, *I Remember Mama,* Professor Charles Burnett, *Parlor Story,* Kenneth Bixby, *Goodbye Again,* all 1948; Clark Redfield, *Dream Girl,* Colonel, *The Hasty Heart,* Petruchio, *The Taming of the Shrew,* Doctor, *Life with Father,* Snowflake, *Ruined by Drink,* Bill Paige, *The Voice of the Turtle,* General K.C. Davis, *Command Decision,* Judge, *Happy Birthday,* Lance Corporal, *See How They Run,* Uncle Stanley, *George Washington Slept Here,* all 1949; Tommy Thurston, *Two Blind Mice,* Horatio Channing, *Invitation to a Murder,* Stephen Minch, *Star Wagon,* Father Moynihan, *Jenny Kissed Me,* Colonel, *Jacobowsky and the Colonel,* all 1950.

Continuing at the Erie Playhouse: Elwood P. Dowd, *Harvey,* Matthew Cromwell, *Strange Bedfellows,* Clarke Storey, *The Second Man,* Jonah Goodman, *The Gentle People,* Macauley-Connor, *The Philadelphia Story,* Tom, *The Glass Menagerie,* Ed Devery, *Born Yesterday,* Curley, *Green Grow the Lilacs,* Bluntschli, *Arms and the Man,* all 1951; Mr. Adams, *Junior Miss,* Jeff, *The Curious Savage,* Clarence Day, *Life with Mother,* Preston and Mitchell, *For Love or Money,* Creon, *Antigone,* Pappa Bonnard, *The Happy Time,* Stephen Wayne, *First Lady,* Henderson, *Gramercy Ghost,* Detective McLeod, *Detective Story,* Mr. Brown, *Let Us Be Gay,*

HENDERSON FORSYTHE

Derrick, *Rip Van Winkle*, all 1952; Professor Pearson, *The Velvet Glove*, Clark Redfield, *Dream Girl*, title role, *Mister Roberts*, Sam Stover, *Apple of His Eye*, Jason, *Medea*, Major Joppolo, *A Bell for Adano*, David Slater, *The Moon Is Blue*, Grandpa Vanderhof, *You Can't Take It with You*, Milo Alcott, *Lo and Behold*, all 1953; Sergeant Schultz, *Stalag 17*, title role, *Father Malachy's Miracle*, Walter Burns, *Front Page*, Charles Colborn, *Janie*, Henderson, *Bell, Book and Candle*, Malcolm Bryant, *Point of No Return*, Captain Ernest Caldwell, *At War with the Army*, all 1954; Howard Carol, *Time Out for Ginger*, O'Flingsley, *Shadow and Substance*, Inspector, *Dial M for Murder*, Linus, *Sabrina Fair*, Professor Charles Burnett, *Mother Was a Statesman*, He, *The Fourposter*, all 1955.

At Cain Park, Cleveland Heights, OH: Reverend Jones, *The Barber and the Cow*, Grandpa Vanderhof, *You Can't Take It with You*, Mr. Webb, *Our Town*, Clark Redfield, *Dream Girl*, and *Sing Out, Sweet Land*, all 1947; Tchang, *Lute Song*, Prime Minister of China, *The Reluctant Virgin*, Petruchio, *The Taming of the Shrew*, all 1948; Tommy Turner, *The Male Animal*, Elwood P. Dowd, *Harvey*, and Nat, *Ah, Wilderness!*, all at Penn Playhouse, Meadville, PA, 1951; Friar Laurence, *Romeo and Juliet*, Shakespearean Workshop, New York City, 1956; Larry, *The Iceman Cometh*, Circle in the Square Theatre, New York City, 1956; Ned Gates, *Miss Lonelyhearts*, Music Box Theatre, New York City, 1957; Hickey, *The Iceman Cometh*, Circle in the Square Theatre, New York City, 1957; Peter Stockman, *An Enemy of the People*, Actors Playhouse, New York City, 1959; Banquo, *Macbeth*, Cambridge Drama Festival, MA, 1959.

Title role, *Krapp's Last Tape*, Provincetown Playhouse, New York

City, 1960; G. Bernard Shaw, *A Figleaf in Her Bonnet*, Gramercy Arts Theatre, New York City, 1961; Father Francis, *Someone from Assisi* and Father, *Childhood*, both Circle in the Square Theatre, New York City, 1962; Harry, *The Collection*, Cherry Lane Theatre, New York City, 1962; George, *Who's Afraid of Virginia Woolf?*, Billy Rose Theatre, New York City, 1964; Bert, *Dark Corners*, Actors Playhouse, New York City, 1964; Edward, *A Slight Ache*, Writers Stage, New York City, 1964; Donald Crawford, *The Right Honourable Gentleman*, Billy Rose Theatre, New York City, 1965; Cox, Miles, and Doctor, *Malcolm*, Shubert Theatre, New York City, 1966; Harry, *A Delicate Balance*, Martin Beck Theatre, New York City, 1966; Petey, *The Birthday Party*, Booth Theatre, New York City, 1967; Tobias, *A Delicate Balance*, Studio Arena Theatre, Buffalo, NY, 1967.

William Chumley, *Harvey*, ANTA Theatre, New York City, 1970; Nelson Longhurst, *The Engagement Baby*, Helen Hayes Theatre, New York City, 1970; Dr. Freytak, *The Happiness Cage*, New York Shakespeare Festival, Public Theatre, New York City, 1970; Vladimir, *Waiting for Godot*, Sheridan Square Playhouse, New York City, 1971; Edward, *In Case of Accident*, Eastside Playhouse, New York City, 1972; Austin, *Not I*, Forum Theatre, New York City, 1972; Norris Cummings, *An Evening with the Poet-Senator*, Playhouse II, New York City, 1973; Priest, *The Freedom of the City*, Alvin Theatre, New York City, 1974; L. D. Alexander, *The Last Meeting of the Knights of the White Magnolia*, Arena Stage, Washington, DC, 1975, then Kennedy Center, Washington, DC, 1976; Clarence Sickenger, *The Oldest Living Graduate*, Kennedy Center, 1976; also appeared as L. D. Alexander in "The Last Meeting of the Knights of the White Magnolia," and Clarence Sickenger in "The Oldest Living Graduate," under the combined title of *The Texas Trilogy*, Kennedy Center, then transferred to Broadhurst Theatre, New York City, 1976; Sheriff Ed Earl Dodd, *The The Best Little Whorehouse in Texas*, Entermedia Theatre, New York City, then 46th Street Theatre, New York City, both 1978.

Harry, *Close Relations*, Manhattan Punch Line Theatre, New York City, 1980; Sheriff Ed Earl Dodd, *The The Best Little Whorehouse in Texas*, Drury Lane Theatre, London, 1981; Bishop Cooley, "The Lady or the Tiger Show," and Louis Benjamin Hinkle, "I'm Good to My Doggies," under the combined title of *Wild Life*, VanDam Theatre, New York City, 1983; Hornby, "A Kind of Alaska," and Controller, "Victoria Station," under the combined title of *Other Places*, Manhattan Theatre Club, New York City, 1984; Case, *My Father's House*, American Theatre of Actors, New York City, 1984; Lou, *After the Fall*, Playhouse 91, New York City, 1984; Hastings Hamilton, *A Broadcast Baby*, with the American Jewish Theatre at the 92nd Street YMHA, New York City, 1985; Henry Lowenthal, *Cliffhanger*, Lambs Theatre, New York City, 1985; Sorin, *The Seagull*, Kennedy Center, Washington DC, 1985-86; Charlie, *Seascape*, Coconut Grove Playhouse, FL, 1986.

MAJOR TOURS—Chip Reegan, *The Indoor Sport*, U.S. cities, 1962; Boss Finley, *Sweet Bird of Youth*, U.S. cities, 1986-87.

PRINCIPAL STAGE WORK—Director: *State of the Union*, 1948, *The Taming of the Shrew*, 1949, *The Cellar and the Well*, 1950, *The Women, Charley's Aunt*, and *Montserrat*, all 1952, *I Remember Mama*, 1953, *Be Your Age* and *As You Like It*, all 1954, all at the Erie Playhouse; *The Taming of the Shrew*, Cain Park, Cleveland Heights, OH, 1948; *The Cellar and the Well*, ANTA Theatre, New York City, 1950.

PRINCIPAL FILM APPEARANCES—*Dead of Night*, Universal,

1974; *Silkwood,* Twentieth Century-Fox, 1983; *Concealed Enemies,* 1984; *End of the Line,* 1986.

PRINCIPAL TELEVSION APPEARANCES—Series: David Stewart, *As the World Turns,* CBS.

AWARDS: Outstanding Performance by a Featured Actor, Antoinette Perry Award, 1978, for *The Best Little Whorehouse in Texas.*

MEMBER: Actors' Equity Assocation, Screen Actors Guild, American Federation of Television and Radio Artists, American National Theatre and Academy (ANTA).

SIDELIGHTS: FAVORITE ROLES—Larry and Hickey, *The Iceman Cometh,* Krapp, *Krapp's Last Tape,* Harry, *The Collection,* George, *Who's Afraid of Virginia Woolf?,* Tobias, *A Delicate Balance.* RECREATIONS—Wood carving, golf.

ADDRESSES: HOME—204 Elm Street, Tenafly, NJ 07670.

*   *   *

FOSTER, Julia   1942-

PERSONAL: Born in 1942, in Lewes, Sussex, England; married Lionel Morton (divorced); married Bruce Fogle.

VOCATION: Actress.

CAREER: STAGE DEBUT—Appeared with Brighton Repertory Theatre, U.K. LONDON DEBUT—Tricia Elliott, *Travelling Light,* Prince of Wales Theatre, 1965. PRINCIPAL STAGE APPEARANCES—Geraldine Barclay, *What the Butler Saw,* Queen's Theatre, London, 1969; Dixie, *Flint,* Criterion Theatre, London, 1970; title role, *Lulu,* Playhouse Theatre, Nottingham, U.K., then Royal Court Theatre, London, 1970, then Apollo Theatre, London, 1971; Jenny Hogarth, *Notes on a Love Affair,* Globe Theatre, London, 1972; Anna, *The Day After the Fair,* Lyric Theatre, Hammersmith, London, 1972; title role, *Saint Joan,* New Theatre, Oxford, U.K., 1974; Angie, *Blind Date,* King's Head Theatre, London, 1977; Helen Dawes, *The Singular Life of Albert Nobbs,* New End Theatre, London, 1978; Brigit 1, *Happy Birthday,* Apollo Theatre, London, 1979; Giacinta, *Country Wife,* Citizens Theatre, Glasgow, 1979, then Lyric Theatre, Hammersmith, London, 1980; appeared in *After You with the Milk,* with the Birmingham Repertory Company, U.K., 1980.

MAJOR TOURS—*What the Butler Saw,* number one tour, U.K. cities, 1969; also *The Country Wife,* U.K. cities.

FILM DEBUT—1960. PRINCIPAL FILM APPEARANCES—*Term of Trial,* Warner Brothers, 1963; *The Loneliness of the Long Distance Runner,* Continental, 1963; *The Small World of Sammy Lee,* Seven Arts, 1963; *One Way Pendulum,* Lopert, 1965; *Alfie,* Paramount, 1966; *Half a Sixpence,* Paramount, 1968; also appeared in *The Bargee.*

TELEVISION DEBUT—Ann Carson, *Emergency Ward 10.* PRINCIPAL TELEVISION APPEARANCES—Series: *Good Girl,* BBC. Episodic: *Love Story,* DuMont, 1954; *Taxi,* ABC. Movies: *Crime and Punishment; Moll Flanders; A Cosy Little Arrangement; The Planemakers; Consequences; They Throw It at You; The Image.*

ADDRESSES: AGENT—International Creative Management Ltd., 388 Oxford Street, London W1, England.*

*   *   *

FOWLER, Keith   1939-

PERSONAL: Born February 23, 1939, in San Francisco, CA; son of Jack Franklin (an engineer) and Jaquelin Dorothy (Montgomery) Fowler; married Janet Bell (divorced); children: Jeremy Cay, Matthew Bell. EDUCATION: San Francisco State University, B.A., magna cum laude, 1960; Yale School of Drama, D.F.A., 1969; studied Elizabethan theatre at the Shakespeare Institute, Stratford-upon-Avon, England.

VOCATION: Director, teacher, actor, producer, and writer.

CAREER: STAGE DEBUT—Cottage Cheese, *A Dairy Pageant,* St. Vincent De Paul School, CA, 1944. OFF-BROADWAY DEBUT—The father, *Camille,* New York Theatre Ensemble, 1979. PRINCIPAL STAGE APPEARANCES—Mark Antony, *Julius Caesar,* Oregon Shakespeare Festival, 1960; at the Virginia Museum Theatre, 1969-1976: Brutus, *Julius Caesar,* title role, *Uncle Vanya,* narrator and Fred, *A Christmas Carol,* Aston, *The Caretaker,* Teddy, *The Homecoming,* Roger Casement, *The Royal Rape of Ruri McCasmonde,* title role, *Hamlet,* Stage Manager, *Our Town.*

PRINCIPAL STAGE WORK—Director: *Hamlet,* San Francisco Shakespeare Festival, 1962; *Macbeth,* Festival Theatre, El Paso, TX, 1964. At the Virginia Museum Theatre, produced and directed: *Marat/Sade, The Great Divide, A Taste of Honey,* and *HMS Pinafore,* all 1969, *Threepenny Opera* and *Once in a Lifetime,* 1970, *The Homecoming, America Hurrah,* and *Summertree,* all 1971, *Twelfth Night* and *A Christmas Carol,* 1972, *Indians, The Taming of the Shrew, A Christmas Panto,* and *Macbeth,* all 1973, *Cyrano de Bergerac* and *The Sorrows of Fredrick the Great,* 1974, *The Country Wife, Our Father* (also at the Manhattan Theatre Club), *Guys and Dolls,* and *Children,* all 1975, *Childe Byron,* 1976.

Also directed: *Scenes from American Life,* Temple University, 1976; *Othello, Ashes of Soldiers, El Grande de Coca Cola,* and *A Christmas Carol,* all with the American Revels Company, Richmond, VA; staged reading, *Tales from the Vienna Woods,* Yale Repertory Theatre; *Volpone,* Wayside Theatre, Middletown, VA.

RELATED CAREER— Producing director, Virginia Museum Theatre, 1969-77; head of directing, Yale School of Drama, 1977-78; artistic director, American Revels Company, 1978-81; professor, University of California at Irvine, 1981—.

NON-RELATED CAREER—Certified hypnotherapist.

WRITINGS: PLAYS, PRODUCED—Adaptation of *A Christmas Carol,* Virginia Museum Theatre, 1972.

AWARDS: Borden Prize, 1956; Fulbright Scholarship, 1960; Wilson Fellowship, 1961; John Shubert Directing Fellowship, 1963.

MEMBER: Actors' Equity Association, Society of Stage Directors and Choreographers; Alpha Psi Omega.

SIDELIGHTS: Keith Fowler informs *CTFT* that he has ''studied

German and travels frequently to Germany and Austria.'' He is also involved in reasearch in performance trance funded by university grants.

ADDRESSES: OFFICE—School of Fine Arts, University of California, Irvine, CA 92717.

┄ ┄ ┄

FOXWORTH, Robert   1941-

PERSONAL: Born November 1, 1941, in Houston, TX; son of John Howard (a roofing contractor) and Erna Beth (a writer; maiden name, Seamman) Foxworth; married Marilyn McCormick, September 24, 1964 (divorced, 1974); children: Brendon, Kristyn. EDUCATION: Carnegie-Mellon University, B.F.A.; studied for the theatre at the Arena Stage, Washington, DC. POLITICS: Democrat.

VOCATION: Actor and director.

CAREER: STAGE DEBUT—The leading child, *The Indian Captive*, Little Red School House, Houston, TX, 1950. BROADWAY DEBUT—Chorus, *Henry V*, American National Theatre Academy (ANTA) Theatre, 1969, for thirty performances. PRINCIPAL STAGE APPEARANCES—Ten roles in repertory, Alley Theatre, Houston, TX, 1958-61; eighteen roles in repertory, Arena Stage, Washington, DC, 1965-68; three roles in repertory, American Shakespeare Festival, Stratford, CT, 1969; John Proctor, *The Crucible*, Vivian Beaumont Theatre, Lincoln Center, New York City, 1972;

ROBERT FOXWORTH

McMurphy, *One Flew Over the Cuckoo's Nest*, Huntington Hartford Theatre, Los Angeles, 1975; Earl of Leicester, *Mary Stuart*, Ahmanson Theatre, Los Angeles, 1980; Scott, *Terra Nova*, American Place Theatre, New York City, 1984; also *P.S. Your Cat Is Dead*.

FILM DEBUT—Leading Man, *The Treasure of Matecumbe*, Buena Vista, 1976. PRINCIPAL FILM APPEARANCES—*Damien—Omen II*, Twentieth Century-Fox, 1978; *Airport '77*, Universal, 1977; *Prophecy*, Paramount, 1979; Valnikov, *The Black Marble*, AVCO-Embassy, 1980; Seymour Borde, *The Invisible Stranger*, Trans-World Entertainment, 1984; also, *The Astral Factor*.

TELEVISION DEBUT—"Sadbird," *CBS Playhouse*, 1969. PRINCIPAL TELEVISION APPEARANCES—Series: David Hansen, *Storefront Lawyers*, CBS, 1970-71; Chase Gioberti, *Falcon Crest*, CBS, 1981—. Movies: Alvin Karpis, *The F.B.I. vs. Alvin Karpis*, 1974; Jack Maddock, *Mrs. Sundance*, 1974; Questor, *The Questor Tapes*, 1974; Peter, *Peter and Paul*, 1981. Specials: Narrator, *National Geographic Special: In the Shadow of Vesuvius*, PBS, 1987.

PRINCIPAL TELEVISION WORK—Director of episodes of *Falcon Crest*, CBS, 1981—.

PRINCIPAL RADIO WORK—Producer and host, *American Dialogues*, 1985—.

AWARDS: Theatre World Award, 1972, for *The Crucible;* honored by the League of United Latin American Citizens, 1985.

MEMBER: Actors' Equity Association, American Federation of Television and Radio Artists, Screen Actors Guild; Commission of Concern for Central America, Los Angeles Chapter (board of directors, 1983-85), Disciples of Christ Church, other environmental, antinuclear and nuclear freeze organizations.

SIDELIGHTS: FAVORITE ROLES—Valnikov, *The Black Marble*, and McMurphy in *One Flew Over the Cuckoo's Nest*.

ADDRESSES: OFFICE—Krisbo Productions, 315 S. Beverly Drive, Suite 211, Beverly Hills, CA 90212.*

*   *   *

FRANCE, Richard   1938-

PERSONAL: Born Richard Zagami, May 5, 1938, in Boston, MA; son of N. Roy (a U.S. Army officer) and Rita Foster (France) Zagami; married Rachel Anne Mehr (a writer and designer), March 21, 1969; children: Rebecca, Miriam. EDUCATION: Carnegie-Mellon University, Ph.D., 1973; studied playwrighting with John Gassner at the Yale School of Drama.

VOCATION: Writer and actor.

CAREER: STAGE DEBUT—Boanerges, *The Apple Cart*, Interplayers Theatre, San Francisco, 1961, for twenty-four performances. OFF-BROADWAY DEBUT—Christmas Present, *A Christmas Carol*, Ridiculous Theatrical Company, 1981, for forty-five performances.

FILM DEBUT—Zombie, *Night of the Living Dead*, Continental, 1968. PRINCIPAL FILM APPEARANCES—Dr. Watts, *The Crazies*,

RICHARD FRANCE

Latent Image, 1973; Dr. Rausch, *Dawn of the Dead*, United Artists, 1979. Also appeared in *The Sorrows of Dolores* and *Strong Medicine*.

PRINCIPAL TELEVISION WORK—Film and drama critic, *Newsroom*, WQED, PBS, Pittsburgh, PA, 1969-72; producer, *Jewel Walker's Mime Circus*, PBS.

RELATED CAREER—Assistant professor, Rhode Island College, 1972-73; assistant professor, Lawrence University, 1974-80; vice-chairman, American Theatre Association Playwrights Program, 1972-75, then chairman, 1975-77. Contributor to periodicals, including "Theatre Quarterly," "Theatre Survey," and "Yale/Theatre." Performs voice-over work for radio and television.

WRITINGS: PLAYS, PRODUCED—*The First Word and the Last,* Open Space Theatre Workshop, London, 1968, and Mikery Theatre, Amsterdam, 1968; *Don't You Know It's Raining,* Dallas Theatre Center, Dallas, TX, 1970; *A Day in the Life,* Salt City Playhouse, Syracuse, NY, 1974, Midwest Playwrights Lab, 1976, and Actors Alley Theatre, Los Angeles, 1978; *An End in Sight,* No Smoking Playhouse, New York City, 1981; *Station J,* Body Politic Theatre, Chicago, 1979, East-West Players, Los Angeles, 1981, and 28th Street Playhouse, New York City, 1982.

PLAYS, PUBLISHED—*The Magic Shop,* Baker's Plays, 1972; *Fathers and Sons,* Baker's Plays, 1972; *The Adventure of the Dying Detective,* I. E. Clark, 1974; *One Day in the Life of Ivan Denisovich,* Baker's Plays, 1974; "The Image of Elmo Doyle," *Best Short Plays of 1979,* Chilton, 1979; *Feathertop,* Baker's Plays, 1980; *Station J,* Irvington Press, 1982; *Don't You Know It's Raining,* Arion Press, 1984.

NON-FICTION—*The Theatre of Orson Welles,* Bucknell University Press, 1978, Kodan-sha, Tokyo, 1983.

AWARDS: Sam S. Shubert Playwriting Fellowship Award, 1965; John Golden Playwriting Fellowship Award, 1965; Rockefeller Production Grant Award, 1970; Wisconsin State Council on the Arts Creative Writing Award, 1977; Ford Foundation New American Play Production Grant Award, 1979; National Endowment for the Humanities Fellowship for Independent Study Award, 1979-80; National Endowment for the Arts Creative Writing Fellowship Award, 1974 and 1980; Silver PEN Award for Playwrighting, 1982.

MEMBER: Screen Actors Guild, American Federation of Television and Radio Artists, Dramatists Guild.

ADDRESSES: AGENT—Sydell Albert, 6716 Hill Park Drive, Los Angeles, CA 90068.

*   *   *

FRANCINE, Anne   1917-

PERSONAL: Full name, Anne Hollingshead Francine; born August 8, 1917, in Philadelphia, PA; daughter of Albert Phillip (a physician) and Emilie G. (Ehret) Francine. EDUCATION: Studied singing with Robert Fram, Burt Knepp, and Norman Fields and dancing with Valerie Bettis.

VOCATION: Actress.

CAREER: STAGE DEBUT—Eileen Ellers, *Too Many Girls,* Wilson Theatre, Detroit, MI, 1940. BROADWAY DEBUT—Reena Rowe, *Marriage Is for Single People,* Cort Theatre, 1945. LONDON DEBUT—Octavia Brooks, *Innocent as Hell,* Lyric Theatre, Hammersmith, London, 1960. PRINCIPAL STAGE APPEARANCES—Rena Leslie, *George Washington Slept Here,* Bucks County Playhouse, New Hope, PA, 1944; *Sugar 'n Spice,* Copley Theatre, Boston, 1944; Liz Courtney, *Dinner for Three,* pre-Broadway tryout, 1945; Judith Canfield, *Stage Door,* Stamford, CT, 1945.

Kate, *The Taming of the Shrew,* Equity Library Theatre, New York City, 1950; Olga Katrina, *You Can't Take It with You* and Mrs. George, *Getting Married,* both Equity Library Theatre productions at the Lenox Hill Playhouse, New York City, 1951; appeared in *Hay Fever* and portrayed Janet Archer, *Kiss and Tell,* both Palm Beach Theatre, FL, 1953; Flora Busch, *By the Beautiful Sea,* Majestic Theatre, New York City, 1954; Madeline, *The Wayward Kiss,* Bucks County Playhouse, 1955; Colonel Yerka Bradacova, *The Great Sebastians,* American National Theatre Academy (ANTA) Theatre, New York City, 1956; Queen Elizabeth, *The Dark Lady of the Sonnets* and Marian Hunt, *Made in Heaven,* both Berkshire Festival, Stockbridge, MA, 1956; Mrs. St. Maugham, *The Chalk Garden,* 1956, and Romaine, *Witness for the Prosecution,* 1957, both Robin Hood Theatre, Wilmington, DE; Miss Casewell, *The Mousetrap* and Mrs. Benjamin Gulle, *The Happiest Millionaire,* both Corning Summer Theatre, NY, 1958; Pamela Barry, *Separate Rooms,* Fulton Theatre, Lancaster, PA, 1959; appeared in the revue *Quick Changes,* Chicago, 1959; Ninotchka, *Silk Stockings,* Starlight Musicals, Indianapolis, IN, 1959; Rayna, *Guitar,* Jan Hus House, New York City, 1959.

Mrs. Hurstpierpoint, *Valmouth,* York Theatre, New York City,

1960; *Tenderloin*, 46th Street Theatre, New York City, 1960; Theresa, *Walk Alone Together*, 1961, and appeared in *Critics Choice*, 1962, both at the John Drew Theatre, East Hampton, NY, 1961; Contessa, *If Five Years Pass*, Theatre 73, New York City, 1962; Susan B. Anthony, *Asylum*, Theatre de Lys, New York City, 1962; Fortune Teller, *The Skin of Our Teeth*, Brandeis University, Boston, 1963; Maria, *Twelfth Night*, Playhouse-in-the-Park, Cincinnati, OH, 1963; appeared in *Diary of a Scoundrel*, 1965, and *Mother Courage*, 1966, both at the Milwaukee Repertory Theatre; *The Flies*, Association of Performing Artists (APA), Ann Arbor, MI, 1966; Olga, *You Can't Take It with You*, APA Repertory, Lyceum Theatre, New York City, 1967; understudy Vera Charles, *Mame*, Winter Garden Theatre, New York City, 1967; appeared in *Are You Now or Have You Ever Been?*, Theatre of Riverside Church, New York City, 1973; Mrs. Sprode, *Miss Moffat*, pre-Broadway tryout, 1974; appeared in *The Importance of Being Earnest*, Syracuse Stage, NY, 1975; Vera Charles, *Mame*, Gershwin Theatre, New York City, 1983.

MAJOR TOURS—Ethel Brander, *Rose Marie*, Boston and Montreal, 1941; Martha Ladd, *Without Love*, 1945; Dorothy Shaw, *Gentlemen Prefer Blondes*, New England, 1953; Colonel Yerka Bradacova, *The Great Sebastians*, 1956; Lily Schaeffer, *Time for Elizabeth*, 1957; Vera Charles, *Mame*, U.S. cities, 1968.

PRINCIPAL CABARET APPEARANCES—Coq Rouge, 1938-40; Persian Room at the Plaza Hotel, New York City, 1940; Club Cuba, 1940, Cafe Pierre, 1941; Versailles Club, New York City, 1941, Le Petit Palais, 1941; Embassy Club, 1941-43; Copacabana, New York City, 1942; on the Queen Mary, 1942; Armendo's, 1943-45; Les Ambassadeurs, Paris, 1947; Monseigneur's, Paris, 1947; Ciro's, Paris, 1947; La Martinique, Paris, 1947; Ritz, Montreal, 1949-51; British Colonial, Nassau, Bahamas, 1952; Black Patch, St. Thomas, Virgin Islands, 1961; Upstairs at the Duplex, New York City, 1962; Blue Angel, New York City, 1963.

PRINCIPAL FILM APPEARANCES—*Juliet of the Spirits*, Rizzoli, 1965; *Stand Up and Be Counted*, Columbia, 1972; *Savages*, Angelika, 1972.

PRINCIPAL TELEVISION APPEARANCES—"The Great Sebastians," *Producers Showcase*, NBC, 1957.

MEMBER: Actors' Equity Association, Screen Actors Guild, American Federation of Television and Radio Artists, American Guild of Variety Artists; Episcopal Actors Guild.

ADDRESSES: AGENT—Fifi Oscard Agency, 19 W. 44th Street, New York, NY 10036.

*   *   *

FRANCIS, Ivor   1917-1986

PERSONAL: Born 1917, in Toronto, ON, Canada; died October 22, 1986, in Sherman Oaks, CA; married; children: four. MILITARY: Royal Air Force.

VOCATION: Actor.

CAREER: PRINCIPAL TELEVISION APPEARANCES—Series: Professor Dragon, *Room 222*, ABC, 1969-74. Episodic: *Mary Hartman, Mary Hartman*, syndicated; *Kojak*, CBS; *Starsky and Hutch*,

ABC; *The Six Million Dollar Man*, ABC; *The Waltons*, CBS; *Hawaii Five-0*, CBS; *The Odd Couple*, ABC; *The Jeffersons*, CBS; *Maude*, CBS; *The Flying Nun*, ABC; *Get Smart*, NBC; *Swat*, ABC.

PRINCIPAL STAGE APPEARANCES—Broadway: *Gideon; The Investigation; JB; Fun Couple; The Devil's Advocate; Lorenzo; A Rainy Day in Newark.*

PRINCIPAL RADIO WORK—Joe, *Ma Perkins*.

RELATED CAREER—Acting teacher in both New York City and Los Angeles.*

*   *   *

FRANN, Mary

PERSONAL: Born Mary Luecke, February 27, in St. Louis, MO; daughter of Harry (a sportswriter) and Del Luecke. EDUCATION: Attended Northwestern University for two years.

VOCATION: Actress.

CAREER: PRINCIPAL TELEVISION APPEARANCES—Series: *My Friend Tony*, NBC, 1969; *Return to Peyton Place*, ABC; Amanda Peters, *Days of Our Lives* (four years) ABC; Nan Hollister, *King's Crossing*, ABC, 1982; Joanna Loudon, *Newhart*, CBS, 1982—. Episodic: *The Rockford Files*, NBC; *The Mary Tyler Moore Show*, CBS; *WKRP in Cincinnati*, CBS; *Fantasy Island*, ABC; *Darkroom*,

MARY FRANN

ABC. Movies: *Portrait of an Escort,* ABC, 1986. Specials: Host, *Macy's Thanksgiving Day Parade,* CBS, 1985, 1986. Was a reporter on the staff of KSD-TV News, St. Louis, MO; also co-host for an ABC news affiliate, Chicago.

PRINCIPAL STAGE APPEARANCES—At the Mark Taper Forum, Los Angeles: *Story Theatre, Line,* and *An Evening of Twelve One Acts,* all 1968-70; *Story Theatre,* Broadway production, 1970; also appeared at the Drury Lane and Pheasant Run Theatres, Chicago.

AWARDS: National winner, America Junior Miss Program, full scholarship to Northwestern University.

MEMBER: Actors' Equity Association, American Federation of Radio and Television Artists.

ADDRESSES: PUBLICIST—Rogers & Cowan, Inc., 10000 Santa Monica Blvd. Los Angeles, CA 90067.

*   *   *

FREES, Paul   1919-1986

PERSONAL: Born in 1919; died of heart failure in Tiboron, CA, November 1, 1986; children: a son and daughter.

VOCATION: Actor.

CAREER: PRINCIPAL TELEVISION WORK—Voice-overs: Series —John Beresford Tipton, *The Millionaire,* CBS, 1955-60; Inspector Fenwick and Boris Badenov, *Bullwinkle; The Beatles; The Jackson Five; The Osmonds.* Specials: *The Hobbit; Frosty the Snowman; Rudolph the Red-Nosed Reindeer; Santa Claus Is Coming to Town; The Stingiest Man in Town.*

PRINCIPAL FILM WORK—Narrator: *Day of Trinity; The Case of Dashiell Hammett; The Life of George Pal.*

PRINCIPAL STAGE APPEARANCES—Performed in vaudeville as comic Buddy Green.

AWARDS: Won many Clio and IBA Awards.

SIDELIGHTS: CTFT learned that Paul Frees worked in films by dubbing voices for such stars as Humphrey Bogart, Kirk Douglas, and Toshiro Mifune and provided many voices for the continuing attractions at Disneyland and Disney World.*

*   *   *

FRENCH, Valerie   1932-

PERSONAL: Born Valerie Harrison, March 11, 1932, in London, England; daughter of Frank Orvin Percy and Muriel Clare (Smith) Harrison; married Michael Pertwee (divorced); married Thayer David (died). EDUCATION: Attended Malvern Girls' College; studied dancing with David Lichine and Matt Mattox.

VOCATION: Actress.

CAREER: STAGE DEBUT—*Treasure Hunt,* Theatre Royal, Windsor, U.K., 1951. LONDON DEBUT—*Cockles and Champagne,* Saville Theatre, 1954. BROADWAY DEBUT—Liz, *Inadmissible*

VALERIE FRENCH

Evidence, Belasco Theatre, New York City, 1965. PRINCIPAL STAGE APPEARANCES—Doreen, *It's Different for Men,* Duchess Theatre, London, 1955; Sarah Lord, *Help Stamp Out Marriage,* Booth Theatre, New York City, 1966; Wendy, *The Tea Party,* Eastside Playhouse, New York City, 1968; Griselda, *The Mother Lover,* Booth Theatre, New York City, 1969; Imogen Parrott, *Trelawny of the Wells,* Anspacher Theatre, New York City, 1970; Cecily Hundson, *Studs Edsel,* Ensemble Studio Theatre, New York City, 1974; Dark Marion, *Finn McKool, The Grand Distraction,* Theatre de Lys, New York City, 1975; Alice, *Henry V,* New York Shakespeare Festival, Delacorte Theatre, 1976; Lucy, *Alphabetical Order,* Long Wharf Theatre, New Haven, CT, 1976; Fanny Wilton, *John Gabriel Borkman,* Roundabout Theatre, New York City, 1976; Ruth, *Blithe Spirit,* Meadowbrook Theatre, Detroit, MI, 1979; Sister Ubbidienza, *Bicicletta,* Public Theatre, New York City, 1980; Julie, *Fallen Angels,* Roundabout Theatre, New York City, 1980; Lavinia, *The Cocktail Party,* Chapel Hill, NC, 1980; Helen, *A Taste of Honey,* Roundabout Theatre, New York City, 1981.

Also appeared in *What the Butler Saw,* Arena Theatre, Washington, DC; *Nag's Head,* New Theatre, *Children, Children,* Ritz Theatre, and *The Wayward Stork,* Theatre Guild, all New York City.

MAJOR TOURS—Dominique Beaurevers, *A Shot in the Dark,* national, 1962-63; Madge Larrabee, *Sherlock Holmes,* national, 1975-76.

FILM DEBUT—*The Constant Husband,* British, 1954. PRINCIPAL FILM APPEARANCES—*Maddalena,* I.F.E., 1955; *Jubal,* Columbia, 1956; *The Secret of Treasure Mountain,* Columbia, 1956; *The*

Garment Jungle, Columbia, 1957; *The 27th Day,* Columbia, 1957; *The Hard Man,* Columbia, 1957; *Decision at Sundown,* Columbia, 1957; *The Four Skulls of Jonathan Drake,* United Artists, 1959; *Shalako,* Cinerama, 1968; *Nighthawks,* Universal, 1981.

PRINCIPAL TELEVISION APPEARANCES—Episodic: *The Nurses,* CBS; *Schlitz Playhouse,* CBS; *Have Gun, Will Travel,* CBS; *The Prisoner,* CBS; *Meet McGraw,* NBC; *The Third Man,* syndicated; *The Alaskans,* ABC; *Love Story,* NBC, 1973; *One of the Boys,* NBC, 1981. Movies: *Get Christie Love!,* 1974. Dramatic specials: *Arias and Arabesques; The Detour.* Series: *The Edge of Night,* ABC; *One Life to Live,* ABC; Maureen Teller, *All My Children,* ABC.

Also appeared in *Ten Little Indians, A Time for Us, Brighter Day, Ballad of the Artificial Mash,* and *Champion House.*

MEMBER: Actors' Equity Association, Screen Actors Guild, American Federation of Television and Radio Artists; Crockford's Club.

SIDELIGHTS: RECREATIONS—Chinoiserie and collecting snake jewelry.

ADDRESSES: AGENT—c/o Peter Crouch, Crouch Associates, 59 Frith Street, London W1, England.

*   *   *

FRIEDMAN, Lewis   1948-

PERSONAL: Born October 28, 1948. MILITARY: U.S. Army.

VOCATION: Producer.

CAREER: PRINCIPAL STAGE WORK—Producer, Broadway productions: *A Chorus Line; Zorba; Comedy with Music.* Off-Broadway productions: *Lies and Legends: The Musical Stories of Harry Chapin,* Village Gate Theatre.

Also produced: *Mark Twain Tonight; Diversions and Delights; Mahalia* and concerts of the Preservation Hall Dance Band, Vladimir Horowitz, the Grateful Dead, American Ballet Theatre, Johnny Mathis, Andres Segovia, and Liberace.

MAJOR TOURS—Produced U.S. national tours of: *One Mo' Time; Morning's at Seven; Sophisticated Ladies; Joseph and the Amazing Technicolor Dreamcoat; On Your Toes; Comedy with Music.*

RELATED CAREER—Assistant press agent, public relations director, Theatre Under the Stars, Atlanta, GA; press agent, general manager, Melody Top Theatre, Milwaukee, WI; owner, Kolmar-Luth Entertainment, Inc.

ADDRESSES: OFFICE—The Edgewood Organization, Inc., 1501 Broadway, Suite 201, New York, NY 10036.

*   *   *

FRIEDMAN, Stephen   1937-

PERSONAL: Born March 15, 1937; son of Irving (a retailer) and Dorothy (a teacher; maiden name, Lipsius) Friedman. EDUCATION: University of Pennsylvania, B.S.; Harvard Law School, L.L.B.

VOCATION: Producer, writer, and attorney.

CAREER: FIRST FILM WORK—Producer, *The Last Picture Show,* Columbia, 1971. PRINCIPAL FILM WORK—Producer: *Slap Shot,* Universal, 1977; *Bloodbrothers,* Warner Brothers, 1979; *Fast Break,* Columbia, 1979; *Hero at Large,* United Artists, 1980; *Little Darlings,* Paramount, 1980; *Eye of the Needle,* United Artists, 1981; *All of Me,* Universal, 1984; *Creator,* Universal, 1985; *Enemy Mine,* Twentieth Century-Fox, 1985; *The Best of Times,* Universal, 1986.

NON-RELATED CAREER—Former attorney for the Federal Trade Commission.

WRITINGS: SCREENPLAYS—*Lovin' Molly,* Columbia, 1974.

MEMBER: Academy of Motion Picture Arts and Sciences.

ADDRESSES: HOME—Brentwood, CA. OFFICE—1901 Avenue of the Stars, Suite 605, Los Angeles, CA 90067.

*   *   *

FRIERSON, Monte L.   1930-

PERSONAL: Born February 15, 1930; son of Ambrose Montgomery (an oil producer) and Frances Veronica (Knigge) Frierson. EDUCATION: University of Oklahoma, B.B.A., 1953; trained as a theatrical manager with Lutz and Carr, certified public accountants. POLITICS: Republican. RELIGION: Presbyterian. MILITARY: U.S. Army, 1953-55.

VOCATION: Manager and producer.

CAREER: PRINCIPAL STAGE WORK—Producer: *The Buffalo Skinner,* New York City; also producer for Broadway Summer Musicals, Tulsa, OK, and Tampa Star Theatre, FL; assistant to the producer, the Theatre Guild, New York City; general manager for the Boston Herald Repertory of Classical Drama, MA, McCarter Theatre, Princeton, NJ, Carousel Theatre, Framingham, MA, and the Peninsula Players, Fish Creek, WI; manager, Bridgeport Festival Theater, Beverly, MA; production manager, Oklahoma Symphony Orchestra, Oklahoma City; business manager, St. John Terrell's Music Circus, Lambertville, NJ; concert manager, Elwood Emerick Management, New York City; president, Frierson Management, Tulsa, OK.

RELATED CAREER—Subscription department, American Theatre Society, New York City; treasurer, American Shakespeare Festival, Stratford, CT; treasurer, North Shore Music Theatre, Beverly, MA; assistant to president, American Theatre Wing, New York City; press agent, Westport Country Playhouse, Westport, CT; personal manager for Singer Management Company and Frierson and Durgom Management, both New York City.

MEMBER: Assembly of Community Arts Councils of Oklahoma (board of directors), Association of College, University, and Community Arts Administrators (ACUCAA).

ADDRESSES: HOME—401 W. Sixth Avenue, Bristow, OK 74010. OFFICE—Frierson Management, Williams Center Tower One, Seventh Floor, One W. Third Street, Tulsa, OK 74103.

FURST, Stephen 1955-

PERSONAL: Born Steven Feuerstein, May 8, 1955, in Norfolk, VA; son of Nathan (a salesman) and Lillian (a teacher; maiden name Gish) Feuerstein; married wife Lorraine, June 13, 1976; children: Nathan, Griffith. EDUCATION: Virginia Commonwealth University, B.F.A.; trained for the stage with Richard Newdick. RELIGION: Jewish.

VOCATION: Actor.

CAREER: STAGE DEBUT—Pseudelous, *A Funny Thing Happened on the Way to the Forum,* Cavalier Theatre, Norfolk, VA, 1972, for ninety-two performances.

FILM DEBUT—Kent Dorfman, *Animal House,* Universal, 1978. PRINCIPAL FILM APPEARANCES—*Take Down,* Buena Vista, 1979; *Scavenger Hunt,* Twentieth Century-Fox, 1979; *Soft Explosion,* 1980; *The Unseen,* Triune Films, 1981; *Midnight Madness,* Buena Vista, 1980; *Silent Rage,* Columbia, 1982; *Class Reunion,* Twentieth Century-Fox, 1982; *Up the Creek,* Orion, 1984.

TELEVISION DEBUT—*The Bastard,* syndicated, 1978. PRINCIPAL TELEVISION APPEARANCES—Series: Kent "Flounder" Dorfman, *Delta House,* ABC, 1979; Eliot Axelrod, *St. Elsewhere,* NBC, 1982—.

Episodic: Delivery man, *Family,* ABC, 1979. *Movin' On,* NBC; *CHiPs,* NBC; *Family,* ABC; *The Bob Newhart Show,* CBS; *Lottery!,* ABC; *The Jeffersons,* CBS; *Faerie Tale Theatre,* Showtime. Pilots: *Bizzare,* ABC; *Two Reelers,* NBC; *For Members Only,* CBS. Movies: *The Day After,* ABC, 1983; *Off Sides* (also known as *Pigs vs. Freaks*), NBC, 1984. Specials: *Disneyland 25th Anniversary Show,* NBC.

AWARDS: Honorary Sheriff, Chatsworth, CA, 1986.

MEMBER: Academy of Motion Picture Arts and Sciences, Screen Actors Guild, American Federation of Television and Radio Artists.

ADDRESSES: OFFICE—MTM Enterprises, 4063 Radford Avenue, Studio City, CA 91604. AGENT—Blake Edwards Management, 1888 Century Park East, Los Angeles, CA 90067.

STEPHEN FURST

G

GABEL, Martin 1912-1986

PERSONAL: Born June 19, 1912, in Philadelphia, PA; died of a heart attack in New York City, May 22, 1986; son of Israel (a jeweler) and Ruth (Herzog) Gabel; married Arlene Francis (an actress and broadcaster); trained for the stage at the American Academy of Dramatic Art. EDUCATION: Attended Lehigh University.

VOCATION: Actor, producer, and director.

CAREER: BROADWAY DEBUT—Emmett, *Man Bites Dog,* Lyceum Theatre, 1933. PRINCIPAL STAGE APPEARANCES—Dumkopf, *The Sky's the Limit,* Fulton Theatre, New York City, 1934; Frankie, *Three Men on a Horse,* Chicago, IL, 1935; Hunk, *Dead End,* Belasco Theatre, New York City, 1935; Peter, *Ten Million Ghosts,* St. James Theatre, New York City, 1936; Cassius, *Julius Caesar,* Mercury Theatre, New York City, 1937; title role, *Danton's Death,* Mercury Theatre, New York City, 1938; the Statistician, *Medicine Show,* New Yorker Theatre, New York City, 1940; Earl of Kent, *King Lear,* National Theatre, New York City, 1950; Jonas Astorg, *Reclining Figure,* Lyceum Theatre, New York City, 1954; Irving Lasalle, *Will Success Spoil Rock Hunter?,* Belasco Theatre, New York City, 1955; Stephen A. Douglas, *The Rivalry,* Bijou Theatre, New York City, 1959; Basil Smythe, *Big Fish, Little Fish,* American National Theatre Academy (ANTA) Theatre, New York City, 1961; Melvin Peabody, *Children from Their Games,* Morosco Theatre, New York City, 1963; Professor Moriarty, *Baker Street,* Broadway Theatre, New York City, 1965; Joseph Mayflower, *Sheep on the Runway,* Helen Hayes Theatre, New York City, 1970; Mark Walters, *In Praise of Love,* Morosco Theatre, New York City, 1974.

MAJOR TOURS—Stephen A. Douglas, *The Rivalry,* U.S. cities, 1959.

PRINCIPAL STAGE WORK—Director: *A Young Couple Wanted,* Maxine Elliott Theatre, New York City, 1940; *The Assassin,* National Theatre, New York City, 1945; *The Survivors,* The Playhouse, New York City, 1948; *Men of Distinction,* 48th Street Theatre, New York City, 1953.

Producer: (With Richard Wharton) *Life with Father,* Empire Theatre, New York City, 1939; (with Wharton) *The Medicine Show,* New Yorker Theatre, New York City, 1940; (with Wharton) *Charley's Aunt,* Cort Theatre, New York City, 1941; (with Wharton) *The Cream in the Well,* Booth Theatre, New York City, 1941; (with Wharton) *Cafe Crown,* Cort Theatre, New York City, 1942; *The Survivors,* Playhouse Theatre, New York City, 1948; (with Chandler Cowles) *King Lear,* 48th Street Theatre, New York City, 1953; (with Henry Margolis) *Reclining Figure,* Lyceum Theatre, New York City, 1954; (co-producer) *The Hidden River,* Playhouse

Theatre, New York City, 1957; (co-producer) *Once More with Feeling,* National Theatre, New York City, 1958, then New Theatre, London, 1959; (co-producer) *Sweet Love Remember'd,* Shubert Theatre, New Haven, CT, 1959; *Mrs. Dally,* John Golden Theatre, New York City, 1965.

PRINCIPAL FILM APPEARANCES—*M,* 1931; *Fourteen Hours,* 1951; *The Thief,* 1952; *Deadline U.S.A.,* 1952; *Tip on a Dead Jockey,* Metro-Goldwyn-Mayer (MGM), 1957; *Marnie,* Universal, 1964; *Lord Love a Duck,* United Artists, 1966; *Divorce American Style,* Columbia, 1967; *Lady in Cement,* Twentieth Century-Fox, 1968; *There Was a Crooked Man,* Warner Brothers, 1970; Dr. Eggelhofer, *The Front Page,* Universal, 1974; *The First Deadly Sin,* Filmways, 1980.

PRINCIPAL FILM WORK—Director, *Lost Moment,* Universal, 1947.

PRINCIPAL TELEVISION APPEARANCES—Narrator, *The Making of the President.*

AWARDS: Antoinette Perry Award and *Variety* New York Drama Critics Award, both 1961, for *Big Fish, Little Fish.*

*   *   *

GAGLIANO, Frank 1931-

PERSONAL: Full name, Francis Joseph Gagliano, born November 18, 1931, in Brooklyn, NY; son of Francis Paul and Nancy (LaBarbera) Gagliano; married Sandra Gordon (an operatic soprano), January 18, 1958; children: Francis Enrico. EDUCATION: Attended Queens College of the City University of New York, 1949-53; University of Iowa, B.A., 1954; Columbia University, M.F.A., 1957.

VOCATION: Playwright, teacher, administrator, and journalist.

WRITINGS: PLAYS, PRODUCED—*The Library Raid,* Alley Theatre, Houston, TX, 1961; *Conerico Was Here to Stay* (one-act), Cherry Lane Theatre, New York City, 1965; *Night of the Dunce,* Cherry Lane Theatre, 1966; *Father Uxbridge Wants to Marry,* Eugene O'Neill Theatre Center, Waterford, CT, then American Place Theatre, New York City, 1967; *The Hide-and-Seek Odyssey of Madeline Gimple* (one-act), Eugene O'Neill Theatre Center, then Project Create, New York City, 1967; *Frank Gagliano's City Scene* (two one-acts entitled, "Paradise Gardens East" and "Conerico Was Here to Stay"), Fortune Theatre, New York City, 1969.

The Prince of Peasantmania, Milwaukee Repertory Company, WI, 1970, and O'Neill Theatre Center; (with Lionel Bart) *Quasimodo,* 1971; *Anywhere the Wind Blows,* 1972; *In the Voodoo Parlor of Marie Leveau* and *The Commedia World of Lafcadio Beau.* both Eugene O'Neill Theatre Center, then Phoenix Theatre, New York City, 1974; (with Raymond Benson) *The Resurrection of Jackie Cramer,* E. P. Conkle Workshop for Playwrights, University of Texas at Austin, University of Rhode Island Theatre, and New Dramatists, 1974; (with Claibe Richardson) *Congo Square,* University of Rhode Island Theatre, 1975; *The Total Immersion of Madeleine Favorini,* University of Nevada at Las Vegas, then New Dramatists, New York City, 1979; also *The Humungus Toe Rides Again.* Also represented in anthologies, including *Showcase I,* edited by John Lahr, Grove Press, 1970, and *Scripts III,* Houghton Mifflin Company.

SCREENPLAYS—*The Bel Canto Gang* and *Those Talented Ladies from Suicide Street* (a television movie).

TELEVISION PLAYS—"Big Sur," *Experiment in Television,* NBC, 1969; *The Private Eye of Hiram Bodoni,* 1971; and *Father Uxbridge Wants to Marry,* PBS.

RELATED CAREER—Playwright-in-Residence, Royal Shakespeare Company, London, 1967-68 and Florida State University, 1969-73; director and lecturer, E. P. Conkle Workshop for Playwrights, University of Texas at Austin, 1973-76; Benedam Professor of Playwrighting, West Virginia University, 1975—.

AWARDS: Fellowships: Rockefeller Foundation, 1965-67; O'Neill Foundation-Wesleyan University, 1967; National Endowment for the Arts, for playwriting, 1973; Guggenheim, for playwriting, 1974.

MEMBER: Dramatists Guild, New Dramatists Committee, Eugene O'Neill Theatre Center, Actors Studio, Writers Guild of America.

SIDELIGHTS: RECREATIONS—Reading, listening to music.

ADDRESSES: AGENT—c/o Gilbert Parker, William Morris Agency, Inc., 1350 Avenue of the Americas, New York, NY 10019.*

*   *   *

GARRETT, Betty   1919-

PERSONAL: Born May 23, 1919, in St. Joseph, MO; daughter of Curtis and Elizabeth Octavia (Stone) Garrett; married Larry Parks (died). EDUCATION: Attended schools in Tacoma, WA; trained for the stage at the School of the Theatre and the Neighborhood Playhouse in New York.

VOCATION: Actress and singer.

CAREER: STAGE DEBUT—*Danton's Death,* Mercury Theatre, New York City, 1938. LONDON DEBUT—A program of songs with husband, Larry Parks, Palladium, 1950. PRINCIPAL STAGE APPEARANCES—Lead dancer, *Martha Graham Company,* 1938; *Railroads on Parade,* World's Fair, New York City, 1939; *You Can't Sleep Here,* Barbizon-Plaza Theatre, New York City, 1940; appeared in a musical revue at the Pauline Edwards Theatre, New York City, 1940; *A Piece of Our Mind,* Mail Studios, New York City, 1940; *All in Fun,* Majestic Theatre, New York City, 1941; *Of*

V We Sing, Concert Theatre, New York City, 1942; *Let Freedom Sing,* Longacre Theatre, New York City, 1942; Mary Francis, *Something for the Boys,* Alvin Theatre, New York City, 1943; Sergeant Maguire, *Jackpot,* Alvin Theatre, New York City, 1944; *Laffin' Room Only,* Winter Garden Theatre, New York City, 1944; *Call Me Mister,* National Theatre, New York City, 1946; Ella Peterson, *Bells Are Ringing,* Shubert Theatre, New York City, 1958; Clara, *Beg, Borrow, or Steal,* Martin Beck Theatre, New York City, 1960; appeared in a staged reading of *Spoon River Anthology,* Booth Theatre, New York City, 1963; Penny Moore, *A Girl Could Get Lucky,* Cort Theatre, New York City, 1964; *Who's Happy Now?,* Mark Taper Forum, Los Angeles, CA, 1968; *Betty Garrett and Other Songs,* Los Angeles, 1974-75; Mae, *The Supporting Cast,* Biltmore Theatre, New York City, 1981; Sarah McKendree Bonham, *Quilters,* Mark Taper Forum, Los Angeles, 1984.

MAJOR TOURS—*Meet the People,* U.S. cities, 1941; in vaudeville, U.S. and Canadian cities, 1952; Marion Maxwell, *The Anonymous Lover,* U.S. cities, 1952-53; Gloria, *The Tiger* and Sylvia, *The Typists,* U.S. cities, 1965; Karen Nash, Muriel Tate, and Norma Hubley, *Plaza Suite,* U.S. cities, 1968-70; Catherine Reardon, *And Miss Reardon Drinks a Little,* U.S. cities, 1972.

FILM DEBUT—*The Big City,* 1948. PRINCIPAL FILM APPEARANCES—*Words and Music,* 1948; *On the Town,* Metro-Goldwyn-Mayer (MGM), 1949; *Star of Tomorrow,* 1949; *Neptune's Daughter,* 1949; *My Sister Eileen,* Columbia, 1955; *Shadow on the Window,* Columbia, 1957.

PRINCIPAL TELEVISION APPEARANCES—Series: Irene Lorenzo, *All in the Family,* CBS, 1973-75; Mary Hallen, *Who's Happy Now?,* 1975; Mrs. Edna Babish De Fazio, *Laverne and Shirley,* ABC, 1976-81; Mrs. McCoy, *The Love Boat,* ABC, 1977; Elizabeth Rogers, *Mr. Merlin,* CBS, 1981. Episodic: *The Lloyd Bridges Show,* CBS, 1962; also *The Art Carney Show,* 1959; *Love Is Funny* and *The Best of Anything,* both 1960. Specials: Catherine, *All the Way Home,* 1981; also appeared on *Gene Kelly. . .An American in Pasedena,* 1978.

AWARDS: Best Musical Comedy Performance, Donaldson Award, 1946, for *Call Me Mister.*

MEMBER: Actors' Equity Association, American Federation of Television and Radio Artists.

SIDELIGHTS: RECREATIONS—Painting and ceramics.

ADDRESSES: AGENT—Louis Mendelson, 1880 Century Park East, Suite 1418, Los Angeles, CA 90067.*

*   *   *

GARRISON, David   1952-

PERSONAL: Born June 30, 1952, in Long Branch, NJ; son of Earl B. (a school administrator) and Maude B. (a teacher) Garrison. EDUCATION: Boston University School of Fine Arts, B.F.A., summa cum laude, 1974.

VOCATION: Actor.

CAREER: STAGE DEBUT—Deputy, *The Front Page,* Arena Stage,

Washington, DC, 1974. BROADWAY DEBUT—David, *A History of the American Film,* American National Theatre Academy (ANTA) Theatre, 1978. PRINCIPAL STAGE APPEARANCES—Serge B. Samovar, *A Day in Hollywood/A Night in the Ukraine,* John Golden Theatre, New York City, 1980; Police Sergeant, *The Pirates of Penzance,* Minskoff Theatre, New York City, 1981; Milo McGee McGarr, *Geniuses,* Playwrights Horizons, New York City, 1982; Arnold Beckoff, *Torch Song Trilogy,* Helen Hayes Theatre, New York City, 1983; Frank Finger, *It's Only a Play,* Manhattan Theatre Club, New York City, 1985; Frosch, *Die Fledermaus* and Froissart, *The King Goes Forth to France,* both Santa Fe Opera, NM, 1986.

TELEVISION DEBUT—Cody Patrick, *The Edge of Night,* ABC, 1979. PRINCIPAL TELEVISION APPEARANCES—Series: Norman Lamb, *It's Your Move,* NBC, 1984-85.

AWARDS. Antoinette Perry Award nomination, 1980, for Serge B.Samovar, *A Day in Hollywood/A Night in the Ukraine.*

MEMBER: Actors' Equity Association, American Federation of Radio and Television Artists, Screen Actors Guild, American Guild of Musical Artists, Actors Fund (life member); Sierra Club (life member).

SIDELIGHTS: David Garrison informs *CTFT* that he is a licensed whitewater river guide.

ADDRESSES: AGENT—c/o Elin Flack, Abrams Artists and Associates, 420 Madison Avenue, New York, NY 10017.

DAVID GARRISON

CHRISTIE GAUDET

GAUDET, Christie   1957-

PERSONAL: Surname pronounced "Go-day"; born March 28, 1957, in New Orleans, LA; daughter of Herman Anthony (a teacher) and Carol Ann (an administrator; maiden name Dill) Gaudet. EDUCATION: Attended Tulane University for three years; trained for the stage with Clyde Vinson in New York City.

VOCATION: Actress and singer.

CAREER: NEW YORK DEBUT—Smeraldina, *The Servant of Two Masters,* LaKota Theatre Company, New York City, 1985. OFF-BROADWAY DEBUT—Jeannie, *Lost and Found,* Douglas Fairbanks Theatre, 1986. PRINCIPAL STAGE APPEARANCES—Chorus, *The Trojan Women,* LaKota Theatre Company, New York City, 1986; Andrea, *Staggerlee,* Second Avenue Theatre, New York City, 1987.

MAJOR TOURS—European tour of the works of Shubert, Handel, and Durante, 1978.

FILM DEBUT—*Murder at the Madri Gras,* 1978.

TELEVISION DEBUT—*Search for Tomorrow,* NBC, 1984.

MEMBER: Actors' Equity Association, American Federation of Television and Radio Artists.

ADDRESSES: MANAGER—c/o Dan Nani, 1697 Broadway, Suite 1401, New York, NY 10019.

GAYE, Freda   1907-1986

PERSONAL: Born December 27, 1907, in Hunmanby, England; died 1986, in London; daughter of Wilfrid and Harriet Jane (Pickard) Gaye.

VOCATION: Actress and theatre historian.

CAREER: LONDON DEBUT—A strange shape, *The Tempest,* Aldwych Theatre, 1921. BROADWAY DEBUT—Rose Belcher, *Evensong,* Selwyn Theatre, 1933. PRINCIPAL STAGE APPEARANCES—Miss Lucy, *Brer Rabbit,* Everyman Theatre, London, 1926; joined Birmingham Repertory Theatre, U.K., 1931; Rose Belcher, *Evensong,* Queen's Theatre, London, 1932; Bell Brown, *Gallows Glorious,* Shaftesbury Theatre, London, 1933; Poppy Straight, *Limelight,* Birmingham Repertory Theatre, 1936; Fay Beaudine, *London After Dark,* Apollo Theatre, London, 1937; played leading roles in Matthew Forsyth's Company at the De La Warr Pavilion Theatre, Bexhill, U.K., 1939-40.

Nurse, *Medea,* New Theatre, London, 1941; Nancy Steele, *Sense and Sensibility,* Embassy Theatre, London, 1946; Agatha, *The Family Reunion,* Mercury Theatre, London, 1946; Dr. Jean Linden, *The Linden Tree,* Duchess Theatre, London, 1947; Nurse Secretary, and later as Lavinia Chamberlayne, *The Cocktail Party,* New Theatre, London, 1950.

Gertrude Timms, *Up the Garden Path,* Bolton's Theatre, London, 1952; Lady Melbourne, *Caro William,* Embassy Theatre, London, 1952; Marie Anne, *The Ermine,* Nottingham Playhouse, 1955; Elizabeth Hector-Crammles, *The Strangers,* Bristol Old Vic Theatre, U.K., 1957; also appeared in many productions at the Q Theatre, London.

MAJOR TOURS—Rose Belcher, *Evensong,* U.K. cities, 1932; leading roles, H.V. Neilson Shakespeare Company, U.K. cities, 1934-35; Lady Ursula, *The Zeal of Thy House,* U.K. cities, 1938-39; with the Old Vic Company toured British cities in *Macbeth, Medea, Jacob's Ladder, The Seagull, King John,* and *Shirley,* 1940-42; with the Curtain Theatre Company, toured Scottish and Orkney cities, 1943-44; Ellen Cred, *Ladies in Retirement,* West German cities, 1949; Pitt, *Liberty Bill,* U.K. cities, 1954.

RELATED CAREER—Editor, *Who's Who in the Theatre,* 1958-70; curator, British Theatre Museum, 1963-64.

WRITINGS: RADIO PLAYS—(With Jonquil Antony) *Judith,* 1936.*

*   *   *

GENNARO, Peter   1919-

PERSONAL: Born November 23, 1919, in Metairie, LA; son of Charles (a tavern operator and real estate executive) and Conchetta (a tavern operator; maiden name, Sabella) Gennaro; married Jean Kinsella (a dancer), January 24, 1948; children: Michael, Liza. EDUCATION: Trained for the stage at the American Theatre Wing. RELIGION: Catholic. MILITARY: Served during World War II.

VOCATION: Choreographer, dancer, producer, and director.

CAREER: PRINCIPAL STAGE APPEARANCES—Dancer, San Carlo Opera, 1949; appeared as a dancer in Broadway productions of: *Make Mine Manhattan,* 1949; *Subway Circuit,* 1949; *Kiss Me Kate,*

PETER GENNARO

1950; *Guys and Dolls,* 1950; *Arms and the Girl,* 1950; *Pajama Game,* 1954; *Bells Are Ringing,* 1956.

PRINCIPAL STAGE WORK—Choreographer, Broadway productions of: *Seventh Heaven,* 1955; *Fiorello!,* 1959; *Mr. President,* 1963; *Bajour,* 1964; co-choreographer, *West Side Story,* 1957; *Annie,* 1977; *Little Me,* 1982; also for Broadway productions of *Jimmy, Irene, Carmelina;* choreographer, London productions of: *Bar Mitzvah Boy,* 1978; *Singin' in the Rain,* 1985.

MAJOR TOURS—Choreographer: *Wonderful Town,* 1977; *Singin' in the Rain; On the Town.*

PRINCIPAL CABARET APPEARANCES—Appeared as a dancer at the Aladdin Hotel, Las Vegas, and in *Al Hirt's Salute to New Orleans.*

PRINCIPAL TELEVISION APPEARANCES—In the 1960s, appeared as a dancer on: *Polly Bergen Show; Andy Williams Show; Bob Crosby Show; Perry Como Show; Judy Garland Show; Bing Crosby Show; Academy Awards; Ed Sullivan Show; Mike Douglas Show; A.M. America; Kraft Music Hall.*

PRINCIPAL TELEVISION WORK—Choreographer: *Polly Bergen Show; Andy Williams Show; Bob Crosby Show; Perry Como Show; Judy Garland Show; Bing Crosby Show; Ed Sullivan Show; Ed Sullivan's Tribute to Irving Berlin,* 1968.

Also choreographed: *Robert Goulet and Maurice Chevalier Special; Bob Hope and Phyllis Diller Special; Mitzi Gaynor Special; Bing Crosby and Fred Astaire Special; Salute to Ford's Theatre; Brigadoon; Miss America Pageants,* 1973-76, and 1984.

PRINCIPAL FILM WORK—Choreographer, *The Unsinkable Molly Brown,* Metro-Goldwyn-Mayer, 1964.

RELATED CAREER—Producer, director, and choreographer, Radio City Music Hall productions, New York City, 1971-78.

AWARDS. Drama Desk Award, Antoinette Perry Award, both 1977, for *Annie;* Emmy Award nomination, for *Brigadoon;* Antoinette Perry Award nomination, 1982, for *Little Me;* Dance Educators Award, 1957, 1973; *Dance Magazine* Award, 1965; Boston Dance Association Award, 1963; Eleanor Roosevelt Humanitarian Award, 1974; honorary degrees: Doctor of Fine Arts, Salve Regina College, Newport, RI.

MEMBER: Directors' Guild, American Federation of Television and Radio Artists.

ADDRESSES: AGENT—William Morris Agency, 1350 Avenue of the Americas, New York, NY 10019.

*　　*　　*

GERDES, George　1948-

PERSONAL: Surname rhymes with "birdies;" born February 23, 1948, in New York, NY. EDUCATION: Carnegie-Mellon University, B.F.A., drama, 1969.

VOCATION: Actor and composer.

GEORGE GERDES

CAREER: PRINCIPAL STAGE APPEARANCES—Soutine, *Modigliani,* Astor Place Theatre, New York City, 1980; Eddie, *Fool for Love,* Douglas Fairbanks Theatre, New York City, 1985; Stranger, *To Whom It May Concern,* St. Stephen's Church Theatre, New York City, 1986.

FILM DEBUT—Joe, *Skip Tracer,* Tri-Star Pictures, 1987.

PRINCIPAL TELEVISION APPEARANCES—Episodic: Pete Taylor, *Our Family Honor,* ABC, 1985.

WRITINGS: SONGS—"Steady with the Maestro," featured on the Roaches album *Keep on Doing,* United Artists Records.

RECORDINGS: ALBUMS—*Obituary* and *Son of Obituary,* both Warner Brothers.

MEMBER: Actors' Equity Association, Screen Actors Guild, American Federation of Television and Radio Artists, American Society of Composers, Authors, and Publishers, Affiliated Federation of Musicians.

ADDRESSES: AGENT—Kennth Kaplan, 311 W. 43rd Street, New York, NY 10036.

*　　*　　*

GIAGNI, D. J.　1950-
(Danny Daniels)

PERSONAL: Surname pronounced with silent middle "g"; full name, Daniel Joseph Giagni; born December 3, 1950, in New York, NY; son of Daniel (a choreographer) and Bernice (Grant), Giagni Jr.; married Pamela Mitchell, January 12, 1980; children: Anne Elizabeth. EDUCATION: Studied at the American Ballet Theatre.

VOCATION: Choreographer and dancer.

CAREER: STAGE DEBUT—Lead dancer, *Fiddler on the Roof,* Westbury Music Fair, 1970. PRINCIPAL STAGE WORK—Associate choreographer, *The Tap Dance Kid,* Broadway Theatre, then Minskoff Theatre, New York City, 1983-85; choreographer: *Harrigan n' Hart,* Longacre Theatre, New York City, 1985; *Personals,* Minetta Lane Theatre, New York City, 1986; also: *Girl Crazy,* Seattle Repertory Company, WA; *Carnival,* Goodspeed Opera House, East Haddam, CT; *A Funny Thing Happened on the Way to the Forum,* Alliance Theatre, Atlanta, GA.

MAJOR TOURS—Associate choreographer, *The Tap Dance Kid,* national.

PRINCIPAL FILM WORK—Choreographer: *Exorcist II: The Heretic,* Warner Brothers, 1977; also tap dance instructor, *Pennies from Heaven,* United Artists, 1981.

PRINCIPAL TELEVISION WORK—Choreographer: *Visions,* KCET; *All My Children,* ABC; *How to Be a Man,* CBS.

RELATED CAREER—Teacher for Danny Daniels Dance America School; free-lance teacher for the Broadway Dance Center, New York City.

D. J. GIAGNI

MEMBER: Society of Stage Directors and Choreographers.

ADDRESSES: HOME—323 W. 101st Street, Apt. 2, New York, NY 10025. MANAGER—Scott Shukat Company, Ltd. 340 W. 55th Street, New York, NY 10019.

*   *   *

GILDER, Rosamond de Kay   1891-1986

PERSONAL: Born July 17, 1891, in Marion, MA; died in Tyringham, MA, September 5, 1986; daughter of Richard Watson (a poet and editor of *The Century Magazine*) and Helena (de Kay) Gilder. EDUCATION: Attended public schools and the Brearly School in New York.

VOCATION: Writer, editor, arts administrator, and teacher.

CAREER: PRINCIPAL STAGE WORK—Editorial secretary, National Theatre Conference, 1932-36; director of Bureau of Research and Publication, Federal Theatre, 1934-35; secretary, American National Theatre and Academy, 1945-50, vice-president, 1963; National Theatre on the National Commission for UNESCO, 1948-54; founder and president, International Theatre Institute, 1947-75, honorary president, 1975-86; president, U.S. Center of the International Theatre Institute, 1963-86; chairman, United States delegation to the first World Conference on Theatre, Bombay, India, 1956.

RELATED CAREER—Lecturer, associate in English, Barnard College, New York City, 1948-55; also lectured in Europe, India, and Japan.

WRITINGS: PERIODICALS—Assistant editor, associate editor, and editor-in-chief, ''Theatre Arts Monthly,'' 1945-49. Author of articles and essays on U.S. and international theatre.

BOOKS PUBLISHED—Editor, *Letters of Richard Watson Gilder,* Houghton, 1916; translator of Emma Calve's *My Life,* Appleton, 1922; *Enter the Actress,* Houghton, 1931, and second edition, ''Theatre Arts,'' 1960; compiler, *A Theatre Library,* ''Theatre Arts,'' 1932; (co-author with George Freedly) *Theatre Collections in Libraries and Museums,* ''Theatre Arts,'' 1936; *John Gielgud's Hamlet,* Oxford University Press, 1937; (co-author with R. M. MacGregor) *Stages of the World,* ''Theatre Arts,'' 1949; editor, *Theatre Arts Treasury,* ''Theatre Arts Monthly,'' 1950; editor, *Theatre Arts Anthology,* ''Theatre Arts Monthly,'' 1950, second edition, 1961.

AWARDS: Antoinette Perry Award, 1948; appointed honorary member, New York Drama Critics Circle, 1950; Fulbright award, Paris, 1955-56; L.H.D., University of Denver, CO, 1969; decorated medadille d'Epicdemie, medaille de Reconnaissance, France; officier l'Ordre des Arts et des Lettres, France, 1961; Benjamin Franklin Fellow of the Royal Society of Arts, London, England, 1970.

MEMBER: American National Theatre and Academy (board of directors); Cosmopolitan Club, New York City.*

*   *   *

GILLETTE, Anita   1936-

PERSONAL: Born Anita Luebben, August 16, 1936, in Baltimore, MD; daughter of John Alfred and Juanita (Wayland) Luebben; married Ronald William Gillette (a doctor), October 13, 1957 (divorced, 1967); married Armand Eugene Coullet, July 23, 1982; children: Timothy Ronald, Christopher John. EDUCATION: Trained for the stage at the Peabody Conservatory with Lee Strasberg and Robert Lewis.

VOCATION: Actress and singer.

CAREER: STAGE DEBUT—Sophie, *Roberta,* North Shore Music Theatre, Beverly, MA, 1958. BROADWAY DEBUT—Thelma, *Gypsy,* Broadway Theatre, 1959. LONDON DEBUT—Title role, *Pocohantas,* Lyric Theatre, 1963. PRINCIPAL STAGE APPEARANCES—*Russell Patterson's Sketchbook,* Maidman Theatre, New York City, 1960; Gypsy, then Lili, *Carnival!,* Imperial Theatre, New York City, 1961; Susan, *All American,* Winter Garden Theatre, New York City, 1962; Sarah Browne, *Guys and Dolls,* O'Keefe Center, Toronto, 1962; Leslie Henderson, *Mr. President,* St. James Theatre, New York City, 1962; Angela Crane, *Kelly,* Broadhurst Theatre, New York City, 1965; Sarah Browne, *Guys and Dolls,* City Center, New York City, 1965; appeared in *Meet Me in Saint Louis,* Municipal Opera House, St. Louis, MO, 1965; Resi, *The Great Waltz,* Civic Light Opera Theatre, Los Angeles, 1965; appeared in a revue sponsored by the Festival of American Arts and Humanities, U.S. Embassy, London, 1966; Susan Hollander, *Don't Drink the Water,* Morosco Theatre, New York City, 1966; Sally

Bowles, *Cabaret*, Broadhurst Theatre, New York City, 1968; Betty Compton, *Jimmy*, Winter Garden Theatre, New York City, 1969; Tina Trenhoven, *Knickerbocker Holiday*, Curran Theatre, San Francisco, 1971; female roles, *Rich and Famous*, New York Shakespeare Festival, Public Theatre, New York City, 1976; appeared in stock, *Bus Stop*, 1976; appeared in repertory, *Travesties* and *The Importance of Being Earnest*, Mark Taper Forum, Los Angeles, 1977; Jennie Malone, *Chapter Two*, Ahmanson Theatre, Los Angeles, then Imperial Theatre, New York City, 1977; *Night Is Mother to the Day*, Yale Repertory Theatre, New Haven, CT, 1984; Blanche, *Brighton Beach Memoirs*, Neil Simon Theatre, New York City, 1984.

MAJOR TOURS—Leslie Henderson, *Mr. President*, U.S. cities, 1964; Eliza Doolittle, *My Fair Lady*, U.S. cities, 1966.

TELEVISION DEBUT—1962. PRINCIPAL TELEVISION APPEAR-ANCES—Guest: *The Garry Moore Show*, *The Ed Sullivan Show*, CBS; *The Tonight Show*, NBC; *P.M. East*. Series: panelist, *What's My Line?*, CBS, 1968; panelist, *I've Got a Secret*, CBS, 1972; Liz Reynolds, *Me and the Chimp*, CBS, 1972; Alice Henderson, *Bob & Carol & Ted & Alice*, ABC, 1973; Nancy Baxter, *The Baxters*, syndicated, 1979; Dr. Emily Hanover, *Quincy, M.E.*, NBC, 1982; also appeared on *Brass*, CBS, 1985 and *All That Glitters*. Specials: Blue Fairy, *Pinocchio*, 1968; Ethel, *George M!*, 1970.

AWARDS: Best Actress, Los Angeles Drama Critics Award, 1978, for *Chapter Two*.

MEMBER: Actors' Equity Association, American Federation of Television and Radio Artists.

ADDRESSES: AGENT—Smith-Freedman & Associates, 123 N. San Vincente Blvd., Beverly Hills, CA 90211.*

*   *   *

GIRAUDEAU, Philippe   1955-

PERSONAL: Born November 16, 1955, in La Rochelle, France; son of Rene Jules Pierre (a car salesman) and Claudie (Legoff) Giraudeau. EDUCATION: Lycee Fromentin, La Rochelle, France; studied Ballet with Colette Milner in France and with Brenda Last and Maryon Lane in London; studied the Martha Graham technique at The Place in London; studied voice with Clare Davidson and Bardy Thomas in London.

VOCATION: Dancer and actor.

CAREER: NEW YORK DEBUT—Dancer, with the Second Stride Dance Company, Dance Theatre Workshop, 1983. PRINCIPAL STAGE APPEARANCES—Dancer, Grand Theatre De Bordeaux Ballet Theatre Contemporain, 1973-76; dancer, with the London Contemporary Dance Theatre at Sadlers Wells Theatre, 1977; with the London Comtemporary Dance Theatre, Mantis Dance Company, Second Stride, 1977-86; actor and dancer, *Secret Gardens*, ICA Theatre, London, then Mickery Theatre, Amsterday, 1983; *Song & Dance*, London, 1985; actor, *IQ of Four*, ICA Theatre, London, 1984; Duc de Nemours, *Princess of Cleves*, ICA Theatre, London, 1985; *Bosendorfer Waltzes*, The Place, London, and in Munich, West Germany, 1986; *A Mouthful of Birds*, Royal Court Theatre, London, 1986.

MAJOR TOURS—Dancer: With the London Contemporary Dance Theatre, toured England, Europe and the U.S., 1977; with the Peter Goss Dance Company, Theatre de la Bastille and the Pompidou Centre, Paris; with the London Contemporary Dance Theatre, Theatre de la Ville, Paris, England, and the Middle East, 1979-81; with Second Stride, England and the U.S., 1982; with the Mantis Company, Paris and Indonesia, 1983; with Second Stride, Canada and Europe, 1985.

FILM DEBUT—*Le cri du Silence*, Cinopsis Films.

PRINCIPAL TELEVISION APPEARANCES—Dancer, Channel 4, BBC; *South Bank Show*; LWT.

PRINCIPAL RADIO WORK—*Le Grand Meaulnes*, Radio 4.

RELATED CAREER—Assistant to director Pierre Audi for the opera *Kopernikus*, Almeida Theatre, London.

MEMBER: Amnesty International.

SIDELIGHTS: Philippe Giraudeau informs *CTFT* that he plays the piano, speaks French and English, and that he performs in both languages.

ADDRESSES: HOME—282 Caledonian Road, London M1, England. AGENT—Kate Feast Management, 43A Princess Road, London NW1, England.

PHILIPPE GIRAUDEAU

GISH, Lillian 1893-

PERSONAL: Born Lillian de Guiche, October 14, 1893, in Springfield, OH; daughter of James Lee and Mary (Robinson) de Guiche.

VOCATION: Actress, writer, and film director.

CAREER: STAGE DEBUT—*In Convict Stripes,* Rising Sun Theatre, OH, 1902. PRINCIPAL STAGE APPEARANCES—Performed as a dancer in a Sarah Bernhardt production, New York City; Marganie, *A Good Little Devil,* Republic Theatre, New York City, 1913; Helena, *Uncle Vanya,* Cort Theatre, New York City, 1930; Marguerite Gautier, *Camille,* Central City, CO, then Morosco Theatre, New York City, 1932; Effie Holden, *Nine Pine Street,* Longacre Theatre, New York City, 1933; Christina Farley, *The Joyous Season,* Belasco Theatre, New York City, 1934; Young Whore, *Within the Gates,* National Theatre, New York City, 1934; Ophelia, *Hamlet,* Empire Theatre, New York City, 1936; Charlotte Lovell, *The Old Maid,* King's Theatre, Glasgow, Scotland, 1936; Martha Minch, *The Star Wagon,* Empire Theatre, New York City, 1937; Grace Fenning, *Dear Octopus,* Broadhurst Theatre, New York City, 1939; Vinnie, *Life with Father,* Chicago, IL, 1940.

Jane Gwilt, *Mr. Sycamore,* Guild Theatre, New York City, 1942; Marquise Eloise, *The Marquise* and Leonora, *The Legend of Leonora,* both stock productions, 1947; Katerina Ivanova, *Crime and Punishment,* National Theatre, New York City, 1947; Ethel, *The Curious Savage,* Martin Beck Theatre, New York City, 1950; Mrs. Carrie Watts, *The Trip to Bountiful,* Henry Miller's Theatre, New York City, 1953; appeared in *Portrait of a Madonna* and *The Wreck of the 5:25,* both Congress Hall, Berlin, West Germany, 1957; Agatha, *The Family Reunion,* Phoenix Theatre, New York City, 1958; Catherine Lynch, *All the Way Home,* Belasco Theatre, New York City, 1960; Mrs. Moore, *A Passage to India,* Chicago, 1962-63; Mrs. Mopply, *Too True to Be Good,* 54th Street Theatre, New York City, 1963; Nurse, *Romeo and Juliet,* American Shakespeare Festival, Stratford, CT, 1965; Dowager Empress, *Anya,* Ziegfeld Theatre, New York City, 1965; Margaret Garrison, *I Never Sang for My Father,* Longacre Theatre, New York City, 1968; Marina, *Uncle Vanya,* Circle in the Square Theatre, New York City, 1973; *A Musical Jubilee,* St. James Theatre, New York City, 1975.

MAJOR TOURS—Vinnie, *Life with Father,* U.S. cities, 1941; title role, *Miss Mabel,* U.S. cities, 1950-51; *The Chalk Garden,* U.S. cities, 1956; *Lillian Gish and the Movies—The Art of Film 1900-28,* Moscow, Paris, London, Edinburgh, and U.S. cities, 1969-70.

FILM DEBUT—*An Unseen Enemy,* Biograph, 1912. PRINCIPAL FILM APPEARANCES—*The Musketeers of Pig Alley,* Biograph, 1912, *Judith of Bethulia,* Biograph, 1913. With Griffith Studios: *The Battle of the Sexes, The Escape,* and *Home Sweet Home,* all 1914; *The Lost House, Enoch Arden, The Lily and the Rose,* and *The Birth of a Nation,* all 1915; *Daphne and the Pirate, An Innocent Magdalene, Pathways of Life, Intolerance,* and *Diane of the Follies,* all 1916; *The House Built Upon Sand* and *Souls Triumphant,* both 1917; *Hearts of the World, True Heart Susie,* and *The Great Love,* all 1918; *The Greatest Thing in Life, A Romance of Happy Valley,* and *Broken Blossoms,* 1919; *Way Down East,* 1920; *The Orphans of the Storm,* 1921.

The White Sister, Inspiration, 1923; *Romala,* Inspiration, 1924; for Metro-Goldwyn-Mayer (MGM): *La Boheme* and *The Scarlet Letter,* 1926, *Annie Laurie,* 1927, *The Enemy* and *The Wind,* 1928, *One Romantic Night,* 1930, and *His Double Life,* 1933; *Comman-*

dos Strike at Dawn, 1942; *Miss Susie Slagle's* and *Duel in the Sun,* both 1946; *A Portrait of Jennie,* 1948; *The Night of the Hunter,* United Artists, 1955; *The Cobweb,* MGM, 1955; *Orders of Kill,* 1958; *The Unforgiven,* United Artists, 1960; appeared in the film anthology *The Great Chase,* Continental, 1963; *Follow Me, Boys!,* Buena Vista, 1966; *The Comedians,* MGM, 1967; *A Wedding,* Twentieth Century-Fox, 1978; *Thin Ice,* 1980; *Hambone and Hillie,* New World Pictures, 1984; *Sweet Liberty,* Universal, 1986.

PRINCIPAL FILM WORK—Director, *Remodelling Her Husband,* Griffith Studios, 1920.

PRINCIPAL TELEVISION APPEARANCES—Series: *Silents Please,* ABC, 1960; *The Defenders,* CBS, 1961; hostess, *The Silent Years,* 1975. Episodic: "The Birth of the Movies," *Philco TV Playhouse,* NBC, 1950; *Celanese Theatre,* ABC, 1951; *Campbell Soundstage,* NBC, 1953; *Goodyear TV Playhouse,* NBC, 1953; "The Day Lincoln Was Shot," *Ford Star Jubilee,* CBS, 1955; *The Love Boat,* ABC. Movies: *Infinity in an Hour,* 1978; *Breaking Point.* Teleplays: *Arsenic and Old Lace,* 1969; *Twin Detectives,* 1976; *Sparrow,* 1977; *Hobson's Choice,* 1983; also *The Trip to Bountiful, Mornings at Seven,* and *Ladies in Retirement.*

WRITINGS: BOOKS—Autobiographies: *Lillian Gish: An Autobiography,* 1968; *The Movies, Mr. Griffith, and Me,* Prentice-Hall, 1969; *Dorothy and Lillian Gish,* Scribner's, 1973.

AWARDS: Honorary Academy Award, 1971; Handel Medallion, City of New York, 1973; Royal Command appearance before Elizabeth, the Queen Mother, 1980; Life Achievement Award, American Film Institute, 1984. Honorary degrees: Doctor of Fine Arts, Rollins College; Doctor of Performing Arts, Bowling Green State University; Doctor of Humanities, Mt. Holyoke College.

MEMBER: American Academy of Dramatic Arts (trustee, 1966-67).

SIDELIGHTS: RECREATIONS—Travel and reading.

ADDRESSES: OFFICE—430 E. 57th Street, New York, NY 10022.*

*   *   *

GISONDI, John 1949-

PERSONAL: Born April 7, 1949, in Tucson, AZ. EDUCATION: Southern Methodist University, B.F.A., 1975.

VOCATION: Lighting designer.

CAREER: FIRST NEW YORK STAGE WORK—Lighting design, *The Hairy Ape,* Impossible Ragtime Theatre, 1976. PRINCIPAL STAGE WORK—Lighting design: *Sound & Beauty,* New York Shakespeare Festival, Public Theatre, New York City, 1983; *The Rainmaker,* Tyrone Guthrie Theatre, Minneapolis, MN; *Back in the Race,* Circle Repertory Company, New York City.

MAJOR TOURS—Lighting design, *Whose Life Is It Anyway?,* Kennedy Center, Washington, DC.

PRINCIPAL TELEVISION WORK—Lighting director, *A Christmas Carol, Live from Ford's Theatre,* PBS, 1979.

AWARDS: Emmy Award nomination, Best Lighting, 1979, for *A Christmas Carol, Live from Ford's Theatre,* 1979; Drama Desk Award nomination, Best Lighting, 1983, for *Sound & Beauty.*

MEMBER: United Scenic Artists, Local 829.

ADDRESSES: HOME—21 Cornelia Street, New York, NY 10014.

*   *   *

GLAZE, Susan   1956-

PERSONAL: Born October 9, 1956, in Murfreesboro, TN; daughter of Claire Andrew (a salesman) and Helen (Cooley) Glaze; married Mark Mitchell, October 22, 1983 (divorced, 1987). EDUCATION: University of Tennessee, B.A., 1978; trained as a singer with Dee Marquit in New York City.

VOCATION: Actress and singer.

CAREER: STAGE DEBUT—Ensemble, *Rip Van Winkle,* Kennedy Center, Washington, DC, 1976, for fifty performances. BROADWAY DEBUT—Mary Jane Wilks, *Big River,* Eugene O'Neill Theatre, 1986-87. PRINCIPAL STAGE APPEARANCES—Nelly, *The Playboy of the Western World,* Clarence Brown Theatre Company, Knoxville, TN, 1976; Catherine, *Pippin,* Nat Horne Theatre, New York City, 1980; Sally, *Whoopee,* Coachlight Theatre, Windsor Locks, CT, 1983; Wendy, *Peter Pan,* Cinncinati Playhouse in the Park, OH, 1983; Aline, *Le Grande Cafe,* Musical

Theatre Works, New York City, 1984; Eleanor, *The Middle Ages,* Gateway Playhouse, NJ, 1985.

MAJOR TOURS—Ensemble, *Rip Van Winkle,* Philadelphia, PA, 1976.

FILM DEBUT—Susie, *Sleepaway Camp,* United, 1983.

TELEVISION DEBUT—Pilots: Ensemble, *Dancing in the Dark,* 1982. PRINCIPAL TELEVISION APPEARANCES—Small roles on many daytime dramas.

MEMBER: Actors' Equity Association, Screen Actors Guild.

ADDRESSES: HOME—Brooklyn, NY. AGENT—c/o Dorothy Scott, Marje Fields, Inc., 165 W. 46th Street, New York, NY 10036.

*   *   *

GLENN, Scott   1942-

PERSONAL: Full name, Theodore Scott Glenn; born January 26, 1942, in Pittsburgh, PA; son of Theodore Glenn and his wife; married Carol Schwartz (an artist), September 10, 1968; children: Dakota, Rio (both girls). EDUCATION: Attended the College of William and Mary; trained for the stage at the Actors' Studio with Lee Strasberg. MILITARY: U.S. Marine Corps.

SUSAN GLAZE   **SCOTT GLENN**

VOCATION: Actor.

CAREER: FILM DEBUT—Tad Jacks, *The Baby Maker,* National General, 1970. PRINCIPAL FILM APPEARANCES—Private Kelly, *Nashville,* Paramount, 1975; *Apocalypse Now,* Zoetrope, 1979; Newt, *More American Graffitti,* Universal, 1978; Dalton, *Cattle Annie and Little Britches,* Universal, 1981; Wes Hightower, *Urban Cowboy,* Paramount, 1980; Terry Tingloff, *Personal Best,* Warner Brothers, 1982; Rick Murphy, *The Challenge,* Embassy, 1982; Alan Shepard, *The Right Stuff,* Warner Brothers, 1983; Glasken, *The Keep,* Paramount, 1983; Joe Wade, *The River,* Universal, 1984; John Haddad, *The Wild Geese II,* Universal, 1985; Emmett, *Silverado,* Columbia, 1985; Creasy, *Man on Fire,* Tri-Star, 1987.

TELEVISION DEBUT—*The Edge of Night,* 1968. PRINCIPAL TELE-VISION APPEARANCES—Movies: Willie, *As Summers Die,* HBO, 1986; *Countdown to Looking Glass.*

STAGE DEBUT—Gentleman Caller, *The Glass Menagerie,* College of William and Mary Theatre. PRINCIPAL STAGE APPEARANCES—*Zoo Story,* Cherry Lane Theatre, New York City, 1966; *Alice and Wonderland,* Actors' Studio Theatre, 1968; Edmund, *Long Day's Journey into Night,* Actors Studio, New York City, 1968; Larry, *Angelo's Wedding,* Circle Repertory Company, New York City, 1985; also appeared as Smitty in *Fortune in Men's Eyes;* in *Collision Course,* Actors Playhouse, New York City; as title role, *Jack Street,* Perry Street Theatre, New York City.

MEMBER: Actors' Equity Association, Screen Actors Guild, American Federation of Television and Radio Artists, Academy of Motion Picture Arts and Sciences.

ADDRESSES: AGENT—Deborah Dozier, P.O. Box 1902, Santa Fe, NM 87504.

         *   *   *

GLOVER, John   1944-

PERSONAL: Born August 7, 1944, in Kingston, NY; son of John S. and Cade (Mullins) Glover. EDUCATION: Attended Towson State College.

VOCATION: Actor.

CAREER: STAGE DEBUT—Eugene Gant, *Look Homeward, Angel,* Barter Theatre, Abingdon, VA, 1963. BROADWAY DEBUT—Ward Nichols, *The Selling of the President,* Shubert Theatre, New York City, 1972. PRINCIPAL STAGE APPEARANCES—Godfrey, *A Scent of Flowers,* Martinique Theatre, New York City, 1969; Prince Myshkin, *Subject to Fits,* New York Shakespeare Festival (NYSF), Public Theatre, New York City, 1971; Ronnie, *House of Blue Leaves,* Truck and Warehouse Theatre, New York City, 1971; William Brown, *The Great God Brown* and Pierrot, *Don Juan,* both with the New Phoenix Company, Lyceum Theatre, New York City, 1972; Teacher, *The Visit,* Planteloup, *Chemin de Fer,* and Johnny Case, *Holiday,* all at the Ethel Barrymore Theatre, New York City, 1973; Dr. Samuel Sutler, *Rebel Women,* NYSF, Public/Newman Theatre, New York City, 1976; Algernon Moncrieff, *The Importance of Being Earnest,* Circle in the Square, New York City, 1977; Patrick, *Treats,* Hudson Guild Theatre, New York City, 1977; *A Man for All Seasons,* Ahmanson Theatre, Los Angeles, 1979.

Henry Clerval, *Frankenstein,* Palace Theatre, New York City, 1981; *Hedda Gabler,* Yale Repertory Theatre, New Haven, CT, 1981; with the National Shakespeare Festival, San Diego, CA, 1981; John Wilkes Booth, *Booth,* South Street Theatre, New York City, 1982; *The Doctor's Dilemma,* Long Wharf Theatre, New Haven, 1982; *A Doll's House,* Yale Repertory Theatre, 1982; Roger Dashwell, *Whodunnit,* Biltmore Theatre, New York City, 1982-83; Renfro, *Criminal Minds,* Production Company, New York City, 1984; Leo, *Design for Living,* Circle in the Square, New York City, 1984; Roman, ''The Fairy Garden,'' *Linda Her and The Fairy Garden,* Second State Theatre, New York City, 1984; Nelson Worth, *Digby,* with the Manhattan Theatre Club at The Space at City Center, New York City, 1985.

Also appeared with the American Shakespeare Festival in 1975 and Off-Broadway in *Government Inspector.*

PRINCIPAL FILM APPEARANCES—Johnnie, *Shamus,* Columbia, 1972; the actor boyfriend, *Annie Hall,* United Artists, 1977; Sammy, *Julia,* Twentieth Century-Fox, 1977; Hubert Little, *Somebody Killed Her Husband,* Columbia, 1978; Richard Peabody, *The Last Embrace,* United Artists, 1979; Ernst, *American Success Company,* 1979; Nathan Wyeth, *Mountain Men,* Columbia, 1980; Attorney Freese, *Melvin and Howard,* Universal, 1980; Ackroyd, *Brubaker,* Twentieth Century-Fox, 1980; Tom Keller, *The Incredible Shrinking Woman,* Universal, 1981; Walter, *A Little Sex,* Universal, 1982; Briggs, *The Evil that Men Do,* Tri-Star, 1984; Ross Halley, *A Flash of Green,* Spectrafilm, 1985; Wynn Scott, *White Nights,* Columbia, 1985; Mr. Niceman, *Willy/Milly,* 1985; also *My Sister's Keeper,* 1986.

PRINCIPAL TELEVISION APPEARANCES—Movies: Clifford, *The Face of Rage,* 1983; Pierre Lafitte, *Ernie Kovacs: Between the Laughter,* ABC, 1984; Victor DiMato, *An Early Frost,* 1985. Mini-Series: William Walton, *Kennedy,* 1983; Scanlon, *Rage of Angels,* 1983; General Charles Lee, *George Washington,* ABC, 1984; Richard Behrens, *Nutcracker,* NBC, 1987. Specials: Mr. Stewart, *Don't Touch,* 1985.

ADDRESSES: AGENT—Triad Artists, 10100 Santa Monica Blvd., Los Angeles, CA 90067.*

         *   *   *

GLOVER, Julian   1935-

PERSONAL: Born March 27, 1935, in St. John's Wood, London, England; son of C. Gordon and Honor (Wyatt) Glover; married second wife, Isla Blair. EDUCATION: Attended St. Paul's School, Hammersmith and Alleyn's, Dulwich; trained for the stage at the Royal Academy of Dramatic Art.

VOCATION: Actor.

CAREER: STAGE DEBUT—Pantomime, New Theatre, Bromley, U.K., 1953. LONDON DEBUT—S.S. Officer, *Altona,* Royal Court Theatre, then Saville Theatre, 1961. PRINCIPAL STAGE APPEAR-ANCES—Albany, *King Lear,* Stratford-Upon-Avon, U.K., 1959; Knight, *Luther,* Royal Court Theatre, then Phoenix Theatre, London, 1961; Orsino, *Twelfth Night,* Royal Court Theatre, London, 1962; the Baron, *The Lower Depths,* New Arts Theatre, London, 1962; Franco Laspiga, *Naked,* Royal Court Theatre, London, 1963; Brutus, *The Ides of March,* Haymarket Theatre, London, 1963;

portrayed Hotspur in Joan Littlewood's version of *Henry IV,* Edinburgh Festival, Scotland, 1964.

Title role, *The Pastime of M. Robert,* Hampstead Theatre, London, 1966; Standard, *The Constant Couple,* New Theatre, London, 1967; Harry, *The Family Reunion,* Arnaud Theatre, Guildford, U.K., 1968; Don John, *Much Ado About Nothing* and Boswell, *Boswell's Life of Johnson,* Edinburgh Festival, Scotland, 1970; Mr. Medley, *The Man of Mode,* with the Royal Shakespeare Company, Aldwych Theatre, London, 1971; Rogozhin, *Subject to Fits,* with the Royal Shakespeare Company, The Place Theatre, London, 1971; Captain Starkey, *We Bombed in New Haven,* Forum Theatre, Billingham, U.K, 1973; Antony, *Antony and Cleopatra,* Bankside Globe Theatre, London, 1973; Mr. Manningham, *Gaslight,* Arnaud Theatre, Guildford, 1974; Sherlock Holmes, *Sherlock's Last Case,* Open Space Theatre, London, 1974.

Mirabell, *The Way of the World,* Arnaud Theatre, Guildford, 1975; Jeff, *Otherwise Engaged,* Queen's Theatre, London, 1975; Archie, *Jumpers,* National Theatre, London, 1976; Warwick, *Henry VI,* Parts I, II and III, Tullus Aufidius, *Coriolanus,* with the Royal Shakespeare Company, Stratford-Upon-Avon, 1977; King Charles VI of France, *Henry V* and Warwick, *Henry VI* both at the Aldwych Theatre, London, 1978; appeared in *Great English Eccentrics,* Old Vic Theatre, London, 1978; Gordon, *Cousin Vladimir* and Alonzo, *The Changeling,* both at the Aldwych Theatre, London, 1978; Claudius, *Hamlet,* Old Vic Theatre, London, 1979.

MAJOR TOURS—Demetrius, *A Midsummer Night's Dream,* South American and European cities, 1964; with Prospect Productions: Hector, *Thieves' Carnival* and Boswell, *Boswell's Life of Ben Johnson,* U.K. cities, both 1967, Boswell, *Boswell's Life of Ben Johnson,* Pierre, *Venice Preserved,* and Benedick, *Much Ado About Nothing,* U.K. cites, 1970.

FILM DEBUT—*Tom Jones,* Lopert, 1963. PRINCIPAL FILM APPEARANCES—*Nicholas and Alexandra,* Columbia, 1971; *Juggernaut,* United Artists, 1974.

PRINCIPAL TELEVISION APPEARANCES—Series: *Q.E.D.,* CBS, 1982; also appeared in *An Age of Kings.*

SIDELIGHTS: RECREATIONS—Carpentry and writing. FAVORITE ROLES—Boswell, from *Boswell's Life of Ben Johnson,* and Benedick, from *Much Ado About Nothing.*

ADDRESSES: AGENT—Norman Boyack, Nine Cork Street, London W1, England.*

*　　*　　*

GODUNOV, Alexander　1949-

PERSONAL: Born November 28, 1949, in Ujno-Sakalin, Union of Soviet Socialist Republics; immigrated to the United States, 1979; son of Boris Ilaryion and Lydia Nicolaivna (Studensova) Godunov; married Ludmilla Vlasova, October 1971 (divorced). EDUCATION: Attended Riga Music School, 1958-67; trained for the dance at the Riga Choreography School and for the stage at the Stella Adler Acting School.

VOCATION: Dancer and actor.

CAREER: PRINCIPAL STAGE APPEARANCES—Dancer, Igor

ALEXANDER GODUNOV

Moiseyev's Young Ballet Company, Union of Soviet Socialist Republics (U.S.S.R.), 1958-66; principal dancer, Bolshoi Dance Company, U.S.S.R., 1967-79; principal dancer, American Ballet Theatre (ABT), New York City, 1979-82; also appeared in *Spell* with the Alvin Ailey Dance Company.

MAJOR TOURS—Principal dancer, Bolshoi Ballet, U.S. cities, 1974, 1979; with "Godunov and Friends."

FILM DEBUT—Daniel Hochleitner, *Witness,* Paramount, 1985. PRINCIPAL FILM APPEARANCES—Max Beissart, *The Money Pit,* Universal, 1986.

TELEVISION DEBUT—Dancer, *Godunov: The World to Dance In,* PBS, 1983.

AWARDS: First Prize Gold Medal Award, International Ballet Competition, Moscow, 1973.

MEMBER: Screen Actors Guild, American Federation of Television and Radio Artists, American Guild of Musical Artists.

SIDELIGHTS: "With his mane of long blond hair and powerful tall build, [Alexander] Godunov may well be the premier danseur of the rock generation," wrote Anna Kisselgoff in an August 24, 1979, *New York Times* article. Once the youngest male principal dancer of the Bolshoi Ballet, Godunov has also been called "the most flamboyant of the Soviet ballet defectors" (*New York Times,* September 6, 1981). Even before his dramatic and internationally publicized defection in 1979, Godunov thrilled critics with his Prince Valiant look, "his prodigious athleticism," and a "fire-breathing stage presence that recalls the young Nureyev'' (*Newsweek,* August 26, 1974).

Godunov began training for ballet when he was nine. Eight years later, he joined Igor Moiseyev's Young Ballet Company and gained three years of stage experience before joining the Bolshoi Ballet in 1970. He was immediately cast for the lead in *Swan Lake,* and Jennifer Dunning reports that a Soviet critic described Godunov's first performance in that role as "'an evening of poetic discovery'" (*New York Times,* August 27, 1979). Soon after his debut, Maya Plisetskaya, the company's prima ballerina, chose Godunov to be her partner in *Carmen, La Rose Malade,* and her own full-length production of *Anna Karenina.* "Within three years, Godunov established himself as a premier danseur of immense popularity," wrote John Gruen in a September, 1982, *Dancemagazine* article. Godunov extended his reputation by winning the Moscow International Ballet Competition's gold medal in 1973.

Godunov toured America with the company that same year, but as Gruen reports, the dancer's individuality, his long-hair-and-blue-jeans style, and "his enthusiasm for touring abroad" aroused the suspicion of Russian authorities. Godunov was not allowed to tour again until 1979, when conflicts within the company made Godunov's presence on tour necessary. In August, after successful performances in New York, Godunov became the first dancer to defect from the Bolshoi Ballet. Soviet authorities quickly escorted his wife to Kennedy Airport to return to Moscow, but U.S. officials detained the plane at Godunov's request to inquire if Ludmila Vlasova was leaving voluntarily. The delay lasted more than twenty-four hours and became a foreign policy issue between the two nations before the plane was allowed to depart with Vlasova aboard.

Since his defection, Godunov has made several difficult adjustments. He became a member of the American Ballet Theatre (ABT) in New York City, but his three-year tenure was complicated by a dancer's strike; in 1982, he was let go by artistic director Mikhail Baryshnikov for a season because the company's repertoire did not require Godunov's presence. Baryshnikov had been Godunov's classmate at the Riga Ballet School in Latvia, and he told Gruen that though their relationship during that time was competitive, it was good because "it makes you work harder" (*Dancemagazine,* September, 1982). But Godunov, who had become "a top drawing card at ABT" (*New York Times,* September 6, 1981), sees more behind his dismissal than the stated reasons, and he "is the first to point out that ABT must 'still be playing the same repertoire,' because they have not requested his return" (*Dancemagazine,* February, 1985).

Before his last season with ABT, directors from Hollywood had approached Godunov with movie offers. In his first major screen role, Godunov played Daniel Hochleitner, Harrison Ford's Amish rival in the movie *Witness.* In 1985, he starred in *The Money Pit.* Norma McLain Stoop noted in the February, 1985, issue of *Dancemagazine* that a Broadway appearance may be pending for Godunov, who looks forward to more acting, but the popular ballet star told her, "of course, I'll also continue to dance."

As a "gypsy" performer not attached to an established ballet company, Godunov has performed in Japan and Brussels and has crossed dance genres to partner Judith Jamison in Alvin Ailey's jazz work, *Spell.* He also tours with his own group, "Godunov and Friends," which is, as he told Gruen, "a big success." Stoop concluded that whatever Godunov's future in films may be, "there'll always be another *Giselle* somewhere waiting for his long-honed dynamic partnering and his newly-sharpened acting ability."

ADDRESSES: OFFICE—Godunov Inc., 9887 Santa Monica Blvd., Suite B, Beverly Hills, CA 90212. AGENT—c/o Joan Hyler, William Morris Agency, 151 El Camino Drive, Beverly Hills, CA 90212. PUBLICIST—Evelyn Shriver, 501 Madison Avenue, New York, NY 10022.

*   *   *

GOLDSMITH, Merwin   1937-

PERSONAL: Born August 7, 1937, in Detroit, MI; son of Max Harold (a corrugated box salesman) and Alice Flora (an elementary science teacher; maiden name, Singer) Goldsmith; married Susan Leigh Benson (a cosmetologist) March, 1966 (divorced, 1969). EDUCATION: University of California, Los Angeles, B.A., theatre arts, 1960; studied acting for two years and completed course at the Bristol Old Vic Theatre School, London, England. MILITARY: U.S. Air Force Reserve.

VOCATION: Actor and director.

CAREER: STAGE DEBUT—Ralph Devine, *Auntie Mame,* Northland Playhouse, Detroit, MI, for eight performances, 1958. OFF-BROADWAY DEBUT—Rossencraft, *The Naked Hamlet,* New York Shakespeare Festival (NYSF), Public Theatre, for forty-six performances, 1967. PRINCIPAL STAGE APPEARANCES—At the Liverpool Playhouse, U.K., 1964-65: Dr. Grenock, *The Scandalous Affair of Mr. Kettle & Mrs. Moon;* wicked chancellor, *The Heartless Princess;* Sir Charles Freeman, *The Beaux Stratagem;* Jimmy, *Playboy of the Western World;* Lt. O'Brien, *License to*

MERWIN GOLDSMITH

Murder; Fat Prince, *The Caucasian Chalk Circle;* Streetsinger, *La Mandragola;* R.O. Man, *Sparrers Can't Sing;* Embezzler, *The Quare Fellow;* Boatswain, *The Tempest;* Lt. Espoir, *My Three Angels.*

At the Ashton Pavilion Theatre, St. Anne's-on-Sea, U.K., 1965: Robert Freeman, *Semi-Detached;* Edward, *Roar Like a Dove,* Oscar, *Miss Pell Is Missing;* Reverend Toop, *Pools Paradise;* Daniel, *Trap for a Lonely Man;* Jitters, *No Time for Love;* and Charlie, *Never Too Late.* At the Theatre of the Living Arts, Philadelphia, PA, 1965-67: Aufschnitt, *The Last Analysis;* Phillipe, Louis XVI, *Poor Bitos;* Sir Christopher Hatton, the justice, and the Italian singer, *The Critic;* various roles, *U.S.A.;* Nick, *The Time of Your Life;* Theramenes, *Phaedra;* transvestite singer, *Beclch;* Harry Binion, *Room Service;* the milkman, *Dream of Love;* appeared as Sir Francis Beekman, *Gentlemen Prefer Blondes,* Music Fairs, 1965.

Captain Vere, *Billy Budd,* Bucks County Playhouse, New Hope, PA, 1967; Pottsy Granger, *Leda Had a Little Swan,* Cort Theatre, New York City, 1968; Mr. Hochmeister, *Minnie's Boys,* Imperial Theatre, New York City, 1970; Fishmonger, *King of Schnorrers,* Goodspeed Opera House, East Haddam, CT, 1971; Wicked Magician, *Comedy,* Colonial Theatre, Boston, 1972; Jacob Hooper, *Wanted,* Cherry Lane Theatre, New York City, 1972; Dogberry, *Much Ado About Nothing,* American Shakespeare Festival, Stratford, CT, 1973. At the Goodman Theatre, Chicago, 1973: Ludlow Lowell, *Pal Joey,* Hebble Tyson, *The Lady's Not for Burning,* and Owen O'Malley, *On the Twentieth Century.* Pastor, *The Visit* and Lapige, *Chemin de Fer,* both Ethel Barrymore Theatre, New York City, 1973; Papa, *Laugh a Little, Cry a Little,* Music Fairs, 1974; Barney Cashman, *Last of the Red Hot Lovers,* Four Seasons Dinner Theatre, 1974.

At the Syracuse Stage, Syracuse, NY, 1974-75: Nicolla, *Arms and the Man,* first king and brute, *The Butterfingers Angel,* Judge Brack, *Hedda Gabler,* and the Husband, *La Ronde.* Mr. Ablett, *Trelawny of the Wells,* Vivian Beaumont Theatre, New York City, 1975; House Speaker, *Rubbers* and *Yanks,* both American Place Theatre, New York City, 1975; Comus, *Rex,* Lunt-Fontanne Theatre, New York City, 1976; Chairman Withenshaw, *Dirty Linen,* John Golden Theatre, New York City, 1977; Ali Hakim, *Oklahoma!,* Artpark, 1978; Gabriel Astruc, *Chinchilla,* Phoenix Theatre, New York City, 1979; Lou Cohn, *The 1940's Radio Hour,* St. James Theatre, New York City, 1979.

Various roles, *Real Life Funnies,* Manhattan Theatre Club, New York City, 1981; Uncle Ben, *Death of a Salesman,* Sharon Playhouse, Sharon, CT, 1982; Reverend Chausible, *The Importance of Being Earnest* and Father, *Holiday,* both Sharon Playhouse, 1982; Harry Costello, *The Great Magoo,* Hartford Stage Company, CT, 1982; Willy Curry, *Slab Boys,* Playhouse Theatre, New York City, 1983; Horace Vandergelder, *Hello, Dolly!,* Artpark, 1983; Mayor Shinn, *The Music Man,* Artpark, 1984; Semyon, *The Bathers,* Long Wharf Theatre, New Haven, CT, 1984; Alcindoro, *La Boheme,* NYSF, Public Theatre, New York City, 1984; Joe Josephson, *Merrily We Roll Along,* La Jolla Playhouse, CA, 1985; Gremio, *The Taming of the Shrew,* American Shakespeare Festival, CT, 1985; Mr. Van Daan, *Yours, Anne,* Playhouse 91, New York City, 1985; Polonius, *Hamlet,* American Shakespeare Festival, 1986; Pittalaluga, *Idiot's Delight,* American National Theatre, Kennedy Center, Washington, DC, 1986.

MAJOR TOURS—Lazar Wolf and understudy Tevya, *Fiddler on the Roof,* First National Company, 1968-69.

PRINCIPAL STAGE WORK—Director: *Vanities,* Beverly Hills Playhouse, CA, 1980; industrial shows: Pulsar Watches, 1982; Arrow Shirts, 1983.

FILM DEBUT—Jerk at the bar, *Shamus,* Columbia, 1972. PRINCIPAL FILM APPEARANCES—Maxie, *Hercules in New York,* independent, 1972; Charley, *Boardwalk,* independent, 1979; boutique owner, *Soup for One,* Warner Brothers, 1981; Dave Lewis, *So Fine,* Warner Brothers, 1981; Sid, *Blue Heaven,* independent, 1984; the producer, *Lily in Love,* Robert Halmi Productions, 1984; Lou, *Making Mr. Right,* Orion Pictures, 1986.

PRINCIPAL TELEVISION APPEARANCES—Series: George Coolidge, *The Goodtime Girls,* ABC, 1980. Episodic: *All My Children,* ABC; *Ryan's Hope,* ABC; *The Guiding Light,* CBS; *Search for Tomorrow,* NBC; *The Doctors,* ABC; *As the World Turns,* CBS; *Another World,* NBC; *Love of Life,* CBS; Sergeant Janowitz, *Wide World of Mystery,* ABC, 1974; TV Stage Manager, *Love, Sydney,* NBC, 1982. Mini-Series: Ambassador Zorin, *Kennedy,* NBC, 1983. Movies: The process server, *The Connection,* ABC, 1972; top buyer, *Sessions,* NBC, 1982.

PRINCIPAL RADIO WORK—General Rieekan, *The Empire Strikes Back,* various roles, *A Canticle for Liebowitz,* Cajun Johnny, *Happiness,* and Victor Dallas, *Middleman Out,* all for National Public Radio.

RELATED CAREER—Instructor of musical theatre, Jandora International Opera Seminar, Ghent, Belgium, 1977, Inter-Action, Ltd., London, England, 1979 and 1981, and at the National Theatre Institute, O'Neill Theatre Center, 1984.

AWARDS: Best Actor in a Musical, *Variety* Critics Poll Award nomination, 1972, for *Wanted;* Best Supporting Actor in a Musical, Joseph Jefferson Award nomination, 1973, for *Pal Joey.*

MEMBER: Actors' Equity Association, American Federation of Radio and Television Artists, Screen Actors Guild; The Players Club.

SIDELIGHTS: Merwin Goldsmith informs *CTFT* that he works occasionally as a professional still photographer. He speaks and studies French and Hebrew.

ADDRESSES: HOME—66 W. 88th Street, New York, NY 10024. AGENT—Monty Silver Agency, 200 W. 57th Street, New York, NY 10019.

*   *   *

GOODMAN, Dody

PERSONAL: Born Dolores Goodman, October 28, in Columbus, OH; daughter of Dexter and Leona G. Goodman. EDUCATON: Studied dance at the Jorg Fasting School, Columbus, OH, the School of American Ballet, and the Metropolitan Opera Ballet School in New York City, 1939-43.

VOCATION: Actress, dancer, and writer.

CAREER: PRINCIPAL STAGE APPEARANCES—Dancer in the corps de ballet, Radio City Music Hall, 1940; chorus, *High Button Shoes,* Century Theatre, New York City, 1947; chorus, *Miss*

Liberty, Imperial Theatre, New York City, 1949; chorus, *Call Me Madam*, Imperial Theatre, New York City, 1950; Violet, *Wonderful Town*, Winter Garden Theatre, New York City, 1953; *Shoestring Revue*, President Theatre, New York City, 1955; *Shoestring '57*, Barbizon Plaza, New York City, 1957; *Parade*, Players Theatre, New York City, 1960; Dora, *Fiorello!*, City Center, New York City, 1962; Elizabeth Lamb, *A Rainy Day in Newark*, Belasco Theatre, New York City, 1963; first woman, *A Thurber Carnival*, Bucks County Playhouse, New Hope, PA, 1965; *Ben Bagley's Cole Porter Revue*, Square East Theatre, New York City, 1965; Sally Ellis, *My Daughter, Your Son*, Booth Theatre, New York City, 1969; Jenny, *The Front Page*, Ethel Barrymore Theatre, New York City, 1969; Dolly Gallagher Levi, *The Matchmaker*, Mummers Theatre, Oklahoma City, OK, 1972; Mrs. Ella Spofford, *Lorelei*, Palace Theatre, New York City, 1974; Miss Ronberry, *Miss Moffat*, Shubert Theatre, Philadelphia, 1974; Miss Leighton, *Once in a Lifetime*, Mark Taper Forum, Los Angeles, 1975; appeared in *George Washington Slept Here*, summer stock, 1976; appeared in *Side by Side by Sondheim*, Charles Playhouse, Boston, 1978.

MAJOR TOURS—Winnifred, *Once upon a Mattress*, U.S. cities, 1960-61; Sally Ellis, *My Daughter, Your Son*, U.S. cities, 1971.

FILM DEBUT—*Bedtime Story*, Universal, 1964. PRINCIPAL FILM APPEARANCES—*Silent Movie*, Twentieth Century Fox, 1976; *Grease*, Paramount, 1978; *Grease II*, Paramount, 1982; also *Valentine Day on Love Island*.

PRINCIPAL TELEVISION APPEARANCES—Series: Martha Shumway, *Mary Hartman, Mary Hartman*, syndicated, 1976-78; Martha Shumway, *Fernwood Forever*, syndicated and on CBS, 1977-80; Ruby Bell, *Mary Tyler Moore Hour*, CBS, 1979. Episodic: *Sergeant Bilko*, CBS; *The Love Boat*, ABC. Guest: *The Jack Paar Show*, NBC; *The Tonight Show*, NBC; *The Sid Caesar Show*, ABC; *The Martha Raye Show*, NBC.

WRITINGS: PLAYS, PRODUCED—*Mourning in a Funny Hat*, Ogunquit Playhouse, Ogunquit, ME, 1972. SCREENPLAYS—*Women, Women, Women!*

MEMBER: Actors' Equity Association, Screen Actors Guild, American Federation of Television and Radio Artists.

ADDRESSES: AGENT—Robert G. Hussong Agency Inc., 721 N. La Brea Ave., Suite 201, Los Angeles, CA 90038.*

* * *

GOSS, Bick 1942-

PERSONAL: Born Richard Gosso, February 10, 1942, in San Francisco, CA; son of Luigi Gonsaga (a certified public accountant) and Erma Ruthlee (a singer; maiden name, Stewart) Gosso. EDUCATION: San Jose State College, B.F.A. RELIGION: Protestant.

VOCATION: Choreographer, director, writer, and dancer.

CAREER: STAGE DEBUT—Tulsa, *Gypsy*, package tour. BROADWAY DEBUT—Gypsy dancer, *Bajour*, Shubert Theatre, 1965-66.

MAJOR TOURS—Appeared in *Dancin'*, *Little Me*, *A Christmas Carol*. Directed and choreographed *Babes in Toyland*.

PRINCIPAL STAGE WORK—Choreographer and director at: Alley Theatre, Houston, TX; Pennsylvania Stage Company, Allentown, PA; George Street Playhouse, New Brunswick, NJ; The Attic Theatre; Stage 4, New York City; The Village Gate, New York City; Provincetown Playhouse, New York City; *Vagabond Stars*, Jewish Repertory Theatre, New York City, 1982.

FILM DEBUT—Dancer, *Sweet Charity*, Universal, 1969.

TELEVISION DEBUT—Dancer, *The Ed Sullivan Show*, CBS, 1968-72.

WRITINGS: PLAYS, PRODUCED—*Possessions*, workshop production.

MEMBER: Actors' Equity Association, Society of Stage Directors and Choreographers, Directors Guild of America, Screen Actors Guild, American Federation of Radio and Television Artists.

ADDRESSES: HOME—201 W. 85th Street, New York, NY 10024. AGENT—Honey Sanders Agency, Ltd., 229 W. 42nd Street, New York, NY 10036.

* * *

GOULET, Robert 1933-

PERSONAL: Full name, Robert Gerard Goulet; born November 26, 1933, in Lawrence, MA; son of Joseph (a laborer) and Jeanette (Gauthier) Goulet; married Louise Longmore, 1956 (divorced, March 12, 1963); married Carol Lawrence (an actress), August 12, 1963 (divorced); children: (first marriage) Nicolette; (second marriage) Christopher, Michael. EDUCATION: Studied music at the Royal Conservatory of Music, Toronto, 1952-54; studied singing with Joseph Furst and Dr. Ernesto Vinci.

VOCATION: Actor and singer.

CAREER: STAGE DEBUT—*The Messiah*, Edmonton, Alberta, Canada, 1951. BROADWAY DEBUT—Lancelot, *Camelot*, Majestic Theatre, 1960. PRINCIPAL STAGE APPEARANCES—*Thunder Rock* and *Visit to a Small Planet*, both Crest Theatre, Toronto, Canada; Captain MacHeath, *The Beggar's Opera*, Shakespeare Festival, Stratford, Ontario, Canada, 1958; *South Pacific*, *Finian's Rainbow*, and *Gentlemen Prefer Blondes*, all at the Theatre-under-the-Stars, Vancouver, British Columbia, Canada, 1958; Sid Sorokin, *The Pajama Game* and Jeff, *Bells Are Ringing*, both at the Packard Music Hall, Warren, OH, 1959; Jacques Bonnard, *The Happy Time*, Broadway Theatre, New York City, 1968; Lancelot, *Camelot*, Dorothy Chandler Pavilion, Los Angeles, 1975; Bill, *Carousel*, Westbury Music Fair and Valley Forge, PA, 1979.

PRINCIPAL NIGHT CLUB APPEARANCES—Persian Room, Plaza Hotel, New York City, 1962, 1964, 1971; Shoreham Hotel, Washington, DC, 1962; Empire Room, Waldorf-Astoria Hotel, New York City, 1969, 1973; Frontier Hotel, Las Vegas, 1969; Cafe Cristal, Hotel Diplomat, Miami Beach, 1970; Sands Hotel, Las Vegas, 1975; Nanuet Star Theatre, NY, 1975; also Coconut Grove Playhouse, Los Angeles; Fairmont Hotel, San Francisco; Sahara Hotel, Las Vegas.

FILM DEBUT—Voice-over, *Gay Purr-ee*, Warner Brothers, 1962. PRINCIPAL FILM APPEARANCES—*His and Hers*, Metro-Goldwyn-Mayer (MGM), 1964; *The Richest Girl in Town*, MGM, 1964; *Honeymoon Hotel*, MGM, 1964; *I'd Rather Be Rich*, Universal,

1964; *I Deal in Danger,* Twentieth Century-Fox, 1966; *Underground,* United Artists, 1970; *Atlantic City,* Paramount, 1981.

PRINCIPAL TELEVISION APPEARANCES—Series: David March, *Blue Light,* ABC, 1966. Episodic: *The Danny Thomas Show,* CBS, 1961; *The Bell Telephone Hour,* NBC, 1962; *Spotlight,* CBS, 1967; also, *Omnibus,* CBS; *The Jack Benny Show,* CBS, *The Patty Duke Show,* ABC; *Showtime,* CBC (Canada); *That's Life,* ABC.

Specials: *Little Women,* CBC (Canada), 1955; *The Enchanted Nutcracker,* ABC, 1961; *The Broadway of Lerner and Loewe,* NBC, 1962; *Rainbow of Stars,* NBC, 1962; *The Robert Goulet Hour,* CBS, 1964; *Brigadoon,* ABC, 1966; *Carousel,* ABC, 1967; *Kiss Me, Kate,* ABC, 1968; *The Robert Goulet Show, Starring Robert Goulet,* ABC, 1970; *Monsanto Night Presents Robert Goulet and Carol Lawrence,* NBC, 1973.

Guest: *The Jack Paar Show,* NBC; *The Red Skelton Show,* NBC; *The Dean Martin Show,* NBC; *The Bob Hope Show,* NBC; *The Judy Garland Show,* CBS; *The Garry Moore Show,* CBS; *The Ed Sullivan Show,* CBS; *Andy Williams Show,* NBC; *Hollywood Palace,* ABC; also appeared on Granada television in England.

RELATED CAREER—Disc jockey, CKUA radio, Edmonton, Alberta.

RECORDINGS: ALBUMS—*Always You; Two of Us; Sincerely Yours; The Wonderful World of Love; Robert Goulet in Person; This Christmas I Spend with You; Manhattan Tower; Without You; My Love Forgive Me; Travelling On; Robert Goulet on Tour; Robert Goulet on Broadway; Robert Goulet on Broadway II.* Original cast albums: *Camelot; The Happy Time.*

AWARDS: Best New Artist, Grammy Award, 1962; Gold Medal Award, 1964; Best Actor in a Musical, Antoinette Perry Award, 1968, for *The Happy Time.*

MEMBER: Actors' Equity Association, American Federation of Television and Radio Artists, Screen Actors Guild, American Guild of Musical Artists.

SIDELIGHTS: RECREATIONS—Music and body building.

ADDRESSES: OFFICE—c/o American Guild of Musical Artists, 1841 Broadway, New York, NY 10023. AGENT— International Creative Management, 8899 Beverly Blvd., Los Angeles, CA 90048.*

*   *   *

GRAHAM, Charlotte Akuyoe   1959-

PERSONAL: Born 1959, in Accra, Ghana, West Africa; daughter of Leonard Yao (an accountant) and Gladys Lamiokor (an executive secretary; maiden name, Boye) Graham. EDUCATION: High School of the Performing Arts, New York City; attended Hunter College for one year; trained for the stage with Herbert Berghof and Sanford Meisner. POLITICS: Humanist. RELIGION: Humanist.

VOCATION: Actress.

CAREER: PRINCIPAL STAGE APPEARANCES—Gillian, *House of Mirth,* Herbert Berghof Playwrights' Foundation, New York City, 1978; Elina, *The Winds,* Perry Street Theatre, New York City, 1979; Beverly, *I Can't Hear the Birds Singing,* LaMama Expermental

CHARLOTTE AKUYOE GRAHAM

Theatre Company (E.T.C.), New York City, 1980; Seinnie Pegues, *Sweet Dreams,* New Dramatists, New York City, 1981; Sally, *Murder One,* Royal Court Repertory Company, New York City, 1981; Mildred Hall, *Testimonies,* Trinity Church Theatre, New York City, 1982; Celeste, *Terrain,* New Voices at the Ensemble Studio Theatre, New York City, 1983; Cindy, *Teens Today,* Young Playwrights Festival, Circle Repertory Company, New York City, 1983; Kuumba, *Bedlam Moon,* Walnut Street Theatre, Philadelphia, 1983; Rosaline, *Love's Labours Lost,* Circle Repertory Company, New York City, 1984; Beneatha, *A Raisin in the Sun,* Pioneer Memorial Theatre, University of Utah, 1985.

MAJOR TOURS—Beneatha, *A Raisin in the Sun,* 1985-86.

PRINCIPAL FILM APPEARANCES—Billie, *Alcoholism in Teenagers,* Guidance Associates-Documentary Films, 1977; Nicole, *French Postcards,* Paramount, 1978; various roles, *Black Theatre Now,* Institute of New Cinema Artists, 1981; Sabina, *Rock 'n' Roll Woman,* MTV, 1982; Princess Angela, *Fairytales,* Columbia Independent Films, 1985.

PRINCIPAL TELEVISION APPEARANCES—Voice over, *Miss Universe Pageant,* television news broadcasts, 1981; Patsy Cole, *Search for Tomorrow,* NBC, 1982-84; Paulette, *The Good Life,* Centre for the Media Arts, 1985.

NON-RELATED CAREER—Director of the Police Athletic League's After-School Program, group named themselves, "The Misfits," South Bronx, NY.

AWARDS: Scholarship to study with Herbert Berghof and Uta Hagen.

MEMBER: Actors' Equity Association, Screen Actors Guild, American Federation of Television and Radio Artists; Circle Repertory Company.

SIDELIGHTS: In materials submitted to *CTFT* for this volume, Charlotte Akuyoe Graham tells us, "I love the work. Much of the profession excites me. As an artist I have the chance to speak to people in a different way. I have the chance to reach and touch people through my work, in ways which the usual communicative channels cannot reach and touch them. With a smile, a frown, or a gesture, a spell is cast over an audience and a heart is moved. This is real soul food. This is why I do what I do. The beauty, too, is that when the work is the focus, as it should be, regardless of success, one becomes very humble."

ADDRESSES: OFFICE—c/o Circle Repertory Company, 99 Seventh Avenue S., New York, NY 10013.

*   *   *

GRANGER, Percy   1945-

PERSONAL: Born August 8, 1945, in Ithaca, NY; son of Bruce Ingham (a professor) and Rosemary (an artist; maiden name, Jemne) Granger; married Helen Wright (a florist) July 11, 1975; children: Andrew, Jamie. EDUCATION: Harvard University, B.A., English literature, cum laude, 1967.

VOCATION: Writer.

WRITINGS: PLAYS, PRODUCED—*Vivien,* as part of the One Act Play Festival, Mitzi E. Newhouse Theatre, New York City, 1981; *Eminent Domain,* Circle in the Square Theatre, New York City, 1982; *Unheard Songs,* Ark Theatre Company, New York City, 1982; *The Dolphin Position,* Ensemble Studio Theatre, New York City, 1984.

PLAYS, PUBLISHED—*Eminent Domain* and *The Dolphin Position,* both published by Samuel French.

TELEVISION—Series: *Loving,* ABC, 1983-85; *As the World Turns,* CBS, 1985—. Movies: *Vital Signs,* 1986; *The Comeback,* 1986.

SCREEENPLAYS—*A Dime to Dance By,* 1986.

RELATED CAREER—Playwright-in-Residence, Arizona State University, 1986-88.

AWARDS: National Playwrights Conference, 1977.

ADDRESSES: HOME—650 West End Avenue, New York, NY 10024. AGENT—c/o Rick Leed, Agency for the Performing Arts, 888 Seventh Avenue, New York, NY 10106.

*   *   *

GRANICK, Harry   1898-
(Harry Taylor)

PERSONAL: Born January 23, 1898, in Nova Kraruka, Russia; came to the United States in 1905, naturalized citizen, 1918; son of Joseph (a teacher in Russia, factory worker in United States) and

Lisa (Tishkofsky) Granick; married Ray Weiss (a librarian), February 3, 1924; children: David. EDUCATION: "Formal education ceased at age 14—self-acquired, still at it." MILITARY: British Army, Jewish Legion, Royal Fusiliers, 1918-19.

VOCATION: Writer and critic.

WRITINGS: PLAYS, PRODUCED—(Co-author) *Dear Mother,* Roerich Theatre (now the Equity Library Theatre), New York City, 1937; *Age of the Common Man* (tone poem, choral), Carnegie Hall, New York City, 1943; *Warsaw Ghetto* (tone poem), Carnegie Hall, New York City, 1947; *Reveille Is Always,* Young Men's Hebrew Association, New York City, 1947; *The Criminals,* Smithtown, NY, 1949; *Witches' Sabbath,* Syracuse University, NY, 1951, Madison Avenue Playhouse, New York City, 1962; *The Guilty,* Margo Jones Theatre, Dallas, TX, 1954; *The Hooper Law,* Margo Jones Theatre, 1955; *The Bright and Golden Land,* PAF Playhouse, Huntington, NY, 1977, Shelter West Theatre, New York City, 1979. With the Morningside Players, New York City (one-acts): *The Man Who Knew Ole Abe, Florabelle for President, Shall We Ever Know, Let's All Take a Ride,* 1983-87; *And Still Is Love,* Valley Players, VT, 1984; *The Long Smoldering,* Riverside Church, New York City, 1985.

PLAYS UNPRODUCED—"Promenade and Around We Go," 1968; "Hells of Dante," 1968; "Pigeons," 1972; "The Jew of Venice," 1975; "Two for One," 1978.

BOOKS PUBLISHED—*Run, Run!,* Simon & Schuster, 1939; *Underneath New York,* Rinehart & Company, 1947; (contributor to anthology) *American Stuff,* Viking, 1937; "Witches' Sabbath," *First Stage,* Purdue University, 1961-62.

RADIO—Series: *Great Adventure,* 1934-54. Free-lance radio writer, 1934-46.

TELEVISION—Writer, 1950-52.

CRITICISM—As Harry Taylor, in *New Theatre Magazine,* London, 1945-51; *New Masses, Masses and Mainstream,* 1938-48.

PERIODICALS—Contributor of poems, stories, and articles to magazines.

RECORDINGS: Yank and Christopher Columbus, Keystone, 1937; *Are You the One,* 1960.

AWARDS: Peabody Award, 1944, for *Great Adventures* radio program; Sergel Prize from the National Theatre Conference, and first prize from Five Arts Contest, 1952, for *Witches' Sabbath.*

MEMBER: Authors League of America, Dramatists Guild, American Society of Composers, Authors, and Publishers (ASCAP); New Playwrights Committee.

SIDELIGHTS: Harry Granick continues to be active writing plays. He told *CTFT:* "I have written five plays in the last five years. At eighty-plus, I'm still being pushed to it and hopeful."

ADDRESSES: HOME—100 La Salle St. New York, NY 10027. AGENT—c/o Bertha Klausner, International Literary Agency, Inc., 71 Park Ave., New York, NY 10016.

GRANT, Cary 1904-1986

PERSONAL: Born Archibald Alexander Leach, January 18, 1904, in Bristol, England; immigrated to the United States, 1921, became a naturalized citzen, 1942; died of a stroke just prior to a performance of his one man show, in Davenport, IA, November 29, 1986; son of Ellas (a pants presser in a clothing firm) and Elsie (Kingdom) Leach; married Virginia Cherill (an actress), February, 1934 (divorced, September, 1934); married Barbara Hutton (Woolworth heiress), July 8, 1942 (divorced, August, 1945); married Betsy Drake (an actress), 1949 (divorced, 1962); married Dyan Cannon (an actress), July 22, 1965 (divorced, 1968); married Barbara Harris (an actress), 1981; children: (fourth marriage) Jennifer. EDUCATION: Attended Fairfield Academy, Somerset, England, 1914-19.

VOCATION: Actor and business executive.

CAREER: STAGE DEBUT—Performed with the Bob Pender Troupe of comics and acrobats, touring England and Europe, 1917-20. PRINCIPAL STAGE APPEARANCES—With the Bob Pender Troupe, Hippodrome Theatre, 1920; *Golden Dawn*, New York City, 1927; *Polly with a Past*, New York City; *Boom, Boom*, New York City; *A Wonderful Night*, New York City; *Street Singer*, New York City; season with the St. Louis Municipal Opera Company, 1931; *Cary, Nikki*, New York City, 1931.

FILM DEBUT—*This Is the Night*, Paramount, 1932. PRINCIPAL FILM APPEARANCES—*Sinners in the Sun*, Paramount, 1932; *Merrily We Go to Hell*, Paramount, 1932; *The Devil and the Deep*, Paramount, 1932; *Blonde Venus*, Paramount, 1932; *Hot Saturday*, Paramount, 1932; *Madame Butterfly*, Paramount, 1932; *She Done Him Wrong*, Paramount, 1933; *I'm No Angel*, Paramount, 1933; *The Woman Accused*, Paramount, 1933; *The Eagle and the Hawk*, Paramount, 1933; *Gambling Ship*, Paramount, 1933; Mock Turtle, *Alice in Wonderland*, Paramount, 1933; *Born to Be Bad*, Paramount, 1934; *Sylvia Scarlett*, RKO, 1935; *Suzy*, Metro-Goldwyn-Mayer (MGM), 1936; *Big Brown Eyes*, Paramount, 1936; *Wedding Present*, Paramount, 1936; George Kerby, *Topper*, MGM, 1937; *The Awful Truth*, Columbia, 1937; *When You're in Love*, RKO, 1937; *The Toast of New York*, Columbia, 1937; *Bringing Up Baby*, Columbia, 1938; *Holiday*, Columbia, 1938; *Gunga Din*, RKO, 1939; *In Name Only*, RKO, 1939; *Only Angels Have Wings*, RKO, 1939.

The Philadelphia Story, MGM, 1940; *My Favorite Wife*, RKO, 1940; *The Howards of Virginia*, 1940; *His Girl Friday*, Columbia, 1940; *Penny Serenade*, Columbia, 1941; *Suspicion*, RKO, 1941; *The Talk of the Town*, 1942; *Once Upon a Honeymoon*, RKO, 1942; *Mr. Lucky*, RKO, 1943; *Destination Tokyo*, 1943; *Once Upon a Time*, 1944; *None But the Lonely Heart*, RKO, 1944; Mortimer Brester, *Arsenic and Old Lace*, Warner Brothers, 1944; *Notorious*, RKO, 1946; Cole Porter, *Night and Day*, Warner Brothers, 1946; *The Bachelor and the Bobbysoxer*, RKO, 1947; *The Bishop's Wife*, RKO, 1947; *Every Girl Should Be Married*, RKO, 1948; title role, *Mr. Blandings Builds His Dreamhouse*, RKO, 1948; *I Was a Male War Bride*, 1949; *You Can't Sleep Here*, 1949.

Crisis, MGM, 1950; *People Will Talk*, 1951; *Room for One More*, 1952; *Monkey Business*, 1952; *Dream Wife*, MGM, 1953; *To Catch a Thief*, Paramount, 1955; *The Pride and the Passion*, United Artists, 1957; *An Affair to Remember*, Twentieth Century-Fox, 1957; *Kiss Them for Me*, Twentieth Century-Fox, 1957; *Indiscreet*, 1957; *Houseboat*, Paramount, 1958; *North by Northwest*, MGM,

1959; *Operaton Petticoat*, Universal, 1959; *The Grass Is Greener*, Universal, 1961; *That Touch of Mink*, Universal, 1962; *Charade*, Universal, 1964; *Father Goose*, Universal, 1965; *Walk, Don't Run*, Columbia, 1966.

PRINCIPAL TELEVISION APPEARANCES—*All Star Party for Clint Eastwood*, CBS, November 30, 1986 (videotaped September 28, 1986).

RELATED CAREER—Director, Metro-Goldwyn-Mayer.

NON-RELATED CAREER—Director, Faberge Inc.; director, Hollywood Park, Inc.; director emeritus, Western Airlines.

AWARDS: Academy Award nominations, Best Actor, 1941, for *Penny Serenade* and *None but the Lonely Heart*, 1944; one of the ten best Money Making Stars in *Motion Picture Herald-Fame* Poll, 1944, 1949, 1965-66; special Academy Award for his "sheer brilliance and contributions to the film industry," 1970; Kennedy Center Honors Medal, 1981.

MEMBER: Actors' Equity Association, Screen Actors Guild; U.S.O. (board of govenors).

SIDELIGHTS: Described by Todd McCarthy in the December 3, 1986, issue of *Variety* as a "consummate leading man of the screen who represented the epitome of debonair sophistication for 50 years," Cary Grant appeared over seventy films, wooed an international roster of more than fifty leading ladies, and exhibited an agelessness that enabled him to play romantic roles despite the silver-gray in his hair.

On screen, Grant appeared a born aristocrat. In fact, his real name was Archibald Alexander Leach, and he was the product of a poverty-stricken environment. His father worked in the British garment industry, and his mother suffered a nervous breakdown and entered a mental hospital when her son was twelve; he did not see her again for twenty years.

While still in school, Archie Leach ran away from home and joined a troupe of comic acrobats with whom he toured England and Europe for a year. After a New York City engagement in 1920, he left the troupe and for several years held a variety of odd jobs. He also appeared in supporting roles iln several musical comedies. In 1932, he travelled to Hollywood and was signed by Paramount Studios. It was then that he changed his name to the more euphonious Cary Grant.

His first movies, including *This Is the Night, She Done Him Wrong*, and *I'm No Angel* established him as a romantic lead. He went on to display a mastery of sophisticated comedy in a series of classic films during the 1930s and 1940s, including *Topper, Bringing Up Baby, Holiday*, and *Arsenic and Old Lace*.

His most notable dramatic roles, played with his inimitable light touch, included four films directed by Alfred Hitchcock: *Suspicion, Notorious, To Catch a Thief*, and *North by Northwest*. According to Pauline Kael in her book *When the Lights Go Down* (Holt & Co., 1983), in these romantic suspense comedies, Grant played "the glamourous, worldly figure that 'Cary Grant' had come to mean: he was cast as Cary Grant, and he gave a performance as Cary Grant."

Even in his later films, Grant lost none of his romantic appeal or pure command of gesture and expression that was his hallmark. His personal style, as described by Eric Pace in the December 1, 1986,

New York Times, was marked by "a Cockney-flavored but cosmopolitan manner of speaking, a knack for lifting his eyebrows to register comic disbelief, and a flair for managing to seem irresistible to the heroine while remaining rather passive and indifferent to her at the same time."

Although Grant was twice nominated for an Academy Award—for his portrayal of a star-crossed newspaperman in *Penny Serenade,* a 1941 drama, and for his role as a London street tough in the 1944 film *None But the Lonely Heart*—it was not until 1970 that he received a special Oscar for his total contribution to film and in recognition of his having been one of the most popular stars in Hollywood for more than three decades. Retiring from the screen in 1966, Grant became an executive of Faberge, a large cosmetics firm.

Even in retirement, however, Cary Grant remained a star. Television reruns of his films and promotional appearances for Faberge kept him before the public eye. And his youthful charm and worldly, fun-loving lifestyle seemed but an extension of his screen personality. As Kael observed, "He has lived up to his screen image, and then some."

Grant "was everyone's favorite uncle, brother, best friend and ideal lover; more than most stars he belonged to the public," wrote David Shipman in his book *The Great Movie Stars: The Golden Years* (Hill & Wang, 1981). "He stayed young," added Shipman. "We loved [Clark] Gable, [Bing] Crosby, [Gary] Cooper as much, but they aged. The appeal of many of them lay in familiarity: unlike us and the world, Grant was changeless."

Kael concurred. "Everyone likes the idea of Cary Grant," she posited. "Everyone thinks of him affectionately, because he embodies what seems a happier time—a time when we had a simpler relationship to a performer. We could admire him for his timing and nonchalance. . . . We didn't want depth from him; we asked only that he be handsome and silly and make us laugh."

Grant died of a stroke November 29, 1986, in Davenport, Iowa, where he was scheduled to appear in a one-man show of filmclips and reminiscences. Among his many eulogies was a tribute from President Ronald Reagan that read, "[Grant] was one of the brightest stars in Hollywood, and his elegance, wit and charm will endure forever on film and in our hearts." Similarly, in a *Newsweek* article of December 8, 1986, David Ansen called Grant "The embodiment . . . of charm and elegance and effortless accomplishment" and mourned the loss of the world's "quintessential romantic icon, probably the most purely likable leading man in the history of the movies."*

*   *   *

GRAY, Dolores   1924-

PERSONAL: Born June 7, 1924, in Chicago, IL; daughter of Harry and Barbara Marquerite Gray; married Andrew Crevolin. EDUCATION: Trained as a singer and actress with her mother and at the Royal Academy of Dramatic Art.

VOCATION: Actress and singer.

CAREER: BROADWAY DEBUT—*Seven Lively Arts,* Ziegfeld Theatre, 1944. LONDON DEBUT—Annie Oakley, *Annie Get Your Gun,* Coliseum Theatre, 1947-50. PRINCIPAL STAGE APPEARANCES—Bunny La Fleur, *Are You with It?,* Century Theatre, New York City, 1945; Diana Janeway, *Sweet Bye and Bye,* pre-Broadway tryout, Shubert Theatre, New Haven, CT, then Erlanger Theatre, Philadelphia, 1946; Nell Gwynne, *Good King Charles's Golden Days,* Drury Lane Theatre, London, 1948.

Two on the Aisle, Mark Hellinger Theatre, New York City, 1951; Eliza Doolittle, *Pygmalion,* Westport Country Playhouse, CT, 1952; Cornelia, *Carnival in Flanders,* New Century Theatre, New York City, 1953; Pistache, *Can-Can,* Municipal Opera House, St. Louis, MO and Municipal Auditorium, Dayton, OH, 1957; Ninotchka, *Silk Stockings,* Pittsburgh Civic Opera, and Municipal Opera House, St. Louis, 1958; Liza Elliot, *Lady in the Dark,* Municipal Opera House, St. Louis, 1958; singer, Palladium Theatre, London, 1958; Frenchie, *Destry Rides Again,* Imperial Theatre, New York City, 1959; Babe, *The Pajama Game* and Annie, *Annie Get Your Gun,* both at the Municipal Opera House, St. Louis, 1962; repeated role, Pistache, *Can-Can,* Theatre under the Stars, Atlanta, 1962; title role, *The Unsinkable Molly Brown,* Municipal Opera House, then repeated role with the Pittsburgh Light Opera Company, 1963; Wildcat Jackson, *Wildcat,* Owens Auditoruium, Charlotte, NC, 1963; Louraine Sheldon, *Sherry!,* Alvin Theatre, New York City, 1967; Rose, *Gypsy,* Piccadilly Theatre, London, 1973; *Brothers and Sisters,* New York City, 1975; Maggie Jones, *42nd Street,* Majestic Theatre, 1986-87; also appeared in summer theatre productions of: *Wildcat, The Unsinkable Molly Brown, The Pajama Game, Gypsy.*

MAJOR TOURS—Frenchie, *Destry Rides Again,* European cities, 1959; Annie Oakley, *Annie Get Your Gun,* U.S. cities, 1966; Maggie Jones, *42nd Street,* U.S. cities, 1985-86.

PRINCIPAL CABARET PERFORMANCES—Singer, restaurants and supper clubs, San Francisco, 1940; Copacabana, New York City, 1944; Empire Room, Waldorf-Astoria Hotel, New York City, 1962; The Cork Club, Houston, TX, 1962; Talk of the Town, London, 1963; Tivoli Gardens, Copenhagen, Denmark, 1964.

PRINCIPAL FILM APPEARANCES—*It's Always Fair Weather,* Metro-Goldwyn-Mayer (MGM), 1954; *Kismet,* MGM, 1955; *The Opposite Sex,* MGM, 1956; *Designing Woman,* MGM, 1957.

PRINCIPAL TELEVISION APPEARANCES—Episodic: *The Milton Berle Show, The Buick Circus Hour, The Ed Sullivan Show, The U.S. Steel Hour, The Bell Telephone Hour.* Specials: *Salute to Cole Porter,* CBS, 1957; *Sid Caesar Special,* CBS, 1959; *The Good Old Days* and *Sunday Night at the Palladium,* both Leeds Television, U.K., 1974. Guest: *The Tonight Show, The Steve Allen Show, The Mike Douglas Show, The Perry Como Show.*

PRINCIPAL RADIO PERFORMANCES—Singer, *The Rudy Vallee Show,* 1940.

AWARDS: Antoinette Perry Award, 1953, for *Carnival in Flanders;* Film Exhibitors Laurel Medallion, 1956, for *The Opposite Sex.*

MEMBER: Actors' Equity Association, Screen Actors Guild, American Federation of Television and Radio Artists, American Guild of Variety Artists.*

RICHARD GRAYSON

GRAYSON, Richard 1925-

PERSONAL: Born Richard Andrew Rosenblatt; changed name to Richard Martin, 1942-1950; changed name to Richard Grayson, 1950; born May 2, 1925, in San Francisco, CA; son of Martin S. (a business executive) and Margaret (Cohn) Rosenblatt. EDUCATION: Attended Stanford University, 1942-43. MILITARY: U.S. Navy, 1943-44.

VOCATION: Actor, director, manager, and producer.

CAREER: STAGE DEBUT—Cheshire Cat and Humpty Dumpty, *Alice in Wonderland,* community theatre, San Francisco, CA, 1932. PRINCIPAL STAGE APPEARANCES—Hertibise, *Orphee,* Provincetown Playouse, New York City, 1945; the juvenile, *The Shining Hour,* Equity Library Theatre, 1946; Loutec, *Red Gloves,* Mansfield Theatre, New York City, 1948; *Yes, My Darling Daughter,* Town Hall Theatre, Fairhaven, MA, and at the Bucks County Playhouse, New Hope, PA, 1949; *The Barker,* Town Hall Theatre, Fairhaven, MA, and Lake Hopatcong, NJ, 1949; the tutor, *Cry of the Peacock,* Mansfield Theatre, New York City, 1950; understudy Michel, *The Immoralist,* Royale Theatre, New York City, 1954.

MAJOR TOURS—Victor Sellers, *The Ryan Girl,* opened at the Shubert Theatre, Philadelphia, PA, closed at the Blackstone Theatre, Chicago, IL, 1945; *Any Wednesday,* Curtain-Up Dinner Theatre, St. Louis, MO, 1974.

PRINCIPAL STAGE WORK—Stage manager, (opera) *The Devil and Daniel Webster,* Veteran's Auditorium, San Francisco, CA, 1942;

assistant stage manager, *Catherine Was Great,* Shubert Theatre, New York City, 1944; stage manager, *Sleep, My Pretty One,* Playhouse Theatre, 1944; assistant to the director, *Signature,* Forrest Theatre, New York City, 1945; business manager, Provincetown Playhouse, 1945; assistant stage manager, *The Ryan Girl,* Plymouth Theatre, New York City, 1945; co-producer, *Live Life Again* and *This Property Condemned,* Equity Library Theatre, New York City, 1945-46; stage manager, *The Royal Family,* John Drew Theatre, East Hampton, L.I., NY, 1946; business manager, Hilltop Summer Theatre, Lutherville, MD, 1946; assistant stage manager, *Ballet Ballads,* American National Theatre Academy (ANTA) experimental production at Maxine Elliot's Theatre, New York City, 1948; stage manager, *The Red Gloves,* Mansfield Theatre, New York City, 1948; stage manager, Town Hall Theatre, Fairhaven, MA, 1949; stage manager, *The Cry of the Peacock,* Mansfield Theatre, New York City, 1950; stage manager, *The Live Wire,* Playhouse Theatre, New York City, 1950; co-producer, *Ballet Ballads,* Century Theatre, Hollywood, 1950; was associated with Lawrence Langner with assignments encompassing all of Mr. Langner's theatrical activities, including the Theatre Guild, New York City and the Westport Country Playhouse, CT.

Assistant stage manager, *The Immoralist,* Royale Theatre, New York City, 1954; advance stage manager for American Shakespeare Festival East Coast tour, *An Evening with Will Shakespeare,* 1953; executive coordinator, American Shakespeare Festival, Stratford, CT, 1955; assistant stage manager, *No Time for Sergeants,* Alvin Theatre, New York City, 1955; production manager for Maurice Evans Productions, Inc., 1955-57; stage manager, *The Apple Cart,* Plymouth Theatre, New York City, 1956, and on tour, 1957; stage manager, *The Reluctant Debuante,* West Coast tour, 1957; apprentice company manager, *The Body Beautiful,* Broadway Theatre, New York City, 1957; apprentice house manager, New Locust Theatre, Philadelphia, PA, 1958; general manager, *Heartbreak House,* Billy Rose Theatre, New York City, 1959; *Little Mary Sunshine,* Orpheum Theatre, New York City, 1959; company manager, *Take Me Along,* Shubert Theatre, New York City, 1959; company manager, *Gypsy,* Broadway Theatre, New York City, 1959, and national tour, 1961; company manager, *La Plume de Ma Tante,* Royale Theatre, New York City and on tour, 1960; company manager, *Carnival,* Imperial Theatre, New York City, 1961; company manager second tour of *Gypsy,* 1961-62; company manager, *Do Re Mi,* tour, 1962; company manager, *Irma La Douce,* national tour, 1962; company manager, *Anything Goes,* Orpheum Theatre, 1962; *Tovarich,* Broadway Theatre, 1963; company manager, *The Sound of Music,* national tour, 1964; general manager, *Roar Like a Dove,* Booth Theatre, New York City, 1964; stage manager, Dupont Pavilion, New York World's Fair, 1964.

General manager, *Oliver!* and *Camelot,* bus and truck tours, 1964-65; company manager, *The Glass Menagerie,* Broadway revival and *Kismet,* national tour, 1965; company manager, *Mame,* Broadway production, 1966-69; company manager, *The Boys in the Band,* New York City, 1970; company manager, *Sensations,* Off-Broadway production, 1970; general manager, *Bob & Ray: The Two and Only,* Broadway production, 1970; company manager, *The Joffrey Ballet,* New York City production and tour, 1971; company manager, *Hair,* national tour, 1972; company manager, *Disney on Parade,* national tour, 1973; company manager, *The Alvin Ailey Dance Theatre,* 1973-75; co-produced *Broadway in Concert,* Town Hall Theatre, New York City, *She Loves Me,* New York City production, and *Knickerbocker Holiday,* New York City production, all 1977.

Since 1978, has worked with the affiliated corporations of Kolmar/

Luth Entertainment, Inc., KL Management, Inc., The Edgewood Organization, Inc.

As comptroller, company manager, general manager, and associate producer for *Lies & Legends, The Musical Stories of Harry Chapin,* Off-Broadway production, national tours of *Beehive, On Your Toes, Sophisticated Ladies, Peter Pan, Mornings at Seven,* and *One Mo' Time,* and for *Victor Borge,* Broadway production and tour; company manager, *Gertrude Stein and a Companion,* Lucille Lortel Theatre, New York City, 1986.

PRINCIPAL FILM APPEARANCES—*Down Among the Sheltering Palms,* Twentieth Century-Fox, 1951; *Chain of Circumstance,* Columbia, 1951; *Flat Top,* Mono, 1952; *Thunderbirds,* Republic, 1952; *Bonzo Goes to College,* Universal, 1952; *Eight Iron Men,* Columbia, 1952; *Lili,* Metro-Goldwyn-Mayer (MGM), 1952; *Above and Beyond,* MGM, 1952.

PRINCIPAL TELEVISION APPEARANCES—Episodic: Quartermaster, "Battleship Bismark," *Studio One,* CBS, 1949; Cotton Candy Operator, "The Barker," *Ford Theatre,* CBS, 1950; Jimmy, "Fable of Honest Harry," *Armstrong Circle Theatre,* NBC, 1952; Thompson, "Dial 'M' for Murder," *Hallmark Hall of Fame,* NBC, 1958.

PRINCIPAL TELEVISION WORK—Was associated with Lawrence Langner with assignments encompassing all of Mr. Langner's productions including *U.S. Steel Hour,* 1953-55.

PRINCIPAL RADIO WORK—John Royal, "Quiet Wedding," *Theatre Guild of the Air,* NBC, 1953.

NON-RELATED CAREER—Co-owner of La Bottega Ltd., manufacturers of men's toiletries.

MEMBER: Actors' Equity Association, Screen Actors Guild, American Federation of Television and Radio Artists, American Guild of Variety Artists, Association of Theatrical Press Agents and Managers (vice-president).

ADDRESSES: OFFICE—1501 Broadway, Suite 201, New York, NY 10036.

*   *   *

GREENE, Ellen

BRIEF ENTRY: Born in Brooklyn, raised on Long Island, NY. Father, a dentist; mother, a guidance counselor. Actress and singer. Although she'd been taking singing lessons since she was seven years old, it wasn't until after her first year in Rider College that Ellen Greene decided to join a musical road show and dedicate her efforts toward professional performing. After appearing in a cabaret act at The Brothers & The Sisters Club and Reno Sweeney's in New York City, she was discovered by the New York Shakespeare Festival, and performed in such productions as *In the Boom Boom Room, The Sorrows of Steven,* and as a vengeful whore in a 1976 Broadway revival of *The Threepenny Opera,* which won her an Antoinette Perry Award nomination. Also in 1976, she made her film debut playing the female lead in *Next Stop, Greenwich Village,* which earned her critical attention. After playing in the film, *I'm Dancing as Fast as I Can,* and working in both New York City and regional productions, she appeared on television in the unsuccessful

pilot, *Rock Follies.* What followed next was a period of unemployment that wasn't broken until 1982, when she auditioned for and won the part of Audrey in *Little Shop of Horrors,* a part that she's played since, not only onstage at the Orpheum Theatre in New York City, and in Los Angeles and London, but also in the 1986 Warner Brothers movie of the same title (she is the only member of the original stage production to be cast in the movie).*

*   *   *

GREENWOOD, Jane   1934-

PERSONAL: Born April 30, 1934, in England; daughter of John Richard and Florence Sarah Mary (Humphries) Greenwood; married Ben Edwards (a set designer); children: two daughters. EDUCATION: Attended Merchant Taylor's Girls School, Liverpool and Central School of Arts and Crafts.

VOCATION: Costume designer.

CAREER: FIRST STAGE WORK—Costume design for Pirandello's *Henry IV,* Oxford Repertory, U.K., 1958. FIRST LONDON STAGE WORK—*The Hamlet of Stepney Green,* Lyric Theatre, Hammersmith, 1958. PRINCIPAL STAGE WORK—Costume design: *The Importance of Being Earnest,* Madison Avenue Playhouse, New York City, 1963; *The Ballad of the Sad Cafe,* Martin Beck Theatre, New York City, 1963; *Hamlet,* Lunt-Fontanne Theatre, New York City, 1964; *Incident at Vichy,* American National Theatre Academy (ANTA), New York City, 1964; *Tartuffe,* ANTA, 1965; (costume supervisor) *Half a Sixpence,* Broadhurst Theatre, New York City, 1965; *A Race of Hairy Men,* Henry Miller's Theatre, New York City, 1965; *Tartuffe,* American Conservatory Theatre (ACT), Pittsburgh, 1965.

Nathan Weinstein, Mystic, Connecticut, Brooks Atkinson Theatre, New York City, 1966; *Where's Daddy?,* Billy Rose Theatre, New York City, 1966; *Murder in the Cathedral* and *Twelfth Night,* both for the American Shakespeare Festival, Stratford, CT, 1966; (costume supervisor) *The Killing of Sister George,* Belasco Theatre, New York City, 1966; *How's the World Treating You?,* Music Box Theatre, New York City, 1966; *What Do You Really Know About Your Husband?,* pre-Broadway tryout, 1967; *More Stately Mansions,* Broadhurst Theatre, New York City, 1967; *The Comedy of Errors* and (co-designer with Alvin Colt) *She Stoops to Conquer,* both with the National Repertory Theatre at Ford's Theatre, Washington, DC, 1968; *The Prime of Miss Jean Brodie,* Helen Hayes Theatre, New York City, 1968; *The Seven Descents of Myrtle,* Ethel Barrymore Theatre, New York City, 1968; *I'm Solomon,* Mark Hellinger Theatre, New York City, 1968; *The Wrong Way Light Bulb,* Booth Theatre, New York City, 1969; *Much Ado About Nothing, Hamlet,* and *The Three Sister,* all for the American Shakespeare Festival, 1969; *Episode in the Life of an Author* and *The Orchestra,* both Studio Arena, Buffalo, NY, 1969; *The Penny Wars,* Royale Theatre, New York City, 1969; *Crimes of Passion,* Astor Place Theatre, New York City, 1969; *Angela,* Music Box Theatre, New York City, 1969.

All's Well That Ends Well, The Devil's Disciple, and *Othello,* American Shakespeare Festival, 1970; *Othello,* ANTA, New York City, 1970; *Hay Fever,* Helen Hayes Theatre, New York City, 1970; *Les Blancs,* Longacre Theatre, New York City, 1970; *Sheep on the Runway,* Helen Hayes Theatre, New York City, 1970; *Gandhi,* Playhouse Theatre, New York City, 1970; *Seventy Girls*

Seventy, Broadhurst Theatre, New York City, 1971; *The House of Blue Leaves*, Truck and Warehouse Theatre, New York City, 1971; *The Merry Wives of Windsor*, *The Tempest*, and *Mourning Becomes Electra*, all with the American Shakespeare Festival, 1971; *Wise Child*, Helen Hayes Theatre, New York City, 1971; *That's Entertainment*, Edison Theatre, New York City, 1972; *Julius Caesar*, *Anthony and Cleopatra*, and *Major Barbara*, American Shakespeare Festival, 1972; *Look Away*, Playhouse Theatre, New York City, 1973; *Finishing Touches*, Plymouth Theatre, New York City, 1973; *The Country Wife*, *Measure for Measure*, and *Macbeth*, American Shakespeare Festival, 1973; *The Head Hunters* and *The Prodigal Daughter*, both at the Eisenhower Theatre, John F. Kennedy Center for the Performing Arts, Washington, DC, 1973; *A Moon for the Misbegotten*, Morosco Theatre, New York City, 1973; *Getting Married*, Hartford State Company, CT, 1973; *Finishing Touches*, Ahmanson Theatre, Los Angeles, 1973.

Twelfth Night, *Romeo and Juliet*, and *Cat on a Hot Tin Roof*, American Shakespeare Festival, 1974; *Cat on a Hot Tin Roof*, ANTA, 1974; *Beyond the Horizon*, McCarter Theatre, Princeton, NJ, 1974; *Same Time Next Year*, Brooks Atkinson Theatre, New York City, 1975; *King Lear* and *A Winter's Tale*, American Shakespeare Festival, 1975; *A Long Day's Journey into Night*, Brooklyn Academy of Music, NY, 1976; *A Matter of Gravity*, Broadhurst Theatre, New York City, 1976; *Who's Afraid of Virginia Woolf?*, Music Box Theatre, New York City, 1976; *California Suite*, Ahmanson Theatre, Los Angeles, then Eugene O'Neill Theatre, New York City, 1976; *A Texas Trilogy*, Broadhurst Theatre, New York City, 1976; *Otherwise Engaged*, Plymouth Theatre, New York City, 1977; *Caesar and Cleopatra*, Palace Theatre, 1977; *Anna Christie*, Imperial Theatre, 1977; *Vieux Carre*, St. James Theatre, New York City, 1977; *The Night of the Tribades*, Helen Hayes Theatre, New York City, 1977; *An Almost Perfect Person*, Belasco Theatre, New York City, 1977; *Cheaters*, Biltmore Theatre, 1978; *Knockout*, Helen Hayes Theatre, New York City, 1979; *Happy Days*, Newman Theatre at the Public Theatre, New York City, 1979; *Father's Day*, American Place Theatre, New York City, 1979; *Romantic Comedy*, Ethel Barrymore Theatre, New York City, 1979; *A Month in the Country*, Roundabout Stage One, New York City, 1979.

Judgement, Theatre at St. Peter's Church, New York City, 1980; *Summer*, Hudson Guild Theatre, New York City, 1980; *The Seagull*, New York Shakespeare Festival, Newman Theatre, New York City, 1980; *To Grandmother's House We Go*, Biltmore Theatre, New York City, 1981; *Hedda Gabler* and *Misalliance*, both Roundabout Theatre, Stage One, New York City, 1981; *Faces of Love*, Roundabout Theatre, Stage Two, 1981; *The Millionairess*, Hartman Theatre Company, Stamford, CT, 1981; *The Supporting Cast*, Biltmore Theatre, New York City, 1981; *West Side Waltz*, Ethel Barrymore Theatre, New York City, 1981-82; *Duet for One*, Royale Theatre, New York City, 1981-82; with the Los Angeles Actors' Theatre, 1981-82; costume advisor to the Yale Repertory Theatre, New Haven, CT, 1981-84; *Medea*, Cort Theatre, New York City, 1982; *The Queen and the Rebels*, Plymouth Theatre, New York City, 1982; *Plenty*, New York Shakespeare Festival, Newman Theatre, New York City, 1982, then Plymouth Theatre, New York City, 1983.

Tartuffe, American Place Theatre, New York City, 1983; *The Guardsman* and *The Lady and the Clarinet*, both at the Long Wharf Theatre, New Haven, 1983; *Heartbreak House*, Circle in the Square Theatre, New York City, 1983-84; *The Garden of Earthly Delights*, St. Clement's Theatre, New York City, 1984; *The Golden Age*, Jack Lawrence Theatre, New York City, 1984; *Cinders*, New York Shakespeare Festival, LuEsther Theatre, New York City, 1984; *Found a Peanut* and *La Boheme*, both at the New York Shakespeare Festival, Anspacher Theatre, New York City, 1984; *Alone Together*, Music Box Theatre, New York City, 1984-85; *Jacques and His Master*, American Repertory Theatre, Cambridge, MA, 1984-85; with the Long Wharf Theatre, New Haven, CT 1984-85.

Also designed costumes for New York City productions of *Figures in the Sand*, *Finn McKool*, *The Grand Distraction*, *The Prince of Grand Street*, *The Kingfisher*, *The Umbrellas of Cherbourg*, and *Faith Healer*. Has also designed costumes for the Metropolitan Opera and City Center Opera Company in New York City, and the Guthrie Theatre, Minneapolis, MN.

MAJOR TOURS—Costume designer: *What Do You Really Know About Your Husband?*, U.S. cities, 1967; *West Side Waltz*, U.S. cities, 1980-81.

PRINCIPAL FILM WORK—Costume designer: *Last Embrace*, United Artists, 1979; *Can't Stop the Music*, Associated Film Distributors, 1980.

PRINCIPAL TELEVISION WORK—Teleplays: Costume designer— *A Touch of the Poet*, PBS; *Look Homeward, Angel*, CBS; *The House without a Christmas Tree*, NBC; *The Thanksgiving Treasure*, NBC; *Moon for the Misbegotten*.

RELATED CAREER—Teacher of design at the Lester Polakov Design Studio, New York City; lecturer at Juilliard School Department of Drama, New York University, and at Yale University.

ADDRESSES: OFFICE—321 W. 19th Street, New York, NY 10011.*

*   *   *

GREENWOOD, Joan   1921-1987

PERSONAL: Born March 4, 1921, in Chelsea, London, England; died of an apparent heart attack in London, February 28, 1987; daughter of Sydney Earnshaw and Ida (Waller) Greenwood; married Andre Morell (died).

VOCATION: Actress.

CAREER: STAGE DEBUT—Louisa, *The Robust Invalid*, Apollo Theatre, London, 1938. NEW YORK DEBUT—Lucasta Angel, *The Confidential Clerk*, Morosco Theatre, 1954. PRINCIPAL STAGE APPEARANCES—Timpson, *Little Ladyship*, Strand Theatre, London, 1939; Little Mary, *The Women*, Lyric Theatre, London, 1939, then Strand Theatre, London, 1940; Pamela Brent, *Dr. Brent's Household*, Richmond Theatre, London, 1940; *Rise Above It*, Q Theatre, London, 1941; Wendy, *Peter Pan*, Adelphi Theatre, London, 1941; Netta, *Striplings*, Q Theatre, London, 1943; Henriette, *Damaged Goods*, Whitehall Theatre, London, 1943; Ellie Dunn, *Heartbreak House*, Cambridge Theatre, London, 1943; performed with the Worthing Repertory Company, U.K., 1944.

Lady Teazle, *School for Scandal*, title role, *Cleopatra*, Nora Helmer, *A Doll's House*, all at the Oxford Playhouse, U.K., 1945;

Bertha, *Frenzy*, St. Martin's Theatre, London, 1948; Sabina Pennant, *Young Wives' Tale*, Savoy Theatre, London, 1949; title role, *Peter Pan*, Scala Theatre, London, 1951; Noel Thorne, *The Uninvited Guest*, St. James's Theatre, London, 1953; a visitor, *The Moon and the Chimney*, Lyceum Theatre, Edinburgh, Scotland, 1955; Gillian Holroyd, *Bell, Book, and Candle*, Phoenix Theatre, London, 1955; Mrs. Mallett, *Cards of Identity*, Royal Court Theatre, London, 1956; title role, *Lysistrata*, Royal Court Theatre, 1957, then Duke of York's Theatre, London, 1958; Hattie, *The Grass Is Greener*, St. Martin's Theatre, London, 1958.

Title role, *Hedda Gabler*, Oxford Playhouse, 1960; Hedda Rankin, *The Irregular Verb to Love*, Criterion Theatre, London, 1961; Calantha, *The Broken Heart* and Elena, *Uncle Vanya*, both at the Chichester Festival, U.K., 1962; title role, *Hedda Gabler*, New Arts Theatre, then St. Martin's Theatre, London, 1964; Olga, *Oblomov*, New Lyric Theatre, Hammersmith, then transferred as *Son of Oblomov* to the Comedy Theatre, London, 1964; Valentina Ponti, *Those That Play the Clowns*, American National Theatre Academy (ANTA) Theatre, New York City, 1966; Julia Sterroll, *Fallen Angels*, Vaudeville Theatre, London, 1967; title role, *Candida*, Richmond Theatre, London, 1968; Mrs. Rogers, *The Au Pair Man*, Duchess Theatre, London, 1969; Lady Kitty, *The Circle*, New Theatre, Bromley, U.K., 1970; Miss Madrigal, *The Chalk Garden*, Arnaud Theatre, Guildford, U.K., 1970; the Diva, ''Before Dawn,'' Lydia Crutwell, ''After Lydia,'' both part of *In Praise of Love*, Duchess Theatre, London, 1973; Madame Ranevsky, *The Cherry Orchard*, Leeds Playhouse, U.K., 1976.

MAJOR TOURS—Wendy, *Peter Pan*, U.K. cities, 1942; Ellie Dunn, *Heartbreak House*, with the Entertainment National Service Association (ENSA), U.K. cities, 1943; Ophelia, *Hamlet* and Celia, *Volpone*, both U.K. cities, 1944; *It Happened in New York*, U.K. cities, 1945; Stella, *Eden End*, U.K. cities, 1972.

FILM DEBUT—*My Wife's Family*, 1941. PRINCIPAL FILM APPEARANCES—*Whiskey Galore*, Ealing, 1948; *The Man in the White Suit*, Universal, 1951; *Father Brown (The Detective)*, Columbia, 1955; *Moonfleet*, Metro-Goldwyn-Mayer (MGM), 1955; *Stage Struck*, Buena Vista, 1958; *The Hound of the Baskervilles*, United Artists, 1959; *The Mysterious Island*, Columbia, 1961; *Tom Jones*, Lopert, 1963. Also appeared in *Girl in a Million*, 1946; *The October Man*, 1947; *Saraband for Dead Lovers* (also known as *Saraband*), 1948; *Flesh & Blood*, 1949; Sibella, *Kind Hearts and Coronets*, 1949; *Bad Lord Byron*, 1951; *The Young Wives' Tale*, 1951; *The Importance of Being Earnest*, 1952; *Knave of Hearts* (also known as *Lovers, Happy Lovers!*), 1954; *The Amorous Mr. Prawn*, 1962; *The Water Babies*, 1978. Also: *The Gentle Sex*, *They Knew Mr. Knight*, *Latin Quarter*, *The Man Within*, *The White Unicorn*, *Train of Events*, *Mr. Peek-a-Boo*, *The Moonshiners*, *Boy Stroke Girl*, and *The Uneasy*.

PRINCIPAL TELEVISION APPEARANCES—All British television: *King & Mrs. Candle*, *Man and Superman*, *Fat of the Land*, *Good King Charles*, *Golden Days*, *Love Is the Flame*, *Love Among the Artists*, *Wainwright's Law*, *Bognor*, *Strangers and Brothers*, *One by One*, *The Best of Friends*, *Country*, *Triangle*, and *Wagner*.

Mini-Series: *Ellis Island*, CBS, 1985.

SIDELIGHTS: RECREATIONS—Ballet dancing, sleeping, reading, and talking.

ADDRESSES: OFFICE—c/o The Spotlight, 42 Cranbourn Street, London WC2, England.*

GREY, Joel   1932-

PERSONAL: Born Joel Katz, April 11, 1932, in Cleveland, OH; son of Mickey (a comedian) and Grace Katz; married Jo Wilder, June 29, 1958; children: Jennifer, Jimmy. EDUCATION: Attended Alexander High School, Los Angeles, CA; trained for the stage at the Cleveland Playhouse, OH, and the Neighborhood Playhouse, New York City.

VOCATION: Actor, dancer, and singer.

CAREER: STAGE DEBUT—Pud, *On Borrowed Time*, Cleveland Playhouse, OH, 1941. BROADWAY DEBUT—*The Littlest Revue*, Phoenix Repertory Theatre, 1956. PRINCIPAL STAGE APPEARANCES—Buddy Baker, *Come Blow Your Horn*, Brooks Atkinson Theatre, New York City, 1961; Arthur Kipps, *Half a Sixpence*, Broadhurst Theatre, New York City, 1965; *Harry, Noon and Night*, 1965; Master of Ceremonies, *Cabaret*, Broadhurst Theatre, New York City, 1966; title role, *George M!*, Palace Theatre, New York City, 1968, then Curran Theatre, San Francisco, CA, 1969; *1776*, Maddox Hall, Atlanta, GA, 1972.

Title role, *Goodtime Charley*, Palace Theatre, New York City, 1975; *The Joel Grey Show*, Nanuet, NY, 1975; Stony McBride, *Marco Polo Sings a Solo*, New York Shakespeare Festival, Public Theatre, New York City, 1977; title role, *Platonov*, Williamstown Theatre Festival, MA, 1977; S. L. Jacobowsky, *The Grand Tour*, Palace Theatre, New York City, 1979; Olim, *Silverlake*, New York City Opera, New York City, 1980; *Night of 100 Stars*, Radio City Music Hall, New York City, 1982; Ned Weeks, *The Normal Heart*, New York Shakespeare Festival, Public Theatre/LuEsther Hall, New York City, 1985.

Also appeared in *Finian's Rainbow; Mardi Gras; Tom Sawyer, West Side Story*, and *Joy Ride*.

CABARET—Appearances in cabaret include the Fairmont Hotel, San Francisco, CA, 1972, the Riviera Hotel, Las Vegas, NV, 1972, the Caribe Hilton, San Juan, PR, 1973, the Empire Room, Waldorf Astoria Hotel, New York City, 1973; concert appearance at the Music Hall, Cleveland, OH, 1973; Variety Revue, Westbury Music Fair, Long Island, NY, 1974.

MAJOR TOURS—Littlechap, *Stop the World—I Want to Get Off*, U.S. cities, 1963-64; variety revue, U.S. cities, 1974.

FILM DEBUT—*About Face*, 1952. PRINCIPAL FILM APPEARANCES—*Calypso Heat Wave*, Columbia, 1957; *Come September*, Universal, 1961; Master of Ceremonies, *Cabaret*, Allied Artists, 1972; *Man on a Swing*, Paramount, 1974; *Buffalo Bill and the Indians*, United Artists, 1976; *The Seven Per Cent Solution*, Universal, 1976; Chiun, *Remo Williams: The Adventure Begins*, Orion, 1985.

PRINCIPAL TELEVISION APPEARANCES—Series: Host, *Live from Wolf Trap*, PBS. Episodic: *Maverick*, ABC; *December Bride*, CBS; *Ironside*, NBC; *Night Gallery*, NBC; *The Carol Burnett Show*, CBS; *The Julie Andrews Hour*, ABC; *The Engelbert Humperdinck Show*, ABC; *This Is Tom Jones*, ABC; *The Burt Bacharach Show*.

Pilots: Joe Brown, *Man on a String*, 1972; *Don't Call Me Mama Anymore*, 1973. Teleplays: Theodore Lawrence, *Little Women*, 1958. Specials: *Jack and the Beanstalk* and *George M!*, 1970; *T'was the Night Before Christmas*, 1974; *Jubilee!*, 1976; *Merry Christmas. . .with Love, Julie*, 1979; host, *Paddington Bear*, 1981; *Night of 100 Stars*, 1982; *Yeoman of the Guard*, 1984; host,

Christmas at Radio City Music Hall, 1986; *The Kraft All-Star Salute to Ford's Theatre,* 1986.

AWARDS: Best Actor in a Musical, Antoinette Perry Award and New York Critics Poll Award, both 1967, both for *Cabaret;* Best Supporting Actor, Academy Award, 1972, for *Cabaret;* honorary degree: Cleveland State University, Doctor of Literature.

ADDRESSES: AGENT—International Creative Management, 40 W. 57th Street, New York, NY 10019.*

* * *

GROSS, Shelly   1921-

PERSONAL: Born May 20, 1921, in Philadelphia, PA; son of Samuel W. (a physician) and Anna (a teacher; maiden name, Rosenblum) Gross; married Joan Seidel, May 1, 1946; children: Byron, Frederick, Daniel. EDUCATION: University of Pensylvania, A.B., 1942; Northwestern University, M.S., 1947. MILITARY: U.S. Navy, 1942-46.

VOCATION: Producer and writer.

CAREER: FIRST BROADWAY WORK—Producer (with Lee Guber and Frank Ford), *Catch Me If You Can,* Morosco Theatre, March 9, 1965. PRINCIPAL STAGE WORK—Producer (with Lee Guber): *Sherry!,* Alvin Theatre, New York City, 1967, *The Grand Music Hall of Israel,* Palace Theatre, New York City, 1968; *Inquest,* Music Box Theatre, New York City, 1970; *Lorelei, or Gentlemen Still Prefer Blondes,* Palace Theatre, New York City, 1974; (also co-produced with Joseph Harris) *Charles Aznavour on Broadway* and *Tony Bennett and Lena Horne Sing,* both at the Minskoff Theatre, New York City, 1974; at the City Center, New York City, presented *The Monty Python Show* and the Pennsylvania Ballet, both 1976, also presented productions of *A Man and a Woman* and *Peter Pan; The King and I,* Uris Theatre, New York City, 1977; *Annie Get Your Gun,* Jones Beach, NY, 1978; *Murder at the Howard Johnson's,* New York City, 1979; *Bruce Forsyth on Broadway,* Winter Garden Theatre, New York City, 1979; *Bring Back Birdie,* Martin Beck Theatre, New York City, 1981; *Painting Churches,* Lambs Theatre, New York City, 1983-84; *Shirley MacLaine on Broadway,* Gershwin Theatre, New York City, 1984.

MAJOR TOUR WORK—Producer (with Lee Guber and Frank Ford), all U.S. cities: *Li'l Abner,* 1958; *The Pleasure of His Company,* 1960; *The Andersonville Trial,* 1960-61; *A Thurber Carnival,* 1961-62; *Carnival!,* 1962-63; *Lorelei,* 1973.

PRINCIPAL TELEVISION WORK—With Lee Guber, as Music Fair Group, obtained the franchise to broadcast the 1971 heavyweight boxing championship between Muhammed Ali and Joe Frazier.

RELATED CAREER—Local news director and announcer, WFPG, Atlantic City, NJ, 1948-49; special events director and announcer, WFIL-AM and FM radio and television, Philadelphia, 1949-58; owner (with Lee Guber) and chief executive officer, Music Fair Group, Inc., Devon, PA, 1955—, New York City, 1955—, which owns and operates the following theatres: Valley Forge Music Fair, Devon, PA; Westbury Music Fair, Long Island, NY; Camden County Music Fair, Haddonfield, NJ; Shady Grove Music Fair, Gaithersburg, MD; Painters Mill Music Fair, Owings Mills, MD, and Storrowtown Music Fair, West Springfield, MA; operator, John B. Kelly Playhouse in the Park, Philadelphia; with Lee Guber, as Music Fair Group, Inc., has presented limited-engagement

productions, including the Newport Jazz Festival, at the City Center, New York City.

NON-RELATED CAREER—With Lee Guber, as Music Fair Group: operates the American Wax Museum, Independence Hall, Philadelphia; also owns Taft Advertising Agency.

WRITINGS: BOOKS—*The Crusher,* Curtis Books, 1970; *Havana X,* Arbor House, 1978.

AWARDS: Outstanding Commercial Announcer Award, *TV Guide,* 1954; Super Achiever Award, Juvenile Diabetes Foundation, 1976.

MEMBER: League of New York Theatres and Producers, Musical Arena Theatre Association (vice president); Young Men's Hebrew Association, Philadelphia (board of directors, 1962—); Phi Beta Kappa, Phi Gamma Mu, Sigma Delta Chi.

ADDRESSES: OFFICE—Music Fair Group, Inc., 176 Swedeford Road, Devon, PA 19333 and 41 E. 57th Street, New York, NY 10022.*

* * *

GROVE, Barry   1951-

PERSONAL: Born November 19, 1951, in Madison, CT; son of Herbert Frank and Cecelia Irene (Sullivan) Grove, married Maggie Blackmon, (a development director), October 8, 1973. EDUCATION: Dartmouth College, B.A., theatre, 1973.

BARRY GROVE

© *Ann Chwatsky*

VOCATION: Manager.

CAREER: PRINCIPAL STAGE WORK—General manager, New Repertory Project, University of Rhode Island, 1973-75; faculty, theatre administration, University of Rhode Island, 1973-75; managing director, Manhattan Theatre Club, New York City, 1975—.

RELATED CAREER—Onsite consultant for National Endowment for the Arts; theatre management consultant for the Foundation for the Extension and Development of American Professional Theatre.

AWARDS: Marcus Heiman Award for Contribution to the Creative Arts, Dartmouth College, 1973.

MEMBER: League of Off-Broadway Theatres (board), Alliance of Resident Theatres, New York (board), New York State Council of the Arts (advisory panel); Dartmouth Alumni Association (executive committee), Yale Club.

ADDRESSES: OFFICE—Manhattan Theatre Club, 453 W. 16th Street, New York, NY 10011.

* * *

GUBER, Lee   1920-

PERSONAL: Full name, Leon M. Guber; born November 20, 1920, in Philadelphia, PA; son of Jack (a motel operator and realtor) and Elizabeth (Goldberg) Guber; married Barbara Walters (a broadcast journalist), December 8, 1963 (divorced, March 23, 1976); children: one daughter. EDUCATION: Temple University, B.S., 1942, M.A., 1949; also attended University of Michigan and the University of Pennsylvania, 1952-55; studied directing at the American Theatre Wing, 1957, and film production at the New School for Social Research, 1962. MILITARY: U.S. Army, World War II.

VOCATION: Producer and theatre executive.

CAREER: FIRST BROADWAY STAGE WORK—Producer, *The Happiest Girl in the World,* Martin Beck Theatre, 1961. PRINCIPAL STAGE WORK—Producer (with Shelly Gross and Frank Ford), *Catch Me If You Can,* Morosco Theatre, New York City, March 9, 1965; with Shelly Gross: *Sherry!,* Alvin Theatre, New York City, 1967; *The Grand Music Hall of Israel,* Palace Theatre, New York City, 1968; *Inquest,* Music Box Theatre, New York City, 1970; *Lorelei, or Gentlemen Still Prefer Blondes,* Palace Theatre, New York City, 1974; (also co-produced with Joseph Harris) *Charles Aznavour on Broadway* and *Tony Bennett and Lena Horne Sing,* both at the Minskoff Theatre, New York City, 1974; at the City Center, New York City, presented *The Monty Python Show* and the Pennsylvania Ballet, both 1976, also presented productions of *A Man and a Woman* and *Peter Pan; The King and I,* Uris Theatre, New York City, 1977; *Annie Get Your Gun,* Jones Beach, NY, 1978; *Murder at the Howard Johnson's,* New York City, 1979; *Bruce Forsyth on Broadway,* Winter Garden Theatre, New York City, 1979; *Bring Back Birdie,* Martin Beck Theatre, New York City, 1981; *Painting Churches,* Lambs Theatre, New York City, 1983-84; *Shirley MacLaine on Broadway,* Gershwin Theatre, 1984. Also produced (with Madeline Gilford) *The World of Sholom Aleichem,* Rialto Theatre, New York City, 1982; (with Martin Heinfling and Marvin A. Krauss) *Rags,* Mark Hellinger Theatre, New York City, 1986.

MAJOR TOUR WORK—Producer (with Shelly Gross and Frank Ford), all U.S. cities: *Li'l Abner,* 1958; *The Pleasure of His Company,* 1960; *The Andersonville Trial,* 1960-61; *A Thurber Carnival,* 1961-62; *Carnival!,* 1962-63; *Lorelei,* 1973; also has presented tours of *Mame, Fiddler on the Roof, Hello, Dolly!,* and *Camelot.*

PRINCIPAL TELEVISION WORK—With Shelly Gross, as Music Fair Group, obtained the franchise to broadcast the 1971 heavyweight boxing championship between Muhammed Ali and Joe Frazier.

RELATED CAREER—Owner (with Shelly Gross and Frank Ford), operator and vice-president, Music Fair Group, Inc., Devon, PA, 1955—, New York City, 1955—, which owns and operates the following theatres: Valley Forge Music Fair, Devon, PA; Westbury Music Fair, Long Island, NY; Camden County Music Fair, Haddonfield, NJ; Shady Grove Music Fair, Gaithersburg, MD; Painters Mill Music Fair, Owings Mills, MD, and Storrowtown Music Fair, West Springfield, MA; operator, John B. Kelly Playhouse in the Park, Philadelphia, 1964—; with Shelly Gross, as Music Fair Group, Inc., has presented limited-engagement productions, including the Newport Jazz Festival, City Center, New York City.

NON-RELATED CAREER—With Shelly Gross, as Music Fair Group: operates the American Wax Museum, Independence Hall, Philadelphia; also owns Taft Advertising Agency. Pre-theatre: Night club owner and research assistant.

AWARDS: Awarded the Battle Star, for distinguished service, U.S. Army.

MEMBER: New York State Council on the Arts, League of American Theatres and Producers (governor), Musical Arena Theatres Association.

ADDRESSES: OFFICE—Music Fair Group, Inc., 176 Swedeford Road, Devon, PA 19333 and 41 E. 57th Street, New York, NY 10022.*

* * *

GUNN, Moses   1929-

PERSONAL: Born October 2, 1929, in St. Louis, MO; son of George and Mary (Briggs) Gunn; foster child of Jewel C. Richie; married Gwendolyn Landis, July 25, 1955; children: Kirsten Sarah. EDUCATION: Tennessee State University, A.B., 1959. MILITARY: U.S. Army, 1954-57.

VOCATION: Actor.

CAREER: OFF-BROADWAY DEBUT—Governor, *The Blacks,* St. Mark's Playhouse, 1962. PRINCIPAL STAGE APPEARANCES—*In White America,* Sheridan Square Playhouse, New York City, 1963; Banquo, *Macbeth,* Prospero, *The Tempest,* Jacques, *As You Like It,* all with Antioch Shakespeare Festival, Yellow Springs, OH, 1964; First Citizen, Industrialist, Pious, and Rastus, *Day of Absence,* St. Mark's Playhouse, New York City, 1965; Able and Coke, *Bohikee Creek,* Stage 73, New York City, 1966; Provost, *Measure for Measure,* New York Shakespeare Festival, Delacorte Theatre, New York City, 1966; *A Hand Is on the Gate,* Longacre Theatre, New

York City, 1966; Muslim, *Junebug Graduates Tonight!*, Chelsea Theatre Center, New York City, 1967; Aaron, *Titus Andronicus*, New York Shakespeare Festival, Delacorte Theatre, New York City, 1967; with the Negro Ensemble Company, appeared in *Song of the Lusitanian Bogey*, St. Mark's Playhouse, New York City, 1968; Roo Webber, *Summer of the Seventeenth Doll*, New York City, 1968; title role, *Kongi's Harvest*, New York City, 1968; title role, *Daddy Goodness*, New York City, 1968; Capulet, *Romeo and Juliet*, New York Shakespeare Festival, Delacorte Theatre, New York City, 1968; Goddam Passmore, Dead White Father, and Reverend Passmore, "The Owl Answers," Man Beast, "A Beast's Story," both part of *Cities in Bezique*, New York Shakespeare Festival, Public Theatre, New York City, 1969; Nick, *The Perfect Party*, Tambellini's Gate Theatre, New York City, 1969; various parts, *To Be Young, Gifted, and Black*, Cherry Lane Theatre, New York City, 1969.

Title role, *Othello*, American Shakespeare Festival, Stratford, CT, 1970, then American National Theatre Academy (ANTA) Theatre, New York City, 1970; Blind Jordan, *The Sty of the Blind Pig*, St. Mark's Playhouse, New York City, 1971; Orsino, *Twelfth Night*, Vivian Beaumont Theatre, New York City, 1972; Benjamin Hurspool, *The Poison Tree*, Westport Country Playhouse, CT, 1973; Milton Edward, *The First Breeze of Summer*, St. Mark's Playhouse, New York City, 1975; Blind Jordan, *The Sty of the Blind Pig*, Playhouse in the Park, Philadelphia, PA, 1975; Benjamin Hurspool, *The Poison Tree*, Ambassador Theatre, New York City, 1976; Martin Luther King, Jr., *I Have a Dream*, Ambassador Theatre, New York City, 1976; Joshua Tain, *Our Lan'*, Dartmouth, NH, 1977; Jacques, *As You Like It*, Yale Repertory Theatre, New Haven, CT, 1979.

PRIINCIPAL STAGE WORK—Director, *Contributions*, Tambellini's Gate Theatre, New York City, 1970.

PRINCIPAL FILM APPEARANCES—*Nothing but a Man*, Cinema V, 1965; *W.U.S.A.*, Paramount, 1970; *The Great White Hope*, Twentieth Century-Fox, 1970; Bumpy Jonas, *Shaft*, Metro-Goldwyn-Mayer (MGM), 1971; Ben, *Wild Rovers*, MGM, 1971; Bumpy Jonas, *Shaft's Big Score*, MGM, 1972; General Gourgaud, *Eagle in a Cage*, National General, 1972; Ambassador Amusa, *Hot Rock*, Twentieth Century-Fox, 1972; Joe Mott, *The Iceman Cometh*, American Film Theatre, 1973; Welton J. Waters, *Amazing Grace*, United Artists, 1974; Blackwell, *Cornbread, Earl, and Me*, American International, 1975; Cletus, *Rollerball*, United Artists, 1975; Ike, *Aaron Loves Angela*, Columbia, 1975; Pike, *Remember My Name*, 1978; Major Nammack, *Twinkle, Twinkle, "Killer" Kane*, 1979; *The Ninth Configuration*, 1980; Booker T. Washington, *Ragtime*, Paramount, 1981; Turner, *Amityville II: The Possession*, Orion, 1982; Carion, *The Neverending Story*, Warner Brothers, 1984; Dr. Pynchot, *Firestarter*, Universal, 1984; Dr. Freedman, *A Certain Fury*, New World, 1985; Sergeant Webster, *Heartbreak Ridge*, Warner Brothers, 1986.

PRINCIPAL TELEVISION APPEARANCES—Series: Cal Dickson, *Good Times*, CBS, 1974; George Beifus, *The Contender*, CBS, 1980; Moses Gage, *Father Murphy*, NBC, 1981-84. Movies: *The Borgia Stick*, 1967; Doc, *Carter's Army*, 1970; Cliff Wilder, *The Sheriff*, 1971; Seacrist, *Haunts of the Very Rich*, 1972; Mr. Nightlinger, *The Cowboys*, 1974; Jacob, *Law of the Land*, 1976; also *If You Give a Dance, You Gotta Pay the Band*. Dramatic Specials: Crooks, *Of Mice and Men*, 1968; Milton Edwards, *The First Breeze of Summer*, 1976. Mini-Series: Kintango, *Roots*, ABC, 1977; *Charlotte Forten's Mission: Experiment in Freedom*, 1985. Episodic: *Hawaii Five-O*, CBS; *The F.B.I.*, ABC; *Kung-Fu*, ABC.

NON-RELATED CAREER—Speech and drama teacher, Grambling College.

AWARDS: Obie Award, 1967-68; Best Actor, *Jersey Journal* Award, 1967-68.

MEMBER: Actors' Equity Association, Screen Actors Guild; Theta Alpha Phi.

ADDRESSES: AGENT—Blake Agency, Ltd., 409 N. Camden Road, Suite 202, Beverly Hills, CA 90210.*

*   *   *

GUNTER, John 1938-

PERSONAL: Born October 31, 1938, in Billericay, Essex, U.K.; son of Herbert Carl and Charlotte Rose (Reid) Gunter; married Micheline McKnight. EDUCATION: Trained for the stage at the Central School of Speech and Drama, London.

VOCATION: Set designer.

CAREER: PRINCIPAL STAGE WORK—Designer, with the Royal Court Theatre, London: *Saved*, 1965; *The Knack*, 1966; *The Soldier's Fortune* and *Marya*, both 1967; *The Double Dealer, The Contractor*, and *Insideout*, all 1969; *AC/DC* and *The Philanthropist* (also designer for Broadway production), both 1970; *West of Suez*, 1971; *Entertaining Mr. Sloane*, 1975; *Flying Blind* and *Inadmissable Evidence*, both 1978. Also designer, *Comedians*, Nottingham Playhouse, U.K., 1975.

With the Royal Shakespeare Company: *God Bless* and *Julius Caesar*, both produced in London, 1968; *Jingo*, 1975; *The White Devil*, 1976; *Stevie* and *The Old Country*, 1977; *Tishoo*; 1979; *Death of a Salesman*, National Theatre, London, 1979; *Born in the Gardens*, National Theatre, 1979; *Rose*, London production, then Cort Theatre, New York City, 1981; *Plenty*, London Production, then New York Shakespeare Festival, Public Theatre, then transferred to the Plymouth Theatre, New York City, 1983; *All's Well That Ends Well*, Martin Beck Theatre, New York City, 1983. Also has designed extensively in Germany, Vienna and Buenos Aires.

RELATED CAREER—Resident designer, Zurich Schauspielhaus, 1972-74; Head of Theatre Design Department, Central School of Art and Design, 1974—.

MEMBER: Arts Council Training Committee.

SIDELIGHTS: RECREATIONS—Travelling and fishing.

ADDRESSES: HOME—25 Hillfield Park, Muswell Hill, London N10, England.*

*   *   *

GURNEY, A.R., Jr. 1930-

PERSONAL: Full name, Albert Ramsdell Gurney, Jr.; born November 1, 1930, in Buffalo, NY; son of Albert Ramsdell (a real estate businessman) and Marion (Spaulding) Gurney; married Mary Goodyear, June 8, 1957; children: George, Amy, Evelyn, and

Benjamin. EDUCATION: Attended Williams College, B.A., 1952; Yale School of Drama, M.F.A., 1958. MILITARY: U.S. Naval Reserve, 1952-55.

VOCATION: Playwright, novelist, and educator.

WRITINGS: PLAYS, PRODUCED AND PUBLISHED—"Three People," in *Best Short Plays, 1955-56,* edited by Margaret Mayorga, Beacon Press, 1956; *Love in Buffalo,* Yale School of Drama, New Haven, CT, 1958; (co-author) *Tom Sawyer,* Kansas City Starlight Theatre, KS, 1959; "Turn of the Century," in *Best Short Plays, 1957-58,* edited by Mayorga, Beacon Press, 1958; *Around the World in Eighty Days,* Dramatic Publishing Company, 1962; *The Bridal Dinner,* Massachusetts Institute of Technology (M.I.T.) Community Players, Cambridge, MA; *The Comeback,* Cambridge Image Theatre, 1965; *The Open Meeting,* New Theatre Co-operative, Atma Coffeehouse, Boston, MA, 1965; *The Rape of Bunny Stuntz,* Playwright's Unit, Cherry Lane Theatre, New York City, 1964; *The David Show,* Boston University Playwrights Workshop, Tanglewood, MA, 1966; *The Golden Fleece,* Mark Taper Forum, Los Angeles, CA, 1968.

Represented in *Best Short Plays, 1969,* 1970, and *Best Short Plays, 1970,* 1971, both edited by Stanley Richards, both Chilton; *Tonight in Living Color,* (includes "The David Show" and "The Golden Fleece"), Actors Playhouse, New York City, 1969; *The Love Course,* Theatre Company of Boston, 1970; *Scenes from American Life,* Forum Theatre, Lincoln Center Repertory Theatre, New York City, 1971, and Alley Theatre, Houston, TX, 1983; *The Old One-Two,* Spingold Theatre, Brandeis University, MA, 1973; *Children,* Mermaid Theatre, London, 1974; *Who Killed Richard Cory?,* Circle Repertory Company, New York City, 1975; *The Problem,* King's Head Theatre, London, 1976; *The Wayside Motor Inn,* Manhattan Theatre Club, New York City, 1977; *The Middle Ages,* Hartman Theatre, Stamford, CT, 1978, Ark Theatre, New York City, 1982, and Theatre at St. Peter's Church, 1983; *The Golden Age,* Greenwich Theatre, London, 1980 and Jack Lawrence Theatre, New York City, 1984; *The Dining Room,* Playwrights Horizons Theatre, then Astor Place Theatre, both New York City, 1982; *What I Did Last Summer,* Circle Repertory Theatre, New York City, 1983; *The Perfect Party,* Playwrights Horizons, New York City, 1986; *Sweet Sue,* Music Box Theatre, New York City, 1987; *Another Antigone,* Old Globe Theatre, San Diego, CA, 1987.

Also wrote *Another Aida,* produced at the Theatre Company of Boston.

SCREENPLAYS—*The House of Mirth,* 1972. TELEVISION—(Adaptation) *O Youth and Beauty,* 1979. BOOKS—*The Gospel According to Joe,* Harper & Row, 1974; *Entertaining Strangers,* Doubleday, 1976; *The Snow Ball,* Arbor House, 1985.

RELATED CAREER—Teacher of English and Latin at high school in Belmont, MA, 1959-60; member of the faculty, Massachusetts Institute of Technology, 1960—, professor of literature, 1970—.

AWARDS: Everett Baker Teaching Award, Massachusetts Institute of Technology, 1969; Vernon Rice Drama Desk Award, 1971; Rockefeller Playwright-in-Residence Award, 1977; Playwriting Award, National Endowment of the Arts, 1981-82.

MEMBER: Dramatists Guild (council), Authors League of America, Writers Guild; Phi Beta Kappa.

ADDRESSES: HOME—Wellers Bridge Road, Roxbury, CT 06783.

OFFICE—120 W. 70th St., Suite 3C, New York, NY 10023. AGENT—c/o Gilbert Parker, William Morris Agency, Inc., 1350 Avenue of the Americas, New York, NY 10019.

*   *   *

GUTIERREZ, Gerald   1952-

PERSONAL: Born February 3, 1952, in Brooklyn, NY; son of Andrew (a New York City police detective) and Obdulia (a flamenco dancer; maiden name, Concheiro) Gutierrez. EDUCATION: State University of New York at Stony Brook, 1967-68; Juilliard School, New York City, B.S. (theatre arts); studied musical theatre with Lehman Engel.

VOCATION: Director, writer, and actor.

CAREER: PRINCIPAL STAGE WORK—Director: *The Apple Tree,* Juillard School, New York City, 1970; *A Life in the Theatre,* Theatre de Lys, New York City, 1977; *Elegy for Young Lovers,* San Francisco Opera, 1978; *You Can't Take It with You,* 1978; *No Time for Comedy,* McCarter Theatre, Princeton, NJ, 1978; *Meetings,* Phoenix Theatre Company, New York City, 1981; *The Curse of an Aching Heart,* Little Theatre, New York City, 1982; *Terra Nova,* American Place Theatre, New York City, 1984; *Much Ado About Nothing,* the Acting Company, New York City, 1986-87; also, *The Primary English Class.*

Directed at Playwrights Horizons, New York City: *She Loves Me,* 1980, *Geniuses,* 1982, *The Rise and Rise of Daniel Rocket,* 1982, *Isn't It Romantic,* 1983-84, *Miami,* 1986.

PRINCIPAL STAGE APPEARANCES—*The Three Sisters, Beggars Opera, The Time of Your Life,* and *The Cradle Will Rock,* all with the Acting Company, New York City.

MAJOR TOURS—Director, *Broadway,* with the Acting Company, U.S. cities, 1979.

PRINCIPAL FILM WORK—Director, *A Bag of Shells,* 1981.

PRINCIPAL TELEVISION WORK—Director, *A Life in the Theatre,* PBS, 1979; director, *Comedy Zone,* CBS, 1984; consultant, *A Musical Toast,* PBS, 1987.

RELATED CAREER—Directing instructor, New York University; instructor in comedy technique, Juilliard School, New York City; co-artistic director, the Acting Company, 1986—.

WRITINGS: SCREENPLAY—*A Bag of Shells.*

AWARDS: Best Director, Joseph Jefferson Award, 1978, for *You Can't Take It with You;* New York Drama Desk nomination, 1984, for *Isn't It Romantic;* Joseph Jefferson Award nominations for *The Curse of an Aching Heart, The Primary English Class.*

MEMBER: Actors' Equity Association, Society of Stage Directors and Choreographers, Directors Guild; The Players Club.

ADDRESSES: AGENT—Flora Roberts, 157 W. 57th Street, New York, NY 10019.

H

HAGUE, Albert 1920-

PERSONAL: Born Albert Marcuse, October 13, 1920, in Berlin, Germany; son of Harry (a psychiatrist) and Mimi (a champion chess player; maiden name, Heller) Marcuse; adopted son of Eliott B. Hague; married Renee Orin (an actress). EDUCATION: University of Cincinnati College of Music, Bachelor of Music, 1942; studied at the Royal Conservatory, Rome. MILITARY: U.S. Army, World War II.

VOCATION: Composer and actor.

CAREER: FIRST STAGE WORK—Composer, *Reluctant Lady,* Cain Park, Cleveland, OH, 1948. FIRST BROADWAY WORK—Composer, *The Madwoman of Chaillot,* Belasco Theatre, 1948. PRINCIPAL STAGE WORK—Composer: *Dance Me a Song,* Royale Theatre, New York City, 1950; *All Summer Long,* Coronet Theatre,

ALBERT HAGUE

New York City, 1954; *Plain and Fancy,* Mark Hellinger Theatre, New York City, 1955; *Redhead,* 46th Street Theatre, New York City, 1959; *Cafe Crown,* Martin Beck Theatre, New York City, 1964; *The Fig Leaves Are Falling,* Broadhurst Theatre, New York City, 1969; *Miss Moffat,* Philadelphia, PA, 1974; *Surprise! Surprise!,* New York City, 1979; *Flim Flam* (upcoming).

PRINCIPAL FILM WORK—Composer: *Coney Island U.S.A.,* 1951; *The Funniest Man in the World,* Grove, 1969.

PRINCIPAL FILM APPEARANCES—Professor Shorofsky, *Fame,* United Artists, 1980; actor, *Nightmares,* Universal, 1983.

FIRST TELEVISION WORK—Composer, *The Mercer Girls,* 1953. PRINCIPAL TELEVISION WORK—Composer, *How the Grinch Stole Christmas,* CBS, 1966.

PRINCIPAL TELEVISION APPEARANCES—Series: Mr. Benjamin Shorofsky, *Fame,* NBC, 1982-83; independent, 1983—. Movies: *Not Just Another Affair,* CBS, 1982; *Passions,* CBS, 1984. Episodic: "Rip Van Winkle," *Faerie Tale Theatre,* Showtime, 1986.

PRINCIPAL CABARET APPEARANCES—*Hague and Hague: His Hits and His Mrs.,* New York City, 1976, and on board the Queen Elizabeth II on a voyage to London.

WRITINGS: SONGS—Composer: (with Langston Hughes) *Early Blue Evening;* wrote the songs for the video *What Every Child Should Know,* SQN.

RECORDINGS: ALBUM—*Albert Hague Sings for Children,* SQN.

AWARDS: Antoinette Perry Award, 1959, for *Redhead.*

MEMBER: Lambs Club, Dutch Treat Club, Players Club.

SIDELIGHTS: RECREATIONS—Table tennis, bridge, poker.

ADDRESSES: OFFICE—c/o American Society of Composers, Authors and Publishers, 1 Lincoln Plaza, New York, NY 10023. PUBLICIST—Gutman and Pam, 8500 Wilshire Blvd., Suite 801, Beverly Hills, CA 90211.

* * *

HALL, Lois 1926-

PERSONAL: Full name Lois Grace Hall; born August 22, 1926, in Grand Rapids, MI; daughter of Ralph Stewart (an inventor and buisinessman) and Lois Grace (a teacher; maiden name, Lambert) Hall; married Maurice Willows, January 31, 1953; children: Debo-

LOIS HALL

rah, Kimberly, Christina. EDUCATION: Trained for the stage at the Pasadena Playhouse and with Jeff Corey and Gail Kobe. RELIGION: Baha'i Faith.

VOCATION: Actress.

CAREER: PRINCIPAL FILM APPEARANCES—*Every Girl Should Be Married,* RKO, 1948; young bride, *Family Honeymoon,* Universal, 1948; show girl, *Love Happy,* independent, 1948; society woman, *Duke of Chicago,* Republic, 1948; title role, *Daughter of the Jungle,* Republic, 1948; Lady of the Lake, *Adventures of Sir Galahad,* Columbia, 1948; stewardess, *Woman of Distinction,* Columbia, 1949; peasant girl, *Rogues of Sherwood Forrest,* Columbia, 1949; young mother, *My Blue Heaven,* Twentieth Century-Fox, 1949; *Roaring Westward,* Monogram, 1949; *Frontier Outpost,* Columbia, 1949; *Texas Dynamo,* Columbia, 1949; Miss Coca-Cola, *Petty Girl,* Columbia, 1950; secretary, *Kill the Umpire,* Columbia, 1950; secretary, *When You're Smiling,* Columbia, 1950; secretary, *The Tougher They Come,* Columbia, 1950; Lola, *Sister Carrie,* Paramount, 1950; *Cherokee Uprising,* Monogram, 1950; Ann, *The Squared Circle,* Monogram, 1950; *Blazing Bullets,* Monogram, 1950; *Colorado Ambush,* Monogram, 1950; *Pirates of the High Seas,* Columbia, 1950.

Stewardess, *Cuban Fireball,* Republic, 1951; young mother, *A Baby for Midge,* Warner Brothers, 1951; *The Congregation,* Protestant Films, 1951; *Slaughter Trail,* RKO, 1951; English girl, *Secrets of Monte Carlo,* Republic, 1951; *Texas City,* Monogram, 1951; *Night Raiders,* Monogram, 1951; showgirl, *Leave It to the Girls,* Paramount, 1952; Mary of Bethany, *Life of Jesus,* Scripture Films, 1952; townswoman, *Seven Brides for Seven Brothers,*

Metro-Goldwyn-Mayer, 1953; Sarah, *A Woman for All Men,* 1974; Faye Bader, *Being Born Again,* Family Films, 1978.

PRINCIPAL TELEVISION APPEARANCES—Episodic: "The Shot" and "Of Thee I Love," both 1949, and "Canterville Ghost," 1950, all *Fireside Theatre,* NBC; *Wild Bill Hickock,* syndicated, 1950; "Quicksilver Murder," "Vigilante Story," and "Sleeping Gas," all on *Cisco Kid,* syndicated, 1951; "Fight Town," "The Fatal Bullet," and "Showdown at Sunrise," all *Range Rider,* syndicated, 1951; "Fury and Sound," *Unexpected,* syndicated, 1951; "The Treasure Map," *Dick Tracy,* ABC, 1951; "Kite High," *Racket Squad,* CBS, 1951; *The Beulah Show,* ABC, 1951; "Nathanial Hawthorne," *Cavalcade,* NBC, 1952; *Boston Blackie,* syndicated, 1952; *Mr. and Mrs. North,* CBS, 1952 and 1953; "Danger Hill," *The Adventures of Kit Carson,* syndicated, 1952; "Law of the Frontier," "Gold Fever," and "Let 'er Buck,"all *Range Rider,* syndicated, 1952; "Operation Underground," *Lone Ranger,* ABC, 1952; "Flight to Nowhere," *Unexpected,* syndicated, 1952; "The Mystic Pawn," *Ramar of the Jungle,* syndicated, 1952; *Superman,* syndicated, 1953; *Annie Oakley,* syndicated, 1954 and 1955; *Hallmark Playhouse,* NBC, 1954; *Man Called X* and *Highway Patrol,* both syndicated, 1956; "Jack Be Nimble," *Marcus Welby, M.D.,* ABC, 1972; "Bear That Bit Me," *Father Murphy,* NBC; "A New Beginning," *Little House on the Prairie,* NBC; *Divorce Court.*

Series: Beth Holly, *One Man's Family,* NBC, 1954-55; Kate Mulligan, *Days of Our Lives,* NBC, 1975.

Movies: Dour nun, "A Home Run for Love," *Afterschool Special,* ABC, 1978; "Schoolboy Father," *Afterschool Special,* ABC; *Rage,* CBS.

PRINCIPAL STAGE APPEARANCES—At the Pasadena Playhouse, CA: Miriamne, *Winterset,* 1947, Christina, *The Silver Cord,* 1948, Tracy, *Philadelphia Story,* 1948, title role, *Mellony Holtspur,* 1948, *Glamour Preferred,* 1949, and *Holiday,* 1949; *The Square Needle,* Los Angeles and San Francisco, CA, 1951.

MEMBER: Pasadena Playhouse Alumni Association.

ADDRESSES: AGENT—Tyler Kjar Agency, 8961 Sunset Blvd., Suite B, Los Angeles, CA 90069.

*   *   *

HALL, Monty   1924-

PERSONAL: Born Monty Halparin, August 25, 1924, in Winnipeg, Manitoba, Canada; son of Maurice Harvey and Rose (Rusen) Halparin; married Marilyn Plottel (an actress, writer, and producer) on September 28, 1947; children: Joanna Gleason (an actress), Richard David, Sharon Fay. EDUCATION: University of Manitoba, B.S. MILITARY: Canadian Army, served as emcee of Canadian Army shows, WWII.

VOCATION: Television producer, performer, actor, and writer.

CAREER: PRINCIPAL STAGE APPEARANCES—Musicals and plays in college.

MAJOR TOURS—Lead role, *High Button Shoes,* national tour, 1978.

MONTY HALL

PRINCIPAL CABARET APPEARANCES—At the Sahara Hotel, Las Vegas.

TELEVISION DEBUT—Subsitute emcee, *Strike It Rich*, CBS. PRINCIPAL TELEVISION APPEARANCES—Series: Anchor, *Monitor*, NBC, 1955-60; host and narrator, *Cowboy Theatre*, NBC, 1956-57; emcee, *Keep Talking*, CBS, 1958; host, *Byline: Monty Hall*, CBS, 1959; emcee, *Video Village*, CBS, 1960; emcee, *Let's Make a Deal*, NBC, 1963-68, ABC 1968-77, revived from Vancouver, British Columbia, 1980, and again on CBS, 1984-86; host, *NBC Comedy Playhouse*, NBC, 1968; host, *Beat the Clock*, CBS, 1979; host, *Split Second*, in syndication, 1986-87. Episodic: *The Odd Couple*, ABC; *Love, American Style*, ABC; *That Girl*, ABC; *The Flip Wilson Show*, NBC; *The Dean Martin Show*, NBC; *The Love Boat*, ABC. Movies: *The Courage and the Passion*, ABC, 1978. Specials: Host of numerous ABC specials.

PRINCIPAL TELEVISION WORK—Producer/packager, *Your First Impression*, NBC, 1960; *Let's Make a Deal*, 1963-86; *Split Second*, 1986.

NON-RELATED CAREER—Cedars-Sinai Medical Center (board of directors); United Jewish Appeal (co-chairman); Israel Bonds (national board of directors, entertainment division); Guardians of Courage (board of directors); B'nai B'rith (board of directors); Anti-Defamation League (board of directors); Technion University (vice president, board of directors); Israel Tennis Centers (international board of directors); American Friends of Hebrew University (vice president, board of directors); American Friends of Tel Aviv University (advisory board); Far West Financial Corporation (board of directors); Far West Savings and Loan (board of directors).

WRITINGS: BOOKS—*Emcee: Monty Hall*, Grosset, 1973.

AWARDS: Lifetime title of International Chairman, Variety Clubs International, 1981; Humanitarian Award, Variety Clubs International, 1983; inducted into the Television Hall of Fame, Hollywood, CA; read into the Congressional Record for organizing the all-star show for families of the victims of the Wichita State University and Marshall University air disasters; Spirit of Life Award, City of Hope; Medallion Award, Cedars-Sinai Hospital; Louis Pasteur Award, Intra-Science Foundation; Menachem Begin Award, Bar-Ilan University; Canadian Award, Canadian Hadassah; Centennial Awards, University of Manitoba and Winnipeg, Canada; Susie Award, (Eddie Cantor Lodge) B'nai B'rith; Torch of Liberty Award, Anti-Defamation League; Variety Heart Award of Los Angeles, and Toronto, Canada; Sword of Haganah Award, Israel Bonds; two King David Awards, Israel Bonds; Johns Hopkins Medical Center dedication of the "Monty Hall Room for Pediatric Oncology Therapy"; "Monty Hall Variety Children's Pavilion," Hahnemann Hospital, Philadelphia; "Monty Hall Variety Center for Children," University of California Medical Center; Honorary Mayor, Hollywood, CA, for seven years; "Monty Hall Week," proclaimed by Mayor Tom Bradley of Los Angeles, CA.

Awards from the following organizations: Boys Club of America, Big Brothers of America, Leukemia Foundation, Muscular Dystrophy Foundation, Multiple Sclerosis Foundation, Arthritis Foundation, Kidney Foundation, Christmas Seal Campaign, Easter Seal Campaign, TEACH Foundation, CARE Village USA, National Foundation for Ileitis and Colitis, Alcohol and Drug Abuse Program, Special Olympics, Sunair Home for Asthmatic Children, CEDU (Associates for Troubled Children), Gateways, Los Angeles Free Clinic, Los Angeles Music Center, National Conference of Christians and Jews, Guardians of Courage, Technion University, American Friends of Hebrew University, American Friends of Tel Aviv University, Simon Wiesenthal Center.

MEMBER: American Guild of Variety Artists, Actors' Equity Association, Screen Actors Guild, American Federation of Television and Radio Artists, Association of Canadian Television and Radio Artists; Variety Clubs International (international chairman, past chairman of the board, past international president); Variety Club of Southern California (former chief barker, emcee of annual telethon).

SIDELIGHTS: Monty Hall makes over one-hundred appearances every year, in the United States, Canada, and the United Kingdom for charitable organizations representing hospitals, diseases, the handicapped, and the underprivileged. He has raised over two-hundred-fifty-million dollars for these organizations.

ADDRESSES: HOME—Beverly Hills, CA. OFFICE—Monty Hall Enterprises, 7833 Sunset Blvd., Los Angeles, CA 90028.

*   *   *

HALLETT, Jack   1948-

PERSONAL: Born November 7, 1948, in Philadelphia, PA; son of George and Marie R. (Cullen) Hallett.

VOCATION: Actor.

JACK HALLETT

CAREER: STAGE DEBUT—George M. Cohan, *George M.!*, Rochester Music Theatre, Rochester, NH, 1969. BROADWAY DEBUT—Wally Ferguson, *1940's Radio Hour*, St. James Theatre, 1979, for ninety-four performances. PRINCIPAL STAGE APPEARANCES—*1940's Radio Hour*, Arena Stage, Washington, DC, 1978; *The Suicide*, Goodman Theatre, Chicago, 1979; *The First*, Martin Beck Theatre, New York City, 1981; *American Comedy*, Mark Taper Forum, Los Angeles, 1983; *The Vinegar Tree*, Berkshire Theatre Festival, Stockbridge, MA, 1984; *Mandrake* and *Wedding*, Seattle Repertory Theatre, WA, 1985; title role, *Fiorello!*, Goodspeed Opera House, East Haddam, CT, 1985; at the Humana Playwrighting Festival, Actors Theatre of Louisville, KY, 1987; also appeared as Sir Toby Belch, *Twelfth Night*, Triplex Theatre, New York City.

MAJOR TOURS—Luther Billis, *South Pacific*, Montreal, Toronto, Ottawa, Pittsburgh, Valley Forge, and Westbury, Long Island, NY.

PRINCIPAL FILM APPEARANCES—Philo Bartley, *Puddin' Head Wilson;* Lieutenant Carson, *Raw Deal;* also appeared in *Critical Condition*, Paramount, 1987.

TELEVISION DEBUT—*We've Got Each Other*, CBS, 1977. PRINCIPAL TELEVISION APPEARANCES—*Love, Sidney*, NBC; *The Ellen Burstyn Show*, ABC; *Texas*, NBC.

RELATED CAREER—Co-owner, Village Dinner Theatre, Raliegh, NC, 1980-83.

NON-RELATED CAREER—President, Beach Cove Realty, North Wildwood, NJ, 1978—; president, Mermaid Realty, North Wildwood, NJ, 1983—.

MEMBER: Society of Stage Directors and Choreographers; Players Club.

ADDRESSES: HOME—New York City. AGENT—Don Buchwald and Associates, Ten E. 44th Street, New York, NY 10017.

*   *   *

HAMLISCH, Marvin   1944-

PERSONAL: Born June 2, 1944, in New York, NY; son of Max and Lily (Schachter) Hamlisch. EDUCATION: Queen's College, B.A., 1967; graduate, preparatory division, Juilliard School of Music.

VOCATION: Composer, pianist, and actor.

CAREER: STAGE DEBUT—Toured as straight man and accompanist with Groucho Marx, 1974-75. PRINCIPAL STAGE APPEARANCES—Pianist with the Minneapolis Symphony Orchestra, 1975.

PRINCIPAL STAGE WORK—Composer: *A Chorus Line*, Shubert Theatre, New York City, 1975; *They're Playing Our Song*, Imperial Theatre, New York City, 1979; *Smile*, Lunt-Fontanne Theatre, New York City, 1986; *Blithe Spirit*, Neil Simon Theatre, New York City, 1987.

PRINCIPAL FILM WORK—Composer: *The Swimmer*, Columbia, 1968; *Take the Money and Run*, Cinerama, 1969; *Bananas*, United Artists, 1971; *Kotch*, Cinerama, 1971; *Save the Tiger*, Paramount, 1972; *The Way We Were*, Columbia, 1973; musical adaptation, *The Sting*, Universal, 1973; *The Fan*, 1976; *The Spy Who Loved Me*, United Artists, 1977; *Same Time Next Year*, Universal, 1979; *Ice Castles*, Columbia, 1979; *Chapter Two*, Columbia, 1979; *Starting Over*, Paramount, 1979; *Ordinary People*, Paramount, 1980; *Seems Like Old Times*, Columbia, 1980; *Sophie's Choice*, Universal, 1982; *Romantic Comedy*, Metro-Goldwyn-Mayer/United Artists, 1983; *D.A.R.Y.L.*, Paramount, 1985.

PRINCIPAL TELEVISION APPEARANCES—Guest: *The Tonight Show; Late Night with David Letterman*.

PRINCIPAL TELEVISION WORK—Composer, theme music to *Good Morning, America*, ABC, 1975; *The Two Mrs. Grenvilles*, NBC, 1987.

WRITINGS: SONGS—(In addition to the songs written for the plays and films mentioned above) "Sunshine, Lollipops and Rainbows," 1960; "Nobody Does It Better," 1977.

AWARDS: Best Original Song and Best Original Dramatic Score, Academy Award, 1973, for *The Way We Were;* Best Scoring, Academy Award, 1973, for *The Sting;* Best Musical, Antoinette Perrry Award, and Pulitzer Prize, both 1975, for *A Chorus Line.*

MEMBER: American Society of Composers, Authors and Publishers (ASCAP).

ADDRESSES: HOME—New York, NY. OFFICE—c/o Rastar Films Inc., Columbia Plaza West, Burbank, CA, 91505.*

HAMMER, Ben

PERSONAL: Born in Brooklyn, NY; son of Morris and Mollie (Nadler) Hammer; married Dorothea (a potter), December 21, 1958; children: Marlayna, Paula. EDUCATION: Brooklyn College, B.A., 1948. MILITARY: U.S. Army, Staff Sergeant, 1945-46.

VOCATION: Actor.

CAREER: BROADWAY DEBUT—Pavlat, *The Great Sebastians*, 1955. PRINCIPAL STAGE APPEARANCES—Broadway productions: *The Royal Hunt of the Sun, The Tenth Man, The Deputy, The Crucible, In the Matter of J. Robert Oppenheimer, Mother Courage, The Diary of Anne Frank,* and *Golda; Henry IV*, Part I, Mark Taper Forum, Los Angeles; *Tamara*, Los Angeles, CA.

MAJOR TOURS—*Come Back, Little Sheba*, 1950-51; *The Diary of Anne Frank*, Theatre Guild tour, 1957-58.

PRINCIPAL FILM APPEARANCES—*Zabriskie Point*, Metro-Goldwyn-Mayer (MGM), 1970; *Johnny Got His Gun*, Marketing & Distributing Company, 1971; *The First Family*, Warner Brothers, 1980; *The Competition*, Columbia, 1980; *The Beastmaster*, MGM, 1982; *Jagged Edge*, Columbia, 1985; *Mannequin*, Twentieth Century-Fox, 1987; also *Survival Quest*.

PRINCIPAL TELEVISION APPEARANCES—Series: *Days of Our Lives*, NBC; *The Young and the Restless*, CBS; *One Life to Live*, ABC. Episodic: *Hart to Hart*, ABC; *Jennifer Slept Here*, NBC; *The Incredible Hulk*, CBS; *Quincy*, NBC; *Six Million Dollar Man*, ABC; *CHiPS*, NBC; *Simon and Simon*, CBS; *Barney Miller*, ABC; *Kojak*, CBS; *Streets of San Francisco*, ABC; *Mannix*, CBS; *Barnaby*

BEN HAMMER

Jones, CBS; *Fame*, NBC; *The A Team*, NBC. Movies: *The Execution of Private Eddie Slovick*, 1974; *Collision Course*, 1975; *Griffin and Phoenix: A Love Story*, 1976; *The Howard Hughes Story*, 1978; *The Winds of War*, 1982; also *An Affair to Forget*.

MEMBER: Actors' Equity Association, Screen Actors Guild, American Federation of Television and Radio Artists, Academy of Motion Picture Arts and Sciences, Academy of Television Arts and Sciences.

SIDELIGHTS: RECREATIONS—Motorcycles, airplanes, and travel.

ADDRESSES: AGENT—c/o Michael Hartig Agency, 114 E. 28th Street, New York, NY 10016.

*   *   *

HANDMAN, Wynn   1922-

PERSONAL: Born May 19, 1922; son of Nathan and Anna Handman. EDUCATION: City College of New York, B.A.; Columbia University, M.A.; trained for the stage at the Neighborhood Playhouse School of Theatre, 1948. MILITARY: U.S. Coast Guard, 1943-46.

VOCATION: Producer, artistic director, and teacher.

CAREER: PRINCIPAL STAGE WORK—Producer and artistic director at the American Place Theatre, New York City: *The Old Glory, My Kinsman Major Molineaux Benito Cereno*, all 1964; *Harry, Noon and Night, Hogan's Goat*, both 1965; *Jonah, The Journey of the Fifth Horse, Who's Got His Own, The Displaced Person*, all 1966; *La Turista, Posterity for Sale, Father Uxbridge Wants to Marry, The Ceremony of Innocence*, all 1967; *The Electronic Nigger and Others* (three plays entitled "A Son Come Home," "The Electronic Nigger," and "Clara's Ole Man"), *Endicott and the Red Cross, The Cannibals, The Acquisition* (three plays entitled "Trainer," "Dean," and "Liepolt and Company"), *This Bird of Dawning Singeth All Night Long, The Young Master Dante*, all 1968; *Boy on the Straight Back Chair, Papp, Mercy Street*, all 1969.

Continuing at the American Place Theatre: *Five on the Black Hand Side, Two Times Two* (two plays entitled "The Last Straw" and "Duet for Solo Voice"), *The Pig Pen, Sunday Dinner, The Carpenters*, all 1970; *Pinkville, Black Bog Beast Bait, Fingernails Blue as Flowers, Lake of the Woods*, all 1971; *The Chickencoop Chinaman, The Kid, The Little Theater of the Dear*, all 1972; *Freeman, The Karl Marx Play, Baba Goya*, all 1973; *Bread, A Festival of Short Plays* (including "Shearwater," "Cream Cheese," "Dr. Kheal," and "Love Scene"), *The Year of the Dragon, The Beauty Part, At Sea with Benchley, Kalmar and Ruby*, all 1974; *Killer's Head, Action, Rubbers, Yanks 3 Detroit 0 Top of the Seventh, Gorky*, all 1975; *Every Night When the Sun Goes Down, The Old Glory, Rehearsal, Comanche Cafe/Domino Courts*, all 1976; *Isadora Duncan Sleeps with the Russian Navy, Hold Me!, Cold Storage, Cockfight, Passing Game*, all 1977; *Fefu and Her Friends, Conjuring an Event, Touching Bottom*, all 1978; *Seduced, Tunnel Fever, Letters Home, Smart Aleck*, all 1979.

At the American Place Theatre: *Paris Lights, SIM, or One Night with a Lonely Undertaker from Texas, Killings on the Last Line, The Impossible H.L. Mencken, After the Revolution*, all 1980;

Memory of Whiteness, Still Life, The Amazin' Casey Stengel, The Fuehrer Bunker, Grace, Behind the Broken Words, all 1981; *Lydie Breeze, The Death of a Miner, The Brothers, Twelfth Night, The Country Wife, The Regard of Flight, A Crowd of Two, The Stage That Walks, Do Lord Remember Me,* all 1982; *Little Victories, Buck, Pericles, Tartuffe, Play and Other Plays, The Cradle Will Rock, Heart of a Dog, Territorial Rites, Great Days, The Vi-Ton-Ka Medicine Show,* all 1983; *Breakfast Conversations in Miami,* repeat performance of *Do Lord Remember Me, A. . .My Name Is Alice, The Danube, Festival of One-Act Plays, To Heaven in a Swing, Pay Attention, Terra Nova, What's a Nice Country Like You Still Doing in a Place Like This?,* all 1984; *Four Corners, Rude Times, Paducah, Jubilee!,* all 1985.

Directed *The Power of Darkness,* York Theatre, New York City, 1959.

RELATED CAREER—Acting teacher and director of productions, Neighborhood Playhouse School of Theatre, 1950-55; founder and acting teacher, Wynn Handman Studio, 1955—; co-founder and artistic director, American Place Theatre, New York City, 1963—.

MEMBER: Actors' Equity Association, Society of Stage Directors and Choreographers.

ADDRESSES: OFFICE—The American Place Theatre, 111 W. 46th Street, New York, NY 10019.*

*   *   *

HANSEN, Nina

VOCATION: Actress.

CAREER: PRINCIPAL STAGE APPEARANCES—Fraulein Schneider, *I Am a Camera;* Mama, *Come Back, Little Sheba; The Deputy,* Broadway production; *Autumn Crocus,* Philadelphia; *The Dragon,* Phoenix Theatre, New York City; also: *Anastasia; The Guardsman; The Madwoman of Chaillot; Anyone for Love?*

PRINCIPAL FILM APPEARANCES—*Stage Struck,* RKO Pictures, 1936; *A Likely Story,* RKO Pictures, 1947; *The Sweet Smell of Success,* Hecht-Lancaster Production, 1957; *That Kind of Woman,* Paramount, 1959; *Middle of the Night,* Hecht-Lancaster Production, 1959; *The Pawnbroker,* Landau Productions, 1965; *The Incident,* Moned Associates, 1967; *The Gambler,* Paramount, 1974; *The Last Angry Man,* Hecht-Lancaster Production, 1974; grandmother, *Saturday Night Fever,* Paramount, 1977; also: *The Woman in Brown,* Republic Pictures; *Guerilla Girl,* United Artists; *Turned On,* Deb Corporation.

PRINCIPAL TELEVISION APPEARANCES—Episodic: Kasturbai, *You Are There,* CBS; Elsa, *Robert Montgomery Presents,* NBC; *The Doctors,* ABC.

PRINCIPAL RADIO WORK—*Modern Romance,* ABC; *Eternal Light,* NBC.

MEMBER: Actors' Equity Association, American Federation of Television Artists, Screen Actors Guild.

NINA HANSEN

SIDELIGHTS: Nina Hansen is proficient in all Continental dialects from French and Polish to German and Italian.

ADDRESSES: HOME—350 W. 24th Street, New York, NY 10011.

*   *   *

HARE, David   1947-

PERSONAL: Born June 5, 1947, in Sussex, England; son of Clifford Theodore Rippon (a sailor) and Agnes (Gilmour) Hare; married Margaret Matheson, August, 1970 (divorced, 1980); children: Joe, Lewis, Darcy. EDUCATION: Attended Lancing College, Sussex; Cambridge University, M.A., 1968.

VOCATION: Playwright, director, and filmmaker.

CAREER: PRINCIPAL STAGE WORK—Playwright (see below); director: *Inside Out,* produced in London, 1968; *Christie in Love,* Portable Theatre Company, Brighton, U.K., 1969, London, 1970; *Purity,* produced in Canterbury, U.K., 1969; *Fruit,* produced in London, 1970; *Blow Job,* produced in Edinburgh, Scotland and London, 1971; *England's Ireland,* Mickery Theatre, Amsterdam, and Roundhouse Theatre, London, 1972; *The Provoked Wife,* produced in Watford, Hertfordshire, U.K., 1973; *Brassneck,* Nottingham Playhouse, U.K., 1973; *The Pleasure Principle,* Theatre Upstairs, London, 1973; *Teeth 'n' Smiles,* Royal Court Theatre, 1975; *Weapons of Happiness,* National Theatre, London, 1976; *Devil's Island,* Royal Court Theatre, 1977; *Plenty,* National Theatre, London, New York Shakespeare Festival (NYSF), Public Theatre, 1982, then transferred to the Plymouth Theatre, New York City, 1983.

MAJOR TOURS—Director, *The Party*, National Theatre tour, U.K. cities, 1974.

PRINCIPAL FILM WORK—Writer (see below); director, *Wetherby*, Metro-Goldwyn-Mayer/United Artists (MGM/UA), 1985.

PRINCIPAL TELEVISION WORK—Movies: writer (see below); director, *Dreams of Leaving*, BBC, 1980.

RELATED CAREER—Film editor, A.B. Pathe, London, 1968; director, Portable Theatre, 1968-71; director, Joint Stock Theatre, England, 1974; literary manager, Royal Court Theatre, London, 1969-70; resident dramatist, Royal Court Theatre, 1970-71; resident dramatist, Nottingham Playhouse, U.K., 1973; associate director, National Theatre, 1984.

WRITINGS: PLAYS, PRODUCED AND PUBLISHED—(With Tony Bicat) *Inside Out* (one-act), Arts Laboratory, London, 1968; *How Brophy Made Good* (one-act), Brighton Combination Theatre, 1969, published in *Gambit*, London, 1970; *Slag*, Hampstead Theatre Club, London, 1970, NYSF, Public Theatre, New York City, 1971, Royal Court Theatre, London, 1971, published by Faber & Faber, London, 1971; *What Happened to Blake?*, Royal Court Theatre, London, 1970; adaption of Luigi Pirandello's *The Rules of the Game*, National Theatre, London, 1971; *Lay By* (one-act), Traverse Theatre, Edinburgh, Scotland, 1971, Open Space Theatre, London, 1971, published by Calder and Boyars, 1972; *Deathsheads* (one-act), Traverse Theatre, Edinburgh, 1971; *The Great Exhibition*, Hampstead Theatre Club, London, 1972, published by Faber & Faber, 1972; *England's Ireland*, Mickery Theatre, Amsterdam, the Netherlands, 1972, Roundhouse Theatre, London, 1972; (with Howard Brenton) *Brassneck*, Nottingham Playhouse, U.K., 1973, published by Eyre Methuen, 1974; *Knuckle*, Comedy Theatre, London, 1974, Phoenix Theatre, New York City, 1975, published by Faber & Faber, 1974; adaptation of William Hinton's *Fanshen*, ICA Theatre, London, 1975, published by Faber & Faber, 1976; *Teeth 'n' Smiles*, Royal Court Theatre, London, 1975, Wyndams Theatre, London, 1976, published by Faber & Faber, 1976.

Plenty, National Theatre, London, 1978, Public Theatre, New York City, 1982, then transferred to the Plymouth Theatre, New York City, 1982, published by Faber & Faber, 1982; *A Map of the World*, Adelaide Festival, 1982, National Theatre, London, 1983, NYSF, Public Theatre, New York City, 1984, published by Faber & Faber, 1983; *Pravda*, National Theatre, London, 1985, published by Faber & Faber, 1986.

SCREENPLAYS—*The Butter Mountain*, 1984; *Wetherby*, MGM/UA, 1985; *Plenty*, Twentieth Century-Fox, 1985.

TELEPLAYS—*Man Above Men*, BBC, 1973; *Licking Hitler*, BBC, 1978, published by Faber & Faber, 1978; *Dreams of Leaving*, BBC, 1980; *Saigon: Year of the Cat*, BBC, 1983.

AWARDS: Most Promising Playwright, London *Evening Standard* Award, 1971, for *Slag;* John Llewellyn Rhys Memorial Award, 1975, for *Knuckle;* Best Television Play of the Year, British Academy of Film and Television Arts Award, 1979, for *Licking Hitler;* New York Critic's Circle Award, 1983, for *Plenty;* Golden Bear Award, 1985.

MEMBER: Dramatists Guild.

SIDELIGHTS: RECREATIONS—Golf.

ADDRESSES: HOME—33 Ladbroke Road, London W11, England. AGENT—Margaret Ramsay Ltd., 14a Goodwin's Court, St. Martin's Lane, London WC2N 4LL, England.*

*   *   *

HARRIS, Barbara   1935-

PERSONAL: Born 1935, in Evanston, IL; daughter of Oscar (a restauranteur) and Natalie (a piano teacher; maiden name, Densmoor) Harris; married Paul Sills (a director and teacher). EDUCATION: Attended the University of Chicago; trained for the stage at the Goodman School of Drama and with Paul Sills.

VOCATION: Actress and director.

CAREER: STAGE DEBUT—Playwrights Theatre Club, Chicago, 1959. BROADWAY DEBUT—*From the Second City*, Royale Theatre, September 26, 1961. PRINCIPAL STAGE APPEARANCES—Rosalie, *Oh Dad, Poor Dad, Mama's Hung You in the Closet and I'm Feelin' So Sad*, Phoenix Repertory Theatre, New York City, 1962; *Seacoast of Bohemia* and *Alarums and Excursions*, with the Second City group, Square East Theatre, New York City, 1962; Yvette Pottier, *Mother Courage and Her Children*, Martin Beck Theatre, New York City, 1963; *When the Owl Screams*, with the Second City group, Square East Theatre, New York City, 1963; appeared in *Open Season at Second City*, with the Second City group, Square East Theatre, New York City, 1964; Tlimpattia, *Dynamite Tonight*, York Theatre, New York City, 1964; Daisy Gamble and Melinda, *On a Clear Day You Can See Forever*, Mark Hellinger Theatre, New York City, 1965; Eve, ''The Diary of Adam and Eve,'' Passionella and Ella, ''Passionella'' and Princess Barbara, ''The Lady or the Tiger,'' in a program with the overall title, *The Apple Tree*, Shubert Theatre, New York City, 1966; Jenny, *The Rise and Fall of the City of Mahagonny*, Anderson Theatre, New York City, 1970.

PRINCIPAL STAGE WORK—Director, *The Penny Wars*, Royale Theatre, New York City, 1969.

PRINCIPAL FILM APPEARANCES—Sandra Markowitz, *A Thousand Clowns*, United Aritsts, 1966; Rosalie, *Oh Dad, Poor Dad, Mama's Hung You in the Closet and I'm Feelin' So Sad*, Paramount, 1967; Allison, *Who Is Harry Kellerman and Why Is He Saying All Those Terrible Things About Me?*, National General, 1971; Muriel Tate, *Plaza Suite*, Paramount, 1971; Terry Koslenko, *The War Between Men and Women*, National General, 1972; Kathy, *Mixed Company*, United Artists, 1974; Albuquerque, *Nashville*, Paramount, 1975; *Family Plot*, Universal, 1976; *Freaky Friday*, Buena Vista, 1979; *Movie, Movie*, Warner Brothers, 1979; *The Seduction of Joe Tynan*, Universal, 1979; *The North Avenue Irregulars*, Buena Vista, 1979; *Second Hand Hearts*, Paramount, 1981.

AWARDS: New York Drama Critics Award, 1961, 1962; Obie and *Theatre World* awards, 1962, both for *Oh Dad, Poor Dad, Mama's Hung You in the Closet and I'm Feelin' So Sad;* Best Actress in a Musical, Antoinette Perry Award, 1966, for *The Apple Tree;* Entertainer of the Year Award, *Cue* magazine, 1966.

MEMBER: Actors' Equity Association, Screen Actors Guild, American Federation of Television and Radio Artists, American Guild of Variety Artists.

ADDRESSES: AGENT—Robinson and Associates, Inc., 132 S. Rodeo Drive, Beverly Hills, CA 90212.*

*   *   *

HARRISON, Rex   1908-

PERSONAL: Born March 5, 1908, in Huyton, Lancaster, U.K.; son of William Reginald and Edith (Carey) Harrison; married Noel Marjorie Collette Thomas (divorced); married Lilli Palmer (divorced); married Kay Kendall (died); married Rachel Roberts (divorced); married Elizabeth Harris (divorced); married Mercia Tinker. MILITARY: Royal Air Force Volunteer Reserve (RAFVR), 1942-44.

VOCATION: Actor.

CAREER: STAGE DEBUT—Husband, *Thirty Minutes in a Street,* Liverpool Repertory Theatre, September, 1924. LONDON DEBUT—Honorable Fred Thrippleton, *Getting George Married,* Everyman Theatre, 1930. BROADWAY DEBUT—Tubbs Barrow, *Sweet Aloes,* Booth Theatre, March 2, 1936. PRINCIPAL STAGE APPEARANCES—Member, Liverpool Repertory Theatre, 1924-27; Rankin, *The Ninth Man,* Prince of Wales's Theatre, London, 1931; *Another Language,* Lyric Theatre, London, 1933; Peter Featherstone, *No Way Back,* Whitehall Theatre, London, 1934; John Murdock, *Our Mutual Father,* Piccadilly Theatre, London, 1934; Anthony Fair, *Anthony and Anna,* Fulham Theatre, 1934; Paul Galloway, *Man of Yesterday,* St. Martin's Theatre, London, 1935; Mark Kurt, *Short Story,* Queen's Theatre, London, 1935.

Rodney Walters, *Charity Begins. . .,* Aldwych Theatre, London, 1936; Tom Gregory, *Heroes Don't Care,* St. Martin's Theatre, London, 1936; Honorable Alan Howard, *French without Tears,* Criterion Theatre, London, 1936; Leo, *Design for Living,* Haymarket Theatre, London, 1939; Gaylord Easterbrook, *No Time for Comedy,* Haymarket Theatre, London, 1941; Henry VIII, *Anne of a Thousand Days,* Shubert Theatre, New York City, 1948; Unidentified Guest, *The Cocktail Party,* New Theatre, London, 1950; Shepherd Henderson, *Bell, Book and Candle,* Barrymore Theatre, New York City, 1950; Hereward, *Venus Observed,* New Century Theatre, New York City, 1952; directed and appeared as The Man, *The Love of Four Colonels,* Shubert Theatre, New York City, 1953; directed and appeared as Anthony Henderson, *Bell, Book and Candle,* Phoenix Theatre, London, 1954; Henry Higgins, *My Fair Lady,* Mark Hellinger Theatre, New York City, 1956-58, then Drury Lane Theatre, London, 1958; General, *The Fighting Cock,* American National Theatre Academy (ANTA) Theatre, New York City, 1959.

Title role, *Platonov,* Royal Court Theatre, London, 1960; Sir Augustus Thwaites, *August for the People,* Royal Court Theatre, London, and Edinburgh Festival, Scotland, 1961; Lionel Fairleigh, *The Lionel Touch,* Lyric Theatre, London, 1969; title role, *Henry IV,* Her Majesty's Theatre, London, 1974; Sebastian Crutwell, *In Praise of Love,* Morosco Theatre, New York City, 1974; title role, *M Perichon's Travels,* Chichester, U.K., 1976; Caesar, *Caesar and Cleopatra,* Palace Theatre, New York City, 1977; Cecil, *The Kingfisher,* Biltmore Theatre, New York City, 1978; Captain Hushabye, *Heartbreak House,* Haymarket Theatre, London, 1982,

then Circle in the Square Theatre, New York City, 1983; Lord Grenham, *Aren't We All,* Haymarket Theatre, London, then Brooks Atkinson Theatre, New York City, 1984-85.

PRINCIPAL STAGE WORK—Director: *The Love of Four Colonels,* Shubert Theatre, New York City, 1953; *Bell, Book and Candle,* Phoenix Theatre, London, 1954; *Nina,* Haymarket Theatre, London, 1955; *The Bright One,* Winter Garden Theatre, New York City, 1958.

MAJOR TOURS—Ralph, *After All,* U.K. cities, 1931; *Other Men's Wives* and *For the Love of Mike,* U.K. cities, 1932; *Road House* and *Mother of Pearl,* U.K. cities, 1933-34; title role, *Henry IV,* U.S. cities, 1973; Higgins, *My Fair Lady,* U.S. cities, 1980-81; Lord Grenham, *Aren't We All,* U.S. cities, 1985-86. Also toured U.K. in *Charley's Aunt, Potiphar's Wife, Alibi, The Chinese Bungalow,* and *A Cup of Kindness.*

FILM DEBUT—*The Great Game,* 1929. PRINCIPAL FILM APPEARANCES—*Leave It to Blanche,* 1934; *All at Sea,* 1935; *Men Are Not Gods,* 1936; *Storm in a Teacup,* 1937; *St. Martin's Lane,* 1938; *The Citadel,* 1938; *Over the Moon,* 1939; *Ten Days in Paris,* 1939; *Night Train to Munich,* 1940; *Major Barbara,* 1940; *Blithe Spirit,* 1945; *I Live in Grosvenor Square,* 1945; *The Rake's Progress,* 1945; *Anna and the King of Siam,* Twentieth Century-Fox, 1946; *The Ghost and Mrs. Muir,* Twentieth Century-Fox, 1947; *The Foxes of Harrow,* Twentieth Century-Fox, 1947; *Unfaithfully Yours,* Twentieth Century-Fox, 1948; *Escape,* Twentieth Century-Fox, 1948; *The Four Poster,* 1952; *Main Street to Broadway,* 1953; *King Richard and the Crusaders,* 1954; *The Constant Husband,* 1955.

The Reluctant Debutante, Metro-Goldwyn-Mayer (MGM), 1958; *Midnight Lace,* Universal, 1960; *The Happy Thieves,* United Artists, 1962; *Cleopatra,* Twentieth Century-Fox, 1963; *The Yellow Rolls-Royce,* MGM, 1964; *My Fair Lady,* Warner Brothers, 1964; *The Agony and the Ecstasy,* Twentieth Century-Fox, 1965; *The Honey Pot,* United Artists, 1967; *Dr. Dolittle,* Twentieth Century-Fox, 1967; *A Flea in Her Ear,* Twentieth Century-Fox, 1968; *Staircase,* Twentieth Century-Fox, 1969. Also appeared in *The Prince and the Pauper,* 1976; *Behind the Iron Mask,* 1977; *Ashanti,* 1978.

PRINCIPAL TELEVISION WORK—Episodic: *Chevrolet Tele-Theatre,* NBC, 1948-49; "Excerpts from the Mikado," *Omnibus,* CBS, 1952; "The Man in Possession," *U.S. Steel Hour,* ABC, 1953.

Dramatic Specials: *Don Quixote,* 1972; *The Kingfisher,* 1982. Mini-Series: Grand Duke Cyril Romanov, *Anastasia: The Story of Anna,* NBC, 1986.

WRITINGS: BOOKS—(Autobiography) *Rex,* 1974; *If Love Be Love.*

AWARDS: *Evening Standard* Award, 1961, for *Platonov;* Best Film Actor, Academy Award, 1964, for *My Fair Lady;* New York Film Critics Award, Golden Globe Award, and David di Donatello Award, all 1965; Order of Merit, Italy, 1966; recipient of a special New York Drama Desk Award, 1985; honorary degrees: Boston University.

MEMBER: Actors' Equity Association, British Actors' Equity Association, Screen Actors Guild; Green Room Club, Garrick Club, Beefsteak Club, all in London; Players Club, in New York; Travellers' Club, in Paris.

SIDELIGHTS: FAVORITE ROLES—Henry Higgins, from *My Fair Lady,* and Caesar, from *Caesar and Cleopatra.*

Actor Rex Harrison, perhaps best remembered for his portrayal of the irascible Professor Henry Higgins in the stage and screen versions of the musical *My Fair Lady,* began his stage career in London during the 1930s, a period when, as he later put it, the theatre was dominated by "tail-coat actors, who used to wander about the stage as if it were their dressing room." After playing a number of supporting parts, Harrison became a star with his 1936 performance in Terence Rattigan's drawing room comedy *French without Tears.* From then until World War II, he appeared in several other sophisticated comedies, including S. N. Behrman's *No Time for Comedy* and Noel Coward's *Design for Living.* Coward called Harrison "the best light comedian in the world—after me."

While appearing in those plays at night, Harrison was frequently making movies during the day for Alexander Korda and other British producers. His performances in such English films as *Night Train to Munich* and *Blithe Spirit* brought him to the attention of the American studio Twentieth Century-Fox, which signed him to a seven-year contract in 1946. Coming to Hollywood for the first time, Harrison immediately scored a triumph as the nineteenth-century Siamese King Mongkut in *Anna and the King of Siam.* Reviewer Alton Cook of the *New York World-Telegram* (June 20, 1946) wrote, "This characterization is so vividly and imaginatively detailed, [that] the whole emphasis of the story is changed, and it is the King, not Anna, who becomes the central figure . . . Harrison . . . works his portrait of the King from a set of small, elaborate and exotic mannerisms. There is a wonderful variety to them as he sweeps through the picture, ranging from his blind rages to whimsical jest." The reviewer called Harrison's creation "one of the most fascinating characters ever seen on a movie screen." Several years later, Richard Rodgers and Oscar Hammerstein II offered Harrison the role of the King in their musical version of the same tale, *The King and I,* but he was forced to turn it down due to other commitments.

Harrison followed Anna with another successful film, *The Ghost and Mrs. Muir* (1947), but his next three pictures for Fox were all box office failures (although one, *Unfaithfully Yours,* the story of a symphony conductor who suspects that his wife is unfaithful to him, has since achieved cult status). The actor's stay in Hollywood was also marred by fights with the press, especially following the 1948 death of actress Carole Landis, who had been with Harrison the night before she committed suicide. Shortly after that, Harrison's contract with Fox was terminated by mutual agreement.

Returning to the stage, Harrison won the Tony Award for his 1948 performance on Broadway as King Henry VIII in Maxwell Anderson's *Anne of the Thousand Days,* and received acclaim for his performances in T. S. Eliot's *The Cocktail Party* in London and John van Druten's comedy *Bell, Book and Candle* on both sides of the Atlantic. His greatest success came in his first musical role, in the Broadway production of *My Fair Lady,* Alan Jay Lerner and Frederick Loewe's adaptation of George Bernard Shaw's *Pygmalion.* Because Harrison's singing was, as he himself admitted in a 1956 *New York Herald Tribune* interview, "dismal," he invented his own method of "talking in pitch" for the musical numbers.

After viewing Harrison's 1956 Broadway opening night performance in *My Fair Lady,* Brooks Atkinson of the *New York Times* (March 16, 1956) wrote, "Mr. Harrison is perfect in the part—crisp, lean, complacent and condescending until at last a real flare of human emotions burns the egotism away." Harrison remained with *My Fair Lady* for two years in New York and another year at London's Drury Lane Theatre.

As a result of his success in *My Fair Lady,* Harrison once again began receiving important film offers, and during the next decade he appeared in such major Hollywood productions as *Cleopatra* (1963) and *The Agony and the Ecstacy* (1965). Although not all of these films were well received by critics, Harrison generally garnered excellent personal notices in them. A number of reviewers felt that his performance as Julius Caesar stole Twentieth Century-Fox's forty-million dollar epic *Cleopatra* away from his more famous co-stars, Elizabeth Taylor and Richard Burton. Harrison was the only cast member to earn an Academy Award nomination.

Harrison's most popular movie was the 1964 film version of *My Fair Lady,* for which he won most major cinema awards, including the Oscar. A majority of critics hailed the movie as a faithful representation of the stage musical, and some, such as Judith Crist of the *New York Herald Tribune,* went so far as to say that Harrison's Higgins was "not only intact but, thanks to the intimate camera-eye, exposed in larger-than-life detail in all its brilliance. Every nuance . . . can be seen and heard as it never was on stage."

Harrison's subsequent films did not equal the success of *My Fair Lady.* After 1969, he devoted most of his energy to the stage, taking parts in such diverse plays as Luigi Pirandello's *Henry IV* and Terence Rattigan's sentimental comedy *In Praise of Love.* His 1978 return to drawing-room comedy in William Douglas-Home's *The Kingfisher* on Broadway prompted Martin Gottfried to remark in *Cue:* "Style has gone out of style, out of the theater, and out of our lives . . . I think you'd better see these two [Harrison and co-star Claudette Colbert] while you have the chance."

What may have been the most critically acclaimed performance of Harrison's acting career came in 1983, when he portrayed the aging Captain Shotover in a Broadway revival of Shaw's *Heartbreak House.* As the *New Republic*'s Robert Brustein (January 9, 1984) saw it, Harrison "proves once again that he is our supreme Shavian actor." To Walter Kerr of the *New York Times* (January 8, 1984), Harrison's Shotover was "the best work the actor has ever done," asserting that even *My Fair Lady* "was a one-note job by comparison." Kerr particularly admired Harrison's refusal to milk Shaw's lines for easy laughs.

In appraising his career in *Films in Review* (December, 1965), Rudy Behlmer wrote: "Rex Harrison has a unique acting style, and one that gives the illusion of being without pressure. But it is the craft of a hardworking perfectionist who approaches and rehearses a role with both thought and care. His stage and screen performances rank with the best acting of this generation."

ADDRESSES: AGENT—International Creative Management, Ltd., 22 Grafton Street, London W1, England.

*　　*　　*

HART, Charles   1961-

PERSONAL: Born June 3, 1961, in London, England; son of George Wilson (an antiquarian book dealer) and Juliet Lavinia (Byam-Shaw) Hart. EDUCATION: Robinson College, Cambridge University, B.A., music, 1983; studied advanced composition with Robert Saxon at the Guildhall School of Music and Dramatic Art, London, 1983-84.

CHARLES HART

VOCATION: Lyricist, composer, and writer.

WRITINGS: LYRICS—*The Phantom of the Opera* (additional lyrics by Richard Stilgoe), Her Majesty's Theatre, London, 1986; published by R.U.G., England; recorded and released by Polydor Records.

AWARDS: Best Musical (co-recipient), Laurence Olivier Award and *Evening Standard*, both 1986, for *The Phantom of the Opera*.

MEMBER: Society for the Promotion of New Music (United Kingdom), musicians union (United Kingdom), Performing Right Society, Dramatists Guild.

ADDRESSES: HOME—London, England. AGENT—Morgan & Goodman, One Old Compton Street, London W1, England.

*   *   *

HARTLEY, Mariette   1940-

PERSONAL: Born June 21, 1940; daughter of Paul Hembree (an account executive) and Mary Ickes (a saleswoman and manager; maiden name, Watson) Hartley; married Patrick Francois Boyriven (a producer), August 13, 1978; children: Sean Paul, Justine Emelia. EDUCATION: Attended Carnegie-Mellon University; studied for the theatre with Eva LeGallienne at the American Shakespeare Festival, Stratford, CT. RELIGION: Methodist.

VOCATION: Actress, television journalist, and spokeswoman.

CAREER: STAGE DEBUT—Perdita, *A Winter's Tale,* American Shakespeare Festival, Stratford, CT, 1956-57. OFF-BROADWAY DEBUT—Isabella, *Measure for Measure,* New York Shakespeare Festival in the Park, 1958-59. PRINCIPAL STAGE APPEARANCES— Portia, *The Merchant of Venice,* Goodman Theatre, Chicago, 1959; title role, *Antigone,* UCLA Theatre Group, Los Angeles, 1961-62; Marianna, *The Miser,* Mark Taper Forum, Los Angeles, 1968; Maggie, *Put Them All Together,* McCarter Theatre, Princeton, NJ, 1978 and at the Coronet Theatre, Los Angeles, 1982; Mary, *Detective Story,* Ahmanson Theatre, Los Angeles, 1984.

MAJOR TOURS—Helena, *A Midsummer Night's Dream,* and Perdita, *A Winter's Tale,* American Shakespeare Festival tour, 1959-60.

FILM DEBUT—*Ride the High Country,* 1962. PRINCIPAL FILM APPEARANCES—*Marooned,* Columbia, 1969; *Skyjacked,* Metro-Goldwyn-Mayer, 1972; *Improper Channels,* 1979.

TELEVISION DEBUT—*Gunsmoke,* CBS, 1962. PRINCIPAL TELEVISION APPEARANCES—Series: Dr. Claire Morton, *Peyton Place,* ABC, 1965; Ruth Garret, *The Hero,* NBC, 1966; Jennifer Barnes, *Goodnight, Beantown,* CBS, 1983-84; guest host, *Good Morning, America,* ABC; co-host, *The Morning Program,* CBS, 1986—. Movies: Candy Lightner, *M.A.D.D.: Mothers Against Drunk Drivers,* 1982; *Silence of the Heart,* CBS, 1984; Erica Bovza, *To Love, Honor, and Arrest,* ABC, 1986. Episodic: "Married," *The Incredible Hulk,* CBS, 1978.

RELATED CAREER—Formerly appeared on numerous television

MARIETTE HARTLEY

commercials, including award-winning roles for Polaroid cameras; founder Maraday Production company.

AWARDS: Outstanding Lead Actress in a Series, Emmy Award, 1978, for "Married," *The Incredible Hulk;* six Emmy Award nominations; three Clio Awards.

MEMBER: Actors' Equity Association, Screen Actors Guild, American Federation of Television and Radio Artists; Mothers Against Drunk Drivers (M.A.D.D.).

ADDRESSES: OFFICE—c/o *The Morning Program,* CBS Broadcast Center, Studio 43, 524 W. 57th Street, New York, NY 10019.*

*   *   *

HAUPTMAN, William   1942-

PERSONAL: Born November 26, 1942, in Wichita Falls, TX; son of Herman Ray (a geologist) and Arlene (Vanderhook) Hauptman; married Marjorie Erdreich (an actress), June 22, 1984; children: Sarah Olivia. EDUCATION: University of Texas, B.F.A., drama, 1966; Yale University School of Drama, M.F.A., playwriting, 1973.

VOCATION: Playwright.

WRITINGS: PLAYS, PRODUCED/PUBLISHED—*Shearwater,* American Place Theatre, New York City, 1974, published in *Performance* magazine, 1974; *Heat,* New York Shakespeare Festival, Public Theatre, New York City, 1975, published in *Yale/Theatre* magazine and by Samuel French, Inc.; *Domino Courts/Commanche Cafe,* American Place Theatre, 1976, published in *Performing Arts Journal* and Stanley Richards' *Best Short Plays of 1977,* also by Samuel French Inc.; *Durango Flash,* Yale Repertory Theatre, 1977; *Big River,* American Repertory Theatre, 1984, La Jolla Playhouse, 1984, Eugene O'Neill Theatre, New York City, 1985—, published by Grove Press; *Gillette,* American Repertory Theatre, 1985, La Jolla Playhouse, 1986, published by Theatre Communications Group, *Plays in Progress.*

In addition, numerous off-off Broadway and Equity Waiver showcases and regional productions by the Empty Space Theatre, Seattle, WA, St. Nicholas Theatre of Chicago, and theatres in Canada, England, and France.

TELEPLAYS—*Denmark Vesey,* PBS.

SHORT STORIES—Published in *Playboy, Atlantic Monthly,* and *The Best American Short Stories of 1982.*

NON-FICTION—Contributor to the *Atlantic Monthly.*

AWARDS: CBS grant in playwriting, 1977; National Endowment for the Arts grant in playwriting, 1977; Guggenheim grant in playwriting, 1978; Distinguished Playwriting, Obie Award, 1978, for *Domino Courts/Comanche Cafe;* Best Book of a Musical, Boston Theatre Critic's Circle Award for Best New Musical, San Diego Theatre Critic's Circle Award for Best New Play, and Antoinette Perry Award, all 1985, for *Big River;* National Association for the Advancement of Colored People (NAACP) Freedom Foundation Award and Emmy Award nomination, for *Denmark Vesey.*

MEMBER: Writers Guild of America East, Dramatists Guild.

ADDRESSES: AGENT—c/o Rick Leed, Agency for the Performing Arts, 888 Seventh Avenue, New York, NY 10106.

*   *   *

HAYDU, Peter   1948-

PERSONAL: Born June 7, 1948, in Mineola, NY; son of Bela William (a physician) and Mary Elizabeth (a flutist; maiden name, Miles) Haydu. EDUCATION: Parsons College, B.A., 1969; trained for the stage with Mira Rostova, Michael Shurtleff, and H. Neill Whiting and as a dancer with Andre Eglevski, Walter Rains, Sandy Hagaen, Jeanette Neill, and Luigi.

VOCATION: Actor and singer.

CAREER: STAGE DEBUT—Sir Evelyn, *Anything Goes,* Theatre 369, Boston, 1974. PRINCIPAL STAGE APPEARANCES—Mickey Maloy, *A Touch of the Poet,* Lyric Stage, Boston, 1980; *Forbidden Broadway,* Park Plaza Theatre, Boston, 1985-86; title role, *Billy Bishop Goes to War,* Nickerson Theatre, Boston, 1986; Orin, *Little Shop of Horrors,* Charles Playhouse, Boston, 1987.

Also, Sparkish, *The Country Wife,* Loeb Drama Center, Cambridge, MA; Florindo and Capo Comico, *A Servant of Two Masters,* Romeo, *Romeo and Juliet,* Joseph Surface, *A School for Scandal,* and Cleante, *Tartuffe,* all at Theatre of Monmouth, ME;

PETER HAYDU

various roles, *A Child's Christmas in Wales,* Eilert Loevborg, *Hedda Gabler,* and Frank Gardner, *Mrs. Warren's Profession,* all at Lyric Stage, Boston; Fred, Young Scrooge, *A Christmas Carol,* Charles Playhouse, Boston; Cratchit and Fezziwig, *A Christmas Carol,* Nickerson Theatre, Boston; Jonathan Harker, *The Passion of Dracula,* Theatre by the Sea, Portsmouth, NH; Jigger, *Carousel,* Wheelock Family Theatre; Dick Deadeye, *H.M.S. Pinafore,* Castle Hill Festival; various roles, *If the Falls Could Speak,* Merrimack Regional Theatre.

MAJOR TOURS—Narrator, *Pepsi-Cola Skate,* U.S. cities; *The Spirit of Challenge,* U.S. cities.

TELEVISION DEBUT—Defendant, "For Love or Money," *Miller's Court,* Metromedia, 1982. PRINCIPAL TELEVISION APPEAR-ANCES—Episodic: Wayne, "And Give Up Show Biz?," *Spenser for Hire,* ABC, 1986; plaintiff, "Honor Thy Parents," *Miller's Court,* Metromedia. Movies: Chauffeur, *Robert F. Kennedy and His Times,* CBS. Specials: Narrator, *Enterprize: Run for the Money,* PBS, 1986. Voice overs: *Vietnam, a Television History,* PBS; *Frontline,* PBS; *Comrades,* PBS.

PRINCIPAL FILM APPEARANCES—*Starting Over,* Paramount, 1979; *Whose Life Is It Anyway?,* United Artists, 1981; *The Bostonians,* ALMI Pictures, 1984.

PRINCIPAL RADIO WORK—Series: *The Spider's Web,* National Public Radio.

AWARDS: Commendation Awards: Actors' Equity Association and American Federation of Television and Radio Artists, for organizational work to amend tax reform legislation, 1986.

MEMBER: Actors' Equity Association, Screen Actors Guild, American Federation of Television and Radio Artists.

ADDRESSES: HOME—352 Harvard Street, Cambridge, MA 02138.

*   *   *

HAYES, Catherine Anne   1958-

PERSONAL: Born November 21, 1958, in Brooklyn, NY; daughter of Francis X. (an accountant) and Loddie (a pediatric nurse; maiden name, Krynski) Hayes; married Walter A. Ulasinski (an actor, designer, and technical director), June 16, 1979. EDUCA-TION: Trained for the theatre at the Herbert Berghof Studios and the Riverside Shakespeare Company; studied voice with Raymond McDermott.

VOCATION: Actress and model.

CAREER: STAGE DEBUT—Daisy, *The Giant, Jack & the Beanstalk Show,* Academy Arts Theatre, New York City, 1978. PRINCIPAL STAGE APPEARANCES—Sara, old woman, and lifeguard, *Red Letter Days,* Coney Island, NY, 1986; Rose Beef, *Sainte Carmen of the Main,* Cubiculo Theatre, New York City, 1986; Hedda Gabler, *The Hedda Enigma,* Manhattan Ensemble, New York City, 1987.

PRINCIPAL FILM APPEARANCES—Big Lady, *Love You to Death,* Poundridge Productions, 1987; Pharmacy clerk, *Weeds,* DeLaurentiis Entertainment Group, 1987.

CATHERINE ANNE HAYES

TELEVISION DEBUT—Mimi, "If the Shoe Fits," *Tales from the Dark Side,* syndicated, 1986.

RELATED CAREER—Has appeared in many television commercials and works as a singer and model.

MEMBER: Actors' Equity Association, Screen Actors Guild, American Federation of Television and Radio Artists, Catholic Actors Guild.

SIDELIGHTS: Catherine Anne Hayes writes to *CTFT,* "I own one Yellow Cheek Amazon parrot and I love birds. My family owns and operates 'Marlas Dogs,' specializing in mastiffs, English bulldogs, and sharpeis."

ADDRESSES: HOME—70-47 67th Street, Glendale, NY 11385.

*   *   *

HECKART, Eileen   1919-

PERSONAL: Full name, Anna Eileen Heckart; born March 29, 1919, in Columbus, OH; daughter of Leo Herbert and Esther (Stark) Heckart; married John Harrison Yankee, Jr. (an insurance broker), June 26, 1943; children: five sons. EDUCATION: Attended Ohio State University; trained for the stage at the American Theatre Wing.

VOCATION: Actress.

CAREER: BROADWAY DEBUT—Understudy and assistant stage manager, *The Voice of the Turtle*, Morosco Theatre, December 8, 1943. LONDON DEBUT—Mrs. Baker, *Butterflies Are Free*, Apollo Theatre, November 4, 1970. PRINCIPAL STAGE APPEARANCES— *Tinker's Dam*, Blackfriars Guild Theatre, 1943; appeared in *Our Town*, City Center Theatre, New York City, 1944; performed with the Shorewood Players, Milwaukee, WI, 1944-45; understudy, *Brighten the Corner*, Lyceum Theatre, New York City, 1945; Elaine, *Waltz Me Around Again*, Brighton Theatre, Brooklyn, NY, 1948; understudy, *They Knew What They Wanted*, Music Box Theatre, New York City, 1949; appeared in *The Stars Weep*, Boston, 1949; Eva Mckeon, *The Traitor*, 48th Street Theatre, New York City, 1949; Nell Bromley, *Hilda Crane*, Coronet Theatre, New York City, 1950; Valerie McGuire, *In Any Language*, Cort Theatre, New York City, 1952; Rosemary Sidney, *Picnic*, Music Box Theatre, New York City, 1953; Mrs. Daigle, *The Bad Seed*, 46th Street Theatre, New York City, 1954; Beatrice, *A View from the Bridge* and Agnes, *A Memory of Two Mondays*, both at the Coronet Theatre, New York City, 1955; Lottie Lacey, *The Dark at the Top of the Stairs*, Music Box Theatre, New York City, 1957; *Before Breakfast*, Congress Hall Theatre, Berlin, West Germany, then Theatre de Lys, New York City, 1959.

Deedee Grogan, *Invitation to a March*, Music Box Theatre, New York City, 1960; Melba Snyder, *Pal Joey*, City Center, New York City, 1961; title role, *Everybody Loves Opal*, Longacre Theatre, New York City, 1961; Tilly Siegel, *A Family Affair*, Billy Rose Theatre, New York City, 1962; Nurse Sweetie, *Too True to Be Good*, 54th Street Theatre, New York City, 1963; Regina Giddens, *The Little Foxes*, Stadium Theatre, Columbus, OH, 1964; Ruby, *And Things That Go Bump in the Night*, Royale Theatre, New York City, 1965; Mrs. Banks, *Barefoot in the Park*, Biltmore Theatre, New York City, 1965; Harriet, Edith, and Muriel, *You Know I Can't Hear You When the Water's Running*, Ambassador Theatre, New York City, 1967; Mrs. Haber, *The Mother Lover*, Booth Theatre, New York City, 1969; Mrs. Baker, *Butterflies Are Free*, Booth Theatre, New York City, 1969.

Martha, *Remember Me*, Westport Country Playhouse, CT, 1972; the woman, *Veronica's Room*, Music Box Theatre, New York City, 1973; title role, *Mother Courage and Her Children*, McCarter Theatre, Princeton, NJ, 1975; Mrs. Gibbs, *Our Town*, Stratford, CT, 1975; Bella Gardner, *Ladies at the Alamo*, Martin Beck Theatre, New York City, 1977; Thelma Cates, *'Night, Mother*, Westport Country Playhouse, CT, 1985.

MAJOR TOURS—*Janie*, U.S. cities, 1944; *Windy Hill*, U.S. cities, 1945; Leora Samish, *The Time of the Cuckoo*, U.S. cities, 1964; Beatrice, *The Effect of Gamma Rays on Man-in-the-Moon Marigolds*, U.S. cities, 1971; Eleanor Roosevelt, *Eleanor*, U.S. cities, 1976.

FILM DEBUT—*Miracle in the Rain*, Warner Brothers, 1956. PRINCIPAL FILM APPEARANCES—*Bad Seed*, Warner Brothers, 1956; *Bus Stop*, Twentieth Century-Fox, 1956; *Somebody Up There Likes Me*, Metro-Goldwyn-Mayer, 1957; *Hot Spell*, Paramount, 1958; *Heller in Pink Tights*, Paramount, 1960; *My Six Loves*, Paramount, 1963; *Up the Down Staircase*, Warner Brothers, 1967; *No Way to Treat a Lady*, Paramount, 1968; *Butterflies Are Free*, Columbia, 1972; *Zandy's Bride*, Warner Brothers, 1974; *The Hiding Place*, World Wide Pictures, 1975; *Burnt Offerings*, United Artists, 1976.

TELEVISION DEBUT—1947. PRINCIPAL TELEVISION APPEARANCES—Series: Aunt, *The Mary Tyler Moore Show*, CBS, 1976;

Eleanor Roosevelt, *Back Stairs at the White House*, NBC, 1979; Boss Angel, *Out of the Blue*, ABC, 1979; Amy Decker, *Trauma Center*, ABC, 1983; Jeanine, *Partners in Crime*, NBC, 1984.

Episodic: *The New Breed*, ABC, 1964; *The Fugitive*, ABC, 1964; *Eleventh Hour*, NBC, 1964; *The Doctors and Nurses*, CBS, 1965; *Naked City*, ABC, 1965; *Gunsmoke*, CBS, 1965; *The F.B.I.*, ABC, 1965; *Girl Talk*, ABC, 1966; *Ben Casey*, ABC, 1966; *Felony Squad*, ABC, 1966; *The Defenders*, CBS, 1967; "Secrets" and "The Web," both on *CBS Playhouse*, CBS, 1968; also appeared on *Kraft Suspense Theatre*, NBC; *Philco Playhouse*, NBC. Teleplays: Clara, "Save Me a Place at Forest Lawn," and Beatrice, "The Effect of Gamma Rays on Man-in-the-Moon Marigolds," both *New York Television Theatre*, PBS, 1966.

AWARDS: Outer Circle Award, Daniel Blum Citation Award, both 1953, for *Picnic;* Character Actress of the Year, Sylvania Award, 1954; Donaldson Award, 1955, for *Bad Seed;* Foreign Press Award, Academy Award nomination, Film Daily Citation Award, all 1956, for *Bad Seed;* Best Supporting Actress, New York Drama Critics Award, 1958, for *Dark at the Top of the Stairs;* Emmy Award, 1967, for "Save Me a Place at Forest Lawn," *New York Television Theatre;* Antoinette Perry Award nomination, 1970, for *Butterflies Are Free;* Strawhat Award, 1972, for *Remember Me*, also 1975, 1977; Best Supporting Actress, Academy Award, 1973, for *Butterflies Are Free;* also received the March of Dimes Award, Ohio State University Centennial Award, and the Aegis Award, all 1970; Governor's Award, Ohio, 1977, Ohiana Library Award, 1978. Honorary degrees: Doctor of Laws, Sacred Heart University, 1973.

MEMBER: Actors' Equity Association, American Federation of Radio and Television Artists, Screen Actors Guild; Phi Beta (pledge president, 1938, rush chairman, 1940, president, 1941).

ADDRESSES: HOME—135 Comstock Hill Road, New Canaan, CT 06840. AGENT—International Creative Management, 40 W. 57th Street, New York, NY 10019.*

*   *   *

HEFFERNAN, John   1934-

PERSONAL: Born May 30, 1934, in New York, NY. EDUCATION: Attended City College of New York and Columbia University; Boston University, B.F.A.

VOCATION: Actor.

CAREER: OFF-BROADWAY DEBUT—Arthur Olden, *The Judge*, Masque Theatre, 1958. PRINCIPAL STAGE APPEARANCES—At the Charles Street Playhouse, Boston: Judge Cool, *The Grass Harp* and Eddie Carbone, *A View from the Bridge*, also in *Blood Wedding*, *The Iceman Cometh*, *Hotel Paradiso*, *Shadow of a Gunman*, and *The Crucible;* Lepidus, *Julius Caesar*, New York Shakespeare Festival (NYSF), New York City, 1959; Older Draftsman, *The Great God Brown*, Coronet Theatre, New York City, 1959; with the Phoenix Theatre, New York City: Lykon, *Lysistrata*, 1959, Aase's Father, *Peer Gynt*, various roles, *Henry IV, Part I*, Robert Shallow and a Drawer, *Henry IV, Part II*, Tony Lumpkin, *She Stoops to Conquer*, and Young Covey, *The Plough and the Stars*, all 1960, Jacob McCloskey, *The Octoroon*, Polonius, *Hamlet*, and Androcles, *Androcles and the Lion*, all 1961.

Tailor and Pedant, *The Taming of the Shrew*, NYSF, New York City, 1960; Galy Gay, *A Man's a Man*, Masque Theatre, New York City, 1962; Old Shepherd, *The Winter's Tale* and Touchstone, *As You Like It*, both NYSF, New York City, 1963; Weinard, *Luther* and later the title role, St. James Theatre, New York City, 1963; Subtle, *The Alchemist*, Gate Theatre, New York City, 1964; Butler, *Tiny Alice*, Billy Rose Theatre, New York City, 1964; *Postmark Zero*, Brooks Atkinson Theatre, New York City, 1965; Kermit, *Malcolm*, Shubert Theatre, New York City, 1966; Captain Bluntschli, *Arms and the Man*, Sheridan Square Playhouse, New York City, 1967; the Inquisitor, *Saint Joan*, Vivian Beaumont Theatre, New York City, 1968; Chorus Leader, *Final Solutions*, Felt Forum Theatre, New York City, 1968; Jan Ballas, *The Memorandum*, NYSF, Anspacher Theatre, New York City, 1968; John Rocky Park, *Woman Is My Ideal*, Belasco Theatre, New York City, 1968; Tillich, "Morning," Kerry, "Noon" and Robin Breast Western, "Night," in the play *Morning, Noon, and Night*, Henry Miller's Theatre, New York City, 1968; Cincinnatus the Prisoner, *Invitation to a Beheading*, NYSF, Public Theatre, New York City, 1969; Solveig's Father, Priest, and Button Moulder, *Peer Gynt*, NYSF, Delacorte Theatre, New York City, 1969.

Old Captain, *Purlie*, Broadway Theatre, New York City, 1970; Seumas Shields, *The Shadow of a Gunman*, Sheridan Square Playhouse, New York City, 1972; Bernard Shaw, *Dear Liar*, Syracuse Repertory Company, NY, 1973; Jason Pepper, "Ravenswoood" and Hugh Gumbo, "Dunelawn," together in a double bill entitled *Bad Habits*, Booth Theatre, New York City, 1974; Hatch, *The Sea*, Manhattan Theatre Club, New York City, 1975; Professor Arnholm, *The Lady from the Sea*, Circle in the Square, New York City, 1976; Abe, *Knock Knock*, Biltmore Theatre, New York City, 1976; Lawyer Craven, *Sly Fox*, Broadhurst Theatre, New York City, 1976.

Aristarkh Dominikovich Grand-Skubik, *The Suicide*, American National Theatre and Academy (ANTA) Theatre, 1980; Old Actor, *The Fantasticks*, Sullivan Street Playhouse, New York City, 1981; Caterpiller and Sheep, *Alice in Wonderland*, Virginia Theatre, New York City, 1982-83.

MAJOR TOURS—Title role, *Luther*, U.S. cities, 1963.

PRINCIPAL STAGE WORK—Co-producer, *The Shadow of a Gunman*, Sheridan Square Playhouse, New York City, 1972, and Syracuse Repertory Company, NY, 1973.

PRINCIPAL FILM APPEARANCES—*The Sting*, Universal, 1973; *The Time of the Heathen*.

PRINCIPAL TELEVISION APPEARANCES—Episodic: *Camera Three*, CBS; *Look Up and Live*, CBS; *Hawk*, ABC; *New York Television Theatre*, PBS; *Experiment in TV*, NBC; *The Catholic Hour*, NBC; *Directions '66*, ABC.

RELATED CAREER—Co-founder, Charles Street Playhouse, Boston.

AWARDS: Obie Award, 1960; Best Performance by an Actor in a Supporting Role, *Variety* Critics Poll Award, 1965, for *Tiny Alice*.

MEMBER: Actors' Equity Association, Screen Actors Guild, American Federation of Television and Radio Artists.

ADDRESSES: AGENT—Triad Artists, 888 Seventh Avenue, Suite 1602, New York, NY 10106.*

HEMINGWAY, Alan 1951-

PERSONAL: Born September 2, 1951, in Salt Lake City, UT. EDUCATION: Portland State University, B.A., 1973, M.A., 1976; Ph.D. candidate, City University of New York; trained for the theatre with Nikos Psacharapolous at the Circle in the Square Professional Theatre Workshop.

VOCATION: Actor, stage manager, and choreographer.

CAREER: STAGE DEBUT—Prince, *The King and I*, Billings Theatre, Billings, MT, 1962. OFF-BROADWAY DEBUT—The Mute, *The Fantasticks*, Sullivan Street Playhouse, 1978. PRINCIPAL STAGE APPEARANCES—Ed Devery, *Born Yesterday*, Thunderbird Dinner Theatre, NJ, 1978; Officer Klien, *Arsenic & Old Lace*, Angie and Patsy, *Gypsy*, and Protean, *A Funny Thing Happened on the Way to the Forum*, all at the Meadowbrook Theatre, Rochester, MI, 1979; Knave, *The Passion of Alice*, Greenwich Mews Theatre, New York City, 1979; Young Scrooge, *Mr. Scrooge*, Trinity Theatre, New York City, 1980; Mortimer, *The Fantasticks*, Barter Theatre, Abingdon, VA, 1981; Jonathan Wilde, *Children of Darkness*, Trinity Theatre, New York City, 1981.

MAJOR TOURS—Mortimer, *The Fantasticks*, toured Virginia with the Barter Theatre Company, 1981.

FILM DEBUT—Tophat, *The Warriors*, Paramount, 1979.

PRINCIPAL STAGE WORK—Stage manager for: *The Fantasticks*, TheatreWorks USA, New York City Ballet; choreographer: *You Never Know*, *The Boyfriend*, *Anything Goes*, *The Fantasticks*, *Man of La Mancha*.

AWARDS: Award for Excellence in the Theatre, Kennedy Center, 1972.

MEMBER: Actors' Equity Association.

ADDRESSES: HOME—370 Columbus Ave. New York, NY 10024.

* * *

HEWITT, Alan 1915-1986

PERSONAL: Born January 21, 1915, in New York, NY; died of cancer in New York, NY, November 7, 1986; son of William M. (an advertiser and publisher) and Hortense J. (a manufacturer; maiden name, Baum) Hewitt. EDUCATION: Dartmouth College, B.A., 1934; studied acting with Benno Schneider, 1937, and at the American Theatre Wing, 1946-51; also studied voice with Clytie Hine Mundy, 1947-51. MILITARY: U.S. Army, 1943-46.

VOCATION: Actor and director.

CAREER: STAGE DEBUT—*The Death of Bad Grammar*, P.S. 6, New York City, 1925. BROADWAY DEBUT—Lucentio, *The Taming of the Shrew*, Guild Theatre, 1935. PRINCIPAL STAGE APPEARANCES—Mose, *The Pursuit of Happiness*, Douglas Helder, *Interference*, Tom Crosby, *Song and Dance Man*, Philip, *You Never Can Tell*, Al Diamond, *Minick*, and Lord Clinton, *Mary Tudor*, all in Cohasset, MA, 1934; CT, Dorilant, *The Country Wife*, Sergeant Duval, *Ode to Liberty*, and interned officer, *The Coward*, all Westport Country Playhouse, NY, 1935.

First Officer, *Idiot's Delight,* Shubert Theatre, New York City, 1936; Jeremy, *Love for Love,* Pat, *Dr. Knock,* Juggins, *Fanny's First Play,* and music master, *The Would-Be Gentleman,* all at the Westport Country Playhouse, 1936; Clayton Herrick, *The Golden Journey,* Booth Theatre, New York City, 1936; Fritzi, *The Masque of Kings* and Warrior, *Amphitryon 38,* both Shubert Theatre, New York City, 1937; Yacov, *The Seagull,* Shubert Theatre, New York City, 1938; Martin Holme, *The Ghost of Yankee Doodle,* Wolf Beifeld, *Liliom,* Honorable Alan Howard, *French without Tears,* and Clendon Wyatt, *Rain from Heaven,* all at the Lydia Mendelsohn Theatre, Ann Arbor, MI, 1938; Bill Chapman, *Away from It All,* Rockridge Theatre, Carmel, NY, 1938; David Kingsley, *Stage Door* and *One for the Money,* both Suffern, NY, 1938; Toby Cartwright, *Ways and Means,* Alec Harvey, *Still Life,* Homer Sampson, *Grandpa,* Honorable Alan Howard, *French without Tears,* and Corbier, *Cognac,* all Casino Theatre, Newport, RI, 1938; Mago, *The Road to Rome,* Maplewood, NJ, and Albany, NY, 1938; Alex Hewitt, *The American Way,* Center Theatre, New York City, 1939; Philip Graves, *Here Today,* Berkshire Playhouse, Stockbridge, MA, 1939; David F. Winmore, *Love's Old Sweet Song,* Plymouth Theatre, New York City, 1940.

Lawrence Vail, *Once in a Lifetime,* Suffern, NY, 1941; Wilfred Marks, *The Walrus and the Carpenter,* Cort Theatre, New York City, 1941; Captain Loft, *The Moon Is Down,* Martin Beck Theatre, New York City, 1942; Tony Kenyon, *Skylark* and Captain Jensen, *The Skull Beneath,* both stock productions, 1947; Morgan Kilpatrick, *The Gentleman from Athens,* Mansfield Theatre, New York City, 1947; Howard Wagner, *Death of a Salesman,* Morosco Theatre, New York City, 1949; Pemberton Maxwell, *Call Me Madam,* Imperial Theatre, New York City, 1950.

Valentine, *You Never Can Tell* and Lord Allan Frobisher, *Jane,* both at the Berkshire Playhouse, 1953; Lord Chamberlain and First Judge, *Ondine,* 46th Street Theatre, New York City, 1954; Cardinal Richelieu, *The Three Musketeers,* St. Louis Municipal Opera Theatre, MO, 1956; E.K. Hornbeck, *Inherit the Wind,* National Theatre, New York City, 1955; Angelo, *Measure for Measure,* Library of Congress Theatre, Washington, DC, 1958; Judge Michael Lengel, *Outrage,* Eisenhower Theatre, Kennedy Center, Washington, DC, 1982.

MAJOR TOURS—Delivery boy, *Bring on the Girls,* U.S. cities, 1934; third huntsman and Philip, *The Taming of the Shrew,* U.S. cities, 1935; Sir James Fenton, *Petticoat Fever,* Frederick Ogden, *The Virginian,* and Boze Hertzlinger, *The Petrified Forest,* all U.S. cities, 1937; Lucentio, *The Taming of the Shrew,* U.S. cities, 1939-40; Warwick Wilson, *Biography,* Brooks, *The Bat,* Alastair Fitzfassenden, *The Millionairess,* and Philip Graves, *Here Today,* all 1940; Rudd Kendall, *Old Acquaintance,* 1942.

PRINCIPAL STAGE WORK—Director: *Bus Stop,* Berkshire Playhouse, 1957; *Inherit the Wind,* Grist Mill Playhouse, Andover, NJ, 1957; *Who Was That Lady I Saw You With?,* Bucks County Playhouse, New Hope, PA, 1959.

FILM DEBUT—Matt Helmsley, *Career,* 1959. PRINCIPAL FILM APPEARANCES—*A Private's Affairs,* Twentieth Century-Fox, 1959; *The Absent Minded Professor,* Buena Vista, 1961; *Bachelor in Paradise,* Metro-Goldwyn-Mayer (MGM), 1961; *Follow That Dream,* United Artists, 1962; Dr. Gruber, *That Touch of Mink,* Universal, 1962; *Days of Wine and Roses,* Warner Brothers, 1962; *Son of Flubber,* Buena Vista, 1963; *The Misadventures of Merlin Jones,* Buena Vista, 1964; *How to Murder Your Wife,* United Artists, 1965; *The Monkey's Uncle,* Buena Vista, 1965; *The Horse in the Gray Flannel Suit,* Buena Vista, 1968; *The Brotherhood,* Paramount, 1968; *Sweet Charity,* Universal, 1969; *The Computer Wore Tennis Shoes,* Buena Vista, 1970; *R.P.M.,* Columbia, 1970; *The Barefoot Executive,* Buena Vista, 1971; *Now You See Him, Now You Don't,* Buena Vista, 1972; *The Seniors,* 1978.

PRINCIPAL TELEVISION APPEARANCES—Series: Det. Bill Brennan, *My Favoriet Martian,* CBS, 1964-66. Episodic: *Alfred Hitchcock Presents; The Defenders; Dr. Kildare; Perry Mason; U.S. Steel Hour; Omnibus; Bewitched; Gomer Pyle; I Dream of Jeannie; Lost in Space; Love, American Style; Daktari; Bob Newhart Show; Slattery's People; Hec Ramsay; Wild, Wild West; Felony Squad; Movie of the Week; NBC World Premier.* Movies: *Pueblo.* Mini-Series: *The Adams Chronicles.*

PRINCIPAL RADIO WORK—*Theatre Guild on the Air; NBC Calvalcade; The Greatest Story Ever Told; Famous Jury Trials; Radio Reader's Digest.*

RELATED CAREER—Actors' Equity Association council, 1940-51, House Affairs Committee, 1963-81; Drama League advisory committee, 1972-82; Actors Fund board of trustees, 1971-86, executive committee, 1977-86, chairman, 1981-86; Friends of Dartmouth Library executive committee, 1970-80.

WRITINGS: ESSAYS—Wrote an essay on American acting in the twentieth century in the *The American Theatre: A Sum of Its Parts,* Samuel French. Essays have also been included in *The New Republic, Theatre Arts, Equity Magazine, Equity News, Screen Actor, The New York Times.*

RECORDINGS: ALBUMS—More than 225 books for the blind and physically handicapped for the American Foundation for the Blind, Talking Book Program of the Library of Congress.

MEMBER: Actors' Equity Association, Screen Actors Guild, American Federation of Television and Radio Artists, Drama League; Actors Fund.

SIDELIGHTS: Alan Hewitt served as the Actors' Equity Association's unofficial archivist and statistician. He compiled valuable annual charts tabulating Equity employment. He also prepared the chronology of the careers of Alfred Lunt and Lynn Fontanne that was printed in the program book for the American National Theatre Academy (ANTA)/West tribute to the Lunts on June 11, 1972. He compiled the same type of chronology for Helen Hayes on the ocassion of the ANTA/West salute to her on July 6, 1976.

*   *   *

HILL, Ann Stahlman   1921-

PERSONAL: Born April 15, 1921, in Nashville, TN; daughter of James Geddes (a newspaper publisher) and Mildred Porter (Thornton) Stahlman; married George de Roulahac Hill (a public relations executive), September 23, 1947; children: Mary, George Jr., Margaret, Thomas. EDUCATION: Vanderbilt University, B.A., 1943. POLITICS: Republican. RELIGION: Episcopalian. MILITARY: U.S. Naval Reserve, Lieutenant (j.g.), 1943-46.

VOCATION: Arts administrator.

CAREER: PRINCIPAL THEATRE WORK—With the Nashville Academy Theatre (formerly Nashville Children's Theatre): Set and costume designer, 1947; member of board of directors, thirty-three years, secretary, treasurer, and president, 1956-58; persuaded city to provide $250,000 bond issue to build theatre, 1960. With the Southeastern Theatre Conference: First chairman, Children's Theatre Division; administrative vice-president, vice-president, and president, 1962-63; chairman, New Play Project; chairman, Honors and Nominations; member, Ways and Means Committee; member, Endowment Fund Committee; member, Ethics Committee.

With the Children's Theatre Association of America: Chairman, Ways and Means Committee, 1959-62; member, governing board, 1960-63; comptroller, 1962-66; vice-president, 1967-69; president, 1969-71; delegate to White House Conference on Children, 1970; chairman, Future Policy Committee, 1972-73; chairman, Winifred Ward Scholarship Committee, 1978-80.

U.S. Center for ASSITEJ, (International Association of Theatre for Children and Youth): Executive Secretary-Treasurer, 1967-73; U.S. delegate to congresses and meetings in London, Moscow, The Hague, Venice, Montreal, Albany, NY, Madrid.

Tennessee Theatre Association: Founder and first program chairman, 1968; vice-president for Middle Tennessee, 1968-69; member, Curriculum Committee; member, By-laws Committee.

American Educational Theatre Association/American Theatre Association: Member, Awards and Honors Committee, 1962-63; member, Finance Committee, 1969-71, chairman, 1971; member, Structure Committee, 1967-71; vice-president for administration,

1972-73; president, 1975; member, executive committee and board of directors, 1969-78; elected to College of Fellows, 1975, chairman, 1980-82.

Member, board of trustees, American National Theatre and Academy (ANTA), 1961-64; member, board of trustees, Children's Theatre Foundation, 1967—; member, theatre advisory panel, Tennessee Arts Commission, 1968-76; member, drama advisory panel, Kentucky Arts Commission, 1975; vice-chairman, Tennessee Alliance for Arts Education, 1975-82; vice-chairman, Nashville Institute for the Arts, 1978; member, board of directors, Tennesseans for the Arts, 1981, secretary, 1984; Women's Advisory Committee, Tennessee Performing Arts Foundation, 1975-80; U.S. delegate for theatre to joint Roumanian-U.S. Conference on Arts Education, 1975.

RELATED CAREER—Reporter and drama writer, "Nashville Banner," 1964-73.

AWARDS: Distinguished Service Award, Southeastern Theatre Conference, 1973; Distinguished Service Award, Tennessee Theatre Association, 1975; Jennie Heiden Award for Service to Professional Children's Theatre, 1975; Main auditorium of Nashville Academy Theatre named the Ann Stahlman Hill Auditorium, 1979.

MEMBER: American Theatre Association, Southeastern Theatre Conference, Tennessee Theatre Association.

ADDRESSES: HOME—201 Lynwood Blvd., Nashville, TN 37205.

*   *   *

ANN STAHLMAN HILL

HILLARY, Ann   1930-

PERSONAL: Born Ann-Margaret Francis, January 8, 1930; daughter of Paul (a coal operator) and Sally (Bailey) Francis; married Frederick Knott (a playwright), November 10, 1953; children: Anthony Frederick. EDUCATION: Attended University of Kentucky and Northwestern University; American Academy of Dramatic Arts, 1949; studied at the Herbert Berghof Studio in New York and with Sanford Meisner.

VOCATION: Actress.

CAREER: STAGE DEBUT—Judy, *Junior Miss,* Fitchburg Playhouse, MA, 1941. BROADWAY DEBUT—Vicki Holly, *Be Your Age,* 48th Street Theatre, 1953. PRINCIPAL STAGE APPEARANCES—Agnes Sorel, *The Lark,* Longacre Theatre, New York City, 1955; Jean Stratton, "Table Number Seven" and Jean Tanner, "Table by the Window," both part of *Separate Tables,* Music Box Theatre, New York City, 1956; Barbara Allen, *Dark of the Moon,* Carnegie Hall Playhouse, New York City, 1958.

Mme. Maute der Fluerville, *Total Eclipse,* West Side Arts Theatre, New York City, 1984; Mrs. McPhail, *Rain,* Bertha Katz, *Paradise Lost,* standby for Geraldine Page, *The Inheritors,* Constance, *The Madwoman of Chaillot,* standby, Mrs. Martyn, *Clarence,* all with the Mirror Repertory Company, New York City, 1984-85; replaced the role of Soot, *The Marriage of Bette & Boo,* New York Shakespeare Festival, Public Theatre, New York City, 1985; standby Lady Kitty, *The Circle,* Mirror Repertory Company, 1986; has also appeared as the Aunt, *South,* H.B. Playwrights Foundation and

ANN HILLARY

in *Tobacco Road*, White Barn Theatre, Irwin, PA; appeared at the Elitch Gardens Theatre, Denver, CO, Newport Playhouse, RI, and the Worcester Playhouse in MA.

PRINCIPAL FILM APPEARANCES—Sister Mary E. Fellows, *The Rosary Murders*, upcoming.

PRINCIPAL TELEVISION APPEARANCES—Series: Henry's girl, *The Aldrich Family*, NBC, 1949-53; *The Brighter Day*, NBC. Episodic: *Tales from the Darkside*, 1985; *Playhouse 90*, CBS; *Kraft Theatre*, NBC; *Armstrong Circle Theatre*, NBC; *Broadway TV Theatre*, NBC; *The Verdict Is Yours*, CBS; *The Paul Winchell Show*, CBS.

MEMBER: Actors' Equity Association, Screen Actors Guild, American Federation of Radio and Television Artists.

ADDRESSES: HOME—108 Westerly Road, Princeton NJ, 08540.

*   *   *

HIRSCH, Judd   1935-

PERSONAL: Born March 15, 1935, in New York, NY; son of Joseph Sidney (an electrician) and Sally (Kitzis) Hirsch; children: Alexander. EDUCATION: Studied architecture at Cooper Union, NY, 1957; City College of New York, B.S., physics, 1960; studied for the theatre at the American Academy of Dramatic Arts and at the

Herbert Berghof Studios and at the Gene Frankel Studio, with Bill Hickey and Viveca Lindfors. RELIGION: Jewish. MILITARY: U.S. Army.

VOCATION: Actor and director.

CAREER: STAGE DEBUT—Villain, *Crisis in the Old Sawmill*, Back Room, Estes Park, CO, 1962. OFF-BROADWAY DEBUT—Lead role, *On the Necessity of Being Polygamous*, Gramercy Arts Theatre, 1964. PRINCIPAL STAGE APPEARANCES—*Diary of a Madman, The Fantasticks, The Threepenny Opera,* and *My Fair Lady,* all Woodstock Playhouse, Woodstock, NY, 1964; telephone man, *Barefoot in the Park,* Biltmore Theatre, New York City, 1966-67; Harold Wonder, *Scuba Duba,* New Theatre, New York City, 1967-69; member of the acting company, Theatre of the Living Arts, Philadelphia, 1969-70.

Senator, *King of the United States,* Westbeth Theatre, New York City, 1972; Senator, *Mystery Play,* Cherry Lane Theatre, New York City, 1972; Bill, *Hot L Baltimore,* Circle Repertory Company, New York City, 1972, then Circle in the Square, New York City, 1973; Wiseman, *Knock, Knock,* Circle Repertory Theatre, New York City, 1975, then Biltmore Theatre, New York City, 1976; George Schneider, *Chapter Two,* Ahmanson Theatre, Los Angeles, 1977, then Imperial Theatre, New York City, 1978; Matt Friedman, *Talley's Folly,* Circle Repertory Company, New York City, 1979, Mark Taper Forum, Los Angeles, 1979, Brooks Atkinson Theatre, New York City, 1980, and Elitch Theatre, Denver, 1981; Trigorin, *The Seagull,* Circle Repertory Company, New York City, 1983; Nat, *I'm Not Rappaport,* American Place

JUDD HIRSCH

Theatre, New York City, 1985, then Booth Theatre, New York City, 1986.

MAJOR TOURS—Peter, *Peterpat,* Houston and Fort Worth dinner theatre, 1970; Wilson, *Harvey,* Chicago, 1971; Nat, *I'm Not Rappaport,* U.S. cities, 1986-87.

PRINCIPAL STAGE WORK—Director: *Squaring the Circle,* Back Room, Estes Park, CO, 1962; *Not Enough Rope,* Circle Repertory Company, New York City, 1974; *Talley's Folly,* Elitch Theatre, Denver, 1981.

FILM DEBUT—*King of the Gypsies,* 1978. PRINCIPAL FILM APPEARANCES—Dr. Berger, *Ordinary People,* 1980; Detective Al Minetti, *Without a Trace,* 1983; Arthur Korman, *The Goodbye People,* 1984; Roger Reubel, *Teachers,* 1984.

TELEVISION DEBUT—Murray Stone, *The Law,* 1974. PRINCIPAL TELEVISION APPEARANCES—Series: Sergeant Dominick Delvecchio, *Delvecchio,* CBS, 1976-77; Alex Rieger, *Taxi,* ABC 1978-1983, then NBC, 1982-1983. Movies: *The Keegans,* 1975; *The Legend of Valentino,* 1975; *Medical Story,* 1975; *Fear on Trial,* 1975; *Sooner or Later,* 1978; *Marriage Is Alive and Well in the U.S.A.,* 1980; Dr. Petrofsky, *First Steps,* CBS, 1984; *Brotherly Love,* CBS, 1984; *Detective in the House,* CBS, 1985.

Specials: Dracula, *The Halloween That Almost Wasn't;* Pontius Pilate, *The Resurrection.*

NON-RELATED CAREER—Worked as a busboy, hospital bill collector, summer camp driver, library page, and law office clerk.

WRITINGS: ARTICLES—"Andy Kaufman, 1949-84," *Rolling Stone,* July 5, 1984.

AWARDS: Drama Desk Award, 1976, for *Knock, Knock;* Obie Award, and Antoinette Perry Award nomination, both 1979, for *Talley's Folley;* Best Supporting Actor, Academy Award nomination, 1980, for *Ordinary People;* Best Actor in a Comedy Series, Emmy Awards, 1981 and 1983, for *Taxi;* Best Actor, Antoinette Perry Award, 1986, for *I'm Not Rappaport.*

MEMBER: Actors' Equity Association, American Federation of Television and Radio Artists, Screen Actors Guild; Circle Repertory Company, 1972—.

ADDRESSES: AGENT—Mort Leavy, 79 Madison Avenue, New York, NY 10016.

*   *   *

HOCHWAELDER, Fritz   1911-1986

PERSONAL: Born May 28, 1911, in Vienna, Austria; emigrated to Switzerland, 1938; died of a heart attack in Zurich, Switzerland, October 20, 1986; son of Leonhard (an upholsterer) and Therese (Koenig) Hochwaelder; married Ursula Buchi, July 26, 1951 (marriage ended); married Susan Schreiner, July 20, 1960; children: (second marriage) Monique. EDUCATION: Attended elementary school in Vienna, Austria and later studied in evening classes at Volkshochschule.

VOCATION: Writer.

CAREER: PRINCIPAL STAGE WORK—Playwright. Plays performed in small theatres in Vienna, Austria, 1932, 1936; writer in Zurich, Switzerland, 1945—.

NON-RELATED CAREER—Served as an apprentice upholsterer as his first plays were being produced in Vienna.

WRITINGS: PLAYS, PRODUCED AND PUBLISHED—*Das heilige Experiment,* first produced as five-act, 1943, subsequently presented in two acts in Paris as *Sur La Terre comme au Ciel,* then in London and New York as *The Strong Are Lonely,* published by Volksverlag Elgg, 1947, translation of the French play by Eva le Gallienne published as *The Strong Are Lonely,* Samuel French, 1954, German version in *Oesterreichisches Theatre,* published by Buechergilde Gutenbert, 1964; *Der Unschuldige (The Innocent),* first produced, 1958, privately printed in Zurich, 1949, published by Volksverlag Elgg, 1958.

Donadieu, first produced, 1953, published by Paul Zsolnay, Hamburg, 1953, and Harrap, England, 1967; *Der oeffentliche Anklaeger,* first produced, 1948, published by Paul Zsolnay, 1954, translation by Kitty Black published as *The Public Prosecuter,* Samuel French, 1958, edition in German published by Methuen, 1962; *Hotel du commerce,* first produced, 1944, published by Volksverlag Elgg, 1954; *Der Fluechtling (The Fugitive),* first produced, 1945, published by Volksverlag Elgg, 1955; *Die Herberge (The Shelter),* first produced, 1956, published by Volksverlag Elgg, 1956; *Meier Helmbrecht,* first produced, 1946, published by Volksverlag Elgg, 1956; *Dramen I* (a collection including "Das heilige Experiment," "Die Herberge," and "Donnerstag"; "Donnerstag" first produced at Salzburg Festival, Vienna, Austria, 1959), published by Albert Langen/Georg Mueller, 1959; *Esther,* first produced, 1940, published by Volksverlag Elgg, 1960.

Dramen II (a collection including "Der oeffentliche Anklaeger," "Der Unschuldige," and "1003"; "1003" first produced, 1963), published by Albert Langen/Georg Mueller, 1964; *Der Himbeerpfluecker,* first produced, 1964, translation by Michael Bullock produced in London as *The Raspberry Picker,* 1967, published by Albert Langen/Georg Mueller, 1965, English translation by Martin Esslin published in *The New Theatre of Europe,* Delta, 1970; *Dramen* (a collection including "Esther," "Das heilige Experiment," "Hotel du commerce," "Meier Helmbrecht," "Der oeffentliche Anklaeger," "Donadieu," "Die Herberge," "Der Unschuldige," "Der Himbeerpfluecker," and "Der Befehl"), published in two volumes by Verlag Styria, Graz, 1975; *Lazaretti: oder, Der Sae beltiger,* produced at the Saltzburg Festival, 1975, published by Verlag Styria, 1975.

Also *Die Prinzessin von Chimay,* 1981; *Der Verschwundene Mond,* 1982; *Die Burgschaft,* 1984.

TELEPLAYS—"The Public Prosecuter," *U.S. Steel Hour,* CBS, 1958; *Der Befehl,* Eurovisions-Zentrale, Stiasny, 1967, English translation by Robin Hirsch published in *Modern International Drama,* Volume III, Number 2, Pennsylvania State University Press, 1970.

AWARDS: Literary Prize Award, City of Vienna, 1955; Grillparzer Prize Award, Austrian Academy of Sciences, 1956; Anton Wildgans Prize of Austrian Industry, Austria, 1963; Austrian State Prize for Literature, 1966; Oesterreichisches Ehrenkreuz fuer Kunst und Wissenschaft, 1971; Ehrenring der Stadt Wien, 1972.

MEMBER: P.E.N. (Austria), Societe des Auteurs (Paris), Schweizer Schriftsteller-Verein, Vereinigung oesterreichischer Dramatiker.*

JANE HOFFMAN

HOFFMAN, Jane 1911-

PERSONAL: Full name, Jane Ruth Hoffman; born July 24, 1911, in Seattle, WA; daughter of Samuel Lewis (a salesman) and Marguerite (Kirschbaum) Hoffman; married James W. McGlone, Jr. (a businessman), July, 1936 (divorced, 1945); married William Friedberg (a writer), December 9, 1945 (divorced, 1950); married Richard McMurray (an actor), September 9, 1950 (divorced, 1969); children: (third marriage) Samuel. EDUCATION: University of California, B.A., 1931; studied with Maria Ouspenskaya and Tamara Daykarhanova, New York City, 1934-35; and at the Actors Studio, New York City; studied voice with Robert Fram, 1940-50.

VOCATION: Actress and teacher.

CAREER: STAGE DEBUT—The kid, *The Poor Nut,* Henry Duffy Stock Company, Seattle, 1926. BROADWAY DEBUT—*'Tis of Thee,* revue, Maxine Elliott Theatre, October 26, 1940. PRINCIPAL STAGE APPEARANCES—*Crazy with the Heat,* Lowes State Theatre, New York City, then Buffalo, NY, 1941; appeared in *The Desert Song* and *The New Moon,* both at the Paper Mill Playhouse, Millburn, NJ, 1942; understudy, Betty-Jean, *Something for the Boys,* Alvin Theatre, New York City, 1943; Rose and understudy Molly, *One Touch of Venus,* Imperial Theatre, New York City, 1943; Lotus, *Calico Wedding,* National Theatre, New York City, 1945; Mrs. James, *Mermaids Singing,* Empire Theatre, New York City, 1945; Sister, *The Constant Wife,* John Drew Theatre, East Hampton, NY, 1946; Dagmar, *The Trial of Mary Dugan,* Bucks County Playhouse, New Hope, PA, 1947; Marion Froude, *Biography,* Hunterdon Hills Playhouse, NJ, 1947; Miss Evans, *A Temporary Island,* Maxine Elliot Theatre, New York City, 1948; appeared

in *Chicken Every Sunday* and *Twentieth Century,* both Olney Playhouse, MD, 1948; Mrs. Whiting, *A Story for Strangers,* Royale Theatre, New York City, 1948; Miss Johnson, *Two Blind Mice,* Cort Theatre, New York City, 1949; Liz, *The Philadelphia Story* and Stella, *Anna Lucasta,* both at the Cort Theatre, New York City, 1949.

Flora, *The Rose Tattoo,* Martin Beck Theatre, New York City, 1951; Ada Ryan, *Tin Wedding,* Westport Country Playhouse, CT, 1952; Mrs. Putnam and understudy Elizabeth Proctor, *The Crucible,* Martin Beck Theatre, New York City, 1953; appeared in *Affairs of State* and *Life with Father,* both at the Cecil Wood Theatre, Fishkill, NY, 1953; understudy Janet Mackenzie, *Witness for the Prosecution,* Henry Miller's Theatre, New York City, 1954; Mrs. Yang, *The Good Woman of Setzuan,* Phoenix Theatre, New York City, 1956; Amy Underhill, *The Third Best Sport,* Ambassador Theatre, New York City, 1958.

Mommy, *The Sand Box,* Jazz Gallery, 1960; the Housewife, *Rhinoceros,* Longacre Theatre, New York City, 1961; Mommy, *The American Dream,* York Playhouse, New York City, 1961; the Mother, *Picnic on a Battlefield,* Mrs. Peep, *The Killer,* Mommy, *The Sandbox,* and Mommy, *The American Dream,* all in a program of one-acts entitled, *The Theatre of the Absurd,* Cherry Lane Theatre, New York City, 1962; *The World of Jules Feiffer,* Hunterdon Hills Playhouse, 1962; old woman and peasant woman, *Mother Courage and Her Children,* Martin Beck Theatre, New York City, 1963; repeated role, Mommy, *The American Dream,* Cherry Lane Theatre, New York City, 1963; Emilie Ducotel, *My Three Angels,* Playhouse-on-the-Mall, Paramus, NJ, 1963; Mrs. Bennington, *Fair Game for Lovers,* Cort Theatre, New York City, 1964; Mlle. Suisson, *A Murderer Among Us,* Morosco Theatre, New York City, 1964; repeated role of Mommy, *The American Dream,* Cherry Lane Theatre, New York City, 1964; Nurse, *Medea,* at the Library of Congress, Washington, DC, 1964; Charity Perrin, *The Child Buyer,* Garrick Theatre, New York City, 1964.

With the Stanford Repertory Theatre, University of Stanford, CA: Mrs. Antrolius, *The Skin of our Teeth,* Nerine, *The Scoundrel Scapin,* the countess, *All's Well that Ends Well,* the old woman, *The Chairs,* Flora, *A Slight Ache,* all 1965-1966; the wife, *Inadmissible Evidence,* the gossip columnist, *Once in a Lifetime,* Mrs. Peachum, *The Beggar's Opera,* all 1966-67; Mrs. Coffman, *Come Back, Little Sheba* and Stella, *Light Up the Sky,* both with the Long Island Festival Repertory Theatre at the Mineola Theatre, NY, 1968; Grandma, *The Corner of the Bed,* Gramercy Arts Theatre, New York City, 1969; Mrs. Gershon, *Someone's Comin' Hungry,* Pocket Theatre, New York City, 1969; Mrs. Croft, *The Killing of Sister George,* Tappan Zee Playhouse, NY, 1969; appeared in *The American Hamburger League,* New Theatre Workshop, 1969; Duchess of York, *Richard III,* New Theatre Workshop, 1969; Vlasta Huml, *The Increased Difficulty of Concentration,* Forum Theatre, Lincoln Center, 1969.

Mother, *Slow Memories,* Theatre de Lys, New York City, 1970; Tante Frumkah, *The Last Analysis,* Circle in the Square, New York City, 1971; Lady Mount-Temple, *Dear Oscar,* Playhouse Theatre, New York City, 1972; Gertrude Saidenberg, *Murder Among Friends,* Biltmore Theatre, New York City, 1975; standby, *Wings,* Lyceum Theatre, New York City, 1978-79; Hannah Galt, *The Art of Dining,* New York Shakespeare Festival, Newman Theatre, New York City, 1979, then at the Eisenhower Theatre, Kennedy Theatre, Washington, DC, 1980.

Lena Benz, *One Tiger to Kill,* Manhattan Theatre Club, New York

City, 1980; Mrs. Weinblatt, *Second Avenue Rag,* Marymount Manhattan Theatre, New York City, 1980; Tasha Blumberg, *Isn't It Romantic,* Marymount Manhattan Theatre, New York City, 1981; Grandma Fortune, *The House Across the Street,* Ensemble Studio Theatre, 1982; *I Love You, Love You Not,* 1983; Ethel, *The Alto Part,* WPA Theatre, New York City, 1983; *Remember Crazy Zelda?,* Ensemble Studio Theatre, New York City, 1984; *The Torch-Bearers,* Hartman Theatre, Stamford, CT, 1984; *The Golden Windows,* Brooklyn Academy of Music, 1985; *Alteratons,* WPA Theatre, New York City, 1986.

MAJOR TOURS—Secretary, *Personal Appearance,* Eastern cities, 1936; *Crazy with the Heat,* New York state cities, 1941; *Pal Joey,* U.S. cities, 1942; Stella, *Anna Lucasta,* Lakewood Theatre, Barnsville, PA, and Hartford Actors Theatre, CT, 1949; Agnes, *A Delicate Balance,* U.S. cities, 1967.

FILM DEBUT—Voice-over, Chemda, *My Father's House,* Kline-Levin, 1947. PRINCIPAL FILM APPEARANCES—*A Hatful of Rain,* 1957; Mrs. Hayworth, *Laydbug, Ladybug,* United Artists, 1964; interviewer, *Where's Poppa?,* United Artists, 1971; information operator, *They Might Be Giants,* Universal, 1971; Mother, *Up in the Sandbox,* Columbia, 1972; *The Day of the Locusts,* Paramount, 1975; *The Sentinel,* Universal, 1977; *Tattoo,* Twentieth Century-Fox, 1981; *Batteries Not Included,* upcoming; also, *Black Harvest* and *Static.*

PRINCIPAL TELEVISION APPEARANCES—Series: Mrs. Shannon, *Love of Life,* NBC, 1971-75. Episodic: *Actors Studio,* ABC, 1948; *Goodyear Television Playhouse,* NBC, 1953; *Alcoa Hour,* NBC, 1957; *Camera Three,* CBS, 1958; *The Big Story,* NBC, 1958; *Look Up and Live,* CBS, 1959; *The Edge of Night,* CBS, 1960; *Route 66,* CBS, 1961; *The Defenders,* CBS, 1962; *Naked City,* ABC, 1962; *East Side/West Side,* CBS, 1963; *Popi,* CBS, 1976; also *Kojak,* CBS. Teleplays: Housekeeper, "The Waltz of the Toreadors," *Play of the Week,* WNTA-TV, 1959; Mommy, "The Sandbox," *Fierce, Funny and Far Out,* 1961.

RELATED CAREER—Director and teacher, Ensemble Studio Theatre, New York City.

NON-RELATED CAREER—Prior to acting, was a saleslady and restaurant hostess.

MEMBER: Actors' Equity Association, Screen Actors Guild, American Federation of Television and Radio Artists, American Guild of Variety Artists, Ensemble Studio Theatre, New York City (board of directors), Actor's Studio (charter member).

SIDELIGHTS: FAVORITE ROLES— Mommy, *The American Dream,* Agnes, *A Delicate Balance,* and Vlasta Huml, *The Increased Difficulty of Concentration.* RECREATIONS—Gardening and tennis.

ADDRESSES: HOME—New York, NY.

*   *   *

HOFFMAN, William M.   1939-

PERSONAL: Born April 12, 1939, in New York, NY; son of Morton (a caterer) and Johanna (a jeweler; maiden name, Papiermeister) Hoffman. EDUCATION: City College of New York, B.A., Latin (cum laude), 1960.

VOCATION: Playwright, director, producer, and editor.

CAREER: PRINCIPAL STAGE WORK—Artist-in-residence, Lincoln Center Student Program, 1971-72; visiting lecturer of theatre arts, University of Massachusetts, 1973; playwriting consultant, CAPS Program, New York State Council on the Arts, 1975-77; playwriting consultant, Massachusetts Arts and Humanities Foundation, 1978; playwright-in-residence, American Conservatory Theatre, San Francisco, 1978; playwright-in-residence, LaMama Experimental Theatre Company (E.T.C.), New York City, 1978-79; star adjunct professor in Playwriting, Hofstra University, 1980-83.

RELATED CAREER—Editor, Hill and Wang, 1961-68; literary advisor, *Scripts,* magazine, 1971-74.

WRITINGS: PLAYS, PRODUCED—*The Children's Crusade* and *From Fool to Hanged Man,* both Playwrights Horizons, New York City, 1972; *A Nut Bread to Make Your Mouth Water* (also known as *Spontaneous Combustion*), Manhattan Theatre Club, New York City, 1973; *Gilles de Rais,* Gate Theatre, New York City, 1975; *Cornbury,* staged reading, Public Theatre, New York Shakespeare Festival, New York City, 1976; *Shoe Palace Murray,* American Conservatory Theatre, San Francisco, 1978; *Gulliver's Travels,* LaMama E.T.C., New York City, 1978; *X's,* La Mama E.T.C., New York City, 1981; *A Book of Etiquette,* s.n.a.f.u. Theatre, New York City, 1983; *As Is,* Circle Repertory Company Theatre, New York City, then Lyceum Theatre, New York City, 1985.

PLAYS, PUBLISHED—*Thank You Miss Victoria,* 1970; *From Fool to Hanged Man,* 1970; *Saturday Night at the Movies,* 1973; *A Quick Nut Bread to Make Your Mouth Water* (also known as *Spontaneous*

WILLIAM M. HOFFMAN

Combustion), 1973; *The Last Days of Stephen Foster,* 1978; (with Anthony Holland) *Cornbury,* 1979; *As Is,* published by Dramatists Play Service.

TELEVISION—"Notes from the New World: Louis Moreau Gottschalk," *Camera Three,* CBS, 1976; scripts for WNET, Channel 13, 1976-77; (pilot) *Pink Panther's Magic Music Hall,* 1977; "The Last Days of Stephen Foster," *Camera Three,* CBS, 1977; "Whistler, Five Portraits," *Camera Three,* CBS, 1978.

POEMS AND LYRICS—*The Cloisters,* song cycle, 1968 included in anthology, *31 New American Poets* and *Fine Frenzy,* 1972; *Wedding Song,* 1979.

AWARDS: MacDowell Fellowship, 1971; Guggenheim Fellowship, 1974-75; librettists grant, National Endowment for the Arts, 1975-76; Creative Writing Fellowship, National Endowment for the Arts, 1976-77; commission for libretto for one hundreth anniversary opera, *A Figaro for Antonia,* Metropolitan Opera, New York City, 1983.

MEMBER: Dramatists Guild, American Society of Composers, Authors and Publishers (ASCAP), PEN, Circle Repertory Company's Playwrights Workshop, New York Theatre Strategy; Phi Beta Kappa.

ADDRESSES: AGENT—c/o Luis SanJuro, International Creative Management, 40 W. 57th Street, New York, NY 10019.*

*   *   *

HOLDGRIVE, David   1958-

PERSONAL: Born David Holdgreiwe, July 26, 1958, in Cincinnati, OH; son of Alvin C. and Suzzane R. (Kinsey) Holdgreiwe. EDUCATION: Attended the University of Cincinnati Conservatory of Music.

VOCATION: Choreographer, designer, and writer.

CAREER: FIRST STAGE WORK—Choreographer, *Day by Day,* Ford's Theatre, Washington, DC, Charles Playhouse, Boston, MA, and Cincinnati Playhouse, 1979. FIRST OFF-BROADWAY STAGE WORK—Choreographer, *Can-Can,* Equity Library Theatre, 1979. PRINCIPAL STAGE WORK—Director, *Sister Aimee,* Gene Frankel Theatre, New York City, 1981; choreographer, *The Baker's Wife,* Cincinnati Playhouse, 1981; choreographer, *Lola,* York Theatre Company, 1982; choreographer, *Applause,* Equity Library Theatre, 1982; director, *I'm Getting My Act Together and Taking It on the Road,* Cincinnati Playhouse, 1983; choreographer, *Fanny,* Berkshire Theatre Festival, Stockbridge, MA, 1983; director and choreographer, *Tallulah,* West Side Arts Theatre, New York City, 1983, then John Drew Theatre, New York City, 1984; choreographer, *The 1940's Radio Hour,* Repertory Theatre of St. Louis, MO, 1984; director and choreographer, *Maybe I'm Doing It Wrong,* Cincinnati Playhouse, 1984; director, *Lady Liberty,* Theatreworks, USA, 1985; choreographer, *Dori,* Leah Poslins Theatre, Toronto Canada, 1985; director and choreographer, *The Wonder Years,* Coronet Theatre, Los Angeles, 1986; director and choreographer, *On the Couch,* Roundabout Theatre, New York City, 1986.

Also directed and/or choreographed productions of: *Vanities,*

Oklahoma!, South Pacific, Carousel, Fiddler on the Roof, Shenandoah, Camelot, Anything Goes, No No Nanette, By Strouse, How to Succeed in Business without Really Trying, Sugar, Company, The Pirates of Penzance, Side by Side by Sondheim, Pippin, The Music Man, Oh Coward, Grease, Annie Get Your Gun, Mack & Mabel, Something's Afoot, Over Here, Is There Life After High School?, Tintypes, Baby.

PRINCIPAL TELEVISION WORK—Choreographer, *The Edge of Night,* NBC, 1984.

RELATED CAREER—Stage Directors and Choreographers Workshop Foundation, member, board of trustees.

WRITINGS: PLAYS, PRODUCED—(With David Levy, Steve Liebman, and Terry LaBolt), *The Wonder Years,* Coronet Theatre, Los Angeles, 1986.

MEMBER: Society of Stage Directors and Choreographers.

ADDRESSES: AGENT—Helen Merrill, 361 W. 17th Street, New York, NY 10011.

*   *   *

HOLLAND, Tom   1943-

PERSONAL: Born July 11, 1943, in Poughkeepsie, NY; son of Tom and Lee Holland.

VOCATION: Writer.

WRITINGS: SCREENPLAYS—*The Beast Within,* United Artists, 1982; (with Mark Lester) *The Class of 1984,* 1982; *Psycho II,* Universal, 1983; *Cloak and Dagger,* Universal, 1984; *Scream for Help,* Lorimar, 1984; *Fright Night,* Columbia, 1985.

AWARDS: Best Horror Film Writer, Saturn Award, Academy of Science Fiction, Fantasy, and Horror, 1985, for *Fright Night;* Best Writer, Saturn Award, 1985.

ADDRESSES: OFFICE—Columbia Pictures, Producer's 8, No. 226, Burbank, CA 91505. AGENT—c/o Joel Gotler, The Agency, 10351 Santa Monica Blvd., Los Angeles, CA 90025.

*   *   *

HOPPER, Dennis   1936-

PERSONAL: Born May 17, 1936, in Dodge City, KS. EDUCATION: Trained for the stage at the Old Globe Theatre School, San Diego, CA.

VOCATION: Actor, writer, director, and photographer.

CAREER: FILM DEBUT—*Rebel without a Cause,* Warner Brothers, 1955. PRINCIPAL FILM APPEARANCES—*Giant,* Warner Brothers, 1956; *Gunfight at the O.K. Corral,* Paramount, 1957; *From Hell to Texas,* Twentieth Century-Fox, 1958; *Key Witness,* Metro-Goldwyn-Mayer, 1960; *Night Tide,* American International, 1963; *The Sons of Katie Elder,* Paramount, 1965; *Glory Stompers,*

American International, 1967; *The Trip,* American International, 1967; *Cool Hand Luke,* Warner Brothers, 1967; *Hang 'em High,* United Artists, 1968; *Easy Rider,* Columbia, 1969; *True Grit,* Paramount, 1969; *The Last Movie,* Universal, 1971; *The American Dreamer,* 1971; *Kid Blue,* Twentieth Century-Fox, 1973; *Hex,* 1973; *The Sky Is Falling,* 1975; *Tracks,* 1976; *Mad Dog Morgan,* Australian, 1976; *The American Friend,* New Yorker Films, 1977; *Apocalypse Now,* United Artists, 1979; *Wild Times,* 1980; *King of the Mountain,* 1981; *Human Highway,* 1981; *The Osterman Weekend,* 1983; *Rumblefish,* Universal, 1983; *My Science Project,* Touchstone, 1985; *Blue Velvet,* DEG, 1986; *Hoosiers,* Orion, 1986; *River's Edge,* Orion, 1987; Ben, *Black Widow,* Twentieth Century-Fox, 1987; *Blood Red,* upcoming; *Pick-up Artist,* upcoming.

PRINCIPAL FILM WORK—Writer and director, *Easy Rider,* Columbia, 1969; director: *The Last Movie,* Universal, 1971; *Out of the Blue,* Canadian, 1980; *Colors,* Orion, upcoming.

PRINCIPAL TELEVISION APPEARANCES—Episodic: *Loretta Young Show,* NBC, 1954; *Medic,* NBC, 1955. Specials: *Out of the Blue and into the Black,* U.K. production, 1987.

RELATED CAREER—Photographer; works have been exhibited at the Fort Worth Art Museum, Denver Art Museum, Wichita Art Museum, Cochran Art Museum, and the Spileto Museum.

WRITINGS: SCREENPLAYS—*Easy Rider,* Columbia, 1969; *The Last Movie,* Universal, 1971.

AWARDS: Best New Director, Cannes Film Festival Award, 1969, for *Easy Rider;* Best Film Award, Venice Film Festival, 1971; Best Film Award, Cannes Film Festival, 1980; Best Supporting Actor, Academy Award nomination, 1987, for *Hoosiers;* Best Supporting Actor, Los Angeles Film Critics and National Society of Film Critics Awards, 1987, for *Blue Velvet.*

ADDRESSES: AGENT—Artists Agency, 10,000 Santa Monica Blvd., Suite 305, Los Angeles, CA 90067.*

*　　*　　*

HOWARD, Ken 1944-

PERSONAL: Born March 28, 1944, in El Centro, CA; son of Kenneth Joseph and Martha Carey (McDonald) Howard. EDUCATION: Amherst College, A.B., 1966; trained for the stage at the Yale Drama School, 1968.

VOCATION: Actor and composer.

CAREER: PRINCIPAL TELEVISION APPEARANCES—Series: Adam Bonner, *Adam's Rib,* ABC, 1973; Dave Barrett, *Manhunter,* CBS, 1975; Ken Reeves, *The White Shadow,* CBS, 1978-81; Jack Long, *It's Not Easy,* ABC, 1983; Garrett Boydston, *Dynasty II: The Colbys,* ABC, 1985. Episodic: *Bonanza,* NBC; *Medical Center,* CBS; *Mary Tyler Moore Hour,* CBS. Movies: Major Gandiner, *The Court Martial of George Armstrong Custer,* 1977; Danny Boy Mitchell, *Real American Hero,* 1978; Nels Freiberg, *The Critical List,* 1978; Dave Walecki, *Superdome,* 1978; title role, *Damien: The Leper Priest,* 1980; Joe Buckley, *Victims,* 1982; Michael Saunders, *He's Not Your Son,* 1984. Mini-Series: Adam Warner, *Rage of Angels,* 1983; Ranier Hartheim, *The Thorn Birds,* 1983; Adam Warner, *Rage of Angels: The Story Continues,* 1986. Pilots:

Dave Barrett, *Manhunter,* CBS, 1974. Specials: *Celebrity Football Classic,* 1979.

PRINCIPAL TELEVISION WORK—Music composer, *The Flame Trees of Thika,* 1982; *Q.E.D.,* CBS, 1982; *By Sword Divided,* 1986.

FILM DEBUT—*Tell Me That You Love Me Junie Moon,* Paramount, 1970. PRINCIPAL FILM APPEARANCES—*Such Good Friends,* Paramount, 1971; *1776,* Columbia, 1972; *The Strange Vengence of Rosalie,* 1972; Jefferson, *Independence,* 1975; John Michael Tombs, *Second Thoughts,* Universal, 1983.

STAGE DEBUT—Buffalo Bill, *Annie Get Your Gun,* Congregational Church, Manhasset, Long Island, NY, 1960. BROADWAY DEBUT—Karl Kubelik, *Promises, Promises,* Shubert Theatre, 1968. PRINCIPAL STAGE APPEARANCES—Thomas Jefferson, *1776,* 46th Street Theatre, New York City, 1969; Paul Reese, *Child's Play,* Royale Theatre, New York City, 1970; *Volpone,* Philadelphia Drama Guild, PA, 1972; Jerry Ryan, *Seesaw,* Uris Theatre, New York City, 1973, and later Theatre Under the Stars, Atlanta, GA, 1975; Jack Hassler, *Little Black Sheep,* Vivian Beaumont Theatre, New York City, 1975; Tom, *The Norman Conquests,* Morosco Theatre, New York City, 1976; the President, *1600 Pennsylvania Avenue,* Mark Hellinger Theatre, New York City, 1976; *Fatal Attraction,* Center Stage, Toronto, 1984, then in a New York City production, 1985; also appeared in *Equus.*

AWARDS: Theatre World Award, 1969, for *1776;* Antoinette Perry Award, 1970, for *Child's Play.*

ADDRESSES: HOME—New York, NY. AGENT—Creative Artists Agency, 1888 Century Park East, Suite 1400, Los Angeles, CA 90067.*

*　　*　　*

HOWARD, Ron 1954-

PERSONAL: Born March 1, 1954, in Duncan, OK; son of Rance (an actor and writer) and Jean (Speegle) Howard; married Cheryl Alley (a writer), June 7, 1975; children: Bryce Dallas. EDUCATION: Attended University of Southern California.

VOCATION: Actor and director.

CAREER: STAGE DEBUT—Rickie Sherman, *The Seven Year Itch,* Hilltop Summer Theatre, Baltimore, 1956. PRINCIPAL STAGE APPEARANCES—Ally, *Hole in the Head,* Bridge Bay Summer Theatre, Redding, PA, 1963.

FILM DEBUT—Billy, *The Journey,* Metro-Goldwyn-Mayer (MGM), 1959. PRINCIPAL FILM APPEARANCES—Winthrop, *The Music Man,* Warner Brothers, 1962; Eddie, *The Courtship of Eddie's Father,* MGM, 1963; *The Village of the Giants,* Embassy, 1965; *American Graffiti,* Universal, 1973; *Happy Mother's Day. . .Love George,* 1973; *The Spikes Gang,* United Artists, 1974; *Eat My Dust,* 1976; *The Shootist,* Paramount, 1976; *Grand Theft Auto,* 1977; *More American Graffiti,* Universal, 1979.

PRINCIPAL FILM WORK—Director: *Night Shift,* Warner Brothers, 1982; *Splash,* Buena Vista, 1984; *Cocoon,* Twentieth Century-

RON HOWARD

Fox, 1985; director and executive producer, *Gung Ho*, Paramount, 1986.

TELEVISION DEBUT—*Police Station*, 1958. PRINCIPAL TELEVISION APPEARANCES—Series: Opie Taylor, *The Andy Griffith Show*, CBS, 1960-63; Bob Smith, *The Smith Family*, ABC, 1971-72; Richie Cunningham, *Happy Days*, ABC, 1974-80. Movies: *The Migrants*, ABC, 1974; *The Locusts*, NBC, 1974; *Huck Finn*, CBS, 1975; *Act of Love*, NBC, 1980; *Bitter Harvest*, NBC, 1981; *Return to Mayberry*, CBS, 1985; also, *Fire on the Mountain*, ABC.

Episodic: *The Red Skelton Show*, CBS; *Dennis the Menace*, CBS; *Dobie Gillis* syndicated; *General Electric Theatre*, NBC; *Playhouse 90*, CBS; *Dinah Shore Show*, NBC; *Five Fingers*, NBC; *Johnny Ringo*, CBS; *Danny Thomas Show*, ABC; *Hennessey*, CBS; *The Twilight Zone*, CBS; *Cheyenne*, ABC; *June Allyson Show*, syndicated; *The New Breed*, ABC; *The Eleventh Hour*, NBC; *Dr. Kildare*, NBC; *Route 66*, CBS; "The Plague," *The Great Adventure*, CBS; *The Fugitive*, ABC; *The Big Valley*, ABC; *Gomer Pyle, U.S.M.C.*, CBS; *The Danny Kaye Show*, CBS; *I Spy*, NBC; *The Monroes*, ABC; "A Boy Called Nothing" and "Smoke," both *Disney*, NBC; *Gentle Ben*, CBS; *Mayberry RFD*, CBS; *Land of the Giants*, ABC; *Lancer*, CBS; *Daniel Boone*, NBC; *Judd for the Defense*, ABC; *The F.B.I.*, ABC; *Gunsmoke*, CBS; *Disney*, NBC; *Partner for Lassie*, ABC.

MEMBER: American Federation of Television and Radio Artists, Screen Actors Guild, Writers Guild.

ADDRESSES: AGENT—c/o Michael Ovitz, Creative Artists Agency, 1888 Century Park E., Suite 1400, Los Angeles, CA 90067.

HOWARD, Trevor   1916-

PERSONAL: Born September 29, 1916, in Cliftonville, Margate, Kent, England; son of Arthur John and Mabel Grey (Wallace) Howard; married Helen Cherry. EDUCATION: Attended Clifton College; trained for the stage at the Royal Acadmey of Dramatic Art. MILITARY: British First Airborne Division, 1940-43.

VOCATION: Actor.

CAREER: LONDON DEBUT—*Revolt in a Reformatory*, Gate Theatre, 1934. PRINCIPAL STAGE APPEARANCES—Schwenck, *The Drums Begin*, Embassy Theatre, London, 1934; *Androcles and the Lion*, Winter Garden Theatre, London, 1934; Sagisaka, *The Faithful* and Harry Conway, *Alien Corn*, both at the Westminster Theatre, London, 1934; Jack Absolute, *The Rivals*, Q Theatre, London, 1935; Dmitri, *Crime and Punishment*, Embassy Theatre, London, 1935; Honorable Willie Tatham, *Aren't We All?*, Court Theatre, London, 1935, Walter How, *Justice*, Charles Hornblower, *The Skin Game*, and the journalist, *A Family Man*, all at the Playhouse Theatre, London, 1935; William O'Farrell, *Lady Patricia*, Westminster Theatre, London, 1935; Fred Johnson, *Legend of Yesterday*, Aldwych Theatre, London, 1935; Lucullus, *Timon of Athens*, Westminster Theatre, London, 1935.

Appeared at the Memorial Theatre, Stratford-on-Avon, U.K., 1936 season; Kenneth Lake, *French without Tears*, Criterion Theatre, London, 1936; Bryan Elliott, *Waters of Jordan*, Arts Theatre, London, 1937, Ronnie Dent, *A Star Comes Home*, Arts Theatre, London, 1938; appeared at the Memorial Theatre, Stratford-Upon-Avon, 1939 season; also appeared in seasons at Colchester and Harrogate, U.K.; Captain Plume, *The Recruiting Officer* and Joachim Bris, *On Life's Sunny Side*, both at the Arts Theatre, 1943; Ronald Vines, *A Soldier for Christmas*, Wyndham's Theatre, London, 1944; Mat Burke, *Anna Christie*, Arts Theatre, London, 1944; Petruchio, *The Taming of the Shrew*, with the Old Vic Company at the New Theatre, London, 1947; General Harras, *The Devil's General*, Savoy Theatre, London, 1953; Lopakin, *The Cherry Orchard*, Lyric Theatre, Hammersmith, London, 1954.

Sam Turner, *Two Stars for Comfort*, Garrick Theatre, London, 1962; captain, *The Father*, Piccadilly Theatre, London, 1964; General St. Pe, *The Waltz of the Toreadors*, Haymarket Theatre, London, 1974; appeared in *Scenario*, Toronto, Canada, 1977.

FILM DEBUT—*The Way Ahead*, 1943. PRINCIPAL FILM APPEARANCES—*Brief Encounter*, 1945; *Way to the Stars*, 1945; *The Third Man*, 1949; *Golden Salamander*, 1951; *Odette*, 1951; *Outcast of the Islands*, 1951; *The Clouded Yellow*, 1951; *The Heart of the Matter*, Associated Artists, 1954; *Les amants du Tage*, 1955; *Cockleshell Heros*, Columbia, 1956; *Run for the Sun*, United Artists, 1956; *Around the World in Eighty Days*, United Artists, 1956; *The Key*, Columbia, 1958; *Roots of Heaven*, Twentieth Century-Fox, 1958; *Sons and Lovers*, Twentieth Century-Fox, 1960; *Malaga*, Warner Brothers, 1962; *The Lion*, Twentieth Century-Fox, 1962; *Mutiny on the Bounty*, Metro-Goldwyn-Mayer (MGM), 1962; *Man in the Middle*, Twentieth Century-Fox, 1964; *Father Goose*, Universal, 1965; *The Great Spy Mission*, American International, 1966; *Von Ryan's Express*, Twentieth Century-Fox, 1966; *A Matter of Innocence*, Universal, 1968; *The Charge of Light Brigade*, United Artists, 1968; *Battle of Britain*, United Artists, 1969.

Ryan's Daughter, MGM, 1970; *Mary Queen of Scots*, Universal, 1971; *Pope Joan*, 1972; *Ludwig*, MGM, 1973; *The Offence*, United Artists, 1973; *A Doll's House*, Paramount, 1973; *11 Harrowhouse*,

Twentieth Century-Fox, 1974; *Who?*, 1974; *Hennessy*, American International, 1975; *Conduct Unbecoming*, Allied Artists, 1975; *Bawdy Adventures of Tom Jones*, Universal, 1976; *The Count of Monte Cristo*, 1976; *The Last Remake of Beau Geste*, Universal, 1977; *Eliza Frazer*, 1977; *Superman*, Warner Brothers, 1978; *Night Flight*, 1978; *Hurricane*, Paramount, 1979.

Sir Henry at Rawlinson End, 1980; *Sea Wolves*, Paramount, 1981; *Les Annees Lumieres*, 1981; *Windwalker*, Pacific International, 1982; *Light Years Away*, 1982; *Gandhi*, Columbia, 1982; *The Missionary*, Columbia, 1982; *Dust*, 1985; *In the Heart of the Country*, 1986.

Also appeared in: *Friends, Lovers of Lisbon, Interpol, Manuela, Pretty Polly, The Sabateur, Code Name Morituri*.

PRINCIPAL TELEVISION APPEARANCES—Dramatic specials: Lovberg, *Hedda Gabler*, 1962; *The Invincible Mr. Disraeli*, 1963; *Napoleon at St. Helena*, 1966; *Catholics, The Shillingbury Blowers, Night Flight* and *Staying On*, all 1980; *The Long Exile of Jonathan Swift*, 1981; *Inside the Third Reich* and *A Dangerous Game*, both 1982; *Christmas Eve*, NBC, 1987; also appeared in *George Washington*.

AWARDS: BBC Prize Award, 1934; British Academy Award, 1959, for *The Key;* Television Award, 1963, for *The Invincible Mr. Disraeli*.

ADDRESSES: HOME—Rowley Green, Arkley, Hertfordshire, England.*

*   *   *

HUBLEY, Season

PERSONAL: Born March 14, in New York, NY; daughter of Grant Shelby (a writer and entrepreneur) and Julia Kaul (Paine) Hubley; married Kurt Russell, March 17, 1979 (divorced, 1983); children: Boston Oliver-Grant Russell. EDUCATION: Attended Quintanos School for Young Professionals, New York City; trained for the theatre at the Herbert Berghof Studios with Uta Hagen and Walt Whitcover; studied with Jose Quintero and Tracy Roberts at the Corner Loft Studios in New York City. POLITICS: Democrat.

VOCATION: Actress.

CAREER: TELEVISION DEBUT—Bobbie Joe, *Bobbie Joe & the Big Time Apple Band*, CBS, 1971. PRINCIPAL TELEVISION APPEARANCES—Series: Margit McLean, *Kung Fu*, NBC, 1974-75; Salina Magee, *Family*, ABC, 1976-77. Episodic: *Good Heavens*, ABC, 1975; "All I Could See From Where I Stood," *Visions*, KCET, 1975; *Westside Medical*, Marstar Productions, 1976; *Loose Change*, NBC, 1978; *Black Carrion*, Fox Mystery Theatre/Hammer Productions/Fox TV, 1984; premiere episode, *The Twilight Zone*, CBS, 1985; "Final Escape," *Alfred Hitchcock Presents*, NBC, 1985. Movies: Pam, *She Lives*, ABC, 1973; *Flight of the Maiden*, ABC, 1976; Priscilla, *Elvis*, ABC, 1978; daughter, *Mrs. R's Daughter*, NBC, 1979; *Caribbean Mystery*, CBS, 1983; *London & Davis*, CBS, 1984; *Billy Grier*, ABC, 1984; Anne, *Under the Influence*, CBS, 1985; *Christmas Eve*, NBC, 1986. Mini-Series: Eleni, *Key to Rebecca*, Independent/OPT, 1985. Pilot: *The City*, 1986.

SEASON HUBLEY

FILM DEBUT—Lolly Madonna, *The Lolly Madonna War*, Metro-Goldwyn-Mayer (MGM), 1972. PRINCIPAL FILM APPEARANCES—*Catch My Soul*, Metro Media, 1972; Niki, *Hardcore*, Columbia, 1978; girl in the Chock-Full-of-Nuts, *Escape from New York*, AVCO-Embassy, 1980; Princess, *Vice Squad*, AVCO-Embassy, 1981; Heather, *Twist of Fate*, Lorimar, 1986.

STAGE DEBUT—Billie, *Heat*, Landmark Theatre, Hollywood, 1984. PRINCIPAL STAGE APPEARANCES—Emily, "Strawberry Envy," *Triplet Collection*, Matrix Theatre, Hollywood, 1985.

WRITINGS: BOOKS—*From Spandex to Tennis Shoes*, private publication.

MEMBER: Screen Actors Guild, American Federation of Television and Radio Artists, American Film Intitute.

ADDRESSES: OFFICE—c/o Gelfand Rennert & Feldman, 1880 Century Park East, Suite 900, Los Angeles, CA 90067. AGENT—c/o Alan Lezman, William Morris Agency, 151 El Camino Drive, Beverly Hills, CA 90212.

*   *   *

HUDIS, Norman   1922-

PERSONAL: Born July 27, 1922; son of Isaac (a tailoring production manager) and Beulah (Reuben) Hudis; married Marguerita Robinson (a registered nurse and technical advisor), April 28, 1956; children: Stephen Robin, Kevin Franklin. EDUCATION: Attended

County School, Willesden, London, England for five years. POLITICS: "Variable, as cynicism increases." RELIGION: Jewish. MILITARY: Royal Air Force, 1940-46.

VOCATION: Writer.

WRITINGS: SCREENPLAYS—*Carry on Sergeant,* 1959; *Carry on Nurse,* Governor, 1960; *Carry on Constable,* Governor, 1961; *Carry on Cleo,* Governor, 1965; *Carry on Spying,* Governor, 1965; *Carry on Doctor,* American International, 1968.

TELEVISION—Extensive writing for British and U.S. television since 1966. He has written scripts for U.S. television series (including *Baretta*), pilots, and specials (including *Esther*) and for British television mini-series.

AWARDS: Best Teleplay, Edgar Allan Poe Award, Mystery Writers of America, for *Baretta;* Best Religious Special, Religion in Media, 1981, for *Esther.*

MEMBER: Writers Guild of Great Britian, Writers Guild of American West, Association of Cinemato-Graph Television and Allied Technicians (Great Britain).

SIDELIGHTS: Norman Hudis wrote to *CTFT* about his career: "From childhood I always wanted to write. A newspaper reporter at sixteen in London, war correspondent while in the Royal Air Force, and publicity director for post war British films, I moved on to scripting and have been there ever since. To sum up, I have been fortunate enough to write everything, seemingly satisfactorily, from broad farce to the Bible. I intend to write 'till I die."

ADDRESSES: AGENT—Triad Artists Inc., 10100 Santa Monica Blvd., Los Angeles, CA 90067; England: Eric Glass Ltd., 28 Berkeley Square, London W1X 6HD, England.

*　　*　　*

HURT, Mary Beth

PERSONAL: Born Mary Beth Supinger, September 26, in Marshalltown, IA; daughter of Forrest Clayton and Delores Lenore (Andre) Supinger; married William Hurt (an actor; divorced, 1982); married Paul Schrader (a director and screenwriter), August 6, 1983; children: (second marriage) Molly. EDUCATION: Attended the University of Iowa; studied for the theatre at New York University's School of the Arts.

VOCATION: Actress.

CAREER: STAGE DEBUT—Lily, *New Girl in Town,* Equity Library Theatre, New York City, 1963. PRINCIPAL STAGE APPEARANCES—Lucy Schmieler, *On the Town* and lead, *The Drunkard,* both Gatlinburg, TN; Tirsa, *Three Wishes for Jamie,* Off-Broadway concert; Celia, *As You Like It,* Delacorte Theatre, New York Shakespeare Festival (NYSF), New York City, 1973; Nurse and Uncle Remus, *More Than You Deserve,* Public Theatre, NYSF, 1974; Marina, *Pericles,* Delacorte Theatre, NYSF, 1974; Miss Prue, *Love for Love,* 1974, and Frankie Adams, *Member of the Wedding,* both with the New Phoenix Theatre Company at the Helen Hayes Theatre, New York City, 1975; Rose Trelawney, *Trelawney of the Wells,* Susie, *Boy Meets Girl,* Caroline Mitford, *Secret Service,* and *The Cherry Orchard,* all at the Vivian Beau-

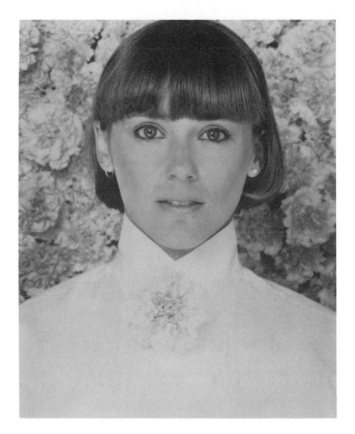

MARY BETH HURT

mont Theatre, Lincoln Center, New York City, 1977; Vi, *Dusa, Fish, Stas and Vi,* Mark Taper Forum, Los Angeles, 1978; *All-Shakespeare Concert,* Alice Tully Hall, New York City, 1978; Estelle, *Father's Day,* American Place Theatre, New York City, 1979.

Lizzie, *The Rainmaker,* Berkshire Theatre Festival, Stockbridge, MA, 1981; Meg McGrath, *Crimes of the Heart,* Manhattan Theatre Club, 1981, transferring to the John Golden Theatre, New York City, 1982, and then the Ahmanson Theatre, Los Angeles, 1983; Celimene, *The Misanthrope,* Circle in the Square Theatre, New York City, 1983; *The Nest of the Woodgrouse,* Public Theatre, NYSF, 1984; Sheila, *Benefactors,* Brooks Atkinson Theatre, New York City, 1985.

MAJOR TOURS—Mazeppa, *Gypsy.*

FILM DEBUT—Joey, *Interiors,* 1978. PRINCIPAL FILM APPEARANCES—*Head Over Heels* (re-released in 1982 as *Chilly Scenes of Winter*), United Artists, 1979; *A Change of Seasons,* Twentieth Century-Fox, 1980; Helen Garp, *The World According to Garp,* Warner Brothers, 1982; *D.A.R.Y.L.,* Paramount, 1985; *Compromising Positions,* Paramount, 1985.

TELEVISION DEBUT—*The Bette Lee Show,* Birmingham, AL. PRINCIPAL TELEVISION APPEARANCES—Caroline Mitford, "Secret Service," *American Playhouse,* PBS, 1977; *The Five Forty Eight,* PBS; also, *Theatre in America,* PBS.

AWARDS: Clarence Derwent Award, 1974, for *Love for Love;* Antoinette Perry Award nomination, 1975, for *Trelawney of the*

Wells; Obie Award, Antoinette Perry Award nomination, and Drama Desk nomination, all 1981, for *Crimes of the Heart.*

MEMBER: Actors' Equity Association, Screen Actors Guild.

ADDRESSES: AGENT—c/o Paul Martino, International Creative Management, Inc., 40 W. 57th Street, New York, NY 10019.*

*   *   *

HUSAIN, Jory

PERSONAL: EDUCATION: Graduated from high school in India; trained for the stage at the Santa Monica Playhouse, CA.

VOCATION: Actor.

CAREER: PRINCIPAL TELEVISION APPEARANCES—Series: *Head of the Class,* ABC, 1986—.

STAGE DEBUT—*Moonlight Madness,* Young People's Professional Productions, Santa Monica Playhouse, CA. PRINCIPAL STAGE APPEARANCES—*Cyrano De Bergerac, Oklahoma!,* and *My Fair Lady,* all productions in Minneapolis, MN; *Bye Bye Birdie, The Odd Couple,* and *Don't Drink the Water,* all productions in India.

SIDELIGHTS: RECREATIONS—Moviegoing, writing, tennis, ping pong.

JORY HUSAIN

From material supplied by his agent, *CTFT* learned that Jory Husain speaks fluent Pakistani and has also mastered other dialects.

ADDRESSES: PUBLICIST—Guttman and Pam, Ltd., 120 El Camino Drive, Beverly Hills, CA 90212.

*   *   *

HUSTON, Anjelica   1951-

PERSONAL: Born July 8, 1951, in Los Angeles, CA; daughter of John Marcellus (a director, actor, and writer) and Enrica (a ballet dancer; maiden name, Soma) Huston. EDUCATION: Attended schools in England; trained for the stage at the Loft Studio and with Peggy Furey, David Craig, and Martin Landau.

VOCATION: Actress.

CAREER: STAGE DEBUT—Ophelia, *Hamlet,* Roundhouse Theatre, London. PRINCIPAL STAGE APPEARANCES—Title role, *Tamara,* Il Vittorale Theatre, Los Angeles.

MAJOR TOURS—Ophelia, *Hamlet.*

FILM DEBUT—*A Walk with Love and Death,* Twentieth Century-Fox, 1967. PRINCIPAL FILM APPEARANCES—*Sinful Davey,* 1969; *Swashbuckler,* Universal, 1976; *Postman Always Rings Twice,* Paramount, 1981; *This Is Spinal Tap,* Embassy, 1984; *The Ice Pirates,* Metro-Goldwyn-Mayer/United Artists, 1984; *Prizzi's Honor,* ABC Motion Pictures/Twentieth Century-Fox, 1985; *Captain Eo,* Walt Disney Productions, 1986; *Gardens of Stone,* upcoming.

PRINCIPAL TELEVISION APPEARANCES—Episodic: *Laverne and Shirley,* ABC; *Faerie Tale Theatre,* Showtime. Movies: *The Cowboy and the Ballerina,* 1984; *A Rose for Emily,* PBS.

AWARDS: Best Supporting Actress, Academy Award, New York Film Critics Award, Los Angeles Film Critics Award, National Board of Review Award, and *Drama-Logue* Award, all 1985, for *Prizzi's Honor.*

SIDELIGHTS: For many years, Anjelica Huston was labeled as either director John Huston's daughter or as actor Jack Nicholson's girlfriend. But with the 1985 film *Prizzi's Honor,* Huston came into her own as an actress. For her role as the granddaughter of an organized crime boss, Huston won several prestigious honors, including an Academy Award, a New York Film Critics Award, and a National Board of Review Award.

Huston made her acting debut at the age of fifteen in 1967's *A Walk with Love and Death,* a film her father directed. Although she had no acting training or experience at the time, her father was convinced that she had natural talent, particularly a gift for mimicry. The elder Huston explained to Aljean Harmetz (*New York Times,* June 27, 1985) that "as a seven-year-old she had shown an extraordinary talent, a gift of revealing a truth with such power it would stagger you." Unfortunately *A Walk with Love and Death* was "a dismal film," as Marie Brenner described it (*Vanity Fair,* September, 1985). The merciless reviews hurt Anjelica deeply, and when, during the film's promotional tour, her mother died in an auto accident, Huston was emotionally devasted. She told Brenner, "I simply checked out of life for a long, long time."

For several years she lived in new York City, where she modeled for photographers Helmut Newton, Richard Avedon, and others. After meeting actor Jack Nicholson, Huston moved into his California

ANJELICA HUSTON

home. A brief dabbling with drugs ended with her arrest for drug possession in the early 1970s. It was Nicholson who finally suggested she take acting classes, a move Huston believes helped her to develop a positive self-image. Soon she was taking small parts in theatrical productions. By the mid-1970s, she was appearing in films again. And in 1985, with *Prizzi's Honor,* Huston gained critical acclaim for her abilities

To play the role of a mafia princess, Huston had to develop a Brooklyn accent, something she did by wandering Brooklyn streets, strolling in and out of the shops, and listening to passersby. Harmetz found the accent to be extremely effective. "With her swanlike neck, chiseled bones, chignoned hair and two-inch-long crimson fingernails," Harmetz wrote, "she glides like an Italian Contessa among peasants. Until she opens her mouth and the elegance dissolves is a thick Brooklyn accent." Ruth La Ferla (*Women's Wear Daily,* June 4, 1985) notes the same effect. Huston is a "straightbacked, shrewd-eyed contemporary Borgia decked out in black and crimson," La Ferla states. "Suddenly her lips part. 'I'm duh fam-ly scandal,' she brays in plaintive Brooklynese, and the regal illusion is crashingly shattered." Brenner called Huston's performance "astonishing," while Harmetz claims that she "ran off with the picture."

The success of *Prizzi's Honor* has changed Huston's perception of herself and her career. As Nicholson tells Brenner, the film "dropped a lot of dead weight off Anjelica's psyche." She has roles in two upcoming films and has returned to the stage as well, portraying a Polish artist in the experimental play *Tamara.* Although she has played a number of offbeat roles during her career, Huston does not see herself as a character actress. She explained her acting goal to La Ferla, "What I really would like is to bring back the character to leading roles."

ADDRESSES: OFFICE—9911 W. Pico Blvd., Penthouse, Los Angeles, CA 90035. AGENT—c/o Toni Howard, William Morris Agency, 151 El Camino Drive, Beverly Hills, CA 90212.

I

IMPERATO, Carlo   1963-

PERSONAL: Full name, Anthony Imperato; born August 30, 1963, in New York, NY; son of Richard Anthony (a salesman) and Leah (a secretary; maiden name Pollack) Imperato. EDUCATION: Attended the Professional Children's School, New York City; studed voice with Richard Dorr.

VOCATION: Actor.

CAREER: OFF-BROADWAY DEBUT—A.J., *Runaways*, Public Theatre, New York Shakespeare Festival, 1977. BROADWAY DEBUT—A.J., *Runaways*, Plymouth Theatre, 1978. LONDON DEBUT—Danny Amatulo, *The Kids from Fame*, Prince Albert Hall, 1983. PRINCIPAL STAGE APPEARANCES—Damis, *Tartuffe*, Whole Theatre Company, Montclair, NJ; *One on One*, Ensemble Studio Theatre, New York City; *Table Settings*, Playwrights Horizons, New York City.

CARLO IMPERATO

PRINCIPAL FILM APPEARANCES—*Enormous Changes; Someone's in the Kitchen with Jamie; Shoeshine Girl;* principal role in a film made for UNICEF.

PRINCIPAL TELEVISION APPEARANCES—Series: Danny Amatullo, *Fame*, NBC, 1982-83, syndicated, 1983—. Episodic: *Angie*, ABC. Guest: *The Match Game*, NBC; *Star Games '85*, ABC; *Good Morning America*, ABC; *The Alan Thicke Show*, ABC; *Bloopers & Blunders*, NBC; *The Mike Douglas Show*, NBC; *Camera Three*, CBS. Specials: *Christmas Special*, NBC; *Tony Awards Show*, CBS; *Christmas in New York*, HBO. Movies: *The Man in the Santa Suit*, 1978; *Hayburners*.

MEMBER: Actors' Equity Association, Screen Actors Guild, American Federation of Television and Radio Artists, Academy of Television Arts and Sciences, American Film Institute; American Lung Association, World Vision, Children's Diabetes Association, Hands Across America.

SIDELIGHTS: RECREATIONS—Singing, karate (black belt), dirt bike riding, gymnastics, basketball, football, baseball, skiing, water skiing, swimming.

ADDRESSES: OFFICE—Carlo Imperato, Inc., 6120 Cartwright Ave., N. Hollywood, CA 91606. AGENT—The Agency, 10351 Santa Monica Blvd., Los Angeles, CA 90025.

*   *   *

INNAURATO, Albert   1948-

PERSONAL: Born June 2, 1948, in Philadelphia, PA; son of Albert and Mary (Walker) Innaurato. EDUCATION: California Institute of the Arts, B.F.A., 1972; Yale University School of Drama, M.F.A., 1975.

VOCATION: Playwright and director.

CAREER: PRINCIPAL STAGE WORK—Playwright (see below); director, *The Transfiguration of Benno Blimpie*, Broadway production, New York City, 1973.

RELATED CAREER—Playwright in residence, New York Shakespeare Festival, Public Theatre, New York City, 1977, Circle Repertory Company, New York City, 1979, and Playwright's Horizons, New York City, 1983.

WRITINGS: PLAYS, PRODUCED AND PUBLISHED—"Summit," and "Lytton Strachey Lucubrates de Rerum Sexualium," unproduced;

(with Christopher Durang) *I Don't Generally Like Poetry but Have You Read 'Trees'?* (musical), Yale Cabaret, 1972; *The Transfiguration of Benno Blimpie*, Yale, 1973, Playwrights Horizons, New York City, 1976, Astor Place Theatre, New York City, 1977, produced in London, 1978, produced again at Playwrights Horizons, New York City, 1983, published by Dramatists Play Service, 1977; *Earthworms*, produced, 1974; *Gemini*, Little Theatre (now the Helen Hayes Theatre), New York City, 1976-80, published by Dramatists Play Service, 1977; *Ulysses in Traction*, Circle Repertory Theatre, New York City, 1977; published by Dramatists Play Service, 1978; (with Christopher Durang) *The Idiots Karamazov* (musical), produced in New York City, 1974, published by Dramatists Play Service, 1980; *Passione*, Morosco Theatre, New York City, 1980, published by Dramatists Play Service, 1981; also, *Coming of Age in Soho*, produced at the Public Theatre, New York City.

BOOKS—(With an introduction by the playwright) *Bizarre Behavior: Six Plays*, Avon Books, 1980.

AWARDS: Guggenheim grant in playwriting, 1976; two Obie Awards, both 1977, for *The Transfiguration of Benno Blimpie* and *Gemini;* Rockefeller Grant in Playwriting, 1977.

MEMBER: Dramatists Guild, Writers Guild of America.

ADDRESSES: HOME—325 W. 22nd Street, New York, NY 10011. AGENT—c/o George Lane, William Morris Agency, 1350 Avenue of the Americas, New York, NY 10019.*

*   *   *

IONESCO, Eugene   1912-

PERSONAL: Born November 26, 1912, in Slatina, Romania; became a French citizen, 1938; son of Eugene (a lawyer) and Marie-Therese (Icard) Ionesco; married Rodika Burileano, July 12, 1936; children: Marie-France. EDUCATION: Attended University of Bucharest, Romania; University of Paris, Sorbonne, licencie es lettres, agrege des lettres.

VOCATION: Writer, director, actor, and educator.

CAREER: PRINCIPAL STAGE WORK—Playwright (see below); director, *Victims of Duty*, produced in Zurich, Switzerland; acted in a production of Dostoevsky's *The Possessed*, and in his own *Lecons de francais pour Americains*, in 1965.

RELATED CAREER—Professor of French in Romania, 1936-39.

WRITINGS: PLAYS, PRODUCED—*La Cantatrice chauve* (one-act), first produced at the Theatre des Noctambules, Paris, France, 1950, produced as *The Bald Soprano*, Sullivan Street Playhouse, New York City, 1958; *La Lecon* (one-act), first produced at the Theatre de Poche-Montparnasse, Paris, 1951, produced as *The Lesson*, Phoenix Theatre, New York City, 1958; *Les Chaises*, first produced at the Theatre Nouveau-Lancry, Paris, 1952, produced as *The Chairs*, Phoenix Theatre, New York City, 1958; *Victimes du devoir* (one-act), first produced at the Theatre du Quartier Latin, Paris, 1953, produced as *Victims of Duty*, Theatre de Lys, New York City, 1960; *Les Grandes Chaleurs, Le Connaissez-vou?*, and *Le Rhume Onirique*, all produced in 1953; *La Jeune Fille a marier*, first produced at the Theatre de la Huchette, Paris, 1953, then later

at the Barbizon-Plaza Theatre and at the Theatre Upstairs, New York City, 1970; *Le Maitre*, first produced at the Theatre de la Huchette, 1953, then later at the Royal Court Theatre, London, 1970; *La Niece-Epouse*, first produced at the Theatre de la Huchette, Paris, 1953, produced as *The Niece-Wife*, London, 1971; *Amedee, ou Comment s'en debarasser*, Theatre de Babylone, Paris, 1954, produced as *Amedee, or How to Disentangle Yourself*, Tempo Playhouse, New York City, 1955.

Jacques, ou la soumission (one-act), Theatre de la Huchette, Paris, 1955, produced as *Jack*, Sullivan Street Playhouse, New York City, 1958; *Le Nouveau Locataire* (one-act), first produced in Helsinki, Finland, 1955, Theatre d'Aujourd'hui, Paris, 1957, produced as *The New Tenant*, Royale Playhouse, New York City, 1960; *L'Impromptu de l'Alma, ou Le Cameleon du berger*, Studio des Champs-Elysses, Paris, 1956, produced as *Improvisation, or the Shepherd's Chameleon*, Theatre de Lys, New York City, 1960; *L'Avenir est dans les oeufs (The Future Is in Eggs)*, first produced, 1957; *Impromptu pour la Duchesse de Windsor*, performed privately for the Duke and Duchess of Windsor, 1957; *Tuer sans gages*, Theatre Recamier, Paris, 1959, produced as *The Killer*, Seven Arts Theatre, New York City, 1960; *Rhinoceros*, first produced in Dusseldorf, 1959, Theatre l'Odeon, Paris, 1960, Royal Court Theatre, London, 1960, Longacre Theatre, New York City, 1961.

Le Jeune Homme a marier and *Apprendre a marcher*, (scenario for ballet by Deryk Mendal), Theatre de l'Etoile, Paris, 1960; *Le Pieton de l'air* (ballet-pantomime), Theatre l'Odeon, Paris, 1963, New York City Center, 1964; *Delire a deux* (one-act), Studio des Champs-Elysses, Paris, 1962; *Le Tableau*, Theatre de la Huchette, Paris, 1955, later produced as *The Painting*, Cafe Deja-vu, New York City, 1969; *Scene a quatre*, first produced in Italy at the Spoleto Festival, 1959, later produced at Theatre Upstairs, London, 1970; *Les Saluations*, Theatre Upstairs, London, 1970; *Le Roi se meurt* (one-act), first produced in Paris, 1962, produced as *Exit the King*, Royal Court Theatre, London, 1963, then by the Association of Performing Artists (APA)-Phoenix Repertory Company at the Lydia Mendelsshon Theatre, Ann Arbor, MI, 1967; *La Soif et la faim*, Comedie-Francaise, Paris, 1966, produced as *Hunger and Thirst*, Berkshire Theatre Festival, Stockbridge, MA, 1969.

La Lacune, Theatre l'Odeon, Paris, Barbizon-Plaza Theatre and Theatre Upstairs, New York City, 1970; *La Salon de l'automobile (The Motor Show)*, *L'Oeuf dur, pour preparer un oeuf dur*, and *Ches le docteur*, all Theatre Upstairs, 1970; *Le Cocotire en flammes*, *D'Isidione, Histoire des bandits*, *Il y eut d'abord*, and *Lecons de francais pour Americains*, all produced at Theatre Upstairs, London, 1970; *Jeux de massacre*, first produced in Dusseldorf, Germany, 1970, Theatre Montparnasse, Paris, 1970, produced as *Wipeout Games*, Arena Stage, Kreeger Theatre, Washington, DC, 1971; *Macbett*, Theatre Rive Gauche, Paris, 1972; *Ce Formidable Bordel*, Theatre Moderne, Paris, 1973; *L'homme aux valises (The Man with the Suitcase)*, first produced, 1975; *Entre la Vie et le Reve* and *Antidotes*, both 1977.

PLAYS, PUBLISHED—*The Chairs* (acting edition), translated by Donald Watson, Samuel French, 1958; *The Lesson* (acting edition), translated by Watson, Samuel French, 1958, French version published as "La Lecon," in Samuel Beckett, *Fin de Partie*, 1957; *Le Rhinoceros*, Gallimard, 1959, edited by Reuben Y. Elliseon and Stowell C. Gooding, Holt, 1961, translation by Derek Prouse, *Rhinoceros: A Play in Three Acts* (acting edition), Samuel French, 1960; *La Cantarice, chauve*, Gallimard, 1962, enlarged edition, 1964, published with "La Lecon," 1970, translation by Watson published as *The Bald Prima Donna: A Pseudo-play* (acting edition), Samuel French, 1961, published as *The Bald Soprano: Anti-play*, Grove Press, 1965, published in England as *The Bald Prima Donna: Anti-play*, J.Calder, 1966; *Le Roi se meurt*, Gallimard, 1963, translation by Watson published as *Exit the King*, Grove Press, 1963, French edition with notes in English, edited by Robert J. North, Harrap, 1966; *Le Soif et la faim* published in Paris, 1966; *Delire a deux*, Gallimard, 1966, *Jeux de massacre*, Gallimard, 1970; *The Niece-Wife* ("La Niece-Epouse"), in Richard N. Coe, *Ionesco: A Study of His Plays*, Methuen, 1971; *Victimes du devoir* and *Une Victime du devoir*, edited by Vera Lee, Houghton, 1972; *Macbett*, Gallimard, 1972.

Omnibus volumes in translation: *Plays*, Volumes I-VII, translated by Donald Watson, Grove Press.

SCREENPLAYS—(Author of text) *Monsieur Tete*, 1959; (co-author) *Seven Capital Sins*, Embassy, 1962; also *La Vase*, 1972.

TELEPLAYS—Ballet version, *The Lesson*, Eurovision, 1963.

RADIO PLAYS—*The Picture* (English translation of "Le Tableau" by Donald Watson), BBC, 1957; *Rhinoceros*, BBC 1959.

BOOKS—(Translator with G. Gabrin) Pavel Dan, *Le Vieil Urcan*, Editions Jean Vigneau, 1945; *Ionesco: Les Rhinoceros au theatre* (with a short story and selections from his journal), R. Julliard, 1960; *La Photo du Colonel* (narratives, includes "Oriflamme," "La Photo du Colonel," "Le Picton de Vase," and "Printomps, 1939"), Gallimard, 1962, new edition, 1970, translation by Jean Stewart published as *The Colonel's Photograph*, Faber & Faber, 1967, Grove Press, 1969; *Notes et contre-notes* (essays, addresses, lectures on drama), Gallimard, 1962, translation by Donald Watson published as *Notes and Counter-notes*, Grove Press, 1964; (author of notes) Joan Miro, *Quelques fleurs pour des amis*, Societe International d'Art, 1964; *Journal en miettes* (autobiography), Mercure de France, 1967, translation by Stewart published as *Fragments of a Journal*, Grove Press, 1968; *Story Number 1: For Children under Three Years of Age* (illustrated by Etienne Delessert), translated by Calvin K. Towle, Harlin Quist, 1968; *Present passe, passe present* (autobiography), Mercure de France, 1968, translation by Helen R. Lane published as *Present Past, Past Present*, Grove Press, 1971; (with Michael Benamou) *Mise en Train: Premiere Annee de francais* (textbook for children, grades 11 12), Macmillan, 1969; *Story Number 2: For Children under Three Years of Age* (illustrated by Delessert), Harlin Quist, 1970; (author of text) Gerard Schneider, *Catalogo* (art exhibit), Torino, 1970; *Story Number 3: For Children over Three Years of Age* (illultrated by Philippe Corentin), translated by Ciba Vaughn, Harlin Quist, 1971; (with Jean Delay) *Discours de reception d'Eugene Ionesco a l'Academie francaise et reponse de Jean Dalay*, Gallimard, 1971; also *The Hermit* (novel), 1974.

PERIODICALS—Contributor: *Les Lettres nouvelles; Les Lettres francaises; Encore; Evergreen Review; Mademosielle; L'Express; Tulane Drama Review; Theatre Arts; Commentary, London Magazine*, and others.

AWARDS: Chevalier Legion of Honor, Commander, ordre des Arts et des Lettres, 1961; Prix de la Critique, Tours Festival, for film *Monsieur Tete*, 1959; Grand Prix Italia, ballet version of *The Lesson*, as shown on Eurovision, 1963; Grand Prix du Theatre de la Societe des Auteurs, for total body of work, 1966; Le Prix National du Theatre, 1969; Prix Litteraire de Monaco, 1969; Austrian Prize for European Literature, 1971; Jerusalem Prize, 1973; International Writers Fellowship, Welsh Arts Council, 1973.

MEMBER: Academie Francaise, 1970—.

ADDRESSES: HOME—96 Boulevard du Montparnasse, 75014 Paris, France. PUBLISHER—c/o Editions Gallimard, 5 rue Sebastien-Bottin, 75007 Paris, France.*

*   *   *

IRVING, Amy   1953-

PERSONAL: Born September 10, 1953, in Palo Alto, CA; daughter of Jules (a director and co-founder of Actor's Workshop, San Francisco) and Prisilla Pointer (an actress) Irving; married Steven Spielberg (a director and producer); children: one daughter. EDUCATION: American Conservatory Theatre, San Francisco, 1971-72; London Academy of Music and Dramatic Art, London, England, 1972-75.

VOCATION: Actress.

CAREER: STAGE DEBUT—As a nine-month-old baby, *Rumpelstilskin*, Actor's Workshop, San Francisco, 1954. BROADWAY DEBUT—Constanza Weber, *Amadeus*, Broadhurst Theatre, 1981. PRINCIPAL STAGE APPEARANCES—Juliet, *Romeo and Juliet*, Los Angeles Free Shakespeare Theatre, 1975, repeated role at the Seattle Repertory Theatre, 1982; Elvira, *Blithe Spirit*, Santa Fe Festival Theatre, 1983; Ellie Dunn, *Heartbreak House*, Circle in the Square Theatre, New York City, 1983.

FILM DEBUT—Sue Snell, *Carrie*, United Artists, 1976. PRINCIPAL FILM APPEARANCES—Gillian, *The Fury*, Twentieth Century-Fox, 1978; Rosemary, *Voices*, United Artists, 1979; Lily Ramsey, *Honeysuckle Rose*, Warner Brothers, 1980; Heidi, *The Competition*, Columbia, 1980; Hadass, *Yentl*, Metro-Goldwyn-Mayer/United Artists, 1983; Micki, *Micki and Maude*, Columbia, 1984; *Rumpelstilskin* and *Soft Target*, both upcoming.

TELEVISION DEBUT—*The Rookies*, ABC. PRINCIPAL TELEVISION APPEARANCES—Episodic: passenger, "Ghost Train," *Amazing Stories*, NBC, 1985; Ellie Dunn, "Heartbreak House," *Great Performances*, PBS, 1986. Movies: *Panache*, 1976; Anna Anderson, *Anastasia: The Mystery of Anne*, 1986; also, *I'm a Fool; Once an Eagle*. Mini-Series: Anjuli, *The Far Pavilions*, Home Box Office, 1984.

MEMBER: Actors' Equity Association, American Federation of Television and Radio Artists, Screen Actors Guild.

ADDRESSES: AGENT—Triad Artists, Inc., 888 Seventh Avenue, Suite 1602, New York, NY 10106.*

*   *   *

IRVING, George S.   1922-

PERSONAL: Born George Irving Shelasky, November 1, 1922, in Springfield, MA; son of Abraham and Rebecca (Sack) Shelasky; married Maria Karnilova. EDUCATION: Attended Classical High

School, Springfield, MA and Leland Powers School, Boston, MA; trained as a singer with Cora Claiborne, Henry Jacobi, Max Rudolph, William Tarrasch, and Elena Gerhardt. MILITARY: U.S. Army, 1943-46.

VOCATION: Actor and singer.

CAREER: STAGE DEBUT—Suitor, *The Marriage Proposal,* 1940. BROADWAY DEBUT—Chorus, *Oklahoma!,* St. James Theatre, 1943. LONDON DEBUT—Ben, *The Telephone* and Mr. Gobineau, *The Medium,* Aldwych Theatre, 1948. PRINCIPAL STAGE APPEARANCES—Stock: *Dark Victory* and *The Student Prince,* both at the Casino Theatre, Sandwich, MA, 1941; with the St. Louis Municipal Opera Company, MO: *Glamorous Night, Sally, Song of the Flame, Girl Crazy, Show Boat,* and *The New Moon,* all 1942.

The Vagabond King, Babes in Toyland, and *Robin Hood,* all at the Papermill Playhouse, Milburn, NJ, 1942; chorus, *Lady in the Dark,* Broadway production, New York City, 1943; *Call Me Mister,* National Theatre, New York City, 1946; Ben, *The Telephone* and Mr. Gobineau, *The Medium,* Theatre de La Renaissance, Paris, 1948; *Along Fifth Avenue,* Broadhurst Theatre, New York City, 1949; Senator, *That's the Ticket,* Shubert Theatre, Philadelphia, 1949; Mr. Gage, *Gentlemen Prefer Blondes,* Ziegfeld Theatre, New York City, 1949.

Harry, *A Tree Grows in Brooklyn,* Dr. Engel, *The Student Prince,* and Jigger, *Carousel,* all at the State Fair Music Hall, Dallas, TX, 1952; *Two's Company,* Alvin Theatre, New York City, 1952; Dario, *Me and Juliet,* Majestic Theatre, New York City, 1953; Varlaam, *Boris Godunov,* Her Majesty's Theatre, Montreal, Quebec, Canada, 1953; Boris, *Can-Can,* Shubert Theatre, New York City, 1954; Larry Hastings, *Bells Are Ringing,* Shubert Theatre, New York City, 1956; Mr. Peachum, *The Beggar's Opera,* City Center, New York City, 1957; Big Bill, *Shinbone Alley,* Broadway Theatre, New York City, 1957.

Various roles, *The Good Soup,* Plymouth Theatre, New York City, 1960; Setmore, *Lock Up Your Daughters,* Shubert Theatre, New Haven, CT, 1960; McGee, *Oh Kay,* East 74th Street Theatre, New York City, 1960; Inspector, *Irma la Douce,* Plymouth Theatre, New York City, 1960; Metallus, *Romulus,* Music Box Theatre, New York City, 1962; Signor Bellardi, *Bravo Giovanni,* Broadhurst Theatre, New York City, 1962; Rosenzweig, *Seidman and Son,* Belasco Theatre, New York City, 1962; Charles Davis, *Tovarich,* Broadway Theatre, New York City, 1963; Marolles, *A Murderer Among Us,* Morosco Theatre, New York City, 1964; Mr. Smith, *Alfie!,* Morosco Theatre, New York City, 1964; Chernov, *Anya,* Morosco Theatre, New York City, 1964; ballad singer, *Galileo,* Vivian Beaumont Theatre, New York City, 1967; Phillippe Bonnard, *The Happy Time,* Broadway Theatre, New York City, 1968; Hannibal Beam, *Up Eden,* Jan Hus Playhouse, New York City, 1968; Mayor, *Promenade,* Promenade Theatre, New York City, 1969.

TV repairman and real estate agent, *Four on a Garden,* Broadhurst Theatre, New York City, 1971; Richard M. Nixon, *An Evening with Richard Nixon and. . .,* Shubert Theatre, New York City, 1972; Capitano Cockalorum, *Comedy,* Colonial Theatre, Boston, MA, 1972; Madame Lucy, *Irene,* Minskoff Theatre, New York City, 1973; Elbert C. Harland, *Who's Who in Hell,* Lunt-Fontanne Theatre, New York City, 1974; the Mayor, *The Government Inspector,* Hartman Theatre, Stamford, CT, 1975; three roles, *So Long 174th Street,* Harkness Theatre, New York City, 1976;

Chairman, *Down at the Old Bull and Bush,* PAF Playhouse, Huntington, Long Island, NY, 1978; Herman Glogamer, *Once in a Lifetime,* Circle in the Square Theatre, New York City, 1978; Uncle Chris, *I Remember Mama,* Majestic Theatre, New York City, 1979.

Mr. Micawber, *Copperfield,* American National Theatre Academy (ANTA) Theatre, New York City, 1981; Major-General Stanley, *The Pirates of Penzance,* Minskoff Theatre, New York City, 1981; Sergei Alexandrovitch, *On Your Toes,* Virginia Theatre, New York City, 1983; *Me and My Girl,* Marquis Theatre, New York City, 1986—.

Stock: *South Pacific, The Remarkable Mr. Pennypacker, Annie Get Your Gun, The Soft Touch, Silk Stockings, Fledermaus, The Boy Friend, Li'l Abner, Oh Captain!.*

MAJOR TOURS—*The Student Prince,* U.S. cities, 1941; Boris, *Can-Can,* U.S. cities, 1954; Bob, *Irma la Douce,* with the Los Angeles Civic Light Opera Company, U.S. cities, 1977.

PRINCIPAL TELEVISION APPEARANCES—Episodic: *Barry Wood's Variety Show,* 1948; also appeared in operas: Chicken Little,'' ''The Mighty Casey,'' and ''The Sleeping Beauty,'' all on *Omnibus,* CBS.

AWARDS: Antoinette Perry Award, 1973, for *Irene.*

MEMBER: Actors' Equity Association.*

*   *   *

Photography by Paul Hoffman

MARK ISHAM

ISHAM, Mark   1951-

PERSONAL: Born September 7, 1951, in New York, NY; son of Howard Fuller (a humanities professor) and Patricia (a violinist; maiden name, Hammond) Isham; married Margaret Johnstone (a music publicist), May 24, 1986. EDUCATION: Attended University of California at Santa Barbara, studied classical trumpet with John Cappola, Joyce Johnson, and Joe Alessi.

VOCATION: Musician and composer.

CAREER: FIRST FILM WORK—Composer: *Never Cry Wolf*, Buena Vista, 1983. PRINCIPAL FILM WORK—Composer: *Mrs. Soffel*, Metro-Goldwyn-Mayer/United Artists, 1984; *The Times of Harvey Milk*, Teleculture, 1984; *Country*, Buena Vista, 1984; also, *Trouble in the Mind*.

PRINCIPAL STAGE APPEARANCES—Trumpeter: Oakland Symphony, San Francisco Symphony, and San Francisco Opera.

MAJOR TOURS—With Arte Lande, European and U.S. cities.

RECORDINGS: ALBUMS—(With Charles Jankel) *Charles Jankel*, A & M; (with Tom Fogerty) *Deal It Out*, Fantasy; (with America) *View from the Ground*, Capitol; (with Van Morrison) *Live at the Belfast Opera House, Into the Music, Inarticulate Speech of the Heart, Common One,* and *Beautiful Vision*, all Warner Brothers; (with Art Lande) *Story of Baku* and *Eccentricities of Earl Dant*, both Arch Street and *Rubisa Patrol* and *Desert Marauders*, both ECM; (with Group 87) *Group 87*, Columbia and *A Career in Dada Processing*, Capitol; (with Steve Miller) *Singing Whale Songs in a Low Voice*, Hip Pocket/Windham Hill and *Sampler 84* and *Country*, both Windham Hill; (with Liz Story) *Unaccountable Effect*, Windham Hill; (with Will Ackerman) *Past Light, Film Music*, and *Vapor Drawings*, all Windham Hill.

MEMBER: American Society of Composers, Authors and Publishers.

ADDRESSES: OFFICE—3395 Deronda Drive, Hollywood, CA 90068. AGENT—c/o Brian Loucks, Creative Artists Agency, 1888 Central Park E., Century City, CA 90067.

J

JACKNESS, Andrew 1952-

PERSONAL: Born September 27, 1952, in New York, NY; son of Jack (in advertising) and Meredith (an education administrator) Jackness. EDUCATION: Studio and Forum of Stage Design, certificate, 1975; Yale University School of Drama, M.F.A., 1979.

VOCATION: Scenic designer.

CAREER: PRINCIPAL STAGE WORK—Scenic designer, Broadway productions: *Wings,* Lyceum Theatre, 1979; *John Gabriel Borkman,* Circle in the Square, 1980; *The Little Foxes,* Martin Beck Theatre, 1981; *Grownups,* Lyceum Theatre, 1981; *Beyond Therapy,* Brooks Atkinson Theatre, 1982; *Whodunnit,* Biltmore Theatre, 1982; *Precious Sons,* Longacre Theatre, New York City, 1986.

Off-Broadway: At the Playwrights Horizons Theatre: *Justice,* 1979, *Coming Attractions,* 1980, *Geniuses,* 1982, *The Rise and Rise of Daniel Rocket,* 1982, *Christmas on Mars,* 1983, and *Isn't It Romantic,* 1984; *The White Devil,* Acting Company, 1979; *Emigres,* Dodger Theatre Group, 1979; *Barbarians,* Brooklyn Academy of Music Theatre Company, 1980; *American Days,* Manhattan Theatre Club, 1980; *The Man & the Fly,* Puetro Rican Travelling Theatre, 1982; *Sound & Beauty,* New York Shakespeare Festival (NYSF), 1983; *Cinders,* NYSF, 1984; *Linda Her* and *The Fairy Garden,* Second Stage, 1984; *Isn't It Romantic,* Lucille Lortel Theatre, 1984; *Salonika,* NYSF, 1985; *Before the Dawn,* American Place Theatre, 1985; *The Vienna Notes,* Second Stage, 1985; *Mrs. Warren's Profession,* Roundabout Theatre, 1985; *The Adventures of Kathy & Mo,* Second Stage, 1986; *Tent Meeting,* Astor Place Theatre, 1987; *Little Murders,* Second Stage, 1987.

Regional: *Wings,* Yale Repertory Theatre, New Haven, CT, 1978; *The Bundle,* Yale Repertory Theatre, 1979; at the Williamstown Theatre Festival, MA: *Idiot's Delight,* 1979, *Whose Life Is It Anyway?* and *The Cherry Orchard,* both 1980, *Trelawny of the Wells,* 1982, *Uncle Vanya,* 1984, *The Glass Menagerie,* 1985, and *School for Scandal,* 1986; *The Cherry Orchard,* American Stage Festival, Milford, NH, 1980; *Terry by Terry,* American Repertory Theatre, Cambridge, MA, 1980; *Grownups,* American Repertory Theatre, 1981; *Trilogy,* Spoleto Festival, U.S.A., Charleston, SC, 1981; *Molly,* Long Wharf Theatre, New Haven, CT, 1982; *Dog Eat Dog,* Hartford Stage Company, CT, 1983; *Not Quite Jerusalem,* Long Wharf Theatre, 1983; *An American Comedy,* Mark Taper Forum, Los Angeles, 1983; *Isn't It Romantic,* Los Angeles Stage Company, 1985; *The Taming of the Shrew,* American Shakespeare Festival, Stratford, CT, 1985; *Die Fledermaus,* Santa Fe Opera Company, 1986; *Present Laughter,* Center Stage, Baltimore, 1986; *A Doll's House,* Hartford Stage Company, 1986; *Isn't It Romantic,* Ivanhoe Theatre, Chicago, 1986.

International: *Wings,* National Theatre of Great Britain, 1979, and at the Schiller Theatre, Berlin, West Germany, 1981; *Caritas,* National Theatre of Great Britain, 1981.

MAJOR TOURS—Scenic designer: *South Pacific,* Los Angeles Civic Light Opera, national tour, 1985.

PRINCIPAL TELEVISION WORK—Scenic designer, "Grownups," *Great Performances,* PBS, 1985; "Blue Window," *American Playhouse,* PBS, 1986; music videos for Motley Crue, Kool & the Gang, Kiss, and April Wine, 1984.

RELATED CAREER—Instructor of scenic design: Bard College, 1975-77, Studio Forum of Stage Design, 1980—, Lester Polakov Studio of Stage Design, 1981-85, Playwrights Horizons Theatre School, 1983.

AWARDS: Donald Oenslager Prize, 1978; Best Set Design, Carbonell Award, 1980, for *The Little Foxes;* Japan Society Travel Grant, 1980; Drama Desk Award nomination, 1983, for *Whodunnit;* National Endowment for the Arts Artistic Associate at Playwrights Horizons, 1983; NISCA Artistic Associateship at Second Stage, New York City, 1983.

MEMBER: United Scenic Artists, Local 829.

ADDRESSES: HOME—503 E. Sixth Street, New York, NY 10009. AGENT—c/o Paul Martino, International Creative Management, 40 W. 57th Street, New York, NY 10019.

*   *   *

JACKSON, Glenda 1936-

PERSONAL: Born May 9, 1936, in Birkenhead, Cheshire, England; married Roy Hodges, 1958 (divorced, 1976); children: Daniel. EDUCATION: Trained for the stage at the Royal Academy of Dramatic Art.

VOCATION: Actress.

CAREER: STAGE DEBUT—*Separate Tables,* Worthing, U.K., 1957. LONDON DEBUT—Ruby, *All Kinds of Men,* Arts Theatre, September, 1957. BROADWAY DEBUT—Charlotte Corday, *Marat/Sade,* Martin Beck Theatre, 1965. PRINCIPAL STAGE APPEARANCES—Alexandra, *The Idiot,* Lyric Theatre, Hammersmith, London, 1962; Siddie, *Alfie,* Mermaid Theatre, then Duchess Theatre, London, 1963; appeared in "Theatre of Cruelty" season with the Royal Shakespeare Company at the London Academy of Music and Dramatic Art (LAMDA), 1964; Princess of France, *Love's Labour's Lost* and Ophelia, *Hamlet,* both with the Royal Shakespeare Company, Stratford-Upon-Avon, U.K., 1965; Eva,

Puntila, reader, *The Investigation,* and Charlotte Corday, *Marat/ Sade,* all with the Royal Shakespeare Company at the Aldwych Theatre, London, 1965; Masha, *Three Sisters,* Royal Court Theatre, London, 1967; Tamara Fanghorn, *Fanghorn,* Fortune Theatre, London, 1967.

Katherine Winter, *Collaborators,* Duchess Theatre, London, 1973; Solange, *The Maids,* Greenwich Theatre, London, 1974; title role, *Hedda Gabler,* with the Royal Shakespeare Company at the Aldwych Theatre, London, 1975; Vittoria Corombona, *The White Devil,* Old Vic Theatre, London, 1976; title role, *Stevie,* Vaudeville Theatre, London, 1977; Cleopatra, *Antony and Cleopatra,* with the Royal Shakespeare Company, Stratford-Upon-Avon, 1978, then at the Aldwych Theatre, London, 1979; title role, *Rose,* Duke of York's Theatre, London, 1980, then Cort Theatre, New York City, 1981; appeared in *Phedra,* 1984; Nina Leeds, *Strange Interlude,* Nederlander Theatre, New York City, 1985.

MAJOR TOURS—Title role, *Hedda Gabler,* with the Royal Shakespeare Company, U.S., Australian, and U.K. cities, 1975.

PRINCIPAL FILM APPEARANCES—*Marat/Sade,* United Artists, 1967; *Negatives,* Continental, 1968; *Women in Love,* United Artists, 1970; *The Music Lovers,* United Artists, 1971; *Mary Queen of Scots,* Universal, 1971; *Sunday Bloody Sunday,* United Artists, 1971; *The Nelson Affair,* Universal, 1972; *Triple Echo,* Altuna, 1973; *A Touch of Class,* AVCO-Embassy, 1973; *The Tempter,* 1974; *The Maids,* American Film Theatre, 1975; *The Romantic Englishwoman,* New World, 1975; *Hedda Gabler,* Brut Productions, 1976; *Incredible Sarah,* 1976; *Nasty Habits,* Brut Productions, 1977; *Stevie,* 1978; *The Class of Mrs. MacMichael,* Brut Productions, 1978; *House Calls,* Universal, 1978; *Lost and Found,* Columbia, 1979; *Health,* 1979; *Hopscotch,* AVCO-Embassy, 1980; *Giro City,* 1982; *Return of the Soldier,* 1982; *Summit Conference,* 1982; *Great and Small,* 1983; *And Nothing But the Truth,* Castle Hill, 1984; *Turtle Diary,* Samuel Goldwyn Co., 1986; Charlotte, *Beyond Therapy,* New World Productions, 1987.

PRINCIPAL TELEVISION APPEARANCES—Series: "Elizabeth R," *Masterpiece Theatre,* PBS, 1971. Movies: Title role, *The Patricia Neal Story,* 1981; *Sakharov,* Home Box Office, 1984.

AWARDS: Most Promising Actress, *Variety* Award, 1965, for *Marat/Sade;* Best Actress, Academy Award, 1970, for *Women in Love;* Outstanding Single Performance by an Actress in a Leading Role, Emmy Award, 1972, for "Elizabeth R.," *Masterpiece Theatre;* Best Actress, Academy Award, 1973, for *A Touch of Class.* Honorary degrees: Doctor of Literature, Liverpool University, 1978.

SIDELIGHTS: RECREATIONS—Gardening, reading, listening to music, and travel.

ADDRESSES: AGENT—Crouch Associates, 59 Frith Street, London W1, England; Robinson Luttrell and Associates, 141 El Camino Drive, Suite 110, Beverly Hills, CA 90212; Lionel Larner, Ltd., 850 Seventh Avenue, New York, NY 10019.*

* * *

JAFFE, Michael   1945-

PERSONAL: Born January 9, 1945, in New York, NY; son of Henry (a producer) and Jean (an acting teacher; maiden name, Muir) Jaffe; married Jann Dutmer (an assistant director). EDUCA-

TION: Yankton College, B.A., 1967; attended University of Chicago, 1968-69; Cornell University, M.A., 1971.

VOCATION: Producer.

CAREER: PRINCIPAL TELEVISION WORK—Movies: Executive in charge of production, *Alexander, the Other Side of Dawn,* ABC, 1977; producer, "Emily, Emily," *Hallmark Hall of Fame,* NBC, 1977; producer, *The Death of Richie,* NBC, 1977; co-producer, *A Woman Called Moses,* NBC, 1978; producer, *Battered,* NBC, 1978; co-producer, *When She Was Bad,* ABC, 1979; producer, "Aunt Mary," *Hallmark Hall of Fame,* CBS, 1979; producer, *Escape,* CBS, 1980; co-executive producer, *Incident at Crestridge,* CBS, 1981; co-executive producer, *I Was a Mail Order Bride,* CBS, 1982; producer, *The Seduction of Gina,* CBS, 1983. Series: Financier and co-executive producer, *Emergency Plus Four,* NBC, 1976.

PRINCIPAL FILM WORK—Producer, *Better Off Dead,* Warner Brothers, 1985; co-executive producer, *Bad Medicine,* Twentieth Century-Fox, 1985; producer, *One Crazy Summer,* Warner Brothers, 1986; producer, *Disorderlies,* Warner Brothers, 1987.

RELATED CAREER—President, Michael Jaffe Films, Ltd.

AWARDS: Arc of Excellence Award, 1977, for "Emily, Emily," *Hallmark Hall of Fame;* Lonne Elder Award, Writers Guild of America Award, and Christopher Award, all 1978, for *A Woman Called Moses;* American Women in Film Certificate of Commendation, 1978, for *Battered;* Award of Excellence, Film Advisory Board, 1979, for *When She Was Bad;* Christopher Award, 1979, for "Aunt Mary," *Hallmark Hall of Fame.*

MEMBER: Academy of Motion Picture Arts and Sciences, Academy of Television Arts and Sciences.

ADDRESSES: HOME—Los Angeles, CA. OFFICE—1145 N. McCadden Place, Los Angeles, CA 90038.

* * *

JANIS, Conrad   1928-

PERSONAL: Born February 11, 1928, in New York, NY; son of Sidney (an art dealer and writer) and Harriet (a writer) Janis; married Vicki Quarles (a model) May 20, 1948 (divorced, June 1957); married Ronda Copland, April 22, 1979 (divorced, April, 1982); children: (first marriage) Christopher, Carin.

VOCATION: Actor, musician, and art dealer.

CAREER: BROADWAY DEBUT—Haskell Cummings III, *Junior Miss,* Lyceum Theatre, November 18, 1941. LONDON DEBUT—Timothy Bertram, *The Velvet Shotgun,* Duchess Theatre, 1958. PRINCIPAL STAGE APPEARANCES—Floyd Allen, *Dark of the Moon,* 46th Street Theatre, New York City, 1945; Barney Brennen, *The Next Half Hour,* Empire Theatre, New York City, 1945; Charlie, *The Brass Ring,* Lyceum Theatre, New York City, 1952; Eddie Davis, *Time Out for Ginger,* Lyceum Theatre, New York City, 1952; Waldo, *Remains to Be Seen,* Clinton Theatre, CT, 1952; Cantrell, *The Terrible Swift Sword,* Phoenix Repertory

Theatre, New York City, 1955; *Joy Ride,* Huntington Hartford Theatre, Los Angeles, 1956; Conrad, *Visit to a Small Planet,* Booth Theatre, New York City, 1957; Johnny King, *Make a Million,* Playhouse Theatre, New York City, 1958.

Adam, *Sunday in New York,* 48th Street Theatre, New York City, 1961; provided music with his band, "The Tail Gate Five" and appeared as emcee and Rudy, *Marathon '33,* American National Theatre Academy (ANTA) Theatre, New York City, 1963; Kruger, *The Front Page,* Ethel Barrymore Theatre, New York City, 1969; Jimmy Skouras, *No Hard Feelings,* Mark Hellinger Theatre, New York City, 1973; George, *Same Time Next Year,* Brooks Atkinson Theatre, New York City, 1975.

MAJOR TOURS—Barlow Adams, *Junior Miss,* U.S. cities, 1942; George, *Same Time, Next Year,* U.S. cities, 1975.

FILM DEBUT—Ronald, *Snafu,* Columbia, 1945. PRINCIPAL FILM APPEARANCES—Johnikins, *Margie,* Twentieth Century-Fox, 1946; *That Hagen Girl,* Warner Brothers, 1947; *The Brasher Doubloon,* Twentieth Century-Fox, 1947; *Beyond Glory,* Paramount, 1948; *Airport '75,* Universal, 1974; *The Happy Hooker,* 1975; *The Duchess and the Dirtwater Fox,* Twentieth Century-Fox, 1976; *Roseland,* Cinema Shares, 1977; *The Buddy Holly Story,* Columbia, 1978; *Oh God, Book II,* Warner Brothers, 1980; band leader, *Nothing in Common,* Tri-Star, 1986.

PRINCIPAL TELEVISION APPEARANCES—Series: Title role, *Jimmy Hughes, Rookie Cop,* DuMont, 1953; Edward, *Bonino,* NBC, 1953; Otto Palindrome, *Quark,* NBC, 1978; Frederick McConnell, *Mork and Mindy,* ABC, 1978-82. Episodic: *Kraft Theatre,* NBC; *Studio One,* CBS; *Gulf Playhouse,* NBC; *The Untouchables,* ABC; *The Nurses,* NBC; *Colgate Comedy Hour,* NBC; *CBS-TV Workshop,* CBS; *Actors Studio Theatre,* CBS; *Philco Theatre,* NBC; *Suspense,* CBS; *Barnaby Jones,* CBS; *Maude,* CBS, *St. Elsewhere,* NBC.

Movies: *The Virginia Hill Story,* NBC, 1974. Guest: *Arthur Godfrey Show,* CBS; *The Stork Club Show,* NBC; *The Home Show,* NBC; *The Tonight Show,* NBC; with his band, *The Steve Allen Show,* NBC.

RELATED CAREER—Leader and jazz trombonist, "Conrad Janis and the Tailgaters," performed in New York City at Carnegie Hall, Town Hall, Jimmie Ryans, Central Plaza, Child's Paramount, Basin Street and the Metropole Cafe. Also performed at Beverly Caverns, Hollywood, The Savoy Club, Boston, Jazz, Ltd., Chicago, Yale University, University of Pennsylvania, University of Virginia, and touring U.S. cities, 1951—; leader, Beverly Hills Unlisted Jazz Band, 1978—.

NON-RELATED CAREER—Co-director, Janis Gallery, New York City.

AWARDS: Best Supporting Performance, Silver World Award, 1950; *Theatre World* Award, 1952, for *The Brass Ring;* Best Jazz Trombonist, *Playboy* Jazz Poll Award, 1960, 1961.

MEMBER: Actors' Equity Association, Screen Actors Guild, American Federation of Television and Radio Artists, American Federation of Musicians, Local 802; Nautico Club.

ADDRESSES: OFFICE—Janis Gallery, Six W. 57th Street, New York, NY 10019.*

MARTIN JARVIS

JARVIS, Martin   1941-

PERSONAL: Born August 4, 1941, in Cheltenham, England; son of Denys Harry and Margot Lillian Jarvis; married second wife Rosalind Ayres (an actress); children: two sons. EDUCATION: Attended the Royal Academy of Dramatic Art, London.

VOCATION: Actor and writer.

CAREER: STAGE DEBUT—Title role, *Henry V,* National Youth Theatre, Royal Academy of Dramatic Art, London. PRINCIPAL STAGE APPEARANCES—Sebastian, *Twelfth Night,* Library Theatre, Manchester, U.K., 1962; Drummer, *Cockade,* New Arts Theatre, London, 1963; Franz Delanoue, *Poor Bitos,* New Arts Theatre, 1963, then Duke of York's Theatre, both London, 1964; Octavius Robinson, *Man and Superman,* New Arts Theatre, then Vaudeville Theatre, both London, 1966; Owen Gereth, *The Spoils of Poynton,* May Fair Theatre, London, 1969; Piers Cramp, *The Bandwagon,* Mermaid Theatre, London, 1969; Jack Absolute, *The Rivals,* Thorndike Theatre, Leatherhead, U.K., and University Theatre, New York City, 1972; title role, *Hamlet,* Festival of British Theatre, Theatre Royal, Windsor, U.K., 1973; Adam, *Paradise Lost,* recitals at Chichester, U.K., then the Old Vic Theatre Company, London, 1975; Arnold Champion-Cheney, *The Circle,* Chichester Festival, U.K., then Haymarket Theatre, London, 1976; Edward VIII, *The Woman I Love,* Churchill Theatre, Bromely, U.K., 1978; appeared in production of *Woman in Mind,* 1986-87.

Also: *Caught in the Act,* Garrick Theatre, London; Ernest, *The*

Importance of Being Earnest, "274," *Victoria Station,* and Hector, *The Trojan War Will Not Take Place,* all at the National Theatre, London.

MAJOR TOURS—Father Michael, *The Prodigal Daughter,* British cities, 1974; Young Marlow, *She Stoops to Conquer,* Canadian cities and at the Hong Kong Arts Festival, 1978.

FILM DEBUT—*The Last Escape,* United Artists, 1970.

TELEVISION DEBUT—Jon, *The Forsyte Saga,* BBC. PRINCIPAL TELEVISION APPEARANCES—Series: *Rings on Their Fingers,* BBC; *Breakaway;* Wildred Anstey, *The Black Tower,* BBC. Movies: King George VI, *Ike: The War Years,* 1978; *The Bunker,* CBS, 1981; Mr. Stone, *The Business of Murder,* BBC; *Make and Break,* BBC; also Uriah Heep, *David Copperfield; Nicholas Nickleby.*

PRINCIPAL RADIO WORK—Series: *Jarvis' Frayn.*

WRITINGS: RADIO—*Bright Boy,* BBC; also short stories for BBC Radio.

MEMBER: British Actors' Equity Association; National Youth Theatre (council member), U.K.

SIDELIGHTS: FAVORITE ROLES—Arnold, *The Circle.* RECREATIONS—Cooking and music.

ADDRESSES: AGENT—(British) Michael Whitehall Ltd., 125 Gloucester Road, London SW7, England; (American) Irv Swartz, Agency for the Performing Arts, 9000 Sunset Blvd. Suite 315, Los Angeles, CA 90069.

*   *   *

JEANS, Michael

PERSONAL: Son of Ronald Jeans (a playwright). EDUCATION—Trained at the London Mask Theatre School. MILITARY—Royal Naval Air Serivce, 1941-46.

VOCATION: Writer, producer, and educator.

CAREER: PRINCIPAL TELEVISION WORK—Developed a drama/music format for educational television programs in England. Using comedy and satire to encourage serious thought and discussion concerning social issues and textbook skills, he wrote and produced *The Living of It* and *Rules, Rules, Rules,* for ATV. More recently, he has developed a pre-school program called *Pipkins,* which gives small children the opportunity of seeing actors develop an idea into a play using minimal props and costumes.

WRITINGS: BOOKS—*Let's Pretend* (based on his television show *Pipkins*), Oxford University Press, 1987.

MEMBER: Union Society, Cambridge University; Wig and Pen Club, London.

SIDELIGHTS: Michael Jeans told *CTFT* that his program *Pipkins* "is designed to help mothers of children living in areas where outdoor play is difficult. It encourages creativity and inventiveness in an ordinary surrounding."

ADDRESSES: AGENT—Eric Glass Ltd., 28 Berkeley Square, London W1X 6HD, England.

*   *   *

JECKO, Timothy   1938-

PERSONAL: Born January 24, 1938, in Washington, DC; son of Perry Joseph and Cora Elizabeth (Timothy) Jecko; married Mary Louise Long, October 20, 1962 (divorced, 1982); married Margaret Ann Oksner, August 1, 1982; children: Christopher, Nicholas, Sara. EDUCATION: Yale University, B.A., 1959, Yale School of Drama, M.F.A., 1967. MILITARY: U.S. Naval Reserve, 1959-63.

VOCATION: Actor.

CAREER: STAGE DEBUT—Matt, *The Fantasticks,* Theatre-in-the-Rink, New Haven, CT, 1964. BROADWAY DEBUT—Louis Howe, *Annie,* Alvin Theatre, 1980-82 for eight hundred performances. PRINCIPAL STAGE APPEARANCES—Georg Nowack, *She Loves Me* and Sir Evelyn, *Anything Goes,* both Mt. Southington Theatre, CT, 1965; Lt. Lansing, *The Good Lieutenant,* Yale Drama School, 1967; Harry Paddington, *The Beggars' Opera,* Yale Drama School, 1967; El Gallo, *The Fantasticks,* Cavanaugh Productions, Washington, DC, 1968; Frank Butler, *Annie Get Your Gun,* Smithsonian Mall Theatre, Washington, DC, 1969; Dr. Engel, *The Student Prince,* Allenberry Playhouse, PA, 1978; Alfred, *The Friday Bench,* Quaigh Theatre, New York City, 1979; Dr. Higgins, *Where the Cross Is Made,* Nameless Theatre, New York City, 1979.

TIMOTHY JECKO

Larry, *Woman of the Year*, Palace Theatre, New York City, 1982-83; Sam Craig, *Waitin' in the Wings*, Town Hall Theatre, New York City, 1983; Rev. Peabody, *Shakespeare and the Indians*, State University of New York, Summerfare, 1983; Dr. Robinson, *Downriver*, Musical Theatre Works, New York City, 1984.

FILM DEBUT—*Power*, Film Ventures, 1985.

TELEVISION DEBUT—Colton, *Movin' On*, NBC, 1976. PRINCIPAL TELEVISION APPEARANCES—Series: Father Mulcahy, *The Doctors*, NBC; Mr. Scott, *The Guiding Light*, CBS; Martin Trevor, *Divorce Court*, CBS; Senator Whitestone, *Capitol*, CBS; Tom Hayes, *General Hospital*, ABC; Sam Haggarty, *Starman*, ABC; Gene Woodall, *Knots Landing*, CBS; Richard Blakely, *The Judge*, CBS, 1986.

Episodic: "Out on a Limb," *St. Elsewhere*, NBC, 1985; "Heroes," *Hotel*, ABC, 1985; "When a Body," *Murder, She Wrote*, CBS, 1986; "Fagin, 1986," *Hunter*, NBC, 1986. Mini-Series: Captain Johnson, *Eleanor and Franklin*, NBC, 1977; Brady, *Washington: Behind Closed Doors*, CBS, 1983.

RELATED CAREER—Deputy director, Division of Performing Arts, Smithsonian Institution, Washington, DC, 1967-70; teacher and drama director, Arlington County Public Schools, Arlington, VA, 1970-78.

MEMBER: Actors' Equity Association, Screen Actors Guild, American Federation of Television and Radio Artists.

SIDELIGHTS: Timothy Jecko was the captain of the Yale swim team in 1958-59 and became a national and world record holder on the collegiate level. He was a member of the U.S. Olympic swimming team during the Melbourne, Australia games in 1956.

ADDRESSES: HOME—17132 Palisades Circle, Pacific Palisades, CA 90272.

*   *   *

JENRETTE, Rita

PERSONAL: Born Rita Carpenter; daughter of C.H. (a businessman) and Reba (Garlington) Carpenter; married John Jenrette (a former U.S. Congressman; divorced).EDUCATION: University of Texas, B.A., 1971; trained for the stage at Harvey Lembeck Comedy Workshop and Parmount Studios and with Stella Adler, Marilyn Freed, Tracey Roberts, Lurene Tuttle, and David Collyer. POLITICS: Independent. RELIGION: Catholic.

VOCATION: Actress.

CAREER: PRINCIPAL TELEVISION APPEARANCES—Episodic: *Kate and Allie*, CBS; *Fantasy Island*, ABC; *Edge of Night*, ABC; *The Girls in the Office*, Canadian Cable. Specials: *Comedy Tonight*, Fox Television; *Dick Clark Special*, ABC; *David Steinberg Special*, HBO; *Club Med Special*, HBO.

Guest: *Oprah Winfrey Show; Lifestyles of the Rich and Famous; Today Show; P.M. Magazine; A.M. New York; Phil Donohue Show; Hour Magazine; Merv Griffin Show; A.M. L.A.; Nightline; Good Morning America; Tomorrow Show; 20/20; People Are Talking*, San Francisco, CA; *Live at Five*, WNBC, New York City.

RITA JENRETTE

Host: *Mid-Morning L.A.; Tomorrow Show*, NBC; *Variety Special; Leave It to the Women*.

PRINCIPAL FILM APPEARANCES—Sandy, *Island Massacre;* Ida, *Aunt Ida's Place*, Wescom, 1987; Sharon, *End of the Line*, Orion, 1987.

PRINCIPAL STAGE APPEARANCES—Albee, *On with the Show*, Austin, TX; Celia, *Hatful of Rain* and Liz, *The Philadelphia Story*, both Los Angeles productions; Nina, *The Pact*, Dramatists Guild, New York City; Rita, *A Girl's Guide to Chaos*, American Place Theatre, New York City.

WRITINGS: BOOKS—*My Capitol Secrets*, Bantam; *Conglomerate*, Richardson-Steirman.

AWARDS: Best Actress, *Drama-Logue* Critics' Award, 1982, for *The Philadelphia Story*.

ADDRESSES: AGENT—c/o Steve Carson, Phoenix Agency, 250 W. 57th Street, Suite 2530, New York, NY 10019.

*   *   *

JETT, Joan

BRIEF ENTRY: Best known as a rock and roll musician, singer, and composer, Joan Jett was raised in a family that had moved around the United States fifteen times, before finally settling in Los

Angeles. It was here, in 1975, that she formed her first group, "The Runaways," which recorded six successful albums for Mercury Records and toured around the world. In 1981, when "The Runaways" disbanded, Jett formed another group and called it, "Joan Jett and the Blackhearts." With the immediate success of the group's first album, *Bad Reputation,* she resumed a busy touring schedule, with her group averaging over two hundred dates per year. Her 1981 album, *I Love to Rock and Roll,* included the top-ten hit, "Crimson and Clover," which was a platinum-selling single and was number one on the pop charts for over eight weeks. The group's other works include the gold-selling record, *Album,* in 1983, *Glorious Results of a Misspent Youth,* and her latest release, *Good Music.* Her popularity and talent made her a natural choice for her film debut as a rock and roll musician in *Light of Day,* released in 1987, by Tri-Star. Although she initially resisted the idea of entering the acting profession by playing a rock and roll star, it occured to her after reading the script that *Light of Day* wasn't simply a rock and roll movie, but an opportunity for her to act as well as to perform her music. Seeing that made all the difference. "Once I could tell that," she said, "then I was interested in it."*

*   *   *

JETTON, Lisbeth   1962-

PERSONAL: Born January 27, 1962, in Charlotte, NC; daughter of Thomas Lawrence (a salesman) and Elizabeth C. Jetton. EDUCATION: North Carolina School of the Arts, B.F.A., theatre.

VOCATION: Actress.

LISBETH JETTON

CAREER: STAGE DEBUT—Elvira, *Blithe Spirit,* Little Theatre of Charlotte, NC, 1978. PRINCIPAL STAGE APPEARANCES—North Carolina School of the Arts, DeMille Theatre: Ela, *Charley's Aunt,* Arlie, *Getting Out,* Hattie, *Laundry and Bourbon,* Patsy, *The Rimers of Eldritch;* also appeared in *Far From the Madding Crowd, St. Patrick's Day, Richard III, School for Wives, The Little Foxes, The Hostage,* and *The Devils;* Martha, *A Christmas Carol,* North Carolina Shakespeare Festival.

PRINCIPAL FILM APPEARANCES—Kirsten, *Landscape Suicide,* independent film, 1986.

PRINCIPAL TELEVISION APPEARANCES—As day player, *All My Children,* ABC; *The Guiding Light,* CBS; *Another World,* NBC; *The Edge of Night,* NBC.

MEMBER: Actors' Equity Association, American Federation of Television and Radio Artists, Screen Actors Guild.

ADDRESSES: HOME—305 W. 45th Street, New York, NY 10036.

*   *   *

JILLIAN, Ann   1951-

PERSONAL: Born Ann Jura Nauseda, January 29, 1951; daughter of Joseph (a pilot) and Margaret Nauseda; married Andrew L. Murcia (a police sergeant and personal manager). EDUCATION: Pierce Junior College, A.A.; trained for the musical theatre with the Los Angeles Civic Light Opera and studied with Len Bledso and Paul Gleason. RELIGION: Catholic.

VOCATION: Actress and singer.

CAREER: STAGE DEBUT—Dainty June, *Gypsy,* Melodyland, Anaheim, CA, 1963. BROADWAY DEBUT—Soubrette, *Sugar Babies,* Mark Hellinger Theatre, 1979-80. PRINCIPAL STAGE APPEARANCES—Daughter, *Anniversary Waltz,* Pasadena Playhouse, CA, 1964; Tintinabula, *A Funny Thing Happened on the Way to the Forum,* Ahmanson Theatre, Los Angeles, 1970; torch singer, *Sammy Cahn's Words and Music,* 1976; Madam Labouche, *Goodnight Ladies,* Drury Lane Theatre, Chicago, 1977.

MAJOR TOURS—*Sugar Babies,* San Francisco, Los Angeles, Chicago, Detroit, Philadelphia, 1979; *I Love My Wife,* Chicago, 1979.

FILM DEBUT—Little Bo Peep, *Babes in Toyland,* Buena Vista, 1961. PRINCIPAL FILM APPEARANCES—Dainty June, *Gypsy,* Warner Brothers, 1963; Joan, *Mr. Mom,* Twentieth Century-Fox, 1983.

TELEVISION DEBUT—*Art Linkletter's House Party,* NBC. PRINCIPAL TELEVISION APPEARANCES—Series: Millie Ballard, *Hazel,* CBS, 1965-66; Cassie Cranston, *It's a Living* (re-titled *Making a Living*), ABC, 1980-82 and 1985-86; Jennifer Farrell, *Jennifer Slept Here,* NBC, 1983-84; also, Joan, *Malibu,* CBS. Episodic: *The Love Boat,* ABC; *Fantasy Island,* ABC; *Ben Casey,* ABC; *The Twilight Zone,* CBS; *Wagon Train,* ABC; *The Partridge Family,* ABC. Movies: Title role, *Mae West,* 1982; *Death Ride to Osaka* (also known as *Girls of the White Orchid*), 1983; *This Wife for Hire,* ABC, 1985; Red Queen *Alice in Wonderland,* CBS, 1985; *Convicted: A Mother's Story,* NBC, 1987. Mini-Series: *Ellis Island,* CBS, 1984.

Guest: *Good Morning America,* NBC; *The Tonight Show,* NBC; *Merv Griffin Show,* ABC; *The Mike Douglas Show,* CBS; *Today Show,* NBC; *Nightline,* ABC. Specials: *Battle of the Network Stars,* ABC, 1980 and 1981; *Night of 100 Stars,* 1982; *Parade of Stars,* 1983; *Black Achievement Awards Special,* 1983; also, three Bob Hope specials; *Perry Como Special.*

NON-RELATED CAREER—Before and between acting jobs, worked as a saleslady, answering-service employee, and cocktail waitress.

WRITINGS: SONG—''Most Beautiful Ghost,'' theme song for television series, *Jennifer Slept Here.*

AWARDS: Dramalogue Award, 1979, for *Sugar Babies;* Best Actress in a Limited Series or Special, Emmy Award nomination, Golden Globe Award nomination, and Bronze Halo Award, all 1982, for *Mae West.*

MEMBER: Actors' Equity Association, Screen Actors Guild, American Federation of Television and Radio Artists.

ADDRESSES: AGENT—c/o Eddie Bondy and Jerry Katzman, William Morris Agency, 151 El Camino Drive, Beverly Hill, CA 90212.*

*   *   *

JOHNSON, Van   1916-

PERSONAL: Born August 25, 1916, in Newport, RI; son of Charles (a plumber) and Loretta (Snyder) Johnson; married Eve Abbott Wynn, January 25, 1947 (divorced); children: a daughter, Schuyler Van.

VOCATION: Actor.

CAREER: BROADWAY DEBUT—In the chorus, *New Faces of 1936,* Vanderbilt Theatre, May 19, 1936. LONDON DEBUT—Harold Hill, *The Music Man,* Adelphi Theatre, 1961. PRINCIPAL STAGE APPEARANCES—*Eight Men in Manhattan,* Rainbow Room, New York City, 1936; the student, *Too Many Girls,* Imperial Theatre, New York City, 1939; understudy Joey Evans, played Victor, and danced, *Pal Joey,* Barrymore Theatre, New York City, 1941; Herbert H. Lundquist, *Come on Strong,* Morosco Theatre, New York City, 1962; Bruce Barrett, *Mating Dance,* Eugene O'Neill Theatre, New York City, 1965; Robert Danvers, *There's a Girl in My Soup,* Coconut Grove Playhouse, Miami, 1968, and repeated role at the Studio Arena Theatre, Buffalo, NY, 1974; Jeff Moss, *Bells Are Ringing,* State Fair Music Hall, Dallas, TX, 1968.

Billy Boylen, *Forty Carats,* Morosco Theatre, 1970; appeared in *Help Stamp Out Marriage,* Country Dinner Playhouse, Dallas, 1974; Paul Friedman, *6 Rms Riv Vu,* Drury Lane Theatre, Chicago, 1974; Scottie Templeton, *Tribute,* Hanna Theatre, Cleveland, OH, then Blackstone Theatre, Chicago, 1980; appeared in *Night of 100 Stars,* Radio City Music Hall, New York City, 1982; Georges, *La Cage aux Folles,* Palace Theatre, New York City, 1985; appeared in *Night of 100 Stars II,* Radio City Music Hall, New York City, 1985.

MAJOR TOURS—All U.S. cities: In vaudeville, 1936; *Damn Yankees,* 1963; Dr. Mark Bruckner, *On a Clear Day You Can See Forever,* 1966; Robert Danvers, *There's a Girl in My Soup,* 1971; *Help Stamp Out Marriage,* 1972; Robert, *Boeing Boeing,* 1975.

FILM DEBUT—The Student, *Too Many Girls,* 1940. PRINCIPAL FILM APPEARANCES—*The War Against Mrs. Hadley,* 1942; *Dr. Gillespie's New Assistant,* 1942; *Pilot No. 5,* 1943; *Dr. Gillespie's Criminal Case,* 1943; *A Guy Named Joe,* 1943; *The Human Comedy,* 1943; *Madame Curie,* 1943; *Till the Clouds Roll By,* 1944; *Three Men in White,* 1944; *Two Girls and a Sailor,* 1944; *Thirty Seconds Over Tokyo,* 1944, *Between Two Women,* 1944; *Thrill of Romance,* 1945; *Weekend at the Waldorf,* 1945; *Ziegfeld Follies,* 1946; *The Romance of Rosy Ridge,* 1947; *The Bride Goes Wild,* 1948; *The State of the Union,* 1948; *Command Decision,* 1948; *In the Good Old Summertime,* 1949; *Scene of the Crime,* 1949; *Battleground,* 1949.

The Big Hangover, 1950; *Grounds for Marriage,* 1950; *Three Guys Named Mike,* 1951; *Go for Broke,* 1951; *Too Young to Kiss,* 1951; *It's a Big Country,* 1951; *Invitation,* 1952; *When in Rome,* 1952; *Washington Story,* 1952; *Plymouth Adventure,* 1952; *Confidentially Connie,* 1953; *Remains to Be Seen,* 1953; *Easy to Love,* 1953; *The Caine Mutiny,* Columbia, 1954; *Siege at Red River,* 1954; *Men of the Fighting Lady,* 1954; *Brigadoon,* Metro-Goldwyn-Mayer (MGM), 1954; *The Last Time I Saw Paris,* 1954; *The End of the Affair,* Columbia, 1955; *The Bottom of the Bottle,* 1956; *Miracle in the Rain,* 1956; *23 Paces to Baker Street,* 1956; *Slander,* 1956; *Kelly and Me,* 1957; *The Last Blitzkrieg,* 1958; *Beyond This Place,* 1958; *Subway in the Sky,* 1959; *Web of Evidence,* 1959; *The Mating Game,* 1959.

The Enemy General, 1960; *Wives and Lovers,* 1963; *Where Angels Go, Trouble Follows,* 1968; *Eagles Over London,* 1970; *The Kidnapping of the President,* 1980; *The Purple Rose of Cairo,* Orion, 1985.

TELEVISION DEBUT—Title role, *The Pied Piper of Hamlin,* November 26, 1957. PRINCIPAL TELEVISION APPEARANCES—Episodic: *I Love Lucy,* CBS; *The Love Boat,* ABC; *Murder, She Wrote,* CBS, 1984. Mini-Series: Marsh Goodwin, *Rich Man, Poor Man—Book I,* ABC, 1976-77. Guest: *Shower of Stars,* CBS; *The Tonight Show,* and others.

NON-RELATED CAREER—Prior to acting career, worked in his father's plumbing office.

ADDRESSES: AGENT—William Morris Agency, Inc., 151 El Camino Drive, Beverly Hills, CA 90212.*

*   *   *

JONES, James Earl   1931-

PERSONAL: Born January 17, 1931, in Arkabutla, MI; son of Robert Earl (an actor) and Ruth (a tailor; maiden name, Williams) Jones; married Cecilia Hart, March 15, 1982. EDUCATION: University of Michigan, B.A., 1953; studied with the American Theatre Wing in New York City, diploma, 1957; also studied with Lee Strasberg and Tad Danielewsky. MILITARY: U.S. Army.

VOCATION: Actor.

CAREER: STAGE DEBUT—Brett, *Deep Are the Roots,* University of Michigan, 1949. BROADWAY DEBUT—Understudy Perry Hall, *The Egghead,* Ethel Barrymore Theatre, 1957. LONDON DEBUT—One man show, *Paul Robeson,* Her Majesty's Theatre, 1978.

PRINCIPAL STAGE APPEARANCES—At the University of Michigan: Verges, *Much Ado About Nothing*, King, *The Birds*, and David King, *A Sleep of Prisoners;* at the Manistee Michigan Summer Theatre: *Stalag 17, The Caine Mutiny, Velvet Gloves, The Tender Trap, Arsenic and Old Lace, The Desparate Hours*, title-role, *Othello*, 1955-59; Sergeant Blunt, *Wedding in Japan*, Greystone Hotel, New York City, 1957; Edward, *Sunrise at Campobello*, Cort Theatre, New York City, 1958.

Harrison Thurston, *The Cool World*, Eugene O'Neill Theatre, New York City, 1960; Williams, *Henry V*, Abhorson, *Measure for Measure*, both with the New York Shakespeare Festival (NYSF) at Belvedere Lake, New York City, 1960; Deodatus Village, *The Blacks*, St. Marks Playhouse, New York City, 1961; Oberon, *A Midsummer Night's Dream* and Lord Marshall, *Richard II*, both NYSF at Wolman Memorial Theatre, 1961; Roger Clark, *Clandestine on the Morning Line*, Actors Playhouse, New York City, 1961; *The Apple*, Living Theatre, New York City, 1961; Ephraim, *Moon on a Rainbow Shawl*, East Eleventh Street Theatre, New York City, 1962; Cinna, *Infidel Caesar*, Music Box Theatre, New York City, 1962; Caliban, *The Tempest* and Prince of Morocco, *The Merchant of Venice*, both NYSF, New York City, 1962; Mario Saccone, *PS 193*, Writer's Stage, New York City, 1962; George Gulp, *The Love Nest*, Writer's Stage, New York City, 1963; Camillo, *The Winters Tale*, NYSF, Delacorte Theatre, New York City, 1963; title role, *Mister Johnson*, Equity Library Theatre, New York City, 1963; Rudge, *Next Time I'll Sing to You*, Phoenix Theatre, New York City, 1963; Zachariah Pieterson, *The Blood Knot*, Cricket Theatre, New York City, 1964; title role, *Othello*, NYSF, Delacorte Theatre then Martinque Theatre, New York City, 1964.

Ekart, *Baal*, Martinque Theatre, New York City, 1965; Junius Brutus, *Coriolanus* and Ajax, *Troilus and Cressida*, both NYSF, Delacorte Theatre, New York City, 1965; Philippeau, *Danton's Death*, Vivian Beaumont Theatre, New York City, 1965; title role, *Macbeth*, NYSF, New York City, 1966; *A Hand Is on the Gate*, revue, Longacre Theatre, New York City, 1966; Jack Jefferson, *The Great White Hope*, Arena Stage, Washington, DC, 1967, transferred to Alvin Theatre, New York City, 1968; Lennie, *Of Mice and Men*, Purdue University Theatre, Lafayette, IN, 1968; Boesman, *Boesman and Lena*, Circle in the Square, New York City, 1970; Tshembe Matoseh, *Les Blancs*, Longacre Theatre, New York City, 1970; title role, *Othello*, Mark Taper Forum, Los Angeles, 1971; Claudius, *Hamlet*, NYSF, Delacorte Theatre, New York City, 1972; Lopakin, *The Cherry Orchard*, NYSF, Anspacher Theatre, New York City, 1973; title role, *King Lear*, NYSF, Delacorte Theatre, New York City, 1973; Theodore Hickman (Hicky), *The Iceman Cometh*, Circle in the Square, New York City, 1973; appeared in a gala benefit show for the Circle in the Square, New York City, 1974; Lennie, *Of Mice and Men*, Brooks Atkinson Theatre, New York City, 1974; one man show, *Paul Robeson*, Lunt-Fontanne Theatre, then Booth Theatre, New York City, 1978.

Steve Daniels, *A Lesson from Aloes*, Playhouse Theatre, New York

City, 1980; *Hedda Gabler*, Yale Repertory Theatre, New Haven, CT, 1980; title role, *Othello*, with the American Shakespeare Theatre, Stratford, CT, 1981; repeated title role, *Othello*, Winter Garden Theatre, New York City, 1982; *The Day of the Picnic*, Yale Repertory Theatre, 1983; *Fences*, Yale Repertory Theatre, 1985; *Night of 100 Stars II*, Radio City Music Hall, New York City, 1985; Troy Maxson, *Fences*, 46th Street Theatre, New York City, 1987.

MAJOR TOURS—Sam, *Master Harold. . .and the Boys*, U.S. cities, 1983.

FILM DEBUT—*Dr. Strangelove*, Columbia, 1964. PRINCIPAL FILM APPEARANCES—*The Comedians*, Metro-Goldwyn-Mayer, 1967; *The End of the Road*, Allied Artists, 1970; Jack Jefferson, *The Great White Hope*, Twentieth Century-Fox, 1970; *The Man*, Paramount, 1972; *Claudine*, Twentieth Century-Fox, 1974; *The River Niger*, 1975; *The Swashbuckler*, Universal, 1976; *The Bingo Long Traveling All-Stars and Motor Kings*, Universal, 1976; *The Greatest*, Columbia, 1977; *The Last Remake of Beau Geste*, Universal, 1977; *A Piece of the Action*, Warner Brothers, 1977; voice of Darth Vader, *Star Wars*, Twentieth Century-Fox, 1977; *Exorcist II: The Heretic*, Warner Brothers, 1977; voice of Darth Vader, *Empire Strikes Back*, Twentieth Century-Fox, 1980; *The Bushido Blade*, 1981; *Conan, the Barbarian*, Universal, 1982; *Blood Tide*, 1982; voice of Darth Vader, *Return of the Jedi*, Twentieth Century-Fox, 1983; Umslopogaas, *Allan Quartermain and the Lost City of Gold*, Cannon, 1987; *My Little Girl*, independent, 1987.

PRINCIPAL TELEVISION APPEARANCES—Series: Detective Andrews, *The Defenders*, CBS, 1962; Woody Paris, *Paris*, CBS, 1979-80. Episodic: Joe, "Who Do You Kill?," *East Side/West Side*, CBS, 1963; *Camera 3*, 1963; *Look Up and Live*, 1963; *Me & Mom*, 1985. Movies: Narrator, *Malcolm X*, 1972; *The Cay*, 1974; *King Lear*, 1974; *Big Joe and Kansas*, 1975; *The UFO Incident*, 1975; *Sojourner*, 1975; *A Day without Sunshine*, 1976; *Jesus of Nazareth*, 1976; *The Greatest Thing That Almost Happened*, 1977; *Guyana Tragedy—The Story of Jim Jones*, 1980; *The Golden Moment: An Olympic Love Story*, 1980; *Philby, Burgess and MacLean*, 1981; *The Atlanta Child Murders*, CBS, 1984; *The Vegas Strip War*, NBC, 1984. Mini-Series: *Roots: The Next Generations*, ABC, 1979.

AWARDS: Obie Awards, all 1962, for *Clandestine on the Morning Line*, *The Apple*, and *Moon on a Rainbow Shawl; Theatre World* Award, 1962, for *Moon on a Rainbow Shawl;* Obie Award, 1965, for *Baal;* Vernon Rice Award, 1965, for *Othello;* Best Actor, Antoinette Perry Award, 1969, for *The Great White Hope;* Grammy Award, 1976; Medal for spoken language, 1981, American Academy of Arts and Letters.

MEMBER: Actors' Equity Association, Screen Actors Guild, American Federation of Television and Radio Artists; National Council of the Arts.

ADDRESSES: AGENT—Lucy Kroll Agency, 390 West End Avenue, New York, NY 10024.*

K

KALEMBER, Patricia

PERSONAL: Daughter of Robert James (an executive) and Viven Daisy (Wright) Kalember; married Daniel Gerroll (an actor), February 25, 1986; children: Rebecca Anne Olivia. EDUCATION: Indiana University, B.A.; Temple University, M.F.A.

VOCATION: Actress.

CAREER: STAGE DEBUT—Orange Girl, *Cyrano de Bergerac*, Center Stage, Baltimore, 1980, for over thirty performances. OFF-BROADWAY DEBUT—Linda Tipton, *The Butler Did It*, Players Theatre, 1981, for one-hundred-twenty performances. PRINCIPAL STAGE APPEARANCES—*The Front Page*, Center Stage, Baltimore, 1980; *Two Gentlemen of Verona*, Pennsylvania Stage Company, 1982; *The Foreigner*, Astor Place Theatre, New York City, 1984; *The Nerd*, Helen Hayes Theatre, New York City, 1987.

FILM DEBUT—Marcia, *Cat's Eye*, Dino de Laurentiis, 1984.

TELEVISION DEBUT—Merrill Vochek, *Loving*, ABC, 1983. PRINCIPAL TELEVISION APPEARANCES—Series: Title role, *Kay O'Brien*, CBS, 1986. Episodic: Colleen, *The Equalizer*, CBS, 1985; Stephanie Davis, *The Equalizer*, CBS, 1987.

AWARDS: Outstanding Debut of an Actress, Outer Critics Circle Award nomination, 1985.

MEMBER: Actors' Equity Association, Screen Actors Guild, American Federation of Television and Radio Artists.

ADDRESSES: HOME—Brooklyn, NY. AGENT—Gersh Agency, 130 W. 42nd Street, New York, NY 10036.

*   *   *

PATRICIA KALEMBER

KANIN, Fay

PERSONAL: Born Fay Mitchell, in New York, NY; married Michael Kanin (a writer); children: Josh. EDUCATION: University of Southern California, B.A.

VOCATION: Writer and producer.

CAREER: PRINCIPAL TELEVISION WORK—Movies: Producer—*Friendly Fire*, ABC, 1979; *Fun and Games*, ABC, 1980; *Heartsounds*, ABC, 1984.

WRITINGS: SCREENPLAYS—*Blondie for Victory*, 1942; *The Outrage*, 1950; *My Pal Gus*, 1952; *Rhapsody*, 1953; *The Opposite Sex*, Metro-Goldwyn-Mayer (MGM), 1956; (with Michael Kanin) *Teacher's Pet*, Paramount, 1958; *The Right Approach*, Twentieth Century-Fox, 1961; *Swordsman of Siena*, MGM, 1962.

PLAYS, PRODUCED: Broadway productions: *Goodbye My Fancy*, 1949; (with Michael Kanin) *His and Hers*, 1950; (with Michael Kanin) *Rashomon*, 1957; (with Michael Kanin) *The Gay Life* (later retitled, *The High Life*), 1962; *Grind*, 1985. PLAYS, PUBLISHED—*Goodbye, My Fancy*, *His and Hers*, *Rashomon*, and *The High Life*, all published by Samuel French.

TELEVISION—Movies: *Heat of Anger*, CBS, 1972; *Tell Me Where It Hurts*, CBS, 1974; *Hustling*, ABC, 1975; *Friendly Fire*, ABC, 1979; *Heartsounds*, ABC, 1984.

FAY KANIN

AWARDS: Best Original Screenplay, Academy Award nomination, 1959, for *Teacher's Pet;* Emmy Award and Christopher Award, both 1974, for *Tell Me Where It Hurts;* Best Television Drama, Writers Guild Award and Best Original Drama, Emmy Award nomination, both 1975, for *Hustling;* Emmy Award, Christopher Award, San Francisco Film Festival Award, Peabody Award, all 1979, for *Friendly Fire;* National Commission on Working Women Broadcast Award, 1980, for *Fun and Games;* Peabody Award, for 1984, for *Heartsounds;* has also won the Valentine Davies Award and the Crystal Award.

MEMBER: Academy of Motion Picture Arts and Sciences (past president, current vice-president), Writers Guild of America West (president of Screen Branch), American Film Institute (board of trustees), National Center for Film and Video Preservation (co-chairman), American College Theatre Festival (board of directors and judge).

ADDRESSES: HOME—653 Ocean Front, Santa Monica, CA 90402.

*   *   *

KARPF, Merrill H.   1940-

PERSONAL: Born October 11, 1940, in New York, NY; son of Stuart J. (a film editor) and Mary (Rosenfeld) Karpf; married Susan L. Geffen (a gourmet cooking instructor); children: Erin Rochelle, Ryan Douglas. EDUCATION: University of California at Los Ange-

les, B.A.; University of California School of Law, L.L.B. MILITARY: U.S. Air Force National Guard, 1957-62.

VOCATION: Producer and lawyer.

CAREER: Entertainment lawyer, O'Melveny and Myers, Los Angeles, 1966-74, executive vice-president, 1975; president and chief operating officer, Quinn Martin Productions, Los Angeles, 1976-82; partner, Schaefer/Karpf Productions, Studio City, CA, 1982—(now Schaefer/Karpf/Eckstein, Toluca Lake, CA).

PRINCIPAL TELEVISION WORK—Series: As producer, with Quinn Martin Productions, *The Streets of San Francisco,* ABC; *Cannon,* CBS; *Barnaby Jones,* CBS; also others; with Schaefer/Karpf/Eckstein Productions, *The Booth,* PBS; *Freemont Place,* CBS. Movies: with Quinn Martin Productions, *Help Wanted: Male,* CBS, 1982; with Schaefer/Karpf/Eckstein Productions, *Right of Way,* HBO, 1983; *The Best Christmas Pageant Ever,* 1983; *Children in the Crossfire,* NBC, 1984; *Stone Pillow,* CBS, 1985; *Mrs. Delafield Wants to Marry,* CBS, 1986; *Six Against the Rock,* NBC, upcoming.

NON-RELATED CAREER—Editor of Law Review during law school attendance University of California at Los Angeles.

AWARDS: ACE Award nomination, 1983, for *Right of Way;* Angel Award, Monte Carlo Film Festival Award, Wilbur Award, and Golden Halo Award, all 1985, for *Children in the Crossfire;* also, Emmy Award nomination, for *The Best Christmas Pageant Ever.*

MEMBER: Academy of Television Arts and Sciences, CAUCUS,

MERRILL H. KARPF

American Film Institute, Hollywood Radio and Television Society, NCTA.

ADDRESSES: OFFICE—3500 W. Olive Ave., Suite 730, Toluca Lake, CA 91505. AGENT—Creative Artists Agency, 1800 Century Park East, Los Angeles, CA 90067.

*   *   *

KASHA, Lawrence N.   1933-

PERSONAL: Born December, 1933, in Brooklyn, NY; son of Irving (a hair stylist) and Rose (a hair stylist; maiden name, Katz) Kasha. EDUCATION: New York University, B.A., 1954, M.A., 1955; studied at the American Theatre Wing, 1957; studied acting with Harold Clurman and Robert Lewis, 1956-57. MILITARY: U.S. Air Force, 1951-54.

VOCATION: Producer, director, and playwright.

CAREER: FIRST BROADWAY STAGE WORK—Production assistant, *Silk Stockings,* Imperial Theatre, 1955. PRINCIPAL STAGE WORK—Stage manager, *Li'l Abner,* St. James Theatre, New York City, 1956; stage manager, *Whoop-Up,* Shubert Theatre, New York City, 1958; stage manager, *Happy Town,* 54th Street Theatre, New York City, 1959; stage manager, *How to Succeed in Business without Really Trying,* 46th Street Theatre, New York City, 1961.

Director, musical comedies at the Colonie Summer Theatre, Latham, NY, 1959; producer, *Parade,* Players Theatre, New York City, 1960, then producer and director, same production, Hollywood Center Theatre, CA, 1961; producer, *Future Perfect,* Cape Playhouse, Dennis, MA, 1961; director, *Guys and Dolls* and *The Most Happy Fella,* O'Keefe Center, Toronto, Ontario, Canada, 1962; director, *Anything Goes,* Orpheum Theatre, New York City, 1962; producer and director, "The Con Edison Show" (industrial), New York City, 1963; producer and director, *Plain and Fancy,* Westchester Theatre, NY, 1963; co-producer, *She Loves Me,* Eugene O'Neill Theatre, New York City, 1963; directed musicals at the Dallas Summer Musicals, State Fair Music Hall, 1963; director, *A More Perfect Union,* La Jolla Playhouse, CA, 1963; associate director, *Funny Girl,* Winter Garden Theatre, New York City, 1964; *The Sound of Music,* San Bernardino Civic Light Opera, CA, 1964; director, *Bajour,* Shubert Theatre, New York City, 1964.

Director, *Funny Girl,* Prince of Wales Theatre, London, 1966; director, *Showboat,* New York State Theatre, New York City, 1966; co-producer, *A Mother's Kisses,* Shubert Theatre, New Haven, CT, 1968; producer, *Hadrian VII,* Helen Hayes Theatre, New York City, 1969; director, *Mame,* London production, 1969; co-producer, *Applause,* Palace Theatre, New York City, 1970; director, *Lovely Ladies, Kind Gentlemen,* Majestic Theatre, New York City, 1970; co-producer, *Father's Day,* John Golden Theatre, New York City, 1971; co-producer, *Inner City,* Ethel Barrymore Theatre, New York City, 1971; co-producer, *Seesaw,* Uris Theatre, New York City, 1973; co-producer, *No Hard Feelings,* Martin Beck Theatre, New York City, 1973; co-writer, producer, and director, *Heaven Sent,* New Las Palmas Theatre, Los Angeles, 1978; co-producer, *Woman of the Year,* Palace Theatre, New York City, 1981; co-writer and co-producer, *Seven Brides for Seven Brothers,* Alvin Theatre, New York City, 1982.

MAJOR TOURS—Stage manager, *Silk Stockings,* U.S. cities, 1956;

director, *Li'l Abner,* U.S. cities, 1956; director, *Silk Stockings, High Button Shoes, The Male Animal, South Pacific, Desert Song,* summer tours, 1960; director, *Gentlemen Prefer Blondes,* summer tour, 1961; director, *Camelot,* U.S. cities, 1964; co-producer, *The Coffee Lover,* pre-Broadway tour, 1966; director, *Cactus Flower,* U.S. cities, 1968; director, *Star Spangled Girl,* 1968; co-writer, producer, and director, *Seven Brides for Seven Brothers,* U.S. cities, 1978.

PRINCIPAL TELEVISION WORK—Specials: Producer— *Applause,* CBS, 1973; *Another April,* CBS, 1974; *Rosenthal & Jones,* CBS, 1975. Series: Producer—*Busting Loose,* CBS, 1977; *Komedy Tonite,* NBC, 1978.

WRITINGS: PLAYS, PRODUCED—(With Hayden Griffin) *The Pirate,* 1968; (with Lionel Wilson) *Where Have You Been, Billy Boy,* 1969; (with David S. Landay) *Heaven Sent,* New Las Palmas Theatre, Los Angeles, 1978; (with Landay) book, *Seven Brides for Seven Brothers,* toured, 1978, Alvin Theatre, New York City, 1982.

AWARDS: For direction, Outer Critics Circle Award, 1962, for *Anything Goes;* Antoinette Perry Award, 1970; Outer Critics Circle Award, 1973.

MEMBER: Society of Stage Directors and Choreographers, Actors' Equity Association, Writers Guild of America, West; Kappa Nu.

ADDRESSES: HOME—2229 Gloaming Way, Beverly Hills, CA 90210.*

*   *   *

KAWALEK, Nancy

PERSONAL: Born February 25, in Brooklyn, NY; daughter of Cy (a salesman and designer of business forms) and Addie Kawalek. EDUCATION: Northwestern University, B.S.; trained for the stage at the Neighborhood Playhouse with Robert Modica.

PERSONAL: Actress and playwright.

CAREER: STAGE DEBUT—*Story Theatre,* Hunter Drama Festival, New York City, 1972. BROADWAY DEBUT— *Strider,* Helen Hayes Theatre, 1979. PRINCIPAL STAGE APPEARANCES—Koryphaios, *The Birds,* Drama Committee Repertory, New York City, 1976; Smitanka III, *Strider,* Chelsea Westside Theatre, New York City, 1979; Sarah, *Success Story,* Jewish Repertory Theatre, New York City, 1980; Wilma Green, *What a Life,* Manhattan Punch Line Theatre, New York City, 1982; resident actress, "Punch Line Players," Manhattan Punch Line; Alice Burger, *Something Creative for the Inmates,* New York City.

Regional: Buttercup, *Winnebago,* Goodman Theatre, Chicago, IL; Becky and Anita, *Dreams,* Victory Gardens Theatre, Chicago and Evanston Theatre Company, IL; actress number one, *Walt Whitman,* The Playhouse, Chicago; Lady Larken, *Once Upon a Mattress,* Antonia, *Man of La Mancha,* and resident actress for Gershwin, Porter, and Berlin music revues, all at the Green Mountain Guild, VT; Little Nun, *The House of Blue Leaves,* Benson Street Theatre, Evanston, IL; Evelyn, *Paris Was Yesterday* and Sofia Ivanovna, *Dead Souls,* both at the McCormick Theatre, Evanston, IL; Bride, *Robber Bridegroom,* Hunter Drama Festival, New York City; Stage

NANCY KAWALEK

Manager, *Our Town* and April, *Company,* both with the Troupe Repertory, CO; actress number one, *The Works of Saroyan,* Syracuse, NY.

WRITINGS: PLAYS, PRODUCED—*Alice Without,* Colonnades Theatre, New York City.

MEMBER: Actors' Equity Association, Screen Actors Guild, American Federation of Television and Radio Artists; National Women's Health Network, National Abortion Rights Action League (NARAL).

ADDRESSES: HOME—New York, NY.

* * *

KAY, Beatrice   1907-1986

PERSONAL: Born Hannah Beatrice Kuper (performed as Honey Kuper and Honey Day), April 21, 1907, in New York, NY; died of complications developing from a previous stroke in North Hollywood, CA, November 8, 1986; married: four times (all ending in divorce).

VOCATION: Actress and singer.

CAREER: STAGE DEBUT—Title role, *Little Lord Fauntleroy,* McCauley Stock Company, Louisville, KY. PRINCIPAL STAGE APPEARANCES—Singer, Diamond Horseshoe Club, New York City; Mayfair Music Hall, Santa Monica, CA; also appeared as a

singer in most of the major clubs in the U.S. and was one of the first headliners to play Las Vegas, NV; also appeared at the Moulin Rouge in Paris.

MAJOR TOURS—Australian and European cities.

PRINCIPAL FILM WORK—Double for Madge Evans in many silent films at Fort Lee, NJ, Studios; *Sweet Adelaine,* Gotham, 1935; *Diamond Horseshoe,* 1945; *Underworld, U.S.A.,* Columbia, 1961.

PRINCIPAL TELEVISION APPEARANCES—Episodic: *Bonanza,* NBC; *Hawaiian Eye,* ABC; also appeared with Rosemary Clooney, Milton Berle and many others.

RECORDINGS: Twelve albums for Columbia and RCA including *Mention My Name in Sheboygan* for Columbia.

SIDELIGHTS: CTFT learned that Beatrice Kay ran her own guest ranch outside Reno, NV, called the Lazy B.K., which attracted many showbusiness personalities in the 1950's.*

* * *

KAZAN, Lainie   1942-

PERSONAL: Born Lainie Levine, May 15, 1942, in Brooklyn, NY; divorced; children: Jennifer. EDUCATION: Hofstra University, B.A.; trained for the stage at the Actors Studio with Lee Strasberg, Sanford Meisner, and Joseph K. Scott, Jr.

LAINIE KAZAN

VOCATION: Actress and singer.

CAREER: FILM DEBUT—*Lady in Cement*, Twentieth Century-Fox, 1968. PRINCIPAL FILM APPEARANCES—*Romance of a Horse Thief*, Allied Artists, 1971; Maggie, *One from the Heart*, Columbia, 1982; Belle Steinberg Carroca, *My Favorite Year*, Metro-Goldwyn-Mayer/United Artists (MGM/UA), 1982; *Lust in the Dust*, New World Pictures, 1985; *The Journey of Natty Gann*, Buena Vista, 1985; *Delta Force*, Cannon, 1986.

PRINCIPAL TELEVISION APPEARANCES—Series: Regular, *Dean Martin Summer Show*, NBC, 1966; Rose Samuels, *Tough Cookies*, CBS. Episodic: *Hotel*, ABC, 1984; *Columbo*, NBC; *Sunset Limousine*, CBS; "Pinocchio," *Fairie Tale Theatre*, Showtime; *Two Close for Comfort*; *Amazing Stories*; *Paper Chase*. Pilots: *Halfway Home*, CBS; *Family Business*. Movies: *Obsessive Love*, CBS, 1984; Sophie Tucker, *My Luke and I*, CBS. Guest: *Dean Martin Show*, NBC; *The Ed Sullivan Show*, CBS; *Tonight Show*, NBC; *Carol Burnett Show*, CBS; *Dinah Shore Show*, NBC; *Merv Griffin Show*; *Tom Jones Show*; *Mike Douglas Show*. Specials: *Come Fly with Me*, BBC.

STAGE DEBUT—Understudy Fanny Brice, *Funny Girl*, Broadway production. PRINCIPAL STAGE APPEARANCES—Gittel Mosca, *Seesaw*, Broadway production; Crystal, *The Women*, Broadway production; Aldonza, *Man of La Mancha*, New York production; Daisy, *On a Clear Day You Can See Forever*, New York production; *Jacques Brel Is Alive and Well and Living in Paris*, New York production; also appeared in *Plaza Suite*, *Who's Afraid of Virginia Woolf*, *House of Blue Leaves*, and *Orpheus Descending*, all New York City productions. Has appeared regionally as Dolly Gallagher Levi, *Hello, Dolly!*, Claridge Hotel, Atlantic City, NJ.

CABARET—Sahara, Hilton, Riviera, and Flamingo Hotels, all Las Vegas, NV; the Empire Room, Mr. Kelly's, the Blue Max, and the Hyatt Regency House, all Chicago, IL; the Persian Room at the Plaza, the Royal Box at the Americana Hotel, the Empire Room at the Waldorf Astoria, and the Rainbow Grill at Rockefeller Plaza, all New York City; the Westside Room at the Century Plaza Hotel and the Backlot at Studio One, both Los Angeles; the Fairmont hotels in Dallas, San Francisco, and New Orleans; Harrah's at Lake Tahoe, Reno, NV; and appeared at and managed "Lainie's Room" at the Playboy Clubs, Los Angeles and New York City.

RECORDINGS: ALBUMS—Four albums for MGM Records including *The Chanteuse Is Loose*, 1984.

AWARDS: National Academy of Recording Arts and Sciences New Artist of the Year Award, 1968.

SIDELIGHTS: RECREATIONS—Horseback riding, writing poetry.

ADDRESSES: HOME—Los Angeles, CA.

*   *   *

KEACH, Stacy   1941-

PERSONAL: Born Stacy Keach, Jr., June 2, 1941, in Savannah, GA; son of Stacy (an actor) and Mary Cain (an actress; maiden name, Peckham), Keach; married Malgosia Tomassi, 1986. EDUCATION: University of California at Berkeley, A.B., English and

drama, 1963; trained for the stage at the Yale School of Drama, 1963-64, and at the London Academy of Dramatic Art, 1964-65.

VOCATION: Actor, director, writer, and producer.

CAREER: STAGE DEBUT—Played in a production of *Rip Van Winkle* in elementary school. OFF-BROADWAY DEBUT—Marcellus and the First Player, *Hamlet*, New York Shakespeare Festival (NYSF), Delacorte Theatre, 1964. PRINCIPAL STAGE APPEARANCES—At the University of California, Berkeley, 1959-63, appeared in: *The Antifarce of John and Leporello*, *To Learn to Love*, *Galileo*, *Purple Dust*, *The Changeling*, *Bartholomew Fair*, *Escurrial*, *A Touch of the Poet*, and *Don Juan*; Armand, *Camille*, Tufts Arena, CA, 1961. At the Ashland, Oregon Shakespeare Festival: Westmoreland, *Henry IV, Part II* and Antiopholus, *The Comedy of Errors*, both 1962; Mercutio, *Romeo and Juliet*, Berowne, *Love's Labour's Lost*, and title role, *Henry V*, all 1963. Appeared in *The Voyage*, Yale School of Drama, New Haven, CT, 1963; Cutler and Turnkey, *Danton's Death* and Mr. Horner, *The Country Wife*, 1965 and appeared in various roles, *The Caucasian Chalk Circle*, 1966, all with the Repertory Theatre of Lincoln Center at the Vivian Beaumont Theatre, New York City; appeared in *Annie Get Your Gun*, *You Can't Take It with You*, *The Lion in Winter*, and *Marat/Sade*, all at the Williamstown Summer Theatre Festival, MA, 1966; Baron Tusenbach, *The Three Sisters* and Master of Ceremonies, *Oh, What a Lovely War*, Long Wharf Theatre, New Haven, CT, both 1966.

Title role, *MacBird!*, Village Gate Theatre, New York City, 1967; Captain Starkey, *We Bombed in New Haven*, Yale Repertory Theatre, New Haven, CT, 1967; August, "The Demonstration" and the man, "Man and Dog," in a production with the overall title, *The Niggerlovers*, Orpheum Theatre, New York City, 1967; appeared in *Henry IV*, *Coriolanus*, and *The Three Sisters*, with the Yale Repertory Theatre, 1968; Sir John Falstaff, *Henry IV*, Parts I and II, NYSF, Delacorte Theatre, 1968; Edmund, *King Lear*, Vivian Beaumont Theatre, New York City, 1968; Buffalo Bill, *Indians*, Arena Stage, Washington, DC, then Brooks Atkinson Theatre, New York City, 1969; title role, *Peer Gynt*, NYSF, Delacorte Theatre, 1969; Benedict, *Beatrice and Benedict*, Los Angeles Music Center, 1970; James Tyrone, Jr., *Long Day's Journey into Night*, Promenade Theatre, New York City, 1971; title role, *Hamlet*, Long Wharf Theatre, 1971, then NYSF, Delacorte Theatre, New York City, 1972, repeated the role for the Center Theatre Group at the Mark Taper Forum, Los Angeles, 1974; title role, *Cyrano de Bergerac*, Long Beach Theatre Festival, CA, 1978; Sydney Bruhl, *Deathtrap*, Music Box Theatre, New York City, 1979; Eric Smith, *Hughie*, with the National Theatre Company, Cottesloe Theatre, U.K., 1980; Harry Van, *Idiot's Delight*, Kennedy Center, Washington, DC.

MAJOR TOURS—*Playing with Fire*, U.K. cities, 1965; Phineas Taylor Barnum, *Barnum*, U.S. cities, 1981.

PRINCIPAL STAGE WORK—Director, *The American Dream* and *C'est la vie*, both at the University of California at Berkeley, 1959-63; director and writer, *The 1960 Axe Revue*, University of California at Berkeley, 1960; director, *Pullman Car Hiawatha*, *The Stronger*, and *The Maids*, all at the London Academy of Music and Dramatic Art, 1964-65.

FILM DEBUT—*The Heart Is a Lonely Hunter*, Warner Brothers-Seven Arts, 1968. PRINCIPAL FILM APPEARANCES—*The Traveling Executioner*, Metro-Goldwyn-Mayer (MGM), 1968; *The End of the Road*, Allied Artists, 1970; *Brewster McCloud*, MGM, 1970;

Doc Holiday, *Doc*, United Artists, 1971; Bad Bob, *The Life and Times of Judge Roy Bean*, National General, 1971; Roy Fehler, *The New Centurions*, Columbia, 1972; Tully, *Fat City*, Columbia, 1972; Mike Mandell and Sonny, *Watched*, Palmyra Films, 1973; narration, *One by One*, 1974; Calvin, *The Gravy Train*, Columbia, 1974; Martin Luther, *Luther*, American Film Theatre, 1974; Adjutant, *Conduct Unbecoming*, Allied Artists, 1975; narration, *James Dean, the First American Teenager*, 1975; Charlie and Phil, *Street People*, American International, 1976; Lou Ford, *The Killer Inside Me*, 1976; Naboth, *The Squeeze*, 1976; *The Greatest Battle*, 1977; narration, *The Duelists*, 1977; *Two Solitudes*, 1977; Captain Bennett, *Gray Lady Down*, Universal, 1978; Sergent Stedenko, *Up in Smoke*, Paramount, 1978; Dr. Edward Foster, *La Montagna del dio Cannibale*, 1978; narration, *The Search for Solutions*, 1979; Colonel Hudson Kane, *Twinkle, Twinkle, 'Killer' Kane*, 1979; *The Ninth Configuration*, 1980; Frank James, *The Long Riders*, United Artists, 1980; Patrick Quid, *Road Games*, AVCO-Embassy, 1981; Jess Tyler, *Butterfly*, 1981; Sarge, *Cheech & Chong's Nice Dreams*, Columbia, 1981; James Daley, *That Championship Season*, Cannon Films, 1982.

PRINCIPAL FILM WORK—Producer and screenwriter, *The Long Riders*, United Artists, 1980.

PRINCIPAL TELEVISION APPEARANCES—Series: Landlord, *How to Marry a Millionaire*, syndication, 1957; Carlson, *Get Smart*, NBC, 1966-67; Dr. Grey, *Johnny Belinda*, 1967; Lt. Ben Logan, *Caribe*, ABC, 1975; Mike Hammer, *Mickey Spillane's Mike Hammer*, CBS, 1984-85; Mike Hammer, *The New Mike Hammer*, CBS, 1986-87. Episodic: *The Sheriff of Cochise*, syndication; "The Repeater," *The Great American Dream Machine*, PBS, 1971.

Pilots: Dr. Eberly, *Kingston: The Power Play*, 1976. Movies: *Orville and Wilbur*, PBS, 1971; *Particular Men*, PBS, 1972; *Classics for Today*, PBS, 1972; *Man of Destiny*, PBS, 1973; Jimmy Wheeler, *All the Kind Strangers*, ABC, 1974; Matt Blackwood, *James A. Michener's "Dynasty"*, NBC, 1975; Barabbas, *Jesus of Nazareth*, 1977; Major Ball, *A Rumor of War*, CBS, 1979; Harry Roat, *Wait Until Dark*, 1982; *Mickey Spillane's Mike Hammer: Murder Me, Murder You*, CBS, 1983; Prince Stash Valensky, *Princess Daisy*, NBC, 1983; Mike Hammer, *Mickey Spillane's Mike Hammer: More than Murder*, CBS, 1984; Dr. Jeffrey Bierston, *Intimate Strangers*, CBS, 1986; Mike Hammer, *The Return of Mickey Spillane's Mike Hammer*, CBS, 1986.

Mini-Series: Jonas Steele, *The Blue and the Gray*, 1981; *Mistral's Daughter*, CBS, 1985. Dramatic specials: Appeared in *Antigone*, 1974; Merchant, *Beauty and the Beast*, 1983; also Banquo, *Macbeth*, Feste, *Twelfth Night*, and Autolycus, *The Winter's Tale*, for the Shakespeare Repertory Theatre, PBS.

PRINCIPAL TELEVISION WORK—Producer, director, and writer, "The Repeater," *The Great American Dream Machine*, PBS, 1971; director, *Six Characters in Search of an Author*, PBS; director, "A Blinding Fear," *The New Mike Hammer*, CBS, 1987.

RELATED CAREER—Founder and president, Positron Productions Ltd.; associate professor of drama, Yale University School of Drama, 1967-68.

WRITINGS: PLAYS, PRODUCED—*The 1960 Axe Revue*, University of California at Berkeley, 1960. TELEPLAYS—"The Repeater," *The Great American Dream Machine*, PBS, 1971. ARTICLES—

"The Take: A Screen Actor in Search of His Character," *New York Times Magazine*, August 24, 1970.

RECORDINGS: *Earth Day*, Caedmon, 1974.

AWARDS: Best Actor Award, University of California, 1963; Best Actor Award, Oregon Shakespeare Festival, 1963; Oliver Thorndike Acting Award, Yale University School of Drama, 1963-64; Fulbright scholarship, 1964-65; Obie Awards and Vernon Rice Drama Desk Awards, 1967, for *Macbird!* and 1972, for *Long Day's Journey into Night;* Antoinette Perry Award and Drama Desk Award, both 1970, for *Indians;* Cine Golden Eagle Award, 1971, and Outstanding Film, London Film Festival, 1972, both for "The Repeater"; Obie Award and Vernon Rice Award, both 1972, for *Hamlet;* David Award, 1983; voted one of the ten Most Watchable Men of 1984 by Man Watchers of America; Best Actor in a Television Series, Golden Globe Award nomination, 1985, for *Mike Hammer;* Veterans Appreciation Award, 1986, for *Mike Hammer*.

MEMBER: Actors' Equity Association, Screen Actors Guild, American Federation of Television and Radio Artists, Academy of Motion Picture Arts and Sciences, Lincoln Center Repertory Company, The Long Wharf Theatre, National Repertory Foundation (sponsor, National Play Award Committee), Kennedy Center Honors Committee (Artists Committee), Yale Theatre Circle (charter member); Academy of Television Arts and Sciences (panelist, Substance Abuse Conference), Entertainment Industry Council before the House Select Committee on Drug Abuse (1985), Artists and Athletes Against Aparteid, National Humane Education Society, United Indian Development Association, National Citizens Communication Lobby, America Cleft Palate Association (spokesman).

SIDELIGHTS: While still in his twenties, Stacy Keach was described as "America's most formidable classical actor," according to Patricia Bosworth in October 19, 1969's *New York Times*. During the 1960s, Keach had leading roles in a score of Shakespearean plays ranging from *Hamlet* and *King Lear* to *Romeo and Juliet*.

It is suprising, then, that Keach is best known today for his role as hard-boiled detective Mike Hammer on the hit television show *Mickey Spillane's Mike Hammer* and *The New Mike Hammer*. The difference between classical actor and television pulp hero may seem enormous, but Keach insists that the acting challenge remains the same. He told Stephen Farber (*New York Times*, March 26, 1984): "From an acting point of view, I think Hammer is every bit as complicated as Hamlet." Hammer is a tough guy detective in the classic 1950s tradition who wears a porkpie hat, a knit tie, and a crumpled suit. (Keach's clothes are deliberately left on the floor to acquire the proper look.) Hammer also carries the obligatory forty-five caliber automatic, which he enjoys using. Keach told Farber that Hammer is "a cross between Dirty Harry and James Bond." Despite the striking differences between the actor and the character he plays, they share a common outlook on one important point. "Hammer and I both have little patience for injustice and the games fat cats and bureaucrats play," Keach explained to Michael Singer in the August 25, 1984 *TV Guide*.

Mickey Spillane's Mike Hammer suffered a serious setback in 1984 when Keach was arrested on drug charges while visiting England. More than an ounce of cocaine was found in Keach's luggage at Heathrow Airport, and the actor was sentenced to nine months in prison. As James Brady pointed out (*Parade*, August 24, 1986), Keach "could have broken his parole and not gone back to England to do his time, [but he] returned to pay his debts.'' In addition to his jail sentence, Keach also put in community work with youth drug awareness programs, something he was not required to do. He told Brady that being arrested probably saved his life: ''I was on the verge of real trouble.'' Speaking to Sharon Rosenthal in *Us* (March 10, 1986), Keach explained that ''the drug had begun to dominate my life.''

In the summer of 1985, Keach left prison and returned to the United States to pick up the pieces of his acting career. After appearing in the television movie *Intimate Strangers,* Keach made two special Mike Hammer television movies. When these proved popular with audiences, CBS signed Keach to star in *The New Mike Hammer* series beginning in the fall of 1986.

Both *Mike Hammer* shows have been extremely popular, consistently placing high in the weekly Nielsen ratings. Of all programs shown in the 10:00 p.m. to 11:00 p.m. time slot, *Mike Hammer* scores the highest ratings among male viewers. The show is popular with female viewers as well. When Keach was experiencing his legal problems in England, more than a quarter of a million women wrote to CBS on his behalf.

After all the tribulations of the past few years, Keach's life seems to have reached an equilibrium. Shortly after leaving prison in 1985, he married Malgosia Tomassi. He is scheduled to play Ernest Hemingway in an upcoming television mini-series. But most important, he is back on the show that made him a household name. As he told Rosenthal, ''I'm just very glad to be doing *Mike Hammer* again. That's the bottom line.''

RECREATIONS—Tennis, bicycle riding, and skiing.

ADDRESSES: MANAGER—James R. Palmer & Associates, 1875 Century Park East, Suite 1600, Los Angeles, CA 90067.

*   *   *

KEEGAN, Donna

PERSONAL: Born in NJ; married. EDUCATION: Attended Indiana University; studied acting with Tepper-Gallegos.

VOCATION: Actress, stunt double, and stunt coordinator.

CAREER: PRINCIPAL FILM WORK—Stunt double, *Scarface,* Universal, 1983; assistant stunt coordinator, *Indiana Jones and the Temple of Doom,* Paramount, 1984; stunt coordinator, *Wild Life,* Universal, 1984; stunt double, *Cannonball Run II,* Warner Brothers, 1984; *Top Gun,* Paramount, 1986; *Legal Eagles,* Universal, 1986; stunt double and stunt coordinator, *Space Camp,* 1986; *To Live and Die in L.A.,* Metro-Goldwyn-Mayer/United Artists, 1986; also stunt double for *Trancers,* Empire Productions, *Love of a Soldier, Inside Adam Swift.*

PRINCIPAL TELEVISION WORK—Episodic: Stunt coordinator, *Joe Bash,* ABC; *Hardcastle and McCormick,* ABC; *Scarecrow and Mrs. King,* CBS; *Paper Chase,* CBS; *Lottery!,* ABC; *Riptide,* NBC; *Mike Hammer,* CBS; *Hunter,* CBS; *Magnum P.I.,* CBS; *Hawaiian Heat,* ABC; *Falcon Crest,* CBS; *T.J. Hooker,* ABC; *Miami Vice,* NBC; *Fantasy Island,* ABC; *Hill Street Blues,* ABC; *Remington Steele,* NBC; *Cover Up,* CBS; *Moonlighting,* ABC; also *Eye to Eye; Suburban Beat; Stingray; Trauma Center; Shadow*

DONNA KEEGAN

Chasers; The Insiders; Sky Terror; Sister Mary and the Saturday Night Girls. Pilots: Stunt double, *Me & Mom,* Viacom.

AWARDS: Miss Golden Globe USA; Miss Hempshire. Also holds thirty gold medals and twenty-two trophies and plaques from state, national, and international competitions in springboard and tower diving.

MEMBER: Screen Actors Guild, American Federation of Television and Radio Artists.

SIDELIGHTS: In addition to her special skills in numerous water sports, Donna Keegan told *CTFT* that she is adept at horseback riding, high falls, fencing, trampoline, rapelling, rollerskating, ice skating, wire work, precision driving, motorcycling, snow skiing, and martial arts.

ADDRESSES: HOME—Los Angeles, CA. PUBLICIST—Nan Herst Public Relations, 8733 Sunset Blvd., Suite 103, Los Angeles, CA 90069.

*   *   *

KEESHAN, Robert J.   1927-
   (Captain Kangaroo)

PERSONAL: Born June 27, 1927, in Lynbrook, Long Island, NY; son of Joseph (a chain grocery supervisor) and Margaret (Conroy) Keeshan; married Anne Jeanne Laurie (a speech therapist and television studio receptionist), December 30, 1950; children: Michael Derek, Laurie Margaret, Maeve Jeanne. EDUCATION: Attended Fordham University, 1947-50. MILITARY: U.S. Marine Corps Reserve, 1945-46.

VOCATION: Actor, producer, director, and writer.

CAREER: PRINCIPAL TELEVISION WORK—Page, 1943-45 and fourth floor receptionist, 1946-47, for NBC Television, New York City; stagehand, *Howdy Doody Show,* NBC, 1947; Clarabelle the Clown, *Howdy Doody Show,* NBC, 1947-52; Corny the Clown, *Time for Fun,* ABC, New York City, 1953-55; producer and Tinker, *Tinker's Workshop,* ABC, 1954-55; creator, writer, and star, *Captain Kangaroo,* 1955-1985; creator and portrayed title role and Town the Clown, *Mr. Mayor Show,* CBS, 1964-65; producer, "Revenge of the Nerd," *CBS Afternoon Playhouse,* CBS.

PRINCIPAL RADIO WORK—Commentator: *The Subject Is Young People,* CBS, 1980-82; CBS News, 1981-82; *CBS Morning News,* 1982—.

WRITINGS: BOOKS—Juvenile: *She Loves Me, She Loves Me Not,* Harper, 1963; editor, *Captain Kangaroo's Storybook,* Random House, 1963. PERIODICALS—Columnist for *New York Herald Tribune, Good Housekeeping, Parade, McCall's.*

AWARDS: Sylvania Award, 1956; Outstanding Television Program for Children, Peabody Awards, 1958, 1972, 1979; Freedoms Foundation Awards, 1962, 1972; Page One Special Award, 1965; Newspaper Guild of New York Award, 1965; Man of the Year Award, National Association of Television Program Executives, 1967; Emmy Awards, Outstanding Children's Entertainment Series, 1978, 1981, 1982, 1983, 1984, all for *Captain Kangaroo;* Emmy Award, Outstanding Performer in Children's Programming, 1982, for *Captain Kangaroo;* National Audience Board Award and National Congress of Parents and Teachers Award, both for *Captain Kangaroo.*

Gabriel Awards, Special Award in Children's Programming, 1974, and Certificate of Merit Award for Youth Oriented Programming, 1978, Outstanding Personal Achievement, 1982; American Education Award, 1978; DeWitt Carter Reddick Award, University of Texas, 1978; James E. Allen Memorial Award, New York State Board of Regents, 1978; Broadcaster of the Year Award, International Radio and Television Society, 1979; Television Father of the Year Award, 1980.

Distinguished Service to Children Award, Parents without Partners, 1981; Sadie Award, University of Alabama, 1981; Humanitarian Award, Telephone Pioneers, 1981; National Education Award for the Advancement of Learning Through Broadcasting, 1982; Special Award for Outstanding Contribution to Early Childhood Development, Massachusetts Society for Prevention of Cruelty to Children, 1982; Suffolk Early Childhood Education Council Award, 1982; Abe Lincoln Award, Southern Baptist Radio and Television Commission, 1983; Joseph E. Conner Award, Phi Alpha Tau Fraternity, Emerson College, 1983; Golden Anniversary Director's Award, State of Ohio, 1986; Centennial Achievement Award, Local One, 1986.

Honorary degrees: Rhode Island College, 1969; Alfred University, 1969; Fordham University, 1975; Dartmouth College, 1975; Southhampton College, Long Island University, 1977; Indiana State University, 1978; College of New Rochelle, 1980; Elmira

College, 1980; Bucknell University, 1981; Le Mouyne College, 1983; Marquette University, 1983; Mount St. Mary College, 1984; Central Michigan University, 1984; Stonehill College, 1986.

MEMBER: West Islip Board of Education (member, 1953-58), Suffolk County Hearing and Speech Center (president, 1967-71), National Association of Hearing and Speech Agencies (director, 1968-72), Suffolk Good Samaritan Hospital (director, 1969-78; president 1978-80), Suffolk County Police Athletic League (president, 1973-77), College of New Rochelle (board of trustees, 1973—), Bank of Babylon (director, 1973-80), Suffolk Child Development Center (director, 1974-75), Anchor Savings Bank, Brooklyn, NY (director, 1977—), Long Island Philharmonic (member, 1979-80), National Council for Children and Television (1982—), National Children and Television Week (co-chairman, 1983), National Committee for Prevention of Child Abuse (board of directors, 1984—), American Heart Association of Suffolk County (honorary chairman), Save the Children Valentine Tree School Project (honorary chairperson), Dartmouth College Parents' Committee (vice-chairman), New York State Voluntary Hospitals Trustees (founding director).

Long Island Yacht Club (commodore, 1964-65), Friars Club, Southward Ho Country Club.

SIDELIGHTS: RECREATIONS—Photography, fishing, sailing.

ADDRESSES: HOME—Babylon, NY 11702. OFFICE—Robert Keeshan Associates, Inc., 524 W. 57th Street, New York, NY 10019. AGENT—Marvin Josephson, 1271 Avenue of the Americas, New York, NY 10019.

*   *   *

KEITH, David   1954-

PERSONAL: Full name, David Lemuel Keith; born May 8, 1954, in Knoxville, TN; son of Lemuel Grady, Jr. (a personnel division worker for the Tennessee Valley Authority) and Hilda Earle (a worker for the Knoxville County Board of Education; maiden name, Coulter) Keith. EDUCATION: University of Tennessee, B.A., 1985. RELIGION: Methodist.

VOCATION: Actor and director.

CAREER: FILM DEBUT—Private Malcolm Harris, *The Rose,* Twentieth Century-Fox, 1980. PRINCIPAL FILM APPEARANCES— *The Great Santini,* Warner Brothers, 1979; *Brubaker,* Twentieth Century-Fox, 1980; *Back Roads,* Warner Brothers, 1981; *Take This Job and Shove It,* AVCO-Embassy, 1981; Sid Worley, *An Officer and a Gentleman,* 1982; *Independence Day,* Warner Brothers, 1982; *The Lords of Discipline,* Paramount, 1983; *Firestarter,* 1984; also: *White of the Eye; Sacrifice.*

PRINCIPAL FILM WORK—Director: *The Farm; Sacrifice.*

TELEVISION DEBUT—Fred Collins, *Happy Days,* ABC, 1978. PRINCIPAL TELEVISION APPEARANCES—Series: Tuck, *Co-Ed Fever,* CBS, 1979. Episodic: *The Runaways,* NBC. Movies: *Are You in the House Alone?,* 1978; *Friendly Fire,* 1978; *The Golden Moment,* 1980; *Gulag,* HBO, 1985; *If Tomorrow Comes,* 1986.

STAGE DEBUT—Scotty, *Red Bluegrass Western Flyer Show,* Goodspeed Opera House, East Haddam, CT, 1977. PRINCIPAL

DAVID KEITH

STAGE APPEARANCES—Duane Wilson, *Harvey,* Elitch Garden Theatre, Denver, and Westport, CT, 1985; multiple roles, *Greater Tuna,* Down Home Theatre, Johnson City, TN, 1986; Bo, *Bus Stop,* Clarence Brown Theatre, University of Tennessee, Knoxville, 1986.

RELATED CAREER—Singer and guitarist.

RECORDINGS: ALBUM—Two songs on the soundtrack of *The Farm.*

AWARDS: Best Supporting Actor and New Star of the Year, Golden Globe Award nomination, 1982, for *An Officer and a Gentleman.*

MEMBER: Screen Actors Guild, American Federation of Television and Radio Artists, Director's Guild.

ADDRESSES: HOME—Knoxville, TN. AGENT—c/o Toni Howard, William Morris Agency, 151 El Camino Drive, Beverly Hills, CA 90212. MANAGER—Peluce Accountants, 449 S. Beverly Drive, Beverly Hills, CA 90212.

*   *   *

KELLY, Vivian   1922-

PERSONAL: Born February 12, 1922, in Brooklyn, NY; daughter of Frederick G. (a businessman) and Jeannette L. (Cox) Hoppe; married Francis C. Kelly, Jr (a government clerk), April 12, 1947 (died, 1958). EDUCATION: Attended City College of New York;

trained for the stage at the Strasberg Institute and with Mitchell Nestor, former artistic director of the Actors Studio.

VOCATION: Actress, writer, and painter.

CAREER: PRINCIPAL STAGE APPEARANCES—Ethel, *Call It a Day,* Eleanor Cody Gould's Theatre, Allen Street, New York City, 1960; Laura Tremp, Trolly, and Marie, *Telemacus Clay,* Pad Theatre, New York City, 1977; Miss Mabel, *J.B.,* Park Avenue South Theatre, New York City, 1981; Madame Pe, *Waltz of the Torreadors,* Irene Moore's Studio Theatre, New York City, 1983; also: Mabel Lamston, *Lemonade,* Pad Theatre, New York City; Flo, *Alice Doesn't Live Here Anymore;* Mrs. Moorhead, *The Women;* Amanda, *Glass Menagerie;* Lily, *The Children's Hour.*

FILM DEBUT—Prospective tenant, *Rent Control,* independent, 1980. PRINCIPAL FILM APPEARANCES—Store customer, *Just Tell Me What You Want,* Warner Brothers, 1980; bag lady, *No Room of Her Own,* independent, 1981; bag lady, *Senior Trip,* independent, 1981; *Falling in Love,* Paramount, 1984; *Broadway Danny Rose,* Orion, 1984; *Nothing Lasts Forever,* Metro-Goldwyn-Mayer/ United Artists, 1984; customer, *Forever Lulu,* independent, 1986; also, *Doctor's Story.*

TELEVISION DEBUT—*The Guiding Light,* CBS, 1978. PRINCIPAL TELEVISION APPEARANCES—*As the World Turns,* CBS, 1984, 1985; *The Guiding Light,* CBS, 1987; *Saturday Night Live,* NBC.

NON-RELATED CAREER—Secretary, Department of Social Services, 1965-72.

VIVIAN KELLY

WRITINGS: PLAYS, PRODUCED—A one-act play produced at Eccentric Circles Theatre workshop, New York City, 1985; reading of a two-act play at the Roundabout Theatre, New York City, 1987. SCREENPLAYS—*No Room of Her Own,* State University of New York at Purchase, 1980.

AWARDS: London International Film Festival Award; Victoria Film Festival Award, Melbourne, Australia; Costa Brevo Film Festival Award, Spain, 1980, for *No Room of Her Own.*

MEMBER: Actors' Equity Association, Screen Actors Guild, American Federation of Television and Radio Artists; Twelfth Night Club.

ADDRESSES: HOME—New York City. AGENT—Michael Amato, 1650 Broadway, New York, NY 10019.

*   *   *

KEMPER, Victor J. 1927-

PERSONAL: Born April 14, 1927, in Newark, NJ; son of Louis and Florence (Freedman) Kemper; married wife Claire, May 24, 1953; children: Jan, Steven, Florence. EDUCATION: Seton Hall University, B.A.

VOCATION: Cinematographer.

CAREER: PRINCIPAL FILM WORK—Cinematographer: *Husbands,* Columbia, 1970; *The Magic Garden of Stanley Sweetheart,* Metro-Goldwyn-Mayer (MGM), 1970; *They Might Be Giants,* Universal, 1971; *Who Is Harry Kellerman and Why Is He Saying Those Terrible Things About Me?,* National General, 1971; *The Hospital,* United Artists, 1971; *The Candidate,* Warner Brothers, 1972; *Last of the Red Hot Lovers,* Paramount, 1972; *Shamus,* Columbia, 1973; *The Friends of Eddie Coyle,* Paramount, 1973; *Gordon's War,* Twentieth Century-Fox, 1973; *The Hideaways,* Cinema 5, 1973; *The Gambler,* Paramount, 1974; *The Reincarnation of Peter Proud,* American International Pictures, 1975; *Dog Day Afternoon,* Warner Brothers, 1975.

Stay Hungry, United Artists, 1976; *The Last Tycoon,* Paramount, 1976; *Mikey and Nicky,* Paramount, 1976; *Slapshot,* Universal, 1977; *Audrey Rose,* United Artists, 1977; *Oh God!,* Warner Brothers, 1977; *The One and Only,* Paramount, 1978; *Coma,* MGM, 1978; *Eyes of Laura Mars,* Columbia, 1978; *Magic,* Twentieth Century-Fox, 1978; . . .*And Justice for All,* Columbia, 1979; *The Jerk,* Universal, 1979; *The Final Countdown,* United Artists, 1980; *Night of the Juggler,* Columbia, 1980; *Xanadu,* Universal, 1981; *The Four Seasons,* Universal, 1981; *Chu Chu and the Philly Flash,* Twentieth Century-Fox, 1981; *Partners,* Paramount, 1982; *Author! Author!,* Twentieth Century-Fox, 1982; *National Lampoon's Vacation,* Warner Brothers, 1983; *Mr. Mom,* Twentieth Century-Fox, 1983; *The Lonely Guy,* Universal, 1984; *Cloak and Dagger,* Universal, 1984; *Secret Admirer,* Orion, 1984; *Pee Wee's Big Adventure,* Warner Brothers, 1985; *Clue,* Paramount, 1985; *BoBo,* MGM, 1986.

MEMBER: American Society of Cinematographers.

ADDRESSES: AGENT—Gersh Agency, 222 N. Canon Drive, Beverly Hills, CA 90210.

SHEPPARD KERMAN

KERMAN, Sheppard 1928-

PERSONAL: Born August 26, 1928, in Brooklyn, NY; son of Louis (a businessman) and Leila (a poet; maiden name, Benowitz) Kerman; married Ilona Morai (a ballet dancer and teacher), January 19, 1957; children: Christina. EDUCATION: City College (now City University of New York), B.S.S., English, 1950.

VOCATION: Actor, writer, director, producer, and multi-media designer.

CAREER: STAGE DEBUT—Title role, *Edward II,* Pauline Edwards Theatre, New York City, 1947. BROADWAY DEBUT—Czech diplomat and radio announcer, *The Prescott Proposals,* Eugene O'Neill Theatre, 1953, for six to eight months. PRINCIPAL STAGE APPEARANCES—Marc Antony, *All for Love,* Off-Broadway production, 1950-51; Mario, *Tonight in Samarkand,* Broadway production, 1954; Dr. Balzar and third soldier, *The Great Sebastians,* Broadway production, 1956; British police sergeant, *Listen to the Mockingbird,* Broadway production, 1957; Cord Elam, *Oklahoma!,* City Center, New York City, 1958; Uncle Max, *The Sound of Music,* Broadway production, 1959-63; narrator, *Caprichos,* American Ballet Theatre, New York City, 1965.

Off-Broadway productions: Oliver, *As You Like It* and Hastings, *Richard III,* both New York Shakespeare Festival; *The Projection Room* Theatre de Lys; title role, *Everyman;* Grandpa, *Trouble in July;* title role, *Santa Claus;* Herod, *Salome;* Diego, *Fools Are Passing Through;* title role, *Faust;* the film director and Ptolemy, *The Thirteenth God;* Dwornitshek, *The Play's the Thing.*

Stock productions: Doc, *Come Back Little Sheba;* Keller, *All My Sons;* Jussac, *Can Can;* Senator Phogbound, *Li'l Abner;* Kendal Nesbit, *Lady in the Dark;* Dr. Serensky, *Anastasia;* Captain Queeg, *The Caine Mutiny Court Martial;* Ali Hakim, *Oklahoma!;* Ed Devery, *Born Yesterday;* Mitch, *A Streetcar Named Desire.*

PRINCIPAL STAGE WORK—Multi-media designer. *Seesaw,* Broadway production, 1973; *Beatlemania,* Winter Garden Theatre and on tour, 1977; *Platinum,* Broadway production, 1978; has also designed for speeches and motivational pieces.

PRINCIPAL FILM APPEARANCES—*Boss Tweed;* has also appeared in industrial and U.S. Army training films.

RELATED CAREER—Writer and producer, Kenyon & Eckhardt Advertising Company, New York City, 1964-69; writer and producer, Charisma Organization, New York City, 1969-71; creative director, Stage Right (multi-media producers), New York City, 1971-72; president and creative director, In-Perspective Communications, Inc., New York City, 1973—.

WRITINGS: PLAYS, PRODUCED AND PUBLISHED—*The Dark and the Day,* New Dramatists, New York City, 1952; *Bilby's Doll,* New Dramatists, New York City, 1953; *Cut of the Axe,* Ambassador Theatre, New York City, 1960, published by Samuel French Inc, 1961; *Players on a Beach,* Masters Institute Theatre, New York City, 1961; *Mr. Simian,* Astor Place Playhouse, New York City, 1963; *The Tune of the Time,* Atlanta Civic Theatre, GA, 1969; *Distant Relations,* 1978. One-act musicals: *Orgy on Park Avenue, Roast, Mamma, The Mood Synthesizer, Lady Collona, Funny Business,* all between 1977-82. PLAYS, UNPUBLISHED—"Nine Rebels," 1962; "The Husband-in-Law," 1968.

TELEVISION—Scripts for *Danger,* CBS; *Studio One,* CBS; *Camera Three,* CBS; *Philco Playhouse,* CBS; *Kraft Playhouse,* CBS; *Matinee Theatre;* "Opportunity Unlimited." RADIO—*Jacob Rils,* WNYC, 1946. LYRICS—For songwriters Marvin Hamlisch, Lee Pockriss, and John Strauss. POETRY, UNPUBLISHED—"The Candy Man," single volume.

AWARDS: Best radio play, WNYC student awards, 1946, for *Jacob Rils;* Best Actor Award, *Show Business,* 1950, for *Everyman* and 1951, for *Love for Love;* Obie Award, *Village Voice* 1964, for *Mr. Simian;* Los Angeles Drama Critics Circle Award for overall visual design concept, 1978, for *Beatlemania;* International Film and Television of New York's Grand Award, for *Opportunity Unlimited.*

MEMBER: New Dramatists, American Federation of Television and Radio Artists, Actors' Equity Association, Screen Actors Guild, American Society of Composers, Authors, and Publishers; Players Club.

ADDRESSES: HOME—41B Dunes Lane, Port Washington, NY 11050. AGENT—Bret Adams & Associates, 448 W. 44th St., New York, NY 10036.

*   *   *

KERR, Deborah   1921-

PERSONAL: Full name, Deborah Jane Kerr-Trimmer; born September 30, 1921, in Helensburgh, Scotland; immigrated to the United States, 1947; daughter of Arthur Charles (a civil engineer) and Kathleen Rose (Smale) Kerr-Trimmer; married Anthony Charles Bartley, November 28, 1946 (divorced, July, 1959); married Peter Viertel (a screenwriter), July 23, 1960; children: Melanie, Francesca, and one step daughter. EDUCATION: Studied dance and acting with her aunt, Phyllis Smale, at her school of dramatic art in England, 1930-38; studied dance at Sadler's Wells.

VOCATION: Actress.

CAREER: STAGE DEBUT—Harlequin, *Harlequin and Columbine,* Knightstone Pavilion, Weston-Super-Mare, U.K., 1937. LONDON DEBUT—In the corps de ballet, *Prometheus,* Sadler's Wells Opera House, 1938. BROADWAY DEBUT—Laura Reynolds, *Tea and Sympathy,* Ethel Barrymore Theatre, September 30, 1953. PRINCIPAL STAGE APPEARANCES—Appeared in repertory, various Shakespeare plays, Open Air Theatre, Regents Park, London, 1939; Margaret, *Dear Brutus* and Patty Moss, *The Two Bouquets,* both with the Oxford Repertory Theatre, Oxford Playhouse, U.K., 1940; Ellie Dunn, *Heartbreak House,* Cambridge Theatre, London, 1943.

Edith Harnham, *The Day After the Fair,* Lyric Theatre, London, 1972; Nancy, *Seascape,* Shubert Theatre, New York City, then Shubert Theatre, Los Angeles, 1974-75; Julie Stevens, *Souvenir,* Shubert Theatre, Los Angeles, 1975; Mary Tyrone, *Long Day's Journey into Night,* Ahmanson Theatre, Los Angeles, 1977; title role, *Candida,* Albery Theatre, London, 1977; title role, *The Last of Mrs. Cheney,* Eisenhower Theatre, Kennedy Center, Washington, DC, 1978, *Overheard,* London production, 1981; *The Corn Is Green,* London production, 1985.

MAJOR TOURS—Ellie Dunn, *Heartbreak House,* U.K. cities, 1943; Mrs. Manningham, *Angel Street,* Holland, Belgium, France, for ENSA, 1945; Laura Reynolds, *Tea and Sympathy,* U.S. cities, 1955; Edith Harnham, *The Day After the Fair,* U.S. cities, 1973-74; title role, *The Last of Mrs. Cheyney,* U.S. cities, 1978; *Overheard,* U.K. cities, 1981.

FILM DEBUT—Hatcheck girl, *Contraband,* British National, 1939. PRINCIPAL FILM APPEARANCES—Jenny Hill, *Major Barbara,* Universal, 1940; *Love on the Dole,* Universal, 1940; *Penn of Pennsylvania,* British National, 1940; *Hatter's Castle,* 1941; *The Day Will Dawn,* Denham, 1941; *Perfect Strangers,* 1944; *The Life and Death of Colonel Blimp,* United Artists, 1945; *I See a Dark Stranger,* 1945; *Black Narcissus,* Universal, 1946; *The Hucksters,* Metro-Goldwyn-Mayer (MGM), 1947; *If Winter Comes,* MGM, 1947; *The Adventuress,* Eagle-Lion, 1947; *Hatter's Castle,* Paramount, 1948; *Edward, My Son,* MGM, 1949.

King Solomon's Mines, MGM, 1950; *Please Believe Me,* MGM, 1950; *Quo Vadis,* MGM, 1951; *Rage of the Vulture,* 1951; *Prisoner of Zenda,* MGM, 1952; *Young Bess,* MGM, 1953; *Dream Wife,* MGM, 1953; *Julius Caesar,* MGM, 1953; *Thunder in the East,* Paramount, 1953; Karen Holmes, *From Here to Eternity,* Columbia, 1953; *The End of the Affair,* Columbia, 1955; *Tea and Sympathy,* MGM, 1956; *The Proud and the Profane,* Paramount, 1956; *The King and I,* Twentieth Century-Fox, 1956; *Heaven Knows, Mr. Allison,* Twentieth Century-Fox, 1957; *An Affair to Remember,* Twentieth Century-Fox, 1957; *Separate Tables,* Universal, 1958; *Bonjour Tristesse,* Columbia, 1958; *Count Your Blessings,* MGM, 1959; *The Journey,* MGM, 1959; *Beloved Infidel,* Twentieth Century-Fox, 1959.

Ida, *The Sundowners,* Warner Brothers, 1960; *The Grass Is Greener,* Universal, 1960; *The Innocents,* Twentieth Century-Fox, 1961; *The Naked Edge,* United Artists, 1961; *The Chalk Garden,* Universal, 1964; *The Night of the Iguana,* MGM, 1964; *Marriage on the Rocks,* Warner Brothers, 1965; *Casino Royale,* Columbia, 1967; *The Eye of the Devil,* MGM, 1967; *The Gypsy Moths,* MGM, 1969; *The Arrangement,* Warner Brothers, 1969; *The Assam Garden,* Moving Picture Company, 1985.

TELEVISION DEBUT—Moira Shepleigh, Grace Annesly, and Miranda Watney, *Three Roads to Rome,* BBC, 1961. PRINCIPAL TELEVISION APPEARANCES—Movies: *A Song at Twilight,* 1981; *Witness for the Prosecution,* 1982; *Ann & Debbie,* 1984; *Reunion at Fairborough,* Home Box Office, 1985. Mini-Series: *A Woman of Substance,* syndicated, 1985; *Emma Harte, Hold the Dream,* syndicated, 1986.

AWARDS: Voted "Star of Tomorrow," Motion Picture *Herald-Fame* Poll, 1942; voted one of the top ten British money making stars, Motion Picture *Herald-Fame* Poll, 1947; New York Film Critics Awards, 1947, for *Black Narcissus* and *The Adventuress,* 1957, for *Heaven Knows, Mr. Allison,* and 1960, for *The Sundowners;* Academy Award nominations, 1949, for *Edward, My Son,* 1953, for *From Here to Eternity,* 1956, for *The King and I,* 1957, for *Heaven Knows, Mr. Allison,* 1958, for *Separate Tables,* and 1960, for *The Sundowners;* Donaldson Award, New York Publicists Guild Award, *Variety* Drama Critics Poll Award, all 1954, and Sarah Siddons Award, 1955, all for *Tea and Sympathy;* Golden Globe Award, 1956, for *The King and I* and 1958, for *Separate Tables;* Box Office Blue Ribbon Awards, 1950, for *King Solomon's Mines* and 1956, for *The King and I;* Star of the Year Award, Theatre Owners of America, 1958; Variety Club of Great Britain Award, 1961.

MEMBER: British Actors' Equity Association, Actors' Equity Association, Screen Actors Guild, Academy of Motion Picture Arts and Sciences.

SIDELIGHTS: Deborah Kerr's stage and screen career spans more than four decades, during which she has appeared in over forty-five films. She has won four New York Film Critics's best actress awards and six Academy Award nominations—for *Edward, My Son, From Here to Eternity, The King and I, Heaven Knows, Mr. Allison, Separate Tables,* and *The Sundowners.* She has yet to win an Oscar and admits she minds missing out on the one in 1960 for Ida, the deprived but tolerant wife of Robert Mitchum's itinerant Australian sheep farmer in *The Sundowners.* Yet, despite her enduring appeal, according to Ken Doeckel in the *Films in Review* issue of January, 1978, Kerr "still defies classification today. All her gifts—classically chiseled features, expressive voice, charm, wit, intelligence and literacy—serve to challenge the usual Hollywood actress image."

Trained as a dancer at her aunt's drama school in Bristol, England, Kerr won a scholarship to the Sadler's Wells ballet school and at seventeen made her London debut among the corps-de-ballet in *Prometheus.* She soon discovered, however, that she was more interested in drama and began playing small roles in various Shakespearean productions. In the early 1940s, she made her British film debut as the Salvation Army girl, Jenny Hill, in the movie version of George Bernard Shaw's *Major Barbara.* Other film roles followed in which she typically played cool and reserved well-bred ladies. In 1946, on the strength of her sensitive portrayal of a nun in *Black Narcissus,* she was brought to Hollywood by Metro-Goldwyn-Mayer to play the lead opposite Clark Gable in *The Hucksters.* She retained her serene, ladylike image on the American screen through a series of genteel roles in such films as *If Winter Comes, Young Bess, King Solomon's Mines,* and *Quo*

Vadis. Then in 1953, she was given the opportunity to play, on loan to Columbia, the part of Karen Holmes, the alcoholic nymphomaniac Army wife in *From Here to Eternity.* Her scene on the beach with Burt Lancaster in their classic love scene from that movie made it clear that a real woman existed beneath that cool exterior. "Suddenly I could act," Kerr told Richard Lee in an interview that appeared in the January 25, 1975, *New York Post.* "Suddenly I had sex appeal."

Soon thereafter Kerr made her Broadway debut as Laura Reynolds, the compassionate wife in Robert Anderson's *Tea and Sympathy.* The part looked like just another "teacup" role, she related to Lee, "another goody-goody lady." It took director Elia Kazan, Kerr explained, to show her that Laura was "a symbol of so many things that I myself believe in . . . compassion and tenderness, for instance, and the idea that a man need not conform to a schoolboy image of masculinity to be a man." Kerr's sensitive, dazzling performance won both critical and popular acclaim. She remained a full season with the hit drama and later went on a national tour with it.

Following *Tea and Sympathy,* Kerr became an internationally respected star. Among her most notable film performances of the next decade were those in *The King and I, Tea and Sympathy, Separate Tables, Beloved Infidel,* and the Australian-filmed *The Sundowners.* She was also the tormented governess in an adaptation of Henry James's novella *Turn of the Screw* titled *The Innocents,* an unconventional governess in *The Chalk Garden,* the frustrated spinster awakened to life by Richard Burton in *The Night of the Iguana,* and Kirk Douglas's unsatisfied wife in *The Arrangement.*

Kerr returned to the London stage in the fall of 1972 in *The Day After the Fair* and took the play on a tour of the United States in 1973. Since then she has appeared in numerous other plays, anmong them Edward Albee's *Seascape,* Eugene O'Neill's *Long Day's Journey into Night,* and Shaws's *Candida.* Kerr made her television debut in the BBC production *Three Roads to Rome.* Other television appearances have included roles in *Witness for the Prosecution, A Woman of Substance,* and *Reunion at Fairborough.* The actress has also graced a few Oscar broadcasts, hosted the Tony Awards in 1972, and narrated several documentaries.

ADDRESSES: AGENT—The Lantz Office, 9255 Sunset Blvd., Suite 505, Los Angeles, CA 90069.*

*   *   *

KERR, Walter 1913-

PERSONAL: Full name, Walter Francis Kerr; born July 8, 1913, in Evanston, IL; son of Walter Sylvester (a carpenter and forcman) and Esther M. (Daugherty) Kerr; married Jean Collins (an author and playwright), August 9, 1943; children: Christopher, Colin and John (twins), Gilbert, Gregory, Katharine. EDUCATION: Attended De Paul University, 1931-33; Northwestern University, B.S., 1937, M.A., 1938. POLITICS: Democrat. RELIGION: Roman Catholic.

VOCATION: Dramatic critic and writer.

CAREER: PRINCIPAL STAGE WORK—Co-writer (see below) and director: *Sing Out, Sweet Land,* International Theatre, New York City, 1944; *Touch and Go,* Broadhurst Theatre, New York City,

1949; *King of Hearts*, Lyceum Theatre, 1954; *Goldilocks*, Lunt-Fontanne Theatre, New York City, 1958.

PRINCIPAL TELEVISION WORK—Series: Host, *Esso Repertory Theatre*, 1965.

RELATED CAREER—Movie and drama critic, *Evanston Review* and *Evanston News-Index*, IL, 1920s; instructor of speech and drama, Catholic University of America, 1938-45, associate professor of drama, 1945-49; drama critic, "Commonweal," New York City, 1950-52; drama critic, *The New York Herald Tribune*, New York City, 1951-66; consultant, Robert Saudek Associates, 1956—; with the *The New York Times*, drama critic for daily editions, 1966-67, drama critic for Sunday editions, 1967-79, and chief drama critic for daily and Sunday editions, 1979—.

WRITINGS: PLAYS, PRODUCED AND PUBLISHED—*Murder in Reverse*, published by Dramatic Publishing, 1935; *Denison's Variety Revue*, published by Denison, 1935; *Harmony Minstrel First-Part*, published by Denison, 1936; *Mystery Minstrel First-Part*, published by Denison, 1937; adapter, *Rip Van Winkle*, published by Samuel French, 1937; adapter, *The Vicar of Wakefield*, published by Samuel French, 1938; *Movie Minstrel First-Part*, published by Denison, 1938; *Hyacinth on Wheels*, published by Row, Peterson, 1939; *Christmas, Incorporated*, published by Samuel French, 1939; (with Leo Brady and Nancy Hamilton) *Count-Me-In* (revue), Ethel Barrymore Theatre, New York City, 1942; adapter, *The Miser*, published by Samuel French, 1942, *Stardust*, published by Dramatic Publishing, 1946; *Sing Out, Sweet Land: A Musical Biography of American Song*, International Theatre, New York City, 1944, published by Baker, 1949; (with Jean Kerr) *Thank You, Just Looking* (revue), Catholic University of America, Washington, DC, 1949, produced as *Touch and Go*, Broadhurst Theatre, New York City, 1949, then Prince of Wales Theatre, London, 1950; adapter, *The Birds*, published by Catholic University of America Press, 1952; (with Jean Kerr) *Goldilocks*, Lunt-Fontanne Theatre, New York City, 1958, published by Doubleday, 1959; also author of *From Julia to Joe*, 1937.

BOOKS—*How Not to Write a Play*, Simon & Schuster, 1955, reprinted by Writer, Inc., 1972; *Criticism and Censorship*, Bruce, 1956; *Pieces at Eight*, Simon & Schuster, 1957; *The Decline of Pleasure*, Simon & Schuster, 1962; *The Theater in Spite of Itself*, Simon & Schuster, 1963; (with V. Louise Higgins) editor, *Five World Plays*, Harcourt, 1964; *Harold Pinter*, Columbia University Press, 1967; *Tragedy and Comedy*, Simon & Schuster, 1967; *Thirty Plays Hath November: Pain and Pleasure in the Contemporary Theatre*, Simon & Schuster, 1969; *God on the Gymnasium Floor and Other Theatrical Adventures*, Simon & Schuster, 1971; *The Silent Clowns*, Knopf, 1975; *Journey to the Center of the Theater*, Knopf, 1979; *The Shabunin Affair: An Episode in the Life of Leo Tolstoy*, Cornell University Press, 1982.

PERIODICALS—Contributor: "Horizon," "Harper's," "Saturday Evening Post," "Life," "Theatre Arts," "American Scholar."

AWARDS: Best Drama Criticism, George Jean Nathan Award, 1963, for *The Theater in Spite of Itself;* Dineen Award, National Catholic Theater Conference, 1965; Iona Award, 1970; Campion Award, 1971; Laetare Medal Award, University of Notre Dame, 1971; National Institute of Arts and Letters Award, 1972; Pulitzer Prize Award, 1978, for drama criticism; Theatre Hall of Fame Award, 1982.

Honorary degrees: Doctor of Law, St. Mary's College, 1956,

Fordham University, 1965; Doctor of Literature, LaSalle College, 1956, University of Notre Dame, 1968, University of Michigan, 1972; Doctor of Humane Letters, Northwestern University, 1962.

MEMBER: Authors League of America, Dramatists Guild, Newspaper Guild, American Society of Composers, Authors and Publishers (ASCAP), New York Drama Critics Circle (president, 1955-56); Players Club.

ADDRESSES: HOME—One Beach Avenue, Larchmont, NY 10538. OFFICE—c/o *The New York Times*, 229 W. 43rd Street, New York, NY 10036. AGENT—Brandt & Brandt Literary Agents, Inc., 1501 Broadway, New York, NY 19936.*

*   *   *

KERT, Larry   1930-

PERSONAL: Full name, Frederick Lawrence Kert; born December 5, 1930, in Los Angeles, CA; son of Harry and Lillian (Pearson) Kert. EDUCATION: Attended Los Angeles City College; trained for the stage at the Neighborhood Playhouse with Sanford Meisner and studied singing with Keith Davis.

VOCATION: Actor and director.

CAREER: STAGE DEBUT—*Bill Norvas and the Upstarts*, cabaret and variety theatres and the Roxy Theatre, New York City, 1950. BROADWAY DEBUT—Chorus, *Tickets, Please*, Coronet Theatre,

LARRY KERT

1950. LONDON DEBUT—Robert, *Company,* Her Majesty's Theatre, 1972. PRINCIPAL STAGE APPEARANCES—*Look Ma, I'm Dancin',* Players Ring Theatre, Los Angeles, 1952; chorus, *John Murray Anderson's Almanac,* Imperial Theatre, New York City, 1953; *The Ziegfeld Follies Revue,* Shubert Theatre, Boston, MA, 1956; Tony, *West Side Story,* Winter Garden Theatre, New York City, 1957 and 1960.

Singer, *The Medium* and *The Telephone,* both in Palm Springs, CA, 1961; Gerry Siegel, *Family Affair,* Billy Rose Theatre, New York City, 1962; Harry Bogen, *I Can Get It for You Wholesale,* Shubert Theatre New York City, 1962; Carlos, *Breakfast at Tiffany's,* Majestic Theatre, New York City, 1966; Clifford Bradshaw, *Cabaret,* Broadway Theatre, New York City, 1968; Mario the Fool, *La Strada,* Lunt-Fontanne Theatre, New York City, 1969; Robert, *Company,* Alvin Theatre, New York City, 1970.

Sondheim: A Musical Tribute, Shubert Theatre, New York City, 1973; *Music! Music!,* City Center, New York City, 1974; Joe, *Sugar,* Los Angeles, 1974; *A Musical Jubilee,* St. James Theatre, New York City, 1975; *Side by Side by Sondheim,* Music Box Theatre, New York City and Huntington-Hartford Theatre, Los Angeles, 1978; Mr. Harris, *Rags,* Mark Hellinger Theatre, New York City, 1986.

MAJOR TOURS—Tony, *West Side Story,* U.S. and Canadian cities, 1959-60; *West Side Story, Pal Joey,* and *The Merry Widow,* U.S. cities, 1961; Harry Bogen, *I Can Get It for You Wholesale,* U.S. and Canadian cites, 1962-63; Proteus, *Two Gentlemen of Verona,* U.S. and Canadian cities, 1973; *A Musical Jubilee,* U.S. cities, 1975.

PRINCIPAL CABARET APPEARANCES—Appeared at the Cole Room, St. Regis Hotel, New York City, for twenty-two weeks.

PRINCIPAL STAGE WORK—Stage Manager, *Mr. Wonderful,* Broadway Theatre, New York City, 1956.

FILM DEBUT—*New York, New York,* United Artists, 1977.

TELEVISION DEBUT—Chorus, *Ed Sullivan Show,* CBS, 1950. PRINCIPAL TELEVISION APPEARANCES—Episodic: *Kojak,* CBS; *Hawaii Five-O,* CBS; *Three Girls, Three,* NBC. Mini-Series: *Rich Man, Poor Man,* ABC. Guest: *The Tonight Show,* NBC.

AWARDS: Antoinette Perry Award nomination, 1970, for *Company.*

SIDELIGHTS: FAVORITE ROLES—Tony from *West Side Story,* Mario from *La Strada,* and Robert from *Company.* RECREATIONS—Raising Ibizan hounds and jumping horses.

ADDRESSES: HOME—69 Horatio Street, New York City, 10014. AGENT—International Creative Management, 40 W. 57th Street, New York, NY 10019.

* * *

KETRON, Larry 1947-

PERSONAL: Born July 27, 1947, in Kingsport, TN. EDUCATION: Attended University of Tennessee and East Tennessee State University. MILITARY: U.S. Army.

VOCATION: Playwright.

CAREER: PRINCIPAL STAGE WORK—Playwright in Residence, WPA Theatre, New York City 1979-86; peer review panelist, New York Creative Artists Public Service Program, 1981-82; guest artist, Aspen Playwrights Conference, CO, 1982; panelist, Artists Foundation, Massachusetts state fellowship program for artists, 1983-84.

WRITINGS: PLAYS, PRODUCED—*Cowboy Pictures,* Playwrights Horizons, New York City, 1974; *Augusta,* Playwrights Horizons, then Theatre de Lys, New York City, 1975; *Stormbound,* Playwrights Horizons, New York City, 1975; *Patrick Henry Lake Liquors,* Manhattan Theatre Club, New York City, 1975; *Quail Southwest,* Manhattan Theatre Club, 1977; *Rib Cage,* Stage West, West Springfield, MA, 1978; *The Frequency,* American Conservatory Theatre, San Francisco, 1978, then WPA Theatre, New York City, 1979; *Character Lines,* WPA Theatre, 1979, St. Nicholas Theatre, Chicago, 1980, then The Show Room, Los Angeles, 1982; *The Trading Post,* WPA Theatre, 1981, then Odyssey Theatre, Los Angeles, 1983; *A Tinker's Damn,* Hershel Zohn Theatre, New Mexico State University, Las Cruces, 1981; *Ghosts of the Loyal Oaks,* WPA Theatre, 1981; *Asian Shake,* WPA Theatre, 1983; *The Hitch-Hikers* (commissioned adaptation of Eudora Welty's short story), WPA Theatre, 1985; *Fresh Horses,* WPA Theatre, 1986; *Rachel's Fate,* Denver Theatre Centre, 1987.

PLAYS, PUBLISHED—All published by Dramatists Play Service: *Patrick Henry Lake Liquors,* 1977; *Quail Southwest,* 1977; *Rib Cage,* 1978; *Character Lines,* 1980; *The Trading Post,* 1981; *Ghosts of the Loyal Oaks,* 1982; *Asian Shade,* 1983; *Eudora Welty's The Hitch-Hikers,* 1986; *Fresh Horses,* 1986.

AWARDS: Best New Play, *Show Business* Award, 1977, for *Patrick Henry Lake Liquors;* Excellence in Playwriting, Villager Award, 1979, for *The Frequency;* John Simon Guggenheim Memorial Foundation Fellowship for Playwriting, 1985.

MEMBER: Dramatists Guild, Writers Guild of America.

ADDRESSES: AGENT—c/o Gilbert Parker, William Morris Agency, 1350 Avenue of the Americas, New York, NY 10019.

* * *

KHEEL, Lee 1918-

PERSONAL: Born October 24, 1918, in Springfield, MA; married Julian Kheel (divorced); children: Richard, Thomas, Wendy, Claudia, Vickey. EDUCATION: Ithaca College, B.S., 1940; University of Rochester, M.A., 1948; trained for the stage at the Herbert Berghof Studio.

VOCATION: Actress.

CAREER: PRINCIPAL STAGE WORK—*If Walls Could Talk,* Manhattan Punchline Theatre, New York City; Mrs. McIlhenny, *The Time of the Cuckoo,* Equity Library Theatre, New York City; Mrs. Levett, *Solomon's Fish,* Strategy Theatre, New York City; Pearl, *Lady of Means,* Troupe Theatre, New York City; Myrtle, *The Laboratory,* Cubiculo Theatre, New York City; Agnes, *Brainwashed,* Equity Library Theatre Informal Series, Lincoln Center, New York City; Grandmere, *Tartuffe,* Theatre East, Rochester, NY; *A Christmas Carol,* Stage Arena, Buffalo, NY.

LEE KHEEL

MEMBER: Actors' Equity Association, Screen Actors Guild, American Federation of Television and Radio Artists.

ADDRESSES: HOME—450 E. 20th Street, New York, NY 10010.

* * *

KINGSLEY, Ben 1943-

PERSONAL: Born Krishna Bahji, December 31, 1943, in Snaiton, Yorkshire, England; son of Rahimutlla Harji (a physician) and Ann Lyna Mary (a fashion model) Bahji; married Gillian Alison Macauley Sutcliffe (a theatre director); children: Edmund. EDUCATION: Manchester Grammar School.

VOCATION: Actor.

CAREER: STAGE DEBUT—On a schools-tour for Theatre Centre, 1964. LONDON DEBUT—The Wigmaker, *The Relapse,* Royal Shakespeare Company, Aldwych Theatre, 1967. BROADWAY DEBUT—Title role, *Edmund Kean,* Brooks Atkinson Theatre, 1984. PRINCIPAL STAGE APPEARANCES—Doolittle, *Pygmalion,* Stoke-on-Trent, U.K., 1965; Narrator, *A Smashing Day,* Arts Theatre, London, 1966; First Murderer, *Macbeth* and party guest, *The Cherry Orchard,* both Chichester Theatre Festival, U.K., 1966; Amiens, *As You Like It,* Royal Shakespeare Company, Stratford-on-Avon, U.K., 1967; Oswald, *King Lear,* Aeneas, *Troilus and Cressida,* and Conrade, *Much Ado About Nothing,* all Royal Shakespeare Company, Stratford-on-Avon, 1968, also performed

the last two plays at the Aldwych Theatre, London, 1969; the Croucher, *The Silver Tassie* and Winwife, *Bartholomew Fair,* both Royal Shakespeare Company, Aldwych Theatre, London, 1969.

Ratcliff, *Richard III,* Claudio, *Measure for Measure,* Demetrius in Peter Brook's production of *A Midsummer Night's Dream,* and Ariel, *The Tempest,* all Royal Shakespeare Company, Stratford-on-Avon, 1970; Demetrius, *A Midsummer Night's Dream* and Sinsov, *Enemies,* both Aldwych Theatre, London, 1971; Gramsci, *Occupations* and Ippolit, *Subject to Fits,* Place Theatre, London, 1971; Puck, *The Faery Queen,* Newcastle, U.K., 1972; Johnnie, *Hello and Goodbye,* Kings Head Theatre, then Place Theatre, London, 1973; Fritz, *A Lesson in Blood and Roses,* Place Theatre, London, 1973; Errol Philander, *Statements,* Royal Court Theatre, London, 1974; Slender, *The Merry Wives of Windsor,* Bronze Wan, *Man Is Man,* and Hamlet in Buzz Goodbody's Other Place Production of *Hamlet,* all Royal Shakespeare Company, Stratford-on-Avon, 1975, and at the Round House, London, 1976.

Danilo, *Dimetos,* Nottingham Playhouse, then Comedy Theatre, London, 1976; Mosca, *Volpone,* Vukhov, *Judgement,* and Trofimov, *The Cherry Orchard,* Royal Shakespeare Company, Stratford-on-Avon, 1979; Frank Ford, *The Merry Wives of Windsor,* Iachimo, *Cymbeline,* Brutus, *Julius Caesar,* and title role, *Baal* (this last also at Other Place), all Royal Shakespeare Company, Stratford-on-Avon, 1979; *Baal,* Warehouse Theatre, London, 1980; Wackform Squeers, *Nicholas Nickleby,* Aldwych Theatre, London, 1980; title role, *Dr. Faustus,* Manchester Royal Exchange Theatre; title role, *Edmund Kean,* Harrogate, 1981, then Lyric Hammersmith, Haymarket Theatre, London, 1983; title role, *Othello,* Royal Shakespeare Company, 1986; also, *Melons,* U.K production, 1986; Shylock in *The Merchant of Venice.*

MAJOR TOURS—Demetrius, *A Midsummer Night's Dream,* United States tour, 1971; Errol Philander, *Statements,* European tour, 1974.

FILM DEBUT—*Fear Is the Key,* 1972. PRINCIPAL FILM APPEARANCES—Title role, *Gandhi,* Columbia, 1982; Robert, *Betrayal,* Twentieth Century-Fox, 1983; *Turtle Diary,* Samuel Goldwyn Co., 1986.

PRINCIPAL TELEVISION APPEARANCES—Episodic: Rossitti, *The Love School.* Movies: *Barbara of Grebe House; Thank You, Comrades; Every Good Boy Deserves Favour; Feel Free; Edmund Kean; The Merry Wives of Windsor; Camille,* CBS, 1984; title role, *Silas Marner,* 1984 (U.S. airing on *Masterpiece Theatre,* PBS, 1987).

AWARDS: Best Actor, Academy Award, British Academy Award, Variety Club Award, and Best Newcomer Award, Golden Globe Award, all 1982, for *Gandhi;* Best Actor, *London Standard* Award, 1983, for *Betrayal;* Padma Shree, Government of India; Honorary M.A., Safford University.

MEMBER: British Actors' Equity Association.

SIDELIGHTS: After a long and successful career in the British theatre, actor Ben Kingsley achieved international prominence in 1982 for his starring role in *Gandhi.* Kingsley—whose father is of Indian ancestry—portrayed Mahatma Gandi in the three-and-a-half hour movie saga that follows the Indian leader's activities through fifty-four years. Kingsley's performance earned him a Golden Globe Award, a New York Film Critics Award, and the coveted "Oscar" for best actor from the Academy of Motion

Picture Arts and Sciences. Undaunted by the notoriety, he has since returned to the stage and has taken roles in other acclaimed movies. Asked by *New York Times* reporter Leslie Bennetts if the "Gandhi" experience had changed his life, Kingsley replied on September 18, 1983: "I profoundly believe there is nothing else in the world I should be than an actor. I can now see the tip of the iceberg, I know it's there and it's real."

Kingsley was born in Great Britain on December 31, 1943. He was named Krishna Bahji by his parents, a physician whose own father was born in India, and a British fashion model. Growing up in Manchester, Kingsley aspired to follow his father into medicine and evinced little interest in his Indian heritage. He was unable to pass the entrance examinations for medical school, however, so instead he joined an amateur dramatic society and then took a job with a children's theatre company in London. By 1967, he was performing with the prestigious Royal Shakespeare Company. Kingsley's stage performances since that time, both within and outside the Royal Shakespeare Company, have run the gamut of classical and modern drama. He has appeared as Demetrius in *A Midsummer's Night Dream*, Mosca in *Volpone*, Trofimov in *The Cherry Orchard*, Shylock in *The Merchant of Venice*, as Hamlet, and as the evil Wackform Squeers in *Nicholas Nickleby*. It was his 1975 performance as Hamlet that caught the eye of director Richard Attanborough, who had long cherished the idea of filming Mahatma Gandhi's life.

Although Attenborough was advised to sign a "big name" American actor to the role of Gandhi, he became convinced that Kingsley would best suit the demanding part after viewing the actor's screen test. "From the moment Ben came on the screen, he was absolutely mesmeric," Attenborough told Bennetts. "There was no question he was the one." Kingsley embraced the role wholeheartedly. He spent months in India dieting, pouring over photographs, absorbing newsreel footage of Gandhi, and mastering the spinning wheel that Gandhi worked at almost daily. In the process he discovered that his own roots trace back to Gujarat, the Indian state in which Gandhi was born. While he told Bennetts that the responsibility of playing Gandhi was a great weight on his sholders and the preparation was extremely difficult, he nonetheless added: "I've never been happier in my life, in terms of exercising my craft on something I utterly believed in."

Reaction to *Gandhi*, and to Kingsley performance, were almost universally positive. *New York* magazine critic David Denby perhaps sums up the film's reception in his preview of Septmeber 20, 1982: "[*Gandhi*] is a stirringly old-fashioned movie, an epic vision of the birth of modern India made with great detail and love for its subject and also an honorable seriousness about a most difficult theme—the discipline of nonviolence." Denby continued: "And when it opens, moviegoers will greet yet another great British actor. . . . Kingsley's affinity for Gandhi is startling. . . . He prevents the movie from becoming a dutiful exercise in hero worship."

Kingsley's performances since *Gandhi* reflect his ever-present desire for challenging roles. Late in 1983, he appeared on Broadway in a one-man show about the nineteenth-century English actor Edmund Kean. In 1986, he returned to the Royal Shakespeare to star in Shakespeare's *Othello* and Bernard Pomerance's play about an American Indian, *Melons*. These accomplishments led *New York Times* critic Benedict Nightingale to comment on January 26, 1986: "Ben Kingsley the man may go about the globe on a British passport; Ben Kingsley the actor likes to travel with more exotic documentation. As much as any performer now living, he can claim to be a citizen of the world."

A modest man who has brought many years of hard work to the perfection of his craft, Kingsley is both pleased with and challenged by the acclaim he has received. He told Leslie Bennetts: "I am a storyteller. I recognize the need and thrive on the level of compressed association with my fellow human beings that only the theatrical event can bring. With essential truth in mind, it doesn't really matter what the story is."

ADDRESSES: HOME—New Pebworth House, Pebworth, Stratford-on-Avon, Warwickshire, England.*

*　　　*　　　*

KLEINER, Harry   1916-

PERSONAL: Born September 10, 1916, in the Union of Soviet Socialist Republics; son of Abraham and Ida (Neshnikov) Kleiner; married Sophie Risenberg, June 15, 1943; children: Stephanie. EDUCATION: Temple University, B.S.; Yale School of Drama, M.F.A. RELIGION: Jewish.

VOCATION: Writer and producer.

CAREER: PRINCIPAL FILM WORK—Writer (see below); producer, *Garment Jungle*, Columbia, 1957; *Cry Tough*, United Artists, 1959.

WRITINGS: SCREENPLAYS—*Fallen Angel*, Twentieth Century-Fox, 1948; *The Street with No Name*, Twentieth Century-Fox, 1948; *Kangaroo*, Twentieth Century-Fox, 1952; *Salome*, Columbia, 1953; *Miss Sadie Thompson*, Columbia, 1953; *Carmen Jones*, United Artists, 1954; *The House of Bamboo*, Twentieth Century-Fox, 1955; *Garment Jungle*, Columbia, 1957; *Cry Tough*, United Artists, 1959; *Fever in the Blood*, Warner Brothers, 1961; *Fantastic Voyage*, Twentieth Century-Fox, 1966; *Bullitt*, Warner Brothers, 1968; *Extreme Prejudice*, Tri-Star, 1986; also *The Judgement of Corey*, United Artists; *The Valiant Men*, Columbia; *Twenty Four Hours of Le Mans*, Tri-Star.

TELEVISION—Dramatic specials: *The Rosenberg Trial*, CBS; *Robin Hood*, NBC. Episodic: *Bus Stop*, ABC; *The Virginian*, NBC.

AWARDS: Best Screenplay, Academy Award nomination, 1949, for *The Street with No Name;* Best Adaptation, Academy Award nomination, 1955, for *Carmen Jones.*

MEMBER: Screen Writers Guild.

ADDRESSES: OFFICE—8721 W. Sunset Blvd., West Hollywood, CA 90069. AGENT—Jerome Siegel Associates, 8723 W. Sunset Blvd., West Hollywood, CA 90069. PUBLICIST—Nan Herst, 8733 Sunset Blvd. Suite 103, Los Angeles, CA 90069.

*　　　*　　　*

KOMAROV, Shelley   1949-

PERSONAL: Born February 8, 1949, in Odessa, Union of Soviet Socialist Republics; married Boris Komarov, January 21, 1972; children: Dimitry. EDUCATION: Leningrad Industrial Engineering College, M.A., 1972; Repin Institute, Leningrad Academy of Fine Arts, M.F.A., 1977.

VOCATION: Costume designer and former dancer.

CAREER: PRINCIPAL TELEVISION WORK—Mini-series: Costume designer—*Blue Light,* Union of Soviet Socialist Republics Television; *Peter the Great,* NBC, 1983-84. Movies: *Murder: By Reason of Insanity,* CBS, 1985; *Christmas Eve,* NBC, 1986; *Roses Are for the Rich,* CBS, 1987.

PRINCIPAL FILM WORK—Costume designer: *The Cage,* Cannon, 1985; *Murphy's Law,* Cannon, 1986; *The President's Wife,* Cannon, 1986.

PRINCIPAL STAGE APPEARANCES—Dancer: *Swan Lake, Sleeping Beauty, Don Quixote,* White Nights Festivals and in the annual competition at the Vaganova School of Ballet, all with the Leningrad Kirov Ballet, U.S.S.R.

PRINCIPAL STAGE WORK—Costume designer: *The Cherry Orchard,* Pan Andreas Theatre, Los Angeles, 1984.

MAJOR TOURS—Costume designer: *Karmen* and *Katherina Izmailova,* Leningrad Kirov Opera and Ballet Theatre, Soviet and European cities.

RELATED CAREER—Costume designer, "The Russian Collection of Fashion," an exhibition touring Yugoslavia, Germany, Poland, Italy, and France; teacher, Leningrad Design College; lecturer, Stamford University seminars, 1983; instructor, Otis Parsons Institute of Design, 1983-86; lecturer, University of Southern California School of Cinema Seminar, 1986.

AWARDS: Best Design, Leningrad Competition Award, 1973; Best Design, V.D.N.H. National Competition, 1974; Best Costumes, *Drama-Logue* Award, 1984, for *The Cherry Orchard.*

MEMBER: Costume Designers Guild, Costume Society of America.

ADDRESSES: HOME—Santa Monica, CA. AGENT—Gersh Agency, 222 N. Canon Drive, Beverly Hills, CA 90210.

*   *   *

KONDAZIAN, Karen

PERSONAL: Born January 27, in Boston, MA; daughter of Edward (a lawyer) and Lillian M. (a teacher; maiden name, Mosesian) Kondazian. EDUCATION: San Francisco State College, B.A., 1963; also studied as an exchange student at the University of Vienna; trained for the stage at the London Academy of Music and Dramatic Art and at the Actors Studio with Lee Strasberg, Jose Quintero, and Milton Katselas.

VOCATION: Actress and writer.

CAREER: OFF-BROADWAY DEBUT—Chorus, *The Trojan Women,* Circle in the Square Theatre, 1964, for ninety-six performances. LONDON DEBUT—*Playing with Fire.* PRINCIPAL STAGE APPEARANCES—Serafina, *The Rose Tattoo,* Beverly Hills Playhouse, CA, 1978; Alexandra Del Lago, *Sweet Bird of Youth,* Gene Dynarski Theatre, Los Angeles, 1979; *Lady House Blues,* South Coast Repertory Company, Los Angeles, 1980; *Vieux Carre,* Beverly Hills Playhouse, 1983; *Andorra,* American Jewish Thea-

tre, New York City, 1984; *Broken Eggs,* Ensemble Studio Theatre, New York City, 1984; *Aelis, Tamara,* Il Vittoriale Theatre, Los Angeles, 1985; also appeared in Los Angeles in: *Richard II,* Ahmanson Theatre, *Hamlet,* Mark Taper Forum, *Museum,* Los Angeles Actors Theatre, and *Kiss Me Good Morning,* Theatre West.

TELEVISION DEBUT—Kate Holiday, "Shootout at the OK Corral," *Appointment with Destiny,* CBS, 1972. PRINCIPAL TELEVISION APPEARANCES—Series: Mrs. Luciano, *The Gangster Chronicles,* NBC; *Shannon,* CBS, 1981-82. Episodic: *Hill Street Blues,* NBC; *Cagney and Lacey,* CBS; *Moonlighting,* ABC. Movies: *The Bride of Boogedy,* ABC.

FILM DEBUT—*Yes Giorgio,* Metro-Goldwyn-Mayer/United Artists, 1982.

WRITINGS: TELEPLAYS—Treatment: "The Whip," Universal, 1985-86.

AWARDS: Los Angeles Drama Critics Circle Award, 1978, for *The Rose Tatoo;* Distinguished Performance, *Drama-Logue* Award, 1979, for *Sweet Bird of Youth;* Best Actress in a Leading Role, *L.A. Weekly* Award, 1983, for *Vieux Carre;* Distinguished Performance, *Drama-Logue* Award, 1985, for *Tamara.*

MEMBER: Actors Studio (life member); Women in Film.

ADDRESSES: HOME—Los Angeles, CA. AGENT—Fred Amsel and Associates, 6310 San Vicente Blvd., Los Angeles, CA 90048.

KAREN KONDAZIAN

KOPIT, Arthur 1937-

PERSONAL: Born May 10, 1937, in New York, NY; son of George (a business executive) and Maxine (Dubin) Kopit; married Leslie Ann Garis, 1968; children: Alexander, Benjamin, Kathleen. EDUCATION: Harvard University, B.A., 1959.

VOCATION: Writer.

CAREER: PRINCIPAL STAGE WORK—Director: *Oh Dad, Poor Dad, Mama's Hung You in the Closet and I'm Feelin' So Sad,* Theatre des Bouffes-Parisiens, Paris, 1963.

PRINCIPAL TELEVISION WORK—Writer (see below); director, *The Questioning of Nick,* WNHC, 1959.

RELATED CAREER—Adjunct professor of playwriting, Yale University, 1977-80; teacher of playwriting, City College of New York, 1980-84.

WRITINGS: PLAYS, PRODUCED—Productions at Harvard University: *The Questioning of Nick,* 1957; *Gemini,* 1957; (with Wally Lawrence) *Don Juan in Texas,* 1957; (with Lawrence) *On the Runway of Life You Never Know What's Coming Off Next,* 1957; *Across the River and into the Jungle,* 1958; *Sing to Me Through Open Windows* and *To Dwell in a Palace of Strangers,* both 1959.

Oh Dad, Poor Dad, Mama's Hung You in the Closest and I'm Feelin' So Sad, Harvard University, 1960, then Lyric Theatre, Lonon, 1961, Phoenix Theatre, New York City, 1962, transferring to the Morosco Theatre, New York City, 1963, then produced at the Theatre des Bouffes-Parisiens, Paris, 1963; *Asylum, or What the Gentlemen Are Up to, and as for the Ladies,* Theatre de Lys, New York City, 1963; *Chamber Music,* Society Hill Playhouse, Philadelphia, 1965; *Sing to Me Through Open Windows* and *The Day the Whores Came Out to Play Tennis,* both at the Players Theatre, New York City, 1965; *Indians,* with the Royal Shakespeare Company at the Aldwych Theatre, London, 1968, then Arena Stage, Washington, DC, and transferring to the Brooks Atkinson Theatre, New York City, 1969; *The Conquest of Everest* and *The Hero,* both at the New York Theatre Ensemble, New York City, 1973; *The Questioning of Nick,* Manhattan Theatre Club, New York City, 1974; *Secrets of the Rich,* 1976; *Wings,* New York Shakespeare Festival, Public Theatre, New York City, 1978; (libretto) *Nine,* 46th Street Theatre, New York City, 1982-83; (translation of Ibsen's *Ghosts*) *End of the World,* Music Box Theatre, New York City, 1984. Also *Mhil'daim,* 1963, *Ghosts* (translation) and *Good Help is Hard to Find* (one-act), all produced in New York City.

PLAYS, PUBLISHED—*Oh Dad, Poor Dad, Mama's Hung You in the Closet and I'm Feelin' So Sad: A Tragifarce in a Bastard French Tradition,* Hill & Wang, 1960; *The Day the Whores Came Out to Play Tennis, and Other Plays* (contains "The Questioning of Nick," "Sing to Me Through Open Windows," "Chamber Music," "And as for the Ladies," "The Hero," "The Conquest of Everest," and "The Day the Whores Came Out to Play Tennis"), Hill & Wang, 1969 (published in England as *Chamber Music & Other Plays,* Methuen, 1969); *Indians,* Hill & Wang, 1969; *Wings,* Hill & Wang, 1978; *End of the World,* Samuel French, 1985; *Ghosts,* Samuel French.

TELEVISION PLAYS—*The Questioning of Nick,* WNHC, 1959; "The Conquest of Everest," *New York Television Theatre,* NET, 1966; also "Promontory Point Revisited," *New York Television Theatre,* NET.

SCREENPLAYS—*Oh Dad, Poor Dad. . .,* Paramount, 1967; *Indians; Wings.* BOOKS—His work is represented in *Pardon Me, Sir, But is My Eye Hurting Your Elbow?,* edited by Bob Booker and George Foster, published by Geis, 1968. PERIODICALS—First act of *To Dwell in a Palace of Strangers* published in the *Harvard Advocate,* May, 1959.

AWARDS: Vernon Rice Award, Outer Critics Circle Award, both 1960, for *Oh Dad, Poor Dad. . .;* Antoinette Perry Award nomination, 1969, for *Indians;* Antoinette Perry Award nomination, 1978, for *Wings;* Award of Merit, 1971, American Institute of Arts and Letters. Grants: Rockefeller Foundation, National Endowment for the Arts, Guggenheim Fellowship, and CBS Fellowship.

MEMBER: Dramatists Guild (council, 1982—), Writers Guild of America, Actors Studio, Playwrights' Cooperative (founding member, 1973), P.E.N.; Hasty Pudding Club, Signet Society, Harvard Club, Masons.

SIDELIGHTS: RECREATIONS—Playing the piano and photography.

ADDRESSES: AGENT—c/o Bridget Aschenberg, International Creative Management, 40 W. 57th Street, New York, NY 10019.

*   *   *

KORNFELD, Robert 1919-

PERSONAL: Full name, Robert Jonathan Kornfeld; born March 3, 1919, in Newton, MA; son of Lewis F. (a broker) and Lillian S. (an actress and painter) Kornfeld; married Celia Seiferth (a writer and arts administrator), August 23, 1945; children: Robert J., Jr. EDUCATION: Harvard University, A.B., 1941; graduate study at Harvard University, New York University, Tulane, New School for Social Research, College of Mount Saint Vincent, and Columbia University; studied playwriting with Edward Albee at the Circle in the Square School of Drama in New York. POLITICS: Democrat. MILITARY: U.S. Army, 211th Coast Artillery, 1940.

VOCATION: Writer and photographer.

WRITINGS: PLAYS, PRODUCED—*Je suis homme (I Am Man),* Paris, 1953; *Passage in Purgatory* (one-act), Virginia Little Theatre, Norfolk, 1962, in a one-act series at Circle in the Square, New York City, 1963, and at Riverdale Contemporary Theatre, New York City, 1970; *Kicking the Castle Down,* Gramercy Arts Theatre, New York City, 1962; *Minutes of the Meeting,* Virginia Little Theatre, Norfolk, 1963; *Clementina* (one-act), Circle in the Square Theatre, New York City, 1963, Riverdale Contemporary Theatre, New York City, 1970; *Tell The Stars,* O'Neill Memorial Theatre, New London, CT, 1969; (with Melvin Freedman) *Reunion* (musical), Cubiculo Theatre, New York City, 1973-74; *An Hour with Poe: Out of Space, Out of Time,* Lincoln Center Mall series, 1977, Gould Memorial Theatre, New York City, 1977, and Rome Theatre, New York City, 1978; *The Passion of Frankenstein,* New York Stage Works, 1980, Network Theatre, New York City, 1982; (book and lyrics) *Glory Hallelujah!,* (two-act musical) 18th Street Playhouse, New York City, 1980-81; *A Dream within a Dream* (libretto, opera), Wave Hill Center for the Performing Arts, New York City, 1984, and Merkin Hall, New York City, 1986; *Mrs. Bullfrog,* Lehman Center for the Performing Arts, New York City, 1985, and Wave Hill Center for the Performing Arts, New York City, 1985.

ROBERT KORNFELD

PLAYS, UNPRODUCED—"Queen of Crags"; "Playing Ludwig"; "The Bridge"; "The Art of Love."

SCREENPLAYS, UNPRODUCED—"The Diplomat."

RADIO—Series: XEQ, Mexico City, Mexico, mystery series in Spanish, 1941.

BOOKS—*Great Southern Mansions,* Samuel Walker, 1977.

RELATED CAREER—Reporter and photographer, *San Francisco Examiner,* 1942-43; contributor to *The New York Times* Travel section, "Morocco," 1977, "The Panama Canal," 1979; photography work exhibited at museums and galleries including the Addison Gallery of Art, the Metropolitan Museum of Art and others.

AWARDS: Best New Play Award, Norfolk Little Theatre, 1962, for *Passage in Purgatory,* and *Minutes of the Meeting,* 1963; Second Place Award, New York Writers Conference, 1963, for "Queen of Crags"; Best Play Award, Broadway Drama Guild, 1979, for "The Art of Love"; commissions for opera librettos, Bronx Arts Ensemble, 1984-86.

MEMBER: Dramatists Guild, Authors League; National Arts Club (literary committee), Kesselring Theatre Committee (board member), Bronx Arts Ensemble (chairman), Riverdale Contemporary Theatre (board member); Historic Districts Council (secretary).

SIDELIGHTS: Mr. Kornfeld told *CTFT* that his travels take him to Italy, France, Asia, and Africa where he continues his photography.

ADDRESSES: OFFICE—5286 Sycamore Avenue, Riverdale, NY 10471. AGENT—c/o Emilie Jacobson, Curtis Brown, Ltd., Ten Astor Place, New York, NY 10003.

*   *   *

KRABBE, Jeroen   1944-

PERSONAL: Second syllable of Christian name rhymes with "Spoon"; surname pronounced "Crabay"; born December 5, 1944, in Amsterdam, The Netherlands; son of Maarten (a painter) and Margreet (a film translator; maiden name, Reiss) Krabbe; married Herma Van Geemert (a social worker); children: Martyn, Jasper, Jakob. EDUCATION: Trained for the stage at the De Toneelschool, Academy of Dramatic Art, Amsterdam, certificate of graduation, 1965, and as a painter at the Academy of Fine Arts, Amsterdam, certificate of graduation, 1981.

VOCATION: Actor, director, painter, and writer.

CAREER: FILM DEBUT—Sims, *Soldier of Orange,* Mouwer Films, 1979. PRINCIPAL FILM APPEARANCES—Maarten and alter ego, *A Flight of Rainbirds,* Meiningen Films, 1979; *Spetters,* Joop Van Der End, 1980; Gerard, *The Fourth Man,* Mouwer Films, 1982; *Turtle Diary,* Samuel Goldwyn Company, 1985; *Jumpin' Jack Flash,* Twentieth Century-Fox, 1986; *No Mercy,* Tri-Star, 1987; *The Living Daylights,* upcoming; also appeared in *Shadow of Victory.*

TELEVISION DEBUT—Camille Desmoulins, *Danton's Death,*

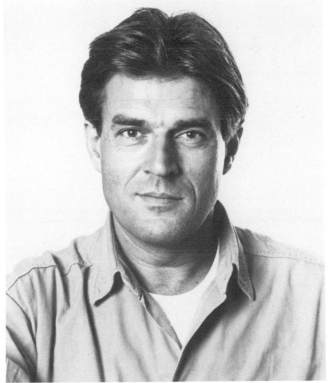

© 1986 Danjaq S. A.

JEROEN KRABBE

AVRO Television, 1966. PRINCIPAL TELEVISION APPEARANCES—Mini-Series: Title role, *William of Orange,* AVRO Television, 1985; *World War Three.* Movies: *One for the Dancer,* upcoming; also hosted a television talk show on Dutch television.

STAGE DEBUT—Berowne, *Love's Labor's Lost,* Stadssdrouwburg Theatre, Haarlem, Netherlands, 1965, for one-hundred-and-fifty performances. PRINCIPAL STAGE APPEARANCES—At the Stadssdrouwburg Theatre, Haarlem, Netherlands: Bosola, *The Duchess of Malfi,* Cassio, *Othello,* Milo, *Sleuth,* Bri, *A Day in the Death of Joe Egg,* Chance Wayne, *Sweet Bird of Youth,* Elyot, *Private Lives,* Jesse, *Mann Ist Mann,* various roles, *Furcht und Elend.*

MAJOR TOURS—Dutch cities: Gregory, *Relatively Speaking,* William, *How the Other Half Loves,* Christian, *Cyrano de Bergerac,* Jerry, *Two for the Seesaw,* Otto Frank, *Diary of Anne Frank.*

PRINCIPAL STAGE WORK—Director, *The Diary of Anne Frank,* tour of Dutch cities.

PRINCIPAL RADIO WORK—Hosted his own music program on Dutch radio.

RELATED CAREER—Founder of a theatre company which toured Dutch cities; translator of plays into Dutch; costume designer.

NON-RELATED CAREER—As a painter his work has been widely exhibited, notably at the Singer Museum in Amsterdam in a showing of paintings by his father and great grandfather.

WRITINGS: BOOKS—*The Economy Cookbook.*

AWARDS: Best Actor Award in Italy, Spain, and England, for *The Fourth Man.*

MEMBER: British Actors' Equity, Screen Actors Guild.

ADDRESSES: HOME—107 Vajn Eeghen Straat, Amsterdam 1071EZ, The Netherlands. AGENT—c/o Marion Rosenberg, The Lantz Office, 9255 Sunset Blvd., Los Angeles, CA 90069.

*   *   *

KRAMER, Bert

PERSONAL: Raised in La Mesa, CA. EDUCATION: Graduated from University of California at Los Angeles; trained for the stage at the Group Repertory Theatre, New York City, with Peggy Feury and with Lee Strasberg. MILITARY: U.S. Army.

VOCATION: Actor.

CAREER: PRINCIPAL TELEVISION APPEARANCES—Series: Emmet Ferguson, *Sara,* CBS, 1976; Mike Fitzpatrick, *The Fitzpatricks,* CBS, 1977-78; Alex Wheeler, *Texas,* NBC; Brent Davis, *The Young and the Restless,* CBS.

Episodic: *Sea Hunt,* syndicated; *Playhouse 90,* CBS; *The Hardy Boys,* ABC; *The Bionic Woman,* NBC; *The Six Million Dollar Man,* ABC; *The Rockford Files,* NBC; *CHiPS,* NBC; *Dallas,* CBS; *Dynasty,* ABC; *M*A*S*H,* CBS; *Little House on the Prairie,* NBC; *The Fall Guy,* ABC.

BERT KRAMER

PRINCIPAL FILM APPEARANCES—*Raintree County,* Metro-Goldwyn-Mayer, 1957; *Lady Sings the Blues,* Paramount, 1972; *Earthquake,* Universal, 1974; *Moment by Moment,* Universal, 1978; *Thunder Alley,* upcoming.

PRINCIPAL STAGE APPEARANCES—*Happy Days Are Here Again,* Group Repertory Theatre, New York City; also appeared on stage as Noah in *110 in the Shade;* Harry Brock in *Born Yesterday;* Emil DeBeque in *South Pacific;* Willie Stark in *All the King's Men;* Gus in *Three by Tennessee;* Von Trapp in *The Sound of Music;* MacDuff in *Macbeth* and appeared in *The Trip Back Down,* 1978.

AWARDS: Drama-Logue Award, 1978, for *The Trip Back Down;* also nominated three times for the Drama Critics Award.

SIDELIGHTS: RECREATIONS—Illustrating, writing, body surfing, gardening, and softball.

ADDRESSES: HOME—Los Angeles, CA. PUBLICIST—Chris Costello and Company Public Relations, P.O. Box 2084, Toluca Lake Station, North Hollywood, CA 91602.

*   *   *

KRAMER, Marsha

PERSONAL: Born June 19, in Chicago, IL; daughter of Allen T. (a tobacconist) and Tina (a tobacconist; maiden name, Braverman) Kramer; married Jim Keller (a photographer), March 23, 1986. EDUCATION: Univeristy of California at Los Angeles, B.A., secondary teaching credential; trained for the stage at the Royal Academy of Dramatic Art and the Los Angeles Civic Light Opera Workshop and with David Craig, Bobby Lewis, Curt Conway, and Ella Gerber.

VOCATION: Actress and singer.

CAREER: PRINCIPAL STAGE APPEARANCES—Wendy, *Peter Pan,* Lunt-Fontanne Theatre, New York City; *Noah,* Pan Asian Repertory Theatre, New York City; Helen, *Out of This World,* Equity Library Theatre, New York City; Marsha, *Victory Canteen* and Lucy, *Charlie Brown,* both at the Ivar Theatre, Los Angeles; Melissa, *Funny You Should Ask,* Sebastian's Theatre, Los Angeles; Sylvia, *The Great American Backstage Musical,* Los Angeles and San Francisco productions; Ella, *The Cradle Will Rock,* Dupree Studio Theatre, Los Angeles; Jenny, *Shenandoah* and Wendy, *Peter Pan,* both at the Long Beach Civic Light Opera, CA; Ruby, *Dames at Sea,* La Mirada Civic Theatre, CA; Wendy, *Peter Pan,* Studio Arena Theatre, Buffalo, NY; June, *Gypsy,* Canal Fulton Theatre, OH; Chava, *Fiddler on the Roof,* Carousel Theatre, OH; Agnes, *George M!* and Jenny, *Shenandoah,* both at the Sacramento Music Circus; Amy, *Company,* Dorothy, *Wizard of Oz,* and title role, *Gigi,* all at the Milwaukee Melody Top Theatre, WI.

MAJOR TOURS—Wendy, *Peter Pan,* national; Sally, *On a Clear Day You Can See Forever,* national.

PRINCIPAL TELEVISION APPEARANCES—Episodic: *The Waltons,* CBS; *Barnaby Jones,* CBS; *The Bob Newhart Show,* CBS; *Lucas Tanner,* NBC; *Code R,* CBS; *The Bill Cosby Show,* NBC; also appeared on *Jambo; Superior Court; The Judge.*

MARSHA KRAMER

AWARDS: Drama-Logue Awards: 1984, 1986, both for Wendy, *Peter Pan.*

MEMBER: Actors' Equity Association, Screen Actors Guild, American Federation of Television and Radio Artists, American Guild of Variety Artists.

ADDRESSES: HOME—Burbank, CA. AGENT—c/o Joan Kovats, Exclusive Artists, 2501 Burbank Blvd., Suite 304, Burbank, CA 91505.

*   *   *

KRAMER, Stanley E.   1913-

PERSONAL: Born September 29, 1913, in New York, NY; married Ann Pearce, 1950 (divorced); married Karen Sharpe, 1966; children: (first marriage) Casey, Larry; (second marriage) Katharine, Jennifer . EDUCATION: New York University, B.S., 1933. MILITARY: U.S. Army.

VOCATION: Producer and director.

CAREER: PRINCIPAL FILM WORK—Producer: *So This Is New York,* 1948; *Home of the Brave,* United Artists, 1949; *Champion,* United Artists, 1949; *The Men,* United Artists, 1950; *Cyrano de Bergerac,* United Artists, 1950; *Death of a Salesman,* United Artists, 1951; *High Noon,* United Artists, 1952; *The Happy Time,* 1952; *The Sniper,* 1952; *My Six Convicts,* 1952; *Eight Iron Men,* 1952; *The Four Poster,* 1952; *The 5000 Fingers of Dr. T.,* 1952; *The Wild One,* 1953; *The Member of the Wedding,* 1953; *The Juggler,* 1953; *The Caine Mutiny,* Columbia, 1954.

Producer and director: *Not as a Stranger,* United Artists, 1955; *The Pride and the Passion,* United Artists, 1957; *The Defiant Ones,* United Artists, 1958; *On the Beach,* United Artists, 1959; *Inherit the Wind,* United Artists, 1960; *Judgement at Nuremberg,* United Artists, 1961; *It's a Mad, Mad, Mad, Mad World,* United Artists, 1963; *Ship of Fools,* Columbia, 1965; *Guess Who's Coming to Dinner,* Columbia, 1967; *The Secret of Santa Vittoria,* United Artists, 1969; *R.P.M.,* Columbia, 1970; *Bless the Beasts and the Children,* Columbia, 1971; *Oklahoma Crude,* Columbia, 1973; *The Domino Principle* (also known as *The Domino Killings*), AVCO-Embassy, 1977; *The Runner Stumbles,* Twentieth Century-Fox, 1979.

RELATED CAREER—Researcher, Metro-Goldwyn-Mayer; film cutter; film editor; writer for radio and film; formed Stanley Kramer Productions, 1949; formed Stanley Kramer Company, 1950 (merged with Columbia Pictures, 1951).

AWARDS: Best Director, *Look* Achievement Award, 1950; Academy Award nomination, Best Picture, 1952, for *High Noon;* Best Picture and Best Director, New York Film Critics Awards and Best Picture and Best Director, Academy Awards, all 1958, for *The Defiant Ones;* Best Picture and Best Director, Academy Award nominations, 1961, for *Judgment at Nuremberg;* Irving Thalberg Award, 1961; Best Picture, Academy Award nomination, 1965, for *Ship of Fools;* Best Picture and Best Director, Academy Award nominations, 1967, for *Guess Who's Coming to Dinner;* Gallatin Medal Award, New York University, 1968.

SIDELIGHTS: A press release for director-producer Stanley Kramer's

STANLEY E. KRAMER

film *The Runner Stumbles* asserts that "More than any other producer of major motion pictures. . . Kramer has demonstrated courage and integrity in selecting challenging, controversial and thought-provoking themes in his films." Specifically, Kramer's films explore "such elements as race relations (*Home of the Brave, The Defiant Ones, Pressure Point,* and *Guess Who's Coming to Dinner*); fascism and the abuse of political power (*Judgement at Nuremberg* and *Ship of Fools*); the right to teach Darwinian evolution (*Inherit the Wind*); human greed (*It's a Mad, Mad, Mad, Mad World*); the military chain of command (*The Caine Mutiny*); and nuclear extinction (*On the Beach*)."

The first film Kramer produced, however, was the 1948 comedy *So This Is New York,* which he made just after finishing his service in World War II. His first hit came the next year with the boxing drama *Champion.* With *Home of the Brave* in 1949, his third film, he began to address social issues; this picture was one of the first Hollywood movies to deal with racial relations. Over the next few years, Kramer produced such commercially and critically successful movies as *High Noon* and *The Caine Mutiny,* as well as several prestigious adaptations of stage plays, including *Cyrano de Bergerac, Death of a Salesman,* and *The Member of the Wedding.*

Until 1955, Kramer hired other directors to film his pictures, but in that year he made his own directorial debut with *Not as a Stranger,* an adaptation of a best-selling novel about corruption in the medical industry. It was financially successful, but he later admitted that "I don't think it was very good." His second directorial effort, the expensive Spanish epic *The Pride and the Passion,* failed at the box office and in reviews when it was released in 1957, but *The Defiant Ones* (1958), the story of two convicts—one black, one white—

who make their escape while chained together, was well-received by both critics and the public. As Bosley Crowther of the *New York Times* (September 25, 1958) saw it, the film "rips right into the subject with ferocity and flails it about with merciless fury until all the viciousness in conflict is spent . . . Mr. Kramer has a strong, stark symbolization of an abstract theme."

Kramer's 1959 film *On the Beach* depicted the world facing destruction in a nuclear holocaust. The producer-director, who intended the movie as a warning for mankind, arranged for it to open simultaneously in eighteen different cities, including Moscow. In his *New York Times* review, Crowther said, "The great merit of this picture . . . is the fact that it carries a passionate conviction that man is worth saving, after all." The noted scientist and anti-nuclear advocate Linus Pauling speculated, "It may be that some years from now we can look back and say that *On the Beach* is the movie that saved the world."

Both of Kramer's next two movies were fictionalized versions of famous trials from the past—the 1925 Tennessee "monkey trial" on the teaching of evolution (*Inherit the Wind,* 1960) and the prosecution of German war criminals following World War II (*Judgement at Nuremberg,* 1961).

Characterizing the latter film as an intellectual drama, but one with an obvious emotional involvement on the part of Kramer and his cast, Paul Beckley wrote in the *New York Herald Tribune* (December 20, 1961), "Throughout one feels no desire to vilify but rather to understand, to know, and this gives the film an intellectual integrity rare in cinematic examination of events so close to the emotions of living men." He further surmised, "One feels Kramer saw his theme, not as a mere historical re-enactment, but as an identification of the forces, psychological and social, that made up our past and could shape our future." *New Yorker*'s Brendan Gill found that the director and his screenwriter Abby Mann "have posed some formidable questions, and they plainly intend that everyone who sees the picture should make a conscientious effort to answer them." Assuring his readers that the film was not at all "schoolmarmish," the critic assessed, "The questions are among the biggest that can be asked and are no less fresh and healthy for being thousands of years old."

At the Los Angeles premiere of *It's a Mad, Mad, Mad, Mad World* in 1963, the first comedy Kramer directed, he explained that "I wanted to made a comedy to end all comedies." The resulting film cost over nine-and-a-half million dollars and had a running time of three hours and twelve minutes, prompting Judith Crist in the *Herald Tribune* to call it "a bit much in the madness department." Crist went on, however,to dismiss her own criticism as "perfection-seeking" and to conclude, "The cheers are not only for Mr. Kramer's *Mad World* but basically for its having appreciated and reminded us of the fundamentals of pure American comedy and the glories of exploiting true comedians . . . it's a joyous reminder of our heritage."

Kramer returned to serious themes as he worked again with screenwriter Abby Mann to bring Katherine Anne Porter's bestselling novel *The Ship of Fools* to the screen. The story presents a number of characters aboard a German luxury liner sailing from Mexico to Germany in 1931. In an essay on Kramer that was included in her book *Kiss Kiss Bang Bang* (Atlantic Monthly Press, 1968), Pauline Kael felt the director and writer had exaggerated Porter's anti-Nazi message and complained "If this ship is supposed to be a cross-section of the German people—and obviously this is what Mann intends—then he has failed . . . to make the characters representative of the major elements in that society; and even more significantly, he has failed. . . to demonstrate how the flaws in character and outlook even in a representative group might have led to the specific consequence of Nazism.''

On the other hand, Arthur Knight of the *Saturday Review* (July 3, 1965) wrote that ''given at least a dozen characters of depth and substance, [Kramer] manages to sustain not only a high level of interest in all of them throughout, but also to suggest that, like icebergs, there is considerably more to them than shows on the surface.'' Knight went on: ''This is a new Stanley Kramer, not hitting each scene head-on or underscoring every significant statement. He has become more oblique, more willing to imply, and more deft in cutting quickly to another sequence, another character, before the scene has fully played itself out.''

In the *Herald Tribune* (July 29, 1965), Judith Crist took a position between those two extremes, calling the film, ''one of the classiest soap operas-cum-social significance to come our way since the original *Grand Hotel.*'' She felt that the characters were ''stripped to stereotype,'' but added, ''Mr. Kramer has, in a number of instances, cast them so shrewdly and evoked such overwhelming performances that one is disarmed for the duration of scene after scene.''

The acting was also generally regarded as the best aspect of Kramer's 1967 comedy *Guess Who's Coming to Dinner,* which deals with the reactions of a liberal couple when they learn that their daughter wishes to marry a black man. Katharine Houghton and Sidney Poitier play the engaged pair. Like most critics, Joseph Morgenstern of *Newsweek* (December 25, 1967) felt that the Poitier character had been made so virtuous as to rob the movie's plot of any sociopolitical meaning it might have possessed: ''What these two propose is no interracial marriage but an unprecedented cross-breeding of nobility and virtue.''

The on-screen reunion of Spencer Tracy and Katharine Hepburn as the bride's parents, however, won critics' acclaim. The veteran performers had starred together in a number of popular films of the 1940s and 1950s. Tracy died just after principal photography for this film was completed. Morgenstern, again typical of most of his fellow reviewers, savored Tracy and Hepburn ''doing their lovely stuff for the last time together,'' and concluded, ''When Tracy gives his blessings to the lovers in a novel speech that was written as a melodrama's climax and may now serve as an artists's epitaph . . . then everything wrong with the film is right and we can see . . . an authentically heroic man.'' Despite the critical reservations, *Guess Who's Coming to Dinner* was a major financial success, earning $25,500,000 in film rentals in the United States and Canada.

Kramer's later films did not repeat the success of *Guess Who's Coming to Dinner* and its predecessors, and since 1979 he has made no pictures, largely because of an inability to secure financial backing. In 1978, he moved from California to the area of Seattle, Washington, explaining: ''I guess everything is a search for oneself. I was hopeful that being out of Hollywood I could . . . think. Time, after all, is limited. One may live to be one hundred, but you never know. How does one occupy oneself in the time one has left so that those ensuing years become important? I found it necessary to shake my very foundations.''

ADDRESSES: OFFICE—Stanley Kramer Productions, P.O. Box 158, Bellevue, WA 98009.

ALEX KUBIK

KUBIK, Alex

PERSONAL: Born November 11, in Pittsburg, PA; son of Alexander A. (a steelworker) and Susan (Montagna) Kubik. EDUCATION: University of Northern Colorado, B.A.; trained for the stage with West Coast Repertory. MILITARY: U.S. Air Force, 1963-67.

VOCATION: Actor and writer.

CAREER: STAGE DEBUT—John, *Silent Screams,* Aruada Playhouse, Denver, CO, 1972, for twenty-one performances. PRINCIPAL STAGE APPEARANCES—Sir Dinaden, *Camelot,* LTR Theatre, Denver, 1972; Atahualpa, *Royal Hunt of the Sun,* Studio Theatre, Los Angeles, 1976.

MAJOR TOURS—Bill Sykes, *Oliver,* Adam, *Diary of Adam and Eve,* and *Butterflies Are Free,* Colorado cities, 1972-73.

FILM DEBUT—*Stunts,* New Line Cinema, 1977. PRINCIPAL FILM APPEARANCES—*Inside Moves,* Associated, 1980; *Second Thoughts,* Universal, 1983.

TELEVISION DEBUT—Robot gunfighter, *Beyond Westworld,* 1978. PRINCIPAL TELEVISION APPEARANCES—Movies: *The Legend of Walks Far Woman,* 1979; *Stagecoach,* NBC, 1986.

Episodic: *The Fall Guy,* ABC; *Knight Rider,* NBC; *Cagney and Lacey,* CBS; *Airwolf,* CBS; *Dukes of Hazzard,* CBS; *Jessie,* ABC; *Benson,* ABC.

WRITINGS: SCREENPLAYS—*Shadows of Children at Play; Pros-*

pector; *Squirrel at My Window;* (with Bev Ross) *Schoolmarm;* (with Patti Hyde) *The Taxidermist.* PLAYS—*Freedom Bird,* 1986.

AWARDS: Military: Purple Heart and other medals.

MEMBER: Screen Actors Guild, American Federation of Radio and Television Artists, Writers Guild West.

SIDELIGHTS: RECREATIONS—Writing country and western music.

ADDRESSES: AGENT—Mark Levin and Associates, 328 S. Beverly Drive, Suite E, Beverly Hills, CA 90212.

*   *   *

KURNITZ, Julie 1942-

PERSONAL: Born September 8, 1942, in Mount Vernon, NY. EDUCATION: Trained as a singer with Annette Havens.

VOCATION: Actress and singer.

CAREER: OFF-BROADWAY DEBUT—*In Circles,* Cherry Lane Theatre. PRINCIPAL STAGE APPEARANCES—Mother, *Peace,* Astor Place Theatre, New York City, 1969; Mrs. McNish, *Minnie's Boys,* Imperial Theatre, New York City, 1970; Mother Superior, *Joan,* Circle in the Square Downtown Theatre, New York City, 1971; Catherine the Great, *The Faggot,* Truck and Warehouse Theatre, New York City, 1972; Lady Celia, *Gorey Stories,* Booth

Theatre, New York City, 1979; also appeared as Arnalta, *The Coronation of Poppea,* with the New York Lyric Opera Company, New York City.

PRINCIPAL CABARET APPEARANCES—In New York City at Don't Tell Mama, the Ballroom, the Duplex, and Les Mouches, 1979-87.

PRINCIPAL FILM WORK—Irene, *Radio Days,* Orion, 1987.

TELEVISION DEBUT—Singer, *Caught in the Act,* CBS, 1979. PRINCIPAL TELEVISION APPEARANCES—Carrie Nation, *The Drunkard,* Arts and Entertainment Cable Network.

WRITINGS: BOOKS—(With John P. Eaton) *The Disgusting Despicable Cat Cookbook,* New Century, 1982.

ADDRESSES: HOME—New York City. AGENT—Barry Douglas Talent Agency, 1650 Broadway, New York, NY 10019.

*   *   *

KURTH, Juliette 1960-

PERSONAL: Full name, Juliette Elizabeth Kurth; born July 22, 1960, in Madison, WI; daughter of Richard Herbert (an engineer) and Barbara Joan (a psychiatric nurse; maiden name, Frampton) Kurth. EDUCATION: State University of New York at Purchase, B.F.A.; trained for the stage with Joan Potter.

VOCATION: Actress.

JULIE KURNITZ   JULIETTE KURTH

CAREER: BROADWAY DEBUT—Anne, *La Cage Aux Folles,* Palace Theatre, 1986. PRINCIPAL STAGE APPEARANCES—Elsie, *The Miser,* York Theatre Company, New York City; Lisa, *The Majestic Kid,* Delaware Repertory Theatre; Lady Utterword, *Heartbreak House,* Lady Sullen, *The Beaux Strategem,* Anna Livia, *Finnegan's Wake,* Lillian Farmer, *God's Peculiar Care,* Lady Capulet, *Romeo and Juliet,* and Olga, *Three Sisters,* all New York City productions.

MAJOR TOURS—Anne, *La Cage Aux Folles,* national, 1986; also Lisa, *The Majestic Kid,* with the Delaware Theatre Company, U.S. cities.

PRINCIPAL TELEVISION APPEARANCES—*One Life to Live,* ABC.

RELATED CAREER—Dancer with the: American Dance Machine, American Ballet Theatre, the Joffrey Ballet, San Francisco Ballet.

AWARDS: June Helmers Acting Award, State University of New York at Purchase.

MEMBER: Actors' Equity Association, Screen Actors Guild.

ADDRESSES: AGENT—c/o Bob Beseda, Coleman-Rosenberg, 210 E. 58th Street, Suite 2F, New York, NY 10022.

*   *   *

KURTZ, Swoosie

PERSONAL: Born September 6, in Omaha, NE; daughter of Frank (an Air Force colonel and three time Olympic diver) and Margo (a writer) Kurtz. EDUCATION: Attended the University of Southern California; trained for the stage at the London Academy of Dramatic Arts.

VOCATION: Actress.

CAREER: STAGE DEBUT—*Charley's Aunt* and *The Skin of Our Teeth,* in repertory at the Cincinnati Playhouse in the Park, OH, 1966. OFF-BROADWAY DEBUT—*The Effect of Gamma Rays on Man-in-the-Moon Marigolds,* Mercer Arts Theatre and New Theatre, 1970. PRINCIPAL STAGE APPEARANCES—Muriel, *Ah, Wilderness!,* Circle in the Square Theatre, New York City, 1975; Mariane, *Tartuffe,* Circle in the Square Theatre, New York City, 1977; Rita, *Uncommon Women and Others,* Phoenix Theatre Company, New York City, 1977; Bette, *A History of American Film,* American National Theatre Academy (ANTA) Theatre, New York City, 1978; Gwen, *The Fifth of July,* New Apollo Theatre, New York City, 1980-81; Bananas, *The House of Blue Leaves,* Mitzi Newhouse Theatre and the Vivian Beaumont Theatre, both Lincoln Center, New York City, 1986.

SWOOSIE KURTZ

FILM DEBUT—*Slapshot,* Universal, 1977. PRINCIPAL FILM APPEARANCES—Hooker, *The World According to Garp,* Warner Brothers, 1982; Edie, *Against All Odds,* Columbia, 1984.

PRINCIPAL TELEVISION APPEARANCES—Series: Regular, *Mary,* CBS, 1978; Laurie Morgan, *Love, Sidney,* ABC, 1981-83. Movies: *A Caribbean Mystery,* 1983; *Guilty Conscience,* CBS, 1985.

AWARDS: Antoinette Perry Award nomination, 1978, for *Tartuffe;* Obie Award, 1978, for *Uncommon Women and Others;* Drama Desk Award, 1978, for *A History of American Film;* Antoinette Perry Award, Outer Critics Circle Award, and Drama Desk Award, all 1981, for *The Fifth of July;* Emmy Award nominations, 1982 and 1983, for *Love, Sidney.*

MEMBER: Actors' Equity Association, American Federation of Television and Radio Artists, Screen Actors Guild.

ADDRESSES: AGENT—Creative Artists Agency, 1888 Century Park E., Suite 1400, Los Angeles, CA 90067.*

L

LAHTI, Christine 1950-

PERSONAL: Born April 4, 1950, in Detroit, MI; daughter of Paul Theodore (a surgeon) and Elizabeth Margaret (an artist; maiden name, Tabar) Lahti; married Thomas Schlamme (a director), September 4, 1983. EDUCATION: University of Michigan, M.F.A.; trained for the stage at the Herbert Berghof Studios with William Esper and Uta Hagen.

VOCATION: Actress.

CAREER: STAGE DEBUT—*The Zinger.* OFF-BROADWAY DEBUT—Ruth, *The Woods,* Public Theatre, 1978. PRINCIPAL STAGE APPEARANCES—*Division Street,* Ambassador Theatre, New York City, 1980; *Loose Ends,* Circle in the Square, New York City, 1981; *Present Laughter,* Circle in the Square, New York City, 1983; Betty, *Landscape of the Body,* Walter McGinn/John Cazale Theatre, New York City, 1984; Georgie Elgin, *The Country Girl,* Chelsea Playhouse, New York City, 1984; *Cat on a Hot Tin Roof,* Long Wharf Theatre, New Haven, CT, 1985.

FILM DEBUT—*And Justice for All,* Columbia, 1979. PRINCIPAL FILM APPEARANCES—Dr. Scott, *Whose Life Is It Anyway?,* United Artists, 1981; *Swing Shift,* Warner Brothers, 1984; *Just Between Friends,* Orion, 1986; Kathleen Morgan, *Season of Dreams,* Spectrafilms, 1987.

PRINCIPAL TELEVISION APPEARANCES—Movies: *The Last Tenant,* 1978, *The Executioner's Song,* 1982. *Singles Bars, Single Women,* ABC, 1984. Mini-Series: Aletha Milford, *Amerika,* ABC, 1987.

AWARDS: Theatre World Award, 1978, for *The Woods.;* Academy Award nomination and New York Film Critics Award, Best Supporting Actress, both 1984, for *Swing Shift.*

MEMBER: Actors' Equity Association; Ensemble Studio Theatre.

ADDRESSES: AGENT—Triad Artists Inc., 888 Seventh Avenue, Suite 1602, New York, NY 10106.*

*   *   *

LaLOGGIA, Frank

PERSONAL: Born in Rochester, NY. EDUCATION: Attended State University of New York, University of Miami, and University of Southern California.

VOCATION: Producer, director, writer, composer, and actor.

CAREER: PRINCIPAL FILM WORK—Writer, director, and producer, *Gabriel;* director and composer, *Fear No Evil,* AVCO-Embassy, 1981; writer and (with Charles LaLoggia) co-producer, *Lady in White,* upcoming.

PRINCIPAL TELEVISION APPEARANCES—Pilots: *Salt and Pepe,* CBS; *Mixed Nuts,* ABC; *Snavely,* ABC.

AWARDS: Gold Medal from the Atlanta International Film Festival Award, Francis Scott Key Award from the Baltimore Film Festival, and the Photographic Society of America Award, all for *Gabriel.*

ADDRESSES: PUBLICIST—Chris Costello and Company Public Relations, P.O. Box 2084, Toluca Lake Station, North Hollywood, CA 91602.

FRANK LaLOGGIA

ZOHRA LAMPERT

LAMPERT, Zohra   1937-

PERSONAL: Born May 13, 1937, in New York, NY; daughter of Morris (an ironworker and architect) and Rachil (a hatmaker and draper; maiden name, Eriss) Lampert. EDUCATION: Attended the High School of the Performing Arts in New York City; attended the University of Chicago; continues to study with Mira Rostova.

VOCATION: Actress.

CAREER: STAGE DEBUT—Conchita, *Dancing in the Chequered Shade,* McCarter Theatre, Princeton, NJ, 1955. OFF-BROADWAY DEBUT—*Venice Preserv'd,* Phoenix Theatre Company, 1955-56. PRINCIPAL STAGE APPEARANCES—Mashenka, *Diary of a Scoundrel,* Phoenix Theatre Company, New York City, 1956; Maid to Lady Britomart, *Major Barbara,* Morosco Theatre, New York City, 1956, later portrayed Rummy Michens in the same production; Adele, *Maybe Tuesday,* Playhouse Theatre, New York City, 1958; Jennifer Lewison, *Look: We've Come Through,* Hudson Theatre, New York City, 1961; Illyona, *First Love,* Morosco Theatre, New York City, 1961; member of the Second City troupe, Square East, New York City, 1962-63; Kattrin, *Mother Courage and Her Children,* Martin Beck Theatre, New York City, 1963; Felice, *After the Fall* and Princess Jukachin, *Marco Millions,* both Lincoln Center Repertory Company, American National Theatre Association, Washington Square East Theatre, New York City, 1964; Rachel, *Nathan Weinstein, Mystic, Connecticut,* Brooks Atkinson Theatre, New York City, 1966; Jane, *The Natural Look,* Longacre Theatre, New York City, 1967; Brenda, *Lovers and Other Strangers,* Brooks Atkinson Theatre, New York City, 1968.

Iris, *The Sign in Sidney Brustein's Window,* Longacre Theatre, New York City, 1972; Joan, *Drinks Before Dinner,* Mitzi E. Newhouse Theatre, Lincoln Center, New York City, 1978-79; Mother, *Gifted Children,* Jewish Repertory Theatre, New York City, 1983; Annie, *My Poppa's Wine,* South Street Theatre, New York City, 1986; Mrs. Frank, *The Diary of Anne Frank,* American Stage Theatre, Teaneck, NJ, 1987.

FILM DEBUT—*Pay or Die,* 1960. PRINCIPAL FILM APPEARANCES—Angelina, *Splendor in the Grass,* Warner Brothers, 1961; *A Fine Madness,* Warner Brothers, 1966; *Bye Bye Braverman,* Warner Brothers, 1968; Jessica, *Let's Scare Jessica to Death,* Paramount, 1971; *Alphabet City,* Atlantic Releasing, 1984; *The Cafeteria,* 1986.

PRINCIPAL TELEVISION APPEARANCES—Series: Ellie, *Where the Heart Is,* 1970-71; Anne, *The Girl with Something Extra,* NBC, 1973-74; Dr. Norah Purcell, *Doctors' Hospital,* NBC, 1975-76. Episodic: Jenny, *Better Luck Next Time,* London, ITV, 1964; *The F.B.I.,* ABC, 1970; *Love, American Style,* ABC, 1972-73; Janine, *The Bob Newhart Show,* CBS, 1973; also, *Doctor Kildare,* NBC; *The Defenders,* CBS; *Sam Benedict,* NBC; *Alfred Hitchcock Presents,* NBC. Movies: Hannah, *The Connection,* 1972; Esther, *Izzy & Moe,* 1985. Specials: Leonard Bernstein's "Carmen," *Omnibus,* PBS.

RELATED CAREER—Radio commercials for Bankers Trust; television commercials, Enkasheer, 1970; Eve, Cranapple juice, Goya Beans.

AWARDS: Variety, New York Drama Critics Poll Award, 1973, for Kattrin, *Mother Courage and Her Children;* Antoinette Perry Award nominations, 1961, for *Look, We've Come Through* and 1963, for *Mother Courage and Her Children;* Andy Awards, for Bankers Trust radio commercials and an Enkasheer television commerical, 1970.

MEMBER: Actors' Equity Association, Screen Actors Guild, American Federation of Television and Radio Artists, American Guild of Variety Artists.

SIDELIGHTS: Zohra Lampert's early stage name was Zohra Alton. She began using the name Lampert in 1956 in the production of *Major Barbara* at the Morosco Theatre. Her uncle, Samuel Iris, was an actor.

ADDRESSES: AGENT—c/o Sheila Robinson, International Creative Management, 40 W. 57th Street, New York, NY 10019.

*   *   *

LANCHESTER, Elsa   1902-1986

OBITUARY NOTICE: See index for *CTFT* sketch: Born Elsa Sullivan, October 28, 1902, in Lewisham, London, England; died of bronchio-pneumonia, in Woodland Hills, CA, December 26, 1986; married Charles Laughton (an actor), February 10, 1929 (died, 1962). Elsa Lanchester's career spanned silent films to contemporary television. She was noted for her individual and eccentric characterizations as well as her comic ability. She will perhaps be best remembered for her film role as the mate of Dr. Frankenstein's monster in *The Bride of Frankenstein.* Lanchester starred opposite her husband, actor Charles Laughton, on stage and screen. She moved with him to Los Angeles in 1934, and became a United States citizen in 1950. Incapacited by heart problems since suffering a stroke in 1983, she was hospitalized December 17, 1986 and died nine days later.*

*   *   *

LANDERS, Audrey

PERSONAL: Daughter of Ruth Landers (an agent). EDUCATION: Barnard College, B.A.

VOCATION: Actress and singer.

CAREER: PRINCIPAL CONCERT APPEARANCES—As a singer, has toured Europe.

TELEVISION DEBUT—Guest singer, *The Merv Griffin Show*, independent. PRINCIPAL TELEVISION APPEARANCES—Series: *The Secret Storm*, CBS; *Somerset*, ABC; Afton Cooper, *Dallas*, CBS, 1981-84.

FILM DEBUT—Val, *A Chorus Line*, Columbia, 1985. PRINCIPAL FILM APPEARANCES—*Getting Even*, 1986.

RELATED CAREER—Writes songs with her sister, Judy Landers. Has recorded singles as well as albums.

SIDELIGHTS: In her publicity biography, Audrey Landers reviews

her singing and recording career: ''We intentionally planned to go to Europe first to gain recognition musically. People here tend not to give credence to television personalitics as singers, so we took the long way around. But I know it will be worth it.''

ADDRESSES: PUBLICIST—Jo-Ann Geffen & Associates, 3151 Cahuenga Blvd. West, Suite 235, Los Angeles, CA 90068.

*   *   *

LANDERS, Judy

PERSONAL: Daughter of Ruth Landers (an agent). EDUCATION: Attended the American Academy of Dramatic Arts, New York City.

VOCATION: Actress and singer.

CAREER: PRINCIPAL CONCERT APPEARANCES—As a singer, toured the United States and Europe in an act with her sister, Audrey.

FILM DEBUT—Wanda the Bod, *What Really Happened to the Class of '65?* PRINCIPAL FILM APPEARANCES—*Hellhole*, Arkoff International Pictures, 1985; *Armed and Dangerous*, Columbia, 1986; *Stewardess School*, Columbia, 1986.

PRINCIPAL TELEVISION APPEARANCES—Series: Angie Turner, *Vegas*, ABC, 1978-79; Stacks, *B.J. and the Bear*, 1981; Sara Joy,

AUDREY LANDERS

JUDY LANDERS

275

Madame's Place, 1982. Specials: Two appearances, *Circus of the Stars*, ABC.

RELATED CAREER—Has recorded singles and albums with her sister Audrey Landers.

AWARDS: New York State Tumbling Championship.

SIDELIGHTS: From her publicity biography submitted to *CTFT*, Judy Landers tells us that she began her performing career as a gymnast while still in high school.

ADDRESSES: PUBLICIST—Jo-Ann Geffen & Associates, 3151 Cahuenga Blvd. West, Suite 235, Los Angeles, CA 90068.

*   *   *

LANDSBURG, Valerie   1958-

PERSONAL: Born August 12, 1958; daughter of Alan (a producer) and Sally (a therapist and author) Landsburg; married James R. McVay (a composer and performer), December 1, 1984; children: Taylor.

VOCATION: Actress, writer, and director.

CAREER: TELEVISION DEBUT—Series: Doris Schwartz, *Fame*, NBC and syndicated, 1981-85. PRINCIPAL TELEVISION APPEARANCES—Series: Lorraine Elder, *All Is Forgiven*, NBC, 1985-86; Pam, *You Again*, NBC, 1986.

PRINCIPAL TELEVISION WORK—Director, "Reflections," *Fame*, NBC.

BROADWAY DEBUT—Libby, *I Ought to Be in Pictures*, Eugene O'Neill Theatre, 1980, for sixty performances. PRINCIPAL STAGE APPEARANCES—*The Floating Light Bulb*, Vivian Beaumont Theatre, Lincoln Center, New York City, 1981.

FILM DEBUT—*Thank God It's Friday*, Columbia, 1977.

WRITINGS: TELEVISION—(With Mike Hoey) "Signs " *Fame*, NBC.

AWARDS: Best Dramatic Episode, Governor's Media Award, for "Signs," *Fame*.

MEMBER: Actors' Equity Association, Screen Actors Guild, American Federation of Television and Radio Artists, Directors Guild of America.

ADDRESSES: AGENT—Smith-Freedman, 123 N. San Vincente Blvd., Beverly Hills, CA 90211.

*   *   *

LANE, Genette   1940-

PERSONAL: Born Genette Lebowitz, October 13, 1940, in Baltimore, MD; daughter of Isaac (a grocery store owner) and Tani (a grocery store owner; maiden name, Shapiro) Lebowitz; married

GENETTE LANE

Leopold Kaplan (an attorney), June 10, 1961; children: Elissa, Evonne. EDUCATION: Attended the Peabody Preparatory School of Music and the Peabody Conservatory of Music; trained for the stage at the American Theatre Wing with Helen Mencken and Jay Gorney.

VOCATION: Actress.

CAREER: PRINCIPAL STAGE APPEARANCES—Broadway productions: *The Rothschilds, Ambassador,* and Mistress Schermerhorn, *Knickerbocker Holiday*. Regional and stock productions: Gittel, *Topele,* Zorah, *Ruddigore,* Mrs. Wilson, *The Drunkard,* Golda and Shandel, *Fiddler on the Roof,* Mme. Grimaldi, *George M!,* Olivia, *Your Own Thing,* Bloody Mary, *South Pacific,* Fran, *The Only Game in Town,* Catherine, *A View from the Bridge,* Joan and Susan, *Lovers and Other Strangers,* Eulalie Mackecknie Shinn, *The Music Man,* understudied several roles, *Fanny*.

MAJOR TOURS—*Bye, Bye Birdie, Song for Cyrano, Man of La Mancha, Fiorello!*

PRINCIPAL FILM APPEARANCES—*Once upon a Time in America*, Warner Brothers, 1984.

PRINCIPAL TELEVISION APPEARANCES—Guest, *The Joe Franklin Show*, 1980.

PRINCIPAL CABARET APPEARANCES—With the group Grace Notes Trio at Reno Sweeney's, Grand Finale, The Bushes of Central Park West, and Concord-Grossingers; also toured with the trio.

MEMBER: Actors' Equity Association, Screen Actors Guild, American Federation of Television and Radio Artists.

ADDRESSES: AGENT—c/o Dorothy Scott, Marje Fields, Inc., 165 W. 46th St., Suite 1205, New York, NY 10036.

*   *   *

LANG, Andre   1893-1986

PERSONAL: Born January 12, 1893, in Paris, France; died in Paris, October 4, 1986; married Lise Clemenceau, 1920 (died, 1921); married Sari de Megyery (a poet) 1939 (died, 1983); children: (first marriage) one son (died, 1977).

VOCATION: Playwright, critic, and novelist.

WRITINGS: PLAYS, PRODUCED—*Fantaisie amoureuse*, 1925; *The Three Henrys*, Comedie-Francaise, 1930; *La paix est pour Hemain*, 1937; *L'impure*, 1948; *Le voyage a Turin*, 1956; *Le sac*, 1962; *La dame de Coppet*, 1964.

SCREENPLAYS—*Tarakanowa*, 1929; adaptor, *Les Miserables*, 1933; *Anne-Marie*, 1936; (co-writer) *Volpone*, 1939; *Le tableau blanc*, 1948.

BOOKS, PUBLISHED—Novels: *Le responsable*, 1921; *Fausta*, 1922; *Mes deux femmes*, 1931; *Le septieme ciel*, 1958. Biography: *Une vie d'orages: Germaine de Stael*, 1958; *Pierre Brisson*, 1967. Autobiography: *Bagage a la consigne*, 1960.

RELATED CAREER—Literary and film critic, *Les Annales*, 1927-34, and for *France-Soir*, 1946-58.

AWARDS: Officier Legion d'honneur, Croix de guerre.

MEMBER: Association of Cinema and Television Critics, Paris (honorary president).*

*   *   *

LAPIS, Peter

PERSONAL: Born in Standardville, UT. EDUCATION: California State University at Fullerton, B.A., political science; attended one year of law school; trained for the stage with Wynn Handman, David Proval, and others.

VOCATION: Actor.

CAREER: PRINCIPAL FILM APPEARANCES—*Starhops*, Grodnick Films, 1978; *Sextette*, Briggs and Sullivan, 1978; *Ghoulies*, Empire Pictures, 1985; *Swordkill* (upcoming); also appeared in *Ghost Warrior*.

PRINCIPAL TELEVISION APPEARANCES—Episodic: *Beyond Westworld*, CBS; *The Misadventures of Sheriff Lobo*, NBC; *Flamingo Road*, NBC; also, *Capitol*; *The Young and the Restless*; *Romance Theatre*.

PRINCIPAL STAGE APPEARANCES—*A Loss of Roses*, Zephyr

PETER LAPIS

Theatre, Los Angeles, CA; *To Serve, to Protect and Kill*, Los Angeles City College; *The Night of the Broken Glass*, MET Theatre, Los Angeles.

SIDELIGHTS: In material provided by his agent, Peter Lapis lists a number of special skills, including boxing, bareback riding, western riding, auto racing, dirt bike racing, snow and water skiing, hang gliding, billiards, baseball, basketball, and football.

ADDRESSES: PUBLICIST—Nan Herst Public Relations, 8733 Sunset Blvd., Suite 103, Los Angeles, CA 90069.

*   *   *

LAWRENCE, Carol   1935-

PERSONAL: Born Carol Laraia, September 5, 1935, in Melrose Park, IL; married Robert Goulet (a singer and actor), August 12, 1963 (divorced); children: Christopher, Michael.

VOCATION: Actress and singer.

CAREER: BROADWAY DEBUT—*New Faces of 1952*, Royale Theatre, 1952. PRINCIPAL STAGE APPEARANCES—Liat, *South Pacific*, City Center, New York City, 1955; Arana, *Shangri-La*, Winter Garden Theatre, New York City, 1956; *The Ziegfeld Follies*, New York City, 1957; Maria, *West Side Story*, New York City, 1957 and a revival in 1960; Clio Dulaine, *Saratoga*, New York City, 1959; Angela McKay, *Subways Are for Sleeping*, St.

James Theatre, New York City, 1961; Gia, *Night Life,* Brooks Atkinson Theatre, New York City, 1962; Agnes, *I Do! I Do!,* 46th Street Theatre, New York City, 1967; Guinevere, *Camelot,* Dorothy Chandler Pavilion, Los Angeles, CA, 1975.

MAJOR TOURS—Fanny Brice, *Funny Girl,* U.S. cities, 1967; Maria Rainer, *The Sound of Music,* U.S. cities, 1971; temporary replacement for Ann Miller, *Sugar Babies,* U.S. cities, 1983.

PRINCIPAL CABARET APPEARANCES—Flamingo Hotel, Las Vegas, 1963; Persian Room, New York City, 1971.

PRINCIPAL TELEVISION APPEARANCES—Series: Regular, *The Dean Martin Summer Show,* NBC, 1967. Episodic: *Oldsmobile Music Theatre,* NBC, 1959; *The Bell Telephone Hour,* NBC.

AWARDS: *Theatre World* Award, 1958, for *West Side Story.**

*   *   *

LAWRENCE, Darrie

PERSONAL: Daughter of James F. (a U.S. Marine Corps officer) and Diana Harrison (a social worker; maiden name, Foote) Lawrence. EDUCATION: University of North Carolina at Greensboro, B.A., 1967; Pennsylvania State University, M.F.A., 1974.

VOCATION: Actress.

CAREER: STAGE DEBUT—Elizabeth Proctor, *The Crucible,*

DARRIE LAWRENCE

Playmakers Repertory Theatre, Chapel Hill, NC, 1977. PRINCIPAL STAGE APPEARANCES—At the Playmakers Repertory Theatre, Chapel Hill: May Daniels, *Once in a Lifetime,* Bette, *History of American Film,* Hester, *Equus,* all 1977; Nettie, *The Subject Was Roses,* Stage South, Columbia, SC, 1978; at the Denver Center Theatre Company: Belise, *Learned Ladies,* 1979-80, Emily Stilson, *Wings,* Nurse, *Medea,* all 1980-81, Meg, *The Hostage,* Olga, *The Three Sisters,* both 1982-83, and Hannah, *Night of the Iguana,* Nurse, *Romeo and Juliet,* both 1983-84; Miss Fellows, *Night of the Iguana,* McCarter Theatre, Princeton, NJ, 1981; Mrs. Davidson, *Rain,* Indiana Repertory Company, 1982; Ina, *Miss Lulu Bett,* Milwaukee Repertory Company, 1982; Linda, *Death of a Saleman,* Arizona Theatre Company, 1984; actress, *La Ronde,* Ohio Theatre, New York City, 1984; Fanny, *Painting Churches,* Weathervane Theatre, Whitefield, NH, 1986.

MAJOR TOURS—Jenny, *Quilters,* with the Denver Center Theatre Company, international and western U.S. cities, 1983; Miss Havisham, *Great Expectations,* with the Guthrie Theatre of Minneapolis, national tour, 1985-86.

PRINCIPAL TELEVISION APPEARANCES—Episodic: *The Doctors,* NBC; *One Life to Live,* CBS; *Another World,* NBC; *Loving,* ABC. Movies: *How to Survive a Marriage.*

RELATED CAREER—Adjunct faculty, Marymount Manhattan College, 1974—.

MEMBER: Actors' Equity Association, American Federation of Television and Radio Artists.

ADDRESSES: AGENT—Ambrosio & Mortimer, 165 W. 46th St., Suite 1109, New York, NY 10036.

*   *   *

LAWRENCE, Lawrence Shubert, Jr.   1916-

PERSONAL: Born February 18, 1916, in Philadelphia, PA; son of Lawrence Shubert, Sr. (general manager, Shubert Theatrical Organization) and Frances (Von Summerfeld) Lawrence; married; children: five. EDUCATION: University of Pennsylvania, B.A., 1938. MILITARY: U.S. Naval Reserve, 1944-46.

VOCATION: Executive.

CAREER: PRINCIPAL STAGE WORK—As president and chief executive officer of the Shubert Theatre Enterprises and president of the Shubert Foundation from 1962 to 1972, presided over the administration and developement of the company owned theatres: the Ambassador, Ethel Barrymore, Belasco, Booth, Broadhurst, Broadway, Cort, John Golden, Imperial, Longacre, Lyceum, Majestic, Music Box (50% interest), Plymouth, Royale, Shubert, and the Winter Garden in New York City and the Forrest Theatre in Philadelphia, the Blackstone Theatre in Chicago, the Shubert Theatres in Boston, Cincinnati, and Los Angeles, and the Cox Theatre in Los Angeles. During his tenure, was directly responsible for the interior and exterior renovations of almost every Shubert owned theatre. Instituted the sale of theatre tickets through Macy's Department store; established ticket distribution programs for lower echelon members of the United Nations and high school students in New York City as well as for the New York City Police Athletic League. Assumed leadership of a project to clean up the Times

Square district in New York City. Began playwriting fellowships in some sixty colleges and universities across the country along with an international playwriting contest. He is currently retired from the organization.

MEMBER: Association of Theatrical Producers and Managers, Broadway Association (former director), Council of the Living Theatre (play selection committee); Actors Fund; The Lambs Club; Kappa Sigma.

ADDRESSES: HOME—2500 Maya Palm Drive E., Boca Raton, FL 33432.

*   *   *

LAZARIDIS, Stefanos   1944-

PERSONAL: Born July 28, 1944, in Dire-Dawa, Ethiopia. EDUCATION: Studied in Geneva, Switzerland and London, England.

VOCATION: Scenic designer.

CAREER: FIRST STAGE WORK—Scenic designer, *Eccentricities of a Nightingale*, Guildford, U.K., 1967. PRINCIPAL STAGE WORK—Scenic designer; *The Taming of the Shrew*, Royal Shakespeare Company, 1987; also, *The Possessed*, Theatre de l'Europe, Paris, also produced in London and Milan; *Little Tragedies*, Bologna and Rome.

Photography by Clive Barda

STEFANOS LAZARIDIS

Opera: at the English National Opera, London: *Rusalka, Katya Kabanova, Osud, Madama Butterfly, Dalibor, Tosca, The Mikado, Doctor Faust* all prior to 1987; also, *Lady Macbeth of Mtsensk* and *Hansel and Gretel*, 1987.

Carmen, Opera North, England, 1987; also designed *Rigoletto, Don Giovanni, Les Pêcheurs De Perles, Prince Igor, Oedipus Rex, Tristan Und Isolde, Der Fliegende Hollander, The Bartered Bride, Nabucco, Don Carlos, Fidelio*, for various companies including Maggio Musicale Fiorentino, Scottish Opera, San Francisco Opera, Houston Opera, Opera North Leeds, Teatro Comunale Bologna, Opera de Nice, Deutsche Oper Berlin, and the Stuttgart Opera.

ADDRESSES: HOME—7A Lansdowne House, Lansdowne Road, London W11, England. AGENT—William Morris U.K. Ltd., 147 Wardour Street, London W1, England.

*   *   *

LAZARUS, Paul   1954-

PERSONAL: Born October 25, 1954, Philadelphia, PA; son of Steven (a business executive) and Arlene (a teacher; maiden name, Travin) Lazarus. EDUCATION: Dartmouth College, B.A., 1976; trained for the stage as an apprentice with the Royal Shakespeare Company.

VOCATION: Director.

CAREER: PRINCIPAL STAGE WORK—Director: *Scooter Thomas*, Lincoln Center Institute, Juilliard School, New York City, 1982; *The Baker's Wife*, Woodstock Opera House, Woodstock, IL, 1983; *You Never Know*, American Stage Festival, Milford, NH, Huntington Theatre Company, Boston, MA, 1984, and Goodspeed Opera House, East Haddam, CT; *Follies in Concert*, New York Philharmonic, Avery Fisher Hall, Lincoln Center, New York City, 1985; *Personals*, Minetta Lane Theatre, New York City, 1985; *God Bless You Mr. Rosewater*, Cincinatti Conservatory of Music, 1986.

Director: *Henry V* and *Henry IV*, Parts I, II and III, all Royal Shakespeare Company, London and Stratford-Upon-Avon; *Working*, Dartmouth Summer Repertory, Hanover, NH; *Escurial* and *Gray Spades*, both Actors Studio, New York City; artistic director, "New Plays Festival," Westbeth Theatre Center, New York City; director and co-conceiver, *Harry Ruby's Songs My Mother Never Sang*, the Production Company and Manhattan Theatre Club, New York City; *Chinamen* and *Acceptance*, both No Smoking Playhouse, New York City; director and co-conceiver, *Rearranging Deck Chairs*, Playwrights Horizons, New York City; *A Stephen Sondheim Evening* Composer's Showcase, Whitney Museum, New York City; *Barnum's Last Life*, La Mama Experimental Theatre Club (E.T.C.), New York City; *An Evening with Stephen Sondheim and Friends*, American Music Theatre Festival, Philadelphia, PA; *Rapunzel*, Promenade Theatre and Town Hall, New York City; *A Marc Blitzstein Tribute*, Alice Tully Hall, Lincoln Center, New York City; *The Emperor's New Clothes*, Theaterworks USA and Town Hall, New York City; *The Divine Orlando*, Classic Stage Company, New York City; *Hot L Baltimore*, Dartmouth Summer Repertory, Hanover, NH.

PRINCIPAL TELEVISION WORK—Director, *Whispers from the White House*, HBO, 1980; creative consultant, *Nightcap*, ARTS, 1982.

PRINCIPAL RADIO WORK—Series: Producer and host, *Anything Goes*, WBAI-FM, New York City and National Public Radio, 1978—.

AWARDS: Armstrong Award, for *Anything Goes;* Best Director, Drama Desk nomination, 1985, for *Personals.*

MEMBER: Dramatists Guild, Society of Stage Directors and Choreographers.

ADDRESSES: AGENT—c/o Gilbert Parker, William Morris Agency, 1350 Avenue of the Americas, New York, NY 10019.

*   *   *

LEACHMAN, Cloris   1930-

PERSONAL: Born June 30, 1930, in Des Moines, IA; married George England, 1953 (divorced, 1979); children: five. EDUCATION: Attended Northwestern University.

VOCATION: Actress.

CAREER: PRINCIPAL TELEVISION APPEARANCES—Dramatic Specials: *Kraft Television Theatre*, NBC, 1949; *Screen Director's Playhouse*, NBC and ABC, 1956; *Ladies of the Corridor*, 1975; "Breakfast with Les and Bess," *American Playhouse Theatre*, PBS. Episodic: *Danger*, CBS; *Suspense*, CBS; *Telephone Time*, ABC; *Twilight Zone*, CBS; *Route 66*, CBS; *Laramie*, NBC; *Trials*

CLORIS LEACHMAN

of O'Brien, CBS. Mini-Series: Mrs. Jaffrey, *Backstairs at the White House*, NBC, 1979. Specials: *Screen Actors' Guild 50th Anniversary Celebration*, CBS, 1984.

Series: Effie Perrine, *Charlie Wild, Private Detective*, CBS, then ABC, then DuMont, 1951-52; *Bob and Ray*, NBC, 1952; Ruth Martin, *Lassie*, CBS, 1957-58; Phyllis Lindstrom, *Mary Tyler Moore Show*, CBS, 1970-75; title role, *Phyllis*, CBS, 1977; Beverly Ann, *The Facts of Life*, NBC, 1986—.

Movies: *Brand New Life*, 1972; *The Migrants*, 1974; *Death Scream*, 1975; *It Happened One Christmas*, ABC, 1975; *A Girl Named Sooner*, 1975; *The New Original Wonder Woman*, 1975; *The Love Boat*, 1976; *Deadly Intentions*, ABC, 1985.

PRINCIPAL FILM APPEARANCES—*Kiss Me Deadly*, United Artists, 1955; *Butch Cassidy and the Sundance Kid*, Twentieth Century-Fox, 1969; *W.U.S.A.*, Paramount, 1970; *The Last Picture Show*, Columbia, 1971; *The Steagle*, AVCO-Embassy, 1971; *Dillinger*, American International, 1973; *Daisy Miller*, Paramount, 1974; *Young Frankenstein*, Twentieth-Century Fox, 1974; *Crazy Mama*, New World, 1975; *High Anxiety*, Twentieth Century-Fox, 1979; *The North Avenue Irregulars*, Buena Vista, 1979; *Scavenger Hunt*, Twentieth Century-Fox, 1979; *Herbie Goes Bananas*, Buena Vista, 1980; *History of the World, Part I*, 1981.

PRINCIPAL STAGE APPEARANCES—*A Fatal Weakness*, Monaco, 1985.

AWARDS: Best Supporting Actress, Academy Award, 1971, for *The Last Picture Show;* Outstanding Performance by an Actress, Emmy Award, 1972-73, for *A Brand New Life;* Best Supporting Actress in a Comedy Series, Emmy Award, 1973-74, for "The Lars Affair," *Mary Tyler Moore Show;* Outstanding Supporting Actress in a Comedy Series, Emmy Award, 1974-75, for *Mary Tyler Moore Show;* Outstanding Individual Performance in a Variety or Musical Special, Emmy Award, 1984, for *Screen Actors' Guild 50th Anniversary Celebration.*

ADDRESSES: OFFICE—NBC Television, 3000 W. Alameda Avenue, Burbank, CA 91523.

*   *   *

LEBOWSKY, Stanley   1926-1986

PERSONAL: Full name, Stanley Richard Lebowsky; born November 26, 1926, in Minneapolis, MN; died of a heart attack in New York City, October 19, 1986; son of Morris (a merchant) and Katy (Sorkin) Lebowsky; married Barbara Warden (an actress, dancer, and choreographer), March 8, 1959; children: one son and one daughter. EDUCATION: University of California, Los Angeles, B.A., 1949; studied at MacPhail College of Music, 1939; studied voice with Seymour Osborne, New York City, 1959, conduction with Leon Barzan, New York City, 1958. MILITARY: U.S. Army Medical Corps, 1945-46.

VOCATION: Conductor, composer, arranger, and pianist.

CAREER: PRINCIPAL STAGE WORK—Musical director, *I Love Lydia*, Players Ring Theatre, Los Angeles, 1950; pianist and assistant musical director, *Jollyanna*, 1952, and *Carousel*, 1953, both at the Philharmonic Auditorium, Los Angeles, and then

Curran Theatre, San Francisco; musical director and pianist, *Look Ma, I'm Dancin'* Players Ring Theatre, Los Angeles, 1952-53; musical director, *The Boy Friend* and *Best of Friends,* both Coconut Grove Playhouse, Miami, 1957; musical director and vocal arranger, *Whoop-Up,* Shubert Theatre, New York City, 1958; musical director at the Carousel Theatre, Framingham, MA, for *Kiss Me Kate, Show Boat, Damn Yankees!, Annie Get Your Gun* and *Kismet,* all 1960.

Musical director and vocal arranger, *Irma La Douce,* Plymouth Theatre, New York City, 1960; musical director and vocal arranger, *A Family Affair,* Billy Rose Theatre, New York City, 1961; musical director and vocal arranger, *Tovarich,* Broadway Theatre, New York City, 1963; musical director and vocal arranger, *Wonder World,* New York World's Fair, 1964; musical director, *Half a Sixpence,* Broadhurst Theatre, New York City, 1965; musical director and vocal arranger, *Holly Golightly,* pre-Broadway tour, name changed to *Breakfast at Tiffany's,* closed in previews, Majestic Theatre, New York City, 1966.

Musical director and vocal arranger, *Ari,* Mark Hellinger Theatre, New York city, 1971; conductor, *Jesus Christ Superstar,* Mark Hellinger Theatre, 1971; conductor, *Pippin,* Imperial Theatre, 1972-77; musical director, *Chicago,* 46th Street Theatre, New York City, 1975-77; musical director, *The Act,* Majestic Theatre, New York City, 1977-78; musical director and supervisor, *The 1940s Radio Hour,* St. James Theatre, New York City, 1979-80; musical routining, *Musical Showboat,* Radio City Music Hall, 1980; musical director and vocal arranger, *Can-Can,* Minskoff Theatre, New York City, 1981; musical supervisor, *The Moony Shapiro Songbook,* Morosco Theatre, New York City, 1981; production musical director, *Cats,* Winter Garden Theatre, 1982-86; music supervisor, *Singin' in the Rain,* Gershwin Theatre, New York City, 1985-86, and London production; musical director, *Me And My Girl,* Marquis Theatre, New York City, 1986.

MAJOR TOURS—Assistant musical director and then music director, *Guys and Dolls,* national, 1951-54; pianist, *Silk Stockings,* pre-Broadway tour, 1954-55; musical director, *Can-Can,* 1955; musical director, *The Boy Friend,* national, 1955-57; musical director, *1958 Ford Show,* West Coast cities, 1957; musical director for six companies of *Cats,* 1983-86.

PRINCIPAL STAGE APPEARANCES—Zoot Doubleman, *The 1940s Radio Hour,* St. James Theatre, New York City, 1979-80.

PRINCIPAL TELEVISION WORK—Pianist, *Bob McLaughlin Show,* KLAC, Los Angeles, 1949; musical director, *Best of New Faces,* WNTA, 1961; worked with the Ballet de Marseilles, *Salute to Ford's Theatre,* 1985; *Quincy's Quest,* Thames TV.

WRITINGS: COMPOSITIONS—Stage: *Mile a Minute Malone,* Los Angeles, 1962-63; music for *Gantry,* George Abbott Theatre, New York City, 1970; music for *Nobody Starts Out to Be a Pirate,* Whole Theatre Company, Montclair, NJ, 1983.

Television: *Let There Be Stars,* ABC, 1949.

Songs: *The Wayward Wind;* 50th Anniversary song for Radio City Music Hall; more than thirty-five of Lebowsky's songs were recorded between 1950-53.

RECORDINGS: ALBUMS—*Me And My Girl,* original American cast recording.

AWARDS: Blue Ribbon Citation, BMI, 1956, for *The Wayward Wind;* Best Musical Director, Antoinette Perry Award nomination, 1961, for *Irma La Douce.*

MEMBER: American Federation of Musicians, American Guild of Authors and Composers, Dramatists Guild.*

*   *   *

LEE, Ming Cho   1930-

PERSONAL: Born October 3, 1930, in Shanghai, China; son of Tsufa F. (an insurance representative) and Ing (Tang) Lee; married Elizabeth Rapport, March 21, 1958; children: three sons. EDUCATION: Occidental College, Los Angeles, B.A., 1953, attended the University of California at Los Angeles, 1953-54; studied art with the water-colorist Kuo-Nyen Chang; studied scene design as an apprentice and assistant designer with Jo Mielziner for five years.

VOCATION: Scenic and lighting designer.

CAREER: FIRST STAGE WORK—Scenic designer, *The Silver Whistle,* Occidental College, 1951. FIRST BROADWAY STAGE WORK—Costume supervisor, *Madama Butterfly,* Metropolitan Opera Company, 1958. PRINCIPAL STAGE WORK—Scenic designer (unless otherwise stated): *Guys and Dolls,* Grist Mill Playhouse, Andover, NJ, 1955; *The Infernal Machine,* Phoenix Theatre, New York City, 1958; *The Crucible,* Martinique Theatre, New York City, 1958; *Triad,* Theatre Marquee, New York City, 1958; scenic and lighting designer, *The Moon Besieged,* Lyceum Theatre, New York City, 1962; scenic and lighting designer, *Walk in Darkness,* Greenwich Mews Theatre, New York City, 1963; *Mother Courage,* Martin Beck Theatre, New York City, 1963; scenic and lighting designer, *Conversations in the Dark,* Walnut Street Theatre, Philadelphia, 1963; *Slapstick Tragedy,* Longacre Theatre, New York City, 1966; *A Time for Singing,* Broadway Theatre, New York City, 1966; *Little Murders,* Broadhurst Theatre, New York City, 1967; *Here's Where I Belong,* Billy Rose Theatre, New York City, 1968; *King Lear,* Vivian Beaumont Theatre, New York City, 1968; *Billy,* Billy Rose Theatre, New York City, 1969; *La Strada,* Lunt Fontanne Theatre, New York City, 1969.

Gandhi, Playhouse Theatre, New York City, 1970; *All God's Chillun Got Wings,* Circle in the Square, New York City, 1975; *The Glass Menagerie,* 1975; *Romeo and Juliet,* Circle in the Square, New York City, 1977; *Caesar and Cleopatra,* Palace Theatre, New York City, 1977; *The Shadow Box,* Morosco Theatre, New York City, 1977; *Mother Courage and Her Children* and *King Lear,* both at the American Place Theatre, New York City, 1978; *Angel,* 1978; *The Grand Tour,* Palace Theatre, 1979; *For Colored Girls Who Have Considered Suicide/When the Rainbow Is Enuf,* Booth Theatre, New York City, 1979; *Glass Menagerie,* Eugene O'Neill Theatre, New York City, 1983; *K2,* Brooks Atkinson Theatre, New York City, 1983; also *The Shadow Box,* 1983.

As principal designer for the New York Shakespeare Festival, New York City: *The Merchant of Venice, The Tempest, King Lear, Macbeth,* all 1962; *Antony and Cleopatra, As You Like It, A Winter's Tale, Twelfth Night,* all 1963; *Hamlet, Othello, Electra, A Midsummer Night's Dream,* all 1964; *Love's Labour's Lost, Coriolanus, Troilus and Cressida, The Taming of the Shrew, Henry V,* all 1965; *All's Well That Ends Well, Measure for Measure, Richard III,* all 1966; *The Comedy of Errors, Titus Andronicus,*

Hair, all 1967; *Henry IV*, Parts I and II, *Romeo and Juliet*, *Ergo*, all 1968; *Peer Gynt*, *Electra*, *Cities in Bezique*, *Invitation to a Beheading*, all 1969; *The Wars of the Roses* ("Henry VI" Parts I, II and III and "Richard III"), *Sambo*, *Jack MacGowran in the Works of Samuel Beckett*, all 1970; *Timon of Athens*, *Two Gentlemen of Verona*, *The Tale of Cymbeline*, all 1971; *Older People*, *Hamlet*, *Much Ado About Nothing*, *Wedding Band*, all 1972; *The Sea Gull*, all 1975; *Colored Girls*, all 1976.

For the Arena Stage, Washington, DC: *The Crucible*, 1967; *The Tenth Man*, *Room Service*, *The Iceman Cometh*, all 1968; *The Night Thoreau Spent in Jail*, 1970; *Our Town*, 1972; *Julius Caesar*, 1975; *Waiting for Godot*, 1976; *Don Juan*, 1978; also designed during the 1979-80 and 1982-83 seasons. Also, *Lolita, My Love*, Philadelphia production, 1971; *Remote Asylum*, Ahmanson Theatre, Los Angeles, 1971; *Henry IV*, Part I, Los Angeles, 1972; *Two Gentlemen of Verona*, London, 1973; *King Lear*, Yale School of Drama, New Haven, CT, 1973.

Designs for ballet troupes of Jose Limon, Martha Graham, Gerald Arpino, and Alvin Ailey include: *Missa Brevis*, 1958; *Three Short Dances*, 1959; *A Look at Lightning*, 1962; *Sea Shadow*, 1963; *Ariadne, The Witch of Endor*, 1965; *Olympics, Night Wings*, 1966; *Elegy*, 1967; *The Lady of the House of Sleep*, *Secret Places*, *A Light Fantastic*, 1968; *Animus*, *The Poppet*, 1969.

Designs for opera companies include: Peabody Arts Theatre, Peabody Institute, Baltimore, MD, 1959-63: *The Turk in Italy*, *The Old Maid and the Thief*, *The Fall of the City*, *La Boheme*, *Amahl and the Night Visitors*, *The Pearl Fishers*, *Werther*, and *Hamlet*; for the Empire State Music Festival, NY: *Katya Kabanova*, *Peter Ibbetson*, 1960, *The Pearl Fishers*, 1961; for the Baltimore Civic Opera: *Tristan and Isolde*, 1962; for the Opera Company of Boston: *Madama Butterfly*, 1962; for the Metropolitan Opera National Company, New York City: *Madama Butterfly*, 1965, and *The Marriage of Figaro*, 1966; for the Opera Society of Washington, DC: *Bombarzo*, *Faust*, 1968, and *Roberto Devereaux*, 1970; for the Hamburgische Staatscoper, Hamburg, Germany: *Julius Caesar*, 1969, and *Lucia di Lammermoor*, 1971; for the Juilliard Opera Theatre and the American Opera Center of the Juilliard School of Music: *Katya Kabanova*, *Il Tabarro*, *Gianni Schicchi*, 1964, *Fidelio*, *The Magic Flute* and *The Trial of Lucullus*, 1965, *The Rape of Lucrezia*, 1967, *L'Ormando*, 1968, *The Rake's Progress*, and *Il Giuramento*, 1970.

RELATED CAREER—Art director and designer in residence, San Francisco Opera, 1961; teacher of set design: Yale Drama School and New York University; building designer, New York Shakespeare Festival: The Mobile Unit, Florence Sutro Anspacher Theatre, and the Estelle R. Newman Theatre; building designer, The Garage Theatre, Harlem Center of the Arts; consultant, Performing Arts Center of the State University of New York at Purchase; consultant designer, Cincinnati Music Hall's acoustical shell and proscenium arch and for the Patricia Corbett Pavilion of the University of Cincinnati School of Music; water colors and designs displayed in one-man shows in Los Angeles and New York City.

AWARDS: Recipient, Maharam Award, 1965, for *Electra*; Antoinette Perry Award, 1983, for *K2*.

MEMBER: United Scenic Artists, Local 829 (vice-president, 1969-71); Theatre Projects Committee of New York City (planning commission), American Theatre Planning Board; California Water Color Society.

ADDRESSES: HOME—12 E. 87th Street, New York, NY 10028. OFFICE—Yale University Drama School, 205 Park Street, New Haven, CT 06520.*

*   *   *

LEE, Robert E. 1918-

PERSONAL: Full name, Robert Edwin Lee; born October 15, 1918, in Elyria, OH; son of C. Melvin (an engineer) and Elvira (a teacher; maiden name, Taft) Lee; married Janet Waldo (an actress), March 29, 1948; children: Jonathan Barlow, Lucy Virginia. EDUCATION: Attended Northwestern University, 1934, Ohio Wesleyan University, 1935-37, Western Reserve University, 1938 and Drake University, 1943-44. POLITICS: Democrat. RELIGION: Congregationalist. MILITARY: U.S. Air Force, 1943-44.

VOCATION: Writer, director, producer, and educator.

CAREER: PRINCIPAL STAGE WORK—Writer (see below); director, *Ten Days That Shook the World*, MacGowan Hall, University of California, Los Angeles, 1973.

PRINCIPAL TELEVISION AND RADIO WORK—(With Jerome Lawrence) Producer, director, and writer: *Hollywood Showcase*, 1940-41; *I Was There*, 1941-42; *They Live Forever*, 1942; *Columbia Workshop*, 1942-43; *Request Performance*, 1945-46; *Orson Welles Theatre*, 1945-46; *Favorite Story*, 1945-48; *Frank Sinatra Show*, 1947; *The Railroad Hour*, 1948-54; *Hallmark Hall of Fame*, 1949-51; *Halls of Ivy*, 1950-51; *Date with Judy*; *The Unexpected*; *Times Square Playhouse*; *Song of Norway*; *West Point*; *Lincoln: The Unwilling Warrior*; also adaptations for television of *Shangri-La* and *Inherit the Wind*.

RELATED CAREER—Director, WHK-WCLE, Cleveland, OH, 1937-38; with Jerome Lawrence, founder and director of partnership, Lawrence & Lee, 1942, vice president, Lawrence & Lee, New York City and Los Angeles, 1955—; professor of playwriting, College of Theatre Arts, Pasadena Playhouse, CA, 1963; lecturer in playwriting, University of California, Los Angeles, 1966—, also guest lecturer at other national and international universities; speaker at national convention of American Theatre Association (ATA), 1972; founder, with Jerome Lawrence, of the Lawrence and Lee Collection of Theatre Manuscripts and Transcriptions, Lincoln Center Library of the Performing Arts, New York City.

NON-RELATED CAREER—Observer and technician, Perkins Observatory, Delaware, OH, 1936-37; with Young & Rubicam advertising, New York City, then director of Hollywood office, 1938-42.

WRITINGS: PLAYS, PRODUCED AND PUBLISHED—(All with Jerome Lawrence, except as indicated) "Laugh, God!," published in *Six Anti-Nazi Plays*, Contemporary Play Publications, 1939; "Inside a Kid's Head," published in *Radio Drama in Action*, edited by Eric Barnouw, published by Farrar and Rinehart, 1945; book, *Look Ma, I'm Dancin'!*, Adelphi Theatre, New York City, 1948; *The Laughmaker*, Players Ring Theatre, Los Angeles, 1952, rewritten and produced as *Turn on the Night*, Playhouse in the Park, Philadelphia, 1961, rewritten and produced as *The Crocodile Smile*, State Theatre of North Carolina, Flat Rock, NC, 1970, published by Dramatists' Play Service, 1972; *Inherit the Wind*, National Theatre, New York City, 1955, published by Random

House, 1955, reprinted by Bantam, 1969, Dramatists' Play Service, 1958, revised edition, 1963; (with Lawrence and James Hilton) *Shangri-La*, Winter Garden Theatre, New York City, 1956, published by Morris Music, 1956; *Auntie Mame*, Broadhurst Theatre, New York City, 1956, published by Vanguard, 1957, Dramatists' Play Service, 1960; *The Gang's All Here*, Ambassador Theatre, New York City, 1959, published by World Publishing, 1960, Samuel French, 1961; *Only in America*, Cort Theatre, New York City, 1959, published by Samuel French, 1960.

A Call on Kuprin, Broadhurst Theatre, New York City, 1961, published by Samuel French, 1962; *Diamond Orchid*, Henry Miller's Theatre, New York City, 1965, rewritten and produced as *Sparks Fly Upward*, McFarlin Auditorium Theatre, Dallas, TX, 1967, published by Dramatists' Play Service, 1967; *Mame*, Winter Garden Theatre, New York City, 1966, published by Random House, 1967; *Dear World*, Mark Hellinger Theatre, New York City, 1969; *The Incomparable Max!*, Barter Theatre, Abingdon, VA, 1969, Royale Theatre, New York City, 1971, published as a "Fireside Theatre Play-of-the-Month," Hill and Wang, 1972.

The Night Thoreau Spent in Jail, Ohio State University Theatre, Columbus, 1970, Arena Theatre Washington, DC, 1970, published by Hill and Wang, 1971; by himself, *Ten Days That Shook the World*, MacGowan Hall, University of California, Los Angeles, 1973; *Jabberwock: Improbabilities Lived and Imagined by James Thurber In the Fictional City of Columbus, Ohio*, Thurber Theatre, Columbus, OH, 1972, Dallas Theatre Center, TX, 1973, published by Samuel French, 1974; *First Monday in October*, produced in Cleveland, OH, 1975, Kennedy Center, Washington, DC, 1977, Majestic Theatre, New York City, 1978; *Sounding Brass*, New York City production, 1975, published by Samuel French, 1976.

PLAYS, UNPRODUCED—(All with Jerome Lawrence) "Top of the Mark," "Paris, France," "Eclipse," "Dilly," "Some Say Ice," "Houseboat in Kashmir," "Short and Sweet," "The Angels Weep."

OPERAS—(All with Jerome Lawrence): *Annie Laurie*, published by Harms, Inc., 1954; *Roaring Camp*, published by Harms, Inc., 1955; *Familiar Strangers*, published by Harms, Inc., 1956.

SCREENPLAYS—(All with Jerome Lawrence, except as indicated) *My Love Affair with the Human Race*, 1962; *The New Yorkers*, 1963; *Joyous Season*, 1964; *The Night Thoreau Spent in Jail*, 1976; (with John Sinn) *Quintus*, 1971.

TELEPLAYS AND RADIO PLAYS—(With Jerome Lawrence) *Hollywood Showcase*, 1940-41; *I Was There*, 1941-42; *They Live Forever*, 1942; *Columbia Workshop*, 1942-43; *Request Performance*, 1945-46; *Orson Welles Theatre*, 1945-46; *Favorite Story*, 1945-48; *Frank Sinatra Show*, 1947; *The Railroad Hour*, 1948-54; *Hallmark Hall of Fame*, 1949-51; *Halls of Ivy*, 1950-51; *Date with Judy; The Unexpected; Times Square Playhouse; Song of Norway; West Point; Lincoln: The Unwilling Warrior;* also adaptations for television of *Shangri-La* and *Inherit the Wind*.

BOOKS—*Television: The Revolution*, Essential Books, 1944. Also, with Jerome Lawrence, contributes articles to various periodicals.

RECORDINGS:ALBUMS—(With Jerome Lawrence) Dramatized and directed *Rip Van Winkle, The Cask of Amontillado*, and *A Tale of Two Cities*, all Decca; *One God*, Kapp.

AWARDS: New York Press Club Award, 1942; Peabody Award,

1948, for radio series on the United Nations; *Radio-TV Life* Award, 1948, 1952; *Radio-TV Mirror* Award, 1952, 1953; (with Jerome Lawrence) Donaldson Award, Outer Circle Award, *Variety* New York Drama Critics Poll, all 1955, Best Foreign Play, Critics Award and British Drama Critics Award, both 1960, all for *Inherit the Wind;* Antoinette Perry Awards, 1955, 1966; Moss Hart Memorial Award, 1967; citation for distinguished service, 1979, American Theatre Association. Honorary degrees: Doctor of Literature, Ohio Wesleyan University, 1962; M.A. in Theatre, Pasadena Playhouse College of Theatre Arts, CA, 1963; Doctor of Humanities, Ohio State University, 1979; Doctor of Literature, Wooster College, 1983.

MEMBER: Dramatists Guild, Writers Guild of America West, Academy of Motion Picture Arts and Sciences, National Academy of Television Arts and Sciences, American Playwright's Theatre (president, 1973); National Council of Churches (Broadcasting and Film Commission, 1962-72), Players Club, Theta Alpha Phi, Ohio Wesleyan University Alumni Association (president, 1963-64); Cultural Exchange Mission to Union of Soviet Socialst Republics, 1971.

ADDRESSES: HOME—15725 Royal Oak Road, Encino, CA 91436. OFFICE—MacGowan Hall, University of California at Los Angeles, Los Angeles, CA 90024.*

*   *   *

LeFRAK, Francine   1950-

PERSONAL: Born October 18, 1950; daughter of Samuel I. (a real estate developer) and Ethel (Stone) LeFrak. EDUCATION: Finch College, B.A., 1970.

VOCATION: Producer.

CAREER: PRINCIPAL STAGE WORK—Producer or co-producer: *They're Playing Our Song*, London, 1980; *March of the Falsettos*, Playwrights Horizons Theatre, New York City, 1981; *Crimes of the Heart*, Music Box Theatre, New York City, 1981; *Nine*, 46th Street Theatre, New York City, 1982; *My One and Only*, St. James Theatre, New York City, 1983; *Noises Off*, Brooks Atkinson Theatre, New York City, 1983; *Leader of the Pack*, New York City, 1985; also, associated with *Les Liaisons Dangereuses*, London, 1986.

PRINCIPAL FILM WORK—Production associate, *The Eyes of Laura Mars*, 1977; currently developing feature film projects for Twentieth Century-Fox, Disney, Warner Brothers, and New World.

PRINCIPAL TELEVISION WORK—Co-ordinator of segments for *Bob Hope's 80th Birthday*, 1983; *Royal Variety Show*, London, 1983; producer, "This Year in Jerusalem: 'Americans Living in Israel,'" *Eyewitness News;* producer, "If There's a Cure for This?," *Midday Live;* projects consultant, WNET Channel 13.

RELATED CAREER—President, LeFrak Productions, Inc. Ms. LeFrak was instrumental in bringing a number of productions to the Broadway stage, including *Ain't Misbehavin'* and *Children of a Lesser God;* Lee Strasberg Theatre Institute Creative Center (advisory board).

NON-RELATED CAREER—Vice president, Sotheby Parke Bernet

Auction Galleries, 1970-74; guest lecturer, New School for Social Research, 1970-74; art appraiser and advisor, 1974-77; guest instructor, Hunter College, "The Art of the Creative Process," 1978; president, The Whole Picture Company Ltd; teacher, private aerobics dance class.

AWARDS: Outer Critics Circle Award, 1982, for *March of the Falsettos;* Best New Broadway Musical, Outer Critics Circle Award, 1982, for *Nine;* Best Musical, Drama Desk Award and Antoinette Perry Award, 1982, for *Nine.*

MEMBER: League of New York Theatres and Producers; Art Appraisers Association of America.

ADDRESSES: OFFICE—LeFrak Productions Inc., 40 W. 57th Street, New York, NY 10019.

*   *   *

LESTER, Terry

PERSONAL: Born April 13, in Indianapolis, IN; son of Ernest (an industrialist) and Carol Lester. EDUCATION: DePauw University, B.A. MILITARY: U.S. Army.

VOCATION: Actor.

CAREER: PRINCIPAL TELEVISION APPEARANCES—Series: Jack Abbott, *The Young and the Restless,* CBS; *Ark II,* CBS. Episodic:

McMillan and Wife, NBC; *Dallas,* CBS; *Flying High,* CBS; *Eight Is Enough,* ABC. Movies: *KISS Meets the Phantom,* 1978; *Once Upon a Spy,* 1980; Joe Blade, *Blade in Hong Kong,* CBS, 1985.

PRINCIPAL FILM APPEARANCES—*Airport 1975,* Universal, 1974.

PRINCIPAL STAGE APPEARANCES—Singer, Glendale Symphony Orchestra, CA.

SIDELIGHTS: RECREATIONS—Motorcycle riding, tennis, skiing, computers, and studying philosophy.

ADDRESSES: PUBLICIST—c/o C. Moyers, Guttman and Pam, Ltd., 120 El Camino Drive, Suite 104, Beverly Hills, CA 90212.

*   *   *

LEVEN, Boris   1908-1986

PERSONAL: Born August 13, 1908, in Moscow; died in Los Angeles, CA, October 11, 1986; son of Israel and Zinaida (Narkirier) Leven; married Vera Glooshkoff, February 8, 1948. EDUCATION: University of Southern California, B. Arch., 1932; received design certificate from the Beaux Arts Institute, 1932, in New York City. MILITARY: U.S. Army Air Force, 1942-45.

VOCATION: Art director and production designer.

CAREER: PRINCIPAL FILM WORK—Art director: *Alexander's*

Photography by Timothy Fielding

TERRY LESTER   **BORIS LEVEN**

Ragtime Band, 1938; *Just Around the Corner,* 1938; *The Flying Deuces,* 1939; *Second Chorus,* 1940; *Shanghai Gesture,* 1941; *Hello Frisco Hello,* 1942; *Tales of Manhattan,* 1942; *Thunderbirds,* 1942; *Girl Trouble,* 1942; *Life Begins at 8:30,* 1942; *Dollface,* 1945; *I Wonder Who's Kissing Her Now,* 1946; *The Senator Was Indiscreet,* 1947; *The Shocking Miss Pilgrim,* 1947; *Crisscross,* 1948; *Mr. Peabody and the Mermaid,* 1948; *The Prowler,* 1951; *Sudden Fear,* 1952; *The Star,* 1952; *Silver Chalice,* Warner Brothers, 1955; *Giant,* Warner Brothers, 1956; *The Courage of Black Beauty,* 1957; *Zero Hour,* Paramount, 1957; *John Paul Jones,* Warner Brothers, 1959; *Anatomy of a Murder,* Columbia, 1959.

West Side Story, United Artists, 1961; *Two for the Seesaw,* United Artists, 1962; *The Sound of Music,* Twentieth Century-Fox, 1964; *The Sand Pebbles,* Twentieth Century-Fox, 1965; *Star!,* Twentieth Century-Fox, 1968; *A Dream of Kings,* National General, 1969; *The Andromeda Strain,* Universal, 1971; *The New Centurions,* Columbia, 1972; *Jonathan Livingston Seagull,* Paramount, 1973; *Mandingo,* Paramount, 1975; *New York, New York,* United Artists, 1977; *The Last Waltz,* United Artists, 1978; *Matilda,* American International, 1978; *The King of Comedy,* Twentieth Century-Fox, 1983; *Fletch,* Universal, 1985; *The Color of Money,* Touchstone Pictures, 1986; *Wildcats,* Warner Brothers, 1986; *The Last Temptation of Christ.*

RELATED CAREER—Sketch artist, designer, Paramount Studios, 1933-35; traveled, painted abroad, 1935-36; art director, Twentieth Century-Fox, 1937-38, 1941-42, 1945-46; art director, Universal International Picutres, 1947-48; traveled, sketched in Europe and Russia, 1959-60, 1968 and 1970; exhibited water colors and paintings in private collections.

AWARDS: First Emerson Prize, 1932; First Prize, Beaux Arts Ball, 1932; First Prize, American Institute of Steel Construction, 1932; First Prize, National Scarab Traveling Sketch competition, 1933; First Prize, Art Direction, American Institute of Decorators, 1947, for *The Senator Was Indiscreet;* Photoplay Magazine medal, 1956, for *Giant;* Best Art Direction, Academy Award nominations, 1938, for *Alexander's Ragtime Band,* 1941, for *Shanghai Gesture,* 1956, for *Giant,* 1964, for *The Sound of Music,* 1965, for *The Sound Pebbles,* 1968, for *Star!,* and 1971, for *The Andromeda Strain;* Best Art Direction, Academy Award, 1961, for *West Side Story.*

MEMBER: Society of Motion Picture Art Directors, United Scenic Artists, Academy of Motion Picture Arts and Sciences; Scull and Dagger, Delta Phi Delta, Tau Sigma Delta.

*   *   *

LEVINE, Michael   1952-

PERSONAL: Born April 17, 1952; son of Arthur (a publisher) and Marilyn (a columnist; maiden name, Beck) Levine. EDUCATION: Rutgers University. POLITICS: Republican. RELIGION: Jewish.

VOCATION: Public relations agent and editor.

CAREER: PRINCIPAL WORK—President of Michael Levine Public Relations Company, 1983—; publicist for television actors, film actors, film producers, sports personalities, variety artists, musical artists, musical groups, and others.

WRITINGS: BOOKS—*The Address Book: How to Reach Anyone*

Who's Anyone, Putnam-Perigee, 1980, 1984, 1986; *The Corporate Address Book: How to Reach the Thousand Most Important Businesses in America,* Putnam-Perigee, 1987.

MEMBER: Academy of Television Arts and Sciences, Entertainment Industries Council, The Father Center, Inc. (board member), Nell Bogart Association (board member).

ADDRESSES: HOME—Los Angeles, CA. OFFICE—Michael Levine Public Relations, 8730 Sunset Blvd., Los Angeles, CA 90069.

*   *   *

LEVIT, Ben   1949-

PERSONAL: Born February 9, 1949, in Bridgeton, NJ; son of Isai Levit. EDUCATION: Florida State University, M.F.A.

VOCATION: Director.

CAREER: PRINCIPAL STAGE WORK—Director: *The Wakefield Trilogy, Alfred the Great, Our Father's Failing, Alfred Dies,* all at the Actors' Studio, New York City; *A Flea in Her Ear* and *Alfred Dies,* both at the American Stage Festival; *Streamers* and *Emigres,* both at the Theatre by the Sea; *Flight to the Fatherland, Terra Nova,* and *Pantomine,* all at GeVa Theatre, Rochester, NY; *A Servant of Two Masters,* Kenyon Festival, OH; *Chieftains,* St. Clements Theatre, New York City; *Native Speech,* Juilliard Theatre Center, New York City; *The Comedy of Errors,* McCarter Theatre, Princeton, NJ, then at the Shakespeare Festival of Dallas, TX; *Whose Life Is It Anyway?,* Kennedy Center, Washington, DC; *A Midsummer Night's Dream,* Northshore Music Theatre; *The Birthday Party,* Young Playwrights Festival; *America Kicks Up Its Heels* and *Herringbone,* Playwrights Horizons, New York City; *The Genius,* Mark Taper Forum, Los Angeles, CA.

RELATED CAREER—Faculty, Playwrights Horizons Theatre Studio, New York University, NY; director in residence at the McCarter Theatre and Mark Taper Forum.

ADDRESSES. HOME—55 W. 76th Street, New York, NY 10023. AGENT—c/o George Lane, William Morris Agency, 1350 Avenue of the Americas, New York, NY 10019.

*   *   *

LEWIS, Jenny   1976-

PERSONAL: Born 1976, in Las Vegas, NV; father is a member of the Harmonica Gang and mother is a professional singer.

VOCATION: Actress.

CAREER: PRINCIPAL STAGE APPEARANCES—*The Wiz; Peter Pan; Cinderella.*

TELEVISION DEBUT—*Baby Makes Five,* ABC, 1983. PRINCIPAL TELEVISION APPEARANCES—Series: Becky McGibbon, *Life with Lucy,* CBS, 1986. Episodic: *Hell Town,* ABC; *Webster,* ABC. Movies: *Convicted,* 1985; Little Eva, *Uncle Tom's Cabin,* Showtime, 1987.

JENNY LEWIS

MARY RIO LEWIS

RELATED CAREER—Over 125 national commercials.

SIDELIGHTS: Jenny Lewis' public relations coordinators inform *CTFT* that Jenny has won several blue ribbons in gymnastics and plays on her school soccer team which had won two championships. She also collects dolls.

ADDRESSES: PUBLICIST—Neal and Handler Public Relations, 6311 Romaine Street, Los Angeles, CA 90038.

*   *   *

LEWIS, Mary Rio   1922-

PERSONAL: Born Mary Rio McGee, in 1922, in Lancaster, SC; daughter of Peter (a blacksmith) and Nancy (Clyburn) McPherson. EDUCATION: Studied acting with Herbert Berghof and Al Saxe and musical theatre with Charles Nelson Reilly in New York City. POLITICS: Democrat. RELIGION: Protestant.

VOCATION: Actress and singer.

CAREER: BROADWAY DEBUT—Actress and dancer, *Memphis Bound*, Broadway Theatre, 1946. PRINCIPAL STAGE APPEARANCES—*God's Favorite*, O'Neill Theatre, New York City, 1978; *Life in Louisiana, Another Part of the Forest,* and *Lost in the Stars,* all at the Equity Library Theatre, New York City; *The Crucible, What Color Goes with Brown,* and *A Streetcar Named Desire,* all at the Lane Theatre Workshop, New York City.

MAJOR TOURS—With the Katherine Dunham Company.

PRINCIPAL FILM APPEARANCES—*The Pawnbroker*, Allied Aritsts, 1965; *The Group*, United Aritsts, 1966; *Up the Down Staircase*, Warner Brothers, 1967; *Goodbye Columbus*, Paramount, 1969; *The Hospital*, United Artists, 1971; *A Place Called Today*, 1972.

PRINCIPAL TELEVISION APPEARANCES—Episodic: *Philco Playhouse*, NBC; *Frontiers of Faith*, NBC; *You Are There*, CBS; *Armstrong Circle Theatre*, CBS; *The Nurses & Doctors*, CBS; *The Guiding Light*, CBS; *As the World Turns*, CBS; *Search for Tomorrow*, CBS; *The Good Life*, CBS; *The Defenders*, CBS; *For the People*, CBS; *Trials of O'Brien*, CBS; *The Gene Kelly Show*, CBS; *Another World*, NBC; *Look Up & Live*, CBS; *Love Is a Many Splendored Thing*, CBS. Movies: *Dr. Webb of Horseshoe Bend*, ABC; *The Witness*, CBS; *John Brown's Body*, CBS.

MEMBER: Actors' Equity Association, American Federation of Television and Radio Artists, Screen Actors Guild.

ADDRESSES: HOME—1026 E. 219th Street, New York, NY 10469.

*   *   *

LEYDEN, Leo   1929-

PERSONAL: Born January 28, 1929, in Dublin, Ireland; son of Leo (a chemist) and Adalaide (Cox) Leyden; divorced; children: Vanessa. EDUCATION: Catholic University School, Dublin, Ireland, 1938-47; trained for the stage at the Abbey Theatre School in Dublin.

VOCATION: Actor.

CAREER: STAGE DEBUT—Channon, *The Dybbuk*, Gaiety Theatre, Dublin, 1947. BROADWAY DEBUT—Bevill Higgins, *Love and Libel*, Martin Beck Theatre, 1959. LONDON DEBUT—Clergyman, *Tom Jones*, Leatherhead Theatre, 1965. PRINCIPAL STAGE APPEARANCES—Member of the Gate Theatre Company in Dublin for ten years; Broadway productions: *Darling of the Day, The Mundy Scheme, The Rothchilds, Captain Brassbound's Conversion, Habeus Corpus*, Sir Jasper, *Me and My Girl*, Marquis Theatre, New York City, 1986-87.

The Plough and the Stars, Edward II, A Moon for the Misbegotton, Sleuth, Comedians, Bent, Charley's Aunt, A Child's Christmas in Wales, The Seagull, Striptease, The Doctor's Dilemma, The Comedy of Errors, Wild Oats, Arsenic and Old Lace, The Prisoner of Zenda, Timon of Athens, Polonius, *Hamlet* (rock music adaptation), all in productions throughout the U.S. and Canada; has appeared at the Shaw Festival in Canada and the American Shakespeare Festival, Stratford, CT.

MAJOR TOURS—Touchstone, *As You Like It*, Canadian Players, 1957-58; Aslaksen, *Enemy of the People*, Canadian Players, 1962-63; Major General, *Pirates of Penzance*, U.S. cities, 1981-82.

FILM DEBUT *The Gentle Gunman*, 1949. PRINCIPAL FILM APPEARANCES—*The Luck of Ginger Coffey*, Reade-Sterling, 1964; *Naked Runner*, Warner Brothers/Seven Arts, 1967; *1776*, Columbia, 1972; *Circle of Two*, 1980; also, *Quiet Day in Belfast*.

LEO LEYDEN

TELEVISION DEBUT—Policeman, *The Telltale Heart*, CBC, 1957. PRINCIPAL TELEVISION APPEARANCES—*The Importance of Being Earnest; The Lady's Not for Burning; The Apple Cart; Sarah; Evangeline Deusse; She Stoops to Conquer* (musical version); *The Misanthrope* (musical version).

RECORDINGS: PLAYS—*Juno and the Paycock, The Quare Fellow; King Lear; Julius Caesar*.

MEMBER: Actors' Equity Association, Canadian Actors' Equity Association, American Federation of Television and Radio Artists, Association of Canadian Television and Radio Artists, Screen Actors Guild.

*   *   *

LICHTERMAN, Victoria   1940-

PERSONAL: Born Victoria Rauch (surname sounds like "now"), January 10, 1940; daughter of Frank Xavier (a businessman) and Allison (a businesswoman) Rauch; married Marvin Lichterman (an actor), September 10, 1969; children: a daughter, Courtney Paige. EDUCATION: Ohio University, Athens, B.F.A., 1961; Yale School of Drama, M.F.A., 1964.

VOCATION: Writer, teacher, and actress.

CAREER: OFF-BROADWAY DEBUT—Principal role, *Route One*, 1964. PRINCIPAL STAGE APPEARANCES—*I Stand Here Ironing*, Bruno Walter Theatre, Lincoln Center Library, New York City; performed eight years in Off-Broadway, Off-Off Broadway, and stock.

TELEVISION DEBUT—*Trials of O'Brien*, NBC, 1965. PRINCIPAL TELEVISION APPEARANCES—Series: Dorothy Royce, *Search for Tomorrow*, CBS.

RELATED CAREER—Teacher, Brooklyn College, 1967-77; teacher, director, and owner, Victoria Rauch Acting School, New York City, 1978-83; curriculum designer, Brooklyn College; curriculm designer and teacher, Pritikin Better Health Program; communication teacher, People Resources; curriculum designer and acting teacher, Burnley Associates; curriculum designer and speech teacher, Woman Unlimited.

NON-RELATED CAREER—In partnership with husband, Blithe Spirits, a manufacturer and dealer of decorative architectural objects.

WRITINGS: TELEVISION—"The Safe Caper," *Kate and Allie*, CBS, 1984; (pilot) *The John and Sandy Show*. PLAYS, PRODUCED—*Lifestyles*, Valerie Bettis Foundation Theatre. SCREENPLAYS, UNPRODUCED—"No, for An Answer." PERIODICALS—(Published under pseudonym, Victoria Robinson) "The Late Bloomer," *Redbook;* "As Pretty Does It," *Redbook*.

MEMBER: Writers Guild of America, Screeen Actors Guild, Actors Equity Association, American Federation of Television and Radio Artists.

ADDRESSES: HOME—311 E. 23rd Street, New York, NY 10010.

LIFAR, Serge   1905-1986

PERSONAL: Born April 2, 1905, in Kiev, Russia; died in Lausanne, Switzerland, December 15, 1986; son of Michel Lifar; married. EDUCATION: Studied with Bronislava Nijinska, Diaghilev, and Cecchetti.

VOCATION: Dancer, choreographer, producer, writer.

CAREER: STAGE DEBUT—With the Diaghilev company, Paris, 1923. LONDON DEBUT—*Cimarosiana* and *Les facheux*, Coliseum, 1924. PRINCIPAL STAGE APPEARANCES—Dancer, *Cochran's 1930 Revue*, London Pavilion, 1930; produced and danced in Paris: *Bacchus and Ariadne; Le spectre de la rose; Giselle*, 1931; *Icare*, 1935; *David triomphant*, 1936; *Le chevalier et demoiselle*, 1941; *Jean de Zarissa*, 1942; *Suite en blanc*, 1943; *Chota Roustavelli, Dramma per Musica*, 1946; *Lucifer*, 1948; *Septour, Le chevalier errant, Phedre*, 1950; *Blanche neige*, 1951; *Fourberies de Scapin*, 1952; *Noces fantastiques*, 1955; *Romeo et Juliette*, 1955.

FIRST STAGE WORK—Choreographer, *Le Renard*, Ballets Russe, 1929. PRINCIPAL STAGE WORK—Founder and director, Institute Choreographique, Opera National de Paris, 1947-58, 1962-63; Ballet Master, Paris Opera, 1947-58, 1962-63; organizer of ballet for the coronation of the Shah of Iran, 1967.

PRINCIPAL FILM APPEARANCES—*Testament of Orpheus*, 1960; *Le Crime ne paie pas.*

PRINCIPAL FILM WORK—Choreographer, *Nuits de feu; La Mort du cygne.*

WRITINGS: BOOKS, PUBLISHED—*Traditional to Modern*, 1938; *Diaghilev, a Biography*, 1940; *Traite de la danse academique*, 1950; *Histoire du ballet russe*, 1951; *Vestris*, 1951; *Reflexions sur la danse*, 1952; *Traite de choreographie*, 1952; *The Three Graces*, 1959; *Ma vie* (autobiography), 1969.

AWARDS: International Film Prize, 1937; First Prize for Dance, 1955; Gold Medal, 1956, Scarlet Medal, Paris, 1978; Karina Ari Gold Medal (Sweden); Chevalier, l'ordre de Vasa (Sweden); ordre do l'Etoile rouge (Yugoslavia).

MEMBER: Academie des Beaux-Arts, 1970.*

*   *   *

LITHGOW, John   1945-

PERSONAL: Born June 6, 1945, in Rochester, NY; son of Arthur W. (a producer) and Sarah Jane (a teacher; maiden name, Pride) Lithgow; married Jean Taynton, September 10, 1966 (divorced, 1980); married Mary Yeager (a professor); children: Ian, Phoebe, Nathan. EDUCATION: Harvard College, 1967; trained for the stage at the London Academy of Music and Dramatic Arts.

VOCATION: Actor, director, and writer.

CAREER: STAGE DEBUT—Mustardseed, *A Midsummer Night's Dream*, Antioch Shakespeare Festival, OH, 1953. BROADWAY DEBUT—Kendall, *The Changing Room*, Morosco Theatre, 1973. PRINCIPAL STAGE APPEARANCES—At the Great Lakes Shakespeare Festival, OH, appeared in fifteen Shakespearean roles,

1963-64; Bunthorne, *Patience*, Peachum, *The Beggar's Opera*, Don Andres, *La Perichole*, and Lord Chancellor, *Iolanthe*, all at the Highfield Theatre, Falmouth, MA, 1965; Henry Higgins, *Pygmalion*, Lennie, *Of Mice and Men*, and Achilles, *Troilus and Cressida*, all at the McCarter Theatre, Princeton, NJ, 1969-70.

Sir, *The Roar of the Greasepaint, the Smell of the Crowd*, Dr. Talacryn, *Hadrian VII*, and Captain Vale, *The Magistrate*, all at the Bucks County Playhouse, New Hope, PA, 1970; Kendall, *The Changing Room*, Kiper, *What Price Glory?*, and Arthur, *Trelawny of the Wells*, all at the Long Wharf Theatre, New Haven, CT, 1972; James, *My Fat Friend*, Brooks Atkinson Theatre, New York City, 1973; Ged Murray, *Comedians*, Music Box Theatre, New York City, 1976; Mat Burke, *Anna Christie*, Imperial Theatre, New York City, 1977; George Lewis, *Once in a Lifetime*, Circle in the Square, New York City, 1978; Frank, *Spokesong*, Circle in the Square Theatre, New York City, 1979; Trevor, *Bedroom Farce*, Brooks Atkinson Theatre, New York City, 1979.

Joe Hill, *Salt Lake City Skyline*, New York Shakespeare Festival, Public Theatre, New York City, 1980; Chris, *Division Street*, Ambassador Theatre, New York City, 1980; George S. Kaufman, *Kaufman at Large*, Phoenix Theatre, New York City, 1981; Bruce, *Beyond Therapy*, Brooks Atkinson Theatre, New York City, 1982; Harlan "Mountain" McClintock, *Requiem for a Heavyweight*, Long Wharf Theatre, New Haven, CT, 1984, then Martin Beck Theatre, New York City, 1985; also acted with the Royal Shakespeare Company, London, and appeared in *Hamlet, Secret Service*, and *Boy Meets Girl*, all Off-Broadway productions, New York City.

PRINCIPAL STAGE WORK—Director: *As You Like It, Much Ado About Nothing*, and *The Way of the World*, all at the McCarter Theatre, Princeton, 1970; *The Magistrate* and *Barefoot in the Park*, both at the Bucks County Playhouse, New Hope, 1970; *Abduction from the Seraglio*, New Jersey Opera Theatre, Princeton, 1970; *The Beaux Strategem*, Center Stage, Baltimore, MD, 1972; *A Pagan Place*, Long Wharf Theatre, New Haven, 1973; *Kaufman at Large*, Phoenix Theatre, New York City, 1981; also directed with the Royal Shakespeare Company, London.

FILM DEBUT—La Salle, *Obsession*, Columbia, 1976. PRINCIPAL FILM APPEARANCES—*All That Jazz*, Twentieth Century-Fox, 1979; *Rich Kids*, United Artists, 1979; *Blow Out*, Filmways, 1981; *The World According to Garp*, Warner Brothers, 1982; *Twilight Zone: The Movie*, Warner Brothers, 1983; *Terms of Endearment*, Paramount, 1983; *The Adventures of Buckeroo Banzai: Across the Eighth Dimension*, Twentieth Century-Fox, 1984; *Footloose*, Paramount, 1984; *2010*, Metro-Goldwyn-Mayer/United Artists, 1984; *Santa Claus: The Movie*, Tri-Star, 1985; *The Manhattan Project*, Twentieth Century-Fox, 1986; also, *Mesmerized.*

TELEVISION DEBUT—"The Country Girl," *Hallmark Hall of Fame*, 1973. PRINCIPAL TELEVISION APPEARANCES—Movies: *The Day After*, ABC, 1983; *The Glitter Dome*, Home Box Office, 1984; *The Resting Place*, CBS, 1986. Episodic: Host, *Saturday Night Live*, NBC, 1987.

PRINCIPAL RADIO WORK—Producer, writer, and actor, *Under the Gun*, WBAI-FM, New York City, 1972-73.

NON-RELATED CAREER—Printmaker and founder of Lithgow Graphics.

WRITINGS: ADAPTATIONS—*Kaufman at Large*, from the letters of George S. Kaufman, produced at the Phoenix Theatre, New York City, 1981.

AWARDS: Best Supporting Actor, Antoinette Perry Award, 1973, for *The Changing Room;* Best Supporting Actor, Academy Award nominations, 1982, for *The World According to Garp* and 1983, for *Terms of Endearment,* graduated magna cum laude, Harvard College, 1967, Fulbright Study Grant, London, 1967-69.

MEMBER: Actors' Equity Association, American Federation of Television and Radio Artists, Screen Actors Guild.

SIDELIGHTS: RECREATIONS—Music, guitar, banjo, art and painting, drawing, and "my family."

ADDRESSES: AGENT—Contemporary Artists Agency, 1888 Century Place, Los Angeles, CA 90048.*

*   *   *

LITTLE, Cleavon   1939-

PERSONAL: Born June 1, 1939, in Chickasha, OK; son of Malachi (a gardener) and DeEtta (Jones) Little; married Valerie Wiggins, February 19, 1972 (divorced, 1974). EDUCATION: San Diego College, B.A., 1965; trained for the stage at the American Academy of Dramatic Art, 1965-67.

VOCATION: Actor.

CAREER: PRINCIPAL FILM APPEARANCES—*What's So Bad About Feeling Good,* Universal, 1968; *Cotton Comes to Harlem,* United Artists, 1970; *Vanishing Point,* Twentieth Century-Fox, 1971; *Blazing Saddles,* Warner Brothers, 1974; *Greased Lightning,* Warner Brothers, 1977; *FM,* Universal, 1978; *Scavenger Hunt,* Twentieth Century-Fox, 1979; *High Risk,* Metro-Goldwyn-Mayer, 1981; *Jimmy the Kid,* Zephyr, 1982; *Once Bitten,* Samuel Goldwyn Company, 1985.

PRINCIPAL TELEVISION APPEARANCES—Series: Regular, *The David Frost Revue,* syndicated, 1971-73; Jerry Noland, *Temperature's Rising,* ABC, 1972-74. Episodic: "Uptown Saturday Night," *Comedy Theatre,* NBC, 1981; *All in the Family,* CBS; *Felony Squad,* ABC; *Loveboat,* ABC. Pilots: *Mr. Dugan,* CBS. Movies: *The Homecoming—A Christmas Story,* CBS, 1971; *The Brothers Grimm,* 1977; *Don't Look Back,* 1981; also *The Day the Earth Moved.*

STAGE DEBUT—*A Raisin in the Sun,* Globe Theatre, San Diego, CA. OFF-BROADWAY DEBUT—*Americana,* American National Theatre Academy (ANTA) matinee series, Theatre de Lys, January 8, 1966. PRINCIPAL STAGE APPEARANCES—*The Skin of Our Teeth,* La Jolla Playhouse, CA; *Macbeth,* New York Shakespeare Festival (NYSF), Mobile Theatre, 1966; Muslim Witch and a conspirator, *MacBird!,* Village Gate Theatre, New York City, 1967; Foxtrot, *Scuba Duba,* New Theatre, New York City, 1967; title role, *Hamlet,* NYSF, Mobile Theatre, New York City, 1968; Lee Haines, *Jimmy Shine,* Brooks Atkinson Theatre, New York City, 1968; Paul Odum, *Someone's Comin' Hungry,* Pocket Theatre, New York City, 1969; Rufus, *The Ofay Watcher,* Stage 73 Theatre, New York City, 1969; Father Xavier, *Kumaliza,* The Other Stage Theatre, New York City, 1969.

Title role, *Purlie,* Broadway Theatre, New York City, 1970; Shogo, *Narrow Road to the Deep North,* Vivian Beaumont Theatre, New York City, 1972; title role, *The Great Macdaddy,* with the Negro Ensemble Company, St. Mark's Playhouse, 1974; Corpie, *The Charlatan,* Mark Taper Forum Theatre, Los Angeles, 1974; Lewis, *All Over Town,* Booth Theatre, New York City, 1974; Willy Stopp, *The Poison Tree,* Ambassador Theatre, New York City, 1976; Narrator, *Joseph and the Amazing Technicolor Dreamcoat,* Brooklyn Academy Theatre, New York City, 1976; *Same Time Next Year,* 1977; Oberon, *A Midsummer Night's Dream,* with the Los Angeles Shakespeare Festival, 1978; Simon Able, *Sly Fox,* San Diego production, 1978; Lester Young, *The Resurrection of Lady Lester,* Manhattan Theatre Club, New York City, 1981; Meadowlark Rachel Warner, *Two Fish in the Sky,* Theatre at St. Peter's Church, New York City, 1982; title role, *Keyboard,* with the Henry Street Settlement, Louis Abrons Arts for Living Center, New York City, 1982; Midge, *I'm Not Rappaport,* Seattle Repertory Theatre, WA, 1985, American Place Theatre, New York City, 1985, and Booth Theatre, New York City, 1986.

AWARDS: Recipient of scholarship to the American Academy of Dramatic Arts, 1965, sponsored by ABC-TV; Best Actor in a Musical, Antoinette Perry Award, New York Critics Poll Award, Drama Desk Award, F. and M. Schaeffer Brewing Company Award, all 1970, for *Purlie;* presented with Key to the City of San Diego, 1973; Image Award, National Association for the Advancement of Colored People (NAACP), 1976.

MEMBER: Actors' Equity Association, Screen Actors Guild.

ADDRESSES: AGENT—Jack Fields Agency, 9255 Sunset Blvd., Los Angeles, CA 90069; William Morris Agency, 151 El Camino Drive, Beverly Hills, CA 90212.*

*   *   *

LITTLE, Stuart W.   1921-

PERSONAL: Born December 19, 1921, in Hartford, CT; son of Mitchell (a manufacturer) and Elizabeth (Hapgood) Little; married Anastazia Raben-Levetzau (a writer), September 25, 1945; children: Caroline, Christopher, Suzanne. EDUCATION: Attended the Kingswood School in Hartford; Groton School; Yale University, B.A., 1944. MILITARY: U.S. Air Force, 1943-45.

VOCATION: Writer and editor.

CAREER: PRINCIPAL WORK—Reporter and assistant city editor, 1946-54, theatre news reporter, 1958-66, *New York Herald Tribune;* freelance writer, 1966—; editor, *The Authors Guild Bulletin.*

RELATED CAREER—President, Buckley-Little Book Catalogue Company, Inc., 1983-86; director of communications, Theatre Development Fund, 1986—.

WRITINGS: TELEVISION—*Report from America,* NBC, 1954-56; *Project 20,* NBC, 1955; writer, NBC, New York City, 1954-58. NON-FICTION—(With Arthur Cantor) *The Playmakers,* Norton, 1970; *Off-Broadway: The Prophetic Theater,* Coward, 1972; *Enter Joseph Papp,* Coward, 1974; *After the Fact,* Arno, 1975. PERIODICALS—Regular columnist, "Books in Communication," *Saturday Review,* 1966-72.

MEMBER: Drama Desk (vice president, 1960-62; president, 1962-64); Century Association.

ADDRESSES: HOME—131 Prince Street, New York, NY 10012. OFFICE—Theatre Development Fund, 1501 Broadway, New York, NY 10036.

*   *   *

LITTLEWOOD, Joan

VOCATION: Director, actress, and writer.

CAREER: FIRST LONDON STAGE WORK—Director, *Operation Olive Branch* (re-titled from *Lysistrata*), Rudolf Steiner Hall, October, 1947. FIRST BROADWAY STAGE WORK—Director, *The Hostage,* Cort Theatre, September, 1960. PRINCIPAL STAGE WORK—Director, *Uranium 235,* Embassy Theatre, transferred to the Comedy Theatre, London, 1952.

Director: With the Theatre Workshop, at the Theatre Royal, Stratford, London: *The Dutch Courtesan, The Fire Eaters, The Flying Doctor, Johnny Noble, The Cruel Daughters, The Chimes, The Prince and the Pauper, The Good Soldier Schweik* (the lasst transferred to the Embassy Theatre), all 1954; *Richard II, The Other Animals, Volpone, The Midwife, The Legend of Pepito, The Sheep Well, The Italian Straw Hat,* all 1955; *The Good Soldier Schweik, Edward II, The Quare Fellow,* all 1956; *You Won't Always Be on Top, And the Wind Blew, Macbeth,* all 1957; *Celestina, Unto Such Glory, The Respectable Prostitute, A Taste of Honey, The Hostage, A Christmas Carol,* all 1958; *Fings Ain't Wot They Used T'Be, The Dutch Courtesan, Make Me an Offer,* all 1959; *Ned Kelly, Every Man in His Humour, Sparrers Can't Sing,* all 1960; *We're Just Not Practical, They Might Be Giants,* both 1961; *Oh, What a Lovely War!,* 1963 (also at the Broadhurst Theatre, New York City, 1964), *A Kayf Up West,* both 1964; *Macbird!, Intrigues and Amours, Mrs. Wilson's Diary, The Marie Lloyd Story,* all 1967; *Forward, Up Your End, The Projector,* all 1970; *The Londoners, The Hostage, Costa Packet,* all 1972; *So You Want to Be in Pictures,* 1973.

Also directed: *Mother Courage and Her Children,* Devon Festival, Barnstaple, U.K., 1955; *Unternehmen olzweig,* Maxim Gorki Theatre, Berlin, Germany, 1960; *Henry IV,* Edinburgh Festival, Scotland, 1964.

MAJOR TOURS—Director, Theatre Workshop on tour, 1945-53, British Isles, Scandinavia, Germany, and Czechoslovakia, 1945-53.

PRINCIPAL STAGE APPEARANCES—Witch, *Uranium 235,* Comedy Theatre, London, 1952; with the Theatre Workshop, Theatre Royal, Stratford, London: Marinette, *The Flying Doctor,* 1954, Duchess of Gloucester, *Richard II,* 1955, and Mrs. Kepes, *The Midwife,* 1955.

PRINCIPAL FILM WORK—Director, *Sparrers Can't Sing,* 1963.

RELATED CAREER—Founder and director, Theatre of Action, Manchester, England, 1933; founder, Theatre Union, Manchester, 1934; with Gerry Raffles, founder and director, Theatre Workshop, Stratford, London, 1945, artistic director, 1945-75; with Theatre

Royal, Stratford, London 1953-75; director to Theatre of Nations, Paris, France, 1955—; with Centre Culturel, Hammamet, Tunisia, 1965-67; with Image India, Calcutta, 1968; created children's entertainments outside Theatre Royal, Stratford, 1968-75; seminar, Relais Culturel, Aix-en-Provence, 1976.

WRITINGS: STAGE ADAPTATIONS—All produced at the Theatre Workshop, Theatre Royal, Stratford, London: *The Cruel Daughters, The Chimes, The Prince and the Pauper,* all 1954; *A Christmas Carol,* 1958.

AWARDS: Outstanding Direction, Gold Medal, Berlin, German Democratic Republic, 1958, for *Lysistrata;* Olympic Award for Theatre, 1959; Society of West End Theatres Award, 1983; Best Production of the Year, awarded three times, Theatre of the Nations, Paris, France. Honorary Doctorate, Open University, 1977.

MEMBER: French Academy of Writers.

SIDELIGHTS: CTFT has learned that because of her political opinions, Joan Littlewood was banned as a freelance writer from the BBC and Entertainments National Service Association from 1939-45.

ADDRESSES: OFFICE—One place Louis Revol, 38200 Vienne, France.*

*   *   *

LIVINGSTON, Ruth   1927-

PERSONAL: Born March 25, 1927, in New Haven, CT; daughter of Alan V. (a real estate and insurance broker) and Theresa A. (Kieffer) Livingston; married Leslie Barrett (an actor), June 19, 1977. EDUCATION: University of Michigan, B.A., speech; trained for the theatre at the American Theatre Wing and with Uta Hagen and William Ball.

VOCATION: Actress.

CAREER: STAGE DEBUT—Stella, *A Streetcar Named Desire,* Manitoba Theatre Centre, Winnipeg, Manitoba, Canada, 1960. BROADWAY DEBUT—Lady Montague, *Romeo and Juliet,* Circle in the Square Theatre, 1977. PRINCIPAL STAGE APPEARANCES—Isabelle's Mother, *Ring 'Round the Moon,* Barter Theatre, Abingdon, VA, 1963; at the Neptune Theatre, Halifax, Nova Scotia: Abigail, *The Crucible,* Josefa, *A Shot in the Dark,* Lady Percy, *Henry IV, Part I,* Fran Rose, *The Physicist,* and Aunt Martha, *Arsenic and Old Lace,* all 1966; Susan, *The Little Hut,* Citadel Theatre, Edmonton, Alberta, Canada, 1966; Stella, *A Streetcar Named Desire,* Edgecliff Theatre, Cincinnati, OH, 1967; Gwendolyn, *The Odd Couple,* Music Fair Theatre, Philadelphia, PA, 1968; Mrs. Banks, *Barefoot in the Park,* Lazy Susan Dinner Theatre, Woodbridge, VA, 1975; Flipote, *Tartuffe,* Circle in the Square Theatre, New York City, 1977; understudy Ethel, *On Golden Pond,* New Apollo Theatre, then Century Theatre, New York City, 1978; Nora, *The Octette Bridge Club* and Aunt Lucy, *Courtship,* both Actors Theatre of Louisville, 1984; standby, *The Octette Bridge Club,* Biltmore Theatre, then Music Box Theatre, New York City, 1985; Marge, *Baby Grand,* Long Island Stage, Hampstead, NY, 1985.

RUTH LIVINGSTON

MAJOR TOURS—Reporter, *Advise & Consent,* national, 1961-62; Nettie, *The Subject Was Roses,* Country Dinner Playhouse, St. Petersburg, FL, Dallas TX, Austin, TX; Edith, *Never Too Late,* Beef 'n Boards Dinner Theatre, Lexington, KY, Indianapolis, IN, Simpsonvill, KY, 1973.

FILM DEBUT—Kay's nurse, *The Group,* 1963.

TELEVISION DEBUT—Nurse/housekeeper, *As the World Turns,* CBS, 1970. PRINCIPAL TELEVISION APPEARANCES—Harriet McFadden, *All My Children,* ABC, 1978-80.

MEMBER: Actors' Equity Association, American Federation of Television and Radio Artists.

ADDRESSES: HOME—203 W. 81st Street, New York, NY 10024.

*   *   *

LLOYD, Christopher   1938-

PERSONAL: Born October 22, 1938, in Stamford, CT; married wife, Kay (an actress). EDUCATION: Trained for the stage at the Neighborhood Playhouse, New York City.

VOCATION: Actor.

CAREER: PRINCIPAL STAGE APPEARANCES—Bill Cracker, *Happy*

End, Martin Beck Theatre, New York City, 1977; also *Red White and Maddox,* New York City; *Macbeth,* New York Shakespeare Festival, New York City; *Hot'L Baltimore,* Mark Taper Forum, Los Angeles; *The Possessed* and *A Midsummer Night's Dream,* both with the Yale Repertory Theatre, New Haven, CT; *Kaspar,* New York City.

PRINCIPAL FILM APPEARANCES—*One Flew Over the Cuckoo's Nest,* United Artists, 1975; *Another Man, Another Chance,* United Artists, 1977; *Three Warriors,* United Artists, 1978; *Goin' South,* Paramount, 1978; *The Onion Field,* AVCO-Embassy, 1979; *Butch and Sundance: The Early Days,* Twentieth Century-Fox, 1979; *The Lady in Red* (also known as *Guns, Sin and Bathtub Gin*), 1979; *Pilgrim Farewell,* 1980; *The Black Marble,* AVCO-Embassy, 1980; *The Postman Always Rings Twice,* Paramount, 1981; *The Legend of the Lone Ranger,* Universal, 1981; *National Lampoon Goes to the Movies,* 1981; *To Be or Not to Be,* Twentieth Century-Fox, 1983; *Mr. Mom,* Twentieth Century-Fox, 1983; *Star Trek III: The Search for Spock,* Paramount, 1984; *The Adventures of Buckaroo Banzai: Across the Eighth Dimension,* Twentieth Century-Fox, 1984; Dr. Emmett Brown, *Back to the Future,* Universal, 1985; *Clue,* Paramount, 1985; also *Acts of a Young Man, Miracles, White Dragon.*

PRINCIPAL TELEVISION APPEARANCES—Series: Jim, *Taxi,* ABC and NBC, 1979-83. Episodic: *Barney Miller,* ABC; *Twilight Zone,* CBS, 1986. Movies: *Visions,* 1972; *Lacy and the Mississippi Queen,* 1978; *Stunt Seven,* 1979; *The Cowboy and the Ballerina,* CBS, 1984.

AWARDS: Obie Award and Drama Desk Award, both for *Kaspar.*

MEMBER: Actors' Equity Association, Screen Actors Guild, American Federation of Television and Radio Artists.

SIDELIGHTS. Mr. Lloyd has performed extensively in summer stock and Off-Broadway productions in addition to his Broadway, film, and television performances.

ADDRESSES: AGENT—c/o Phil Gersh, The Gersh Agency Inc., 222 Canon Drive, Beverly Hills, CA 90210.*

*   *   *

LLOYD, Sharon

PERSONAL: EDUCATION: Trained for the stage at the Academy of Live and Recorded Artists, London.

VOCATION: Actress.

CAREER: STAGE DEBUT—Mary, *Angel Knife,* Soho Poly Theatre, London, 1983. PRINCIPAL STAGE APPEARANCES—Gemini, *A Funny Thing Happened on the Way to the Forum,* Bristol Old Vic Theatre, 1984; Ramandu's daughter, *Voyage of the Dawn Treader,* Sadlers Wells Theatre, London, 1987.

MAJOR TOURS—With Vanessa Ford Productions: Witch, *Macbeth & Alfred,* Rosencrantz, *Rosencrantz and Guildenstern Are Dead,* both 1985; Wolf, *The Lion, the Witch and the Wardrobe* and Ramandu's daughter, *Voyage of the Dawn Treader,* both 1986.

SHARON LLOYD

ADDRESSES: AGENT—Eric Glass Ltd. 28 Berkeley Square, London W1X 6HD, England.

*   *   *

LLOYD PACK, Roger   1944-

PERSONAL: Born August 2, 1944, in London, England; son of Charles (an actor) and Ulrike (a travel agent; maiden name, Pulay) Lloyd Pack; married J'ehane Markham (a writer), April 24, 1975; children: Emily, Spencer, Hartley. EDUCATION: Studied at the Royal Academy of Dramatic Art, London.

VOCATION: Actor, writer, and director.

CAREER: STAGE DEBUT—*The Shoemakers Holiday,* Northampton Repertory Company. LONDON DEBUT—Policeman, *Staircase,* Aldwych Theatre, 1967. PRINCIPAL STAGE APPEARANCES—The Lover, *The Lover,* St. Martin's Theatre; Lloyd, *The Prime of Miss Jean Brodie,* Lyceum Theatre, Edinburgh; Rosencrantz, *Hamlet,* Roundhouse Theatre, London; Valverde, *The Royal Hunt of the Sun,* Watford Palace Theatre; French mercenary, *Paradise,* Royal Court Theatre, London; Aston, *The Caretaker,* Shaw Theatre; title role, *The Trial of Bukovsky,* Young Vic Theatre Company; Joey, *The Homecoming* and Errol Philander, *Statements,* both Leeds Playhouse, U.K.; Dave, *Otherwise Engaged* and Philip, *Relatively Speaking,* both Vienna English Theatre; John, *Summer Party,* Crucible Theatre, Sheffield, U.K.; Jimmy, *Moving,* Queen's Theatre, London; Will, *Caritas,* National Theatre, London; Tim, *Noises*

Off, Lyric Theatre, Hammersmith, then Savoy Theatre, London; Andy, *Fly Away Home,* Controller, *Victoria Station,* and Victor, *One for the Road,* all Lyric Theatre, Hammersmith, London; Osip, *Wild Honey* and Tabs, *Garden of England,* both National Theatre; Cmielewski, *The Deliberate Death of a Polish Priest,* Almeda Theatre; Mandelstam, *The Futurists,* National Theatre, London; Kafka, *Kafka's Dick,* Royal Court Theatre, London; Crysaldus, *School for Wives* and Juan, *Yerma,* both National Theatre, London, 1986.

MAJOR TOURS—Harry, *The Speakers,* ICA, and British tour; Fanshen, ICA and British tour; Joey, *The Homecoming,* Garrick Theatre and tour of Israel; Jimmy, *Moving,* British tour.

PRINCIPAL STAGE WORK—Writer and director, *The End,* King's Head Theatre, 1976.

FILM DEBUT—Young Magus, *The Magus,* Twentieth Century-Fox, 1969. PRINCIPAL FILM APPEARANCES—A soldier, *The Virgin Soldiers;* flat cleaner, *Secret Ceremony;* Rosencrantz, *Hamlet;* Pavlov, *Meetings with Remarkable Men;* Nunez, *Cuba;* Doctor, *Bloody Kids;* Charles, *The Go-Between,* Columbia, 1971; Rabbi, *Fiddler on the Roof,* United Artists, 1971; Waiter, *1984,* 1985.

TELEVISION DEBUT—*Softly Softly,* BBC. PRINCIPAL TELEVISION APPEARANCES—Villian, *Dixon of Dock Green,* BBC; revolutionary, *Survivors,* BBC; Sydney Bagley, *Brassneck,* BBC; Liz, *The Naked Civil Servant,* Thames TV; Earl of Glouchester, *Shakespeare,* ATV; Ramos, *The Professionals: Longshot,* Mark 1; second gentleman, *Henry VIII,* BBC; Corsican, *Turtle's Progress,*

ROGER LLOYD PACK

ATV; Melvyn, *Private Shultz,* BBC; Chambers, *The Crime of Captain Colthurst,* BBC; Trigger, *Only Fools and Horses,* BBC; Eddie Stone, *Making Good,* BBC; Roy Scarper, *Bouncing Back,* Central TV; P.C., *I Thought You'd Gone,* Central TV; Bus fanatic, *Video Stars,* BBC; Noble, *Miracles Take Longer,* Thames TV; Manders, *The Brief,* TVS; Jimmy, *Moving,* Thames TV; Ronald Selser, *In a Secret State,* BBC; *The Silent World of Nicholas Dunn,* Central TV.

AWARDS: Best Supporting Actor, Drama Theatre Award, for Osip in *Wild Honey* and Victor in *One for the Road,* 1984.

MEMBER: British Actors' Equity Association.

SIDELIGHTS: RECREATIONS—Chess, reading, playing the piano and travel.

ADDRESSES: AGENT—Kate Feast Management, 43A Princess Road, Regents Park, London NW1, England.

*　　＊　　＊　　＊*

LOGAN, Joshua　1908-

PERSONAL: Full name, Joshua Lockwood Logan, born October 5, 1908, in Texarkana, TX; son of Joshua Lockwood and Susan (Nabors) Logan; married Barbara O'Neill, 1940 (divorced, 1941); married Nedda Harrigan (an actress), 1945; children: Thomas Heggen, Susan Harrigan. EDUCATION: Attended Culver Military Academy, 1927, graduated Princeton University, 1931; trained for the stage on a scholarship to the Moscow Art Theatre with Constantin Stanislavsky, 1931. MILITARY: U.S. Air Force, 1942-45.

VOCATION: Producer, director, actor, and writer.

CAREER: BROADWAY DEBUT—Mart Strong, *Carrie Nation,* Biltmore Theatre, 1932. PRINCIPAL STAGE APPEARANCES—Robert Humphreys, *A Room in Red and White,* 46th Street Theatre, New York City, 1936.

PRINCIPAL STAGE WORK—Assistant stage manager, *She Loves Me Not,* New York City, 1933; assistant stage manager, *It's You I Want,* New York City, 1935; worked with summer stock company, Suffern, NY, 1935.

Director: With the University Players, Falmouth, MA, 1928-32, and in Baltimore, 1931-33; *Camille,* Colonial Theatre, Boston, 1933; *The Day I Forgot,* Globe Theatre, London, 1933; *To See Ourselves,* Ethel Barrymore Theatre, New York City, 1935; *Hell Freezes Over,* Ritz Theatre, New York City, 1935; *On Borrowed Time,* Longacre Theatre, New York City, 1938; *I Married an Angel,* Shubert Theatre, New York City, 1938; *Knickerbocker Holiday,* Ethel Barrymore Theatre, New York City, 1938; *Stars in Your Eyes;* Majestic Theatre, New York City, 1939; *Mornings at Seven,* Longacre Theatre, New York City, 1939; *Two for the Show,* Booth Theatre, New York City, 1939; *Higher and Higher,* Shubert Theatre, New York City, 1939.

Continuing as director: *Charlie's Aunt,* Cort Theatre, New York City, 1940; *By Jupiter,* Shubert Theatre, New York City, 1942; *This Is the Army,* Broadway Theatre, New York City, 1942; *Annie Get Your Gun,* Imperial Theatre, New York City, 1946; *Happy Birthday,* Broadhurst Theatre, New York City, 1945; *John Loves Mary,* Booth Theatre, New York City, 1946; *Mister Roberts,* Alvin

Theatre, New York City, 1948, then at the Coliseum Theatre in London, 1950; *South Pacific,* Majestic Theatre, New York City, 1949, then at the Drury Lane Theatre, London, 1951; *The Wisteria Trees,* Martin Beck Theatre, New York City, 1950; *Wish You Were Here,* Imperial Theatre, New York City, 1952; *Picnic,* Music Box Theatre, New York City, 1953; *Kind Sir,* Alvin Theatre, New York City, 1953; *Fanny,* Majestic Theatre, New York City, 1954; *Middle of the Night,* American National Theatre Academy (ANTA) Theatre, New York City, 1956; *Blue Denim,* Playhouse Theatre, New York City, 1958; *The World of Suzie Wong,* Broadhurst Theatre, New York City, 1958; *There Was a Little Girl,* Cort Theatre, New York City, 1960; *All American,* Winter Garden Theatre, New York City, 1961; *Mr. President,* St. James Theatre, New York City, 1962; *Tiger, Tiger, Burning Bright,* Booth Theatre, New York City, 1962; *Ready When You Are, C.B.!,* Brooks Atkinson Theatre, New York City, 1964; *Hot September,* 1965; *Look to the Lilies,* Lunt-Fontanne Theatre, New York City, 1970; *Miss Moffatt,* Shubert Theatre, Philadelphia, 1974.

Producer: (With J.H. Del Bondio) *To See Ourselves,* Ethel Barrymore Theatre, New York City, 1935; (with Richard Rodgers and Oscar Hammerstein II) *John Loves Mary,* Booth Theatre, New York City, 1947; (with Leland Hayward) *Wish You Were Here,* Imperial Theatre, New York City, 1951; *Kind Sir,* Alvin Theatre, New York City, 1953; *Middle of the Night,* ANTA Theatre, New York City, 1956; (with David Merrick) *Epitaph for George Dillon,* John Golden Theatre, New York City, 1958; co-producer, *Miss Moffatt,* Shubert Theatre, Philadelphia, 1974; producer, *Trick,* Playhouse Theatre, New York City, 1979.

PRINCIPAL FILM WORK—Dialogue director, *The Garden of Allah,* United Artists, 1936; dialogue director, *History Is Made at Night,* United Artists, 1937; co-director, *I Met My Love Again,* United Artists, 1937; director, *Picnic,* Columbia, 1955; director, *Bus Stop,* Twentieth Century-Fox, 1956; director, *Sayonara,* Warner Brothers, 1957; director, *South Pacific,* Twentieth Century-Fox, 1958; director and producer, *Tall Story,* Warner Brothers, 1960; director and producer, *Fanny,* Warner Brothers, 1961; director and producer, *Ensign Pulver,* Warner Brothers, 1964; director, *Camelot,* Warner Brothers/Seven Arts, 1967; director, *Paint Your Wagon,* Paramount, 1969.

WRITINGS: PLAYS, PRODUCED AND PUBLISHED—(With Gladys Hurlbut) *Higher and Higher,* Shubert Theatre, New York City, 1940; (with Thomas Heggen) *Mister Roberts,* Alvin Theatre, New York City, 1948, published by Random House, 1948; (with Oscar Hammerstein II) *South Pacific,* Majestic Theatre, New York City, 1949, published by Random House, 1949; *The Wisteria Trees,* Martin Beck Theatre, New York City, 1950, published by Random House, 1950; (with Harold Rome and Arthur Kober) *Wish You Were Here,* Imperial Theatre, New York City, 1952; (with S.N. Behrman) *Fanny,* Majestic Theatre, New York City, 1954, published by Random House, 1955; (with Emlyn Williams) *Miss Moffatt,* Shubert Theatre, Philadelphia, 1974; *Rip Van Winkle,* Kennedy Center, Washington, DC, 1976; a play of his is also published in *American Plays,* edited by Allan G. Halline, AMS Press, 1976.

SCREENPLAYS—(With Frank Nugent) *Mister Roberts,* Warner Brothers, 1955; (with Peter S. Feibleman) *Ensign Pulver,* Warner Brothers, 1964.

NON-FICTION—(Autobiographies) *Josh: My Up and Down, In and Out Life,* Delacorte, 1976; *Movie Stars, Real People and Me,* Delacorte, 1978.

AWARDS: Pulitzer Prize Award, 1950, for *South Pacific;* was saluted by a *A Gala Tribute to Joshua Logan,* in which he also peformed at the Imperial Theatre, New York City, 1975. Honorary M.A., 1953, from Princeton University.

MEMBER: Screen Directors Guild of America, Society of Stage Directors and Choreographers; Players Club, New York Athletic Club, River Club.

SIDELIGHTS: RECREATIONS—Photography and sculpture.

ADDRESSES: OFFICE—435 E. 52nd Street, New York, NY 10022.*

*   *   *

LOGGIA, Robert   1930-

PERSONAL: Surname pronounced "low-jah"; born January 3, 1930, in New York, NY; son of Benjamin (a shoe designer) and Elena (Blandino) Loggia; married second wife, Audrey O'Brien (a business executive), December 27, 1982; children: (first marriage) Tracey, John, Kristina; (second marriage) Cynthia Marlette (stepdaughter). EDUCATION: Attended Wagner College, Staten Island, NY, 1947-49; University of Missouri, Bachelor of Journalism, 1951; studied acting with Stella Adler at the Actors Studio in New York City. RELIGION: Catholic. MILITARY: U.S. Army, Panama Caribbean Forces Network.

ROBERT LOGGIA

VOCATION: Actor.

CAREER: STAGE DEBUT—Petruchio, *The Taming of the Shew,* Wagner College, Staten Island, NY, 1948. OFF-BROADWAY DEBUT—Frankie Machine, *Man with the Golden Arm,* Cherry Lane Theatre, 1955. LONDON DEBUT—Solyony, *The Three Sisters,* World Theatre Festival, Aldwych Theatre, 1964. PRINCIPAL STAGE APPEARANCES—Julian, *Toys in the Attic,* Hudson Guild Theatre, New York City, 1960; Solyony, *The Three Sisters,* Morosco Theatre, New York City, 1963; *In the Boom Boom Room,* New York City, 1973-74.

FILM DEBUT—Frankie Peppo, *Somebody Up There Likes Me,* 1956. PRINCIPAL FILM APPEARANCES—Joseph, *The Greatest Story Ever Told,* United Artists, 1956; Tulio Renata, *The Garment Jungle,* 1956; *S.O.B.,* Paramount, 1981; Byron Mayo, *An Officer and a Gentleman,* Paramount, 1982; *The Trail of the Pink Panther,* United Artists, 1982; Dr. Raymond, *Psycho II,* Universal, 1983; Frank Lopez, *Scarface,* Universal, 1983; *Prizzi's Honor,* Twentieth Century-Fox, 1985; *Jagged Edge,* Columbia, 1985; *Hot Pursuit,* RKO Pictures, 1987; *Gaby,* Gaby Brimmer Productions, 1987; *The Believers,* Orion, 1987; Jason Cutler, *Over the Top,* Warner Brothers, 1987; voice characterization, *Oliver,* Disney, 1987.

PRINCIPAL TELEVISION APPEARANCES—Series: "The Nine Lives of Elfego Baca," *Walt Disney Productions,* ABC, 1957-59; Thomas Hewitt Edward Cat, *T.H.E. Cat,* NBC, 1966-67. Movies: *Streets of Justice,* NBC, 1985.

AWARDS: Best Supporting Actor, Academy Award nomination, 1985, for *Jagged Edge.*

ADDRESSES: AGENT—Blake Edwards Entertainment, 1888 Century Park East, Suite 1616, Los Angeles, CA 90067.*

*   *   *

LONDON, Chuck   1946-

PERSONAL: Born February 5, 1946, in New York, NY; son of Robert L. (an attorney) and Frances A. (a teacher; maiden name, Abes) London. EDUCATION: University of Michigan, radio and television production, 1962-66.

VOCATION: Sound designer, producer, and director.

CAREER: FIRST STAGE WORK—Sound designer, *Hot L Baltimore,* Circle Repertory Company, New York City, 1972. PRINCIPAL STAGE WORK—Sound designer: *Fifth of July, Knock, Knock,* and other productions at the Circle Repertory Company, New York City, 1972—.

PRINCIPAL FILM WORK—Producer and director of industrial films for Pepsi Cola, *America Laughs,* Pepsi Cola School Assembly Program; Hoffman La Roche training program.

PRINCIPAL TELEVISION WORK—Producer and director of industrial videos and commercials including Canon Copiers and Broadway shows, *Gemini,* and others.

RELATED CAREER—Director of productions, 1492 Productions Ltd., New York City, 1966-71; vice president, Motiva Ltd., New

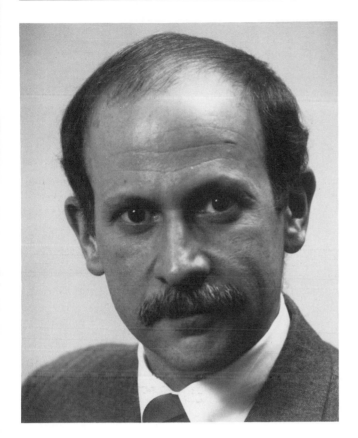

CHUCK LONDON

Photography by Alex Ely

ROBERT LORD

York City, 1971-76; president and chief executive officer, London Multimedia Ltd., New York City, 1978—.

AWARDS: Silver Medals from the International Film and Television Festival, New York City, 1980 and 1984; Grammy Award nomination, for the commercial for Broadway show, *Gemini*.

MEMBER· National Academy of Television Arts and Sciences, National Academy of Recording Arts and Sciences, Directors Guild of America, Theatrical Sound Designers Association; Association for Multi-Image.

SIDELIGHTS: Chuck London told *CTFT:* ''I acted in radio plays at age eight and fell in love with electronic communications. I have travelled all over the U.S. and England.''

ADDRESSES: OFFICE—London Multi-Media Ltd., 381 Fifth Avenue, New York, NY 10016. MANAGER—c/o Mr. Gerald Delet, TWM, 641 Lexington Avenue, New York, NY 10022.

*   *   *

LORD, Robert 1945-

PERSONAL: Born July 18, 1945, in Rotorua, New Zealand; son of Richard H. (a banker) and Bebe Lord. EDUCATION: Victoria University, Wellington, New Zealand, B.A.

VOCATION: Playwright.

WRITINGS: PLAYS, PRODUCED—*It Isn't Cricket,* Downstage Theatre, Wellington, New Zealand, 1971, Unity Theatre, Wellington, 1972, Playwrights' Conference, Canberra, Australia, 1973, Gateway Players, Tauranga, New Zealand, 1973, and IRT Theatre, New York City, 1978; *Balance of Payments,* Downstage Theatre, Wellington, 1972, Unity Theatre, Wellington, 1973, Gateway Players, Tauranga, 1973, Q Theatre, Sydney, Australia, 1975, and Independent Theatre, Auckland, New Zealand, 1977; *Meeting Place,* Downstage Theatre, Wellington, 1973, Centerpoint Theatre, Palmerston North, New Zealand, 1975, and Phoenix Theatre, New York City, 1975; *Well Hung,* Trinity Square Repertory, Providence, RI, 1974, Nimrod Theatre, Sydney, Australia, 1974, Downstage Theatre, Wellington, 1976, Fortune Theatre, Dunedin, New Zealand, 1977, and the Hole in the Wall Theatre, Perth, Australia, 1978.

Nativity, Theatre Corporate, Auckland, 1973; *Heroes and Butterflies,* Mercury Theatre, Auckland, 1974 and Downstage Theatre, Wellington, 1977; *Dead and Never Called Me Mother,* O'Neill Playwrights Conference, Waterford, CT, 1975; *I'll Scream If I Want To,* Provincetown Playhouse, Cape Cod, MA, 1976; *The Kite Play,* Downstage Theatre, Wellington, 1978, and at the Production Company, New York City, 1978; *Cop Shop,* St. Lawrence Center, Toronto, Canada, 1979 and Mana Little Theatre, Wellington, 1983; *Glitter and Spit,* Ranfurly Little Theatre, New Zealand, 1982 and Takaka Drama Society, New Zealand, 1984; *Unfamiliar Steps,* Court Theatre, Christchurch, New Zealand, 1983; *Bert and Maisy,* Stables Theatre, Sydney, Australia, 1984 and at the Old Globe Theatre, San Diego, CA, the Mercury Theatre, Auckland, the Circa Theatre, Wellington, and Newcastle Repertory Theatre, Newcastle, Australia, all 1986; *Country Cops,* Circa Theatre, Wellington, 1985.

PLAYS, UNPRODUCED—China Wars; The Travelling Squirrel.

AWARDS: Katherine Mansfield Young Writers' Award, 1969; CAPS Grant Award, 1984.

MEMBER: PEN, New Dramatists, Dramatists Guild.

ADDRESSES: HOME—250 W. 85th Street, New York, NY 10024. AGENT—c/o Gilbert Parker, William Morris Agency, 1350 Avenue of the Americas, New York, NY 10019.

*   *   *

LOUDON, Dorothy   1933-

PERSONAL: Born September 17, 1933, in Boston, MA; daughter of James E. (an advertising manager for a machine company) and Dorothy Helen (a sheet music demonstrator at Filene's department store; maiden name, Shaw) Loudon; married Norman Paris (a composer, music arranger, and conductor), December 18, 1971 (died, 1977). EDUCATION: Attended Syracuse University; trained for the stage at the American Academy of Dramatic Arts, and studied for the theatre with Sawyer Falk, Lola Allbee, and Gertrude Binley Kay.

VOCATION: Actress and singer.

CAREER: BROADWAY DEBUT—In a vaudeville show, Palace Theatre, 1953. PRINCIPAL STAGE APPEARANCES—Passionella, *The World of Jules Feiffer,* pre-Broadway tryout, 1962; Wilma Risque, *Nowhere to Go But Up,* Winter Garden Theatre, 1962; *Sweet Potato,* Barrymore Theatre, New York City, 1968; Lillian Stone, *The Fig Leaves Are Falling,* Broadhurst Theatre, New York City, 1969; Mabel, *Three Men on a Horse,* Lyceum Theatre, New York City, 1969; Charlotte Haze, *Lolita, My Love,* Shubert Theatre, Philadelphia, 1971; Beatrice, *The Effect of Gamma Rays on Man-in-the-Moon Marigolds,* American Conservatory Theatre, San Francisco, 1972; Edith Potter, *The Women,* 46th Street Theatre, New York City, 1973; Miss Hannigan, *Annie,* Alvin Theatre, New York City, 1977; Bea Asher, *Ballroom,* Majestic Theatre, New York City, 1978; Mrs. Lovett, *Sweeney Todd,* Uris Theatre, New York City, 1980; Cara Varnum, *West Side Waltz,* Barrymore Theatre, New York City, 1981; Dottie Otley, *Noises Off,* Brooks Atkinson Theatre, New York City, 1983-84, then Ahmanson Theatre, Los Angeles, 1985.

MAJOR TOURS—Title role, *The Unsinkable Molly Brown,* stock tour, 1963; Reno Sweeney, *Anything Goes,* stock tour, 1964; Ellen Manville, *Luv,* national tour, 1965; Eve, Bar-bara, and Passionella, *The Apple Tree,* national tour, 1970; *You Know I Can't Hear You When the Water's Running,* national tour, 1970; Karen Nach, Muriel Tate, and Norma Hubley, *Plaza Suite,* national tour, 1971; Beatrice, *The Effect of Gamma Rays on Man-in-the-Moon Marigolds,* 1972; Cara Varnum, *West Side Waltz,* national tour, 1981-82.

FILM DEBUT—*Garbo Talks,* Metro-Goldwyn-Mayer/United Artists, 1984.

PRINCIPAL TELEVISION APPEARANCES—Series: Regular, *It's a Business,* DuMont, 1952; panelist, *Laugh Line,* NBC, 1959; regular, *The Garry Moore Show,* CBS, 1962-64; Dorothy Banks,

Dorothy, CBS, 1979. Guest: *The Ed Sullivan Show,* CBS; *The Kraft Music Hall,* NBC; *The Dinah Shore Show,* NBC. Episodic: "Those Ragtime Years," 1960, "Music of the Thirties," 1961, and "Regards to George M. Cohan," 1962, all on the *DuPont Show of the Month,* NBC; also appeared on British television on *Gradada at 9:00* and *Sunday at the Palladium.*

PRINCIPAL CABARET APPEARANCES—Nightclub singer and satirist, Ruban Bleu, 1953-58, The Blue Angel, 1953-62, Flamingo Hotel, 1962, Harrah's, Lake Tahoe, NV, 1963; also Mister Kelly's and The Palmer House, both in Chicago, and the Persian Room, Plaza Hotel, New York City, 1964.

RECORDINGS: ALBUMS—*Dorothy Loudon at the Blue Angel,* Decca, 1960; also cast albums of *Annie* and *Ballroom,* and others; also is a "cover" records singer for RCA.

AWARDS: Most Promising Newcomer, *Theatre World* Award, 1962; Drama Desk Award, 1969, for *The Fig Leaves Are Falling;* Drama Desk Award, 1970, for *Three Men on a Horse;* Antoinette Perry Award, Drama Desk Award, and Outer Critics Circle Award, all 1977, for *Annie;* Antoinette Perry Award nomination and Drama Desk Award nomination, both 1979, for *Ballroom;* Actress of the Year, Sarah Siddons Award, 1982, for *West Side Waltz;* Woman of the Year, Yeshiva University's Albert Einstein College of Medicine, 1979.

MEMBER: Actors' Equity Association, American Guild of Variety Artists, Screen Actors Guild, American Federation of Television and Radio Artists, Musicians Union, Local 802.

SIDELIGHTS: RECREATIONS—Writing, painting, sewing (she makes most of her own clothes), and playing the piano.

Dorothy Loudon can be heard singing the best songs of the great masters of theatre music on the series of Ben Bagley "Revisited" albums, many conducted by her late husband, Norman Paris.

She told *CTFT:* "I'm happiest when I'm onstage. I think that's probably why most people act: it's because they get to be somebody else. I find a strength onstage that I don't have offstage. It's when I have my confidence."

ADDRESSES: AGENT—Lionel Larner, Ltd., 850 Seventh Avenue, New York, NY 10019.*

*   *   *

LOUIS, Barbara

PERSONAL: Born February 3, in Latrobe, PA; daughter of Ben (a salesman) and Elizabeth (an office worker; maiden name, Glenn) Louis. EDUCATION: Studied at the George Heid School of Radio Announcing; trained for the stage with Bill Putch at the Pittsburgh Playhouse School and with Lee Grant at the Herbert Berghof Studio in New York City. POLITICS: Democrat. RELIGION: Jewish.

VOCATION: Actress and singer.

CAREER: STAGE DEBUT—Clarisse Carter, *Goodbye My Fancy,* Pittsburgh Playhouse, 1952. OFF-BROADWAY DEBUT—Lucy Brown, *The Threepenny Opera,* Theatre de Lys, 1960-61. PRINCI-

PAL STAGE APPEARANCES—Emilia, *Othello*, 1952; title role, *The Heiress*, 1953; Gail Joy, *Best Foot Forward*, 1953; Madam Parole, *My Three Angels*, 1953; Shirley, *High Button Shoes*, 1954; Irene, *Light Up the Sky*, 1954; Crystal, *The Women*, 1954; Gillian, *Bell, Book and Candle*, 1955; Leila Tree, *Panama Hatti*, 1955; Elie, *Transfers*, Off-Broadway, New York City, 1973; Jenny *The Threepenny Opera*, 1980, Myra, *Deathtrap*, 1985.

MAJOR TOURS—Francy, *Uncle Willie*, 1956; Mrs. Durant, *Cactus Flower*, 1967-68; Ruth, *Blithe Spirit*, 1976; Gert, *Murder Among Friends*, 1976; Vera, *Mame* (two productions), 1972, 1981.

FILM DEBUT—*Never Love a Stranger*, Allied Artists, 1958. PRINCIPAL FILM APPEARANCES—*Star!*, 1968; *Report to the Commissioner*, United Artists, 1975; also, *Run Across the River*.

TELEVISON DEBUT—Hostess, *The Weather Show*, KDKA-TV, Pittsburgh, 1954. PRINCIPAL TELEVISION APPEARANCES—Series: *As the World Turns*, CBS, 1959; *Another World*, NBC, 1960. Movies: *Miracle on 34th Street*, 1962.

MEMBER: Actors' Equity Association, Screen Actors Guild, American Federation of Television and Radio Artists.

SIDELIGHTS: Barbara Louis commented to *CTFT* about the motivation of her career, "I started singing on a local radio show a the age of five, my interest continued from then on. I was one of ten outstanding seniors of my graduation class and was honored for my acting."

ADDRESSES: HOME—200 W. 16th Street, New York, NY 10011.

BARBARA LOUIS

LUCAS, George   1944-

PERSONAL: Born 1944, in Modesto, CA; married Marcia Griffin, 1969 (divorced). EDUCATION: University of Southern California, 1944.

VOCATION: Producer, director, and writer.

CAREER: PRINCIPAL FILM WORK—Assistant to the director, *The Rain People*, 1969; director of documentary on making *The Rain People*, 1970; director and co-writer, *THX-1138*, Warner Brothers, 1971; director and co-writer, *American Graffiti*, Universal, 1973; director and writer, *Star Wars*, Twentieth Century-Fox, 1977; executive producer, *More American Graffiti*, Universal, 1979; executive producer, *The Empire Strikes Back*, Twentieth Century-Fox, 1980; executive producer, *Raiders of the Lost Ark*, Paramount, 1981; executive producer, *Return of the Jedi*, Twentieth Century-Fox, 1982; executive director and story, *Indiana Jones and the Temple of Doom*, Paramount, 1984; executive producer (with Francis Ford Coppola), *Mishima: A Life in Four Chapters*, Warner Brothers, 1985; executive producer, *Labyrinth*, Tri-Star, 1986; executive producer, *Howard the Duck*, Universal, 1986; executive producer, *Captain EO*, Disney Productions, 1986; upcoming: executive producer, *The Land Before Time Began*, executive producer, *Tucker: A Man and His Dream*, producer, *Michael Bye Fall Down*, executive producer, *Willow*, producer, *Indiana Jones Three*, producer, *North-South*.

PRINCIPAL TELEVISION WORK—Movies: Executive producer, *The Ewok Adventure*, ABC, 1984; *Ewoks, The Battle for Endor*, ABC, 1985. Animated: *Droids: The Adventures of R2D2 and 3CP0*, 1985; *Ewoks: The Cartoon*, 1985; *The Great Heep*, 1986.

AWARDS: Grand Prize for Film, National Student Film Festival, 1967, for *THX-1138*.

SIDELIGHTS: Director George Lucas made cinematic history with his 1977 film, *Star Wars*, a swashbuckling science fiction adventure that set new records at the box office. Shortly after its release, *Star Wars* became the highest-grossing film of all time. Its characters—Luke Skywalker, the robots R2D2 and C3PO, and the villain Darth Vader—are familiar to millions of moviegoers. In 1980, Lucas followed *Star Wars* with a sequel, *The Empire Strikes Back*, another commercial smash. The two films currently hold the second and third spots for all-time top-grossing films, just behind Steven Spielberg's *E.T.* The subsequent films *Raiders of the Lost Ark, The Return of the Jedi*, and *Indiana Jones and the Temple of Doom*, all released by Lucas's own company, Lucasfilm, have also proven tremendously popular.

This phenomenal success was foreshadowed by Lucas's earlier film work. His first movie, *THX-1138*, was a science fiction story about a repressive society of the future where people are deprived of their names and given numbers. A critical but not a commerical success, the film won Lucas a loyal cult following. This changed with *American Graffiti*, Lucas's 1973 effort about teenage life in the early 1960s. This film was "one of the most profitable films in Hollywood history," Gerald Clarke reported in the May 23, 1983, issue of *Time*. "It cost Universal Pictures only $780,000 to produce, but it . . . returned $145 million worldwide."

With the release of *Star Wars*, however, Lucas became a household name—as did a host of his movie characters. Essentially a "space opera," as Lucas described it to Donald Goddard in the September 12, 1977, *New York Times, Star Wars* tells of a rebellion against the evil Darth Vader, who has usurped the throne of the galaxy government and imprisoned the Princess Leia. "I was trying to say," Lucas explained to Clarke, "in a very simple way, knowing that the film was made for a young audience, that there is a God and there is both a good side and a bad side. You have a choice between them, but the world works better if you're on the good side."

The sequels to *Star Wars—The Empire Strikes Back* and *The Return of the Jedi*—continue the original story to form a trilogy. Lucas claimed at one point that he would make a total of ten *Star Wars* films by the year 2004, detailing an imaginary history spanning decades. The success of the first three films would seem to guarantee that the series will continue. *Star Wars* has grossed over $500 million worldwide, with *Empire* and *Jedi* racking up several million more each in ticket sales. Sales of such related products as games, toys, and clothing total a staggering $1.5 billion. But "besides making money," Clarke maintained, "the *Star Wars* pictures changed the way moviemakers look at film and created a new vision of ancient mythological themes that has deeply affected a whole generation of children. What Walt Disney was to the children of the '30s, '40s and '50s, Lucas is to those of the late '70s and '80s."

As one of the wealthiest men in the film industry—with an estimated personal fortune of $100 million—Lucas is intent now on giving himself the freedom to pursue whatever film projects he desires. "Lucas is using his increasing asset base to attain a unique degree of independence from the industry establishment he holds in contempt," maintained Stratford P. Sherman of *Fortune* in the October 6, 1980 issue. "Lucas's ultimate goal is to buy himself the creative freedom he hasn't enjoyed since he left film school."

To achieve this goal, Lucas has established Lucasfilm, Ltd., a film production company with studios in northern California. The company now has over two hundred employees and a $30 million film complex set on three thousand acres. The complex will serve as a center where other directors can make their films away from the giant Hollywood studios. "I'm going to bring together a group of filmmakers who are friends," Lucas told Tom Nicholson of *Newsweek* (June 15, 1981), "and give us a place to work. It's just luck that I was the one who could do this."

Since directing *Star Wars* in 1977, Lucas has assumed a more comprehensive role in his films. He writes the script, oversees production, and serves as executive producer supervising the work of his directors. The work load has been enormous. *Star Wars* has grabbed my life and taken it over against my will," he told Clarke. Lucas has spoken of taking some time off the think things over, explaining to Paul Scanlon in the July 21-August 4, 1983 *Rolling Stone:* "I may move on to something else or find out after a while that the only think I really love to do is make movies."

ADDRESSES: OFFICE—Lucasfilm, P.O. Box 2009, San Rafael, CA 94912.

*   *   *

LYNCH, Brian   1954-

PERSONAL: Born February 18, 1954, in Gary, IN; son of John Bernard and Agnes Mary (Ott) Lynch; married Mary Jean Craig (an academic psychologist), September 1, 1979; children: Jonathon Craig. EDUCATION: Northwestern University, B.S., speech and

BRIAN LYNCH

theatre, 1976; trained in voice with Douglas Susu-Mago, Calvin Snyder, and Maureen Parzybok and in dance with Gus Giordano, Lou Conte, and Lea Darwin; studied acting with David Downs and Bonnie Raphael. RELIGION: Roman Catholic.

VOCATION: Actor, dancer, and choreographer.

CAREER: STAGE DEBUT—Randolph MacAfee, *Bye Bye Birdie,* Morrillville High School, Morrillville, IN, 1965, for four performances. PRINCIPAL STAGE APPEARANCES—At the Candlelight Dinner Playhouse, Chicago: Alter Ego of Phil and understudy for Vernon Gersch, *They're Playing Our Song;* Anagnosti and understudy for Niko, *Zorba;* Sir Sagramore and understudy for Lancelot and Arthur, *Camelot;* Young Vincent, *Follies;* Jacey Squires, *The Music Man;* Tulsa, *Gypsy;* Tommy Keeler, *Annie Get Your Gun;* Frank Wyman, *Mack and Mabel;* Frank Schultz, *Show Boat;* Dream Curly and understudy for Curly, *Oklahoma!;* Lt. Joe Cable, *South Pacific;* Fyedka, *Fiddler on the Roof;* Rooster, *Annie;* Sky Masterson, *Guys and Dolls;* Riff, *West Side Story;* Dany Zuko (also choreographer), *Grease;* Pirate King, *Pirates of Penzance;* Che and Magaldi, *Evita;* Zach, *A Chorus Line;* Audrey II, *Little Shop of Horrors.* Appeared as Prince Charming, *Sleeping Beauty,* McCormack Playhouse, Chicago; Jacey Squires, *The Music Man,* Tin Tree Theatre, New Buffalo, MI.

RELATED CAREER—Jazz dance instructor: Giordano Dance Center, Evanston, IL, 1976-78; Illinois Academy of Ballet, Glenbrook, IL, 1976-78; Columbia College Dance Center, Chicago, 1977-78. Choreographer, Glenbrook South High School, IL, 1977—. Has performed as a singer, actor, dancer, and choreographer for industrial and trade shows sponsored by McDonald's, Eureka vacuum cleaners, Jovan, and Whirlpool Corporation. Also appeared as a singer and dancer at the International Trade Fair.

AWARDS: Outstanding Choreography, Joseph Jefferson Award, 1984, for *Grease.*

ADDRESSES: HOME—9359 Bay Colony Dr., Des Plaines, IL, 60016. OFFICE—Candlelight Dinner Playhouse, 5620 S. Napley, Summit, IL, 60501. AGENT—Shirley Hamilton, Inc., 620 N. Michigan Avenue, Chicago, IL, 60611.

*   *   *

LYNNE, Gillian

PERSONAL: Born in Bromley, Kent, U.K.; daughter of Leslie Pyrke and Barbara (Hart) Lynne; married Patrick St. John Back (divorced). EDUCATION: Attended the Arts Educational School.

VOCATION: Dancer, director, and choreographer.

CAREER: STAGE DEBUT—Dancer, with Sadler's Wells Ballet Company, U.K., 1944. PRINCIPAL STAGE APPEARANCES—Queen of the Wilis, *Giselle,* Lilac Fairy, *Sleeping Beauty,* both with the Sadler's Wells Ballet; lead dancer, with the London Palladium, 1951-52, in repertory at Hythe Windsor and the Devon Festival, U.K., 1953; Claudine, *Can Can,* Coliseum, 1954; narrator and mimic of characters, *Peter and the Wolf,* London Philharmonic Orchestra, 1958; *Becky Sharp,* Windsor, U.K., 1959; *New Cranks,* Lyric Theatre, Hammersmith, London, 1960.

PRINCIPAL STAGE WORK—Choreographer: *Owl and the Pussycat* (ballet), Western Theatre Ballet, 1961; *England Our England,* 1962; also director, *Round Leicester Square* and *Collages,* both in Edinburgh, Scotland, 1963; *The Roar of the Greasepaint, the Smell of the Crowd* and *Pickwick,* both in New York City, 1965; *Ambassador,* 1971; *The Card,* 1973; *Hans Andersen,* 1974; *The Trojans* and *Parsifal* (operas), both at Covent Gardent, London, 1977; *The Yeoman of the Guard,* Tower of London, England, 1978; *My Fair Lady* and *Songbook,* both 1979.

Director: *The Matchgirls,* 1966; *Bluebeard,* Sadler's Wells Opera, London, 1969; *Love on the Dole,* Nottingham, U.K., 1971; *Once Upon a Time* and *Liberty Ranch,* 1972; *The Papertown Chase,* 1973; with the Royal Shakespeare Company: *A Comedy of Errors,* 1976, *As You Like It,* 1977, *Once in a Lifetime,* 1978, *The Way of the World,* 1979, co-director, *A Midsummer Night's Dream,* 1977, *The Greeks,* 1980; also choreographer, *Cats,* Winter Garden Theatre, New York City, 1982—; *Jeeves Takes Charge,* City Center, New York City, 1983.

MAJOR TOURS—Director, *Home Is Best,* Amsterdam, Holland, 1978; director and choreographer, *Cats,* U.S. cities, 1983—.

PRINCIPAL FILM WORK—Choreographer, *Half a Sixpence,* 1969; *Man of La Mancha,* United Artists, 1972; *Quilp.*

SIDELIGHTS: RECREATIONS—Rehearsing and cooking.

ADDRESSES: HOME—25 The Avenue, Bedford Park, Chiswick, London W4, England.*

M

MACAULAY, Pauline

PERSONAL: Married Donald McWhinnie; children: Paul. EDUCA-
TION: Attended Herbert Strutt School. POLITICS: Green Party.
RELIGION: Church of England.

VOCATION: Writer.

WRITINGS: PLAYS, PRODUCED, PUBLISHED—*The Creeper*,
Nottingham Playhouse, also in London and Berlin, 1965; *The
Astrakhan Coat*, Washington, DC and New York City, 1967,
published by Samuel French; *Monica*, produced, 1970, published
by Samuel French.

TELEPLAYS—*Monica*, BBC; *A Man Inside*, LWT; *Alfred Potter's
Story*, Thames; "A Little Bit of Wildlife," *Jemima Shore*, Thames;
(adaptation) *A Room with a View*, BBC; (adaptation) *Howard's
End*, BBC; *The Obelisk*, BBC; *The Guest*, BBC.

MEMBER: Writers Guild, Theatre Writers Union; International
Fund for Animal Welfare, C.A.P.A.

SIDELIGHTS: RECREATIONS—Table Tennis, swimming, and
travel.

ADDRESSES: HOME—16 Cherstow Place, London W2, England.
AGENT—Eric Glass, Ltd., 28 Berkeley Square, London W1X
6HD, England.

* * *

MacCORKINDALE, Simon   1952-

PERSONAL: Born February 12, 1952, in Ely, Cambridge, Eng-
land; son of Peter Bernard (in the Royal Air Force) and Gilliver
Mary (Pendered) MacCorkindale; married Fiona Elizabeth Fullerton,
July 10, 1976 (divorced, September, 1983); married Susan Melody
George (an actress and producer), October 5, 1984. EDUCATION:
Attended Haileybury College, England, 1965-70; trained for the
stage at the Studio of Theatre Arts, London.

VOCATION: Actor, director, producer, and writer.

CAREER: TELEVISION DEBUT—Lieutenant Carter, *Hawkeye the
Pathfinder*, BBC, 1973. PRINCIPAL TELEVISION APPEARANCES—
Episodic: Rolf, "Skin Game," *BBC Play of the Month*, BBC,
1974; *General Hospital*, ABC, 1974; Houseman, *Hunter's Walk*,
1975; Lucius, *I, Claudius*, BBC, 1976; *Doomdolt Chase*, HTV,
1977; *Just William*, 1977; *Dukes of Hazzard*, CBS, 1979; *Fantasy

Island, ABC, 1981; Billy Dawson, *Hart to Hart*, ABC, 1982;
Dynasty, ABC, 1982; *Matt Houston*, ABC, 1984.

Series: Ian Sutherland, *Sutherland's Law*, BBC, 1975; Peter Gilke,
Baby for Beasts, 1976; Dr. Dady, *Within These Walls*, 1977;
Jonathan Chase, *Manimal*, NBC, 1983; Greg Reardon, *Falcon
Crest*, CBS, 1984—. Dramatic Specials: Sir Thomas Walsingham,
Will Shakespeare, 1976; Paris, *Romeo and Juliet*, Thames, 1976;
MacDuff, *Macbeth*, 1981; narrator, *Future Probe II*, PBS, 1985.

Movies: The Pilot, *Time and Again*, 1975; Lucius, *Jesus of Nazareth*,
NBC, 1975; Paul Verdayne, *Three Weeks*, Thames, 1976; Sieg-
fried Sassoon, *Out of Battle*, BBC, 1977; *The Hammer House of
Horror* (also known as *Visitor from the Other Side*), 1980; Hank
Richards, *Falcon's Gold*, 1982; Glen Stevens, *Obsessive Love*,
CBS, 1984.

SIMON MacCORKINDALE

301

Mini-Series: Joe Kapp, *Quatermass,* Thames, 1978; David Clement, *The Manions of America,* ABC, 1980. Pilots: *Scalpels,* NBC, 1980. Guest Appearances: *This Is Your Life,* Thames, 1977.

PRINCIPAL TELEVISION WORK—Director, *Falcon Crest* (one episode), CBS, 1985.

FILM DEBUT—Helmsman, *Juggernaut,* United Artists, 1974. PRINCIPAL FILM APPEARANCES—Lawrence Gibbons, *The Road to Mandalay,* Chatsworth Films, 1977; Simon Doyle, *Death on the Nile,* Paramount, 1977; Arthur Davies, *The Riddle of the Sands,* Rank, 1978; Joe Kapp, *The Quatermass Conclusion,* Euston, 1978; Lewis Clarkson, *Cabo Blanco,* AVCO-Embassy, 1979; Richard Kayertz, *Outpost of Progress,* AFI, 1981; Prince Mikah, *The Sword and the Sorcerer,* Group One, 1982; Philip Fitzroyce, *Jaws 3-D,* Universal, 1982.

STAGE DEBUT—Captain Blackwood, *Bequest to the Nation,* Belgrade Theatre, Coventry, U.K., 1973, for twenty-four performances. LONDON DEBUT—Sarcastic Bystander, *Pygmalion,* Albery Theatre, 1974, for two hundred eighteen performances. PRINCIPAL STAGE APPEARANCES—Captain Hardy, *Journey's End,* Geoff, *Getting On,* Woodenshoes Elchorn, *The Front Page,* all at Coventry, U.K., 1973; Adam, *Back to Methuselah,* Shaw Festival, 1973; Russian Soldier, *The Potsdam Quartet,* Yvonne Arnaud Theatre, London, 1973; Jeremy, *B-B-Que,* Soho Poly, U.K., 1974; Alan Howard, *French without Tears,* Thorndike Theatre, then Yvonne Arnaud Theatre, London, 1975; Shakespeare, *The Dark Lady of the Sonnets,* Cockpit Theatre, London, 1975, then National Theatre, London, 1977; title role, *The Gayden Chronicles,* CAST Theatre, Los Angeles, CA, 1980.

One Man Show: *The Importance of Being Oscar,* Cambridge Festival, 1977, 1981; at Questors Theatre, Blandford, Haileybury, Oakington, Upavon, U.K.; Globe Playhouse and CAST Theatre, Hollywood, CA; the Ludlow Festival, 1980; the Stage Company, West Palm Beach, FL, 1982; the Westwood Playhouse, Los Angeles, 1985.

PRINCIPAL STAGE WORK—Director: *The Happiest Days of Your Life,* Oakington, U.K.; *Relatively Speaking,* Oakington, 1974 and at the Questors Theatre, London, 1977; *The Merchant of Venice,* Globe Playhouse, Los Angeles, 1981; *A Doll's House,* Matrix Theatre, Hollywood, CA, 1982; *Sleuth,* Houston and Dallas, TX, both 1982. Producer: *Relatively Speaking,* Questors Theatre, London, 1977; *A Doll's House,* Matrix Theatre, Hollywood, CA, 1982; *Sleuth,* La Mirada, Fresno, and Santa Barbara, CA, all 1982.

WRITINGS: PLAYS, PRODUCED—(With John Byrne Cooke) *Woden's Day,* 1986.

AWARDS: Most Promising Newcomer, *British Evening News* Award, 1979.

MEMBER: Academy of Motion Picture Arts and Sciences, British Academy of Film and Television Arts, Screen Actors Guild, Directors Guild of America, British Actors' Equity, American Film Institute; Stars Organization for Spastics, St. James Club.

ADDRESSES: HOME—Los Angeles, CA. OFFICE—AMY International Productions, Inc., 9903 Santa Monica Blvd., Beverly Hills, CA, 90210. AGENT—c/o John Gaines, Agency for the Performing Arts, 9000 Sunset Blvd., Los Angeles, CA, 90069.

SHIRLEY MacLAINE

MacLAINE, Shirley   1934-

PERSONAL: Born Shirley MacLean Beaty, April 24, 1934, in Richmond, VA; daughter of Ira O. (a realtor) and Kathlyn (MacLean) Beaty; married Steve Parker (a businessman), September 17, 1954 (divorced, 1977); children: Stephanie Sachiko. EDUCATION: Attended high school in Washington, DC. POLITICS: Democrat.

VOCATION: Actress and writer.

CAREER: PRINCIPAL STAGE APPEARANCES—Chorus girl and dancer, 1950-53. Appeared on Broadway in: *Me and Juliet,* 1953, *Pajama Game,* 1954, *A Gypsy in My Soul,* 1976; also, *Shirley MacLaine on Broadway,* Gershwin Theatre, New York City, 1984.

FILM DEBUT—*Trouble with Harry,* Paramount, 1956. PRINCIPAL FILM APPEARANCES—*Artists and Models,* Paramount, 1956; *Around the World in 80 Days,* United Artists, 1956; *Hot Spell,* Paramount, 1957; *The Matchmaker,* Paramount, 1958; *The Sheepman,* Metro-Goldwyn-Mayer (MGM), 1957; *Some Came Running,* MGM, 1958; *Ask Any Girl,* MGM, 1959; *Career,* 1959.

Can-Can, Twentieth Century-Fox, 1960; *The Apartment,* United Artists, 1960; *Two Loves,* MGM, 1961; *The Loudest Whisper,* 1962; *My Geisha,* Paramount, 1962; *Children's Hour,* United Artists, 1962; *Two for the Seesaw,* United Artists, 1963; *Irma la Douce,* United Artists, 1963; *What a Way to Go,* Twentieth Century-Fox, 1964; *The Yellow Rolls Royce,* MGM, 1964; *John Goldfarb Please Come Home,* Twentieth Century-Fox, 1965; *Gambit,* Universal, 1966; *Woman Times Seven,* Embassy, 1967;

Sweet Charity, Universal, 1968; *The Bliss of Mrs. Blossom*, Paramount, 1968; *Two Mules for Sister Sara*, Universal, 1969.

(Also co-producer) *Desperate Characters*, Paramount, 1970; (also co-producer) *The Possession of Joel Delaney*, Paramount, 1971; *The Turning Point*, Paramount, 1977; *Being There*, United Artists, 1979; *A Change of Seasons*, Twentieth Century-Fox, 1980; *Loving Couples*, Prominent, 1980; *Terms of Endearment*, Paramount, 1983.

PRINCIPAL TELEVISION WORK—Series: Shirley Logan, *Shirley's World*, ABC, 1971-72. Specials: Produced and performed in *If They Could See Me Now*, 1974, *Amelia*, 1975, *Gypsy in My Soul*, 1976, and *Shirley MacLaine at the Lido*, 1980; produced and co-wrote *Shirley MacLaine. . .Every Little Movement*, CBS, 1980; co-directed (with Claudia Weill), produced, and wrote narrative for the documentary *The Other Half of the Sky: A China Memoir*, PBS, 1975; appeared in *Shower of Stars*, CBS. Guest: *David Frost Show*, CBS. Movies: Produced, directed, co-wrote, and appeared as herself in *Out on a Limb*, ABC, 1987.

WRITINGS: AUTOBIOGRAPHY—*Don't Fall Off the Mountain*, Norton, 1970; *You Can Get There from Here*, Norton, 1975; *Out on a Limb*, Bantam, 1983; *Dancing in the Light*, Bantam, 1985. NONFICTION—Editor, *McGovern: The Man and His Beliefs*, Norton, 1972; editor and author of introduction, *The New Celebrity Cookbook*, Price, Stern, 1973.

TELEVISION—(With Buz Kohan) *Shirley MacLaine. . .Every Little Movement*; author of narration, *The Other Half of the Sky: A China Memoir*, documentary, 1975, PBS; (co-writer) *Out on a Limb*, ABC, 1987.

AWARDS: International Stardom Award, Hollywood Foreign Press Association, both 1954; Best Actress, Golden Globe Awards, 1958, 1961, and 1963; Best Actress, Academy Award nomination, 1958 and Golden Globe Award, 1959, both for *Some Came Running;* Best Actress, Silver Bear Award, International Berlin Film Festival, 1959, for *Ask Any Girl;* Best Actress, Academy Award nomination, Venice Film Festival Award, and British Film Academy Award, all 1960, for *The Apartment;* Best Actress, Academy Award nomination, 1963 and Golden Globe Award, 1964, both for *Irma la Douce;* Best Actress, Italian Film Festival Award, 1964; Star of the Year Award, Theater Owners of America, 1967; Best Actress, Berlin Film Festival Award, 1971, for *Desperate Characters;* Emmy Award, 1974, for *If They Could See Me Now;* Female Musical Star of the Year, Las Vegas Entertainment Award, 1976; Best Actress, Academy Award nomination, 1977, for *The Turning Point;* Outstanding Writing of Variety or Music Program, Emmy Award, 1980, for *Shirley MacLaine. . .Every Little Movement;* Best Actress, Academy Award and New York Film Critics Circle, both 1983, for *Terms of Endearment.*

SIDELIGHTS: By 1971, Shirley MacLaine could boast sixteen years of movie stardom and three Academy Award nominations, but she was also active in so many other diversified pursuits that *Saturday Review* critic Hollis Alpert deemed her "a restless source of energy" (February 27, 1971). "It's not enough for her to be an actress," Alpert related. At that time, MacLaine was also a political activist, a best-selling author, a film and television producer, and a world traveller in fascinated pursuit of mystical experiences. Albert quoted her explanation: "I need to activate, to change, to create."

MacLaine began to take dancing lessons before she was three years old and impressed New York audiences with her dancing while still

in high school. Too tall to play the lead in her dance school's production of *Cinderella*, MacLaine auditioned for a dance part in a City Center production of *Oklahoma!* She was chosen for the center spot in the ballet. After watching her dance, the show's creators, Richard Rodgers and Oscar Hammerstein, invited MacLaine to perform in the London production. Instead, her father persuaded her to stay home and finish school. MacLaine was eighteen when she danced her next stage role in the chorus of the Broadway show *Me and Juliet;* she was nineteen and Carol Haney's understudy in *Pajama Game* when Haney broke a leg, compelling the teen to step in. "MacLaine went out a chorus girl and came back a star," William A. Henry wrote in *Time* magazine (May 14, 1984).

Producer Hall Wallis, who was in the audience that night, quickly signed MacLaine to a multiyear movie contract. A short time later she played the lead in Alfred Hitchcock's film *The Trouble with Harry* (1956). In *The Great Movie Stars: The International Years* (Hill and Wang, 1981), David Shipman reported that the movie lost money, but the press "liked it" and "warmly welcomed MacLaine." Critics generally admired MacLaine's performances in the more than thirty films she was to make before 1983, but few of the films impressed Hollywood. MacLaine received Oscar nominations for *Some Came Running* (with Frank Sinatra in 1958), *The Apartment* (a huge box office success with Jack Lemmon in 1960), *Irma La Douce* (with Lemmon and Ricardo Montalban in 1963)—but no Oscar.

MacLaine's "early glory had faded in bad films and a scatter-shot career" in the 1960s and 1970s observed Henry. During those years, however, her restless energy found expression in her increasing involvement in politics, travel, and the pursuit of self-awareness. MacLaine became an outspoken supporter of civil rights, the anti-war movement, and legalized abortion; she campaigned for presidential candidates Robert Kennedy in 1968 and George McGovern in 1972, when she became the first woman speaker in the history of the National Democratic Club. That year, the Peking government invited MacLaine to lead the first delegation of American women to their newly opened country. She accepted, found financial support, and made a documentary of her trip to China with filmmaker Claudia Weill. The film, *The Other Side of the Sky: A China Memoir*, was aired on public television in 1975 and nominated for an Oscar. Her other travels, more closely linked to her "relentless quest for self-knowledge," Henry noted, "led her to the Masai tribe of [Nairobi,] Africa, the mountaintop villages of Bhutan [an obscure kingdom in the Himalayas, and] the Indians of Peru, often at the spur of the moment." MacLaine also became a television and film producer when the industry's studio system slowed production at the end of the 1960s. As the partner of British television magnate Sir Lew Grade, MacLaine produced *Desperate Characters* (about a troubled couple in New York City) and *The Possession of Joel Delaney*, which she described, according to Alpert, as "'an elegant mixture of the psychological and the occult.'" The amount of time devoted to these activities helps explain a five-year absence from the screen that ended with her role in the 1977 feature film *The Turning Point.*

MacLaine's own turning point in terms of public appreciation came in 1984, when the star turned fifty. In that year, her third book, *Out on a Limb*, topped the best seller list; she show *Shirley MacLaine on Broadway* brought in record receipts of $475,000 a week; and her role in *Terms of Endearment* earned her an Oscar. With all these achievements, Henry noted, "Shirley the survivor [had] become Shirley the Superstar."

Combining her fame as an actress and her fascination with inner life, MacLaine developed a second career as an author. Nearly all of her books have been best sellers, but the most successful so far is *Out on a Limb,* which had 2.5 million copies in print in 1985 and became an ABC-TV mini-series starring its author in 1987. The book focuses on topics highlighted in her earlier books, *Don't Fall Off the Mountain* (1970) and *You Can Get There from Here* (1975), such as out-of-body experiences, conversations with the dead through mediums, and reincarnation. One reviewer described *Out on a Limb* as MacLaine's "psychic autobiography . . . . An enthusiastic disciple of channeling—the process of contacting spirits beyond the grave and the galaxy—she has done more than anyone to focus attention on this suddenly chic phenomenon" (*People,* January 26, 1987).

"People who claim their bodies are taken over by spirits from another dimension" have given MacLaine her "understanding of metaphysics," according to an article in the January 25, 1987, *Washington Post,* which also announced the opening of MacLaine's seminars on spiritual experience. But her "fascination with the spirit may, like her past absorbtion with politics and travel, turn out to be a 'phase that she will exhaust, in the same way an actor exhausts a part,'" suggested Pete Hamill, who lived with MacLaine for seven years. "I have thought of that," MacLaine explained to Henry. Continuing her self-assessment, she noted her propensity for change. "My strongest personality trait is the way I keep unsettling my life when most other people are settling down." Indeed, the public should "Look for further diversification," Alpert observed, since "MacLaine is a doer, a shaker, a maker, a *Monstre sacre,* a human dynamo, and something of a prodigy in our time."

ADDRESSES: AGENT—Chasin-Park-Citron Agency, 9244 Sunset Blvd., Los Angeles, CA 90069.

*   *   *

MACY, Bill   1922-

PERSONAL: Born William Macy Garber, May 18, 1922, in Revere, MA; son of Michael (a manufacturer) and Mollie (Friedopfer) Garber; married Samantha Harper (an actress). EDUCATION: New York University School of Education, B.S., 1954; trained for the stage at New York University and studied with Lee Strasberg. MILITARY: U.S. Army Engineers, 1943-46.

VOCATION: Actor.

CAREER: PRINCIPAL STAGE APPEARANCES—Gus Mizzy, *The Roast,* Winter Garden, New York City, 1980; Joe Williams, *An American Comedy,* Mark Taper Forum, Los Angeles, 1983; *The Man Who Came to Dinner,* Long Beach, CA; also in New York City: *Once More with Feeling, And Miss Reardon Drinks a Little, I Ought to Be in Pictures, America Hurrah, Oh! Calcutta!, The Balcony, Machinal, Threepenny Opera, The Cannibals, Awake and Sing.* In London: *The Tempest, America Hurrah, Oh! Calcutta!*

MAJOR TOURS—Herb, *I Ought to Be in Pictures,* U.S. cities, 1980-81.

PRINCIPAL FILM APPEARANCES—*The Producers,* Embassy, 1968; *The Late Show,* Warner Brothers, 1977; *The Jerk,* Universal, 1979; *Serial,* Paramount, 1980; *My Favorite Year,* Metro-Goldwyn-Mayer/United Artists (MGM/UA), 1982; *Movers and Shakers,* MGM/UA, 1985; *Bad Medicine,* Twentieth Centiury-Fox, 1985.

BILL MACY

PRINCIPAL TELEVISION APPEARANCES—Series: Walter Findlay, *Maude,* CBS, 1972-78; Louis Harper, *Hanging In,* CBS, 1979; *Nothing in Common,* NBC, 1987—. Movies: Myron Selznick, "The Scarlett O'Hara War," *Movieola,* 1980; Mr. Goldberger, *The Day the Bubble Burst.*

MEMBER: Actors' Equity Association, Screen Actors Guild, American Federation of Television and Radio Artists.

SIDELIGHTS: RECREATIONS—Photography, tennis, and reading.

ADDRESSES: AGENT—Harry Gold Associates, 12725 Ventura Blvd., Suite E, Studio City, CA 91604.

*   *   *

MAKEPEACE, Chris   1964-

PERSONAL: Born April 22, 1964, in Montreal, Quebec, Canada; son of Harry and Doreen Makepeace. EDUCATION: Attended Jarvis Collegiate Institute; trained for the stage at the Second City Workshop with Alan Guttman.

VOCATION: Actor.

CAREER: FILM DEBUT—Rudy Gerner, *Meatballs,* Cinepix/Paramount, 1979. PRINCIPAL FILM APPEARANCES—Clifford, *My Bodyguard,* Twentieth Century-Fox, 1980; Ring, *The Last Chase,*

CHRIS MAKEPEACE

© *BBC. Photography by DavidEdwards*

PATRICK MALAHIDE

Argosy, 1981; Darryl, *The Terry Fox Story,* Twentieth Century-Fox, 1983; Matt, *The Oasis,* Titan, 1984; David, *The Falcon and the Snowman,* Orion, 1984; Mike, *Hanauma Bay,* Hanauma Bay Productions, 1984; Keith, *Vamp,* New World, 1986.

TELEVISION DEBUT—August, *The Mysterious Stranger,* PBS, 1981. PRINCIPAL TELEVISION APPEARANCES—Movies: Jay Jay, *Mazes and Monsters,* CBS, 1982; Dennis and Jody, *The Undergrads,* Disney, 1985. Series: Host, *Going Great,* CBC, 1982-84.

MEMBER: Screen Actors Guild, Alliance of Canadian Television and Radio Artists.

ADDRESSES: AGENT—c/o Bob Gersh, The Gersh Agency, 222 N. Canon Drive, Suite 202, Beverly Hills, CA 90210. MANAGER—c/o Michael Oscars, Oscars-Abrams Agency, 59 Berkeley Street, Toronto, Canada M5A 2W5.

*　　　*　　　*

MALAHIDE, Patrick 1945-

PERSONAL: Born March 24, 1945, in Berkshire, England; married Rosi Wright, June 10, 1970; children: Liam, Mairi. EDUCATION: Attended Edinburgh University, 1963-65.

VOCATION: Actor and director.

CAREER: PRINCIPAL STAGE APPEARANCES—At the Royal Lyceum Theatre Company, Edinburgh, Scotland: Jimmy, *Look Back in Anger,* Proteus, *Two Gentlemen of Verona,* Sergius, *Arms and the Man,* Guildenstern, *Rosencrantz and Guildenstern Are Dead,* Adolphus Cusins, *Major Barbara,* Clov, *Endgame,* Teddy, *The Homecoming,* The Doctor, *Woyzeck,* and Antonio, *Twelfth Night.* the Fool, *King Lear,* Bristol Old Vic; Alexander Ivanov, *Every Good Boy Deserves Favour,* Traverse Theatre and the Scottish National Orchestra; Captain Andrei Vukhov, *Judgement,* Liverpool Playhouse, Edinbrugh Theatre Festival, Mickery Theatre in Amsterdam, and the Dublin Theatre Festival; Rev. Hale, *The Crucible* and Ariel, *The Tempest,* both with the Birmingham Repertory Company, 1979; Sneed, *Operation Bad Apple,* Royal Court Theatre, London, 1982; the Maniac, *The Accidental Death of an Anarchist,* Bristol Old Vic, U.K., 1982; Kenneth Halliwell, *Cockups,* Manchester Royal Exchange, U.K., 1983.

PRINCIPAL FILM APPEARANCES—*A Month in the Country; Comfort and Joy,* Universal, 1984; *The Killing Fields,* Warner Brothers, 1984.

PRINCIPAL TELEVISION APPEARANCES—England: Colin Anderson, *The Standard;* Mr. Chisholm, *Minder;* Mr. Jingle, *The Pickwick Papers;* title role, *Our Geoff;* Saul, *Charlie;* Binney, Finney, and Raymond, *The Singing Detective;* also: *Love Lies Bleeding; Snacker; Dying Day; The Black Adder; Videostars; Pity in History; The Russian Soldier; The December Rose.*

RELATED CAREER—Stage manager, Byre Theatre, St. Andrews Scotland, became director of productions, 1969-72.

AWARDS: Best Solo Performance, Edinburgh Festival Fringe.

SIDELIGHTS: RECREATIONS—Sailing and tennis.

ADDRESSES: AGENT—Kate Feast Management, 43A Princess Road, Regents Park, London NW1, England.

*   *   *

MALM, Mia   1962-

PERSONAL: Born October 18, 1962, in Ann Arbor, MI; daughter of William P. (an ethnomusicolgist) and Joyce A. (a modern dancer; maiden name, Rutherford) Malm. EDUCATION: Attended San Francisco School of the Arts, 1976-78; studied ballet with Maria Vegh at the Marin Ballet Company; trained for the stage at the Herbert Berghof Studios in New York City.

VOCATION: Actress and dancer.

CAREER: STAGE DEBUT—Dancer, *Make Mine Disco* (cabaret revue), Harrah's Lake Tahoe, NV, 1979. BROADWAY DEBUT—Chorus, *42nd Street,* Majestic Theatre, 1986. PRINCIPAL STAGE APPEARANCES—Soloist with the Marin Ballet Company, San Francisco; several roles, *Kicks: The Showgirl Musical,* workshop production, New York City; Joanne Marshall and Kate Gardner, *Smile,* workshop production and at the Lunt-Fontanne Theatre, New York City, 1986; singer, *A Celebration Honoring Jule Styne,* Avery Fisher Hall, New York City, 1987.

MIA MALM

MAJOR TOURS—Dancer and singer, *Dancin',* U.S., Italy, Paris, and Tokyo, Osaka, Fukuoka, and Nagoya, Japan, 1981-83.

FILM DEBUT—Extra, *Moscow on the Hudson,* Columbia, 1984. PRINCIPAL FILM APPEARANCES—Dream Girl, *Curtain Call,* Kadokawa Films, 1984; Apostle, *Joan-Lui,* Silver Films, 1985; dancer, *A Chorus Line,* Columbia, 1985; Maitre d', *Ishtar,* Columbia.

TELEVISION DEBUT—Dancer, *Dance Through Time,* Channel 11, San Francisco, 1978. PRINCIPAL TELEVISION APPEARANCES—Episodic: Girl in dance hall, *Capitol,* CBS, 1982. Videos: *Subway Surfin'.*

RELATED CAREER—Dance teacher, Marin Ballet School, 1978-79.

MEMBER: Actors' Equity Association, Screen Actors Guild, American Federation of Television and Radio Artists; Planned Parenthood (sustaining member), National Organization of Women.

SIDELIGHTS: Mia Malm told CTFT, "I became interested in dance as a small child. At 13, I went to study seriously in California, under the tutelage of Maria Vegh. However, at 16, I began to see that the ballet world was very sheltered and insular, and I wanted freedom of expression beyond the movement of my body in space. I discovered that I could sing and act, and that need for total expression brought me to New York. I enjoy drawing, watercolors, and reading of all sorts."

ADDRESSES: MANAGER—Landslide Management, 928 Broadway, New York, NY 10019.

*   *   *

MALTBY, Richard, Jr.   1937-

PERSONAL: Full name, Richard Eldridge Maltby, Jr.; born October 6, 1937, in Ripon, WI; son of Richard Eldridge and Virginia (Hosegood) Maltby; married Barbara Black Sudler (a script consultant), June 5, 1965; children: Nicholas Avery, David Stevenson. EDUCATION: Attended Phillips Exeter Academy; Yale University, B.A., 1959.

VOCATION: Director, writer, and lyricist.

CAREER: PRINCIPAL STAGE WORK—Director, *The Glass Menagerie,* Walnut Street Theatre, Philadelphia, 1975; director, *Long Day's Journey into Night,* Walnut Street Theatre, Philadelphia, 1976; adaptor and co-lyricist, *Daarlin' Juno,* Long Wharf Theatre, New Haven, CT, 1976; director and lyricist, *Starting Here, Starting Now,* Manhattan Theatre Club, New York City, 1977; director and conceiver, *Ain't Misbehavin',* Manhattan Theatre Club, then transferred to the Longacre Theatre, New York City, 1978, then Plymouth Theatre, New York City, 1979; director, *Street Songs,* Roundabout Theatre, New York City, 1980; director, *Livin' Dolls,* Manhattan Theatre Club, New York City, 1982; director, *An Evening of Sholom Aleichem,* Ballroom Theatre, New York City, 1983; director and lyricist, *Baby,* Ethel Barrymore Theatre, New York City, 1983; director and co-writer, *Hang on to the Good Times,* Manhattan Theatre Club, New York City, 1985.

MAJOR TOURS—Director, *Street Songs,* U.S. cities, 1975-79.

RELATED CAREER—Lyricist with composer Richard Shire.

NON-RELATED CAREER—Contributor of crossword puzzles to *Harpers Magazine.*

AWARDS: Best Director of a Musical, Antoinette Perry Award, 1978, for *Ain't Misbehavin';* Best Director of a Musical, Best Musical, and Best Musical Score, all Antoinette Perry Award nominations, 1984, for *Baby.*

MEMBER: Dramatists' Guild, Society of Stage Directors and Choreographers, American Society of Composers, Authors and Publishers (ASCAP).

ADDRESSES: AGENT—Flora Roberts, Inc., 157 W. 57th Street, New York, NY 10019.*

*   *   *

MANKIEWICZ, Don   1922-

PERSONAL: Born January 20, 1922, in Berlin, Germany; son of Herman J. (a writer) and Sara (Aaronson) Mankiewicz; married Ilene Korsen, March 26, 1946 (divorced, 1972); married Carol Bell Guidi, July 1, 1972; children: (first marriage) Jane, John; (second marriage) Jan, Sandy. EDUCATION: Columbia University, B.A., 1942, additional study at Columbia Law School. POLITICS: Democrat. MILITARY: U.S. Army, 1942-46.

VOCATION: Writer.

WRITINGS: SCREENPLAYS—(Collaboration) *Fast Company,* Metro-Goldwyn-Mayer (MGM), 1953; *Trial,* MGM, 1955; (with Nelson Gidding) *I Want to Live!,* United Artists, 1958; (collaboration) *The Chapman Report,* Warner Brothers, 1962; (collaboration) *Black Bird,* Columbia, 1975. TELEPLAYS—*Studio One,* CBS; *Playhouse 90,* CBS; *Kraft Television Theatre,* NBC; *Armstrong Circle Theatre,* NBC; *Profiles in Courage,* NBC; also *On Trial* and *One Step Beyond.* Pilot films: *Ironside,* NBC, 1967; *Marcus Welby, M.D.,* ABC, 1968; *Sarge: The Badge or the Cross,* NBC, 1970; (collaboration) *Lanigan's Rabbi,* NBC, 1976; (collaboration) *Rosetti and Ryan,* NBC, 1977.

BOOKS—*See How They Run,* Knopf, 1950; *Trial,* Harper, 1955; *It Only Hurts a Minute,* Putnam, 1967.

RELATED CAREER—Reporter, *New Yorker* magazine, 1946-48; free-lance writer, 1948—; contributor to *Collier's, Cosmopolitan, Esquire, Saturday Evening Post.*

AWARDS: Harper Prize Novel Award, 1955, for *Trial;* Best Screenplay, Academy Award nomination, 1958, for *I Want to Live!;* Emmy Award nominations, 1966, for *Ironside* and 1968, for *Marcus Welby, M.D.;* Edgar Allen Poe Award, 1978, for *Rosetti and Ryan.*

MEMBER: Writers Guild, National Academy of Television Arts and Sciences, Producer's Guild of America (board of directors), American Society of Composers, Authors, and Publishers (ASCAP).

SIDELIGHTS: CTFT learned that Don Mankiewicz is active in Democratic Party politics, having been a Democratic-Liberal candidate for the New York Assembly in 1952, vice-chairman of the Nassau County Democratic Committee, 1953-72, and a delegate-at-large for the New York State Constitutional Convention in 1967.

ADDRESSES: HOME—3944 El Lado Drive, La Crescenta, CA 91214. OFFICE—Two Prospect Avenue, Sea Cliff, Long Island, NY 11579. AGENT—Harold Ober Associates, 40 E. 49th Street, New York, NY 10017.

*   *   *

MARCUS, Lawrence B.   1925-

PERSONAL: Born July 19, 1925, in Beaver, UT; son of Abe (a businessman) and Jenny (Gold) Marcus; children: Andrew. MILITARY: U.S. Air Force, 1943-46.

VOCATION: Writer and teacher.

WRITINGS: SCREENPLAYS—Eighteen feature films including: *Witness for the Prosecution,* United Artists, 1958; *Petulia,* Warner Brothers, 1968; (co-author with Richard Nash) *The Stunt Man,* Twentieth Century-Fox, 1980.

TELEVISION—Over 200 scripts for pilots, series, and specials, for all three major networks.

RELATED CAREER—Instructor, New York University, 1984-86.

AWARDS: Writers Guild of America Award; Christopher Award; Alfred Sloan Award; Golden Globe Award. Five additional award nominations from the Writers Guild of America; Best Screenplay Written Directly for the Screen, Academy Award nomination, 1980, for *The Stunt Man.*

MEMBER: Academy of Motion Picture Arts and Sciences, Writers Guild of America.

SIDELIGHTS: Lawrence B. Marcus wrote *CTFT* that he loved writing and that "of it all, radio writing was most satisfying because it gave me complete freedom."

ADDRESSES: AGENT—c/o Ben Benjamin, International Creative Management, Inc., 8899 Beverly Blvd., Los Angeles, CA 90048.

*   *   *

MARK, Judi

PERSONAL: Born Judith Ann March, March 20, in Chicago, IL; daughter of Leonard (an electronic engineer) and Dorothy (a pianist) March. EDUCATION: Southern Illinois University, B.S., education; graduate work in choreography, San Diego State University and the U.S. International University of Performing Arts. RELIGION: Jewish.

VOCATION: Actress, dancer, and choreographer.

CAREER: OFF-BROADWAY DEBUT—Sicilian woman and choreographer, *Three by Pirandello,* Colonnades Theatre, for twenty-

JUDI MARK

three performances. PRINCIPAL STAGE APPEARANCES—Dancer, U.S. International Dance Theatre, Balboa Park Theatre, San Diego, CA; Anita, *West Side Story*, Rosa, *The Rose Tattoo*, and Lizzie Curry, *The Rainmaker*, all with the Niles Repertory Theatre; *Quindo's Window*, Kennedy Theatre; the Queen, *The Emperor's New Clothes*, Thirteenth Street Theatre, New York City.

PRINCIPAL STAGE WORK—Choreographer and dancer: *Time* and *Involvement*, both at San Diego State University, CA, 1975; *Where's My Friend*, Stage 7, San Diego, 1975; "Judi Mark & Company," San Diego State College, 1977.

PRINCIPAL FILM APPEARANCES—*Deathtrap*, Warner Brothers, 1982; *Turk 182!*, Twentieth Century-Fox, 1985; *Private Resorts*, 1986; also choreographer, *Berlin*, independent.

PRINCIPAL TELEVISION APPEARANCES—Guest: *Miami Vice*, NBC; guest vocalist on cable programs.

PRINCIPAL CABARET PERFORMANCES—Lead dancer, "The Gypsy and the Preacher," Club Meditteranne, Hanalei, Hawaii, 1977; soloist, Byblos Nightclub, Port Au Prince, Haiti, 1979; soloist, Club Meditterannee, Cancun, Mexico, 1979.

RELATED CAREER—Founder and choreographer, Judi Mark & Company Dance Company; dance teacher, P.S. 190, New York City, 1986—.

NON-RELATED CAREER—Elementary school teacher, Dade County Schools, 4th and 5th grades, 1970-74.

MEMBER: American Federation of Television and Radio Artists.

SIDELIGHTS: Judi Mark commented to *CTFT* that her "childhood success in the arts encouraged her professional pursuit." She has travelled to Europe, the Caribbean, and all over the United States.

ADDRESSES: HOME—303 E. 83rd Street, New York, NY 10028.

*　　*　　*

MARSDEN, Les   1957-

PERSONAL: Born Les Marderosian, February 26, 1957, in Fresno, CA; son of Kay (a salesman) and Helen (Boornazian) Marderosian; married Diane Thorson (a conservationist), January 20, 1985. EDUCATION: California State University at Fresno, M.A., 1978; trained for the stage with William Gibson, Anthony Quayle, Donovan Marley, Richard Johnson, Lisa Harrow, James Moll, Laird Williamson, Bernard Lloyd, Charles Keating, and Allen Fletcher.

VOCATION: Actor, composer, and writer.

CAREER: STAGE DEBUT—Ivar Helmer, *A Doll's House*, Fresno Community Theatre, Fresno, CA 1971, for thirty performances. OFF-BROADWAY DEBUT—Chico and Harpo, *Groucho*, Theatre de Lys, 1986. PRINCIPAL STAGE APPEARANCES—At California State University, Fresno: *The Homecoming, The Merchant of*

LES MARSDEN

Venice, The Little Foxes, The Cherry Orchard, What the Butler Saw, The Visit, Tiny Alice, Zorba, and *Macbeth.* Ensemble, *South Pacific* and Diamond Louis, *The Front Page,* both with Pacific Coast Performing Arts, CA; Miklos Kipnos, *Guys Like Me and Bogie,* Edinburgh Festival, Scotland; Groucho, *Minnie's Boys,* Bank Playhouse; Harpo, *A Night at Harpo's,* Bank Playhouse and CAST Theatre, Los Angeles; Arthur Lee, *See My Lawyer,* Little Oscar Theatre, Los Angeles.

MAJOR TOURS—Chico and Harpo, *Groucho,* U.S. cities, 1986.

PRINCIPAL STAGE WORK—Musical director: *Telethon Fool, Annie Get Your Gun, Guys and Dolls.*

TELEVISION DEBUT—Harpo Marx, *Matt Houston,* CBS, 1984. PRINCIPAL TELEVISION APPEARANCES—*New Bob Newhart Show,* CBS, 1985; *T.V. Bloopers and Practical Jokes,* NBC, 1985. Guest: *Good Morning America,* ABC, 1985.

FILM DEBUT—Allen Ginsberg, *Kerouac Looking Back,* Independent, 1979. PRINCIPAL FILM APPEARANCES—*E. Nick: A Legend in His Own Mind,* Independent, 1984.

RELATED CAREER—Portrays Groucho Marx for MCA/Universal Studios publicity, tours, etc., 1984—.

WRITINGS: PLAYS, PRODUCED—Creator (one-man show), A Night at Harpo's, Bank Playhouse and CAST Theatre, Los Angeles.

SCORES—Composer of original scores for: *Telethon Fool, The Country Wife, Tom Jones, The Cherry Orchard.*

SIDELIGHTS: Les Marsden told *CTFT:* "I entered this profession strictly for the money. I can't understand, therefore, what has kept me in this profession."

ADDRESSES: HOME—Seven Pomander Walk, New York, NY 10025. OFFICE—14607 Erwin Street, Suite 306, Van Nuys, CA 91411. AGENT—David Sacks-Mark Levin Associates, 208 S. Beverly Drive, Beverly Hills, CA 90212; c/o Don Schwartz, Don Schwartz Associates, 8721 Sunset Blvd., Los Angeles, CA 90069.

*   *   *

MARTIN, William   1937-

PERSONAL: Born September 6, 1937, in Pueblo, CO; son of William George (a deputy sheriff) and Lois Elaine (Bunner) Martin. EDUCATION: Bob Jones University, B.A., 1962, M.A., 1964; University of Wisconsin, Ph.D., American Theatre History, 1971. MILITARY: U.S. Naval Air Corps, 1956-58.

VOCATION: Director, producer, and writer.

CAREER: FIRST STAGE WORK—Director, *The Student Prince,* Lakewood Musical Playhouse, PA, 1972. PRINCIPAL STAGE WORK—Director: *Iolanthe,* Village Light Opera Company, New York City, 1972; *You Can't Take It with You,* Wilkes College, PA; *Blood Wedding,* Florida Atlantic University; *The Tempest,* Mars Hill College, NC; *Dark of the Moon,* Boston University; *Twelfth Night* and *Alice in Wonderland,* both with the Empire State Youth Theatre, NY; *The Taming of the Shrew,* Columbus College, GA; *Life with Father,* Auburn University, AL; *The Inspector General,*

WILLIAM MARTIN

University of Washington; *A Memory for Saturday,* University of Virginia; *Richard III,* Viterbo College, WI.

Director: *Song of Norway,* Surflight Summer Theatre, NJ; *Finian's Rainbow,* Club Bene Dinner Theatre, NJ; *The Pirates of Penzance,* Florence Little Theatre, SC; *The Waltz of the Toreadors,* Madison Civic Repertory Theatre, WI; *On Golden Pond, Magnets,* and *To Kill a Mockingbird,* all Southern Appalachian Repertory Theatre, NC; *Treemonisha,* Richmond Opera Company, VA; *The Second Greatest Entertainer in the Whole Wide World,* Boston Repertory Theatre, MA.

At the Heritage Repertory Theatre, Charlottesville, VA, 1984-85, directed: *That Man Jefferson, She Would Be a Soldier, The Drunkard, Look Homeward Angel, The Cat and the Canary, Ring Round the Moon, The Crucifer of Blood, Death of a Salesman, George Washington Slept Here, The Three Musketeers.*

Directed: *Murder on the Nile,* Minnesota Repertory Theatre, MN; *The Commedia World of Lafcadio "B",* New York City; *A Shriek to Melt the Texas Moon,* New York City; *Princess Ida,* Village Light Opera Company, New York City; *Sticks and Stones,* Circle in the Square, New York City, then at New York University; *Except in My Memory,* Neighborhood Group Theatre, New York City; *I Used to Be a Rock-'n-Roll Star,* Manhattan Theatre Club; *The Frequency,* WPA Theatre, New York City; *Northern Boulevard,* AMAS Repertory Theatre, New York City; *Cowboy and the Legend,* Burt Reynolds Dinner Theatre, FL; *The Lieutenant,* Lyceum Theatre, New York City, 1974.

Assistant director, *Seascape,* Shubert Theatre, 1975.

Assistant producer: *Noel Coward in Two Keys,* Ethel Barrymore Theatre, 1974 and *Golda,* Morosco Theatre, 1977.

RELATED CAREER—Assistant to Edward Albee as coordinator of his playwright's foundation, the William Flanagan Memorial Center for Creative Persons, Montauk, NY, 1975-76. Critic, lecturer, and instructor: Usdan Center for the Performing Arts, NY, 1975-76; Madison Civic Repertory Theartre Classes, WI; Henrico County Schools and Humanitites Center, teacher in-service training, Richmond, VA, 1978; Tennessee Theatre Association Convention, 1978-79; International Thespians Society Conference, 1980; Delaware State Play Festival, 1979-80; South Carolina Theatre Conference, 1980-81; North Carolina Theatre Conference, 1981; Alabama Theatre League, 1982; Town Theatre Acting Festivals, Charlotte, NC, 1982; American College Theatre Festivals, 1978-83; American Theatre Association, National Conventions, 1978-83; Virginia High School League, State Festival, 1984; United States Institute of Theatre Technology Conference, 1985; Furman University, SC, 1986; Community Theatre Association, 1984-86; New England Theatre Conference, 1983-86; Southeastern Theatre Conference, 1979-86; artistic director, Heritage Repertory Theatre, Charlottesville, VA, 1984-85.

WRITINGS: PLAYS, PRODUCED—(with David Cupp) *That Man Jefferson,* Heritage Repertory Theatre, Charlottesville, VA, 1976; *Some Day Just Began,* Henrico County Schools, 1983; adaptation, *The Three Musketeers,* Heritage Repertory Theatre, 1985.

AWARDS: Best Director, Drama Desk Award nomination, 1975, for *The Lieutenant.*

MEMBER: Society of Stage Directors and Choreographers (board of trustees; past member of the executive board); John Philip Sousa Operetta Company, Inc. (vice-president).

ADDRESSES: HOME—222 W. 83rd Street, Apt. 32, New York, NY 10024.

*   *   *

MARVIN, Mel   1941-

PERSONAL: Born November 24, 1941, in Walterboro, SC; son of Melvin Williams (a farmer) and Louise Strother (a teacher; maiden name, Smalley) Marvin; married Angela Harman Wigan (a writer), December 18, 1965; children: Katharine Lesley. EDUCATION: Attended the College of Charleston, B.S., 1962; Columbia University, M.A., 1965.

VOCATION: Composer and director.

CAREER: PRINCIPAL STAGE WORK—As composer: *Jubilee,* Dock Street Theatre, Charleston, 1962; *Shoemakers' Holiday,* Orpheum Theatre, New York City, 1967; *Rare Fine Towne,* Dock Street Theatre, Charleston, 1970; *Horatio,* Loretto Hilton Center, St. Louis, MO, 1971, then restaged at the Arena Stage, Washington, DC, and at the American Conservatory Theatre, San Francisco, 1974; *Amerikan Schrapnel,* American Shakespeare Festival, Stratford, CT, 1971; *The Elinor Glyn Love Regatta,* Repertory Theatre of New Orleans, 1972; *Prizewinning Plays of the 1920's,*

Manhattan Theatre Club, New York City, 1973; *Variety Obit,* Cherry Lane Theatre, New York City, 1973; *I, Said the Fly,* Tyrone Guthrie Theatre, Minneapolis, 1973; *The Portable Pioneer and Prairie Show,* first produced at the Tyrone Guthrie Theatre, Minneapolis, 1974, restaged at Ford's Theatre, Washington, DC, 1975, later produced at the Portland Stage Company, ME, 1984, and at the Manhattan Theatre Club, New York City, 1985; *Yentl,* Chelsea Theatre Center, New York City, 1974, then at the Eugene O'Neill Theatre, New York City, 1976; *Polly,* Chelsea Theatre Center, New York City, 1975; *Gorky,* American Place Theatre, New York City, 1975.

Composer: *The Prince of Homburg* and *Lincoln,* both at the Chelsea Theatre Center, New York City, 1976; *Marvin's Garden,* Manhattan Theatre Club, New York City, 1976; *An American Mass,* Episcopal Diocese of South Carolina, 1976; *The National Health,* Arena Stage, Washington, DC, 1976; *A History of the American Film,* Arena Stage, Washington, DC, 1977, then at the American National Theatre and Academy (ANTA) Theatre, New York City, 1978; *Green Pond,* Stage South and Spoleto Festival, Charelston, 1977; *Tales from the Vienna Woods* and *Ah Wilderness!,* 1978, and *The Winter's Tale,* 1979, all Arena Stage, Washington, DC; *Das Lusitania Songspiel,* Chelsea Westside Theatre, New York City, 1979; *Back County Crimes,* Temple University Theatre, Philadelphia, 1979; *Tintypes,* Arena Stage, Washington, DC, 1979, then at the John Golden Theatre, New York City, 1980, and at the Mark Taper Forum, Los Angeles, 1981; *The Glass Menagerie,* Tyrone Guthrie Theatre, 1980; *Funeral March for a One-Man Band,* St. Nicholas Theatre, Chicago, 1980.

Composer: *Constance and the Musician,* American Place Theatre, New York City and the GeVa Theatre, Rochester, NY, 1982; *Cymbeline,* Arena Stage, Washington, DC, 1982; *The Great Magoo,* 1982, and *As You Like It,* 1983, both Hartford Stage Company; *The Empress of China,* Cincinnati Playhouse in the Park, Cincinnati, 1984; *Beloved Friend,* Hartman Theatre Company, Stamford, CT, 1984; *The Hoffman Project* and *The Tempest,* both Hartford Stage Company, 1985; *Twelfth Night,* St. Louis Repertory Theatre, 1985; *The Cherry Orchard,* Portland Stage Company, 1985; *Legs,* Musical Theatre Works, New York City, 1985; *The Haunted Palace,* staged reading, Chelsea Theatre Center, New York City, 1986; *The Gilded Age* and *A Doll's House,* both at the Hartford Stage Company, 1986.

As director: *The Curse of the Starving Class* and *The Real Thing,* both at the Portland Stage Company, 1986.

WRITINGS: COMPOSITIONS, PUBLISHED—Musicals: *Variety Obit,* Samuel French, Inc., 1973; *Gorky,* Samuel French, Inc., 1976; *A History of the American Film,* Samuel French, Inc., 1978; *Back County Crimes,* Samuel French, Inc., 1980; *Tintypes,* Music Theatre International, 1981; *The Portable Pioneer and Prairie Show,* Music Theatre International, 1985. SONGS, PUBLISHED—*Green Pond,* G. Schimer, Inc., 1977.

RECORDINGS: ALBUMS—*Tintypes,* DRG Records, 1981.

AWARDS: National Endowment Associate Artist, 1985.

MEMBER: American Federation of Musicians, Dramatists Guild, National Association of Recording Arts & Sciences.

ADDRESSES: AGENT—Ellen Neuwald, Inc., 905 West End Avenue, New York, NY 10025.

MASSEY, Anna 1937-

PERSONAL: Born August 11, 1937, in Thakeham, Sussex, England; daughter of Raymond Hart (an actor) and Adrianne (Allen) Massey; married Jeremy Brett (an actor; divorced). EDUCATION: Attended schools in London, New York, Switzerland, France, and Italy.

VOCATION: Actress.

CAREER: STAGE DEBUT—Jane, *The Reluctant Debutante,* Theatre Royal, Brighton, U.K., 1955. LONDON DEBUT—Jane, *The Reluctant Debutante,* Cambridge Theatre, 1955. BROADWAY DEBUT—Jane, *The Reluctant Debutante,* Henry Miller's Theatre, 1956. PRINCIPAL STAGE APPEARANCES—Penelope Shawn, *Dear Delinquent,* Westminster Theatre, London, 1957; Monica Claverton-Ferry, *The Elder Statesman,* Lyceum Theatre, Edinburgh Festival, Scotland, and at the Cambridge Theatre, London, 1958; Jane, *Special Providence,* St. Martin's Theatre, London, 1960; Rose, *The Last Joke,* Phoenix Theatre, London, 1960; Annie Sullivan, *The Miracle Worker,* Royalty Theatre, London, 1961; Lady Teazle, *School for Scandal,* Haymarket Theatre, London, 1962; Jennifer Dubedat, *The Doctor's Dilemma,* Haymarket Theatre, London, 1963; Virginia Crawford, *The Honourable Gentleman,* Her Majesty's Theatre, London, 1964; Laura Wingfield, *The Glass Menagerie,* Yvonne Arnaud Theatre, Guildford, U.K., and at the Haymarket Theatre, London, 1965.

Title role, *The Prime of Miss Jean Brodie,* Wyndham's Theatre, London, 1966; Julia, *First Day of a New Season,* Yvonne Arnaud Theatre, Guilford, 1967; Candida, *The Flip Side,* Apollo Theatre, London, 1967; Rowena Highbury, *This Space Is Mine,* Hampstead Theatre Club, London, 1969; Ophelia, *Hamlet,* Birmingham Repertory Theatre, U.K., 1970; Joanna, *Spoiled,* Haymarket Theatre, London, 1971; Ann, *Slag,* Royal Court Theatre, London, 1971; Ariadne Utterword, *Heartbreak House,* with the Old Vic Theatre Company at the National Theatre, London, 1975; Gwendoline, *Jingo,* with the Royal Shakespeare Company at the Aldwych Theatre, London, 1975; First Woman, *Play,* Royal Court Theatre, London, 1976; Lady Driver, *Donkey's Years,* Globe Theatre, London, 1977; Marianne, *Close of Play,* National Theatre, London, 1979.

FILM DEBUT—Sally, *Gideon's Day,* 1957. PRINCIPAL FILM APPEARANCES—*Peeping Tom,* 1960; *Bunny Lake Is Missing,* Columbia, 1965; *The Looking Glass War,* Columbia, 1970; *Frenzy,* Universal, 1972; *A Doll's House,* Paramount, 1973; *A Little Romance,* Orion, 1979; *Sweet William,* Kendon Films, 1979.

TELEVISION DEBUT—Jacqueline, *Green of the Year,* 1955. PRINCIPAL TELEVISION APPEARANCES—Movies: *David Copperfield,* 1970; *The Corn Is Green,* 1979; also *Remember the Germans; Wicked Woman; Sakharov; The Mayor of Casterbridge; Rebecca; You're Not Watching Me, Mummy.*

MEMBER: British Actors' Equity Association.

ADDRESSES: AGENT—c/o Norman Boyack, Nine Cork Street, London, W1, England.*

*   *   *

MASTRANTONIO, Mary Elizabeth 1958-

PERSONAL: Born November 17, 1958, in Lombard, IL; daughter of Frank A. (a foundry owner) and Mary D. (Pagone) Mastrantonio.

EDUCATION: Attended University of Illinois, 1976-78; studied in New York City.

VOCATION: Actress and singer.

CAREER: STAGE DEBUT—Lady Sybil, *Camelot,* Marriot Lincolnshire, IL, 1979. BROADWAY DEBUT—Understudy, Maria, *West Side Story,* 1980. PRINCIPAL STAGE APPEARANCES—Dore Spenlow, *Copperfield* and Musica, *Oh, Brother!,* both at the American National Theatre and Academy (ANTA) Theatre, New York City, 1981; Katerina Cavalieri and Constanza, *Amadeus,* Broadhurst Theatre, New York City, 1982; Celeste number two, *Sunday in the Park with George,* Playwrights Horizons, New York City, 1983; Bess Macauley, *The Human Comedy,* New York Shakespeare Festival (NYSF), Public/Anspacher Theatre, then Royale Theatre, New York City, 1984; Katharine, *Henry V,* NYSF, Delacorte Theatre, New York City, 1984; *Figaro,* Circle in the Square, New York City, 1985; Isabella, *Measure for Measure,* NYSF, Delacorte Theatre, New York City, 1985; *The Knife,* NYSF, Public/Newman Theatre, New York City, 1987.

FILM DEBUT—Gina Montana, *Scarface,* Universal, 1983. PRINCIPAL FILM APPEARANCES—*The Color of Money,* Touchstone Films, 1986.

PRINCIPAL TELEVISION APPEARANCES—*Mussolini: The Untold Story,* NBC, 1985.

AWARDS: Best Supporting Actress, Academy Award nomination, 1986, for *The Color of Money.*

ADDRESSES: AGENT—J. Michael Bloom, 400 Madison Avenue, New York, NY 10019.*

*   *   *

MAY, Winston 1937-

PERSONAL: Born February 3, 1937; son of John B. (a farmer) and Eula (Newsom) May. EDUCATION: Arkansas State University, B.F.A., 1957; trained for the stage at the American Theatre Wing. MILITARY: U.S. Army Reserves, 1959-60.

VOCATION: Actor.

CAREER: STAGE DEBUT—Gentleman Caller, *The Glass Menagerie,* Cape Playhouse, Dennis, MA, 1959, for nine performances. OFF-BROADWAY DEBUT—Judge, *The Bond,* Roundabout Theatre, 1967, for twenty-one performances. PRINCIPAL STAGE APPEARANCES—Edmund, *King Lear,* Morell, *Candida,* Plume, *Trumpets and Drums,* Sandor, *The Play's the Thing,* The Count, *The Fan,* Captain, *The Father,* and Astrov, *Uncle Vanya,* all at the Roundabout Theatre, New York City, 1968-74; Brad, *Everybody Loves Opal,* Meadowbrook Theatre, Detroit, 1972; *Servant of Two Masters,* Equity Library Theatre, New York City, 1973; Nick, *The Autumn Garden,* Joseph Jefferson Theatre, Chicago, 1975; Dr. Lyman, *Bus Stop,* Playhouse on the Mall, Paramus, NJ, 1975; Steve, *How Do You Live with Love,* White Barn Theatre, 1975; Daugherty, *Villager,* Lion Theatre, New York City, 1982. Also Mott, *Madmen,* Walden Theatre Conservatory, New York City.

PRINCIPAL FILM APPEARANCES—Jeweler, *A Little Sex,* Universal, 1982; businessman, *Ghostbusters,* Columbia, 1984.

WINSTON MAY

TELEVISION DEBUT—Dr. Marshall, *Search for Tomorrow*, NBC, 1974. PRINCIPAL TELEVISION APPEARANCES—Sergeant Murphy and Jack Kincaid, *All My Children*, ABC, 1980; Dr. Brown and maitre'd at L'Auberge, *Another World*, NBC, 1981; D.A. Reidy, *Search for Tomorrow*, NBC, 1984; Mr. Hanson, *One Life to Live*, ABC, 1985.

RELATED CAREER—Has also acted and been featured in commericals and industrial films for A.T.& T., Minolta, J.C. Penney, and Metropolitan Life, among others.

ADDRESSES: HOME—261 Broadway, New York, NY 10007. AGENT—Roxy Horen Management, 300 W. 17th Street, New York, NY 10011.

*   *   *

MAYSLES, David   1933-1987

PERSONAL: Born 1933, in Boston, MA; died following a stroke in New York, NY, January 3, 1987; married; children: one son, one daughter. EDUCATION: Attended Boston University. MILITARY: U.S. Army, intelligence school.

VOCATION: Film producer.

CAREER: PRINCIPAL FILM WORK—Assistant to producer, *Bus Stop*, Twentieth Century-Fox, 1956; *The Prince and the Showgirl*,

1957. (All with his brother, Albert) Producer of documentaries: *Showman*, 1962; producer and co-director, *Salesman*, 1968; *Gimme Shelter*, Cinema V, 1970; *Christo's Valley Curtain*, 1973; (also with Ellen Hovde, Muffie Meyer, and Susan Froemke) *Grey Gardens*, 1976; *Running Fence*, 1976; (also with Froemke, Deborah Dickson, and Pat Jaffe) *Vladimir Horowitz: The Last Romantic*, 1983; (also with Froemke and Dickson) *Ozawa*, 1984; *Islands*, 1985; also *What's Happening! The Beatles in the U.S.A.*, *Meet Marlon Brando*, and other nonfiction features and television films, including *Blue Yonder*, upcoming.

RELATED CAREER—Founder with his brother Albert, Maysles Production Company, 1962.

AWARDS: Best Short Story Documentary, Academy Award nomination, 1973, for *Christo's Valley Curtain*.

SIDELIGHTS: David Maysles and his brother became known for their "direct cinema" approach to filmmaking. Utilizing hand held cameras to capture slices of daily life, they made over two dozen nonfiction features since forming their company.*

*   *   *

McCALL, Kathleen

PERSONAL: Born January 11, in Denver, CO; daughter of Donald Leon (a high school principal) and Jo Ann (a grade school principal; maiden name, Hickman) McCall; married Kim R. Morerer (an

KATHLEEN McCALL

actor) May 31, 1981 (divorced, 1987). EDUCATION: Moorehead State University, B.A., theatre arts; graduate, London Academy of Music and Dramatic Art, London. POLITICS: Independent.

VOCATION: Actress.

CAREER: STAGE DEBUT—Minnie Fay, *The Matchmaker,* Straw Hat Players, Moorhead, MN, 1979. PRINCIPAL STAGE APPEARANCES—Sonya, *Uncle Vanya,* Mistress Quickly, *The Merry Wives of Windsor,* Lady Anne, *Richard III,* and Lady Brute, *The Provoked Wife,* all at the London Academy of Music and Dramatic Art; title role, *Colette,* Bianca, *The Taming of the Shrew,* Leilah, *Uncommon Women and Others,* and Viola, *Twelfth Night,* all at the Center for the Arts, Moorhead; Sandy, *The Prime of Miss Jean Brodie* and Abigail, *The Crucible,* both at the Straw Hat Players Theatre, Moorhead.

Chrissy, *In the Boom Boom Room,* Theatre in the Round, Minneapolis, 1984; Irena, *The Three Sisters,* Park Square Theatre, St. Paul, 1984; Carol, *Thanksgiving,* Manhattan Class Company, New York City, 1985; Joyce, *And a Nightingale Sang,* Cincinnati Playhouse in the Park, OH, 1986.

MAJOR TOURS—Heather, *Doubles,* U.S. cities, 1986-87.

TELEVISION DEBUT Nurse Dottie, *The Guiding Light,* CBS, 1984-85. PRINCIPAL TELEVISION APPEARANCES—Zona Boocham, *Loving,* ABC, 1985-86.

NON-RELATED CAREER—Certified lifeguard and instructor, 1976—.

AWARDS: Finalist, University Resident Theatre Association.

MEMBER: Actors' Equity Association, Screen Actors Guild, American Federation of Television and Radio Artists.

SIDELIGHTS: Kathleen McCall informed *CTFT,* "My mom got me into this business." RECREATIONS—"Very athletic, outdoors person."

ADDRESSES: AGENT—Ambrosio & Mortimer and Associates, 165 W. 46th Street, Suite 1109, New York, NY 10036.

*   *   *

McCARTHY, Frank   1912-1986

PERSONAL: Born June 8, 1912, in Richmond, VA; died of cancer in Woodland Hills, CA, December 1, 1986; son of Frank J. (an insurance broker) and Lillian (Binford) McCarthy. EDUCATION: Virginia Military Institute, A.B., 1933; University of Virginia, M.A., 1940. RELIGION: Episcopalian. MILITARY: U.S. Army, 1933-45.

VOCATION: Producer.

CAREER: PRINCIPAL FILM WORK—Technical advisor, *Brother Rat,* 1938; producer: *Decision Before Dawn,* Twentieth Century-Fox, 1951; *Sailor of the King* (also known as *Single Handed*), Twentieth Century-Fox, 1953; *A Guide for the Married Man,* Twentieth Century-Fox, 1967; *Patton,* Twentieth Century-Fox, 1970; *MacArthur,* Universal, 1977.

PRINCIPAL TELEVISION WORK—Movies: Producer, *Fireball Forward,* 1972.

RELATED CAREER—Press agent for theatrical producer George Abbott, New York City, 1937-39; representative, Motion Picture Association of America, Hollywood and European cities, 1946-49; executive and producer, Twentieth Century-Fox Studios, 1949-62, 1965-72; producer, Universal Studios, 1963-65, 1972-77.

NON-RELATED CAREER—Instructor and tactical officer, Virginia Military Institute 1933-35, 1936-37; reporter, *Richmond News Leader,* VA, 1935-36; brigadier general, U.S. Army, 1940-45; secretary of War Department, general staff, 1944-45; assistant secretary of state, United States Department of State, 1945-46; alternate delegate, United Nations Conference on Freedom of Information, Geneva, 1948.

AWARDS: Order of the British Empire; Best Picture, Academy Award, 1970, for *Patton;* Virginian of the Year, Virginia Press Association, 1970; One of America's Ten Outstanding Young Men Award, U.S. Junior Chamber of Commerce, 1945; Distinguished Service Medal, Legion of Merit.

MEMBER: Academy of Motion Picture Arts and Sciences, Los Angeles Center Theatre Group; Motion Picture and Television Relief Fund, Motion Picture Permanent Charities Commission, Norton Simon Museum of Art (vice president, board of directors); George C. Marshall Research Foundation (trustee), Virginia Military Institute Society, Virginia Historical Society.

SIDELIGHTS: CTFT learned that Frank McCarthy rose from the rank of second lieutenant in the Army Reserves in 1933, to the rank of brigadier general in the U.S. Army.*

*   *   *

McCARTHY, Kevin   1914-

PERSONAL: Born Feburary 14, 1914, in Seattle, WA; son of Roy Winfield and Martha Therese (Preston) McCarthy; married Augusta Dabney (divorced). EDUCATION: Attended School of Foreign Service, Georgetown University, 1933-34; attended University of Minnesota, 1936-38; trained for the stage at the Actors Studio. MILITARY: U.S. Air Force and U.S. Military Police, 1942-45.

VOCATION: Actor.

CAREER: FILM DEBUT— Biff, *Death of a Salesman,* Columbia, 1951. PRINCIPAL FILM APPEARANCES—*Drive a Crooked Road,* Columbia, 1954; *Gambler from Natchez,* Twentieth Century-Fox, 1954; *Stranger on Horseback,* United Artists, 1955; *Annapolis Story,* Allied Artists, 1955; *Nightmare,* United Artists, 1956; *Invasion of the Body Snatchers,* Allied Artists, 1956; *Nightmare,* United Artists, 1956; *Forty Pounds of Trouble,* Universal, 1962; *A Gathering of Eagles,* Universal, 1963; *The Prize,* Metro-Goldwyn-Mayer (MGM), 1963; *An Affair of the Skin,* Zenith, 1964; *The Best Man,* Warner Brothers, 1964; *Mirage,* Universal, 1965; *A Big Hand for the Little Lady,* Warner Brothers, 1966; *Hotel,* Warner Brothers, 1967; *To Hell with Heroes,* Universal, 1968; *If He Hollars, Let Him Go!,* Paramount, 1968; *Ace High,* Paramount, 1969; *Kansas City Bomber,* MGM, 1972; *Buffalo Bill and the Indians,* United Artists, 1976; *Invasion of the Body Snatchers* (remake), United Artists, 1978; *Hero at Large,* United Artists,

1980; *Those Lips, Those Eyes,* United Artists, 1980; *The Howling,* 1981; *Dark Tower,* Spectrafilm (upcoming).

PRINCIPAL TELEVISION APPEARANCES—Series: Philip Hastings, *The Survivors,* ABC, 1970; Claude Weldon, *Flamingo Road,* NBC, 1981-82; Zack Cartwright, *Amanda's,* ABC, 1983. Episodic: Romeo, "Romeo and Juliet," *Cameo Theatre,* NBC, 1949; "Antigone," *Omnibus,* CBS; *Studio One,* CBS; *U.S. Steel Hour,* ABC; *Goodyear Playhouse,* NBC; *Climax,* CBS; *DuPont Theatre,* ABC; *Kraft Television Theatre,* NBC; *Twilight Zone,* CBS; *Ben Casey,* ABC; *Breaking Point,* ABC; *Dr. Kildare,* NBC; *Burke's Law,* ABC; *Alfred Hitchcock,* CBS; *The Fugitive,* ABC; *The F.B.I.,* ABC; *The Man from U.N.C.L.E.,* NBC; *Judd for the Defense,* ABC; *Hawaii Five-O,* CBS; *Mission: Impossible,* CBS; *The Name of the Game,* NBC.

Movies: *U.M.C.,* CBS, 1969; *A Great American Tragedy,* ABC, 1972; *The Making of a Male Model,* ABC, 1983; *Deadly Intentions,* ABC, 1985; *The Midnight Hour,* ABC, 1985; *A Masterpiece of Murder,* NBC, 1986; Joe Kennedy, *LBJ: The Early Years,* NBC, 1987; *Home,* ABC, 1987. Mini-Series: Franklyn Hutton, *Poor Little Rich Girl,* NBC, 1987.

BROADWAY DEBUT—Jasp and Phil, *Abe Lincoln in Illinois,* Plymouth Theatre, 1938. LONDON DEBUT—Biff, *Death of a Salesman,* Phoenix Theatre, 1949. PRINCIPAL STAGE APPEARANCES—Dan Crawford, *Brother Rat,* Wharburton Square Playhouse, Yonkers, NY, 1938; Richard Banning, *Flight to the West,* Guild Theatre, New York City, 1940; *Mexican Mural,* Chanin Building, Penthouse Theatre, New York City, 1942; Ronny Meade, *Winged Victory,* 44th Street Theatre, New York City, 1943; Maurice, *Truckline Cafe,* Belasco Theatre, New York City, 1946; Dunois, *Joan of Lorraine,* Alvin Theatre, New York City, 1946; Morgan Decker, *The Survivors,* Playhouse Theatre, New York City, 1948; Kurt Heger, *Bravo!,* Lyceum Theatre, New York City, 1948; Matt Burke, *Anna Christie,* City Center Theatre, New York City, 1952; Berowne, *Love's Labour's Lost,* City Center, New York City, 1953; Freddie Page, *The Deep Blue Sea,* Morosco Theatre, New York City, 1953; Boris Trigorin, *The Seagull,* Phoenix Theatre, New York City, 1954; Ayamonn Breydon, *Red Roses for Me,* Booth Theatre, New York City, 1955; Richard Morrow, *The Day the Money Stopped,* Belasco Theatre, New York City, 1958; Jerry Ryan, *Two for the Seesaw,* Booth Theatre, New York City, 1959; Rupert Forster, *Marching Song,* Gate Theatre, New York City, 1959.

Van Ackerman, *Advise and Consent,* Cort Theatre, New York City, 1960; Captain Dodd, *Something About a Soldier,* Ambassador Theatre, New York City, 1962; appeared in *Brecht on Brecht,* Theatre de Lys, New York City, 1962, and at the University of California at Los Angeles Theatre, 1963; Reverend Shannon, *Night of the Iguana,* Festival Theatre, Louisville, KY, 1964; Vershinin, *The Three Sisters,* Morosco Theatre, New York City, 1964; Homer, *A Warm Body,* Cort Theatre, New York City, 1967; Julian, *Cactus Flower,* Royale Theatre, New York City, 1967.

Harold Ryan, *Happy Birthday, Wanda June,* Theatre de Lys and then at the Edison Theatre, New York City, 1970; Dan, *The Children,* New York Shakespeare Festival, The Other Stage Theatre, New York City, 1972; Trigorin, *The Seagull,* Williamstown Festival Theatre, MA, 1974; Gerte, *The Rapists,* New Dramatists Theatre, New York City, 1974; Harry Harrison, *Harry Outside,* Circle Repertory Theatre, New York City, 1975; *Poor Murderer,* Ethel Barrymore Theatre, New York City, 1976; George Butler, *Alone Together,* Music Box Theatre, New York City, 1984; Presi-

dent Harry S. Truman, *Give 'Em Hell, Harry,* Pasadena Playhouse, Pasadena, CA, 1987. Summer stock: *The Lion in Winter,* 1976; *Equus,* 1978.

MAJOR TOURS—Ronny Meade, *Winged Victory,* U.S. cities, 1944; Jerry Ryan, *Two for the Seesaw,* U.S. cities, 1960 and 1965-66.

MEMBER: Actors' Equity Association, Screen Actors Guild, American Federation of Television and Radio Artists.

ADDRESSES: AGENT—William Morris Agency, 1350 Avenue of the Americas, New York, NY 10019.*

*   *   *

McCLANAHAN, Rue

PERSONAL: Born February 21, in Healdton, OK; daughter of William Edwin and Dreda Rheua-Nell (Medaris) McClanahan. EDUCATION: Attended University of Tulsa; trained for the stage with Uta Hagen and Perry Mansfield.

VOCATION: Actress.

CAREER: TELEVISION DEBUT—*Malibu Run,* also titled *The Aquanauts,* CBS, 1960. PRINCIPAL TELEVISION APPEARANCES—Series: Vivian Cavender Harmon, *Maude,* CBS, 1972-78; Ginger Nell-Hollyhock, *Apple Pie,* ABC, 1978; Aunt Fran Crowley, *Mama's Family,* NBC, 1983-84; Blanche, *The Golden Girls,* NBC, 1986—. Episodic: *All in the Family,* CBS. Movies: *Topper,* 1979. Dramatic Specials: *Hogan's Goat, The Rimers of Eldritch; Picnic,* Showtime, 1986.

STAGE DEBUT—Rachel, *Inherit the Wind,* Erie Playhouse, PA, 1957. BROADWAY DEBUT—Hazel, *The Secret Life of Walter Mitty,* Players Theatre, 1964. PRINCIPAL STAGE APPEARANCES—Understudy of female leads, *The Best Laid Plans,* Brooks Atkinson Theatre, New York City, 1966; Lady MacBird, *MacBird!,* Village Gate Theatre, New York City, 1967; *The Hostage* and *The Threepenny Opera,* both with the Hartford Stage Company, CT, 1967-68; Sally Weber, *Jimmy Shine,* Brooks Atkinson Theatre, New York City, 1968; Betty, *The Golden Fleece,* Actors Playhouse, New York City, 1969; Faye Precious, *Who's Happy Now?,* Village South Theatre, New York City, 1969.

Caitlin Thomas, *Dylan,* Mercer-O'Casey Theatre, New York City, 1972; Harriet, *Sticks and Bones,* John Golden Theatre, New York City, 1972; Crystal, *Crystal and Fox,* McAlpin Rooftop Theatre, New York City, 1973; Hannah, Diana, and Gert, *California Suite,* Eugene O'Neill Theatre, New York City, 1977; Fortuneteller, *The Skin of Our Teeth,* Old Globe Theatre, San Diego, 1983; *In the Sweet Bye and Bye,* Back Alley Theatre, Los Angeles, 1985; stock appearances include: *After the Fall, Who's Afraid of Virginia Woolf?, Death of a Salesman,* and *Critic's Choice.*

FILM DEBUT—*They Might Be Giants,* Universal, 1970. PRINCIPAL FILM APPEARANCES—*The People Next Door,* AVCO-Embassy, 1970.

SIDELIGHTS: RECREATIONS—Hiking, reading, sewing, beachcombing, and writing.

ADDRESSES: OFFICE—c/o *Golden Girls,* Sunset Gower Studios, 1438 N. Gower, Los Angeles, CA 90028. AGENT—c/o Sylvia Gold, International Creative Management, 8899 Beverly Blvd., Los Angeles, CA 90048.*

*   *   *

McCLORY, Sean   1924-

PERSONAL: Born March 8, 1924, in Dublin, Ireland; son of Hugh Patrick (an architect and civil engineer) and Mary Margaret (a model; maiden name, Ball) McClory; married P. Souris (divorced); married M. B. Morrison (divorced); married Sue Alexander (died, 1979); married Peggy Webber (an actress and producer), March 17, 1983; children: Duane, Kevin, Cathleen. EDUCATION: Graduated from St. Ignatius Jesuit College, Galway, Ireland, 1942; also attended National University of Ireland Medical School, Galway, 1942-45; trained for the stage at the Gaelic Theatre of Galway and at the Abbey Theatre, Dublin. RELIGION: Roman Catholic. MILITARY: Irish Army Medical Corps.

VOCATION: Actor, producer, director, and writer.

CAREER: STAGE DEBUT—Mickey Linden, *The Shining Hour,* La Jolla Playhouse, CA, 1947. BROADWAY DEBUT Rory Commons, *King of Friday's Men,* Playhouse Theatre, 1951, for three performances.

PRINCIPAL STAGE WORK—Member of the resident company,

SEAN McCLORY

Abbey Theatre, Dublin, for two and one half years; member of resident company, Gaelic Theatre, Galway, for twelve years; also performed at: Ahmanson Theatre, Los Angeles; Mark Taper Forum, Los Angeles; La Jolla Playhouse; Valley Music Theatre; Sombrero Theatre; Lobero Theatre; member of the John Ford Stock Company; appeared as Seamus Shields, *Shadow of a Gunman,* C.A.R.T. Theatre, 1984. Founded, managed, and acted for Tara Theatre, San Francisco.

MAJOR TOURS—*The Lady's Not for Burning, Dial M for Murder,* West Coast cities.

TELEVISION DEBUT—*The O'Branigans of Boston,* ABC, 1950. PRINCIPAL TELEVISION APPEARANCES—Series: Jack McGivern, *The Californians,* NBC, 1959; *Overland Trail,* NBC, 1960; Pat McShane, *Kate McShane,* CBS, 1975; *General Hospital,* ABC, 1980; Myles Delany, *Bring 'em Back Alive,* CBS, 1982.

Episodic: *Lux Video Theatre,* CBS; *Shirley Temple Theatre,* NBC; *Climax,* CBS; *Four Star Playhouse,* CBS; *The Islanders,* ABC; *Convoy,* NBC; *Sugarfoot,* ABC; *Daniel Boone,* NBC; *Cavalcade of America,* NBC; *Surfside Six,* ABC; *Westinghouse Desilu Playhouse,* CBS; *Have Gun Will Travel,* CBS; *Restless Gun,* NBC; *General Electric True Theatre,* CBS; *Adventures in Paradise,* ABC; *Iron Horse,* ABC; *Here Come the Brides,* ABC; *The Real McCoys,* ABC; *The Life and Legend of Wyatt Earp,* ABC; *My Three Sons,* ABC; *Make Room for Daddy,* ABC; *Rawhide,* CBS; *Stagecoach West,* ABC; *This Is the Life,* DuMont; *Wagon Train,* NBC; *Matinee Theatre.*

Beverly Hillbillys, CBS; *Suspense Playhouse,* CBS; *Death Valley Days,* syndicated; *Lancer,* CBS; *Medic,* NBC; *The Rifleman,* ABC; *Lost in Space,* CBS; *Mannix,* CBS; *One Step Beyond,* syndicated; *Tarzan,* NBC; *Broken Arrow,* ABC; *My Favorite Martian,* CBS; *Wanted Dead or Alive,* CBS; *Family Affair,* CBS; *The Untouchables,* ABC; *High Chaparral,* NBC; *Men from Shiloh,* NBC; *Bonanza,* NBC; *The Virginian,* NBC; *Honey West,* ABC; *Alfred Hitchcock Presents,* CBS; *Thriller,* NBC; *The Monroes,* ABC; *Gunsmoke,* CBS; *Kung Fu,* ABC; *S.W.A.T.,* ABC; *Little House on the Prairie,* NBC; *Columbo,* NBC; *Fish,* ABC; *The Battlestar Galactica,* ABC; *The Blue Knight,* CBS; *Trapper John, M.D.,* CBS; *Strike Force,* ABC; *Fantasy Island,* ABC; *Lottery,* ABC; *Simon and Simon,* CBS; *Falcon Crest,* CBS.

Movies: *The New Daughters of Joshua Cabe,* 1976. Mini-Series: *Captains and the Kings,* NBC; *Once an Eagle,* NBC; *How the West Was Won,* ABC. Specials: *The Women of Ballybunion.*

FILM DEBUT—Irish-American Cop, *Dick Tracey vs. the Claw,* RKO, 1946. PRINCIPAL FILM APPEARANCES—*Dick Tracy vs. Cueball,* RKO, 1946; *Daughter of Rosie O'Grady,* 1950; *Anne of the Indies,* 1951; *Lorna Doone,* 1951; *The Quiet Man,* Republic, 1952; *Island in the Sky,* 1953; *Plunder of the Sun,* 1953; *Ring of Fear,* 1954; *Them,* Warner Brothers, 1954; *The Long Grey Line,* Columbia, 1955; *Moonfleet,* Metro-Goldwyn-Mayer (MGM), 1955; *I Cover the Underworld,* Republic, 1955; *The King's Thief,* MGM, 1955; *Diane,* MGM, 1956; *Guns of Fort Petticoat,* Columbia, 1957; *Valley of the Dragons,* Columbia, 1961; *Cheyenne Autumn,* Warner Brothers, 1964; *Mara of the Wilderness,* Allied Artists, 1965; *Follow Me Boys,* Buena Vista, 1966; *The Gnome-Mobile,* Buena Vista, 1967; *The Happiest Millionaire,* Buena Vista, 1967; *Two of a Kind,* Twentieth Century-Fox, 1983; *My Chauffeur,* Crown International, 1986; also: *The Secret Sharer; Well of the Saints; My Pal Rusty; Beyond Glory; Roughshod; Botany Bay; Niagara; Rogues March; Storm Warning; Les*

Miserables; What Price Glory?; Man in the Attic; Day of the Wolves; Roller Boogie.

RELATED CAREER—Has worked under contract with Warner Brothers, RKO, and Batjac Productions, Inc.

WRITINGS: PLAYS, PRODUCED—*Moment of Truth,* Masquers Theatre, Hollywood, CA, 1970.

ARTICLES—Feature writer and co-editor, "The Jester," Masquers Club, Hollywood, 1976; editor, "American National Theatre Academy (ANTA) Monthly," 1977-79; feature writer and photo editor, "The Benedictine Annual," 1980, and editor, *Pax,* "Benedictine Commemorative Annual," 1981, both St. Andrews, CA.

AWARDS: Best Actor, Dramalogue Award, 1984, for *Shadow of a Gunman,* C.A.R.T. Theatre; also received Emmy nomination for performance on *Lost in Space.*

MEMBER: Screen Actors Guild, American Federation of Television and Radio Artists, Actors' Equity Association, Directors Guild of America; Masquers Club, Variety Arts Center.

ADDRESSES: HOME—6612 Whitley Terrace, Los Angeles, CA 90068. AGENT—c/o Steve Stevens, Twentieth Century Artists, 3518 Cahuenga Blvd. West, Suite 316, Los Angeles, CA 90068.

*   *   *

McCRANE, Paul   1961-

PERSONAL: Born January 19, 1961, in Phildelphia, PA; son of James J. (a writer and actor) and Eileen C. (a nurse; maiden name, Manyak) McCrane. EDUCATION: Attended Holy Ghost Preparatory School; studied for the theatre with Uta Hagen at the Herbert Berghof Studios, New York City; studied stage combat with B.H. Barry.

VOCATION: Actor.

CAREER: OFF-BROADWAY DEBUT—Bert, *Landscape of the Body,* Public Theatre, New York Shakespeare Festival (NYSF), 1977. PRINCIPAL STAGE APPEARANCES—Ensemble, *Dispatches,* Public Theatre, NYSF, New York City, 1978; Eddie, *Runaways,* Plymouth Theatre, New York City, 1978; Jeff and waiter, *Split,* Second Stage Theatre, New York City, 1979; Christopher, *Sally's Gone, She Left Her Name,* Center Stage Theatre, Baltimore, MD, 1981; Ronnie, *The House of Blue Leaves,* Berkshire Theatre Festival, Stockbridge, MA, 1981; Rovo, *Hunting Scenes from Lower Bavaria* and Carlo, *Crossing Niagara,* both at the Manhattan Theatre Club, 1981; Alvin Coolidge, *The Palace of Amateurs,* Berkshire Theatre Festival, 1982; Ricky, *Hooters,* Hudson Guild Theatre, New York City, 1982; Wishy Burke, *The Curse of an Aching Heart,* Little Theatre, New York City, 1982; Leslie, *The Hostage,* Long Wharf Theatre, New Haven, CT, 1983; Chick, Kit, Vinnie, Bernard, Clay, and Andy, *Fables for Friends,* Playwrights Horizons, New York City, 1984; Don Parritt, *The Iceman Cometh,* Lunt-Fontanne Theatre, New York City, 1985.

FILM DEBUT—Young Patient, *Rocky II,* United Artists, 1979. PRINCIPAL FILM APPEARANCES—Montgomery, *Fame,* United Artists, 1980; Brenner, *Purple Hearts,* Warner Brothers, 1984; Frank Berry, *The Hotel New Hampshire,* Orion Pictures, 1984.

PAUL McCRANE

TELEVISION DEBUT—Joey Rodick, *Death Penalty,* 1979. PRINCIPAL TELEVISION APPEARANCES—Movies: Bobby Moore, *And Baby Comes Home,* 1980; Preacher, *We're Fighting Back,* 1981; Iggy Vile, *Moving Right Along,* 1982; George Nicholas, *Nurse—Fevers,* 1982.

AWARDS: Best Supporting Actor, Joseph Jefferson Award nomination, 1077, for *Landscape of the Body;* Best Young Disc Artist, Youth in Entertainment Award, 1980; Best Motion Picture Album, Grammy Award Nomination, 1981, for *Fame.*

MEMBER: Actors' Equity Association, Screen Actors Guild, American Federation of Television and Radio Artists; Amnesty International.

SIDELIGHTS: Paul McCrane told *CTFT,* "My favorite role, to date, is Leslie in *The Hostage;* my motivation : Uta Hagen and her book, *Respect for Acting.*"

ADDRESSES: AGENT—Alan Willig & Associates, 47A Horatio Street, New York, NY 10014; The Artists Agency, 10000 Santa Monica Blvd., Los Angeles, CA 90067.*

*   *   *

McDERMOTT, Keith   1953-

PERSONAL: Born September 28, 1953, in Houston, TX; son of James E. and Betty Ray (Rees) McDermott. EDUCATION: Ohio University, B.A.; trained for the stage with Robert Lewis at the Actors Studio.

VOCATION: Actor.

CAREER: PRINCIPAL STAGE APPEARANCES—Alan Strang, *Equus,*
Plymouth Theatre, New York City; Harold, *Harold and Maude,*
Martin Beck Theatre, New York City; Tom, *A Meeting by the
River,* Palace Theatre, New York City; Billy, *The Poker Session,*
Theatre Off-Park, New York City; Romeo, *Romeo and Juliet,* Lion
Theatre, New York City; Bentley, *Misalliance,* Roundabout Thea-
tre, New York City; Mooney, *Life Class,* Manhattan Theatre Club,
New York City; Marqualis, *End as a Man,* title role, *Edison,* and
Ferdinand, *The Tempest,* all Off-Broadway productions.

Young Charlie, *Da,* Studio Arena Theatre, Buffalo, NY; Fleance,
Macbeth and Lucius, *Julius Caesar,* both with the American
Shakespeare Festival; Man, *I Was Sitting on My Patio. . .,* San
Francisco production; John, *A Life in the Theatre,* Kenyon Festival
Theatre, OH.

PRINCIPAL FILM APPEARANCES—*Tourist Trap,* Charles Band
Productions, 1979; Philippe, *Without a Trace,* Twentieth Century-
Fox, 1983.

PRINCIPAL TELEVISION APPEARANCES—Mini-Series: *How the
West Was Won,* NBC.

MEMBER: Actors' Equity Association, Screen Actors Guild, American Federation of Television and Radio Artists.

ADDRESSES: HOME—29 W. 12th Street, New York, NY 10011.
AGENT—Mary Day Agency, 305 W. 44th Street, New York, NY
10036.

*   *   *

McINTOSH, Marcia

PERSONAL: Daughter of Fred (a lawyer) and Sue McIntosh.
EDUCATION: West Virginia University, B.F.A., 1975; trained for
the stage with Susanne Shepherd, Tom Brennan, Mel Shapiro, and
Joe Bova.

VOCATION: Actress and stage manager.

CAREER: STAGE DEBUT—Laura, *The Glass Menagerie,* Appala-
chian Actor's Theatre, 1974, for thirty performances. LONDON
DEBUT—Nancy Reagan, *The Bottom Line,* Battersea Arts Theatre,
1983, for one hundred performances. PRINCIPAL STAGE APPEAR-
ANCES—Factory worker, *Dying to Make It,* Labor Theatre, 1980;
Galileo Project, Pittsburgh Public Theatre, PA, 1981; Nora
Greenbaum, *Ball,* Green Street Cafe, New York City, 1984; also:
From Hair to Dispatches, New York Shakespeare Festival, Public
Theatre, New York City; Gail, *Fly Blackbird,* Richard Allen Center
for Culture and Art, New York City; Nancy Reagan, *The Bottom
Line,* Labor Theatre, New York City; *Scripts in Comedy,* Manhat-
tan Punch Line, New York City.

Stock: Puck, *A Midsummer Night's Dream,* Appalachian Actor's
Theatre; *Working Our Way Down,* Boars Head Theatre, MI;
Morgan Le Fay, *Sir Gawain and the Green Knight,* Ringling
Museum, FL; Agnes Gooch, *Mame,* Beef n' Boards Dinner Thea-
tre; *Grandfather Tales,* Roadside Theatre. Also appeared in *Cele-
bration, Madame Butterfly,* as Maria in *Twelfth Night,* and as
Masha in *The Seagull,* all at the Creative Arts Center, Morgantown,
WV.

MARCIA McINTOSH

MAJOR TOURS—Nancy Reagan, *The Bottom Line,* U.K. cities,
1983; *I Just Wanted Someone to Know,* Labor Theatre Repertory
Company.

PRINCIPAL STAGE WORK—Stage manager, Broadway: *Sante Fe
on Broadway,* Shubert Theatre. Off-Broadway: *Potholes,* Cherry
Lane Theatre; *The New World Monkey,* American Place Theatre;
Chase a Rainbow, Theatre Four; *From Hair to Dispatches,* Public
Theatre. Regional: *A Flea in Her Ear, As You Like It, Streamers,
The Drunkard, Violano Virtuoso,* and *A Member of the Wedding,* all
at the Players State Theatre, Miami, FL. Assistant stage manager,
stock: *Bell, Book and Candle, California Suite, Fiddler on the
Roof,* and *I Do, I Do,* all at the Corning Summer Theatre, NY.
Production stage manager, tours: *Jack London—The Man from
Eden's Grove, Workin' Our Way Down, I Just Wanted Someone to
Know,* all with the Labor Theatre, New York City. Wardrobe
assistant and dresser, *42nd Street,* Majestic Theatre, New York
City.

PRINCIPAL FILM APPEARANCES—Hippie Mom, *Four Friends,*
Film Ways, 1981.

PRINCIPAL TELEVISION APPEARANCES—Beatrice, ''Staus,''
Realizations - Growing Old in America, PBS, 1984.

NON-RELATED CAREER—Masseuse, reflexologist, shiatsu specialist.

MEMBER: Actors' Equity Association, Screen Actors Guild.

SIDELIGHTS: CTFT has learned that among Marcia McIntosh's

skills is her ability to play the washtub string bass, and that she enjoys mountain folk dancing, jogging, and jestering.

ADDRESSES: HOME—233 W. 99th Street, Apt. 6E, New York, NY 10025.

*   *   *

McKELLEN, Ian   1939-

PERSONAL: Born May 25, 1939, in Burnley, England; son of Denis Murray (a civil engineer) and Margery Lois (Sutcliffe) McKellen. EDUCATION: St. Catherine's College, Cambridge University, B.A., 1961.

VOCATION: Actor and director.

CAREER: STAGE DEBUT—Roper, *A Man for All Seasons,* Belgrade Theatre, Coventry, U.K., 1961. LONDON DEBUT—Godfrey, *A Scent of Flowers,* Duke of York's Theatre, 1964. BROADWAY DEBUT—Leonidik, *The Promise,* Henry Miller's Theatre, 1967. PRINCIPAL STAGE APPEARANCES—Repertory, including title roles in *Henry V* and *Luther,* 1962-63; in repertory, including Aufidius, *Coriolanus,* Arthur Seaton, *Saturday Night and Sunday Morning,* title role, *Sir Thomas More,* all in Nottingham, England, 1963-64; Claudio, *Much Ado About Nothing,* Protestant Evangelist, *Armstrong's Last Goodnight,* and Captain de Foenix, *Trelawny of the Wells,* all with the National Theatre Company, Chichester Festival, U.K., 1965; Alvin, *A Lily in Little India,* Hampstead Theatre, then St. Martin's Theatre, London, 1965-66; Andrew Cobham, *Their Very Own* and *Golden City,* both at the Royal Court Theatre, London, 1966; title role, *O'Flaherty, VC* and Bonaparte, *The Man of Destiny,* all at the Mermaid Theatre, London, 1966; Leonodik, *The Promise,* Oxford Playhouse, 1966, then Fortune Theatre, London, 1967; Tom, *The White Liars* and Harold Gorringe, *Black Comedy,* Lyric Theatre, London, 1968; Pentheus, *The Bacchae,* Liverpool Playhouse, U.K., 1969.

Darkly, *Billy's Last Stand,* Theatre Upstairs, London, 1970; title role, *Hamlet,* Prospect Theatre Company, Cambridge, U.K., 1971; Svetovidov, *Swan Song,* Michael, *The Wood Demon,* Footman, *The Way of the World,* Edgar, *King Lear,* all at the Edinburgh Festival, Scotland, then Brooklyn Academy of Music, New York City, 1973; repeated above plays in addition to *Giovanni,* Wimbledon, England, 1974; title role, *Dr. Faustus,* with the Royal Shakespeare Company at the Edinburgh Festival and the Aldwych Theatre, London, 1974; title role, *The Marquis of Keith,* Aldwych Theatre, London, 1974; Philip the Bastard, *King John,* Aldwych Theatre, London, 1975; Colin, *Ashes,* Young Vic Theatre Company, London, 1975; Aubrey Bagot, *Too True to Be Good,* with the Royal Shakespeare Company at the Globe Theatre, 1975; Romeo, *Romeo and Juliet,* Leontes, *The Winter's Tale,* and title role, *Macbeth,* all Stratford-on-Avon, England, 1976; solo show, *Words, Words, Words,* Edinburgh Festival, 1977; title role, *Macbeth* and Face, *The Alchemist,* both with the Royal Shakespeare Company, Stratford-on-Avon, 1977; Alex, *Every Good Boy Deserves Favor,* Festival Hall, England, 1977; solo show, *Acting Shakespeare,* Edinburgh Festival, 1977; Karsten Bernick, *Pillars of the Community* and Face Langevin, *Days of the Commune,* both Aldwych Theatre, London, 1977-78; Sir Toby, *Twelfth Night* and Andrei, *The Three Sisters,* both with the Royal Shakespeare Company, 1978; Max, *Bent,* Royal Court Theatre, then Criterion Theatre, London, 1979.

Salieri, *Amadeus,* Broadhurst Theatre, New York City, 1980; *Cowardice,* Ambassadors Theatre, London, 1983; Pierre, *Venice Preserv'd,* Platonov, *Wild Honey,* and title role, *Coriolanus,* all at the National Theatre, London, 1984; *Wild Honey,* Ahmanson Theatre, Los Angeles, and the Virginia Theatre, New York City, 1986-87.

MAJOR TOURS—Title role, *Richard III,* Prospect Theatre, 1968; title role, *Richard II* and title role, *Edward II,* Prospect Theatre tour including the Mermaid Theatre and the Picadilly Theatre, London, 1969; Captain Plume, *The Recruiting Officer* and Corporal Hill, *Chips with Everything,* Cambridge Theatre Company, 1971; Giovanni, *'Tis Pity She's a Whore,* Page-Boy, *Ruling the Roost,* and Prince Yoremitsu, *The Three Arrows,* with the Actors Company at the Edinburgh Festival and subsequent tour, 1972; *Acting Shakespeare,* Israel, Scandinavia, Spain, France, Cyprus, Romanina, Los Angeles, CA, and the Ritz Theatre, New York City, 1980-83; (recital) *Eagle in New Mexico,* Santa Fe, 1980; *The Duchess of Malfi, The Real Inspector Hound, The Critic,* and *The Cherry Orchard,* all with the National Theatre of Great Britain at the Blackstone Theatre, Chicago, 1986.

PRINCIPAL STAGE WORK—Director: *The Prime of Miss Jean Brodie,* Liverpool Playhouse, 1969; *The Erpingham Camp,* Palace Theatre, Watford, U.K., 1972; *A Private Matter,* Vaudeville Theatre, London, 1973; *The Clandestine Marriage,* Savoy Theatre, London, 1975; directed and also appeared in *Twelfth Night* and *The Three Sisters,* Royal Shakespeare Company tour, 1978.

PRINCIPAL FILM APPEARANCES—*Alfred the Great,* 1969; *A Touch of Love,* 1969; *The Promise,* 1969; *Prince of Love,* 1981; *The Scarlet Pimpernel,* 1982; *The Keep,* Paramount, 1983; *Plenty,* 1985.

PRINCIPAL TELEVISION APPEARANCES—Movies: *David Copperfield; Ross; Hedda Gabler; Macbeth; Every Good Boy Deserves Favor; Walter; Acting Shakespeare,* 1982.

WRITINGS: PLAYS, PRODUCED—*Acting Shakespeare.*

AWARDS: Awarded the Commander of the British Empire, 1979. Clarence Derwent Award, 1964, for *The Promise;* "Plays and Players" Award for most promising actor, 1976; Actor of the Year Award, 1976, for *Macbeth;* Society of West End Theatres awards, for 1977, for *Pillars of the Community,* 1978, for *The Alchemist,* and 1979, for *Bent;* Antoinette Perry Award, New York Drama League Award, Outer Critics Circle Award, all 1981, for *Amadeus;* Drama Desk Award, 1983, for *Acting Shakespeare;* Antoinette Perry Award nomination, 1984, for *Acting Shakespeare,* 1984; Actor of the Year, *London Standard* Award, 1985, for *Coriolanus.* Honorary fellow, St. Catherine's College, Cambridge, 1982.

SIDELIGHTS: In publicity material submitted to *CTFT,* Ian McKellen reflected on his career. "As a child, I went regularly to the local theatres in South Lancashire, where I was born and brought up: first with my parents (who were keen theatre-goers) and by the time I was twelve, increasingly on my own. I also acted a great deal at school and with local amateur dramatic societies. As a family we rarely went to the cinema—perhaps my parents, who were devoted churchgoers, slightly disapproved of the movies! They preferred the theatre or to stay at home and listen, as a family, to plays on the radio. They could not afford a television. So in those days, when I thought of actors I thought of the stage-actors who walked past out house on their way home from the local repertory theatre. And any ambitions I had about becoming an actor myself never included the fantasy of being a film-star. When I turned professional, after acting a great deal with my fellow undergraduates at Cambridge University, I started as I meant to go on—in the theatre. I put all my energies into training myself for the stage rather than in waiting to be 'discovered' by a movie mogul and whisked off to Hollywood.''

ADDRESSES: AGENT—James Sharkey, Fifteen Golden Square, Third Floor, London W1R 3AG, England.

* * *

McKENNA, David   1949-

PERSONAL: Born November 5, 1949; son of Joseph P. and Elizabeth (Nash) McKenna. EDUCATION: University of Texas, B.A., 1971; Carnegie Mellon University, M.F.A., 1976.

VOCATION: Director.

CAREER: FIRST OFF-BROADWAY STAGE WORK—Director, *Jekyll and Hyde,* La Mama Experimental Theatre Club (ETC), June, 1976, for sixteen performances. PRINCIPAL STAGE WORK—Director: *The Boys in the Band,* First Repertory Theatre, San Antonio, TX, 1974; *Steambath,* The Country Theatre, San Antonio, 1974; *What the Butler Saw,* Nat Horne Theatre, New York City, 1977; *R,* Westbeth Theatre Center, New York City, 1978; *Cabaret,* Yale University School of Drama, New Haven, CT, 1978; *Comeback of a One-Eyed Lion,* Walden Theatre, New York City, 1980; *Arsenic and Old Lace,* South Jersey Regional Theatre, NJ, 1980; *Who's Afraid of Virginia Woolf?,* University of South Dakota, 1980; *Sleuth,* South Jersey Regional Theatre, 1981; *Millers' Tale,* No Smoking Playhouse, New York City, 1983; *Immorality Play,* Alliance Theatre, Atlanta, GA, 1983; *Cliffhanger,* Lamb's Theatre, New York City, 1985; *The Miss Firecracker Contest,* South of Broadway Theatre, Miami, FL, 1985; *Richard II,* Ensemble Studio Theatre, New York City, 1986.

RELATED CAREER—Script analyst for Twentieth Century-Fox Films, CBS-Fox Video, Home Box Office, and Cinecom Films. Guest artist: University of South Dakota, Yale School of Drama, New York University, Circle in the Square Theatre, New York City, Stella Adler Studio; moderator for National Academy of Television Arts and Sciences (NATAS) Actors' Workshop; director, industrial films; voice-over artist.

MEMBER: Society of Stage Directors and Choreographers, National Academy of Television Arts and Sciences.

ADDRESSES: OFFICE—400 W. 43rd Street, Apt. 19G, New York, NY 10036.

* * *

McKENNA, Siobhan   1923-1986

PERSONAL: Born May 24, 1923, in Belfast, Northern Ireland; died of a heart attack following surgery for lung cancer in Dublin, Ireland, November 16, 1986; daughter of Owen (a mathematical physics professor) and Margaret (a designer and buyer of millinery; maiden name, O'Reilly) McKenna; married Denis O'Dea (an

actor), July 7, 1946 (died, 1978); children: a son. EDUCATION: Attended the National University of Ireland.

VOCATION: Actress.

CAREER: STAGE DEBUT—Title role, *Mary Rose* and *Tons of Money,* both with the Gaelic Repertory Theatre at the An Taibhdhearc Theatre, Galway, Ireland, 1940. LONDON DEBUT—Nora Fintry, *The White Steed,* Embassy Theatre, 1947. BROADWAY DEBUT—Miss Madrigal, *The Chalk Garden,* Ethel Barrymore Theatre, 1955. PRINCIPAL STAGE APPEARANCES—With the Gaelic Repertory Theatre at the An Taibhdherarc Theatre, Galway: Mrs. Grigson, *Shadow of a Gunman* and Bessie Burgess, *The Plough and the Stars,* both 1940, the wife, *Tons of Money,* Miriam, *Winterset,* and Lady Macbeth, *Macbeth,* all 1941, and Bella, *Gaslight* and appeared in *The White Scourge,* both 1942; Nicole, *Le Bourgeois Gentilhomme,* and appeared in *The Countess Cathleen, The End House, Marks and Mabel, The Far-off Hills,* and *Thy Dear Father,* all with the Abbey Players at the Abbey Theatre, Dublin, 1943-46; Helen Pettigrew, *Berkeley Square,* Q Theatre, London, 1949.

Title role, *Saint Joan,* Gaiety Theatre, Dublin, and An Taibhdhearc Theatre, Galway, 1950; Maura Joyce, *Fading Mansion,* Duchess Theatre, London, 1951; Regina, *Ghosts,* Embassy Theatre, London, 1951; appeared in *The White-Headed Boy* and as Pegeen Mike, *The Playboy of the Western World,* both at the Edinburgh Festival, Scotland, 1951; title role, *Heloise,* Duke of York's Theatre, London, 1951, then at the Memorial Theatre, Stratford-Upon-Avon, 1952; Avril, *Purple Dust,* Royal Glasgow Theatre, Scotland, 1953; Beauty, *The Love of Four Colonels* and title role, *Anna Christie,* both at the Gaiety Theatre, Dublin, 1953; Luka, *Arms and the Man* and Pegeen Mike, *The Playboy of the Western World,* both at the Gaiety Theatre, 1954; title role, *Saint Joan,* Gate Theatre, Dublin, 1954, then later at the Arts Theatre, London and St. Martin's Theatre, London, 1955; title role, *Saint Joan,* Sanders Theatre, Cambridge, MA, 1956, then Phoenix Theatre, New York City, 1956; title role, *Hamlet,* Theatre de Lys, New York City, 1957; Viola, *Twelfth Night,* Stratford Shakespeare Festival, Ontario, Canada, 1957; Margaret Hyland, *The Rope Dancers,* Cort Theatre, New York City, 1957; Viola, *Twelfth Night* and Lady Macbeth, *Macbeth,* both Cambridge Drama Festival, MA, 1959.

Isobel, *Motel,* Wilbur Theatre, Boston, 1960; Pegeen Mike, *The Playboy of the Western World,* Dublin Theatre Festival, then Piccadilly Theatre, London and St. Martin's Theatre, London, 1960; Joan Dark, *Saint Joan of the Stockyards,* Dublin Festival, Gaiety Theatre, 1961; Anna Freeman, *To Play with a Tiger,* Comedy Theatre, London, 1962; *An Evening with Irish Writers,* Shelbourne Theatre, Dublin, 1963; Joan Dark, *Saint Joan of the Stockyards,* Queen's Theatre, London, 1964; Marie-Jeanne, *The Cavern,* Strand Theatre, London, 1965; Juno Boyle, *Juno and the Paycock,* Gaiety Theatre, Dublin, 1966; title role, *The Loves of Cass Maguire,* Dublin Festival, 1967; Madame Ranevsky, *The Cherry Orchard,* Dublin Festival, 1968; Pearl, *On a Foggy Day,* St. Martin's Theatre, London, 1969.

Josie Connaught, *Best of Friends,* Strand Theatre, London, 1970; *Here Are Ladies,* Playhouse Theatre, Oxford, U.K., then Criterion Theatre, London, 1970; Juno Boyle, *Juno and the Paycock,* Mermaid Theatre, London, 1973; *The Morgan Yard,* Dublin Festival, Olympia Theatre, 1974; *Here Are Ladies,* Gate Theatre, Dublin, 1975; Julia Sterroll, *Fallen Angels,* Gate Theatre, Dublin, 1975; Josie, *A Moon for the Misbegotten,* Gate Theatre, Dublin, 1976; Bessie Burgess, *The Plough and the Stars,* Abbey Theatre, Dublin, and in New York City, 1976; Jocasta, *Sons of Oedipus,* Greenwich

Festival, U.K., 1977; Sarah Bernhardt, *Memoir,* Guelph Festival, Canada, then Olympia Theatre, Dublin, 1977, and Ambassadors Theatre, London, 1978; Margaret, *Meeting by the River,* Palace Theatre, New York City, 1979.

Juno Boyle, *Juno and the Paycock,* Abbey Theatre, Dublin, 1980; Agrippina, *Britannicus,* produced in London, 1981; *Here Are Ladies,* Abbey Theatre, Dublin, 1982; *Bailegangaire,* produced in London, 1985.

MAJOR TOURS—Pegeen Mike, *The Playboy of the Western World,* European cities, 1960; Widow Quinn, *The Playboy of the Western World,* U.K. cities and Hong Kong, 1977.

PRINCIPAL STAGE WORK—Director: *The Playboy of the Western World,* Long Wharf Theatre, New Haven, CT, 1967; *Daughter from Over the Water,* Dublin, 1968; *I'm Getting Out of This Kip,* Dublin, 1968; *Tinker's Wedding, Shadow of the Glen, Riders to the Sea,* all at the Arts Festival, Toronto, Canada, 1973; *Juno and the Paycock,* Mermaid Theatre, London, 1973; *The Playboy of the Western World,* produced in U.K. and U.S., 1977; *The Golden Cradle,* Greenwich Festival, London, 1978.

FILM DEBUT—Kate, *Hungry Hill,* Rank, 1946. PRINCIPAL FILM APPEARANCES—Emmy, *Daughter of Darkness,* Paramount, 1947; the Frenchwoman, *The Lost People,* Gainsborough, 1949; *Fortune in Diamonds* (also known as *The Adventurers*), Rank, 1952; Virgin Mary, *King of Kings,* Metro-Goldwyn-Mayer (MGM), 1961; Pegeen Mike, *The Playboy of the Western World,* Janus, 1963; Nora, *Of Human Bondage,* MGM, 1964; Anna, *Doctor Zhivago,* MGM, 1965; *Philadelphia Here I Come;* 1975; *Here Are Ladies.*

PRINCIPAL TELEVISION APPEARANCES—Episodic: Sister Joanna, "The Cradle Song," *Hallmark Hall of Fame,* NBC, 1957; "The Winslow Boy," *DuPont Show of the Month,* CBS, 1958; Maggie, "What Every Woman Knows," *DuPont Show of the Month,* CBS, 1959; Donna Ana, "Don Juan in Hell," *Play of the Week,* WNTA, 1960; "The Woman in White," *Great Mysteries,* NBC, 1960; "The Rope Dancers," *Play of the Week,* WNTA, 1960; also *Hall of Kings,* ABC, 1967; *Girl Talk,* ABC, 1965. Movies: *The Last Days of Pompeii,* ABC, 1984; also *Cuckoo Spit; A Cheap Bunch of Nice Flowers; The Landlady and Lady Gregory.*

WRITINGS: TRANSLATIONS—Gaelic translations of *Mary Rose* and *Saint Joan.*

AWARDS: Best Actress, London *Evening Standard* Award, 1955, for *St. Joan;* voted best international actress in Italy, 1961, for *The Playboy of the Western World;* awarded gold medal, 1971, from Eire Society, Boston, MA; honorary Doctor of Humane Letters, Wilson College.*

*   *   *

McKEON, Doug   1966-

PERSONAL: Full name, Douglas Jude McKeon; born June 10, 1966, in Pomptain Plains, NJ; son of Richard F. (a stock broker) and Irene Anne (a teacher; maiden name, Kisla) McKeon. EDUCATION: Attending University of Southern California. RELIGION: Roman Catholic.

VOCATION: Actor.

DOUG McKEON

CAREER: BROADWAY DEBUT—Tommy, *Dandelion Wine,* Lyceum Theatre, 1974. PRINCIPAL STAGE APPEARANCES—Leon, *Truckload,* Lyceum Theatre, New York City, 1975; Eugene, *Brighton Beach Memoirs,* Neil Simon Theatre, New York City, 1983.

FILM DEBUT—Robbie, *Uncle Joe Shannon,* United Artists, 1979. PRINCIPAL FILM APPEARANCES—Frank Strelzyk, *Night Crossing,* Buena Vista, 1981; Billy Ray, *On Golden Pond,* Universal, 1981; Jonathan, *Mischief,* Twentieth Century-Fox, 1985; Ben Aitken, *Turnaround,* 1986.

TELEVISION DEBUT—Dirk, *The Silent Eye,* NBC, 1974. PRINCIPAL TELEVISION APPEARANCES—Series: Max Sutter, *Big Shamus, Little Shamus,* CBS, 1979; Timmy Farraday, *The Edge of Night,* ABC, for two years. Episodic: *Murder She Wrote,* CBS; *The Andros Targets,* ABC; *The Little Rascals* (remake), Norman Lear Productions, NBC. Movies: *Desparate Lives,* CBS; *An Innocent Love,* CBS; *The Comeback Kid,* ABC; *Tell Me My Name,* NBC; *Daddy I Don't Like It Like This,* CBS; *Silent Eye,* NBC. Mini-Series: Phillip Wendell, *Centennial,* NBC; Mark Schroeder, *At Mother's Request,* CBS, 1987.

WRITINGS: SCREENPLAYS—(Also director) *The Gang's All Here,* privately produced.

AWARDS: Best Juvenile Actor, Afternoon TV "Soap Box," Award, 1976 and 1978, both for *The Edge of Night;* Best Male Debut, Brussels International Film Festival, 1979, for *Uncle Joe Shannon;* Best Supporting Actor nomination, Youth Film Festival Award and Best Supporting Actor nomination, Golden Apple Award, both 1981, for *The Comeback Kid;* Best Supporting Actor nomination,

National Association of Theatre Owners, 1982, for *On Golden Pond;* Distinguished Youth Achievement Award, Maynard, MA, 1982; Massachusetts State Senate Citation, for distinguished contribution among the youth, on behalf of drug rehabilitation programs in high schools and care centers, 1982; guest speaker at a symposium entitled, "Generations at the Crossroads," sponsored by Representative Claude Pepper at the House of Representatives, Washington, DC, 1982.

MEMBER: Actors' Equity Association, Screen Actors Guild, American Federation of Television and Radio Artists; Young Artists United (board of trustees).

SIDELIGHTS: Doug McKeon told *CTFT* about his aspirations and activities: "I wish to not only act, but to pursue a career in writing and directing as well. Aside from various screenplays in the works, I attend the University of Southern California where I make student films. Outside of school, I completed a personal endeavor entitled 'The Gang's All Here,' which I wrote and directed. I'm active in all sports, particularly swimming, football, baseball and golf. I love to read; favorite authors are John Steinbeck and William Goldman."

ADDRESSES: AGENT—c/o Jeff Witjas, William Morris Agency, 151 El Camino Drive, Beverly Hills, CA 90069.

*　　　*　　　*

McMARTIN, John

PERSONAL: Born in Warsaw, IN. EDUCATION: Attended Columbia University.

VOCATION: Actor.

CAREER: OFF-BROADWAY DEBUT—Corporal Billy Jester, *Little Mary Sunshine*, Orpheum Theatre, 1959. PRINCIPAL STAGE APPEARANCES—Forrest Noble, *The Conquering Hero*, American National Theatre Academy (ANTA) Theatre, New York City, 1961; Captain Mal Malcolm, *Blood, Sweat and Stanley Poole*, Morosco Theatre, New York City, 1961; Mr. Dupar, *A Matter of Position*, Walnut Street Theatre, Philadelphia, PA, 1962; Sidney Balzer, *Children from Their Games*, Morosco Theatre, New York City, 1963; Edward Voorhees, *A Rainy Day in Newark*, Belasco Theatre, New York City, 1963; John Paul Jones, *Pleasures and Palaces*, Fisher Theatre, Detroit, MI, 1965; Oscar, *Sweet Charity*, Palace Theatre, New York City, 1966.

Benjamin Stone, *Follies*, Winter Garden Theatre, New York City, 1971, then Shubert Theatre, Century City, CA, 1972; Dion Anthony, *The Great God Brown* and Sganarelle, *Don Juan*, both at the Lyceum Theatre, New York City, 1972; *Sondheim: A Musical Tribute*, Shubert Theatre, New York City, 1973; *Forget-Me-Not Lane*, Mark Taper Forum, Los Angeles, 1973; Anton Schill, *The Visit* and Fedot, *Chemin de Fer*, both at the Ethel Barrymore Theatre, 1973; Foresight, *Love for Love* and Leone Gala, *The Rules of the Game*, both at the Helen Hayes Theatre, New York City, 1974; *Continental Divide*, ANTA West, Los Angeles, 1975; *The Autumn Garden*, Long Wharf Theatre, New Haven, CT, 1976; Alceste, *The Misanthrope*, New York Shakespeare Festival at the Anspacher Theatre, New York City, 1977; *Absurd Person Singular*, Ahmanson Theatre, Los Angeles, 1978; *Journey's End*, Long Wharf Theatre, New Haven, CT, 1978.

A Little Family Business, Ahmanson Theatre, Los Angeles, then Martin Beck Theatre, New York City, 1982; *Passion*, Mark Taper Forum, Los Angeles, 1983; *Solomon's Child*, Little Theatre, New York City, 1984.

PRINCIPAL FILM APPEARANCES—*What's So Bad About Feeling Good?*, Universal, 1968; *Sweet Charity*, Universal, 1969; *All the President's Men*, Warner Brothers, 1976; *Thieves*, Paramount, 1977; *Brubaker*, Twentieth Century-Fox, 1980; *Pennies from Heaven*, United Artists, 1981; *Legal Eagles*, Universal, 1986.

PRINCIPAL TELEVISION APPEARANCES—Dramatic Specials: *Murrow;* also appeared on *American Playhouse.* Movies: *Fear on Trial*, 1981. Episodic: *Mary Tyler Moore Show*, CBS.

MEMBER: Actors' Equity Association, Screen Actors Guild.

ADDRESSES: AGENT—Leaverton Associates, 1650 Broadway, New York, NY 10019.

*　　　*　　　*

McNALLY, Terrence　1939-

PERSONAL: Born November 3, 1939, in St. Petersburg, FL; son of Hubert Arthur and Dorothy Katharine (Rapp) McNally. EDUCATION: Columbia University, B.A., 1960.

VOCATION: Playwright.

WRITINGS: PLAYS, PRODUCED—(Adaptation) *The Lady of the Camellias*, Winter Garden, New York City, 1963; *And Things That Go Bump in the Night*, Tyrone Guthrie Theatre, Minneapolis, MN, 1964, then Royale Theatre, New York City, 1965; *Sweet Eros*, Gramercy Arts Theatre, New York City, 1968; *Witness*, Gramercy Arts Theatre, New York City, 1968; *Tour*, Mark Taper Forum, Los Angeles, 1967, then Cafe au Go Go, New York City, 1968; *Noon* (produced in a program with two other one-acts with the overall title, *Morning, Noon, and Night*) Henry Miller's Theatre, New York City, 1968; *Cuba Si!*, Theatre de Lys, New York City, 1968; book for the musical, *Here's Where I Belong*, Billy Rose Theatre, New York City, 1968; *Next*, Greenwich Mews Theatre, New York City, 1969.

Where Has Tommy Flowers Gone?, Yale Repertory Theatre, Eastside Playhouse, New York City, 1971; *Bad Habits* (two one acts, "Ravenswood" and "Dunelawn"), John Drew Theatre, East Hampton, NY, 1971, then Astor Place Theatre, New York City, 1974; *Botticelli*, Old Post Office Theatre, East Hampton, NY, 1971; *Bringing It All Back Home*, Provincetown Playhouse, New York City, 1971; *Sweet Eros* and *Next*, both produced on a double bill at the Open Space Theatre, London, 1971; *Whiskey*, Theatre at St. Clement's Church, New York City, 1973; *The Tubs*, Yale Repertory Theatre, New Haven, CT, 1974, revised version produced as *The Ritz*, Longacre Theatre, New York City, 1975, later revived at Henry Miller's Theatre, New York City, 1983; *The Golden Age*, first produced in New York City, 1975, revived at Jack Lawrence Theatre, New York City, 1984; *Broadway, Broadway*, John Drew Theatre, East Hampton, NY, and Shubert Theatre, Philadelphia, 1979; *It's Only a Play*, with the Manhattan Punch Line at the Actors and Directors Theatre, New York City, 1982; book for the musical, *The Rink*, Martin Beck Theatre, New York City, 1984.

Also author of *The Roller Coaster*, 1960, and *This Side of the Door* and *Let It Bleed*, 1972.

PLAYS, PUBLISHED—*And Things That Go Bump in the Night*, Dramatists Play Service, 1966; *Apple Pie: Three One-Act Plays*, Dramatists Play Service, 1968; *Botticelli*, Dramatists Play Service, 1968; *Sweet Eros and Witness: Two One-Act Plays*, Dramatists Play Service, 1969; *Sweet Eros, Next, and Other Plays* (contains "Sweet Eros," "Next," "Witness," "Cuba Si!," and "Botticelli"), Random House, 1969; *Noon* (one-act, with *Morning*, by Israel Horovitz, and *Night*, by Leonard Melfi), Random House, 1969; *Cuba Si!*, *Bringing It All Back Home*, *Last Gasps: Three Plays*, Dramatists Play Service, 1970; *Where Has Tommy Flowers Gone?: A Play*, Dramatists Play Service, 1972; *Whiskey*, Dramatists Play Service, 1973; *Bad Habits*, Dramatists Play Service, 1974; *The Ritz and Other Plays* (contains "The Ritz," "Where Has Tommy Flowers Gone?," "Bad Habits," "And Things That Go Bump in the Night," "Whiskey," and "Bringing It All Back Home"), Dodd, 1977. Also, *The Ritz*, Samuel French.

SCREENPLAYS—*The Ritz*, Warner Brothers, 1977.

TELEPLAYS—*Apple Pie* and *Last Gasps*, 1966; (adaptation) *The Five Forty-Eight*, PBS, 1979. RADIO PLAYS—*The Lisbon Traviata*, 1979.

RELATED CAREER—Stage manager, Actors' Studio, New York City.

NON-RELATED CAREER—Former newspaper reporter.

AWARDS: Most Distinguished Play, Obie Award, 1974, for *The Ritz*; fellowships: Guggenheim, 1966, 1969.

MEMBER: American Academy of Arts and Letters, Dramatists Guild (vice president, 1981).

ADDRESSES: HOME—218 W. Tenth Street, New York, NY 10014. AGENT—Howard Rosenstone, Rosenstone/Wender, Three E. 48th Street, New York, NY 10017.*

*   *   *

McNAMARA, Dermot   1925-

PERSONAL: Born August 24, 1925, in Dublin, Ireland; son of Peter (a clerk) and Anna Christina (a secretary; maiden name, Dowdall) McNamara; children: Annaleese, Peter Cormac. EDUCATION: Attended St. Joseph's College, Dublin, Ireland; trained for the stage at the Abbey Theatre School. RELIGION: Roman Catholic.

VOCATION: Actor, director, and manager.

CAREER: STAGE DEBUT—Phipps, *An Ideal Husband*, Gate Theatre, Dublin, 1949, for twenty-one performances. OFF-BROADWAY DEBUT—Christie, *Playboy of the Western World*, 1959-60, for three-hundred-six performances. PRINCIPAL STAGE APPEARANCES—Broadway: *Pictures in the Hallway*, Lincoln Center Theatre; Grumio, *The Taming of the Shrew*; Tom, *Philadelphia Here I Come*; Paddy, *A Touch of the Poet*; Drumm, *A Life*; also appeared in *Donnybrook*. Off-Broadway: Leopold Bloom, *Irish Players*; also *The Plough and the Stars*, *The Shadow of a Gunman*, *No Exit*, and *Stephen D*.

DERMOT McNAMARA

Regional: Pat, *The Hostage*, Loretto Hilton; *A Whistle in the Dark*, Long Wharf Theatre, New Haven, CT; Davies, *The Caretaker*, Nassau Repertory Theatre, NY; *Translations*, Alaska Repertory Theatre; Drumm, *DA* and Joxer, *Juno and the Paycock*, both at the Alley Theatre, Houston. Also appeared in *The Contractor*, A Contemporary Theatre, Seattle, WA; *O'Neill's Sea Plays* and *A Memory of Two Mondays*, both at the Cincinnati Playhouse.

MAJOR TOURS—U.S. cities: Christie Mahon, *Playboy of the Western World*; also *Shadow and Substance*, *Happy as Larry*, and *The Wake*.

TELEVISION DEBUT—Patch Keegan, "Little Moon of Alban," *Hallmark Hall of Fame*, NBC, 1965. PRINCIPAL TELEVISION APPEARANCES—Movies: *A Night to Remember*, NBC; Captain Matt Corcoran, *From Sea to Shining Sea*, NBC. Episodic: *One Life to Live*, ABC; *All My Children*, ABC. Dramatic Specials: Joxer, *Juno and the Paycock*, PBS; Sean O'Casey, *The Creative Person*, PBS; *The Best of Families*, PBS.

PRINCIPAL FILM APPEARANCES—*Ragtime*, Paramount, 1981; Scappy Peck, *The Year of the Dragon*, Metro-Goldwyn-Mayer/United Artists, 1985.

MEMBER: Actors' Equity Association, Screen Actors Guild, American Federation of Television and Radio Artists.

SIDELIGHTS: Among his skills, Dermot McNamara lists tennis, swimming, equestrian, soccer, and hurling.

ADDRESSES: HOME—556 Main Street, Roosevelt Island, NY

10044. AGENT—Hartig Agency, 114 E. 28th Street, New York, NY 10016.

*   *   *

McQUIGGAN, John   1935-

PERSONAL: Born January 12, 1935, in Detroit, MI. EDUCATION: Graduated from Washington and Lee University; trained for the stage at the Neighborhood Playhouse with Sanford Meisner and Martha Graham, 1957-59.

VOCATION: Producer.

CAREER: PRINCIPAL STAGE WORK—Producer and founder, APA Phoenix Repertory Company, NY, 1960; founder and producer, Milwaukee Repertory, WI, 1962-66; co-director and producer, *Project Discovery,* Trinity Square Repertory, RI; producer, *Horseman, Pass By,* New York City, 1969; producer, *The Foreigner,* Astor Place Theatre, New York City, 1983; producer, *Quartermaine's Terms,* Playhouse 90, New York City, 1983-84; producer, *The Common Pursuit,* Promenade Theatre, New York City, 1986-87; producer, *Money in the Bank* (upcoming).

PRINCIPAL TELEVISION WORK—Producer: Two plays for *Exxon's Theatre U.S.A.*

RELATED CAREER—Director of development, Performing arts division, Smithsonian Institution; developer, Arena Stage, Washington DC, 1974; organizer, Arts Counterparts, Inc., New York City; head consultant and production co-ordinator, Joffrey Ballet in Residence, Lincoln, NE.

ADDRESSES: OFFICE—New Roads Productions, 311 W. 43rd Street, Suite 702, New York, NY 10036.

*   *   *

McRAE, Glory

PERSONAL: Born October 26, in Jacksonville, FL; daughter of step-parents Walter Adams (an automobile dealership owner) and Glory Sims (Mott) McRae; married Frederick Hardy Bowen, Jr. (a vicepresident and head of research for a brokerage house), April 7, 1972; childen: Glory, Frederick Hardy III, Thomas Jefferson Mott. EDUCATION: Sweet Briar College, B.A., music and voice; trained for the stage at the American Academy of Dramatic Art and the Weist Barron School in New York City. RELIGION: Unitarian.

VOCATION: Actress, singer, and writer.

CAREER: STAGE DEBUT—Dream Sharon and Barbara Tyler, *Play It Again Sam,* first national touring company. PRINCIPAL STAGE APPEARANCES—Off-Broadway productions: Amamda and Annie, *The Second Coming;* Magdalena and Prudencia, *The House of Bernada Alba;* Susan Dunham, *A Nice Place to Visit.* Stock and repertory productions: Lady Percy, *Henry IV,* Part I; title role, *Antigone;* multiple roles, *Spoon River Anthology;* Mme. Ernestine

JOHN McQUIGGAN

GLORY McRAE

Von Liebedicht, *Little Mary Sunshine;* Corie, *Barefoot in the Park;* Poppie, *The Tender Trap;* Fair Witch and Miss Metcalf, *Dark of the Moon;* Sophie, *Star-Spangled Girl;* Gloria, *Everybody Loves Opal;* Maisie, *The Boyfriend.* Opera: Marguerite, *Faust* and first soprano, *Pagliacci,* both with the Jacksonville Opera Association. Dinner theatre: Toni Simmons, *Cactus Flower,* Carousel Dinner Theatre; Jenny Jones and Mrs. Waters, *Tom Jones,* Beef 'n Boards Dinner Theatre; Peggy Evans, *Come Blow Your Horn,* Chateau de Ville Dinner Theatre; Katrin Sveg, *The Marriage-Go-Round,* Westgate and Curtain-Up Dinner Theatres.

MAJOR TOURS—Packages: Flora Latham, *No, No, Nanette* and Katrin Sveg, *Marriage-Go-Round.*

PRINCIPAL TELEVISION APPEARANCES—Guest: *Carolina Today,* WNCT; *The Jim Gerard Show,* WRTZ; *The Diane Leeds Show,* WISH; *The Darell Travis Show,* WBLG; *The June Rollings Show,* WKYT; *The Marilyn Moosnik Show,* WLEX; *The Reed Farrell Show,* KPLR.

NON-RELATED CAREER— Florida State Welfare worker, Jacksonville, FL, 1967; also taught art appreciation to an elementary school.

MEMBER: Actors' Equity Association, Screen Actors Guild, American Federation of Television and Radio Artists; American Association of University Women, League of Women Voters; Town Club; Dog Obedience Club.

ADDRESSES: HOME—145 Lake Drive, Mountain Lakes, NJ 07046.

*   *   *

McROBBIE, Peter   1943-

PERSONAL: Born January 31, 1943, in Hawick, Scotland; son of William (a storekeeper) and Mary Fleming (a writer; maiden name, Heigh) McRobbie; married Charlotte Bova (an actress), September 15, 1977; children: Oliver William, Andrew Peter. EDUCATION: Yale School of Drama, B.A., 1966; studied acting with Uta Hagen at the Herbert Berghof Studios in New York City. MILITARY: U.S. Army, 1966-68.

VOCATION: Actor.

CAREER: STAGE DEBUT—James Anderson, *My Fat Friend,* Westport Country Playhouse, CT, 1975. BROADWAY DEBUT— Dr. Travers, *Whose Life Is It Anyway?,* Nederlander Theatre, 1979, for two hundred performances. PRINCIPAL STAGE APPEARANCES— Richard, *Rattle of a Simple Man,* Huntington Hartford Theatre, Los Angeles, 1975; Nebeker, *The Wobblies,* Labor Theatre, New York City, 1976; member of the resident company, Meadow Brook Theatre, Rochester, MI, 1977-79; standby, Dennis Quinlan, *Last Licks,* Longacre Theatre, New York City, 1979; Major Swindon, *The Devil's Disciple,* Equity Library Theatre, New York City, 1980; standby, *Mixed Couples,* Brooks Atkinson Theatre, New York City, 1980; member of the resident company, Tyrone Guthrie Theatre, Minneapolis, MN, 1981-83; murderer and doctor, *Macbeth,* Circle in the Square Theatre, New York City, 1982; member of the resident company, Shakespeare & Co., Lenox, MA, 1982; the Inspector, *Cinders,* New York Shakespeare Festival (NYSF), Public Theatre, New York City, 1984; Captain Gower, *Henry V,*

NYSF, Delacorte Theatre, New York City, 1984; Doc, *The Ballad of Soapy Smith,* NYSF, Public Theatre, New York City, 1984; standby Sam Evans, *Strange Interlude,* Nederlander Theatre, New York City, 1985; James Throttle, *The Mystery of Edwin Drood,* Imperial Theatre, New York City, 1985.

MAJOR TOURS—Sea captain and priest, *Twelfth Night,* Chicago and East coast tour, 1978.

FILM DEBUT—George Cooke, *A Jury of Her Peers,* independent, 1977. PRINCIPAL FILM APPEARANCES—Communist, *Zelig,* Warner Brothers, 1981; Milhauser, *The Beniker Gang,* Lorimar Productions, 1983; Twilly, *The Purple Rose of Cairo,* Orion Pictures, 1984; Electronics N.E.S.T., *The Manhattan Project,* Twentieth Century-Fox, 1986.

TELEVISION DEBUT—Dr. Steele, *As The World Turns,* CBS, 1980. PRINCIPAL TELEVISION APPEARANCES—Episodic: *New Show,* NBC, 1984; Thurmond Yoder, *The Guiding Light,* CBS, 1985.

MEMBER: Actors' Equity Association, Screen Actors Guild, American Federation of Radio and Television Artists.

ADDRESSES: AGENT—Abrams Artists, Inc., 420 Madison Avenue, New York, NY 10017.

*   *   *

MEADOW, Lynne   1946-

PERSONAL: Full name, Lynne Carolyn Elizabeth Meadow; born November 12, 1946, in New Haven, CT; daughter of Franklin Raymond and Virginia (Ribakoff) Meadow. EDUCATION: Bryn Mawr College, B.A., 1968; Yale School of Drama, 1968-70.

VOCATION: Artistic director, director, and producer.

CAREER: PRINCIPAL STAGE WORK—Artistic director, Manhattan Theatre Club, New York City, 1972—.

Director, Manhattan Theatre Club: *Jesus as Seen by His Friends, Shooting Gallery,* both 1973; *The Wager, Bits and Pieces,* both 1974; *Golden Boy,* 1975; *The Pokey, Ashes,* both 1976; *Chez Nous,* 1977; *Catsplay,* 1978; *Artichoke, The Jail Diary of Albie Sachs,* both 1979; *Vikings,* 1980; *Close of Play,* 1981; *Sally and Marsha, The Three Sisters,* both 1982; *Park Your Car in Harvard Yard,* 1984; also directed *Marco Polo,* Phoenix Theatre, New York City, 1976.

(All at the Manhattan Theatre Club, unless otherwise noted) As artistic director of Manhattan Theatre Club, has produced, among others: *Starting Here, Starting Now,* 1977; *Ain't Misbehavin',* Longacre Theatre, New York City, 1978; *Vikings, Crimes of the Heart, One Tiger to Kill, American Days, Close of Play, Real Life Funnies,* 1980-81; *Mass Appeal,* Booth Theatre, New York City, 1981; *Hunting Scenes from Bavaria, Harry Ruby's Songs My Mother Never Sang, The Resurrection of Lady Lester, Crossing Niagara, And I Ain't Finished Yet, No End of Blame, Strange Snow, Sally and Marsha, Livin' Dolls,* 1981-82; *The Singular Life of Albert Nobbs, Talking With, Standing on My Knees, Don't Start Me Talkin' or I'll Tell Everything I Know, The Three Sisters, Skirmishes, Summer, Triple Feature, Elba, Early Warnings, On the Swing*

Shift, 1982-83; *The Philanthropist, Blue Plate Special, Friends, A Backers' Audition, Mench Meier, Park Your Car in Harvard Yard, Other Places, The Miss Firecracker Contest*, 1983-84; *In Celebration, Husbandry, Messiah, Hang onto the Good Times, What's Wrong with this Picture?*, 1984-85.

RELATED CAREER—Director, New York Shakespeare Festival, New York City, 1977; adjunct professor, State University of New York at Stony Brook, 1975-76; director, Eugene O'Neill Playwrights' Conference, Waterford, CT, 1975-77; director, Yale University and Circle in the Square, New York City, 1977-80; theatre and music theatre panelist, National Endowment for the Arts, 1977—.

AWARDS: Outer Circle Crites Award, Drama Desk Award, and Obie Award, all 1977, for *Ashes*.

SIDELIGHTS: RECREATIONS—Tennis and skiing.

ADDRESSES: OFFICE—Manhattan Theatre Club, 453 W. 16th Street, New York, NY 10011.*

*   *   *

MEDOFF, Mark   1940-

PERSONAL: Born March 18, 1940, in Mount Carmel, IL; son of Lawrence R. (a physician) and Thelma Irene (a psychologist; maiden name, Butt) Medoff; married Vicki Eisler, 1967 (divorced); married Stephanie Thorne, June 29, 1972; children: Debra Ann, Rachel Celeste, Jessica Lynn. EDUCATION: University of Miami, B.A., 1962; Stanford University, M.A., 1966.

VOCATION: Playwright, director, actor, and educator.

CAREER: Playwright (see below). STAGE DEBUT—Teddy, *When You Comin' Back, Red Ryder?*, First Chicago Center Theatre, 1974. PRINCIPAL STAGE APPEARANCES—Andrei Bolkonski, *War and Piece;* Marat, *Marat/Sade;* Pozzo, *Waiting for Godot;* Harold Gorringe, *Black Comedy;* Bro Paradock, *A Resounding Tinkle.*

PRINCIPAL STAGE WORK—Director: *When You Comin' Back Red Ryder?; Waiting for Godot; The Effect of Gamma Rays on Man-in-the-Moon Marigolds; Jacques Brel Is Alive and Well and Living in Paris; The Birthday Party; One Flew Over the Cuckoo's Nest.*

RELATED CAREER—Supervisor of publications and assistant director of admissions, Capitol Radio Engineering Institue, Washington, DC, 1962-66; associate professor of English, New Mexico University, Las Cruces, NM, 1966-79, dramatist in residence, 1974, chairman of drama department, 1978, professor of drama, 1979.

WRITINGS: PLAYS, PRODUCED—*Doing a Good One for the Red Man*, Las Cruces, NM, 1969; *The Froegle Dictum*, Albuquerque, NM, 1971; *The Kramer*, American Conservatory Theatre, San Francisco, 1972, and Mark Taper Forum, Los Angeles, 1973; *The Wager*, H.B. Playwright's Foundation Theatre, 1972, then Eastside Playhouse, New York City, 1974; *War on Tatem*, Las Cruces, 1972; (with Carleene Johnson) *The Odyssey of Jeremy Jack*, New Mexico State University, 1974; *When You Comin' Back, Red Ryder?*, Circle Repertory Theatre, New York

City, Eastside Playhouse, New York City, 1973, First Chicago Center Theatre, 1974; *The Conversion of Aaron Weiss*, Guthrie Theatre, Minneapolis, 1977; *The Firekeeper*, Kalita Humphreys Theatre, Dallas, 1978; *The Halloween Bandit*, PAF Playhouse, Huntington, LI, then Jewish Repertory Theatre, New York City, 1978; *Children of a Lesser God*, New Mexico State University, then Longacre Theatre, New York City, 1980; *The Hands of Its Enemy*, Manhattan Theatre Club at City Center, New York City, 1986.

PLAYS, PUBLISHED—*Four Short Plays* ("Doing a Good One for the Red Man," "The Froegle Dictum," "The War on Tatem," and "The Ultimate Grammar of Life"), Dramatists Play Service, 1974; *The Odyssey of Jeremy Jack*, Dramatists Play Service, 1974; *When You Comin' Back, Red Ryder?*, Dramatists Play Service, 1974; *The Wager*, Dramatists Play Service, 1975; *The Wager: A Play in Three Acts, with Two Short Plays, Doing a Good One for the Red Man and The War on Tatem*, J.T. White, 1976; *Children of a Lesser God*, J.T. White, 1981; also *The Majestic Kid*, Dramatists Play Service; plays appear in *Best Plays, 1973-74, 1974-75, 1979-80* and *Best Short Plays, 1975.*

SCREENPLAYS—Co-adaptor, *Children of a Lesser God*, Paramount, 1986.

RADIO PLAYS—"The Disintegration of Aaron Weiss," *Earplay* Minnesota Public Radio, 1977.

AWARDS: Obie Award, Joseph Jefferson Award, Outer Critics Circle Award, John Gasner Award, 1973-74, all for *When You Comin' Back Red Ryder?;* Distinguished Playwrighting, Drama Desk Award, 1974; Westhofer Award, New Mexico State University, 1974, for excellence in creativity; Best Play, Antoinette Perry Award, Drama Desk Award, Outer Critics Circle Award, 1980, all for *Children of a Lesser God;* Governor's Award for the Arts, State University of New Mexico, 1981; Media Award, Presidential Commission on Employment for the Handicapped, 1981, for *Children of a Lesser God;* Best Screenplay Adaptation, Academy Award nomination, 1986, for *Children of a Lesser God;* honorary degrees: Gallaudet College, Doctor of Humane Letters, 1981; fellowships: Guggenheim, 1974-75.

MEMBER: Writers Guild of America, Dramatists Guild, Actors' Equity Association.

ADDRESSES: HOME—Las Cruces, NM. OFFICE—c/o Department of Drama, New Mexico State University, Box 3072, Las Cruces, NM 88001. AGENT—c/o Gilbert Parker, William Morris Agency, 1350 Avenue of the Americas, New York, NY 10019.*

*   *   *

MEREDITH, Burgess   1909-

PERSONAL: Born November 16, 1909, in Cleveland, OH; son of William George (a physician) and Ida Beth (Burgess) Meredith; married Helen Berrian Derby, 1932 (divorced, 1935); married Margaret H. Frueauff (also known as Margaret Perry), 1936 (divorced, July, 1938); married Paulette Goddard, May 23, 1944 (divorced, July, 1948); married Kaja Sundsten (a ballet dancer), 1950; children: Jonathan Sanford, Tala Beth. EDUCATION: Attended Amherst College, 1926-28. RELIGION: Episcopalian. MILITARY: U.S. Army Air Corps, World War II.

VOCATION: Actor, director, producer, and writer.

CAREER: FILM DEBUT—Mio, *Winterset*, RKO, 1936. PRINCIPAL FILM APPEARANCES—*There Goes the Groom*, RKO, 1937; *Spring Madness*, Metro-Goldwyn-Mayer (MGM), 1938; *Idiot's Delight*, MGM, 1939; *Of Mice and Men*, United Artists, 1939; *Castle on the Hudson*, Warner Brothers, 1940; *San Francisco Docks*, Universal, 1941; *Second Chorus*, Paramount, 1941; *That Certain Feeling*, 1941; *The Forgotten Village*, Mayer-Burstin, 1941; *Tom, Dick and Harry*, 1941; *Street of Chance*, Paramount, 1942; *Welcome to Britain*, 1943; *Salute to France*, 1944; *The Yank Comes Back*, 1945; *Story of G.I. Joe*, United Artists, 1945; *Diary of a Chambermaid*, United Artists, 1946; *Magnificent Doll*, Universal, 1946; *A Miracle Can Happen*, Paramount, 1947; *Mine Own Executioner*, 1948; *The Man on the Eiffel Tower*, RKO, 1949; *On Our Merry Way*, 1948; *Jigsaw*, 1949.

The Gay Adventure, Allied Artists, 1953; *Joe Butterfly*, Universal, 1957; *Universe*, 1961; *Advise and Consent*, Columbia, 1962; *The Cardinal*, Columbia, 1963; *In Harm's Way*, 1965; *Madonna X*, Universal, 1966; *A Big Hand for the Little Lady*, Universal, 1966; *The Torture Garden*, Columbia, 1966; *Hurry Sundown*, Paramount, 1967; *Stay Away, Joe*, MGM, 1968; *Hard Contract*, Twentieth Century-Fox, 1968; *MacKenna's Gold*, Columbia, 1969.

There Was a Crooked Man, Warner Brothers, 1970; *The Yin and the Yang*, 1970; *A Fan's Notes*, 1970; *The Clay Pigeon*, MGM, 1971; *Such Good Friends*, Paramount, 1971; *The Man*, Paramount, 1972; *B for Murder*, 1973; *Golden Needles*, American International, 1974; *The Day of the Locust*, Paramount, 1975; *92 in the Shade*, United Artists, 1975; *The Hindenburg*, Universal, 1975; *Burnt Offerings*, United Artists, 1976; *Rocky*, United Artists, 1976; *The Sentinel*, Universal, 1977; *The Manitou*, AVCO-Embassy, 1978; *Foul Play*, Paramount, 1978; *Magic*, Twentieth Century-Fox, 1978; *The Great Georgia Bank Hoax*, Warner Brothers, 1978; *Golden Rendezvous*, 1977; *Rocky II*, United Artists, 1979; *The Day the World Ended*, 1979; *Final Assignment*, 1979; *The Last Chase*, 1979.

When Time Ran Out, 1980; *Clash of the Titans*, United Artists, 1981; *True Confessions*, United Artists, 1981; *Rocky III*, Metro-Goldwyn-Mayer/United Artists, 1982; *Santa Claus, the Movie*, Tri-Star, 1985.

PRINCIPAL FILM WORK—Producer, *Diary of a Chambermaid*, United Artists, 1946; producer, *On Our Merry Way*, 1947; director, *Man on the Eiffel Tower*, RKO, 1949.

PRINCIPAL TELEVISION APPEARANCES—Series: Host, *Junior Ford Omnibus*, NBC, 1953; narrator, *The Big Story*, syndicated, 1957; Martin Woodridge, *Mr. Novak*, NBC, 1964-65; Penguin, *Batman*, ABC, 1965-66; Cameron, *Search*, NBC, 1972-73; host, *Those Amazing Animals*, ABC, 1981; Dr. Willard Adams, *Gloria*, CBS, 1983; also a frequent host on *Your Show of Shows*, NBC.

Episodic: *The Billy Rose Show*, ABC, 1951; "One Sunday Afternoon," *Ford Theatre*, CBS, 1951; "The Human Comedy," *DuPont Show of the Month*, CBS, 1959; *Springtime Pause to Refresh*, CBS, 1959; "Ah, Wilderness!," *Hallmark Hall of Fame*, NBC, 1959; "Freedom Sings," *Bell Telephone Hour*, NBC, 1960; "Waiting for Godot," *Play of the Week*, WNTA, 1961; also *Lights Out*, NBC; *Silver Theatre*, CBS; "Time Enough at Last," *Twilight Zone*, CBS; "Edison the Man," *General Electric Theatre*, CBS.

PRINCIPAL TELEVISION WORK—Director, "The Christmas Tie," *Omnibus*, CBS, 1952; producer, *Junior Ford Omnibus*, NBC, 1953; director, "Jet Propelled Couch," *Playhouse 90*, CBS, 1958.

RADIO DEBUT—Red Davis, Beechnut Company, 1934. PRINCIPAL RADIO PERFORMANCES—Title role, *Hamlet*, WABC, 1937; "Something about Love," *The Overcoat*, WABC, 1939; *Fall of the City*, CBS, 1939; *Pursuit of Happiness*, CBS, 1939; *Spirit of '41* and *Listen America!*, both for the War Department, 1941-42; *Cavalcade of America*, NBC, 1941; *Adventure*, ABC, 1951.

STAGE DEBUT—Walk on, Civic Repertory Theatre, New York City, 1929. PRINCIPAL STAGE APPEARANCES—Peter, *Romeo and Juliet*, Civic Repertory Theatre, New York City, 1930; various roles, Civic Repertory Theatre, New York City, 1930-33; Wick Martin, *People on the Hill*, Comedy Theatre, New York City, 1931; Peon, *Night Over Taos*, 48th Street Theatre, New York City, 1932; Crooked Finger Jack, *Threepenny Opera*, Empire Theatre, New York City, 1933; Red Barry, *Little Ol' Boy*, Playhouse Theatre, New York City, 1933; appeared in *I Am Laughing*, summer stock, Red Bank, NJ, 1933; appeared in *Jack Be Nimble*, Westchester County Playhouse, Mt. Kisco, NY, 1933; Buzz Jones, *She Loves Me Not*, 46th Street Theatre, New York City, 1933; Jim Hipper, *Hipper's Holiday*, Maxine Elliott Theatre, New York City, 1934; Seaman Jones, *Battleship Gertie*, Lyceum Theatre, New York City, 1935; Octavius Moulton, *The Barretts of Wimpole Street*, Martin Beck Theatre, New York City, 1935; Leonard Dobie, *The Flowers of the Forest*, Martin Beck Theatre, New York City, 1935; appeared in *Noah*, Central School Theatre, Glencove, NY, 1935; Mio, *Winterset*, Martin Beck Theatre, New York City, 1935; Van Van Dorn, *High Tor*, Martin Beck Theatre, New York City, 1937; Stephen Minch, *The Star Wagon*, Empire Theatre, New York City, 1937.

Title role, *Liliom*, 44th Street Theatre, New York City, 1940; Eugene Marchbanks, *Candida*, Shubert Theatre, New York City, 1942; speaker, *Lincoln Portrait*, Royal Albert Hall, London, 1943; Christopher Mahon, *The Playboy of the Western World*, Booth Theatre, New York City, 1946; Mio, *Winterset*, Gaiety Theatre, Dublin, Ireland, 1947.

Larry, *Happy as Larry*, Coronet Theatre, New York City, 1950; Gandersheim, *The Little Blue Light*, American National Theatre Academy (ANTA) Playhouse, New York City, 1951; Oliver Ertwenter, *The Silver Whistle*, summer stock, 1951; Michael, *The Fourposter*, Ethel Barrymore Theatre, New York City, 1952; Pa Pennypacker, *The Remarkable Mr. Pennypacker*, Coronet Theatre, New York City, 1953; Sakini, *Teahouse of the August Moon*, New York City, 1955; title role, *Hamlet*, Baylor University Theatre, Waco, TX, 1956; Adolphus Cusins, *Major Barbara*, Martin Beck Theatre, New York City, 1956; title role, *The Circus of Dr. Lao*, Edgewater Beach Playhouse, Chicago, 1957; Pa Pennypacker, *The Remarkable Mr. Pennypacker*, Edgewater Beach Playhouse, Chicago, 1958; title role, *Enrico*, Erlanger Theatre, Philadelphia, 1958; old man, *The Death of Cuchulain*, Beekman Tower Hotel Theatre, New York City, 1959; *The Vagabound King*, State Fair Theatre, Dallas, 1959; Arnold St. Clair, *The Plaster Bambino*, Marine's Memorial Theatre, San Francisco, 1959.

Mr. Kicks, *Kicks and Company*, Arie Crown Theatre, Chicago, 1961; Erie Smith, *Hughie*, Duchess Theatre, London, 1963; Daniel Considine, *I Was Dancing*, Lyceum Theatre, New York City, 1964; appeared in *The Little Foxes*, Westwood Playhouse, CA, 1976; summer stock: Marchbanks, *Candida*.

MAJOR TOURS—Prince Hal and King Henry V, *Five Kings*, pre-Broadway tour, Boston, Washington, DC, and Philadelphia, 1939; Elwood P. Dowd, *Harvey*, U.S. citics, 1950; *Teahouse of the August Moon*, U.S. cities, 1955; *An Evening with Burgess Meredith*, U.S. cities, 1960; Erie Smith, *Hughie*, U.K. cities, 1963.

PRINCIPAL STAGE WORK—Director: *Happy as Larry*, Coronet Theatre, New York City, 1950; *Season in the Sun*, Cort Theatre, New York City, 1950; *Let Me Hear the Melody*, Wilmington Theatre, DE, 1951; *Lo and Behold*, Booth Theatre, New York City, 1951; *Macbeth*, Bermuda, 1954; *Ulysses in Nighttown*, Rooftop Theatre, New York City, 1958; *God and Kate Murphy*, 54th Street Theatre, New York City, 1959; also conceiver, *A Thurber Carnival*, ANTA Theatre, New York City, 1960; *A Whiff of Melancholy*, Bucks County Playhouse, New Hope, PA, 1961; *Blues for Mr. Charlie*, ANTA Theatre, New York City, 1964, then, with the Actors Studio Company at the Aldwych Theatre, London, 1965; *Of Love Remembered*, ANTA Theatre, New York City, 1967; *The Latent Heterosexual*, Kalita Humphreys Theatre, Dallas, 1968; *Ulysses in Nighttown*, Winter Garden Theatre, New York City, 1974.

Co-producer, *Speaking of Murder*, Royale Theatre, New York City, 1956, then St. Martin's Theatre, London, 1958.

CONCERT WORK—Host and narrator, Honolulu Symphony Orchestra, 1961; director, New York Symphony Orchestra, Carnegie Hall, New York City, 1969.

RELATED CAREER—Artistic director, Merle Oberon Theatre, Los Angeles, 1972—.

WRITINGS: SCREENPLAYS—*The Diary of a Chambermaid*, United Artists, 1946; *The Yin and the Yang*, 1979. RADIO PLAYS—"Something about Love," *The Overcoat*, WABC, 1939.

RECORDINGS: ALBUMS—Narrator: *The Gold Rush*, Epic-Columbia, 1961; *The Ray Bradbury Stories*, Prestige, 1962; *The Wonderful O*, Colpix, 1965; also *Puff the Magic Dragon, Part II*, 1979; producer and director, *The Declaration of Independence*, 1963.

AWARDS: Best Director, Antoinette Perry Award nomination, 1974, for *Ulysses in Nighttown;* Best Supporting Actor, Academy Award nomination, 1976, for *Rocky;* Best Supporting Actor in a Dramatic Special, Emmy Award, 1977, for *Tail Gunner Joe;* honorary degrees: Amherst College, 1939.

MEMBER: Actors' Equity Association (vice-president and acting president, 1938), Actors Studio West (executive director, 1972), Screen Actors Guild, American Federation of Television and Radio Artists; Player's Club.

SIDELIGHTS: FAVORITE ROLES—Mio, *Winterset*. RECREATIONS—Farming and writing.

ADDRESSES: AGENT—Jack Fields Agency, 9255 Sunset Blvd., Suite 1105, Los Angeles, CA 90069.*

*   *   *

MEYERS, Ari   1969-

PERSONAL: Born Ariadne Meyer, in 1969, in Puerto Rico; daughter of Taro Meyer (an actress).

ARI MEYERS

VOCATION: Actress.

CAREER: PRINCIPAL TELEVISION APPEARANCES—Series: Emma McArdle, *Kate and Allie*, CBS, 1984—. Movies: *Running Out*, 1983; *License to Kill*, CBS, 1984; *Kid's Don't Tell*, CBS, 1985; *Picking Up the Pieces*, CBS, 1985; also *Haunted*, PBS. Pilots: *Full House*, CBS.

PRINCIPAL FILM APPEARANCES—*Author! Author!*, Twentieth Century-Fox, 1982.

SIDELIGHTS: RECREATIONS—Aerobic exercise, scuba-diving, movie-going and jewelry making.

Ari Meyers told *CTFT* that some of her original jewelry has been worn on screen by the stars of *Kate and Allie*.

ADDRESSES: AGENT—c/o Monique Moss, Michael Levine Public Relations, 9123 Sunset Blvd., Los Angeles, CA 90069.

*   *   *

MIDLER, Bette   1945-

PERSONAL: Born December 1, 1945, in Honolulu, HI; married Martin Von Haselberg, December, 1984; children: Sophie. EDUCATION: Attended University of Hawaii.

VOCATION: Actress, singer, and writer.

CAREER: FILM DEBUT—Extra, *Hawaii*, United Artists, 1966. PRINCIPAL FILM APPEARANCES—*The Rose*, Twentieth Century-Fox, 1979; *Divine Madness*, Warner Brothers, 1980; *Jinxed*, Metro-Goldwyn-Mayer/United Artists, 1982; *Down and Out in Beverly Hills*, Touchstone, 1986; *Ruthless People*, Touchstone, 1986; Sandy, *Outrageous Fortune*, Touchstone, 1987.

PRINCIPAL TELEVISION APPEARANCES—Specials: *Bette Midler: Old Red Hair Is Back*, NBC, 1978; also appeared in other specials of her own. Guest: *The Tonight Show*, NBC; *People*, CBS, 1978.

BROADWAY DEBUT—Chorus, *Fiddler on the Roof*, Imperial Theatre, 1966. PRINCIPAL STAGE APPEARANCES—Tzeitel, *Fiddler on the Roof*, Majestic Theatre, New York City, 1967-69; *Salvation*, New York City, 1970; *Tommy*, Seattle Opera Company, WA, 1971; *Clams on the Half Shell Revue*, Palace Theatre, New York City, 1973-74 and later at the Minskoff Theatre, New York City, 1975.

PRINCIPAL CONCERT APPEARANCES—At the Continental Baths in New York City; in Las Vegas, NV, with Johnny Carson, 1972; at Philharmonic Hall, New York City, 1972; *Bette! Divine Madness*, Majestic Theatre, New York City, 1979; appeared at Radio City Music Hall, New York City, 1983.

MAJOR TOURS—*Divine Madness*, U.S., European, and African cities.

WRITINGS: BOOKS—*A View from a Broad*, Simon & Schuster, 1980; *The Saga of Baby Divine*, 1983.

RECORDINGS: The Divine Miss M, 1972; *Bette Midler*, 1973; *Broken Blossom*, 1977; *Live at Last*, 1977; *Thighs and Whispers*, 1979; *New Depression*, 1979; *Divine Madness*, 1980; *No Frills*, 1984; *Mud Will Be Flung Tonight*, 1985.

AWARDS: After Dark Ruby Award, 1973; Grammy Award, 1973; Special Antoinette Perry Award, 1973; Outstanding Special, Emmy Award, 1978, for *Bette Midler: Old Red Hair Is Back;* Best Actress, Academy Award nomination, 1979, for *The Rose*.

SIDELIGHTS: In the two decades since Bette Midler decided to enter show business, her search for fulfillment—personal and professional—has had both fruitful and fallow periods. The highs have ranged from the enthusiasm with which her first audiences greeted her when her flamboyant stage persona burst into view in the early 1970s to a best actress nomination for her film debut in 1979 and critical and popular acclaim for the two books she authored. But she has had her share of lows as well, including a stormy business partnership and romance with her ex-manager; a disastrous second movie in 1982 that led to a long period of exhaustion and depression; the emotional fallout of an unhappy childhood; and a reputation—not entirely deserved—for being difficult to work with.

At the age of forty-one, however, she is riding high in both her private and professional lives. Marriage in December, 1984, to Martin von Haselberg, a commodities trader and occasional performance artist, and the birth of her daughter, Sophie, in late 1986, have given direction and joy to Midler's offstage life, and her once-stalled movie career is in high gear.

Named after her mother's favorite screen star, Bette Davis, Midler

credited her own youthful diversion of watching old Hollywood musicals which inspired her adult musical style. In 1965, she got her first acting job as an extra on the set of *Hawaii*. When the company moved to Hollywood to finish filming, she went along. After the shooting was completed, Midler travelled to New York City. She landed a job in the chorus of the Broadway play *Fiddler on the Roof*, eventually graduating to a featured role. It was also at this time that Midler was hired to sing at Manhattan's Continental Baths, a homosexual health spa and cabaret on the city's west side. Billing herself as "the divine Miss M.," Midler created the campy, bawdy, energetic style that became her trademark. Dressed in platform shoes, calf-length trousers, strapless tops, sequined gowns, and rhinestone girdles, she gestured and strutted and wisecracked as she sang songs from the 1940s, 1950s, and 1960s—novelty songs, blues, and rock. "I was able to take chances on that stage that I could never have taken anywhere else," Midler wrote in her book *A View from a Broad*. "The more outrageous I was, the more they liked it. It loosened me up."

As her fame spread, Midler began to receive offers from nightclubs, television shows, concert agents, and record companies. Signed for *The Tonight Show*, she proved so popular with late-night audiences that she played the show regularly for the next eighteen months, and in April, 1972, she appeared with host Johnny Carson in his nightclub act in Las Vegas. Her return to the New York nightclub circuit brought packed houses—and something of a cult status among the city's underground chic. In November, 1972, her first album, *The Divine Miss M.*, scored an impressive success, selling more than one hundred thousand copies in the first month of its release. By the end of the year Midler was performing at the Lincoln Center's Philharmonic Hall. At a special New Year's Eve event she entertained two sellout crowds and, with her usual irreverence, rose on to the stage dressed in a diaper and vinyl sash that read "1973."

In her act she sang songs from a wide variety of sources, prompting critics to comment on her musical scope. Chris Chase, for instance, maintained that "there's nothing she can't sing" (*New York Times*, January 14, 1973). Richard Poirier likewise noted in *New Republic* (August 2, 1975) that "she has the vocal resources to sing in the style of any woman vocalist of the past 30 years." He further observed: "Midler doesn't imitate or parody a specific singer through an entire song, however. Rather, like a person truly haunted, Midler in the phrasing of a song will suddenly veer off from one coloration into another. It sometimes happens with an air of true discovery. As with most great jazz singers, she therefore never does a song exactly the same way twice. The avenue of experimentation is always left open."

In 1972, Midler met Aaron Russo, who became her manager. When she told him to make her a legend, he took charge of her career with what some detractors have called the dominance of a Svengali. Their personal relationship quickly deteriorated, but Midler admired his business savvy and kept him as her manager until 1979. During that time he acquired a film property, *The Rose*, for Midler's first starring motion picture role. A serious portrayal of a self-destructive rock star, modeled on Janis Joplin, the film was a popular and critical triumph and brought Midler an Academy Award bid for best actress.

It was to be three years, however, before the diminutive diva was to see another film offer, and her acceptance of it led to what she described to interviewer Nancy Collins of *Rolling Stone* (December 9, 1982) as "the worst experience of my life. It drove me to a nervous breakdown." The power struggle between Midler, co-star Ken Wahl, and director Don Siegel was a constant source of friction, and the movie itself, appropriately titled *Jinxed*, was a box-office flop.

The next several years were largely unproductive ones for Midler. She still made records and took concert tours, but the zest that fans remembered from the early days was gone. It took meeting and marrying von Haselberg to snap the artist out of the sleepwalk that her life had become. She reset her priorities and began a career overhaul. The urge to be in pictures reasserted itself, so Midler set up her own production company to insure a steady supply of appealing film projects. She also signed a three-picture deal with Touchstone Films, an adult-oriented subdivision of Disney Studios. Midler's first movie from Touchstone was *Down and Out in Beverly Hills*, a 1986 production that co-starred Richard Dreyfuss and Nick Nolte. The film not only reignited Midler's career but went on to become tenth among 1986's box-office winners. In this comedy satirizing the conspicuous consumption of the super-rich, the actress played a wealthy, neurotic matron who is, according to movie reviewer Susan Stark in the *Detroit News* (January 31, 1986), "the antithesis of the trashy, flashy persona that brought Ms. Midler to fame."

The second of the Touchstone trilogy showcasing Midler's talent as a comic player, *Ruthless People*, was also released in 1986 and paired the actress with actor Danny DeVito in a complex, vulgar black comedy that impressed critics and moviegoers alike. Midler's role was that of a shrew whose husband is only too happy to see her kidnapped. When the kidnappers lower their ransom demand rather than do away with his wife, DeVito's greedy, lecherous Sam is enraged. "Midler hurls herself into this monster with unabashed glee," remarked David Ansen in *Newsweek* (June 30, 1986). "her expression when she discovers the nightmare truth—that she's been *marked down*—deserves to be preserved in amber."

The last of the trio of Midler films for Touchstone, *Outrageous Fortune*, opened in early 1987, likewise to favorable reviews. Described by David Ansen and Peter McAlevey in *Newsweek* (January 26, 1987), as "a buddy movie with two *women* in the leads," Midler and Shelley Long, *Outrageous Fortune* is a comedy thriller set in motion when a couple of rival New York actresses discover that they share a lover, who has mysteriously disappeared. Their frantic efforts to tract him down force them to become partners and, according to the two reviewers, provide "a servicable framework for a brash and clever entertainment about acting, friendship, and the delights of unfettered female vulgarity."

In a recent *Newsweek* interview with Midler (June 30, 1986), Cathleen McGuigan asked her if—with two movie successes within one year behind her and at least two more projects well under way, with a new husband and a new baby—she were happy now. Smiling broadly, Midler replied, "Of course I am. I'm delirious."

ADDRESSES: OFFICE—c/o Kathy Acquavna, Atlantic Records, 75 Rockefeller Plaza, New York, NY 10019. AGENT—c/o Rick Nicita, Creative Artists Agency, 1888 Century Park East, Suite 1400, Los Angeles, CA 90067.*

*   *   *

MILANO, Alyssa   1972-

PERSONAL: Born December 19, 1972, in New York, NY; daughter of Thomas M. (a music editor) and Lin (a fashion designer) Milano. EDUCATION: Attending Bel Air Preparatory School, Los Angeles.

VOCATION: Actress.

CAREER: STAGE DEBUT—July, *Annie*, national tour, June, 1980. OFF-BROADWAY DEBUT—Adele, *Jane Eyre*, Theatre Opera Music Institute (T.O.M.I.). PRINCIPAL STAGE APPEARANCES—Lisa, *Tender Offer*, New York Ensemble Theatre, New York City; Terry, *All Night Long*, with the Second Stage Theatre Company at the McGinn/Cazale Theatre, New York City, 1984; *Warning Signals*, Manhattan Theatre Club, New York City.

MAJOR TOURS—July and understudy Molly, *Annie*, U.S. cities, 1980-81.

FILM DEBUT—Lisa, *Old Enough*, Orion, 1982. PRINCIPAL FILM APPEARANCES—Jenny, *Commando*, Twentieth Century-Fox, 1985.

TELEVISION DEBUT—Samantha, *Who's the Boss*, ABC, 1984—. PRINCIPAL TELEVISION APPEARANCES—Movies: Jenny, *The Canterville Ghost*, HTV.

AWARDS: Best Supporting Actress in a Television Series, Youth Films Award, for *Who's the Boss*.

MEMBER: Actors' Equity Association, Screen Actors Guild, American Federation of Television and Radio Artists.

ADDRESSES: HOME—Studio City, CA. OFFICE—AJM Productions, 500 S. Sepulveda Blvd., Los Angeles, CA 90049. AGENT—c/o Stu Ehrlich, International Creative Management, 8899 Beverly Blvd., Los Angeles, CA 90048.

*   *   *

MILLER, Ann   1919-

PERSONAL: Born Lucille Ann Collier, April 12, 1919, in Houston, TX; daughter of John and Clara Emma (Birdwell) Collier; married Reese Milner (divorced); married William Moss (divorced); married Arthur Cameron (divorced). EDUCATION: Attended Lawler Professional School, Hollywood, CA; trained as a dancer when a child.

VOCATION: Actress, singer, dancer, and writer.

CAREER: FILM DEBUT—*New Faces of 1937*, 1937. PRINCIPAL FILM APPEARANCES—*Life of the Party*, 1937; *Stage Door*, 1937; *Room Service*, 1939; *You Can't Take It with You*, 1939; *Too Many Girls*, 1940; *Time Out for Rhythm*, 1941; *Reveille with Beverly*, 1943; *Eve Knew Her Apples*, 1945; *Thrill of Brazil*, 1946; *The Kissing Bandit*, Metro-Goldwyn-Mayer (MGM), 1948; *Easter Parade*, MGM, 1948; *On the Town*, MGM, 1949; *Watch the Bride*, MGM, 1950; *Texas Carnival*, MGM, 1951; *Two Tickets to Broadway*, 1951; *Lovely to Look At*, MGM, 1952; *Hit the Deck*, 1952; *Small Town Girl*, MGM, 1952; *Kiss Me, Kate*, MGM, 1953; *Deep in My Heart*, MGM, 1954; *The Opposite Sex*, MGM, 1956; *The Great American Pastime*, MGM, 1956; *That's Entertainment*, United Artists, 1974; *That's Entertainment, II*, United Artists, 1976; *Won Ton Ton*, Paramount, 1976; also appeared in *Radio City Revels*; *Having a Wonderful Time*; *Priorities on Parade*; *Jam Session*.

BROADWAY DEBUT—*George White Scandals*, Alvin Theatre,

1939. PRINCIPAL STAGE APPEARANCES—Title role, *Mame*, Winter Garden Theatre, New York City, 1969-70; Ann, *Sugar Babies*, Mark Hellinger Theatre, New York City, 1979-82; also appeared in *Can Can, Hello, Dolly!, Panama Hattie, Blithe Spirit.*

MAJOR TOURS—*Mame*, U.S. cities, 1970-71; *Hello, Dolly!*, Ohio and Indiana cities, 1971; Reno Sweeney, *Anything Goes*, U.S. cities, 1974, then again in 1976; *Cactus Flower*, U.S. cities, 1978-79; Ann, *Sugar Babies*, U.S. cities, 1982-86.

PRINCIPAL TELEVISION APPEARANCES—Specials: *The Magic of Christmas*, 1968. Guest: *Ed Sullivan Show*, CBS, 1958, 1959; *The Perry Como Show*, NBC, 1961; *The Bob Hope Show*, 1961; *Palace Shows*, between 1966 and 1968; *The Jonathan Winters Show*, CBS, 1969.

WRITINGS: BOOKS—*Miller High Life*, Doubleday, 1972; *Tops in Taps*, 1981.

AWARDS: Antoinette Perry Award nomination, 1980, for *Sugar Babies;* Israeli Cultural Award, 1980; Woman of the Year Award, Anti-Defamation League, 1980; also created Dame of the Knights of Malta.

SIDELIGHTS: Ann Miller, the dancer, the actress, the singer, is known today for never quite making it big as a star. David Shipman says in *The Great Movie Stars: The International Years* (Hill & Wang, 1981) that Miller "used to refer to herself as the near-click of show business." In a more positive vein, Miller is remembered for her zestiness, her long, sexy legs, her "classy chassis and sequined tights" (*The MGM Stock Company: The Golden Era*, Arlington House, 1973), and particularly for her machine-gun tapping which is known to top five hundred taps per minute. In addition, Miller has been labeled Queen of the B movies, "those wonderful nonsense movies of the 1930s and '40s," writes Jerry Tallmer for the *New York Post* (June 7, 1969).

Ann Miller was born Lucille Ann Collier (though some sources cite her name as Johnnie Lucille, with the implication that her father wanted a son). At age five she was sent to dancing school by her mother as therapy for a case of rickets. Since her mother and father separated when Miller was still a child, she started tap dancing at the Elks and Rotary Clubs to help support her mother and herself. When she won a personality contest at age ten, her mother took her to Hollywood. While tap dancing at the Bal Tabarin, Miller was discovered by Lucille Ball and Benny Rubin, who notified RKO talent scouts. RKO was interested and Miller's first movie, made while she was still a teenager, was *New Faces of 1937*. In close succession she appeared in *Stage Door* with Katharine Hepburn and Ginger Rogers, in *Too Many Girls* with Lucille Ball and Desi Arnaz, and in *Room Service* with the Marx brothers. Ephraim Katz remarked in *The Film Encyclopedia* (Crowell, 1979) that "for a decade . . . her talents were wasted on mainly minor comedy musicals."

It was not until the late 1940s that Miller entered her golden period. She acted in such musicals as *Easter Parade* with Judy Garland and Fred Astaire, *On the Town* with Gene Kelly and Frank Sinatra, and as Bianca in her favorite, *Kiss Me Kate*. Only in *Kiss Me Kate* did Miller get a high billing, but her show-stopping dancing numbers kept her alive in film for nearly two decades. When her film career ended in the mid-1950s, she appeared in nightclubs, on television, and occasionally on the stage. Blake Green for the *San Francisco Chronicle* (May 24, 1979) recorded Miller's remarks regarding her early career: "I've seen Hollywood at the top and at the bottom . . .

and I still think it is one of the most fascinating places on earth. I came along at the tail end of the golden era, and I don't think we'll ever see its likes again."

Miller acted on the stage once during 1939 in George White's *Scandals of 1939*. She returned as Mame in the Broadway production of the same name in 1969, and according to Louis Botto for *Playbill* (October, 1981), on opening night when she took her tap shoes from her bag she immediately received an ovation. Tallmer observed that "as the new leading lady, [Miller has] injected a whole new shot of plasma into the tired Broadway bloodstream." Describing her appearance in *Mame* to Tallmer, Miller said: "I had three marriages, did 40 movies, played the top TV shows, but in my personal life I never found happiness. It took Broadway to fix that up. I've never felt better in my life." And ten years later, in 1979, Miller was starring on Broadway again, this time with Mickey Rooney in *Sugar Babies*, a Broadway musical about the heyday of Burlesque. As she enthusiastically told Green, "I have the strangest feeling I'll be tapping when I'm 80."

ADDRESSES: AGENT—c/o Contemporary Korman Agency, 132 Lasky Drive, Beverly Hills, CA 90212.*

*   *   *

MILLER, Jason 1939-

PERSONAL: Born April 22, 1939, in Scranton, PA; son of John (an electrician) and Mary (a teacher) Miller; married Linda Gleason, 1963 (divorced, 1973); children: Jennifer, Jason, Jordan. EDUCATION: Attended University of Scranton, B.A., 1961; Catholic University.

VOCATION: Actor and writer.

CAREER: OFF-BROADWAY DEBUT—Pip, *Pequod*, Mercury Theatre, 1969. PRINCIPAL STAGE APPEARANCES—The assistant, *The Happiness Cage*, New York Shakespeare Festival (NYSF), Estelle Newman Theatre, New York City, 1970; appeared at the Windmill Dinner Theatre, Fort Worth, TX, 1970; Paryfon Rogozhin, *Subject to Fits*, NYSF, Public Theatre, New York City, 1971; Edmund Tyrone, *Long Day's Journey into Night* and appeared in *Juno and the Paycock*, both at the Hartke Theatre, Catholic University, Washington, DC, 1971; Coach, *That Championship Season*, Montage, PA, 1987; also performed with the Champlain Shakespeare Festival, Burlington, VT, Cincinnati Shakespeare Festival, OH, and at the Baltimore Center Stage, MD.

PRINCIPAL FILM APPEARANCES—Father Karras, *The Exorcist*, Warner Brothers, 1973; Cooper, *Nickel Ride*, Twentieth Century-Fox, 1975; *The Ninth Configuration*, 1980; *Monsignor*, Twentieth Century-Fox, 1982.

PRINCIPAL TELEVISION APPEARANCES—Movies: *F. Scott Fitzgerald in Hollywood*, 1976; *The Dain Curse*, 1978; *Vampire*, 1979; *Henderson Monster*, 1980; *A Touch of Scandal*, CBS, 1984; Dr. Miles Keefer, *Deadly Care*, CBS, 1987; also *A Home of Our Own*.

WRITINGS: PLAYS, PRODUCED—*Lou Gehrig Did Not Die of Cancer, Perfect Son,* and *The Circus Lady*, all performed on a triple-bill at the Triangle Theatre, New York City, 1967; *Nobody Hears a Broken Drum*, Fortune Theatre, New York City, 1970; *That Championship Season*, NYSF Estelle Newman Theatre, then

Booth Theatre, New York City, 1972 and Garrick Theatre, London, 1974; also wrote *It's a Sin to Tell a Lie*. PLAYS, PUBLISHED—*Lou Gehrig Did Not Die of Cancer, It's a Sin to Tell a Lie*, and *The Circus Lady*, all published in one volume, Dramatists Play Service, 1971; *Nobody Hears a Broken Drum*, Samuel French; *That Championship Season*, Dramatists Play Service, 1972.

SCREENPLAYS—*That Championship Season*, Cannon, 1982. TELEVISION—Movies: *Marilyn: The Untold Story*, 1980; *The Reward*, 1980.

POETRY—*Stone Step*, printed privately, 1968.

AWARDS: Best Play, New York Drama Critics Circle Award, 1972, and Antoinette Perry Award and Pulitzer Prize Award, both 1973, all for *That Championship Season*; Best Supporting Actor, Academy Award nomination, 1974, for *The Exorcist*.

ADDRESSES: AGENT—c/o Earl Graham, The Graham Agency, 311 W. 43rd Street, New York, NY 10036.*

*   *   *

MILLER, June   1934-

PERSONAL: Born June 10, 1934, in West Lawn, PA; daughter of Ralph Walter (a factory worker) and Grace Emma (a factory worker; maiden name, Bickel) Miller. EDUCATION: Pennsylvania State University, B.A., 1960; studied acting with William Hickey at the Herbert Berghof Studios in New York City.

JUNE MILLER

VOCATION: Actress.

CAREER: STAGE DEBUT—Lila, *The Whole Town's Talking*, Gretna Playhouse, Gretna, PA, 1956. PRINCIPAL STAGE APPEARANCES—Joey's mother, *Where People Gather*, Gramercy Arts Theatre, New York City, 1967; over twenty productions at the Shady Lane Playhouse, PA, including: Karen, Muriel, and Norma, *Plaza Suite*, Clea, *Black Comedy*, Lena, *Take My Wife*, Clara, *In One Bed*, and Jessica, *The Tender Trap*; Gillian, *Bell, Book & Candle*, Royal Victoria Playhouse, Nassau, Bahamas; Judy, *Send Me No Flowers*, Bolton Hill Dinner Theatre; Grace, *Under Papa's Picture*, Old Log Theatre; Mrs. Bradman, *Blithe Spirit*, Highlands Playhouse; *Voice of the Turtle*, Outer Banks Theatre. *The Solid Gold Cadillac*, Gretna Playhouse.

MAJOR TOURS—Standby, *Plaza Suite*, Bus & Truck tour.

PRINCIPAL TELEVISION APPEARANCES—Series: Nurse, *The Doctors*, NBC, 1971; Lorraine Caton, *As the World Turns*, CBS; Erma, *Another World*, NBC.

MEMBER: Actors' Equity Association, American Federation of Television and Radio Artists, Screen Actors Guild.

ADDRESSES: HOME—400 W. 43rd Street, Apt. 350, New York, NY 10036.

*   *   *

MINER, Jan   1917-

PERSONAL: Full name, Janice Miner; born October 15, 1917, in Boston, MA; daughter of Walter Curtis (a dentist) and Ethel Lindsey (a painter; maiden name, Chase) Miner; married Richard Merrell (a writer), May 5, 1963. EDUCATION: Attended Vesper George School of the Arts, Boston, MA; trained for the stage with Lee Strasberg, David Craig, Ira Cirker, and Don Richardson.

VOCATION: Actress.

CAREER: STAGE DEBUT—*Street Scene*, Copley Theatre, Boston, 1945. BROADWAY DEBUT—Maria Louvin, *Obligato*, Theatre Marquee, 1958. PRINCIPAL STAGE APPEARANCES—With the Copley Theatre Company, Boston, 1945-48; Frances Black, *Light Up the Sky*, Playhouse Theatre, Cincinnati, OH, 1958; Peggy, *Viva Madison Avenue!*, Longacre Theatre, New York City, 1960; Lottie Lacey, *The Dark at the Top of the Stairs*, Cape Playhouse, Dennis, MA, 1960; Pampina, *The Decameron*, 74th Street Playhouse, New York City, 1961; Alice Lambkin, *Dumbbell People in a Barbell World*, Cricket Theatre, New York City, 1962; Reporter, *There Must Be a Pony*, Mineola Playhouse, Long Island, NY, 1962; Yvonne, *Intimate Relations*, Mermaid Theatre, New York City, 1962; standby and appeared for Hermione Baddeley, *The Milk Train Doesn't Stop Here Anymore*, Morosco Theatre, New York City, 1963; Prudence, *The Lady of the Camellias*, Winter Garden Theatre, New York City, 1963; appeared in *Long Distance*, Palace Vaudeville Theatre, New York City, 1963; third woman, *The Wives*, Stage 73 Theatre, New York City, 1965; Mistress Quickly, *Henry IV Part I* and a woman of Canterbury, *Murder in the Cathedral*, both at the American Shakespeare Festival, Stratford, CT, 1966; Nancy Reed, *The Freaking Out of Stephanie Blake*, Eugene O'Neill Theatre, New York City, 1967; Megaera, *Androcles and the Lion,* American Shakespeare Festival, Stratford, 1968; Mabel, *Lemonade* and Lila, *The Autograph Hound,* both at the Jan Hus Playhouse, New York City, 1968.

Emilia, *Othello* and widow of Florence, *All's Well That Ends Well,* both with the American Shakespeare Festival, Stratford, 1970; Emilia, *Othello,* American National Theatre Academy (ANTA) Theatre, New York City, 1970; Mistress Quickly, *The Merry Wives of Windsor,* American Shakespeare Festival, Stratford, 1971; Mrs. Baker, *Butterflies Are Free,* Booth Theatre, New York City, 1971; Lady Britomart Undershaft, *Major Barbara,* American Shakespeare Festival, Stratford, 1972; Countess de Lage, *The Women,* 46th Street Theatre, New York City, 1973; Aunt Meme, *Saturday, Sunday, Monday,* Martin Beck Theatre, New York City, 1974; Amanda Wingfield, *The Glass Menagerie* and Mrs. Fisher, *The Show-Off,* Olney Theatre, Olney, MD, 1975; repeated role of Mrs. Fisher, *The Show-Off,* Long Wharf Theatre, New Haven, CT, 1975; Lavinia, *The Heiress,* Broadhurst Theatre, New York City, 1976; Nurse, *Romeo and Juliet,* Circle in the Square, New York City, 1977; Madame Arcati, *High Spirits,* Darien Dinner Theatre, CT, 1977; Margaret Lord, *The Philadelphia Story,* Long Wharf Theatre, New Haven, 1978; Bodey, *A Lovely Sunday for Creve Coeur,* for the Sports Festival, USA, 1978; Fanny Farrelly, *Watch on the Rhine,* Long Wharf Theatre, New Haven, 1979, then John Golden Theatre, New York City, 1980.

Appeared in *Eve,* Repertory Theatre of St. Louis, MO, 1980; Frau Winifred Wagner, *The Music Keeper,* South Street Theatre, New York City, 1982; appeared in *The Glass Menagerie,* with the Hartford Stage Company, CT, 1982; appeared in *Astopovo,* Yale Repertory Theatre, New Haven, CT, 1982-83; Nurse Guiness, *Heartbreak House,* Circle in the Square, New York City, 1983; appeared in *The Torch-Bearers,* Hartman Theatre, Stamford, CT, 1984; appeared in *Cat on a Hot Tin Roof,* Long Wharf Theatre, 1985; *Gertrude Stein and a Companion,* White Barn Theatre, Westport, CT, 1985.

PRINCIPAL FILM APPEARANCES—*Ten Girls Ago,* unreleased, 1962; *The Swimmer,* Columbia, 1968; *Lenny,* United Artists, 1974; *Willie and Phil,* Twentieth Century-Fox, 1980.

PRINCIPAL TELEVISION APPEARANCES—Series: Ann Williams, *Crime Photographer,* CBS, 1951-52; regular, *Robert Montgomery Presents,* NBC, 1954-56; *Our Father's House,* 1978. Episodic: *The Jackie Gleason Show,* CBS; *N.Y.P.D.,* WPIX; *The Defenders,* CBS; *The Nurses,* CBS; *Naked City,* ABC; *Alcoa Playhouse,* NBC; *Lux Video Theatre,* CBS; *Schlitz Playhouse of Stars,* CBS; also *Friends and Lovers.*

PRINCIPAL RADIO WORK—Appeared on *Boston Blackie, Casey, Crime Photographer,* and *Dimension X.*

RELATED CAREER—Has appeared since 1965 as Madge the Manicurist for Colgate-Palmolive Liquid, doing commercials in French, German, and Italian, in addition to English.

AWARDS: Best dramatic actress award, nine consecutive years, for radio work.

MEMBER: Actors' Equity Association, Screen Actors Guild (board member), American Federation of Television and Radio Artists; Variety Arts.

ADDRESSES: AGENT—Hester Lewis Agency, 156 E. 52nd Street, New York, NY 10022.*

MITCHELL, David   1932-

PERSONAL: Born May 12, 1932, in Honesdale, PA; son of Amos D. and Ruth (Cole) Mitchell; married Emily Jon Fouts, September 9, 1961; children: Jennifer Lee, David Nathaniel. EDUCATION: Attended Pennsylvania State University at Kutztown, 1950-54, and Boston University, 1957-60. MILITARY: U.S. Army, 1955-57.

VOCATION: Scene and costume designer.

CAREER: FIRST STAGE WORK—Scene designer, *Henry V,* New York Shakespeare Festival (NYSF), 1965. PRINCIPAL STAGE WORK—Scene designer (unless otherwise indicated): *Medea,* Martinique Theatre, New York City, 1965; *Macbeth,* 1966, *Volpone* and *Hamlet,* 1967, all for the NYSF, New York City; *A Cry of Players,* Berkshire Theatre Festival, 1968; also costume designer, for the Repertory Theatre of Lincoln Center, New York City: *The Increased Difficulty of Concentration,* 1969, *Steambath, Dolette, Trelawny of the Wells,* 1970, *How the Other Half Loves, The Basic Training of Pavlo Hummel, The Incomparable Max,* 1971.

The Cherry Orchard, 1972, *Barbary Shore,* 1973, *Short Eyes,* Public Theatre and Vivian Beaumont Theatre, New York City, 1974, all for the New York Shakespeare Festival; *The Cherry Orchard,* Goodman Theatre, Chicago, 1974; *The Wager, In the Boom Boom Room,* and *Enter a Free Man,* 1974; *Little Black Sheep* and *Trelawny of the Wells,* both at the Vivian Beaumont Theatre, New York City, and *Shoe Shine Parlor,* 1975; *Apple Pie, Mrs. Warren's Profession, Henry V, Mondongo* and *A Photograph,* 1976; *Annie, I Love My Wife, The Marriage Proposal,* 1977; other designs include *The Gin Game,* Long Wharf Theatre, New Haven, CT, and New York City, 1976; *I Love My Wife,* London, 1977; *Working,* 46th Street Theatre, New York City, 1978; *End of the War,* Ensemble Studio Theatre, New York City, 1978; *Annie,* London, 1978; *I Remember Mama,* Majestic Theatre, New York City, 1979; *The Price,* Playhouse Theatre, New York City, 1979; *The Gin Game,* London, 1979.

Barnum, St. James Theatre, New York City, 1980; *Can-Can,* Minskoff Theatre, New York City, 1981; *Foxfire,* Ethel Barrymore Theatre, New York City, 1982; *Brighton Beach Memoirs,* Alvin Theatre, New York City, 1983; *Dance a Little Closer,* Minskoff Theatre, New York City, 1983; *Private Lives,* Lunt-Fontanne Theatre, New York City, 1983; *La Cage aux Folles,* Palace Theatre, New York City, 1983; *The Old Flag,* George Street Playhouse, New Brunswick, NJ, 1984; *Harrigan 'N Hart,* Longacre Theatre, New York City, 1985; *Biloxi Blues,* Ahmanson Theatre, Los Angeles, then Neil Simon Theatre, New York City, 1985.

Operas: *Madame Butterfly* and *Lord Byron,* Juilliard School, New York City; *Aida* and *Falstaff,* Teatro Municipal Theatre, Santiago, Chile; *Pelleas et Melisande,* New England Conservatory Theatre; *Manon,* San Francisco Opera; *Macbeth,* Washington Opera and Houston Grand Opera, TX; *Boris Godunov,* Cincinnati Opera and Canadian Opera; *The Italian Straw Hat,* Santa Fe Opera, NM; *Mephistophele,* New York City Opera; *Aida,* Deutsche Oper, Berlin, Germany; *Il Trovatore,* Paris Opera.

Ballets: *Ravel Festival,* New York City Ballet, 1974; *Journeys,* Pennsylvania Ballet; also costume designer, *The Steadfast Tin Soldier,* New York City Ballet, 1979; *The Magic Flute,* New York City Ballet, 1983; *Rossini Quartets,* New York City Ballet, 1983; *Liebeslieder Walzer,* New York City Ballet, 1984.

PRINCIPAL FILM WORK—Designer, *Rich Kids,* United Artists, 1979; *One Trick Pony,* Warner Brothers, 1980; *My Dinner with Andre,* 1981.

PRINCIPAL TELEVISION WORK—Scene and costume designer, "The Steadfast Tin Soldier," *Dance in America,* PBS.

AWARDS: Drama Desk Award, 1974, for *Short Eyes;* Antoinette Perry Award nomination, 1976, for *Trelawny of the Wells;* Antoinette Perry Award, Outer Critics Circle Award, both 1977, for *Annie;* Antoinette Perry Award nomination, 1978, for *Working;* Antoinette Perry Award, Joseph Maharan Award, both 1980, for *Barnum;* Antoinette Perry Award nominations, 1981, for *Can-Can* and 1982, for *Foxfire.*

MEMBER: United Scenic Artists Union.

ADDRESSES: AGENT—International Creative Management, 40 W. 57th Street, New York, NY 10036.*

*   *   *

MITCHELL, John H.   1918-

PERSONAL: Born April 27, 1918, in New York City; son of Ralph and Lillian II. (Heidelberg) Mitchell; married Patricia W., November 29, 1969; children: Joan E. Fletcher. EDUCATION: Universtiy of Michigan, A.B., economics, 1939. MILITARY: U.S. Navy, 1942-45.

JOHN H. MITCHELL

VOCATION: Studio executive and television consultant.

CAREER: Vice-president of sales, Screen Gems-Columbia Pictures Television, 1952-77, president, 1969-77; board of directors, Columbia Pictures Industries; president, John H. Mitchell Company, Inc., 1977—.

AWARDS: Liberty Award, B'Nai Brith Anti-Defamation League; Man of the Year Award, Conference of Personal Managers, West.

MEMBER: Hollywood Radio and Television Society (president, 1975-76), Academy of Television Arts and Sciences (president, 1980-83), Television Academy Hall of Fame (founder and chairman, 1983—); vice-president, Beverly Hills/Trousdale Homeowners Association.

ADDRESSES: HOME—1039 Wallace Ridge, Beverly Hills, CA 90210. OFFICE—1801 Avenue of the Stars, Suite 312, Los Angeles, CA 90067.

*   *   *

MOFFAT, Donald   1930-

PERSONAL: Born December 1930, in Plymouth, England; son of Walter George (an insurance agent) and Kathleen Mary (Smith) Moffat; married Anne Murray Elisperman (an actress), May 22, 1954 (divorced, August, 1968); married Gwen Arner (an actress), May, 1969; children: (first marriage) Kathleen Wendy, Gabriel Robin; (second marriage) Lynn Marie, Catherine Jean. EDUCATION: Attended King Edward VI School, Totnes and Dartington Hall, Devon, 1951-52; trained for the stage at the Royal Academy of Dramatic Art, 1952-54. MILITARY: Royal Artillary, 1949-51.

VOCATION: Actor and director.

CAREER: STAGE DEBUT—Earl of Loam, *The Admirable Crichton,* school production, U.K., 1947. LONDON DEBUT—First murderer, *Macbeth,* Old Vic Theatre, 1954. BROADWAY DEBUT—Mr. Ogmore and Nogood Boyo, *Under Milkwood,* Henry Miller's Theatre, 1957. PRINCIPAL STAGE APPEARANCES—First murderer, *Macbeth,* Edinburgh Festival, Scotland, 1954; Sir Stephen Scroop, *Richard II,* Old Vic Theatre, London, 1955; Earl of Douglas, *Henry IV, Part I,* Old Vic Theatre, London, 1955; Earl of Warwick, *Henry IV, Part II,* Old Vic, London, 1955; Mr. Martin, *The Bald Soprano* and Grandfather Jack, *Jack,* both at the Sullivan Street Playhouse, New York City, 1958; Detective Inspector Bruton, *Listen to the Mockingbird,* Colonial Theatre, Boston, then Shubert Theatre, Washington, DC, 1958; Shabyelsky, *Ivanov,* Renata Theatre, New York City, 1959; Verges, *Much Ado About Nothing,* Lunt-Fontanne Theatre, New York City, 1959.

George, *The Tumbler,* Helen Hayes Theatre, New York City, 1960; Clerk of the Court, *Duel of Angels,* Helen Hayes Theatre, New York City, 1960; Ohio Shakespeare Festival, Akron, 1960: title role, *Richard II,* Earl of Worcester, *Henry IV, Part I,* Justice Shallow, *Henry IV, Part II* and Chorus, *Henry V;* for the Association of Producing Artists (APA), McCarter Theatre, Princeton, NJ, 1961: Laudisi, *Right You Are. . .If You Think You Are,* Geronte, *Scapin,* Dr. Dorn, *The Seagull* and Reverend Canon Chasuble, *The Importance of Being Earnest;* for the Akron Shakespeare Festival, 1961: title role, *Macbeth,* Malvolio, *Twelfth Night,* and Gremio, *The Taming of the Shrew;* Mr. Tarlton, *Misalliance,* Sheridan

Square Playhouse, New York City, 1961; Sam McBryde, *A Passage to India*, Ambassador Theatre, New York City, 1962; title role, *Richard II* and Touchstone, *As You Like It*, both at the Great Lakes Shakespeare Festival, Cleveland, OH, 1962; Julian Skeffington, *The Affair*, Henry Miller's Theatre, New York City, 1962; Dick Dudgeon, *The Devil's Disciple*, A and B, *Act without Words*, and Henry IV, *The Emperor*, all at the Playhouse in the Park, Cincinnati, OH, 1963; Gremio, *The Taming of the Shrew*, Phoenix Theatre, New York City, 1963; title role, *Henry V* and Duke Vincentio, *Measure for Measure*, both at the Great Lakes Shakespeare Festival, Cleveland, OH, 1963; Aston, *The Caretaker*, Players Theatre, New York City, 1964; Octavius Robinson and Jack Tanner, *Man and Superman*, University of Michigan and Phoenix Theatre, New York City, 1964.

Andrei, *War and Peace*, New York City production, 1965; Martin Vanderhof, *You Can't Take It with You*, Lyceum Theatre, New York City, 1965; Lamberto Laudisi, *Right You Are. . .If You Think You Are*, Lyceum Theatre, New York City, 1966; Joseph Surface, *School for Scandal*, Lyceum Theatre, New York City, 1967; also Hjalmar Ekdal, *The Wild Duck*, Martin Vanderhof, *You Can't Take It with You*, and Andrei, *War and Peace*, all New York City, 1967; Lopahin, *The Cherry Orchard* and Jack Mohan, *Cock-a-Doodle Dandy*, both at the Lyceum Theatre, New York City, 1969; Horatio, *Hamlet*, 1969; Chanal, *Chemin de Fer*, Mark Taper Forum, Los Angeles, 1969.

Richard, *Father's Day*, New Theater for Now, Los Angeles, 1970, then John Golden Theatre, New York City, 1971; title roles, *Hadrian VII* and *The Magistrate*, Bucks County Playhouse, New Hope, PA, 1970-71; Thomas Melville, *The Trial of the Catonsville Nine*, Mark Taper Forum, Los Angeles, 1971; Boniface, *Hotel Paradiso*, Seattle Repertory Theatre, WA, 1971; *The Crucible*, Ahmanson Theatre, Los Angeles, 1972; *Forget-Me-Not Lane*, Mark Taper Forum, Los Angeles, 1973; Vagabond, *The Tavern*, Seattle Repertory, 1973; Joseph Malley, *Child's Play*, 1973, Harpagon, *The Miser*, 1974, and Moricet, *13 Rue de l'Amour*, 1975, all Studio Arena Theatre, Buffalo, NY; *The Kitchen* and *Cock-a-Doodle Dandy*, both at the Los Angeles Actors' Theatre, 1975; Captain Shotover, *Heartbreak House*, Westwood Playhouse, Los Angeles, 1976; John Tarleton, *Misalliance*, Academy Festival Theatre, Chicago, 1976; Estragon, *Waiting for Godot* and *Krapp's Last Tape*, both at the Los Angeles Actors Theatre, 1977; Scott, *Terra Nova*, Mark Taper Forum, Los Angeles, 1979.

Gardner Church, *Painting Churches*, South Street Theatre, New York City, 1983; Cam MacMillan, *Play Memory*, Longacre Theatre, New York City, 1984; James, *Passion Play*, Mark Taper Forum, Los Angeles, 1985; also appeared in *The Iceman Cometh*, New York City and Los Angeles, 1986.

MAJOR TOURS—Pat, *The Hostage*, U.S. and Canadian cities, 1961.

PRINCIPAL STAGE WORK—Stage manager: *Salad Days*, Vaudeville Theatre, London, 1954; *Romanoff and Juliet*, Piccadilly Theatre, London, 1955; *The Skin of Our Teeth*, University Players, Princeton, NJ, 1957.

Director: *A Midsummer Night's Dream*, Akron Shakespeare Festival, OH, 1961; *Julius Caesar* and *The Merry Wives of Windsor*, Great Lakes Shakespeare Festival, Cleveland, OH, 1964; *Miss Julie*, McCarter Theatre, Princeton, NJ, 1966; *New York. . .and Who to Blame It On*, for the APA Phoenix Theatre, New York City, 1968; *Cock-a-Doodle Dandy*, New York City, 1969; *Father's*

Day, John Golden Theatre, New York City, 1971; *13 Rue de l'Amour*, Studio Arena Theatre, Buffalo, 1975; *Cock-a-Doodle Dandy*, Los Angeles Actors Theatre, 1975; *Wakefield Mystery Plays*, Los Angeles Actors Theatre, CA, 1977.

FILM DEBUT—Swanson, *Pursuit of the Graf Spee*, Rank, 1957. PRINCIPAL FILM APPEARANCES—The father, *Rachel, Rachel*, Warner Brothers, 1968; Thomas Manning, *The Trial of the Catonsville Nine*, Columbia, 1970; *R.P.M.*, Columbia, 1970; Manning, *Great Northfield Minnesota Raid*, Universal, 1972; Art, *Showdown*, Universal, 1973; McPherson, *Terminal Man*, Warner Brothers, 1974; *Earthquake*, Universal, 1974; *On the Nickel*, 1979; *Strangers*, 1979; *Health*, 1979; *Promises in the Dark*, Warner Brothers, 1979; *Popeye*, Paramount, 1980; *License to Kill*, 1983; *The Right Stuff*, Warner Brothers, 1983; *Alamo Bay*, Tri-Star, 1985.

PRINCIPAL TELEVISION APPEARANCES—Series: Reverend Lundstrom, *The New Land*, ABC, 1974; Rem, *Logan's Run*, CBS, 1977-78. Episodic: "Ad Astra," *Camera Three*, CBS, 1958; Jimmy, "You Can't Have Everything," *U.S. Steel Hour*, CBS, 1961; also appeared on *Armstrong Circle Theatre*, NBC; *DuPont Show of the Month*, NBC; *Bonanza*, NBC; *High Chaparral*, NBC. Movies: *Eleanor and Franklin*, 1977; *Sergeant Matlovich Vs. the U.S. Air Force*, 1977; *Forget-Me-Not Lane*, 1979; *Tartuffe*, 1979; *Who Will Love My Children*, 1982.

AWARDS: Best Featured Performance, Los Angeles Drama Critics Award nomination, 1986, for *The Iceman Cometh*.

MEMBER: Actors' Equity Association, Screen Actors Guild, American Federation of Television and Radio Artists, Society of Stage Directors and Choreographers.

SIDELIGHTS: FAVORITE ROLES—Hjalmar Ekdal, Estragon and Lamberto Laudisi. RECREATIONS—Photography.

ADDRESSES: HOME—223 33rd Street, Hermosa Beach, CA 90254. AGENT—Triad, 10100 Santa Monica Blvd., 16th Floor, Los Angeles, CA 90067.

*   *   *

MOLL, Richard   1943-

PERSONAL: Full name, Charles Richard Moll; born January 13, 1943, in Pasadena, CA; son of Harry Findley (a lawyer) and Violet Anita (a nurse; maiden name, Grill) Moll. EDUCATION: University of California at Berkeley, B.A.; trained for the stage with Jack Kosslyn and Lawrence Parke.

VOCATION: Actor and writer.

CAREER: TELEVISION DEBUT—Lohr Khan 1, *Bigfoot and Wildboy*, ABC, 1978. PRINCIPAL TELEVISION APPEARANCES—Series: Milo Beaudry, *Dukes of Hazzard*, CBS, 1979-81; Bull, *Night Court*, NBC, 1984—.

Episodic: *Laverne and Shirley*, ABC; *Just Our Luck*, ABC; *Nine to Five*, ABC; *Remington Steele*, NBC; *Happy Days*, ABC; *Alice*, CBS; *Fall Guy*, ABC; *Fantasy Island*, ABC; *T.J. Hooker*, ABC; *Bret Maverick*, NBC; *Buck Rogers in the Twenty-Fifth Century*, NBC; *The Misadventures of Sheriff Lobo*, NBC; *The Rockford*

RICHARD MOLL

Files, NBC; *The Gangster Chronicles,* NBC; *How the West Was Won,* ABC; *The A-Team,* NBC; *Santa Barbara,* NBC.

Movies: *The Jericho Mile,* ABC, 1979; *Combat High,* NBC, 1987.

FILM DEBUT—Joseph Smith, *Brigham,* Sunset, 1977. PRINCIPAL FILM APPEARANCES—*Caveman,* United Artists, 1981; *Hard Country,* Marble Arch, 1981; *Liar's Moon,* Hanna, 1981; *The Sword and the Sorcerer,* Group 1, 1982; *Metalstorm,* Universal, 1983; *Dungeonmaster,* Empire, 1985; *House,* New World, 1986; *Survivor,* Flangeport, London; also appeared in *Evilspeak; Ragewar; The Horror Star; American Pop; Cataclysm.*

STAGE DEBUT—Squire Cribbs, *The Drunkard,* San Francisco, CA, 1967, for ten performances. PRINCIPAL STAGE APPEARANCES—Oberon, *As You Like It;* Northumberland, *Richard II;* Friar Francis, *Much Ado About Nothing,* and appeared in *Cymbeline,* all at the Globe Theatre, San Diego, CA; Oberon, *A Midsummer Night's Dream* and Caliban, *The Tempest,* both at Will Geer's Theatricum Botanicum; Abraham Lincoln, *The Lincoln-Douglas Debates,* The American Living History Theatre, Los Angeles.

WRITINGS: PLAYS—(co-author) *The Lincoln-Douglas Debates.*

AWARDS: Golden Scroll Award, Academy of Science Fiction, Fantasy and Horror Films.

MEMBER: American Federation of Television and Radio Artists, Screen Actors Guild; Friars Club (honorary), National Child Passenger Safety Association (honorary chariman).

SIDELIGHTS: Richard Moll told *CTFT* that his decision to become an actor came to him, "by asking myself what I *wanted* to do, not what I *should* do, or was *supposed* to do."

ADDRESSES: AGENT—Jack Rose Talent Agency, 6430 Sunset Blvd., Suite 1203, Hollywood, CA 90028. PUBLICIST—Laurence Frank & Company Public Relations, 4605 Lankershim Blvd., North Hollywood, CA 91602.

*   *   *

MOONEY, Debra

PERSONAL: Born Debra Vick; daughter of Henry M. and Isabel (Smith) Vick; children: Kirstin. EDUCATION: Auburn University, B.A.; University of Minnesota, M.F.A., acting.

VOCATION: Actress.

CAREER: OFF-BROADWAY DEBUT—Vee Talbott, *Battle of Angels,* Circle Repertory Theatre, 1975. PRINCIPAL STAGE APPEARANCES—All New York City: Wendy, *The Farm,* Circle Repertory Theatre, 1976; Jan Atwater, *Stargazing,* Circle Repertory Theatre, 1978; Faye Medwick, *Chapter Two,* Imperial Theatre, 1978; Sally, *Talley's Folly,* Brooks Atkinson Theatre, 1980; *The Dining Room,* Playwrights Horizons, 1982; Betty, *A Think Piece,* Circle Repertory Theatre, 1982; Leah Heron, *Wonderland,* Hudson Guild Theatre, 1982; Lillian Cornwall, *Isn't It Romantic,* Lucille Lortel Theatre, 1984; Mickey, *The Odd Couple,* Broadhurst Thea-

DEBRA MOONEY

tre, 1985-86; Sally, *The Perfect Party,* Playwrights Horizons, 1986. Also appeared as Ada, *Childe Byron,* Frau Wolf, *The Beaver Coat,* Debra, *George and Rosemary,* Alma, *Summer and Smoke,* Blanche, *A Streetcar Named Desire;* also *What I Did Last Summer, Death of a Salesman.*

PRINCIPAL FILM APPEARANCES—*Chapter Two,* Columbia, 1979; *Tootsie,* Columbia, 1982; *Cross Creek,* Universal, 1983; also Mrs. Kirkpatrick, *Agent on Ice.*

TELEVISION DEBUT—Dr. Petrie, *Delvecchio,* CBS, 1976. PRINCIPAL TELEVISION APPEARANCES—Grace, *All My Children,* ABC; Molly, *The Guiding Light,* CBS; "Don't Touch" *ABC Afterschool Special;* also appeared in *The Cradle Will Fall.*

RELATED CAREER—Instructor, University of Minnesota; announcer, KUOM Radio.

AWARDS: Dramalogue Award, for *Talley's Folly.*

MEMBER: Actors' Equity Association, Screen Actors Guild, American Federation of Television and Radio Artists, Circle Repertory Company.

ADDRESSES: AGENT—Gage Group, 1650 Broadway, New York, NY 10019.

*   *   *

MOORE, Melba   1945-

PERSONAL: Born Melba Hill, October 29, 1945, in New York City; daughter of Teddy and Melba (Smith) Hill; married George Brewingston. EDUCATION: Montclair State Teachers College, B.A.

VOCATION: Actress and singer.

CAREER: PRINCIPAL TELEVISION APPEARANCES—Series: *Melba Moore-Clifton Davis Show,* CBS, 1972; title role, *Melba,* CBS, 1986. Mini-Series: *Ellis Island,.* CBS, 1984. Episodic: *Hotel,* ABC. Specials: Harriet Tubman, *The American Woman: Portraits of Courage.*

PRINCIPAL FILM APPEARANCES—*Lost in the Stars,* American Film Theatre, 1974.

PRINCIPAL STAGE APPEARANCES—Chorus and Sheila, *Hair,* Broadway production; *Purlie,* Broadway production, 1970.

NON-RELATED CAREER—Teacher, New York City Public Schools.

RECORDINGS: ALBUMS—*Melba Moore; Peach Melba; This Is It; A Portrait of Melba; The Other Side of the Rainbow; Never Say Never; Read My Lips; A Lot of Love.*

AWARDS: Antoinette Perry Award, New York Drama Critics' Award, and Drama Desk Award, all 1970, for *Purlie;* Grammy Award nomination, 1985, for *Read My Lips,* and previously for *This Is It.*

MELBA MOORE

Photography by Carol Weinberg

ADDRESSES: AGENT—c/o Monique Moss, Michael Levine Agency, 9123 Sunset Blvd., Los Angeles, CA 90069.

*   *   *

MORIARTY, Michael   1941-

PERSONAL: Born April 5, 1941, in Detroit, MI; son of George and Elinor (Paul) Moriarty; married Francoise Martinet, June, 1966 (divorced); married Anne Hamilton Martin; children: (first marriage) Matthew. EDUCATION: Attended Dartmouth College; trained for the stage at the London Academy of Music and Dramatic Art.

VOCATION: Actor, director, writer, and composer.

CAREER: OFF-BROADWAY DEBUT—Octavius Caesar, *Antony and Cleopatra,* New York Shakespeare Festival (NYSF), Delacorte Theatre, 1963. PRINCIPAL STAGE APPEARANCES—Jack, *As You Like It* and Floritzel, *The Winter's Tale,* 1963, Longaville, *Love's Labour's Lost* and Helenus, *Troilus and Cressida,* 1965, all at the NYSF, Delacorte Theatre, New York City; *Major Barbara,* Charles Street Playhouse, Boston, 1966; with the Tyrone Guthrie Theatre Company, Minneapolis, MN: *Enrico IV,* Crawford Livingston Theatre, St. Paul, MN, 1968, chorus, *The House of Atreus* and Ted Ragg, Charles Fish, and Ignatius Dullfeet, *The Resistable Rise of Arturo Ui,* both at the Tyrone Guthrie Theatre, Minneapolis, and at the Billy Rose Theatre, New York City, 1968, *Mourning Becomes Electra,* Tyrone Guthrie Theatre, 1969.

The Alchemist, Crawford Livingston Theatre, St. Paul, 1970; *In the Jungle of Cities,* Charles Street Playhouse, Boston, 1970; Man, *Peanut Butter and Jelly,* University of the Streets Theatre, New York City, 1970; Thoreau, *The Night Thoreau Spent in Jail,* Alley Theatre, Houston, TX, 1970; George Mische, *The Trial of the Catonsville Nine,* Good Shepherd Church, then Lyceum Theatre, New York City, 1971; Julian Weston, *Find Your Way Home,* Brooks Atkinson Theatre, New York City, 1974; title role, *Richard III,* Mitzi E. Newhouse Theatre, Lincoln Center, New York City, 1974; Edmund Tyrone, *Long Day's Journey into Night,* Brooklyn Academy of Music, NY, 1976; chorus, *Henry V,* NYSF, Delacorte Theatre, 1976; Scoutmaster Hennessey, *Dirty Jokes,* Lake Forest Theatre, Chicago, 1976; Micah, *G. R. Point,* Playhouse, New York City, 1979; Kenneth Harrison, *Whose Life Is It Anyway?,* Kennedy Center, Washington, DC; *The Ballad of Dexter Creed* and Astrov, *Uncle Vanya,* both NYSF, at the Public Theatre, New York City, 1982; Captain Queeg and Barney Greenwald, *The Caine Mutiny Court Martial,* Circle in the Square, New York City, 1983; *The Night of the Iguana,* Broadway production, 1985-86.

PRINCIPAL STAGE WORK—Director: *Love's Labour Lost and Psalm to the Son of Man,* both at St. John's Cathedral, New York City, 1979; producer, *What Everywoman Knows,* NYSF, Public Theatre, New York City, 1982.

PRINCIPAL FILM APPEARANCES—*Bang the Drum Slowly,* Paramount, 1973; *The Last Detail,* Columbia, 1974; *Report to the Commissioner,* United Artists, 1975; *Who'll Stop the Rain?,* United Artists, 1978; *Shoot It Black, Shoot It Blue,* Thorn/EMI, 1974; *Winged Serpent,* 1982; *The Link,* 1982; *Reborn,* 1984; *Pale Rider,*

MICHAEL MORIARTY

Warner Brothers, 1985; *Troll,* Empire Pictures, 1986; *The Stuff,* New World Pictures, 1986; Williamson, *Hanoi Hilton,* Cannon, 1987; also, *Dark Tower,* Spectrafilms, upcoming.

PRINCIPAL TELEVISION APPEARANCES—Movies: Wilbur Wright, *The Winds of Kitty Hawk,* ABC, 1978; *Too Far to Go,* 1979; Dorf, *Holocaust,* NBC. Specials: Gentleman Caller, *The Glass Menagerie,* PBS.

WRITINGS: PLAYS, PRODUCED—*Flight to the Fatherland,* GeVa Theatre, Rochester, NY, 1979; *The Ballad of Dexter Creed,* NYSF, Public Theatre, New York City, 1982.

MUSIC—*Symphony for String Orchestra,* Greenwich House Orchestra, New York City, 1984.

AWARDS: Best Actor, Antoinette Perry Award, *Theatre World* Award, and Drama Desk Award, all 1974, for *Find Your Way Home;* Best Supporting Actor in a Drama, Emmy Award, 1974, for *The Glass Menagerie;* San Sebastian International Film Festival Award, 1979, for *Too Far to Go;* Outstanding Creative Versatility Award, Yeshiva University.

ADDRESSES: AGENT—Estelle Lasher Management, 75-11 147th Street, Kew Garden Hills, NY 11367.

*   *   *

MOSS, Jeffrey B.   1945-

PERSONAL: Born January 8, 1945; son of Seymour L. (a manufacturer) and Shirley R. (Bach) Moss; married Susan Schulman; children: Amanda, Shaun. EDUCATION: Pennsylvania State University, B.A.; Columbia University, M.F.A.

VOCATION: Director and designer.

CAREER: PRINCIPAL STAGE WORK—Director: *Mayor,* Top of the Gate, Village Gate, New York City; *Some Enchanted Evening,* King Cole Room, St. Regis-Sheraton Hotel, New York City, then Kennedy Center, Washington, DC; *This Must Be Love* and *Hooray for Hollywood,* both at the King Cole Room, St. Regis-Sheraton Hotel, New York City; also directed *The Drunkard; Fiddler on the Roof; On the Twentieth Century; Golden Boy; South Pacific; I Do, I Do; Pal Joey; Ain't Misbehavin'; An Evening with Romberg; Hair.* Associate director: *Big Apple Country.* Scenic and costume designer for Broadway productions.

MAJOR TOURS—Director, *A New Road to Freedom,* U.S. cities.

PRINCIPAL TELEVISION WORK—Director: *The Drunkard;* scenic and costume designer for network television.

ADDRESSES: OFFICE—205 Lexington Avenue, New York, NY 10016.

*   *   *

MOTTA, Bess

BRIEF ENTRY: Actress, singer, and dancer. Bess Motta currently plays host and instructor on the television aerobic show *20 Minute Workout.* She appeared in London in *The Great American Back-*

stage Musical for six months before returning to the United States where she enrolled in an aerobic class to lose weight. Using her dance and theatre training, she became the instructor of the class and was seen by a producer who then arranged her televison program. She sings in concert and has appeared in two films, *The Terminator* and *You Talkin' to Me?* Motta has also appeared in television commercials as spokesperson for Converse Aerobic and Fitness Shoes, Kraft Foods, Coppertone, and the Crystal Light National Aerobic Championship. She told *CTFT,* "Most people get into singing after acting—I started in music and although I love to do films as well, singing is really my first passion."

*   *   *

MULLIGAN, Richard   1932-

PERSONAL: Born November 13, 1932, in the Bronx, NY; married wife Lenore; children: James.

VOCATION: Actor.

CAREER: PRINCIPAL TELEVISION APPEARANCES—Series: Sam Garrett, *The Hero,* NBC, 1966-67; Jeff Harmon, *Diana,* NBC, 1973-74; Burt Campbell, *Soap,* ABC, 1978-81; Reggie Potter, *Reggie,* ABC, 1983. Episodic: *Kate McShane,* CBS; *Charlie's Angels,* ABC; *Medical Story,* NBC; *Dog and Cat,* ABC; *Doctor's Hospital,* NBC; *Knowledge; Little House on the Prairie,* NBC; *The Love Boat,* ABC; *Switch,* CBS; *Kingston: Confidential,* NBC. Movies: *Jealousy, Malibu, Harvey, The Pueblo Incident, Having Babies II.* Guest: *The Mike Douglas Show, The Merv Griffin Show, The Dinah Shore Show, Hollywood Squares.*

PRINCIPAL FILM APPEARANCES—*One Potato Two Potato,* Cinema V, 1964; *The Group,* United Aritsts, 1966; *Little Big Man,* National General, 1970; *A Change in the Wind,* Cinerama, 1972; *Irish Whiskey Rebellion,* 1972; *From the Mixed-Up Files of Mrs. Basil E. Frankweiler,* Cinema V, 1973; *Visit to a Chief's Son,* 1974; *The Big Bus,* Paramount, 1976; *Scavenger Hunt,* Twentieth Century-Fox, 1979; *S.O.B.,* Paramount, 1981; *The Trail of the Pink Panther,* Metro-Goldwyn-Mayer/United Artists (MGM/UA), 1982; *Summertime,* 1983; *Teachers,* MGM/UA, 1984; *Micki and Maude,* Columbia, 1984; *The Heavenly Kid,* Orion, 1985; *A Fine Mess,* Columbia, 1986; *Quicksilver,* Columbia, 1986; *The Music Box,* Columbia, upcoming.

BROADWAY DEBUT—Understudy to Arthur Hill and Tom Wheatley, *All the Way Home,* Belasco Theatre, 1960. PRINCIPAL STAGE APPEARANCES—Phil Matthews, *Nobody Loves an Albatross,* Lyceum Theatre, New York City, 1963; Max, *Everybody Out, the Castle Is Sinking,* Colonial Theatre, Boston, MA, 1964; Charlie, *Never Too Late,* The Playhouse, New York City, 1965; Roger MacDougall, *Mating Dance,* Eugene O'Neill Theatre, New York City, 1965; Matthew Stanton, *Hogan's Goat,* American Place Theatre, New York City, 1966; Joe Grady, *The Only Game in Town,* Mechanic Theatre, Baltimore, MD, 1968; with the Repertory Theatre, New Orleans, LA, 1970 season; Bob Phillips, *How the Other Half Loves,* Royale Theatre, New York City, 1971; Dan Train, *Ring Round the Bathtub,* Martin Beck Theatre, New York City, 1972; Martin Cramer, *Thieves,* Broadhurst Theatre, New York City, 1974; Michael Ruskin, *Special Occasions,* Music Box Theatre, New York City, 1982; also appeared in *The Crucible; Luv; Other People; Pound on Demand; Beyond the Horizon; Glass Menagerie; The Great God Brown; Never Too Late.*

AWARDS: Theatre World Award, 1965; Outstanding Lead Actor in a Comedy, Emmy Award, 1980, for *Soap.*

MEMBER: Actors' Equity Association, Screen Actors Guild, American Federation of Television and Radio Artists.

ADDRESSES: AGENT—Litke-Grossbart Management Ltd., 8500 Wilshire Blvd., Beverly Hills, CA 90210.*

*   *   *

MURPHY, Donn B.   1930-

PERSONAL: Born July 21, 1930, in San Antonio, TX; son of Arthur Morton (a college president) and Clare Frances (a writer; maiden name, McCarthy) Murphy. EDUCATION: Benedictine College, KS, B.A., sociology, 1954; Catholic University of America, M.F.A., speech and drama, 1956; University of Wisconsin, Ph.D., theatre and psychology, 1965. POLITICS: Democrat. RELIGION: Roman Catholic. MILITARY: U.S. Army, 1950-52.

VOCATION: Actor, director, writer, educator, and administrator.

CAREER: FIRST STAGE WORK—Lighting director, Starlight Theatre, Kansas City, MO, 1955-56. PRINCIPAL STAGE WORK—Professor of theatre, chairman of department of Fine Arts, Georgetown University, Washington, DC, 1954—. Directed at Georgetown University: *Stalag 17,* 1955; *Macbeth, Banned in Boston,* and *The*

DONN B. MURPHY

First Legion, all 1956; *The Importance of Being Earnest, The Most Happy Jet*, and *Teahouse of the August Moon*, all 1957; *Julius Caesar, The Natives Are Restless, The Madwoman of Chaillot*, and *The Caine Mutiny Court Martial*, all 1958; *Anyone Mind?* and *Detective Story*, both 1959; *Captain Brassbound's Conversion, The Thirties Girl*, and *The Firstborn*, all 1960; *My Three Angels, Down the Hatch*, and *Othello*, all 1961; *Show Me the Way to Go, Homer*, and *The Visit*, both 1962, *One in a Million* and *Bonaparte!*, both 1963; *Pantagleize*, 1964; *Man Alive, They Went That-a-Way*, and *Summer and Smoke*, all 1965; *The Twelve-Pound Look, One Sleepless Knight*, and *Richard III*, all 1966; *Come Back, Little Phoenix* and *Ivory Tower*, both 1967; *My Son, Hamlet* and *The Fantasticks*, both 1968; *The Wasp That Ate Cleveland and the Rest of the World* and *Royal Hunt of the Sun*, both 1969; *If I Had a Yardstick I Could Rule the World*, 1970; *Death of a Salesman, I Lost It at the Movies, Cop-Out*, and *Home Fires*, all 1971, *Senior Prom* and *The Resistable Rise of Arturo Ui*, both 1972; *Paradise: Lost and Found* and *Man of La Mancha*, both 1973; *Diva* and *The Skin of Our Teeth*, both 1974; *When You Comin' Back, Red Ryder?*, 1975; *Leonardo!*, 1976; *The Exiled*, 1983.

Directed at Chestnut Lodge, Rockville, MD: *Scanarelle's Journey into the Land of the Philosophers*, 1960; *A View from the Bridge* and *You Can't Take It with You*, both 1961; *Under Milk Wood*, 1962; *The Glass Menagerie*, 1963; *Hay Fever* and *The Importance of Being Earnest*, both 1964; *Picnic*, 1965; *John Brown's Body*, 1966; *Dark of the Moon*, 1975; *Chatauqua Tonight!*, 1977; *The Last of My Solid Gold Watches* and *The Unsatisfactory Supper*, both 1979.

Directed at the Trinity Theatre, Washington, DC: *Show Boat*, 1961; *Finian's Rainbow*, 1962; *South Pacific*, 1963. Also directed *The King and I*, 1964 and *Camelot*, 1965, both at the Lisner Auditorium, Washington, DC; *West Side Story*, Duke Ellington School, Washington, DC, 1966; *A Tribute to the Veterans of Vietnam*, Ford's Theatre, Washington, DC, 1979; *The Ephemeral Is Eternal*, Hirshhorn Museum, Washington, DC, 1982; *Eleanor Roosevelt: First Lady of the World*, The National Museum of American History, Washington, DC, 1984, then Georgetown University, 1985; also directed *The Women Speak*, 1984.

PRINCIPAL STAGE APPEARANCES—Organ Morgan, *Under Milk Wood*, 1966, the Ambassador, *Romanoff and Juliet*, 1969, both University of Wisconsin; the Chaplain, *Senior Prom*, Washington Theatre Club, 1972, also appeared as Sir Pearce Madigan, *O'Flaherty, V.C.*, sponsored by the Embassy of Ireland, 1983.

FILM DEBUT—Major Andrew Ellicott, *Washington: City Out of Wilderness*, National Capitol Historical Society, 1973.

RELATED CAREER—Stage manager, Erika Thimey Dance Theatre, Washington, DC, 1956; assistant director, WRC-Channel 4, Washington, DC, 1957; applied psychology field researcher, Century Research Corporation, Arlington, VA, 1957; speech consultant, Department of Internal Revenue, Washington, DC, 1958; speech consultant, American Savings and Loan Association, Washington, DC, 1959-60; supervisor for special productions at the White House, Washington, DC, 1961-1965; production coordinator and director of film festival, United States Pavilion, Montreal, Canada, 1971; teacher, workshop for professional actors, Mara Theatre, Athens, Greece, 1973; theatre reviewer and interviewer, WETA, National Public Radio, 1976; critic for theatre and music programs, Department of the Army, 1976-80; lecturer, Smithsonian Institution Associates, 1980; lecturer for U.S. International Communications Agency, Germany, 1981; faculty member, Salzburg Seminar in American Studies: "Contemporary Theatre," 1981;

festival manager, opening ceremonies, Kingdom of Morocco, EPCOT Center, Walt Disney World, Orlando, FL, 1983; consultant on stage installations, lighting, and magic effects, The Great Foodini, Inc., 1984.

WRITINGS: PLAYS, PRODUCED—*Papers of Fire*, Future Farmers of America, 1960; *Concentration Camp*, Georgetown University, 1969; *Creation of the World*, American Theatre Association, National Music Educators National Conference, 1970; *Something of a Sorceress*, National Collection of Fine Arts, Folger Shakespeare Library, 1971; (with Kathleen Barry) *Creation of the World II*, 1975, *Creation of the Nation*, 1976 and *Happy Landings*, 1977, all produced at Wolf Trap Farm Park, VA; *Tyger/Tyger*, the Theatre Wagon, Staunton, VA, New Playwrights' Theatre, Washington, DC, Northern Michigan State University and the Corner Theatre, Baltimore, MD, all 1977; (with Kathleen Barry) *The Curious Computer from Planet Z*, 1978 and *The Magic Falcon*, 1979, both produced at Wolf Trap Farm Park.

Edited narration: *The Nutcracker Suite*, Georgetown University Symphony, 1983. Adapation: *The Exiled*, Georgetown University Intercultural Center, 1983.

TELEPLAYS—(With Kathleen Barry) *You, the People*, NBC, 1976.

BOOKS—*A Director's Guide to Good Theatre*, National Contemporary Theatre Conference, Washington, DC, 1968; (with D. Lee and R. Meersman) *Stage for a Nation*, University Press of America, Washington, DC, 1985.

ARTICLES—"The Director as Vector," *Catholic Theatre Magazine* (December, 1959); "Acting and Self-Concept," *Catholic Theatre Magazine* (November-December, 1960); "Turn on the Tape," *Players Magazine* (March, 1960); "Projection Techniques in Three Theatres," *Catholic Theatre Magazine* (January, 1967); "Make Workshops Fun," *Catholic Theatre Magazine* (May, 1968); "Georgetown Theatre: Alive and Well," *Georgetown Today Magazine* (September, 1969); "Theatre and the Contemporary World," *Players Magazine* (October, 1969); "Directing Questions to the Actor," *Stage* (October, 1977); "Involvement Theatre for the Disabled," *Creative Drama News* (Spring-Summer, 1978); "Counterpart," (poem) *The Bear Flag News* (April, 1978); "Gift Exchange," (poem) *The Bear Flag News* (August, 1978); "Theatrical Special Effects: Food, Fire and Flying," *Secondary School Theatre Journal* (Fall, 1978); "New Life for the Grande Dame of E Street," *National Theatre Program* (February, 1980); "Writing in Fine Arts," *Georgetown University Writing Program Newsletter* (April, 1985); (with S. Moore) "Making Music-Makers," *Journal Papers* (April, 1985) and "The Grand Old Banjo Man of Broadway," *Good Reading* (June, 1985).

AWARDS: Best Director award, Washington Theatre Alliance, 1960-61; Fellowship in International Theatre, Ford Foundation, 1963-64; Outstanding Young Men of America, 1965; Invitation from President Johnson to attend the signing of the Arts and Humanities Bill in the Rose Garden, 1965; special award, Army Theatre Project, American Theatre Association, 1968 and 1970; national winner, American College Theatre Festival, 1969; Vicennial Medal, years of service, Georgetown University, 1974; Personal Citation, Congressional Record, 1974; regional winner, American College Theatre Festival, 1974; Outstanding Teachers of America, 1975; national finalist, Forest Roberts Playwriting Contest, Northern Michigan University, 1977; Iron Mike Award, U.S. Army, Fort Bragg, 1980; Outstanding Service to Theatre, American Theatre

Association, Mid-Atlantic Chapter, 1984; Award for University Service, Georgetown University Alumni Association, 1985.

MEMBER: American Theatre Association, Mid-Atlantic Chapter (president, 1971-72 and 1983-84, chairman, Special Arrangements, National Convention, 1975), American Light Opera Company (board of directors, 1962-65), Workshops for Careers in the Arts (board of advisors, 1967-69), Alliance for Arts Education (Virginia representative, 1972-75), Arlington Theatre Associates (board of directors, 1973-74), The New Direction Educational Foundation (board of directors, 1973—), National Theatre, Washington, DC (secretary, 1974-79, vice-president, 1979-82, president, 1982—), American Association of University Professors (1975—), New Playwrights' Theatre, Washington, DC (board of advisors, 1975—), InterPlay Productions, Inc. (president, 1975-1979), Dramatists Guild, Authors League of America (1976—), United States Institute for Theatre Technology (1977—), Cultural Alliance of Washington (1977—), International Theatre Institute (1979-81), International Children's Festival, Wolf Trap Farm Park (artistic advisory panel, 1982—), Richard L. Coe Award (honorary committee, 1980-84), Actors' Center of Washington (board of advisors, 1983—), Axolotyl Theatre Company (board of advisors, 1984—), Washington Theatre Wing (board of advisors, 1985—); Food for the Holidays (board of advisors, 1980-82), Offender Aid and Restoration (inmate counselor, 1982); National Council of Catholic Men (vice-president, 1970-71), Benedictine College (board of governors, 1980—).

SIDELIGHTS: In the September-October, 1984, issue of *Georgetown Magazine*, Donn Murphy offers the following quote: "What I hope to give to my students is a sense of the vitality of the performing arts and the awesome impact they can have on our lives."

ADDRESSES: HOME—2323 N. Utah Street, Arlington, VA 22207. OFFICE—The National Theatre, 1321 Pennsylvania Avenue, NW, Washington, DC 20004.

*   *   *

MURRAY, Brian   1937-

PERSONAL: Born Brian Bell, September 10, 1937, in Johannesburg, South Africa; son of Alfred (a professional golfer) and Mary Dickson (Murray) Bell. EDUCATION: Attended King Edward VII School, Johannesburg.

VOCATION: Actor, director, and writer.

CAREER: STAGE DEBUT—Taplow, *The Browning Version*, Hofmeyer Theatre, Cape Town, South Africa, 1950. LONDON DEBUT—Harry Lomax, *Last Day in Dreamland*, Lyric Theatre, Hammersmith, 1959. BROADWAY DEBUT—Tolen, *The Knack*, Royale Theatre, New York City, 1964. PRINCIPAL STAGE APPEARANCES—Appeared as a child actor in Johannesburg, 1950-54; continued in South Africa until 1957, playing such parts as: Bo Decker, *Bus Stop*, Bruno, *Dear Charles*, Peter, *The Diary of Anne Frank*, and Father Oros, *The Strong Are Lonely;* Conrad Mayberry, *Visit to a Small Planet*, Westminster Theatre, London, 1960; Wade, *Roger the Sixth*, Westminster Theatre, London, 1960; with the Royal Shakespeare Company, Stratford-upon-Avon: Horatio, *Hamlet*, Earl of Richmond, *Richard III*, Romeo, *Romeo and Juliet*, and Cassio, *Othello*, all 1961, Malcolm, *Macbeth*, Edgar, *King*

Lear, Guiderius, *Cymbeline*, and Lysander, *A Midsummer Night's Dream*, all 1962, repeated roles of Lysander, *A Midsummer Night's Dream* and Edgar, *King Lear*, both at the Aldwych Theatre, London, 1962, then repeated Edgar, *King Lear*, at the Theatre Sarah Bernhardt, Paris, 1963, Edgar, *King Lear*, State Theatre, New York City, 1964, Arthur Fitton, *All in Good Time*, Royale Theatre, New York City, 1965; with the Bristol Old Vic Theatre, U.K., appeared as Philip, *The Spiral Bird* and Bassanio, *The Merchant of Venice*, 1965, and Claudio, *Measure for Measure*, 1966.

Mike, *Wait Until Dark*, Strand Theatre, London, 1966; Rosencrantz, *Rosencrantz and Guildenstern Are Dead*, Alvin Theatre, New York City, 1967, moving to the Eugene O'Neill Theatre, New York City, 1968, then repeated role at the O'Keefe Theatre, Toronto, Canada, 1969; BBC voice, *The Real Inspector Hound*, Theatre Four, New York City, 1972; Milo Tindle, *Sleuth*, Music Box Theatre, New York City, 1973; Philip, *The Philanthropist*, Goodman Theatre, Chicago, 1975; Gibson McFarland, *Artichoke*, Long Wharf Theatre, New Haven, CT, 1975; appeared in *The Devil's Disciple* and *Design for Living*, both at the Goodman Theatre, 1976; Colin, *Ashes*, Manhattan Theatre Club, and later moving to the New York Shakespeare Festival (NYSF), Public/Anspacher Theatre, New York City, 1977; Charlie Now, *Da*, Hudson Guild Theatre, then moving to the Morosco Theatre, New York City, 1978; title role, *The Jail Diary of Albie Sachs*, Manhattan Theatre Club, New York City, 1979.

Monakhov, *Barbarians*, Brooklyn Academy Theatre, NY, 1980; Oberon, *A Midsummer Night's Dream*, Brooklyn Academy of Music, NY, 1981; appeared in *Summer*, Royal Poinciana Playhouse, Palm Beach, FL, 1981; Theodore Gunge, *The Acrata Promise*, No Smoking Playhouse, New York City, 1982; appeared in *Terra Nova*, Center Stage Theatre, Baltimore, MD, 1981; appeared in *Pantomime*, Goodman Theatre, 1981; Lloyd Dallas, *Noises Off*, Brooks Atkinson Theatre, New York City, 1983, then repeated role at the Ahmanson Theatre, Los Angeles, 1985.

PRINCIPAL STAGE WORK—Director: *Beauty and the Beast*, Civic Theatre, Torquay, U.K., 1965; *Thea Ruffian on the Stair*, New York City production, 1968; *Mephistopheles* and *Pigeons*, both New York City, 1968; *The Private Ear* and *The Public Eye*, both Sullivan, IL, 1969; *A Scent of Flowers*, Martinique Theatre, New York City, 1969; *A Slight Ache* and *Oldenburg*, both Playhouse in the Park, Cincinnati, OH, 1969; *A Place without Doors*, Stairway Theatre, New York City, 1970, then Goodman Theatre, Chicago, 1971; *Bedtime and Butter* and *Charley's Aunt*, both London, 1971; *Ride a Cock-Horse*, London, 1972; *The Waltz of the Toreadors*, Philadelphia Drama Guild, then Kennedy Center, Washington, DC, then Circle in the Square, New York City, 1973; *Fanny's First Play*, Niagara-on-the-Lake Theatre, Canada, 1973; *The Ruffian on the Stair*, New York City, 1974; *The Cherry Orchard*, Goodman Theatre, 1974; *Enter a Free Man*, Theatre at St. Clements, New York City, 1974; *Downriver*, New York City, 1975; "Endicott and the Red Cross," and "My Kinsman, Major Mollineux," a double-bill entitled, *The Old Glory*, American Place Theatre, New York City, 1976; *The Dream Watcher*, Seattle, WA, 1977; *Hobson's Choice*, Philadelphia, 1978; *Stevie*, New York City, 1979; *Summer*, Hudson Guild Theatre, New York City, 1980; *Tartuffe*, American Place Theatre, New York City, 1983; *Hay Fever*, Music Box Theatre, New York City, 1985-86; *Blithe Spirit*, Neil Simon Theatre, New York City, 1987.

MAJOR TOURS—Edgar, *King Lear*, U.K., European, Soviet, and Canadian cities, 1964; Rosencrantz, *Rosencrantz and Guildenstern*

Are Dead, U.S. cities, 1970; Donny, *A Present from Harry,* U.K. cities, 1970. As director, *The Waltz of the Toreadors,* U.S. cities, 1974.

FILM DEBUT—1959. PRINCIPAL FILM APPEARANCES—*The Angry Silence,* 1960; *The League of Gentlemen,* 1960.

TELEVISION DEBUT—1959. PRINCIPAL TELEVISION APPEAR-ANCES—Movies: Title role, *Kipps;* Jed, *Shadow of a Pale Horse; Kojack: The Price of Justice,* CBS, 1987.

WRITINGS: PLAYS, PRODUCED—*On the Inside, on the Outside,* staged reading at the Long Wharf Theatre, 1975.

SIDELIGHTS: FAVORITE ROLES—Edgar, Romeo, and Rosencrantz. RECREATIONS—Music of every sort, writing, travelling, and thinking.

ADDRESSES: AGENT—International Creative Management, 22 Grafton Street, London W1, England.*

* * *

MUSKY, Jane   1954-

PERSONAL: Born May 27, 1954, in New Jersey; daughter of John Peter (a musician) and Olga (a real estate broker; maiden name, Badaukus) Musky; married Tony Goldwyn (an actor) May 30, 1987. EDUCATION: Boston University School for the Arts, B.F.A.

VOCATION: Designer.

CAREER: PRINCIPAL STAGE WORK—Assistant designer, *Barnum,* St. James Theatre, New York City, 1980; production designer, Williamstown Theatre Festival, Second Company, 1981; assistant designer, Williamstown Theatre Festival, main stage, 1982; set designer, *Marathon 1984,* Ensemble Studio Theatre, New York City, 1984; designer, *The News,* Helen Hayes Theatre, New York City, 1985.

PRINCIPAL FILM WORK—Production designer, *The Little Sister,* American Playhouse, art director, *Split Cherry Tree,* 1983; *Blood Simple,* River Road Productions, 1985; *Raising Arizona,* Circle Arizona Productions, 1985.

PRINCIPAL TELEVISION WORK—Movies: Production designer, *Rockabye,* NBC; *L.B.J.,* NBC; art director, *Johnny Bull,* ABC. Mini-Series: *Murrow,* HBO. Specials: Production designer, "Alfred G. Graebner Handbook of Rules and Regulations," *ABC After School Special,* Highgate Pictures.

VIDEOS—Art director, *Pink House Party,* Music Television; art director, *State Your Mind,* Nile Rogers Video.

RELATED CAREER—Assistant designer, scenic artist, Harker's Studio, London, in association with the English National Opera, Glyndebourne Opera, and Pinewood Studios.

AWARDS: Best Production Design, Emmy Award nominaton, for "Alfred G. Graebner Handbook of Rules and Regulations," *ABC Afterschool Special.*

MEMBER: United Scenic Artists, Local 829.

SIDELIGHTS: Jane Musky commented on her career to *CTFT,* "I enjoy the chance to constantly watch my world around me and relate the environments of all types to the public."

ADDRESSES: HOME—Hoboken, NJ. AGENT—The Gersh Agency, 222 N. Canon Drive, Beverly Hills, CA 90210.

N

NALLON, Steve 1960-

PERSONAL: Born December 8, 1960, in Leeds, England; son of Joseph (an office worker) and Christine (an office worker; maiden name, Oddy) Nallon. EDUCATION: Attended St. Michael's College, Leeds, England; Birmingham University, B.A., drama, theatre, arts, and English.

VOCATION: Actor.

CAREER: STAGE DEBUT—Burt, *The Cloggies,* Theatre Llwyd, 1983. LONDON DEBUT—Margaret Thatcher, *Pop Concert,* Royal Albert Hall, 1986. PRINCIPAL STAGE APPEARANCES—Pierre, *As from a Miser to a Fool,* Birmingham, U.K., 1984; *Mouthing Off,* Edinburgh, Scotland, 1985; *Englishmen and a Broad,* Edinburgh, Scotland, 1986; *Maggie's Last Night,* Bournemouth, U.K., 1986;

additional personal appearances as British Prime Minister Margaret Thatcher include a performance of "her version of" *Peter and the Wolf,* with the Bournemouth Symphony Orchestra.

TELEVISION DEBUT—Dave, *Frankie and Johnnie,* British, 1985. PRINCIPAL TELEVISION APPEARANCES—In the U.S.: *The Mike Nesmith Show,* 1985; *Spitting Image,* 1986. In the U.K.: *The Krankies,* 1985; *Mike Yarwood Show,* 1985; *Fame Game,* 1985; *Pet Hates,* 1985; *Time of Your Life,* 1985; *Lenny Henry Show,* 1985; *Now Something Else,* 1986; *Cinderella,* 1986; *Get Fresh,* 1986; *Little and Large,* 1986; *Saturday Live,* 1986; *Roland Rat: The Series,* 1986.

RELATED CAREER—Lecturer on comedy.

AWARDS: Emmy Award, 1985, for *Spitting Image;* Bronze Rose of Montreux.

ADDRESSES: AGENT—Eric Glass Ltd., 28 Berkeley Square, London W1X 6HD, England.

*　　*　　*

NASSAU, Paul 1930-

PERSONAL: Born January 30, 1930, in New York, NY; son of Harry (in the textile industry) and Lillian (an antique store owner) Nassau; married Chloe Anderson, December 23, 1953; children: Robert, Julie. EDUCATION: Oberlin College, B.A., 1953.

VOCATION: Composer and lyricist.

WRITINGS: PLAYS, PRODUCED—Composer and lyricist (with Oscar Brand): *A Joyful Noise,* Broadway production, 1966; *The Education of H*Y*M*A*N K*A*P*L*A*N,* Broadway production, 1968. SONGS—*New Faces of 1956* (two songs).

NON-RELATED CAREER—Owner-manager, Lillian Nassau, Ltd., antique store, 1971—.

SIDELIGHTS: Mr. Nassau told *CTFT* that he "retired from show business in 1971. I can remember what motivated me to leave my profession: the desire to make some money so I could support my wife (who supported me for a long time) and send my kids to good schools."

ADDRESSES: HOME—201 W. 86th Street, New York, NY 10024. OFFICE—Lillian Nassau, Ltd., 220 E. 57th Street, New York, NY 10022.

STEVE NALLON

NASSIVERA, John 1950-

PERSONAL: Born July 28, 1950, in Glen Falls, NY; son of Charles J. and Ruth (Holmquest) Nassivera. EDUCATION: Boston University, B.A., 1972; McGill University, Ph.D., 1977.

VOCATION: Writer and producing director.

CAREER: PRINCIPAL STAGE WORK—In addition to the playwriting activity listed below: literary manager, New Dramatists, New York City, 1979-80; producing director, Dorset Theatre Festival, Dorset, VT, 1976—; director, Dorset Colony House, 1980—.

RELATED CAREER—Teacher, McGill University, Montreal, Quebec, Canada, 1973-77 and at Columbia University, New York City, 1977-79.

WRITINGS: PLAYS, PRODUCED AND PUBLISHED—*The Penultimate Problem of Sherlock Holmes,* Dorset Theatre Festival, VT, 1978, Hudson Theatre, NY, 1980, published by Samuel French, 1980; *Sweeney Todd, or the String of Pearls,* Dorset Theatre Festival, VT, 1980; *Phallacies,* Dorset Theatre Festival, VT, 1980, then New Playwright's Theatre, Washington, DC, 1982; *Four of a Kind,* Dorset Theatre Festival, VT, 1981; *Making a Killing,* Dorset Theatre Festival, VT, published by Samuel French.

TELEVISION—*Electra* (documentary).

AWARDS: National Endowment for the Arts Fellowship, 1982.

MEMBER: Dramatists Guild, New Dramatists; Players Club.

ADDRESSES: HOME—Church Street, Dorset, VT 05251. OFFICE—Dorset Colony House, Dorset, VT 05251.

*   *   *

NEAGLE, Anna 1904-1986

PERSONAL: Born Florence Marjorie Robertson, October 20, 1904, in Forest Gate, London, England; died in Surrey, England, June 3, 1986; daughter of Herbert William and Florence (Neagle) Robertson; married Herbert Wilcox (a producer and director), 1944 (died, 1977). EDUCATION: Trained as a dancer with Madame Espinosa and Gladys Dillon.

VOCATION: Actress, dancer, and producer.

CAREER: STAGE DEBUT—Child dancer, *The Wonder Tales,* Ambassadors Theatre, London, 1917. BROADWAY DEBUT—Dancer, *Wake Up and Dream,* Selwyn Theatre, 1929. PRINCIPAL STAGE APPEARANCES—Chorus, *Bubbly,* Duke of York's Theatre, London, 1925; chorus, *Charlot's Revue,* Prince of Wales Theatre, London, 1925; chorus, *Rose Marie,* Drury Lane Theatre, London, 1926; chorus, *The Desert Song,* Drury Lane Theatre, London, 1927; chorus, *This Year of Grace,* Pavilion Theatre, London, 1928; dancer in cabaret, Trocadero Restaurant, London, 1926-29; dancer, *Wake Up and Dream,* Pavilion Theatre, London, 1929; Mary Clyde-Burkin, *Stand Up and Sing,* Southampton, U.K., 1930, then at the Hippodrome, London, 1931; Rosalind, *As You Like It* and Olivia, *Twelfth Night,* both at the Open Air Theatre, London, 1934; *Peter Pan,* Palladium, London, 1937; Carol Beaumont, Nell Gwynn, Queen Victoria, and Lilian Grey, *The Glorious*

Days, Palace Theatre, London, 1953; Stella Felby, *The More the Merrier,* Strand Theatre, London, 1960.

Ruth Peterson, *Nothing Is for Free,* Lyceum Theatre, Edinburgh, Scotland, 1961; Jane Canning, *Person Unknown,* Pavilion Theatre, Bournemouth, U.K., 1963; Lady Hadwell, *Charlie Girl,* Adelphi Theatre, London, 1965; Sue Smith, *No, No, Nanette,* Drury Lane Theatre, London, 1972; Dame Sibyl Hathaway, *The Dame of Sark,* Duke of York's Theatre, London, 1975; Janet Fraser, *The First Mrs. Fraser,* Arnaud Theatre, Guildford, U.K., 1976; *Most Gracious Lady,* Theatre Royal, Windsor, for the Silver Jubilee, 1977; Comtesse de la Briere, *Maggie,* Shaftesbury Theatre, London, 1977; *Relative Values,* English Theatre, Vienna, 1978; Mrs. Higgins, *My Fair Lady,* Haymarket Theatre, Leicester, London, 1978, then Adelphi Theatre, London, 1979.

MAJOR TOURS—*Victoria Regina* and *French without Tears,* U.K. and European cities, during World War II; Emma Woodhouse, *Emma,* U.K. cities, 1944; Carol Beaumont, Nell Gwynn, Queen Victoria, and Lilian Grey, *The Glorious Days,* U.K. cities, 1952; Lady Hadwell, *Charlie Girl,* Melbourne, 1971 and Auckland, 1972; Janet Fraser, *The First Mrs. Fraser,* U.K. cities, 1976; Mrs. Higgins, *My Fair Lady,* U.K. cities, 1978.

PRINCIPAL FILM APPEARANCES—*Sixty Glorious Years,* 1938; *Nurse Edith Cavell,* 1939; *Irene,* 1940; *Bittersweet,* 1940; *The Yellow Canary,* 1943; *I Live in Grosvenor Square,* 1945; *Picadilly Incident,* 1946; *The Courtneys of Curzon Street,* 1947; *Spring in Park Lane,* 1947; *Odette,* 1951; *Lady with a Lamp,* 1951; *Derby Day,* 1952; *Maytime in Mayfair,* 1952; *Lilacs in the Spring,* 1953; also *Goodnight Vienna; Nell Gwynn; Victoria the Great; Elizabeth of Ladymead; King's Rhapsody; My Teenage Daughter; No Time for Tears; The Man Who Couldn't Talk; The Lady Is a Square.*

PRINCIPAL FILM WORK—Producer, *Those Dangerous Years,* 1957; (with husband Herbert Wilcox:) *Wonderful Things; The Heart of a Man.*

WRITINGS: AUTOBIOGRAPHY—*There's Always Tomorrow,* 1974.

AWARDS: Created Commander of the British Empire, 1952, made Dame of the British Empire, 1969; Honorable Ensign Award, FANY Award, both 1950.

MEMBER: FANY Regimental Club; King George VI Memorial Foundation (executive council), King George's Fund for Actors and Actresses.

SIDELIGHTS: CTFT learned from published material that Dame Anna Neagle played Lady Hadwell in *Charlie Girl* for over two thousand performances.*

*   *   *

NEIPRIS WILLE, Janet 1936-

PERSONAL: Born March 11, 1936; daughter of Samuel and Dorothy (Damis) Brown; married Donald Wille (a writer and engineer); children: Cynthia, Carolyn, Ellen. EDUCATION: Tufts University, B.A., 1957; Simmons College, M.A., 1971; Brandeis University, M.F.A., 1975.

VOCATION: Writer.

CAREER: PRINCIPAL STAGE WORK—Playwright-in-residence, University of Montana, 1975; visiting faculty member, Brandeis University, 1978; visiting faculty, Continuing Education, Harvard University, 1978-80; playwright-in-residence, Smith College, 1980; chairman, dramatic writing program, New York University, 1983—.

RELATED CAREER—Panelist: "Women in the Media," Harvard University, 1979; "Radio Drama in America and England," WGBH, Boston, 1979; "American Drama," Theatre Communications Group, Yale University, 1980.

WRITINGS: PLAYS, PRODUCED—*A Time to Remember* (A History of Women in Education), Statler Hilton, Boston, MA, 1967; *Abe Lincoln* (musical), Winchester Public Schools, Winchester, MA, 1969; *The Princess and the Dragon* (musical), Boston Arts Festival, 1969; *The Little Bastard* (musical), Simmons College, 1971; *Statues, Exhibition,* and *The Bridge at Belharbour* (one-acts), Brandeis University, 1973-75, Cubiculo Theatre, New York City, 1975, Goodman Theatre, Chicago, 1976, Center Stage, Baltimore, MD, 1976, and Manhattan Theatre Club, New York City, 1976; *Exhibition* (one-act), Arena Stage, Washington, DC, 1977, Invisible Theatre, AZ, 1977, Cape Ann Theatre, Gloucester, MA, 1978, and Kalamazoo College, MI, 1978; (co-author) *Jeremy and the Thinking Machine* (musical), Cape Ann Theatre, Gloucester, MA, 1977, then 13th Street Theatre, New York City, 1977-78; *Flying Horses,* University of Montana, 1977, Goddard College, 1978; *The Bridge at Belharbour* (one-act), Invisible Theatre, AZ, 1977, Brandeis University, 1980, Hampshire College Performing Arts Center, MA, 1981.

Separations, Arena Stage, Washington, DC, 1978, Smith College, 1980, staged reading, Playwright's Horizons, New York City, 1980, and Playwrights Platform, Boston, MA, 1980; *The Desert,* Milwaukee Repertory Theatre, WI, 1979, American Premier Stage, Boston, MA, 1980, workshop production at the American Place Theatre, New York City, 1980, scenes done at Boston University, 1980, Pittsburgh Public Theatre, PA, 1981, scenes done at the Charles Playhouse, Boston, MA, 1982, Sharon Playhouse, CT, 1982, and a staged reading at the Manhattan Punchline Theatre, New York City, 1983; *Out of Order,* Harold Clurman Theatre, New York City, 1980, University of Massachusetts, Fine Arts Center, 1981, and Circle Repertory Company's Plays in Progress series, 1983; *The Agreement,* staged reading, Circle Repertory Company, New York City, 1982, Town Hall Playwrights series, Westport, CT, 1982; *The Southernmost Tip,* staged reading, Circle Repertory Company, New York City, 1982-83; *Almost in Vegas,* Manhattan Punchline Theatre, New York City, 1985.

PLAYS, PUBLISHED—In collections at the Lincoln Center Library for the Performing Arts branch of the New York Public Library and the Schlessinger Library, Radcliffe College, Cambridge, MA.

TELEVISION—*The Baxters,* ABC, 1977-80; *How Does Your Garden Grow,* ABC, WCVB-TV, Boston, MA, 1977; (contributing writer) *Women '77,* CBS, WBZ-TV, Boston, MA, 1977; (pilot) *The President's Assistants,* ABC, 1978; (contributing writer) *Impact,* CBS, WJZ-TV, Baltimore, MD; *Our Place, Senior Scouts,* and *The Cowboy and the Lady,* CBS-Weinstein-Skyfield Productions development projects.

RADIO—*The Desert,* Earplay, PBS, 1980; *The Agreement,* Earplay, PBS, 1981; *The Piano,* Earplay, PBS, 1982; *The Agreement,* Australian Broadcasting System, 1983.

MUSIC—Orginal music for piano, flute and cello to accompany "Black Milk of Morning," a poem by Paul Celan, Simmons College, Boston, MA, 1973; incidental music, *Requiem,* play, by Kevin O'Morrison, produced at the University of Montana, 1976; incidental music, piano and flute, *Death of a Salesman,* Sharon Playhouse, CT, 1982; incidental music for ten short plays presentation called "First Annual Playwrights Benefit," Circle Repertory Company, New York City, 1983.

ARTICLES—"For John Holmes," *Sidelines,* Vol. 2, 1977; "How a Playwright Experimenting Finds a Special Life Upon the Stage," *The Washington Star,* 1978; "Writing a Stage Play," *The Writer,* 1978, and *The Writers Handbook,* 1980.

AWARDS: Sam Shubert Playwriting Fellowship, Brandeis University, 1974-75; National Endowment for the Arts Literary Fellowship, Playwriting, 1979-80.

MEMBER: Dramatists Guild, Authors League of America, Writers Guild of America East; Circle Repertory Company's Playwright's Lab, American Place Theatre's Women's Project.

SIDELIGHTS: Janet Neipris Wille lists as works in progress a musical called "Notes on a Life" and a full length play titled "The Perfect Way to Live."

ADDRESSES: OFFICE—712 Broadway, Fourth Floor, New York, NY 10003. AGENT—Lois Berman, 240 W. 44th Street, New York, NY 10036.

*   *   *

NELSON, Judd

BRIEF ENTRY: Born in Portland, ME. Judd Nelson appeared in summer repertory theatres as a member of the Shoestring Theatre Company, touring throughout New England. He continued summer repertory appearances after enrolling at Bryn Mawr College, but soon left school to work and study acting in New York City at the Stella Adler Conservatory. During this time, he performed in numerous plays, including appearances as Mozart in *Mozart and Salieri* and Roy in *Domino Courts.* Nelson's film debut came in 1984, with the Metro-Goldwyn-Mayer/United Artists release of *Making the Grade.* Since then, he's been working steadily, appearing as a troubled outcast in the 1985 film, *The Breakfast Club,* as a "Yuppie" in *St. Elmo's Fire,* as a heroic young man suddenly forced into adulthood in the 1986 Paramount film *Blue City.* His most recent work appears in the 1987 movie, *From the Hip.* Television audiences may remember Nelson from his appearances on an episode of *Moonlighting,* the popular ABC series.

*   *   *

NETTLETON, Lois

PERSONAL: Full name, Lois June Nettleton; born in Oak Park, IL; daughter of Edward L. (a stationary engineer) and Virginia (Schaffer) Nettleton; married Jean Shepherd (an actor, humorist, and writer), December 3, 1960 (divorced). EDUCATION: Trained for the stage at the Goodman Theatre School, Chicago, IL, and the Actors Studio, 1951.

VOCATION: Actress.

CAREER: STAGE DEBUT—Father, Hansel and Gretel, Greenbriar Community Center, Chicago. BROADWAY DEBUT—Laurie Hutchins, The Biggest Thief in Town, Mansfield Theatre, 1949. PRINCIPAL STAGE APPEARANCES—Luba, Darkness at Noon, Alvin Theatre, New York City, 1951; understudy Maggie, Cat on a Hot Tin Roof, Morosco Theatre, New York City, 1955; Nerissa, The Merchant of Venice and Hero, Much Ado About Nothing, both with the American Shakespeare Festival, Stratford, CT, 1957; Shelagh O'Connor, God and Kate Murphy, 54th Street Theatre, New York City, 1959; Janet, Silent Night, Lonely Night, Morosco Theatre, New York City, 1959.

Title role, Elektra, Olney Playhouse, MD, 1960; Julia Stevens, The Wayward Stork, 46th Street Theatre, New York City, 1966; Catherine, Diane, Dorothy, and Maria, The Hemingway Hero, Shubert Theatre, New Haven, CT, 1967; The Only Game in Town, Arlington Park, IL, 1972; Blanche DuBois, A Streetcar Named Desire, St. James Theatre, New York City, 1973; Amy, They Knew What They Wanted, Playhouse Theatre, New York City, 1976; Compliments of Cole, Chicago, 1978; Dorothy Thompson, Strangers, John Golden Theatre, New York City, 1979; Irene, Light Up the Sky, Coconut Grove Playhouse, FL, 1983-84; also appeared in The Rainmaker.

FILM DEBUT—Period of Adjustment, Metro-Goldwyn-Mayer (MGM), 1962. PRINCIPAL FILM APPEARANCES—Come Fly with Me, MGM, 1963; Mail Order Bride, MGM, 1964; Valley of Mystery, Universal, 1967; Bamboo Saucer, NTA, 1967; The Good Guys and the Bad Guys, Warner Brothers, 1969; Dirty Dingus Magee, Metro-Goldwyn-Mayer, 1970; The Sidelong Glances of a Pigeon Kicker (also known as Pigeons), MGM, 1970; The Honkers, United Artists, 1972; Echoes of a Summer, Cine Artists, 1976; Butterfly, Analysis Films, 1982.

TELEVISION DEBUT—The Brighter Day, 1954. PRINCIPAL TELEVISION APPEARANCES—Episodic: Medical Center, CBS; Hawaii Five-0, CBS; Route 66, CBS; Gunsmoke, CBS; The Nurses, CBS; Alfred Hitchcock Presents, CBS; Twilight Zone, CBS; Dupont Show, NBC; Eleventh Hour, NBC; Armstrong Circle Theatre, NBC; Naked City, ABC; Doctor Kildare, NBC; "From the Heart," Finder of Lost Loves, ABC; "Lost and Found," Hotel, ABC; Murder, She Wrote, CBS; "A Minor Miracle," Glitter, ABC. Movies: Dolly and the Great Little Madisons, 1979; Brass, CBS, 1985; also No Hiding Place, Portrait of Emily Dickinson, Emanuel, Duet for Two Hands, Hidden River, Woman in White, The Light That Failed, Incident of Love.

AWARDS: Clarence Derwent Award, 1959, for God and Kate Murphy; included in "top ten new female movie personalities," Laurel Award, 1963.

MEMBER: Actors' Equity Association, Screen Actors Guild, American Federation of Television and Radio Artists.

ADDRESSES: AGENT—William Morris Agency, 1350 Avenue of the Americas, New York, NY 10019.*

*			*			*

NEVILLE, John   1925-

PERSONAL: Born May 2, 1925, in Willesden, London, England; son of Reginald Daniel (a truck driver) and Mabel Lillian (Fry) Neville; married Caroline Hooper (an actress), December 9, 1949;

children: two sons, three daughters. EDUCATION: Trained for the stage at the Royal Academy of Dramatic Arts. MILITARY: Served in the Royal Navy for two years during World War II.

VOCATION: Actor and director.

CAREER: STAGE DEBUT—Walk-on, Richard III, New Theatre, London, 1947. BROADWAY DEBUT—Romeo, Romeo and Juliet, Winter Garden Theatre, 1956. PRINCIPAL STAGE APPEARANCES—Lysander, A Midsummer Night's Dream, Chatillon, King John, Open Air Theatre, London, 1948; with the Lowestoft Repertory Company, U.K., 1948; with the Birmingham Repertory Company, U.K., 1949-50.

With the Bristol Old Vic Company, U.K.: Gregers Werle, Ring Round the Moon, Marlow, She Stoops to Conquer, Richard, The Lady's Not for Burning, Dunois, Saint Joan, Edgar, Venus Observed, Valentine, Two Gentlemen of Verona, the Duke, Measure for Measure, and title role, Henry V, 1950-53; with the Old Vic Company, London: Fortinbras, Hamlet, Bertram, All's Well That Ends Well and Ferdinand, The Tempest, 1953-54, Macduff, Macbeth, title role, Richard II, Berowne, Love's Labour's Lost, Orlando, As You Like It, and Henry Percy, Henry IV Part I, 1954-55, Marc Antony, Julius Caesar, Autolycus, The Winter's Tale, alternated as Othello and Iago, Othello, Troilus, Troilus and Cressida, Romeo, Romeo and Juliet, and title role, Richard II, 1955-56, title role, Richard II, Macduff, Macbeth, Thersites, Troilus and Crissida (also at the Winter Garden Theatre, New York City), 1956, title role, Hamlet, Angelo, Measure for Measure, and Sir Andrew Aguecheek, Twelfth Night, 1957-58.

With the Nottingham Playhouse Company, U.K.: Title role, Macbeth and Sir Thomas More, A Man for All Seasons, 1961, Petruchio, The Taming of the Shrew, Joseph Surface, The School for Scandal (also at the Haymarket Theatre, London), and D'Artagnan, The Three Musketeers, 1962, title role, Coriolanus and John Worthing, The Importance of Being Earnest, 1963, Bernard Shaw, The Bashful Genius, Moricet, The Birdwatcher, and title role, Oedipus the King, 1964, title role, Richard II and Corvino, Volpone, 1965, Barry Field, The Spies Are Singing and title role, Doctor Faustus, 1966, Willy Loman, Death of a Salesman, Iago, Othello, and Kolpakov and others, Beware of the Dog (also St. Martin's Theatre, London), 1967.

Other appearances include Victor Fabian, Once More with Feeling, New Theatre, London, 1959; Nestor, Irma La Douce, Lyric Theatre, London, 1959; Jacko, The Naked Island, Arts Theatre, London, 1960; the Stranger, The Lady from the Sea, Queen's Theatre, London, 1961; the Evangelist, The Substitute, Palace Theatre, London, 1961; Don Frederick, The Chances and Orgilus, The Broken Heart, Chichester Festival, U.K., 1962; title role, Alfie, Mermaid Theatre, London, then Duchess Theatre, London, 1963; Henry Gow, "Mr." and Alec Harvey, "Mrs." in the double bill, Mr. and Mrs., Palace Theatre, London, 1968; King Magnus, The Apple Cart, Mermaid Theatre, London, 1970; Garrick, Boswell's Life of Johnson and Benedick, Much Ado About Nothing, Edinburgh Festival, Scotland, 1970; Macheath, The Beggars' Opera, Sir Colenso Ridgeon, The Doctor's Dilemma, Chichester Festival, U.K., 1972; Prospero, The Tempest, National Arts Centre Theatre, Canada, 1972; Judge Brack, Hedda Gabler, Manitoba Theatre Centre, Winnipeg, Canada, 1972; Oh, Coward, Bethune, Pygmalion, and Happy Days, all at the Citadel Theatre, Edmonton, Alberta, Canada, 1972; Sherlock Holmes, New York City, 1975; Othello and Staircase, both at the Neptune Theatre, Halifax, Nova Scotia,

1978; appeared with the Stratford Theatre Festival, Ontario, Canada, 1984.

MAJOR TOURS—Romeo, *Romeo and Juliet,* title role, *Richard II,* Macduff, *Macbeth,* Thersites, *Troilus and Cressida,* U.S. cities, 1956; title role, *Hamlet,* Sir Andrew Aguecheek, *Twelfth Night,* with the Old Vic Company, U.S. cities, 1958-59; title role, *Macbeth* and Thomas More, *A Man for All Seasons,* Malta, 1961; title role, *Macbeth,* with the Nottingham Playhouse Company, West African cities, 1963; Humbert Humbert, *Lolita,* U.S. cities, 1970.

PRINCIPAL STAGE WORK—Director: *Henry V,* Old Vic Theatre, London, 1960; with the Nottingham Playhouse: *Twelfth Night, A Subject of Scandal,* and *Concern,* 1962; *The Importance of Being Earnest,* 1963; *Memento More, The Mayor of Zalamea,* and *Listen to the Knocking Bird,* 1964; *Richard II, Collapse of Stout Party,* and *Measure for Measure,* 1965; *Saint Joan, Moll Flanders, Antony and Cleopatra,* and *Jack and the Beanstalk,* 1966; *Honour and Offer,* Fortune Theatre, London, 1969; *The Rivals,* National Arts Centre Theatre, Ottawa, 1972; *Romeo and Juliet,* Citadel Theatre, Edmonton, Alberta, Canada, 1972; *Les Canadiens* and *The Seagull,* Neptune Theatre, Halifax, Nova Scotia, Canada, 1978; also directed the opera *Don Giovanni,* Festval Theatre of Canada.

PRINCIPAL FILM APPEARANCES—*Oscar Wilde,* FAW, 1960; *Mr. Topaz,* 1961; *Billy Budd,* Allied Artists, 1962; *The Unearthly Stranger,* American International, 1964; Sherlock Holmes, *A Study in Terror,* Columbia, 1966; *Adventures of Gerrard,* British production, 1970.

PRINCIPAL TELEVISION APPEARANCES—Dramatic Specials: *Henry V,* BBC, 1957; *Romeo and Juliet,* NBC, 1957; "Hamlet," *DuPont Show of the Month,* CBS, 1959; Duke of Marlborough, "The First Churchills," *Masterpiece Theatre,* PBS.

RELATED CAREER—Director, Nottingham Playhouse, U.K., 1963-68; artistic director, Citadel Theatre, Edmonton, Alberta, Canada, 1973-78; artistic director, Neptune Theatre, Halifax, Nova Scotia, 1978—, director, Stratford Festival Theatre, Canada, 1983—.

AWARDS: Order of the British Empire, Birthday Honors, 1965; honorary degrees: Lethbridge University, Alberta, Canada, Doctor of Fine Arts (D.F.A.), 1979; Nova Scotia College of Art and Design, D.F.A., 1981.

MEMBER: British Actors' Equity Association.

SIDELIGHTS: FAVORITE ROLES—Gregers Werle, *The Wild Duck,* title role, *Richard II,* and Pistol, *Henry IV, Part II.* RECREATIONS—Music and opera.

ADDRESSES: AGENT—Larry Dalzell Associates Ltd., Three Goodwin's Court, St. Martins Lane, London, WC2, England.*

*   *   *

NEW, Babette 1913-

PERSONAL: Born November 7, 1913, in New York, NY; daughter of William Francis (a performer; stage name William Francis Nugent) and Elizabeth Brown Lee (a poetess; maiden name,

MacCarley) New; married Harold Kovner (a lawyer and hospital director), February 23, 1943 (divorced); children: Amy; (step-son) Victor. EDUCATION: Studied dancing with Martha Graham and acting with Maria Ouspenskaya, Herbert Berghof, and Stella Adler.

VOCATION: Actress.

CAREER: STAGE DEBUT—Penny, *Dear Octopus,* Peterborough Players, NH, 1939. PRINCIPAL STAGE APPEARANCES—Barbara, Duchess of Cleveland, *In Good King Charles' Golden Days,* New York City production, 1957; Baroness, *The Italian Straw Hat,* New York City, 1959; at the Carriage House Theatre, Little Compton, RI: Aunt, *Hedda Gabler,* 1962, mother, *Dark of the Moon,* 1964, Aunt, *Sweet Bird of Youth,* 1965, Baroness, *Sleeping Prince,* 1966, Aunt, *The Miracle Worker,* 1969, Maud, *Forty Carats,* 1972, and Prudence, *Camille,* 1974; *Tsk, Mary, Tsk,* New York City, 1970; *Orestes,* American Academy of Dramatic Art, 1970; *Brand,* New York City, 1971; *Abbott & Son,* Roundabout Theatre, New York City, 1971; *Cybele* and *Petty Bourgeois,* both W.P.A. Theatre, New York City, 1972; *Il Manifesto,* Provincetown Theatre, 1974; *Peril at End House,* Impossible Ragtime Theatre, New York City, 1978.

FILM DEBUT—*The Stoolie,* 1972. PRINCIPAL FILM APPEARANCES—*The Godfather, Part II,* Paramount, 1974; *Marathon Man,* Paramount, 1976; *The Next Man,* Allied Artists, 1976; *The Front,* Columbia, 1976; *Audrey Rose,* United Artists, 1977; *Roseland,* Cinema Shares, 1977; *Superman,* Warner Brothers, 1978; *Seventh Avenue,* 1978; *Circle of Two,* 1979; *Stardust Memories,* United Artists, 1980; *Paternity,* Paramount, 1981; *Dogs of War,* United Artists, 1981; *Only When I Laugh,* Columbia, 1981; *Zelig,* Warner Brothers, 1983.

PRINCIPAL TELEVISION APPEARANCES—Episodic: *Calucci's Department,* CBS, 1973.

MEMBER: Screen Actors Guild.

SIDELIGHTS: Babette New told *CTFT* that she studied sculpture in Paris in 1932 and served as a model for painters. She speaks French and has travelled in France, Greece, Italy, England, and Ireland.

ADDRESSES: HOME—155 W. 68th Street, New York, NY 10023. AGENT—Peter Beilin, 230 Park Avenue South, New York, NY 10169.

*   *   *

NICHOLAS, Anna

PERSONAL: Born January 22, in Boston, MA; daughter of John Cary and Susanne (an antiques dealer; maiden name, Britton) Nicholas. EDUCATION: Mills College, B.A.; Benjamin Cardero School of Law, J.D.; attended the Image Theatre School of Drama; trained for the stage at the London Academy of Music and Dramatic Art.

VOCATION: Actress and writer.

CAREER: STAGE DEBUT—Samantha, *Lloyd Adams Chronicles,* Off-Broadway production, 1985.

FILM DEBUT—*Hot Resorts,* Cannon Films, 1986.

TELEVISION DEBUT—Louise, *One Life to Live*, ABC, 1981. PRINCIPAL TELEVISION APPEARANCES—Episodic: Linda, *Perfect Strangers*, ABC; Lizetta, *The New Mike Hammer*, CBS; Danielle, *Remington Steele*, NBC; *Mary*, CBS.

WRITINGS: PLAYS—"Stuffing," produced in workshop.

MEMBER: Actors' Equity Association, American Federation of Television and Radio Artists.

SIDELIGHTS: Anna Nichols tells *CTFT* that she speaks French and has travelled to France, Spain, Italy, Greece, Switzerland, England, Wales, and Japan.

ADDRESSES: AGENT—Ambrosio-Mortimer & Associates, 165 W. 46th Street, New York, NY 10036.

*   *   *

NICHOLS, Peter   1927-

PERSONAL: Born July 31, 1927; son of Richard George and Violet Annie (Poole) Nichols; married Thelma Reed (a painter), December 26, 1959; children: Abigail (died), Louise, Daniel, Catherine. EDUCATION: Attended Trent Park Teachers College.

VOCATION: Writer.

CAREER: Writer (see below), 1959—; member of Greenwich Theatre, U.K., 1971-75; visiting playwright, Guthrie Theatre, Minneapolis, MN, 1976.

RELATED CAREER—Professional actor, 1950-55.

WRITINGS: PLAYS, PRODUCED AND PUBLISHED—*The Hooded Terror*, first produced in U.K., 1964; *A Day in the Death of Joe Egg*, Citizens Theatre, Glasgow, Scotland, 1967, published by Samuel French, 1967, and Grove Press, 1968; *The National Health*, Old Vic National Theatre, London, 1969, published by Samuel French, 1970, and Grove Press, 1975; *Forget-Me-Not Lane*, Greenwich Theatre, London, 1971, published by Samuel French, 1971; *Chez Nous: A Domestic Comedy in Two Acts*, Globe Theatre, London, 1974, published by Faber & Faber, 1974; *The Freeway*, Old Vic National Theatre, London, 1974, published by Faber & Faber, 1975; *Hardin's Luck*, Greenwich Theatre, London, 1977; *Privates on Parade*, Aldwych Theatre, London, 1977, published by Faber & Faber, 1977, and Samuel French; *Born in the Gardens*, Bristol Old Vic Theatre Royal, U.K., 1979, then Globe Theatre, London, 1980, published by Faber & Faber, 1980, and Samuel French; *Passion Play*, Aldwych Theatre, London, 1981, then later at the Seattle Repertory Company, WA, 1984, Hartford Stage Company, CT, 1984, Dallas Theatre Center, TX, 1984, Mark Taper Forum, Los Angeles, 1985, Arena Stage, Washington, DC, 1985, published by Methuen, 1981; *Passion*, Longacre Theatre, New York City, 1983, published by Methuen, 1983, and Samuel French, 1984; also *Poppy*, published by Methuen, 1982; *The Pope's Divisions*, published by Brown.

SCREENPLAYS—*Georgy Girl*, Columbia, 1966; *Joe Egg*, Columbia, 1972; *The National Health*, Columbia, 1974; also *Changing Places*.

TELEPLAYS—Has written twenty television plays since 1959.

AWARDS: Best Play, *Evening Standard* Awards, 1967, for *A Day in the Death of Joe Egg* and 1969, for *The National Health;* Best Comedy, *Evening Standard* Award and Society of West End Theatres Award, and Best British Musical, Ivor Novello Award, 1978, for *Privates on Parade*.

MEMBER: British Arts Council (drama panel), 1973-76.

ADDRESSES: AGENT—Margaret Ramsay, 14a Goodwin's Court, St. Martin's Lane, London WC2N 4LL, England.*

*   *   *

NICHOLS, Robert   1924-

PERSONAL: Born July 20, 1924, in Oakland, CA; son of Ray D. (a real estate broker) and Edna (Beemer) Nichols; married Jennifer Napier (a film costumier), October 1, 1950; children: Christie, David. EDUCATION: College of the Pacific, Stockton, CA, 1942-43 and 1946-47; studied acting at the Royal Academy of Dramatic Arts, London. MILITARY: U.S. Army, Special Services (entertainer), 1943-46.

VOCATION: Actor.

CAREER: LONDON DEBUT—Song and dance man, *Late Joys*, Players Theatre, 1948. BROADWAY DEBUT—Hector Malone, *Man and Superman*, Circle in the Square Theatre, 1978. PRINCIPAL STAGE APPEARANCES—Ensign Pulver, *Mister Roberts*, Las Palmas Theatre, Los Angeles, 1953; Woody Twigg, *Great to Be Alive*, Las Palmas Theatre, 1954; comic, *That's Life*, Las Palmas Theatre, 1955; Jimmy, *The Rainmaker*, Player's Ring Theatre, Los Angeles, 1955; Mr. Macafee, *Bye Bye Birdie*, Her Majesty's Theatre, London, 1961; Henry, *The Summer People* and Morris, *Dark at the Top of the Stairs*, both at the Pembroke Theatre, London, 1962; Mr. Bratt, *How to Succeed in Business without Really Trying*, Shaftsbury Theatre, London, 1963; Pemberton Maxwell, *Call Me Madam*, Valley Music Theatre, 1966; Felix Unger, *The Odd Couple*, Ivar Theatre, Los Angeles, 1968; Frank Kennedy, *Gone with the Wind*, Dorothy Chandler Pavilion, Los Angeles, 1971; Uncle Jimmy, *No No Nanette*, Casa Manana Dinner Theatre, Ft. Worth, TX, 1973; Oscar, *The Little Foxes*, Syracuse Stage, NY, 1974; Chairman Huac, *Are You Now or Have You Ever Been*, Promenade Theatre, New York City, 1978; Boss Mangan, *Heartbreak House*, McCarter Theatre, Princeton, NJ, 1979; Psychiatrist, *Medal of Honor Rag*, Pittsburgh Public Theatre, PA, 1979.

Capn' Andy, *Showboat*, Coachlight Theatre, E. Windsor, CT, 1980; Charlie, *Einstein and the Polar Bear*, Cort Theatre, New York City, 1981; Uncle Sid, *Ah! Wilderness*, Roundabout Theatre, New York City, 1983; Nat Miller, *Take Me Along*, Martin Beck Theatre, New York City, 1984.

FILM DEBUT—Pig soldier, *Red Badge of Courage*, Metro-Goldwyn-Mayer (MGM), 1950. PRINCIPAL FILM APPEARANCES—Lt. MacPherson, *The Thing*, RKO, 1950; Henry, *Sally and St. Anne*, Universal, 1952; *Johnny Dark*, Universal, 1953; *This Island Earth*, Universal, 1954; *The Command*, Warner Brothers, 1954; Pinky, *Giant*, Warner Brothers, 1955; *Bomber's B-52*, Warner Brothers, 1957; Sam, *The Amorous Prawn*, Warner Brothers, 1962; *The Yellow Rolls Royce*, Warner Brothers, 1963; *The Victors*, Columbia, 1963; *Man in the Middle*, Columbia, 1963; *The Out of*

Towners, Paramount, 1970; Pycroft, *Reuben, Reuben,* Paramount, 1983.

TELEVISION DEBUT—Henry, *My Little Margie,* CBS, 1952. PRINCIPAL TELEVISION APPEARANCES—Episodic: *Life and Legend of Wyatt Earp,* ABC; *Gunsmoke,* CBS; *Bonanza,* NBC; *Maverick,* ABC; *Sugarfoot,* ABC; *Trackdown,* CBS; *The Real McCoys,* ABC; *The Ann Sothern Show,* CBS; *The Ray Miland Show,* CBS; *The John Forsythe Show,* NBC; *Medic,* NBC; *Four Star Playhouse,* CBS; *Matinee Theatre,* CBS; *The Addams Family,* ABC; *Green Acres,* CBS; *The Dick Van Dyke Show,* CBS.

MEMBER: Actors' Equity Association, Screen Actors Guild, American Federation of Radio and Television Artists; Players Club.

SIDELIGHTS: FAVORITE ROLES—Nat Miller, *Ah! Wilderness,* Capn' Andy, *Showboat,* Uncle Sid, *Ah! Wilderness,* and Ben Hubbard, *The Little Foxes,* some of which he has yet to portray.

ADDRESSES: AGENT—Fifi Oscard and Associates, 19 W. 44th Street, New York, NY 10036.

O

O'CALLAGHAN, Richard 1940-

PERSONAL: Born Richard Brooks, March 4, 1940, in London, England; son of Valentine Ernest Cozens and Patricia Lawlor (Hayes) Brooks; married Juliet Elizabeth Alliston. EDUCATION: Attended Wimbledon College; trained for the stage at the London Academy of Music and Dramatic Art.

VOCATION: Actor.

CAREER: LONDON DEBUT—Moritz, *Spring Awakening,* Royal Court Theatre, 1965. PRINCIPAL STAGE APPEARANCES—At the Royal Court Theatre, London: Appeared in four roles, *Ubu Roi,* Brother Ched, *Three Men for Colverton,* Fleance, *Macbeth,* and Ivan Cheprakov, *A Provincial Life,* all 1966; Gerald Popkiss, *Rookery Nook,* Swan Theatre, Worcester, U.K., 1969; Alvin Hanker, *Three Months Gone,* Royal Court Theatre, then Duchess Theatre, London, 1970.

Joey Keyston, *Butley,* Criterion Theatre, London, 1971; Worsely, *Owners,* Theatre Upstairs, London, 1972; Peter, *Kingdom Cottage,* The Howff Theatre, London, 1973; Guildenstern, *Rosencrantz and Guildenstern Are Dead,* also appeared in other productions with the Young Vic Theatre Company, London, 1974-75; Eugene Grimley, *The Great Caper,* Royal Court Theatre, London, 1974; Guildenstern, *Rosencrantz and Guildenstern Are Dead,* with the Young Vic Company at the Criterion Theatre, London, 1975; appeared in *Dirty Linen,* Almost Free Theatre, London, 1976; Konstantin, *The Seagull,* Derby Playhouse, then Duke of York's Theatre, London, 1976; appeared in *Mr. Whatnot,* Orange Tree Theatre, Richmond, U.K., 1977; Martin Taylor, *Brimstone and Treacle,* Open Space Theatre, London, 1979.

FILM DEBUT—*The Bofors Gun,* Universal, 1968. PRINCIPAL FILM APPEARANCES—*Butley,* American Film Theatre, 1974; *Galileo,* American Film Theatre, 1975; also *Carry on Loving.*

PRINCIPAL TELEVISION APPEARANCES—Dramatic Specials: *Professional Foul; Born and Bred; Renoir My Father.*

SIDELIGHTS: FAVORITE ROLES—Alvin Hanker, Joey Keyston, Guildenstern. RECREATIONS—Going to the movies, dropping in on friends.

ADDRESSES: AGENT—Duncan Heath Associates, Ltd., Paramount House, 162-170 Wardour Street, London W1, England.*

O'CONNOR, Kevin 1938-

PERSONAL: Born May 7, 1938, in Honolulu, HI. EDUCATION: Attended University of Hawaii, University of California and San Francisco State University; trained for the stage at the Neighborhood Playhouse, and with Uta Hagen and Lee Strasberg.

VOCATION: Actor, director, and producer.

CAREER: OFF-BROADWAY DEBUT—Harry, *Up to Thursday,* Cherry Lane Theatre, 1965. PRINCIPAL STAGE APPEARANCES—Office boy, "Thank You, Miss Victoria," Frankie Basta, "Birdbath," Younger Actor, "War," Stu, "Chicago," and appeared in "This Is Rill Speaking," in a production with the overall title, *Six from La Mama,* Martinique Theatre, New York City, 1966; Bill Maitland, *Inadmissible Evidence,* Woodstock Summer Theatre, NY, 1966; Walter, *The Rimers of Eldritch,* Cherry Lane Theatre, New York City, 1967; Sir Andrew Aguecheek, *Twelfth Night,* Baltimore Center Stage, MD, 1968; title role, *Tom Paine,* Stage 73 Theatre, New York City, 1968; Dionysus, *The Bacchae,* Charles Playhouse, Boston, 1968; Toby, *Boy on a Straight-Back Chair,* Theatre at St. Clement's Church, New York City, 1969.

Julius Esperanza, *Gloria and Esperanza,* American National Theatre Academy (ANTA) Theatre, New York City, 1970; Alex Koonig, *Dear Janet Rosenberg, Dear Mr. Koonig,* and Jake, *Jakey Fat Boy,* both at the Gramercy Arts Theatre, New York City, 1970; with the Milwaukee Repertory Theatre, WI, 1970-71 season; with the Eugene O'Neill Memorial Theatre Playwright's Unit, Waterford, CT: man three, *American Triptych,* Sir Owen Hopton, *Campion,* B, *African Star,* William Wallace, *Bruce,* and cop, Lonnie, *James Bernhardt and Zoowolski,* all 1971, Antrocius, *The General Brutus,* number three, *The Executioners,,* street vendor, *Artists for the Revolution,* title role, *Warren Harding,* and Will, *Alfred the Great,* all 1972, Mr. Ryan, *A Grave Undertaking,* Marc, *She's Bad Today,* and Aaron Burr, *Founding Father,* all 1974.

Douglas Two, "Grail Green" and Douglas, "Three Street Koans," under the overall title, *Kool Aid,* Forum Theatre, New York City, 1971; Abe, *Eyes of Chalk,* Theatre at St. Clement's Church, New York City, 1972; appeared in "The Funny Men Are in Trouble," in a double bill with the overall title, *Two by Paul Austin,* Theatre at St. Clement's Church, New York City, 1973; Glendenning, *The Contractor,* Chelsea Theatre of Manhattan, New York City, 1973; the Kid, *Alive and Well in Argentina* and Man, *Duet and Trio* (retitled *Figures in the Sand*), both at the Theatre at St. Clement's Church, New York City, 1974; James, *The Morning After Optimism,* Manhattan Theatre Club, New York City, 1974; Jesse James, *Jesse and the Bandit Queen,* The Other Stage Theatre, New York City, 1975; appeared in *Gauguin in Tahiti,* Theatre of the Open Eye, New York City, 1976; appeared in *Memphis Is Gone,*

Theatre at St. Clement's Church, New York City, 1977; appeared in *Natures,* Theatre of the Open Eye, New York City, 1977; appeared in *Scenes from a Country Life,* Perry Street Theatre, New York City, 1978; Fallon, *Devour the Snow,* John Golden Theatre, New York City, 1979.

Appeared in *Rocket to the Moon,* Indiana Repertory Theatre, Indianapolis, IN, 1980; Chucky Craydon, *Chucky's Hunch,* and repeated role of Frankie Basta, *Birdbath,* both at the Harold Clurman Theatre, New York City, 1982; Count Henri de Toulouse-Lautrec, *Jane Avril,* Provincetown Playhouse, New York City, 1982; Boy Wonder, *Inserts,* Actors and Directors Theatre, New York City, 1982; the director, "Catastrophe" and Bam, "What Where," in a trilogy of plays with the overall title, *Samuel Beckett Plays,* Harold Clurman Theatre, New York City, 1983; Tarzan, *Last of the Knucklemen,* American Theatre of Actors, New York City, 1983; Bogart, *A Kiss Is Just a Kiss,* Manhattan Punch Line Theatre, New York City, 1983; Van Amburgh, *Planet Fires,* GeVa Theatre, Rochester, NY, 1984.

PRINCIPAL STAGE WORK—Artistic director, Theatre at St. Clement's Church, New York City, 1972-75; director, Theatre at St. Clement's Church: *Whiskey* and *Winging It!,* both 1973, *Alive and Well in Argentina,* 1974, *Virility,* 1976; *The Day Roosevelt Died,* Theatre Genesis, New York City, 1978.

Producer, Theatre at St. Clement's Church, New York City: *Of Mice and Men, Ceremony for a Murdered Black* and *Two by Paul Austin,* all 1972, *The White Whore* and *The Bit Player,* produced in English and Spanish, *The Golden Daffodil Dwarf, Nightwalk, Terminal, The Mutation Show, The Richard Morse Mime Theatre, Secrets of the Citizens Correction Committee, Babel—Babel, Moon Mysteries,* and *The Greatest Story Ever Told,* all 1973, *The Petrified Forest, Disquieting Muses, Studio II, La Ramera de la Cueva (The Harlot of the Cave), First Garbagemen Cantata, or the Grey Lady Cantata Number 4, The Meadow Green, In Our Time Electra, Nuts, The Fall and Redemption of Man, The Robber Bridegroom, The King of the United States, Enter a Free Man* and *Icarus's Mother,* all 1974, *War Babies, Joe's Opera, Workers, Frogs, Waking Up to Beautiful Things,* and *The Red Blue-Grass Western Flyer Show,* all 1975.

PRINCIPAL FILM APPEARANCES—*Coming Apart,* independent, 1969; *Let's Scare Jessica to Death,* Paramount, 1971; *Welcome to the Club,* Columbia, 1971; title role, *Bogie: The Last Hero,* Charles Fries Productions, 1980.

PRINCIPAL TELEVISION APPEARANCES—*Apple Pie,* PBS; also *Hidden Faces* and *The Doctors.*

AWARDS: Obie Award and Drama Desk Vernon Rice Award, both 1966, for *Six from La Mama;* Drama Desk Award, 1974, for *The Contractor.*

ADDRESSES: AGENT—Leaverton Associates Ltd., 1650 Broadway, New York, NY 10019.*

* * *

O'DONOGHUE, Michael

VOCATION: Writer, producer, director, and actor.

CAREER: PRINCIPAL FILM APPEARANCES—Dennis, *Manhattan,* United Artists, 1979.

MICHAEL O'DONOGHUE

PRINCIPAL FILM WORK—Producer and director, *Mr. Mike's Mondo Video,* 1979.

PRINCIPAL TELEVISION WORK—Series: Performer and writer, *Saturday Night Live,* NBC, 1975-80; 1985-86. Movies: Co-executive producer, *Single Bars, Single Women,* 1984.

PRINCIPAL RADIO WORK—*National Lampoon Radio Hour,* 1973.

WRITINGS: SCREENPLAYS—*Savages,* 1972; (also lyrics) *La Honte de la Jungle,* 1975; *Gilda Live,* 1979; *Mr. Mike's Mondo Video,* 1979. RADIO—*National Lampoon Radio Hour.* SONGS—"Single Women."

AWARDS: Outstanding Writing in a Comedy-Variety or Music Series, co-winner, Emmy Award, 1975-76 and 1976-77, both for *Saturday Night Live.*

ADDRESSES: AGENT—c/o John Burnham, William Morris Agency, 151 El Camino Drive, Beverly Hills, CA 90212.

* * *

O'HARA, David   1965-

PERSONAL: Born July 9, 1965, in Glasgow, Scotland; son of Patrick (a construction worker) and Martha (Scott) O'Hara. EDUCATION: Central School of Speech and Drama, London. RELIGION: Roman Catholic.

DAVID O'HARA

VOCATION: Actor.

CAREER: STAGE DEBUT —Tybalt, *Romeo and Juliet*, Open Air Theatre, Regents Park, London.

MAJOR TOURS—*A Midsummer Night's Dream*, Munich, Almagro, Malaga, and Florence.

FILM DEBUT—Michael, *Comfort and Joy*, Universal, 1985. PRINCIPAL FILM APPEARANCES—Tom, *Wink*, Warner Brothers, upcoming.

TELEVISION DEBUT—Scots boy, *The Monicled Mutineer*, BBC, 1986. PRINCIPAL TELEVISION APPEARANCES—Andy, *One by One*, BBC.

SIDELIGHTS: David O'Hara told CTFT that his primary reason for entering the show business profession was "to find a better life than Glascow had to offer."

ADDRESSES: AGENT—Kate Feast Management, 43A Princess Road, Regents Park, London NW1, England.

　　　　　*　　　*　　　*

O'LEARY, William

PERSONAL: Born October 19, in Chicago, IL; son of John Arthur (a lawyer and Federal Bureau of Investigation operative) and Eileen (Carroll) O'Leary. EDUCATION: Illinois State University, B.S.; University of Washington, M.F.A.

VOCATION: Actor.

CAREER: STAGE DEBUT—Charlie Then, *Da*, A Contemporary Theatre, Seattle, WA, 1982. BROADWAY DEBUT—Artie, *Precious Sons*, Longacre Theatre, 1986. PRINCIPAL STAGE APPEARANCES—Betty/Gerry, *Cloud 9*, A Contemporary Theatre, Seattle, 1983; Tom, *The Adventures of Huck Finn*, Seattle Repertory Theatre, 1983; Donay, *Side Effects*, Philadelphia Festival Theatre, PA, 1985; Ariel, *The Tempest*, Hartford Stage Company, CT, 1985; Pascal, *Antique Pink*, Project Theatre, MI, 1985; *Self Torture and Strenuous Exercise*, Circle Repertory Theatre Directors' Lab, New York City, 1985; *Spring Awakening*, Double Image Theatre, New York City, 1986; Mesron, *The Dispute*, New York Workshop Theatre, New York City, 1986.

FILM DEBUT—Andy, *Nice Girls Don't Explode*, New World, 1987.

MEMBER: Actors' Equity Association, Society of American Fight Directors.

ADDRESSES: AGENT—c/o Mary Sames, Sames-Rollnick, 250 W. 57th Street, New York, NY 10107.

WILLIAM O'LEARY

County, ABC, 1981. Animation: *M.A.S.K.*, Dic Enterprises, twelve episodes in syndication, 1984-84.

BOOKS—(With Rod Baker)*The Adventures of Gabby Bear*, ten young adult books with accompanying cassette recordings, Select Merchandising, Inc., 1986-87.

RELATED CAREER—Lecturer on writing for television at New Mexico State University and the University of Wisconsin.

AWARDS: Best Adaptation, Youth in Film Award, Cine Golden Eagle Award 1981-82, for *The Notorious Jumping Frog of Calaveras County;* National Association for the Advancement of Colored People Image Award and Emmy Award nomination, 1983-84, for "All the Money in the World," *ABC Weekend Special.*

MEMBER: Writers Guild of America West.

ADDRESSES: AGENT—c/o Gary Salt, Paul Kohner Agency, 9169 Sunset Blvd., Los Angeles, CA 90069.

*　　*　　*

O'NEAL, Patrick   1927-

PERSONAL: Born September 26, 1927, in Ocala, FL; son of Coke Wisdom (a citrus grower) and Martha (Hearn) O'Neal; married Cynthia Baxter; children: two sons. EDUCATION: Attended Riverside Military Academy and the University of Florida, B.A.; trained for the stage at the Actors Studio and the Neighborhood Playhouse. MILITARY: U.S. Air Force, 1952-53.

VOCATION: Actor and director.

CAREER: TELEVISION DEBUT—1949. PRINCIPAL TELEVISION APPEARANCES—Series: Dick Starrett, *Dick and the Duchess*, CBS, 1958; Dr. Daniel Coffee, *Diagnosis: Unknown*, CBS, 1960; Samuel Bennett, *KAZ*, CBS, 1978-79; Harlan Adams, *Emerald Point N.A.A.*, CBS, 1983-84.

Episodic: *Gruen Playhouse*, DuMont, 1952; also appeared on *Hallmark Hall of Fame*, NBC; *Philco Playhouse*, NBC; *Studio One*, CBS; *ABC Playhouse*, ABC; *The Alcoa Hour*, NBC; *The Millionaire*, CBS; *The Ann Sothern Show*, CBS; *Play of the Week*, syndicated; *The Naked City*, ABC; *The Defenders*, CBS; *Dr. Kildare*, NBC; *Route 66*, CBS; *The Twilight Zone*, CBS; *The F.B.I.*, ABC; *McCloud*, NBC; *Columbo*, NBC; *Marcus Welby, M.D.*, ABC; *Cannon*, CBS.

Movies: *Companions in Nightmare*, NBC, 1968; *Cool Million*, NBC, 1972.

FILM DEBUT—1954. PRINCIPAL FILM APPEARANCES—*The Mad Magician*, Columbia, 1954; *The Black Shield of Falworth*, Universal, 1954; *From the Terrace*, Twentieth Century-Fox, 1960; *A Matter of Morals*, 1961; *The Cardinal*, Columbia, 1963; *In Harm's Way*, Paramount, 1965; *King Rat*, Columbia, 1965; *Chamber of Horrors*, Warner Brothers/Seven Arts, 1966; *A Fine Madness*, Warner Brothers, 1966; *Alvarez Kelley*, Columbia, 1966; *Matchless*, United Artists, 1967; *A Big Hand for the Little Lady*, Warner Brothers/Seven Arts, 1967; *Where Were You When the Lights Went Out*, Metro-Goldwyn-Mayer (MGM), 1968; *The Secret Life of an American Wife*, Twentieth Century-Fox, 1968; *Castle Keep*, Co-

GLEN OLSON

OLSON, Glen   1945-

PERSONAL: Born May 16, 1945, in Minneapolis, MN; son of Russell Merle and Evangeline Olive (Hanson) Olson; married Sheilah May Cocoran, October 19, 1963; children: Kimberly, Erica. EDUCATION: Long Beach State University, B.A., drama, 1973. MILITARY: U.S. Navy, 1964-68.

VOCATION: Writer.

WRITINGS: TELEVISION—(All with Rod Baker) Episodes of *Hawaii Five-O*, CBS: "Hookman," 1973, "Right Grave—Wrong Body," 1974, "The Flip Side Is Death," 1974, "A Woman's Work Is with a Gun," 1974, and "A Sentence to Steal," 1975; "A Covenant with Evil," *Petrocelli*, NBC, 1974; "The Night of the Strangler," *Charlie's Angels*, ABC, 1976; "The Cannibals," *The Streets of San Francisco*, ABC, 1976; "Plastique," *Jigsaw John*, NBC, 1976; *Baa Baa Blacksheep*, NBC: "Last One for Hutch," 1977, and "Operation Standown," 1978; story editor, *CHiPs*, NBC, 1977, writer, "Rainey Day," 1978; "The Starships Are Coming," *The New Adventures of Wonder Woman*, CBS, 1979; "Oil and Water," *240 Robert*, ABC, 1979; "Death Fare," *Strike Force*, ABC, 1982.

Novel adaptations for television: *ABC Weekend Specials:* "The Ghost of Thomas Kempe," 1979, "The Joke's on Mr. Little," 1981, "The Haunted Mystery Mansion," 1982, "All the Money in the World," 1983, and "The Dog Days of Arthur Kane," 1983. Short story adaptations: *The Notorious Jumping Frog of Calaveras*

lumbia, 1969; *Stilleto,* AVCO-Embassy, 1969; *Assignment to Kill,* Warner Brothers, 1969; *The Kremlin Letter,* Twentieth Century-Fox, 1970; *Joe,* Cannon, 1970; *El Condor,* National General, 1970; *The Sporting Club,* AVCO-Embassy, 1971; *Corky,* MGM, 1972; *The Way We Were,* Columbia, 1973; *Silent Night, Bloody Night,* Cannon, 1974; *The Stepford Wives,* Columbia, 1975.

PRINCIPAL FILM WORK—Director, *Circle Back,* 1970.

STAGE DEBUT—Marchbanks, *Candida,* PK Yonge Theatre, Gainesville, FL, 1944. BROADWAY DEBUT—Arthur Turner, *Oh Men! Oh, Women!,* Henry Miller's Theatre, 1954. PRINCIPAL STAGE APPEARANCES—Walter Schwarz, *Lulu,* Fourth Street Theatre, New York City, 1958; Reverend T. Lawrence Shannon, *Shannon* (later titled *The Night of the Iguana*), Spoleto Festival, Italy, 1959; John Gilbert, *Laurette,* Shubert Theatre, New Haven, CT, 1960; Frederick Wohlmuth, *A Far Country,* Music Box Theatre, New York City, 1961; Reverend T. Lawrence Shannon, *The Night of the Iguana,* Royale Theatre, New York City, 1961; Sebastian Dangerfield, *The Ginger Man,* Orpheum Theatre, New York City, 1963.

MAJOR TOURS—Juvenile lead, *The Violin Messiah,* U.S. cities, 1951.

NON-RELATED CAREER—In partnership with other members of his family, owns several restaurants in New York City, including O'Neal's Balloon, O'Neal's at Fifty-Seventh, and The Ginger Man.

MEMBER: Actors' Equity Association, Screen Actors Guild, American Federation of Television and Radio Artists, Actors Studio.

SIDELIGHTS: FAVORITE ROLES—Reverend T. Lawrence Shannon and Sebastian Dangerfield. RECREATIONS—Boating and his restaurant, The Ginger Man.

ADDRESSES: AGENT—Perry and Naidorf, 315 S. Beverly Drive, Beverly Hills, CA 90212.*

*   *   *

OSBORNE, Kipp   1944-

PERSONAL: Born October 17, 1944, in Jersey City, NJ. EDUCATION: Attended the University of Michigan; trained for the stage at the Neighborhood Playhouse.

VOCATION: Actor.

CAREER: BROADWAY DEBUT—Don Baker, *Butterflies Are Free,* Booth Theatre, 1970. PRINCIPAL STAGE APPEARANCES—W.S., the salesman, *Love Gotta Come by Saturday Night,* Theatre de Lys, New York City, 1973; Arthur Kindred, *Detective Story,* Shubert Theatre, Philadelphia, 1973; Jimmy, *The Children's Mass,* Theatre de Lys, New York City, 1973; repeated role of Don Baker, *Butterflies Are Free,* Studio Arena Theatre, Buffalo, NY, 1973; the young man, *Veronica's Room,* Music Box Theatre, New York City, 1973; appeared in *Lyngstrand,* Circle in the Square, New York City, 1976.

MAJOR TOURS—Ricky Fleisher, *The Impossible Years,* U.S. cities, 1967-68.

AWARDS: *Theatre World* Award, 1970, for *Butterflies Are Free.*

ADDRESSES: AGENT—Triad Artists, 888 Seventh Avenue, Suite 1602, New York, NY 10106.*

*   *   *

OSMUN, Betsy   1954-

PERSONAL: Born April 6, 1954, in Orange, NJ; daughter of William Robert and Jane Catherine (Switzer) Osmun. EDUCATION: Boston University, B.S., human movement, 1976; studied acting at the Actors' Playhouse with Jim Baffico and at the Nico Hartos Workshop in New York City. RELIGION: Spiritual studies.

VOCATION: Actress, dancer, and singer.

CAREER: PRINCIPAL STAGE APPEARANCES— Performed one-act plays and scenes from: *A Streetcar Named Desire, Chapter Two, A Hatful of Rain,* and *Androcles and the Lion* at the Actors Playhouse, New York City; original material for children with the Actors Club Theatre, Inc., Brooklyn and Queens, NY; also performed scenes at the 18th Street Theatre, New York City.

PRINCIPAL CABARET APPEARANCES—The Duplex, Don't Tell Mama, The Fives, New York Hilton, The Feedbag, Palsson's, and Oliver's, all in New York City, and the Parsippany Hilton, NJ.

BETSY OSMUN

PRINCIPAL FILM APPEARANCES—Nurse Higgins, *Winter Cowboy*, New York University student film; *Turk 182!*, Twentieth Century-Fox, 1985; *Killer Clown*.

PRINCIPAL TELEVISION APPEARANCES—Episodic: *Search for Tomorrow*, NBC; *Another World*, NBC; *All My Children*, ABC; host, *The Big O Show*, Manhattan Cable. Guest: *Soap Factory Disco*, WNEW; *Regis Philbin Lifestyles*.

NON-RELATED CAREER—Certified paralegal, real estate and antitrust litigation; teacher, ballroom dancing; advertising salesperson, New York City.

MEMBER: Actors' Equity Association, American Federation of Television and Radio Artists.

SIDELIGHTS: Betsy Osmun wrote to *CTFT* concerning her career and interests: "Show business is in my blood. My mother was a concert pianist on radio at the age of ten. The more I experienced and viewed the real world, the more I found myself driven to show business to find growth, pleasure, and escape. I love any role that provides a challenge for me and enables me to express myself in one form or another."

ADDRESSES: HOME—P.O. Box 6466, Yorkville Station, New York, NY 10128.

*   *   *

OSTERMAN, Lester   1914-

PERSONAL: Born Lester Osterman, Jr., December 31, 1914, in New York, NY; son of Lester (a merchandising executive) and Adrienne (an actress; maiden name, Pinover) Osterman; married Marjorie Ruth Korn (a writer), June 3, 1937; children: Patricia Ann, Lester Thomas. EDUCATION: Attended the University of Virginia.

VOCATION: Producer and theatre owner.

CAREER: PRINCIPAL STAGE WORK—Producer: (With Jule Styne and George Gilbert) *Mr. Wonderful*, Broadway Theatre, New York City, 1956; (with Ethel Linder Reiner) *Candide*, Martin Beck Theatre, New York City, 1956; (with Alfred R. Glancy, Jr.) *Lonelyhearts*, Music Box Theatre, New York City, 1957; *Brouhaha*, Aldwych Theatre, London, 1958; (with Jule Styne) *Say Darling*, American National Theatre Academy (ANTA) Theatre, New York City, 1958; *A Loss of Roses*, Eugene O'Neill Theatre, New York City, 1959; *The Cool World* and *Face of a Hero*, both at the Eugene O'Neill Theatre, New York City, 1960; (with Shirley Bernstein) *Isle of Children*, Cort Theatre, New York City, 1962; (with Robert Fletcher and Richard Horner) *High Spirits*, Alvin Theatre, New York City, 1964; *Fade Out-Fade In*, Mark Hellinger Theatre, New York City, 1964; *Something More*, Eugene O'Neill Theatre, New York City, 1964; (with Lawrence Kasha) *The Coffee Lover*, Westport Country Playhouse, CT, 1966; co-producer, *Dinner at Eight*, Alvin Theatre, New York City, 1966; (with Saint-Subber) *Weekend*, Broadhurst Theatre, New York City, 1968; *Hadrian VII*, Helen Hayes Theatre, New York City, 1969.

The Rothschilds, Lunt-Fontanne Theatre, New York City, 1970; *Butley*, Morosco Theatre, New York City, 1972; *The Women*, 46th Street Theatre, New York City, 1973; co-producer, *Crown Matrimonial*, Helen Hayes Theatre, New York City, 1973; *A Moon for the Misbegotten*, Morosco Theatre, New York City, 1973; *James Whitmore in Will Rogers' USA*, Helen Hayes Theatre, New York City, 1974; *Sizwe Banzi Is Dead* and *The Island*, New York City productions, 1974; *The Norman Conquests, Rockabye Hamlet*, and *Rodgers and Hart*, New York City productions, 1975; (with Ken Marsolais, Allan Francis, and Leonard Soloway) *The Shadow Box*, Morosco Theatre, New York City, 1977; (with Marilyn Strauss and Marc Howard) *Da*, Morosco Theatre, New York City, 1978; *The Crucifer of Blood* and *Getting Out*, New York City productions, 1979.

Co-producer, *The Lady from Dubuque*, Morosco Theatre, New York City, 1980; co-producer, *Watch on the Rhine*, John Golden Theatre, New York City, 1980; co-producer, *A Life*, Morosco Theatre, New York City, 1980; co-producer, *One Night Stand*, Nederlander Theatre, New York City, 1980; co-producer, *Lyndon*, Wilmington Playhouse, DE, then Shubert Theatre, Philadelphia, PA, 1984; co-producer, *Execution of Justice*, Virginia Theatre, New York City, 1986.

MAJOR TOURS—Co-producer, *A Mother's Kisses*, U.S. cities, 1968; producer, *The Rothschilds*, U.S. cities, 1972.

PRINCIPAL TELEVISION WORK—Producer: *The Littlest Angel; Raggedy Ann*.

RELATED CAREER—Former owner and operator of the Eugene O'Neill Theatre, the Alvin Theatre, the 46th Street Theatre, the Helen Hayes Theatre, and the Morosco Theatre, all in New York City; president of L.O. Management Corporation, which still owns and operates the Morosco and Helen Hayes Theatres; president, Lester Osterman Productions.

NON-RELATED CAREER—Owner of the Bristol Owls (a minor league baseball club), 1946-49.

AWARDS: Antoinette Perry Awards: 1969, for *Hadrian VII*, 1970, for *The Rothschilds*, 1972, for *Butley*, 1973, for *Moon for the Misbegotten*, 1974, for *Sizwe Banzi Is Dead* and *The Island*, 1977, for *The Shadow Box*, and 1978, for *Da;* Pulitzer Prizes, 1977, for *The Shadow Box*, and 1978, for *Da;* Drama Critics Award, 1978, for *Da*.

MEMBER: League of New York Theatres and Producers (board of governors).

SIDELIGHTS: RECREATIONS—Football, harness racing, and baseball.

ADDRESSES: OFFICE—111 Field Point Drive, Fairfield, CT 06430.*

*   *   *

O'TOOLE, Peter   1932-

PERSONAL: Born August 2, 1932, in Connemara, County Galway, Ireland; son of Patrick Joseph and Constance Jane (Ferguson) O'Toole; married Sian Phillips, 1959 (divorced, 1979); children: Kate, Pat. EDUCATION: Trained for the stage at the Royal Academy of Dramatic Art. MILITARY: Royal Navy.

VOCATION: Actor.

CAREER: PRINCIPAL FILM APPEARANCES—*Kidnapped*, Buena Vista, 1960; *The Day They Robbed the Bank of England*, Metro-Goldwyn-Mayer (MGM), 1960; *The Savage Innocents*, Paramount, 1961; *Lawrence of Arabia*, Columbia, 1962; *Becket*, Paramount, 1964; *Lord Jim*, Columbia, 1965; *What's New Pussycat*, United Artists, 1965; *How to Steal a Million*, Twentieth Century-Fox, 1966; *The Night of the Generals*, Columbia, 1967; *The Bible. . .in the Beginning*, Twentieth Century-Fox, 1966; *Great Catherine*, 1968; *A Lion in Winter*, AVCO-Embassy, 1968; *Goodbye Mr. Chips*, MGM, 1969; *Brotherly Love*, MGM, 1970; *Murphy's War*, Paramount, 1971; *The Ruling Class*, AVCO-Embassy, 1972; *Man of LaMancha*, United Artists, 1972; *Under Milk Wood*, 1973; *Rosebud*, United Artists, 1975; *Man Friday*, 1975; *Foxtrot*, 1975; *Coup d'Etat*, 1977; *Power Play*, 1978; *Caligula*, 1979; *Zulu Dawn*, 1979; *Stunt Man*, Twentieth Century-Fox, 1981; *The Antagonists*, 1981; *My Favorite Year*, MGM, 1982; *Supergirl*, Tri-Star, 1984; *Creator*, Universal, 1985; *Club Paradise*, Warner Brothers, 1986; *Hidden Talent*, upcoming.

PRINCIPAL TELEVISION APPEARANCES—Mini-Series: *Masada*, 1981. Movies: *Rogue Male*, BBC, 1976; *Strumpet City*, RTE, 1979; *Svengali*, 1982; *Kim*, 1984. Guest: *Monitor*, NBC, 1983.

STAGE DEBUT—Civic Theatre, Leeds, U.K., 1949. LONDON DEBUT—Peter Shirley, *Major Barbara*, with the Bristol Old Vic Company at the Old Vic Theatre, 1956. BROADWAY DEBUT—Henry Higgins, *Pygmalion*, Plymouth Theatre, 1987. PRINCIPAL STAGE APPEARANCES With the Bristol Old Vic Company, U.K.: Cabman, *The Matchmaker*, and Corvino, *Volpone*, both 1955, Duke of Cornwall, *King Lear*, Hebert, *The Empty Chair*, Bullock, *The Recruiting Officer*, Maupa, *The Queen and the Rebels*, Cardinal Malko Barberini, *Lamp at Midnight*, Lodovico, *Othello*, and Baron Parsnip, *The Sleeping Beauty*, all 1956, Mr. Jaggers, *Great Expectations*, Alfred Doolittle, *Pygmalion*, Lysander, *A Midsummer Night's Dream*, Jimmy Porter, *Look Back in Anger*, Uncle Gustave, *Oh, My Papa!* (also later at the Garrick Theatre,

London, 1957), the Angel, *Sodom and Gomorrah*, the General, *Romanoff and Juliet*, and Mrs. Millie Baba, *Ali Baba and the Forty Thieves*, all 1957, John Tanner, *Man and Superman*, title role, *Hamlet*, Paddy, *The Pier*, and Jupiter, *Amphitryon 38*, all 1958, Private Bamforth, *The Long and the Short and the Tall*, Royal Court Theatre, then New Theatre, London, 1959.

Shylock, *The Merchant of Venice*, Petruchio, *The Taming of the Shrew*, and Thersites, *Troilus and Cressida*, all with the Shakespeare Memorial Theatre Company, Stratford-upon-Avon, U.K., 1960; title role, *Baal*, Phoenix Theatre, London, 1963; title role, *Hamlet*, with the National Theatre Company at the Old Vic Theatre, London, 1963; Peter, *Ride a Cock Horse*, Piccadilly Theatre, London, 1965; Captain Jack Boyle, *Juno and the Paycock*, Gaiety Theatre, Dublin, Ireland, 1966; John Tanner, *Man and Superman*, Gaiety Theatre, Dublin, 1969; Vladimir, *Waiting for Godot*, Abbey Theatre, Dublin, 1969; title role, *Uncle Vanya*, D'Arcy Tuck, *Plunder*, King Magnus, *The Apple Cart*, and solo reader, *Justice*, all with the Bristol Old Vic Company, U.K., 1973-74; appeared in three roles, *Dead-Eyed Dicks*, Dublin Festival Theatre, Ireland, 1976; appeared in *Macbeth*, Old Vic Theatre, London, 1978; also appeared in London in *Man and Superman*, 1982-83 and Henry Higgins, *Pygmalion*, 1984.

MAJOR TOURS—Roger Muir, *The Holiday*, U.K. cities, 1958; appeared in *Present Laughter* and *Uncle Vanya*, with the Royal Alexandra Theatre, U.S. cities, 1978.

RELATED CAREER—Artistic director, Royal Alexandra Theatre, U.S. tour, 1978; partner, Keep Films Ltd.

MEMBER: The Garrick Club.

ADDRESSES: AGENT—Veerline, Ltd., 54 Baker Street, London W1, England.*

P-Q

PAGE, Geraldine 1924-

PERSONAL: Full name, Geraldine Sue Page; born November 22, 1924, in Kirksville, MO; daughter of Leon Elwin (an osteopathic physician and surgeon) and Edna Pearl (Maize) Page; married Alexander Schneider (a violinist; divorced); married Rip Torn (an actor and director); children: one daughter, twin sons. EDUCATION: Studied at the Goodman Theatre School, 1942-45; trained for the stage with Sophia Swanstrom Young, Chicago, 1940; studied acting with Mira Rostova, New York City, 1950, and with Uta Hagen, New York City, 1949-56; studied voice with Alice Hermes, New York City.

VOCATION: Actress.

CAREER: STAGE DEBUT—*Excuse My Dust,* Englewood Methodist Church, Chicago, 1940. LONDON DEBUT—Lizzie Currie, *The Rainmaker,* St. Martin's Theatre, 1956. PRINCIPAL STAGE APPEARANCES—Sophomore, *Seven Mirrors,* Blackfriars Guild, New York City, 1945; summer stock productions at Lake Zurich Summer Playhouse, IL, 1945-48, Woodstock Winter Playhouse, IL, 1947-49, and Shadylane Summer Playhouse, IL, 1950-51; Pagan Crone, *Yerma* and Alma, *Summer and Smoke,* both at the Circle in the Square Theatre, New York City, 1951-52; Lily Barton, *Midsummer,* Vanderbilt Theatre, New York City, 1953; Marcelline, *The Immoralist,* Royale Theatre, New York City, 1954; Lizzie Currie, *The Rainmaker,* Cort Theatre, New York City, 1954; Amy McGregor, *The Innkeepers,* John Golden Theatre, New York City, 1956; Abbie Putnam, *Desire Under the Elms,* Natalia Islaev, *A Month in the Country,* and Marcelline, *The Immoralist,* all in repertory at the Studebaker Theatre, Chicago, 1956; Mrs. Shankland and Miss Railton-Bell, *Separate Tables,* Music Box Theatre, New York City, 1957; Alexandra del Lago, *Sweet Bird of Youth,* Martin Beck Theatre, New York City, 1959.

Sister Bonaventure, *The Umbrella,* Locust Theatre, Philadelphia, 1962; Nina Leeds, *Strange Interlude,* Hudson Theatre, New York City, 1963; Olga, *The Three Sisters,* Morosco Theatre, New York City, 1964; Julie Cunningham, *P.S. I Love You,* Henry Miller's Theatre, New York City, 1964; Oriane Brice, *The Great Indoors,* Eugene O'Neill Theatre, New York City, 1966; Baroness Lemberg, *White Lies* and Clea, *Black Comedy,* both at the Ethel Barrymore Theatre, New York City, 1967; Angela Palmer, *Angela,* Music Box Theatre, New York City, 1969.

The Marriage Proposal and *The Boor,* both at the Playhouse in the Park, Philadelphia, 1971; Mary Todd Lincoln, *Look Away,* Playhouse Theatre, New York City, 1973; performed for a benefit gala at Circle in the Square Theatre, New York City, 1974; Regina Giddens, *The Little Foxes,* Academy Festival Theatre, Lake Forest, IL, and at the Walnut Street Theatre, Philadelphia, 1974; Marion, *Absurd Person Singular,* Music Box Theatre, New York City, 1974; Blanche DuBois, *A Streetcar Named Desire,* Academy Festival Theatre, Lake Forest, 1976; Tekla, *Creditors,* Hudson Guild Theatre, and at the Public/Newman Theatre, New York Shakespeare Festival, New York City, 1977.

Elberta, *Mixed Couples,* Brooks Atkinson Theatre, New York City, 1980; appeared in *Clothes for a Summer Hotel,* Cort Theatre, New York City, 1980; Mother Miriam Ruth, *Agnes of God,* Music Box Theatre, 1982; with the Mirror Repertory Company at the Theatre at St. Peter's Church, New York City, 1983-85; Madame Arcati, *Blithe Spirit,* Neil Simon Theatre, New York City, 1987; also appeared as Mama, *Papa Is All,* New York City production.

MAJOR TOURS—U.S. cities: *The Rainmaker,* 1955; *Separate Tables,* 1957; *Sweet Bird of Youth,* 1959; *Marriage and Money,* 1971; *Slightly Delayed,* 1979; Madame Arcati, *Blithe Spirit,* pre-Broadway tour, 1987.

FILM DEBUT—*Out of the Night,* Moody Bible Institute, Chicago, 1947. PRINCIPAL FILM APPEARANCES—*Taxi,* Twentieth Century-Fox, 1953; *Hondo,* Warner Brothers, 1953; *Summer and Smoke,* Paramount, 1961; *Sweet Bird of Youth,* Metro-Goldwyn-Mayer (MGM), 1962; *Toys in the Attic,* United Artists, 1963; *Dear Heart,* Warner Brothers, 1964; *The Three Sisters,* Ely Landau Productions, 1965; *You're a Big Boy Now,* Seven Arts, 1966; *The Happiest Millionaire,* Buena Vista, 1967; *Trilogy,* Associated Artists, 1969; *Whatever Happened to Aunt Alice?,* Cinerama, 1969; *Beguiled,* Universal, 1971; *J.W. Coop,* Columbia, 1972; *Pete 'n Tillie,* Universal, 1972; *The Day of the Locust,* Paramount, 1974; *The Abbess of Crewe,* 1976; *Nasty Habits,* Brut Productions, 1977; *Interiors,* 1978; *Honky Tonk Freeway,* Universal, 1980; *Harry's War,* 1980; *I'm Dancing as Fast as I Can,* Paramount, 1982; *The Pope of Greenwich Village,* MGM/United Artists, 1984; *The Bride,* Columbia, 1985; *White Nights,* Columbia, 1985; *A Trip to Bountiful,* Island, 1986; *Native Son,* Cinecom, 1986; *My Little Girl,* 1987; also, *Flanagan.*

TELEVISION DEBUT—The Virgin Mary, *Easter Story,* WBBM, Chicago, 1946. PRINCIPAL TELEVISION APPEARANCES—Dramatic Specials: *The Turn of the Screw,* CBS, 1955; Xantippe, "Barefoot in Athens," *Hallmark Hall of Fame,* NBC, 1966; Miss Sook, "A Christmas Memory," *Stage 67,* ABC, 1966, and again as Miss Sook in *A Thanksgiving Visitor,* ABC, 1968; "Montserrat," *Hollywood Television Theatre,* KCET, PBS, 1971; "Look Homeward Angel," *CBS Playhouse,* and on *Playhouse 90,* CBS, 1972. Episodic: *Goodyear Playhouse,* NBC; *Omnibus,* CBS; *Studio One,* CBS; *Kraft Television Theatre,* NBC; *U.S. Steel Hour,* CBS; *Robert Montgomery Presents,* NBC; *Philco Playhouse,* NBC; *Windows,* CBS; *Sunday Showcase,* NBC; *The Long Hot Summer,*

ABC; *The Name of the Game,* NBC; *Night Gallery,* NBC; *Medical Center,* CBS; *Ghost Story,* NBC.

AWARDS: Best Supporting Actress, Academy Award nomination, 1953, for *Hondo;* Donaldson Award, *Theatre World* Award, and co-winner of the *Variety* New York Drama Critics Poll, all 1953, for *Midsummer;* winner, *Variety,* New York Critics Poll, 1959, and the Sarah Siddons Award, 1960, both for *Sweet Bird of Youth;* Who's Who of American Women Award as outstanding woman of the year in the theatre, 1960; Best Actress Award, *Cue* magazine, 1961; Best Actress, Academy Award nominaton, 1961, for *Summer and Smoke;* Cinema Nuova Gold Plaque, Venice, 1961, National Board of Review of Motion Pictures Award, 1961, Golden Globe Award, 1962, Best Actress, Academy Award nomination, 1962, and Donatello Award, 1963, all for *Sweet Bird of Youth;* Golden Globe Award, 1964, for *Dear Heart;* Best Actress, Emmy Awards, 1967, for *A Christmas Memory* and 1969, for *The Thanksgiving Visitor;* British Academy of Film and Television Arts Award, 1979, for *Interiors;* Best Actress, Academy Award, 1986, for *A Trip to Bountiful.*

MEMBER: Actors' Equity Association, Screen Actors Guild, American Federation of Television and Radio Artists, Actors Studio; Phi Beta Kappa.

SIDELIGHTS: FAVORITE ROLES—Alma, *Summer and Smoke,* Sadie Thompson, *Rain,* Blanche, *A Streetcar Named Desire,* Mama, *Papa Is All.* RECREATIONS—Studying acting.

ADDRESSES: AGENT—The Gage Group, 1650 Broadway, New York, NY 10019.*

*   *   *

PARKINSON, Dian

PERSONAL: EDUCATION: Studied for the stage at the Lee Strasberg Studio, Los Angeles.

VOCATION: Model and actress.

CAREER: PRINCIPAL TELEVISION APPEARANCES—Talk Show: Hostess, *The Women's Side.* Game Shows: *The Price Is Right.* Guest: *The Tonight Show, Starring Johnny Carson,* NBC. Episodic: *Vegas,* ABC. Specials: *Bob Hope's Desert Classic; The Bob Hope Christmas Show.*

MAJOR TOURS—*Bob Hope's Christmas Show,* Vietnam and Far East tour.

RELATED CAREER—Modeled with photographer Bert Stern and featured on the cover of his book, *Bert Stern, Master of Contemporary Photography;* featured on the cover of *Cosmopolitan;* also modeled for commericals, posters, billboards, and other magazines including *Los Angeles Magazine.*

AWARDS: Miss U.S.A.; Emmy Award Citation for *The Bob Hope Christmas Show.*

DIAN PARKINSON

ADDRESSES: PUBLICIST—Jo-Ann Geffen & Associates, 3151 Cahuenga Blvd. West, Suite 235, Los Angeles, CA 90068.

*   *   *

PARLAKIAN, Nishan   1925-

PERSONAL: Born July 11, 1925, in New York, NY; son of Raphael (a jeweler) and Rose (O'Hanion) Parlakian; married Florence B. Mechtel (a librarian), December 27, 1952; children: Nishan Payel, Elizabeth Rose. EDUCATION: Syracuse University, B.A., 1948; Columbia University, M.A, 1952, Ph.D., 1967. MILITARY: U.S. Army.

VOCATION: Writer and director.

CAREER: PRINCIPAL STAGE WORK—Playwright; artistic director, the Diocesan Players, Armenian Church of America.

RELATED CAREER—Professor of drama and speech, John Jay College, City University of New York, 1970—.

WRITINGS: PLAYS, PRODUCED—*Their Hills Are Scarred,* Master Theatre, New York City, 1949; *Plagiarized,* Pace University, New York City, 1965; *What Does Greta Garbo Mean to You?,* Churchyard Playhouse, 1976; *Cast the First Stone,* Quaigh Theatre, New York City, 1975; *For the Sake of Honor,* Classic Theatre, New York City, 1976; *Evil Spirit,* Classic, New York City, 1980.

NISHAN PARLAKIAN

PLAYS, PUBLISHED—*Plagiarized,* First Stage, 1965; *What Does Greta Garbo Mean to You?,* Drama and Theater, 1976.

MEMBER: Pirandello Society (first vice-president).

AWARDS: Honorable Mention Award, Wagner Writers Conference, 1961, for *Plagiarized;* Excellence in Teaching Award, Pace University, 1969.

ADDRESSES: OFFICE—New York, NY.

*   *   *

PATRICE, Teryn   1956-

PERSONAL: Born Joanna Patrice, April 8, 1956, in Cincinnati, OH; daughter of Irwin (a fashion industry worker) and Mildred Barie (a fashion industry worker; maiden name, Barrett) Patrice. EDUCATION: Trained for the stage with Charles Conrad, Lee Strasberg, Sandy Meisner, Milton Katselas, Alan Miller, and Jeff Corey.

VOCATION: Actress.

CAREER: STAGE DEBUT—Flora, *27 Wagons Full of Cotton,* Lee Strasberg Theatre, Los Angeles, 1976. PRINCIPAL STAGE AP-

PEARANCES—The Girl, *Hello Out There,* Artists Repertory Company, 1976; Sabrina, *The Skin of Our Teeth,* Equity Library Theatre, New York City, 1976; Stepdaughter, *Six Characters in Search of an Author* and Ophelia, *Hamlet,* both at the Pittsburgh Playhouse, 1976; Sandra, *A Thousand Clowns* and Jo, *A Taste of Honey,* both at the Three Arts Theatre, 1976; Flora, *27 Wagons Full of Cotton,* Odyssey Theatre and at the South Coast Repertory Company, Costa Mesa, CA, 1976; Jean Harlow, *The Beard,* Century City Playhouse, Los Angeles, 1977.

TELEVISION DEBUT—*Quincy,* NBC, 1979. PRINCIPAL TELEVISION APPEARANCES—Episodic: *The Seekers,* ABC, 1979; *Simon and Simon,* CBS, 1981; *Quincy,* NBC, 1981; *Simon and Simon,* CBS, 1984; *Call to Glory,* NBC, 1986; *Divorce Court,* NBC, 1986.

FILM DEBUT—*A Place Like This,* independent, 1980. PRINCIPAL FILM APPEARANCES—*Days of Wrath,* independent, 1981; *Walk the Walk,* independent, 1982; *Night Song,* independent, 1984.

RELATED CAREER—Singer with various rock and roll gropus recording at Columbia and Chatahoochee Records.

MEMBER: Actors' Equity Association, Screen Actors Guild, American Federation of Television and Radio Artists; Windfeather (to aid Native Americans).

ADDRESSES: HOME—12659 Moorpark Avenue, Studio City, CA 91604. AGENT—CTC Agency, 8439 Sunset Blvd., Suite 406, Los Angeles, CA 90069.

TERYN PATRICE

PEEK, Brent

PERSONAL: Son of Elmer and Dolores Mae (Boyer) Peek. EDUCATION: University of California at Los Angeles, B.A., M.F.A.

VOCATION: Manager, producer, and director.

CAREER: FIRST STAGE WORK—Stage manager, *Hair*, Moore Theatre, Seattle, WA, 1968. FIRST BROADWAY WORK—Stage manager, *Equus*, Plymouth Theatre, 1972. PRINCIPAL STAGE WORK—Production stage manager: *The Merchant*, Plymouth Theatre, New York City, 1975; *The Gin Game*, John Golden Theatre, New York City, 1979; *The Elephant Man*, Booth Theatre, New York City, 1981.

Production coordinator for McCann and Nugent Producers (all New York City productions): *Home*, Cort Theatre, 1980; *Mornings at Seven*, Lyceum Theatre, 1980; *The Floating Light Bulb*, *Macbeth*, and *The Philadelphia Story*, all Vivian Beaumont Theatre, 1981; *Crimes of the Heart* and *Tintypes*, both John Golden Theatre, 1981; *Amadeus*, Broadhurst Theatre, 1981; *The Elephant Man*, Booth Theatre, 1981; *Rose*, Cort Theatre, 1982; *Piaf*, Plymouth Theatre, 1982; *The Adventures of Nicholas Nickleby*, Plymouth Theatre, 1982; *The Dresser*, Brooks Atkinson Theatre, 1982; *Mass Appeal*, Booth Theatre, 1982; *Lydie Breeze*, American Place Theatre, 1982.

General manager (all New York City productions): *Red Eye of Love*, Playwright's Horizons, 1982; *Quartermaine's Terms*, Playhouse 91, 1982; *Passion*, Longacre Theatre, 1983; *The Golden Age*, Jack Lawrence Theatre, 1984; *Zelda*, American Place Theatre, 1984; *Balm in Gilead*, Minetta Lane Theatre, 1984; *Comic Relief*, Shubert Theatre, 1985; *Short Change*, Harold Clurman Theatre, 1985; *Curse of the Starving Class*, Promenade Theatre, 1985; *Corpse*, Helen Hayes Theatre, 1985; *Perfect Party*, Astor Place Theatre, 1986; *The Adventures of Nicholas Nickleby*, Broadhurst Theatre, 1986.

Associate producer, *Polobolus*, American National Theatre Academy (ANTA) Theatre, New York City, 1982; producer (all New York City productions): *Quartermaine's Terms*, Playhouse 91, 1982; *The Golden Age*, Jack Lawrence Theatre, 1984; *Balm in Gilead*, Minetta Lane Theatre, 1984.

Director and re-stager: *Truman Capote at Lincoln Center*, Mitzi Newhouse Theatre, New York City, 1980.

MAJOR TOURS—Re-staging: *Hair*, national cities, 1969; *Equus*, first and second national tours and bus and truck tour, 1975; *The Elephant Man*, national cities, Spoleto, Italy, and bus and truck tour, 1981.

MEMBER: Actors' Equity Association, League of American Theatre Owners and Producers, The Production Group.

ADDRESSES: HOME—25 W. Eighth Street, New York, NY 10011. OFFICE—311 W. 43rd Street, Suite 702, New York, NY 10036.

*   *   *

PEMBER, Ron   1934-

PERSONAL: Born April 11, 1934, in Plaistow, London, England; son of William Henry and Gladys Emily Martha (Orchard) Pember; married Yvonne Tylee. EDUCATION: Attended Eastbrook Secondary Modern School.

VOCATION: Actor, writer, and director.

CAREER: STAGE DEBUT—Fabian, *Twelfth Night*, tour of Durham Mining District, U.K., 1949. LONDON DEBUT—Harry, *Treasure Island*, Mermaid Theatre, 1959. PRINCIPAL STAGE APPEARANCES—Bird, *Blitz!*, Adelphi Theatre, London, 1962; with the National Theatre Company, London, 1965-68; at the Mermaid Theatre, London, appeared in productions of *Treasure Island*, Staff, *Lock Up Your Daughters*, Bernard, *The Bandwagon*, both 1969, and Trinculo, *The Tempest*, 1970; Third Workman, *King Lear*, Royal Court Theatre, London, 1971; Bert Brown, *At the End of the Day*, Savoy Theatre, London, 1973; Feste, *Twelfth Night*, Porter and Sergeant, *Macbeth*, both with the Royal Shakespeare Company, Stratford-upon-Avon, U.K., 1974, then Aldwych Theatre, London, 1975; Fingers Philips, *Liza of Lambeth*, Shaftesbury Theatre, London, 1976; the Stranger, *The Cherry Orchard*, Riverside Studio Theatre, London, 1978.

MAJOR TOURS—Director, *Treasure Island*, New York City and Canadian cities, 1969; Shylock, *The Merchant of Venice*, U.K. cities, 1980.

PRINCIPAL STAGE WORK—Director, *The Goblet Game*, Mermaid Theatre, London, 1968; director, *Lock Up Your Daughters*, Mermaid Theatre, London, 1969; director, *Treasure Island*, Mermaid Theatre, 1969; director, *Enter Solly Gold*, *Henry IV*, Parts I and II, and *Dick Turpin*, 1970; co-director, *King and Country*, Mermaid Theatre, London, 1976; co-adaptor and director, *The Point*, Mermaid Theatre, London, 1976; co-director, *1900* and *Froze to Death*, both with the CVI Theatre Company, Coventry, U.K., 1978; director, *Jack the Ripper*, Providence, RI, 1979.

FILM DEBUT—1960. PRINCIPAL FILM APPEARANCES—*Oh What a Lovely War*, Paramount, 1969; *Young Winston*, Columbia, 1972; *Murder by Decree*, AVCO-Embassy, 1979; *Bullshot*, Island Alive, 1985.

PRINCIPAL TELEVISION APPEARANCES—Dramatic Specials: *Nicholas Nickleby; Secret Army*.

RELATED CAREER—Co-founder, CVI Theatre Company, Coventry, U.K., 1978, appointed artistic director, 1980.

WRITINGS: PLAYS, PRODUCED—*Dick Turpin*, Mermaid Theatre, London, 1970; composer and co-author, *Jack the Ripper*, London, 1974; *1900* and *Froze to Death*, CVI Theatre Company, Coventry, U.K., 1978. PLAYS, PUBLISHED—*Jack the Ripper*, Samuel French.

SIDELIGHTS: RECREATIONS—Chess, writing.

ADDRESSES: HOME—11 Glencoe Drive, Dagenham, Essex, England.*

*   *   *

PENDLETON, Austin   1940-

PERSONAL: Born March 27, 1940, in Warren, OH; married Katina Commings; children: one daughter. EDUCATION: Yale University, B.A., 1961; trained for the stage at the Williamstown Theatre Festival, MA, 1957-58.

VOCATION: Actor and director.

CAREER: OFF-BROADWAY DEBUT—Jonathan, *Oh Dad, Poor Dad, Mama's Hung You in the Closet and I'm Feelin' So Sad,* Phoenix Theatre, 1962. PRINCIPAL STAGE APPEARANCES—Motel, *Fiddler on the Roof,* Imperial Theatre, New York City, 1964; Irwin Ingham, *Hail Scrawdyke!,* Booth Theatre, New York City, 1966; Leo Hubbard, *The Little Foxes,* Vivian Beaumont Theatre, Lincoln Center, New York City, then at the Ethel Barrymore Theatre, New York City, 1967; with the Studio Arena Theatre Company, Buffalo, NY, 1968-69.

Isaac, *The Last Sweet Days of Isaac,* Eastside Playhouse, New York City, 1970, then at the Cincinnati Playhouse in the Park, OH, 1971; with the Long Wharf Theatre, New Haven, CT, 1971-72; Charles, *American Glands,* New Dramatists, Inc., New York City, 1973; Professor Bobby Rudetsky, *An American Millionaire,* Joseph E. Levine Theatre, Circle in the Square, New York City, 1974; title role, *Tartuffe,* Cincinnati Playhouse in the Park, 1974; *The Government Inspector,* Hartman Theatre, Stamford, CT, 1975; Frederick, *The Sorrows of Frederick the Great,* American Repertory, New York City, 1976; title role, *Tartuffe,* Hartman Theatre, Stamford, CT, 1977; Tusenbach, *The Three Sisters* and Mark Antony, *Julius Caesar,* both at the Brooklyn Academy of Music, NY, 1977; Estragon, *Waiting for Godot,* Brooklyn Academy of Music, 1978; Jack, *The Office Murders,* Quaigh Theatre, New York City, 1979.

Bashmachkin, *The Overcoat,* Westside Mainstage Theatre, New York City, 1982; *Uncle Vanya,* The Whole Theatre, Montclair, NJ, 1982; Adam, *Up from Paradise,* Jewish Repertory Theatre, New York City, 1983; *After the Fall,* Williamstown Theatre Festival, 1984; *The Sorrows of Frederick,* The Whole Theatre, Montclair, 1985; Arnie, *Doubles,* Ritz Theatre, New York City, 1985.

MAJOR TOURS—With the American Conservatory Theatre, San Francisco, 1966-67.

PRINCIPAL STAGE WORK—Director: *Shelter,* John Golden Theatre, New York City, 1973; *The Master Builder,* Long Wharf Theatre, New Haven, 1973; *The Runner Stumbles,* Manhattan Theatre Club, New York City, 1974; *The Scarecrow,* Eisenhower Theatre, Kennedy Center, Washington, DC, 1975; *The Runner Stumbles,* Hartman Theatre, Stamford, CT, and at the John Golden Theatre, New York City, 1976; *Benito Cereno,* American Place Theatre, New York City, 1976; *Misalliance,* Academy Festival Theatre, Lake Forest, IL, 1976; *The Gathering,* Manhattan Theatre Club, New York City, 1977; *Say Goodnight, Gracie,* 78th Street Theatre Lab, New York City, 1979; *The Little Foxes,* Martin Beck Theatre, New York City, 1981; with the Mirror Repertory Company at the Theatre at St. Peter's Church, New York City, 1984; *Mass Appeal,* with the York Theatre Company at the Chancel of the Church of Heavenly Rest, New York City, 1984; *After the Fall,* Williamstown Theatre Festival, 1984.

PRINCIPAL FILM APPEARANCES—*Skidoo,* 1968; *Catch-22,* Paramount, 1970; *Oven 350,* 1970; *What's Up Doc?,* Warner Brothers, 1972; *Every Little Crook and Nanny,* Metro-Goldwyn-Mayer (MGM), 1972; *The Thief Who Came to Dinner,* Warner Brothers, 1972; *The Front Page,* Universal, 1974; *Lovesick,* Warner Brothers, 1974; *The Great Smokey Roadblock,* 1976; *The Muppet Movie,* Associated Film Distributors, 1979; *Starting Over,* Paramount, 1979; *Simon,* Warner Brothers, 1980; *First Family,* Warner Brothers, 1980.

RELATED CAREER—Acting teacher, Herbert Berghof Studios and at the Circle in the Square Theatre School, both New York City.

AWARDS: Clarence Derwent Award, 1966, for *Hail Scrawdyke!;* Obie Award, New York Drama Critics Poll Award, and Drama Desk Award, all 1970, for *The Last Sweet Days of Isaac.*

MEMBER: Actors' Equity Association, Screen Actors Guild, American Federation of Television and Radio Artists, Society of Stage Directors and Choreographers.

ADDRESSES: AGENT—The Artists Agency, 190 N. Canon Drive, Beverly Hills, CA 90210.*

                               *   *   *

PENNINGTON, Janice

PERSONAL: Married Carlos de Abrue (a jeweler and watch manufacturer).

CAREER: PRINCIPAL TELEVISION APPEARANCES—Game Shows: *The Price Is Right,* NBC, Series: *Playboy After Dark; Rowan and Martin's Laugh-In,* NBC, two seasons. Episodic: *Ironside,* NBC.

PRINCIPAL FILM APPEARANCES—*I Love My Wife,* Universal, 1970; *The Other Side of the Wind,* upcoming.

PRINCIPAL CABARET APPEARANCES—Desert Inn, Las Vegas, NV; Seattle World's Fair; with Liza Minnelli in Paris and Monte Carlo.

JANICE PENNINGTON

RELATED CAREER—Model with the Ford Modeling Agency; featured in *Vogue;* modeled in television commercials.

RECORDINGS: SINGLES—"Bend Me Shape Me," The Models, Metro-Goldwyn-Mayer Records.

ADDRESSES: PUBLICIST—Jo-Ann Geffen and Associates, 3151 Cahuenga Blvd. West, Suite 235, Los Angeles, CA 90068.

*   *   *

PERSKY, Lisa Jane

PERSONAL: Daughter of Mort and Jane Holley (Wilson) Persky.

VOCATION: Actress.

CAREER: PRINCIPAL STAGE APPEARANCES—Cordelia Wells, *Grandmother Is in the Strawberry Patch,* La Mama Experimental Theatre Company (E.T.C.), New York City; Mary Eleanor, *Women Behind Bars,* Truck & Warehouse Theatre, New York City; Maryclare, *Catholic Girls,* Mark Taper Forum, Los Angeles; Debbie, *Passing Game,* Denver Center Theatre Company, CO; Mary Clare, *Hearts on Fire,* Odyssey Theatre Ensemble; Cloris, *These Men,* Los Angeles Actors Theatre; Dawn, *Steaming,* Brooks Atkinson Theatre, New York City; Nancy Spungen, *Vicious,* Steppenwolf Theatre Company, Chicago.

PRINCIPAL FILM APPEARANCES—Mary Ann Meechum, *The Great Santini,* Orion, 1979; Dirty Dee, *KISS Meets the Phantom,* 1980; Bella, *American Pop,* Columbia, 1981; Miss Beasley, *Breathless,* Orion, 1983; Frances Flegenheimer Schultz, *The Cotton Club,* Orion, 1985; Mary Anne, *The Sure Thing,* 1985; Dolores Dodge, *Peggy Sue Got Married,* Tri-Star, 1986; McCabe, *The Big Easy,* Kings Road Productions, 1986.

PRINCIPAL TELEVISION APPEARANCES—Series: *The Fitzpatricks,* Warner Brothers Television; Monica, *Shirley,* NBC; Lola, *Billy,* CBS; Laurie, *Open All Night,* ABC; Joanne Goldman, *Crime Story,* NBC. Episodic: Penny, *Quincy,* NBC; Rita, *The Hulk,* NBC; Shirley Crater, *Amazing Stories,* NBC; Sandra, *The Twilight Zone,* CBS; Sally, *Trapper John, M.D.,* CBS; Shelly, *E/R,* CBS; Kate, *The Golden Girls,* NBC.

Pilots: Henry, *The Mississippi,* CBS; Dora, *Back Together,* CBS; Sheila, *All the Way Home,* NBC. Movies: Emmy, *The Choice,* Finnegan Associates/Greene Production, 1981; Linda, *Desperate Intruder,* ComWorld Productions, 1983; Sister Cathy, *Shattered Vows,* NBC, 1984; also, Cindy, *Snowbound,* NBC; *A Matter of Time,* CBS. Videos: Idy (voiceover), *3-D Captain EO,* Lusacfilm/ Disney Pictures; Jasmine, *Motown's Mustang,* Motown/Modern Productions.

AWARDS: Drama-Logue and *L.A. Weekly* awards, for *These Men* and *Hearts on Fire;* Outstanding Performance, Drama Critics Circle nomination, for *These Men.*

MEMBER: Actors' Equity Association, Screen Actors Guild, American Federation of Radio and Television Artists.

ADDRESSES: AGENT—The Gage Group, 9229 Sunset Blvd., Los Angeles, CA 90069.

ROBERTA PETERS

PETERS, Roberta 1930-

PERSONAL: Born Roberta Peterman, May 4, 1930, in New York, NY; daughter of Sol and Ruth (Hirsch) Peterman; married Bertram Fields (a private investor), April 10, 1955; children: Paul Adam, Bruce Eric. EDUCATION: Studied with William Herman.

VOCATION: Actress and operatic and concert singer.

CAREER: NEW YORK DEBUT—Zerlina, *Don Giovanni,* Metropolitan Opera. LONDON DEBUT—*The Bohemian Girl,* Covent Garden. PRINCIPAL STAGE APPEARANCES—Continually with the Metropolitan Opera from her debut until the present in well over five hundred performances of operas including: Marzelline, *Fidelio, Lucia di Lammermoor,* Gilda, *Rigoletto,* Rosina, *Il Barbiere de Siviglia,* and Kitty, *The Last Savage.* Also, *La Boheme* and *La Traviata.* In the legitimate theatre, has performed throughtout the U.S. as Anna in *The King and I,* Maria in *The Sound of Music,* and in *Bittersweet* and *The Merry Widow.*

MAJOR TOURS—Opera: Performed in cities in the Soviet Union, People's Republic of China, and Israel.

TELEVISION DEBUT—*Ed Sullivan Show,* CBS, 1950. PRINCIPAL TELEVISION APPEARANCES—Guest: *Ed Sullivan,* CBS; *Milton Berle,* NBC; *Jackie Gleason,* NBC; *Jimmy Durante,* NBC; *Perry Como,* NBC; *Garry Moore,* CBS; *Johnny Carson,* NBC; *Merv Griffin,* CBS; *Mike Douglas; Dinah Shore,* NBC. Episodic: *Medical Center,* CBS; *Hotel,* ABC; *13 Clocks.*

FILM DEBUT—*Tonight We Sing,* Twentieth Century-Fox, 1952.

PRINCIPAL RADIO WORK—*The Voice of Firestone.*

WRITINGS: BOOKS—*Debut at the Met.*

RECORDINGS: ALBUMS Many albums for RCA, DG, CBS, and Decca Records.

AWARDS: Bolshoi Medal Award, Moscow, 1972; Woman of the Year Award, Federation of Women's Clubs, 1964. Honorary Degrees: D. Litt, Elmira College, 1967; D.M., Ithaca College, 1968; D.H., Westminister College, 1974; L.H.D., Lehigh University, 1977; D.M., Colby College, 1981; D.M., St. John's University, 1982.

SIDELIGHTS: RECREATIONS—Tennis.

In material provided by Roberta Peters, *CTFT* learned that her career as an operatic and concert performer has been highlighted by long runs and multiple appearances. Her career with the Metropolitan Opera is the longest continuous association with a coloatura soprano in its history. She appeared on the *Ed Sullian Show* sixty-five times and with *The Voice of Firestone* twenty-five times.

ADDRESSES: HOME—Scarsdale, NY. AGENT—International Creative Management, 40 W. 57th Street, New York, NY 10019.

*   *   *

PETERSEN, Erika   1949-

PERSONAL: Born March 24, 1949, in New York, NY; daughter of E. Peter (a painter) and Mary Ruth (a teacher and writer; maiden name, Layton) Petersen; married Robert F. Strohmeier (a lighting designer), May 7, 1983. EDUCATION: Attended New York University School of the Arts; trained for the stage with Allan Miller and Felix Knight and dance with Matt Mattox, Frank Pietri, and Nanatte Glushack.

VOCATION: Actress.

CAREER: OFF-BROADWAY DEBUT—*One Is a Lonely Number,* Mermaid Theatre, 1964. PRINCIPAL STAGE APPEARANCES—Broadway: Standby to lead, *Nuts,* Biltmore Theatre. Off-Broadway: Linda, *I Dreamt I Dwelt in Bloomingdales,* Provincetown Playhouse; Lydia Languish, *The Rivals,* Perry Street Theatre; Bride, *F. Jasmine Addams* and Kate, *P.S. Your Cat Is Dead,* both Circle in the Square Downtown; four roles, *Dubliners,* Roundabout Theatre; Ronda, *Hooters,* Playwrights Horizons; Bride, *Frankenstein* and Agnes, *Brand,* CSC Repertory Theatre.

Regional: Raymonde, *A Flea in Her Ear,* Walnut Street Theatre, Philadelphia; Marianne, *The Miser,* Emily, *Our Town,* and Celia, *As You Like It,* all at the Great Lakes Shakespeare Festival, IL; Curly's Wife, *Of Mice and Men,* Cohoes Music Hall; Sissy, *Come Back to the Five and Dime, Jimmy Dean, Jimmy Dean,* Alliance Theatre, Atlanta; Gloria, *You Never Can Tell,* Pittsburgh Public Theatre; Lady Teazle, *School for Scandal,* Meadow Brook Theatre, Detroit; Celia, *The Cocktail Party,* Hartford Stage Company, CT; Nora, *A Doll's House* and Portia, *The Merchant of Venice,* both Syracuse Stage Company, NY; Blanche, *A Streetcar Named Desire* and Sally, *Talley's Folly,* both Stage West; Jane, *Absurd Person Singular,* Whole Theatre Company, Montclair, NJ.

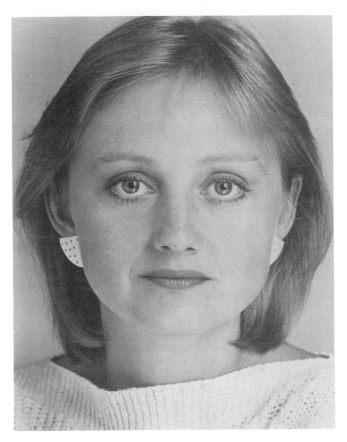

ERIKA PETERSEN

TELEVISION DEBUT—Sally Field, *The Doctors,* NBC, 1971. PRINCIPAL TELEVISION APPEARANCES—*Feeling Good,* PBS.

FILM DEBUT—Lead, *Life Study,* Independent, 1971. PRINCIPAL FILM APPEARANCES—*Heaven's Gate,* United Artists, 1980; *Rent Control,* Ader/Dennis, 1984.

ADDRESSES: HOME—New York, NY. AGENT—Ambrosio-Mortimer, 165 W. 46th Street, New York, NY 10036; Cunningham, Escott and Depine, 118 E. 25th Street, New York, NY 10010.

*   *   *

PHILLIPS, Arlene   1943-

PERSONAL: Born May 22, 1943, in London, England; daughter of A.E. and R. Phillips; children: Alana Roxanne. EDUCATION: Trained as a dancer in the United States and England.

VOCATION: Dancer.

CAREER: PRINCIPAL FILM APPEARANCES—*Escape to Athena,* Associated Film, 1979; *Can't Stop the Music,* Associated Film, 1980; *The Fan,* 1981; *Annie,* Columbia, 1982; *Monty Python's Meaning of Life,* Universal, 1983; *Legend,* British, 1985; *Highlander,* Twentieth Century-Fox, 1986; *Duran Duran Arena.*

PRINCIPAL TELEVISION APPEARANCES—Great Britain: *The Kenny Everett Video Show; Benny Hill Show; The Very Hot Gossip*

ARLENE PHILLIPS

Show; Kiri Te Kenawa; Leo Sayer Series; Leo Sayer Special; David Essex Series; Golden Oldie Picture Show; Hot Shoe Show; A Royal Gala Performance for the Queen. U.S.: *Dancing to the Hits; Duran Duran,* HBO; *Donna Summer Special,* HBO; *Tina Turner,* HBO.

PRINCIPAL RADIO WORK—Series: *Out on the Floor.*

RELATED CAREER—Dancer for many television commercials.

VIDEOS—Danced in music videos made by: Elton John, Joan Jett, Cliff Richard, The Bee Gees, Donna Summer, Duran Duran, Culture Club, Tina Turner, Olivia Newton John, Go West, Paul Young, Freddie Mercury, Elton John and Millie Jackson, Moody Blues, AC/DC, Kiss, Queen, Aretha Franklin, Diana Ross, Elton John and George Michael, Feargal Sharkey, Whitney Houston.

MEMBER: British Actors' Equity Association, Royal Academy of Dancing.

ADDRESSES: AGENT—Michael Summerton, London, England.

*   *   *

PHILLIPS, Bob   1953-

PERSONAL: Full name, Robert Thomas Phillips, Jr.; born December 3, 1953, in Worcester, MA; son of Robert Thomas (a firefighter) and Norma Anne (Lawless) Phillips. EDUCATION: Simon's Rock College, A.A; New York University, B.S.

VOCATION: Scenic designer.

CAREER: FIRST STAGE WORK—Scene designer, *Jumpcrow,* Lenox Arts Center, Lenox, MA, 1972. PRINCIPAL STAGE WORK—Scenic designer (all New York City productions): *Journey's End,* Classic Theatre, 1980; *Knitters in the Sun,* Theatre de Lys, 1980; *Mecca,* Quaigh Theatre, 1980; *Naomi Court,* Players Theatre, 1980; *Hughie* and *The Stronger,* Harold Clurman Theatre, 1982; *The Two Character Play,* Open Space Theatre, 1982; *Confluence,* Circle Repertory Theatre, 1982; *It's Only a Play,* Manhattan Punchline Theatre, 1982; *Knight of the Burning Pestle,* Classic Theatre, 1983; *The Beautiful LaSalles,* Wonderhorse Theatre, 1984; *Sacraments,* Harold Clurman Theatre, 1984; *Robin and Marion* and *City of Women,* both Mannes Camerata Theatre, 1985; *Manoa Valley,* Pan Asian Repertory Theatre, 1985; *Jack and Jill,* Riverwest Theatre, 1985; *Gertrude Stein and a Companion,* Lucille Lortel Theatre, 1986; *Spanish Tragedy,* Riverside Shakespeare Theatre, 1986; *Kobo Abe,* St. Clements Church Theatre, 1986; *Big Time,* Lambs Theatre, 1986.

Regional: Scenic design work at: Theatre by the Sea, Portsmouth, NH, 1976—; *School for Wives,* George Street Playhouse, New Brunswick, NJ, 1978; American Shaw Festival, Mt. Gretna, PA, 1981—; *Ashes,* Studio Arena Theatre, Buffalo, NY, 1980; *Talley's Folly,* Barter Theatre, Abingdon, VA, 1981; *Frankenstein,* Post Opera Theatre, 1982; *To Gillian on Her 37th Birthday,* Summerfest Theatre, 1986.

MAJOR TOURS—Scenic designer: National Shakespeare Company, national, 1980-81, 1983-84; *The Bon Voyage,* East Coast Ocean Tour, 1980; *For Colored Girls Who Have Considered Suicide When the Rainbow Is Enuf,* national, 1980; *Viaduct,* New Jersey and Pennsylvania cities and New York City, 1981; with the South Street Repertory Company, Austrian and Swedish cities, 1982; with the National Opera Institute, New York City and Washington DC, 1983.

PRINCIPAL TELEVISION WORK—Scenic designer: *Soap Opera Review,* 1981; *My Piece of the Pie, A Media Fable,* New York City, 1984; *Another World,* NBC, 1981-86; *Video Hits One,* cable, 1986; *Gertrude Stein and a Companion,* New York City, 1986.

RELATED CAREER—Resident designer, New Triangle Theatre, New York City.

AWARDS: Downtown Theatre Award, 1980, for *Knitters in the Sun;* Outstanding Contribution to the Season, Outer Critics Circle Award, 1981; Audelco Award nomination, 1985, for *The Beautiful LaSalles.*

MEMBER: United Scenic Artists, Local 829.

ADDRESSES: HOME—201 E. Tenth Street, New York, NY 10003. AGENT—John Giroux, 575 Madison Avenue, New York, NY 10022.

*   *   *

PICKRELL, Piper   1950-

PERSONAL: Born November 19, 1950, in Joplin, MO; daughter of Lewis Clinton (a physician) and Mary Ann (a dance instructor; maiden name, Hatley) Pickrell; married Stephen Bonnell (a director), April 12, 1986; children: Carrie Clinton. EDUCATION: Texas Christian University, B.F.A., 1972; California Institute of the Arts, M.F.A., 1975. RELIGION: Nicherin Shoshu Buddhist.

VOCATION: Choreographer.

CAREER: FIRST STAGE WORK—Choreographer, *Oklahoma!*, Playhouse on Broadway, Pittsburgh, PA, 1972. FIRST OFF-BROADWAY WORK—Choreographer, *Salford Road*, Washington Square Church, 1979. PRINCIPAL STAGE WORK—Choreographer: *A Midsummer Night's Dream*, Theatre of the Riverside Church, New York City, 1979; *Benjamin Poe*, No Smoking Playhouse, New York City, 1981; *A Time to Remember*, SoHo Repertory, New York City, 1981; *Space Cadets*, Ohio Theatre, New York City, 1981; *High Heeled Women*, 1982; *Acts*, 1982; *Our American Girl*, Westside Arts Theatre, New York City, 1982; *Going Down*, Third Street Playhouse, New York City, 1982; *Winter Shakers*, Circle Repertory Theatre, New York City, 1982; *On Hold*, Manhattan Theatre Club, New York City, 1982; *Street Scene*, Equity Library Theatre, New York City, 1982; *First Comes Love*, Musical Theatre Works, New York City, 1983; *Dickens' Reflections on the Carol*, Equity Library Theatre Informal Series, 1983; *Bette Midler "De Tour,"* Radio City Music Hall, New York City, 1984; *Pal Joey*, Equity Library Theatre, 1984; *The Gifts of the Magi*, Lambs Theatre, New York City, 1984-85; *Jacques Brel Is Alive and Well and Living in Paris*, Equity Library Theatre, New York City, 1985; *Merry Christmas Dude*, 1985, and *Attack of the Yuppie Aliens*, 1986, both Strasberg Institute Young People's Program, New York City; *Anything Goes*, Post Theatre Company, Long Island, NY, 1986; *Brand*, American Musical and Dramatic Academy (AMDA), New York City, 1986.

Director and choreographer, *An Evening of Cole Porter*, AMDA, New York City, 1985.

Also, choreographed stock productions of: *The Threepenny Opera, They're Playing Our Song, Robber Bridegroom, Oklahoma!, The Music Man, Lady in the Dark, Jacques Brel Is Alive And Well and Living in Paris, Happy End, Gypsy, Guys and Dolls, George M!, Dames at Sea, Company, Chicago, Cabaret, Brigadoon, Anything Goes, Annie Get Your Gun, Ain't Misbehavin'*. Directed and choreographed *Ain't Misbehavin'*, Country Dinner Playhouse, St. Petersburg, FL, 1986.

MAJOR TOURS—*Bette Midler "De Tour,"* national, 1983-84.

PRINCIPAL TELEVISION WORK—Choreographer: *Rockin' and Rollin' with Phil Spector*, PBS and ITV, London, 1982; *Dance Baby*, 1984; *Bette Midler "No Frills,"* HBO, 1984; *Bette Midler "Art or Bust,"* HBO, 1984; *Subway Surfing*, 1985.

RELATED CAREER—Movement specialist, National Educational Association, 1973-79; dance teacher, Strasberg Institute, New York City, 1983—; dance teacher, American Musical Dramatic Academy, New York City, 1984—.

AWARDS: Festival Fringe First Award, 1979, for *Salford Road*.

MEMBER: Actors' Equity Association, American Federation of Television and Radio Artists, Society of Stage Directors and Choreographers.

ADDRESSES: AGENT—c/o Dan Mizell, William Morris Agency, 1350 Avenue of the Americas, New York, NY 10019.

GEOFFREY PIERSON

PIERSON, Geoffrey   1949-

PERSONAL: Born June 16, 1949, in Chicago, IL; son of Roy J. (a businessman) and Helen T. (McGinness) Pierson; married Catherine Daly, January 23, 1971; children: Norah, Elizabeth, Roy. EDUCATION: Fordham University, B.A., philosophy, 1971; Yale School of Drama, M.F.A., 1980.

VOCATION: Actor.

CAREER: STAGE DEBUT—Season of plays, Shady Land Summer Theatre, Marengo, IL, 1976. OFF-BROADWAY DEBUT—Doctor, *Wings*, New York Shakespeare Festival, Public Theatre, 1978. PRINCIPAL STAGE APPEARANCES—*I Won't Dance*, Broadway production; *Tricks of the Trade*, Circle in the Square, New York City; with the Yale Repertory Theatre, New Haven, CT: Lord Lucius, *Timon of Athens*, Wang, *The Bundle*, Angelo and Pompey, *Measure for Measure*, Hildy, *The Front Page*, also appeared in *Ubu Rex*.

At the Yale School of Drama: Harris, *After Magrite*, General Custer, *Custer*, James, *Long Day's Journey into Night*, Buckingham, *Richard III*, Alfred, *Tales from the Vienna Woods*.

Stanley, *A Streetcar Named Desire*, Center Stage, PA; *Miss Julie* and *Playing with Fire*, both at the Roundabout Theatre, New York City; *Crossing Delancy*, Jewish Repertory Theatre, New York City.

FILM DEBUT—T.J., *Without a Trace*, Twentieth Century-Fox, 1983.

TELEVISION DEBUT—Lt. Donovan, *Texas*, NBC, 1980. PRINCIPAL TELEVISION APPEARANCES—Series: Frank Ryan, *Ryan's Hope*, ABC, 1983-85. Episodic: *Another World*, NBC; *Kate & Allie*, NBC; *The Equalizer*, NBC. Movies: *The Mating Season*, 1980, NBC.

MEMBER: Actors' Equity Association, American Federation of Television and Radio Artists.

SIDELIGHTS: FAVORITE ROLES—Angelo, *Measure for Measure*, Jean, *Miss Julie*, and Stanley, *A Streetcar Named Desire*.

ADDRESSES: HOME—Pelham, NY. AGENT—Bret Adams Ltd., 448 W. 44th Street, New York, NY 10036.

*   *   *

PINE, Robert   1928-

PERSONAL: Born February 21, 1928, in New York, NY; son of Robert (a salesman) and Lillian (Levine) Pine. EDUCATION: New York University, B.A., civil engineering, 1949; Pratt Institute, M.S., city planning, 1968; attended School of Dramatic Arts, Columbia University.

VOCATION: Writer.

WRITINGS: PLAYS, PRODUCED AND PUBLISHED—*Landscape with Waitress*, Ensemble Studio Theatre, 1981, published by Samuel French, 1981; fourteen additional plays which have received readings and workshop productions.

MEMBER: Dramatists Guild; Ensemble Studio Theatre, NY.

SIDELIGHTS: Robert Pine told *CTFT* "I see the theatre as a force for change."

ADDRESSES: AGENT—Susan Schulman, 454 W. 44th Street, New York, NY 10036.

*   *   *

PLIMPTON, Martha   1970-

PERSONAL: Born November 16, 1970; daughter of Keith Carradine (an actor) and Shelley Plimpton. EDUCATION: Attended the Professional Children's School, New York City.

VOCATION: Actress.

CAREER: STAGE DEBUT—*The Runaways*, Public Theatre, 1979. PRINCIPAL STAGE APPEARANCES—*The Haggadah*, Public Theatre, New York City.

FILM DEBUT—*The River Rat*, 1984. PRINCIPAL FILM APPEARANCES—*Mosquito Coast*, Warner Brothers, 1986; *Shy People*, Cannon, 1987.

TELEVISION DEBUT—"The Hand Me Down Kid," *Afterschool Special*, ABC, 1983.

MEMBER: Nature Conservancy.

ADDRESSES: AGENT—c/o Jenny Delaney, Triad Artists, 10100 Santa Monica Blvd., 16th Floor, Los Angeles, CA 90067.

*   *   *

PLOWRIGHT, Joan   1929-

PERSONAL: Born October 28, 1929, in Scunthorpe, Brigg, Lincolnshire, England; daughter of William Ernest and Daisy Margaret (Burton) Plowright; married Roger Gage (an actor), September, 1954 (divorced, 1960); married Lord Laurence Olivier (an actor and director), March 17, 1961; children: one son, two daughters. EDUCATION: Trained for the stage at the Laban Art of Movement Studio, 1949-50, Old Vic Theatre School, 1950-52, and with Michel St. Denis, Glen Byam Shaw, and George Devine.

VOCATION: Actress.

CAREER: STAGE DEBUT—Hope, *If Four Walls Told*, Grand Theatre, Croydon, U.K., 1951. LONDON DEBUT—Donna Clara, *The Duenna*, Westminster Theatre, 1954. BROADWAY DEBUT—Jean Rice, *The Entertainer*, Royale Theatre, 1958. PRINCIPAL STAGE APPEARANCES—With the Bristol Old Vic Repertory Theatre, U.K., 1952; Allison, *The Merry Gentlemen*, Bristol Old Vic Repertory Theatre, 1954; Pip, *Moby Dick*, Duke of York's Theatre, London, 1955; leading roles, Nottingham Playhouse, U.K., 1955-56; Mary Warren, *The Crucible*, English Stage Company, Royal Court Theatre, London, 1956; Baptista, *Don Juan*, the Receptionist, *The Death of Satan*, Miss Tray, *Cards of Identity*, Mrs. Shin, *The Good Woman of Setzuan*, with the English Stage Company at the Royal Court Theatre, London, 1956; Margery Pinchwife, *The Country Wife*, Royal Court Theatre, London, 1956, then Adelphi Theatre, London, 1957; old woman, *The Chairs* and Elizabeth Compton, *The Making of Moo*, both at the Royal Court Theatre, London, 1957; Jean Rice, *The Entertainer*, Palace Theatre, London, 1957; repeated role of the old woman, *The Chairs* and pupil, *The Lesson*, Phoenix Theatre, New York City, 1958; title role, *Major Barbara*, Royal Court Theatre, London, 1958; Arlette, *Hook, Line and Sinker*, Piccadilly Theatre, London, 1958; Beatie Bryant, *Roots*, Belgrade Theatre, Coventry, U.K., 1959.

Daisy, *Rhinoceros*, Royal Court Theatre, London, 1960; Josephine, *A Taste of Honey*, Lyceum Theatre, New York City, 1960; Another Constatia, *The Chances* and Sonya, *Uncle Vanya*, both at the Chichester Festival, U.K., 1962; title role, *Saint Joan*, Chichester Festival, 1963; repeated title role, *Saint Joan*, Edinburgh Festival, Scotland, 1963; repeated title role, *Saint Joan* and Sonya, *Uncle Vanya*, with the National Theatre at the Old Vic Theatre, London, 1963; at the National Theatre, London: Maggie Hobson, *Hobson's Choice* and Hilda Wangel, *The Master Builder*, 1964, Beatrice, *Much Ado About Nothing*, Masha, *The Three Sisters*, and Dorine, *Tartuffe*, 1967, Teresa, *The Advertisement* (National Theatre and Royal Theatre, London), and Rosaline, *Love's Labour's Lost*, all 1968, voice of Lilith, *Back to Methuselah*, Part II, 1969.

Portia, *The Merchant of Venice*, New Theatre, London, 1970; Mistress Anne Frankford, *A Woman Killed with Kindness*, New Theatre, 1971; Silla, *The Rules of the Game*, New Theatre, London, 1971; Jennifer Dubedat, *The Doctor's Dilemma* and Katharina, *The Taming of the Shrew*, both at the Chichester Festival, 1972; Rebecca West, *Rosmersholm*, Greenwich Theatre, U.K., 1973;

Rosa, *Saturday, Sunday, Monday,* Old Vic Theatre, London, 1973 and later at the Queen's Theatre, London, 1974; Stella Kirby, *Eden End,* Old Vic Theatre, then National Theatre, London, 1974; with the Lyric Theatre Company, London: Irena Arkadina, *The Seagull,* Alma, *The Bed Before Yesterday,* 1975; Filumena Marturano, *Filumena,* 1977, then St. James Theatre, New York City, 1980.

Also appeared at the National Theatre, London in *Enjoy,* 1980, *Who's Afraid of Virginia Woolf?,* 1981, *Cavell,* 1982, *The Cherry Orchard,* 1983, *The Way of the World,* 1984, *Mrs. Warren's Profession,* 1985.

MAJOR TOURS—With the Old Vic Company, South African cities, 1952.

PRINCIPAL STAGE WORK—With the National Theatre, London, co-director, *An Evasion of Women* and *The Travails of Sancho Panza,* 1969; director, *Rites,* 1969.

PRINCIPAL FILM APPEARANCES—*Moby Dick,* Warner Brothers, 1956; *Time without Pity,* Astor, 1957; *The Entertainer,* Continental, 1960; *Three Sisters,* Brandon, 1969; *Equus,* Warner Brothers, 1977; *Richard Wagner,* 1982; *Brimstone and Treacle,* Namara, 1982; *Britannica Hospital,* United Artists Classics, 1983.

PRINCIPAL TELEVISION APPEARANCES—Episodic: *Odd Man In,* BBC, 1958; *Secret Agent,* BBC, 1959. Dramatic Specials: *The School for Scandal,* BBC, 1959, then repeated on U.S. television, 1961; *Twelfth Night,* BBC, 1967, *Merchant of Venice,* BBC, 1973. Movies: *Daphne Laureola,* 1977; *Saturday, Sunday, Monday,* 1977.

AWARDS: Created Commander of the British Empire (CBE), Birthday Honors, 1970; Best Actress, Antoinette Perry Award, 1960, for *A Taste of Honey;* Best Actress, *Evening Standard* Award, 1964, for *St. Joan;* Variety Club Award, 1976, for *The Bed Before Yesterday;* Best Actress, Society of West End Theatres Award, 1978, for *Filumena.*

ADDRESSES: AGENT—LOP Ltd., 33-34 Chancery Lane, London WC2A 1EN, England.*

*   *   *

PLUMMER, Christopher   1927-

PERSONAL: Full name, Arthur Christopher Orme Plummer; born December 13, 1927, in Toronto, Ontario, Canada; son of John (a secretary to the dean of science, McGill University) and Isabella Mary (Abbott) Plummer; married Tammy Lee Grimes (an actress), 1956 (divorced); married Patricia Audrey Lewis (a journalist), May 4, 1962 (divorced); married Elaine Regina Taylor, 1970; children: (first marriage) Amanda. EDUCATION: Attended Jennings Private School.

VOCATION: Actor.

CAREER: STAGE DEBUT—Faulkland, *The Rivals,* Canadian Repertory Theatre, Ottawa, Ontario, Canada, 1950. BROADWAY DEBUT—George Phillips, *The Starcross Story,* Royale Theatre, 1954. LONDON DEBUT—King Henry II, *Becket,* Aldwych Theatre, London, 1961. PRINCIPAL STAGE APPEARANCES—Played nearly one hundred roles for the Canadian Repertory Theatre, Ottawa,

Ontario, Canada, 1950-52; with the Bermuda Repertory Theatre, 1952: Old Mahon, *The Playboy of the Western World,* Gerard, Nina, Anthony Cavendish, *The Royal Family,* Ben, *The Little Foxes,* Duke Manti, *The Petrified Forest,* Father, *George and Margaret,* Hector Benbow, *Thark,* and Bernard Kersal, *The Constant Wife;* Manchester Monaghan, *Home Is the Hero,* Booth Theatre, New York City, 1954; Count Peter Zichy, *The Dark Is Light Enough,* American National Theatre Academy (ANTA) Theatre, New York City, 1955; Jason, *Medea,* International Festival, Sarah Bernhardt Theatre, Paris, 1955; Mark Antony, *Julius Caesar* and Ferdinand, *The Tempest,* both at the Shakespeare Festival, Stratford, CT, 1955; Earl of Warwick, *The Lark,* Longacre Theatre, New York City, 1955.

Title role, *Henry V,* Stratford Shakespeare Festival, Ontario, Canada, then Assembly Hall Theatre, Edinburgh Festival, Scotland, 1956; narrator, *L'Histoire du Soldat,* City Center, New York City, 1956; Lewis Rohnen, *Night of the Auk,* Playhouse Theatre, New York City, 1956; at the Stratford Shakespeare Festival, Ontario, Canada: title role, *Hamlet* and Sir Andrew Aguecheek, *Twelfth Night,* both 1957, Benedick, *Much Ado About Nothing,* Leontes, *The Winter's Tale,* and Bardolph, *Henry IV, Part I,* all 1958; Nickles, *J.B.,* ANTA Theatre, New York City, 1958; Philip the Bastard, *King John* and Mercutio, *Romeo and Juliet,* both at the Stratford Shakespeare Festival, Ontario, Canada, 1960; Benedick, *Much Ado About Nothing* and title role, *Richard III,* with the Royal Shakespeare Company, Stratford-on-Avon, U.K., 1961; King Henry II, *Becket,* Aldwych Theatre, then transferred to the Globe Theatre, London, 1961; title role, *Cyrano de Bergerac* and title role, *Macbeth,* both with the Stratford Shakespeare Festival, Ontario, Canada, 1962; title role, *Arturo Ui,* Lunt-Fontanne Theatre, New York City, 1963; Francisco Pizzaro, *The Royal Hunt of the Sun,* ANTA Theatre, New York City, 1965.

Mark Antony, *Antony and Cleopatra,* Stratford Shakespeare Festival, Ontario, Canada, 1967; Jupiter and Amphitryon, *Amphitryon 38* and Danton, *Danton's Death,* both with the National Theatre Company at the New Theatre, London, 1971; title role, *Cyrano,* Guthrie Theatre, Minneapolis, MN, then Palace Theatre, New York City, 1973; Anton Chekov, *The Good Doctor,* Eugene O'Neill Theatre, New York City, 1973; appeared in *Love and Master Will,* Opera House, Kennedy Center, Washington, DC, 1975; Edgar, *Drinks Before Dinner,* New York Shakespeare Festival (NYSF), Public/Newman Theatre, New York City, 1978.

Title role, *Henry V,* American Shakespeare Festival, Stratford, CT, 1981; Iago, *Othello,* Winter Garden Theatre, New York City, 1982; appeared in *Parade of Stars Playing the Palace,* Palace Theatre, New York City, 1983; *Peccadillo,* Florida, 1985.

PRINCIPAL FILM APPEARANCES—*Stage Struck,* Buena Vista, 1958; *The Fall of the Roman Empire,* Paramount, 1964; *The Sound of Music,* Twentieth Century-Fox, 1965; *Inside Daisy Clover,* Warner Brothers, 1966; *Triple Cross,* Warner Brothers/Seven Arts, 1967; *Oedipus the King,* Universal, 1968; *The High Commissioner,* Cinerama, 1968; *Lock Up Your Daughters,* Columbia, 1969; *The Royal Hunt of the Sun,* National General, 1969; *Battle of Britain,* United Artists, 1969; *Waterloo,* Paramount, 1971; *The Pyx,* Cinerama, 1973; *Spiral Staircase,* 1975; *Conduct Unbecoming,* Allied Artists, 1975; *Return of the Pink Panther,* United Artists, 1975; *The Man Who Would Be King,* Allied Artists, 1975; *Aces High,* 1976; *Disappearance,* 1977; *International Velvet,* United Artists, 1978; *Silent Partner,* 1978; *Hanover Street,* 1979; *Murder by Decree,* AVCO-Embassy, 1980; *Somewhere in Time,* Universal, 1980; *Eyewitness,* Twentieth Century-Fox, 1981; *Dis-*

appearance, 1981; *The Janitor,* 1981; *The Amateur,* Twentieth Century-Fox, 1982; *Dreamscape,* Twentieth Century-Fox, 1984; *Ordeal by Innocence,* 1984; *Lily in Love,* New Line Cinema, 1985; *The Boy in Blue,* Twentieth Century-Fox, 1986; voice of Henri, *An American Tail,* Universal Pictures, 1986; also *Across the Everglades.*

TELEVISION DEBUT—Montano, *Othello,* CBC, Canada, 1951. PRINCIPAL TELEVISION APPEARANCES—Episodic: Title role, "Oedipus Rex," *Omnibus,* CBS, 1956; Miles Hendon, "The Prince and the Pauper," *DuPont Show of the Month,* NBC, 1957; soldier, "Little Moon of Alban," *Hallmark Hall of Fame,* NBC, 1958; Thomas Mendip, "The Lady's Not for Burning," *Omnibus,* CBS, 1958; Doctor, "Johnny Belinda," *Hallmark Hall of Fame,* NBC, 1958; Agamemnon and Orestes, "The Orestia," *Omnibus,* CBS, 1959; Mike, "The Philadelphia Story," *DuPont Show of the Month,* NBC, 1959; Helmer, "A Doll's House," *Hallmark Hall of Fame,* NBC, 1959; title role, "Captain Brassbound's Conversion," *Hallmark Hall of Fame,* NBC, 1960; Prince, "Time Remembered," *Hallmark Hall of Fame,* NBC, 1961; Rassendyl, "The Prisoner of Zenda," *DuPont Show of the Month,* NBC, 1961; title role, "Cyrano de Bergerac," *Hallmark Hall of Fame,* NBC, 1962; title role, *Macbeth,* for the Stratford Shakespeare Festival, Ontario, Canada, televised by satelite transmission, 1962; title role, *Hamlet at Elsinore,* BBC, 1964.

Mini-Series: *The Moneychangers,* 1977; *Jesus of Nazareth,* 1977; *The Thornbirds,* 1983. Movies: *The Shadow Box,* 1980.

AWARDS: Best Actor, *Theatre World* Award, 1955, for *The Dark Is Light Enough;* Best Actor, *Evening Standard* Award, 1961, for *Becket;* citation for performance, *Best Plays,* 1963-64, for *Arturo Ui;* Best Actor in a Musical, Antoinette Perry Award, Outer Circle and Drama Desk Awards, and *Best Plays* citation, all 1973, for *Cyrano;* Emmy Award, 1977, for *The Moneychangers;* named Companion of the Order of Canada, 1969, for performance in *Cyrano de Bergerac.*

MEMBER: Actors' Equity Association, American Federation of Television and Radio Artists, Screen Actors Guild; The Players Club, The Garrick Club.

SIDELIGHTS: RECREATIONS—Skiing, tennis, and playing piano.

ADDRESSES: AGENT—International Creative Management, 8899 Beverly Blvd., Los Angeles, CA 90048; Stanley, Gorrie, Whitson and Company, Nine Cavendish Square, London W1, England.*

*   *   *

POGGI, Jack   1928-

PERSONAL: Full name, Emilio John Poggi, Jr.; born June 14, 1928, in Oakland, CA; son of Emilio J. (a salesman) and Josephine (Giani) Poggi; married Jeanlee M. Mathey (a teacher) January 14, 1967; children: David B. EDUCATION: University of San Francisco, B.A., 1950; Harvard University, M.A., 1951; Columbia University, Ph.D., 1966; studied acting with Mira Rostova and at the Herbert Berghof Studios in New York. POLITICS: Democrat. MILITARY: U.S. Army, 1951-53.

VOCATION: Actor, writer, and acting coach.

CAREER: STAGE DEBUT—Professor Talbot, *Leave It to Jane,*

Gateway Playhouse, Bellport, Long Island, NY, 1960. OFF-BROADWAY DEBUT—*This Side of Paradise,* Sheridan Square Playhouse, 1962. PRINCIPAL STAGE APPEARANCES—*Uncle Vanya,* Actors Alliance Theatre, New York City, 1977; one man show, *Dostoevsky's Forgotten People,* 1978-1981; Teleygin, *Uncle Vanya,* Huntington Theatre Company, Boston, 1985; *The Orchard,* Dorset Theatre Festival, VT, 1986.

FILM DEBUT—Cardinal, *Zelig,* Warner Brothers, 1983.

TELEVISION DEBUT—Dr. Eli Stern, *One Life to Live,* ABC, 1983.

RELATED CAREER—Part-time instructor, Cooper Union and Manhattan School of Music, 1956-63; professor, department of theatre and film, C.W. Post Center of Long Island University, 1963-83; acting and audition coach, New York City, 1986—.

WRITINGS: NON-FICTION—*Theatre in America: The Impact of Economic Forces, 1870-1967,* Cornell University Press, 1968. PLAYS—(Translation) *Uncle Vanya,* 1977. ARTICLES—"Stanislavsky Today," *The Drama Review,* 1973; "Second Thoughts on the Theory of Action," *Actor Training 2,* 1976; "The Monologue Shop," regular feature in *Back Stage,* 1985-86.

MEMBER: Actors' Equity Association, American Federation of Television and Radio Artists.

ADDRESSES: HOME—880 W. 181st Street, New York, NY 10033.

JACK POGGI

POLAND, Albert 1941-

PERSONAL: Born April 30, 1941; son of Lloyd O. and Bessie Berniece (Seymour) Poland. EDUCATION: Studied acting and musical comedy at the American Theatre Wing. POLITICS: Democrat.

VOCATION: Producer, manager, press agent, writer, actor, and singer.

CAREER: STAGE DEBUT—Understudy, Rolf, *The Sound of Music*, Bus and Truck tour, 1961-62. PRINCIPAL STAGE APPEARANCES—Soloist, *Lotte Lenya at Carnegie Hall*, Carnegie Hall, New York City, 1965; Brandon De Wilde, *Eye on New York*, La Mama Experimental Theatre Club (ETC), New York City, 1970; Hans, *If Time Has a Stop, Space Is Where It's At, Here at Dead Center of America*, Old Reliable Theatre Tavern, 1970; Polly Parrot, *Elegy to a Down Queen*, La Mama ETC, New York City, 1972; Professor, *The Faggot*, Judson Poet's Theatre, New York City, 1973; Master of Ceremonies, *The Peaches Intimate Revue*, Judson Memorial Church Garden, New York City, 1973; Pope Pius XII, *Religion*, Judson Poet's Theatre, New York City, 1974.

PRINCIPAL CABARET APPEARANCES—With the Winged Victory Chorus, various nightclubs, 1961; as a soloist, has appeared at the Latin Quarter and the Village Barn, New York City, 1961-63.

PRINCIPAL STAGE WORK—Press agent: For the American Conservatory Theatre, San Francisco, CA, 1966; for the Ravinia Festival, Chicago, 1966; for the Maharishi Mahesh Yogi and Beach Boys tour, 1968. Company manager: *Sweet Bird of Youth*, Harkness Theatre, New York City, 1976; *Who's Afraid of Virginia Woolf?*, Music Box Theatre, New York City, 1976; *Happy End*, Martin Beck Theatre, New York City, 1977; *Are You Now or Have You Ever Been*, Promenade and Century Theatres, New York City, 1978-79.

Producer: *Now Is the Time for All Good Men*, Theatre de Lys, New York City, 1967; *Peace*, Astor Place Theatre, New York City, 1969; *The Unseen Hand* and *Forensic and the Navigators*, both Astor Place Theatre, New York City, 1970; *Acrobats* and *Line*, Theatre de Lys, New York City, 1971; *The Bar That Never Closes*, Astor Place Theatre, New York City, 1972; *The Peaches Intimate Revue*, Judson Memorial Church Garden, 1973; *Dear Nobody*, Cherry Lane Theatre, New York City, 1974; *Modigliani*, Astor Place Theatre, New York City, 1979.

General manager: (Also associate producer) *Futz*, Theatre de Lys, New York City, 1968; *The Dirtiest Show in Town*, Astor Place Theatre, New York City, 1970; *Touch*, Village Arena Theatre, New York City, 1970; *Rain*, Astor Place Theatre, New York City, 1971; *And They Put Handcuffs on the Flowers*, Mercer Arts Center, New York City, 1972; San Francisco Mime Troupe, *The Dragon Lady's Revenge*, Astor Place Theatre, New York City, 1973; *The Faggot*, Truck and Warehouse Theatre, New York City, 1973; *Let My People Come*, Village Gate, New York City, 1974-75; *Why Hanna's Skirt Won't Stay Down*, Top of the Gate, New York City, 1974; *The Charles Pierce Show* and *Tommy Tune Atop the Village Gate*, both Top of the Gate, New York City, 1975; *A Life in the Theatre*, Theatre de Lys, New York City, 1977-78; *Patio* and *Porch*, both Century Theatre, New York City, 1978; *The Neon Woman*, Hurrah Theatre, New York City, 1978; *Crimes Against Nature*, Actors' Playhouse Theatre, New York City, 1978; *Lone Star* and *Pvt. Wars*, both Century Theatre, 1979; *Vanities*, Chelsea Theatre Center, New York City, 1979-80; *The Price*, Playhouse

Theatre, New York City, 1979; *One Mo' Time*, Village Gate, New York City, 1979-82.

General Manager: *Table Settings*, with Playwrights Horizons at the Chelsea Theatre Center, New York City, 1980; *Das Lusitania Songspiel*, Chelsea Theatre Center, New York City, 1980; *An Evening with W.S. Gilbert* and *To Bury a Cousin*, both Cherry Lane Theatre, New York City, 1980; *Harlem Swing* (also known as *Ain't Misbehavin*), Theatre de la Porte St. Martin, Paris, France, 1980; *Forty-Deuce*, Perry Street Theatre, New York City, 1981; *The Buddy System*, Circle in the Square Downtown, New York City, 1981; *Marry Me a Little*, Actors Playhouse Theatre, New York City, 1981; *One Mo' Time*, Cambridge Theatre, London, England, 1981-82; *Entertaining Mr. Sloan*, Cherry Lane Theatre, New York City, 1981-82; *Tomfoolery*, Top of the Gate, New York City, 1981-82; *Little Shop of Horrors*, Orpheum Theatre, New York City, 1982—; *Weekend* and *The Middle Ages*, both Theatre at Saint Peter's Church, New York City, 1983; *Little Shop of Horrors*, Westwood Playhouse, Los Angeles, 1983; *One Mo' Time*, Village Gate, Toronto, Canada, 1983-84; *The Vampires*, Astor Place Theatre, New York City, 1984; *Orphans*, Westside Arts Theatre, New York City, 1985; *As Is*, Lyceum Theatre, New York City, 1985; *A Lie of the Mind*, Promenade Theatre, New York City, 1985; *El Grande de Coca Cola*, Village Gate, New York City, 1986.

MAJOR TOURS—Producer and press agent, *The Fantasticks*, national, 1966-68.

WRITINGS: NON-FICTION—*The Off Off-Broadway Book. The Plays, People, Theatre*, 1974. PLAYS, UNPRODUCED—*Normal*, 1975.

MEMBER: Actors' Equity Association, National Academy of Recording Arts and Sciences, League of Off-Broadway Theatres and Producers (board of governors); Association of Theatrical Press Agents and Managers (board of governors).

ADDRESSES: OFFICE—226 W. 47th Street, New York, NY 10036.

*   *   *

POPPENGER, Carol 1937-

PERSONAL: Born November 17, 1937, in Plymouth, MI. EDUCATION: Florida State University, B. of Music, 1959; New England Conservatory of Music, M.A., 1961; trained for the stage with Michael Shurtleff, William Woodman, Barnet Kellman, Joan Evans, and Daniel Gerroll.

VOCATION: Actress and singer.

CAREER: PRINCIPAL STAGE APPEARANCES—Mrs. Smith, *Men in White*, Quaigh Theatre, New York City; Mrs. Conway, *Time and the Conways*, St. Clement's Theatre, New York City; Helen Baird, *A Loss of Roses*, Strasberg Institute Theatre, New York City; leading roles, *Landscape* and *Night*, All Soul's Players Theatre, New York City; Mrs. Newquist, *Little Murders*, Frankel Theatre, New York City; Miss Crews, *Boy Meets Girl*, Directors' Loft Theatre, New York City.

Regionally: Godmother and Queen, *Cinderella*, Theatre of Light; Paula, *The Girl in the Freudian Slip*, Laura, *The Second Time*

CAROL POPPENGER

Around, and Maggie, *The Indoor Sport*, all at the Shady Lane Theatre, IL; Mabel, *Little Mary Sunshine*, Charles Playhouse, Boston; Alice, *The Impossible Years*, Alhambra Dinner Theatre, Jacksonville, FL; Shaindel, *Fiddler on the Roof*, Club Bene, Sayreville, NJ; Mrs. Baker, *Come Blow Your Horn*, Mrs. Rogers, *Ten Little Indians*, and *Promenade All*, all at the Wolfeboro Playhouse, NH.

MAJOR TOURS—*The Sound of Music*, national.

MEMBER: Actors' Equity Association, American Federation of Television and Radio Artists, American Guild of Musical Artists.

ADDRESSES: AGENT—Chalek and Chalek, 380 Lexington Avenue, New York, NY 10017.

*   *   *

PORTER, Stephen   1925-

PERSONAL: Full name, Stephen Winthrop Porter; born July 24, 1925, in Ogdensburg, NY; son of Charles Talbot (an engineer) and Anna Martin (a teacher; maiden name, Newton) Porter. EDUCATION: Attended Yale University and Yale School of the Drama.

VOCATION: Director, designer, producer, and translator.

CAREER: PRINCIPAL STAGE WORK—Director and designer, for McGill University, Montreal, Quebec, Canada: *Hippolytus*, 1952,

Measure for Measure and *The Caprice of Marianne*, both 1953, *The Cenci* and *The Seagull*, both 1954, *Much Ado About Nothing*, 1955; producer and director, *The Misanthrope*, Theatre East, New York City, 1956; producer, director, and designer, *The Country Wife*, Renata Theatre, New York City, 1957; director of summer stock productions of: *Mr. Roberts, Cat on a Hot Tin Roof, The Matchmaker, Inherit the Wind, Auntie Mame*, and *Room at the Top*, all at the Red Barn Theatre, Northport, NY, 1958-59; director, *Two Philoctetes*, 1959; director, *Dark of the Moon* and *Our Town*, both at the Fred Miller Theatre, Milwaukee, WI, 1959.

Director for the Playhouse in the Park, Cincinnati, OH: *The Lady's Not for Burning, The Hostage, The Devil's Disciple, The Burnt Flower Bed, The Doctor in Spite of Himself, Major Barbara*, and *Sodom and Gomorrah*, all 1962-65.

Director for the Association of Producing Artists (APA), at the McCarter Theatre, Princeton, NJ: *Right You Are (If You Think You Are)* and *Scapin*, both 1960, *King Lear* and *Twelfth Night*, both 1961, *The Alchemist* and *Antigone*, both 1962, *Caligula, Galileo*, and *Julius Caesar*, all 1963; also directed for the APA: *Scapin*, Phoenix Theatre, New York City, 1963; *A Phoenix Too Frequent*, Trueblood Theatre, Ann Arbor, MI, 1963, *Right You Are (If You Think You Are)*, Trueblood Theatre, 1963, then Phoenix Theatre, New York City, 1964, then Lyceum Theatre, New York City, 1966, *Impromptu at Versailles*, Phoenix Theatre, New York City, 1964, *The Hostage*, and *Man and Superman*, both 1964, *The Wild Duck*, 1965, *The Show-Off*, 1967, and *The Misanthrope*, 1968, all at the Trueblood Theatre; *Krapp's Last Tape, King Lear, Twelfth Night*, and *Private Lives*, all at Trueblood Theatre, then transferring to Billy Rose Theatre, New York City, 1969.

As the artistic director of the New Phoenix Repertory Company, New York City, directed: *The School for Wives*, Ann Arbor, then Lyceum Theatre, New York City, 1971, *Don Juan*, Lyceum Theatre, New York City, 1972, *Chemin de Fer*, Ethel Barrymore Theatre, New York City, 1973, *Rules of the Game*, Helen Hayes Theatre, New York City, 1974, *They Knew What They Wanted* and *Days in the Trees*, 1976, produced: *The Great God Brown* and *A Meeting by the River*, 1972, *Strike Heaven on the Face, Games, After Liverpool, The Government Inspector, Holiday*, and *The Visit*, all 1973, *The Removalists, Love for Love, In the Voodoo Parlor of Marie Leveau*, and *Pretzels*, all 1974, *The Member of the Wedding, Knuckle, Dandelion Wine*, and *Meeting Place*, all 1975.

Director for other managements: *The Alchemist*, Gate Theatre, New York City, 1964; *Tartuffe*, Fred Miller Theatre, Milwaukee, WI, 1964; *The Tempest* and *Diary of a Scoundrel*, both at the Fred Miller Theatre, 1965; *The Birds* and *School for Wives*, both at the McCarter Theatre, 1965; *Phaedra*, Theatre of the Living Arts, Philadelphia, 1967; *Thieves Carnival*, Tyrone Guthrie Theatre, Minneapolis, MN, 1967; *As You Like It*, American Shakespeare Festival, Stratford, CT, 1968; *Enrico IV*, Studio Arena Theatre, Buffalo, NY, 1968; *The Master Builder*, Tyrone Guthrie Theatre, 1968; *The Wrong Way Light Bulb*, John Golden Theatre, New York City, 1969; *Chemin de Fer*, Mark Taper Forum, Los Angeles, 1969; *The Guardsman*, Shaw Festival, Niagara-on-the-Lake, Ontario, Canada, 1969; *Harvey*, American National Theatre Academy (ANTA) Theatre, New York City, 1970; *Richard II*, Old Globe Theatre, San Diego, CA, 1970.

The Italian Straw Hat, Avon Theatre, Stratford Shakespeare Festival, Ontario, Canada, 1971; *Captain Brassbound's Conversion*, Kennedy Center, Washington, DC, then Ethel Barrymore Theatre, New York City, 1972; *The Enchanted* and *The Prodigal Daughter*, both at the Kennedy Center, Washington, DC, 1973; *The School for Wives* and *Born Yesterday*, both at the Royal Poinciana Playhouse, Palm Beach, FL, 1973; *End of Summer*, John Drew Theatre, East Hampton, NY, 1975; *The Importance of Being Earnest* and *Tartuffe*, both at the Circle in the Square, New York City, 1977; *Man and Superman*, Circle in the Square, New York City, 1978; *The Circle*, American Conservatory Theatre, San Francisco, 1978; *Absurd Person Singular*, Ahmanson Theatre, Los Angeles, 1978; *Catsplay*, Studio Arena Theatre, 1979; *Major Barbara* and *The Man Who Came to Dinner*, both at the Circle in the Square, New York City, 1980; *My Husband's Wild Desires Almost Drove Me Mad*, Studio Arena Theatre, 1980; *Misalliance*, *The Twelve Pound Look*, and *The Browning Version*, all at the Roundabout Theatre, New York City, 1981; *Mrs. Warren's Profession*, Yale Repertory Theatre, New Haven, CT, 1981; *The Misanthrope*, Circle in the Square, New York City, 1983; *The Madwoman of Chaillot*, with the Mirror Repertory Company at the Theatre at St. Peter's Church, New York City, 1985.

MAJOR TOURS—Director, *Harvey*, 1971, and *Present Laughter*, both with the New Phoenix Repertory Company, U.S. cities, 1975.

PRINCIPAL TELEVISION WORK—Director, *A Touch of the Poet*, PBS, 1974.

RELATED CAREER—Formerly an assistant professor of theatre, McGill University, Montreal, Canada.

WRITINGS: ADAPTATIONS—(Translated, with Ellis Rabb) *Two Philoctetes*, 1959; (translated, with Ellis Rabb) *Scapin*, for the APA at the McCarter Theatre, 1963; *Man and Superman*, Ann Arbor, 1964; (translated) *Don Juan*, for the New Phoenix Repertory Company at the Lyceum Theatre, New York City, 1972.

AWARDS: Best Direction, Antoinette Perry Award nomination, 1971, for *School for Wives*.

MEMBER: Actors' Equity Association, Society of Stage Directors and Choreographers, Directors Guild of America.

ADDRESSES: OFFICE—44 Gramercy Park North, New York, NY 10010.*

*   *   *

POSTON, Tom   1921-

PERSONAL: Born October 17, 1921, in Columbus, OH; son of George (a dairy chemist and liquor salesman) and Margaret Poston; married Jean Sullivan, 1955 (marriage ended); married Kay Hudson, June 8, 1968; children: (first marriage) one daughter, (second marriage) one daughter, one son. EDUCATION: Attended Bethany College, 1938-40; trained for the stage at the American Academy of Dramatic Arts. MILITARY: U.S. Army Air Force pilot, World War II.

VOCATION: Actor.

CAREER: PRINCIPAL TELEVISION APPEARANCES—Series: Emcee, *Entertainment*, ABC, 1955; regular, *The Steve Allen Show*, NBC, ABC, 1956-59, 1961; regular panelist, *To Tell the Truth*, CBS, 1958-67; panelist, *Pantomime Quiz*, CBS; Mr. Sullivan, *On*

the Rocks, ABC, 1975-76; Damon Jerome, *We've Got Each Other*, CBS, 1977-78; Franklin Delano Bickley, *Mork and Mindy*, ABC, 1978-82; George Utley, *Newhart*, CBS, 1982—.

Episodic: "You Sometimes Get Rich," *Playwrights '56*, NBC; title role, "The Change in Chester," *U.S. Steel Hour*, CBS; "The Enchanted," *Play of the Week*, PBS; "The Tempest," *Hallmark Hall of Fame*, NBC. Specials: *Merman on Broadway*, NBC.

STAGE DEBUT—As a tumbler, *The Flying Zebleys*, 1930. BROADWAY DEBUT—Title role, *Cyrano de Bergerac*, Alvin Theatre, 1947. PRINCIPAL STAGE APPEARANCES—Otakar, *The Insect Comedy*, City Center, New York City, 1948; the Herald, *King Lear*, National Theatre, New York City, 1950; Private Turnipseed, *Stockade*, President Theatre, New York City, 1954; Edward Martin, *The Grand Prize*, Plymouth Theatre, New York City, 1955; George MacCauley, *Will Success Spoil Rock Hunter?*, Belasco Theatre, New York City, 1955; Arthur Westlake, *Goodbye Again*, Helen Hayes Theatre, New York City, 1956; Hermes, *Maiden Voyage*, Forrest Theatre, Philadelphia, 1957; *The Best of Burlesque Revue*, Carnegie Hall, New York City, 1957; the General, *Romanoff and Juliet*, Plymouth Theatre, New York City, 1958; Miles Pringle, *Drink to Me Only*, 54th Street Theatre, New York City, 1958; Ferguson Howard, *Golden Fleecing*, Henry Miller's Theatre, New York City, 1959; Cornelius, *Come Play with Me*, York Playhouse, New York City, 1959.

Woodrow Truesmith, *The Conquering Hero*, American National Theatre Academy (ANTA) Theatre, New York City, 1961; Alan Baker, *Come Blow Your Horn*, Brooks Atkinson Theatre, New York City, 1962; Bob McKellaway, *Mary, Mary*, Helen Hayes Theatre, New York City, 1962; *Easy Does It*, Yonkers Playhouse, New York City, 1964; Jeremy Troy, *The Well-Dressed Liar*, Coconut Grove Playhouse, New York City, 1966; *The Butter and Egg Man*, Ivanhoe Theatre, Chicago, 1967; Walter London, *But, Seriously. . .*, Henry Miller's Theatre, New York City, 1969.

Billy Boylan, *Forty Carats*, Morosco Theatre, New York City, 1970; *Play It Again, Sam*, Falmouth Playhouse, MA, 1971; Prologus and Pseudolus, *A Funny Thing Happened on the Way to the Forum*, Lunt-Fontanne Theatre, New York City, 1972; title role, *Cyrano de Bergerac* and *Anything Goes* both Bucks County Playhouse, New Hope, PA, 1972; *Lovers and Other Strangers*, Playhouse in the Park, Philadelphia, 1973; Lenny, *Of Mice and Men* and Nick, *The Inn People*, both Bucks County Playhouse, New Hope, PA, 1973; Chaplain, *Mother Courage and Her Children* and appeared in *Romeo and Juliet*, both at the McCarter Theatre, Princeton, NJ, 1975.

MAJOR TOURS—Title role, *Destry Rides Again*, U.S. cities, 1961; *Any Wednesday*, U.S. cities, 1967; F. Sherman, *The Owl and the Pussycat*, U.S. cities, 1971; Sam Nash, Jesse Kiplinger, and Roy Hubley, *Plaza Suite*, U.S. cities, 1971; *Lovers and Other Strangers*, U.S. cities, 1973.

PRINCIPAL FILM APPEARANCES—*The City That Never Sleeps*, Republic, 1953; *Zotz!*, Columbia, 1962; *The Old Dark House*, Columbia, 1963; *Cold Turkey*, United Artists, 1971; *The Happy Hooker*, 1975.

AWARDS: Best Supporting Actor as a Continuing Character in a Comedy Series, Emmy Award, 1959, for *The Steve Allen Show*.

MEMBER: Actors' Equity Association, Screen Actors Guild, American Federation of Television and Radio Artists.

ADDRESSES: AGENT—c/o Jack Rollins, Rollins and Joffe, Inc, 130 W. 57th Street, New York, NY 10019.*

*   *   *

PRICE, Lonny   1959-

PERSONAL: Born March 9, 1959, in New York, NY; son of Murray A. (an owner of a car-leasing company) and Edie L. (a merchandise manager; maiden name, Greene) Price. EDUCATION: Graduated from the High School of the Performing Arts, New York City; studied at the Juilliard School. RELIGION: Jewish.

VOCATION: Actor.

CAREER: STAGE DEBUT—Young Amshel, *The Rothchilds,* Camden County Music Fair, Camden, NJ. OFF-BROADWAY DEBUT—Racks, *Class Enemy,* Players Theatre, 1979. PRINCIPAL STAGE APPEARANCES—Rudy, *The Survivor,* Morosco Theatre, New York City, 1981; Charley Kringas, *Merrily We Roll Along,* Alvin Theatre, New York City, 1981; Hally, *Master Harold. . .and the Boys,* Lyceum Theatre, New York City, 1982; Abel, *Up from Paradise,* Jewish Repertory Theatre, New York City, 1983; Private Ackenbaum, *Rommel's Garden,* Harold Clurman Theatre, New York City, 1985; *Amateurs,* Cincinnati Playhouse in the Park, OH, 1985.

FILM DEBUT—Steven Levy, *Headin' for Broadway,* 1980. PRINCIPAL FILM APPEARANCES—David, *The Chosen,* 1981; Ronnie Crawford, *The Muppets Take Manhattan,* 1984.

LONNY PRICE

TELEVISION DEBUT—*Make-Believe Marriage,* 1979.

AWARDS: Theatre World Award, 1979-80, for *Class Enemy.*

ADDRESSES: AGENT—Lionel Larner, Ltd., 850 Seventh Avenue, New York, NY 10019.*

*   *   *

PRICE, Vincent   1911-

PERSONAL: Born May 27, 1911, in St. Louis, MO; son of Vincent Leonard (a businessman) and Marguerite Cobb (Wilcox) Price; married Edith Barrett, 1938 (divorced); married Mary Grant, 1939 (divorced); married Coral Browne, 1974; children: (first marriage) one son; (second marriage) one daughter. EDUCATION: Attended St. Louis Country Day School; Yale University, B.A.; University of London, M.A., fine arts; also attended the California College of Arts and Sciences; studied art at the Courtauld Institute in London.

VOCATION: Actor and writer.

CAREER: STAGE DEBUT—Charles Murdock and the Judge, *Chicago,* Gate Theatre, London, 1935. BROADWAY DEBUT—Prince Albert, *Victoria Regina,* Broadhurst Theatre, 1935-37. PRINCIPAL STAGE APPEARANCES—Prince Albert, *Victoria Regina* and Max, *Anatol,* both at the Gate Theatre, London, 1935; summer stock, 1937, leading roles in: *What Every Woman Knows, Elizabeth the Queen, Parnell, The Wild Duck, The Passing of the Third Floor Back, Romance, Eden End, Turandot,* and *The Lady of La Paz;* Jean, *The Lady Has a Heart,* Longacre Theatre, New York City, 1937; Master Hammon, *The Shoemaker's Holiday,* Mercury Theatre, New York City, 1938; Hector Hushabye, *Heartbreak House,* Mercury Theatre, New York City, 1938; Reverend William Duke, *Outward Bound,* Playhouse Theatre, New York City, 1938.

Saint, *Mamba's Daughters,* Biltmore Theatre, Los Angeles, 1941; Mr. Manningham, *Angel Street,* John Golden Theatre, New York City, 1941; Arthur Winslow, *The Winslow Boy,* Playhouse Theatre, Las Palmas, CA, 1950; unidentified guest, *The Cocktail Party,* Curran Theatre, San Francisco, 1951; Thomas Mendip, *The Lady's Not for Burning,* La Jolla Playhouse, CA, 1952; Duke of Buckingham, *Richard III,* City Center, New York City, 1953; Dr. Nicholas Marsh, *Black-Eyed Susan,* Playhouse Theatre, New York City, 1954; Priam Farel, *Darling of the Day,* George Abbott Theatre, New York City, 1968; the Count, *Ardele,* Queen's Theatre, London, 1975; Fagin, *Oliver!,* Music Fair Theatre, Dallas, TX, 1976; Sebastian Melmoth, *Oscar Wilde: Diversions and Delights,* Marines Memorial Theatre, San Francisco, 1977, then Eugene O'Neill Theatre, New York City, 1978; appeared in *Night of 100 Stars II,* Radio City Music Hall, New York City, 1985.

Also appeared as narrator with various symphony orchestras in the following operas: *Moses, Peter and the Wolf, A Lincoln Portrait.*

MAJOR TOURS—*Goodbye Again,* U.S. cities, 1952; Devil, *Don Juan in Hell,* Curran Theatre, San Francisco, Civic Opera House, Chicago, 1952; *Charley's Aunt,* U.S. cities, 1976; Sebastian Melmoth, *Oscar Wilde: Diversions and Delights,* U.S. cities, 1977.

PRINCIPAL FILM APPEARANCES—*Service de Luxe,* Universal,

1938; *The Private Lives of Elizabeth and Essex*, Warner Brothers, 1939; *The Tower of London*, Universal, 1939; *Green Hell*, Universal, 1940; *House of Seven Gables*, Universal, 1940; *The Invisible Man Returns*, Universal, 1940; *The Song of Bernadette*, Twentieth Century-Fox, 1943; *Buffalo Bill*, 1944; *The Eve of St. Mark*, Twentieth Century-Fox, 1944; *Wilson*, Twentieth Century-Fox, 1944; *The Keys of the Kingdom*, Twentieth Century-Fox, 1944; *Laura*, Twentieth Century-Fox, 1944; *A Royal Scandal*, Twentieth Century-Fox, 1945; *Leave Her to Heaven*, 1945; *Dragonwyck*, Twentieth Century-Fox, 1946; *Shock*, Twentieth Century-Fox, 1946; *The Long Night*, RKO, 1947; *Moss Rose*, 1947; *The Web*, Universal, 1947; *The Three Musketeers*, Metro-Goldwyn-Mayer (MGM), 1948; *Rogue's Regiment*, 1948; *The Bribe*, 1949; *Bagdad*, 1949.

Baron of Arizona, 1950; *Curtain Call at Cactus Creek*, Universal, 1950; *Champagne for Caesar*, Universal, 1950; *His Kind of Woman*, RKO, 1951; *Adventures of Captain Fabian*, Republic, 1951; *Las Vegas Story*, RKO, 1952; *House of Wax*, Warner Brothers, 1953; *Dangerous Mission*, RKO, 1954; *Mad Magician*, Columbia, 1954; *Son of Sinbad*, RKO, 1955; *Serenade*, Warner Brothers, 1956; *The Ten Commandments*, Paramount, 1957; *Story of Mankind*, Warner Brothers, 1957; *While the City Sleeps*, RKO Radio Pictures, 1958; *The Fly*, Twentieth Century-Fox, 1958; *The Return of the Fly*, Twentieth Century-Fox, 1959; *The Big Circus*, Allied Artists, 1959; *The Bat*, Allied Artists, 1959; *The Tingler*, Columbia, 1959; *House on Haunted Hill*, Allied Artists, 1959.

House of Usher, American International, 1960; *The Pit and the Pendulum*, American International, 1961; *Poe's Tales of Terror*, American International, 1962; *The Raven*, 1962; *Confessions of an Opium Eater*, Allied Artists, 1962; *The Tower of London*, United Artists, 1962; *Convicts 4*, Allied Artists, 1962; *The Comedy of Terrors*, American International, 1963; *The Masque of the Red Death*, American International, 1964; *The Last Man in the World*, 1964; *War Gods of the Deep*, American International, 1965; *The Tomb of Ligeia*, American International, 1965; *Dr. Goldfoot and the Bikini Machine*, American International, 1965; *Dr. Goldfoot and the Girl Bombs*, American International, 1966; *The House of 1000 Dolls*, American International, 1967; *The Conqueror Worm*, American International, 1968; *More Dead Than Alive*, United Artists, 1969; *The Oblong Box, American International, 1969*.

Scream and Scream Again, American International, 1970; *The Abominable Dr. Phibes*, American International, 1971; *Dr. Phibes Rises Again*, American International, 1972; *Theatre of Blood*, United Artists, 1973; narrated, *The Devil's Triangle*, Maron, 1974; *Madhouse*, American International, 1974; *Scavenger Hunt*, Twentieth Century-Fox, 1979; *The House of the Long Shadows*, 1983.

PRINCIPAL TELEVISION APPEARANCES—Series: Jason, *Time Express*, CBS, 1979; host, *Mystery!*, PBS, 1979-83; also appeared in over two thousand programs including: "Angel Street," *Matinee Theatre*, NBC; "The Three Musketeers," *Family Classics*, CBS; *Alfred Hitchcock Presents*, CBS; *The Man from U.N.C.L.E.*, NBC; *Night Gallery*, NBC; *The Tonight Show*, NBC; *The Saint*, NBC; *CBS Playhouse*. Movies: *What's a Nice Girl Like You. . .?*, ABC, 1971. Panelist: *The $64,000 Challenge*, CBS; *Hollywood Squares*, NBC.

PRINCIPAL RADIO WORK—Torvald, "A Doll's House," *Great Plays*, WJZ Radio, 1939; *The Saint*, 1947-50; *Lux Radio Theatre*.

NON-RELATED CAREER—Art consultant to Sears, Roebuck & Company.

WRITINGS: BOOKS—(Author of introduction and catalogue notes) *Vincent Price Collects Drawings*, Oakland Art Museum, 1957; (author of introduction) *Drawings of Five Centuries*, Santa Barbara Museum of Art, 1959; *I Like What I Know* (autobiography), Doubleday, 1959; (with Mary Price) *The Book of Joe: About a Dog and His Man*, Doubleday, 1961; (with Mary Price) *Michelangelo Bible*, 1964; (editor with Chandler Brossard) *Eighteen Best Stories by Edgar Allan Poe*, Dell, 1965; (with Mary Price) *A Treasury of Great Recipes: Famous Specialties of the World's Foremost Restaurants Adapted for the American Kitchen*, Geis, 1965; (author of introduction) Eugene Delacroix, *Drawings*, Borden, 1966; (with Mary Price) *Mary and Vincent Price Present a National Treasury of Cookery*, Heirloom, 1967; (with Mary Price) *Mary and Vincent Price's Come into the Kitchen Cookbook: A Collector's Treasury of America's Great Recipes*, Stravon, 1969; *The Vincent Price Treasury of American Art*, Country Beautiful, 1972; *Vincent Price: His Movies, His Plays, His Life*, Doubleday, 1978; (co-author) *The Monsters*, 1981; also author of introduction, *Nineteeth and Twentieth Century European Master Graphics*, Sears Vincent Price Gallery, Chicago.

MEMBER: Actors' Equity Association, Screen Actors Guild; Elizabethan Club; Yale Club, United States Indian Arts and Crafts Board (commissioner), Archives of American Art (board of directors), University of California at Los Angeles (president, art council), Whitney Museum Friends of American Art, Royal Academy of Arts, Fine Arts Commission of the White House, Washington, DC, Royal Society of Art.

SIDELIGHTS: The name Vincent Price has become synonymous with cinematic terror through such horror classics as *House of Wax*, *The Fly*, and *The Abominable Dr. Phibes*. Price plays arch-fiends with such relish that he was once dubbed a "goose-pimple grandee, . . . the last of the venerable horror stars whose creepy roles make kids cry for a night light," in a *Newsweek* feature of June 14, 1971. According to Tony Thomas in *Cads and Cavaliers*, Price has worked for three decades "in a celluloid world of wierd science fiction, populated by . . . monsters, demented doctors, perverted scientists, Satan worshipers, torturers, necromancers, and tormented spirits. He has prospered in this milieu of haunded houses, crypts, and dungeons." Thomas is quick to add an observation that many film critics share; namely, that Price is a skilled actor of uncommon intelligence whose best work has been obscured in rarely-seen films and stage plays.

Thomas notes of Price: "The difference between the private man and his ghoulish screen image is extreme; in fact there is a distinct dichotomy." On the one hand lies Vincent Price, the film star, torturing and murdering his way through horror films in ever more creative ways. On the other hand lies Vincent Price, the connoisseur of fine art, delivering lectures and making educational television programs of every meduim of art from paintings to African masks. In his book *The Horror People*, John Brosnan comments: "As an actor, one way Vincent Price has coped with the horror tag is by putting his tongue firmly in his cheek and leaving it there." Another way Price has coped is by admitting honestly that he enjoys both the paychecks he garners from horror film work and the amount of work he is invited to do. "I'm not at all ashamed to be in entertainment pictures," he told Thomas. "I like to be seen, I love being busy and I believe in being active. I know some people think I've lowered myself as an actor—well, my idea of professional decline is not working."

By his own admission, Price has never lacked for activities. He was born in St. Louis, Missouri, on May 27, 1911, one of four children of a wealthy confectionary company president. Raised in an environment that encouraged an appreciation of the fine arts, Price immersed himself in music and painting. He was so curious about so many artistic fields that his family allowed him to travel alone to Europe when he was sixteen. He visited the British Museum, the Louvre, and other art galleries from Amsterdam to Rome, and he returned home determined to become an artist. He attended Yale University, receiving a Bachelor of Arts degree in art history, then earned his Master's degree in fine arts from the University of London.

Acting was definitely a secondary occupation for Price at first, but he achieved a measure of success almost immediately on the London stage. Just out of graduate school, he auditioned for the role of Prince Albert in *Victoria Regina*, a play about Britain's Queen Victoria. The play received good notices, and its cast, including Price, was invited to repeat the work on Broadway. It opened in New York on December 26, 1935, and since that day Price has labored almost exclusively as an actor. In the more than fifty years of his career, he has appeared in over one hundred films, over two thousand television shows, nearly one thousand radio shows, and in numerous commercial advertisements as diverse as Burger King and the United States Treasury Department.

From 1938 until 1953, Price carved out a precarious niche in Hollywood playing character roles; his few top-billed films were box-office failures. He was better known on Broadway, where he appeared in notable plays such as *Outward Bound, Heartbreak House,* and *Angel Street*. In the latter vehicle he played his first villain, and the audiences responded enthusiastically. Returning to Hollywood, he took a wide variety of parts and is best remembered for his portrayals of Sir Walter Raleigh in *The Private Lives of Elizabeth and Essex* (1939) and Cardinal Richelieu in *The Three Musketeers* (1948). According to Thomas, after 1942, Price "started to specialize in roles of cruelty—and to build a solid livelihood on the weaknesses of the human species."

Price's career received a momentous boost in 1953 when he signed to star in *House of Wax*. The movie, which reveals the sordid life of a demented sculptor whose wax figures conceal human corpses, was filmed in 3-D and proved quite popular. Thomas notes that with *House of Wax*, Price established himself as "one of the few actors who has ever been capable of essaying macabre humor in a richly florid style without being totally ridiculous." After *House of Wax*, Price returned to playing character villains, but his equally successful 1958 horror film *The Fly* cast him firmly into the horror genre. *The Fly* concerns a scientist whose experiments mix his body parts with those of an insect. Recalling the film, Price remembers experiencing moments of uncontrollable laughter over the absurd situations in the story.

In the 1960s, Price abandoned himself almost totally to low-budget horror films. He teamed with director Roger Corman of American International Pictures on a series of movies based loosely on stories by Edgar Allan Poe. Some of these, such as *The Fall of the House of Usher, The Pit and the Pendulum, Tales of Terror,* and *The Raven* were significant moneymakers for the fledgling movie company. The June 14, 1971 *Newsweek* article quotes Price as saying during this period: "The best parts are the heavies. The hero is usually someone who has really nothing to do. He comes out on top, but it's the heavy who has all the fun."

Price is perhaps best remembered for *The Abominable Dr. Phibes* (1971) and *Theatre of Blood* (1973). In *Dr. Phibes*, Thomas notes, Price "was even more wide-ranging in his mayhem than in

previous guises . . . He brings upon his victims various plagues . . .—the ravages of rats, bats, beasts, boils, locusts and hail." Similar in plot, *Theatre of Blood* casts Price as a bad actor who murders his critics by using methods borrowed from Shakespeare. Thomas contends that such films established Price as "one of Hollywood's best examples of an actor coming to terms with life in a highly commercial system."

Price, who has used some of his lucrative film work to pay for a personal collection of fine art, feels his works are not horror films so much as pure escapist fare. "To me films that deal with drug addiction, crime, and war are horror films," he told Thomas. Mine are fairy tales. . . . My main concern in playing these strange roles is in making them believable, which is not easy. Neither is it easy to scare people in a world where actual slaughter and vicious crimes are common, daily occurrences. Compared to current warfare practices, a good ghoulish movie is comic relief."

In recent years Price has added two achievements to his long and successful career. In 1977, he toured America in the stage play *Diversions and Delights,* a one-man show about the eccentric playwright Oscar Wilde. And in 1983, he lent his eerie voice to the title song on Michael Jackson's *Thriller* album, which has since become the best-selling record in history. As Christopher Buckley noted in the April 25, 1978, issue of *Esquire*, Vincent Price's oeuvre, "such as it is, will play on and on to endless millions of adoring insomniacs, adolescents, and afficionados, and he will endure forever as the high priest of lowbrow."

ADDRESSES: OFFICE—315 S. Beverly Drive, Beverly Hills, CA 90212.*

*   *   *

PURCELL, Lee   1953-

PERSONAL: Born June 15, 1953, in North Carolina; married Gary A. Lowe (a producer and production manager); children: Dylan and a step-daughter. EDUCATION: Trained for the stage at the Royal Academy of Dramatic Art with Margot Lister; also with Milton Katselas, Jeff Corey and Robert F. Lyons.

VOCATION: Actress.

CAREER: FILM DEBUT—Jerri Jo Hopper, *Adam at Six A.M.,* National General, 1970. PRINCIPAL FILM APPEARANCES—Karen, *Stand Up and Be Counted,* Columbia, 1971; teenage witch, *The Toy Factory,* Group Three, 1971; Berle, *Dirty Little Billy,* Warner Brothers, 1972; Molly, *Kid Blue,* Twentieth Century-Fox, 1973; Wiley, *Mr. Majestyk,* United Artists, 1974; Peggy, *Big Wednesday,* Warner Brothers, 1978; Christine, *Almost Summer,* 1978; Susan, *Stir Crazy,* Columbia, 1980; Beth, *Valley Girl,* Atlantic, 1983; Jilly, *Eddie Macon's Run,* Universal, 1983; *Trackers,* Vestron 1986; *Laura's Dream,* Opera Films, 1986.

TELEVISION DEBUT—Local television, Memphis, TN, age five years. PRINCIPAL TELEVISION APPEARANCES—Episodic: *Magnum, P.I.,* CBS, 1985; *Murder, She Wrote,* CBS, 1985. Pilots: *The Secret War of Jackie's Girls,* NBC, 1980; *Of Men and Women,* ABC; *My Wife Next Door,* CBS.

Movies: *Hijack,* CBS, 1973; *Stranger in Our House,* 1978; *Kenny Rogers as the Gambler,* 1980; *The Girl, the Gold Watch and Dynamite,* 1981; *Killing at Hell's Gate,* CBS, 1981; Olivia de Havilland, *My Wicked, Wicked Ways: The Legend of Errol Flynn,*

LEE PURCELL

CBS, 1986; Billy Dove, *Howard: The Amazing Mr. Hughes; Death Works Overtime,* ABC; *Betrayed by Innocence,* upcoming; *Summer of Fear.*

PRINCIPAL STAGE APPEARANCES—Lady Anne, *Richard III;* Barbara Allen, *Dark of the Moon;* Stella, *A Streetcar Named Desire;* Katharina, *The Taming of the Shrew;* Titania, *A Midsummer Night's Dream;* Brenda, *Lovers and Other Strangers;* Sopie, *Star-Spangled Girl;* Madge, *Picnic.*

AWARDS: Bronze Halo Career Achievement Award, Southern California Motion Picture Council, 1985.

MEMBER: Actors' Equity Association, Screen Actors Guild, American Federation of Television and Radio Artists, Academy of Motion Picture Arts and Sciences, Academy of Television Arts and Sciences.

SIDELIGHTS: RECREATIONS: Writing, collecting antiques and music boxes.

ADDRESSES: AGENT—Abrams, Harris, and Goldberg, 9220 Sunset Blvd., Suite 101B, Los Angeles, CA 90069.

*　　*　　*

QUAYLE, Anna　1937-

PERSONAL: Born October 6, 1937, in Birmingham, England; daughter of John Douglas Stuart (an actor) and Kathleen (Parke)

Quayle; children: Katy Nova. EDUCATION: Attended the Convent of Jesus and Mary, Harlesden, UK; trained for the stage at the Royal Academy of Dramatic Art.

VOCATION: Actress and writer.

CAREER: STAGE DEBUT—*Better Late,* Edinburgh Festival, Scotland, 1956. LONDON DEBUT *Look Who's Here!,* Fortune Theatre, 1960. BROADWAY DEBUT—Evie, *Stop the World I Want to Get Off,* Shubert Theatre, 1962. PRINCIPAL STAGE APPEARANCES—*Ridgeway's Late Joys,* Players' Theatre, London, 1958; *Do You Mind?,* Palladium Theatre, Edinburgh, Scotland, 1959; *And Another Thing,* Fortune Theatre, London, 1960; Evie, *Stop the World I Want to Get Off,* Queen's Theatre, London, 1961; Doris, *Homage to T. S. Eliot,* Globe Theatre, London, 1965; *Full Circle,* Apollo Theatre, London, 1970.

Miss Dyott, *Out of Bounds,* Bristol Old Vic Theatre, UK, 1973; Melba, *Pal Joey,* Edinburgh Festival for the Oxford Playhouse, 1976; Anne of Cleves, *Kings and Clowns,* Phoenix Theatre, London, 1978; Lady Tremurrain, *The Case of the Oily Levantine,* Her Majesty's Theatre, London, 1979; Madame Dubonnet, *The Boy Friend,* Old Vic and Albery Theatres, London, 1984.

MAJOR TOURS—Lucie, *A Fig for Glory,* U.K. cities, 1958.

PRINCIPAL FILM APPEARANCES—*Chitty Chitty Bang Bang,* United Artists, 1968; *The Seven Per Cent Solution,* Universal, 1976; also *The Sinking of the Titanic.*

PRINCIPAL TELEVISION APPEARANCES—Dramatic Specials:

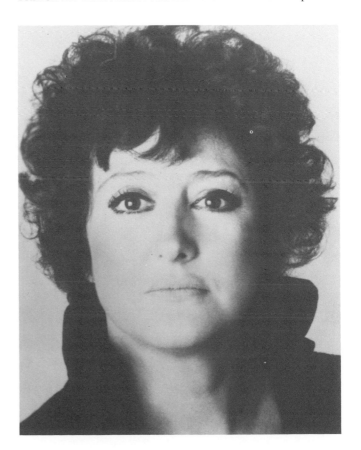

ANNA QUAYLE

CONTEMPORARY THEATRE, FILM, AND TELEVISION ● Volume 4

Brideshead Revisited, PBS, 1982; *Rollins Home,* 1982; Olga Braceley, *Mapp and Lucia,* 1986; *Lytton's Diary,* 1986; *Marjorie and Men,* 1986. Series: Mother Superior, *Father Charlie,* 1982. Teleplays: *Henry V.* All BBC.

WRITINGS: PLAYS, PRODUCED—*Full Circle,* Apollo Theatre, London, 1970.

AWARDS: Best Supporting Actress, Antoinette Perry Award, London Critics Circle Award, *Saturday Review* Award, and *Variety* Drama Critics Poll Award, all 1962, for *Stop the World I Want to Get Off.*

ADDRESSES: HOME—Rose Cottage, 4 Guildford Rd., Brighton, Sussex, England.

R

RABB, Ellis 1930-

PERSONAL: Born June 20, 1930, in Memphis, TN; son of Clark Williamson and Mary Carolyn (Ellis) Rabb; married Rosemary Harris, December 4, 1959 (divorced, 1967). EDUCATION: University of Arizona, B.A., 1950; Carnegie Institute of Technology, B.F.A., 1953; also attended Yale University.

VOCATION: Actor, director, and producer.

CAREER: STAGE DEBUT—Dauphin, *King John*, Antioch Arena Theatre, Yellow Springs, OH, 1952. OFF-BROADWAY DEBUT—Robin Starveling, *A Midsummer Night's Dream*, Jan Hus Playhouse, 1956. PRINCIPAL STAGE APPEARANCES—Antioch Arena Theatre, Yellow Springs, OH: Duke of York, *Richard II*, Earl of Worcester, *Henry IV, Part I*, Shallow, *Henry IV, Part II*, Archbishop of Canterbury and Lewis, *Henry VI* Parts I, II, and III, a murderer, *Richard III*, Cardinal Wolsey, *Henry VIII*, Troilus, *Troilus and Cressida*, a citizen, *Coriolanus*, Ventidius, *Timon of Athens*, Lysimachus, *Pericles*, Cassius, *Julius Caesar*, Eros, *Antony and Cleopatra*, all 1953, Gremio, *The Taming of the Shrew*, Speed, *Two Gentlemen of Verona*, Herald, *Othello*, Bassanio, *The Merchant of Venice*, Palemon, *Two Noble Kinsmen*, Ariel, *The Tempest*, all 1954, Leontes, *The Winter's Tale*, Lucius, *Titus Andronicus*, Sir Andrew Aguecheek, *Twelfth Night*, First Lord, *Cymbeline*, old man, *Macbeth*, all 1955, Benedick, *Much Ado About Nothing*, title role, *King Lear*, both 1956, Malvolio, *Twelfth Night*, 1957.

Alceste, *The Misanthrope*, Theatre East, New York City, 1956; Sir William Davidson, *Mary Stuart*, Phoenix Theatre, New York City, 1957; Player King, *Hamlet*, Starveling, *A Midsummer Night's Dream*, and Camillo, *The Winter's Tale*, all with the American Shakespeare Festival, Stratford, CT, 1958; General Koschnadieff, *Look After Lulu*, Henry Miller's Theatre, New York City, 1959; Octavius, *Man and Superman*, Smee, *Peter Pan*, Tiresias, *Oedipus Rex*, all with the Group 20 Theatre, Wellesley, MA, 1959; Reverend Furze, *Jolly's Progress*, Longacre Theatre, New York City, 1959.

With the Association of Producing Artists (APA) Phoenix Repertory, New York City, between 1960-70: John Tanner and Don Juan, *Man and Superman*, Gremio, *The Taming of the Shrew*, Matthew Skips, *The Lady's Not for Burning*, the vagabond, *The Tavern*, Algernon Moncrieff, *The Importance of Being Earnest*, title role, *King Lear*, William, *As You Like It*, Malvolio, *Twelfth Night*, Robin Starveling, *A Midsummer Night's Dream*, Mr. Tiffany, *Fashion*, Joseph Surface, *The School for Scandal*, Oberon, *A Midsummer Night's Dream*, title role, *Richard II*, Benedick, *Much Ado About Nothing*, Governor of the Province, *Right You Are (If You Think You Are)*, the Vagabond, *The Tavern*, Geronte, *Scapin*, La Thorilliere, *Impromptu at Versailles*, the Baron, *The Lower Depths*, Jack Tanner, *Man and Superman*, Joseph Surface, *The School for Scandal*, title role, *Pantagleize*, Shanaar, *Cock-a-Doodle Dandy*, title role, *Hamlet*.

Tony Cavendish, *The Royal Family*, Helen Hayes Theatre, New York City, 1976; Robert, *A Life in the Theater*, Theatre de Lys, New York City, 1977; Sheridan Whiteside, *The Man Who Came to Dinner*, Circle in the Square Theatre, New York City, 1980; Prospero, *The Tempest*, Old Globe Theatre, San Diego, CA, 1982; appeared with the Mirror Repertory Theatre at the Theatre at St. Peter's Church, 1983-84; voice-over as "Operator," *Isn't It Romantic*, Lucille Lortel Theatre, New York City, 1983-84; with the Mirror Repertory Company at the Theatre at St. Peter's Church, New York City, 1985.

MAJOR TOURS—Verges and Don Pedro, *Much Ado About Nothing*, U.S. cities, 1958; as artistic director of APA, toured U.S. and Bermuda annually, 1960-70.

PRINCIPAL STAGE WORK— Director: *A Midsummer Night's Dream*, *Measure for Measure*, and *Julius Caesar*, all with the Antioch Arena Theatre, Yellow Springs, OH, 1957; *Much Ado About Nothing* and *A Streetcar Named Desire*, both with the Group 20 Theatre, Wellesley, MA, 1959. Founder and artistic director APA Phoenix Repertory Company; directed: *The School for Scandal*, *The Tavern*, *The Seagull*, *Right You Are (If You Think You Are)*, *Box and Cox*, *The Cat and the Moon*, and *Scapin*, all at the Folksbiene Theatre, New York City, 1960; for the APA, also directed: *Hamlet*, *As You Like It*, *A Midsummer Night's Dream*, *Anatol*, 1961; *The School for Scandal*, *The Tavern*, *A Penny for a Song*, *We Comrades Three* and *The Seagull*, 1962; *Richard II*, 1963; *War and Peace*, *Judith*, and *You Can't Take It with You*, 1965; *The School for Scandal*, 1966; (co-director) *Pantagleize*, 1967; *Hamlet*, 1969.

For other companies directed: *Antony and Cleopatra*, American Shakespeare Festival, Stratford, CT, 1963; *A Midsummer Night's Dream*, Old Globe Theatre, San Diego, CA, 1963; *Orpheus in the Underworld*, Kansas City Opera, MO, 1967; *Dido and Aneas* and *Aida*, Dallas Civic Opera, TX, 1969; *Hamlet*, Old Globe Theatre, San Diego, 1968; *The Grass Harp*, 1971; *Twelfth Night* and *Enemies*, 1972; *The Merchant of Venice*, *A Streetcar Named Desire*, and *Veronica's Room*, 1973; *Who's Who in Hell*, 1974; *Edward II* and *The Royal Family*, 1975; *A Midsummer Night's Dream*, Theatre Memphis, TN, 1976; *Caesar and Cleopatra*, Palace Theatre, New York City, 1977; *The Philadelphia Story*, Vivian Beaumont Theatre, New York City, 1980; (co-director) *Chekhov in Yalta*, Mark Taper Forum, Los Angeles, 1981; *You Can't Take It with You*, Paper Mill Playhouse, Millburn, NJ, then Plymouth Theatre, New York City, 1983; *Clap Your Hands*, Old Globe Theatre, San Diego, 1983; *The Loves of Anatol*, Circle in the

Square, New York City, 1985; *Light Up the Sky,* Ahmanson Theatre, Los Angeles, 1987.

Producer for the APA Repertory, New York City: *Right You Are (If You Think You Are), Box and Cox, The Cat and the Mouse,* and *Scapin,* 1960; *As You Like It,* 1961; *The Seagull* and *Ghosts,* 1962; *The Merchant of Venice, A Phoenix Too Frequent,* and *Right You Are (If You Think You Are),* 1963 and 1966; *Exit the King, The Cherry Orchard,* and *Show-Off,* 1967 and all again in 1968.

PRINCIPAL TELEVISION APPEARANCES—Dramatic Specials: *Bartleby the Scrivener,* 1958. Movies: *The Dain Curse,* 1978. Episodic: *Cheers,* NBC, 1987; *St. Elsewhere,* NBC, 1987.

PRINCIPAL TELEVISION WORK—Dramatic Specials: Director— *The Royal Family; Enemies; You Can't Take It with You.*

WRITINGS: PLAYS, PRODUCED—(With Nicholas Martin) *Clap Your Hands,* Old Globe Theatre, San Diego, 1983. ADAPTA- TIONS—(Translated, with Stephen Porter) *Two Philoctetes,* 1959; (translated, with Stephen Porter) *Scapin,* for the APA, 1963; (with Nicholas Martin) *The Loves of Anatol,* Circle in the Square, New York City, 1985.

AWARDS: Clarence Derwent Award, 1957, for *The Misanthrope;* Obie Award and Vernon Rice Award, for his season with the APA, 1962-63; Obie Award, 1962; Outer Critics Circle Award, 1965; Best Director, Antoinette Perry Award and Lola D'Annunzio Award, 1976.*

*   *   *

RAPPOPORT, David Steven   1957-

PERSONAL: Born August 14, 1957, in Pasadena, CA; son of Stanley (a physician) and Lonette (a social worker; maiden name, Shepps) Rappoport. EDUCATION: Attended the University of South- ern California in Los Angeles; studied at Norman Corwin's Writing Workshop.

VOCATION: Playwright.

WRITINGS: PLAYS, PRODUCED—*Ode to a Scenic Northwest,* various amateur productions, 1973; (with Joannie Fritz) *Lily Frog* (children's musical), Las Palmas Theatre, Los Angeles, 1976; *The Styx Border,* 13th Street Theatre, New York City, 1977; *Play in the Dark,* staged readings and workshop production, Actors Playhouse Productions, 1978; *Medusa in the Suburbs,* staged readings and workshop production, Actors Playhouse, New York City, 1978, then 13th Street Theatre, New York City, 1978, Chelsea Theatre Center New Yorks Project, New York City, 1980, Fordham Uni- versity, 1980, Theatre-by-the-Grove, Indiana, PA, 1981, Equity Library Theatre Informal Series, New York City, 1983, Quaigh Dramathon, New York City, 1984, and The Actors Space, New York City, 1985; *The Upper Depths,* Chelsea Theatre Center, 1982; *Proteus in Repose,* The Actors Space, New York City, 1985; *The Rapids,* Playwrights Preview Productions Ltd., 1985, then Circle Repertory Company, New York City, 1985, Summer Solstice Theatre Conference, 1986, staged reading and workshop produc- tion, Capitol Repertory New Plays Festival, Albany, NY, 1986, and International City Theatre, Long Beach, CA, 1986; *Cave Life,* staged reading and workshop productions, Circle Repertory Com-

pany and The Actors Space, New York City, 1986; *Buying Win- dows,* Circle Repertory Company Director's Lab, 1987.

PLAYS, UNPRODUCED—(Book and lyrics) "Nana," 1983.

RELATED CAREER—Contributing editor, *Pasadena Magazine,* 1975-76; writer of a syndicated radio news insert, *Oddities in the News,* Ribar Productions, Los Angeles, 1976-77; associate produc- er and writer, *Hynopsis Hotline,* radio talk show, Los Angeles, 1976-77; writer for stand-up comics in Los Angeles and New York City, 1976-80; teacher of playwriting, 13th Street Theatre, 1978- 79, American Playwrights' Theatre, 1980-81; associate artistic director, American Playwrights' Theatre, 1980-84; writer, *The Big Apple Report,* New York Telephone phone-in tape about activities in New York City, 1980-81; artist-in-residence, Indiana Universi- ty, PA, 1983; editorial assistant, *The Adoption Newsletter,* 1985; contributor, City University of New York's *Computer Newsletter,* 1985.

AWARDS: National Student Playwriting Competition, *Dramatics Magazine,* honorable mention, 1972, second place, 1973, third place, 1974; Residency Fellowship, Edward F. Albee Foundation, 1980; grant, Cheryl Crawford Fund, 1982; nomination for best play of the season, Chelsea Theatre Center as part of Theatre Communi- cations Group Plays in Progress series, 1983, for *The Upper Depths;* grant from Drama League of New York, 1986; play commission, Circle Repertory Company, for their Director's Lab series, 1987.

MEMBER: Dramatists Guild; Circle Repertory Company Play- wright's Lab.

ADDRESSES: HOME—301 Tenth Avenue, New York, NY 10001.

*   *   *

RAWLS, Eugenia   1916-

PERSONAL: Full name, Mary Eugenia Rawls; born September 11, 1916, in Macon, GA; daughter of Hubert Fields (a lawyer) and Louise (a pianist; maiden name, Roberts) Rawls; married Donald R. Seawell (a lawyer, producer, and publisher), April 5, 1941; children: Brockman and Brook (daughter). EDUCATION: Attended Wesleyan Conservatory and University of North Carolina, 1932- 33; trained for the stage with the Carolina Playmakers and with Frederick Koch, Anne Chenauet Wallace, and Edna West.

VOCATION: Actress and writer.

CAREER: STAGE DEBUT—Clare Tree Major's Children's Thea- tre, New York City, 1933. BROADWAY DEBUT—Peggy, *The Children's Hour,* Maxine Elliott's Theatre, 1934-35, for eight- hundred-twenty-two performances. LONDON DEBUT—Title role, *Affectionately Yours, Fanny Kemble* and title role, *Tallulah, a Memory,* British National Theatre at the Arts Theatre. PRINCIPAL STAGE APPEARANCES—Tomassa, *To Quito and Back,* Guild Theatre, New York City, 1937; Dene Horey, *Journeyman,* Fulton Theatre, New York City, 1938; *Susannah and the Elders* and *The Inner Light,* both Westport Country Playhouse, CT, 1938; Celia, *As You Like It,* Titania, *A Midsummer Night's Dream,* and Bianca, *The Taming of the Shrew,* all New York World's Fair Theatre, New York City, 1939; Alexandra, *The Little Foxes,* National Theatre, New York City, 1939.

Photography by Cris Alexander

EUGENIA RAWLS

Ellean, *The Second Mrs. Tanqueray*, 1940; Alexandra, *The Little Foxes*, Newport Playhouse, RI, 1941; ingenue, *Curtain Going Up*, Westport Country Playhouse, CT, 1941; title role, *Harriet*, University of Syracuse Theatre, NY, 1942; Evelyn Heath, *Guest in the House*, Plymouth Theatre, New York City, 1942; Connie, *Cry Havoc*, Studebaker Theatre, Chicago, 1943; Mrs. de Winter, *Rebecca*, Ogunquit Playhouse, ME, 1944; Hester Falk, *The Man Who Had All the Luck*, Forrest Theatre, New York City, 1944; Harriet Harris, *Strange Fruit*, Royale Theatre, New York City, 1945.

Ann Downs, *The Shrike*, Cort Theatre, New York City, 1952; Mrs. Czerney, *The Great Sebastians*, American National Theatre Academy (ANTA) Theatre, New York City, 1956.

Catherine, *All the Way Home*, Playhouse in the Park, Philadelphia, 1961; standby for role of Nina Kecew, *First Love*, Morosco Theatre, New York City, 1961; Emily Bindix, *A Case of Libel*, Longacre Theatre, New York City, 1963; Amanda, *The Glass Menagerie*, Playhouse in the Park, Cincinnati, OH, 1965; *Our Town*, Repertory Theatre of New Orleans, 1967; Mrs. Beavis, *The Poker Session*, Martinique Theatre, New York City, 1967.

Title role, *Affectionately Yours, Fanny Kemble*, Abbey Theatre, Dublin, Ireland, 1972, and later at the Bath Festival, U.K., 1972, School for Social Research Theatre, London, 1974; title role, *Tallulah, a Memory*, American Embassy Theatre, Dublin, Ireland, 1972; Amanda Mangebois, *The Enchanted*, Kennedy Center, Washington, DC, 1973; also *Women of the West*, Kennedy Center, Washington, DC.

MAJOR TOURS—Jane Bennett, *Pride and Prejudice*, U.S. cities, 1934; Alexandra, *The Little Foxes*, U.S. cities, 1940-41; Evelyn Heath, *Guest in the House*, U.S. cities, 1942; Mrs. de Winter, *Rebecca*, U.S. cities, 1944; title roles, *Affectionately Yours, Fanny Kemble* and *Tallulah, a Memory*, U.S. cities including Washington, DC, Chapel Hill, NC, 1974; also *Women of the West*, U.S. and European cities as well as on board the Queen Elizabeth II ocean liner.

TELEVISION DEBUT—Mrs. Elvsted, "Hedda Gabler," *The U.S. Steel Hour*, CBS, 1954. PRINCIPAL TELEVISION APPEARANCES—Series: Margaret, *On the Road to Reality*, ABC, 1960-61; Elaine Harris, *Love of Life*, CBS, 1966-67; Grace Burton, *As the World Turns*, CBS, 1972-73. Episodic: *Armstrong Circle Theatre*, NBC; *Dupont Show of the Month*, NBC; *The Great Sebastians*, NBC, 1957; *The Doctors*, NBC, 1963; *Nurses*, CBS, 1963; "The Magnificent Yankee," *Hallmark Hall of Fame*, NBC, 1965; "A Punt, a Pass, and a Prayer," *Hallmark Hall of Fame*, NBC, 1968. Guest: *The Joe Franklin Show*.

PRINCIPAL FILM APPEARANCES—Has appeared in many documentary films.

PRINCIPAL RADIO WORK—"Look Homeward Angel," *Voice of America*.

RELATED CAREER—Artist in residence: University of Denver, University of Northern Colorado, University of Tampa.

WRITINGS: PLAYS, PRODUCED AND PUBLISHED—*Tallulah, a Memory*, University of Alabama Presss, 1979; *A Moment Ago*, Denver Center for the Performing Arts Presss, 1984.

NON-FICTION—Contributed to two published cookbooks and cooperated with Brendan Gill in preparing the book *Tallulah*, published in 1973.

RECORDINGS: DRAMA—*Arrowsmith; Look Homeward Angel;* also recorded ninety-six talking books for the sightless.

AWARDS: Gold Chair Award, Central City Opera Association; honorary degrees: University of Northern Colorado, Doctor of Humane Letters; Wesleyan College, Doctor of Fine Arts.

MEMBER: Actors' Equity Association, Screen Actors Guild, American Federation of Television and Radio Artists; Cosmopolitan Club.

SIDELIGHTS: RECREATIONS—Writing poetry, travelling, and farming.

ADDRESSES: AGENT—Talent Representatives, 20 E. 53rd Street, New York, NY 10019.

*   *   *

RAYE, Martha 1916-

PERSONAL: Born Margaret Theresa Yvonne Reed, August 27, 1916, in Butte, MT; daughter of Peter (a vaudevillain) and Mabelle (a vaudevillian; maiden name, Hooper) Reed; married Hamilton Buddy Westmore (divorced); married David Rose (divorced); married Neal Lang (divorced); married Nick Condos (divorced); married Edward Thomas Begley (divorced); married Robert O'Shea. EDUCATION: Attended the Professional Children's School, New York City.

VOCATION: Actress and singer.

CAREER: PRINCIPAL TELEVISION APPEARANCES—Series: Regular, *All Star Revue,* NBC, 1951-53; regular, *Max Liebman Presents,* NBC, 1954-56; host, *The Martha Raye Show,* NBC, 1955-56; regular, *Milton Berle Show,* NBC, 1954-56; *The Bugaloos,* 1970-72; Agatha, *McMillan and Wife,* NBC, 1976-77; Carrie Sharples, *Alice,* CBS, 1982-84. Mini-Series: Duchess, *Alice in Wonderland,* CBS, 1986. Episodic: *Club Oasis,* NBC; *Carol Burnett Show,* CBS; *Love, American Style,* ABC; "Anything Goes," *Musical Comedy Time,* NBC, 1950.

FILM DEBUT—In short subjects, 1934. PRINCIPAL FILM APPEARANCES—*Rhythm on the Range,* 1936; *The Big Broadcast of 1937,* 1936; *College Holiday,* 1936; *Waikiki Wedding,* 1937; *Mountain Music,* 1937; *Artists and Models,* 1937; *Double or Nothing,* 1937; *The Boys from Syracuse,* 1940; *Navy Blues,* 1942; *Keep 'Em Flying,* 1942; *Hellzapoppin,* 1942; *Pin-Up Girl,* 1944; *Four Jills and a Jeep,* 1944; *Monsieur Verdoux,* 1947; *Annie Get Your Gun,* 1952; *The Solid Gold Cadillac,* Columbia, 1956; *Pufnstuff,* Universal, 1970; *The Concorde: Airport 1979,* Universal, 1979. Also *Hideaway Girl* and *Par.*

STAGE DEBUT—As a member of her parents vaudeville act, 1919. BROADWAY DEBUT—*Calling All Stars,* Hollywood Theatre, 1934. LONDON DEBUT—*Variety,* Palladium Theatre, 1948. PRINCIPAL STAGE APPEARANCES—Loew's State Theatre, 1934; *Earl Carrol's Sketchbook Revue,* Winter Garden Theatre, New York City, 1935; Mamie, *Hold on to Your Hats,* Shubert Theatre and Loew's State Theatre, New York City, 1941; Annie Oakley, *Annie Get Your Gun,* Miami Beach, FL, 1952.

Laura Partridge, *The Solid Gold Cadillac,* Drury Lane Theatre, Chicago, 1960; Carole Arden, *Personal Appearance,* Sombrero Playhouse, Phoenix, AZ, 1961; title role, *Calamity Jane,* with the Pittsburgh Light Opera Company, 1961; Dolly Gallagher Levi, *Hello Dolly!,* St. James Theatre, New York City, 1967; Pauline, *No, No, Nanette,* 46th Street Theatre, New York City, 1972; Opal, *Everybody Loves Opal,* Sardi Dinner Theatre, Franklin Square, Long Island, NY, 1975.

PRINCIPAL CABARET APPEARANCES—Since 1929, has appeared as a singer and comedienne in cabaret, including performances with Nick Condos, Five O'Clock Club, Miami Beach, FL, 1949-53; also at the Shamrock Hotel, Houston, TX, 1972.

MAJOR TOURS—Worked extensively in vaudeville with such companies as: The Benny Davis Revue, the Ben Blue Company, Paul Ash's Orchestra, and the Will Morrissey Company, 1919-1929; with the United Service Organization (U.S.O.), World War II theatre of operations tour; Pam, *Separate Rooms,* U.S. cities, 1961; title role, *Wildcat,* U.S. cities, 1962; Sally Adams, *Call Me Madam,* U.S. cities, 1963; toured Minsky's Burlesque Theatres, U.S. cities, 1972; Opal, *Everybody Loves Opal,* U.S. cities, 1975; with the U.S.O., Vietnam theatre of operations, yearly until 1974.

AWARDS: Jean Hersholt Humanitarian Award.

MEMBER: Actors' Equity Association, Screen Actors Guild, American Federation of Television and Radio Artists.

SIDELIGHTS: CTFT learned Martha Raye appeared with her parents in vaudeville from the age of three until she was thirteen years old.

ADDRESSES: AGENT—c/o Ruth Webb, 7500 DeVista Drive, Los Angeles, CA 90046.*

*   *   *

REES, Roger   1944-

PERSONAL: Born May 5, 1944, in Aberystwyth, Wales, U.K.; son of William John and Doris Louise (Smith) Rees. EDUCATION: Attended Balham Secondary Modern School; Camberwell School of Art; Slade School of Fine Art.

VOCATION: Actor, director, and playwright.

CAREER: STAGE DEBUT—Alan, *Hindle Wakes,* Wimbledon, U.K., 1964. PRINCIPAL STAGE APPEARANCES—Yasha, *The Cherry Orchard,* Pitlochry, U.K., 1965. With the Royal Shakespeare Company, Stratford, U.K.: *The Taming of the Shrew* and *As You Like It,* 1967; Volumnius, *Julius Caesar* and Fenton, *The Merry Wives of Windsor,* 1968; Patchbreech, *Pericles,* Curio, *Twelfth Night,* Guildford, *Henry VIII,* and *The Winter's Tale,* 1969; *The Winter's Tale, Twelfth Night,* Damaschke, *The Plebeians Rehearse the Uprising,* and Stephen Undershaft, *Major Barbara,* 1970; Claudio, *Much Ado About Nothing* and Roderigo, *Othello,* 1971, also at the Aldwych Theatre, London, 1971-72; Benvolio, *Romeo and Juliet,* Young Shepherd, *The Winter's Tale,* Malcolm, *Macbeth,* and Antipholus, *The Comedy of Errors,* 1976.

Gratiano, *The Merchant of Venice* and Balin, *The Island of the Mighty,* both at the Aldwych Theatre, London, 1971-72; Marchbanks, *Candida,* Neptune Theatre, Halifax, Nova Scotia, 1973; Vosco, *Paradise* and Q, *Moving Clocks Go Slow,* both at the Theatre Upstairs, London, 1975; Ananias, *The Alchemist,* Other Place Theatre, then at the Aldwych Theatre, London, 1977; Malcolm, *Macbeth* and Nazzer, *Factory Birds,* both at the Warehouse Theatre, London, 1977; Petulant, *The Way of the World,* Aldwych Theatre, London, 1978; Posthumus, *Cymbeline,* with the Royal Shakespeare Company, Stratford, and at the Other Place Theatre, London, 1979.

Semyon Podsekalnikov, *The Suicide,* Other Place, then at the Newcastle, The Warehouse, and the Aldwych Theatres, London, 1980; title role, *The Adventures of Nicholas Nickleby,* Aldwych Theatre, London, 1980, then at the Plymouth Theatre, New York City, 1981; *The Real Thing,* Strand Theatre, London, 1983; David, *Cries from the Mammaz House,* Royal Court Theatre, London, 1983; title role, *Hamlet* and Berowne, *Love's Labour's Lost,* both with the Royal Shakespeare Company, Stratford, 1984, then Newcastle Theatre and Barbican Theatre, London, 1985; Duncan McFee, *Double-Double,* Watford Palace and Fortune Theatres, London, 1986; Lofty, *Archangels Don't Play Pinball,* with the Bristol Old Vic Theatre Company at the Theatre Royal, London, 1986.

MAJOR TOURS—Fabian, *Twelfth Night,* Pierre, *Aunt Sally or the Triumph of Death,* Young Marlowe, *She Stoops to Conquer,* Brother, *Fear and Misery in the Third Reich,* and Simple Simon, *Jack and the Beanstalk,* all with the Cambridge Theatre Company, U.K. cities, 1973-74; Charles Courtly, *London Assurance,* with the Royal Shakespeare Company, U.S. cities, 1974-75; Algernon, *The Importance of Being Earnest* and Stanley, *The Birthday Party,* both with the Cambridge Theatre Company, U.K. cities, 1975; Sir Andrew, *Twelfth Night,* Tusenbach, *The Three Sisters,* and appeared in *Is There Honey Still for Tea?,* all with the Royal Shakespeare Company, U.K. cities, 1978.

PRINCIPAL STAGE WORK—Director, with the Bristol Old Vic Theatre Company at the Theatre Royal and the New Vic Theatre, London: *Turkey Time,* 1986, *Julius Caesar* and *John Bull,* 1987.

PRINCIPAL FILM APPEARANCES—*Star 80,* Warner Brothers, 1983.

PRINCIPAL TELEVISION APPEARANCES—Movies: *A Christmas Carol,* CBS, 1984; also *Place of Peace; Under Western Eyes; Bouquet of Barbed Wire; Saigon; Imaginary Friends; The Adventures of Nicholas Nickelby; The Comedy of Errors; Macbeth; The Voysey Inheritance;* David Williams, "The Ebony Tower," *Great Performances,* PBS, 1987.

RELATED CAREER—Associate director, Bristol Old Vic Theatre Company, 1986—.

WRITINGS: PLAYS—(With Eric Elice) *Double-Double,* produced at the Watford Palace Theatre and the Fortune Theatre, London, 1986; (with Eric Elice) *Elephant Manse.*

AWARDS: Best Actor, Antoinette Perry Award, 1982, for *The Adventures of Nicholas Nickleby.*

SIDELIGHTS: RECREATIONS—Horse riding and tap dancing.

ADDRESSES: AGENT—International Creative Management, 22 Grafton Street, London W1, England.

*   *   *

REICH, Richard

VOCATION: Writer.

WRITINGS: PLAYS, PRODUCED—*The Tin Cup,* retitled, *To Murder with Love,* Dallas, TX, New Lindsey Theatre, London, Theatre Royal, Windsor, U.K., as well as in South African cities and many regional theatres in the U.S.; *Girls Are the Funniest,* Pheasant Run Playhouse, St. Charles, IL, and under the title *Departemento De Soltero,* in Buenos Aires, Argentina and U.S. cities; *Semilla,* Buenos Aires, Argentina; *Pets,* Provincetown Playhouse, MA; *Nordland,* Akademic Theatre, Vienna, Austria; *Orchestra,* Der Josefstadt Theatre, Vienna, Austria; *Night Shake,* Straight Wharf Theatre, Nantucket, MA.

TELEVISION—*Girls Are the Funniest.*

SCREENPLAYS—*Submission,* independent.

MEMBER: Dramatists Guild, National Writers Club.

ADDRESSES: HOME—875 West End Avenue, New York, NY 10025.

REID, Frances   1918-

PERSONAL: Born December 9, 1918, in Wichita Falls, TX; daughter of Charles William (a banker) and Anna May (Priest) Reid; married Philip Bourneuf, June 27, 1940. EDUCATION: Trained for the stage at the Pasadena Playhouse School of the Theatre.

VOCATION: Actress.

CAREER: STAGE DEBUT—Helene Dupont, *Tovarich,* Lobero Playhouse, Santa Barbara, CA, then Curran Theatre, San Francisco and Biltmore Theatre, Los Angeles, 1938. BROADWAY DEBUT—Juliette Lecourtois, *Where There's a Will,* John Golden Theatre, 1939. PRINCIPAL STAGE APPEARANCES—Stock productions in Maplewood, NJ, and Ridgefield, CT, 1939; understudy for Catherine Daly and Cora Bedell, *Young Couple Wanted,* Maxine Elliott's Theatre, New York City, 1940; stock performances in Ridgefield, CT, 1940; *The White-Haired Boy,* Plymouth Theatre, Boston, 1940.

Western Union Please, Paper Mill Playhouse, Milburn, NJ and Studebaker Theatre, Chicago, 1941; Julia, *The Rivals,* Theatre Guild, Shubert Theatre, New York City, 1942; Martha, *The Patriots,* National Theatre, New York City, 1943; Jeannie Mackenzie, *A Highland Fling,* Plymouth Theatre, New York City, 1944; Beth, *Little Women,* City Center, New York City, 1944; *Clover Ring,* Plymouth Theatre, Boston, 1945; Sally Jones, *Star Spangled Family,* Biltmore Theatre, New York City, 1945; Jean, *The Wind Is 90,* Booth Theatre, New York City, 1945; Ophelia, *G.I. Hamlet,* Columbus Circle Theatre, New York City, 1945; Roxanne, *Cyrano de Bergerac,* Alvin Theatre, New York City, 1946; Minnie, *Rip Van Winkle,* City Center, New York City, 1947; Elena Popova, *The Bear,* City Center, New York City, 1948; Raina, *Arms and the Man,* Utah Drama Festival, University of Utah, 1948; Gwendolyn, *The Importance of Being Earnest,* Olney Theatre, MD, 1948; Ann, *Richard III,* Booth Theatre, New York City, 1949; Viola, *Twelfth Night,* Ann Arbor Drama Festival, Lydia Mendelssohn Theatre, MI, 1949, then Empire Theatre, New York City, 1949.

Lady Utterwood, *Heartbreak House,* Brattle Theatre, Cambridge, MA, 1953; Mrs. Antrobus, *The Skin of Our Teeth,* Boston Arts Festival, Public Gardens Theatre, Boston, 1955; Lavinia, *Androcles and the Lion,* Studebaker Theatre, Chicago, 1956; Renata, *Last Five Minutes,* Columbia University Theatre, New York City, 1957; Ranata, *Lease on Love,* Bucks County Playhouse, New Hope, PA, 1957; Comtesse Louise de Clerambard, *Clerambard,* Rooftop Theatre, New York City, 1957.

Nora, *A Touch of the Poet,* Solange, *The Maids,* and Lina, *Misalliance,* Marine's Memorial Theatre, San Francisco, 1960-61; *When the Bear Goes National,* Bucks County Playhouse, New Hope, 1962; Mrs. Russell, *The Best Man,* Kelley Memorial Theatre, Fairmont Park, Philadelphia, 1962.

MAJOR TOURS—Ophelia, *G.I. Hamlet,* U.S. cities, 1945; Judith, *The Devil's Disciple,* U.S. cities, 1950; Lavinia, *Androcles and the Lion,* U.S. cities, 1956; Madmoiselle de St. Euverte, *The Waltz of the Toreadors,* U.S. cities, 1958; Miss Swanson, *Lord Pengo,* U.S. cities, 1963.

PRINCIPAL TELEVISION APPEARANCES—Series: Grace Baker, *As the World Turns,* CBS, 1959-60; Dear Rose Pollack, *Edge of Night,* 1964; Mrs. Thomas Horton, *The Days of Our Lives,* NBC, 1963—. Episodic: *Suspense,* CBS; *Danger,* CBS; *You Are There,* CBS; *Cameo Theatre,* NBC; *Philco Television Playhouse,* NBC;

Hallmark Hall of Fame, NBC; *Matinee Theatre*, NBC; *Telephone Time*, NBC; *Alfred Hitchcock Presents*, CBS; *Wagon Train*, NBC; *Ben Casey*, ABC; *Eleventh Hour*, NBC; *The Defenders*, CBS; *Perry Mason*, CBS; *Armstrong Circle Theatre*, CBS. Dramatic Specials: Roxanne, *Cyrano de Bergerac*, NBC, 1948; Olivia, *Twelfth Night*, NBC, 1949; Portia, *Portia Faces Life*, CBS, 1954. Movies: Emily Gilbert, *Mercy or Murder*, NBC, 1986.

PRINCIPAL FILM APPEARANCES—*Seconds*, Paramount, 1966.

RADIO DEBUT—*Charlotte Corday*, NBC, 1939. PRINCIPAL RADIO WORK—*Prologue to Glory*, NBC, 1939-40; *Little Women*, NBC, 1939-40.

AWARDS: Fanny Morrison Award from the Pasadena Playhouse.

MEMBER: Actors' Equity Association, Screen Actors Guild, American Federation of Television and Radio Artists.

ADDRESSES: AGENT—Progressive Artists Agency, 400 S. Beverly Drive, Beverly Hills, CA 90212.

* * *

REINGLAS, Fred

PERSONAL: Son of Jacob (an actor) and Sofia (an actress; maiden name, Gorlicki) Reinglas.

VOCATION: Stage manager.

CAREER: PRINCIPAL STAGE WORK—Production stage manager: *Hair*, Biltmore Theatre, New York City, 1977; *Gemini*, Little Theatre, New York City 1979; *Talley's Folly*, Brooks Atkinson Theatre, New York City, 1980; *Fifth of July*, New Apollo Theatre, New York City, 1982; *Angels Fall*, Circle Repertory Theatre, then Longacre Theatre, New York City, 1983; *Passion*, Longacre Theatre, New York City, 1983; *As Is*, Lyceum Theatre, New York City, 1985. Also, assistant stage manager, *Ghosts*, Fourth Street Theatre.

Resident production stage manager, Circle Repertory Company, New York City, 1975—.

ADDRESSES: HOME—222 E. Tenth Street, New York, NY 10001. OFFICE—Circle Repertory Company, 161 Avenue of the Americas, New York, NY 10017.

* * *

REINKING, Ann   1949-

PERSONAL: Born November 10, 1949, in Seattle, WA; daughter of Walton F. and Frances (Harrison) Reinking. EDUCATION: Trained as a dancer with the San Francisco Ballet Company.

VOCATION: Actress, dancer, and singer.

CAREER: BROADWAY DEBUT—Lulu, *Cabaret*, Broadway Theatre, 1969. PRINCIPAL STAGE APPEARANCES—Coco, Mark Hellinger Theatre, New York City, 1969; *Wild and Wonderful*,

Lyceum Theatre, New York City, 1971; Player, *Pippin*, Imperial Theatre, New York City, 1972; Maggie, *Over Here!*, Shubert Theatre, New York City, 1974; Joan of Arc, *Goodtime Charley*, Palace Theatre, New York City, 1975; Cassie, *A Chorus Line*, Shubert Theatre, New York City, 1976; Roxie Hart, *Chicago*, 46th Street Theatre, New York City, 1977; *Dancin'*, Broadhurst Theatre, New York City, 1978; appeared in *Parade of Stars Playing the Palace*, Palace Theatre, New York City, 1983; appeared in *One More Song/One More Dance*, Joyce Theatre, New York City, 1983; appeared in *Ann Reinking. . .Music Loves Me*, Joyce Theatre, New York City, 1984; title role, *Sweet Charity*, Minskoff Theatre, New York City, 1986-87.

PRINCIPAL FILM APPEARANCES—"Troubles" Moran, *Movie, Movie*, Warner Brothers, 1979; Kate Jagger, *All That Jazz*, Twentieth Century-Fox, 1979; Grace, *Annie*, Columbia, 1982; Micki Salinger, *Micki & Maude*, Columbia, 1984.

PRINCIPAL TELEVISION APPEARANCES—Episodic: *Ellery Queen*, NBC. Specials: *Doug Henning: Magic on Broadway*, 1982; *Parade of Stars*, 1983; host, *American Treasury*, 1985; *The Fortieth Annual Tony Awards*, 1986.

AWARDS: Clarence Derwent Award, Outer Critics Circle Award, *Theatre World* Award, 1974; Dance Educators Award, 1979; Harkness Dance Award, 1979; also nominated for two Antoinette Perry Awards; scholarships: Ford Foundation, 1964-66; Robert Joffrey Award, 1967.

MEMBER: Actors' Equity Association, Screen Actors Guild, American Federation of Television and Radio Artists.

SIDELIGHTS: FAVORITE ROLES—Joan of Arc and Roxie Hart.

ADDRESSES: AGENT—Allan Willig & Associates Ltd., 165 W. 46th Street, New York, NY 10036.*

* * *

RHODES, Leah   1902-1986

PERSONAL: Born 1902, in Port Arthur, TX; died after a brief illness in Burbank, CA, October 17, 1986; married: twice.

VOCATION: Costume designer.

CAREER: PRINCIPAL FILM WORK—Costume designer: *Old Acquaintance, Mission to Moscow, Northern Pursuit*, all 1943; *Passage to Marseilles, Experiment Perilous*, both 1944; *God Is My Co-Pilot, Hotel Berlin, Confidential Agent, Saratoga Trunk*, all 1945; *The Big Sleep, Cloak and Dagger*, both 1946; *Pursued, Stallion Road, The Voice of the Turtle*, all 1947; *Key Largo, June Bride, One Sunday Afternoon*, all 1948; *Colorado Territory, Girl from Jones Beach, White Heat, Task Force*, all 1949; *The Adventures of Don Juan*, 1949; *Caged, Bright Leaf, The Breaking Point*, all 1950.

Strangers on a Train, Come Fill the Cup, both 1951; *Starlift, April in Paris*, both 1952; *The Desert Song*, 1953; *Forty Guns*, Twentieth Century-Fox, 1957; *Kings Go Forth*, United Artists, 1958; *Tickle Me*, Allied Artists, 1965; *Village of the Giants*, Embassy, 1965; *Picture Mommy Dead*, Embassy, 1966; *Good Times*, Columbia, 1967; *The Fox*, Claridge, 1968; *Five Card Stud*, Paramount, 1968.

AWARDS: (With Travilla and Majorie Best) Best Costumes, Academy Award, 1949, for *The Adventures of Don Juan.**

* * *

RIBEIRO, Alfonso 1971-

PERSONAL: Born September 21, 1971, in New York, NY; son of Michael (a manager) and Joy Ribeiro. EDUCATION: Attended Valley Professional School, Los Angeles.

VOCATION: Actor, dancer, and singer.

CAREER: BROADWAY DEBUT—Willie, *The Tap Dance Kid*, Broadhurst Theatre, then Minskoff Theatre, 1983-84.

PRINCIPAL TELEVISION APPEARANCES—Series: Alfonso Spears, *Silver Spoons*, NBC, 1984—. Episodic: *Magnum P.I.*, CBS; *Mighty Pawns*, PBS.

Guest: *Merv Griffin Show*, CBS; *Good Morning America; Live at Five*, WNBC; *Phil Donahue Show; The Star's Table; Puttin' on the Kids.*

Specials: Pee Wee, *O Yee Willie*, PBS; *NBC 60th Anniversary Special; 1984 Emmy Awards; NBC Fall Preview Special; KHQ-TV Variety Telethon; 1985 Golden Globe Awards; Wildest Wild West Show of the Stars; Andy Williams Christmas Special; Circus of the Stars; Night of 100 Stars II; 1986 Tony Awards.*

RECORDINGS: SINGLES—*Dance Baby*, Prism; *Not Too Young*, Prism; *Time Bomb*, Prism; *Sneak Away with Me*, Prism.

AWARDS: Hollywood Press Club's Rising Star Award, 1985.

SIDELIGHTS: Alfonso Ribeiro is involved in the "Say No to Drugs" and "Hands Across America" programs.

ADDRESSES: AGENT—c/o Aaron Cohen and Bryan Lourd, William Morris Agency, 151 El Camino Drive, Beverly Hills, CA 90212.

* * *

RICH, John 1925-

PERSONAL: Born July 6, 1925, in Rockaway Beach, NY; son of Louis and Jennie Rich; married Andrea Louise; children: Catherine Lee, Anthony Joseph, Robert Lawrence. EDUCATION: University of Michigan, B.A., 1948, M.A., 1949. MILITARY: U.S. Air Force, 1943-46.

VOCATION: Director and producer.

CAREER: PRINCIPAL TELEVISION WORK—Episodic: Director—*Ezio Pinza Show, Joan Davis Show, The Ray Bolger Show, Our Miss Brooks*, all between 1952-55; *Gunsmoke*, CBS, *Bonanza*, NBC, *Twilight Zone*, CBS, *G.E. Theatre*, CBS, all between 1956-60; *The Dick Van Dyke Show*, CBS, 1960-63.

Series: Producer and director, *All in the Family*, CBS, 1971-74; producer and director, *On the Rocks*, ABC, 1975-76; executive producer and director, *Benson*, ABC, 1980-82; *Mr. Sunshine*,

1985-86; *MacGyver*, NBC, 1985-87. Pilots: Director—*Maude*, CBS, 1973; *The Jeffersons*, CBS; *Barney Miller*, ABC; *Newhart*, CBS; *Condo*, ABC. Specials: Director, *Henry Fonda as Clarence Darrow*, 1974.

PRINCIPAL FILM WORK—Director: *Wives and Lovers*, Paramount, 1963; *The New Interns*, Columbia, 1964; *Roustabout*, Paramount, 1964; *Boeing Boeing*, Paramount, 1965; *Easy Come, Easy Go*, Paramount, 1967.

AWARDS: Outstanding Directorial Achievement, Emmy Awards, 1963, for *The Dick Van Dyke Show*, and 1971, for *All in the Family*; Director of the Year, Directors Guild of America, 1971; Best Comedy Series, Emmy Award, 1972, for *All in the Family*; Image Award, National Association for the Advancement of Colored People, 1973; Golden Globe Awards, 1972-73 and 1973-74, both for *All in the Family*; Christopher Award, 1974, for *Henry Fonda as Clarence Darrow*; Phi Beta Kappa, University of Michigan.

MEMBER: Directors Guild of America (former vice-president, secretary, and treasurer), Directors Guild of America Producer Pension Plan (founding member), Writers Guild of America, Producers Guild of America, Screen Actors Guild, American Federation of Television and Radio Artists, Caucus for Writers, Producers, and Directors; Phi Kappa Phi.

SIDELIGHTS: RECREATIONS—Swimming, reading, and bicycling.

ADDRESSES: OFFICE—Henry Winkler/John Rich Productions, Paramount Television, 5555 Melrose Avenue, Los Angeles, CA 90038. MANAGER—FKB, 1801 Avenue of the Stars, Los Angeles, 90067.

* * *

RICHARDS, Jess 1943-

PERSONAL: Born December 23, 1943, in Seattle, WA; son of Jack Earl and Permelia (Dunn) Sederholm. EDUCATION: Attended University of Washington.

VOCATION: Actor.

CAREER: STAGE DEBUT—Chorus, *Finian's Rainbow*, Hyatt Music Theatre, San Francisco, CA, 1965. BROADWAY DEBUT —*Walking Happy*, Lunt-Fontanne Theatre, 1966. PRINCIPAL STAGE APPEARANCES—Dick, *Dames at Sea*, Theatre de Lys, New York City, then The Hungry I Theatre, San Francisco, CA, 1969; Dudley, *Chronicle*, Chelsea Theatre Company, New York City, 1969; Billy Cockcroft, *Blood Red Roses*, John Golden Theatre, New York City, 1970; standby Jam and Japheth *Two by Two*, Imperial Theatre, New York City, 1970; Ariel, *The Tempest*, American Shakespeare Festival, Stratford, CT, 1971; Chip, *On the Town*, Imperial Theatre, New York City, 1971; (revue) *One for the Money*, East Side Playhouse, New York City, 1972; Hal, *Loot*, McCarter Theatre, Princeton, NJ, 1973; Constantine, *The Seagull*, Seattle Repertory Theatre, WA, 1974; Frank Wyman, *Mack and Mabel*, Majestic Theatre, New York City, 1974; (revue) *Lovesong*, Village Gate, New York City, 1976; Joshua Logan's *Muscial Scrapbook*, Rainbow Grill, New York City and Studio One, Los Angeles, 1977-78; Edward Middleton, *The Drunkard*, Players State Theatre, Maimi, FL, 1978; *Side by Side by Sondheim*, Seattle Repertory Theatre, 1979; *The All Night Strut*, Theatre Four, New York City, 1979.

JESS RICHARDS

Gary, *Musical Chairs*, Rialto Theatre, New York City, 1980; *A Reel American Hero*, Rialto Theatre, New York City, 1981; P.T. Barnum, *Barnum*, St. James Theatre, New York City, 1981, Pioneer Memorial Theatre, Salt Lake City, UT, 1983, and Norwegian Carribean Lines, 1984; Frederick Egerman, *A Little Night Music*, Alliance Theatre, Atlanta, GA, 1983; Pseudolus, *A Funny Thing Happened on the Way to the Forum*, Coconut Grove Playhouse, Miami, FL, 1983; Digger, *The Hasty Heart*, Theatre Guild, New York City, 1984; Fred Graham, *Kiss Me, Kate*, Alley Theatre, Houston, TX, 1985; Nestor, *Irma La Douce*, Claridge Hotel, Atlantic City, 1986.

MAJOR TOURS—Barnaby Tucker, *Hello, Dolly!*, national, 1967-68; Ozzie, *Irene*, national, 1974-75.

AWARDS: Theatre World Award, 1972, for Chip, *On the Town*.

MEMBER: Actors' Equity Association.

ADDRESSES: HOME—175 W. 76th Street, New York, NY 10023.

*   *   *

RICHE, Robert   1925-

PERSONAL: Born September 23, 1925, in Pittsfield, MA; son of Leon L. (an insurance salesman) and Ruth (Savery) Riche; married Fran Schmidt (a photographer), February 21, 1964; children: Pierre, Michele. EDUCATION: Yale University, B.A., 1947. POLITICS: Independent liberal.

VOCATION: Writer.

CAREER: PRINCIPAL STAGE WORK—Playwright.

RELATED CAREER—Staff correspondent and editor, United Press International, New York City, 1948-50; free lance commercial writer, metal worker, labor organizer, temporary typist, and has worked in advertising and public relations, 1966—.

WRITINGS: PLAYS, PRODUCED AND PUBLISHED—*Message from the Grassroots*, Bristol Old Vic, U.K., 1968, and Weldon Theatre, New York City, 1970, published by Samuel French, 1970; *The Great Two Hundredth Anniversay H-Bomb Crisis*, Magic Theatre, Berkeley, CA, 1972; *Thanksgiving at Aunt Betty's*, Washington Theatre Club, 1973; *We Hold These Truths*, Theatre Off Park, New York City, 1976; *Why Is That Dumb Son of a Bitch Down the Street Happier Than I Am?*, New Playwrights Theatre, Washington, DC, 1977, and Harbor Repertory Theatre, Staten Island, NY, 1981; (staged reading) *Last Dance Before the Music*, Walden Theatre, New York City, 1982; (staged reading) *The Stag at Eve*, Alliance Theatre, GA, 1984.

PLAYS, UNPRODUCED—Daddy Beautiful, Hot Pants and Little Blue Jewel.

TELEVISION—Pilots: *Angela*, CBS, 1979; *Studio 84*, ABC, 1980. Movies: *Run for Your Wife*, NBC, 1981. Series: *Cereal*, Viacom, 1982.

NON-FICTION—*The Nine Most Troublesome Teen-Age Problems* (*And How to Solve Them*), Lyle Stuart, 1986.

ROBERT RICHE

AWARDS: Play production grant, Office for Advanced Drama Research, Rockefeller Foundation, 1972; grant from the National Endowment for the Arts, 1974; playwriting grant, Connecticut Foundation for the Arts, 1976; Stanley Drama Award from Wagner College, 1979, for *The Stag at Eve.*

MEMBER: Dramatists Guild, Writers Guild of America East; The Players Club.

SIDELIGHTS: Robert Riche told *CTFT:* "The increasing escalation of craziness in life can only be dealt with in wildly comic ways."

ADDRESSES: HOME—45 New Street, Ridgefield, CT 06877. AGENT—Robert A. Freedman Dramatic Agency, 1501 Broadway, New York, NY 10036.

*   *   *

RINEHIMER, John   1951-

PERSONAL: Born November 3, 1951; son of John (a physician) and Angela (Hunt) Rinehimer. EDUCATION: Boston University, Berklee College of Music, B.A., English and music.

VOCATION: Composer and musical director.

CAREER: FIRST STAGE WORK—Guitar player, *Hair,* Boston.

PRINCIPAL STAGE WORK—Arranger, *People Magazine's Tenth Anniversary,* Lincoln Center, New York City, 1986.

MAJOR TOURS—Worked on tour with the Supremes and with a production of *Grease.*

PRINCIPAL FILM WORK—Produced parts of soundtrack for *Stripper,* Twentieth Century-Fox, 1986.

RELATED CAREER—Director, Wellesley School, 1972-76; music director and jingles writer, P.P.X., Inc., 1979-84.

AWARDS: Carbonelle Award, Best Conductor, Florida Theatre Association.

ADDRESSES: HOME—429 W. 45th Street, New York, NY 10036.

*   *   *

ROBBE, Scott D.   1955-

PERSONAL: Born February 16, 1955; son of James D. (a contractor) and Helen J. (Coffeen) Robbe. EDUCATION: University of Wisconsin, B.A., 1977; trained for the stage at the Herbert Berghof Studio and with Bill Hickey. POLITICS: Democratic Socialist. RELIGION: "Agnostic" Lutheran.

VOCATION: Production manager, stage manager, and producer.

CAREER: STAGE DEBUT—James Callaghan, *Left Out Lady,* St. Peter's Performing Arts Labor Theatre, New York City, 1982, for seventy-two performances. PRINCIPAL STAGE APPEARANCES—

Mike O'Keefe, *The Bayside Boys,* St. Peter's Performing Arts Theatre, New York City, 1983.

PRINCIPAL STAGE WORK—Production stage manager, *Yours for the Revolution, Jack London,* The Labor Theatre, New York City; associate producer, *Left Out Lady* and *Railroad Bill,* Labor Theatre, New York City; house manager and company manager, *The Passion of Dracula,* Cherry Lane Theatre, New York City; producer, *The San Francisco Mime Troupe,* Orpheum Theatre and Entermedia Theatre, New York City; associate producer, *Comedy Week at the Orpheum,* production stage manager, *The Kids from New Jersey,* producer, *Julianna Osinchuk,* and general manager, *Big Bad Burlesque,* all at the Orpheum Theatre; house manager, *Fugue in a Nursery;* production stage manager, *2,000 R.P.M.,* Labor Theatre; producer, *Safe Sex,* Lyceum Theatre, New York City, 1987.

MAJOR TOURS—Production stage manager, *Railroad Bill,* U.S. cities.

PRINCIPAL FILM WORK—Portrayed Detective J.A. Bolling and was production manager, *In the King of Prussia,* 1982.

PRINCIPAL TELEVISION APPEARANCES—Yush Meskovak, *Staus,* PBS, 1983.

PRINCIPAL TELEVISION WORK—Location manager, *The Struggle to Survive,* PBS, 1983; production manager, *Hard Winter,* PBS, 1984; production manager, *A Dream of Empire,* 1984; executive in charge of production, "The House of Dies Drear," *Wonderworks,* PBS, 1984; production manager, *Realizations: Growing Old in America,* 1984; production manager, *Jack London: The Man from Eden's Grove,* PBS, 1984; production manager, *The 30 Second Seduction,* HBO, 1985; production manager, *Running Great with Grete Waitz,* 1985; associate producer, *The Best of National Geographic Specials,* 1986; production manager, *The Independents: Ordinary People,* 1986; line producer and production manager, "A Mistaken Charity," *American Playhouse,* PBS, 1986. Series: Production manager, *It's Your World,* 1986; unit production manager, *Tales from the Darkside,* 1986.

RELATED CAREER—Associate producer, Shubert Organization, New York City.

MEMBER: Actors' Equity Association, Association of Independent Video and Film Makers.

ADDRESSES: OFFICE—Scott Robbe Management Services, 102 E. Fourth Street, New York, NY 10003.

*   *   *

ROBBINS, Jerome   1918-

PERSONAL: Born Jerome Rabinowitz, October 11, 1918, in New York, NY; son of Harry (a corset manufacturer) and Lena (Rips) Rabinowitz. EDUCATION: Attended New York University, 1935-36; studied ballet with Ella Daganova, H. Platova, Anthony Tudor, and Eugene Loring; studied modern dance with the New Dance League, and Spanish dance with Helen Veola.

VOCATION: Director, choreographer, producer, writer, and dancer.

CAREER: STAGE DEBUT—Dancer with Sandor-Sorel Dance

Center, 1937. PRINCIPAL STAGE APPEARANCES—Dancer: *Great Lady*, Majestic Theatre, New York City, 1939; *The Straw Hat Review*, Ambassador Theatre, New York City, 1939; *Keep Off the Grass*, Broadhurst Theatre, New York City, 1940; dancer and choreographer, Camp Tamiment, PA, 1938-41; with the corps de ballet of the Ballet Theatre, New York City, appeared as: Hermes, *Helen of Troy*, Detroit, MI, 1942, and Moor, *Petrouchka*, the youth, *Three Virgins and a Devil*, and Benvolio, *Romeo and Juliet*, Metropolitan Opera House, New York City, 1944; created and appeared in "Interplay," in *Concert Varieties*, Ziegfeld Theatre, New York City, 1945; appeared with the Ballet Theatre at the Metropolitan Opera House, New York City, 1945; at the City Center, New York City, appeared in *Bouree Fantasque*, 1949, title role, *The Prodigal Son*, and appeared in *The Age of Anxiety*, both 1950, appeared in *The Pied Piper*, 1951, and Ringmaster, *Circus Polka*, City Center, then Paris Opera, France, 1971; dancer, *Pulcinella*, 1972.

PRINCIPAL STAGE WORK—Creator and choreographer, *On the Town*, Adelphi Theatre, New York City, 1944; creator, "Interplay," in *Concert Varieties*, Ziegfeld Theatre, New York City, 1945; choreographer, *Billion Dollar Baby*, Alvin Theatre, New York City, 1945; choreographer, *Pas de Trois*, for the Original Ballet Russe at the Metropolitan Opera House, New York City, 1947; choreographer, *High Button Shoes*, Century Theatre, New York City, 1947; author of book, director, and choreographer, *Look Ma, I'm Dancin'*, Adelphi Theatre, New York City, 1948; director, *That's the Ticket*, Shubert Theatre, Philadelphia, 1948; choreographer, *The Guests*, for the New York City Ballet at the City Center, New York City, 1949; choreographer, *Miss Liberty*, Imperial Theatre, New York City, 1949; choreographer, *The Age of Anxiety* and *Jones Beach*, both at the City Center, New York City, 1950.

Associate artistic director, City Ballet Company; choreographer, *Call Me Madam*, Imperial Theatre, New York City, 1950; choreographer, *The King and I* and creator of *The Small House of Uncle Thomas*, both at the St. James Theatre, New York City, 1951; choreographer, *The Cage*, for the New York City Ballet Company at City Center, 1951; choreographer, *The Pied Piper*, City Center, 1951; choreographer, *Two's Company*, Alvin Theatre, New York City, 1952; choreographer, *Wonderful Town*, for the New York City Ballet Company at the Winter Garden Theatre, New York City, 1953; choreographer, *Afternoon of a Faun*, City Center, 1953; choreographer, *Fanfare*, City Center, 1953, then later restaged for the Royal Danish Ballet, 1956; choreographer, *Quartet*, City Center, 1954; co-director, *The Pajama Game*, St. James Theatre, New York City, 1954; choreographer and director, *Peter Pan*, Winter Garden Theatre, New York City, 1954; choreographer, *The Tender Land*, for the New York City Opera Company at City Center, 1954; director and arranger of choreography, *Bells Are Ringing*, Shubert Theatre, New York City, 1956; creator, director, and choreographer, *West Side Story*, Winter Garden Theatre, New York City, 1957, then at Her Majesty's Theatre, London, 1958.

Founder of ballet company, Ballets: U.S.A., performed at the Alvin Theatre, New York City, 1958, and later at the American National Theatre Academy (ANTA) Theatre, New York City, 1961; director and choreographer, *Gypsy*, Broadway Theatre, New York City, 1959; director, *Oh Dad, Poor Dad, Mama's Hung You in the Closet and I'm Feelin' So Sad*, Phoenix Theatre, New York City, 1962; co-producer and director, *Mother Courage and Her Children*, Martin Beck Theatre, New York City, 1963; production supervisor, *Funny Girl*, New York City production, 1964; director and choreographer, *Fiddler on the Roof*, Imperial Theatre, New York City, 1964, and later produced in London, 1967; production

supervisor, *West Side Story*, Nissei Theatre, Tokyo, Japan, 1964; choreographer, *Les Noces*, American Ballet Theatre, New York City, 1965, and later at the Royal Swedish Ballet, 1969; choreographer, *Moves*, Joffrey Ballet, New York City, 1967, then later for the Batsheva Dance Company, 1969, and for the Nederlands Dans Theatre at the Venice Festival, 1973; choreographer, *Dances at a Gathering*, New York City Ballet, 1969, and The Royal Ballet, London, 1970.

Choreographer, *In the Night*, for the New York City Ballet at the City Center, 1970, then for the Royal Ballet, 1973; choreographer, *Firebird*, City Center, 1970; *The Goldberg Variations*, City Center, 1971; choreographer, *Watermill* and *Scherzo Fantastique*, both for the New York City Ballet at the City Center, 1972; choreographer, *Circus Polka*, for the New York City Ballet at City Center, 1972, then at the Paris Opera, France, 1974; choreographer, *Dunbarton Oaks*, for the New York City Ballet at the City Center, 1972; (with George Ballanchine) choreographer, *Pulcinella*, for the New York City Ballet at the City Center, 1972; choreographer, *Requiem Canticles*, City Center, 1972, then Bayerischen Staadsper, Munich, Germany, 1974; choreographer, *Interplay*, Joffrey Ballet, New York City, 1972; choreographer, *An Evening's Waltzes* and *Four Bagatelles*, City Center, 1973; choreographer, *Celebration: The Art of the Pas de Deux*, Spoleto Festival, Italy, 1973; choreographer, *The Dybbuk*, 1974; choreographer, *Concert for the Royal Ballet*, Covent Garden, London, 1975; choreographer, *In G Major*, *Introduction, Allegro for Harp, Mother Goose, Und Barque Sur L'Ocean*, and *Chansons Madecasses*, all for the New York City Ballet Ravel Festival, 1975; choreographer, *Other Dances*, American Ballet Theatre, New York City, 1976; (with Peter Martins and Jean-Pierre Bonnefous) choreographer, *Tricolore*, 1978; choreographer, *The Four Seasons* and *Opus 19*, for the New York City Ballet at the City Center, 1979; choreographer for the revival, *Fiddler on the Roof*, New York State Theatre, New York City, 1981.

Also choreographer of: *Facsimile*, 1947; *The Concert*, 1956; *Events*, 1961; *The Dreamer*, 1979; *Suite of Dances*, 1980; *Rondo*, 1981; *Andantino*, 1981; *Pas de Deux from Tchaikovsky First Piano Concerto*, 1981; (with Balanchine and Taras) *Piano Pieces*, 1981; *Allegro con Grazia*, 1981; *The Gershwin Concerto*, 1982; *Four Chamber Works*, 1982; *Glass Pieces*, 1983; *I'm Old Fashioned*, 1983.

Other ballets in the repertories of: Boston Ballet, National Ballet of Canada, Harkness Ballet, Australian Ballet, San Francisco Ballet, Pennsylvania Ballet, Dance Theatre of Harlem, La Scala Opera Ballet, and Opernhaus Zurich.

MAJOR TOURS—Ballets: U.S.A., Spoleto Festival, Italy, then World's Fair, Brussels, Belgium, then U.S. cities, 1958; *Gypsy*, European cities, 1959, also 1981; with Ballets: U.S.A., for the U.S. State Department, European cities, 1959, 1961; *Fiddler on the Roof*, U.S. and European cities, 1964, 1980; *Peter Pan*, U.S. and European cities, 1981; *Jerome Robbins Chamber Dance Company*, Peoples Republic of China, 1981.

PRINCIPAL TELEVISION WORK—Choreographer: *Ford 50th Anniversary Show*, 1953; *Peter Pan*, NBC, 1955, 1956, and 1960; also *Two Duets*, 1980; *Live from Studio 8H*, 1980.

PRINCIPAL FILM WORK—Choreographer, *The King and I*, Twentieth Century-Fox, 1956; choreographer and co-director, *West Side Story*, United Artists, 1961.

WRITINGS: PLAYS, PRODUCED—Book, *Look Ma, I'm Dancin'*, Adelphi Theatre, New York City, 1948.

AWARDS: Donaldson Award, 1946, for *Billion Dollar Baby;* New York Drama Critics Award, 1948, for *High Button Shoes;* Emmy Award, 1957, for *Peter Pan; Evening Standard* Award, 1959, for *West Side Story,* Best Director, Best Choreographer, Academy Award, 1961, for *West Side Story;* Chevalier de Arts Award, 1964; Best Choreographer, Best Director, Antoinette Perry Awards, 1966, for *Fiddler on the Roof;* Handel Medallion of the City of New York, 1976; Capezio Dance Award, 1976; American-Israel Arts, Sciences, and Humanities Award, 1979; Screen Directors Guild Award; Laurel Award; Sylvania Award; *Dance* Magazine Award; *Box Office* Blue Ribbon Award; City of Paris Award; Kennedy Center Honors Award, 1981; Creative Arts Award, Brandeis University, 1984; honorary degrees: D.F.A., Ohio University, 1974.

MEMBER: Actors' Equity Association, American Guild of Musical Artists, Directors Guild of America; New York State Council on the Arts, 1973-77; National Council of the Arts, 1974-79; Theatre Advisory Group of the Hopkins Center at Dartmouth College.

SIDELIGHTS: RECREATIONS—Photography.

ADDRESSES: OFFICE—New York City Ballet, New York State Theatre, Lincoln Center Plaza, New York, NY 10023.*

*   *   *

ROBERTS, Doris   1930-

PERSONAL: Born November 4, 1930, in St. Louis, MO; daughter of Ann Meltzer; married William Goyen (a novelist); children: Michael. EDUCATION: Attended New York University; trained for the stage at the Actors Studio with Lee Strasberg and at the Neighborhood Playhouse with Stanford Meisner.

VOCATION: Actress.

CAREER. BROADWAY DEBUT—Prostitute, *The Time of Your Life,* City Center, New York City, 1955. PRINCIPAL STAGE APPEARANCES—Miss Rumple, *The Desk Set,* Broadhurst Theatre, New York City, 1955; Nurse, *The Death of Bessie Smith* and Mommy, *The American Dream,* both at the York Playhouse, New York City, 1961, the latter revived at the Cherry Lane Theatre, New York City, 1971; *Color of Darkness* and *Cracks,* both at the Writers Stage Theatre, New York City, 1963; Rae Wilson, *Marathon '33,* American National Theatre and Academy (ANTA) Theatre, New York City, 1963; understudied Madame Girard and Eloisa, *Malcolm,* Shubert Theatre, New York City, 1966; Miss Punk, *The Office,* Henry Miller's Theatre, New York City, 1966; Edna, *The Natural Look,* Longacre Theatre, New York City, 1967; Jeanette Fisher, *Last of the Red Hot Lovers,* Eugene O'Neill Theatre, New York City, 1969.

May, *Felix,* Actors Studio, New York City, 1972; Miss Manley, *The Secret Affairs of Mildred Wild,* Ambassador Theatre, New York City, 1972; Dolly Scupp, "Ravenswood" and Becky Hedges, "Dunelawn," in the double bill *Bad Habits,* Astor Place Theatre, then Booth Theatre, New York City, 1974; Dede, *Ladies at the Alamo,* Actors Studio, New York City, 1975; Grace, *Cheaters,* Biltmore Theatre, New York City, 1978.

DORIS ROBERTS

MAJOR TOURS—Claudia, *The Opening,* U.S. cities, 1972; *Mornings at Seven,* U.S. cities, 1976.

PRINCIPAL FILM APPEARANCES—*No Way to Treat a Lady,* Paramount, 1968; *A Lovely Way to Die,* Universal, 1968; *The Honeymoon Killers,* Cinerama, 1970; *Such Good Friends,* Paramount, 1971; *Little Murders,* Twentieth Century-Fox, 1971; *A New Leaf,* Paramount, 1971; *The Taking of Pelham 1-2-3,* United Artists, 1974; *Hester Street,* Midwest, 1975; *The Rose,* Twentieth Century-Fox, 1979; also appeared in *Rabbit Test,* 1978; *Good Luck Miss Wykoff,* 1979; *An Ordinary Hero; Number One with a Bullet.*

TELEVISION DEBUT—1952. PRINCIPAL TELEVISION APPEARANCES—Series: Theresa Falco, *Angie,* ABC, 1979-80; Loretta, *Maggie,* ABC, 1981-82; Mildred Krebs, *Remington Steele,* NBC, 1983—. Episodic: *Soap,* ABC; *Barney Miller,* ABC; *Alice,* CBS; *Mary Hartman, Mary Hartman,* syndicated; *St. Elsewhere,* NBC.

Movies: *It Happened One Christmas,* 1977; *Ruby and Oswald* (also known as *Four Days in Dallas*), 1978; *Jennifer: A Woman's Story,* 1979; *Diary of Anne Frank,* 1980; *A Letter to Three Wives,* 1985; *California Girls,* 1985; also, *Three Little Pigs.*

AWARDS: Best Supporting Actress, Emmy Award, 1984, for "Cora and Arnie," St. Elsewhere; Best Supporting Actress, Emmy Award nomination, 1985, for *Remington Steele;* Outer Critics Circle Award; *Los Angeles* Weekly Award.

MEMBER: Actors' Equity Association, Screen Actors Guild, American Federation of Television and Radio Artists.

SIDELIGHTS: RECREATIONS—Painting, re-doing old furniture, and needlepoint.

ADDRESSES: AGENT—William Morris Agency, 151 El Camino Drive, Beverly Hills, CA 90212.*

*   *   *

ROBERTS, Julie   1966-

PERSONAL: Born Julie Deliso, November 20, 1966, in Huntington, NY; daughter of John Vincent (an accountant) and Marie Vincenza (a business manager in car sales; maiden name, Merolla) Deliso. EDUCATION: Trained for the theatre with Francesca DeSapio and at the Actors and Directors Lab, Actors Institute, the Weist Barron School, and the New York Academy of Theatrical Arts. RELIGION: Catholic.

VOCATION: Actress and dancer.

CAREER: PRINCIPAL STAGE APPEARANCES—*The Frankie Avalon Show,* 1981; dancer, *The Jerry Vale Show,* 1981; dancer, *Encore,* Hofstra University Theatre, 1984; dancer, *Dancin',* Hofstra University Theatre, 1985; dancer, *Cats,* Hofstra University Theatre, 1985.

PRINCIPAL FILM APPEARANCES—*Times Square,* Associated Film

JULIE ROBERTS

Distributors, 1980; Betsy, *Sleepaway Camp,* 1981; *Blow Out,* Filmways, 1981; *Heaven Help Us,* Tri-Star, 1985.

PRINCIPAL TELEVISION APPEARANCES—Episodic: Student, "High School Narc," *After School Special,* ABC, 1985; dancer, *Fame,* ABC, 1986; *Star Search,* NBC, 1986; *As the World Turns,* CBS, 1986-87.

NON-RELATED CAREER—Aerobic instructor, head of physical fitness group for three years.

MEMBER: Actors' Equity Association, Screen Actors Guild, American Federation of Television and Radio Artists.

SIDELIGHTS: Julie Roberts told *CTFT:* "I started dancing when I was five and I loved being in front of an audience. I went to see Liza Minnelli in *The Act* and knew then I wanted show business as a career. I love the theatre and that is what I want to do. I have lots of hobbies but the ones I do most are aerobics and bike riding."

ADDRESSES: HOME—754 Blue Ridge Drive, Medford, NY 11763. MANAGER—Michele Donay Talent, 236 E. 74th Street, New York, NY 10021.

*   *   *

ROBERTSON, Scott   1954-

PERSONAL: Born January 4, 1954, in Stamford, CT. EDUCATION: Attended Drake University, Des Moines, IA; trained for the stage at the O'Neill Theatre Center, Waterford, CT.

VOCATION: Actor.

CAREER: BROADWAY DEBUT—Roger, *Grease,* Royale Theatre. PRINCIPAL STAGE APPEARANCES—Title role, *Mayor, the Musical,* Latin Quarter, New York City, 1985; *It's Only a Play,* Manhattan Theatre Club, New York City, 1985; Gitelson, *The Rise of David Levinsky,* George Street Playhouse, New Brunswick, NJ, 1986. Also in New York City: Frankie, *Pageant,* Riverwest Theatre; *A Lady Needs a Change,* Manhattan Theatre Club; *Hang on to the Good Times,* City Center; *Secrets of the Lava Lamp,* Manhattan Theatre Club; *Not So New Faces of '82,* Westside Mainstage Theatre; *She Loves Me,* Playwright's Horizons; *A Backers' Audition,* Manhattan Theatre Club; *Scrambled Feet,* Village Gate.

Regional: Strouse, *Future of American Musical,* Music Society, MI; Quixote, *Man of La Mancha,* Westport, NY; Truffaldino, *Servant of Two Masters* and *Once in a Lifetime,* both Loretto-Hilton Theatre, St. Louis, MO; Robert, *Company,* Drake University Theatre; *Oh Coward!,* New Jersey Theatre Forum; *Marco Polo Sings a Solo,* Nantucket Stage Company; *Let 'Em Eat Cake,* Berkshire Theatre Festival.

MAJOR TOURS—Title role, *Tom Jones,* St. Louis Repertory Tour, U.S. cities; Herbie, *Godspell,* U.S. cities; *Annie,* U.S. cities, 1984.

PRINCIPAL FILM APPEARANCES—Executive, *Night Hawks,* Universal, 1981; *Zelig,* Warner Brothers, 1983; *Beauty and the Beast,* Cannon.

PRINCIPAL TELEVISION APPEARANCES—*Adam's Chronicles,* PBS; Ephram, *Search for Tomorrow,* CBS.

SCOTT ROBERTSON

ADDRESSES: HOME—New York, NY. AGENT—Ambrosio-Mortimer, 165 W. 46th Street, New York, NY 10036.

*   *   *

ROBERTSON, Toby   1928-

PERSONAL: Born November 29, 1928, in Chelsea, London, England; son of David Lambert and Felicity Douglas (Tomlin) Robertson; married Jane McCulloch. EDUCATION: Attended Stowe and Trinity College, Cambridge.

VOCATION: Director.

CAREER: PRINCIPAL STAGE WORK—*The Iceman Cometh,* New Shakespeare Theatre, Liverpool, U.K., 1958; director of London productions of *The Buskers,* 1959, *The Lower Depths,* by the Royal Shakespeare Company, 1960, *Pitlochry,* 1962, *Henry IV* (by Luigi Pirandello) and *Muir of Huntershill,* both 1963, *The Provok'd Wife,* also in Richmond and Yorkshire, U.K., 1964.

As artistic director for the Prospect Theatre Company, London, director of: *The Soldier's Fortune, You Never Can Tell, The Confederacy,* and *The Importance of Being Earnest,* 1964; *The Square, Howard's End,* and *The Man of Mode,* 1965; *Macbeth, The Tempest,* and *The Gamecock,* 1966; *A Murder of No Importance,* 1967; *A Room with a View,* also produced at the Edinburgh Festival, Scotland, 1967; *Edward II, The Servant of Two Masters, Twelfth*

Night, and *No Man's Land,* 1968; *The Beggar's Opera,* also produced in Edinburgh, 1968; *Edward II,* Edinburgh Festival, Scotland, 1969; *Venice Preserved* and *Much Ado about Nothing* and *Boswell's Life of Johnson,* both also produced in Edinburgh, 1970; *King Lear* and *Love's Labour's Lost,* both produced in Edinburgh, and London, 1971; *Alice in Wonderland,* Ashcroft Theatre, Croydon, U.K., 1971; *Richard III* and *Ivanov,* London productions, 1972; *The Beggars' Opera,* for the Phoenix Opera Company, AZ, 1972; *The Grand Tour, Pericles, The Royal Hunt of the Sun,* and *Twelfth Night,* London productions, 1973; *The Pilgrim's Progress* and *A Month in the Country,* Chichester Festival, U.K., 1975; *Circle of Glory, Pilgrim,* and co-director, *A Room with a View,* London productions, 1975.

For the Prospect Theatre Company, Old Vic Theatre, London, *War Music, Hamlet, Buster,* and *Antony and Cleopatra,* 1977; *Twelfth Night, Great English Eccentrics, Ivanov,* and *King Lear,* 1978; *Hamlet, Romeo and Juliet, The Government Inspector, The Padlock,* and *The Trial of Queen Caroline,* 1979; *Hamlet,* Elsinore Castle, Denmark, 1979; *Next Time I'll Sing to You,* London production, 1980; *Night and Day,* Huntington Theatre Company, Boston, MA, 1982; *Pericles,* American Place Theatre, New York City, 1983; with the Cleveland Playhouse, OH, 1983-84; *Love's Labour's Lost,* Circle Repertory Company, New York City, 1984.

Operas: *A Midsummer Night's Dream,* 1972; *Hermiston,* for the Scottish Opera Company, 1975; *The Marriage of Figaro,* for the Scottish Opera Company, 1977.

MAJOR TOURS—Director: *King Lear* and *Love's Labor's Lost,* Australian cities, 1971; *Pericles, Twelfth Night* and *The Royal Hunt of the Sun,* Moscow, Leningrad, and Hong Kong, 1973; *Great English Eccentrics,* Moscow, Hong Kong, and Australian cities; *Hamlet,* cities in the Republic of China, 1979.

PRINCIPAL FILM WORK—Assistant director, *Lord of the Flies,* Continental, 1963.

PRINCIPAL TELEVISION WORK—Director of over twenty-five productions including: *The Beggar's Opera, Richard II,* and *Edward II.*

RELATED CAREER—Formerly an actor.

AWARDS: Wilson Memorial Lecture Award, Cambridge University, 1974.

MEMBER: Bunbury Club.

SIDELIGHTS: RECREATIONS—Painting and sailing.

ADDRESSES: OFFICE—Five Spencer Park, London SW18, England.*

*   *   *

ROBINSON, Dar   1948-1986

PERSONAL: Born 1948, in Los Angeles, CA; died while filming a stunt sixty-five miles north of Page Arizona, November 21, 1986.

VOCATION: Stuntman and actor.

CAREER: PRINCIPAL FILM APPEARANCES—As stuntman and actor, *Sharkey's Machine,* Warner Brothers, 1981; *Turk 182!,* Twentieth Century-Fox, 1985; *Stick,* Universal, 1985. Robinson died while filming a stunt for the film *Million Dollar Industry,* upcoming.

PRINCIPAL TELEVISON APPEARANCES—Series: *That's Incredible,* ABC. Guest: *The Tonight Show,* NBC.

SIDELIGHTS: Dar Robinson was a record-holding stuntman who once did a free fall from Toronto's nine-hundred foot CN tower with a wire cable that stopped him only two-hundred feet from the ground. He also accomplished a leap from atop the Houston Astrodome, and a two-hundred eighty-six foot jump from a helicopter. He was considered by many to be the world's best stuntman.*

*　　　*　　　*

ROBINSON, Patrick　1963-

PERSONAL: Born November 6, 1963, in London, England; son of Lenval Augustus (an electrician) and Gloria Jean (Downe) Robinson. EDUCATION: South East London College, technical diploma, 1981; studied acting for three years at the London Academy of Music and Dramatic Art.

VOCATION: Actor.

CAREER: STAGE DEBUT—Policeman, *Romeo & Juliet,* Royal Shakespeare Company, Stratford-on-Avon, England, 1986. PRINCIPAL STAGE APPEARANCES—Pastoral servant and Lord, *The Winters Tale,* Royal Shakespeare Company, Stratford-on-Avon, 1986; Biskey, *The Rover,* Royal Shakespeare Company, Swan Theatre, 1986; Seyton, *Macbeth,* Royal Shakespeare Company, 1986.

MEMBER: British Actors' Equity Association.

ADDRESSES: HOME—29 Deloraine House, Tanners Hill, Deptford, London SE8 4PY, England. AGENT—Kate Feast Management, 43A Princess Road, Regents Park, London NW1, England.

*　　　*　　　*

ROGERS, Melody

PERSONAL: Born in Kentucky. EDUCATION: Attended Northwestern University; trained for the stage at the Actors Studio with Lee Strasberg and studied piano at the Chicago Conservatory of Music.

VOCATION: Actress, dancer, and television hostess.

CAREER: STAGE DEBUT—*Showboat.* PRINCIPAL STAGE APPEARANCES—*Coco,* Broadway production; title role, *Hedda Gabler;* Sheila, *A Chorus Line,* Los Angeles, 1977; also appeared in a

PATRICK ROBINSON

MELODY ROGERS

concert version of *Damn Yankees* as Lola, 1985; *Scorchers*, Whitefire Theatre, Sherman Oaks, CA, 1986.

PRINCIPAL TELEVISION APPEARANCES—Weather reporter, WBBM, CBS affiliate, Chicago; host, *Two on the Town*, KCBS, Los Angeles, 1980—. Episodic: *Buck Rogers in the 25th Century*, NBC; *Nobody's Perfect*, ABC, 1980.

AWARDS: Four Emmy Awards, for *Two on the Town*.

ADDRESSES: PUBLICIST—Jo-Ann Geffen and Associates, 3151 Cahuenga Blvd. West, Suite 235, Los Angeles, CA 90068.

* * *

ROMANO, John 1948-

PERSONAL: Born October 2, 1948, in Newark, NJ; son of John and Mildred Romano; married Nancy Forbes (a writer), May 22, 1977; children: Clarissa, Juliana. EDUCATION: Colgate University, A.B., 1970; Yale University, Ph.D., 1975.

VOCATION: Writer.

CAREER: PRINCIPAL TELEVISION WORK—Writer, executive story editor, *Hill Street Blues*, NBC, 1986-87.

RELATED CAREER—Assistant professor of English, Columbia University, New York City, 1975-81; book reviewer, *New York Times Sunday Book Review*, 1975-83.

WRITINGS: SCREENPLAYS—*Key Exchange*, Twentieth Century-Fox, 1984; *Trail of the Fox*, Orion, 1987.

ADDRESSES: AGENT—c/o Jim Berkus, Leading Artists, 445 N. Bedford Drive, Beverly Hills, CA 90210.

* * *

ROSE, George 1920-

PERSONAL: Full name, George Walter Rose; born February 19, 1920, in Bicester, England; son of Walter John Alfred (a butcher) and Eva Sarah (Rolfe) Rose. EDUCATION: Attended private schools and Oxford High School in the United Kingdom; trained for the stage at the Central School of Speech and Drama; studied with Gwynneth Thurburn and Audrey Bullard.

VOCATION: Actor.

CAREER: LONDON DEBUT—*Peer Gynt*, Old Vic Company, New Theatre, 1944. BROADWAY DEBUT—Peto, *Henry IV, Part I*, Century Theatre, 1946. PRINCIPAL STAGE APPEARANCES—With the Old Vic Company, at the New Theatre, London: Peto, *Henry IV, Part I*, Thomas, Duke of Clarence, Lord Bardolph, and Mouldy, *Henry IV, Part II*, Sir Christopher Hatton, *The Critic*, and appeared in the chorus of *Oedipus Rex*, all 1945; the Duke of Burgundy and a captain, *King Lear*, and Montfleury, *Cyrano de Bergerac*, both 1946; Kastril, *The Alchemist*, the Duke of Surrey and Keeper, *Richard II*, Lucentio, *The Taming of the Shrew*, and an English Soldier, *Saint Joan*, all 1947; Zemlyanika, *The Government Inspector*, and a Roman herald, *Coriolanus*, both 1948.

Dickie Miles, *People Like Us*, Wyndham's Theatre, London, 1948; Tiresias, *Oedipus Rex*, and George, *Peace Comes to Peckham*, both with the High Wycombe Repertory Company at the High Wycombe Repertory Theatre, U.K., 1948; appeared in the revue, *1066 and All That*, with the Royal Artillery Repertory Company, at the Royal Artillery Theatre, Woolwich, U.K., 1948.

With the Royal Shakespeare Company, at the Memorial Theatre, Stratford-on-Avon: Lennox, *Macbeth*, Snug, *A Midsummer Night's Dream*, Dogberry, *Much Ado About Nothing*, Belarius, *Cymbeline*, Brabantio, *Othello*, first gentleman, *Henry VIII*, Pompey, *Measure for Measure*, and Oswald, *King Lear*, all 1949-50.

Harry, *Nothing Up My Sleeve*, Watergate Theatre, London, 1950; William Humpage, *A Penny for a Song*, Haymarket Theatre, London, 1951; Autolycus, *The Winter's Tale*, Phoenix Theatre, London, 1951; Dogberry, *Much Ado About Nothing*, Phoenix Theatre, London, 1952; Sailor Johnston, *The Square Ring*, Lyric Theatre, Hammersmith, London, 1952; Boanerges, *The Apple Cart*, Haymarket Theatre, London, 1953; Nils Krogstad, *A Doll's House*, Lyric Theatre, Hammersmith, London, 1953; Jules, *My Three Angels*, Royal Theatre, Brighton, then Lyric Theatre, Hammersmith, London, 1955; Maitland, *The Chalk Garden*, Haymarket Theatre, London, 1956; *Living for Pleasure*, Garrick Theatre, London, 1958; Magistrate, *The Trial of Cob and Leach*, Royal Court Theatre, London, 1959; Dogberry, *Much Ado About Nothing*, Cambridge Drama Festival, Cambridge, MA, then Lunt-Fontanne Theatre, New York City, 1959; Burgomaster, *The Visit*, Royalty Theatre, London, 1960; Creon, *Antigone*, Magistrate, *The Trial of Cob and Leach*, both under the title, "Trials by Logue," Royal Court Theatre, London, 1960.

Common Man, *A Man for All Seasons* and *On the Avenue*, both Globe Theatre, London, 1961; Common Man, *A Man for All Seasons*, American National Theatre Academy (ANTA) Theatre, New York City, 1961; First Grave Digger, *Hamlet*, Lunt-Fontanne Theatre, New York City, 1964; Glas, *Slow Dance on the Killing Ground*, Plymouth Theatre, New York City, 1964; Martin Ruiz, *The Royal Hunt of the Sun*, ANTA Theatre, New York City, 1965; Henry Horatio Hobson, *Walking Happy*, Lunt-Fontanne Theatre, New York City, 1966; Truscott, *Loot*, Biltmore Theatre, New York City, 1968; Alfred P. Doolittle, *My Fair Lady*, City Center, New York City, 1968; Mr. Peachum, *The Threepenny Opera*, Mankato University, 1968; Reverend Leslie Rankin, *Captain Brassbound's Conversion*, Ahmanson Theatre, Los Angeles, 1968; Steward, Carpenter, and January, *Canterbury Tales*, Eugene O'Neill Theatre, New York City, 1969; Louis Greff, *Coco*, Mark Hellinger Theatre, New York City, 1969.

Mr. Booker, *Wise Child*, Helen Hayes Theatre, New York City, 1972; Andrew Wyke, *Sleuth*, Music Box Theatre, New York City, 1973; Henry, *My Fat Friend*, Brooks Atkinson Theatre, New York City, 1974; Alfred P. Doolittle, *My Fair Lady*, St. James Theatre, New York City, 1976; Mr. Maraczek, *She Loves Me*, Town Hall Theatre, New York City, 1977; General Burgoyne, *The Devil's Disciple*, Almady, *The Play's the Thing*, and title role, *Julius Caesar*, all with the Brooklyn Academy of Music Theatre Company, NY, 1978; Hawkins, *The Kingfisher*, Biltmore Theatre, New York City, 1978; Mr. Darling and Captain Hook, *Peter Pan*, Lunt-Fontanne Theatre, New York City, 1979; Major General Stanley, *The Pirates of Penzance*, New York Shakespeare Festival (NYSF), Delacorte Theatre, New York City, 1980, then Uris Theatre, New York City, 1981; appeared in *Hey, Look Me Over!*, Avery Fisher Hall, Lincoln Center, New York City, 1981; Boris Kolenkhov, *You Can't Take It with You*, Plymouth Theatre, New York City, 1983;

Dr. Josef Winkler, *Dance a Little Closer*, Minskoff Theatre, New York City, 1983; Stephen Frauldgate, *Beethoven's Tenth*, Nederlander Theatre, New York City, 1984; *Die Fledermaus*, San Francisco Opera Company, 1984; Reverend Ernest Lynton, *Aren't We All?*, Brooks Atkinson Theatre, New York City, 1985; Baron Von Epp, *A Patriot for Me*, Ahmanson Theatre, Los Angeles, 1985; appeared in *Side by Side by Sondheim*, Papermill Playhouse, Milburn, NJ, 1985; Mayor Thomas Sapsea/Chairman, Mr. William Cartwright, *The Mystery of Edwin Drood*, NYSF, Delacorte Theatre, then Imperial Theatre, New York City, 1985-86.

MAJOR TOURS—U.S. cities: Common man, *A Man for All Seasons*, 1961; Louis Greff, *Coco*, 1971; Andrew Wyke, *Sleuth*, 1972; Lutz, *The Student Prince*, 1973; Henry, *My Fat Friend*, 1975.

FILM DEBUT—Coachman, *The Pickwick Papers*, Kingsley, 1952. PRINCIPAL FILM APPEARANCES—*The Square Ring*, Rank, 1953; *The Wicked Wife*, Allied Artists, 1955; *The Sea Shall Not Have Them*, United Artists, 1955; *The Shiralee*, Rank, 1955; *Barnacle Bill*, Metro-Goldwyn-Mayer (MGM), 1956; *Panic in the Parlor*, DCA, 1956; *The Third Key*, Rank, 1957; *A Tale of Two Cities*, Rank, 1958; *The Good Companions*, Stratford, 1958; *A Night to Remember*, Lopert, 1958; *The Devil's Disciple*, United Artists, 1959; *The Heart of a Man*, Rank, 1959; *Jack the Ripper*, Paramount, 1960; *No Love for Johnnie*, Embassy, 1961; *Hawaii*, United Artists, 1966; *A New Leaf*, Paramount, 1971; *From the Mixed-Up Files of Mrs. Basil E. Frankweiler*, Cinema V, 1973.

PRINCIPAL TELEVISION APPEARANCES—Series: Mr. Hacker, *Beacon Hill*, CBS, 1975. Mini-Series: *Holocaust*. Episodic: appeared on *Stage 2*, CBS, 1964. Dramatic Specials: Noah, *Before the Flood*, BBC, 1951; the sergeant, *The Face of Love*, ATV, 1954; the tax inspector, *Both Ends Meet*, ATV, 1955; Trock, *Winterset*, ATV, 1957; the prisoner, "The Dock Brief" and the husband, "What Shall We Tell Caroline?," both on *Play of the Week*, WNTA, 1959; the magistrate, "Oliver Twist," *DuPont Show of the Month*, NBC, 1959; George, "The Fifth Column," *Buick Electra Playhouse*, CBS, 1960; Owen, "The Citadel," *DuPont Show of the Month*, NBC, 1960; Ben Gunn, "Treasure Island," *DuPont Show of the Month*, NBC, 1960; Drinkwater, "Captain Brassbound's Conversion," *Hallmark Hall of Fame*, NBC, 1960; Ericson, *The Family First*, ATV, 1960; Salinas, *Top Secret*, ARTV, 1961; Raguneau, "Cyrano de Bergerac," *Hallmark Hall of Fame*, NBC, 1962; Doolittle, "Pygmalion," *Hallmark Hall of Fame*, NBC, 1963; appeared in "Eagle in a Cage," *Hallmark Hall of Fame*, NBC, 1965.

RELATED CAREER—Artist in residence, Mankato University, 1968.

AWARDS: Best Supporting Actor in a Musical, Antoinette Perry Award nomination, 1969, for *Coco*; Outstanding Performance, Drama Desk Award, Best Supporting Actor, Antoinette Perry Award nomination, both 1974, for *My Fat Friend*; Antoinette Perry Award, Drama Desk Award, 1976, both for *My Fair Lady*; Outstanding Featured Actor in a Play, Drama Desk Award, 1979, for *The Kingfisher*; Antoinette Perry Award nomination, 1981, for *Pirates of Penzance*; Best Actor in a Musical, Antoinette Perry Award, 1986, for *The Mystery of Edwin Drood*.

MEMBER: Actors' Equity Association, British Actors' Equity Association, American Federation of Television and Radio Artists.

SIDELIGHTS: RECREATIONS—Collecting gramophone records, reading, photography, and cats.

ADDRESSES: AGENT—International Creative Management, 40 W. 57th Street, New York, NY 10019.*

*   *   *

ROSE, Maxine   1928-

PERSONAL: Born Maxine Bercholz, June 6, 1928, in New York, NY; daughter of Benjamin and Claire (Berler) Bercholz; children: Leonard, Lewis. EDUCATION: Studied at the American Academy of Dramatic Arts, New York City and at the Stella Adler Studios.

VOCATION: Actress, producer, and writer.

CAREER: PRINCIPAL STAGE APPEARANCES—Performed with the Gold Coast Players, FL, and at the Tamarac Art Theatre, Oakland West Dinner Theatre, Marco Polo Dinner Theatre, Sea Ranch Dinner Theatre, and Viking Dinner Theatre.

PRINCIPAL STAGE WORK—Co-founder and director, Professional Actor's Workshop, Boca FL.

PRINCIPAL FILM APPEARANCES—*Hot Stuff*, Columbia, 1979; *Harry and Son*, Orion, 1984.

PRINCIPAL TELEVISION APPEARANCES—Pilots: *Matchmaker*; *Green Card*. Special: *The Great Voice*, Channel 2.

Photography by Scott Singer

MAXINE ROSE

PRINCIPAL TELEVISION WORK—Producer of talk shows for WKAT, Miami, and WCKO, Ft. Lauderdale, FL.

RELATED CAREER—Instructor, Broward Community College; public speaker. Performs voice-over work for Insight for the Blind.

WRITINGS: BOOKS—Success Formula for Aspiring Models; How to Be a Winner in the Game of Life.

ARTICLES—In the following magazines: "Real Estate Pictorial," "International Backgammon," "Gold Coast Journal," "Lifestyles," "Western News," "Fiesta," "Living," "Town Topics," "Singles," "Midnite Sun."

ADDRESSES: HOME—4121 N.W. 26th Street, Townhouse 14, Lauderhill, FL 33313.

*   *   *

ROSS, Stuart   1950-

PERSONAL: Born September 10, 1950; son of George Z. (a lawyer) and Mae E. (a secretary; maiden name, Folb) Ross. EDUCATION: Clark University, B.A., 1972; University of Manchester, England, 1973; trained as a director at the Circle in the Square Theatre School with Nikos Psacharopoulos.

VOCATION: Director and writer.

CAREER: FIRST OFF-BROADWAY STAGE WORK—Director, *The Knight of the Twelve Saucers,* Playwrights Horizons, 1976, for six performances. PRINCIPAL STAGE WORK—Writer and director, *The Heebie Jeebes,* Westside Arts Theatre, New York City and Berkshire Theatre Festival, MA, 1981; writer and director, *Not-So-New Faces,* O'Neals Upstairs Theatre, New York City, 1982, 1983, 1984; director, *Sharing,* Equity Library Theatre and No Smoking Playhouse, New York City, 1983; director, *Lunch Girls,* Courtyard Playhouse, New York City, 1984; writer and director, *Hollywood Opera,* The Ballroom, New York City, 1985; director, *Secrets of the Lava Lamp,* Manhattan Theatre Club, Upstage Theatre, New York City, 1985; writer and director, *Creeps,* New York City, 1985, 1986, 1987.

WRITINGS: PLAYS, PRODUCED—*The Heebie Jeebes,* Westside Arts Theatre, New York City and Berkshire Theatre Festival, 1981; *Not-So-New Faces,* O'Neals Upstairs Theatre, New York City, 1982, 1983, 1984; *Creeps,* New York City, 1985, 1986, 1987; *Fun with Dick and Jane,* Playwrights Horizons, New York City, 1987; *Starmites,* Music Theatre Works, New York City, 1987.

AWARDS: U.S. State Department grant, 1978.

MEMBER: Society of Stage Directors and Choreographers, Dramatist's Guild.

ADDRESSES: HOME—484 W. 43rd Street, Apt. 35T, New York, NY 10036.

*   *   *

ROTH, Ann

VOCATION: Costume designer.

CAREER: FIRST OFF-BROADWAY STAGE WORK—Costume designer, *Maybe Tuesday,* Playhouse Theatre, 1958. PRINCIPAL STAGE WORK—(All New York City, except where noted otherwise) *Edward II, Make a Million, The Disenchanted,* 1958; *A Desert Incident,* 1959; *The Cool World, Gay Divorce, Ernest in Love, Face of a Hero,* 1960; *A Far Country, Purlie Victorious, Look, We've Come Through,* 1961; *This Side of Paradise, Isle of Children, Venus at Large, A Portrait of the Artist as a Young Man, The Barroom Monks,* 1962; *Natural Affection, Hey You, Light Man!, Children from Their Games, A Case of Libel,* 1963; *In the Summer House, The Last Analysis, Slow Dance on the Killing Ground, I Had a Ball,* 1964; *The Odd Couple, Romeo and Juliet, The Impossible Years,* 1965; *The Wayward Stork, The Star-Spangled Girl,* 1966; *The Deer Park, The Beard, Something Different,* 1967; *Happiness Is Just a Little Thing Called a Rolls Royce,* 1968; *Play It Again Sam, My Daughter, Your Son, Tiny Alice, The Three Sisters,* 1969; *Gantry, Purlie, What the Butler Saw, The Engagement Baby,* 1970; *Father's Day,* 1971; *Prettybelle,* Boston, 1971; *Fun City, Rosebloom, Twelfth Night, Children! Children!, 6 Rms Riv Vu, Enemies, Purlie,* 1972; *The Merchant of Venice, Seesaw, The Women,* 1973; *The Royal Family,* 1975; *The Heiress,* 1976.

The Importance of Being Earnest, Circle in the Square, New York City, 1977; *Do You Turn Somersaults,* 46th Street Theatre, New York City, 1978; *The Best Little Whorehouse in Texas,* Entermedia Theatre, New York City, 1978; *The Crucifer of Blood,* Helen Hayes Theatre, New York City, 1978; *First Monday in October,* Majestic Theatre, New York City, 1978; *They're Playing Our Song,* Imperial Theatre, New York City, 1979; *Strangers,* John Golden Theatre, New York City, 1979.

Lunch Hour, Ethel Barrymore Theatre, New York City, 1980; designed costumes with the Hartman Theatre Company, Stamford, CT, 1981; *Gardenia,* Manhattan Theatre Club, New York City, 1982; *Kaufman at Large,* with the Phoenix Theatre at the Marymount Manhattan Theatre, New York City, 1982; designed costumes for the Long Wharf Theatre, New Haven, CT, 1982; *Present Laughter,* Circle in the Square, New York City, 1982; *The Misanthrope,* Circle in the Square Theatre, New York City, 1983; *Yankee Wives,* Old Globe Theatre, San Diego, CA, 1983; *Open Admissions,* Music Box Theatre, New York City, 1984; *Hurlyburly,* Goodman Theatre, Chicago, then Ethel Barrymore Theatre, New York City, 1984; *Design for Living,* Circle in the Square Theatre, New York City, 1984; *Biloxi Blues,* Ahmanson Theatre, Los Angeles, 1984, then Neil Simon Theatre, New York City, 1985; *Arms and the Man,* Circle in the Square, New York City, 1985; *Juno's Swans,* Second Stage Theatre, New York City, 1985.

Designed decor for *We Comrades Three,* New York City, 1962; also designed costumes for: The American Conservatory Theatre, San Francisco, CA; the Kennedy Center, Washington, DC; American Ballet Theatre; American Shakespeare Festival, Stratford, CT; San Francisco Opera Company.

PRINCIPAL FILM WORK—Costume designer: *Up the Down Staircase,* Warner Brothers/Seven Arts, 1967; *Pretty Poison,* Twentieth Century-Fox, 1968; *Midnight Cowboy,* United Artists, 1969; *The Owl and the Pussycat,* Columbia, 1970; *Klute,* Warner Brothers, 1971; *The Pursuit of Happiness,* Columbia, 1971; *They Might Be Giants,* Universal, 1971; *The Valachi Papers,* 1972; *Murder by Death,* 1976; *California Suite,* Columbia, 1978; *Hair,* United Artists, 1979; *The Island,* Universal, 1980; *Honky Tonk Freeway,* Universal, 1981; *Only When I Laugh,* Columbia, 1981; *Rollover,* Warner Brothers, 1981; *The World According to Garp,* Warner Brothers, 1982.

MEMBER: United Scenic Artists Union, Local 829.

ADDRESSES: OFFICE—United Scenic Artists Union, Local 829, AFL-CIO, 575 Eighth Avenue, New York, NY 10018.*

*   *   *

ROTH, Michael S.   1954-

PERSONAL: Born July 23, 1954, in Brooklyn, NY; son of William (a lawyer) and Sophie (Shub) Roth. EDUCATION: University of Michigan, B.A., music and theatre, cum laude, 1975; studied musical composition with William Bolcom.

VOCATION: Composer and musical director.

CAREER: PRINCIPAL STAGE WORK—Music director and orchestrator: *Maybe I'm Doing It Wrong: The Songs of Randy Newman,* Roxy Theatre, Los Angeles, La Jolla Playhouse, CA, and Astor Place Theatre, New York City, 1984; *Big River,* American Repertory Theatre, Cambridge, MA, 1984.

RELATED CAREER—Composer-in-residence, La Jolla Playhouse; guest lecturer, Stanford University, 1985, University of California at San Diego, 1986.

WRITINGS: PRINCIPAL COMPOSITION WORK—*The Dybbuk,* Impossible Ragtime Theatre, New York City, 1977; *Dynamite Tonight,* two piano adaptation of an opera by William Bolcom, 1980; *Theme for a Futuristic Movie,* piano composition, Windham Hill Records, 1980; *Rag for Five Instruments,* commissioned chamber composition, Spectrum Ensemble, New York City, 1981; (co-composer) *Hopi Prophecies,* opera, West Bank Cafe, New York City, 1983; *No End to Stand On,* commissioned chamber composition, New York Quintet, Merkin Hall, New York City, 1983; *The Visions of Simone Machard,* La Jolla Playhouse, 1983; *As You Like It,* La Jolla Playhouse, 1984; *Ghost on Fire* and *The Seagull,* both at the La Jolla Playhouse, 1985; *Streich,* commissioned flute quartet, Carnegie Recital Hall, New York City, Atheneum Theatre, La Jolla, 1986; composer and sound designer, *Cleveland,* BACA Gallery, Brooklyn, NY, 1986; composer and sound designer, *1951,* for the University of California at San Diego at the Perry Street Theatre, New York City, both 1986; composer and sound designer, *The Three Cuckolds,* La Jolla Playhouse, Bill Irwin performer.

Works-in-progress: "Fats," composition for piano; "Accidental Requiem," chamber compostion brass quintet with tape loop; "Imagination Dead Imagine," chamber composition to text by Samuel Beckett.

AWARDS: Best Orchestration Award, Los Angeles Critic's Circle, 1984, for *Maybe I'm Doing It Wrong: The Songs of Randy Newman;* several American Society of Composers, Authors and Publishers (ASCAP) awards.

MEMBER: American Society of Composers, Authors and Publishers, Dramatists Guild, American Music Center.

ADDRESSES: HOME—248 W. 105th Street, New York, NY 10025; 388 Nautilus Street, La Jolla, CA 92037.

ROTHMAN, John   1949-

PERSONAL: Born June 3, 1949, in Baltimore, MD; son of Donald N. (a lawyer) and Elizabeth D. (Davidson) Rothman: married Susan Bolotin (a writer and editor), May 30, 1983; children: Lily. EDUCATION: Wesleyan University, B.A.; Yale School of Drama, M.F.A.; trained for the stage with Michael Howard. RELIGION: Jewish.

VOCATION: Actor and writer.

CAREER: STAGE DEBUT—Tom Hogan, *Trial of the Cantonsville Nine,* Center Stage, Baltimore, MD, 1972. BROADWAY DEBUT—Martin, *Social Security,* Barrymore Theatre, 1986. PRINCIPAL STAGE APPEARANCES—Off-Broadway: Title role, *The Impossible H.L. Mencken,* American Place Theatre, *Rats Nest,* VanDam Theatre; *The Italian Straw Hat,* Manhattan Punchline; *The Hotel Play,* La Mama Experimental Theatre Club (E.T.C.); *The Buddy System,* Circle in the Square Downtown; *The Modern Ladies,* Marathon '83 Festival, Ensemble Studio Theatre; *Becoming Memories,* McCann-Nugent Workshop Theatre.

Regional: Demitry, *Idiots Karamazov, The Possessed,* and *Happy End,* all Yale Repertory Theatre, New Haven, CT; Ernest Wooley, *Admirable Crichton,* Long Wharf Theatre, New Haven, CT; *The Beaux Stratagem,* Center Stage, Baltimore; *Engame,* Williamstown Theatre Festival, MA; *Beauty and the Beast,* PAF Playhouse, Long Island, NY; *A Midsummer Night's Dream,* Kenyon Festival Theatre, Columbus, OH; *The Importance of Being Earnest,* American Stage Festival.

FILM DEBUT—Jack Abel, *Stardust Memories,* United Artists, 1979. PRINCIPAL FILM APPEARANCES—*Sophie's Choice,* Universal, 1982; head librarian, *Ghostbusters,* Columbia, 1984; lawyer, *Purple Rose of Cairo,* Orion, 1985.

TELEVISION DEBUT—Dr. Francis Mitchell, *Nurse,* CBS, 1982. PRINCIPAL TELEVISION APPEARANCES—*Landscape with Waitress,* PBS; *How to Be a Perfect Person in Just Three Days,* PBS; *Tales from the Dark Side; Ryan's Hope.*

WRITINGS: PLAYS, PRODUCED—*The Impossible H.L. Mencken,* American Place Theatre, New York City.

ADDRESSES: HOME—28 E. Tenth Street, New York, NY 10003. AGENT—STE Representation, 888 Seventh Avenue, New York, NY 10106.

*   *   *

ROVEN, Glen   1958-

PERSONAL: Born July 13, 1958. EDUCATION: Attended Columbia University.

VOCATION: Composer and musical director.

CAREER: FIRST BROADWAY WORK—Musical director, *Sugar Babies,* Mark Hellenger Theatre, 1979-83, for eleven hundred performances. PRINCIPAL STAGE WORK—New York City productions: Rehearsal pianist, *Pippin,* 1976; musical director, *Let My People Come,* 1976; musical director, *Joseph and the Amazing Technicolor Dreamcoat,* 1978.

MAJOR TOUR WORK—Musical arranger, *Woman of the Year*, national, 1984.

PRINCIPAL TELEVISION WORK—Musical director, *Flora the Red Menace*, CBS, 1978; musical co-ordinator, *Leonard Bernstein, an Appreciation*, PBS, 1978; musical director, *Kennedy Center Honors*, CBS, 1982.

WRITINGS: COMPOSITIONS, PLAYS—*Meeting by the River*, 1977; *Lydia Breeze*, 1981; *Gardenia*, 1981; *Gotta Getaway*, 1983; *A. . .My Name Is Alice*, 1983.

COMPOSITIONS, TELEVISION—*We Interrupt This Week*, PBS, 1978; *Best of Everything*, 1984; *Antoinette Perry Award Show*, 1985; *Night of 100 Stars II*, 1985; *Placido Domingo Special*, 1985; *Antoinette Perry Award Show*, 1985; *Emmy Award Show*, 1985; *NBC 60th Anniversary Special*, 1986; *Antoinette Perry Award Show*, 1986; *Emmy Award Show*, 1986.

COMPOSITIONS, FILMS—*Cop and the Anthem*, HBO, 1981; *Different Twist*, Scholastic, 1982; *Exchange Student*, Scholastic, 1984.

AWARDS: Emmy Award nomination, 1985, for *Night of 100 Stars II;* Emmy Award, 1986, for *Antoinette Perry Award Show*.

MEMBER: American Society of Composers, Authors, and Publishers, National Academy of Recording Arts and Sciences, Dramatists Guild, Academy of Television Arts and Sciences.

ADDRESSES: OFFICE—2166 Broadway, New York, NY 10024.

* * *

ROWE, Dee Etta   1953-

PERSONAL: Born January 29, 1953, in Lewiston, ME; daughter of Harry Alvan (an officer in the U.S. Air Force) and Elinor Ilene (a professional dancer and owner of a beauty salon; maiden name, Flagg) Rowe. EDUCATION: Hartt College of Music, University of Hartford, B. Music, opera, 1975; studied voice with Pamela Kucenic, assistant to Ellen Faull; studied acting with Alan Savage.

VOCATION: Actress and singer.

CAREER: STAGE DEBUT—Neighbor lady and understudy Cleo, *The Most Happy Fella* (revival), Majestic Theatre, New York City 1979. PRINCIPAL STAGE APPEARANCES—Evie, *Stop the World, I Want to Get Off*, Marion Players, MA; Nancy, *Oliver!*, Falmouth Theatre, MA; Nettie Fowler, *Carousel*, Beef n' Boards Dinner Theatre, IN; Frau Schmidt, *The Sound of Music*, Northstage Theatre, Long Island, NY; Hattie, *Kiss Me, Kate*, An Evening Dinner Theatre, NY; Millie, *Good News*, Beef n' Boards Dinner Theatre, KY; Olga von Sturm and understudy Mama Maddelena, *Nine*, 46th Street Theatre, New York City; Mama Maddelena, *Nine*, An Evening Dinner Theatre, NY.

MAJOR TOURS—Mother Abbess, *The Sound of Music*, bus and truck; Mrs. O'Brian, *Showboat*, Wolftrap Farm Park, Arlington, VA, and national; ensemble, *Sweeney Todd*, national; Lulu, *The*

DEE ETTA ROWE

Jumping Frog of Calaveras County, with the Hartford Symphony at the Bushnell Auditorium, Atlantic City, NJ.

PRINCIPAL OPERA APPEARANCES—With the Hartt Opera Theatre, CT: Constanza, *The Abduction from the Seraglio;* Eurydice, *Orpheus in the Underworld;* Musetta, *La Boheme;* Anne Trulove, *The Rake's Progress;* title role, *Carmen*.

Miss Pinkerton, *The Old Maid and the Thief*, Greater Hartford Civic Arts Festival; High Priestess, *Aida* and Curra, *La Forza Del Destino*, both Connecticut Opera Association; Mrs. Splinters, *The Tender Land*, Encompass Theatre, New York City; soloist, *The Creation*, Chatham Chorale, Cape Cod, MA; Gabriel (soloist), *The Seven Last Words of Christ*, Bethany Covenant Church, CT.

PRINCIPAL TELEVISION APPEARANCES—*Sweeney Todd*, cable; *The Most Happy Fella*, with the Michigan Opera Theatre on PBS.

RELATED CAREER—Teacher of musical theatre, American Musical and Dramatic Academy, 1976—.

AWARDS: Music Award, Cape Cod Conseveratory, 1970; Yorkin Music Award, Hartt College of Music, 1971-72; Royal Dadmund Vocal Award, Hartt College of Music, 1972; Citation of Recognition, Hartt College, 1985.

MEMBER: Actors' Equity Association.

ADDRESSES: HOME—134 W. 93rd Street, New York, NY 10025. AGENT—Richard Cataldi Agency, 180 Seventh Avenue, Suite 1C, New York, NY 10011.

ROWE, Hansford   1924-

PERSONAL: Born May 12, 1924, in Richmond, VA; son of Hansford Herndon (a veterinarian) and Virginia Isabel (Willis) Rowe; married Ales Jackson (divorced, 1972); married Janice Solomon (a public relations consultant), July 7, 1985; children: Hansford III, Blake E. EDUCATION: University of Richmond, B.A., 1950; University of North Carolina, M.A., 1952; trained for the stage with Robert Lewis. MILITARY: U.S. Navy, 1943-46.

VOCATION: Actor.

CAREER: STAGE DEBUT—Dan, *Night Must Fall,* University of Richmond, VA, 1948, for thirty performances. BROADWAY DEBUT—Hunter, *We Bombed in New Haven,* 1967, for one-hundred-twenty performances. PRINCIPAL STAGE APPEARANCES—New York City productions: Simpson, *Singin' in the Rain,* Art Kirk, *Nuts,* understudy title role, *Da,* and detective, *Porgy and Bess;* regional: Murray Burns, *A Thousand Clowns,* Virginia Museum Theatre, Richmond, 1960.

MAJOR TOURS—Detective, *Porgy and Bess,* U.S. and European cities.

FILM DEBUT—Security guard, *Three Days of the Condor,* Paramount, 1975. PRINCIPAL FILM APPEARANCES—Attack dog salesman, *Gordon's War,* Twentieth Century-Fox, 1973; general, *The Osterman Weekend,* Twentieth Century-Fox, 1983; Sam Botts, *Baby Boom.*

PRINCIPAL TELEVISION APPEARANCES—Episodic: *Bob Newhart Show,* CBS; *Remington Steele,* NBC; *Dallas,* CBS; *Love, Sidney,* NBC; *Greatest American Hero,* ABC; *Bare Essence,* NBC. Movies: *Dorothy Parker's Big Blonde.*

AWARDS: Best Actor, Drama Desk Award nomination, 1978, for *Nuts.*

SIDELIGHTS: FAVORITE ROLES—Murray Burns in *A Thousand Clowns.*

ADDRESSES: HOME—New York, NY. AGENT—The Gage Group, 1650 Broadway, New York, NY 10019; J. Michael Bloom, Ltd., 233 Park Avenue South, New York, NY 10003.

*   *   *

ROZAKIS, Gregory   1913-

PERSONAL: Born January 30, 1913, in Brooklyn, NY; son of Stavros (a restaurant manager) and Stella (Tsambarlis) Rozakis. EDUCATION: Attended New York University, 1960-63; trained for the stage with Lee Strasberg and Burt Lanc. POLITICS: Democrat. RELIGION: Greek Orthodox.

VOCATION: Actor and writer.

CAREER: STAGE DEBUT—Son, *Natural Affection.* BROADWAY DEBUT—*Natural Affection,* Booth Theatre, 1963. PRINCIPAL STAGE APPEARANCES—Felipillo, *The Royal Hunt of the Sun,* American National Theatre Academy (ANTA) Theatre, New York City, 1965; Scott, *What Did We Do Wrong?,* Helen Hayes Theatre, New York City, 1967; Laci Racz, *The Cannibals,* Helen Hayes

GREGORY ROZAKIS

Theatre, New York City, 1968; Bambi, *Person Unclaimed,* Theatre Rapport, Los Angeles, 1977; also appeared in *Balm in Gilean,* La Mama Experimental Theatre Club (E.T.C.); *Double Talk,* Theatre de Lys, New York City.

FILM DEBUT—Hohaness, *America, America,* Warner Brothers, 1963. PRINCIPAL FILM APPEARANCES—The murderer, *Deathwish,* Paramount, 1974; Joe, *The Gambler,* Paramount, 1974; *Abduction,* 1975; Charlie Chaplin, *Cotton Club,* Orion, 1984; Detective Mazola, *Five Corners,* 1987; also was featured in *Below the Belt,* Aberdeen Productions.

PRINCIPAL TELEVISION APPEARANCES—Episodic: "The Incident," *Dupont Show of the Week,* NBC; "Inheritance," *Lou Grant,* CBS; "Kojack's Days," *Kojak,* CBS; *Police Story,* CBS; "Murder for Me," *Baretta,* ABC; "Disco Angel," *Charlie's Angels,* ABC; "Pariah" and "Death in a Different Place," *Starsky and Hutch,* ABC; "Count Your Fingers," *Kaz,* CBS; "Death Set," *Hart to Hart,* ABC; "A Touch of Venom," *Cannon,* CBS; "Too Easy to Kill," *Wide World of Mystery.* Series: *The Best of Everything,* ABC; Lou, *One Life to Live,* ABC; Sacha, *All My Children,* ABC. Movies: *Million Dollar Face,* 1981; *The Judgement,* CBS.

WRITING: PLAYS, PRODUCED—(With Barry Bostwick) *The Whores of Broadway,* Cubiculo Theatre, New York City, 1973; *Persons Unclaimed,* Theatre Rapport, Los Angeles, 1977.

TELEVISION—"Chalk Marks on the Wall," *Lamp Unto My Feet,* 1962.

AWARDS: Best Supporting Actor, Golden Globe Award nomination, 1963, for *America, America;* Hollywood Foreign Press Association Variety Award, *Saturday Review* Award, and Critics Poll Award, all 1963, for *Natural Affection.*

MEMBER: Actors' Equity Association, Screen Actors Guild, American Federation of Television and Radio Artists, Dramatists Guild.

ADDRESSES: HOME—Brooklyn, NY. AGENT—Jerry Kahn, 853 Seventh Avenue, New York, NY 10019.

                    *   *   *

RUSSELL, Theresa   1957-

BRIEF ENTRY: Born Theresa Paup in San Diego, CA, in 1957.

Russell began modeling at age twelve and eventually dropped out of Burbank High School to study acting at the Lee Strasberg Institute. In 1977, she appeared in her first feature film as a college girl determined to seduce the head of a motion picture studio in *The Last Tycoon.* One year later, in *Straight Time,* she played an office worker who becomes slowly enveloped by the violent world of an ex-convict. Her performances in these films brought her talents to the attention of English director Nicolas Roeg, who cast her in his 1980 film *Bad Timing/A Sensual Obsession.* They were married in 1986 and have two sons, Stratten Jack and Maxim. She also appeared in other Roeg films, including *Insignificance,* the 1985 film in which she portrays a sexually-charged woman who wants to have an affair with Albert Einstein. She is currently at work with Roeg in the upcoming film *Track 29.* In 1986, she performed as the central character in the critically acclaimed *Black Widow,* a film about a highly sensuous woman who seduces a series of wealthy men and later kills them. She also played Maureen Dean in the miniseries *Blind Ambition.**

S

SAHAGEN, Nikki

PERSONAL: Full name, Nikki Jean Sahagen; born May 22, in Los Angeles, CA; daughter of Armen Nicholas (an inventor and manufacturer of electronics) and Joyce Anne (a legal administrator; maiden name, Mathews) Sahagen. EDUCATION: Trained in dance at the Royal Academy of Dancing, London, and for the stage at the American Academy of Dramatic Arts with Wynn Handman.

VOCATION: Actress, choreographer, dancer, and singer.

CAREER: BROADWAY DEBUT—*42nd Street*, Winter Garden Theatre, 1980. PRINCIPAL STAGE APPEARANCES—Peggy Sawyer, *42nd Street*, Majestic Theatre, New York City, 1983; Belle, *Take Me Along*, Martin Beck Theatre, 1985, Angy Howard, *Follow Thru* and Irma, *Irma La Douce*, both at the Goodspeed Opera House, East Haddam, CT, 1986; Ruby, *Dames at Sea*, Pennsylvannia Stage Company, Allentown, PA, 1986.

FIRST FILM WORK—Assistant choreographer, *Children of a Lesser God*, Paramount, 1985.

TELEVISION DEBUT—Singer and dancer, *The Bob Hope Birthday Special*, 1981. PRINCIPAL TELEVISION APPEARANCES—Performer and associate choreographer, *Gershwin Gala*, WNET-TV, New York City, 1987.

MEMBER: Actors' Equity Association, Screen Actors Guild, American Federation of Television and Radio Artists.

ADDRESSES: HOME—New York, NY.

*   *   *

SALISBURY, Frank   1930-

PERSONAL: Born March 2, 1930, in Ft. Worth, TX; son of Frank Albert (a theatre manager) and Burmah Elizabeth (an actress and drama teacher; maiden name, Pressley) Salisbury; children: Scott Allen. EDUCATION: Attended Los Angeles City College. POLITICS: Democrat. RELIGION: Protestant. MILITARY: U.S. Army.

VOCATION: Writer.

WRITINGS: TELEVISION—Series: *Search for Tomorrow*, NBC; *As the World Turns*, CBS; *General Hospital*, ABC; *The Guiding Light*, CBS; *Dynasty*, ABC; *Capitol*, CBS; *Santa Barbara*, NBC. Also *The Edge of Night*, *Somerset*, and *Rituals*.

Episodic: *Schlitz Playhouse*, CBS; *Science Fiction Theatre* and *Dr. Hudson's Secret Journal*, both syndicated.

PLAYS, PRODUCED—*Venice*, Group Repertory, North Hollywood, CA; *The Ice Cream Sunday*, CAST Theatre, Los Angeles; *The Seagulls of 1933*, Actors Alley Theatre, Sherman Oaks, CA. PLAYS, UNPRODUCED—"Shooting in Scotland."

AWARDS: Los Angeles Drama Critics Award, 1976, for *The Seagulls of 1933*; Emmy Award nomination, 1981, for *General Hospital*; Emmy Award, 1982, for *The Guiding Light*.

MEMBER: Writers Guild of America West, Dramatists Guild, Academy of Television Arts and Sciences.

SIDELIGHTS: RECREATIONS—Tennis and cooking.

FRANK SALISBURY

Frank Salisbury's first job was at the Alvin G. Manuel Literary Agency, which is where he became interested in professional writing.

ADDRESSES: OFFICE—3631 Dixie Canyon Place, Sherman Oaks, CA 91423. AGENT—Jerome Siegel, 8733 Sunset Blvd., Los Angeles, CA 90069; Theatrical Agent: Earl Graham, 311 W. 43rd Street, New York, NY 10036.

*   *   *

SAMMS, Emma   1960-

PERSONAL: Born Emma Samuelson, August 28, 1960, in London, England; daughter of Michael E. W. (a film executive) and Madeliene U. (a ballet dancer; maiden name, White) Samuelson. EDUCATION: Attended Harrow College; trained for the ballet at the Royal Ballet School, London.

VOCATION: Actress.

CAREER: TELEVISION DEBUT—Mini-Series: Lea, *Goliath Awaits,* 1981. PRINCIPAL TELEVISION APPEARANCES—Series: Holly Scorpio, *General Hospital,* ABC, 1982-85; Fallon Carrington Colby, *Dynasty,* ABC, 1985—; Fallon Carrington Colby, *The Colbys,* ABC, 1985—.

Mini-Series: Violet Weiler, *Ellis Island,* CBS, 1984. Movies: Egg Eastman, *Murder in Three Acts,* CBS, 1986.

EMMA SAMMS

FILM DEBUT—Princess Zuleira, *Arabian Adventure,* EMI, 1978.

AWARDS: Discovery of the Year, Golden Apple Award, 1985.

MEMBER: American Foundation of Televison and Radio Artists; Starlight Foundation (co-founder).

SIDELIGHTS: RECREATIONS—Ice skating and dancing.

Emma Samms is a co-founder of the Starlight Foundation, a charity that grants wishes to critically and terminally ill children.

ADDRESSES: AGENT—c/o Peter Giageri, Agency for the Performing Arts, 9000 Sunset Blvd., Suite 315, Los Angeles, CA 90069.

*   *   *

SAMPLES, M. David

PERSONAL: EDUCATION: Lake Forest College, B.A.; University of North Carolina, M.A.

VOCATION: Director, actor, and playwright.

CAREER: PRINCIPAL STAGE WORK—Director: *The Begger's Opera,* Memorial Hall; *Dearie, You're a Dreamer* and *Crown of Choice,* both at the Playmakers Theatre, NC; *A Word in Edgewise* and *There Dies an Adonis,* both at the Playmakers Theatre and at the Rockford Civic Theatre, IL, all with the University of North Carolina Playmakers; *Consider the Heavens,* Moorehead State College, KY; *Mrs. President,* Lincoln College, IL; *The Eleventh Hour,* outdoor symphonic drama, Staunton, VA; *Voice in the Wind,* outdoor symphonic drama, Ruskin, FL; *Queen Anne's Bell,* outdoor symphonic drama, Bath, NC; stock tryouts: *A Delicate Question, The Best Man, Loss of Roses, Summer Brave,* and *On the March to the Sea;* at the Woodstock Opera House, McHenry, IL, the Woodstock Playhouse, NY, and the Hyde Park Playhouse NY, directed more than one hundred productions, including: *Family Portrait, Bye Bye Birdie, A Moon for the Misbegotten, Look Back in Anger, Blue Denim, Romanoff and Juliet, Look Homeward Angel, The Drunkard, Two for the Seesaw, The Diary of Anne Frank, The Dark at the Top of the Stairs, Critic's Choice, The Golden Fleecing, Roshomon, Arsenic and Old Lace, Springtime for Henry, Duet for Two Hands, Sweet Bird of Youth.*

Also directed: *Kataki,* St. Mark's Playhouse, New York City; *My Heart's in the Highlands,* Equity Library Theatre, New York City; *The Beheading,* Lincoln Center Library Theatre, New York City; *Plays for Living,* with Family Service of America, New York City; also *In White America,* and *Boy with a Cart,* both New York City productions.

PRINCIPAL STAGE APPEARANCES—Colonel Jed Willis, *Wilderness Road,* Peter Cartwright, *Forever This Land,* and Father Martin, *The Lost Colony,* all outdoor symphonic dramas; stock productions at the Woodstock Playhouse, NY and the Hyde Park Playhouse, NY: Dr. Sloper, *The Heiress,* Dr. Jacobson, *The Rope Dancers,* Elwood P. Dowd, *Harvey,* Malachi Stack, *The Matchmaker,* Billy Rice, *The Entertainer,* William Russell, *The Best Man,* and Pogo Poole, *The Pleasure of His Company; The Beheading,* Lincoln Center Library Theatre, New York City; *Insufficient Evidence,* Double Image Theatre, New York City; *Night of the Auk,*

Equity Library Theatre, New York City; *Cock-a-Doodle-Dandy,* Carnegie Hall Playhouse, New York City; *Tobias and the Angel,* Theatre East, New York City; *As You Like It,* with the New York Shakespeare Festival, New York City; *Richard III,* New York Shakespeare Festival, New York City; *Wedding in Japan,* Graystone Theatre, New York City.

RELATED CAREER—Executive director, West Side Players, West Side Presbyterian Church, New York City; director for four seasons, Rockford Civic Theatre, IL.

WRITINGS: PLAYS, PRODUCED—*Winter's Harvest* (three one-acts), *Out of Order,* and *The Bereaved,* all at the Rockford Civic Theatre, IL, and produced by the University of North Carolina Playmakers; *Winter's Harvest,* YMCA Players, Joliet, IL. PLAYS, PUBLISHED—*Out of Order* and *Winter's Harvest.*

PERIODICALS—Contributor: *English Journal, Bulletin of Secondary School Principals, Players Magazine, The New York Times,* Sunday edition, *Bulletin of National Theatre Conference,* and *Dramatics Magazine.*

AWARDS: Ford Foundation Fellowship to study as a director and observer under George Abbott.

MEMBER: Society of Stage Directors and Choreographers, Directors Unit of the Actors Studio.

ADDRESSES: HOME—441 14th Street, Brooklyn, NY 11215.

*   *   *

SAND, Paul   1935-

PERSONAL: Born Pablo Sanchez, March 5, 1935, in Los Angeles, CA; son of Ernest Rivera and Sonia Borodiansky (Stone) Sanchez. EDUCATION: Attended Los Angeles City College; trained for the stage at the Young Actors Company Repertory Company, Los Angeles and with Viola Spolins; studied mime with Marcel Marceau in France and Switzerland.

VOCATION: Actor and writer.

CAREER: PRINCIPAL TELEVISION APPEARANCES—Series: *The Carol Burnett Show,* CBS, 1971-73; *The Mary Tyler Moore Show,* CBS, 1972; Robert Dreyfuss, *Friends and Lovers,* CBS, 1974-75; Dr. Michael Ridley, *St. Elsewhere,* NBC, 1982-84; *Gimme a Break,* NBC, 1985—. Movies: *The Last Fling,* ABC, 1987. Guest: *The Ed Sullivan Show,* CBS; *The Jack Paar Show,* NBC; *The Dick Cavett Show,* CBS.

PRINCIPAL FILM APPEARANCES—Morrie, *A Great Big Thing,* Aarofilm, 1968; Moreno, *Viva Max!,* Commonwealth United, 1970; Greenberg, *The Hot Rock,* Twentieth Century-Fox, 1972; Benny Napkins, *Every Little Crook and Nanny,* Metro-Goldwyn-Mayer, 1972; *The Main Event,* Warner Brothers, 1979; *Can't Stop the Music,* Associated, 1980.

STAGE DEBUT—Spolin Troupe, Circle Theatre, Los Angeles. BROADWAY DEBUT—As Paul Sanchez, with the Marcel Marceau Mime Troupe at the City Center, 1956. LONDON DEBUT—*Looking for the Action,* with the Second City Troupe, Prince Charles

Theatre, 1963. PRINCIPAL STAGE APPEARANCES—With the Second City troupe, appeared in *The Third Programme, Too Many Hats, The Seacoast of Bohemia,* all at Square East Theatre, Chicago, 1960.

As Paul Sand: *From the Second City,* Royale Theatre, New York City, 1961; *To the Water Tower,* with the Second City troupe at the Square East Theatre, Chicago, 1963; *Luis,* Festival of the Two Worlds, Spoleto Festival, Italy, 1963; Arthur, *Journey to the Day,* Theatre de Lys, New York City, 1963; *Wet Paint,* Renata Theatre, New York City, 1965; Maxime, *Hotel Passionato,* East 74th Street Theatre, New York City, 1965; *The Mad Show,* New Theatre, New York City, 1966 and PJ Theatre, Los Angeles, 1966; *The Star-Spangled Girl,* Plymouth Theatre, New York City, 1967; *Story Theatre,* Ambassador Theatre, New York City, 1970; *Ovid's Metamorphoses,* Ambassador Theatre, New York City, 1971; *Story Theatre,* Mark Taper Forum, Los Angeles, and John F. Kennedy Center for the Performing Arts, Washington, DC, 1971; *Angel City,* Mark Taper Forum, Los Angeles, 1977; *Tales of the Hasidim,* Public/Martinson Hall Theatre, New York City, 1977.

WRITINGS: PLAYS, PRODUCED—*Luis,* Festival of the Two Worlds, Spoleto, Italy, 1963.

SIDELIGHTS: RECREATIONS—Reading, writing, theatre and movie going, body surfing.

ADDRESSES: OFFICE—2409 Panorama Terrace, Los Angeles, CA. AGENT—Leading Artists Agency, 445 N. Bedford Drive, PH, Beverly Hills, CA 90210.*

*   *   *

SANDRICH, Jay   1932-

PERSONAL: Born February 24, 1932, in Los Angeles, CA; son of Mark (a director) and Freda (Wirtschater) Sandrich; married wife Nina, 1953 (divorced, 1976); children: Eric, Tony, Wendy. EDUCATION: University of California at Los Angeles, B.A., 1953. MILITARY: U.S. Army Signal Corps, 1st Lieutenant, 1953-55.

VOCATION: Director and producer.

CAREER: FILM DEBUT—Director, *Seems Like Old Times,* Columbia, 1980.

PRINCIPAL TELEVISION WORK—Producer, *Get Smart,* NBC, 1965. Director: *He & She,* CBS, 1967; *The Bill Cosby Show,* NBC, 1969; *The Mary Tyler Moore Show,* CBS, 1970-77; *Soap,* ABC, 1977-79; *The Cosby Show,* NBC, 1985—.

AWARDS: Outstanding Directorial Achievement in a Comedy Series, Emmy Awards, 1971, for "Toulouse-Lautrec Is One of My Favorite Artists" and 1973, for "It's Whether You Win or Lose," both episodes from *The Mary Tyler Moore Show;* Directors Guild of American Award, 1986, for *The Cosby Show.*

MEMBER: Directors Guild of America.

ADDRESSES: AGENT—c/o Ron Meyer, Creative Artists Agency, 1888 Century Park East, Los Angeles, CA 90067.

SANTONI, Reni

PERSONAL: Children: Nick.

VOCATION: Actor.

CAREER: PRINCIPAL STAGE APPEARANCES—*The Third Ear,* New York City production, 1964; also performed in improvisational works with the Compass Players and the Premise.

FILM DEBUT—*The Pawnbroker,* Commonwealth United, 1965. PRINCIPAL FILM APPEARANCES—*The Return of the Seven,* United Artists, 1966; *Dirty Harry,* Warner Brothers, 1972; *I Never Promised You a Rose Garden,* New World, 1977; *They Went That-a-Way and That-a-Way,* International Picture Show Company, 1978; *Dead Men Don't Wear Plaid,* Universal, 1982; *Bad Boys,* Universal, 1983; *Cobra,* Warner Brothers, 1986; also *Enter Laughing,* 1967; *Anzio,* 1968.

PRINCIPAL TELEVISION APPEARANCES—Series: *Sanchez of Bel Air,* USA Cable; Danny Paterno, *Owen Marshall, Counselor at Law,* ABC, 1973-74; Captain Rivera, *Manimal,* NBC, 1983. Episodic: *Hill Street Blues,* NBC; *Report to Murphy,* CBS; *The Rockford Files,* NBC; *Charlie's Angels,* ABC; *CHiPs,* NBC. Movies: *The Psychiatrist: God Bless the Children,* 1970; *Indict and Convict,* 1973; *Panic on the 5:22,* 1974; *Second Serve,* CBS, 1986. Guest: *The Merv Griffin Show,* CBS, for forty-nine appearances.

ADDRESSES: AGENT—Shiffrin Artists Inc., 7466 Beverly Blvd., Suite 205, Los Angeles, CA 90036.

CHRIS SARANDON

SARANDON, Chris   1942-

PERSONAL: Born July 24, 1942, in Beckley, WV; married Susan Tomalin (an actress), September 16, 1967 (divorced). EDUCATION: West Virginia University, B.A.; Catholic University, M.F.A.

VOCATION: Actor.

CAREER: STAGE DEBUT—Jack Hunter, *The Rose Tattoo,* 1965-66. BROADWAY DEBUT—Jacob, *The Rothschilds,* Lunt-Fontanne Theatre, 1970. PRINCIPAL STAGE APPEARANCES—Proteus, *Two Gentlemen of Verona,* St. James Theatre, New York City, 1972; Tom Wintermouth, *Marco Polo Sings a Solo* and *A Prayer for My Daughter,* both New York Shakespeare Festival, Public Theatre, New York City, 1977; Dick Dudgeon, *The Devil's Disciple,* Ahmanson Theatre, Los Angeles, CA, 1977, then Brooklyn Academy of Music (BAM), NY, 1978; appeared at the Wilbur Theatre, Boston, MA, 1978; Nick, *The Woods,* New York Shakespeare Festival, Public Theatre, New York City, 1979, Benchgelter, *Censored Scenes from King Kong,* Princess Theatre, New York City, 1980; Laertes, *Hamlet,* American Shakespeare Theatre, Stratford, CT, 1982; Bill Page, *The Voice of the Turtle,* Roundabout Theatre, New York City, 1984. Regional: has appeared at the Long Wharf Theatre, New Haven CT; McCarter Theatre, Princeton, NJ; with the Hartford Stage Company, CT, and the Shaw Festival, Niagara-on-the-Lake, Ontario, Canada.

PRINCIPAL FILM APPEARANCES—*Dog Day Afternoon,* Warner Brothers, 1975; *Lipstick,* Paramount, 1976; *The Sentinel,* Universal, 1977; *Cuba,* United Artists, 1979; *The Osterman Weekend,*

RENI SANTONI

Twentieth Century-Fox, 1983; *Protocol*, Warner Brothers, 1984; *Fright Night*, Columbia, 1984.

PRINCIPAL TELEVISION APPEARANCES—Dramatic Specials: *You Can't Go Home Again*, 1979; *The Day Christ Died*, 1980; *A Tale of Two Cities*, 1980; *Broken Promise*, 1981; *This Child Is Mine*, 1985. Also appeared in *Liberty*.

ADDRESSES: AGENT—Smith-Freedman Agency, 850 Seventh Avenue, Suite 305, New York, NY 10036.

*   *   *

SAVANT, Doug

BRIEF ENTRY: Born in Burbank, CA. Actor. Doug Savant initially became interested in athletics in high school, but after tearing three knee ligaments playing football, he turned his attention toward acting. Later, when he was chosen for a part in a community theatre production of *Hello, Dolly!*, he decided to pursue acting as his profession. On television, he played the role of young Mack Mackenzie on *Knots Landing*. He made his film debut as Brad in *Teen Wolf*, a 1985 comedy about a teenager who suddenly discovers that he's a werewolf. Other film roles for Savant have quickly followed, including a part as Tom Hainey, in *Trick or Treat*, in 1986, and as Ashby in the 1987 film about American prisoners of war in Vietnam, *The Hanoi Hilton*. Other work includes guest-starring television appearances on *Cagney and Lacy* and *Hotel*.*

*   *   *

ALAN SCARFE

SCARFE, Alan   1946-

PERSONAL: Born June 8, 1946, in London, England; son of Neville Vincent (a university professor) and Gladys Ellen (a university professor; maiden name, Hunt) Scarfe; married Barbara March (an actress), August 27, 1979; children: Jonathan, Antonia. EDUCATION: Attended the London Academy of Music and Dramatic Art, 1964-1966.

VOCATION: Actor and director.

CAREER: STAGE DEBUT—Marc Antony, *Julius Caesar*, Vancouver Playhouse, Vancouver, BC, 1964. OFF-BROADWAY DEBUT—Otto, *Africanus Instructus*, Music Theatre Group, January, 1986. LONDON DEBUT—Mott, *Fairy Tales of New York*, Little Theatre Club, Garrick Theatre, 1966. PRINCIPAL STAGE APPEARANCES—At the Stratford Shakespeare Festival, Ontario, Canada: Tony Lumpkin, *She Stoops to Conquer*, title role, *King Lear*, 1972; Petruchio, *The Taming of the Shrew*, 1973; Andrei, *The Three Sisters*, Fainall, *The Way of the World*, 1976; Buckingham, *Richard III*, Bottom, *A Midsummer Night's Dream*, Benedick, *Much Ado About Nothing*, 1977; Ford, *The Merry Wives of Windsor*, Aaron, *Titus Andronicus*, Cassius, *Julius Caesar*, 1978; Barrymore, *Ned & Jack*, title role, *Othello*, 1979; Duke of Vienna, *Measure for Measure*, 1985.

Dick Dudgeon, *The Devil's Disciple*, Shaw Festival, 1974; title role, *Hamlet*, Centaur Theatre, Montreal, Canada, 1975; title role, *Dr. Faustus*, Vancouver, Canada, 1975; Harras, *The Devil's General*, Dallas, TX, 1979; Orsino, *Twelfth Night*, Young People's

Theatre, 1980; Warwick, *The Lark*, Shannon, *The Night of the Iguana*, Theatre Plus, 1980; Bruhl, *Deathtrap*, Theatre Aquarius, Hamilton, 1980; Enrico, *Enrico IV*, Theatre Plus, 1981; Robert, *Betrayal* and ΛΛ, *The Emigrants*, both Saidye Bronfman Centre, 1981; Jimmy Porter, *Look Back in Anger*, Young People's Theatre, 1981; Frederick Treves, *The Elephant Man*, Theatre Aquarius, Hamilton, 1981; Kinsella, *Catholics*, Hartman Theatre, Stamford, CT, 1981; Garry Essendine, *Present Laughter*, Neptune Theatre, 1984; Pepper, Gilpin, and Alex, *Tonight at 8:30*, CentreStage Company, Toronto, Canada, 1984; Otto, *Africanus Instructus*, with the Lenox Music Group, Stockbridge, MA, 1986; Comus, *The Mask of Comus*, Comus Music Theatre, 1986; Stalin, *Black Sea Follies*, with the Lenox Music Group, Stockbridge, 1986.

MAJOR TOURS—Petruchio, *The Taming of the Shrew*, Stratford Festival Production, tour of western Europe, Poland, and the Soviet Union, 1973; Dick Dudgeon, *The Devil's Disciple*, Shaw Festival Production, Maritime provinces tour, 1974; Otto, *Africanus Instructus*, with the Music Theatre Group, tour of Spain and France, 1986.

PRINCIPAL STAGE WORK—Director: *Who's Afraid of Virginia Woolf*, Liverpool, U.K., 1967; *The Dragon*, Liverpool, 1968; *Boesman and Lena* and *The Exception and the Rule*, both Montreal, Canada, 1971; *The Bloodknot*, Montreal, 1972; *Hadrian VII*, Vancouver, Canada, 1972; *Mr. Joyce Is Leaving Paris*, Montreal, 1974; *A Day in the Death of Joe Egg*, Regina, Canada, 1974; *The Rivals*, Toronto, Canada, 1975; *Not I*, Stratford, Canada, 1978; *The Last Meeting of the Knights of the White Magnolia*, Toronto, 1981; *Mass Appeal*, Calgary, Canada, 1981; *Classic Christmas, The*

Crucible, and *Sweet Will,* all Toronto, 1982; *Romeo and Juliet,* Halifax, Nova Scotia, 1983; *The Homecoming,* Toronto, 1983.

PRINCIPAL FILM APPEARANCES—*Cathy's Curse,* Agora Films, 1978; Higgins, *Reservations,* Earl Rosen Associates, 1981; Websole, *Bells,* Robert Cooper Film, 1982; Captain Leather, *The Wars,* Neilsen-Ferns, 1983; Sgt. Hawley, *Deserters,* Exile Productions, 1983; Sgt. Coldwell, *The Bay Boy,* Bay Boy Productions, 1984; Simmons, *Walls,* Jericho Productions, 1984; Simmonds, *Labour of Love,* Primedia Company, 1984; Trimble, *Joshua Then and Now,* RLS Productions, 1984; Numero Uno, *Honour the Dead,* Kinorama Productions, 1985; Vladimir Jezda, *Overnight,* Exile Productions, 1985; Royal Wishart, *Keeping Track,* Telecine Productions, 1985.

PRINCIPAL TELEVISION APPEARANCES—Episodic: Meterman, *Sidestreet,* Canadian Broadcasting Company (CBC), 1978; Harrison, *A Gift to Last,* CBC, 1978; Dr. Brooks, *Certain Practices,* CBC, 1978; Betcherly, "Murder by Proxy," *The Great Detective,* Parts 1 & 2, CBC, 1980; Loomis, "The Final Edition," *For the Record,* CBC, 1980; Morley, "Beyond the Pale," *Judge,* CBC, 1982; Tilley, "Your Secret Servant," *Canada Confidential,* CBC, 1982; The Commissioner, "PL," *For the Record,* CBC, 1982; George Chauvinet, *Pajama Tops,* Lorimar Productions, 1982; Selkirk, *Explorers,* CBC, 1983; Richard, "Genesis," *The Littlest Hobo,* CTV, 1983; Mark Kramer, "An Honourable Man," *Judge,* CBC, 84; Mr. Nesbitt, "The Screaming Woman," *Ray Bradbury,* Home Box Office, 1985; the Governor, *The Execution of Raymond Graham,* ABC, 1985; mysterious stranger, "Heretic," *Tales from the Darkside,* syndicated, 1986.

Dramatic Specials: Capt. Horster, *An Enemy of the People,* CBC, 1977; Ernie, *Home Fires,* CBC, 1983; the brother, *As Is,* Showtime Network, 1986; the doctor, "All My Sons," *American Playhouse,* NET, 1986.

PRINCIPAL RADIO WORK—All CBC Radio: Marlowe, *Assassination of Christopher Marlowe,* 1976; the devil, *Man & Superman,* Chekhov, *Chekhov's Island,* and Duke, *Time Remembered,* all 1978; Barrymore, *Ned & Jack,* 1979; solo reader, *Short Stories,* 1980; principal, *Night Fall,* 1980; Rakitin, *A Month in the Country* and reader, *The Decameron,* both 1981; Gulliver, *Author and Creation* and Fanning, *Loyal Son of War,* both 1984.

RELATED CAREER—Associate director, Stratford Festival, Ontario, 1974-76; consultant to the feature films, *The Deserter* and *Overnight.*

WRITINGS: PLAYS, PRODUCED—(With George Ryga) *Captives of the Faceless Drummer;* (with Eric Green) *The Assassination of Christopher Marlowe.*

AWARDS: Association of Canadian Television and Radio Artists Award, 1976, for *The Assassination of Christopher Marlowe;* Best Actor, Association of Canadian Television and Radio Artists Award nomination, 1980, for *Certain Practices;* Best Actor, Genie Award nominations: 1984, for *Deserters,* 1985, for *The Bay Boy,* and 1986, for *Overnight.*

MEMBER: Actors' Equity Association, Screen Actors Guild, British Actors' Equity Association, Association of Canadian Television and Radio Artists, Canadian Academy of Motion Pictures, Preston Jones Symposium (board member).

ADDRESSES: AGENT—Alan Willig and Associates, 47A Horatio Street, New York, NY 10014.

SCHACHTER, Felice   1963-

PERSONAL: Born November 17, 1963, in New York, NY; daughter of Alex (an accountant and real estate developer) and Suzanne Marion (a theatrical manager; maiden name, Mokotoff) Schachter. EDUCATION: Brown University, B.A., 1985; trained for the stage at the American Academy of Dramatic Art, Corner Loft Studio, School of American Ballet, Roland Dupre Dance Academy, George Balanchine's School of American Ballet, Stella Adler Conservatory, and with Lee Strasberg and Jack Garfein.

VOCATION: Actress, dancer, and sports broadcaster.

CAREER: PRINCIPAL TELEVISION APPEARANCES—Sports commentator: *Sports Sunday,* CBS, 1983-84; *U.S. Open,* CBS, 1984-85; also for Prime Ticket Network, Los Angeles, 1986-87.

Series: Nancy, *Facts of Life,* NBC, 1979-82; young Felicia, *Love of Life;* Jessica, *The Doctors.* Episodic: *Diff'rent Strokes,* NBC; *Alice,* CBS; *Quiz Kids,* NBC; *Love, American Style,* ABC; *Rocky Road,* WTBS. Mini-Series: *The Adams Chronicles.* Guest: *P.M. Magazine; The David Susskind Show; Live at Five; To Life.* Specials: *Steve Martin's Twilight Theatre.*

STAGE DEBUT—Flora, *The Innocents,* Performing Arts Foundation Theatre, Long Island, NY, 1975. PRINCIPAL STAGE APPEARANCES—*Time Again,* Off-Broadway production; dancer: *The Taming of the Shrew,* Stuttgart Ballet; *Sleeping Beauty,* Bolshoi Ballet; *Nutcracker Suite,* New York City Ballet.

FELICE SCHACHTER

PRINCIPAL RADIO WORK—Anchorperson, WBRU, Providence, RI.

PRINCIPAL FILM APPEARANCES—Bernadette, *Zapped!*, Embassy, 1982; Tracy, *Just Posing.*

MEMBER: Actors' Equity Association, Screen Actors Guild, American Federation of Television and Radio Artists.

SIDELIGHTS: Feilice Schachter told *CTFT* that she began her performing career at age three months when she was featured in a television commercial and that she was a "steady wage earner," by the time she was one year old.

ADDRESSES: OFFICE—Box 6547, Fresh Meadows, NY 11365. AGENT—Irv Schechter Company, 9300 Wilshire Blvd., Suite 410, Beverly Hills, CA 90212.

*   *   *

SCHAPIRO, Seth L.   1931-

PERSONAL: Born June 24, 1931, in New York, NY. EDUCATION: Williams College, B.A., 1949-53; Columbia Law School, LL.B., 1955-58.

VOCATION: Entertainment attorney.

MEMBER: The League of American Theatres and Producers, Association of Theatrical Press Agents and Managers, Williamstown Theatre Foundation (board of trustees), New York State Bar Association; Williams Club.

ADDRESSES: OFFICE—122 E. 42nd Street, New York, NY 10068.

*   *   *

SCHATZBERG, Jerry   1927-

PERSONAL: Born June 26, 1927 in the Bronx, NY; son of Abraham (a furrier) and Lillian (Eiger) Schatzberg; married Corinne Loeb, February 4, 1950 (divorced); married Maureen Ann Kerwin (an actress), March 10, 1983; children: (first marriage) Don S., Steven M. EDUCATION: Attended the University of Miami, 1947-48. MILITARY: U.S. Navy Medical Corps.

VOCATION: Film director.

CAREER: FIRST FILM WORK—Director, *Puzzle of a Downfall Child*, Universal, 1970. PRINCIPAL FILM WORK—Director: *The Panic in Needle Park*, Twentieth Century-Fox, 1971; *Scarecrow*, Warner Brothers, 1973; *Dandy, the All-American Girl* (also known as *Sweet Revenge*), United Artists, 1977; *The Seduction of Joe Tynan*, Universal, 1979; *Honeysuckle Rose*, Warner Brothers, 1980; *Misunderstood*, Metro-Goldwyn-Mayer/United Artists, 1984; *No Small Affair*, Columbia, 1984; *Street Smart*, Cannon, 1987.

RELATED CAREER—Still photographer and director of television commercials, 1954-68, with his work featured in various periodicals, including *Life* and *Vogue;* exhibition of his photographs and films at the Beaubourg, Paris, France, 1982; guest lecturer, New York University, School of Cinema Studies.

NON-RELATED CAREER—Worked in family fur business; part owner, the Sevens, A Farm, Inc. (thoroughbred horse breeders), 1984—

AWARDS: Golden Palm Award, Cannes Film Festival, 1973, for *Scarecrow.*

MEMBER: Directors Guild of America, Academy of Motion Picture Arts and Sciences, Writers Guild of America.

SIDELIGHTS: In 1982, a book chronicling Schatzberg's life and career was published, entitled *Schatzberg de la Photo au Cinema,* written by Michel Ciment.

ADDRESSES: OFFICE—Bard & Glassman, 342 Madison Avenue, New York, NY 10173. AGENT—International Creative Management, 8899 Beverly Blvd., Los Angeles, CA 90048.

*   *   *

SCHENKKAN, Robert   1953-

PERSONAL: Surname rhymes with "bank in"; full name, Robert Frederic Schenkkan, Jr.; born March 19, 1953, in Chapel Hill, NC; son of Robert Frederic (a public television executive) and Jean (McKenzie) Schenkkan; married Mary Anne Dorward (an actress), December 1, 1984. EDUCATION: University of Texas at Austin, B.A., 1975; Cornell University, M.F.A., 1977.

VOCATION: Actor and writer.

CAREER: STAGE DEBUT—Captain Tim, *Tobacco Road*, Chicago, 1975, for thirty performances. OFF-BROADWAY DEBUT—Wayne Blossom, Jr., *Last Days at the Dixie Girl Cafe,* Theatre Four, 1979. PRINCIPAL STAGE APPEARANCES—Off-Broadway: Lucentio, *The Taming of the Shrew,* Equity Library Theatre, New York City, 1977; *G.R. Point*, Playhouse Theatre, New York City, 1979; understudy, *Key Exchange*, Orpheum Theatre, New York City, 1981; Sebastian, *The Midnight Visitor*, St. Peter's Hall, New York City, 1981; Reverend David Marshall Lee, *The Foreigner*, Astor Place Theatre, New York City, 1984-85; also appeared in *Henry V* and *New Jerusalem*, both at the New York Shakespeare Festival, Public Theatre, New York City; *The Knack*, Roundabout Theatre, New York City; *Cash* and *Fog*, both in the Marathon Series, Ensemble Studio Theatre, New York City; *The Passion of Dracula*, Cherry Lane Theatre, New York City.

Regional: *Write Me a Murder*, Studio Arena Theatre, Buffalo, NY, 1981; *A Full Length Portrait of America* and *SWOP*, both at the Actors Theatre of Louisville, KY, 1981; also appeared with the Actors Theatre of Louisville, 1982-83; *A Midsummer Night's Dream* and *All the Way Home*, both at the Kenyon Theatre Festival, OH; *Tobacco Road*, Academy Festival Theatre.

TELEVISION DEBUT—*Father Brown, Detective*, NBC, 1979. PRINCIPAL TELEVISION APPEARANCES—Movies: *Murder in*

Cowetta County, CBS, 1980. Mini-Series: *George Washington,* CBS, 1983; *Kane and Abel,* CBS, 1984; *Nutcracker,* CBS, 1987. Episodic: *The Twilight Zone,* CBS.

PRINCIPAL FILM APPEARANCES—*Act of Vengeance* (also known as *Rape Squad*), 1974; *Sweet Liberty,* Universal, 1986; *The Manhattan Project,* Twentieth Century-Fox, 1986; *Bedroom Window,* DEG, 1987; also *Chain Letters; Amazing Grace and Chuck.*

WRITINGS: PLAYS, PRODUCED—*Derelict,* Studio Arena Theatre, Buffalo, NY, 1982; *Final Passages,* Studio Arena, Buffalo, also produced in Miami, Philadelphia, Tacoma, WA, Colorado Springs, CO, published by Theatre Communications Group; *The Survivalist,* one-act, Actors Theatre of Louisville, also produced at the Dumaurion Festival, Canada, Edinburgh Festival, Scotland, and in the Marathon Series of the Ensemble Studio Theatre, New York City; also *Intermission, Lunchbreak,* and *Tall Tales.*

PLAYS, PUBLISHED—*Final Passages,* published in *Plays in Progress,* Theatre Communications Group, New York City.

AWARDS: Best of the Fringe Award, Edinburgh Festival, 1984, for *The Survivalist;* CAPS Grant, 1985, for *Final Passages.*

MEMBER: Actors' Equity Association, Screen Actors Guild, American Federation of Television and Radio Artists, Ensemble Studio Theatre (New York City and Los Angeles).

ADDRESSES: AGENT—The Agency, 10351 Santa Monica Blvd., Los Angeles, CA 90025.

Photography by Clare Brett Smith

JAMES SCHEVILL

SCHEVILL, James 1920-

PERSONAL: Born June 10, 1920, in Berkeley, CA; son of Rudolph (a professor of Spanish) and Margaret (a poetess and artist; maiden name, Erwin) Schevill; married Helen Shaner (a piano teacher), December 4, 1942 (divorced, 1966); married Margot Helmuth Blum (a singer and anthropologist), August, 1967; children: (first marriage) Deborah, Susanna. EDUCATION: Harvard University, B.S., 1942; Brown University, M.A. MILITARY: U.S. Army, 1942-46.

VOCATION: Teacher and writer.

WRITINGS: BOOKS—*Tensions* (poems), Bern Porter, 1947; *The American Fantasies,* Bern Porter, 1951; *Sherwood Anderson: His Life and Work,* University of Denver Press, 1951; editor, *Six Histories by Ferdinand Schevill,* University of Chicago Press, 1956; *The Right to Greet,* Bern Porter, 1956; *The Roaring Market and the Silent Tomb* (biography of Bern Porter), Abbey Press, 1956, second edition, 1968; *James Schevill: Selected Poems, 1945-59,* Bern Porter, 1959; *Private Dooms and Public Destinations: Poems 1945-62,* A. Swallow, 1962; *The Stalingrad Elegies,* A. Swallow, 1964; contributor, *Where Is Vietnam?,* Anchor Books, 1967; *Release,* Hellcoal Press, 1968; *Violence and Glory: Poems, 1962-67,* A. Swallow, 1969; *The Buddhist Car and Other Characters,* Swallow Press, 1973; *Breakout: In Search of New Theatrical Environments,* 1973; *Pursuing Elegy: A Poem About Haiti,* Copper Beech Press, 1974; *The Arena of Ants,* Copper Beech Press, 1976; *The Mayan Poems,* Copper Beech Press, 1978; *Fire of Eyes: A Guatemalan Sequence,* Copper Beech Press, 1979; *The American*

ROBERT SCHENKKAN

Fantasies: Collected Poems, 1945-81, Swallow Press, Ohio University Press, 1983; *The Invisible Volcano*, Copper Beech Press, 1985; (with Walter Feldman) *Ghost Names/Ghost Numbers* (poems), 1986; *Ambiguous Dancers of Fame: Collected Poems, 1945-86, Volume II*, upcoming 1987. Also has given numerous readings of works at various educational and community organizations throughout the country, 1960-86.

PLAYS, PRODUCED AND PUBLISHED—*Everyman's History of Love*, California College of Arts and Crafts, Oakland, CA, 1951; *High Sinners, Low Angels*, Theatre San Francisco, published by Bern Porter, 1953; *The Bloody Tenet*, Actor's Workshop, San Francisco, then Goodman Theatre, Chicago, and Shrewsbury Theatre, England, published by Meridian, 1957; (with music by Andrew Imbrie) *Voices of Mass and Capital A*, San Francisco Museum of Art, published by Friendship, 1963; *The Master*, Actor's Workshop, San Francisco, 1963; *The Master and the Fan*, Guthrie Theatre, Minneapolis, MN, 1964; *The Black President and Other Plays*, published by A. Swallow, 1965; *The Stalingrad Elegies*, Actor's Workshop, Berkeley, 1965; libretto, *This Is Not True*, University of Minnesota, Minneapolis, 1966; *The Pilots*, Brown University Theatre, Providence, RI, 1970; *Oppenheimer's Chair*, Brown University Theatre, Providence, 1970, then Magic Theatre, San Francisco, 1971, published by Dancing Bear Productions, 1985; *Lovecraft's Follies*, Trinity Square Repertory Company, Providence, 1970.

The Ushers, Brown University Theatre, 1971; *The American Fantasies*, La Mama Experimental Theatre Club (E.T.C.), New York City, 1972; *Emperor Norton Lives!*, University of Utah, Salt Lake City, UT, 1972; *Fay Wray Meets King Kong* and *Sunset and Evening Stance or Mr. Krapp's New Tapes*, both Wastepaper Theatre, Providence, 1974; *Cathedral of Ice*, Trinity Square Repertory Company, Providence, 1975; *Year After Year*, Barker Playhouse and Wastepaper Theatre, Providence, 1979; *Emperor Norton*, Magic Theatre, San Francisco, 1979; *Mean Man I*, Wastepaper Theatre, Providence, 1980; *Edison's Dream*, Brown University Theatre, Providence, 1981; *Mean Man II*, Wastepaper Theatre, Providence, 1982; *Mother O or The Last American Mother*, Rhode Island Playwrights Theatre, Providence, 1983; *Cult of Youth*, Playwrights' Center Theatre, Minneapolis, 1984; *Old Groucho's Game*, Rhode Island Playwrights Theatre, Providence, 1985; *Monologue on S.J. Perelman*, Providence, 1986; *Time of the Hand and Eye*, Providence College Theatre, 1986; *Collected Short Plays*, Swallow Press, 1986.

TELEPLAYS—*The Cid* (translation), CBC, 1961; *The Space Fan*, WGBH, Boston, 1970; *The Death of Anton Webern*, BBC, 1974.

RADIO PLAYS—*The Sound of a Soldier*, ABC, 1945.

RELATED CAREER—Editor, *Berkeley: A Journal of Modern Culture;* assistant professor of humanities, California College of Arts and Crafts, Oakland, 1951-58; associate professor of English and director of The Poetry Center, San Francisco State College, 1959-68; professor of English, Brown University, 1968—; co-director, then director, Creative Writing Program, Brown University, 1972-75; president, Rhode Island Playwright's Theatre, 1984.

RECORDINGS: (With Margot Schevill) *Performance Poems*, Cambridge Records, 1984.

AWARDS: William Carlos Williams Award, 1965, for *The Stalingrad Elegies;* Best Short Story, *Arizona Quarterly* Annual Award, 1977. Grants and fellowships: Ford Foundation, 1954; National Council

of Churches, 1956; Rockefeller Foundation, National Endowment for the Arts and McKnight Foundation, 1957; Ford Foundation, 1960-61; National Council of Churches, 1961; Trinity Square Repertory Company, 1970; Rhode Island Committee on the Humanities, 1975; Guggenheim, 1981; McKnight Foundation, 1984.

MEMBER: Actor's Workshop (board of directors), San Francisco Regional Arts Council, Trinity Square Repertory Company (board of directors); American Civil Liberties Union.

ADDRESSES: HOME—17 Keene Street, Providence, RI 02906. OFFICE—Department of English, Brown University, Providence, RI 02912.

*   *   *

SCHIMMEL, William   1946-

PERSONAL: Born September 22, 1946, in Philadelphia, PA; son of Leonard F. (a custodian) and Marie F. (Baumkratz) Schimmel; married Micki Goodman (a choreographer), December 1, 1979; children: Michael, Joseph. EDUCATION: Juilliard School of Music, B.A., 1969, M.S., 1970; Doctor of Musical Arts, 1973; also studied music at the Neupauer Conservatory. RELIGION: Roman Catholic.

VOCATION: Composer, musical director, conductor, and performer.

WILLIAM SCHIMMEL

CAREER: FIRST STAGE WORK—Assistant conductor, *Threepenny Opera,* Vivian Beaumont Theatre, Lincoln Center, New York City, 1976, for five-hundred-fifty performances. PRINCIPAL STAGE WORK—Composer, *A Little Wine with Lunch,* No Smoking Playhouse, New York City, 1976; composer, accordionist, pianist, and actor, *The Tennis Game,* Music Theatre Group, Lenox Arts Center, New York City; composer and accordionist, *Jane Avril,* Provincetown Playhouse, New York City; composer, accordionist, and pianist, *Dick Deterred,* No Smoking Playhouse and Westbank Theatre, New York City; composer and accordionist, *Masquerade,* Edinburgh Festival, Scotland, 1979.

MAJOR TOURS—Musical director, Quob Music Theatre, Italian and French cities, 1975; composer and accordionist, *Masquerade,* Long Wharf Theatre, New Haven, CT, Lorretto-Hilton Theatre, St. Louis, MO and other U.S. regional theatres, 1980; also musical consultant, *Frank's Wild Years,* Steppenwolf Theatre, Chicago.

FIRST FILM WORK—Composer and accordionist, *Rivers of the Deep South,* Sunnyside Films, 1982. PRINCIPAL FILM WORK—Composer and accordionist, *An Oasis in Time,* Sunnyside, 1983; composer, *Far from Poland,* 1984.

FIRST TELEVISION WORK—Composer and conductor, *The Hiders,* NBC, 1970. PRINCIPAL TELEVISION WORK—Accordionist, *Holocaust,* NBC, 1978; accordionist, *Late Night with David Letterman,* NBC, 1986.

RELATED CAREER—Professor of composition, Brooklyn College, NY, 1971-76; professor of music theory, Juilliard School, New York City, 1973-74; dean of school of music, Neupauer Conservatory, 1976—; professor of accordion music, Upsala College, 1981—; co-founder (with Micki Goodman), Studio Muse; co-founder (with Michael Sahl), The Tango Project.

WRITINGS: BOOKS—*Improving Aural Skills,* Studio Muse Press, 1983; *Collected Writings,* Studio Muse Press, 1986.

SONGS—Over three-hundred-fifty songs published by April-Blackwood, Sundbury-Dunbar, Chappell, and Schimmel-Norback and four hundred compositions performed and conducted by leading artists around the world, including Leopold Stokowski.

AWARDS: Special Citation, American Accordionists Association Award, 1979; Album of the Year, Stereo Review Award, 1982; Man of the Year, American Accordionists Association.

MEMBER: Accordion Arts Society (founding member, 1976), Composers Concordance (board of directors, 1986).

ADDRESSES: HOME—345 E. 85th Street, New York, NY 10028. OFFICE—242 E. 89th Street, New York, NY 10128.

*   *   *

SCHLARTH, Sharon

PERSONAL: Born January 19, in Buffalo, NY; daughter of J. Don (a journalist) and Sally (a journalist; maiden name, Gallagher) Schlarth. EDUCATION: State University of New York, B.F.A.; studied acting with Ernie Martin, Michael Shurtleff, and Warren Robertson in New York City.

SHARON SCHLARTH

VOCATION: Actress.

CAREER: PRINCIPAL STAGE APPEARANCES—Mildred, *Fahrenheit 451,* Colony Studio, Los Angeles, 1979; Samantha, *Uncommon Women and Others,* Callboard Theatre, Los Angeles, 1980 and the roles of Muffet, Carter, Leilah, and Susie in a production of the same play at the Los Angeles Stage Company, 1981; Curley's wife, *Of Mice and Men,* La Mama Theatre Company, Los Angeles, 1980; Betty Blue, *Hoagy, Bix and Bunkhaus,* Mark Taper forum, Los Angeles, 1981; title role, *Anna Christie,* Actors Federal Theatre, New York City, 1982; Ludmyla, *The Brothers* New Dramatists, New York City, 1982; Laurel, *The Early Girl,* New Dramatists, 1982 and later at Circle Repertory Theatre, New York City, 1986; May, *Fool for Love* and Beth, *Full Hookup,* both Circle Repertory Company, New York City, 1983; Jacquenetta, *Love's Labour's Lost,* Circle Repertory Company, 1984; also: various roles, *Rhino Fat from Red Dog Notes,* Studio Arena Theatre, Buffalo, NY; Jackie, *Hot'L Baltimore,* Michael Rockefeller Theatre; Ismene, *Antigone,* Marvel Theatre; Fran, *Shay,* Arena Theatre, Washington, DC; Nancy, *Oliver!,* Carousel Theatre; title role, *Sweet Charity,* Springside Inn; Kate, *Quiet in the Land,* Jean, *The Mound Builders,* and Lucia *Caligula,* all at the Triplex Theatre, New York City.

MAJOR TOURS—May, *Fool for Love,* with the Circle Repertory Company, Japanese cities, 1985.

PRINCIPAL TELEVISION APPEARANCES—Series: Lois Carney, *Loving,* ABC; Rachel Jolene, *The Young and the Restless,* CBS; featured in four roles, *Omnibus,* BBC (filmed in Los Angeles).

Episodic: Pamela, *Skelton Key*, WKW-TV; *Variety Club Telethon*, PBS; *As the World Turns*, CBS.

PRINCIPAL FILM APPEARANCES—Postgirl, *Fade to Black*, American Cinema, 1980; Linda Regan, *Doorman*, Just Spokes Productions, 1984; *Mangia!*, 1985; Cheryl Cohen, *Eat & Run*, New World Productions

AWARDS: Outstanding Performer, State University of New York.

MEMBER: Actors' Equity Association, Screen Actors Guild, American Federation of Television and Radio Artists, Circle Repertory Company.

ADDRESSES: OFFICE—Circle Repertory Company, 161 Avenue of the Americas, New York, NY 10013.

* * *

SCHMIDT, Marlene

PERSONAL: Born September 7, in Chicago, IL; daughter of Henry Schmidt; married Howard Avedis (a producer, director, and writer) December 26, 1969; children: three step-daughters. EDUCATION: University of Washington, B.A., communications, 1956; studied cinema and law at University of California at Los Angeles and University of Southern California; studied acting with Jeff Corey.

VOCATION: Producer and writer.

CAREER: PRINCIPAL FILM WORK—Producer and co-writer with Howard Avedis: *The Stepmother*, Crown International, 1972; *The Teacher*, Crown International, 1974; *Scorchy*, American International Pictures, 1976; *Texas Detour*, Cinema Shares International, 1977; *The Fifth Floor*, Film Ventures International, 1978; *Separate Ways*, Crown International, 1979; *Mortuary*, Artists Releasing thru Film Ventures International, 1982; *They're Playing with Fire*, New World Pictures, 1984; *Kidnapped*, Fries Entertainment, 1986.

TELEVISION DEBUT—*Ben Casey*, ABC.

PRINCIPAL FILM APPEARANCES—Appeared in films in Rome for five years.

RELATED CAREER—Casting department, Columbia Pictures Television; producer, CBS-TV affiliate news talk show, for five years.

MEMBER: Screen Actors Guild; Women in Film, National Academy of Cable Programming.

ADDRESSES: OFFICE—Hickmar Productions, Burbank Studios, PB4 Room 105, Burbank, CA 91505.

* * *

SCHNABEL, Stefan   1912-

PERSONAL: Born February 2, 1912, in Berlin, Germany; son of Artur (a pianist) and Therese (a concert singer; maiden name, Behr) Schnabel; married Joan Pittman, July 14, 1939 (divorced, 1942; deceased, 1972); married Marion Kohler (an actress), November

26, 1946; children: (first marriage) Susan; (second marriage) Peter, David. EDUCATION: Attended the University of Berlin and the University of Bonn; studied acting with Ilka Gruening in Berlin and at the Old Vic in London, England. MILITARY: OSS in World War II.

VOCATION: Actor.

CAREER: LONDON DEBUT—Off-stage wind noise, *The Tempest*, Old Vic Theatre, London, 1933. BROADWAY DEBUT—Mettulus Cimber, then Decius Brutus, *Julius Caesar*, Mercury Theatre, 1937. PRINCIPAL STAGE APPEARANCES—Third murderer, *Macbeth*, Soothsayer, *Anthony and Cleopatra*, and Lord Willoughby, *King Richard II*, all at the Old Vic Theatre, London, 1934; second player, *The Taming of the Shrew*, Old Vic Theatre, Sadlers Wells, U.K., 1935; Morrison, *Major Barbara* and porter, *Henry IV*, both at the Old Vic Theatre, London, 1935; Krumpaker, *Sweeney Agonestes*, Westminster Theatre, London, 1935; Grabeturn, *The Dog Beneath the Skin*, Westminster Theatre, London, 1936; Bergriffenfeldt, *Peer Gynt*, Sadler's Wells Theatre, London, 1936; messenger, sheriff, and murderer, *King Richard III*, Doctor, *King Lear*, Charles, *As You Like It*, and Hamluc, *The Witch of Endor*, all at the Old Vic Theatre, London, 1936; Dutch skipper, *Shoemaker's Holiday*, Mercury Theatre, New York City, 1938.

Nicholas Jarga, *Glamour Preferred*, Booth Theatre, New York City, 1940; company, *Everyman*, Mercury Theatre, New York City, 1941; Lieutenant Werner, *Land of Fame*, Belasco Theatre, New York City, 1943; Lopakin, *The Cherry Orchard*, National Theatre, New York City, 1944; Avery Jevitt, an Arab spy, a clown,

STEFAN SCHNABEL

and a medicine man, *Around the World in Eighty Days*, Adelphi Theatre, New York City, 1946; M. Hufnagel and Don Modesto, *Now I Lay Me Down to Sleep*, Broadhurst Theatre, New York City, 1950; Dr. Waldersee, *Idiot's Delight*, City Center, New York City, 1951; Col. Alexander Ikonenko, *The Love of Four Colonels*, Shubert Theatre, New York City, 1953; Papa Yoder, *Plain and Fancy*, Mark Hellinger Theatre, New York City, 1955; Gen. Graf Van Donop, *Small War on Murray Hill*, Ethel Barrymore Theatre, New York City, 1957; Baron Gray, *The Grand Duchess of Gerolstein*, Town Hall, New York City, 1958.

Between 1958 and 1965, Schnabel appeared in repertory with the Kammerspiele Muenchen in Munich, West Germany. During that period he also appeared in other theatres throughout Germany, including appearances as *Uncle Vanya*, and in other classic theatre works including *Macbeth*, performed in Berlin in 1962.

Stomil, *Tango*, Pocket Theatre, New York City, 1969; Hans Bethe, *In the Matter of J. Robert Oppenheimer*, Vivian Beaumont Theatre, Lincoln Center, New York City, 1969; Gen. Conrad von Hotzendorf, *A Patriot for Me*, Imperial Theatre, New York City, 1969.

Dubufay, Dunbar, Bubber, Sidney, Bob, and Howardina's brother, *Older People*, New York Shakespeare Festival (N.Y.S.F.) Anspacher/ Public Theatre, New York City, 1972; Gen. Penchakov, *Enemies*, Vivian Beaumont Theatre, New York City, 1972; Ulrik Brendel, *Rosmersholm*, Roundabout-Stage Two, New York City, 1974; Willie Schmidt, *Little Black Sheep*, N.Y.S.F., Vivian Beaumont Theatre, New York City, 1975; Professor von Helsing, *The Passion of Dracula*, Cherry Lane Theatre, New York City, 1978; Glas, *Slow Dance on the Killing Ground*, Alaska Repertory, Anchorage, 1979; title role, *Goodnight, Grandpa*, PAF Playhouse, Huntington, NY, 1979; Rabbi, *Teibele and Her Demon*, Brooks Atkinson Theatre, 1979; Savinet, *Monsieur Ribadier's System; or, How He Did It*, Hudson Guild Theatre, New York City, 1979; *Biography*, Manhattan Theatre Club, New York City, 1980; *Twelve Dreams*, Public Theatre, New York City, 1981; *Firebugs*, Crazy Horse Theatre, New York City, 1982; *Social Security*, Ethel Barrymore Theatre, New York City, 1986-87.

PRINCIPAL FILM APPEARANCES—Purser, *Journey into Fear*, RKO, 1938; *Behind the Iron Curtain* (also known as *The Iron Curtain*), Twentieth Century-Fox, 1947; *The Barbary Pirate*, Columbia, 1949; *Diplomatic Courier*, Twentieth Century-Fox, 1952; *The Great Houdini*, Paramount, 1953; *Crowded Paradise*, Tudor, 1955; *The 27th Day*, Columbia, 1957; *The Mugger*, United Artists, 1959; *The Secret Ways*, Universal, 1962; *The Counterfeit Traitor*, Metro-Goldwyn-Mayer (MGM), 1962; *Freud*, MGM, 1962; *Two Weeks in Another Town*, MGM, 1963; *The Ugly American*, MGM, 1964; *Rampage*, Warner Brothers, 1964; *A Very Rich Woman*, Supervision, 1965; first secretary, *Fire Fox*, Warner Brothers, 1981; psychiatrist, *Lovesick*, Warner Brothers, 1983.

TELEVISION DEBUT—Decius Brutus, *Julius Caesar*, NBC, 1938. PRINCIPAL TELEVISION APPEARANCES—Series: Dr. Steve Jackson, *The Guiding Light*, 1960-62; Wing Firebeard, *Tales of the Vikings*. Episodic: *Kraft Theatre*, NBC; *Ford Theatre*, CBS; *Studio One*, CBS; *Lux Video Theatre*, CBS; *You Are There*, CBS; *Suspense*, CBS. Movies: *Top Brass*, 1984; *Stone Pillow*, CBS, 1985.

PRINCIPAL RADIO WORK—"War of the Worlds," *Mercury Theatre on the Air*, CBS, 1938; Dr. Rheinhardt, *Joyce Jordan, Girl Intern*, retitled, *Joyce Jordan, M.D.*, CBS, 1938-mid 1940s; *Big Sister*, CBS, 1939; Cezar Benedict, *Bright Horizon*, CBS, 1941; *Gangbusters*, CBS, 1940s; the Rattler, *Chick Carter, Boy Detec-*

tive, 1940s; also, *The Story of Mary Marlin*, CBS; *Against the Storm*, NBC; *Columbia Workshop*, CBS; *Portia Faces Life*, CBS; *Second Husband*, CBS; *Revlon Theatre*, NBC; *Theatre Guild*, ABC; others.

MEMBER: Actor's Equity Association, American Federation of Television and Radio Artists, Screen Actors Guild, American Guild of Musical Artists; Players Club.

SIDELIGHTS: RECREATIONS—Sailing and mountaineering.

In a note to *CTFT*, Stefan Schnabel revealed that between 1937 and 1957 he appeared in over five thousand radio shows.

ADDRESSES: AGENT—Alan Willig, 47A Horatio Street, New York, NY 10014.

* * *

SCHRADER, Paul   1946-

PERSONAL: Born July 22, 1946, in Grand Rapids, MI; son of Charles A. (an executive) and Joan (Fisher) Schrader; married Mary Beth Hurt (an actress), August 6, 1983; children: Molly. EDUCATION: Calvin College; University of California at Los Angeles, M.A., film, 1970.

VOCATION: Writer and director.

CAREER: PRINCIPAL FILM WORK—Director: *Blue Collar*, Universal, 1977; *Hardcore*, Columbia, 1978; *American Gigolo*, Paramount, 1979; *Cat People*, Universal, 1981; *Mishima*, Warner Brothers, 1985; *Light of Day*, Taft-British/Tri-Star, 1987. Also, executive producer, *Old Boyfriends*, AVCO-Embassy, 1978.

RELATED CAREER—Wrote film criticism for the *Los Angeles Free Press*, 1968-70; edited the magazine *Cinema* while continuing to freelance for other publications; he wrote briefly for *Coast* and sold articles to *Film Quarterly*.

WRITINGS: SCREENPLAYS—(With Robert Towne) *The Yakuza*, Warner Brothers, 1974; *Taxi Driver*, Columbia, 1976; (with Brian DePalma) *Obsession*, Columbia, 1976; (with Leonard Schrader) *Blue Collar*, Universal, 1977; (with Heywood Gould) *Rolling Thunder*, American-International, 1977; *Hardcore*, Columbia, 1978; (with Leonard Schrader) *Old Boyfriends*, AVCO-Embassy, 1978; *American Gigolo*, Paramount, 1979; (with Mardik Martin) *Raging Bull*, United Artists, 1980; *Cat People*, Universal, 1981; (with Leonard Schrader) *Mishima*, Warner Brothers, 1985; *The Mosquito Coast*, Orion, 1986; *Light of Day*, Taft-British/Tri-Star, 1987.

NON-FICTION—*Transcendental Style in Film: Ozu, Bresson, Dreyer*, University of California Press, 1972.

AWARDS: Two First Place essays, 1968: *Atlantic* and *Story: The Magazine of Discovery*.

MEMBER: Writers Guild of America, West.

ADDRESSES: AGENT—c/o Jeff Berg, International Creative Management, 8899 Beverly Blvd., Los Angeles, CA 90048.

TERRY SCHREIBER

SCHREIBER, Terry 1937-

PERSONAL: Born March 7, 1937, in Winona, MN; son of Walter Milton (a barber) and Vanona Anne Emma (Bielefeldt) Schreiber; married M. Archer Brown, May 5, 1963 (divorced, 1976); married Sara Louise (Sally) Dunn (an actress), July 11, 1981. EDUCATION: St. Thomas College, B.A. POLITICS: Independent. RELIGION: Lutheran. MILITARY: U.S. Naval Reserves.

VOCATION: Director, producer, and acting teacher.

CAREER: PRINCIPAL STAGE WORK—Director: *Does Anybody Here Do the Peabody?*, Wonderhorse Theatre, New York City, 1976; *The Trip Back Down*, Longacre Theatre, New York City, 1977; *Feedlot*, Circle Repertory Theatre, New York City, 1977; *Glorious Morning*, Circle Repertory Theatre, 1978; *Devour the Snow*, John Golden Theatre, New York City, 1979; *K-2*, Brooks Atkinson Theatre, New York City, 1983; *Desire Under the Elms*, Roundabout Theatre, New York City, 1984; also, *Where Do We Go from Here?*, Mama Gail's Theatre, New York City; *The Miracle Worker* and *K-2*, both with the Shochiku Company, Tokyo, Japan; *Bent* and *A Streetcar Named Desire*, both with the Show Company, Tokyo, Japan.

In regional repertory theatres: *A Thousand Clowns, Dark at the Top of the Stairs, The Music Man, Luv, Oliver,* and *Night Must Fall,* all at the Bradford Repertory Theatre; *A Very Private Life,* Buffalo Arena Stage; *Serenading Louie,* George Street Playhouse, New Brunswick, NJ; *Medal of Honor Rag, Slow Dance on the Killing Ground, Ashes,* and *Vanities,* all at the Pittsburgh Public Theatre; *A*

View from the Bridge, Hartman Theatre, Stamford, CT; *Who's Afraid of Virginia Woolf?,* Syracuse Stage and at the Stony Brook Theatre Festival, NY; *A Doll's House, Betrayal, K-2,* and *Passion,* all at Syracuse Stage; *Foxfire,* Guthrie Theatre (Outreach Tour), 1984-85.

At the Terry Schreiber Studio, Off-Off-Broadway, New York City, produced approximately thirty-six plays, including the following, which he also directed: *Suddenly Last Summer, Miss Julie, A Day in the Death of Joe Egg, Hamlet, Of Mice and Men, 49 West 87th Street, Cabin Twelve, The Crucible, The Birthday Party, The Diary of Anne Frank, Alfie, The Lark, You Know I Can't Hear You When the Water's Running, A Midsummer Night's Dream, My Three Angels, The Prime of Miss Jean Brodie, Summer and Smoke,* and *Six Characters in Search of an Author.*

RELATED CAREER—Artistic director: Terry Schreiber Studio, 1969—; Terry Schreiber Theatre, 1969-77; Bradford Repertory Theatre, 1972-73; associate director, Syracuse Stage, 1985-86.

ADDRESSES: HOME—120 Riverside Drive, New York, NY 10024. OFFICE—83 E. Fourth Street, New York, NY 10003. AGENT—c/o Milton Goldman, International Creative Management, 40 W. 57th Street, New York, NY 10019.

*   *   *

SCHWARZENEGGER, Arnold 1947-

PERSONAL: Born July 30, 1947, in Graz, Austria; became naturalized U.S. citizen, September, 1983; son of Karl (a police chief) and Aurelia (Jedrny) Schwarzenegger; married Maria Shriver (a broadcast journalist), April 26, 1986. EDUCATION: University of Wisconsin, Superior, B.A., business and international ecomomics.

VOCATION: Actor, writer, and body-builder.

CAREER: FILM DEBUT—*Stay Hungry,* United Artists, 1976. PRINCIPAL FILM APPEARANCES—*Pumping Iron,* Cinema Five, 1977; *The Villain,* Columbia, 1979; title role, *Conan the Barbarian,* Universal, 1982; title role, *Conan the Destroyer,* Universal, 1983; title role, *The Terminator,* Orion, 1984; *Commando,* Twentieth Century-Fox, 1985; Kalidor, *Red Sonja,* Metro-Goldwyn-Mayer/United Artists, 1985; *Raw Deal,* DeLaurentiis Entertainment Group, 1986.

PRINCIPAL TELEVISION APPEARANCES—Guest: *The Merv Griffin Show,* CBS; *The Tonight Show,* NBC; *The David Letterman Show,* NBC; *Friday Night Videos,* NBC. Specials: *Happy Anniversary and Goodbye,* 1975. Movies: Mickey Hargitay, *The Jayne Mansfield Story.*

RELATED CAREER—Body-builder, 1962-1976; lectures on fitness and body-building; formed his own production company; real estate and mail order businessman. Also is an occasional sports commentator for CBS and ABC television.

WRITINGS: NON-FICTION—*Arnold's Bodyshaping for Women,* Simon & Schuster, Inc., 1979 and (with Douglas K. Hall) 1983; (with Bill Dobbins) *Arnold's Bodybuilding for Men,* Simon & Schuster, Inc., 1981 and 1984; *Arnold's Encyclopedia of Modern Bodybuilding,* Simon & Schuster, Inc., 1984; (with Douglas K. Hall) *Arnold: The Education of a Bodybuilder,* Pocket Books, 1986. PERIODICALS—Articles for "Muscle and Fitness" magazine.

AWARDS: Best Newcomer in Films, Golden Globe, 1976, for *Stay Hungry;* International Star of 1984, National Association of Theatre Owners; thirteen world champion body-building titles won between 1965-1980, including Mr. Universe and Mr. Olympia.

SIDELIGHTS: From material supplied by him, *CTFT* learned that Arnold Schwarzenegger retired from body-building in 1974, only to come out of that retirement to appear in two films, the documentary *Pumping Iron* and the feature film *Stay Hungry.* Both movies deal with the sports of weightlifting and body-building.

Commenting on his movie roles in action-adventure films, Schwarzenegger said, ''I would never alienate people by denying them the things they have come to see from me in the past. I got my breaks in the business because of my physical attributes. What I . . . will continue to do [in my films] is to add on new facets to the characters that I play, exposing new sides of myself. Eventually down the line, I'll play a role where the physical and athletic skills aren't necessary.''

Schwarzenegger spends much of his free time working with the Special Olympics and visiting prisons to implement a prisoner rehabilitation program through weight resistance training.

ADDRESSES: OFFICE—Oak Productions, Inc., 321 Hampton Drive, Suite 203, Venice, CA 90291. PUBLICIST—Guttman and Pam Ltd., 120 El Camino Drive, Beverly Hills, CA 90212.

*   *   *

SCOFIELD, Paul   1922-

PERSONAL: Full name, David Paul Scofield; born January 21, 1922, in Hurstpierpoint, Sussex, England; married Joy Parker (an actress), May 15, 1943; children: one son, one daughter. EDUCATION: Attended the Varndean School for Boys, Brighton, England, 1933-39; trained for the stage at the London Mask Theatre and Drama School, in connection with the Westminster Theatre, London.

VOCATION: Actor.

CAREER: STAGE DEBUT—As one of the crowd, *The Only Way,* Theatre Royal, Brighton, England, 1936. LONDON DEBUT—*Desire Under the Elms,* Westminster Theatre, 1940. BROADWAY DEBUT—Thomas More, *A Man for All Seasons,* American National Theatre Academy (ANTA) Theatre, 1961. PRINCIPAL STAGE APPEARANCES—Third clerk and first soldier, *Abraham Lincoln,* Westminster Theatre, London, 1940; with the Bideford Repertory Theatre Company, U.K., 1941; with the Birmingham Repertory Theatre, U.K., 1942; Alex Morden, *The Moon Is Down,* Whitehall Theatre, London, 1943; with the Birmingham Repertory Theatre: Reginald, *Getting Married,* the Prince, *The Circle of Chalk,* the clown, *The Winter's Tale,* and William D'Albini, *The Empress Maud,* all 1944, Valentine, *Doctor's Delight,* young Marlow, *She Stoops to Conquer,* Konstantin, *The Seagull,* John Tanner, *Man and Superman,* and Philip, *King John,* all 1945; at the Shakespeare Memorial Theatre, Stratford-on-Avon: title role, *Henry V,* Don Armado, *Love's Labour's Lost,* Malcolm, *Macbeth,* Lucio, *Measure for Measure,* Mercutio, *Romeo and Juliet,* Sir Andrew Aguecheek, *Twelfth Night,* Cloten, *Cymbeline,* title role, *Pericles,* and Mephistophilis, *Faust,* all 1946-47; Tegeus-Chromis, *A Phoenix Too Frequent,* with the Shakespeare Memorial Theatre at the Arts Theatre, London, 1946; Mercutio, *Romeo and Juliet* and Sir Andrew Aguecheek, *Twelfth Night,* both with the Shakespeare

Memorial Theatre at Her Majesty's Theatre, London, 1947; Young Fashion, *The Relapse,* Lyric Theatre, Hammersmith, London, 1947, then Phoenix Theatre, London, 1948; with the Shakespeare Memorial Theatre, Stratford-on-Avon: King Philip, *King John,* Bassanio, *The Merchant of Venice,* title role, *Hamlet,* Clown, *The Winter's Tale,* Troilus, *Troilus and Cressida,* and Roderigo, *Othello,* all 1948.

Alexander, *Adventure Story,* St. James Theatre, London, 1949; Treplef, *The Seagull,* Lyric Theatre, Hammersmith, London, 1949; Hugo and Frederic, *Ring 'Round the Moon,* Globe Theatre, London, 1950; title role, *Pericles,* Rudolf Steiner Hall, London, 1950; Don Pedro, *Much Ado About Nothing,* Phoenix Theatre, London, 1952; Philip Sturgess, *The River Line,* Edinburgh Festival, Scotland, then Lyric Theatre, Hammersmith, London, then Strand Theatre, London, 1952; title role, *Richard II,* with Sir John Gielgud's repertory company at the Lyric Theatre, Hammersmith, London, 1952; Witwoud, *The Way of the World* and Pierre, *Venice Preserved,* both with Sir John Gielgud's repertory company at the Lyric Theatre, Hammersmith, London, 1953; Paul Gardiner, *A Question of Fact,* Piccadilly Theatre, London, 1953; Prince Albert Troubiscoi, *Time Remembered,* Lyric Theatre, Hammersmith, London, 1954, and New Theatre, London, 1955; title role, *Hamlet,* Phoenix Theatre, London, 1955; the Priest, *The Power and the Glory,* Phoenix Theatre, London, 1956; Harry, *The Family Reunion,* Phoenix Theatre, London, 1956; Fred Dyson, *A Dead Secret,* Piccadilly Theatre, London, 1957; Johnnie, *Expresso Bongo,* Saville Theatre, London, 1958; Clive Root, *The Complaisant Lover,* Globe Theatre, London, 1959.

Sir Thomas More, *A Man for All Seasons,* Globe Theatre, London, 1960; title role, *Coriolanus* and Don Armado, *Love's Labour's Lost,* both at the Stratford Shakespeare Festival, Ontario, Canada, 1961; title role, *King Lear,* with the Royal Shakespeare Company, Stratford-on-Avon, U.K. then at the Aldwych Theatre, London, 1962, then Sarah Bernhardt Theatre, Paris, France, 1963, and State Theatre, New York City, 1964; title role, *Timon of Athens,* with the Royal Shakespeare Company, Stratford-on-Avon, U.K., 1965; Ivan Alexandrovitch Khlestakov, *The Government Inspector,* Aldwych Theatre, London, 1966; Charlie Dyer, *Staircase,* Aldwych Theatre, London, 1966; the Dragon, *The Thwarting of Baron Bolligrew,* Aldwych Theatre, London, 1966; title role, *Macbeth,* Aldwych Theatre, London, 1967-68; Laurie, *The Hotel in Amsterdam,* Royal Court Theatre, London, then New Theatre, London, and Duke of York's Theatre, London, 1968; title role, *Uncle Vanya,* Royal Court Theatre, London, 1970.

Wilhelm Voigt, *The Captain of Kopenick* and Leone, *The Rules of the Game,* both with the National Theatre Company at the Old Vic Theatre, London, 1971; Alan West, *Savages,* with the National Theatre Company at the Royal Court Theatre, London, then Comedy Theatre, London, 1973; Prospero, *The Tempest,* Leeds Playhouse, U.K., then Wyndham's Theatre, London, 1974; title role, *Dimetos,* Nottingham Playhouse, U.K., then Comedy Theatre, London, 1976; title role, *Volpone,* and Constantine Madras, *The Madras House,* both at the Olivier Theatre, London, 1977; Freddie Kilner, *A Family,* Royal Exchange Theatre, Manchester, U.K., then Haymarket Theatre, London, 1978; Salieri, *Amadeus,* Olivier Theatre, London, 1979; title role, *Othello,* Olivier Theatre, London, 1980; title role, *Don Quixote,* London, 1982.

MAJOR TOURS—Vincentio and Tranio, *The Taming of the Shrew,* with the Entertainments National Service Association (ENSA), U.K. cities, 1941; Stephen Undershaft, *Major Barbara* and Horatio, *Hamlet,* with the Birmingham Repertory Theatre's Traveling Repertory Theatre, U.K. cities, 1942; title role, *Hamlet*, Moscow, U.S.S.R., 1955; title role, *King Lear*, with the Royal Shakespeare Company, West Berlin, Prague, Budapest, Belgrade, Bucharest, Warsaw, Helsinki, Lenningrad, and Moscow, 1964.

PRINCIPAL STAGE WORK—Producer, *Pericles*, Rudolf Steiner Hall, London, 1950.

FILM DEBUT—*Carve Her Name with Pride*, 1954. PRINCIPAL FILM APPEARANCES—Philip II, *That Lady*, Twentieth Century-Fox, 1955; *The Train*, 1963; Sir Thomas More, *A Man for All Seasons*, Columbia, 1966; title role, *King Lear*, 1970; *Bartleby*, 1972; Tobias, *A Delicate Balance*, American Film Institute, 1972; Zharkov, *Scorpio*, United Artists, 1973; Alexander Scherbatov, *1919*, 1974; also, *The Conspiracy*, CAC Productions.

PRINCIPAL TELEVISION APPEARANCES—Movies: *The Ambassadors*, 1977; narrator, *The Curse of King Tut's Tomb*, 1980; James Callifer, *The Potting Shed*, 1981; *If Winter Comes*, 1981; *Song at Twilight*, 1982; *Come into the Garden Maud*, 1982; *A Kind of Alaska*, 1984; Karenin, *Anna Karenina*, CBS, 1985.

RELATED CAREER—Royal Shakespeare Directorate, 1966-68.

AWARDS: Received Commander of the British Empire in New Year's Honors, 1956; *Evening Standard* Drama Award, 1956, for *The Power and the Glory;* Best Actor, Antoinette Perry Award, 1962, for *A Man for all Seasons; Evening Standard* Drama Award, 1962, for *King Lear;* Best Actor, Academy Award, New York Film Critics Award, London Film Academy Award, Saint Genesius Gold Medal, Rome, Italy, all 1966, for *A Man for All Seasons;* Danish Bodil Award, 1967, for *King Lear;* Shakespeare Prize, Hamburg, Germany, 1972; Hon. L.L.D. (Doctor of Letters), Glasgow University, 1968, Hon. D.Litt. (Doctor of Literature), University of Kent, 1973.

MEMBER: Actors' Equity Association (American, Canadian, and British affiliations), Screen Actors Guild.

ADDRESSES: HOME—The Gables, Balcombe, Sussex, England.*

*   *   *

SCULLY, Joe   1926-

PERSONAL: Born March 1, 1926, in Kearny, NJ; son of Joseph B. and Helen A. (Peters) Scully; married Penelope J. Gillette (an actress and teacher); children: Samantha. EDUCATION: Goodman Theatre of the Art Institute of Chicago, 1946. POLITICS: Democrat. RELIGION: Roman Catholic.

VOCATION: Casting director, producer, and writer.

CAREER: PRINCIPAL FILM WORK—Casting director for Twentieth Century-Fox: *In Like Flint*, 1967; *The Valley of the Dolls*, 1967; *The Flim Flam Man*, 1967; *The Secret Life of an American Wife*, 1968; *The Planet of the Apes*, 1968; *Hello, Dolly!*, 1969. Independent casting: *Journey Through Rosebud*, Republic Pictures, 1972; *Play It as It Lays*, Universal, 1972; *Lady Sings the Blues*, Paramount, 1972; *Stone Killer*, Columbia, 1973; *Where the Lilies Bloom*, United Artists, 1974; *Mixed Company*, United Artists, 1974; *The Parallax View*, Paramount, 1974; *Framed*, Paramount,

1975; *The Man in the Glass Booth*, MPT, 1975; *Sounder*, Twentieth Century-Fox, 1975; *Lifeguard*, Paramount, 1976; *A Man, a Woman and a Bank*, AVCO-Embassy, 1979; *Middle Age Crazy*, Twentieth Century-Fox, 1980; *Breakfast in Paris*, John Lamond Films, 1982; *Death Wish II*, Cannon Films, 1982. Casting director for Walt Disney/Touchstone Pictures: *The Black Cauldron*, 1985; *The Great Mouse Detective*, 1986.

PRINCIPAL TELEVISION WORK—Series: Casting director, CBS, 1951-56—*Omnibus, Danger, The Web, Rod Brown of the Rocket Rangers, You Are There*. Casting director, 1965-70: *Peyton Place*, ABC; *Judd for the Defense*, ABC; *Room 222*, ABC. 1970-75: *Bonanza*, NBC; *Nicholas*, NBC; *Search*, NBC; *The Bill Cosby Show*, NBC; *Faraday & Company*, NBC; *The Snoop Sisters*, NBC; *McMillan & Wife*, NBC. 1978-83: *James at 15* (also *James at 16*), NBC; *The Paper Chase*, CBS; *240 Robert*, ABC; *Tales of the Unexpected*, syndicated.

Movies: Casting director—*Doug Selby, D.A.*, 1965; *Along Came a Spider*, 1969; *Murder Once Removed*, CBS, 1971; *The Forgotten Man*, 1971; *Earth II*, ABC, 1971; *The President's Plane Is Missing*, ABC, 1971; *A Tattered Web*, CBS, 1971; *She Waits*, CBS, 1971; *Second Chance*, ABC, 1971; *Thief*, CBS, 1971; *The Morning After*, ABC, 1974; *Men of the Dragon*, 1974; *Get Christie Love!*, 1974; *Strangers: The Story of a Mother & Daughter*, Christianson/Rosenberg Productions, 1979; *The Day the Loving Stopped*, ABC, 1981; *Secrets of a Mother and Daughter*, CBS, 1983; *Gone Are the Days*, Disney Channel, 1985; also *Here We Go Again*. Pilots: *The Ghost & Mrs. Muir*, NBC, 1970; *Julia*, NBC, 1970; *Beyond Westworld*, CBS, 1978; *Side Show*, NBC, 1978; *Misfits of Science*,

JOE SCULLY

NBC, 1985; *Insiders,* ABC, 1986. Mini-Series: *The Missiles of October,* ABC.

Associate producer, CBS, 1956-60: *Playhouse 90, Studio One in Hollywood, Buick Electra Playhouse, Studio One, Dupont Show of the Month, The Time of Your Life.*

RELATED CAREER—Associate producer, Four Star Television, 1960-62; teacher and lecturer: University of California at Los Angeles, California Institute of the Arts, and San Diego State College, 1967—; manager of talent and casting, NBC, 1975-78.

WRITINGS: TELEPLAYS—"The Little Woman," *Danger,* CBS, 1954; "The Young, the Talented and Hopeful," "The Powder Room," and "In the Thurber Room," all on the *Repertoire Workshop,* CBS, 1963.

AWARDS: National Association for Better Radio & Television Award, 1963-64, for producing *Repertoire Workshop;* Award of Merit, Television Academy of Arts and Sciences, 1969-70, for casting *Room 222;* Halo Award for Special Merit, Southern California Motion Picture Council, 1986, for Television and Motion Picture Casting.

MEMBER: Casting Society of America, Academy of Motion Picture Arts and Sciences, Writers Guild of America West.

ADDRESSES: HOME—Studio City, CA.

*   *   *

SEIDELMAN, Arthur Allan

PERSONAL: Born October 11, in New York, NY; son of Theodore and Jeanne (Greenberg) Seidelman. EDUCATION: Whittier College, B.A.; University of California at Los Angeles, M.A.

VOCATION: Producer, director, and writer.

CAREER: FIRST STAGE WORK—Director and producer, *The Beautiful People,* Blue Couch Theatre, Los Angeles, 1960. FIRST OFF-BROADWAY WORK—Director and producer, *The Awakening of Spring,* Pocket Theatre, 1964. PRINCIPAL STAGE WORK— Director: *Hamp, Ceremony of Innocence, The Justice Box, Billy, Vieux Carre, The World of My America, Awake and Sing, The Four Seasons,* and *Inherit the Wind,* all produced in New York City.

Regional productions and national tours: *Romeo and Juliet, The Tempest, A Man for All Seasons, St. Joan, Dear Me, the Sky Is Falling, Cat on a Hot Tin Roof, Irma La Douce, Oh Dad Poor Dad, Mama's Hung You in the Closet and I'm Feelin' So Sad, The Little Foxes, The Roar of the Greasepaint, the Smell of the Crowd,* and *Stop the World, I Want to Get Off.*

FIRST FILM WORK—Director and writer, *Children of Rage,* LSU Productions, 1978. PRINCIPAL FILM WORK—Director: *Echoes,* Herberval Productions, 1984; *The Caller,* Empire State Entertainment, 1986.

PRINCIPAL TELEVISION APPEARANCES—Series: Host, *Actors on Acting,* PBS.

FIRST TELEVISION WORK—Director: *Ceremony of Innocence,*

PBS, 1977. PRINCIPAL TELEVISION WORK—Episodic: Director—*Family,* ABC, 1980; *Magnum, P.I,* CBS; *Murder, She Wrote,* CBS; *Trapper John, M.D.* CBS; *Paper Chase,* CBS; *Knott's Landing,* CBS; *Bay City Blues,* NBC. Movies: Director— *Which Mother Is Mine?, A Special Gift, Schoolboy Father, A Matter of Time, I Think I'm Having a Baby, Sin of Innocence, Kate's Secret, Poker Alice.*

RELATED CAREER—Former staff member of the Repertory Theatre of Lincoln Center and the Phoenix Theatre, New York City.

WRITINGS: SCREENPLAYS—*Children of Rage,* LSU Productions, 1978. TELEPLAYS—(With Richard Alfieri and Norman Lear) *I Love Liberty,* ABC.

AWARDS: Two Emmy Awards; five Emmy Award nominations; Writers Guild Award; Peabody Award; Christopher Award; Golden Halo Award; Silver Plaque Award from both the New York Film Festival and the Chicago Film Festival.

MEMBER: Academy of Television Arts and Sciences, Academy of Cable Television, Actor's Studio; American Civil Liberties Union (board of directors), New Jewish Agenda (board of advisors).

ADDRESSES: OFFICE—Entertainment Professionals, Inc., 1015 Gayley Avenue, Suite 1149, Los Angeles, CA 90024. AGENT—c/o Don Klein, Irv Schechter Company, 9300 Wilshire Blvd., Beverly Hills, CA 90212.

*   *   *

SERRA, Raymond   1936-

PERSONAL: Born Raymond Lacagnina, August 13, 1936, in New York, NY; son of Pietro and Aurelia (Serra) Lacagnina; married Gayle Kaizer; children: Peter, Ralph, Frank, Daralyn. EDUCATION: Attended Rutgers University and Wagner College; trained for the stage with Stella Adler. POLITICS: Republican. RELIGION: Roman Catholic. MILITARY: U.S. Marine Corps, 1956-58.

VOCATION: Actor, producer, and writer.

CAREER: FILM DEBUT—Jay Chasil, *Mr. Inside, Mr. Outside,* 1973. PRINCIPAL FILM APPEARANCES—Benny, *The Gambler,* Paramount, 1974; van driver, *Marathon Man,* Paramount, 1976; Louie, *Looking Up,* Levitt-Pickman, 1977; Tony, *Voices,* United Artists, 1979; detective, *Wolfen,* Warner Brothers, 1981; racetrack owner, *Arthur,* Warner Brothers, 1981; undercover cop, *The Curse of the Pink Panther,* Metro-Goldwyn-Mayer/United Artists, 1983; Bocca, *Prizzi's Honor,* Twentieth Century-Fox, 1984; Shelby, *Purple Rose of Cairo,* Orion, 1984; Gino, *Alphabet City,* Atlantic, 1984; Alfonse, *Forever Lulu* and Vic, *Nasty Hero,* both upcoming.

Also appeared as Frank, *A Time to Remember,* Miam Productions; Chief, *The Rehearsal,* Jules Dassin Films; Mr. Vinnie, *Hooch,* Prudhomme Productions; Bunny, *Hoodlums,* Bonet Productions.

TELEVISION DEBUT—Joe Sweeney, *Mary Hartman, Mary Hartman,* syndicated. PRINCIPAL TELEVISION APPEARANCES—Series: Eddie Lorimer, *The Edge of Night,* ABC; Lt. Al Gambrino, *Powerhouse,* PBS. Episodic: Al Tristero, *Footsteps,* PBS; John, *Love, Sidney,* NBC; Marty Marquietti, *Archie Bunker's Place,*

RAYMOND SERRA

CBS; Joe Broz, *Spencer: For Hire*, ABC; Noah Ganz, *Crime Story*, NBC. Mini-Series: J. Edgar Hoover, *Concealed Enemies*, PBS.

Movies: Jimmy Monks, *Contract on Cherry Street*, NBC, 1977; Vinnie, *Hardhat and Legs*, CBS, 1980; Tony Parisi, *Fight'n Back*, MTM Productions, 1980; Harry, *Bill*, Alan Lansburg Productions, 1981; Joe, *The Dollmaker*, ABC, 1984; Al Dinardi, *Deadly Business*, CBS, 1985; Stan, *Stone Pillow*, CBS, 1985; also Stubby, *Con Sawyer and Hucklemary Finn*, ABC. Dramatic Specials: Mr. Callas, *The House of Ramon Inglesia*, PBS.

OFF-BROADWAY DEBUT—Poppa, *Mr. Jello*, La Mama Experimental Theatre Club (E.T.C.), for eighteen performances. BROADWAY DEBUT—John Morgan, *Wheelbarrow Closers*, Bijou Theatre, 1976, for twenty-eight performances. PRINCIPAL STAGE APPEARANCES—Dr. Carillo, *Momma's Little Angels*, Quaigh Theatre, New York City, 1978; title role, *Manny* (also known as *The Edward G. Robinson Story*), Century Theatre, New York City, 1979; Archbishop Parker, *Marlowe*, Rialto Theatre, New York City, 1981; Chief Bellati, *Accidental Death of an Anarchist*, Belasco Theatre, New York City, 1985; Diamond Louie, *The Front Page*, Vivian Beaumont Theatre, New York City, 1986; also appeared as Tony, *The Honeymoon*, Broadway production. Off-Broadway: *The Shark*, 1975; has appeared in over forty productions at New York City theatres such as La Mama E.T.C., Riverside Church, the Bijou, and the Century.

MAJOR TOURS—*An Evening with Little Caesar*, one-man show, U.S. cities.

RELATED CAREER—President, Buona Serra Productions, Inc., New York City, 1980—.

NON-RELATED CAREER—Vice-president, SNS Building Corporation, New York City, 1983—; vice-president, Hamilton Park Association, New York City, 1984—.

WRITINGS: PLAYS, PRODUCED—*Manny*, Century Theatre, New York City, 1979; *An Evening with Little Caesar*, one-man show, U.S. cities.

TELEVISION—"Cheers," *Powerhouse*, PBS, 1984.

AWARDS: Golden Cine Eagle Award, 1984, for "Cheers," *Powerhouse;* Facts Award, 1985, Australian Commercial Excellence; Humanitarian of the Year, 1985, Cooleys Anemia Foundation.

MEMBER: New York League of Theatres and Producers; American Parkinson's Disease Association (board of directors).

ADDRESSES: HOME—Staten Island, NY. OFFICE—675 Bay Street, Staten Island, NY 10304. AGENT—Fifi Oscard Agency, 19 W. 44th Street, New York, NY 10036.

*   *   *

SEVEN, Johnny 1926-

PERSONAL: Born John A. Fetto, February 23, 1926; son of John Anthony and Marie (Cianci) Fetto; married Edith Patricia Piselli, October 8, 1949; children: John Anthony III, Laura Michelle. EDUCATION: Attended Poe's Institute for Real Estate and Insurance, 1947; studied for the theater with Elia Kazan and Edward Ludlum. MILITARY: U.S. Army, 1944-46.

VOCATION: Actor, director, producer, and writer.

CAREER: STAGE DEBUT—Walters, *The Last Mile*, New England Road Company, 1950. BROADWAY DEBUT—Papa Silvani, *The Storyteller*, President Theatre, 1952, for fourteen performances. PRINCIPAL STAGE APPEARANCES—Stanley, *A Streetcar Named Desire*, Off-Broadway production, 1955; also *Salvage, Winterset, Payment Deferred*, and *Sounds of Hunting*, all Off-Broadway.

MAJOR TOURS—Mangiacavallo, *The Rose Tattoo*, East Coast Road Company, 1954; Stanley, *A Streetcar Named Desire*, East Coast Road Company, 1955.

FILM DEBUT—D'Amore, *The Last Mile*, United Artists, 1958. PRINCIPAL FILM APPEARANCES—*The Sweet Smell of Success*, Hecht-Hill-Lancaster, 1958; *The Cop Hater*, United Artists, 1958; *The Kid Who Caught a Crook*, United Artists, 1958; *Never Steal Anything Small*, Universal International, 1959; *The Music Box Kid*, United Artists, 1960; *Guns of the Timberland*, Paramount, 1960; *Johnny Gunman*, United Artists, 1960; Karl Matuschka, *The Apartment*, United Artists, 1960; Pilate's aide, *The Greatest Story Ever Told*, United Artists, 1965; lead role, *Navajo Run*, American International, 1965; *What Did You Do in the War, Daddy?*, United Artists, 1966; *Gunfight in Abilene*, Universal, 1967; *The Destructors*, United Artists, 1968; *The Love God*, Universal-International, 1969; *Gina & Me*, Johnny Seven Enterprises, 1980.

PRINCIPAL FILM WORK—Producer and director: *Navajo Run*,

1964; *Gina & Me*, 1980; also, *Inhale, Exhale: The New Terror*, documentary.

TELEVISION DEBUT—Reporter, *Suspense*, CBS, 1950. PRINCIPAL TELEVISION APPEARANCES—Series: Lieutenant Carl Reese, *Ironside*, NBC, 1969-75; Lieutenant Contreras, *Amy Prentiss*, NBC, 1974-75. Episodic: *The Untouchables*, ABC; *Naked City*, ABC; *The Verdict Is Yours*, CBS; *Route 66*, CBS; *One Step Beyond*, syndicated; *Get Smart*, NBC; *Bonanza*, NBC; *Gunsmoke*, CBS; *Death Valley Days*, syndicated; *The Jonathan Winters Show*, NBC; *Studio One*, CBS; *The Best of Broadway*, CBS; *Robert Montgomery Presents*, NBC; *Danger*, CBS; *Marcus Welby, M.D.*, ABC; *Police Woman*, NBC; *Switch*, CBS; *CHiPs*, NBC; *Trapper John, M.D.*, CBS; *The Master*, NBC; *Murder, She Wrote*, CBS; also *Hotel Cosmopolitan* and *Lamp Unto My Feet*.

Guest: *The Tonight Show*, NBC.

PRINCIPAL TELEVISION WORK—Producer and director, *The Leprechaun and His Friends*, children's special.

NON-RELATED CAREER—Real estate and investment advisor, 1961-87.

WRITINGS: SCREENPLAYS—*Silent Love; Even Grown Men Cry; Gina & Me.*

PLAYS—*Salvage.*

TELEVISION—*The Leprechaun and His Friends; Alias: The Wheeler;*

JOHNNY SEVEN

The Man Most Likely; The Young Reporters; Property for Sale; Captain Starfish; Slade, and *The Talking Belts.*

AWARDS: Las Vegas International Film Festival Award, 1980, for *Gina & Me;* Los Angeles City Council Humanitarian Award, for *Inhale, Exhale: The New Terror;* Honorary Mayor, Sheriff, and Fire Chief of Granada Hills, CA, 1973-75.

MEMBER: Screen Actors Guild, American Federation of Television and Radio Artists, Actors' Equity Association; National Italian/American Sports Hall of Fame (president, Los Angeles Chapter, 1983-85), California Association of Realtors, San Fernando Board of Realtors.

SIDELIGHTS: Johnny Seven told *CTFT:* "My favorite role was as the Gypsy on *One Step Beyond.* Important to my career: my family and their understanding." He is interested in "the economy, the future of the young, world peace, and ecology."

ADDRESSES: HOME—Granada Hills, CA. OFFICE—Johnny Seven Enterprises, 11024 Balboa Blvd., Granada Hills, CA 91344. AGENT—Alex Brewis Agency, 4721 Laurel Canyon Blvd., Suite 211, North Hollywood, CA 91607.

*   *   *

SEVEN, Marilyn

PERSONAL: Born Marilyn Swartz, March 22; daughter of David (an attorney) and Dorothy (an actress; maiden name, Morris) Swartz; married Richard B. Shull (an actor; divorced, 1985). EDUCATION: Attended Vassar College, B.A, psychology.

VOCATION: Writer.

WRITINGS: PLAYS, PRODUCED—*Life Upon the Wicked Stage*, New York City, 1977; *Double Dutch*, with the Meat and Potatoes Company at the Alvina Krause Theatre, New York City, 1982, then produced in Boston, 1983; *The Ladies Who Lunch*, Minneapolis, MN, 1985-86, Massachusetts, 1987, and on a U.S. midwestern city tour; *The Barber-Surgeon Had a Wife*, Boston, 1986; *The Firebird and the Big T*, Boston, 1987; *N'Yawk N'Yawk. . .Who's There?*, Minneapolis, 1987.

SCREENPLAYS—*Jerry*, commissioned by Media Ventures, Inc., 1986.

RADIO—*Giacomo*, commissioned by KSJN Public Radio, 1985.

AWARDS: Jerome Fellowship, 1983-84; Twin Cities Mayors' Public Art Award, 1985, for *The Ladies Who Lunch;* fellowships: Minnesota Composer-Librettist Opera Studio; Tyrone F. Guthrie Center; PEN America Writer's Fund; The Millay Colony for the Arts; Edward F. Albee Foundation.

MEMBER: Dramatists Guild; National Arts Club, New York City, The Playwrights Center, Minneapolis, and Women in Film, Los Angeles.

ADDRESSES: OFFICE—P.O. Box 331, Radio City Station, New York, NY 10101; and The Playwrights Center, 2301 Franklin

MARILYN SEVEN

Avenue East, Minneapolis, MN 55406. AGENT—c/o Selma Luttinger, Robert A. Freedman Dramatic Agency, Inc., 1501 Broadway, New York, NY 10036.

*   *   *

SHAFFER, Peter   1926-

PERSONAL: Full name Peter Levin Shaffer; born May 15, 1926, in Liverpool, England; son of Jack (a realtor) and Reka (Fredman) Shaffer. EDUCATION: Attended St. Paul's School, London; Cambridge University, B.A., 1950.

VOCATION: Writer and critic.

CAREER: Employed by the New York Public Library, 1951-54, then by Bosey & Hawkes (music publishers), London, 1954-55; writer (see below), 1955—; literary critic, *Truth*, 1956-57; music critic, *Time and Tide*, 1961-62.

WRITINGS: PLAYS, PRODUCED—*Five Finger Exercise*, Comedy Theatre, London, 1958, then Music Box Theatre, New York City, 1959; *The Private Ear* and *The Public Eye*, produced together on a double bill (sometimes entitled *Light Comedies*), Globe Theatre, London, 1962, then Morosco Theatre, New York City, 1963; (with Joan Littlewood and the Theatre Workshop) *The Merry Roosters Panto*, Wyndham's Theatre, London, 1963; *The Royal Hunt of the*

Sun: A Play Concerning the Conquest of Peru, produced by the National Theatre Company at the Chichester Festival, U.K., 1964, then at the American National Theatre Academy (ANTA) Theatre, New York City, 1965; *Black Comedy*, Chichester Festival, 1965, then Old Vic Theatre, London, 1966, then produced with *White Lies*, Ethel Barrymore Theatre, New York City, 1967; *White Lies* retitled *The White Liars*, and revived on a double bill with *Black Comedy*, Lyric Theatre, London, 1967; *A Warning Game*, New York City production, 1967; *It's About Cinderella*, London production, 1969; *The Battle of Shrivings*, Lyric Theatre, London, 1970; *Equus*, Old Vic Theatre, London, 1973, then Plymouth Theatre, New York City, 1974; *Amadeus*, London production, 1979, then Broadhurst Theatre, New York City, 1980; *Yonadab*, London production, 1985.

PLAYS, PUBLISHED—*Five Finger Exercise*, Hamish Hamilton, 1958, Harcourt, 1959, published in *Three Plays*, Penguin, 1968; *The Private Ear* and *The Public Eye*, Hamish Hamilton, 1962, Stein & Day, 1964; *The Royal Hunt of the Sun: A Play Concerning the Conquest of Peru*, Samuel French (London), 1964, Stein & Day, 1965; *Black Comedy* and *White Lies*, Samuel French, 1967, published in *Black Comedy* (including) *White Lies*, Stein & Day, 1967, published in England as *The White Liars* and *Black Comedy*, Hamish Hamilton, 1968; *Equus*, Deutsch, 1973, Bard, 1977, Penguin, 1984, published in *Equus and Shrivings*, Atheneum, 1974, also published by Samuel French; *Shrivings*, published in *Equus and Shrivings*, Atheneum, 1974; *Amadeus*, Harper & Row, 1981, New American Library, 1983, also published by Samuel French.

SCREENPLAYS—"The Lord of the Flies" (not used for the film by that title); *The Public Eye*, Universal, 1972; *Equus*, Warner Brothers, 1977; *Amadeus*, Orion, 1984.

TELEPLAYS—*The Salt Land*, ITN, 1955; *Balance of Terror*, BBC, 1957.

RADIO SCRIPTS—*The Prodigal Father*, BBC, 1955.

FICTION—(All with Anthony Shaffer, published under the joint pseudonym Peter Antony) *How Doth the Little Crocodile?*, Evans Brothers, 1951, published under their own names by Macmillan, 1957; (under joint pseudonym) *Woman in the Wardrobe*, Evans Brothers, 1952; *Withered Murder*, Gollancz, 1955, Macmillan, 1956.

AWARDS: Evening Standard Drama Award, 1958, New York Drama Critics Circle Award, 1960, both for *Five Finger Exercise;* Best Play, Antoinette Perry Award, New York Drama Critics Circle Award, both 1975, for *Equus;* New York Drama Critics Circle Award, 1981, for *Amadeus;* Best Screenplay, Academy Award, 1984, for *Amadeus.*

MEMBER: Dramatists Guild; Dramatists Club (London).

SIDELIGHTS: RECREATIONS—Architecture, walking and music.

CTFT has learned that during World War II, Peter Shaffer was employed as a conscript in coal mines in England, from 1944-47.

ADDRESSES: AGENT—London Management, 235/241 Regent Street, London W1A 2JT, England.*

SHEELEY, Nelson   1942-

PERSONAL: Born August 14, 1942, in Baltimore, MD; son of Donald Brown (a retail merchant) and Jane Lavina (Fleming) Sheeley. EDUCATION: Western Maryland College, B.A., 1964; Yale University School of Drama, M.F.A., 1967.

VOCATION: Director.

CAREER: FIRST STAGE WORK—Director, *The Pursuit of Happiness,* Totem Pole Playhouse, Fayetteville, PA, 1975. PRINCIPAL STAGE WORK—Director: With the Bel Canto Opera Society, New York City: *Le Postillion De Lonjumeau,* 1979; *Stiffelio,* 1980; *Simon Boccenegra,* 1981; *No. 66* and *A Lady in Lottery,* both 1982. Also *The Old Maid and the Thief,* St. Louis Opera Theatre, MO, 1982.

RELATED CAREER—Managing director, Allenberry Playhouse, Boiling Springs, PA, 1978—. Teacher: Baltimore County Public Schools, Essex, MD, 1967-70, and the International School, Bangkok, Thailand, 1970-71.

ADDRESSES: HOME—433 W. 21st Street, Apt. 6D, New York, NY 10011. OFFICE—Box 7, Boiling Springs, PA 17007.

*   *   *

SHEEN, Charlie

BRIEF ENTRY: Born Carlos Irwin Estevez, in New York, Charlie Sheen is the third child of actor Martin Sheen. When his brother, Emilio, entered the acting profession, and used the family name of Estevez, Sheen chose to differentiate himself from his brother by adopting his father's professional name. Growing up in Malibu, California, Sheen attended Santa Monica High School, and was such a distinguished baseball player that he earned a scholarship to the University of Kansas. Because of poor attendance, however, he never received a diploma. "I just couldn't get it together," he told Todd Gold of *People* (March 9, 1987). He returned to Malibu and soon made his film debut in the 1984 thriller, *Grizzly II.* Other film roles followed quickly, including *Red Dawn,* a 1984 action film about a group of teenagers in small-town America who become unwitting heroes during a Soviet invasion of the United States. He also appeared in *Wisdom,* a film that was written and directed by his brother, Emilio. His exposure to movie audiences increased dramatically with his portrayal of Chris Taylor, the naive, wide-eyed recruit in the 1987 Academy Award winning film, *Platoon.* In his forthcoming movie, he will appear as the leader of a car-theft ring.*

*   *   *

SHELLEY, Carole   1939-

PERSONAL: Born August 16, 1939, in London, England; daughter of Curtis (a composer) and Deborah (a singer; maiden name, Bloomstein) Shelley; married Albert G. Woods, July 26, 1967 (died, 1971). EDUCATION: Attended Arts Educational School; trained for the stage at the Royal Academy of Dramatic Art and with Iris Warren and Eileen Thorndike. RELIGION: Jewish.

VOCATION: Actress.

CAREER: STAGE DEBUT—Little Nell, *The Old Curiosity Shop,* George Inn, Southwark, U.K., 1950. LONDON DEBUT—Mabel, *Simon and Laura,* Apollo Theatre, 1955. BROADWAY DEBUT—Gwendolyn Pigeon, *The Odd Couple,* Plymouth Theatre, 1965. PRINCIPAL STAGE APPEARANCES—*For Adults Only,* revue, Lyric Theatre, Hammersmith, London, 1958; *New Cranks,* revue, Lyric Theatre, Hammersmith, London, 1959; *The Art of Living,* revue, Criterion Theatre, London, 1960; Jane, *Boeing-Boeing,* Apollo Theatre, London, 1962; Mary McKellaway, *Mary, Mary,* Globe Theatre, London, 1963; Barbara, *The Astrakhan Coat,* Helen Hayes Theatre, New York City, 1967; Fay, *Loot,* Biltmore Theatre, New York City, 1968; *Noel Coward's Sweet Potato,* revue, Ethel Barrymore Theatre then at the Booth Theatre, New York City, 1968; Patsy Newquist, *Little Murders,* Circle in the Square, New York City, 1969.

Jackie Coryton, *Hay Fever,* Helen Hayes Theatre, New York City, 1970; *Tonight at 8:30, Press Cuttings* and *War, Women and Other Trivia,* all with the Shaw Festival Theatre, Niagara-on-the-Lake, Ontario, Canada, 1971; Rosalind, *As You Like It,* Constance Neville, *She Stoops to Conquer,* Regan, *King Lear,* all with the Stratford Festival, Ontario, Canada, 1972; first witch, *Macbeth,* Margery Pinchwife, *The Country Wife,* both with the American Shakespeare Festival, Stratford, CT, 1973; Nora, *A Doll's House,* Goodman Theatre, Chicago, 1973; Viola, *Twelfth Night* and Lady Capulet, *Romeo and Juliet,* both with the American Shakespeare Festival, Stratford, 1974; Jane, *Absurd Person Singular,* Westport Country Playhouse, CT, then at the Music Box Theatre, New York City, 1974; Ruth, *The Norman Conquests* (a trilogy which included "Table Manners," "Living Together," and "Round and Round the Garden"), Morosco Theatre, New York City, 1975.

Ann Whitefield, *Man and Superman* and Epifania, *The Millionairess,* both Shaw Festival, Niagara-on-the-Lake, 1977; Judith Anderson, *The Devil's Disciple,* Ahmanson Theatre, Los Angeles, 1977 and at the Brooklyn Academy, NY, 1978; Ilona Szabo, *The Play's the Thing,* Brooklyn Academy, NY, 1978; Lady Driver, *Donkey's Years,* New York City, 1978; Madge Kendal, *The Elephant Man,* Theatre of St. Peter's Church and at the Booth Theatre, New York City, 1979.

The Grand Hunt, Seattle Repertory Theatre, WA, 1981; Margaret, *Double Feature,* Theatre at St. Peter's Church, New York City, 1981; Dorothy Trowbridge, *Twelve Dreams,* New York Shakespeare Festival (NYSF), Public Theatre, New York City, 1982; Arsinoe, *The Misanthrope,* Circle in the Square, New York City, 1983; *Blithe Spirit,* with the Stratford Festival, Ontario, 1983; Dotty Otley, *Noises Off,* Brooks Atkinson Theatre, New York City, 1983; *A Little Bit More of Pygmalion,* May Auditorium, Parsons School of Design, New York City, 1984; also appeared in the premiere season of the Robin Phillips Grand Theatre Company, London, Ontario, Canada, 1983-84; *Waltz of the Toreadors,* Roundabout Theatre, New York City, 1985-86.

MAJOR TOURS—Mary McKellaway, *Mary, Mary,* U.S. cities, 1964; Regan, *King Lear,* Bianca, *The Taming of the Shrew,* Denmark, Holland, Poland, and Russia, 1972; Julie Cavendish, *The Royal Family,* U.S. cities, 1975-76.

FILM DEBUT—*Little Nell,* 1942. PRINCIPAL FILM APPEARANCES—*Cure for Love,* British Lion, 1949; *It's Great to Be Young,* Fine Arts, 1957; *Carry On Regardless,* Governor, 1963; *Carry On Cabby,* 1963; *No, My Darling Daughter,* Zenith International,

1964; *The Odd Couple,* Paramount, 1968; *The Boston Strangler,* Twentieth Century-Fox, 1968; provided voices for animated films, *The Aristocats,* Buena Vista, 1971 and *Robin Hood,* Buena Vista, 1974; also appeared in *Give Us This Day.*

PRINCIPAL TELEVISION APPEARANCES—Series: Gwendolyn Pigeon, *The Odd Couple,* ABC, 1970-71. Episodic: ''A Salute to Noel Coward,'' *Camera Three,* CBS; also appeared in England in many of the Brian Rix farces, and on *The Dickie Henderson Show* and *The Avengers.*

AWARDS: Los Angeles Drama Critics Circle Award, 1977, for *The Royal Family;* Best Actress, Antoinette Perry Award, Outer Critics Circle Award, 1979, for *The Elephant Man;* Obie Award, 1982, for *Twelve Dreams.*

MEMBER: Actors' Equity Association, Screen Actors Guild, American Federation of Television and Radio Actors, American Shakespeare Theatre, Stratford, CT (board of trustees).

SIDELIGHTS: RECREATIONS—Needlepoint, dressmaking, cooking, and reading.

ADDRESSES: AGENT—Lionel Larner, 850 Seventh Avenue, New York, NY 10019.*

*   *   *

SHEPARD, Jewel

PERSONAL: Born in New York, NY. EDUCATION: Attended University of California at Berkeley and Los Angeles; studied acting with Charles Conrad, Walter Raneym, Nina Foch, and Jeremiah Comey.

VOCATION: Actress.

CAREER: PRINCIPAL FILM APPEARANCES—*Junkman,* 1982; *Raw Force,* American Panorama, 1982; *Zapped!,* Embassy, 1982; *My Tutor,* Crown, 1983; *Return of the Living Dead,* Orion, 1984; *Christina,* 1984; *Yellow Pages,* upcoming; also *Operation Overkill* and *Hollywood Hot Tubs.*

PRINCIPAL TELEVISION APPEARANCES—Episodic: *Cagney and Lacey,* CBS; *Likely Stories.* Movies: *Sweet Dreams; Body Flash.*

PRINCIPAL STAGE APPEARANCES—Jan Fujaro, *Go Ask Alice,* Oklahoma Civic Theatre; Catherine, *A View from the Bridge* and Daisy, *Lo and Behold,* both with the Community Playhouse Players, Los Angeles; Miss Prothero, *A Child's Christmas in Wales,* Green Mountain Players, Powerhouse Theatre, Los Angeles, 1984.

MAJOR TOURS—Star, *Urban Cowgirls,* fifteen state tour.

RELATED CAREER—Founder, Green Mountain Players, Los Angeles, 1984.

NON-RELATED CAREER—Aerobics teacher.

AWARDS: Golden Scroll Award of Merit, Academy of Science Fiction, Fantasy and Horror, 1985; acknowledgement of service, 1985, from the San Bernardino County Epilepsy Society.

JEWEL SHEPARD

MEMBER: Screen Actors Guild, American Federation of Television and Radio Artists.

SIDELIGHTS: RECREATIONS—Volleyball, photography, horseback riding, demolition derby driving, dancing, and swimming.

ADDRESSES: PUBLICIST—Nan Herst Public Relations, 8733 Sunset Blvd., Suite 103, Los Angeles, CA 90069.

*   *   *

SHERWIN, Mimi

PERSONAL: Born February 25, in New York, NY; daughter of Benjamin (a surgeon) and Hilda (Jacobs) Sherwin. EDUCATION: University of Michigan, B.A.

VOCATION: Actress and singer.

CAREER: STAGE DEBUT—Ballet student, *The Remarkable Mr. PennyPacker.* BROADWAY DEBUT—Prioress, *Canterbury Tales,* Rialto Theatre, 1980. PRINCIPAL STAGE APPEARANCES—Greta Fiorentino, *Street Scene,* Equity Library Theatre, New York City, 1982; Aunt Blanche, *Brighton Beach Memoirs,* Gateway Playhouse, 1986. Also: Prioress, *Canterbury Tales,* Equity Library Theatre, New York City; *She Loves Me,* Playwrights Horizons, New York City.

MIMI SHERWIN

FILM DEBUT—*Trading Places,* Paramount, 1983.

MEMBER: Actors' Equity Association, Screen Actors Guild.

SIDELIGHTS: RECREATIONS—Learning foreign languages and worldwide travel.

ADDRESSES: HOME—New York, NY.

*   *   *

SHERWOOD, Michael
See Weathers, Philip

*   *   *

SHIPLEY, Sandra   1947-

PERSONAL: Born February 1, 1947, in London, England; daughter of Norman and Mildred (Williams) Shipley; married Alfred Wilson, January 3, 1970; children: Alfie, Laura. EDUCATION: Graduated London University, Dramatic Art; also attended the New College of Speech and Drama, London.

VOCATION: Actress.

CAREER: STAGE DEBUT—Title role, *Mary Stuart,* Edinburgh Festival, Scotland, 1968. LONDON DEBUT—Helena, *Look Back in Anger,* Criterion Theatre, 1968-69. PRINCIPAL STAGE APPEARANCES—Ruth Belcher, *Suddenly at Home,* Queens Theatre, London; Sybil, *Private Lives,* with the Exeter Repertory Company, U.K.; Miss Giddens, *The Innocents* and Kate Hardcastle, *She Stoops to Conquer,* both with the Oldham Repertory Company, U.K.; Lady Percy and Doll Tearsheet, *When Thou Art King,* Grace, *London Assurance,* and Jenny, *Major Barbara,* all with the Royal Shakespeare Company, U.K.

Multiple role, *Hard Times,* Gloucester Stage Company, MA; Juno, *Juno and the Paycock* and Helen, *And a Nightingale Sang,* both at the Lyric Stage; Myra, *Deathtrap* and Lizzie, *The Rainmaker,* both at the Nickerson Theatre; Anitra, *Peer Gynt,* with the Boston Symphony Orchestra, MA; Amanda, *Private Lives,* Viola, *Twelfth Night,* Desdemona, *Othello,* Gladys, *A Lesson from Aloes,* Beatrice, *Much Ado About Nothing,* woman one, *Play,* Thaisa, *Pericles,* and Lady Macbeth, *Macbeth,* all with the Boston Shakespeare Company; Estelle Dusseau, *Sweet Table at the Richelieu,* American Repertory Theatre, Cambridge, MA, 1986.

MAJOR TOURS—Ruth Belcher, *Suddenly at Home,* post-West End tour, U.K. cities, 1973.

FILM DEBUT—Pamela, *The Hunting of Lionel Crane,* 1970. PRINCIPAL FILM APPEARANCES—Julia Lennon, *The John Lennon Story,* Newbury Filmworks.

TELEVISION DEBUT—Susan, *Take Three Girls,* BBC, 1971.

SANDRA SHIPLEY

PRINCIPAL TELEVISION APPEARANCES—Miss Phillips, *Spenser: For Hire*, ABC; Carolyn Driscoll, *Miller's Court*, WCVB, Boston.

PRINCIPAL RADIO PERFORMANCES—*The Spider's Web*, WGBH, Boston; also *Monitor Radio*, Boston.

RECORDINGS: DRAMA—Performances for "Novels on Cassettes": *Great Expectations, Wuthering Heights,* and *Roxanna*, Kleos Publications.

AWARDS: Best Performance by an Actress in Resident Non-Profit Theatre, Boston Theatre Critics Circle Award, 1982, for Gladys, *A Lesson from Aloes;* New England Theatre Conference Award, Regional Citation for Excellence in Theatre.

MEMBER: Actors' Equity Association, Screen Actors Guild, American Federation of Television and Recording Artists.

SIDELIGHTS: FAVORITE ROLES—Amanda, *Private Lives,* Lady Macbeth, *Macbeth,* and Gladys, *A Lesson from Aloes.*

ADDRESSES: OFFICE—American Repertory Theatre, Loeb Drama Centre, Brattle Street, Cambridge, MA 02138.

*   *   *

SHIRE, Talia   1946-

PERSONAL: Born Talia Rose Coppola, April 25, 1946, in Jamaica, NY; daughter of Carmine (an arranger and composer) and Italia (Pennino) Coppola; married David Lee Shire, March 29, 1970 (divorced); married Jack Schwartzman (a producer), August 23, 1980; children: (first marriage) Matthew; (second marriage) Jason. EDUCATION: Attended Yale University School of Drama, two years.

VOCATION: Actress and producer.

CAREER: PRINCIPAL FILM APPEARANCES—*The Dunwich Horror*, American International Pictures, 1971; *Gas-s-s*, 1971; *The Christian Licorice Store*, National General, 1971; Connie Corelone, *The Godfather*, Paramount, 1972; *The Outside Man*, United Artists, 1973; Connie Corelone, *The Godfather, Part II*, Paramount, 1974; Adrianne, *Rocky*, United Artists, 1977; *Old Boyfriends*, AVCO-Embassy, 1979; Adrianne, *Rocky II*, United Artists, 1979; *Windows*, United Artists, 1980; Adrianne, *Rocky III*, Metro-Goldwyn-Mayer/United Artists (MGM/UA), 1982; Adrianne, *Rocky IV*, MGM/UA, 1985.

PRINCIPAL FILM WORK —Producer, in partnership with her husband, Jack Schwartzman: *Never Say Never Again*, Taliafilm, Warner Brothers, 1983; *Lionheart*, Taliafilm/Orion, 1986.

PRINCIPAL TELEVISION APPEARANCES—Mini-Series: Teresa Sanjoro, *Rich Man, Poor Man*, ABC, 1976. Movies: *Kill Me If You Can*, 1977.

AWARDS: Best Supporting Actress, Academy Award nomination, 1974, for *The Godfather, Part II;* Best Actress, New York Film Critic's Award and Academy Award nomination, 1976, for *Rocky.*

MEMBER: Screen Actors Guild.

TALIA SHIRE

SIDELIGHTS: CTFT notes that Talia Shire is the sister of director Francis Ford Coppola. From Shire's agent we learned that before starring in *Rocky IV*, she took an acting hiatus to raise her two sons. She is once again working, not in front of the camera, but behind the scenes with her husband, producing such films as *Never Say Never Again* and *Lionheart.*

ADDRESSES: AGENT—Creative Artists Agency, 1888 Century Park East, Los Angeles, CA 90067. PUBLICIST—Guttman and Pam, 8500 Wilshire Blvd., Suite 801, Beverly Hills, CA 90211.

*   *   *

SHOCKLEY, Ed   1957-

PERSONAL: Full name, Edgar Jay Shockley III; born January 26, 1957, in Philadelphia, PA; son of Edgar Jay and Alice L. Shockley. EDUCATION: Columbia University, B.A., 1978; trained for the theatre at the Frank Silvera Writers Workshop. POLITICS: Humanist.

VOCATION: Playwright, composer, and actor.

CAREER: PRINCIPAL STAGE APPEARANCES—Lion, *The Wiz*, Langston Hughes Centre, Seattle, WA; Ross, *Spell Number Seven*, Theatre Center, Philadelphia; John, *The Liar's Contest*, Walt Whitman Center, Camden, NJ; man number one, *Frum Okra to Greens*, Barnard College, New York City; guard, *Cenci/Bardo*, Washington Square Church, New York City.

ED SHOCKLEY

PRINCIPAL RADIO WORK—W.W. Jefferson, *Mumbo Jumbo*, ZBS Foundation; principal, *Silo (Tall Is Best)*; Tecumsa, *Unsung Heroes* (Episode One), Goldman Sound.

WRITINGS: PLAYS, PRODUCED—*Bedlam Moon*, Walnut Street Studio Theatre, Philadelphia; *The Playground* (music by Rico Bimbiri), Madrona Center, Seattle; (with James McBride) *All Roads Lead Home*, Theatre Center, Philadelphia; *The Strange Career of John Hopewell*, Black Spectrum Theatre, New York City; *The Liar's Contest*, Walnut Street Theatre, Philadelphia, Walt Whitman Center, Camden, NJ, and Maryland Historical Society, Baltimore; *Bessie Smith: Empress of the Blues* (also known as *A Nite in the Life of Bessie Smith*), Frank Silvera Writers Workshop, New York City, Kuumba Theatre and Ivanhoe Theatre, both Chicago, Theatre Center, Philadelphia, and Arena Players, Baltimore; also, *The Stalking Horse*.

PLAYS, UNPRODUCED—"Merlin & Vivien"; "Metamorphosis"; "The Bridge"; "The Bottom"; "Badman"; "afterpiece"; "The Box"; "The Gypsy Wagon"; "A Colored Corner of Hell."

SCREENPLAYS—*The Corsairs*, Black Spectrum Films.

AWARDS: Three Audelco Awards (including Best Play) and Joseph Jefferson Award, for *Bessie Smith: Empress of the Blues;* Lorraine Hansberry Award, for *The Strange Career of John Hopewell;* winner, American Minority Playwright's Contest, for *The Stalking Horse.*

SIDELIGHTS: Ed Shockey shared these thoughts with *CTFT:*

"Language is humankind's greatest invention. It is the foundation of science, math and philosophy and our only hope to escape disaster."

ADDRESSES: HOME—Brooklyn, NY. OFFICE—1637 Wharton Street, Philadelphia, PA 19146.

*   *   *

SHUST, William

VOCATION: Actor.

CAREER: PRINCIPAL STAGE APPEARANCES—Broadway: *Arturo Ui*, 1963, *The Owl and the Pussycat*, 1965, and *The Country Girl*, 1972; Milt, *Luv*, Paper Mill Playhouse, Milburn, NJ, 1976; Thomas More, *A Man for All Seasons*, Catholic University, Washington, DC, 1977; *Promenade, All!* and *Dial M for Murder*, both Playhouse on the Hill, NY, 1977; *The Lesson*, Marymount College, New York City, 1977; title role, *Count Dracula*, Equity Library Theatre, 1978; the detective, *The Bat*, Olney Theatre, MD, 1979; one man show, *Chekhov on the Lawn*, Edinburgh Festival, Scotland and Gate Theatre, London, both 1980, and Theatre East, New York City, 1981; *How He Lies to Her Husband* and *Winners*, both Roundabout Theatre, New York City, 1983; *The First Night of Pygmalion*, White Barn Theatre, CT and South Street Theatre, New York City, 1985; title role, *King Lear*, Baldwin-Wallace College,

WILLIAM SHUST

OH, 1985; *Eichmann Interrogated*, Edinburgh Festival, Scotland, 1986.

MAJOR TOURS—*Donkey's Years*, New England cities, 1978.

PRINCIPAL FILM APPEARANCES—*The Rivals*, AVCO-Embassy, 1972; *The Seven-Ups*, Twentieth Century-Fox, 1973; *The Seduction of Joe Tynan*, Universal, 1979.

PRINCIPAL TELEVISION APPEARANCES—Episodic: *Search for Tomorrow*, CBS; *Kojak*, CBS; Patrick Henry, *The Adams Chronicles*, PBS. Specials: *The Last Days of Dillinger; Decades of Decision.*

AWARDS: Best Performance, Edinburgh Festival, Scotland, 1980, for *Chekov on the Lawn*.

MEMBER: Actors' Equity Association, Screen Actors Guild, American Federation of Radio and Television Artists.

ADDRESSES: HOME—13 E. Seventh Street, New York, NY 10003.

* * *

SHUSTER, Rosie 1950-

PERSONAL: Born June 19, 1950, in Toronto, ON, Canada; daughter of Frank (a comedian) and Ruth (an interior designer; maiden name, Burstyn) Shuster; married Lorne Michaels, October 2, 1971 (divorced, 1980); married John Alexander (an artist), January 16, 1987. EDUCATION: Attended University of Toronto and York University School of Art, Toronto.

VOCATION: Writer.

WRITINGS: TELEVISION—Series: *Saturday Night Live*, NBC, 1975-80, 1986-87; Lily Tomlin specials; also many assorted episodic shows. SCREENPLAYS—*The Disappearance*, 1977; *Gilda Live*, Warner Brothers, 1980; also, *Rancho Taboo; Mr. Darling; Just in Time*. BOOKS—Contributor, *Titters One Hundred One: An Introduction to Women's Literature*, 1984.

AWARDS: Outstanding Writing in a Comedy-Variety or Music Series, Emmy Awards, 1975-76 and 1976-77, for *Saturday Night Live*; four Emmy Award nominations, for *Saturday Night Live*; Writers Guild Award.

SIDELIGHTS: Rosie Shuster told *CTFT* that she was recently married in Nepal and that she is a "shrill and strident" left wing feminist and a "world and peace lover."

ADDRESSES: HOME—New York, NY. AGENT—c/o Nancy Blaylock, The Gersh Agency, 130 W. 42nd Street, New York, NY 10036.

* * *

SIFF, Ira 1946-

PERSONAL: Born February 15, 1946, in New York, NY; son of Theodore (a stock broker) and Jeanne (Barth) Siff. EDUCATION: Cooper Union, B.F.A., 1967; studied voice with Randolph Mickelson in New York City.

VOCATION: Actor, writer, singer, and director.

CAREER: OFF-BROADWAY DEBUT—Pablo Picasso, *About Time*, Judson Poet's Theatre, for sixteen performances, 1970. PRINCIPAL STAGE APPEARANCES—Ira, *Joan*, Circle in the Square, New York City, 1972; performed for ten years in various productions Off-Broadway, at the New York Shakespeare Festival, at the Arena Stage in Washington, DC, and in various cabarets in New York City; leading player, La Gran Scena Opera Company (a parody troupe), performed at the Orpheum Theatre, New York City, Entermedia Theatre, New York City, Actors Playhouse, New York City, two seasons at Town Hall, New York City.

MAJOR TOURS—With La Gran Scena Opera Company: Tower Theatre, Houston; Davis Hall, San Francisco; San Diego Opera; Gusman Cultural Center, Miami, FL; Teatro Municipal, Caracas, Venezuela; Theatre Festival, Munich, West Germany.

TELEVISION DEBUT—Pharoah, *The Haggadah*, PBS, 1981. PRINCIPAL TELEVISION APPEARANCES—Live broadcast, Munich Germany with La Gran Scena Opera Company, 1985.

RELATED CAREER—Private voice teacher and coach, 1969-86; founder and artistic director, La Gran Scena Opera Company, 1981.

AWARDS: Manhattan Association of Cabarets Award, 1986.

MEMBER: New York Singing Teachers Association.

IRA SIFF

Photography by John Galluzzi

SIDELIGHTS: Mr. Siff comments on his career in material submitted to *CTFT:* "I began going to the opera at the old Met when I was fifteen. I was struck both by the art form and by the super voices and super egos of the divas. I studied singing privately while obtaining my degree in fine arts and eventually the singing overshadowed the visual arts. I began to teach singing and to sing professionally as a baritone/tenor. I always possessed a strong falsetto and comic ability and so in 1981, I formed La Gran Scena Opera Company as a tribute to the opera diva."

ADDRESSES: OFFICE—La Gran Scena Opera Company, 211 E. Eleventh Street, New York, NY 10003. AGENT—Arthur Shafman International Ltd., 723 Seventh Avenue, New York, NY 10036.

*   *   *

SILBER, Chic

VOCATION: Special effects and lighting designer.

CAREER: PRINCIPAL STAGE WORK—Special effects designer, Broadway productions: *Amadeus; Nicholas Nickleby; Piaf; Sherlock Holmes; The Dresser; Working; Alice in Wonderland; Night and Day; Tintypes; Harold and Maude; Macbeth; Crimes of the Heart; 'Night Mother; The Elephant Man; Dracula.*

MAJOR TOURS—Special effects designer, *Dracula,* London, Mexico City, Amsterdam, and U.S. cities; also lighting designer for *Dracula,* in Venuzuela and for the third National Company that toured the U.S.

RELATED CAREER—Technical director for Barnum and Bailey Circus and the Monte Carlo Circus Festival, Monaco; production co-ordinator, John F. Kennedy Center for the Performing Arts, Washington, DC; also designed effects for many U.S. symphony orchestras, opera companies, and theme parks.

ADDRESSES: OFFICE—Monte Carlo Festival Cirque, 1015 Eighteenth Street, NW, Suite 1100, Washington, DC 20036.

*   *   *

SILVER, Joan Micklin   1935-

PERSONAL: Born May 24, 1935, in Omaha, NE; married Raphael D. Silver, June 28, 1956; children: Dina, Marisa, Claudia. EDUCATION: Sarah Lawrence College, B.A., 1956.

VOCATION: Director and writer.

CAREER: PRINCIPAL STAGE WORK—Director: *Album* and *Maybe I'm Doing It Wrong,* New York City productions; director and co-conceiver (with Julianne Boyd), *A—My Name Is Alice,* Women's Project, New York City.

FIRST FILM WORK—Director, *Immigrant Experience: The Long Long Journey,* Learning Corporation of America, 1972. PRINCIPAL FILM WORK—Director: *Hester Street,* Midwest Films, 1975; *Between the Lines,* Midwest Films, 1976; *Head Over Heels* (also known as *Chilly Scenes of Winter*), United Artists, 1979; also directed several children's films for Midwest Films.

PRINCIPAL TELEVISION WORK—Director: "Bernice Bobs Her Hair," *The American Short Story,* PBS, 1976; *Finnegan, Begin Again,* Home Box Office, 1985.

WRITINGS: SCREENPLAYS—*Hester Street,* Midwest Films, 1975; *Head Over Heels* (also known as *Chilly Scenes of Winter*), United Artists, 1979.

TELEVISION—"Bernice Bobs Her Hair," *The American Short Story,* PBS, 1976.

MEMBER: Directors Guild of America, Writers Guild of America, Dramatists Guild, Society of Stage Directors and Choreographers; Women in Film.

ADDRESSES: OFFICE—Midwest Films, 600 Madison Avenue, New York, NY 10022. AGENT—c/o Elliot Webb, Broder/Kurland/Webb, 9046 Sunset Blvd., Suite 202, Los Angeles, CA 90069.

*   *   *

SILVER, Ron   1946-

PERSONAL: Born July 2, 1946, in New York, NY; son of Irving Roy and May (Zimelman) Silver; married Lynne Miller, December 24, 1975. EDUCATION: University of Buffalo, B.A.; St. John's University (Taiwan), M.A.; trained for the stage at Herbert Berghof Studios with Uta Hagen and at the Actors Studio with Lee Strasberg.

VOCATION: Actor.

CAREER: STAGE DEBUT—*Kaspar* and *Public Insult,* both at the City Center, New York City, 1971. PRINCIPAL STAGE APPEARANCES—Pepe Hernandez, *El Grande de Coca-Cola,* Mercer Arts Center, New York City, 1972; *Lotta* and *More Than You Deserve,* both with the New York Shakespeare Festival, New York City, 1973; repeated role of Pepe Hernandez, *El Grande de Coca-Cola,* Los Angeles, 1975; Ralphie, *Awake and Sing,* Hollywood, CA, 1976; Lanx, *Angel City,* Mark Taper Forum, Los Angeles, 1977; Guy, *In the Boom Boom Room,* Long Beach Shakespeare Festival, CA, 1979; Charlie, *Gorilla,* Goodman Theatre, Chicago, 1983; Mel, *Friends,* Manhattan Theatre Club, New York City, 1983-84; Mickey, *Hurlyburly,* Ethel Barrymore Theatre, New York City, 1984-85; *Social Security,* Ethel Barrymore Theatre, New York City, 1986; *Hunting Cockroaches,* Manhattan Theatre Club, then City Center, New York City, 1987. Also appeared in *The Emperor of Late Night Radio.*

FILM DEBUT—Vlada, *Semi-Tough,* United Artists, 1977. PRINCIPAL FILM APPEARANCES—Dr. Tom Halman, *Silent Rage,* Columbia, 1982; Larry Weisman, *Best Friends,* Warner Brothers, 1982; Dr. Phil Schneiderman, *The Entity,* Twentieth Century-Fox, 1983; Ted Caruso, *Lovesick,* Warner Brothers, 1983; Paul Stone, *Silkwood,* Twentieth Century-Fox, 1983; Eddie Bergson, *The Goodbye People,* Embassy, 1984; *Garbo Talks,* Metro-Goldwyn-Mayer/United Artists, 1984.

TELEVISION DEBUT—Gary Levy, *Rhoda,* CBS, 1976-78. PRINCIPAL TELEVISION APPEARANCES—Series: Regular, *The Mac Davis Show,* NBC, 1976; Detective Schwartz, *Dear Detective,* CBS, 1979; Brad Gabriel, *The Stockard Channing Show,* CBS, 1980; Mike Locasale, *Baker's Dozen,* CBS, 1982. Episodic: *Hill*

Street Blues, NBC. Movies: *Betrayal*, 1978; *Word of Honor*, 1981. Mini-Series: *Kane and Abel*, CBS, 1985.

AWARDS: Best Actor, Joseph Jefferson Award nomination, 1983, for *Gorilla*.

MEMBER: Actors' Equity Association, Screen Actors Guild, American Federation of Television and Radio Artists, Actors Studio, Actors Fund, Academy of Motion Picture Arts and Sciences.

ADDRESSES: AGENT—Litke-Grossbart-Gale Management, 8500 Wilshire Blvd., Suite 506, Beverly Hills, CA 90211; The Gersh Agency, 222 N. Canon, Suite 202, Beverly Hills, CA 90210.*

*　　*　　*

SINCLAIR, Madge

PERSONAL: Born Madge Walters, April 28, in Kingston, Jamaica; daughter of Herbert (an entrepreneur) and Jemima (a school teacher; maiden name, Austin) Walters; married Royston Sinclair (a deputy commissioner of police in Kingston; divorced, 1969); married Dean Compton (a college instructor and manufacturer of women's wear), 1971; children: (first marriage) Garry, Wayne. EDUCATION: Attended Shortwood Women's College, teaching degree.

VOCATION: Actress.

CAREER: STAGE DEBUT—Dark Witch, *Dark of the Moon*, Playhouse on the Green, Columbus, OH, 1969. OFF-BROADWAY DEBUT—Title role, *Kumaliza*, New York Shakespeare Festival (NYSF), Public Theatre, 1969. LONDON DEBUT—Clytemnestra, *Iphigenia*, with the NYSF at the Young Vic Company, 1971. PRINCIPAL STAGE APPEARANCES—Clytemnestra, *Iphigenia*, NYSF, New York City, 1971; Mrs. Bruchinski, *Division Street*, Mark Taper Forum, Los Angeles, 1980; Lena, *Boesman & Lena*, Los Angeles Theatre Center, 1986; Doreen, *Tartuffe*, Los Angeles Theatre Center, 1986; also appeared in *Lady Lazarus*, Mark Taper Forum Lab, Los Angeles; *Mod Donna*, *Ti-Jean and His Brothers*, and *Blood* all with the NYSF; *Lady Day*, Brooklyn Academy of Music, NY.

FILM DEBUT—Mrs. Scott, *Conrack*, Twentieth Century-Fox, 1974. PRINCIPAL FILM APPEARANCES—*Cornbread, Earl & Me*, American International, 1975; Evla, *Leadbelly*, Paramount, 1975; *I Will, I Will. . .For Now*, Twentieth Century-Fox, 1976; Widow Woman, *Convoy*, United Artists, 1978; *Uncle Joe Shannon*, United Artists, 1979; *Star Trek IV*, Paramount, 1986.

PRINCIPAL TELEVISION APPEARANCES—Series: Madge, *Grandpa Goes to Washington*, NBC, 1978-79; Nurse Ernestine Shoop, *Trapper John M.D.*, CBS, 1980-86; "Gussie" Lemmone, *O'Hara*, ABC, 1987. Episodic: *Madigan*, NBC; *Medical Center*, CBS; *The Waltons*, CBS; *Joe Forrester*, NBC; *Doctor's Hospital*, NBC; *Executive Suite*, CBS; *Medical Story*, NBC; *Serpico*, NBC; *A.E.S. Hudson Street*, ABC; *The White Shadow*, CBS; *All in the Family*, CBS.

Mini-Series: Bell, *Roots*, ABC, 1977. Pilots: Hattie, *Divided We Stand*, ABC, 1987. Movies: *I Love You, Goodbye*, 1974; *One in a Million: The Ron LeFlor Story*, 1978; *I Know Why the Caged Bird Sings*, 1979; *High Ice*, 1980; *Jimmy, B and Andre*, 1980; *Guyana*

MADGE SINCLAIR

Tragedy: The Story of Jim Jones, 1980; *Victims*, 1982; also, *Guess Who's Coming to Dinner?*; *Walkin' Walter*; *Three Eyes*; *The Rag Tag Champs*.

NON-RELATED CAREER—School teacher for six years; chairwoman, Madge Walters Sinclair Inc., manufactures and distributes her own line of women's wear, called "'In Focus' by Madge Sinclair"; dealer of Jamaican art, owner of Action Income Tax Service.

AWARDS: Emmy Award nomination, 1977-78, for Belle, *Roots;* Best Supporting Actress, three Emmy Award nominations, all for Nurse Ernestine Shoop, *Trapper John, M.D.;* Best Actress in a Dramatic Series, National Association for the Advancement of Colored People (NAACP) Image Award, 1981 and 1983, for Nurse Ernestine Shoop, *Trapper John, M.D.;* Drama-Logue Critics Award, 1986, for *Boesman & Lena;* Mother of the Year Award, National Mother's Day Committee, 1984. Honorary doctorate, Sierra University.

MEMBER: Actors' Equity Association, Screen Actors Guild, American Federation of Television and Radio Artists, Academy of Television Arts and Sciences, Academy of Motion Picture Arts and Sciences; Museum of African American Art (board of directors), Gwen Bolden Foundation (board of directors).

SIDELIGHTS: RECREATIONS—Travelling, skiing and cycling; also playing the piano and practicing Hatha Yoga.

ADDRESSES: HOME—Hollywood Hills, CA. OFFICE—Madge Sinclair, P.W.W., 850 S. Broadway, Suite 1303, Los Angeles, CA

90014. AGENT—c/o John Kimble, Triad Artists, 10100 Santa Monica Blvd., Los Angeles, CA 90067.

*   *   *

SINGER, Marla   1957-

PERSONAL: Born August 2, 1957, in Oklahoma City, OK; daughter of Charles B. (in the oil business) and Nikki L. (a college instructor; maiden name, Skalovsky) Singer; married Wayne Channer (an executive with a Wall Street firm), June 20, 1986. EDUCATION: Oklahoma City University, B.A., performing arts, 1981; studied acting with Mira Rostova; studied voice with Lee and Sally Sweetland and Kay Cameron.

VOCATION: Actress, dancer, and singer.

CAREER: BROADWAY DEBUT—Lorraine Flemming, *42nd Street,* Majestic Theatre, 1984-85. PRINCIPAL STAGE APPEARANCES—Chastity, *Anything Goes,* Jane Ashton, *Brigadoon,* and Dainty June, *Gypsy,* all at the Music Theatre of Wichita, KS; *Cinderella,* understudy Olga, *Carnival,* and Dodo, *The Merry Widow,* all at the Municipal Theatre of St. Louis; Kit Kat Girl, *Cabaret,* Golden Gate Theatre; Polly, *Funny Girl,* Coachlight Dinner Theatre; nurse and dancer, *Seesaw,* Equity Library Theatre, New York City.

MAJOR TOURS—Hunyak, *Chicago,* production tour, 1982.

PRINCIPAL TELEVISION APPEARANCES—Episodic: *One Life to Live,* ABC; *Another World,* NBC. Guest: *The Merv Griffin Show,* syndicated.

MEMBER: Actors' Equity Association, Screen Actors Guild, American Federation of Television and Radio Artists.

ADDRESSES: AGENT—c/o Marvin Josephson, Gilla Roos Agency, 555 Madison Avenue, New York, NY 10022.

*   *   *

SINKYS, Albert   1940-

PERSONAL: Born July 10, 1940; son of Emil (a real estate executive) and Julia Oha (a real estate executive; maiden name, Galminaitus) Sinkys; married Catherine Eidson (a writer). EDUCATION: Attended Boston University and University of California at Los Angeles; trained for the stage at the Herbert Berghof Studio. RELIGION: Roman Catholic. MILITARY: U.S. Army.

VOCATION: Actor and director.

CAREER: STAGE DEBUT—Oscar, *Mary, Mary,* Carriage House Theatre, Little Compton, RI. OFF-BROADWAY DEBUT—Maske, *The Snob,* English Speaking Theatre. PRINCIPAL STAGE APPEARANCES—Shylock, *The Merchant of Venice,* Columbia University Theatre, New York City; Peter, *The Zoo Story,* English Speaking

MARLA SINGER

ALBERT SINKYS

Theatre, New York City; title role, *Richard III* and Sebastian, *The Tempest*, both American Classical Theatre, Washington, DC; Creon, *Oedipus at Colonus*, Classic Theatre, New York City; Pilate, *From the Memoirs of Pontius Pilate*, title role, *In the Matter of J. Robert Oppenheimer*, Captain Queeg, *The Caine Mutiny Court Martial*, and Goldman, *The Man in the Glass Booth*, all at the American Jewish Theatre, New York City; Givola and Judge Adam, *Concord*, Center Stage, Buffalo, NY; *Arturo Ui*, Hartman Theatre, Stamford, CT.

Regional: Glen, *A Child's Christmas in Wales* and Artie, *Hurlyburly*, both New Jersey Shakespeare Festival; Michael, *Boys in the Band* and Mr. Lowther, *Prime of Miss Jean Brodie*, both Carriage House Theatre, Newport, RI.

MAJOR TOURS—Title role, *Richard III* and Sebastian, *The Tempest*, both U.S. cities.

FILM DEBUT—The Boss, *MS-45*, Navaron, 1980. PRINCIPAL FILM APPEARANCES—Hired killer, *The Watchman*, Watchman Company; fight manager, *Zelig*, Warner Brothers, 1983.

TELEVISION DEBUT—Dr. Archibald Kent, *All My Children*, ABC. PRINCIPAL TELEVISION APPEARANCES—Salieri, *Mozart and Salieri*, Canadian Broadcasting Company; Jules Weatherbee, *One Life to Live*, ABC.

MEMBER: Actors' Equity Association, Screen Actors Guild, American Federation of Television and Radio Artists.

ADDRESSES: HOME—465 West End Avenue, New York, NY 10024.

*   *   *

SISTO, Rocco   1953-

PERSONAL: Born February 8, 1953, in Bari, Italy; son of Joseph and Antoinetta (Armenise) Sisto; married Barbara Allen (a choreographer), December 3, 1984. EDUCATION: University of Chicago, B.A., speech and theatre, 1974; New York University School of the Arts, M.F.A., acting, 1977.

VOCATION: Actor.

CAREER: STAGE DEBUT—Multiple roles, Center Stage, Baltimore tour, 1977. OFF-BROADWAY DEBUT—Capability Brown, *My Uncle Sam*, Public Theatre, 1982. PRINCIPAL STAGE APPEARANCES—*A Flea in Her Ear*, Pennsylvania Stage Company, Allentown, 1980; *Classic Comics*, Virginia Stage Company, Norfolk, 1981; various roles, *Twelfth Night* and *As You Like It*, Shakespeare & Company, Lenox, MA, 1981; Osric, *Hamlet*, Public/Anspacher Theatre, New York City, 1982-83; Malvolio, *Twelfth Night* and Lenox, *Macbeth*, both Shakespeare & Company, Lenox, 1982; *Twelfth Night*, Guthrie Theatre, Minneapolis, MN, 1984; Segismundo, *Life Is a Dream*, Ark Theatre Company, New York City, 1985.

PRINCIPAL FILM APPEARANCES—Lacy Bohle, *Scream for Help*, Lorimar Films, 1983; Daggen, the Wolf, *The Company of Wolves*, Cannon Films, 1986.

PRINCIPAL TELEVISION APPEARANCES—Movies: Tony Portelli, *Doing Life*, NBC.

ROCCO SISTO

ADDRESSES: AGENT—Abrams Artists Associates, 420 Madison Avenue, New York, NY 10012.

*   *   *

SKELTON, Thomas   1927-

PERSONAL: Full name, Thomas Reginald Skelton, Jr.; born September 24, 1927, in North Bridgton, ME; son of Thomas Reginald and Mary Ellen (Anderson) Skelton. EDUCATION: Middlebury College, B.A., 1950. MILITARY: U.S. Army, 1947-48.

VOCATION: Designer, director, educator, and writer.

CAREER: FIRST OFF-BROADWAY STAGE WORK—Lighting designer, *The Enchanted*, Renata Theatre, 1958. PRINCIPAL STAGE WORK—Lighting designer, all New York City productions, unless where noted otherwise: *Calvary, Santa Claus,* and *Escurial,* 1960; *Misalliance,* 1961; *Oh Dad, Poor Dad, Mama's Hung You in the Closet and I'm Feelin' So Sad,* 1962 and 1963; *In the Summer House, Wiener Blut,* and *Zizi,* 1964; *Sing to Me Through Open Windows,* and *The Day the Whores Came Out to Play Tennis,* 1965; *Your Own Thing, Mike Downstairs, Jimmy Shine,* and *Big Time Buck White,* 1968; *Does a Tiger Wear a Necktie?, Come Summer, Henry V, Much Ado About Nothing, Hamlet, The Three Sisters, A Patriot for Me, Indians,* and *Coco,* 1969; *Purlie, Mahagonny, Bob and Ray: The Two and Only,* and *Lovely Ladies, Kind Gentlemen,*

1970; *The Survival of St. Joan*, 1971; *Remote Asylum* and *Design for Living*, both in Los Angeles, 1971; *The Selling of the President, Rosebloom, The Lincoln Mask, The Secret Affairs of Mildred Wild*, and *Purlie*, 1972; *Status Quo Vadis, Gigi*, and *Waltz of the Toreadors*, 1973; *Brainchild*, Philadelphia, 1974; *Where's Charley?* and *Absurd Person Singular*, 1974; *Shenandoah, All God's Chillun' Got Wings, Death of a Salesman, A Musical Jubilee*, and *The Glass Menagerie*, 1975; *A Matter of Gravity, Guys and Dolls*, and *Days in the Trees*, 1976; *Caesar and Cleopatra, Romeo and Juliet*, and *The King and I*, 1977; *The November People* and *The Kingfisher*, 1978; *Peter Pan* and *Oklahoma!*, 1979.

Oklahoma!, Jacksonville Auditorium, FL, 1980; *Brigadoon*, Majestic Theatre, New York City, 1980; *The West Side Waltz*, Spreckels Theatre, Seattle, WA, 1980, then Fifth Avenue Theatre, San Diego, CA, then Ethel Barrymore Theatre, New York City, 1981; *Camelot*, New York State Theatre, New York City, 1980, then Winter Garden Theatre, New York City, 1981; *Can-Can*, Minskoff Theatre, New York City, 1981; *Lena Horne: The Lady and Her Music*, Nederlander Theatre, New York City, 1981; *Family Devotions*, New York Shakespeare Festival, Public Theatre, New York City, 1981; *Little Johnny Jones*, Alvin Theatre, New York City, 1982; *Seven Brides for Seven Brothers*, Alvin Theatre, New York City, 1982; *Show Boat*, Uris Theatre, New York City, 1983; *Dance a Little Closer*, Minskoff Theatre, New York City, 1983; *Mame*, Gershwin Theatre, New York City, 1983; *Peg*, Lunt-Fontanne Theatre, New York City, 1983; *Death of a Salesman*, Broadhurst Theatre, New York City, 1984.

Lighting designer for repertory productions at Boston Opera Company; Yale Repertory Company; American Shakespeare Festival, Stratford, CT; National Opera of Belgium; Circle in the Square, New York City; National Opera of Holland; American Dance Festival; American Spoleto Festival; Jones Beach Repertory Theatre.

Lighting designer, ballets: *Parade*, Massine Company; *The Green Table*, Joos Company; *Astarte*, Joffrey Ballet Company; *Dances at a Gathering*, New York City Ballet Company; *Scenes from Childhood*, Poll Company; *Aurole*, Paul Taylor Dance Company; *The Poor's Pavane*, Jose Limon Company; *Kettentanz*, Arpino Company; *Tiller of the Fields*, Tudor Company; *Rodeo*, DeMille Company; *Rooms*, Anna Sokolow Company; *Concerto Barocco*, Ballanchine Company; *A Footstep of Air*, Eliot Feld Ballet Company.

Set and lighting designer: *Astarte* and *The Beautiful Bait*, both with the Joffrey Ballet Company, 1962; *Sleeping Beauty*, Pennsylvannia Ballet Company; *The Medium and the Telephone, The Passion Play, Dancers of Bali, Compulsions*, all with the Poll Company.

Lighting designer for other dance companies including: Dancers of Bali, Inbal Escudero, Mary Anthony Dance Theatre, Ballet Folklorico de Mexico, Pearl Lang Company, Merce Cunningham Company, Shankar Company, National Ballet of Chile, Ballet of the Twentieth Century, Grand Ballet Canadienne, National Ballet of Canada, Pearl Primus Company, The Royal Ballet, American Ballet Theatre, Boston Ballet, National Ballet of Australia, Nureyev and Friends, Narkarove Company, Ohio Ballet.

Other designs for Bacalor, Haiti; Arirang, Korea; Feux Follet, Canada, and Foo Hsing, Formosa.

Director: *Turn of the Screw*, San Francisco Opera; *The Old Maid and the Thief*, Comic Opera Players; *Come Slowly Eden*, for the American National Theatre Academy (ANTA) Matinee Series, New York City; *Faces*, Berghof Studio, New York City; *Carmen*, Theatre de la Monaie.

MAJOR TOURS—Lighting designer: *Peter Pan*, U.S. cities, 1982-83; *Lena Horne: The Lady and Her Music*, U.S. cities, 1982-84.

RELATED CAREER—Associate professor, Yale University School of Drama, 1978-81; lecturer, Studio and Forum of Stage Design, New York City, University of Washington, University of Ohio, New York University, University of Akron; associate director, Ohio Ballet Company.

WRITINGS: NON-FICTION—*Handbook of Dance Stagecraft and Lighting*, 1955.

AWARDS: Antoinette Perry Award nomination, 1969, for *Indians;* Antoinette Perry Award nomination, 1975, for *All God's Chillun' Got Wings;* Carbonell Award, 1981, for *Peter Pan*.

MEMBER: United Scenic Artists, Studio and Forum of Stage Design (board of trustees); Ohio Ballet Company (executive committee).

ADDRESSES: OFFICE—c/o Ohio Ballet, 354 E. Market Street, Akron, OH 44325.*

*   *   *

SLEZAK, Erika   1946-

PERSONAL: Born August 5, 1946, in Hollywood, CA; daughter of Walter Leo (an actor) and Johanna Elizabeth (Van Rijn) Slezak; married Brian Davies (an actor), August 4, 1978; children: Michael Lawrence, Amanda Elizabeth. EDUCATION: Trained for the stage at the Royal Academy of Dramatic Art in London.

VOCATION: Actress.

CAREER: STAGE DEBUT—Title role, *Electra*, Milwaukee Repertory Theatre, WI, 1966. OFF-BROADWAY DEBUT—Elizabeth, *The Circle*, Roundabout Theatre, 1974. PRINCIPAL STAGE APPEARANCES—With the Milwaukee Repertory Company: Gilda, *Design for Living*, title role, *Hedda Gabler*, Desdemona, *Othello*, Alkmena, *Amphytrion 38*, Queen Elizabeth I, *Mary Stuart*, Cecily, *The Importance of Being Earnest*, Sabina, *The Skin of Our Teeth*, title role, *Dulcy*, Masha, *The Three Sisters*, and Charlotte Corday, *Marat/Sade;* Marianne, *Tartuffe* and Elvira, *Blithe Spirit*, both Alley Theatre, Houston, TX; Desdemona, *Othello*, Studio Arena Theatre, Buffalo, NY.

Stock productions: Liz Imbrie, *The Philadelphia Story*, Corie, *Barefoot in the Park*, and Marian, *The Music Man*.

PRINCIPAL TELEVISION APPEARANCES—Victoria Lord, *One Life to Live*, ABC, 1971—.

AWARDS: Best Actress on Daytime Television, Emmy Award nomination, 1983, for *One Life to Live;* Best Actress on Daytime Television, Emmy Awards, 1984 and 1986, for *One Life to Live*.

ADDRESSES: AGENT—c/o Milton Goldman, International Creative Management, 40 W. 57th Street, New York, NY 10019.

SMITH, Maggie 1934-

PERSONAL: Born December 28, 1934, in Ilford, England; daughter of Nathaniel (public-health pathologist) and Margaret (Hutton) Smith; married Robert Stephens, 1967 (divorced, 1974); married Beverley Cross, 1974; children: (first marriage) two sons. EDUCATION: Attended Oxford High School for Girls; studied for the stage at the Oxford Playhouse School.

VOCATION: Actress.

CAREER: STAGE DEBUT—Viola, *Twelfth Night*, OUDS, 1952. BROADWAY DEBUT—A comedienne, *New Faces '56 Revue*, Ethel Barrymore Theatre, 1956. LONDON DEBUT—Comedienne, *Share My Lettuce*, Lyric Theatre, Hammersmith, then Comedy Theatre, 1957. PRINCIPAL STAGE APPEARANCES—Vere Dane, *The Stepmother*, St. Martin's Theatre, London, 1958; with the Old Vic Theatre Company, 1959-60: Lady Plyant, *The Double Dealer*, Celia, *As You Like It*, Queen, *Richard II*, Mistress Ford, *The Merry Wives of Windsor*, and Maggie Wylie, *What Every Woman Knows;* Daisy, *Rhinoceros*, Strand Theatre, London, 1960; Lucile, *The Rehearsal*, Royal Theatre, then Bristol Old Vic Theatre, Globe Theatre, Queen's Theatre, and Apollo Theatre, London, 1961; Doreen, *The Private Ear* and Belinda, *The Public Eye*, double bill at the Globe Theatre, London, 1962; *Pictures in the Hallway*, dramatic reading, Mermaid Theatre, London, 1962; title role, *Mary, Mary*, Queen's Theatre, London, 1963; with the National Theatre Company at the Old Vic Theatre: Silvia, *The Recruiting Officer*, 1963, Desdemona, *Othello*, also at the Chichester Festival, 1964, Hilda Wangel, *The Master Builder*, Myra, *Hay Fever*, Beatrice, *Much Ado About Nothing*, all 1964, Clea, *Black Comedy*, 1965, title role, *Miss Julie*, 1965-66, Marcela, *A Bond Honoured*, 1966, Margery Pinchwife, *The Country Wife*, 1969, Mrs. Sullen, *The Beaux' Stratagem*, title role, *Hedda Gabler*, 1970, Masha, *The Three Sisters*, also in Los Angeles, 1970.

Amanda Prynne, *Private Lives*, Queen's Theatre, London, 1972; title role, *Peter Pan*, Vaudeville Theatre, London, 1974, then at the 46th Street Theatre, New York City, 1975; with the Stratford Shakespeare Festival, Ontario, Canada, 1976: Cleopatra, *Antony and Cleopatra*, Millamant, *The Way of the World*, Lady Macbeth, *Macbeth*, and Masha, *The Three Sisters;* the actress, *The Guardsman*, Ahmanson Theatre, Los Angeles, 1976; Stratford Shakespeare Festival, Ontario, Canada, 1977-78: Titania and Hippolyta, *A Midsummer Night's Dream*, Queen Elizabeth, *Richard II*, repeated role of the actress, *The Guardsman*, Judith Bliss, *Hay Fever*, Rosalind, *As You Like It*, Lady Macbeth, *Macbeth*, and Amanda, *Private Lives;* Ruth Carson, *Night and Day*, Phoenix Theatre, London, then American National Theatre and Academy (ANTA) Theatre, New York City, 1979; Stratford Shakespeare Festival, Ontario, Canada, 1980: Virginia Woolf, *Virginia*, Beatrice, *Much Ado About Nothing*, and Masha, *The Seagull;* repeated role of Virginia Woolf, *Virginia*, Haymarket Theatre, London, 1981; *Interpreter*, London production, 1986; Halina, *Coming into Land*, Lyttelton Theatre, London, 1987.

PRINCIPAL FILM APPEARANCES—*The V.I.P.s*, Metro-Goldwyn-Mayer (MGM), 1963; Desdemona, *Othello*, Warner Brothers, 1965; *The Honey Pot*, 1967; *Oh! What a Lovely War*, 1968; *Hot Millions*, MGM, 1968; *The Prime of Miss Jean Brodie*, Twentieth Century-Fox, 1969; *Love and Pain (and the Whole Damn Thing)*, Columbia, 1973; *Travels with My Aunt*, MGM, 1972; *Murder by Death*, Columbia, 1976; *Death on the Nile*, Paramount, 1978; *California Suite*, Columbia, 1978; *Quartet*, New World Pictures, 1981; *Clash of the Titans*, United Artists, 1981; *Evil Under the Sun*,

Universal, 1982; *The Missionary*, Columbia, 1982; *Better Late Than Never*, Galaxy, 1983; *Lily in Love*, New Line Cinema, 1985; *A Private Function*, Island Alive, 1985; Charlotte Bartlett, *A Room with a View*, Cinecom International, 1986.

PRINCIPAL TELEVISION APPEARANCES—Dramatic Specials: *Much Ado About Nothing; Man and Superman; On Approval; Home and Beauty*

AWARDS: Received the Commander of the British Empire award in the New Years Honours, 1970; Best Actress, London *Evening Standard* Award, 1962, for *The Private Ear* and *The Public Eye;* Best Actress, Variety Club Award, 1963, for *Mary, Mary;* Best Supporting Actress, Academy Award nomination, 1965, for *Othello;* Best Actress, Academy Award and Best Film Actress, Society of Film and Television Arts, both 1969, for *The Prime of Miss Jean Brodie;* Best Actress, London *Evening Standard* Award, 1970, for *Hedda Gabler;* Best Actress, Variety Club Award, 1972, for Amanda, *Private Lives;* Best Actress, Academy Award nomination, 1972, for *Travels with My Aunt;* Best Supporting Actress, Academy Award, and Golden Globe Award, both 1979, for *California Suite;* Best Actress, London *Evening Standard* Award, 1981, for *Virginia;* Best Supporting Actress, Golden Globe Award and Academy Award nomination, both 1986, for *A Room with a View.*

SIDELIGHTS: A gifted comedienne and dramatic player, Maggie Smith has appeared in numerous stage and screen productions on both sides of the Atlantic during her thirty-five year career in show business. Her extraordinary range and compelling talent have won her a kaleidoscope of roles and considerable public and critical esteem. She won Academy Awards for her performances in *The Prime of Miss Jean Brodie* (best actress, 1969) and *California Suite* (best supporting actress, 1978) and was nominated for Oscars for *Othello* (best supporting actress, 1965) and *Travels with My Aunt* (best actress, 1972).

The daughter of a public-health pathologist, Smith trained for the stage at the Oxford Playhouse School and worked on student productions at the university. She made her stage debut in a revue in 1952 and her first Broadway appearance in Leonard Sillman's *New Faces* in 1956. Back in London she won glowing reviews as the leading comedienne in another revue, Bamber Gascoigne's *Share My Lettuce*, and then joined the Old Vic Company, where she played Lady Plyant in William Congreve's *The Double Dealer* in 1959 and Maggie Wylie in James Barrie's *What Every Woman Knows* in 1960.

Her growing reputation was enhanced by performances in Jean Anouilh's *The Rehearsal* in 1961, in Peter Shaffer's double bill *The Private Ear* and *The Public Eye* in 1963, and in Jean Kerr's *Mary, Mary*, in 1963. In 1964 she joined the National Theatre Company at the invitation of Laurence Olivier and played Desdemona to his Othello. The production, with the original cast, was made into a motion picture, released in 1965 by Warner Brothers, and for her stunning interpretation of Othello's wife, Smith was nominated for an Academy Award.

In the mid to late 1960s Smith gave several outstanding performances in other National Theatre productions, including Hilda Wangel in Ibsen's *Master Builder*, Myra in a revival of Noel Coward's *Hay Fever*, Beatrice in *Much Ado About Nothing* to the Benedick of her first husband, Robert Stephens, the title role in Strindberg's *Miss Julie*, and Hedda Gabler in Ingmar Bergman's production of Ibsen's play. On leaving the National Theatre she played a highly praised Amanda Prynne, again opposite Stephens, in the West End production of Coward's *Private Lives.*

Smith then spent several seasons at the Stratford, Ontario, Shakespeare Festival, where she appeared in many important roles, among them Cleopatra in *Antony and Cleopatra*, Millamant in Congreve's *Way of the World*, Masha in Chekhov's *Three Sisters*, and Lady Macbeth. In 1979 she made a triumphant return to the English stage in Tom Stoppard's *Night and Day* and then played the role in New York. Following that engagement she returned to Stratford, where she starred as Virginia Woolf in Edna O'Brien's *Virginia* in 1980, appearing in the same play in London in 1981. In 1986 she earned rave notices for her role as a neurotic foreign office translator in Ronald Harwood's *Interpreter* at London's Queens Theatre.

It was for her screen work, however, that Smith achieved international acclaim. Her witty and sympathetic portrayal of an eccentric Scots schoolteacher in *The Prime of Miss Jean Brodie* earned the actress splendid notices and tribute as best actress of 1969 by both the Academy of Motion Picture Arts and Sciences in Hollywood and the Society of Film and Television Arts in her native Britain. In 1985 Smith had two films—*A Private Function* and *Lily in Love*—playing in movie houses simultaneously, and in 1986 her portrayal of Charlotte Bartlett, the dutiful aunt and chaperone in the box-office hit *A Room with a View*, adapted from E. M. Forster's 1908 novel, brought new admirers.

Basically a reticent and very private person, Smith is known for her fraigle self-esteem. Admittedly comfortable only on stage, she avoids interviews and talk shows. "It is part of her malaise in her own skin, her admitted sense of being less real, less in command of herself than of the characters she portrays, that makes it extremely difficult for Miss Smith to talk about herself," observed Flora Lewis in the September 12, 1979 *New York Times.* "It is agony for her to walk into a room of strangers, to have to meet people, to be public as a person rather than a part."

Years later Roderick Mann made a similar remark in a *Los Angeles Times* column of May 18, 1986. "Maggie Smith says that if Harrod's sold personalities she'd be first in line to order herself a new one," he remarked. "Nobody else seems to mind her being the funny, self-deprecatory, down-to-earth actress she is—an artist without rival when it comes to playing spinsters, old relatives and maiden aunts—but she does." Disputing her own unflattering judgment of herself as dull, uninteresting, shy, and ordinary, Mann countered, "That's just her opinion. Others find her a delight."

ADDRESSES: AGENT—International Creative Management, 388 Oxford Street, London W1N 9HE, England.*

*   *   *

SMITH, Sukie   1964-

PERSONAL: Born September 23, 1964, in Rochford, England; daughter of David (a banker) and Paddy (a banker; maiden name, Jones) Smith. EDUCATION: Attended the Central School of Speech and Drama, London.

VOCATION: Actress.

CAREER: PRINCIPAL STAGE APPEARANCES—Tiger Lily, *Peter*

SUKIE SMITH

Pan, Palace Theatre, Westcliff, Essex, U.K., 1986; also, Olga, *The Three Sisters;* Ropeen, *The Hostage;* Maxine Faulk, *The Night of the Iguana;* Kitty Maccan, *The Singular Life of Albert Nobbs;* Myrtle, *Still Life;* Julie, *Days to Come;* Dolly, *You Never Can Tell;* title role, *Hedda Gabler;* Queen Elizabeth, *Richard III;* Martha and Mrs. Andrews, *Lark Rise to Candleford;* Martha, *Who's Afraid of Virginia Woolf?;* Polena, *The Seagull;* Isabelle, *Total Eclipse;* Puck, *A Midsummer Night's Dream;* Crusty, *Down the Tube.*

MEMBER: British Actors' Equity Association.

ADDRESSES: AGENT—Kate Feast Management, 43A Princess Road, Regents Park, London NW1, England.

*   *   *

SMITH, Surrey
see Dinner, William

*   *   *

SOMKIN, Steven   1941-

PERSONAL: Born July 8, 1941, in New York, NY; son of Eugene Victor (a physician) and Ida Susan (an artist; maiden name, Marder) Somkin. EDUCATION: Carleton College, B.A., 1963; Tufts Medical School, 1968.

VOCATION: Writer.

WRITINGS: PLAYS, PRODUCED—*Dear John*, WPA Theatre, New York City, 1974; also *The Promotion of Artaud Wistaar; The Grandchild; Lust of Madeleine Leffers; The American Oasis; Beyond Consent; To Marianne with Love; Terminal Relationships; Andahazy, John Anderson.*

SCREENPLAYS—*Steal the Show*, ARC Films, 1986.

MEMBER: Dramatists Guild, New Dramatists Alumni.

SIDELIGHTS: Steven Somkin told *CTFT* that he practiced medicine from 1968 until 1978, and has since been working exclusively as a writer. He has written extensively as a medical specialist for films.

ADDRESSES: HOME—230 Riverside Drive, New York, NY 10025. AGENT—c/o Timothy De Baets, Stults and Marshall, 1370 Avenue of the Americas, New York, NY 10019.

* * *

SORVINO, Paul   1939-

PERSONAL: Born in 1939, in New York, NY EDUCATION: Trained for the stage at the Academy of Musical and Dramatic Arts.

VOCATION: Actor and director.

CAREER: FILM DEBUT—*Where's Poppa*, United Artists, 1970. PRINCIPAL FILM APPEARANCES—*Cry Uncle*, 1971; *Panic in Needle Park*, Twentieth Century-Fox, 1971; *Made for Each Other*, Twentieth Century-Fox, 1971; *The Day of the Dolphin*, AVCO-Embassy, 1973; *A Touch of Class*, AVCO-Embassy, 1973; *Shoot It Black, Shoot It Blue*, Thorn/EMI, 1974; *The Gambler*, Paramount, 1974; *I Will, I Will. . .for Now*, Twentieth Century-Fox, 1976; *Oh God!*, Warner Brothers, 1977; *Slow Dancing in the Big City*, United Artists, 1978; *The Brinks Job*, Universal, 1978; *Blood Brothers*, Warner Brothers, 1979; *Lost and Found*, Columbia, 1979; *Cruising*, United Artists, 1980; *Reds*, Paramount, 1981; *That Championship Season*, Cannon, 1982; *I, the Jury*, Twentieth Century-Fox, 1982; *Off the Wall*, 1983; *Turk 182*, Twentieth Century-Fox, 1984; *Delta Force*, Cannon, 1985; *The Stuff*, New World Pictures, 1985; *The Music Box*, Columbia, upcoming.

PRINCIPAL TELEVISION APPEARANCES—Series: George Platt, *We'll Get By*, CBS, 1975; Sergeant Bert D'Angelo, *Bert D'Angelo: Superstar*, ABC, 1976. Mini-Series: *Seventh Avenue*, NBC, 1977; *Chiefs*, CBS, 1983. Movies: *Tell Me Where It Hurts*, 1974; *Queen of the Stardust Ballroom*, 1975; *With Intent to Kill*, CBS, 1984; *Surviving*, ABC, 1985.

BROADWAY DEBUT—Patrolman, *Bajor*, Shubert Theatre, 1964. PRINCIPAL STAGE APPEARANCES—Officer Lynch, *Mating Dance*, Eugene O'Neill Theatre, New York City, 1965; Francesco, *Skyscraper*, Lunt-Fontanne Theatre, New York City, 1965; Phil Romano, *That Championship Season*, New York Shakespeare Festival (NYSF), Newman Theatre, and then Booth Theatre, New York City, 1972; Gloucester, *King Lear*, NYSF, Delacorte Theatre, New York City, 1973; Nathaniel Schwab, *An American Millionaire*, Circle in the Square, New York City, 1974; Lionel Lane, *For My Last Number*, Westport Country Playhouse, CT, 1975.

MAJOR TOURS—*We'll Get By*, U.S. cities, 1975; *Philemon*, U.S. cities, 1976; Aimable, *The Baker's Wife*, U.S. cities, 1976.

PRINCIPAL STAGE WORK—Director, *The Wheelbarrow Closers*, Bijou Theatre, New York City, 1976.

ADDRESSES: AGENT—Myrna Post, Nine E. 53rd Street, New York, NY 10022.*

* * *

SPACKMAN, Tom   1950-

PERSONAL: Born October 4, 1950, in Johnson City, NY; son of Dayton B. and Patricia M. (an accounting supervisor; maiden name, Wilcox) Spackman; married Lisa A. Angelocci (an actress), June 18, 1983. EDUCATION: Wayne State University, M.F.A.

VOCATION: Actor.

CAREER: TELEVISION DEBUT—Josh Millbank, *Another World*, NBC, 1986. PRINCIPAL TELEVISION APPEARANCES—Jack, *The Guiding Light*, CBS.

STAGE DEBUT—Leo, *Little Foxes*, Meadowbrook Theatre, Rochester, MI, 1975, for thirty performances. OFF-BROADWAY DEBUT—Title role, *Peer Gynt*, Classic Stage Company, 1981, for forty performances. PRINCIPAL STAGE APPEARANCES—Off-

TOM SPACKMAN

Broadway: Tony Williams, *The Servant*, Soho Repertory; Chris, *I Am a Camera*, American Jewish Theatre; *Flirtation*, T.O.M.I. Theatre; *Rum and Coke*, New York Shakespeare Festival; with the City Stage Company, New York City: title role, *Peer Gynt*, Edgar, *King Lear*, the student, *Ghost Sonata*, title role, *Faust*, Parts I and II, Harry Thunder, *Wild Oats*, Camille, *Danton's Death*, Kurt, *Dance of Death*, Victor, *Frankenstein*, Provost, *Brand*.

Regional: Tom, *The Glass Menagerie*, American Shaw Festival, Canada; Blunt, *Henry IV, Part I*, Yale Repertory, New Haven, CT; John, *Becoming Memories*, Pittsburgh Public Theatre; Cherry Evans, *Under Milkwood* and Hotspur, *Henry IV, Part I*, both Denver Center Theatre; Fred, *A Christmas Carol*, Studio Arena, Buffalo, NY; Sebastian, *Twelfth Night* and Lucillus, *Timon of Athens*, both New Jersey Shakespeare Festival; at the Meadowbrook Theatre, Rochester, MI: Dick Dudgeon, *The Devil's Principle*, John, *A Life in the Theatre*, Jack, *The Importance of Being Earnest*, Morgan Evans, *The Corn Is Green*, Stephen, *When You Comin' Back Red Ryder?*

FILM DEBUT—Dr. Fielding, *Brass*, Orion, 1985.

AWARDS: Best Actor, *Detroit Free Press* Award, 1978; St. Clair Bayfield Shakespearean Award, 1982, for *King Lear*.

ADDRESSES: HOME—New York, NY. AGENT—Ambrosio-Mortimer and Associates, 165 W. 46th Street, Suite 1109, New York, NY 10036.

*   *   *

SPINDELL, Ahvi

PERSONAL: Son of Edward (an orthopedic surgeon) and Edith (a sociologist) Spindell. EDUCATION: Attended Ithaca College; trained for the stage at Juilliard Theatre School and the Circle in the Square master class with Jose Ferrer. RELIGION: Jewish.

VOCATION: Actor.

CAREER: PRINCIPAL STAGE APPEARANCES—Lamar, *Godspell*, Cecilwood Theatre; *42 Seconds from Broadway* and *Mind with a Dirty Man*, both Hampton Playhouse; *Grease*, North Carolina Theatre; *Lady Audley's Secret*, Trinity Square Repertory Theatre, Providence, RI; *The Fifth of July, Rosencrantz & Guildenstern Are Dead*, and *Hamlet*, all Cincinnati Playhouse; *American Buffalo*, Milwaukee Repertory Theatre and Berkeley Repertory Theatre; *Private Ear*, Quaigh Theatre Dramathon, New York City; *The Birds*, Greek Theatre of New York; *The Ballgame*, Playwrights Horizon, New York City; *Antony & Cleopatra*, Woman's Interart Theatre, New York City; *Class Enemy*, New York City; *Forty-Deuce*, Theatre de Lys, New York City; *Emma*, New York City; Bruce, *Something Old, Something New*, New York City.

PRINCIPAL FILM APPEARANCES—*Zelig*, Warner Brothers, 1983; *Ten Pin Alley*, AVCO-Embassy.

PRINCIPAL TELEVISION APPEARANCES—*As The World Turns*, CBS.

AWARDS: Drama-Logue Award, for *American Buffalo*.

MEMBER: Actors' Equity Association, Screen Actors Guild, American Federation of Television and Radio Artists; Artists in Action.

AHVI SPINDELL

ADDRESSES: MANAGER—c/o Libby Bush, Landslide Management, 928 Broadway, New York, NY 10010.

*   *   *

STAFFORD-CLARK, Max   1941-

PERSONAL: Born March 17, 1941, in Cambridge, U.K.; son of David (a physician) and Dorothy Crossley (Oldfield) Stafford-Clark; married Carole Hayman (divorced); married Ann Pennington. EDUCATION: Attended Felsted School, Riverdale Country Day School, New York City and Trinity College, Dublin.

VOCATION: Director.

CAREER: FIRST STAGE WORK—Director, *Oh Gloria!*, Traverse Theatre, Edinburgh, Scotland, 1965. FIRST LONDON STAGE WORK—*Dublin Fare*, Arts Theatre, 1965. PRINCIPAL STAGE WORK Associate director, with the Traverse Theatre Company, Edinburgh, 1966; with the Traverse Theatre Company, 1968-70, directed: *The Lunatic, The Secret Sportsman*, and *The Woman Next Door*, also produced in London, all 1968, *Dear Janet Rosenberg, Sawney Bean, Dracula*, and *Dear Mr. Kooning*, also produced in London, all 1969; with the Traverse Theatre Workshop Company, 1970-74, directed: *Mother Earth* and *Our Sunday Times*, both 1970, *Sweet Alice* and *In the Heart of the British Museum*, both 1971, *Hitler Dances* and *Amalfi*, both 1972, *Shivvers* and *X*, both 1974.

With the Royal Court Theatre, London, associate director: *Slag*,

1971, *Magnificence,* 1973, *The Glad Hand, A Prayer for My Daughter,* and *Wheelchair Willie,* all 1978, *Sergeant Ola and His Followers,* 1979.

(With William Gaskill) co-founder and co-director, Joint Stock Theatre Group, London, 1974-76; with the Joint Stock Theatre Group, London, co-directed: *The Speakers,* 1974, *Fanshen,* 1975, *Yesterday's News,* 1976, *Epsom Downs,* 1977, and *Cloud Nine,* 1979; director, *Tea, Sex and Shakespeare,* Abbey Theatre, Dublin, Ireland, 1976; co-director, *A Mad World My Masters,* Young Vic Theatre, London, 1977; with the New York Shakespeare Festival, at the Public Theatre, New York City, directed: *Museum,* 1978, *Top Girls,* 1983, *Tom and Viv,* 1985, *Rat in the Skull,* 1985; *Serious Money,* Royal Court Theatre, London, 1987; also directed, *A Thought in Three Parts.*

RELATED CAREER—Visiting director, La Mama Experimental Theatre Club (E.T.C.), New York City, 1968; associate director, then director, Royal Court Theatre, London, 1971—.

SIDELIGHTS: RECREATIONS—Rugby, travel, and horror movies.

ADDRESSES: HOME—Seven Gloucester Crescent, London NW1, England. OFFICE—Royal Court Theatre, Sloane Square, London SW1, England.*

*   *   *

STAMOS, John

VOCATION: Actor and musician.

JOHN STAMOS

CAREER: PRINCIPAL TELEVISION APPEARANCES—Series: Blackie, *General Hospital,* ABC; Gino Minelli, *Dreams,* CBS, 1984; Matthew Willows, *You Again?,* NBC, 1986—.

PRINCIPAL FILM APPEARANCES—*Never Too Young to Die.*

RELATED CAREER—Musician, plays guitar and drums.

AWARDS: Best Supporting Actor in a Daytime Drama, Emmy Award, for *General Hospital;* two Soapy Awards; Youth in Film Award.

MEMBER: American Federation of Television and Radio Actors; Childhelp, U.S.A. (youth spokesperson).

ADDRESSES: PUBLICIST—Jo-Ann Geffen & Associates, 3151 Cahuenga Blvd. West, Suite 235, Los Angeles, CA 90068.

*   *   *

STAPLETON, Maureen   1925-

PERSONAL: Full name, Lois Maureen Stapleton; born June 21, 1925, in Troy, NY; daughter of John P. and Irene (Walsh) Stapleton; married Max Allentuck (a business manager), July, 1949 (divorced, February, 1959); married David Rayfiel (a playwright), July, 1963 (divorced); children: (first marriage) Daniel, Katharine. EDUCATION: Trained for the stage at the Herbert Berghof Studio.

VOCATION: Actress.

CAREER: BROADWAY DEBUT—Sarah Tansey, *The Playboy of the Western World,* Booth Theatre, 1946. PRINCIPAL STAGE APPEARANCES—Iras, *Antony and Cleopatra,* Martin Beck Theatre, New York City, 1947; Miss Hatch, *Detective Story,* Hudson Theatre, New York City, 1949; Emily Williams, *The Bird Cage,* Coronet Theatre, New York City, 1950; Serafina delle Rose, *The Rose Tattoo,* Martin Beck Theatre, New York City, 1951; Elizabeth Proctor, *The Crucible,* Martin Beck Theatre, New York City, 1953; Bella, *The Emperor's Clothes,* Ethel Barrymore Theatre, New York City, 1953; Anne, *Richard III,* City Center, New York City, 1953; Masha, *The Seagull,* Phoenix Theatre, New York City, 1954; Flora, *Twenty-Seven Wagons Full of Cotton,* Playhouse Theatre, New York City, 1955; Lady Torrance, *Orpheus Descending,* Martin Beck Theatre, New York City, 1957; Aunt Ida, *The Cold Wind and Warm,* Morosco Theatre, New York City, 1958.

Carrie Berniers, *Toys in the Attic,* Hudson Theatre, New York City, 1960; Amanda Wingfield, *The Glass Menagerie,* Brooks Atkinson Theatre, New York City, 1965; Serafina delle Rose, *The Rose Tatoo,* City Center, then Billy Rose Theatre, New York City, 1966; Karen Nash, Muriel Tate, and Norma Hubley, *Plaza Suite,* Plymouth Theatre, New York City, 1968; Beatrice Chambers, *Norman Is That You?,* Lyceum Theatre, New York City, 1970; Evy Meara, *The Gingerbread Lady,* Plymouth Theatre, New York City, 1970; Georgie Elgin, *The Country Girl,* Billy Rose Theatre, New York City, 1972; title role, *The Secret Affairs of Mildred Wild,* Ambassador Theatre, New York City, 1972; Serafina delle Rose, *The Rose Tattoo,* Walnut Street Theatre, Philadelphia, 1973; appeared in a benefit gala at the Circle in the Square, New York City, 1974; Juno Boyle, *Juno and the Paycock,* Mark Taper Forum, Los Angeles, 1974; Amanda Wingfield, *The Glass Menagerie,* Circle in the Square, New York City, 1975; Fonsia Dorsey, *The Gin Game,* John

Golden Theatre, New York City, 1978; Birdie Hubbard, *The Little Foxes,* Martin Beck Theatre, New York City, then Ahmanson Theatre, Los Angeles, 1981.

FILM DEBUT—*Lonely Hearts,* United Artists, 1959. PRINCIPAL FILM APPEARANCES—*Fugitive Kind,* United Artists, 1960; *View from the Bridge,* Continental, 1962; *Bye Bye Birdie,* Columbia, 1963; *Trilogy,* Allied Artists, 1969; *Airport,* Universal, 1970; *Plaza Suite,* Paramount, 1971; *Interiors,* 1978; *The Runner Stumbles,* Twentieth Century-Fox, 1979; *On the Right Track,* Twentieth Century-Fox, 1981; Emma Goldman, *Reds,* Paramount, 1981; *The Fan,* Paramount, 1981; *Johnny Dangerously,* Twentieth Century-Fox, 1984; *Cocoon,* Twentieth Century-Fox, 1985; *The Money Pit,* Universal, 1986; also *Made in Heaven.*

PRINCIPAL TELEVISION APPEARANCES—Episodic: "All the King's Men," *Kraft Theatre,* NBC, 1958; "For Whom the Bell Tolls," *Playhouse 90,* CBS, 1959; "Save Me a Place at Forest Lawn," *New York Television Theatre,* PBS, 1966; "Mirror, Mirror, Off the Wall," *On Stage,* NBC, 1969; also, *Goodyear Playhouse,* NBC; *Philco Playhouse,* NBC; *Armstrong Circle Theatre,* NBC; *Naked City,* ABC; *East Side/West Side,* CBS.

Movies: "Tell Me Where It Hurts," for *General Electric Theatre,* CBS, 1974; *Queen of the Stardust Ballroom,* CBS, 1975; *Cat on a Hot Tin Roof,* 1976; *Little Gloria, Happy at Last,* 1982; *The Electric Grandmother,* 1982; *Mother's Day,* 1984; *Sentimental Journey,* 1984; *Private Sessions,* NBC, 1985; also appeared in *Family Secrets.* Specials: "Among the Paths to Eden," *Xerox Special Event,* ABC, 1967.

AWARDS: Antoinette Perry Award, Peabody Award, *Theatre World* Award, all 1951, for *The Rose Tatoo;* Emmy Awards, 1967, for *Save Me a Place at Forest Lawn,* and 1968, for *Among the Paths to Eden;* Antoinette Perry Award nomination, 1968, for *Plaza Suite;* National Society of Arts and Letters Award, 1969; Best Supporting Actress, Academy Award nomination, 1970, for *Airport;* Antoinette Perry Award, Drama Desk Award, winner of *Variety* New York Drama Critics Poll, all 1971, for *Gingerbread Lady;* Best Supporting Actress, Academy Award nomination, 1978, for *Interiors;* Best Supporting Actress, Academy Award, 1982, for *Reds.*

MEMBER: Actors' Equity Association, Screen Actors Guild, American Federation of Television and Radio Artists.

ADDRESSES: AGENT—International Creative Management, 8899 Beverly Blvd., Los Angeles, CA 90048.*

                    *   *   *

STEELE, Lezley   1944-
(Lezley Havard)

PERSONAL: Born Lezley Morton-Fincham, August 9, 1944, in London, England; daughter of Ernest (a surveyor) and Iris Margaret (a secretary; maiden name, Tobin) Morton-Fincham; married Bernard Havard (a theatrical producer), January 16, 1963; children: Celine, Christiane, Julien.

VOCATION: Playwright.

CAREER: PRINCIPAL STAGE WORK—Formerly wrote under the name Lezley Havard.

LEZLEY STEELE

WRITINGS: PLAYS, PRODUCED—*Only Yesterday,* University of Edmonton, Alberta, Canada, 1976; *Jill,* Citadel Theatre, Edmonton, 1977, Lennoxville Festival, Quebec, 1978, produced as *Hide and Seek,* Wilbur Theatre, Boston, 1980, Belasco Theatre, New York City, 1980, Peachtree Playhouse, Atlanta, 1981, published by Dramatists Play Service; *Victims,* Alliance Theatre, Atlanta, 1978, Windsor, Ontario, 1979, Whitehorse Theatre, Yukon, 1979, published by Playwrights of Canada; *In the Name of the Father,* Alliance Theatre, Atlanta, 1980, toured Amsterdam, Holland, 1985-86; *The Actors,* Alliance Theatre, Atlanta, 1981; staged reading, Wilma Theatre, Philadelphia, 1985; *In the Bag* (one-act), Actors Theatre of Louisville, 1982; *Termination Point* (one-act), Actors Theatre of Louisville, 1983; *A Woman's Place,* staged reading, Alliance Theatre, 1983.

PLAYS, COMMISSIONED—All for the Actors Theatre of Louisville: "Dear John," 1983, "Arrangements," 1984, "The Courting," 1985.

PLAYS, UNPRODUCED—"Session" (one-act), 1986; "What Ever Happened to Charity?," in progress.

RELATED CAREER—Literary manager, Alliance Theatre, Atlanta, 1980-81.

AWARDS: Best Full Length Play, National Competition Women-for-Theatre, Playwrights Co-Op, Toronto, Canada, 1975, for *Victims;* Best Play, Multi-Cultural Association, Toronto, Canada, 1975, for *Only Yesterday;* Clifford E. Lee Playwriting Award, University of Edmonton, Alberta, Canada, 1976, for *Jill;* Senior

Arts Grant and Short Term Grant, both from the Canada Council for the Arts, 1977; Playwriting Fellowship, Georgia Arts Council, 1982; Playwriting Fellowship, Pennsylvania Arts Council, 1985.

MEMBER: Dramatists Guild.

ADDRESSES. OFFICE—Walnut Street Theatre, Ninth and Walnut Streets, Philadelphia, PA 19146. AGENT—Earl Graham Agency, 317 W. 45th Street, New York, NY 10036.

*   *   *

STEIN, Joseph   1912-

PERSONAL: Born May 30, 1912, in New York, NY; son of Charles and Emma (Rosenblum) Stein; married Sadie Singer (divorced); married Elisa Loti (an actress). EDUCATION: College of the City of New York, B.S.S., 1934; attended Columbia University, School of Social Research, 1935-37.

VOCATION: Writer and producer.

CAREER: Writer, 1944— (see below). PRINCIPAL STAGE WORK—Co-producer, *We Bombed in New Haven,* Ambassador Theatre, New York City, 1968.

WRITINGS: PLAYS, PRODUCED—(All with Will Glickman) *Inside U.S.A.,* Century Theatre, New York City, 1948; *Lend an Ear,* National Theatre, New York City, 1948; *Mrs. Gibbons' Boys,* Music Box Theatre, New York City, 1949, then later Westminster Theatre, London, 1956; *Alive and Kicking,* Winter Garden Theatre, New York City, 1950; book, *Plain and Fancy,* Mark Hellinger Theatre, New York City, 1955; book, *Mr. Wonderful,* Broadway Theatre, New York City, 1956; book, *The Body Beautiful,* Broadway Theatre, New York City, 1958.

Author of book, *Juno,* Winter Garden Theatre, New York City, 1959; (with Robert Russell) book, *Take Me Along,* Shubert Theatre, New York City, 1959; *Enter Laughing,* Henry Miller's Theatre, New York City, 1963; book, *Fiddler on the Roof,* Imperial Theatre, New York City, 1964, then Alhambra Theatre, Tel Aviv, Israel, 1965, then Her Majesty's Theatre, London, 1967; book, *Zorba,* Imperial Theatre, New York City, 1968; (with Hugh Wheeler and others) book, *Irene,* Minskoff Theatre, New York City, 1973; book, *King of Hearts,* Minskoff Theatre, New York City, 1978; (with Alan Jay Lerner) *Carmelina,* St. James Theatre, New York City, 1979; book, *The Baker's Wife,* York Theatre Company, New York City, 1985; *Before the Dawn,* American Place Theatre, New York City, 1985; book, *Rags,* Mark Hellinger Theatre, New York City, 1986.

SCREENPLAYS—*Enter Laughing,* Columbia, 1967; *Fiddler on the Roof,* United Artists, 1971.

TELEVISION—Series: *All Star Revue,* NBC, 1950-51; *Your Show of Shows,* NBC, 1952-53; *The Sid Caesar Show,* ABC, 1953-54. Also writer for Phil Silvers, Debbie Reynolds, and others, 1955-62.

RADIO—*Lower Basin Street,* 1944; *Raleigh Room,* NBC, 1944-47; *The Henry Morgan Show,* ABC, 1946-49.

AWARDS: Best Musical, Antoinette Perry Award, New York

Drama Critics Award, both 1964, for *Fiddler on the Roof;* Music and Performing Award, B'nai B'rith, 1965, for "exceptional creative achievement"; Antoinette Perry Award nomination, 1968, for *Zorba.*

MEMBER: Authors League of America, Dramatists Guild (council member, 1970—), Writers Guild of America, Academy of Television Arts and Sciences.

ADDRESSES: OFFICE—250 W. 57th Street, New York, NY 10019.

*   *   *

STEVENS, George, Jr.   1932-

PERSONAL: Full name, George Cooper Stevens, Jr.; born April 3, 1932, in Hollywood, CA; son of George Cooper (a film director) and Yvonne (Shevlin) Stevens; married Elizabeth Guest, July 5, 1965; children: Michael Murrow, David Averell; (step-daughter) Caroline. EDUCATION: Occidental College, B.A., English and speech, 1953. MILITARY: U.S. Air Force, 1954-56.

VOCATION: Writer, producer, director, and motion picture and television executive.

CAREER: PRINCIPAL FILM WORK—Scriptreader for his father, 1950; assisted his father on *A Place in the Sun,* Paramount, 1951; company clerk, *Shane,* Paramount, 1953; assisted on screenplay, editing, and distribution, *Giant,* Warner Brothers, 1956; production assistant to Jack Webb, *The D.I.,* Warner Brothers, 1958; associate producer and director of location scenes, *The Diary of Anne Frank,* Twentieth Century-Fox, 1959; associate producer, *The Greatest Story Ever Told,* United Artists, 1965; co-producer, *Directed by John Ford,* 1970; producer, director, and writer, *George Stevens: A Filmmaker's Journey,* 1985.

PRINCIPAL TELEVISION WORK—Production assistant to Jack Webb on television series, *Dragnet,* NBC, 1952, and *Pete Kelly's Blues,* NBC, 1959; directed various episodes of *Alfred Hitchcock Presents, Peter Gunn,* and *Phillip Marlowe.*

As executive director of the American Film Institute, produced: *American Film Institute Salute to John Ford,* CBS, 1973; *American Film Institute Salute to James Cagney,* CBS, 1974; *American Film Institute Salute to Orson Welles,* CBS, 1975; *American Film Institute Salute to William Wyler,* CBS, 1976; *America at the Movies,* U.S. Bicentennial film, 1976; *American Film Institute Salute to Bette Davis,* CBS, 1977; *The Stars Salute America's Greatest Movies,* CBS, 1977; *American Film Institute Salute to Henry Fonda,* CBS, 1978.

Co-producer and writer, *Kennedy Center Honors,* CBS, 1978; producer and writer: *America Entertains Vice Premier Deng,* PBS, 1979; *American Film Institute Salute to Alfred Hitchcock,* CBS, 1979; *The Kennedy Center Honors,* CBS, 1979; *American Film Institute Salute to James Stewart,* CBS, 1980; *The Kennedy Center Honors,* CBS, 1980; *American Film Institute Salute to Fred Astaire,* CBS, 1981; *The Kennedy Center Honors,* CBS, 1981; *American Film Institute Salute to Frank Capra,* CBS, 1982; *The Kennedy Center Honors,* CBS, 1982; *Christmas in Washington,* NBC, 1982; *American Film Institute Salute to John Huston,* CBS, 1983; *The Kennedy Center Honors,* CBS, 1983; *Christmas in Washington,*

NBC, 1983; *American Film Institute Salute to Lillian Gish,* CBS, 1984; *The Kennedy Center Honors,* CBS, 1984; *Christmas in Washington,* NBC, 1984; *American Film Institute Salute to Gene Kelly,* CBS, 1985; *The Kennedy Center Honors,* CBS, 1985; *Christmas in Washington,* NBC, 1985; *American Film Institute Salute to Billy Wilder,* NBC, 1986; *American Film Institute Salute to Barbara Stanwyck,* ABC, 1987; others.

RELATED CAREER—Director, Motion Picture and Television Service, United States Information Agency (U.S.I.A.), 1962-67, responsible for production and overseas distribution of three hundred films a year and for coordinating special film matters for the U.S. government. Among his U.S.I.A. productions were: *The Five Cities of June, Letter from Colombia, The School at Rincon Santo,* all 1963; *Nine from Little Rock, The March, John F. Kennedy: Years of Lightning, Day of Drums,* all 1964; *Architecture USA,* 1965; *Cowboy,* 1966; *Harvest,* 1967.

Chairman of the U.S. delegations to various film festivals, from 1962—, including festivals in Cannes, Venice, Moscow, and Czechoslovakia; founding director, American Film Institute, 1967-79; member, planning committee, John F. Kennedy Center for the Performing Arts in Washington, DC, 1964-1966; member, advisory committee for the National Endowment for the Arts, 1966; elected a life trustee and co-chairman of the board of the American Film Institute, 1981. Also: produced the gala opening of the Kentucky Center for the Arts, in Louisville, 1983.

NON-RELATED CAREER—Project Hope (chairman, Southern California Committee, 1960).

AWARDS: Best Documentary, Lion of St. Mark, Venice Film Festival, 1963, for *Letter from Colombia;* First Prize for Human Relations, Venice Film Festival, 1963, for *The School at Rincon Santo;* Best Documentary, Academy Award nomination, 1963, for *The Five Cities of June;* Best Documentary, Academy Award, 1964, for *Nine from Little Rock;* Grand Prize, Paris Festival of Architecture, 1965, for *Architecture USA;* San Francisco Festival, Golden Gate Award, 1966, for *Nine from Little Rock;* First Prizes, Documentary Film Festival, Bilbao, Spain and Netherlands Film Festival, both 1966, for *The March;* Best Documentary, International Film Importers and Distributors Award and National Board of Review's selection for one the ten best films of the year, 1966, for *John F. Kennedy: Years of Lightning, Day of Drums;* Best Documentary, Academy Award nominations, 1966, for *Cowboy* and 1967, for *Harvest.*

Outstanding Program and Individual Achievement, Emmy Award, 1974, for *American Film Institute Salute to James Cagney;* Best Variety, Musical or Comedy Program, Emmy Award, 1984, for *The Kennedy Center Honors;* Emmy nominations: 1977, for *American Film Institute Salute to Bette Davis,* 1978, for *American Film Institute Salute to Henry Fonda,* 1979, for *The Kennedy Center Honors,* 1980, for *American Film Institute Salute to James Stewart,* 1981, for *American Film Institute Salute to Fred Astaire,* 1982, for *American Film Institute Salute to Frank Capra,* 1983, for *The Kennedy Center Honors,* 1984, for *The Kennedy Center Honors* and *American Film Institute Salute to Lillian Gish,* two nominations in 1985, for *American Film Institute Salute to Gene Kelly,* and 1985, for *The Kennedy Center Honors.*

Also: Golden Globe Award; Silver Medal, International Film and Television Festival of New York, 1980, for *The Kennedy Center Honors;* various Writers Guild of America awards and nominations for his television specials; a special award from the Berlin Film

Festival, 1976, for *America at the Movies,* which also garnered a special jury award at the Virgin Islands International Film Festival, an award of merit from the National Association of Theatre Owners, and an award from the New School for Social Research; in 1981, awarded the Motion Picture Hall of Fame Annual Award for Outstanding Contribution to Motion Pictures; special "out of competition" presentations at the Cannes, Deauville, and Venice film festivals, 1985, for *George Stevens: A Filmmaker's Journey,* which also received a National Board of Review Award in 1986 and a Distinguished Achievement Award from the International Documentary Association.

Among the earliest tributes paid to George Stevens, Jr., were the Arthur S. Flemming Award as one of the Ten Outstanding Young Men in the Federal Government (1963) and his selection as one of the Ten Outstanding Young Men in the U.S. by the National Junior Chamber of Commerce (1964).

MEMBER: Directors Guild of America, Writers Guild of America, Academy of Motion Picture Arts and Sciences, Academy of Television Arts and Sciences, Caucus for Producers, Writers, and Directors, American Federation of Television and Radio Artists; Century Association, New York.

ADDRESSES: OFFICE—John F. Kennedy Center for the Performing Arts, Washington DC 20566.

*   *   *

STEVENS, Tony   1948-

PERSONAL: Born Anthony Pusateri, May 2, 1948, in New York, NY; son of Anthony A. (a factory worker) and Ruth Ann (owner of a country store; maiden name, Pashia) Pusateri. EDUCATION: Studied dance with Michael Simms and Nanette Charisse.

VOCATION: Choreographer and director.

CAREER: PRINCIPAL STAGE WORK—Choreographer, *Perfectly Frank,* Helen Hayes Theatre, New York City, 1980; director and choreographer, *All Dressed Up,* Whole Theatre Company, Montclair, NJ; director and choreographer, *Get Happy,* Westwood Playhouse, Los Angeles; director and choreographer, *Sing Happy,* Avery Fisher Hall, New York City; director and choreographer, *Sing Happy* and *Godspell,* Burt Reynolds Dinner Theatre, FL; choreographer, *The Yearling,* Atlanta Theatre of Stars; choreographer, *By Bernstein,* Chelsea Theatre, New York City; choreographer, *Music, Music, Music,* City Center, New York City; director and choreographer, *Chicago,* Tokyo, Japan, 1986; also staged Broadway productions of *Wind in the Willows, Spotlight, Rachel Lily Rosenbloom,* and *Rockabye Hamlet.*

PRINCIPAL FILM WORK—Staged party scenes in *The Great Gatsby,* Paramount, 1974; choreographer: *The Best Little Whorehouse in Texas,* Universal, 1982; *Johnny Dangerously,* Twentieth Century-Fox, 1984; *She's Having a Baby,* Paramount, upcoming.

PRINCIPAL CABARET WORK—Choreographer for Chita Rivera, Bernadette Peters, Phyllis Newman, Bette Midler, Liza Minnelli, Dick Van Dyke, and Ann Reinking.

PRINCIPAL TELEVISION WORK—Choreographer: *Broadway Plays*

TONY STEVENS

Washington, PBS, 1982; *Walt Disney's Thirtieth Anniversary,* NBC, 1985.

VIDEO—Choreographer, Lily Tomlin's version of "Maniac," 1986.

RELATED CAREER—Has assisted choreographers Bob Fosse, Gower Champion, and Peter Genarro.

AWARDS: Top Ten Directors of 1986, Tokyo, Japan, for *Chicago;* Best Director, Drama-Logue and *LA Weekly,* for *Get Happy.*

MEMBER: Society of Stage Directors and Choreographers, American Federation of Television and Radio Artists, American Film Institute, Playwrights Horizons.

ADDRESSES: AGENT—c/o Eric Shepard, International Creative Management, 40 W. 57th Street, New York, NY 10019.

*   *   *

STEWART, James   1908-

PERSONAL: Born May 20, 1908, in Indiana, PA; son of Alexander Maitland (a hardware store owner) and Elizabeth Ruth (Jackson) Stewart; married Gloria Hatrick McLean, August 9, 1949; children: Kelly, Judy (twin daughters); (stepsons) Michael, Ronald. EDUCA-

TION: Princeton University, B.S., architecture, 1932; trained for the stage with Joshua Logan. MILITARY: U.S. Army Air Force, 1942-45. RELIGION: Presbyterian.

VOCATION: Actor.

CAREER: FILM DEBUT—*The Murder Man,* Metro-Goldwyn-Mayer (MGM), 1935. PRINCIPAL FILM APPEARANCES—*Next Time We Love,* Universal, 1936; *Rose Marie* (retitled *Indian Love Call*), 1936; *Small Town Girl,* MGM, 1936; *Wife Vs. Secretary,* MGM, 1936; *Speed,* MGM, 1936; *The Gorgeous Hussy,* MGM, 1936; *Born to Dance,* MGM, 1936; *The Last Gangster,* MGM, 1937; *Seventh Heaven,* MGM, 1937; *You Can't Take It with You,* MGM, 1938; *The Shopworn Angel,* MGM, 1938; *Vivacious Lady,* 1938; *Mr. Smith Goes to Washington,* Columbia, 1939; *It's a Wonderful World,* MGM, 1939; *Destry Rides Again,* MGM, 1939; *Philadelphia Story,* MGM, 1940; *The Shop Around the Corner,* 1940; *Mortal Storm,* 1940; George Bailey, *It's a Wonderful Life,* RKO, 1946; *Magic Town,* RKO, 1947; *Call Northside 777,* 1948; *Rope,* 1948; *You Gotta Stay Happy,* 1948; *Stratton Story,* 1949.

Malaga, 1950; *Wincester 73,* Universal, 1950; *Broken Arrow,* Twentieth Century-Fox, 1950; Elwood P. Dowd, *Harvey,* 1950; *Jackpot,* 1950; *No Highway in the Sky,* 1952; *The Greatest Show on Earth,* Paramount, 1952; *Carbine Williams,* 1952; *Bend of the River,* Universal, 1952; *Naked Spur,* MGM, 1953; *Thunder Bay,* Universal, 1953; *The Glenn Miller Story,* Universal, 1954; *Rear Window,* Universal, 1954; *Far Country,* Universal, 1955; *Strategic Air Command,* Paramount, 1955; *The Man from Laramie,* Columbia, 1955; *The Man Who Knew Too Much,* Paramount, 1956; *Spirit of St. Louis,* Warner Brothers, 1957; *Night Passage,* Universal, 1957; *Vertigo,* Paramount, 1958; *Anatomy of a Murder,* Columbia, 1959; *Bell, Book and Candle,* Columbia, 1959; *F.B.I. Story,* Warner Brothers, 1959.

The Mountain Road, Columbia, 1960; *Two Rode Together,* Columbia, 1961; *The Man Who Shot Liberty Valence,* Paramount, 1962; *Mr. Hobbs Takes a Vacation,* Twentieth Century-Fox, 1962; *How the West Was Won,* MGM, 1962; *Take Her, She's Mine,* Twentieth Century-Fox, 1963; *Cheyenne Autumn,* Warner Brothers, 1964; *Dear Brigitte,* Twentieth Century-Fox, 1965; *Shenandoah,* Universal, 1965; *The Rare Breed,* Universal, 1966; *The Flight of the Phoenix,* Twentieth Century-Fox, 1966; *Firecreek,* Warner Brothers/Seven Arts, 1968; *Bandolero!,* Twentieth Century-Fox, 1968.

Cheyenne Social Club, National General, 1970; *Fool's Parade,* Columbia, 1971; *That's Entertainment,* United Artists, 1974; *The Shootist,* Paramount, 1976; *Airport '77,* Universal, 1977; *The Big Sleep,* United Artists, 1978; *The Magic of Lassie,* 1978.

PRINCIPAL TELEVISION APPEARANCES—Series: Professor James K. Howard, *The Jimmy Stewart Show,* NBC, 1971-72; Billy Jim Hawkins, *Hawkins,* CBS, 1973-74. Dramatic Specials: "Flashing Spikes," *Alcoa Premiere,* ABC; "Saddle Tramp in the Old West," *General Electric Theatre,* CBS; "Cindy's Fella," *Startime,* NBC. Movies: *Right of Way,* Home Box Office, 1984; also, *The Late Christopher Bean,* CBS. Guest: *Portrait,* CBS, 1963.

STAGE DEBUT—Chauffeur, *Goodbye Again,* University Players, Falmouth, MA, 1932. BROADWAY DEBUT—Constable Gano, *Carrie Nation,* Biltmore Theatre, 1932. LONDON DEBUT—Elwood P. Dowd, *Harvey,* Prince of Wales Theatre, 1975. PRINCIPAL STAGE APPEARANCES—Chauffeur, *Goodbye Again,* Masque Theatre, New York City, 1932; Johnny Chadwick, *All Good Americans,* Henry Miller's Theatre, New York City, 1932; Jack Breenan,

Spring in Autumn, Henry Miller's Theatre, New York City, 1933; Sergeant O'Hara, *Yellow Jack,* Martin Beck Theatre, New York City, 1934; Teddy Parrish, *Divided by Three,* Ethel Barrymore Theatre, New York City, 1934; Ed Olsen, *Page Miss Glory,* Mansfield Theatre, New York City, 1934; Carl, *A Journey by Night,* Shubert Theatre, New York City, 1935; Elwood P. Dowd, *Harvey,* 48th Street Theatre, New York City, 1947, and later at the American National Theatre Academy (ANTA) Theatre, New York City, 1970; *Festival at Ford's,* Ford's Theatre, Washington, DC, 1970; *Gala Tribute to Joshua Logan,* Imperial Theatre, New York City, 1975; *Night of 100 Stars,* Radio City Music Hall, New York City, 1982; *Night of 100 Stars II,* Radio City Music Hall, New York City, 1985.

PRINCIPAL STAGE WORK—Stage manager, *Camille,* Boston.

AWARDS: New York Critics Award, 1939, for *Mr. Smith Goes to Washington;* Best Actor, Academy Award, 1940, for *Philadelphia Story;* Best Actor, Academy Award nomination, 1946, for *It's a Wonderful Life;* voted one of the top ten money-making stars, *Motion Picture Herald-Fame* Poll, 1950, 1952, 1954, 1957, top money-making star, 1955; Volpi Cup Award, Venice, 1959, for *Anatomy of a Murder;* Berlin Film Award, 1962; American Film Institute Award for Life Achievement, 1980; John F. Kennedy Award for Lifetime Achievement, 1983; Special Academy Award, 1985; Croix de guerre with Palm Award; Presidential Medal of Freedom Award, 1985; also Screen Actors Guild Award; military: Distinguished Flying Cross with Oak Leaf Cluster; Air Medal.

MEMBER: Screen Actors Guild; Princeton University (board of trustees), Claremont College (board of trustees), Los Angeles Council of Boy Scouts of America (executive board), Project Hope (board of directors).

SIDELIGHTS: An affable and modest performer, actor James Stewart has achieved international fame for portraying the quintessential "ordinary man," a gawky hero whose strengths are found amidst the throes of adversity. In a career spanning five decades, Stewart has worked with many of Hollywood's finest directors—including John Ford, Frank Capra, and Alfred Hitchcock—on numerous films that are now considered classics, such as *Mr. Smith Goes to Washington, The Philadelphia Story, It's a Wonderful Life, Destry Rides Again,* and *Vertigo.* As Joseph McBride noted in his June, 1976, *American Film* retrospective, Stewart's "ability to fit with ease into so many directors' worlds attests to the strength of his personality and also to its depth; within the Stewart 'image' there are many Stewarts, but ultimately there is only one, underlying all of the roles." Michiko Kakutani described that one Stewart persona in a January 9, 1985 *New York Times* article. Jimmy Stewart, wrote Kakutani, radiates a "quality of unadorned decency. . .that made him the ideal hero."

Stewart's off-screen life parallels those of some of his "Everyman" on screen creations. He was born in 1908 in tiny Indiana, Pennsylvania, the only child of a hardware store owner. He often recounts his most vivid childhood memory—cleaning the stalls of his father's horses, and learning not to be afraid of them. Stewart attended Princeton University and graduated with a degree in architecture in 1932. Unable to land a job due to the Depression, he accepted work in summer stock theatre with a Princeton friend, Joshua Logan. There he met many struggling actors, including Henry Fonda, Margaret Sullavan, and Myron McCormick, and he decided to try his hand in the theatre. In 1932, Stewart and Fonda shared a room first in New York City and then in Hollywood, where success came gradually for both.

As his fame increased, Stewart provided little grist for Hollywood gossip-mills. He remained a scandal-free bachelor until the age of forty-one, then quietly married a divorced mother of two, Gloria Hatrick McLean. The marriage, which produced twin daughters, has endured for more than thirty-five years. One of the first Hollywood actors to be called for service in World War II, Stewart served honorably as a bomber pilot. He flew twenty missions over Germany, rising from a private to a full colonel. After the war, he continued to serve in the Air Force Reserve, eventually being promoted to brigadier general—the highest military postion ever achieved by an American entertainer. Conservative politically, Stewart supported the American involvement in Vietnam, remaining in favor of the commitment even when his stepson died in that conflict. Stewart's war and family experiences, his well-publicized devotion to pets, including Pie, the feisty horse he rode in most of his Westerns, served to unite him with many members of his audience.

Though his bumbling persona has often been a convenient target for mimics, Stewart has undergone considerable evolution throughtout his performing career. Kakutani described this process in the *New York Times:* "The naifs and country hicks he had become famous playing during the late 30s and 40s slowly gave way to more complicated, subtle roles: grizzled rustlers and bounty hunters in a series of westerns, and the clever, conflicted protagonists of such films as *Rear Window, Vertigo* and *Anatomy of a Murder.* If, in Hitchcock's words, Mr. Stewart continued to stand for 'everyman in bizarre situations,' he had also matured into a new kind of representative hero—still earnest and well-meaning, but less sentimental and a good deal less innocent than he had been in his youth." More recently, Stewart has eschewed retirement for television and movie roles—however small—that allow him to play "a grandfatherly version of what he always was—the *regular* guy," according to James Robert Parish and Ronald L. Bowers in *The MGM Stock Company: The Golden Era* (Arlington House, 1973).

Stewart described his own reaction to his film roles in an October 20, 1983 *Christian Science Monitor* interview: "People have said—and I've felt it at times—there's a certain vulnerability about a lot of my characters. Perhaps this creeps into so many of my pictures because I've tended to select this type of character, because of my feelings about life." Reflecting on the notion of a "typical" Stewart character, he added: "I see nothing wrong with that. Someone asked Spencer Tracy if he got tired of playing himself all the time. He said, 'Who do you want me to play, Humphrey Bogart?' I feel it's all right to bring your own style to a character."

In a career of many varied roles, perhaps two performances remain representative of Jimmy Stewart's screen and stage presence. In *It's a Wonderful Life,* his own favorite film, Stewart plays George Bailey, a struggling small-town businessman whose dreams of a wider world are stymied by the myriad small setbacks of life. On the brink of suicide, George is rescued by a guardian angel who shows him what his town would have been like had he never been born. Though not a box-office success at its release, *It's a Wonderful Life* gained fans when it began to appear on television; it was one of the first films selected for the controversial "colorization" process in 1986. Stewart's other favorite, and somewhat representative, role is that of Elwood P. Dowd, a kindly tippler who keeps company with a six-foot-tall, invisible rabbit named Harvey. Stewart created the lead in *Harvey* on Broadway in 1947, starred in the film version in 1950, and has played in the comedy off and on ever since. "Whenever everything else fails, I can always drag out ol' Harvey," he told the New York *Daily News* on October 23, 1977. "I've played in that so many times that white rabbit has become part of my life. Whenever I feel blue, I turn around and Harvey's always there.''

Stewart's work has been honored by numerous prestigious awards, including lifetime achievement citations from the Cannes Film Festival and the American Academy of Motion Picture Arts and Sciences. On May 24, 1985, he was honored with a Presidential Medal of Freedom, this nation's highest civilian award. Reluctant to talk about his craft in the press, Stewart told *American Film* in June of 1976 that he looks upon acting as a skill, not an art. He concluded: ''Part of the skill, I've always thought, is to make it so the acting doesn't show. As the skill develops, the acting. . .shows less, and believability come sneaking into the thing. This is the magic.'' Stewart brought this ''magic'' to more than seventy feature films, and, nearing the age of eighty, he continues to savor cameo roles. In *The MGM Stock Company: The Golden Era*, he is quoted as saying: ''I am James Stewart, playing James Stewart. I couldn't mess around doing great characterizations. I play variations of myself.''

ADDRESSES: AGENT—Chasin-Park-Citron Agency, 9255 Sunset Blvd., Suite 910, Los Angeles, CA 90069.*

*   *   *

STOCK, Nigel   1919-1985

PERSONAL: Born September 21, 1919, on the island of Malta; died of an apparent heart attack, June 23, 1985, in London; son of W.H. and Margaret Marion (Munro) Stock; married Sonia Williams (marriage ended); married Richenda Carey; children: three. EDUCATION: Trained for the stage at the Royal Academy of Dramatic Art. MILITARY: With the Royal Army, London Irish Rifles, 1939-41, Indian Army, Assam Regiment, 1941-45.

VOCATION: Actor.

CAREER: LONDON DEBUT—The boy Dan, *The Traveller in the Dark*, Savoy Theatre, 1931. BROADWAY DEBUT—Philip, *You Never Can Tell*, Martin Beck Theatre, 1948. PRINCIPAL STAGE APPEARANCES—Mamilius, *The Winter's Tale*, Old Vic Theatre, Sadler's Wells, U.K., 1932; Thomas, *Alice, Thomas and Jane*, Westminster Theatre, London, 1932-33; Young Macduff, *Macbeth*, Old Vic Theatre, London, 1934; Brownie, *Little Ol' Boy*, Arts Theatre, London, 1936; assistant stage manager and Boots, *Farewell Performance*, Lyric Theatre, London, 1936; Jimmy, *Adventure*, Victoria Palace, London, 1936; title role, *Lord Adrian* and Dude Lester, *Tobacco Road*, both at the Gate Theatre, London, 1937; Teddie, *Jenny Frensham*, Q Theatre, London, 1937; Steve, *April Clouds*, Royalty Theatre, London, 1938; Redbrooks and Colley, *Goodbye Mr. Chips*, Shaftesbury Theatre, London, 1938; Peter, *The Mother*, Garrick Theatre, London, 1939; Alfred, *Rolling Stone*, Richmond Theatre, 1939.

Kenneth Tweedie, *And No Birds Sing*, Aldwych Theatre, London, 1946; Jackie Knowles, *Boys in Brown*, Arts Theatre, London, 1947; Dick Tassell, *The Happiest Days of Your Life*, with the Repertory Players at the Strand Theatre, London, 1947; Alexander Montgomerie, *Kate Kennedy*, Mercury Theatre, London, 1947; with the Bristol Old Vic Company, U.K., 1948-49; Miller, *Wilderness of Monkeys*, Embassy Theatre, London, 1949; Dumaine, *Love's Labour's Lost*, Tony Lumpkin, *She Stoops to Conquer*, and Beliayev, *A Month in the Country*, Old Vic Company, New

Theatre, London, 1949; Able Seaman Sims, *Seagulls Over Sorrento*, Apollo Theatre, London, 1950; Albert, *My Three Angels*, Lyric Theatre, London, 1955; Alberto, *Summertime*, Apollo Theatre, London, 1955; Lieutenant Stephen Maryk, *The Caine Mutiny Court-Martial*, London Hippodrome, 1956; Gene Grierson, *Subway in the Sky*, Savoy Theatre, London, 1957; Daniel, *Paddle Your Own Canoe*, Savoy Theatre, London, 1957; Michael Starkwedder, *The Unexpected Guest*, Duchess Theatre, London, 1958.

Werner, *Altona*, Royal Court Theatre, then Saville Theatre, London, 1961; Detective-Sergeant Brown, *How Are You, Johnnie?*, Vaudeville Theatre, London, 1963; Barret, *Brother and Sister*, Piccadilly Theatre, London, 1964; *We Who Are About To. . .*, Hampton Theatre Club, 1969, changed title to *Mixed Doubles*, Comedy Theatre, London, 1969; Roebuck Ramsden, *Man and Superman*, Gaiety Theatre, Dublin, 1969; Serebryakov, *Uncle Vanya*, Prime Minister, *The Apple Cart*, and Oswald Veal, *Plunder*, all at the Theatre Royal, Bristol, 1973-74; Sir Hudson Lowe, *Betzi*, Haymarket Theatre, London, 1975; *Carol's Christmas*, Andrew Crocker-Harris, *The Browning Version*, King's Head Theatre, Islington, 1976; Major Petkoff, *Arms and the Man*, Oxford Festival, 1976; *Sleuth*, Hong Kong Arts Festival, 1977; Proteus, *The Apple Cart*, Chichester Festival, then Phoenix Theatre, London, 1977; Herr Van Putzeboum and Inspector, *Look After Lulu*, Chichester Festival, then Haymarket Theatre, London, 1978; Widdecome, *Stage Struck*, Vaudeville Theatre, London, 1979.

MAJOR TOURS—Barret, *Brother and Sister*, U.K. cities, 1967; Sir Winston Churchill, *A Man and His Wife*, U.K. cities, 1974; Major Petkoff, *Arms and the Man*, U.K. cities, 1977.

PRINCIPAL FILM APPEARANCES—*Dam Busters*, Warner Brothers, 1955; *The Lion in Winter*, AVCO-Embassy, 1968; *The Lost Continent*, Twentieth Century-Fox, 1968; *Cromwell*, Columbia, 1970; *The Nelson Affair*, Universal, 1972; *Russian Roulette*, AVCO-Embassy, 1975; *Eye Witness*, Twentieth Century-Fox, 1981; also, *Seven Men at Daybreak*.

PRINCIPAL TELEVISION APPEARANCES—Series: Dr. Watson, *Sherlock Holmes; Churchhill's People*. Mini-Series: *Tinker, Tailor, Soldier, Spy.*

Movies: *Fall of Eagles*.*

*   *   *

STOLTZ, Eric

PERSONAL: EDUCATION: Attended University of Southern California; trained for the stage at the Loft Studio with Peggy Fury and William Traylor.

VOCATION: Actor.

CAREER: FILM DEBUT—*Fast Times at Ridgemont High*, Universal, 1981. PRINCIPAL FILM APPEARANCES—*Wild Life*, Universal, 1983; *Mask*, Universal, 1984; *Lionheart*, Orion, 1986; Keith Nelson, *Some Kind of Wonderful*, Paramount, 1987.

TELEVISION DEBUT—*Class of '65*, 1980. PRINCIPAL TELEVISION APPEARANCES—Episodic: *Paper Dolls*, ABC, 1982; *St. Elsewhere*, NBC, 1983. Movies: *The Grass Is Greener*, 1980; *The*

Violation of Sarah McDavid, 1982; *Thursday's Child,* 1982; *A Killer in the Family,* 1983.

STAGE DEBUT—Winthrop, *The Music Man,* 1973. PRINCIPAL STAGE APPEARANCES—Billy Bibbitt, *One Flew Over the Cuckoo's Nest,* Santa Barbara, CA, 1978; Barnaby, *Hello, Dolly!,* 1979; Konstantin, *The Seagull,* University of Southern California, 1980; at the Edinburgh Festival, Scotland, 1981: Billy, *Album,* Eddie, *Runaways,* Snoopy, *You're a Good Man, Charlie Brown.*

MAJOR TOURS—Joe Crowell, *Our Town,* 1974; also appeared in *Oliver!,* 1976.

AWARDS: Golden Globe Award nomination, 1985, for *Mask.*

ADDRESSES: AGENT—c/o Paula Wagner, Creative Artists Agency, 1888 Century Park East, Suite 1400, Los Angeles, CA 90067.

*   *   *

STOPPARD, Tom   1937-

PERSONAL: Born Thomas Straussler, July 3, 1937, in Zlin, Czechoslovakia; son of Eugene (a physician) and Martha Straussler; stepson of Kenneth Stoppard; married Jose Ingle, 1965 (divorced, 1972); married Miriam Moore-Robinson, 1972; children: (first marriage) two sons; (second marriage) two sons. EDUCATION: Attended Pocklington Grammar School, Yorkshire, England.

VOCATION: Playwright, director, critic, and journalist.

CAREER: PRINCIPAL STAGE WORK—Director: *Born Yesterday,* Greenwich Theatre, London, 1973; *Every Good Boy Deserves Favour,* Metropolitan Opera House, Lincoln Center, New York City, 1979.

RELATED CAREER—Reporter and critic, *Western Daily Press,* Bristol, U.K., 1954-58; reporter and critic, *Evening World,* Bristol, England, 1958-60; reviewer for *Scene* magazine, 1962; freelance reporter, 1960-63.

WRITINGS: PLAYS, PRODUCED—*The Gamblers,* Bristol Old Vic Theatre, U.K., 1965; *Rosencrantz and Guildenstern Are Dead,* National Theatre, London, then Alvin Theatre, New York City, 1967; *Enter a Free Man,* St. Martin's Theatre, London, and later produced at St. Clement's Church, New York City, 1974; *Tango,* Aldwych Theatre, London, 1968; *The Real Inspector Hound,* Criterion Theatre, London, 1968; *Albert's Bridge,* produced by the Oxford Theatre Group at the Edinburgh Festival, Scotland, 1969; *After Magritte,* Almost Free Theatre, London, 1971, later produced with *The Real Inspector Hound* as a double-bill at Theatre Four, New York City, 1972; *Dogg's Our Pet,* Ambiance Theatre, London, 1972; *Jumpers,* National Theatre, London, 1972, later produced at the Eisenhower Theatre, Kennedy Center, Washington, DC, and at the Billy Rose Theatre, New York City, 1974; (adaptation of a play by Garcia Lorca) *The House of Bernarda Alba,* produced at the Greenwich Theatre, London, 1973; *Travesties,* Aldwych Theatre, London, then Ethel Barrymore Theatre, New York City, 1974.

Dirty Linen and *New-found-land,* double-bill, Ambiance Theatre, London, 1976, then John Golden Theatre, New York City, 1977;

(with music by Andre Previn) *Every Good Boy Deserves Favour,* London, 1977, later produced at the John F. Kennedy Center for the Performing Arts, Washington, DC, and at the Metropolitan Opera House, Lincoln Center, New York City, 1979; *Night and Day,* Phoenix Theatre, London, 1978, then at the John F. Kennedy Center for the Performing Arts, Washington, DC, and at the American National Theatre and Academy (ANTA) Theatre, New York City, 1979; *Dogg's Hamlet* and *Cahoot's Macbeth,* double-bill, Collegiate Theatre, London, then Twenty-Two Steps Theatre, New York City, 1979; (adaptation of a play by Arthur Schnitzler) *Undiscovered Country,* produced at the Hartford Stage Company, CT, 1981; *The Real Thing,* London, 1982, then later produced at the Plymouth Theatre, New York City, 1984; *On the Razzle,* London, 1982, Arena Stage, Washington, DC, 1982; *Rough Crossing,* London, 1984; (adaptation of a play by Arthur Schnitzler) *Dalliance,* London, 1986.

PLAYS, PUBLISHED—*Rosencrantz and Guildenstern Are Dead,* Grove Press, 1967; *The Real Inspector Hound* and *After Magritte,* Grove Press, 1968; *Albert's Bridge,* 1968; *Enter a Free Man,* Grove Press, 1968, also Samuel French; *Jumpers,* Grove Press, 1974, also Samuel French; *Artists Descending a Staircase,* 1973; *Where Are They Now?,* 1973; *Travesties,* Grove Press, 1975; *Dirty Linen* and *New-found-land,* 1976, also published by Samuel French; *Every Good Boy Deserves Favour,* published with *Professional Foul,* Grove Press, 1978; *Dogg's Hamlet* and *Cahoots Macbeth,* Samuel French, 1980; *On the Razzle,* Faber & Faber, 1983, also Samuel French; *The Real Thing,* Faber & Faber, 1984, also Samuel French; (adaptation of a play by Arthur Schnitzler) *Undiscovered Country,* Samuel French, 1984; *Squaring the Circle: Poland, 1980 to 1981,* Faber & Faber, 1985; *Rough Crossing,* Faber & Faber, 1985.

Omnibus editions: *Albert's Bridge & Other Plays* (includes *If You're Glad, I'll Be Frank, Artist Descending a Staircase, Where Are They Now?,* and *A Separate Peace*), Grove Press, 1977; *The Dog It Was That Died & Other Plays,* Faber & Faber, 1983; *Four Plays for Radio,* Faber & Faber, 1985.

SCREENPLAYS—(Co-author) *The Romantic Englishwoman,* New World Pictures, 1975; *Despair,* 1978; *The Human Factor,* United Artists, 1980; (with Terry Gilliam and Charles McKeown) *Brazil,* Universal, 1985.

TELEPLAYS—*A Walk on the Water,* BBC, 1963, revised and retitled, *The Preservation of George Riley,* BBC, 1964; *A Separate Peace,* BBC, 1966; *Teeth,* BBC, 1967; *Another Moon Called Earth,* BBC, 1967; *Neutral Ground,* BBC, 1968; *The Engagement,* NBC, 1970; *One Pair of Eyes,* BBC, 1972; (with Clive Exton) *Eleventh House,* BBC, 1975; *Boundaries,* 1975; *Squaring the Circle,* BBC, 1984.

RADIO PLAYS—*The Dissolution of Dominic Boot,* BBC, 1964; *M Is for Moon Among Other Things,* BBC, 1964; *If You're Glad, I'll Be Frank,* BBC, 1965; *Albert's Bridge,* BBC, 1967; *Where Are They Now?,* BBC, 1970; *Artist Descending a Staircase,* BBC, 1972; *The Dog It Was That Died,* BBC, 1983.

BOOKS—Novel, *Lord Malquist and Mr. Moon,* first published, 1968, Faber & Faber, 1985; contributor of short stories to *Introduction 2,* 1964.

AWARDS: Ford Foundation Grant, 1964; John Whiting Award, 1967; Most Promising Playwright, London *Evening Standard* Award, 1968; Antoinette Perry Award, New York Drama Critics Circle

Award, both 1968, for *Rosencrantz and Guildenstern Are Dead;* *Evening Standard* Award, 1972, for *Jumpers;* Antoinette Perry Award, London *Evening Standard* Award, both 1976, for *Travesties;* London *Evening Standard* Awards, 1978, for *Night and Day* and 1982, for *The Real Thing;* Best Play, Antoinette Perry Award, 1984, for *The Real Thing;* Best Original Screenplay, Academy Award nomination, 1986, for *Brazil.* Honorary degrees: Bristol, 1976; Brunel, 1979; Leeds, 1980; Sussex, 1980.

MEMBER: Committee of the Free World.

SIDELIGHTS: Called England's "most literate and most interesting contemporary playwright" by Peter J. Rosenwald of *Horizon* (November, 1979), Tom Stoppard took the theatrical world by storm in 1967 with *Rosencrantz and Guildenstern Are Dead.* This play, featuring two characters borrowed from Shakespeare's *Hamlet,* established Stoppard as one of the most unconventional of England's playwrights. Kenneth Tynan of the *New Yorker* (December 19, 1977) ranked Stoppard as "one of the two or three most prosperous and ubiquitously adulated playwrights" in England today.

Rosencrantz and Guildenstern Are Dead concerns two friends of Hamlet who, in Shakespeare's play, are put to death for their alleged plotting against Hamlet. But Stoppard saw the two friends in different terms. He explained to Giles Gordon in *Behind the Scenes: Theater and Film Interviews from the Transatlantic Review* (HOH, 1971) that Rosencrantz and Guildenstern "are told very little about what is going on [in *Hamlet*] and much of what they are told isn't true. So I see them much more clearly as a couple of bewildered innocents rather than a couple of henchmen."

When Rosencrantz and Guildenstern are not playing their roles in *Hamlet,* they are shunted to a backroom of the palace where Stoppard shows us their conversations, the word games they play to pass the time, and the decision they make to accept their execution as a way to assert their own identities. "Stoppard's brilliant idea," Jack Kroll wrote in *Newsweek* (January 16, 1984), "was to boldly go where no playwright had ever gone—through the back door of *Hamlet,* to see not the tragic hero but his two ill-starred friends, ordinary slobs chewed up in the grandiose machine of tragedy."

In subsequent plays, Stoppard displays what T. E. Kalem of *Time* (May 6, 1974) called an "intellectual curiosity, verbal agility and quirky sense of humor." These qualities allow Stoppard to play with lanaguage in a dazzling, humorous way. He is, Kroll claims, "the foremost verbal magician of the contemporary theater." His wild word play is meant to celebrate freedom. "From his perspective," Rosenwald writes, "language has an almost paramount importance. If nonsense, puns, tautologies, and word-craftsmanship are the essence of his plays, his work could only exist in an atmosphere where freedom of speech flourishes."

The action of a Stoppard play is often strangely disorienting. Some characters will speak in nonsense language inaccessible to other characters or to the audience. In *Jumpers,* one character carries "a tortoise in one hand and a bow and arrow in the other, his face covered with shaving cream," as Tynan recounted. One play features a corpse in a plastic bag as a character. "There is a definite method in Stoppard's apparent madness," Rosenwald maintains, "but divining it takes some considerable effort on the part of audiences."

Stoppard's continuing theme is the nature of freedom, a topic he has been addressing more openly in recent works. *Every Good Boy*

Deserves Favor, for example, is a "satiric assault on the Soviet Union's nasty trick of putting dissidents into psychiatric hospitals," Kroll related. *Night and Day* examines freedom of the press and the restrictions put on it by censorial governments and press unions. These plays, Rosenwald believes, show "a deep and political commitment."

Stoppard's ability to combine verbal pryrotechnics with a serious theme has been noted by several observers. As Edwin Wilson stated in the *Wall Street Journal* (January 6, 1984), Stoppard is "a verbal and mental juggler supreme. . . . He has proved that his wit can hold its own with Oscar Wilde, G.B. Shaw and Noel Coward. He has also shown a fascination with ideas, and the ability to make them exciting." Speaking of *The Real Thing,* M. D. Aeschliman of *National Review* (April 6, 1984) allows that "Stoppard's plays have always provided feasts of wit, but have often also aroused the suspicion that the elegant and ironic surface is all there is. . . . Yet *The Real Thing* is finally poignant and not merely glib and clever, and its theme is an important one. It is finally 'about' the fate of fidelity in the modern world,. . .the fate of persons in the face of things and of values in the face of facts."

ADDRESSES: AGENT—Fraser and Dunlop, 91 Regent Street, London W1, England.*

*   *   *

STOUT, Paul   1972-

PERSONAL: Born May 12, 1972, in Saugus, CA; son of David Andrew (a policeman) and Deena Kay (a photo journalist; maiden name, Karella) Stout. EDUCATION: Chaminade Prep School; studied acting with Brooke Bundy and David Schaker. RELIGION: Catholic.

VOCATION: Actor.

CAREER: STAGE DEBUT—Nanki Poo, *The Mikado,* Bernadine's, Woodland Hills, CA, 1986 for twelve performances.

FILM DEBUT—Jerry, *Crisis Counselor,* David Rambe Productions, 1981. PRINCIPAL FILM APPEARANCES—*Meatballs, Part II,* Tri-Star, 1984.

TELEVISION DEBUT—Weslie, *The Woman Who Willed a Miracle,* ABC, 1981. PRINCIPAL TELEVISION APPEARANCES—Series: Phillip King, *Scarecrow and Mrs. King,* CBS, 1982— . Episodic: Retarded child, "Special Friends," *Webster,* ABC, 1983; *The Twilight Zone,* CBS, 1986. Movies: *M.A.D.D.: The Candy Lightner Story,* NBC, 1981.

MEMBER: American Federation of Television and Radio Artists, Screen Actors Guild.

SIDELIGHTS: CTFT learned that Paul Stout has studied helicopter piloting and karate and looks after a large family menagerie (approximately twenty pets). He has a large hat collection, enjoys skateboarding and jumping his motorcross bike. His two brothers are also actors.

ADDRESSES: HOME—Woodland Hills, CA. AGENT—Herb Tannen & Associates, 6460 Sunset Blvd, Suite 203, Hollywood, CA

PAUL STOUT

90028. PUBLICIST—Sharp & Associates, 9229 Sunset Blvd. Suite 520, Los Angeles, CA 90069.

*   *   *

STRICKLER, Dan   1949-

PERSONAL: Born February 2, 1949, in Los Angeles, CA; son of Allen (a research scientist) and Beulah (a harpsicordist; maiden name, Friedman) Strickler. EDUCATION: California State University at Fullerton, B.A., 1972; Temple University, M.F.A., 1976.

VOCATION: Actor.

CAREER: OFF-BROADWAY DEBUT—Bernard, *Jules Feiffer's Hold Me!,* American Place Theatre, 1977, for eighty performances. PRINCIPAL STAGE APPEARANCES—Off-Broadway productions, 1980-81: Twelve roles, *Coming Attractions,* Playwrights Horizons; Dan, *Flying Blind,* Harold Clurman Theatre; Lindner, *A Raisin in the Sun,* New Federal Theatre; Holofernes, *Love's Labour's Lost* and Shylock, *The Merchant of Venice,* both with the New York Acting Unit. Clarence, *A Wonderful Life,* Broadway workshop production, New York City; *Suffragette!,* Trinity Theatre, New York City, 1982.

Regional and stock productions, 1982-83: Flunky, *Let 'Em Eat Cake,* Berkshire Theatre Festival; Jocko, *Geniuses,* Arena Stage,

Washington, DC; Marty, *Isn't It Romantic?,* GeVa Theatre, Rochester, NY; Cratchit, *A Christmas Carol,* Hartman Theatre, Stamford, CT; Figet, *A Country Wife,* Sam, *Awake and Sing,* the Duke, *Oh, Kay!,* and Willy, *The Time of Your Life,* all at the Harvard Repertory Theatre, Boston; Austin, *True West* and Bert Lahr, *The Lion and the Lamb,* both at The Philadelphia Company; Jones, *The Basic Training of Pavlo Hummel,* South Coast Repertory Theatre, Costa Mesa, CA; Doolittle, *My Fair Lady* and the Meddlar, *Cyrano de Bergerac,* both at the Pacific Conservatory of the Performing Arts, Santa Maria, CA. Also Ahab, *Moby Dick, Rehearsed.*

MAJOR TOURS—Cratchit, *A Christmas Carol,* with the National Theatre Company, U.S. cities.

PRINCIPAL FILM APPEARANCES—*Cold Feet,* Cinecom International, 1984; *American Moments,* Francis Thompson Productions.

PRINCIPAL TELEVISION APPEARANCES—*Hold Me,* Showtime; also *For Richer, for Poorer.*

AWARDS: Irene Ryan Award finalist, American College Theatre Festival, Kennedy Center, Washington, DC; Temple University Theatre Fellowship.

MEMBER: Actors' Equity Association, Screen Actors Guild, American Federation of Television and Radio Artists.

SIDELIGHTS: RECREATIONS—Photography and making home videos. FAVORITE ROLES—Ahab, in *Moby Dick, Rehearsed,* Holofernes, in *Love's Labor's Lost,* and Austin, in *True West.*

DAN STRICKLER

ADDRESSES: HOME—New York, NY. AGENT—Henderson-Hogan Agency Inc., 405 W. 44th Street, New York, NY 10036.

*   *   *

STYNE, Jule   1905-

PERSONAL: First name pronounced "Julie"; born Julius Kerwin Stein, December 31, 1905, in London, England; immigrated to United States 1912, became a citizen, 1916; son of Isadore (a produce merchant) and Anna (Kertman) Stein; married Ethel Rubenstein, August 9, 1926 (divorced, 1951); married Margaret Brown (an actress and model), June 4, 1962; children: Stanley, Norton, Nicholas, Katharine. EDUCATION: Attended Chicago Music College; Northwestern University, 1927-31.

VOCATION: Composer, producer, and music publisher.

CAREER: PRINCIPAL STAGE WORK—Co-producer, *Make a Wish,* Winter Garden Theatre, New York City, 1950; co-producer, *Pal Joey,* Broadhurst Theatre, New York City, 1952; co-producer, *In Any Language,* Cort Theatre, New York City, 1952; co-producer, *Hazel Flagg,* Mark Hellinger Theatre, New York City, 1953; producer, *Will Success Spoil Rock Hunter?,* Belasco Theatre, New York City, 1955; producer, *Mr. Wonderful,* Broadway Theatre, New York City, 1956; producer, *Say, Darling,* ANTA Theatre, New York City, 1958; co-producer, *Fade Out—Fade In,* Mark Hellinger Theatre, New York City, 1964; co-producer, *High Spirits,* Alvin Theatre, New York City, 1964; co-producer and director, *Something More,* Eugene O'Neill Theatre, New York City, 1964; co-producer, *Jockeys,* 1977; co-producer, *Tiebele and Her Demon,* 1979.

MAJOR TOURS—Pre-Broadway tour, *Lorelei* (revised and later retitled, *Lorelei, or Gentlemen Still Prefer Blondes*) Civic Center Music Hall, Oklahoma City, OK, 1973.

PRINCIPAL TELEVISION WORK—Producer: *Anything Goes,* 1957; *The Best of Broadway,* 1957; *The Eddie Fisher Show,* NBC, 1959; *Panama Hattie,* 1967; co-producer, *The Dangerous Christmas of Red Riding Hood, or Oh Wolf, Poor Wolf,* ABC, 1965.

PRINCIPAL TELEVISION APPEARANCES—Appeared on *A Funny Girl Happened to Me on the Way to the Piano,* London, 1966; *A Salute to Jule Styne,* PBS, 1987. Episodic: *Bilko,* ABC, 1964. Guest: *The Today Show,* NBC, 1966, 1967.

RELATED CAREER—With Lester Osterman, co-founder of On Stage Productions, 1962; composer, "Thrill of a Lifetime," *Ford Industrial Show,* Mark Hellinger Theatre, New York City, 1965.

WRITINGS: PLAYS—Composer: *Glad to See You,* 1944; *High Button Shoes,* Century Theatre, New York City, 1947; *Gentlemen Prefer Blondes,* Ziegfeld Theatre, New York City, 1949, later produced in London, 1962; *Two on the Aisle,* Mark Hellinger Theatre, New York City, 1951; *Hazel Flagg,* Mark Hellinger Theatre, New York City, 1953; (additional music) *Peter Pan,* Winter Garden Theatre, New York City, 1954; *Bells Are Ringing,* Shubert Theatre, New York City, 1956; *Say Darling,* American National Theatre Academy (ANTA) Theatre, New York City, 1958; *Gypsy,* Broadway Theatre, New York City, 1959; *Do Re Mi,* St. James Theatre, New York City, 1960; *Subways Are for Sleeping,* St. James Theatre, New York City, 1962; *Arturo Ui,* Lunt-

Fontanne Theatre, New York City, 1963; *Funny Girl,* Winter Garden Theatre, New York City, 1964, then moved to Majestic Theatre, New York City, 1966; *Fade Out—Fade In,* Mark Hellinger Theatre, New York City, 1964; *Hallelujah, Baby,* Martin Beck Theatre, New York City, 1967; *Darling of the Day,* George Abbott Theatre, New York City, 1968; *Look to the Lilies,* Lunt-Fontanne Theatre, New York City, 1970; *Prettybelle,* Shubert Theatre, Boston, MA, 1971; *Sugar,* Majestic Theatre, New York City, 1972; *Lorelei, or Gentlemen Still Prefer Blondes,* Palace Theatre, New York City, 1974; *Gypsy* (revival), Winter Garden Theatre, New York City, 1974; *Hellzapoppin,* produced 1976; co-composer, *Side by Side by Sondheim,* Stagewest Theatre, West Springfield, MA, 1982; composer, *Treasure Island,* 1985.

FILMS—Collaborator on songs or film scores: *Sailors on Leave,* Republic, 1941; *Sweater Girl,* Paramount, 1942; *Priorities on Parade,* Republic, 1942; *Hit Parade of 1943,* Republic, 1943; *Carolina Blues,* Columbia, 1944; *Follow the Boys,* Universal, 1944; *The Kid from Brooklyn,* RKO, 1945; *Tonight and Every Night,* Columbia, 1945; *Don't Fence Me In,* Republic, 1945; *The Stork Club,* Paramount, 1945; *Anchors Aweigh,* Metro-Goldwyn-Mayer (MGM), 1945; *Tars and Spars,* Columbia, 1946; *Sweetheart of Sigma Chi,* 1946; *Earl Carroll Sketchbook,* Republic, 1946; *It Happened in Brooklyn,* MGM, 1947; *Ladies' Man,* Paramount, 1947; *Romance on the High Seas,* 1947; *Two Guys from Texas,* Warner Brothers, 1948; *It's a Great Feeling,* Warner Brothers, 1949; *The West Point Story,* Warner Brothers, 1950; *Double Dynamite* (also known as *It's Only Money*), RKO, 1951; *Two Tickets to Broadway,* RKO, 1951; *Meet Me After The Show,* Twentieth Century-Fox, 1951; *Macao,* RKO, 1952; *Gentlemen Prefer Blondes,* Twentieth Century-Fox, 1953; *Three Coins in the Fountain,* Twentieth Century-Fox, 1954; *Living It Up,* Paramount, 1954; *My Sister Eileen,* Columbia, 1955; *How to be Very, Very Popular,* Twentieth Century-Fox, 1955; *Bells Are Ringing,* MGM, 1960; *Gypsy,* Warner Brothers, 1962; *What a Way to Go,* Twentieth Century-Fox, 1964; *Funny Girl,* Columbia, 1968; also *Pink Tights.*

TELEVISION—Composer, *The Ruggles of Red Gap,* 1957; contributor, *Peter Pan,* NBC, 1960; composer, *Mr. Magoo's Christmas Carol,* NBC, 1962; co-composer, *The Dangerous Christmas of Red Riding Hood, or Oh Wolf, Poor Wolf,* ABC, 1965; co-composer, *High Button Shoes,* CBS, 1966; composer, "I'm Getting Married," *Stage 67,* ABC, 1967; co-composer, *The Night the Animals Talked,* ABC, 1970.

AWARDS: Donaldson Award and New York Critics Circle Award, 1952, for *Pal Joey;* (with Sammy Cahn) Best Song, Academy Award, 1954, for *Three Coins in the Fountain;* Outstanding Contribution to British Theatre, Anglo-American Award, 1966, for *Funny Girl;* Best Score, Music and Lyrics, and Best Musical, Antoinette Perry Award, 1967, for *Halleujah, Baby.*

Best Song, Academy Award nominations: 1942, for "It Seems I Heard That Song Before," *Youth On Parade;* 1943, for "A Change of Heart," *Hit Parade of 1943;* 1944, for "Anywhere," *Follow the Boys;* 1945, for "I'll Walk Alone," *Tonight and Every Night;* also 1945, for "I Fall in Love Too Easily," *Anchors Aweigh;* 1948, for "It's Magic," *Romance on the High Seas;* 1948, for the title song, *It's a Great Feeling;* 1968, for the title song, *Funny Girl.*

Received tribute in the Congressional Record, 1964; "Jule Styne Day," proclaimed October 19, 1967, U.S. Pavilion, Montreal Expo, '67, Canada; guest of honor, *Jule's Friends at the Palace,* Palace Theatre, New York City, 1974; *A Salute to Jule Styne,* PBS, 1987.

MEMBER: American Society of Composers, Authors and Publishers (ASCAP; board member, board of review, 1963-64), Dramatists Guild (council), Society of Stage Directors and Choreographers, American Federation of Musicians, League of New York Theatres, Academy of Motion Picture Arts and Sciences; Friars Club.

ADDRESSES: OFFICE—237 W. 51st Street, New York, NY 10019.*

*   *   *

SUZMAN, Janet   1939-

PERSONAL: Born February 9, 1939, in Johannesburg, South Africa; daughter of Saul and Betty Suzman; married Trevor Nunn (a director), 1969 (divorced, 1986); children: Joshua. EDUCATION: University of Witwatersand, B.A.; trained for the stage at the London Academy of Music and Dramatic Art.

VOCATION: Actress.

CAREER: STAGE DEBUT—Liz, *Billy Liar,* Tower Theatre, Ipswich, U.K., 1962. LONDON DEBUT—Luciana, *The Comedy of Errors,* with the Royal Shakespeare Company, at the Aldwych Theatre, 1962. PRINCIPAL STAGE APPEARANCES—Joan la Pucelle, *Henry VI* and Lady Anne, *Richard III,* both Stratford, U.K., 1963; Lady Percy, *Henry IV, Parts I and II,* Stratford, U.K., 1964; Lulu, *The*

JANET SUZMAN

Birthday Party, Aldwych Theatre, London, 1964; Rosaline, *Love's Labour's Lost* and Portia, *The Merchant of Venice,* both Stratford, U.K., 1965; Ophelia, *Hamlet* and Berinthia, *The Relapse,* both at the Aldwych Theatre, London, 1965; Kate Hardcastle, *She Stoops to Conquer* and Carmen, *The Balcony,* both at the Playhouse Theatre, Oxford, U.K., 1966-67; Katharina, *The Taming of the Shrew* and Celia, *As You Like It,* both Stratford, U.K., then at the Aldwych Theatre, London, 1967-68; Katharina, *The Taming of the Shrew,* Ahmanson Theatre, Los Angeles, 1968.

Pleasure and Repentance, Edinburgh Festival, Scotland, 1970; Cleopatra, *Antony and Cleopatra,* Lavinia, *Titus Andronicus,* both Stratford, U.K., 1973; Cleopatra, *Antony and Cleopatra,* Aldwych Theatre, London, 1973; Hester, *Hello and Goodbye,* King's Head Theatre, Islington, U.K., then at The Place, London, 1973; Masha, *The Three Sisters,* Cambridge Theatre, U.K., 1976; title role, *Hedda Gabler,* Duke of York's Theatre, London and Edinburgh Festival, Scotland, 1977; Shen Te, *The Good Woman of Setzuan,* Royal Court Theatre, London, 1977; Minerva, *Boo Hoo,* Open Space Theatre, London, 1978.

Clytemnestra, *The War,* Helen, *The Murderers,* and chorus, *The Gods,* all at the Aldwych Theatre, London, 1980; *Cowardice,* Ambassador's Theatre, London, 1983; *Boesman and Lena,* Hampstead Theatre, London, 1984; *Vassa Zheleznova,* Greenwich, U.K., 1985.

Most of Suzman's work has been with the Royal Shakespeare Company.

MAJOR TOURS—Beatrice, *Much Ado About Nothing,* U.S. cities, 1969; *The Duchess of Malfi,* U.K., cities, 1979.

PRINCIPAL FILM APPEARANCES—*Nicholas and Alexandra,* Columbia, 1971; *A Day in the Death of Joe Egg,* Columbia, 1972; *The Priest of Love,* Filmways, 1981; *And the Ship Sails On,* Triumph Films, 1983; *The Draughtsman's Contract,* 1983.

PRINCIPAL TELEVISION APPEARANCES—Dramatic Specials: *The Three Sisters; Hedda Gabler; Twelfth Night; Miss Nightingale; Clayhanger; The Zany Adventures of Robin Hood,* 1983; *Mountbatten, The Last Viceroy,* 1984; *The Singing Detective,* 1986.

AWARDS: Best Actress, Academy Award nomination, 1971, for *Nicholas and Alexandra;* Best Actress, *Evening Standard* Awards, 1973 and 1976; Best Actress, *Plays and Players* Award, 1976; honorary degree, Open University, 1984.

MEMBER: British Actors' Equity Association, Screen Actors Guild, London Academy of Music and Dramatic Art (council member).

ADDRESSES: AGENT—William Morris Agency, 31-32 Soho Square, London, W1 England.

*   *   *

SWAN, William   1928-

PERSONAL: Born February 6, 1928, in Buffalo, NY; son of Earl Bernard (a businessman) and Irene Mildred (Hall) Swan. EDUCATION: Trained for the stage at the Max Reinhardt Theatrical Workshop and with David Craig. RELIGION: Roman Catholic. MILITARY: U.S. Army.

WILLIAM SWAN

VOCATION: Actor.

CAREER: PRINCIPAL TELEVISION APPEARANCES—Series: Dr. David Cahearn, *Dr. Kildare,* NBC, 1961-66; Walter Hines, *All My Children,* ABC, 1982-86; Dr. Ralph Jennings, *The Young and the Restless,* CBS, 1987—. Episodic: *The Guiding Light; Twelve O'Clock High,* ABC; *Twenty-Six Men,* syndicated; *Mike Hammer,* CBS; *Navy Log,* CBS, ABC; *Father Knows Best,* CBS; *Have Gun, Will Travel,* CBS; *How to Marry a Millionaire,* syndicated; *Father of the Bride,* CBS; *The Eleventh Hour,* NBC; *Cannon,* CBS; *Barnaby Jones,* CBS; *The Rockford Files,* NBC; *As the World Turns,* ABC; *Kraft Television Theatre,* CBS; *Studio One,* CBS; *Lux Video Theatre,* CBS; *Producers' Showcase,* NBC; *The Twilight Zone,* CBS; *Mr. Novak,* NBC; *The New Breed,* ABC; *Perry Mason,* CBS; *Felony Squad,* ABC; *Most Wanted,* ABC; *The Streets of San Francisco,* ABC; *Quincy,* NBC; also appeared on *World Premiere* and *Matinee Theatre.* Movies: *Johnny Midnight; Men of Annapolis.*

PRINCIPAL STAGE APPEARANCES—Off-Broadway: *Night Fishing in Beverly Hills,* INTAR Theatre, 1982; also appeared in: *A Delicate Balance, What the Butler Saw, Teahouse of the August Moon, Bus Stop, Mister Roberts, Come Blow Your Horn, Sabrina Fair, Dial M for Murder, Voice of the Turtle, Invitation to a March, All the Way Home, Blithe Spirit, The Rehearsal, Anne of a Thousand Days, Pygmalion, Macbeth, You Never Can Tell, The Lady's Not for Burning, The Matchmaker, Plain and Fancy;* theatres performed at include: Brooklyn Academy of Music, NY; A Contemporary Theatre, Seattle, WA; Berkshire Theatre Festival, Stockbridge, MA; Walnut Street Theatre, Philadelphia; Papermill Playhouse, Millburn, NJ.

PRINCIPAL FILM APPEARANCES—*The Monster That Challenged the World,* United Artists, 1957; *Bombers B-52,* Warner Brothers, 1957; *The Horizontal Lieutenant,* Metro-Goldwyn-Mayer, 1962; *Lady in a Cage,* Paramount, 1964; *Hotel,* Warner Brothers, 1967; *The Parallax View,* Paramount, 1974.

MEMBER: Academy of Television Arts and Sciences; Player's Club.

ADDRESSES: AGENT—Michael Thomas Agency, 305 Madison Agency, New York, NY 10165; First Artists Agency, 427 N. Canon Drive, Beverly Hills, CA 90210.

T-U

TAIKEFF, Stanley 1940-

PERSONAL: Born April 27, 1940, in Brooklyn, NY; son of Irving (an attorney) and Lulu (a milliner; maiden name, Rosenberg) Taikeff; married Lenore Noval (an administrative assistant), August 4, 1968. EDUCATION: Hunter College, B.A., 1963, M.A., theatre, 1971. MILITARY: Army National Guard, NY, 1963-69.

VOCATION: Playwright.

WRITINGS: PLAYS, PRODUCED AND PUBLISHED—*The Coiled Spring,* 13th Street Theatre, New York City, 1968, re-titled, *Denouement,* Hunter College Playhouse, Centennial Celebration, 1970; three one-acts, *Solo Recital, Into That Good Night, The Afflictions of Marlene,* Little Theatre of the 63rd Street YMCA, New York City, 1970; *Don Juan of Flatbush,* reading, Winter

STANLEY TAIKEFF

Playwrights Series, Stockbridge, MA, 1974, Missouri Repertory Theatre, Kansas City, MO, 1976, Jewish Community Center of St. Louis, 1977, The Corner Theatre, Baltimore, MD, 1977, staged reading, The American Jewish Theatre, New York City, 1983; *The Sugar Bowl,* O'Neill Playwrights Conference, Waterford, CT, 1976, workshop production, New Dramatists, New York City, 1978; *In the Modern Style,* reading, Joseph Jefferson Theatre Company, Chicago, 1976, Cricket Theatre, Minneapolis, MN, 1978, also produced in Canada and Europe; *Ah, Eurydice!,* reading, Joseph Jefferson Theatre Company, 1976, production, Shelter West Company at the VanDam Theatre, New York City, 1977, also produced in Canada and Europe, published by Dramatists Play Service in *Best Short Plays of 1978; A Cock to Asclepius,* workshop production, New Dramatists, New York City, 1979.

The Last Ferry to Thebes, workshop production, New Dramatists, New York City, 1980; *Brigitte Berger,* staged reading, New Dramatists, 1981, production, No Smoking Playhouse, New York City, 1983; *The Hermit of Prague,* staged reading, New Dramatists, New York City, 1981, published in "Esprit," State University of New York Journal of Humanities, 1985; *Variations on "To Be or Not to Be",* staged reading, New Dramatists, New York City, 1981; *Dolorosa Sanchez,* staged reading, New Dramatists, New York City, 1982, published in "Esprit," State University of New York Journal of Humanities, 1984; *Civilization and its Malcontents,* and *Shivah,* both readings, New Dramatists, 1984; also, *Duet for Parents,* reading, New Dramatists, New York City.

PLAYS, UNPRODUCED—"Andy Grunnt", "The Creatures of Prometheus"

POEMS—In the periodicals: "Voices of Brooklyn," "Manhattan Review," "Bitterroot," "Writer's Notes & Quotes," "Poetry Parade," "Hyacinths & Biscuits."

SHORT STORIES—In the periodicals: "Abyss," Vol. 1 and 2; "One: A Magazine of Fiction."

ARTICLES—Magazines and journals: "Dramatists Guild Quarterly," "Writers Guild of America West Newsletter."

RELATED CAREER—Part-time instructor in the dramatic writing program at New York University, 1980-84; adjunct English faculty, LaGuardia Community College, City University of New York, 1978—.

AWARDS: Shubert Playwriting Fellowship, 1971; Office for Advanced Drama Research grant, 1976; finalist, National Repertory Theatre Play Award, 1981, for *Brigitte Berger;* CAPS Playwriting Award, 1981.

MEMBER: New Dramatists (executive committee, admissions committee, participant in panel discussions, 1978-85).

SIDELIGHTS: Stanley Taikeff made the following observation to *CTFT:* ''Shakespeare and I were born two days apart in April, he on the 25th and I on the 27th, so I figured I was destined to become a playwright.''

ADDRESSES: HOME—3A Second Place, Brooklyn, NY 11231.

*   *   *

TATUM, Bill   1947-

PERSONAL: Full name, Harold William Tatum, Jr.; born May 5, 1947, in Philadelphia, PA; son of Harold William (a salesman) and Helen Gertrude (Payne) Tatum; married Kay Miner, 1968 (divorced, 1978); married Karen Ziemba, May 6, 1984; children: Will. EDUCATION: Catawba College, B.A., 1970; trained for the stage with Nikos Psacharopoulos and David LeGrant.

VOCATION: Actor.

CAREER: STAGE DEBUT—Boxer, *Animal Farm*, Hedrick Little Theatre, Salisbury, NC, 1966, for twelve performances. OFF-BROADWAY DEBUT—Arthur Zuckerman, *Who's Hungry*, Old Reliable Theatre, 1970, for twenty performances. PRINCIPAL STAGE APPEARANCES—Off-Broadway: Jesse James, *Missouri*

BILL TATUM

Legend, Jerry Ryan, *Seesaw*, and Eddie Yeager, *The Time of the Cuckoo*, all at the Equity Library Theatre; Rink, *Stormbound* and Henry, *Fair Weather Friends*, both at Playwrights Horizons; Streeter, *Thunder Rock*, Joseph Jefferson Theatre; *The Americans: Dorothy Parker*, W.P.A. Theatre; Sandy, *Hay Fever*, Separate Theatre; Jack Nash, *A True Story*, New Vic Theatre; Stan, *Dancers*, Circle Repertory Laboratory Theatre; David, *Our Dancing Daughters*, The Snarks Theatre.

Regional and stock: Paul Verrall, *Born Yesterday*, South Jersey Repertory; George, *Same Time, Next Year* and Wiseman, *Knock, Knock*, both at the Pennsylvania Stage Company, Allentown, PA; *Blue Suede Decade*, Indiana Repertory Cabaret Theatre, Indianapolis; Harry, *The Sea Horse*, New Stages II; Val, *Orpheus Descending*, Rutgers Little Theatre, New Brunswick, NJ; Simon, *The Real Inspector Hound*, Westchester Repertory Theatre; Harbison, *South Pacific*, Playhouse in the Park, Philadelphia; George, *Same Time, Next Year*, Forrestburgh Playhouse; Nevile Strange, *Towards Zero*, Clive, *See How They Run*, William, *How the Other Half Loves*, Wolfeboro Playhouse; John, *Quabbin*, In the Works Theatre, University of Massachusetts.

PRINCIPAL FILM APPEARANCES—Jeff, *Pages of the Heart*, Romantic Movies, Inc.; Detective Henry Burkoff, *Plutonium*, Michael Lawrence Films; *Monkey Grip*, New York University Films, 1982.

PRINCIPAL TELEVISION APPEARANCES—Dave Grace, *The Edge of Night*, ABC; Warren Baker, *One Life to Live*, ABC. Dramatic Specials: Mark, *Kennedy's Children*, PBS.

ADDRESSES: HOME—New York, NY. AGENT—Don Buchwald Associates, Ten E. 44th Street, New York, NY 10017.

*   *   *

TAYLOR, Harry
See Granick, Harry

*   *   *

TEMPERLEY, Stephen   1949-

PERSONAL: Born July 29, 1949, in London, England; son of Joseph (a musician) and Mary (a real estate broker; maiden name, Murray) Temperley. EDUCATION: Attended Alleyn's School, Dulwich, London; trained for the stage at the American Academy of Dramatic Art.

VOCATION: Actor and writer.

CAREER: OFF-BROADWAY DEBUT—Thomas of Clarence, *Henry IV, Part II*, Delacorte Theatre, New York Shakespeare Festival (NYSF), 1968, for forty performances. LONDON DEBUT—Baby Face, *Happy End*, Lyric Theatre, 1975, for sixty-three performances. PRINCIPAL STAGE APPEARANCES—Appeared in England at the Billingham Theatre Company and Oxford Theatre Company; Dick Rivers, *Very Good Eddie*, Piccadilly Theatre, London; Henry, *The Garden*, Hampstead Theatre Club, London; Phillip Hill, *Whose Life Is It Anyway?*, Kennedy Center, Washington, DC; the Lover, *Invitation to a Beheading*, Anspacher/Public Theatre, NYSF, New

York City, 1969; appeared at the Guthrie Theatre, Minneapolis, MN, 1986-87.

Regional and Stock: *Absurd Person Singular,* Hartman Theatre, Stamford, CT, 1978; *Monsieur Ribadier's System,* Hartman Theatre, 1979; *Go Back for Murder,* Player's State Theatre, Coconut Grove, FL, 1981; *Taking Steps,* Virginia Stage Company, Norfolk, VA, 1984; also, Brian Runnicles, *No Sex Please, We're British;* Stanley, *Run for Your Wife.*

TELEVISION DEBUT—Mini-Series: Edward, *Home and Away,* Granada, 1973.

WRITINGS: PLAYS, PRODUCED—*Beside the Seaside,* Hudson Guild Theatre, New York City, 1982; *Money,* Manhattan Punchline Theatre, New York City, 1986.

ADDRESSES: HOME—New York, NY. AGENT—c/o Richard Schmenner, STE Representation, 888 Seventh Avenue, New York, NY 10106.

* * *

THOMAS, Thom 1941-

PERSONAL: Full name, Thomas Neil Thomas; born August 31, 1941, in Lawrence, PA; son of John Edward (a coal miner) and Ruby Christina (Jukes) Thomas. EDUCATION: Attended the Pittsburgh Playhouse School of Theatre, 1958-60; Carnegie-Mellon University, B.F.A., drama, 1966.

VOCATION: Director and writer.

CAREER: PRINCIPAL STAGE WORK—Director: *Camelot, Minnie's Boys, Mame, Annie Get Your Gun, The Prime of Miss Jean Brodie, Bye Bye Birdie, High Button Shoes, Cabaret, The Fantasticks, No Strings, Berlin to Broadway with Kurt Weill, Guys and Dolls, Jacques Brel, The Serpent, Two Gentlemen of Verona, The King and I, Dames at Sea, Hair, All the Way Home, Auntie Mame, Ghost Sonata, The Odd Couple, How the Other Half Loves, Philemon, Once Upon a Mattress, Oh Dad, Poor Dad, Mama's Hung You in the Closet and I'm Feeling So Sad, Dracula;* has also directed fashion shows, industrial shows and tours.

RELATED CAREER—Associate professor of theatre, Point Park College, Pittsburgh, 1966-74; head of department, 1974-77; artistic director, Rabbit Run Summer Theatre, Madison, OH, 1965; artistic director, Pittsburgh Playhouse, 1966-72; artistic director, Odd Chair Playhouse, Bethel Park, PA, 1967-74; artistic director, Pittsburgh Civic Light Opera, 1972—.

WRITINGS: PLAYS, PRODUCED AND PUBLISHED—*The Interview,* Pittsburgh Playhouse, 1976, Academy Festival Theatre, Lake Forest, IL, 1979, Direct Theatre, New York City, 1981, published by Samuel French Inc., 1981; *Approaching Zero,* La Mama Experimental Theatre Club (E.T.C.), New York City, 1978; *The Ball Game,* Open Space Theatre, London, 1978; *I Always Liked Alice Faye,* reading at the Off-Center Theatre, New York City, 1981; *Without Apologies,* reading, Mark Taper Forum, Los Angeles, 1982, Pittsburgh Playhouse, 1983, Theatre 40, Beverly Hills, CA, 1984.

PLAYS IN PROGRESS—"There Was Also David," "Midnight Hearts."

SCREENPLAYS—(In progress) "I'll String Along with You."

PRINCIPAL TELEVISION SCRIPTS—Episodic: "Faith, Hope, and Charity," "Transitions," and two others, *Hotel,* ABC; *Tale of the Gold Monkey,* ABC; "Zen and the Art of Law Enforcement," *Hill Street Blues,* NBC, 1982. Movies: *King of the One Night Stands,* Frank Von Zerneck Productions; *Saturday's Father,* Finnegan Production. Pilots: Writer and producer, *Private Sessions,* NBC, 1984.

AWARDS: Music Corporation of America fellowship, 1964-65; Ford Foundation grant, 1969; Shubert fellow, 1975; National Endowment for the Arts grant, 1978; Cameron Overseas grant; America Conservatory Theatre fellowship in directing; Alliance of Gay and Lesbian Artists Media award, "Faith, Hope, and Charity," and "Transitions," episodes of *Hotel,* ABC, 1984 and 1985.

MEMBER: Actors' Equity Association, Screen Actors Guild, Dramatists Guild, Writers Guild of America West.

SIDELIGHTS: Thom Thomas submitted the the following statement to *CTFT* about his career: "A chance meeting with actor Douglas Watson while he was on tour with *Stalag 17* was when I became interested in acting and theatre. I was thirteen years old. He encouraged me to enter theatre, and was my inspiration. My writing career was first inspired and nurtured by novelist Gladys Schmidt while I attended Carnegie-Mellon University. Then teacher-playwright Arthur Wilmurt continued to encourage and guide me. My big break came when Jose Ferrer read my play *The Interview,* and starred in and directed it. I've traveled a great deal—have spent considerable time in England and Italy—and lived for six months on the island of Gozo in the Maltese Islands where I wrote *The Interview.* I love to read, see films and travel."

ADDRESSES: AGENT—c/o Gilbert Parker, William Morris Agency, 1350 Avenue of the Americas, New York, NY 10019.

* * *

THOMPSON, Sada 1929-

PERSONAL: Full name, Sada Carolyn Thompson; born September 27, 1929, in Des Moines, IA; daughter of Hugh Woodruff and Corlyss Elizabeth (Gibson) Thompson; married Donald E. Stewart, December 18, 1949; children: Liza. EDUCATION: Attended the Carnegie Institute of Technology, B.F.A.

VOCATION: Actress.

CAREER: STAGE DEBUT—Nick's Ma, *The Time of Your Life,* Carnegie Institute of Technology, 1945. PRINCIPAL STAGE APPEARANCES—At the University Playhouse, Mashpee, MA: Harmony Blueblossom, *The Beautiful People,* Lady Bracknell, *The Importance of Being Earnest,* title role, *Peg o' My Heart,* and Adamina Wood, *Dawn from an Unknown Ocean,* all 1947; Eileen, *Where Stars Walk,* Leda, *Amphitryon 38,* Nina, *The Seagull,* and Ruth, *Thunder on the Left,* 1948.

Title role, *Joan of Lorraine,* Pittsburgh Playhouse, 1948; Mrs. Phelps, *The Silver Cord,* Morris Kaufmann Memorial Theatre, Pittsburgh, PA, 1949; in stock, at the Henrietta Hayloft Theatre,

Rochester, NY: Mrs. Higgins, *Pygmalion*, Emily Creed, *Ladies in Retirement*, repeated title role, *Peg o' My Heart*, Mrs. Montgomery, *The Heiress*, Emily, *Our Town*, Raina, *Arms and the Man*, and Madame Arcati, *Blithe Spirit*, 1949, Billie Dawn, *Born Yesterday*, Murial, *Ah, Wilderness!*, Annie Marble, *Payment Deferred*, Jackie Coryton, *Hay Fever*, Birdie Hubbard, *The Little Foxes*, Dona Lucia D'Alvadorez, *Charley's Aunt*, Frances Black, *Light Up the Sky*, Bette Logan, *Heaven Can Wait*, and Hilda Manney, *Room Service*, 1950.

Isabel, *The Enchanted*, stage reading, Pittsburgh Playhouse, 1950; Carmella, *Halloween Bride*, Arena Theatre, Rochester, NY, 1951; repeated title role, *Peg o' My Heart*, Pittsburgh Playhouse, 1952; understudy for Ruth Warrick, *A Certain Joy*, Playhouse Theatre, Wilmington, DE, then Locust Theatre, Philadelphia, PA, 1953; *Under Milk Wood*, (concert reading) Kaufmann Auditorium, New York City, 1953; appeared in *U.S.A.*, White Barn Theatre, Westport, CT, 1953; Patty, *The Moon Is Blue*, Niagara Falls Summer Theatre, Ontario, Canada, 1953; at the Totem Pole Playhouse, Fayetteville, PA: repeated title role, *Peg o' My Heart*, Nita Havemeyer, *For Love or Money*, and Leona Samish, *The Time of the Cuckoo*, 1954; Lizzie Curry, *The Rainmaker* and title role, *Anastasia*, 1956.

Mrs. Heidelberg, *The Clandestine Marriage*, Provincetown Playhouse, New York City, 1954; *Murder in the Cathedral*, stage reading, Kaufmann Auditorium, New York City, 1954; understudy as Sally Ann Peters, *Festival*, Longacre Theatre, New York City, 1955; Cornelia, *The White Devil*, Phoenix Theatre, New York City, 1955; Lavinia Chamberlayne, *The Cocktail Party*, Barter Theatre, Abingdon, VA, 1955; Feng Nan, *The Carefree Tree*, Phoenix Theatre, New York City, 1955; Laura, *The Glass Menagerie*, at the Institute for the Blind, New York City, 1955; gave a reading from the poems of Dylan Thomas, Donnell Memorial Library Theatre, New York City, 1956; Eliante, *The Misanthrope*, Theatre East, New York City, 1956; Isadora Duncan and Eleanor Stoddard, *U.S.A*, with the American National Theatre Academy (ANTA) at the Theatre de Lys, New York City, 1956; Valerie Barton, *The River Line*, Carnegie Hall Playhouse, New York City, 1957; Masha, *The Three Sisters*, Arena Stage, Washington, DC, 1957; Emilia, *Othello* and Margaret, *Much Ado About Nothing*, both with the American Shakespeare Festival, Stratford, CT, 1957; Babakina, *Ivanov*, Renata Theatre, New York City, 1958; Mrs. Coyne, *Juno*, Winter Garden Theatre, New York City, 1959; repeated Isadora Duncan and Eleanor Stoddard, *U.S.A.*, Royal Poinciana Playhouse, Palm Beach, FL, 1959; with the American Shakespeare Festival, Stratford: Mistress Quickly, *The Merry Wives of Windsor* and widow of Florence, *All's Well That Ends Well*, 1959, Maria, *Twelfth Night*, Juno, *The Tempest*, and Octavia, *Antony and Cleopatra*, 1960.

Nastasya Filippovna, *The Idiot*, Chrysler Auditorium, Rye, NY, 1960; appeared in *Under Milk Wood*, Circle in the Square, New York City, 1961; Emma Crosby, *Diff'rent*, New York Playhouse, Hyde Park, NY, 1961; Duchess of York, *Richard II* and Lady Percy, *Henry IV, Part I*, both with the American Shakespeare Festival, Stratford, 1962; Mrs. Rhythm, *The Last Minstrel*, Pocket Theatre, New York City, 1963; Emilia, *Othello*, New York Shakespeare Festival, Delacorte Theatre, New York City, 1964; Dorine, *Tartuffe*, ANTA-Washington Square Theatre, New York City, 1965; repeated Dorine, *Tartuffe* and appeared in *Dear Liar*, both with the American Conservatory Theatre, San Francisco, CA, 1966; Amanda, *The Glass Menagerie*, Milwaukee Repertory Theatre, 1966; Florence Edwards, *Johnny No-Trump*, Cort Theatre, New York City, 1967; Agnes, *A Delicate Balance*, Studio Arena Theatre, Buffalo, NY, 1968; Mommy, *The American Dream* and

Winnie, *Happy Days*, Studio Arena Theatre, Buffalo, then Billy Rose Theatre, New York City, 1968; Mrs. Darlene Finch, *An Evening for Merlin Finch*, The Forum Theatre at Lincoln Center, New York City, 1968; Lady Macbeth, *Macbeth*, San Diego Shakespeare Festival, CA, 1969.

Beatrice, *The Effect of Gamma Rays on Man-in-the-Moon Marigolds*, Mercer-O'Casey Theatre, New York City, 1970; Christine Mannon, *Mourning Becomes Electra*, with the American Shakespeare Festival, Stratford, 1971; title roles, "Emily," "Celia," "Dorothy," and "Ma," presented under the collective title, *Twigs*, Broadhurst Theatre, New York City, 1971, then later at the Westport Country Playhouse, CT, 1973; appeared in *Shay*, Westport Country Playhouse, 1974; Madame Ranevskaya, *The Cherry Orchard*, Geary Theatre, San Francisco, 1974; Rosa, *Saturday, Sunday, Monday*, Martin Beck Theatre, New York City, 1974; *The Vinegar Tree*, Atlanta, GA, 1978; appeared in *The Matchmaker*, Hartford Stage Company, CT, 1978-79; Sal, *Wednesday*, Hudson Guild Theatre, New York City, 1983; Mrs. Antrobus, *The Skin of Our Teeth*, Old Globe Theatre, San Diego, CA, 1983.

MAJOR TOURS—U.S. cities: Mrs. Molloy, *The Matchmaker*, 1962; Emily, Dorothy, and Ma, *Twigs*, 1972-73; *Shay*, 1974.

FILM DEBUT—Margaret, *You Are Not Alone*, 1961. PRINCIPAL FILM APPEARANCES—*The Pursuit of Happiness*, Columbia, 1971; *Desparate Characters*, Paramount, 1971.

PRINCIPAL TELEVISION APPEARANCES—Series: Kate Lawrence, *Family*, ABC, 1976-80. Specials: *Carl Sandburg's Lincoln*, ABC; *The Entertainer*, 1976; also appeared in *Our Town*. Mini-Series: *Marco Polo*, 1982; *Princess Daisy*, 1983. Episodic: *Goodyear Playhouse*, NBC, 1954; *Rocky King, Detective*, DuMont; *Robert Montgomery Presents*, NBC; *Kraft Theatre*, NBC; *Camera Three*, CBS; *The Big Story*, NBC; *Lamp Unto My Feet*, CBS; *The Everlasting Road*, ABC; *The DuPont Show of the Month*, NBC; *The Nurses*, CBS; *Owen Marshall*, ABC; *Love Story*, ABC.

AWARDS: Drama Desk Awards, 1956, for *The Misanthrope* and 1957, for *The River Line*; Obie Award, 1965, for *Tartuffe*; Best Actress, Drama Desk Award, Obie Award, *Variety* Poll of Off-Broadway Critics Award, and *Best Plays* citation, all 1970, for *The Effect of Gamma Rays on Man-in-the-Moon Marigolds*; Antoinette Perry Award, Sarah Siddons Award, Drama Desk Award, *Best Plays* citation, and *Variety* Poll of New York Drama Critics Awards, all 1971, for *Twigs*; Outstanding Lead Actress in a Dramatic Series, Emmy Award, 1978, for *Family*.

MEMBER: Actors' Equity Association (former council member), American Federation of Television and Radio Artists, Screen Actors Guild.

ADDRESSES: AGENT—Bauman, Hiller & Strain, 9220 Sunset Blvd., Suite 202, Los Angeles, CA 90069.*

*   *   *

THORNTON, John   1944-

PERSONAL: Born May 28, 1944, in Gloucester, England; son of John William (an international sportsman) and Betty Joyce (Langford) Thornton. EDUCATION: Studied at the Actors Centre, London; studied dance with Molly Molloy and Matt Maddox at the Dance Centre, Covent Garden, London.

VOCATION: Actor, dancer, singer, and choreographer.

CAREER: LONDON DEBUT—Dancer, London Palladium, 1968. PRINCIPAL STAGE APPEARANCES—*Tommy Steele,* London Palladium; *The Danny La Rue Show, The Val Doonican Show,* and several Royal Galas, Drury Lane Theatre and National Theatre, London; Mungo Jerry, *Cats,* New London Theatre, for eighteen months and later for nine months, 1981-82; *Royal Variety Performance,* 1982; *Jumpers,* Aldwych Theatre, London, 1985; maitre'd, *Cabaret,* Strand Theatre, London, 1986.

MAJOR TOURS—*No Trams to Lime Street,* British tour; *Olde Tyme Music Hall,* Canadian and U.S. cities; maitre'd, *Cabaret,* U.K. cities, 1986.

PRINCIPAL FILM APPEARANCES—*Monty Python and the Holy Grail,* Cinema V, 1975; Hammer, *The Ghoul,* 1975; *Absolute Beginners,* Orion, 1986.

PRINCIPAL FILM WORK—Assistant choreographer, *Absolute Beginners,* 1985.

PRINCIPAL TELEVISION APPEARANCES—Dancer: *Tommy Steele Show; Starburst; Juliet Prowse Show; Marti Caine Show; Shirley Bassey Series; Stanley Baxter Special; Morecambe and Wise Series; Search for a Star Series; Bruce Forsyth Show; The Children's Royal Variety Show,* 1982; actor, Sir Urre, *Morte D'Arthur,* BBC, 1983; *Good Companions,* Yorkshire TV.

JOHN THORNTON

PRINCIPAL TELEVISION WORK—Choreographer, *The Russ Abbott Hogmany Madhouse,* LWT, 1983; also assistant choreographer for LWT.

MEMBER: British Actors' Equity Association.

SIDELIGHTS: John Thornton states, "After seeing *The Red Shoes* at age three, I wanted to dance. I am an expert horse rider. I have worked in Japan, South America, Hong Kong, Korea, Monte Carlo and the United States. I speak French and am interested in conservation."

ADDRESSES: AGENT—Eric Glass Ltd., 28 Berkely Square, London, W1X 6HD, England.

*　　*　　*

THUN, Nancy　1952-

PERSONAL: Born September 27, 1952, in Watseka, IL; daughter of Hans Herman, Jr. (an architect) and Clara Ann (Haberkorn) Thun. EDUCATION: University of Illinois, B.F.A., 1975; Yale School of Drama, M.F.A., 1978; studied design at Brighton Art College of Textile Design, 1973-74 and with Karin Balon at the Bronx Zoo Exhibitions Department, 1986. RELIGION: Presbyterian.

VOCATION. Designer.

CAREER: PRINCIPAL STAGE WORK—Costume designer with the Folger Theatre Group, Washington, DC, 1978-79; costume designer, *On Mount Chimborazo,* Brooklyn Academy of Music, NY, 1979; set and costume designer, *The Glass Menagerie,* Lion Theatre, New York City, 1980; set designer: *Orpheus in the Underworld, Violanta, Florentine Tragedy,* all at the Santa Fe Opera, NM, 1982-83; *True West, Rundown, Boys from Syracuse,* all at the American Repertory Theatre, Cambridge, MA, 1983-85; *Sweeney Todd,* Cleveland, OH, 1985; *Haut Gout,* Virginia Stage Company, Norfolk, 1987.

MAJOR TOURS—Assistant set designer: *Cats,* Boston, Washington, DC, Philadelphia, and Australian cities; *The Adventures of Nicholas Nickleby,* Los Angeles and New York City.

AWARDS: Best Set Design, Cleveland Critics Award, 1985, for *Sweeney Todd.*

MEMBER: Union of Scenic Artists, Local 829.

ADDRESSES: HOME—403 E. 73rd Street, New York, NY 10021. AGENT—Helen Merrill, 361 W. 17th Street, New York, NY 10011.

*　　*　　*

TIMOTHY, Christopher　1940-

PERSONAL: Born October 14, 1940, in Bala, N. Wales; son of Eifion Andrew and Marian Gwladys (Hailstone) Timothy; married Annie Veronica Swatton. EDUCATION: Central School of Speech and Drama, London, 1960-63.

CHRISTOPHER TIMOTHY

VOCATION: Actor.

CAREER: LONDON DEBUT—Corporal M.P., *Chips with Everything,* Royal Court Theatre. BROADWAY DEBUT—Corporal M.P., *Chips with Everything,* Booth Theatre. PRINCIPAL STAGE APPEARANCES—Three years as a member of the National Theatre Company at the Old Vic and Queen's Theatres, London; Sid, *Waiting for Lefty* and Hibbert, *Long Day's Journey into Night,* both at the Cambridge Theatre, London; Alvin, *The Actor's Nightmare,* Ambassador's Theatre, London; Bernard, *Happy Birthday,* Apollo Theatre, London; Clive, *See How They Run,* Shaftesbury Theatre, London; Rosencrantz, *Rosencrantz and Guildenstern Are Dead,* Young Vic Theatre, then Cambridge Theatre, London; Jesus, *The York Mystery Plays,* York Abbey, U.K., 1980; Firk, *The Shoemakers Holiday,* Leicester, U.K.; Petruchio, *The Taming of the Shrew,* Farnham, U.K.

MAJOR TOURS—With the National Theatre Company: tours to Moscow and West Berlin, lead role, *The Cure for Love,* U.K. cities, *The Real Thing,* U.K. cities.

PRINCIPAL FILM APPEARANCES—Spike, *Here We Go Round the Mulberry Bush,* 1968; Cerdic, *Alfred the Great,* 1969; Corporal Brook, *The Virgin Soldiers,* Columbia, 1970; *The Mind of Mr. Soames,* Columbia, 1970; *Spring and Port Wine,* 1970; also *Othello,* with the National Theatre Company; lead role, *Some Sunday; Up the Chastity Belt.*

PRINCIPAL TELEVISION APPEARANCES—Series: James Herriot, *All Creatures Great and Small.* Dramatic Specials: Willis, "Mur-

der Must Advertise," *Lord Peter Wimsy;* Kevin, *The Kitchen;* Corporal, *The Moon Shines Bright on Charlie Chaplin;* Sid Love, "Murder Most English," *The Flaxborough Chronicles;* title role, "Voyzek," *All the World's a Stage; Much Ado About Nothing,* with the National Theatre Company; also *Julius Caesar, Twelfth Night, The Three Sisters, Royal Command Performance of 1982, Mussolini, Take Three Girls, Take Three Women, A History and Its Heritage,* and *A Family and a Fortune.*

AWARDS: John Gielgud Scholarship; Laurence Olivier Award, for Sid *Waiting for Lefty;* Outstanding Male Personality of 1978, Variety Club of Great Britain Award, for *All Creatures Great and Small;* co-winner, BBC-TV Personality of 1979, for *All Creatures Great and Small.*

ADDRESSES: AGENT—c/o Peter Froggatt, Plant and Froggatt Ltd., Four Windmill Street, London W1, England.

*   *   *

TONER, Thomas   1928-

PERSONAL: Born May 25, 1928, in Homestead, PA; son of Peter James (an engineer) and Ann Marie (Connolly) Toner. EDUCATION: University of California at Los Angeles, B.A., 1957. RELIGION: Roman Catholic. MILITARY: U.S. Army, 1950-52.

VOCATION: Actor.

THOMAS TONER

CAREER: STAGE DEBUT—Father, *Come Marching Home,* Catholic Theatre Guild, Pittsburgh, 1945. BROADWAY DEBUT—Geronte, *Tricks,* Alvin Theatre, 1972. PRINCIPAL STAGE APPEARANCES—Shriner, *Light Up the Sky,* Tokyo International Players, Japan, 1951; *The Live Wire,* Gallery Theatre, Los Angeles, 1955; *Romanoff and Juliet,* L. Howe, *Sunrise at Campobello,* janitor, *The Bad Seed, Made in Heaven, The Gazebo,* and *Susan Slept Here,* all at the Deep Well Playhouse, Palm Springs, CA, 1955; *Nina* and *Black Chiffon,* both at the Lobero Playhouse, Santa Barbara, CA, 1959.

At the Alley Theatre, Houston, TX: Janitor, *Library Raid,* Oscar, *Little Foxes, Jane, An Enemy of the People, Six Characters in Search of an Author,* King, *Ondine,* and father, *The Winslow Boy,* all 1960-61; Johnny, *Misalliance;* Corbacchio, *Volpone, Majority of One,* ghost and gravedigger, *Hamlet,* Dan Ponder, *The Ponder Heart,* and *Amphitryon 38,* all 1961-62; Glogower, *The Time of Your Life,* Mr. Pugh, *Under Milkwood,* Corbacchio, *Volpone, Twelve Angry Men,* Pat, *The Hostage,* Joel, *All the Way Home,* and *The Threepenny Opera,* all at the Arena Stage, Washington, DC, 1962-63; Burgomaster, *The Visit,* Ferdinand, *Time Remembered,* and Davies, *The Caretaker,* all at the Olney Theatre, MD, 1963; Friar Mignon, *The Devils, Battle Dream,* Boniface, *Hotel Paradiso, The Wall, The Affair, The Taming of the Shrew,* and Smellicue, *Dark of the Moon,* all at the Arena Stage, Washington, DC, 1963-64; Witherspoon, *Leave It to Jane,* Chaplain, *Mother Courage,* and Dufort, Sr., *Thieves Carnival,* all Olney Theatre, 1964; title role, *Galileo,* Center Stage, Baltimore, MD, 1964.

Ragpicker, *The Madwoman of Chaillot* and Fluther, *The Plough and the Stars,* both Charles Playhouse, Boston, 1965: Danforth, *The Crucible* and Pat, *The Hostage,* both Long Wharf Theatre, New Haven, CT, 1965: Pat, *The Hostage,* Pennyylvannia State Festival, 1965; Swinden, *The Devil's Disciple,* Sid, *Ah, Wilderness!,* Right You Are, Grandpa, *You Can't Take It with You, Duel of Angels,* Bookseller, *Sholem Aleichem,* Mamaev, *Diary of a Scoundrel,* Einstein, *The Physicists,* Dorn, *The Sea Gull,* Davies, *Caretaker,* Harry, *A Delicate Balance,* Harpagon, *The Miser,* Burgess, *Candida,* old Cardinal, *Galileo,* De Stogember, *St. Joan,* and Napoleon, *War and Peace,* all at the Alley Theatre, Houston, TX, 1965-68; title role, *King John,* Polonius, *Hamlet,* Adam, *As You Like It,* title role, *Julius Caesar,* Balthazar and widow, *Comedy of Errors,* and doctor, witch, and porter, *Macbeth,* all at the Old Globe Theatre, San Diego, CA, 1968-69; *Chronicles of Hell* and *The Misanthrope,* both at the A.P.A. Theatre, Ann Arbor, MI, 1969; Dr. Schoenfeld, *Scubba Dubba,* Huntington Hartford Theatre, Los Angeles, 1969.

Monsignor Polycarpe, *Murderous Angels* and Papa, *Crystal and Fox,* both Mark Taper Forum, Los Angeles, 1970; John of Gaunt, *Richard II,* Dogberry, *Much Ado About Nothing,* and title role, *Cymbeline,* all at the Old Globe Theatre, San Diego, 1970; Carlisle, *Richard II,* Seattle Repertory Theatre, WA, 1971; Gremio, *The Taming of the Shrew, A Midsummer Night's Dream,* and *Antony and Cleopatra,* all Old at the Globe Theatre, San Diego, 1971; John of Gaunt, *Richard II,* Ahmanson Theatre, Los Angeles, and Kennedy Center, Washington, DC, 1971; Gloucester, *King Lear,* Dr. Rank, *A Doll's House,* Ben Franklin, *1776,* Pelinore, *Camelot,* and *The Rothschilds,* all at the North Shore Music Theatre, MA, 1973; old man and clerk, *The Good Doctor,* Eugene O'Neill Theatre, New York City, 1974; *Pericles* and *The Merry Wives of Windsor,* both New York Shakespeare Festival (NYSF), Delacorte Theatre, New York City, 1974; Hastings, *Richard III,* Mitzi Newhouse Theatre, Lincoln Center, New York City, 1974.

Quince, *A Midsummer Night's Dream,* Mitzi Newhouse Theatre, Lincoln Center, New York City, 1975; Dr. Morris, *All Over Town,*

Booth Theatre, New York City, 1975; Olin Potts, *A Texas Trilogy,* Kennedy Center, Washington, DC, then Broadhurst Theatre, New York City, 1976; Herdal, *The Masterbuilder,* Kennedy Center, Washington, DC, 1977; *California Suite,* Eugene O'Neill Theatre, New York City, 1977; Archie Lee, *Tiger Tail,* Alliance Theatre, Atlanta, 1978; Senator Jones, *Let 'Em Eat Cake,* Berkshire Theatre Festival, 1978; Judge, *The Inspector General,* Circle in the Square, New York City, 1978; Davies, *The Caretaker,* Olney Theatre, 1979.

Van Buren, *Damn Yankees,* Hartford Stage Company, CT, 1980; Ross, Bishop, and Snork, *The Elephant Man,* Booth Theatre, New York City, 1980; Boyle, *Juno and the Paycock,* Pittsburgh Public Theatre, 1981; title role, *Da,* South Coast Repertory Company, Costa Mesa, CA, 1982; Burns, *The Front Page,* Seattle Repertory Company, 1983; Police Chief, *Accidental Death of an Anarchist,* Mark Taper Forum, Los Angeles, 1983; Nat Danziger, *The Big Knife* and Dr. Chumley, *Harvey,* both at the Berkshire Theatre Festival, 1983; Sir, *The Dresser,* Alley Theatre, Houston, 1983; Weller, *The Gin Game,* Olney Theatre, 1983; Bert Cruckishank, *Over My Dead Body,* Hartman Theatre, Stamford, CT, 1984; Gerry and Grandpa, *Life and Limb,* Playwrights Horizons, New York City, 1985; Elbow, *Measure for Measure,* NYSF, Delacorte Theatre, New York City, 1985; Gilbert, *Sullivan and Gilbert,* Huntington Theatre, Boston, 1985; Gil, *Little Footsteps,* Playwrights Horizons, New York City, 1986; Hethersett the Butler, *Me and My Girl,* New York City, 1986.

MAJOR TOURS—*Murder in the Cathedral,* Vox Poetica Company, U.S. cities, 1958; doctor, witch, and porter, *Macbeth,* U.S. cities, 1968; Dr. Morris, *All Over Town,* U.S. cities, 1975; Ross, Bishop, and Snork, *The Elephant Man,* Florida cities, and other U.S. cities, 1980.

PRINCIPAL FILM APPEARANCES—*Cash McCall,* Warner Brothers, 1960; *Midnight Lace,* Universal, 1960; *Caper of the Golden Bulls,* Embassy, 1967; *I Love My Wife,* Universal, 1970; *Return of Count Yorga,* American International, 1971; *Glass Houses,* Columbia, 1972; *Sunday Dinner,* American Film Institute, 1974; *On the Yard,* Midwest, 1979; *Splash,* Touchstone, 1984.

PRINCIPAL TELEVISION APPEARANCES—Series: H. Bakewell, *Another World,* NBC; Colonel Jamison, *As the World Turns,* CBS; *All My Children; Guiding Light.* Episodic: *Kaz,* CBS; *Kate and Allie,* CBS. Movies: *The Kennedy Project.* Mini-Series: *The Adams Chronicles,* PBS.

AWARDS: Best Actor, Drama-Logue Award nomination, for *Da;* Best Actor, Helen Hayes Award nomination, for *The Gin Game.*

MEMBER: Actors' Equity Association, Screen Actors Guild, American Federation of Television and Radio Artists.

ADDRESSES: AGENT—c/o Sheila Robinson, International Creative Management, 40 W. 57th Street, New York, NY 10019.

*   *   *

TORN, Rip   1931-

PERSONAL: Born Elmore Rual Torn, February 6, 1931, in Temple, TX; son of Elmore Rual (an economist) and Thelma (Spacek) Torn; married Ann Wedgeworth (an actress), January 15, 1955 (divorced, June, 1961); married Geraldine Page (an actress); children: (first marriage) Danae; (second marriage) Angelica, Anthony, Jonathan. EDUCATION: Attended Texas A & M College; University of Texas, B.S.F.A., 1953; trained for the stage with Alice Hermes, Sanford Meisner, Lee Strasberg and the Martha Graham School of the Dance. MILITARY: Served with the National Guard, eight years.

VOCATION: Actor and director.

CAREER: FILM DEBUT—Brick, *Baby Doll,* Warner Brothers, 1956. PRINCIPAL FILM APPEARANCES—*Time Limit,* United Artists, 1957; *A Face in the Crowd,* Warner Brothers, 1957; *Pork Chop Hill,* United Artists, 1959; *King of Kings,* Metro-Goldwyn-Mayer (MGM), 1961; *Hero's Island,* United Artists, 1962; *Sweet Bird of Youth,* MGM, 1962; *Critic's Choice,* Warner Brothers, 1963; *Cincinnati Kid,* MGM, 1965; *One Spy Too Many,* MGM, 1966; *Beach Red,* United Artists, 1967; *You're a Big Boy Now,* Seven Arts, 1967; *Beyond the Law,* Grove, 1968; *Sol Madrid,* MGM, 1968; *Coming Apart,* independent, 1969.

Tropic of Cancer, Paramount, 1970; *Slaughter,* American International, 1972; *Payday,* Cinerama, 1973; *Crazy Joe,* Columbia, 1974; *Birch Interval,* Gamma III, 1976; *Maidstone,* 1976; *The Man Who Fell to Earth,* 1976; *Nasty Habits,* Brut, 1977; *Coma,* United Artists, 1978; *The Seduction of Joe Tynan,* Universal, 1979; *First Family,* Warner Brothers, 1980; *Heartland,* 1980; *One Trick Pony,* Warner Brothers, 1980; *Jinxed,* Metro-Goldwyn-Mayer/United Artists (MGM/UA), 1982; *Airplane II: The Sequel,* Paramount, 1982; *Cross Creek,* Universal, 1983; *Misunderstood,* MGM/UA, 1984; *Dino, Songwriter,* Tri-Star, 1984; *Flashpoint,* Tri-Star, 1984; *City Heat,* Warner Brothers, 1984; *Summer Rental,* Paramount, 1985; *Beer,* Orion, 1985.

PRINCIPAL TELEVISION APPEARANCES—Episodic: "Murder of a Sandflea," *Kraft Television Theatre,* NBC, 1956; "The Blue Hotel," *Omnibus,* ABC, 1956; "Wetback Run," *U.S. Steel Hour,* CBS, 1956; "So Short a Season," *Kaiser Aluminum Hour,* NBC, 1957; "Number Twenty-Two," *Alfred Hitchcock Presents,* CBS, 1957; "The Big Wave," *Alcoa Presents,* NBC, 1957; "The Little Bullfighter," *U.S. Steel Hour,* CBS, 1957; "Hostages to Fortune," *Alcoa Hour,* NBC, 1957; "The Killer Instinct," *Kraft Theatre,* NBC, 1957; "Bomber's Moon," *Playhouse 90,* CBS, 1958; "Johnny Belinda," *Hallmark Hall of Fame,* NBC, 1958; "Murder and the Android," *Producers Showcase,* NBC, 1959; "Epitath for a Golden Girl," *Pursuit,* CBS, 1959; "Face of a Hero," *Playhouse 90,* CBS, 1959; "The Tunnel," *Playhouse 90,* CBS, 1959; *The Untouchables,* ABC, 1961, 1963; *Frontier Circus,* CBS, 1961; "Crazy Sunday," *Dick Powell Theatre,* NBC, 1962; *The Naked City,* ABC, 1962; *Dr. Kildare,* NBC, 1962, 1964; *Route 66,* CBS, 1963; *Channing,* ABC, 1963; *Eleventh Hour,* NBC, 1964; *Ben Casey,* ABC, 1964; *The Man from U.N.C.L.E.,* NBC, 1965; "Monserrat," *Hollywood Television Theatre,* PBS, 1971; *Bonanza,* NBC, 1971; *Mannix,* CBS, 1972; *Actors on Acting,* PRS, 1984.

Dramatic Specials: *Twenty-Four Hours in a Woman's Life,* CBS, 1961; Walt Whitman, *Song of Myself,* PBS, 1976; also Big Daddy, *Cat on a Hot Tin Roof.* Movies: *The President's Plane Is Missing,* 1973; *The FBI Versus the Ku Klux Klan,* 1975; *When She Says No,* 1984; *The Execution,* 1985; *The Atlanta Child Murders,* 1985; Lyndon B. Johnson, *J. Edgar Hoover,* Showtime, 1987.

BROADWAY DEBUT—Brick, *Cat on a Hot Tin Roof,* Morosco

Theatre, 1956. PRINCIPAL STAGE APPEARANCES—Val, *Orpheus Descending,* Coconut Grove Playhouse, Miami, FL, 1958; Bubba John, *Chaparral,* Sheridan Square Playhouse, New York City, 1958; Tom Junior, *Sweet Bird of Youth,* later took over the role of Chance Wayne in this same production, Martin Beck Theatre, New York City, 1959-60.

Carlo, *Daughter of Silence,* Music Box Theatre, New York City, 1961; title role, *Macbeth,* University of Texas, Austin, 1962; Eban Cabot, *Desire Under the Elms,* Circle in the Square, New York City, 1963; Edmund Darrell, *Strange Interlude,* Hudson Guild Theatre, New York City, 1963; Lyle, *Blues for Mr. Charlie,* American National Theatre Academy (ANTA) Theatre, New York City, 1964; Peter, *The Kitchen,* 81st Street Theatre, New York City, 1966; Bernie Dodd, *The Country Girl,* City Center, New York City, 1966; Marion Faye, *The Deer Park,* Theatre de Lys, New York City, 1967; Roberto, *The Cuban Thing,* Henry Miller's Theatre, New York City, 1968; Edward Morris, *Dream of a Blacklisted Actor,* Theatre de Lys, New York City, 1969.

Edgar, *The Dance of Death,* Arena Stage, Washington, DC, 1970, then Ritz Theatre, New York City, 1971; *The Marriage Proposal* and *The Boor,* Playhouse in the Park, Philadelphia, 1971; William McLeod, *Barbary Shore,* New York Shakespeare Festival, Anspacher Theatre, New York City, 1974; gala benefit for Circle in the Square, New York City, 1974; Richard Nixon, *Expletive Deleted,* Theatre of the Riverside Church, New York City, 1974; *The Little Foxes,* Academy Festival Theatre, Lake Forest, IL, then Walnut Street Theatre, Philadelphia, 1974; Captain, *The Father,* Yale Repertory Theatre, New Haven, CT, 1975; Tom, *The Glass Menagerie,* Circle in the Square, New York City, 1975; *A Streetcar Named Desire,* Academy Festival Theatre, Lake Forest, 1976; Gustav, *Creditors,* Hudson Guild Theatre, New York City, 1977; Henry Hackmore, *Seduced,* American Place Theatre, New York City, 1979; Don, *Mixed Couples,* Brooks Atkinson Theatre, New York City, 1980; the man in English, *The Man and the Fly,* Puerto Rican Traveling Theatre, New York City, 1982. Also appeared in *Fever for Life,* 1975; *Night Shift,* 1977.

MAJOR TOURS—Chance Wayne, *Sweet Bird of Youth,* U.S. cities, 1960; *Marriage and Money,* U.S. cities, 1971.

FIRST LONDON STAGE WORK—Director, *The Beard,* Royal Court Theatre, 1968. PRINCIPAL STAGE WORK—Director: *The Beard,* Evergreen Theatre, New York City, 1967; *The Honest-to-God Schnozzola,* Gramercy Arts Theatre, New York City, 1969; *Look Away,* Playhouse Theatre, New York City, 1973; *Creditors,* Hudson Guild Theatre, New York City, 1977.

NON-RELATED CAREER—Oilfield roustabout; architectural draftsman.

AWARDS: Theatre World Award, 1959, for *Chaparral;* Obie Award, 1967, for *The Deer Park;* Best Director, Obie Award, 1968, for *The Beard.*

MEMBER: Actors' Equity Association, Screen Actors Guild, American Federation of Television and Radio Artists, Directors Guild of America, Actors' Studio (board of directors, production board, first chairman of the founding committee); Sigma Chi.

ADDRESSES: OFFICE—Actors Studio, 432 W. 44th Street, New York, NY 10036.*

TRACY, Steve   1952-1986

PERSONAL: Born 1952; died of respiratory failure in conjunction with Kaposi's sarcoma, November 27, 1986, in Tampa, FL. EDUCATION: Attended Los Angeles City College; studied at the Harvey Lembeck Comedy Workshop in Los Angeles.

VOCATION: Actor.

CAREER: PRINCIPAL STAGE APPEARANCES—All in Los Angeles: *The Chicago Conspiracy Trial*, Odyssey Theatre; *Christmas Fantasies, Fractures, The Nuns, Kiss Me Kate,* and *AIDS/Us,* 1985.

PRINCIPAL FILM APPEARANCES—*National Lampoon's Class Reunion*, Twentieth Century-Fox, 1982; *Save the Last Dance for Me; Forever Young.*

PRINCIPAL TELEVISION APPEARANCES—Series: Percival Dalton, *Little House on the Prairie*, NBC, 1980-81. Episodic: *The Jeffersons*, CBS; *Quincy*, NBC; *James at 15*, NBC; *The Frankie and Annette Show.**

*   *   *

TREAT, Martin   1950-

PERSONAL: Born May 9, 1950, in Yreka, CA; son of Harold and Marguerite Treat. EDUCATION: University of Oregon, M.F.A.,

MARTIN TREAT

1975; trained for the stage with Gene Nye and Michael Howard. MILITARY: U.S. Army.

VOCATION: Actor and writer.

CAREER: STAGE DEBUT—*Victims of Duty*, Chico State College, CA. OFF-BROADWAY DEBUT—Aaron Burr, *The Ghost of Spring Street*, La Mama Experimental Theatre Club (E.T.C.). PRINCIPAL STAGE APPEARANCES—Carlin, *A Collier's Friday Night*, Open Space Theatre, New York City, 1981; Hardly Visible, *The Further Inquiry*, American Renaissance Theatre, New York City, 1982; *The Last of Hitler*, Theatre for the New City, New York City, 1984; also, Ned, *Philadelphia Here I Come*, WPA Theatre, New York City; Kovaks, *The Danube* and Alex Gallicin, *Zeks*, both Theatre for the New City, New York City; appeared in classical plays including Shakespeare for the CSC Repertory, New York City.

FILM DEBUT—*Hoodlums*, 1980. PRINCIPAL FILM APPEARANCES—*Easy Money*, Orion, 1983.

PRINCIPAL TELEVISION APPEARANCES—Lead, *Molders of Troy*, PBS, 1982.

WRITINGS: ADAPTATIONS—*Hard Times*, staged reading, Coalition for the Homeless.

MEMBER: Actors' Equity Association, American Theatre Association, Viet Nam Veterans Theatre Company, American Folk Theatre; Common Cause.

ADDRESSES: HOME—30 Saint Mark's Place, New York, NY 10003.

*   *   *

TROLL, Kitty   1950-

PERSONAL: Full name, Kathleen Troll; born December 18, 1950, in New York, NY; daughter of Hans (a physicist) and Lillian Holland (a psychologist; maiden name, Ellman) Troll; married Douglas Getchell (divorced); children: Wyatt Theodore. EDUCATION: Attended the Cambridge School of Weston; studied acting with Lee Strasberg and Michael Howard in New York City.

VOCATION: Actress and writer.

CAREER: STAGE DEBUT—Anitra, *A Grape for Seeing*, Foothill Theatre, CA. OFF-BROADWAY DEBUT—Emmeline, *S.W.A.K.*, Playwrights Horizons. PRINCIPAL STAGE APPEARANCES—At the Commedia Theatre, CA, 1967: Charlotte, *The Night of the Iguana*, Joanna, *Blues for Mr. Charlie*, and Titania, *A Midsummer Night's Dream;* at the Theatre by the Sea, Portsmouth, NH, 1968-70: actress number two, *Spoon River Anthology;* Childie, *The Killing of Sister George*, Tillie, *The Effect of Gamma Rays on Man-in-the-Moon Marigolds*, ingenue, *The Moon Is Blue*, Agnes, *School for Wives*, and mysterious woman, *Victims of Duty.*

Iris, *Beggar's Choice/Johnny Bull*, Eugene O'Neill Playwrights Festival, New London, CT; one-act series, *Day of the Races, Stray Dogs, Old Wives Tale*, No Smoking Playhouse, New York City; *Throckmorton, TX*, Young Playwrights Festival, New York City; Irene and Mable, *Bandits*, St. Peter's Church, New York City; Jane, *After the Ceremony*, Maggie, *Survivors*, and April, *Valen-*

KITTY TROLL

tine, all at the Actor's Studio, New York City; Iris, *Beggar's Choice*, New York Shakespeare Festival; Doris, *Bayside Boys*, Labor Theate, New York City; Sally, *Talley's Folley* and Hero, *Much Ado About Nothing*, both at the Commedia Theatre, CA.

MAJOR TOURS—Children's Theatre tour of New England.

FILM DEBUT—Film critic, *Stardust Memories*, United Artists, 1980. PRINCIPAL FILM APPEARANCES—Carrie, *Nightflowers;* Jane, *The Decision;* narrator of the documentary, *The Last to Know*, 1981; Lynn, *Sun and Moon*, 1986; Selma Lewis, *Permanent Wave*, 1986.

TELEVISION DEBUT—Carol, *As the World Turns*, CBS. PRINCIPAL TELEVISION APPEARANCES—Episodic: Susan Stephens, *For Richer, for Poorer*, NBC; Ilona, *The Best of Families*, PBS; Aggie, *Texas*, NBC; Eve, *All My Children*, ABC.

PRINCIPAL RADIO WORK—Voice overs and commercials; drama, on *Earplay*, National Public Radio.

RELATED CAREER—Drama teacher, Pacific High School, CA; founder, Mixed-Media Theatre, Dallas.

WRITINGS: SCREENPLAYS—*Holding the Bag*.

TELEPLAYS—*Malpractice*.

BOOKS—(With Olauya) *The Party Book;* three children's books.

MEMBER: Actors' Equity Association, Screen Actors Guild, American Federation of Radio and Television Artists.

SIDELIGHTS: Kitty Troll told *CTFT:* "I originally entered this profession to escape being myself. I discovered to my dismay that instead it meant learning about myself as my instrument to an occasionally uncomfortable degree. But without my passion and commitment to acting and the discoveries it required, I would be a very different person, so I am grateful."

ADDRESSES: HOME—203 W. 90th Street, New York, NY 10025.

*   *   *

TUCKER, Forrest Meredith   1919-1986

PERSONAL: Born February 12, 1919, in Plainfield, IN; died of throat cancer in Woodland Hills, CA, October 25, 1986; son of Forrest A. and Doris P. (Heringlake) Tucker; married Marilyn Johnson, March 28, 1950 (died July, 1960); married Marilyn Fisk, October 23, 1961; children: (first marriage) Pamela Brooke; (second marriage) Cynthia, Forrest Sean. EDUCATION: Attended George Washington University. MILITARY: U.S. Army, 1942-45.

VOCATION: Actor.

CAREER: FILM DEBUT—*The Westerner*, 1939. PRINCIPAL FILM APPEARANCES—*The Howards of Virginia*, 1940; *Emergency Landing*, 1941; *New Wave*, 1941; *Keeper of the Flame*, Metro-Goldwyn-Mayer (MGM), 1942; *Counter Espionage*, 1942; *The Yearling*, MGM, 1946; *Renegades*, 1946; *Never Say Goodbye*, 1946; *Rock Island Trail*, 1950; *Sands of Iwo Jima*, 1950; *Warpath*, 1951; *Oh, Susannah!*, 1951; *Crosswinds*, 1951; *The Fighting Coast Guard*, 1951; *Wild Blue Yonder*, 1951; *Flaming Feather*, 1951; *Bugles in the Afternoon*, 1952; *Hoodlum Empire*, 1952; *Ride the Man Down*, 1952; *Hurricane Smith*, 1952; *Montana Belle*, 1952; *Pony Express*, 1953; *Laughing Anne*, 1953; *Trouble in the Glen*, 1953; *Jubilee Trail*, 1954; *San Antone*, 1954; *Flight Nurse*, 1954; *Rage at Dawn*, RKO, 1955; *Vanishing American*, Republic, 1955; *Finger Man*, Allied Artists, 1955; *Night Freight*, Allied Artists, 1955; *Paris Follies of 1956*, Allied Artists, 1956; *Break in the Circle*, Twentieth Century-Fox, 1956; *Auntie Mame*, Warner Brothers, 1958; *Counterplot*, United Artists, 1959; *The Night They Raided Minsky's*, United Artists, 1968; *Barquiero*, United Artists, 1970; *Chisum*, Warner Brothers, 1970; *The Wild McCullocks*, American International, 1975; *The Wackiest Wagon Train in the West*, Topar, 1977; *The Final Chapter: Walking Tall*, 1977; *Thunder Run*, 1985; *Outtakes*, 1985.

PRINCIPAL TELEVISION APPEARANCES—Series: *Crunch and Des*, NBC, 1956; Sergeant Morgan O'Rourke, *F Troop*, ABC, 1965-67; Mr. Callahan, *Dusty's Trail*, syndicated, 1973. Episodic: *Kaiser Aluminum Hour*, NBC; *Filthy Rich*, CBS; *Murder, She Wrote*, CBS. Movies: *Welcome Home Johnny Bristol*, 1971; *Footsteps*, 1972; *Jarrett*, 1973; *The Incredible Rocky Mountain Race*, 1977; *A Real American Hero*, 1978; *The Rebels*, 1979; *Blood Feud*, 1983. Also *Black Beauty; Once an Eagle*.

STAGE DEBUT—Gayety Burlesque Theatre, Washington, DC. PRINCIPAL STAGE APPEARANCES—*Fair Game for Lovers*, Broadway production, 1964; *The Confidence Game*, Drury Lane Theatre, Chicago, 1972-73.

MAJOR TOURS—Professor Harold Hill, *The Music Man,* U.S. cities, for three and one-half years; *Plaza Suite,* U.S. cities, 1971-72; *That Championship Season,* 1972-73; also *Showboat.*

PRINCIPAL RADIO WORK—Host of music and interview show, WCFL, Chicago, 1960s.

RELATED CAREER—Associate producer, Drury Lane Theatre, Chicago, 1969.

AWARDS: Star of Tomorrow Award, 1952.

MEMBER: Screen Actors Guild, American Federation of Television and Radio Artists, Masquers Club (director), Players Club, Lambs Club, Friars Club, Variety International American Stage Golfing (director, London).*

*   *   *

TUGGLE, Richard   1948-

PERSONAL: Born August 8, 1948. EDUCATION: University of Virginia, 1970.

VOCATION: Writer and director.

CAREER: PRINCIPAL FILM WORK—Director, *Tightrope,* Warner Brothers, 1984; director, *Out of Bounds,* Columbia, 1986.

WRITINGS: SCREENPLAYS—*Escape from Alcatraz,* Paramount, 1979; *Tightrope,* Warner Brothers, 1984.

MEMBER: Writers Guild, Directors Guild, Academy of Motion Picture Arts and Sciences.

ADDRESSES: AGENT—c/o Martin Bauer, Bauer-Benedek, 9255 Sunset Blvd., Los Angeles, CA 90069.

*   *   *

TURNER, Douglas
See Ward, Douglas Turner

*   *   *

ULLMAN, Tracey

BRIEF ENTRY: Born in the London suburb of Hackbridge, actress, musician, and singer Tracey Ullman attended the Italia Conti School for four years, until she was expelled. She was soon appearing on British television and onstage in productions of *Grease* and *The Rocky Horror Picture Show.* Her greatest success at that time came when she performed in the improvisational play, *Four in a Million,* in 1981, at the Royal Court Theatre in London. After her work in this play garnered her the London Theatre Critics Award, she returned to working in television. At the same time she starred in a comedy series on the BBC, she also recorded a gold-selling album, *You Broke My Heart in Seventeen Places,* and four of her singles made the British top ten pop charts. But it was her performance as the bohemian Alice Park in *Plenty* that brought Ullman's talents to American audiences. Speaking of the 1985 Twentieth Century-Fox film, Ullman said, "It will be hard to find another script as good." In the meantime, she has made her American television debut with *The Tracey Ullman Show,* a comedy and variety show first broadcast in April, 1987, by the Fox Broadcasting Corporation (FBC).*

V

VAN KAMP, Merete   1961-

PERSONAL: Born Merete Kamp, November 17, 1961; daughter of Kai and Selma Kamp. EDUCATION: Studied acting with Peggy Fury and Lee Strasberg. RELIGION: Protestant.

VOCATION: Actress.

CAREER: FILM DEBUT—*The Osterman Weekend,* Twentieth Century-Fox, 1983.

TELEVISION DEBUT—Mini-Series: *Princess Daisy,* NBC, 1983. PRINCIPAL TELEVISION APPEARANCES—Series: *Dallas,* NBC, 1985-86.

AWARDS: Halo award, for *Princess Daisy.*

MEMBER: Screen Actors Guild, American Federation of Radio and Television Artists.

MERETE VAN KAMP

SIDELIGHTS: RECREATIONS—Dancing, painting and writing.

ADDRESSES: HOME—Los Angeles, CA. AGENT—c/o Caron Shampoo, The Agency, 10351 Santa Monica Blvd., Suite 211, Los Angeles, CA 90025.

*   *   *

VAN PATTEN, Joyce   1934-

PERSONAL: Born March 9, 1934, in New York, NY; daughter of Richard (an interior decorator) and Josephine (a magazine advertising executive; maiden name, Acerno) Van Patten; married Martin Balsam (an actor, divorced); married Dennis Dugan. EDUCATION: Attended the Lodge School in New York City.

VOCATION: Actress.

CAREER: STAGE DEBUT—As the winner in a Shirley Temple look-alike contest, RKO Theatre, Richmond Hill, NY, 1936. BROADWAY DEBUT—Replacement for the role of Mae Yearling, *Love's Old Sweet Song,* Plymouth Theatre, 1940. PRINCIPAL STAGE APPEARANCES—Marie Antoinette Benson, *Popsy,* 48th Street Theatre, New York City, 1941; Zoey, *Family Honeymoon,* Lakewood Theatre, Skowhegan, ME, 1941; Mary, *This Rock,* Longacre Theatre, New York City, 1943; alternated in the role of Patricia Frame, *Tomorrow the World,* Ethel Barrymore Theatre, New York City, 1943, and repeated role at Elitch Gardens Theatre, Denver, CO, 1944; Helen Williams, *The Perfect Marriage,* Ethel Barrymore Theatre, New York City, 1944; Joan, *The Wind Is Ninety,* Booth Theatre, New York City, 1945; Ilka Morgan, *The Bees and the Flowers,* Cort Theatre, New York City, 1946; season at Elitch Gardens Theatre, Denver, 1949; standby for the role of Ruth, *The Man,* Fulton Theatre, New York City, 1950; Judy, *Junior Miss,* Lake Whalon Playhouse, MA, 1951; Joyce Reid, *Put Them All Together,* Shubert Theatre, New Haven, CT, 1954; Elsa, *The Desk Set,* Broadhurst Theatre, New York City, 1955; Julie Gillis, *The Tender Trap* and Myra Hagerman, *Oh, Men! Oh, Women!,* both at the Pocono Playhouse, Mountainhome, PA, 1955; Shirl, *A Hole in the Head,* Plymouth Theatre, New York City, 1957.

Mary Magdalene, *Between Two Thieves,* York Theatre, New York City, 1960, then repeated role at the Theatre West at the University of California at Los Angeles (U.C.L.A.), 1961; *Wild Wicked World,* revue, Interlude Club, Hollywood, CA, 1962; various roles, *Spoon River Anthology,* Theatre West, U.C.L.A., 1963, and repeated various roles in the production, retitled *Spoon River,* Booth Theatre, New York City, 1963; Sarah, *The Lover,* the

Theatre Group, U.C.L.A., 19965; *Who Wants to Be the Lone Ranger,* with the New Theatre for Now at the Mark Taper Forum, Los Angeles, 1971; Canina, *Volpone,* Mark Taper Forum, Los Angeles, 1972; repeated appearance, *Spoon River,* Theatre West, U.C.L.A., 1972; *Twenty-Three Years Later,* with the New Theatre for Now at the Mark Taper Forum, Los Angeles, 1973; *The Kitchen,* Los Angeles Actors Theatre, 1975; replacement for the role of Doris, *Same Time Next Year,* Brooks Atkinson Theatre, New York City, 1975; Marianne, *Gethsemane Springs,* Mark Taper Forum, Los Angeles, CA, 1977; Arlene Miller, *Murder at the Howard Johnson's,* John Golden Theatre, New York City, 1979; *Triptych,* with the U.C.L.A. Theatre Company, Los Angeles, 1979.

Steffy, *I Ought to Be in Pictures,* Eugene O'Neill Theatre, New York City, 1980; Pauline, *The Seagull,* Public Theatre, New York Shakespeare Festival, New York City, 1980; Florrie, *The Supporting Cast,* Biltmore Theatre, New York City, 1981; Blanche, *Brighton Beach Memoirs,* Ahmanson Theatre, Los Angeles, then at the Alvin Theatre, New York City, 1983; *Look Homeward, Angel,* Pasadena Playhouse, CA, 1985.

MAJOR TOURS—Mae Yearling, *Love's Old Sweet Song,* U.S. cities, 1940; Judy, *Junior Miss,* summer theatres, 1946; Miriam, *Dear Ruth,* summer theatres, 1947; Monica, *The Second Man,* summer theatres, 1948; Pat, *The Male Animal,* summer theatres, 1953; *Spice of Life,* U.S. cities, 1955; Karen Nash, Muriel Tate, and Norma Hubley, *Plaza Suite,* U.S. cities, 1971; Ellen Manville, *Luv,* U.S. cities, 1974; *Same Time Next Year,* Canadian cities, 1975.

FILM DEBUT—Mae, *Reg'lar Fellers,* PRC Pictures, 1941. PRINCIPAL FILM APPEARANCES—*14 Hours,* Twentieth Century-Fox, 1951; *The Goddess,* Columbia, 1958; *I Love You, Alice B. Toklas,* Warner Brothers/Seven Arts, 1968; *The Trouble with Girls,* Metro-Goldwyn-Mayer, 1968; *Pussycat, Pussycat, I Love You,* United Artists, 1970; *Making It,* Twentieth Century-Fox, 1970; *Something Big,* National General, 1971; *Thumb-Tripping,* AVCO-Embassy, 1972; *Bone,* Jack Harris Enterprises, 1972; *Unreal,* 1972; *Mame,* Warner Brothers, 1974; *The Bad News Bears,* Paramount, 1976; *Mikey and Nicky,* Paramount, 1977; *The Falcon and the Snowman,* Orion, 1985; *St. Elmo's Fire,* Columbia, 1985.

PRINCIPAL TELEVISION APPEARANCES—Series: Nurse Clara, *Young Dr. Malone,* NBC, 1959-60; *The Brighter Day,* CBS, 1961; regular, *The Danny Kaye Show,* CBS, 1964-67; Claudia Gramus, *The Good Guys,* CBS, 1968-70; Jean Benedict, *The Don Rickles Show,* CBS, 1972; Iris Chapman, *The Mary Tyler Moore Hour,* CBS, 1979.

Episodic: *Hollywood Screen Test,* WJS, 1949; *Martin Kane, Private Eye,* CBS, 1949; *Armstrong Circle Theatre,* 1960; *The Wendy Barrie Show,* WNTA, 1960; *The Law and Mr. Jones,* ABC, 1960; *Ben Casey,* ABC, 1961; *The Verdict Is Yours,* CBS, 1961; *Dobie Gillis,* CBS, 1962; *Bus Stop,* ABC, 1962; *Target: The Corruptors,* ABC, 1962; *Checkmate,* CBS, 1962; *The Detectives,* NBC, 1962; *Dr. Kildare,* NBC, 1962; *The Loretta Young Show,* CBS, 1962; *The Alcoa Hour,* 1963; *Perry Mason,* CBS, 1963; *The Lloyd Bridges Show,* CBS, 1963; *Alfred Hitchcock,* CBS, 1963; *Gunsmoke,* CBS, 1963; *Stoney Burke,* ABC, 1963; *The Untouchables,* ABC, 1963; *Wide Country,* NBC, 1963; *The Twilight Zone,* CBS, 1963; *The Defenders,* CBS, 1963; *The Outer Limits,* ABC, 1963; also, *Philco Television Playhouse* and *Armstrong Circle Theatre,* both NBC.

Mini-Series: *The Martian Chronicles,* ABC. Movies: *Malice in*

Wonderland, CBS, 1985; *Picking Up the Pieces,* CBS, 1985. Dramatic Specials: "The Flattering Word," *Hour Glass,* NBC, 1946; "Dinner at Eight," *Hour Glass,* NBC, 1948; "Brief Music," *Kraft Television Theatre,* NBC, 1951; "The Killers," *Buick Show,* CBS, 1959; "Billy Galvin," *American Playhouse Presents,* PBS, 1987.

RADIO DEBUT—*Let's Pretend,* CBS, 1941. PRINCIPAL RADIO WORK—Series: *Reg'lar Fellers,* CBS, 1941; title role, *Penny* 1946; regular, *My True Story,* ABC, 1957. Episodic: *Theatre Guild of the Air,* 1950-55; also *Grand Central Station; Wendy Warren.*

RELATED CAREER—Co-founder, Theatre West, University of California at Los Angeles.

AWARDS: Donaldson Award, 1944, for *Tomorrow the World.*

MEMBER: Actors' Equity Association, Screen Actors Guild, American Federation of Television and Radio Artists.

SIDELIGHTS: RECREATIONS—Swimming, painting, and cooking.

ADDRESSES: AGENT—Smith-Freedman Associates, 850 Seventh Avenue, New York, NY 10019.*

*   *   *

VERONA, Stephen

PERSONAL: EDUCATION: Attended the School of Visual Arts, New York City, 1958-62. MILITARY: U.S. Army.

VOCATION: Writer, producer, director, editor, and painter.

CAREER: PRINCIPAL FILM WORK—Director, producer, and co-writer, *The Lords of Flatbush,* Columbia, 1974; director, producer, and writer, *Pipe Dreams,* AVCO-Embassy, 1976; director and co-writer, *Boardwalk,* Atlantic, 1979; director and writer, *Talking Walls,* 1983.

PRINCIPAL TELEVISION WORK—Specials: Production designer and animation director, *Class of 1966,* NBC, 1966; director, producer, co-writer, and editor, *Different Strokes,* CBS, 1970; director, producer, and co-writer, *The Music People,* CBS, 1972; director, co-producer, and writer, *Double Exposure,* CBS, 1972. Episodic: Artist, producer, and director, *Sesame Street,* PBS, 1971; producer and director, *Take a Giant Step,* NBC, 1971. Pilots: Producer and co-writer, *Flatbush Avenue J,* ABC, 1976.

VIDEOS—*I Ten,* CBS Epic, 1983; *Natalie Cole,* CBS Epic, 1983; *Mick Fleetwood with Stevie Nicks,* RCA, 1983; *Boy George and Culture Club,* CBS Epic, 1983; *Will Ackerman,* Windham Hill, 1984; *Alex de Grassi,* Windham Hill, 1984; *Liz Story,* Windham Hill, 1984; *Western Light,* Pioneer Classic, 1984; *Where Are You Tonight,* Organically Grown, 1984.

WRITINGS: SCREENPLAYS—*Lapis Lazuli,* independent, 1967; *Forever a Festival,* Alliance, 1969; *Wednesday's Child,* Alliance, 1969; *The Mabinogian,* independent, 1970; *Primary Colors,* Koch-Kirkwood, 1981; *Deception,* independent, 1983; *Dear Diary,* independent, 1985; *The Children of the Lords,* United Artists, 1985; *The Lords of Flatbush 22 Years Later,* Cannon, upcoming; also short subject films: *Life Elektra,* 1960; *Impromt-2,* 1965; *The*

Empty Hand, ACI, 1965; *My Coloring Book,* 1965; *She Said Go,* Apple, London, 1966; *French Provincial,* United Artists, 1966; *Rain on the Roof,* 1967; *Five Will Get You Ten-Sergeant Pepper,* Apple, 1967; *The Rehearsal,* Schoenfeld, 1968; *Most Peculiar Man,* 1969; *Different Strokes,* Schoenfeld, 1970.

TELEVISION—Movies: *Tales of the Nile,* CBS, 1979; *Jack's Video,* CBS, 1986; his work was also featured on *The Art of Film* PBS.

AWARDS: Best Short Subject Live Action, Academy Award nomination, 1972, for *The Rehearsal;* five San Francisco Film Festival Awards; five Chicago Film Festival Awards; three Atlanta Film Festival Awards; five CINE Golden Eagle Awards; Robert Flaherty Documentary Seminar Award; Vancouver, Canada Award; two Pacific Northwest Arts and Crafts Association Film Awards; Adelaide Auckland Film Festival Award; four independent Film Makers Competition Awards; U.S. Industrial Film Festival Award for Creative Excellence; Atlanta Television Special Gold Medal Award; Gold Medal Award, New York Film and Television Festival; Rosenthal Foundation Award; two Pesaro, Italy Awards; Cannes Film Festival Award; Youth Festival Award, Cannes, France; Winterfest Award, Boston, MA; American Film Festival Award, Dallas, TX; Festival de Popoli Award, Florence, Italy; Cork, Ireland Award; Venice, Italy Award; Montivideo, Uruguay Award; Mamaia, Yugoslavia Award; Grenoble Sport Film Festival Award; Animation Festival Award, Museum of Modern Art, New York City; Deauville, France Award; Edward Steichen Photography Award, Museum of Modern Art, New York City; also more than fifty awards for television commercials.

MEMBER: Academy of Motion Picture Arts and Sciences, Directors Guild, Writers Guild of America.

SIDELIGHTS: Stephen Verona told *CTFT* that he painted the official portrait of Governor Jerry Brown of California for the 1980 Presidential election campaign. He also painted the poster for the Music Center Dance Presentations International Ballets at the Dorothy Chandler Pavilion, Los Angeles, in 1981 and the menu cover for Ma Maison Restaurant.

ADDRESSES: HOME—1251 Stone Canyon Road, Bel Air, CA 90024. AGENT—David Shapira and Associates, 15301 Ventura Blvd., Sherman Oaks, CA 91403.

*   *   *

VOIGTS, Richard   1934-

PERSONAL: Full name, Richard Carl Voigts; born November 25, 1934, in Streator, IL; son of Richard Clarence (a farmer) and Lita Alberta (a teacher; maiden name, Brennecke) Voigts. EDUCATION: Attended Augustana College, 1951-53; Indiana University, B.A., 1955; Columbia University, M.A., 1970.

VOCATION: Actor.

CAREER: STAGE DEBUT—Marshall Saidenberg, *Murder Among Friends,* Theatre at the Square, Cambridge, MA, 1979, for eighteen performances. OFF-BROADWAY DEBUT—Major Von Konigswald, *Happy Birthday, Wanda June,* Equity Library Theatre, 1983. PRINCIPAL STAGE APPEARANCES—With the Indiana Repertory Theatre, Indianapolis: Jo, *The Royal Family,* Deputy Winston, *The*

Desperate Hours, and Dr. Bradman, *Blithe Spirit,* all 1980 and Rear Admiral, *The Failure to Zig Zag,* 1981; Northumberland, *Henry IV,* Part I and Antonio, *Much Ado About Nothing,* both at the Alabama Shakespeare Festival, Anniston, 1982; Glas, *Slow Dance on the Killing Ground,* Urban Arts Theatre, 1982; Capulet, *Romeo and Juliet,* Alabama Shakespeare Festival, 1983; Senator Hedges, *Born Yesterday,* South Jersey Regional Theatre, 1983; Hubert Sloane, *Once Is Never Enough,* Pan Asian Repertory Theatre, New York City, 1985; *Black Coffee* and *Rule of Three,* both at the Apple Corps Theatre, New York City, 1986.

MAJOR TOURS—George, *Who's Afraid of Virginia Woolf?,* Germany, Sweden, Holland, and Switzerland, 1985; Dr. Kimborough, *Never Too Late,* Elitch Gardens Theatre, Denver, Cape Playhouse, Dennis, MA, and Westport Country Playhouse, CT, 1986.

FILM DEBUT—Dean Kemper, *Girls' Nite Out,* Aries International Pictures, 1984.

TELEVISION DEBUT—Walter Richards, *The Guiding Light,* CBS, 1980. PRINCIPAL TELEVISION APPEARANCES—Dr. Robinson, *All My Children,* ABC, 1981; Dr. Denton Keats, *One Life to Live,* ABC, 1982; Sloan Ingleby, *Ryan's Hope,* ABC, 1984. Movies: Reverend Sandlock, *Our Family Honor,* Lorimar, NBC, 1986.

MEMBER: Actors' Equity Association, American Federation of Television and Radio Artists; The Players Club.

SIDELIGHTS: FAVORITE ROLES—George in *Who's Afraid of Virginia Woolf?*

RICHARD VOIGTS

Richard Voigts told *CTFT* that he has travelled to Japan, Taiwan, Hong Kong, Thailand, Peru, Guatemala, Morocco, Spain, France, England, Holland, Sweden, Switzerland, Iceland, Egypt, and the Carribean islands.

ADDRESSES: HOME—160 West End Avenue, New York, NY 10023.

* * *

von MAYRHAUSER, Jennifer 1948-

PERSONAL: Born Jennifer Bergin, January 26, 1948, in Ithaca, NY; daughter of Thomas Goddard (a scholar, writer, and teacher) and Florence Theresa (Bullen) Bergin; married Richard Cottrell (an actor), January 11, 1982; children: Julia, Lucy. EDUCATION: Northwestern University, B.S., 1970; studied formal stage design at the Lester Polakov Studios in New York City.

VOCATION: Costume designer.

CAREER: FIRST STAGE WORK—Apprentice, Theatre in the Rink, New Haven, CT, 1964. FIRST OFF-BROADWAY STAGE WORK—Costume design, *Press Cuttings,* Cubiculo Theatre, 1972. PRINCIPAL STAGE WORK—Costume designer, Broadway productions: *Censored Scenes from King Kong, Hide and Seek, Eminent Domain, Solomon's Child, The Father, John Gabriel Borkman, Knock Knock, Da, Talley's Folley, Special Occasions, Beyond Therapy, The Wake of Jamey Foster, Steaming, Angel's Fall, Passion,* *Awake and Sing, The Boys in Autumn, Baby, Execution of Justice, Hayfever.* Costume designer, Off-Broadway: *The Miss Firecracker Contest, Ashes, Uncommon Women and Others.* Costume designer, Regional theatre companies: The Guthrie Theatre, The Long Wharf Theatre, The Williamstown Theatre Festival, The Berkshire Theatre Festival, Syracuse Stage, Cincinnati Playhouse in the Park, The La Jolla Playhouse, The McCarter Theatre, Philadelphia Drama Guild, Arena Stage, Washington, DC. In New York City, she has designed costumes for the Manhattan Theatre Club and over thirty productions for the Circle Repertory Company.

FIRST TELEVISION WORK—Costume design, ''The Mound Builders,'' *Theatre in America,* PBS, 1975. PRINCIPAL TELEVISION WORK—Dramatic Specials: Costume designer—*Looking Back: Edith Wharton,* PBS; *For Colored Girls Who Have Considered Suicide When the Rainbow Is Enuf,* PBS; *The Phantom of the Open Hearth,* PBS; *Elizabeth Cady Stanton in Kansas,* PBS; *Under This Sky,* PBS; *Uncommon Women and Others,* PBS; *Guests of the Nation,* PBS; *The Man That Corrupted Hadleyburg,* PBS; *The Wide Net,* PBS; *The Adventures of Huckleberry Finn,* PBS; *Kennedy's Children,* CBS Cable. Episodic: ''The Open Window,'' *Tales of the Unexpected,* syndication. Movies: *Sunshine's on the Way,* NBC; *The Electric Grandmother,* NBC; *The News in the News,* NBC; *Kingdom Chums,* ABC.

MEMBER: United Scenic Artists Local 829, Circle Repertory Company, Theatre Communications Group (board of directors).

ADDRESSES: HOME—265 W. 254th Street, Riverdale, NY 10471. OFFICE—169 W. 76th Street, Suite 1R, New York, NY 10023. AGENT—c/o George Lane, William Morris Agency, 1350 Avenue of the Americas, New York, NY 10019.

WALLIS, Hal   1898-1986

PERSONAL: Full name, Hal Brent Wallis; born September 14, 1898, in Chicago, IL; died after a long illness in Rancho Mirage, CA, October 5, 1986; son of Jacob and Eva (Blum) Wallis; married Louise Fazenda (an actress), November 24, 1927 (died, 1962); married Martha Hyer (an actress), 1969; children: Hal Brent. EDUCATION: Attended Gregg Business School, 1913.

VOCATION: Film publicist and producer.

CAREER: FIRST FILM WORK—Assistant publicist, then publicist, Warner Brothers, 1923. PRINCIPAL FILM WORK—Publicist, *The Mine with the Iron Door*, Principal Pictures Corporation, 1924; publicist, *Don Juan*, Warner Brothers, 1926; studio manager, then production manager, *The Jazz Singer*, First National (a Warner Brothers subsidiary), 1927.

Producer, Warner Brothers: *Little Caesar*, 1930; *Five Star Final*, 1931; *I Am a Fugitive from a Chain Gang*, 1932; *The World Changes* and *Gold Diggers of 1933*, both 1933; *Flirtation Walk*, 1934; *Captain Blood, Sweet Adeline, A Midsummer Night's Dream, The Story of Louis Pasteur*, and *G Men*, all 1935; *The Charge of the Light Brigade*, 1936; *Stolen Holiday, Green Light, Kid Galahad, The Life of Emile Zola, Confession*, and *Tovarich*, all 1937; *The Adventures of Robin Hood, The Dawn Patrol*, and *The Sisters*, all 1938; *They Made Me a Criminal, Juarez, Daughters Courageous, The Roaring Twenties, The Private Lives of Elizabeth and Essex, We Are Not Alone*, and *The Old Maid*, all 1939; *The Story of Dr. Ehrlich's Magic Bullet, All This, and Heaven Too, The Sea Hawk, They Drive by Night, A Dispatch from Reuters*, and *The Letter*, all 1940; *The Great Lie, The Sea Wolf, The Strawberry Blond, Manpower, The Bride Came C.O.D., Sergeant York, The Maltese Falcon, They Died with Their Boots On*, and *High Sierra*, all 1941; *King's Row, The Male Animal*, and *Desperate Journey*, all 1942; *Yankee Doodle Dandy, Casablanca, Air Force*, and *Watch on the Rhine*, all 1943; *Passage to Marseilles*, 1944; *Love Letters* and *You Came Along*, both 1945; *Saratoga Trunk, The Searching Wind*, and *The Strange Love of Martha Ivers*, all 1946; *I Walk Alone*, 1947.

As producer, at Paramount: *Sorry, Wrong Number*, 1948; *The Accused, My Friend Irma*, and *Rope of Sand*, all 1949; *Paid in Full, The Furies*, and *Dark City*, all 1950; *September Affair, Peking Express*, and *Red Mountain*, all 1951; *Come Back, Little Sheba* and *Scared Stiff*, both 1953; *About Mrs. Leslie*, 1954; *The Rose Tattoo* and *Artists and Models*, both 1955; *Hollywood or Bust* and *The Rainmaker*, both 1956; *Gunfight at the O.K. Corral* and *Loving You*, both 1957; *Last Train from Gun Hill*, 1958; *Wild Is the Wind, Sad Sack, Don't Give Up the Ship*, and *Hot Spell*, all 1959.

Continuing as producer, through Paramount, except where noted

otherwise: *G.I. Blues, King Creole, Visit to a Small Planet*, and *All in a Night's Work*, all 1960; *Blue Hawaii* and *Summer and Smoke*, both 1961; *A Girl Named Tamiko* and *Girls! Girls! Girls!*, both 1962; *Wives and Lovers* and *Fun in Acapulco*, both 1963; *Becket*, 1964; *Roustabout, Wives and Lovers, Boeing Boeing, The Sons of Katie Elder*, and *Easy Come, Easy Go*, all 1965; *Barefoot in the Park* and *Five Card Stud*, both 1966; *Anne of the Thousand Days*, Universal, 1969; *True Grit*, 1969; *Norwood*, 1970; *Mary Queen of Scots* and *Shootout*, both Universal, 1971; *The Public Eye* and *The Nelson Affair*, both Universal, 1972; *Bequest to the Nation* and *The Don Is Dead*, both Universal, 1973; *Rooster Cogburn*, Universal, 1975.

RELATED CAREER—Manager, Garrick Theatre, Los Angeles, 1922-23; publicity manager, Warner Brothers, 1923-26; executive producer in charge of production, Warner Brothers, 1926-1944; with Joseph H. Hazen, founder and partner, Hal Wallis Productions, 1944-53; independent film producer, Hal Wallis, Inc., 1953-86.

NON-RELATED CAREER—Office boy, Cobe & McKinnon, Chicago, 1912; assistant sales and advertising manager, Edison General Electric Company, Chicago, 1916-22.

AWARDS: Best Production, two Irving G. Thalberg Awards, 1938 and 1943.

MEMBER: Masons (thirty-second degree), Shriners.

SIDELIGHTS: Of his four hundred films, one hundred-thirty earned Academy Awards nominations, and thirty-two won Oscars.

In its obituary notice of October 7, 1986, *Variety* quoted Hal Wallis on his success: "I have been a pretty lucky fellow. On the whole, my career is a testimonial to the basic generosity of the human race. Throughout life, I've had the good fortune of knowing people who were ready to give a man a boost up the ladder."*

*   *   *

WALTON, Tony   1934-

PERSONAL: Full name, Anthony John Walton; born October 24, 1934, in Walton-on-Thames, Surrey, England; son of Lancelot Henry Frederick (an orthopedic surgeon) and Hilda Betty (Drew) Walton; married Julie Andrews (a singer and actress), May 10, 1959 (divorced, 1967); children: Emma, Kate. EDUCATION: Attended the Radley College, 1948-52; Oxford School of Technolo-

TONY WALTON

gy, Art and Commerce, 1949-52; Slade School of Fine Arts, 1954-55. MILITARY: Served with the Royal Air Force, 1952-54.

VOCATION: Designer and producer.

CAREER: FIRST STAGE WORK—Designer for Peter Haddon's Company at Wimbledon Theatre, 1955-56. PRINCIPAL STAGE WORK—Designer, *Conversation Piece,* Barbizon-Plaza Theatre, New York City, 1957. Designer of sets and costumes: *Valmouth,* Lyric Theatre, Hammersmith, London, 1958, then York Theatre, New York City, 1960; *Fool's Paradise,* London, 1959; sets only, *The Pleasure of His Company,* London, 1959; *The Ginger Man,* Fortune Theatre, London, 1959; *Pieces of Eight,* Apollo Theatre, London, 1959; *Most Happy Fella,* Coliseum Theatre, London, 1960; *One Over the Eight,* Duke of York's Theatre, London, 1961; *A Wreath for Udomo,* Lyric Theatre, Hammersmith, London, 1961; *Once There Was a Russian,* Music Box Theatre, New York City, 1961; *A Funny Thing Happened on the Way to the Forum,* Alvin Theatre, New York City, 1962, then Strand Theatre, London, 1963; *Cindy-Ella,* Garrick Theatre, London, 1962; *The Love of Three Oranges,* Sadler's Wells Opera Company, U.K., 1963; *The Rape of Lucretia,* Edinburgh Festival, Scotland, then King's Theatre, London, 1963; *Caligula,* Phoenix Theatre, London, 1964; *Golden Boy,* Majestic Theatre, New York City, 1964, then later at the Palladium Theatre, London, 1968; costumes only, *The Rehearsal,* New York City production, 1964; *Otello,* Spoleto Festival, Teatro Nuovo, Italy, 1965; *The Apple Tree,* Shubert Theatre, New York City, 1966; opera, *Midsummer Marriage,* Royal Opera House, Covent Garden, London, 1968; triple bill, *In His Own Write, A Most Unwarrantable Intrusion,* and *The Covent Garden*

Tragedy, National Theatre, London, 1968; *The Travails of Sancho Panza,* National Theatre, London, 1969.

Continuing as set and costume designer: *Pippin,* Imperial Theatre, New York City, 1972, then Her Majesty's Theatre, London, 1973; *Once Upon a Time,* Duke of York's Theatre, London, 1972; *Uncle Vanya,* Circle in the Square, New York City, 1973; *Shelter,* John Golden Theatre, New York City, 1973; *The Good Doctor,* Eugene O'Neill Theatre, New York City, 1974; *Bette Midler's Clams on the Half Shell Revue,* Minskoff Theatre, New York City, 1975; sets only, *Chicago,* 46th Street Theatre, New York City, 1975; opera, *The Cunning Little Vixen,* Santa Fe Opera Festival, NM, 1975; sets only, *Streamers,* Mitzi E. Newhouse Theatre, Lincoln Center, New York City, 1977; sets only, *The Act,* Majestic Theatre, New York City, 1977; *Drinks Before Dinner,* Public Theatre, New York Shakespeare Festival, New York City, 1978; *Double Feature,* Long Wharf Theatre, New Haven, CT, 1979; sets only, *A Day in Hollywood/A Night in the Ukraine,* John Golden Theatre, New York City, 1980; sets only, *Hoagy, Bix and Wolfgang Beethoven Bunkhouse,* Mark Taper Forum, Los Angeles, 1981; sets only, *Sophisticated Ladies,* Lunt-Fontanne Theatre, New York City, 1981; sets only, *Woman of the Year,* Palace Theatre, New York City, 1981; *Little Me,* Eugene O'Neill Theatre, New York City, 1982, then produced in London, 1984; sets only, *The Real Thing,* Plymouth Theatre, New York City, 1984; sets only, *Hurlyburly,* Ethel Barrymore Theatre, New York City, 1984; visual consultant, *Whoopie Goldberg,* Lyceum Theatre, New York City, 1984; sets only, *Leader of the Pack,* New York City, 1985; sets only, *I'm Not Rappaport,* Booth Theatre, New York City, 1985; sets only, *Social Security,* Ethel Barrymore Theatre, New York City, 1986; sets only, *House of Blue Leaves,* Vivian Beaumont Theatre, Lincoln Center, New York City, 1986; sets only, *The Front Page,* Vivian Beaumont Theatre, New York City, 1986.

Ballet: Designer for the San Francisco Ballet: *Harp Concerto,* 1973, *Mother Blues,* 1974, *The Tempest,* 1980, *Stravinsky Piano Pieces,* 1982, *To the Beatles,* 1984, *King Lear,* 1985, and *Hearts,* 1986.

Producer: *The Ginger Man,* Fortune Theatre, London, 1959; co-producer, *New Cranks,* Lyric Theatre, Hammersmith, London, 1960; co-producer, *She Loves Me,* Lyric Theatre, London, 1964.

PRINCIPAL FILM WORK—Costume and production designer: (consultant only) *Mary Poppins,* Buena Vista Productions, 1964; *A Funny Thing Happened on the Way to the Forum,* United Artists, 1965; *Farenheit 451,* MCA/Universal, 1966; *Petulia,* Warner Brothers, 1967; *The Seagull,* Warner Brothers, 1968; *The Boy Friend,* EMI-Metro-Goldwyn-Mayer, 1971; *Murder on the Orient Express,* Paramount-EMI, 1974; *Equus,* United Artists, 1977; *The Wiz,* Universal, 1978; *Just Tell Me What You Want,* Warner Brothers, 1979; (design consultant and fantasy director) *All That Jazz,* Twentieth Century-Fox-Columbia Pictures, 1979; *Prince of the City,* Warner Brothers-Orion Pictures, 1980; *Star 80,* Ladd Company/ Warner Brothers, 1982; *The Goodbye People,* Embassy, 1984; *Death of a Salesman,* Roxbury and Punch Productions, 1985; *Heartburn,* Paramount, 1986; *The Glass Menagerie,* Cineplex, 1987.

PRINCIPAL TELEVISION WORK—Series: Designer, *The Julie Andrews Show,* BBC, 1959. Specials: Designer—*Free to Be. . .You and Me,* NBC, 1976; Diana Ross's New York Central Park Concert, *For One and For All,* 1983; *Whoopi Goldberg Live,* HBO, 1985; *Death of a Salesman,* CBS, 1985.

RELATED CAREER—Book illustrator: *Peacocks and Avarice*, by Joyce Warren, Harper & Row, 1957; *Cindy-Ella*, by Caryl Brahms and Ned Sherrin, W. H. Allen, 1962; *God Is a Good Friend to Have* (children's quotes), Simon and Schuster, 1969; *Witches Holiday*, by Alice Low, Pantheon, 1971; *The Importance of Being Earnest* and *Lady Windemere's Fan*, Limited Editions Club, 1973; *Wonders*, Summit Books/Simon and Schuster, 1980.

Continuing as illustrator, for periodicals: *Playbill*, 1957, *The Reporter*, 1956-57; *Theatre Arts*, 1956-57; *Harpers*, 1956-57; *Vogue*, 1956-57; *The Observer*, 1958.

Exhibitions: Museum of the City of New York; Queens Museum; Museum of the Moving Image, Lincoln Center; The New York Circulation Library of Paintings; The Hazlitt Gallery, London; The Wright-Hepburn Gallery, London and New York; The Gallery at the Watermill Museum.

AWARDS: Outstanding Achievement in Costume Design, Academy Award nomination, 1964, for *Mary Poppins;* Best Costume Design, Antoinette Perry Award nomination, 1966-67, for *The Apple Tree;* Best Scenic Design, Antoinette Perry Award, 1972-73, for *Pippin;* Best Scenic Design, Drama Desk Awards, 1972, for both *Pippin* and *Shelter;* Outstanding Achievement in Costume Design, Academy Award nomination, Best Art Direction and Best Costume Design, two Society of Film and Television Arts nominations, all 1974, for *Murder on the Orient Express;* Most Outstanding Feature Film Title Sequence, Designers and Art Directors Association Silver Award, 1975, for *Murder on the Orient Express;* Best Scenic Design, Antoinette Perry Award nomination, 1975-76, for *Chicago;* Outstanding Costume Design and Outstanding Achievement in Art Direction, two Academy Award nominations, Best Costume Design, Academy of Science Fiction, Fantasy and Horror Films nomination, all 1978, for *The Wiz;* Best Art Direction, All American Press Award, 1979, for *The Wiz.*

Best Scenic Design, Antoinette Perry Award nomination and Drama Desk Award nomination, both 1980, for *A Day in Hollywood/A Night in the Ukraine;* co-winner, Best Art Direction, Academy Award, 1980, for *All That Jazz;* Best Broadway Poster award, New York *Daily News*, 1981, for *Sophisticated Ladies;* Best Scenic Design, Antoinette Perry Award nomination and Drama Desk Award nomination, both 1984, for *The Real Thing;* co-winner, Outstanding Achievement in Set Design, Bay Area Theatre Critics Circle Award, 1985, for *My One and Only;* Outstanding Set Design, Drama Desk Awards, 1985-86, for both *The House of Blue Leaves* and *Social Security;* Best Scenic Design, American Theatre Wing Award and Antoinette Perry Award nomination, both 1985-86, for *House of Blue Leaves;* Best Art Direction, Emmy Award, 1985-86, for *Death of a Salesman.*

MEMBER: United Scenic Artists.

SIDELIGHTS: RECREATIONS—Painting, photography, music, films, and writing.

ADDRESSES: AGENT—c/o Paul Martino, International Creative Management, 40 W. 57th Street, New York, NY 10019.

*   *   *

WALZ, Ken   1942-

PERSONAL: Born April 29, 1942; son of Chester S. and Graye V. Walz; married Joan VanderVeen Dunn (divorced); children: Bryan. EDUCATION: Hope College, B.A., 1966.

VOCATION: Producer.

CAREER: PRINCIPAL TELEVISION APPEARANCES—Guest: *People Are Talking*, Boston; *Moneyline*, cable; *Entertainment Tonight*, syndicated; MTV (Music Television), cable.

PRINCIPAL TELEVISION WORK—Producer: Documentaries for ABC and PBS.

VIDEOS—Produced over one-hundred videos for such performers as Cyndi Lauper, Huey Lewis, Billy Joel, Bette Midler, the Oak Ridge Boys, Run-DMC, and Bruce Springsteen.

RELATED CAREER—Account executive: Foote, Cone and Belding; Ogilvy and Mather; Ted Bates Advertising; president, Ken Walz Productions; panelist: New School, School of Visual Arts, Billboard Convention, Chicago Music Expo, Production East, and the Kodak Professional Forum.

AWARDS: Won sixteen major awards and thirty-six award nominations, including: Gold Medal Award, International Film and Television Festival of New York, 1972, 1981, 1984; Grand Prize Award, International Film and Television Festival of New York, for *Girls Just Want to Have Fun* and *Time After Time; Billboard* awards, 1984; MTV Awards, 1984; American Music Awards, 1985; American Video Awards, 1985.

ADDRESSES: HOME—New York, NY. OFFICE—219 E. 60th Street, New York, NY 10022. AGENT—c/o Steven Starr, William

KEN WALZ

Photography by Arnie Adler/AD AGE

Morris Agency, 1350 Avenue of the Americas, New York, NY 10019.

*   *   *

WARD, Douglas Turner   1930- (Douglas Turner)

PERSONAL: Born May 5, 1930, in Burnside, LA; son of Roosevelt and Dorothy (Short) Ward; married Diana Powell. EDUCATION: Attended Wilberforce University and the University of Michigan; trained for the stage with Paul Mann.

VOCATION: Producer, director, actor, and writer.

CAREER: BROADWAY DEBUT—Joe Mott, *The Iceman Cometh,* Circle in the Square, 1957. PRINCIPAL STAGE WORK—(Appeared under the name of Douglas Turner until 1972; thereafter, used his full name.) Matthew Kumalo, *Lost in the Stars,* City Center, New York City, 1958; Moving Man, understudy Walter Younger, and Bobo, *A Raisin in the Sun,* Ethel Barrymore Theatre, New York City, 1959.

Archibald Wellington, *The Blacks,* St. Mark's Playhouse, New York City, 1961-62; a porter, *Pullman Car Hiawatha,* Circle in the Square, New York City, 1962; understudy Fredericks, *One Flew Over the Cuckoo's Nest,* Cort Theatre, New York City, 1963; Zachariah Pieterson, *The Blood Knot,* Cricket Theatre, New York City, 1964; Fitzroy, *Rich Little Rich Girl,* Walnut Street Theatre, Philadelphia, 1964; roman citizen, *Coriolanus,* New York Shakespeare Festival, Delacorte Theatre, New York City, 1965; Arthur, *Happy Ending* and Mayor and Clan, *Day of Absence,* St. Mark's Playhouse, New York City, 1965.

With the Negro Ensemble Company at the St. Mark's Playhouse, New York City, except where indicated otherwise: Oba Danlola, *Kongi's Harvest,* Thomas, *Daddy Goodness,* both 1968; Russell B. Parker, *Ceremonies in Dark Old Men,* 1969; Black Man, *The Harangues,* 1970; title role, *Frederick Douglas. . . Through His Own Words,* 1972; Johnny Williams, *The River Niger,* 1972, reopened at the Brooks Atkinson Theatre, New York City, 1973; repeated role of Russell B. Parker, *Ceremonies in Dark Old Men,* Walnut Street Theatre, Philadelphia, 1973; repeated role of Johnny Williams, *The River Niger,* New Locust Theatre, Philadelphia, PA, Harper Edwards, *The First Breeze of Summer,* 1975; Mingo Saunders, *The Brownsville Raid,* 1976; Bob Tyrone, *The Offering,* 1977; Jack Hamilton, *Old Phantoms,* 1979; Flick Lacey, *The Michigan,* 1979. Also appeared as Scar, *The Reckoning* (not a Negro Ensemble Company production), St. Mark's Playhouse, New York City, 1969.

Director, with the Negro Ensemble Company at the St. Mark's Playhouse, New York City, except where indicated otherwise: *Daddy Goodness,* 1968; *Contribution, Man Better Man, Brotherhood,* and *Day of Absence,* all 1969; *Perry's Mission* and *Ride a Black Horse,* both 1971; *A Ballet Behind the Bridge,* 1972; *The River Niger,* later reopened at the Brooks Atkinson Theatre, New York City, 1972-73, then opened at the New Locust Theatre, Philadelphia, 1973; *The Great MacDaddy, Black Sunlight,* and *Nowhere to Run, Nowhere to Hide,* all 1974; *The First Breeze of Summer* and *Waiting for Mongo,* both 1975; *Livin' Fat,* 1976; *The Great MacDaddy,* 1977; *The Offering* and *Black Body Blues,* both

1978; *Nevis Mountain Dew, A Season to Unravel, Old Phantoms,* and *Home,* all 1979.

Director, with the Negro Ensemble Company at Theatre Four, New York City: *Zooman and the Sign, Weep Not for Me,* and *Home,* all 1980; *A Soldier's Play,* 1981; *Manhattan Made Me* and *About Heaven and Earth,* both 1983; *District Line* and *Ceremonies in Dark Old Men,* both 1984.

Producer, *Song of the Lusitanian Bogey* and *God Is a (Guess What?),* with the Negro Ensemble Company, Aldwych Theatre, London, 1969.

As artistic director, with the Negro Ensemble Company, St. Mark's Playhouse, New York City: *Summer of the Seventeenth Doll, Kongi's Harvest,* and *Daddy Goodness,* all 1968; *God Is a (Guess What?),* 1968; *Man Better Man,* 1969; *The Harangues, Asura, Brotherhood, Day of Absence, Akokawe,* and *Ododo,* all 1970; *Rosalee Pritchett,* 1971; *The Great MacDaddy, Black Sunlight,* and *Nowhere to Run, Nowhere to Hide, Terraces, Heaven and Hell's Agreement,* and *In the Deepest Part of Sleep,* all 1974; *Eden* and *Livin' Fat,* both 1976; *The Twilight Dinner,* 1978; *Nevis Mountain Dew, A Season to Unravel, Old Phantoms,* and *The Michigan,* all 1979; *Home,* 1979, later moved to the Cort Theatre, New York City, 1980.

As artistic director, with the Negro Ensemble Company, at Theatre Four, New York City, except where indicated otherwise: *The Sixteenth Round, In an Upstate Motel, Zooman and the Sign,* and *Weep Not for Me,* all 1980; *The Rover* and *The Menaechmi,* both 1981; *Colored People's Time,* at the Cherry Lane Theatre, New York City, 1981; *Sons and Fathers of Sons,* 1982; *Abercrombie Apocalypse,* at the Cheryl Crawford Theatre, New York City, 1982; *About Heaven and Earth, Puppetplay,* and *Manhattan Made Me,* all 1983; *American Dreams, Split Second,* and *District Line,* all 1984; *Ceremonies in Dark Old Men,* Ford's Theatre, Washington, DC, 1984, then Theatre Four, 1985; *Henrietta* and *Two Can Play,* and *Ceremonies in Dark Old Men,* all 1985.

MAJOR TOURS—Understudy for Walter Younger and Bobo, succeeding to part of Walter Younger, *A Raisin in the Sun,* U.S. cities, 1960-61. As director and artistic director for the Negro Ensemble Company, *A Soldier's Play,* U.S. cities, 1980-85.

PRINCIPAL FILM APPEARANCES—*Man and Boy,* Levitt-Pickman, 1972.

TELEVISION DEBUT—1958. PRINCIPAL TELEVISION APPEARANCES—Episodic: *Studio One,* CBS; *East Side West Side,* CBS. Specials: Russell B. Parker, *Ceremonies in Dark Old Men,* PBS, 1975; director, and appeared in *The First Breeze of Summer,* 1976.

RELATED CAREER—Co-founder and artistic director, Negro Ensemble Company, New York City, 1967—.

WRITINGS: PLAYS, PRODUCED—*Day of Absence* and *Happy Ending* both at the St. Mark's Playhouse, New York City, 1965; *The Reckoning,* St. Mark's Playhouse, New York City, 1969; plays produced by the Negro Ensemble Company: *Brotherhood,* (produced on a double bill with a revival of *Days of Absence*) St. Mark's Playhouse, New York City, 1970; *The Harangues,* St. Mark's Playhouse, New York City, 1970; *River Niger,* St. Mark's Playhouse, New York City, 1972, then at the Brooks Atkinson Theatre, New York City, 1973, then at the New Locust Theatre, Philadelphia, 1973; *The Brownsville Raid* and *The Offering,* both at the St.

Mark's Playhouse, New York City, 1977; (contributor) *Holidays,* Actors Theatre of Louisville, KY, 1979; "The Redeemer" (one-act, produced in a series of one-acts with the overall title, *About Heaven and Earth*), Theatre Four, New York City, 1983.

PLAYS, PUBLISHED—*Happy Ending* (and) *Day of Absence,* Dramatists Play Service, 1966; *The Reckoning,* Dramatists Play Service, 1970; *Brotherhood,* Dramatists Play Service, 1970; *Two Plays,* Third Press, 1975.

Also represented in anthologies, including *New Black Playwrights,* edited by William Couch, Jr., Louisiana State University Press, 1968; *Black Drama,* edited by William Brasmer and Dominick Consolo, Merrill, 1970; *Contemporary Black Drama,* edited by Clinton Oliver and Stephanie Sills, Scribner & Sons, 1971; *Afro-American Literature,* edited by Robert Hayden, David Burrows, and Frederick Lapides, Harcourt, 1971; *Blackamerican Literature,* edited by Ruth Miller, Free Press, 1971.

AWARDS: Obie Award, 1966, Lambda Kappy Nu citation, 1968, special Antoinette Perry Award and Brandeis University Creative Arts Award, both 1969, all for *Happy Ending;* Best Play, Vernon Rice Drama Desk Award, 1966, for *Day of Absence* and *Happy Ending;* Obie Award, 1973, for *The River Niger;* Best Supporting Actor, Antoinette Perry Award nomination, 1974, for *The River Niger;* co-recipient (with the Negro Ensemble Company), Margo Jones Award, 1973, for contributing to the theatre by producing new plays on a continuing basis.

ADDRESSES: OFFICE—c/o Negro Ensemble Company, 165 W. 46th Street, New York, NY 10036.*

*   *   *

WARD, Jonathan   1970-

PERSONAL: Born February 24, 1970, in Towson, MD; son of John T. (an attorney) and Billye Ward. EDUCATION: Buckley School, Sherman Oaks, CA, 1987.

VOCATION: Actor.

CAREER: STAGE DEBUT—Chorus, orphan, and pickpocket, *Oliver!,* BurnBrae Dinner Theatre, MD, 1979. BROADWAY DEBUT—Michael Darling, *Peter Pan,* Lunt-Fontanne Theatre, 1980, for two years. PRINCIPAL STAGE APPEARANCES—Patrick Dennis, *Mame,* Northstage Theatre, Long Island, NY, 1983; McDuff's son, *Macbeth,* Vivian Beaumont Theatre, Lincoln Center, New York City; Huck, *Huck and Jim on the Mississippi,* Florida Atlantic University.

MAJOR TOURS—Michael Darling, *Peter Pan,* Kennedy Center, Washington, DC, Dallas Music Hall, and Theatre of the Stars, Atlanta.

TELEVISION DEBUT—Jaimie, *Boomer,* NBC, 1981. PRINCIPAL TELEVISION APPEARANCES—Series: Douglas Pembroke, *Charles in Charge,* CBS, 1984—. Movies: *Maid in America,* CBS, 1982; Ben Skinner, *The Great Skinner Strike,* ABC, 1984; Kevin Kennedy, *Heart of the City,* ABC, 1986; title role, *Beans Baxter,* Fox Broadcasting Corporation (FBC), 1987; also: Washington Irving, *Robbers, Rooftops, and Riches,* CBS; Oliver, *Orphans, Waifs, and Wards,* CBS; Junior, *Haunted Mansion Mystery,* ABC; Danny, *Just Another Stupid Kid,* NBC.

JONATHAN WARD

PRINCIPAL FILM APPEARANCES—Mitch, *Rites of Summer,* Columbia, 1985.

MEMBER: Actors and Others for Animals, Greenpeace, Society for the Prevention of Cruelty to Animals.

ADDRESSES: HOME—Studio City, CA. AGENT—The Agency, 10351 Santa Monica Blvd., Los Angeles, CA 90025.

*   *   *

WARFIELD, Joe   1937-

PERSONAL: Full name, Joseph A. Warfield; born November 6, 1937, in Baltimore, MD; son of Alton M. and Hilda L. (Clay) Warfield. EDUCATION: University of Maryland, B.A., 1959; trained for the stage at the Herbert Berghof Studio.

VOCATION: Actor.

CAREER: STAGE DEBUT—Johnny, *My Heart's in the Highlands,* Greenwood Theatre, Baltimore, MD, 1954. OFF-BROADWAY DEBUT—Tex, *Little Mary Sunshine,* Orpheum Theatre, 1959. LONDON DEBUT—Jimmy Currie, *110 in the Shade,* Palace Theatre, 1965. PRINCIPAL STAGE APPEARANCES—First Man, *Jimmy Shine,* Broadway production; the Doctor, *Baby,* Ethel Barrymore Theatre, New York City; Will, *Oklahoma!,* Dallas Musical Theatre, TX; Felix, *The Owl and the Pussycat,* Golden Apple Theatre, FL; Nestor, *Irma La Douce,* Lambertville, NJ; Brad, *The Coldest War of All,* Olney Theatre, MD; various roles, *Ribald Tales,* Story Theatre, Los Angeles; Harvey, *Scandalous Memories,* Mark Taper

JOE WARFIELD

Forum Lab Theatre, Los Angeles; Alfred, *The American Nightmare,* Los Angeles; Papa, *High Button Shoes,* Goodspeed Opera House, East Haddam, CT; Alan, *Baby,* Kenley Players, Akron, OH; Joey, *Oh Say, Can You See,* Off-Broadway production.

FILM DEBUT—Arnold, *That Darn Cat,* Buena Vista, 1965. PRINCIPAL FILM APPEARANCES—Murdoch, *Nickelodeon,* Columbia, 1976; campaign manager, *The Big Fix,* Universal, 1979; also Billy, *The Real Thing;* executive, *Tunnelvision;* various roles, *Jokes My Folks Never Told Me.*

PRINCIPAL TELEVISION APPEARANCES—Episodic: *Columbo,* NBC; *The Mary Tyler Moore Show,* CBS; *Quincy, M.E.,* NBC; *Cannon,* CBS; *Shaft,* CBS; *Marcus Welby, M.D.,* ABC; *The Bob Newhart Show,* CBS; *All My Children; Ryan's Hope; Search for Tomorrow; As the World Turns.* Movies: *Green Eyes,* 1976; *Little Ladies of the Night,* 1977; *Alexander: The Other Side of Dawn,* 1977; *Katherine,* 1979. Specials: *Comedy in America Report.*

MEMBER: Actors' Equity Association, Screen Actors Guild, American Federation of Television and Radio Artists.

ADDRESSES: AGENT—Beverly Chase Management, 162 W. 54th Street, New York, NY 10019.

* * *

WEAKLAND, Kevin L.   1963-

PERSONAL: Born August 14, 1963, in Philadelphia, PA; son of George Walker (a real estate broker) and Helyn Theresa (an accountant; maiden name, Slawecki) Weakland. EDUCATION: Holy Family College, Philadelphia, B.A., international business, 1986. POLITICS: Republican. RELIGION: Roman Catholic.

VOCATION: Entertainment and financial writer.

WRITINGS: ARTICLES—In *Millimeter Magazine, Hollywood Reporter, Billboard, The Wall Street Journal.*

AWARDS: Millimeter Production Buyers Guide Award, 1986.

MEMBER: Association of Independent Video and Filmmakers, National Academy of Video Arts and Sciences, Atlantic States Arts Consortium, National Music Publishers Association.

ADDRESSES: HOME—408 Kathleen Avenue, Cinnaminson, NJ 08077. OFFICE—Lancaster Park & Louisville Road, Hockessin, DE 19707.

* * *

WEATHERS, Philip   1908-
(Michael Sherwood)

PERSONAL: Born November 4, 1908; son of Joesph (a journalist) and Kate Ethel (Nash) Weathers. EDUCATION: Attended Trinty Hall, Cambridge and King's College, London; studied privately with Lena Ashwell. RELIGION: Roman Catholic. MILITARY: British Army, 1940-46.

PHILIP WEATHERS

VOCATION: Actor, director, and writer.

CAREER: STAGE DEBUT—Assistant stage manager and a small role, *The Adventures of Lady Ursula,* Twentieth Century Theatre, London, 1923. PRINCIPAL STAGE APPEARANCES—*Nurse Cavell,* Vaudeville Theatre, London, 1930; understudy, *Cavalcade,* Drury Lane Theatre, London, 1931; one year in repertory at Oxford, Sheffield, York, and Bradford.

PRINCIPAL STAGE WORK—Director: Malvern Festival, England, 1940 (the outbreak of World War II canceled productions at Malvern, but reduced scale productions continued at Arts Theatre, Cambridge, Theatre Royal, Bath, and Theatre Royal, Exeter, U.K.); Theatre Royal, Aldershot, U.K., 1946; Empire Theatre, Swansea, U.K., 1948; Palace Court Theatre, Bournemouth, U.K., 1948; Richmond Theatre, U.K., 1951; Grand Theatre, Swansea, 1952.

Producer, Holiday Shows, Blackpool, Bournemouth, and Torquay, U.K., 1954.

MAJOR TOURS—Lord Fancourt Babberly, *Charley's Aunt,* U.K cities, 1928-30; Ledyard Draper, *The Ninth Man,* U.K. cities, 1930; as a member of Matheson Lang's company, U.K. cities, 1931-33; as a member of Sir John Martin-Harvey's company, U.K. cities, 1934-36.

PRINCIPAL FILM APPEARANCES—*Tell England,* London Films; *City of Song,* in English, French and German.

NON-RELATED CAREER—Personal representative of His Grace the Duke of Northumberland at Syon House, organizing the opening of the house to the public, writing guide books, receiving important visitors, training staff in eighteenth century furniture, painting, and decoration.

WRITINGS: PLAYS, PRODUCED AND PUBLISHED—(All under pen name Michael Sherwood), Experimental theatre productions: *The Weary Heart,* 1936; *Thy Self the Dagger,* 1937; *His Lips Are Not for You to Kiss,* 1938; *Arms and the Woman,* 1947; *Madam Tic-Tac,* published by Samuel French, 1951; *Tell-Tale Murder,* Samuel French, 1952; *Shadow Witness,* Samuel French, 1953; *Proof of the Poison,* Samuel French, 1955; *This Is My Life,* Samuel French, 1957; *Murder Isn't Cricket,* Samuel French, 1959; *Once Upon a Crime,* published by Panopolis Ltd., 1961; *Sometimes It Strikes,* Panopolis Ltd., 1963; *Permit to Kill,* Panopolis Ltd., 1968; *Home or Away?,* Panopolis Ltd., 1969; *Three Shots in the Dark,* Panopolis Ltd., 1970; *O Mistress Mine,* Panopolis Ltd., 1977.

BOOKS—*Syon House,* Clarke and Sherwell, 1968; *Nuns of Syon,* Coates Press, 1975.

MEMBER: British Actors' Equity Association; English Speaking Union.

SIDELIGHTS: Philip Weathers told *CTFT:* "When a child, several of our neighbors were famous stars of silent films. Frequently they would ask my parents if they could take me to the studio to appear in shots requiring children. This played a great part in deciding me to become an actor, although strangely enough I hated working in the early days of the 'talkies' and decided they weren't for me."

ADDRESSES: HOME—Charterhouse, London EC1M 6AN, England. AGENT—Eric Glass Ltd., 18 Berkeley Square, London W1X 6HD, England.

WEBB, Lucy

BRIEF ENTRY: Actress and comedienne. Before she began her career in comedy acting, Lucy Webb was employed as an intern on Washington's Capitol Hill by then-Tennessee Congressman Albert Gore. Ironically, since 1983, Webb has been a regular cast member of the Home Box Office series *Not Necessarily the News,* a show that frequently pokes fun at politicians, "I hear that politicians find the show extremely funny," she said in *The Cable Guide* (April, 1987). The Home Box Office show has been quite popular, spawning several specials, including *Not Necessarily the Year in Review* and *Not Necessarily Television.* Network television audiences have seen Webb's work as Pvt. Luanne Hubble, on the CBS comedy series *Private Benjamin,* and in the movie, *A Few Days at Weasle Creek.* In 1981, Webb also performed in the werewolf comedy *Full Moon High.**

*   *   *

WEISBARTH, Michael L.

PERSONAL: EDUCATION: Queens College, B.A.; University of Michigan, M.A.

VOCATION: Producer.

CAREER: PRINCIPAL TELEVISION WORK—As vice president of production for Tandem Productions/T.A.T., worked on the following series: *All in the Family,* CBS; *Maude,* CBS; *Good Times,* CBS; *The Jeffersons,* CBS; *One Day at a Time,* CBS; *The Facts of Life,* NBC; *Hello, Larry,* NBC; *Highcliff Manor,* NBC; *Archie Bunker's Place,* CBS; *Sanford and Son,* NBC; *What's Happening!!,* ABC; *Joe's World,* NBC; *All's Fair,* CBS; *The Nancy Walker Show,* ABC; *Carter Country,* ABC; *Square Pegs,* CBS; *Silver Spoons,* NBC; *Gloria,* CBS; *Apple Pie,* ABC; *In the Beginning,* CBS; *Palmerstown, U.S.A.,* CBS; *Mary Hartman, Mary Hartman,* syndicated; *Fernwood Tonight,* syndicated; *The Baxters,* syndicated; *All That Glitters.*

As senior vice-president of dramatic programming at Embassy, was responsible for the following television movies: *Eleanor, First Lady of the World,* CBS, 1981; executive producer, *Grace Kelly,* ABC, 1983; *An Invasion of Privacy,* CBS, 1983; as executive vice-president of television for Motown Productions: Series—Executive producer, *Sidekicks,* ABC, 1986. Movies—Executive producer, *The Last Electric Knight,* ABC. Specials—Co-producer, *Motown Returns to the Apollo,* NBC.

RELATED CAREER—Vice president of sales, Vidtronics, 1971-76; vice president of production, executive in charge of production, and senior vice president of dramatic programming, Tandem Productions/T.A.T., now known as Embassy Television, 1976-83; executive vice president of television, Motown Productions, 1983—.

AWARDS: Emmy Award, for *Motown Returns to the Apollo.*

SIDELIGHTS: Currently, Michael Weisbarth is completing two television movies for NBC and one for CBS, in addition to a three hour movie for HBO and developing a prime time dramatic series for CBS.

ADDRESSES: OFFICE—Motown Productions, 6255 Sunset Blvd., Los Angeles, CA 90028.

JOAN WEST

WEST, Joan 1936-

PERSONAL: Full name, Genevieve G. Joan West; born May 30, 1936, in Denver, CO; daughter of Ellsworth Miles (a pharmacist) and Genevieve Louise (a court employee; maiden name, Antonio) West; married John Porfilio Moore (a U.S. Court Judge), August 1, 1959 (divorced, 1983); children: Edward Miles, Joseph Arthur, Jeanne Kathryn. EDUCATION: Attended University of Denver, 1954-56; trained for the stage at the American Academy of Dramatic Art and the Strasberg Theatre Institute with Phil Giberson, Melissa Eddy, Penny Allen, Irma Sandrey, and Monica Hayes. POLITICS: Democrat. RELIGION: Roman Catholic.

VOCATION: Actress, writer, and model.

CAREER: PRINCIPAL TELEVISION APPEARANCES—*Ryan's Hope,* ABC; *As the World Turns,* CBS; *One Life to Live,* ABC; *All My Children,* ABC. Movies: *When She Says No,* ABC, 1984. Episodic: *The Equalizer,* CBS.

PRINCIPAL FILM APPEARANCES—*The Glenn Miller Story,* Universal, 1954.

RELATED CAREER—Fashion model.

NON-RELATED CAREER—Hostess, Continental Airlines; tourguide, U.S. Park Service, New York City.

MEMBER: Actors' Equity Association, American Federation of Television and Radio Artists, Catholic Actors Guild, National

Writers Club; Pi Beta Phi Sorority, Tilden Midtown Democratic Club.

ADDRESSES: HOME—18 Gramercy Park South, New York, NY 10003.

*   *   *

WEST, Timothy 1934-

PERSONAL: Born October 20, 1934; son of Harry Lockwood and Olive (Carleton-Crowe) West; married Jacqueline Boyer, 1956 (divorced); married Prunella Scales (an actress), 1963; children: (first marriage) one daughter; (second marriage) two sons. EDUCATION: Attended John Lyon School, Harrow and Regent Street Polytechnic, England.

VOCATION: Actor and director.

CAREER: STAGE DEBUT—The farmer, *Summertime,* Wimbledon Theatre, U.K., 1956. LONDON DEBUT—Talky, *Caught Napping,* Piccadilly Theatre, 1959. PRINCIPAL STAGE APPEARANCES—In repertory at Salisbury, Hull, Wimbledon, and Northhampton, U.K., 1956-59; the informer, *The Life of Galileo,* Mermaid Theatre, London, 1960; Ginger, *Afore Night Come,* Arts Theatre, London, 1962, then with the Royal Shakespeare Company at the Aldwych Theatre, London, 1964; Hubert, *Gentle Jack,* Queen's Theatre, London, 1963; Arthur, *Trigon,* Arts Theatre, London, 1964; with the Royal Shakespeare Company at the Aldwych Theatre, London: doctor, *Victor,* schoolmaster, *Marat/Sade,* Pilia-Borza, *The Jew of Malta,* Page, *The Merry Wives of Windsor,* Sir Gilbert Boscoe, *The Governor's Lady (Expeditions Two),* all 1964; with the Royal Shakespeare Company at Stratford-on-Avon, U.K.: Sir Nathaniel, *Love's Labour's Lost,* Tubal, *The Merchant of Venice,* Pilia-Borza and Aegeon, *The Comedy of Errors,* Lord Lucius, *Timon of Athens,* all 1965; Korobkin, *The Government Inspector* and Mulka, *The Investigation,* both at the Aldwych Theatre, London, 1966; Alderman Smuggler, *The Constant Couple,* with the Prospect Theatre Company at the New Theatre, London, 1967; Emerson, *A Room with a View,* with the Prospect Theatre Company at the Edinburgh Festival, Scotland, 1967; Otto, *The Italian Girl,* Wyndham's Theatre, London, 1968.

Gilles de Vannes, *Abelard and Heloise,* Wyndham's Theatre, London, 1970; Robert Hand, *Exiles,* Mermaid Theatre, London, 1970; Gilbert, *The Critic as Artist,* Open Space Theatre, London, 1970; Sir William Gower, *Trelawny of the Wells,* Theatre Royal, Bristol, U.K., 1972; Lear and Holofernes, *Love's Labour's Lost,* Aldwych Theatre, London, 1972; Falstaff, *Henry IV,* Parts I and II, Theatre Royal, Bristol, U.K., 1972; Undershaft, *Major Barbara,* Forum Theatre, Billingham, U.K., 1973; George Penny, *The Houseboy,* Open Space Theatre, London, 1973; Shpigelsky, *A Month in the Country,* Chichester Festival, U.K., 1974; title role, *Macbeth* and George, *Jumpers,* both Gardner Centre, Brighton, U.K., 1974; Judge Brack, *Hedda Gabler,* Royal Shakespeare Company, Aldwych Theatre, London, 1975; repeated role of Shpigelsky, *A Month in the Country* and Emerson, *A Room with a View,* both with the Prospect Theatre Company at the Albery Theatre, London, 1975; Claudius, *Hamlet,* Storyteller, *War Music,* and Enobarbus, *Antony and Cleopatra,* all at the Old Vic Theatre Company, London, 1977; Ivan and Gottlieb, *Laughter!,* Royal Court Theatre, London, 1978; Max, *The Homecoming,* Garrick Theatre, London, 1978; *Great English Eccentrics,* Old Vic Theatre Company, London, 1978; *The Undisputed Monarch of the English*

Stage, Old Vic Theatre Company, London, 1979; Creeve, *The Trial of Queen Caroline,* Old Vic Theatre Company, 1979; Sir Thomas Beecham, *Beecham,* Salisbury Theatre, London, 1979, then Apollo Theatre, London, 1980; *Master Class,* Old Vic Theatre Company, 1984; *The War at Home,* Old Vic Theatre Company, 1984, New York City production, 1986.

MAJOR TOURS—Colonel Gray-Balding, *Simple Spymen,* 1961; Peterbono, *Thieves' Carnival,* Samuel Johnson, *Madam, Said Doctor Johnson,* Prospero, *The Tempest,* and Crabbe, *The Gamecock,* all with the Prospect Theatre Company, 1966; Bolingbroke, *Richard II* and Mortimer, *Edward II,* both with the Prospect Theatre Company, at Edinburgh Theatre Festival, Scotland, Mermaid Theatre, London, Piccadilly Theatre, London, and in European cities, 1969; Don Pedro, *Much Ado About Nothing* and Samuel Johnson, *Boswell's Life of Johnson,* both with the Prospect Theatre Company, 1970; title role, *King Lear,* with the Prospect Theatre Company, Edinburgh Theatre Festival, Scotland, then Venice Biennale, 1971; Holofernes, *Love's Labour's Lost,* with the Prospect Theatre Company, Australian and U.K. cities, 1972; Shpigelsky, *A Month in the Country* and Emerson, *A Room with a View,* British tour and the Albery Theatre, London, 1975; Harry, *Staircase,* with the Prospect Theatre Company, 1976; Claudius, *Hamlet,* Storyteller, *War Music,* and Enobarbus, *Antony and Cleopatra,* Germany, Middle East, U.K., and Edinburgh Festival, Scotland; *Great English Eccentrics,* Hong Kong and Australian cities, 1979.

PRINCIPAL STAGE WORK—Director: As artistic director with the Forum Theatre, Billingham, U.K., *We Bombed in New Haven, The National Health,* and *The Oz Trial,* 1973; *The Homecoming,* Gardner Centre, Brighton, U.K., 1975; co-director, Prospect Theatre Company, 1975.

FILM DEBUT—*The Deadly Affair,* Columbia, 1967. PRINCIPAL FILM APPEARANCES—*The Looking Glass War,* Columbia, 1970; *Nicholas and Alexandra,* Columbia, 1971; *The Day of the Jackal,* Universal, 1973; *The Devil's Advocate,* 1975; *The Thirty Nine Steps,* 1978; *Oliver Twist,* Burbank Films, 1982; *Hedda,* Brut Productions, 1983.

PRINCIPAL TELEVISION APPEARANCES—Dramatic Specials: *Edward VII; Hard Times; Crime and Punishment; Churchill and the Generals.*

PRINCIPAL TELEVISION WORK—Produces and appears in recitals throughout the U.K.

RELATED CAREER—Director Old Vic Theatre Company, 1980-81; director in residence, University of West Australia, 1982.

SIDELIGHTS: RECREATIONS—Travel, listening to music and exploring old railways. FAVORITE ROLES—Otto in *The Italian Girl,* Lear, and Samuel Johnson.

ADDRESSES: AGENT—Smith-Freedman Associates, 123 N. San Vincente Blvd., Beverly Hills, CA 90211; James Sharkey Associates, 15 Golden Square, London, W1R 3AG, England.

* * *

WEYAND, Ron 1929-

PERSONAL: Born February 28, 1929; son of William Joseph (a state deputy and constable for Quincy, MA) and Catherine Mae (a beautician; maiden name, Sweeten) Weyand; married Monica Jacqueline Killen (an actress and teacher), September 15, 1955; children: Mercia Ann, Naomi, Damian. EDUCATION: Studied art at the Rhode Island School of Design, 1947-48; Boston College, A.B., English, 1951; Yale Drama School, M.F.A., acting, 1953. POLITICS: Democrat. RELIGION: Roman Catholic. MILITARY: U.S. Army, 1953-55.

VOCATION: Actor and teacher.

CAREER: STAGE DEBUT—Canon, *Shadow and Substance,* Eastern Slope Summer Theatre, North Conway, NH, 1950, for eight performances. BROADWAY DEBUT—Gorky, *The Cave Dwellers,* Bijou Theatre, 1957, for eighty performances. PRINICPAL STAGE APPEARANCES—Tiger Brown, *The Threepenny Opera,* 1957; Ossip, *Country Scandal,* 1959; title role, *The Golem,* 1959; Baron, *Becket,* 1960; the professor, *The Lesson,* 1963; Sawa, *The Caucausian Chalk Circle,* 1965; Cornwall, *King Lear,* 1965; Ajax, *Tiger at the Gates,* 1966; monsigneur, *Galileo,* 1966; captain, *Cyrano de Bergerac,* 1967.

MAJOR TOURS—Bollinger and Esterbrook, *Inherit the Wind,* national tour, including Chicago, Hollywood, CA, Boston, Cleveland and Columbus, OH, Kansas City, MO, Philadelphia, and Pittsburgh, 1956-57.

FILM DEBUT—Larry, *Mad Dog Coll,* Columbia, 1961. PRINCIPAL FILM APPEARANCES—Timoshevsky, *Taras Bulba,* United Artists, 1962; cop, *Alice's Restaurant,* United Artists, 1969; psychiatrist, *They Might Be Giants,* Universal, 1971; Friar Mozian, *Child's Play,* Paramount, 1972; Mr. Hume, *Shamus,* United Artists, 1973;

RON WEYAND

Dr. Fusco, *Man on a Swing,* Paramount, 1974; Schweigen, *The Music School,* 1974; police captain, *Deadly Hero,* AVCO-Embassy, 1976; Dr. Miller, *Ragtime,* Paramount, 1981.

TELEVISION DEBUT—Pedro, "Victory," *Art Carney Show,* NBC, 1959. PRINCIPAL TELEVISION APPEARANCES—Episodic: Ralph, "Color Schemes," *Route 66,* CBS, 1961. Movies: Clerk, *The Friendly Persuasion,* 1975; camp director, *Farewell to Manzanar,* 1975; judge, *The Penalty Killer,* 1977; spokesman, *Old Friends, New Friends,* 1977; Fred Rogers, *The Dain Curse,* 1977; illusionist, *The Blood Hound Gang,* Children's Television Workshop, 1980; psychiatrist, *Svengali,* 1983.

RELATED CAREER—Professor of speech, communications, and member of the drama department, Marymount College, Tarrytown, NY, 1958—; drama department chairman, 1964-83.

AWARDS: Obie Award and Drama Critics Circle Award nomination, both 1964, for *The Lesson.*

MEMBER: Actors' Equity Association, Screen Actors Guild, American Federation of Television and Radio Artists; Alpha Sigma Nu (National Jesuit Honor Society), American Association of University Professors.

ADDRESSES: HOME—34-10 94th Street, Jackson Heights, NY 11372. OFFICE—Marymount College, Tarrytown, NY 10591. AGENT—Monty Silver Agency Ltd., 200 W. 57th Street, New York, NY 10019.

*   *   *

WHITEHEAD, Paxton   1937-

PERSONAL: Born October 17, 1937, in East Malling, Kent, England; son of Charles Parkin (a lawyer) and Louise (Hunt) Whitehead; married Patricia Gage, January 2, 1971 (divorced); married Katherine Robertson; children: (second marriage) Sarah, Charles. EDUCATION: Attended Rugby School; trained for the stage at the Webber-Douglas School of Singing and Dramatic Art.

VOCATION: Actor and director.

CAREER: STAGE DEBUT—Kentish Colt, *The Epilogue,* The Old Stagers Theatre, Canterbury, U.K., 1949. BROADWAY DEBUT—Gilbert Dawson-Hill, *The Affair,* Henry Miller's Theatre, 1962. PRINCIPAL STAGE APPEARANCES—Alphonse, *All for Mary,* Devonshire Park, Eastbourne, U.K., 1956; Francisco, *Hamlet,* with the Royal Shakespeare Company, Stratford, U.K., 1958; *Gallows Humor,* Gramercy Arts Theatre, New York City, 1961; prosecuting counsel, *One Way Pendulum,* East 74th Street Theatre, New York City, 1961; Torvald Helmer, *A Doll's House,* Theatre Four, New York City, 1963; Gower, *Henry V* and King of France, *King Lear,* both with the American Shakespeare Festival, Stratford, CT, 1963; *Beyond the Fringe,* John Golden Theatre, New York City, 1964; Horner, *The Country Wife* and Henry Higgins, *My Fair Lady,* both at the Front Street Theatre, Memphis, TN, 1964; Jack Absolute, *The Rivals,* Charles Playhouse, Boston, 1964; Archie Rice, *The Entertainer,* Hartford Stage Company, CT, 1965; Adolphus Cusins, *Major Barbara,* Playhouse in the Park, Cincinnati, OH, 1965; Randall Underwood, *Heartbreak House,* Christoforou, *The Public Eye,* and Algernon, *The Importance of Being Earnest,* all at the Manitoba Theatre Center, Winnipeg, Canada, 1965; John

Worthing, *The Importance of Being Earnest,* with the Canadian Players, Toronto, Ontario, Canada, 1966; *Charley's Aunt,* Studio Arena Theatre, Buffalo, NY, 1968; *Chemin de Fer,* Mark Taper Forum, Los Angeles, 1969; *Rondelay,* Hudson West Theatre, New York City, 1969; *The Chemmy Circle,* Arena Stage, Washington, DC, 1970; Hector Hushabye, *Heartbreak House,* Goodman Memorial Theatre, Chicago, 1970; the Emperor, *The Brass Butterfly,* Chelsea Theatre Center, New York City, 1970; Reverend Alexander Mill, *Candida,* Longacre Theatre, New York City, 1970.

At the Shaw Festival, Niagara-on-the-Lake, Ontario: Lord Summerhays, *Misalliance* and Magnus, *The Apple Cart,* 1966; Sergius, *Arms and the Man* and Adolphus Cusins, *Major Barbara,* 1967; Hector Hushabye, *Heartbreak House* and Coustilliou, *The Chemmy Circle,* 1968; Dubedat, *The Doctor's Dilemma* and the actor, *The Guardsman,* 1969; Tempest, *Forty Years On,* 1970; Charteris, *The Philanderer* and lead roles, *Tonight at 8:30,* 1971; Valentine, *You Never Can Tell* and Savoyard, *Fanny's First Play,* 1973; Fancourt Babberley, *Charley's Aunt,* 1974; Burgoyne, *The Devil's Disciple,* 1975; Sergius, *Arms and the Man,* Magnus, *The Apple Cart,* and Adrian, *The Millionairess,* 1976; Ronnie Gamble, *Thark,* 1977.

Canon Throbbing, *Habeas Corpus,* Martin Beck Theatre, New York City, 1975; Sherlock Holmes, *The Crucifer of Blood,* Helen Hayes Theatre, New York City, 1978; Henry Carr, *Travesties,* Manitoba Theatre Centre, Winnipeg, Canada, 1979; title role, *The Trials of Oscar Wilde,* The Citadel Theatre, Edmonton, Ontario, 1980; Ronnie Gamble, *Thark* and Malvalio, *Twelfth Night,* both at the Philadelphia Drama Guild, 1980; Pellinore, *Camelot,* State Theatre, New York City, 1980; sergeant of police, *The Pirates of Penzance,* Ahmanson Theatre, Los Angeles, 1981; Harpagon, *The Miser,* Old Globe Theatre, San Diego, CA, 1982; Hector, *Heartbreak House,* Theatre Royal, London, 1983; Anthony Absolute, *The Rivals,* Old Globe Theatre, San Diego, 1983; Freddy, *Noises Off,* Brooks Atkinson Theatre, New York City, 1983-85; title role, *Richard III,* 1985, and Benedick, *Much Ado About Nothing,* 1986, both Old Globe Theatre, San Diego.

MAJOR TOURS—With the Andrew McMaster Company, U.K. cities, 1957; Francisco, *Hamlet,* with the Royal Shakespeare Company, Moscow and Leningrad, U.S.S.R., 1958; lead role, *The Grass Is Greener,* with the Royal Shakespeare Company, U.K. cities, 1959; Freddie, *Pygmalion,* with the Royal Shakespeare Company, U.K. cities, 1960; *Beyond the Fringe,* U.S. cities, 1963; *The Bed Before Yesterday,* U.S. cities, 1976; Pellinore, *Camelot,* U.S. cities, 1980-81.

PRINCIPAL STAGE WORK—Director: *The Circle,* 1967, *The Chemmy Circle,* 1968, *Forty Years On,* 1970, *Misalliance, Getting Married, Charley's Aunt,* 1972, and *Widowers' Houses,* 1977, all at the Shaw Festival, Niagara-on-the-Lake, Ontario.

Continuing as director: *A Flea in Her Ear,* Charles Playhouse, Boston, 1969; *The Secretary Bird,* Main Stage, Vancouver, B.C., Canada, 1970; *The Chemmy Circle* and *The Sorrows of Frederick,* 1971, and *Arms and the Man,* 1973, all at the Main Stage, Vancouver, B.C.; *Misalliance,* Walnut Street Theatre, Philadelphia, then at the Old Globe Theatre, San Diego, 1982; *The Real Thing,* Seattle Repertory Theatre, WA, 1986; *Beyond the Fringe,* Old Globe Theatre, San Diego, transferring to the Los Angeles Theatre Centre, 1986.

PRINCIPAL FILM APPEARANCES—*Back to School,* Orion, 1986; *Jumping Jack Flash,* 1986; *Baby Boom,* 1987.

PRINCIPAL TELEVISION APPEARANCES—Series, Albert, *Marblehead Manor*, 1987—. Episodic: *Hart to Hart*, ABC, 1982-83; *Magnum P.I.*, CBS, 1983; *The A Team*, NBC, 1986; *The Alan King Show*, CNN, 1986; *Silver Spoons*, NBC, 1986. Dramatic Specials: Lord Darlington, *Lady Windermere's Fan*, CBC, 1966; the doctor, *The Wit and World of GBS*, BBC and CBC, 1971; Lord Dufferin, *The National Dream*, CBC, 1973; Z, *The Village Wooing*, CBC, 1974.

RELATED CAREER—Artistic director, Shaw Festival, Niagra-on-Lake, Ontario, 1967-77; artistic director, Playhouse, Vancouver, 1971-73; associate artistic director, Old Globe Theatre, San Diego, 1986.

AWARDS: Antoinette Perry Award nomination, 1980, for *Camelot*. Honorary Doctor of Law, 1986, Trent University.

MEMBER: Actors' Equity Association, Screen Actors Guild, American Federation of Television and Radio Artists; Players Club.

SIDELIGHTS: RECREATIONS—Tennis, skiing, and cards.

ADDRESSES: AGENT—Barna Ostertag Agency, 501 Fifth Avenue, New York, NY 10017.

*   *   *

WILDER, Billy   1906-

PERSONAL: Born June 22, 1906, in Sucha, Austria; immigrated to the U.S., 1934; married Audrey Young (a reporter). MILITARY: U.S. Army, 1945.

VOCATION: Producer, director, and writer.

CAREER: PRINCIPAL FILM APPEARANCES—*Directed By William Wyler*, 1986.

PRINCIPAL FILM WORK—Screenwriter and (with Alexander Esnay) co-director, *Mauvaise Graine*, 1934; director and (with Charles Brackett) co-screenwriter, *The Major and the Minor*, Paramount, 1942; director and (with Brackett) co-screenwriter, *Five Graves to Cairo*, Paramount, 1943; director and (with Raymond Chandler) co-screenwriter, *Double Indemnity*, Paramount, 1944; director and (with Brackett) co-screenwriter, *The Lost Weekend*, Paramount, 1945; director and (with Brackett) co-screenwriter, *The Emperor Waltz*, Paramount, 1948; director and (with Brackett and Richard Breen) co-screenwriter, *A Foreign Affair*, Paramount, 1948.

Director and (with Brackett and D.M. Marshman, Jr.) co-screenwriter, *Sunset Boulevard*, Paramount, 1950; producer, director, and (with Lesser Samuels and Walter Newman) co-screenwriter, *The Big Carnival* (also known as *Ace in the Hole*), Paramount, 1951; producer, director, and (with Edwin Blum) co-screenwriter, *Stalag 17*, Paramount, 1953; producer, director, and (with Samuel Taylor and Ernest Lehman) co-screenwriter, *Sabrina*, Paramount, 1954; producer, director and (with George Axelrod) co-screenwriter, *The Seven Year Itch*, Twentieth Century-Fox, 1955; producer, director, and (with I.A.L. Diamond) co-screenwriter, *Love in the Afternoon*, Allied Artists, 1957; producer, director, and (with Wendell Mayes) co-screenwriter, *The Spirit of St. Louis*, Warner Brothers, 1957; producer, director, and (with Harry Kurnitz) co-screenwriter, *Witness for the Prosecution*, United Artists, 1958; producer, direc-

tor, and (with Diamond) co-screenwriter, *Some Like It Hot*, United Artists, 1959; producer, director, and (with Diamond) co-screenwriter, *The Apartment*, United Artists, 1960.

Producer, director, and (with Diamond) co-screenwriter, *One, Two, Three*, United Artists, 1961; producer, director, and (with Diamond) co-screenwriter, *Irma La Douce*, United Artists, 1963; producer, director, and (with Diamond) co-screenwriter, *Kiss Me, Stupid*, United Artists, 1964; producer, director, and (with Diamond) co-screenwriter, *The Fortune Cookie*, United Artists, 1966; producer, director, and (with Diamond) co-screenwriter, *The Private Life of Sherlock Holmes*, United Artists, 1970; producer, director, and (with Diamond) co-screenwriter, *Avanti*, United Artists, 1972; director and (with Diamond) co-screenwriter, *The Front Page*, Universal, 1974; producer, director, and (with Diamond) co-screenwriter, *Fedora*, United Artists, 1979; director and (with Diamond) co-screenwriter, *Buddy, Buddy*, Metro-Goldwyn-Mayer (MGM)/United Artists, 1981.

WRITINGS: SCREENPLAYS—(In addition to those listed above) *People on Sunday (Menschen am Sonntag)*, Filmstudio Germania, 1929; story *Dodging*, Universal-Germany, 1930; *Emil and the Detectives*, 1931; (with Curt Siodmak and Ludwig Hirschfield) *The Man Who Looked for His Murderer*, UFA, 1931; (with Paul Franck) *The Wrong Husband*, UFA, 1931; (with Franck and Robert Liebmann) *Her Highness' Command*, UFA, 1931; (with Max Kolpe) *The Blue from the Sky*, Aafa-Film AG, 1932; *A Fairer Dream*, UFA, 1932; *Once There Was a Waltz*, Aafa-Film AG, 1932; (with Kolpe) *Scampolo, a Girl of the Street*, German-Austrian, 1932; (with Kolpe) *Madam Wants No Children*, Shaftsproduktion, 1933; (with Franz Schultz) *A Woman's Dreams*, Atrium and Titania Palast, 1933; (with Howard I. Young) *Music In the Air*, Fox, 1934; (with Schultz) *One Exciting Adventure*, Universal, 1943; (with Schultz) *The Lottery Lover*, Fox, 1935; (with H.S. Kraft) story, *Champagne Waltz*, Paramount, 1937; (with Brackett) *Bluebeard's Eighth Wife*, Paramount, 1938; (with Brackett) *Midnight*, Paramount, 1939; (with Brackett and Walter Reisch) *Ninotchka*, MGM, 1939; (with Brackett) *What a Life*, Paramount, 1939; story, *Rhythm on the River*, Paramount, 1940; *Arise My Love*, Paramount, 1940; *Hold Back the Dawn*, Paramount, 1941; (with Brackett) *Ball of Fire*, Paramount, 1941.

TELEVISION—Movies: *Double Indemnity*, 1973.

AWARDS: (With Charles Brackett and Walter Reisch) Best Screenplay, Academy Award nomination, 1939, for *Ninotchka;* Best Director and (with Raymond Chandler) Best Screenplay, Academy Award nominations, both 1944, for *Double Indemnity;* Best Director and (with Charles Brackett) Best Screenplay, Academy Awards, both 1945, for *The Lost Weekend;* Academy Award nomination (with Brackett), Best Screenplay, 1948, for *A Foreign Affair;* Best Director, Academy Award nomination and (with Brackett and D.M. Marshman, Jr.) Best Story and Screenplay, Academy Award, both 1950, for *Sunset Boulevard;* (with Lesser Samuels and Walter Newman) Best Story and Screenplay, Academy Award nomination, 1951, for *The Big Carnival;* Best Director, Academy Award nomination, 1953, for *Stalag 17;* Best Director and (with Samuel Taylor and Ernest Lehman) Best Screenplay, Academy Award nominations, 1954, for *Sabrina;* Best Director, Academy Award nomination, 1957, for *Witness for the Prosecution;* Best Director and (with I.A.L. Diamond) Best Screenplay, Academy Award nominations, 1959, for *Some Like It Hot;* Best Picture, Best Director, and (with I.A.L. Diamond) Best Story and Screenplay, Academy Awards, 1960, for *The Apartment;* (with Diamond) Best Story and Screenplay, Academy Award nomination, 1966, for *The*

Fortune Cookie; Lifetime Achievement Award, American Film Institute, 1986.

SIDELIGHTS: For more than thirty years, producer, director, and writer Billy Wilder reaped commercial and critical success within the Hollywood film industry. He was nominated for nineteen Oscars from the Academy of Motion Picture Arts and Sciences, and he won six—one for producing, two for directing, and three for writing. His screenplays, many of which he also directed, run the gamut from comedy to psychological drama to murder mystery; often the finished projects stirred heated controversy. More than once the flamboyant and temperamental Wilder was berated by critics for tastelessness in his films, possibly because one of his favorite ploys was "to exaggerate the compelling lure of vice and dreary respectability of virtue," according to Louis Giannetti in *Masters of the American Cinema* (Prentice-Hall, 1981). Having written and directed such cinematic classics as *Double Indemnity, Sunset Boulevard, Some Like It Hot,* and *The Apartment,* Wilder never apologized for the cynical or satiric bent of his works. "I'm accused of being vulgar," he told Giannetti. "So much the better. That proves I'm close to life."

Wilder was born in Sucha, Austria (now part of Poland), in 1906. His family was reduced to poverty after the First World War, and Wilder grew up hearing his mother sing the praises of America, a country she had once visited. Giannetti notes that "as a teenager, [Wilder's] passion for American culture exceeded even that of his mother. He loved American movies, jazz, autos, and dances." After graduating from high school, Wilder became a journalist, reporting on sports and crimes and doing celebrity interviews first in Vienna and then in Berlin. His ambition, however, was to break into the screenwriting business, and he was provided the opportunity when a film producer hid in his apartment to avoid violence from a cuckolded fiance. Wilder was offered a contract to write scripts for German movies; his most successful of these, *Menschen am Sonntag* (*People on Sunday*), brought him fame that inevitably led to greater salaries and a more lavish lifestyle.

When the Nazis came to power in Germany, Wilder, a Jew, sensed danger. He fled to Paris and from there to the United States, arriving in Hollywood in 1934. Screenwriting work was difficult for him to obtain, however, because he could not speak or write English. With fellow expatriate Peter Lorre, he struggled to survive on a can of soup a day while learning the language. Wilder's luck improved in 1936 after he met director Ernst Lubitsch at Paramoumt Studios. Lubitsch got Wilder a $125 per week contract and paired him with veteran screenwriter Charles Brackett.

Throughout the 1930s, the Wilder-Brackett writing team produced numerous highly successful comic scripts, including *Bluebeard's Eighth Wife, Midnight,* and the acclaimed *Ninotchka,* starring Greta Garbo. In the *Dictionary of Literary Biography*, Volume 26: *American Screenwriters* (Gale 1984), James Moore describes the methods Wilder and Brackett used to produce scripts: "Wilder created the ideas and tested them on Brackett; Brackett sifted through Wilder's concepts, deciding which were good and which were not usable." The working relationship was a volatile one, "verging on sadomasochism," according to Giannetti, who claims: "Wilder could never resist needling his partner with cruel and nasty insults. When he could no longer endure these taunts, Brackett would literally hurl objects at his tormentor's head." Despite the storms behind the closed doors of their office, Wilder and Brackett became the highest paid writers in Hollywood. Together, notes Giannetti, they also "became notorious for their battles with

Paramount's front office" and "made life miserable for actors and directors who took liberties with their scripts."

Eventually Wilder decided that in order to protect the artistic integrity of his scripts, he would have to direct the films as well as write them. The front office at Paramount agreed to his decision hoping that he would fail; instead, his first two attempts at directing, *The Major and the Minor* (1942) and *Five Graves to Cairo* (1943) were both box office successes. Thereafter, Wilder directed all of his better-known films, including *Double Indemnity* (1944), *The Lost Weekend* (1945), *Sunset Boulevard* (1950), *The Seven Year Itch* (1955), and *Some Like It Hot* (1959). In 1949 the collaboration between Wilder and Brackett ended; Wilder worked with a succession of co-writers, among them Raymond Chandler, until 1957, when he teamed with I.A. L. Diamond. Giannetti feels that Diamond "endured Wilder's mercurial mood shifts better than any other collaborator."

"Throughout his motion picture career," notes Moore, "Billy Wilder has rarely attempted to conform to popular tastes." Indeed, Wilder's cynicism and his grasp of the darker side of human motivation even find voice in his comedies. Giannetti notes that at the beginning of his career, Wilder "found it difficult to convince stars to accept roles in his films, for his antiheroes were a far cry from the moral paragons that most leading men of that era regarded as suitable material." Giannetti finds Wilder's protagonists "moral weaklings who are only too eager to sell out but in the end choose to reclaim their self-respect." In the 1950's, Wilder's most financially successful period, the director signed Jack Lemmon to lead in five films. In Lemmon, writes Giannetti, Wilder discovered his quintessential antihero—"the weak compromiser who's not as smart as he thinks he is." Other actors who achieved fame through controversial Wilder roles were William Holden in *Sunset Boulevard,* Ray Milland in *The Lost Weekend,* and Fred MacMurray in *Double Indemnity.*

Irma La Douce (1963), starring Lemmon and Shirley MacLaine, was Wilder's last box office hit, but he continued to make films until 1981. In 1986 he was honored with the American Film Institute's Life Achievement Award for the body of his work. *American Film* contributor Chris Columbus claims in a March, 1986, piece that Wilder's "iconoclastic filmmaking is a necessary antidote to the sequelmania and cartoon realism of today's films." An exacting and meticulous worker known for bringing movies in on schedule and under budget, Wilder has sometimes been criticized for tempting the harshness of his vision in deference to the box office. But as Stephen Farber notes in (Winter, 1972-73) *Film Comment,* "It is Wilder's delight in the outrageous that is the most distinguishing visual characteristic of his films. In spite of Wilder's cynicism, there is a rather astonishing exuberance in the imagery of his films, an exuberance in the power of art that his films so often celebrate."

ADDRESSES: OFFICE—Equitable Investment Corporation, P.O. Box 93877, Hollywood, CA 90093.

*   *   *

WILLIAMS, Dennis   1944-

PERSONAL: Full name, Dennis Bucher Williams; born August 21, 1944, in Tulsa, OK; son of Paul Dennis (a U.S. Naval Pilot) and Catherine Susan (a secretary; maiden name, Krischan) Bucher.

DENNIS WILLIAMS

EDUCATION: University of Kansas, B.A., 1966; Royal Academy of Dramatic Arts, London, associate degree, 1970; studied acting with Lurene Tuttle at the Pasadena Playhouse, CA.

VOCATION: Actor and writer.

CAREER: STAGE DEBUT Curley, *Oklahoma!*, with a road company, one-hundred-twenty-six city tour, 1959. LONDON DEBUT Cloten, *Cymbeline*, Globe Theatre, 1967.

FILM DEBUT—Movie buff, *Silent Movie*, Twentieth Century-Fox, 1976. PRINCIPAL FILM APPEARANCES—*The Exiles*, Paramount; *Synthetic Fuel Conspiracy*, Longshot Productions; *Truce in the Forest*, Family Films; *Paved with Gold*, independent.

TELEVISION DEBUT—Rob, *Halls of Anger*, United Artists, NBC, 1974. PRINCIPAL TELEVISION APPEARANCES—Series: host, *The Dennis Williams Show*, PBS. Episodic: *Dreams*, CBS; *E/R*, CBS; *Operation Petticoat*, ABC; *The Bionic Woman*, ABC; *Mary Hartman, Mary Hartman*, syndicated; *Maude*, CBS; *The Nancy Walker Show*, ABC. Movies: *Journey from Darkness*, Bob Banner & Associates, 1975; *Gypsy Warriors*, Universal Television; *Born of Water*, PBS; *The Petticoat Affair*, Disney Channel. Specials: *Special Olympics*, CBS.

NON-RELATED CAREER—Owner, Nutritional Needs Company, Hollywood, CA, 1982—.

WRITINGS: SCREENPLAYS—*Sunset Heaven*, 1980.

TELEVISION—Series: *Merlin Meets the Twentieth Century*, 1984.

AWARDS: Best Actor, Munich Film Festival, 1978, and Bronze Halo Award from the Southern California Motion Picture Council, both for *Truce in the Forest;* Best Supporting Actor in a Comedy Series, Emmy Award nomination, 1985, for *E/R;* Celebrity of the Year, Joseph P. Kennedy Foundation; Outstanding Achievement in Acting, American Biographical Institute.

MEMBER: Actors' Equity Association, Screen Actors Guild, American Federation of Television and Radio Artists, Academy of Motion Picture Arts and Sciences, Academy of Television Arts and Sciences, American Film Institute, Pasadena Playhouse Associates; United Services Organization (USO; board of governors).

ADDRESSES: OFFICE—9235 1/2 Doheny Road, Hollywood, CA 90069.

*　　*　　*

WILLIAMS, Hugh Steadman　1935-

PERSONAL: Born June 21, 1935, in London, England; son of Thomas John (a congregational minister) and Margaret (a teacher; maiden name, Hughes) Williams; maried Dell Filmer (a graphic designer), 1965; children: Oliver, Gregory. EDUCATION: University College, Oxford, M.A., modern history, 1959. MILITARY: Royal Corps of Signals, 1954-56.

VOCATION: Writer and director.

HUGH STEADMAN WILLIAMS

CAREER: PRINCIPAL STAGE WORK—Writer (see below); artistic director, Westminster Productions, U.K., 1975—.

WRITINGS: PLAYS, PRODUCED AND PUBLISHED—(With Alan Thornhill) Book and lyrics, *High Diplomacy,* musical, Westminster Theatre, London, 1969; lyrics and sketches, *GB,* musical revue, Westminster Theatre, 1973; (with Thornhill) *Return Trip,* Westminster Theatre, published by Westminster Productions, 1974, German text published by Caux Verlag, 1981; *Fire,* Klein Theatre, Lucerne, Switzerland, 1975, German translation entitled *Das Feuer,* published by Reiss A.G. Basel, 1976, also published by Westminster Productions, London, 1977; *Stranger in the House,* Westminster Theatre, 1979, German translation entitled *Fremder im eigenen Haus,* published by Reiss A.G. Basel, 1979; *Poor Man, Rich Man,* play with music, Edinburgh Fringe Festival, Scotland, 1979, French translation entitled *Un Soleil en pleine Nuit,* Theatre du Ranelagh, Paris, 1982, published by Editions de Caux, 1982, also published by Westminster Productions, 1983; *Everywoman,* verse play, published by Samuel French, 1981; *Gavin and the Monster,* musical, Westminster Theatre, 1981-82, published by Samuel French, 1982; (with Thornhill) *Nehemiah Now,* pop operetta, published by Radius, 1983; *Skeletons,* Caux Theatre, Switzerland, 1986.

RADIO PLAYS—*The Short Sighted Optimist,* BBC Radio 4, 1974; *Diwali Day,* BBC Radio 4, 1974, ABC Radio Australia, 1975.

BOOKS—(With illustrations by Margaret Gray) *Gavin and the Monster,* children's book, Grosvenor, 1981.

ADDRESSES: AGENT—Eric Glass Ltd., 28 Berkeley Square, London W1X 6HD, England.

*   *   *

WILLIAMS, Paul   1940-

PERSONAL: Full name, Paul Hamilton Williams; born September 19, 1940, in Bennington, NE; son of Paul Hamilton (an architectural engineer) and Bertha Mae (Burnside) Williams; married wife Katie; children: two.

VOCATION: Composer, singer, and actor.

CAREER: PRINCIPAL FILM APPEARANCES—*The Loved One,* Metro-Goldwyn-Mayer, 1965; *The Chase,* Columbia, 1966; *Planet of the Apes,* Twentieth Century-Fox, 1968; *Watermelon Man,* Columbia, 1970; *The Phantom of the Paradise,* Twentieth Century-Fox, 1974; *Smokey and the Bandit,* Universal, 1977; *The Cheap Detective,* Columbia, 1978; *Stone Cold Dead,* Canadian, 1980; *Smokey and the Bandit, II,* Universal, 1980; *Smokey and the Bandit, Part Three,* Universal, 1983.

PRINCIPAL TELEVISION APPEARANCES—Episodic: Co-host, *The Mike Douglas Show,* ABC; also hosted four shows of *Midnight Special,* NBC. Guest: *The Merv Griffin Show,* CBS; *The Tonight Show,* NBC; *The Jonathan Winters Show,* NBC; *The Muppet Show,* syndicated. Pilots: *Rooster,* 1982. Movies: *The Night They Saved Christmas,* ABC, 1984.

PRINCIPAL TELEVISION WORK—Musical supervisor, *Sugar Time!,* ABC, 1977-78; (with Pat McCormick) creator and (with Glen A. Larson) co-producer, *Rooster.*

PAUL WILLIAMS

RELATED CAREER—President, Hobbitron Enterprises, 1973—; associate, A & M Records, 1970-77.

WRITINGS: SONGS—(In collaboration with Roger Nichols) "Out in the Country," 1969, "We've Only Just Begun," 1970, "Talk It Over in the Morning," 1970, "Rainy Days and Mondays," 1971, "An Old Fashioned Love Song," 1972, and "Let Me Be the One," 1972; (with Craig Doerge) "Cried Like a Baby," 1970; (with Jack S. Conrad) "Family of Man," 1971 and "The Hell of It," from the film, *The Phantom of the Paradise,* 1974; (with Barbara Streisand) "Evergreen," from the film *A Star Is Born,* 1976; (with composer Michel Colombier) "Wings," a cantata, 1977; (with composer John Williams) "(You're So) Nice to Be Around," from the film, *Cinderella Liberty,* 1973 and "My Fair Share," from the film *One on One,* 1977; (with Kenny Ascher) "The Rainbow Connection," from the film, *The Muppet Movie,* 1979.

FILM SCORES—*The Getaway,* National General, 1972; (with John Williams) *The Man Who Loved Cat Dancing,* Metro-Goldwyn-Mayer (MGM), 1972; (with Williams) *Cinderella Liberty,* Twentieth Century-Fox, 1973; (with Ascher) *The Phantom of the Paradise,* Twentieth Century-Fox, 1974; *The Day of the Locust,* Paramount, 1975; (with Ascher) *A Star Is Born,* Warner Brothers, 1976; *Bugsy Malone,* Paramount, 1976; (with Charles Fox) *One on One,* Warner Brothers, 1977; *The End,* United Artists, 1978; (with Ascher) *The Muppet Movie,* Associated Film Distribution, 1979; *Agatha,* Warner Brothers, 1979; (with Jerry Goldsmith) *The Secret of Nihm,* MGM, 1982; *Ishtar,* Columbia, 1987.

TELEVISION—Series: Theme songs—*The McLean Stevenson Show,* NBC, 1976-77; *The Love Boat,* ABC, 1977-86; *Sugar*

Time!, ABC, 1977-78; *It Takes Two*, ABC, 1982-83. Movies: *No Place to Run*, 1972. Specials: *Emmet Otter's Jug Band Christmas*, ABC, 1980.

RECORDINGS: ALBUMS—With his first group, "Holy Mackerel," one album for Reprise Records; *Someday Man; Just an Old-Fashioned Love Song*, A & M Records, 1971; *Life Goes On*, A & M Records, 1972; *A Little Bit of Love*, A & M Records, 1974; *Here Comes Inspiration*, A & M Records, 1974; *Ordinary Fools*, A & M Records, 1975; *Classics*, A & M Records, 1977; *A Little on the Windy Side*, Portrait Records, 1979; *Crazy for Loving You*, Firstline Records, 1981.

AWARDS: (With John Williams) Best Song, Academy Award nomination, 1973, for "(You're So) Nice to Be Around," from *Cinderella Liberty;* Best Original Motion Picture Score, Academy Award nomination, 1974, for *Phantom of the Paradise;* (with Kenny Ascher) Best Original Motion Picture Score, Golden Globe Award, 1976, for *A Star Is Born;* (with Barbra Streisand) Best Song, Academy Award, 1976, Golden Globe Award and Grammy Award, both 1977, all for "Evergreen," from *A Star Is Born.*

MEMBER: American Society of Composers, Authors and Publishers, National Academy of Recording Arts and Sciences (trustee).

SIDELIGHTS: RECREATIONS—Race car driving.

CTFT learned that Paul Williams began his career in film studios as a set painter and stunt parachutist.

ADDRESSES: HOME—Santa Barbara, CA. OFFICE—Tugboat Productions, Lazy Creek Ranch, 4570 Encino Avenue, Encino, CA 91316; Hobbitron Enterprises, Twentieth Century-Fox Music Corp., 8544 Sunset Blvd., Los Angeles, CA 90069. PUBLICIST—Jo-Ann Geffen & Associates, 3151 Cahuenga Blvd. West, Suite 235, Los Angeles, CA 90068.

*   *   *

WILSON, Mary   1944-

PERSONAL: Born March 6, 1944, in Greenville, MS; daughter of Sam and Johnnie Mae (Lewis) Wilson; married Pedro Antonio Ferrer (divorced); children: Turkessa, Pedro, Raphael, Willie (adopted).

VOCATION: Singer, actress, and writer.

CAREER: PRINCIPAL CONCERT ENGAGEMENTS—(With the "Supremes":) Grand Gala Du Disque Festival, Holland; Lincoln Center, New York City; Madison Square Garden, New York City; Houston Astro Dome, TX; Hollywood Bowl, CA; Stockholm, Sweden; Olympia Theare, Paris, France; Royal Command Performance for the Queen Mother, London; also the Copacabana Club; "USO A Go-Go" Benefit.

FILM DEBUT—*Bikini Beach*, Alta Vista Productions, 1964. PRINCIPAL FILM APPEARANCES—*The Happening*, 1967; *The Girl Groups: The Story of Sound*, Delilah Films, 1983; also *Ready, Steady, Go*, Dave Clark Productions; *That Was Rock; Brown Sugar.*

TELEVISION DEBUT—*The Ed Sullivan Show*, CBS. PRINCIPAL

TELEVISION APPEARANCES—Episodic: Sister Martha, *Tarzan*, NBC. Guest: (With the "Supremes") *The Red Skelton Show*, CBS, *The Dean Martin Show*, NBC, *Hullabaloo*, NBC, *Shindig*, ABC, *Hollywood Palace*, ABC, *American Bandstand*, ABC, *Jackie Gleason*, CBS, *Sammy Davis, Jr.*, NBC, *The Tonight Show*, NBC.

Specials: *TCB (Takin Care of Business)*, NBC; *GIT (Gettin It Together)*, NBC; *Ceremonies in Dark Old Men.*

WRITINGS: BOOKS—*Dream Girl: My Life as a Supreme*, St. Martin's Press, 1986.

RECORDINGS: SONGS—(With "The Supremes") "Where Did Our Love Go?," 1964; "Baby Love," 1964; "Come See about Me," 1964; "I Hear a Symphony," 1965; "Back in My Arms Again," 1965; "Nothing But Heartaches," 1965; "You Can't Hurry Love," 1966; "My World Is Empty without You," 1966; "The Happening," 1967; "Reflections," 1967; "Love Is Here and Now You're Gone," 1967; "I'm Gonna Make You Love Me," 1968; others.

ALBUMS—(With the "Supremes") *Where Did Our Love Go?, More Hits by the Supremes, We Remember Sam Cooke, At the Copa I Hear a Symphony, A Bit of Liverpool, Sing Holland-Dozier-Holland, Sing Rodgers & Hart, A Go-Go, Sing and Perform Funny Girl, Farewell, Anthology, Right On, New Ways But Love Stays, TCB, The Magnificent Seven;* (solo) *Mary Wilson*, all on Motown Records.

AWARDS: With the "Supremes," earned Gold and Platinum Record Awards; New Jersey Citizenship Award, 1967; National

MARY WILSON

Association for the Advancement of Colored People (NAACP) Image Award, 1972; honored, Black History Month, Los Angeles County Library, 1987.

MEMBER: Christian Children's Fund.

ADDRESSES: HOME—Los Angeles, CA. OFFICE—Mary Wilson, Inc., 741 S. Adams, Glendale, CA. AGENT—Sid Craig, The Craig Agency, 8485 Melrose Place, #E, Los Angeles, CA 90069.

*   *   *

WINTERS, Shelley 1922-

PERSONAL: Born Shirley Schrift, August 18, 1922, in East St. Louis, MO; daughter of Jonas (a designer of men's clothing) and Rose (a singer; maiden name, Winters) Schrift; married Mack Paul Mayer (a textile salesman), January 1, 1943 (divorced, October, 1948); married Vittorio Gassman (an actor), April 28, 1952 (divorced, June 2, 1954); married Anthony Francioso (an actor), May 4, 1957 (divorced, November 18, 1960); children: (second marriage) Vittoria. EDUCATION: Attended Wayne University; studied acting at the Drama Workshop of the New School for Social Research, the Actors' Studio, and with Elia Kazan, Michael Chekhov, and Charles Laughton; studied singing with Viola Spers.

VOCATION: Actress and writer.

CAREER: FILM DEBUT—*What a Woman!*, Columbia, 1943. PRINCIPAL FILM APPEARANCES—*The Racket Man*, Columbia, 1944; *Two-Man Submarine*, Columbia, 1944; *She's a Soldier, Too*, Columbia, 1944; *Nine Girls*, Columbia, 1944; *A Double Life*, Universal, 1947; *The Gangster*, Allied, 1947; *Cry of the City*, Twentieth Century-Fox, 1948; *Larceny*, Universal, 1948; *Take One False Step*, 1949; *Johnny Stool Pigeon*, 1949; *The Great Gatsby*, Paramount, 1949; *South Sea Sinner*, Universal, 1950; *Frenchie*, Universal, 1950; *Winchester 73*, Universal, 1950; *A Place in the Sun*, Paramount, 1951; *He Ran All the Way*, United Artists, 1951; *The Raging Tide*, Universal, 1951; *Behave Yourself!*, RKO, 1951; *Untamed Frontier*, Universal, 1952; *Meet Danny Wilson*, Universal, 1952; *Phone Call from a Stranger*, Twentieth Century-Fox, 1952; *My Man and I*, Metro-Goldwyn-Mayer (MGM), 1952; *Tennessee Champ*, MGM, 1954; *Executive Suite*, MGM, 1954; *Saskatachewan*, Universal, 1954; *Playgirl*, Universal, 1954; *Mambo*, Paramount, 1955; *Night of the Hunter*, United Artists, 1955; *I Am a Camera*, Distributing Corporation of America, 1955; *The Big Knife*, United Artists, 1955; *The Treasure of Pancho Villa*, RKO Radio Pictures, 1955; *I Died a Thousand Times*, Warner Brothers, 1955; *Cash on Delivery*, RKO, 1956; *The Diary of Anne Frank*, Twentieth Century-Fox, 1959; *Odds Against Tomorrow*, United Artists, 1959.

Let No Man Write My Epitath, Columbia, 1960; *The Young Savages*, United Artists, 1961; *Lolita*, MGM, 1962; *The Chapman Report*, Warner Brothers, 1962; *A Matter of Conviction*, 1962; *The Balcony*, Continental, 1963; *Wives and Lovers*, Paramount, 1963; *A House Is Not a Home*, Paramount, 1964; *Time of Indifference*, Continental, 1965; *Moving Target*, 1965; *Harper*, Warner Brothers, 1966; *A Patch of Blue*, MGM, 1966; *Alfie*, Paramount, 1966; *Enter Laughing*, Columbia, 1967; *The Scalp Hunters*, United Artists, 1968; *Wild in the Streets*, American International, 1969; *Buona Sera, Mrs. Campbell*, United Artists, 1969; *The Mad Room*, Columbia, 1969; *Arthur, Arthur*, Rank, 1970; *Bloody Mama*,

American International, 1970; *How Do I Love Thee*, Cinerama, 1970; *What's the Matter with Helen?*, United Artists, 1971; *The Poseidon Adventure*, Twentieth Century-Fox, 1972; *Something to Hide*, 1972; *Cleopatra Jones*, Warner Brothers, 1973; *Blume in Love*, Warner Brothers, 1973; *Our Time*, Warner Brothers, 1974; *Diamonds*, AVCO-Embassy, 1975; *Next Stop Greenwich Village*, 1976; *The Tenant*, Paramount, 1976; *An Average Man*, 1976; *Pete's Dragon*, Buena Vista, 1977; *City on Fire*, AVCO-Embassy, 1979.

The Visitor, 1980; *Looping*, 1981; *S.O.B.*, Paramount, 1981; *My Mother My Daughter*, 1981; *Over the Brooklyn Bridge*, MGM/United Artists, 1984; *Delta Force*, Cannon, 1985; also, *Ellie*, Shapiro Entertainment; *Deja Vu*.

PRINCIPAL TELEVISION APPEARANCES—Episodic: "The Women," *Producers Showcase*, NBC, 1955; "A Double Life," *Alcoa Hour*, NBC, 1957; "Beyond This Place," *DuPont Show of the Month*, CBS, 1957; "A Piece of Blue Sky," *Play of the Week*, WNTA, 1960; "Two Is the Number," *Chrysler Theatre*, NBC, 1963; *Ben Casey*, ABC, 1964; "Back to Back," *Bob Hope Chrysler Theatre*, NBC, 1965; *Batman*, ABC, 1966; *That's Life*, ABC, 1968; *McCloud*, NBC, 1974; *Actors on Acting*, PBS, 1984; also appeared on *Wagon Train*, NBC; *Hawaiian Heat*, ABC.

Pilots: *Big Rose*, CBS, 1974. Movies: *Revenge*, 1971; *The Adventures of Nick Carter*, ABC, 1972; *The Vamp*, London TV, 1972; *The Devil's Daughter*, ABC, 1973; *The Death of Her Innocence* (originally released as a feature film entitled, *Our Time* [see above]), 1974; *Double Indemnity*, 1974; *The Sex Symbol*, 1974; *Elvis*, 1978. Mini-Series: *The French Atlantic Affair*, 1979; Do Do Bird, *Alice in Wonderland*, CBS, 1986.

STAGE DEBUT—Edna, *Waiting for Lefty*, Jamaica, NY, 1930. BROADWAY DEBUT—Understudy as Kitty Duval, *The Time of Your Life*, Booth Theatre, 1940. PRINCIPAL STAGE APPEARANCES—Miss Holvaag, *Conquest in April*, Locust Theatre, Philadelphia, 1940; Flora, *The Night Before Christmas*, Morosco Theatre, New York City, 1941; Fifi, *Rosalinda*, 44th Street Theatre, New York City, 1942; Clo-Clo, *The Merry Widow*, Municipal Auditorium, Long Beach, CA, 1946; Ado Annie Carnes, *Oklahoma!*, St. James Theatre, New York City, 1947-48; Stella Kowalski, *A Streetcar Named Desire*, Circle Theatre, Hollywood, CA, 1952; Stella, *Wedding Breakfast*, Triple Cities Playhouse, Binghampton, NY, 1955; Celia Pope, *A Hatful of Rain*, Lyceum Theatre, New York City, 1955; Hilda Brookman, *Girls of Summer*, Longacre Theatre, New York City, 1956; Mrs. Topaz, *The Saturday Night Kid*, Westport Country Playhouse, CT, 1957, then Locust Street Theatre, Philadelphia, 1958; Kay, *A Piece of Blue Sky*, North Jersey Playhouse, Fort Lee, NJ, 1959; Georgie Elgin, *The Country Girl* and Beatrice, *A View from the Bridge*, both at the Paper Mill Playhouse, Millburn, NJ, 1961; Maxine Faulk, *The Night of the Iguana*, Royale Theatre, New York City, 1962; Connie, "Snowangel" and the wife, "Epiphany," two one-acts on a double-bill entitled, *Cages* (also known as *The Last of the Great Jelly Bellies*), York Playhouse, New York City, 1963; Dolores Goodwin, *Days of the Dancing*, Westport Country Playhouse, CT, 1964; Martha, *Who's Afraid of Virginia Woolf?*, Coconut Grove Theatre, Miami, FL, 1965.

Flora Sharkey, "Part I," Marcella Vankuchen, "Part II," and Hilda, "Part III," three one-acts on a triple-bill entitled, *Under the Weather*, Cort Theatre, New York City, 1966, and later at the Spoleto Festival, Italy, 1967; Minnie Marx, *Minnie's Boys*, Imperial Theatre, New York City, 1970; Beatrice, *The Effect of Gamma*

Rays on Man-in-the-Moon Marigolds, Actors Studio, New York City, Westchester Country Playhouse, NY, 1973, and later at the Biltmore Theatre, New York City, 1978; repeated rolls of Connie and the wife, *Cages,* Westwood Playhouse, Los Angeles, 1975; Wanda, *Kennedy's Children,* San Francisco, 1976. Summer stock performances include, *Of Mice and Men, The Male Animal, Gentle People, The Rose Tattoo, and Luv.*

MAJOR TOURS—Member of the company, *Meet the People,* revue, U.S. cities, 1941; Billie Dawn, *Born Yesterday,* summer tour, 1950; Gittel Mosca, *Two for the Seesaw,* summer tour, 1960, and again in 1965-66; Martha, *Who's Afraid of Virginia Woolf?,* U.S. cities, 1965; Beatrice, *The Effect of Gamma Rays on Man-in-the-Moon Marigolds,* U.S. cities, 1973; Connie and the wife, *Cages,* U.S. cities, 1974.

PRINCIPAL CABARET APPEARANCES—La Conga, New York City, 1940; The Flamingo, Las Vegas, 1953; also The Serenade Club, Los Angeles.

RELATED CAREER—Model and vaudeville performer.

NON-RELATED CAREER—Sales clerk in a five and dime store.

WRITINGS: PLAYS, PRODUCED—*One Night Stands of a Noisy Passenger* (three one-act plays), Actors' Studio, New York City, 1973. BOOKS—*Shelley: Also Known as Shirley* (autobiography), Morrow, 1980.

AWARDS: Academy Award nominations, 1948, for *A Double Life* and 1951, for *A Place in the Sun; Holiday* Magazine Award, 1952; Best Supporting Actress, Academy Award, 1958, for *The Diary of Anne Frank;* Best Actress, Emmy Award, 1964, for *Two Is the Number;* Monte Carlo Golden Nymph Award, 1964; Best Actress, Cannes Festival Award, 1965; Best Supporting Actress, Academy Award, 1966, for *A Patch of Blue.*

MEMBER: Actors' Equity Association, Screen Actors Guild, American Federation of Television and Radio Artists, American Guild of Variety Artists.

SIDELIGHTS: RECREATIONS—Swimming, tennis, riding, and politics and civic affairs.

ADDRESSES. AGENT—International Creative Management, 8899 Beverly Blvd., Los Angeles, CA 90048.*

*   *   *

WITCOVER, Walt   1924-

PERSONAL: Born Walter Witcover Scheinman, August 24, 1924, in New York, NY; son of Louis J. (a sculptor and composer) and Juliette T. (a lecturer and critic; maiden name, Benton) Scheinman. EDUCATION: Cornell University, B.A., 1946, M.F.A., 1947; trained for the stage at the American Theatre Wing, at the Actors Studio Directors Unit, and at Hunter College; also studied with Lee Strasberg and Fanny Bradshaw.

VOCATION: Director, actor, producer, teacher, and writer.

CAREER: PRINCIPAL STAGE APPEARANCES—*Outward Bound, Yankee Land, The Choir Rehearsal, Pullman Car Hiawatha, Headin'*

for Havana, and *Love in '76,* all at Cornell University, Ithaca, NY, 1942-46; *You Can't Take It with You, Counsellor-at-Law, A Slight Case of Murder, The Milky Way, Personal Appearance, Janey,* and *Ladies in Retirement,* all at the Priscilla Beach Theatre, 1942; *Twelfth Night, The Barretts of Wimpole Street, The Imaginary Invalid, Count Your Blessings,* and *State of the Union,* all at the Barter Theatre, Abington, VA, 1947 and 1949; *The Miser, Jason, Anatol, L'Arlesienne, The Rivals, Dear Brutus,* and *A Trip to Chinatown,* all at Stanford University, 1948; *Anne Pedersdotter, As You Like It,* and *What Price Glory?,* all at the National Theatre Conference, New York City Showcase, 1948; *Henry IV* and *The Bourgeois Gentleman,* both at the Cherry Lane Theatre, New York City, 1947 and 1949; *Peer Gynt, Paradise Lost, Prologue to Glory, The Merchant of Venice, St. Joan, The World We Make, Misalliance, Finian's Rainbow, Shadow and Substance,* and *The Stages of Love,* all at the Equity Library Theatre, New York City, 1947-55; *Captain Brassbound's Conversion* and *The Royal Family,* both at the New York City Drama Company, 1950-51.

Mr. Roberts, Summer and Smoke, Room Service, and *Tobacco Road,* all at the Smithtown Summer Theatre, 1953; *Lisa and the Lord,* New Dramatists Workshop, New York City, 1953; *Tom Sawyer* and *The Little Red Shoes,* both at the Children's World Theatre, 1953 and 1955; *The Skin of Our Teeth,* for the U.S. State Department at the American National Theatre and Academy (ANTA) Theatre, New York City, 1955; *A Midsummer Night's Dream,* Empire State Music Festival, NY, 1956; *The Seagull,* Actors Studio, New York City, 1964; *Faust, Nathan the Wise, Seize the Day, Manhattan Miracle,* and *A Medley of Native Tunes,* all at the Herbert Berghof Studios, New York City, 1961-71; *The Forced Marriage, Lesons in Love, Boubouroche!, A Serving of Verse,* and *Salon-Comedie,* all at the Masterworks Laboratory Theatre, New York City, 1971-77; moderator, *Talk Show,* with the Masterworks Laboratory Theatre at Lincoln Center Performing Arts Library, New York City, 1976.

PRINCIPAL STAGE WORK—Director: *Once Upon a Hill* and *The Second Shepherds' Play,* both at Cornell University, 1946; *The Philadelphia Story, Kind Lady,* and *Arsenic and Old Lace,* all at the Manor Club Theatre, Pelham, NY, 1949; *The Hasty Heart,* Barter Theatre, 1949; *Light Up the Sky,* Manor Club Theatre, 1950; *Once Upon a Hill,* Cornell University, 1950; *Peter Rabbit, An Airman's Dream,* and *Ten Little Indians,* all at Landsberg Air Force Base, Germany, 1951; *The Stages of Love,* Equity Library Theatre, New York City, 1953; *The Moon Is Blue, John Loves Mary,* and *I Am a Camera,* all at the Old Town Theatre, Smithtown, NY, 1953; *The Hasty Heart,* Equity Library Theatre, New York City, 1954; *The Little Red Shoes,* Children's World Theatre, New York City, 1954; *Maedchen in Uniform,* Equity Library Theatre, New York City, 1955; *The Sun-Dial,* White Barn Theatre, Westport, CT, 1955; *Three Times Three,* Chanin Auditorium, New York City, 1956; *Tea and Sympathy, The Solid Gold Cadillac, The Philadelphia Story,* and *Picnic,* all at the Legion Star Playhouse, Ephrata, PA, 1956; *Exiles,* Renata Theatre, New York City, 1957; *Red Roses for Me,* Stella Adler Studio Theatre, New York City, 1957; *The Glass Menagerie, Overruled, How He Lied to Her Husband, Rocket to the Moon, The Marriage,* and *Thieves' Carnival,* all at the Crystal Lake Theatre, Chestertown, NY, 1959.

Continuing as director: *Born Yesterday,* Club Arena Theatre, Washington, DC, 1960; *Three Modern Noh Plays,* White Barn Theatre, Westport, CT, 1960; *Two Modern Noh Plays,* ANTA Matinee Series at the Theater de Lys, New York City, 1960; *An Evening with Italian Writers,* Brooklyn Public Library, New York City, 1960-61; *Signs Along the Cynic Route,* Actors Studio

Theatre, New York City, 1962; *Talk to Me*, Herbert Berghof Studio Theatre, New York City, 1963; *The Fantasticks*, Bermudiana Hotel Theatre, Bermuda, 1964; *The Exhaustion of Our Son's Love*, Sheridan Square Theatre, New York City, 1964; *What Color Goes with Brown?*, Theatre '65, New York City, 1964; *One of Us Has Been Ignited*, Actors Studio Theatre, New York City, 1965; *The Exhaustion of Our Son's Love*, Cherry Lane Theatre, New York City, 1965; *La Traviata*, Act I, Actors Studio Theatre, New York City, 1966; *Judas Maccabaeus*, Long Island Cultural Festival Theatre, NY, 1966; *The Rivals* and *La Traviata*, Act II, both Actors Studio Theatre New York City, 1967; *La Traviata*, Act II, Sloane House Young Men's Christan Association (YMCA) Theatre, New York Ctiy, 1968; *The Miser*, Syracuse Repertory Theatre, NY, 1968; *La Traviata*, Acts I and II, Actors' Studio Theatre, New York City, 1968; *Next Year in Jerusalem*, Herbert Berghof Playwrights Foundation Theatre, New York Ctiy, 1968; *La Traviata*, Acts III and IV, Actors Studio Theatre, New York City, 1969.

As director: *Experiments in Lyric Theatre*, with the Masterworks Laboratory Theatre at the Theatre-in-the-Courthouse, New York City, 1970; *From the World of Young Chekhov* and *Boubouroche!*, both with the Masterworks Laboratory Theatre at the Theatre-in-the-Courthouse, New York City, 1971; *Marriage*, with the Masterworks Laboratory Theatre at the Madison Avenue Baptist Church, New York City, 1972; *Lyric Theatre '72*, with the Masterworks Laboratory Theatre at Lolly's Theatre Club, New York City, 1972; *A Serving of Verse* and *Mozart as Dramatist*, both with the Masterworks Laboratory Theatre, Brooklyn Heights, NY, 1973; *A Serving of Verse*, Emelin Theatre, Mamaroneck, NY, 1973; with the Masterworks Laboratory Theatre at Spencer Church, Brooklyn Heights, NY: *Salon-Comedie* and *Lovelives*, 1974, *The Gondoliers*, 1975, *Lessons in Love* and *West of Galway*, 1976, and *The Forced Marriage* 1977; at the State University of New York, Purchase, NY: *Brothers and Lovers*, 1978; *Yellow Jack*, and *American Journeys*, 1979; *The Bourgeois Gentleman, A Midsummer Night's Dream*, and *The Other World of Anton Chekhov*, 1980; *Brief Chronicles of the Time*, Actors Studio Theatre, New York City, 1982; *The Misanthrope*, with the Masterworks Labortory Theatre at St. Peter's Performing Arts Center, New York City, 1983; *The Miser*, University of Maryland, College Park, 1983; *She Stoops to Conquer*, Virginia Technical College Theatre, Blacksburg, 1984.

Co-producer, *Three Times Three*, Off-Broadway, New York City, 1956. Producer: *La Traviata*, Actors Studio Theatre, 1968-69; the following all with the Masterworks Laboratory Theatre: *Miss Julie, Boubouroche!, From the World of Young Chekhov, Plays of the Sea, Antigone*, and *Experiments in Lyric Theatre*, all at the Theatre-in-the-Courthouse, 1969-71, *Marriage*, Madison Avenue Baptist Church, 1972, *Lyric Theatre '72*, Lolly's Theatre Club, 1972, *Bastien and Bastienne, The Forced Marriage, The Gaol Gate, The Rising of the Moon, Hyacinth Halvey, Lessons in Love, The Gondoliers, God of Vengeance, The Doctor in Spite of Himself, Lovelives, A Staging of Song Cycles, Bravo Bureaucracy!, One Cannot Think of Everything, A Door Must Be Either Open or Shut, The Magic Flute, Cosi fan Tutte, Don Giovanni, The Marriage of Figaro, Exsultate Jubilate, Press Cuttings, The Man of Destiny, A Serving of Verse*, and *Danton's Death*, all at the Spencer Memorial Church, Brooklyn Heights, NY, 1972-77, *An Evening of Lyric Theatrè* and *The Goose from Cairo*, both at the Masterworks Laboratory Theatre Loft, New York City, 1978-83, *The Misanthrope*, St. Peter's Performing Arts Center, 1983.

MAJOR TOURS—Director: *The Little Red Shoes*, 1954; *The Hasty Heart*, summer theatres, Northeastern U.S., 1954; *The Reluctant Debutant*, summer theatres, Eastern and Southern U.S., 1957; *The Waltz of the Toreadors*, summer theatres, Eastern and Mid-Western U.S., 1958.

PRINCIPAL TELEVISION APPEARANCES—Episodic: "Search for Tomorrow," *Studio One*, CBS.

PRINCIPAL FILM WORK—Documentaries: *Mozart in Motion*, 1973-74.

RELATED CAREER—Staff member, Cornell University Theatre, 1946-47; instructor of improvisation, Stella Adler Studio, New York City, 1946-47; stage manager and lighting designer, Equity Library Theatre, New York City and Barter Theatre, Abingdon, VA, 1947-49; theatrical specialist, U.S. Air Forces in Europe, 1951; acting coach, 1958—; instructor, Herbert Berghof Studio, New York City, 1960-85; artistic director and instructor, Masterworks Laboratory Theatre, 1968—; European visits, with the International Theatre Institute, 1970, 1973-75, 1977, 1981, and 1984; associate professor, State University of New York at Purchase, 1977-81; guest director, University of Maryland, College Park, 1983; guest director, Virginia Technical College, 1984; professional evaluator for the Department of Theatre, University of Maryland, College Park, 1984-86; professor of theatre, University of Maryland, Baltimore County, 1986—.

WRITINGS: BOOKS—*Once Upon a Hill*, 1946. PLAYS—Translations: *Anne Pedesdotter, L'Avanve, Un Caso Clinico, Maedchen in Uniform*, 1955-68.

AWARDS: Rockefeller Foundation Award, Stanford University, 1948; Best Actor, Obie Awards, 1954-55, for *Maedchen in Uniform* and 1956-57, for *Exiles;* Best Off-Broadway New Play Production, Obie Award, 1964-65, for *The Exhaustion of Our Son's Love;* Total Theatre Award, Actors Studio, 1968, for *La Traviata*.

MEMBER: Society of Stage Directors and Choreographers (executive board, 1966-67), Actors' Equity Association, Screen Actors Guild, American Federation of Television and Radio Artists; United University Professions, Phi Beta Kappa.

ADDRESSES: HOME—40 W. 22nd Street, New York, NY 10010.

*   *   *

WOLF, Dick   1946-

PERSONAL: Born December 20, 1946, in New York, NY; son of George (an advertising executive) and Marie G. (Gaffney) Wolf; married Susan Scranton, September 5, 1970 (divorced, 1981) married Christine Harburg, June 29, 1983; children: Olivia Iselin, Sarina Granger. EDUCATION: University of Pennsylvania, B.A., 1969.

VOCATION: Producer and writer.

CAREER: FIRST FILM WORK—Producer, *Skateboard*, Universal, 1978. PRINCIPAL FILM WORK—Producer: *Gas*, Paramount, 1981; *Presented By*, Orion, 1986; *No Man's Land*, Orion, 1986; executive producer, *Dying for Love*, Metro-Goldwyn-Mayer (MGM), 1987.

PRINCIPAL TELEVISION WORK—Executive script consultant, *Hill Street Blues*, NBC, 1985; co-producer, *Miami Vice*, NBC, 1986.

WRITINGS: SCREENPLAYS—*Skateboard*, Universal, 1978; *Gas*, Paramount, 1981; *No Man's Land*, Orion, 1986; *Dying for Love*, MGM, 1987. TELEVISION—Episodic: *Hill Street Blues* (eight episodes), NBC, 1985-86; *Miami Vice* (ten episodes), ABC, 1986-87.

AWARDS: Emmy Award nomination, 1986, for "What Are Friends For," *Hill Street Blues*.

MEMBER: Writers Guild of America West, Academy of Television Arts and Sciences.

ADDRESSES: HOME—Los Angeles, CA. OFFICE—100 Universal City Plaza, Universal City, CA 90069. AGENT—c/o Marty Horwitz and Jim Wiatt, International Creative Management, 8899 Beverley Blvd., Los Angeles, CA 90048.

*   *   *

WOLPER, David   1928-

PERSONAL: Full name, David Lloyd Wolper; born January 11, 1928, in New York, NY; son of Irving S. and Anna (Fass) Wolper; married Margaret Dawn Richard, 1958 (divorced); married Gloria Hill, June 11, 1974; children: (first marriage) Mark, Michael,

DAVID WOLPER

Leslie. EDUCATION: Attended Drake University, 1946; attended University of Southern California, 1949.

VOCATION: Producer.

CAREER: PRINCIPAL FILM WORK—Producer: *The Devil's Brigade*, United Artists, 1968; *The Bridge at Remagen*, United Artists, 1969; *If It's Tuesday, This Must Be Belgium*, United Artists, 1969; *I Love My Wife*, Universal, 1970; *Willy Wonka and the Chocolate Factory*, Paramount, 1971; *Visions of Eight*, Cinema 5, 1973; *Wattstax*, Columbia, 1973; *Birds Do It, Bees Do It*, 1974.

Full length documentaries include: *The Race for Space*, 1958; *The Yanks Are Coming*, 1963; *Four Days in November*, 1964; *Let My People Go*, 1965; *The Really Big Family*, 1966; *Say Goodbye George*, 1970; *The Hellstrom Chronicle*, Cinema 5, 1971; *Journey to the Outer Limits*, 1973.

PRINCIPAL TELEVISION WORK—Producer: Series—*Get Christie Love*, ABC, 1974-75; *Chico and the Man*, NBC, 1974-78; *Welcome Back, Kotter*, ABC, 1975-79.

Movies: *I Will Fight No More Forever*, 1975; *Victory at Entebbe*, 1976; *Moviola*, 1979; *Casablanca*, 1982; *Murder Is Easy*, 1982; *The Betty Ford Story*, ABC, 1987.

Mini-Series: *Roots*, ABC, 1977-78; *Roots: The Next Generations*, ABC, 1979-81; *The Thorn Birds*, 1982; *The Mystic Warrior*, ABC, 1984; *North & South*, 1984; *North & South, Book II*, ABC, 1986.

Specials: National Geographic Specials, 1965-68; George Plimpton Specials, 1970-72; American Heritage Smithsonian Specials, 1973-74; Primal Man Specials, 1973-75; Liberty Weekend Special, 1986.

Documentaries: *The Making of the President*, 1960, 1964, and 1968; *Biography*, syndicated, 1962-63; *Hollywood and the Stars*, NBC, 1963-64; *Men in Crisis*, 1964; *The March of Time*, 1965-66; *The Rise and Fall of the Third Reich*, 1967-68; *The Undersea World of Jacques Cousteau*, 1967-68; *The Unfinished Journey of Robert Kennedy*, 1969; *Appointment with Destiny*, 1971-73.

Other documentaries include: *Project: Man in Space, The Rafer Johnson Story, Biography of a Rookie, Hollywood: The Golden Years, Hollywood: The Fabulous Era, Hollywood: The Great Stars, D-Day, Escape to Freedom, Berlin: Kaiser to Khrushchev, December 7: Day of Infamy, The American Woman in the 20th Century, The Rise and Fall of American Communism, The Legend of Marilyn Monroe, Kreboizen and Cancer, China: Roots of Madness, They've Killed President Lincoln, Sandburg's Lincoln, The First Woman President, Collision Course.*

RELATED CAREER—Vice-president and treasurer, Flamingo Films, 1948-50; vice-president in charge of West Coast operations, Motion Pictures for Television, 1950-54; president and chairman of the board, Wolper Television Sales Company, 1964—; chairman of the board, Metromedia, Inc., 1965-68; president and chairman of the board, Wolper Productions, Los Angeles, 1958—; president, Wolper Pictures Ltd., 1960—; consultant to Warner Brothers and Warner Communications.

AWARDS: San Francisco International Film Festival Award, 1960, for documentaries; Golden Mike Award of the American Legion, 1963; Distinguished Service Award, U.S. Junior Chamber of Commerce, 1963; George Foster Peabody Award, 1963; Monte

Carlo Film Festival Award, 1964; Grand Prix Awards, Cannes Film Festival, 1964 and 1971; forty Emmy Awards, including Outstanding Limited Series, 1977, for *Roots* and 1979, for *Roots: The Next Generations;* one-hundred-forty-five Emmy Award nominations; two Academy Awards and eleven Academy Award nominations, including the following nominations for Best Feature-length Documentary: 1958, for *The Race for Space*, 1963, for *The Yanks Are Coming*, 1964, for *Four Days in November*, 1965, for *Let My People Go*, 1966, for *The Really Big Family*, 1970, for *Say Goodbye George*, 1971, for *The Hellstrom Chronicle*, and 1973, for *Journey to the Outer Limits*.

MEMBER: National Academy of Television Arts and Sciences, Screen Producers Guild, Writers Guild of America, American Film Institute (board of trustees); KCET-TV, Los Angeles (board of trustees), Manuscript Society; Los Angeles County Museum of Art (board of trustees), Hollywood Museum (founding member), President's Advisory Council to American Revolution Bicentennial Administration (chairman), Liberty Weekend Celebration (chairman), Los Angeles Olympic Organizing Committee, Amateur Athletic Foundation of Los Angeles (board of trustees), Cedars of Lebanon-Mt. Siani Hospital (board of directors, Thalia Clinic for Emotionally Disturbed Children), Dodger Baseball Museum (chairman of the board), American Rocket Society.

SIDELIGHTS: David Wolper has been a successful producer of television documentaries, situation comedies, mini-series, and such massive public events as the Twenty-third Olympiad and the Statue of Liberty centennial celebration. He is known, Cynthia Green writes in *Business Week* (December 9, 1985), as "a pioneering documentary filmmaker [and] an originator of the mini-series." Walter Shapiro and Martin Kasindorf of *Newsweek* (April 21, 1986) call Wolper "the Svengali of spectacle [and] the crown prince of crowd pleasers." He has received over 160 awards for his film work.

Wolper's biggest success has been the Statue of Liberty centennial celebration held in New York City over the 1986 Fourth of July weekend. The four-day event included thousands of live performers (including some 1,000 tap dancers), the swearing-in of 15,000 new citizens, 40,000 pleasure boats in the harbor surrounding the statue, speeches by President Ronald Reagan and French President Francois Mitterand, and over seven million spectators (and a live television audience of millions more). The celebration was an immense effort on a scale seldom if ever seen before. Speaking of the work involved in coordinating the affair, Wolper told Bonnie Angelo of *Time* (July 7, 1986): "First you think, wouldn't it be a wonderful thing to do for my country? Second you ask, why the hell am I doing this? And third, after it is over, you say, wasn't it a wonderful experience!"

The Statue of Liberty celebration was a far cry from Wolper's earlier career. He first made his name as a documentary filmmaker in the 1950s and 1960s, producing such award-winning television films as *The Making of the President 1960* and *The March of Time* series. He was "America's most successful producer of film documentaires," as *Newsweek* (November 23, 1964) reported. *Time* (December 7, 1962) explained that "the three largest producers of documentary films for television are NBC, CBS, and David Wolper."

By the 1970s, Wolper had moved into producing feature films and television mini-series. His *Roots*, a mini-series on the history of black Americans, and *The Thorn Birds*, a mini-series set in nineteenth century Australia, earned record ratings when they were aired. The two series are among the top-rated television programs of all time. Wolper also produced such weekly programs as *Welcome Back, Kotter* and *Chico and the Man.*

In 1972 Wolper produced the official film of the Munich Olympic games. This led in 1984 to his being asked to produce the opening and closing ceremonies for the Olympic games in Los Angeles. These televised ceremonies featured singers and dancers on outdoor stages, parades of the athletes, and audience participation events. Because of his experience in producing these live shows involving thousands of people, Wolper was asked by Lee Iacocca, chairman of the planning committee for the 1986 Statue of Liberty centennial celebration, to produce that event as well. Wolper's Statue of Liberty festival was arguably the largest "party" ever staged. It was at least, according to New York mayor Ed Koch in *Time* (July 7, 1986), "the party of the century."

ADDRESSES: OFFICE—c/o Warner Brothers Inc., 4000 Warner Blvd., Burbank, CA 91522.

*   *   *

WYNN, Keenan   1916-1986

PERSONAL: Full name, Francis Xavier Aloysius James Jeremiah Keenan Wynn; born July 27, 1916, in New York, NY; died of cancer in Brentwood, CA, October 14, 1986; son of Ed (an actor) and Hilda (Keenan) Wynn; married Eve Abbott (divorced); married Betty Jane Butler (divorced); married Sharley Jean Hudson; children: (first marriage) two sons; (third marriage) three daughters. EDUCATION: Attended the Horace Mann School, the Harvey School, and St. John's Military Academy.

VOCATION: Actor.

CAREER: FILM DEBUT—*Northwest Rangers*, Metro-Goldwyn-Mayer (MGM). PRINCIPAL FILM APPEARANCES—*For Me and My Gal*, MGM, 1942; *Lost Angel*, MGM, 1943; *See Here, Private Hargrove*, MGM, 1944; *Since You Went Away*, MGM, 1944; *Marriage Is a Private Affair*, MGM, 1944; *Between Two Women*, MGM, 1944; *The Clock*, MGM, 1945; *Without Love*, MGM, 1945; *Weekend at the Waldorf*, MGM, 1945; *What Next, Corporal Hargrove?*, MGM, 1945; *Ziegfeld Follies*, MGM, 1946; *Song of the Thin Man*, MGM, 1947; *The Hucksters*, MGM, 1947; *B.F.'s Daughter*, MGM, 1948; *The Three Musketeers*, MGM, 1948; *Neptune's Daughter*, MGM, 1949.

Annie Get Your Gun, MGM, 1950; *Three Little Words*, MGM, 1950; *Royal Wedding*, MGM, 1951; *Kind Lady*, MGM, 1951; *Angela in the Outfield*, MGM, 1951; *Texas Carnival*, MGM, 1951; *Phone Call from a Stranger*, MGM, 1952; *Fearless Fagan*, MGM, 1952; *Sky Full of Moon*, MGM, 1952; *Desperate Search*, MGM, 1952; *Battle Circus*, MGM, 1953; *Code Two*, MGM, 1953; *All the Brothers Were Valiant*, MGM, 1953; *Kiss Me Kate*, MGM, 1953; *The Long Long Trailer*, MGM, 1954; *Tennesee Champ*, MGM, 1954; *Men of the Fighting Lady*, MGM, 1954; *The Glass Slipper*, MGM, 1955; *The Marauders*, MGM, 1955; *Running Wild*, Universal, 1955; *The Shack Out on 101*, Allied Artists, 1955; *The Man in the Gray Flannel Suit*, Twentieth Century-Fox, 1956; *Johnny Concho*, United Artists, 1956; *The Great Man*, Universal, 1957; *The Perfect Furlough*, 1958; *Some Came Running*, MGM, 1959; *A Hole in the Head*, 1959.

King of the Roaring Twenties, 1960; *The Absent Minded Professor,* Buena Vista, 1961; *Scarface Mob,* 1962; *Dr. Strangelove,* Columbia, 1964; *The Patsy,* Paramount, 1964; *The Americanization of Emily,* MGM, 1964; *Stagecoach,* Twentieth Century-Fox, 1966; *Warning Shot,* Paramount, 1967; *Welcome to Hard Times,* MGM, 1967; *The War Wagon,* Universal, 1967; *Point Blank,* MGM, 1967; *Finian's Rainbow,* Warner Brothers, 1968; *Wild in the Sky,* American International, 1968; *MacKenna's Gold,* Columbia, 1969; *Smith,* Buena Vista, 1969; *Once Upon a Time in the West,* Paramount, 1969; *80 Steps to Jonah,* Warner Brothers, 1969.

The Animals, 1970; *Loving,* Columbia, 1970; *Pretty Maids All in a Row,* MGM, 1971; *B.J. Presents,* 1971; *Cancel My Reservation,* Warner Brothers, 1972; *The Mechanic,* United Artists, 1972; *Herbie Rides Again,* Buena Vista, 1974; *Nashville,* Paramount, 1975; *The Shaggy D.A.,* Buena Vista, 1976; *Orca,* Paramount, 1977; *Piranha!,* New World Pictures, 1978; *Just Tell Me What You Want,* Warner Brothers, 1980; *Best Friends,* Warner Brothers, 1982; *Hyper-Sapien.*

TELEVISION DEBUT—1955. PRINCIPAL TELEVISION APPEARANCES—Series: Kodiak, *Trouble Shooters,* NBC, 1960; panelist, *You're in the Picture,* CBS, 1961; Willard "Digger" Barnes, *Dallas,* CBS, 1979-80; Carl Sarnac, *Call to Glory,* ABC, 1984.

Episodic: "The Rack," *U.S. Steel Hour,* ABC; "Twentieth Century," *Ford Star Jubilee,* CBS, 1956; "Requiem for a Heavy-weight," *Playhouse 90,* CBS, 1957; "The Untouchables," *Westinghouse Desilu Playhouse,* NBC, 1959; *Omnibus,* CBS; *Hallmark Hall of Fame,* ABC; *Alcoa Theatre,* NBC; *Fireside Theatre,* NBC; *The Joseph Cotton Show,* NBC; *Dr. Simon Locke,* Canadian; *Police Woman,* NBC.

STAGE DEBUT—*Ceiling Zero,* Lakewood Summer Theatre, Skowhegan, ME. PRINCIPAL STAGE APPEARANCES—Performed in twenty-one Broadway shows, including *Remember the Day, Hey Diddle Diddle, Star Wagon, Blind Alley,* and *Jason;* appearances in seventy-five stock company shows.

MAJOR TOURS—With the Hollywood Victory Committee for the United Service Organization, U.S. military camps, 1940-57.

PRINCIPAL STAGE WORK—Stage manager, *Room Service,* Broadway production, New York City, 1938.

AWARDS: Best Single Performance in Drama or Comedy Series, Emmy Award nomination, 1978, for *Police Woman;* selected honorary chairman, National Better Hearing and Speech Month, 1980.

SIDELIGHTS: In Keenan Wynn's obituary, *Variety* reported that he held the world hydroplane speed record for circumnavigating the island of Manhattan in a Class A inboard boat from 1934-51.*

Y

YANG, Ginny

PERSONAL: Born April 22, in Korea; adopted daughter of George (a businessman) and Jean Campbell; married Robert D. Cranston (an architect), May 26, 1984. EDUCATION: Catawba College, B.A., drama, 1975; studied acting with William Hickey and Aaron Frankel at the Herbert Berghof Studios in New York City.

VOCATION: Actress.

CAREER: STAGE DEBUT—Grace, *F.O.B.*, Eugene O'Neill National Playwrights Conference, Waterford, CT, 1979. OFF-BROADWAY DEBUT—Grace, *F.O.B.*, Public Theatre, New York Shakespeare Festival (NYSF), New York City, 1980. PRINCIPAL STAGE APPEARANCES—Ruizen, *Peking Man*, Columbia University, New York City, 1980; Mme. Aung, *Plenty*, Public Theatre, NYSF, 1982, transferring to the Plymouth Theatre, New York City, 1983;

GINNY YANG

Yasuko Rokujo, *The Lady Aoi*, Circle Repertory Theatre Lab, New York City, 1985; Ruth, *The Memento*, Yale Repertory Theatre, New Haven, CT, 1986-87; other performances at New Dramatists, the Pan Asian Repertory Theatre, La Mama Experimental Theatre Club (E.T.C.), the Perry Street Theatre, and the Theatre for the New City, all New York City.

MAJOR TOURS—Liat, *South Pacific*, summer stock tour, Ogunquit Playhouse, ME, Pocono Playhouse, PA, Cape Cod Melody Tent, MA, Northshore Music Theatre, MA, and Corning Summer Theatre, NY, 1982.

FILM DEBUT—Grocer, *The Brother from Another Planet*, Cinecon International, 1984.

PRINCIPAL TELEVISION APPEARANCES—Episodic performances in various soap operas; also appearances in specials.

MEMBER: Actors' Equity Association, Screen Actors Guild, American Federation of Television and Radio Artists.

SIDELIGHTS: FAVORITE ROLES—Yasuko Rokujo, from *The Lady Aoi* and Grace, from *F.O.B.* RECREATIONS—Attending dance classes and singing.

ADDRESSES: HOME—Brooklyn, NY.

* * *

YOUNG, David 1928-

PERSONAL: Born May 1, 1928, in New York, NY; son of Maynard (a ship's captain) and Mildred (a theatre assistant; maiden name, Burns) Young; married wife Sheila (divorced); married wife Elizabeth (a teacher), May 24, 1986; children: Michael, Melissa. EDUCATION: Columbia Pacific University, Ph.D.; trained for the stage with Erwin Piscator at the New School for Social Research.

VOCATION: Actor, director, and producer.

CAREER: PRINCIPAL STAGE APPEARANCES—Tilden, *Buried Child*, Actor Center Showcase, Arena Stage, Washington, DC, 1985; *Originals Only*, New York City production; *The Lady from the Sea*, Source Theatre, Washington, DC; also in regional theatre productions: Horatio, *Hamlet*, the wreck, *My Sister Eileen*, Dr. Chumley, *Harvey*, Mr. Manningham, *Angel Street*, Sakini, *Teahouse of the August Moon*, Tom, *The Glass Menagerie*.

MAJOR TOURS—*Angel on the Loose*, pre-Broadway; *Apron Strings*.

DAVID YOUNG

PRINCIPAL STAGE WORK—Director: *Double Solitaire,* Georgetown Theatre Workshop, Washington, DC; *Jacques Brel Is Alive and Well and Living in Paris,* Connecticut Dinner Theatre; *Company* and *Fanny,* both at the Little Theatre, Alexandria, VA; *Amadeus,* Silver Springs Stage, MD, and at the Source Theatre, Washington, DC; two staged readings, Shenan Arts Festival, Staunton, VA; *Grease,* Florida School for the Arts.

Also directed: *That Championship Season, Guys and Dolls, Ah, Wilderness!, The Front Page, The Tenth Man, The Price, The Thirteen Clocks, The Collection, Six Characters in Search of an Author, The Most Happy Fella, Twelfth Night, The Glass Menagerie, Halloween, Kiss Me Kate, One Flew Over the Cuckoo's Nest, Babes in Arms, Private Lives, Hamlet,* and *The Sheep Well;* producer, *Angel on the Loose,* pre-Broadway tour.

PRINCIPAL TELEVISION APPEARANCES—Dramatic Specials: "Lady from the Sea," *Powerhouse,* PBS; "The Man Who Burned Books," *Medallion Theatre,* NBC.

PRINCIPAL RADIO WORK—*F. Scott Fitzgerald,* National Public Radio.

RELATED CAREER—Teacher, University of Hartford, Hartford Conservatory, and Theatre School of Washington, DC; guest lecturer, Smithsonian Institution, Wolf Trap Foundation Education Center, Vienna, VA, and American Association of State Colleges and Universities; artistic advisor, Presidential Scholars in the Arts; national judge, National Society of Arts and Letters; Helen Hayes Theatre Awards (board of directors); producing director, American College Theatre Festival, Kennedy Center, Washington, DC.

AWARDS: National Honor Award, American Community Theatre Association, 1980.

MEMBER: Society of Stage Directors and Choreographers, American Theatre Association, American Community Theatre Association (past president).

ADDRESSES: OFFICE—1249 Derbyshire Road, Potamac, MD 20854.

*   *   *

YOUNG, Dawn

PERSONAL: Born February 19; children: Wolf, Lauren. EDUCATION: Temple University, B.A., M.A.; studied acting with Jack Waltzer, Stella Adler, and Sally Johnson.

VOCATION: Actress.

CAREER: PRINCIPAL STAGE APPEARANCES—Dorine, *Tartuffe* and title role, *The Wisdom of Eve,* both at the Portobello Theatre, New York City; Marianne, *Scenes from a Marriage* and Maria, *Cries and Whispers,* both at the 13th Street Theatre, New York City; Linda, *If You Love Me, Then Stay,* TOMI Theatre, New York City; *Le Bel Indifferent,* Theatre des Calicots, Montreal, Canada; Estelle, *Huis Clos,* Montpellier, France; Agrippine, *Eduard et Agrippine,* Centre Culturel du Languedoc, France; Crystal, *The*

DAWN YOUNG

Women, Connie, *Who Killed Santa Claus?,* and Louise, *Private Lives,* all at the Wyncote Players Theatre, Philadelphia; chorus, *Oklahoma!,* Marion, *The Music Man,* and Karen, *The Children's Hour,* all at the Island Center, St. Croix, VI.

PRINCIPAL FILM APPEARANCES—Friend, *Rich and Famous,* Metro-Goldwyn-Mayer, 1981; prostitute and mother, *The Little Mermaid,* NW Russo, 1981; student in acting class, *Tootsie,* Columbia, 1982.

PRINCIPAL TELEVISION APPEARANCES—Series: Valerie Kripto-poulous, *The Catlins,* WTBS, 1983-85. Episodic: *All My Children,* ABC; *The Edge of Night,* ABC; *One Life to Live,* ABC; *The Guiding Light,* CBS.

RELATED CAREER—Teacher, Temple University, 1971-76.

MEMBER: Actors' Equity Association, Screen Actors Guild, American Federation of Television and Radio Artists.

SIDELIGHTS: RECREATIONS—Scuba diving, sailing, skiing, playing the guitar, and singing.

ADDRESSES: HOME—161 W. 76th Street, New York, NY 10025. AGENT—c/o Doris Mantz, International Creative Management, 40 W. 57th Street, New York, NY 10019.

Z

ZAL, Roxana 1969-

PERSONAL: Born November 8, 1969, in Los Angeles, CA; daughter of Hossein and Maureen Zal. EDUCATION: Attends Santa Monica High School.

VOCATION: Actress.

CAREER: TELEVISION DEBUT—Guest role, *Hart to Hart*, ABC, 1981. PRINCIPAL TELEVISION APPEARANCES—Movies: *Testament*, PBS, 1983; title role, *Something About Amelia*, ABC, 1984; Lesley, *Shattered Spirits*, ABC, 1985. Specials: "God, the Universe and Hot Fudge Sundaes," *CBS Schoolbreak Special*, 1986.

FILM DEBUT—*Table for Five*, Warner Brothers, 1983. PRINCIPAL FILM APPEARANCES—Maggie, *The River's Edge*, 1986.

ROXANA ZAL

AWARDS: Best Actress, Youth in Film, 1982, for *Hart to Hart;* Emmy Award, Golden Globe Award, Golden Apple Award, all 1984, for *Something About Amelia;* Rising Star Award, Hollywood Press, 1985.

MEMBER: Screen Actors Guild, American Federation of Television and Radio Artists.

SIDELIGHTS: RECREATIONS—Playing tennis, snow and water skiing, and reading comic books.

ADDRESSES: PUBLICIST—c/o Monique Moss, Michael Levine Public Relations Company, 9123 Sunset Blvd., Los Angeles, CA 90069.

*   *   *

ZEFFIRELLI, Franco 1923-

PERSONAL: Also known as G. Franco Zeffirelli; born February 12, 1923, in Florence, Italy; son of Ottorino Corsi (a textile importer) and Alaide Cipriani. EDUCATION: Attended University of Architecture, Florence. RELIGION: Roman Catholic.

VOCATION: Director, designer, and actor.

CAREER: PRINCIPAL STAGE APPEARANCES—With the Morelli Stoppa Company, Italy, appeared in *Crime and Punishment*, 1946, *Euridyce*, 1947.

FIRST LONDON STAGE WORK—Director and designer, *Romeo and Juliet*, Old Vic Theatre, 1960. FIRST BROADWAY STAGE WORK—Director and designer, *Romeo and Juliet*, City Center, 1962. PRINCIPAL STAGE WORK—(with Salvador Dali) Scenic designer for the Morelli Stoppa Company: *A Streetcar Named Desire* and *Troilus and Crssida*, 1949; *The Three Sisters*, 1951.

Director and designer, *Othello*, with the Royal Shakespeare Company, Memorial Theatre, Stratford-on-Avon, U.K., 1961; director and designer, *The Lady of the Camelias*, Winter Garden Theatre, New York City, 1963; director, *Who's Afraid of Virginia Woolf?*, Festival del Teatro, Venice and Paris, 1963; director, *After the Fall*, 1964; director and designer, *Amleto*, with the Proclemer-Albertazzi Company, Old Vic Theatre, London, 1964; director and designer, *Much Ado About Nothing*, with the National Theatre Company, Old Vic Theatre, London, 1965; director, *A Delicate Balance*, 1966; director, *Black Comedy*, 1967; director, *Venti Zecchini D'Oro*, 1968; director, *Due Piu Due Non Fanno Quattro*, 1969; director, *La Lupa*, Aldwych Theatre, London, 1969; director and designer,

Saturday, Sunday, Monday, National Theatre Company, Old Vic Theatre, London, 1973, then New York City, 1974; director, *The Dead City,* Italy, 1975; director, *Lorenzaccio,* Comedie Francaise, Paris, 1976; director, *Filumena,* Lyric Theatre, London, 1977, then St. James Theatre, New York City, 1980.

Director, operas: *Cenerentola,* La Scala, Italy, 1954; *I Pagliacci,* 1959; *Cavalleria Rusticana,* 1959; *Lucia Di Lammermoor,* Covent Garden, London, 1959; *La Boheme,* La Scala, Italy, 1963; *Falstaff,* Metropolitan Opera Guild, New York City, 1964; *Tosca,* Covent Garden, London, 1965; *Norma,* Paris Opera, 1965; *Anthony and Cleopatra,* Metropolitan Opera Guild, New York City, 1966; *Otello,* Metropolitan Opera Guild, New York City, 1972; *Don Giovanni,* Staatsoper, Vienna, 1972; *Un Ballo In Maschera,* La Scala, 1972; *Otello,* La Scala, 1975; *Carmen,* Staatsoper, Vienna, 1978; *La Traviata,* 1979; *Turandot,* with the Metropolitan Opera Guild at Lincoln Center, New York City, 1987; also a production of *La Boheme* at the Metropolitan Opera.

MAJOR TOUR WORK—Director: *Romeo and Juliet,* Verona, Paris, Vienna, Rome, Milan, Moscow, and Leningrad, 1964; *La Lupa,* Florence, Rome, Vienna, Zurich, Paris, and Moscow, 1965.

PRINCIPAL FILM WORK—Director: *The Taming of the Shrew,* Columbia/Royal Films, 1967; *Romeo and Juliet,* Paramount, 1968; *Brother Sun, Sister Moon,* Paramount, 1973; *The Champ,* 1979; *Endless Love,* Universal, 1981; *La Traviata,* 1982; *Otello,* 1986.

PRINCIPAL TELEVISION WORK—Director, of specials: *Giorni De Distruzione,* 1966; *Fidelio of Beethoven,* 1970; *Missa Solemnis of Beethoven,* 1970; *I Pagliacci,* PBS, 1984. Mini-Series: *Jesus of Nazareth,* 1977.

AWARDS: Best Director, Academy Award nomination, 1968, for *Romeo and Juliet.*

MEMBER: Directors Guild of America.

SIDELIGHTS: Franco Zeffirelli has had a varied career as a stage actor, a set and costume designer, a director of opera and stage plays, and as a director of a number of successful films. He has "left his mark in stage direction as well as set and costume design for opera, theater, television and cinema," says Lanfranco Rasponi of the *Opera News* (January 16, 1982). "He goes from one to the other with skill, assurance and ease, varying his menu, never growing stale." Although he is most widely known for his films *Romeo and Juliet, Brother Sun, Sister Moon,* and the television production of *Jesus of Nazareth,* Zeffirelli is considered to be, Corby Kummer maintains in *Horizon* (June, 1981), "the world's foremost director of opera."

As a young man, Zeffirelli told Francis Rizzo of *Opera News* (February 13, 1971), he "had no thoughts of a career in the theater." His father was a textile importer in Florence, Italy, and Zeffirelli was encouraged to join the family business. But while still in school he began to design sets for amateur stage productions. This led to acting on the stage and in several films. By the late 1940s, Zeffirelli was an assistant to Italian director Luchino Visconti. During the 1950s he designed sets and directed stage plays and operas. "Zeffirelli's reputation," a *Time* (October 11, 1968) writer explained, "was established at La Scala in Milan, where in 1954 he designed the costumes and sets for, and staged a production of Rossini's *La Cenerentola.* It was the beginning of Zeffirelli style— the flamboyant baroque settings, the epic *brio.*"

Whether directing a stage or film production, Zeffirelli infuses the work with his own distinctive style. "His hallmarks," a writer for the *New Yorker* (September 8, 1972) stated, "are visual splendor, a skillful handling of crowd scenes, and the ability to extract from singers and actors performances that seem direct and spontaneous." Zeffirelli is also known for the lush extravagance of his productions. One set for his production of *Aida* required two hours to assemble. The *New Yorker* critic called him "very extravagant." Kummer notes that Zeffirelli "has made a name for florid showmanship" and has been accused by some critics of "churning out trash disguised with thick coats of varnish."

But Zeffirelli's work has always been successful with audiences. His television production of *Jesus of Nazareth* has been seen by some 600 million people and is a staple of Easter programming around the world. *The Champ,* a 1979 film panned by the critics, has grossed $100 million. None of his films have lost money. Zeffirelli attributes his success to a concern for the audience over the critics. "I always worry," he told Rasponi, "when the critics like my work. . . It is often the kiss of death." Speaking to Kummer, Zeffirelli claims, "You know why I haven't had a commercial flop yet? Because I identify myself with the audience all the time."

ADDRESSES: OFFICE—Via due Macelli 31, Rome, Italy.*

*   *   *

ZIFF, Irwin   1929-

PERSONAL: Born June 7, 1929, in New York, NY; son of Mac (a U.S. marine) and Rose (a dancer and actress; maiden name, Liberoff) Ziff; married Selma Lefkowitz (educator and administrator), October 11, 1953; children: Melody, Amy, Elizabeth, David. EDUCATION: Brooklyn College, B.A., 1951; Boston University, M.A., 1964; studied acting with Marie Moser and Skipper Davidson at the Circle in the Square Actors Workshop, New York City. POLITICS: Republican. RELIGION: Jewish. MILITARY: U.S. Naval Reserve, 1946-51; U.S. Air Force, 1952-73.

VOCATION: Actor.

CAREER: STAGE DEBUT—(As a child actor, known as Bobby Irwin), Flag boy and dancer, *Passing Parade,* Winter Garden Theatre, New York City, 1936. PRINCIPAL STAGE APPEARANCES—Henry, *The Bad Man,* 1950; Dr. Stoner, *Verdict;* Burgomiester, *The Visit;* Alonso, *The Tempest;* Willie Clark, *The Sunshine Boys;* Tubal, *The Merchant of Venice;* Jefferson, *The Man Who Came to Dinner;* Gudgeon the butler, *The Hollow;* Mendele the bookpeddler, *Tales of Sholom Aleichim;* Inspector Lord, *Spider's Web;* Alfred Doolittle, *Pygmalion;* Fintan, *The Patrick Pearse Motel;* the Wizard, *Once Upon a Mattress;* Judd, *Oklahoma!;* Dr. Gribble, *Love from a Stranger;* title role, *Julius Caesar;* Mr. Golden, *Impressario and Abu Hassan;* the Major, *Idiot's Delight;* Buddy, *Hotline to Heaven;* Big Jule, *Guys and Dolls;* Joe Benjamin, *God's Favorite;* John Gonzales, *Crossing the Bar;* King Ferdinand, *Christopher Columbus;* Harry Brock, *Born Yesterday;* Sitting Bull, *Annie Get Your Gun;* Porter, *Deathtrap;* Vandergelder, *Hello, Dolly!;* Anvil salesman, *The Music Man;* Mushnick, *Little Shop of Horrors.*

Has appeared at the following theatres: West End Dinner Theatre, Alexandria, VA; Village Playhouse, NY; Studio Theatre, Wash-

IRWIN ZIFF

ington, DC; Ridgefield Summer Theatre, CT; Second Avenue Theatre, New York City; Arena Stage, Washington, DC; Circle in the Square, New York City; Riverside Theatre, New York City; Kennedy Center, Washington, DC; Folger Theatre, Washington, DC; Brooklyn Academy of Music, NY; Sacramento Music Circus, CA; Center Stage, Baltimore, MD.

MAJOR TOURS—Whitney, *Life with Father*, 1941.

PRINCIPAL FILM APPEARANCES—*Strategic Air Command*, 1955; *The Only Game in Town*, Twentieth Century-Fox, 1970; *And Justice for All*, Columbia, 1979; *Stardust Memories*, United Artists, 1980; *First Family*, Warner Brothers, 1980; *First Monday in October*, Paramount, 1981; *Best Friends*, Warner Brothers, 1982; *Diner*, Metro-Glodwyn-Mayer/United Artists, 1982; *Protocol*, Warner Brothers, 1984; *The Man with One Red Shoe*, Twentieth Century-Fox, 1985; *Violets Are Blue*, 1986; *The Tin Men*, Touchstone, 1987; *Gardens of Stone*, upcoming; also appeared in government and industrial films.

PRINCIPAL TELEVISION APPEARANCES—Episodic: *A Corner of the World*, PBS; *The Bionic Woman*, NBC; *Emergency*, NBC; *Lime Street*, ABC. Mini-Series: *George Washington*, CBS; *Space*, NBC. Movies: *Raid on Entebbe*, NBC, 1977; *Jacqueline Bouvier Kennedy*, CBS, 1981; *Finnegan Begin Again*, HBO, 1985; also, *God Bless America*, Metromedia; *Mirror Image*, BBC/HBO; *The Rehearsal*, Metromedia. Specials: *Sunshine Store*, WRC; *Sherlock Holmes, His Life and Times*, PBS.

RELATED CAREER—Speech, English and drama teacher, Prospect Heights High School, Brooklyn, NY, 1951-52.

NON-RELATED CAREER—Instructor in military history, U.S. Air Force Academy, Colorado Springs, CO, 1963-66; military air attache, U.S. Embassy, Paris, France, 1966-69; military assistant to Assistant Secretary of Defense (Public Affairs), 1970-73.

AWARDS: Kafer Award, Best Supporting Actor, 1950, for *The Bad Man;* Emmy Award nomination, 1983, for *The Life and Times of Sherlock Holmes.*

MEMBER: Actors' Equity Association, American Federation of Television and Radio Artists, Screen Actors Guild; Air Force Association.

ADDRESSES: AGENT—Michael Thomas Agency, 305 Madison Avenue, New York, NY 10017.

*   *   *

ZWERDLING, Allen   1922-

PERSONAL: Born October 11, 1922, in New York, NY; son of William (a wholesale fruit merchant) and Yetta (Nagler) Zwerdling; married Shirley Hoffman, December 2, 1946; children: Sherry, Jan, Gary. EDUCATION: City College of New York, B.S., education, 1940; studied with June Justice at the Players Guild of Manhattan. MILITARY: U.S. Army Air Force, Special Services, 1944-45.

VOCATION: Actor, director, editor, and critic.

CAREER: STAGE DEBUT—At age eight, performed with the Players Guild of Manhattan. PRINCIPAL STAGE WORK—Actor and stage manager, Players Guild of Manhattan; producer and director, the American Players, Zurich, Switzerland, 1946-47; assistant to the director, Zurich State Theatre, Switzerland, 1946-47; director of the Kansas City Resident Theatre, MO, 1947-48; producer and director of ninety-five servicemen shows for the U.S. Air Force Special Services; director of the City College of New York Theatre Workshop.

MAJOR TOURS—Actor and director in Switzerland in *Kiss & Tell* and *Springtime for Henry.*

FILM DEBUT—*One More Time*, 1986.

WRITINGS: NEWSPAPERS—Editor, *Show Business*, 1948-1960; editor and publisher, *Back Stage*, 1960-87; editor of U.S. Army newspaper in Foggia, Italy; syndicated stories on the theatre appearing in over three-hundred-fifty newspapers, published by the U.S. Army. PLAYS—Three short plays published by the U.S. Army.

BOOKS—Editor, *Back Stage Television, Film, Tape & Syndication Directory.*

MEMBER: Drama Desk.

SIDELIGHTS: Mr. Zwerdling writes to *CTFT*, "I am now semi-retired, doing odd acting jobs, odd writing-editing jobs at *Back Stage,* and am an almost fulltime tennis player."

ADDRESSES: HOME—532 Springtown Road. New Paltz, NY 12561. OFFICE—*Back Stage* Publications, 330 W. 42nd Street, New York, NY 10036.

Cumulative Index

To provide continuity with *Who's Who in the Theatre*, this index interfiles references to *Who's Who in the Theatre*, 1st-17th Editions, and *Who Was Who in the Theatre* (Gale Research Co., 1978) with references to *Contemporary Theatre, Film, and Television*, Volumes 1-4.

References in the index are identified as follows:

CTFT and volume number—*Contemporary Theatre, Film, and Television*, Volumes 1-4
WWT and edition number—*Who's Who in the Theatre*, 1st-17th Editions
WWasWT—*Who Was Who in the Theatre*

Cumulative Index

Cumulative Index

Cumulative Index

M

Cumulative Index

S